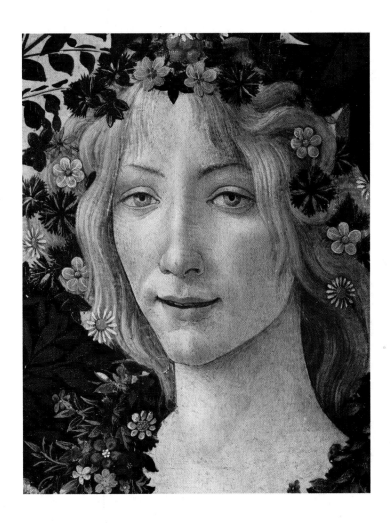

Discovering the Humanities

HENRY M. SAYRE

Oregon State University

Prentice Hall

Upper Saddle River   London   Singapore
Toronto   Tokyo   Sydney   Hong Kong   Mexico City

Editor in Chief: Sarah Touborg
Senior Editor: Amber Mackey
Editor in Chief Development: Rochelle Diogenes
Senior Development Editor: Roberta Meyer
Development Editor: Margaret Manos
Editorial Assistant: Theresa Graziano
Director of Marketing: Brandy Dawson
Senior Marketing Manager: Kate Mitchell
Marketing Assistant: Kyle VanNatter
Senior Managing Editor: Mary Rottino
Senior Project Manager: Barbara Marttine Cappuccio
Project Manager: Marlene Gassler
Copy Editor: Karen Verde
Proofreaders: Barbara DeVries
  and Nancy Stevenson
Text Research: John Sisson
Senior Operations Specialist: Brian Mackey
Senior Art Director: Pat Smythe
Interior Designer: Ximena Tamvakopoulos
Design Adaptation and Cover Design: Laura Gardner
Line Art and Map Program Management: Gail Cocker and
  Mirella Signoretto

Fine Line Art and Cartography: Peter Bull Art Studio
Line Art Studio: Precision Graphics
Pearson Imaging Center
  Site Supervisor: Joe Conti
  Project Coordinator: Corin Skidds
  Scanner Operators: Corin Skidds,
    Robert Uibelhoer, Ron Walko
Manager, Visual Research: Beth Brenzel
Photo Research: Image Research Editorial Services / Francelle
  Carapetyan and Rebecca Harris
Manager, Rights and Permissions: Zina Arabia
Image Permission Coordinator: Debbie Latronica
Manager, Cover Visual Research & Permissions: Karen Sanatar
Cover Art: Erich Lessing / Art Resource, NY
Media Director: Brian Hyland
Media Editor: Alison Lorber
Lead Media Project Manager: Rich Barnes
Composition: Gail Cocker and Wanda España
Printer/Binder: Courier Kendallville
Cover Printer: Phoenix Color Corp.

Discovering the Humanities is a brief version of *The Humanities: Culture, Continuity & Change* ©2008 Pearson Education, Inc.

Credits and acknowledgments borrowed from other sources and reproduced, with permission, in this textbook appear on appropriate page within text or on page Credits-1.

Library of Congress Cataloging-in-Publication Data
Sayre, Henry M.
  Discovering the humanities / Henry M. Sayre
    p. cm.
  Includes bibliographical references and index.
  ISBN 0-205-67230-2 (978-0-205-67230-1 : alk. paper)
  1. Civilization—History. 2. Humanities—History. 3. Social change—History. I. Title.
CB69.S29 2010
909—dc22

                    2008039567

10 9 8 7 6 5

Prentice Hall
is an imprint of

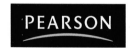

www.pearsonhighered.com

ISBN 10: 0-205-67230-2
ISBN 13: 978-0-205-67230-1
Exam Copy ISBN 10: 0-205-68310-X
ISBN 13: 978-0-205-68310-9

Contents

15 Decades of Change The Plural Self in a Global World 450

See Context and Make Connections...

Discovering the Humanities helps students see context and make connections across the humanities by tying together the entire cultural experience through a narrative storytelling approach. This new brief version of *The Humanities: Culture, Continuity, and Change* was adapted by author Henry Sayre himself. Written around the author's belief that students learn best by remembering stories rather than memorizing facts, it captures the voices that have shaped and influenced human thinking and creativity. And because it is a brief text, *Discovering the Humanities* offers great flexibility by allowing instructors to supplement it with additional readers or other material.

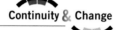

Egyptian and Greek Sculpture

Continuity & Change

Freestanding Greek sculpture of the Archaic period—that is, sculpture dating from about 600–480 BCE—is notable for its stylistic connections to 2,000 years of Egyptian tradition. The Late Period statue of Mentuemhet [men-too-em-het] (Fig. 1.25), from Thebes, dating from around 2500 BCE, differs hardly at all from Old Kingdom sculpture at Giza (see Fig. 1.17), and even though the Anavysos [ah-NAH-vee-sus] *Kouros* (Fig. 1.26), from a cemetery near Athens, represents a significant advance in relative naturalism over the Greek sculpture of just a few years before, it still resembles its Egyptian ancestors. Remarkably, since it follows upon the Anavysos *Kouros* by only 75 years, the *Doryphoros* (Spear Bearer) (Fig. 1.27) is significantly more naturalistic. Although

this is a Roman copy of a lost fifth-century BCE bronze Greek statue, we can assume it reflects the original's naturalism, since the original's sculptor, Polyclitus [pol-ih-KLY-tus], was renowned for his ability to render the human body realistically. But this advance, characteristic of Golden Age Athens, represents more than just a cultural taste for naturalism. As we will see in the next chapter, it also represents a heightened cultural sensitivity to the worth of the individual, a belief that as much as we value what we have in common with one another—the bond that creates the city-state—our *individual* contributions are at least of equal value. By the fifth century BCE, the Greeks clearly understood that individual genius and achievement could be a matter of civic pride. ■

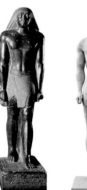 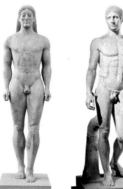

Fig. 1.25 *Mentuemhet*, from Karnak, Thebes, ca. 660 BCE. Granite, height 54". Egyptian Museum, Cairo. Fig.1.26 *Anavysos Kouros*, perhaps young Kroisos, from a cemetery at Anavysos [ah-NAH-vee-sus], near Athens, ca. 525 BCE. Marble with remnants of paint, height 6' 4". National Archaeological Museum, Athens. Fig. 1.27 *Doryphoros* (Spear Bearer), Roman copy after the original bronze by Polyclitus of ca. 450–440 BCE. Marble, height 6' 6". Museo Archeologico Nazionale, Naples

33

CONTINUITY & CHANGE

Full-page essays at the end of each chapter illustrate the influence of one culture upon another and show cultural changes over time.

---

206 ▬▬ CHAPTER 7 THE RENAISSANCE

The task of replacing Old Saint Peter's was a much larger project and Bramante's most important one. Old Saint Peter's was a **basilica**, a type of ancient Roman building with a long central nave, double side aisles set off by colonnades (see Fig. 4.6), an apse in the wall opposite the main door, and a transept near the apse so that large numbers of visitors could approach the shrine to Saint Peter. In his plan for a new Saint Peter's (Fig. 7.22a), Bramante adopted the Vitruvian square, as illustrated in Leonardo's drawing, placing inside it a **Greek cross** (a cross in which the upright and transverse shafts are of equal length and intersect at their middles) topped by a central dome purposely reminiscent of the giant dome of the Pantheon (see Fig. 3.18). The resultant central plan is essentially a circle inscribed within a square. In Renaissance thinking, the central plan and dome symbolized the perfection of God. Construction began in 1506.

Continuity & Change
p. 92

The Pantheon

Julius II financed the project through the sale of **indulgences**, dispensations granted by the Church to shorten an individual's stay in purgatory. This was the place where, in Catholic belief, individuals temporarily reside after death as punishment for their sins. Those wanting to enter heaven faster than they otherwise might could shorten their stay in purgatory by purchasing an indulgence. The

be a very expensive project, but there were also sinners willing to help pay for it. With the deat pope and architect, in 1513 and 1514 respectivel ject came to a temporary halt. Its final plan woul oped in 1546 by Michelangelo (Fig. 7.22b).

Michelangelo and the Sistine Chapel

After the fall of the Medici in 1494, a young Mic not yet twenty years old, had left Florence for Ror must have seemed little prospect for him in Floren a Dominican friar, Girolamo Savonarola [jee-moh sav-oh-nah-ROH-lah] (1452–1498), abb monastery of San Marco, wielded tremendou influence. Savonarola appealed, first and forem moralistic faction of the populace that saw, in th of the city's upper classes, and in their humanistic to classical Greek and Roman culture, clear ev moral decadence. Savonarola railed against the nobility—the Medici in particular—going so far nize troops of children to collect the city's "v everything from cosmetics to books and paint burn them in giant bonfires. Finally, in June 1497 Pope Alexander VI excommunicated him for his preachings and for disobeying his directives for t istration of the monastery of San Marco. Savo commanded not to preach, an order he chose to i

CONTINUITY & CHANGE references provide a window into the past. These eye-catching icons enable students to refer to material in other chapters that is relevant to the topic at hand.

Across the Humanities

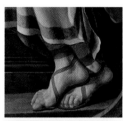
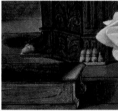
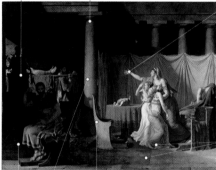

Focus

David's *The Lictors Returning to Brutus the Bodies of His Sons*

The French monarchy commissioned Jacques-Louis David to create *The Lictors Returning to Brutus the Bodies of His Sons*, and it was exhibited in 1789, just six weeks after the storming of the Bastille. As a result, the public closely identified it with the cause of the French republic. The hero of the historical tale that is the subject of this painting is the founder of the Roman republic, Lucius Junius Brutus (6th century BCE; not to be confused with the Brutus who would later assassinate Julius Caesar). He had become head of Rome and inaugurated the republic by eliminating the former monarch, Tarquinius, who had assumed the throne by conspiring with the wife of the former king. She murdered her husband, and he his own wife, and the two married. Brutus's sons had conspired to restore the monarchy—their mother was related to Tarquinius—and under Roman law was required not only to sentence them to death, but to witness the execution.

In David's painting, Brutus sits in shadow at the left, his freshly beheaded sons passing behind him on stretchers carried by his lictors (officers who served rulers). Brutus points at his own head, as if affirming his responsibility for the deed, the sacrifice of family to the patriotic demands of the state. In contrast to the darkened shadows in which Brutus sits, the boys' mother, nurse, and sisters await the bodies in a fully lighted stage space framed by a draperied colonnade. The mother reaches out in a gesture reminiscent of Horatius' in the *Oath of the Horatii*. The nurse turns and buries her head in the mother's robe. One of the sisters appears to faint in her mother's arms, while the other shields her eyes from the terrible sight. Their spotlit anguish emphasizes the human cost of patriotic sacrifice, whereas the *Oath of the Horatii* more clearly celebrates the patriotic sacrifice itself.

This shift in David's emphasis can be at least partly explained by his own biography. Early in 1888, his favorite apprentice, Jean-Germain Drouais, died of smallpox at the age of 25. David was devastated by this loss of one of the best young painters in France. (Drouais was a winner of the Prize of Rome, which sent him to study in that city for five years.) *The Lictors* probably reflects the strength of David's feelings for his young companion.

The **statue of Roma** represents the state and is darkened to suggest the turmoil that Rome is enduring.

The **Doric order** of the architecture underscores the severity of the scene and represents the reasonable and rational order of the Roman republic—the very model of the new French republic about to be born.

David reverses the structure of the *Horatii* by having Brutus' wife extend her hand as Horatius does in the earlier painting. Now the women stand, and the males sit (or lie dead). Female emotion stands triumphant over the demands of reason.

Much of the emotional tension of the painting derives from the contrast between the rigorous scientific perspective of the composition, most explicit in the floor tiles, and the soft, falling curves of the drapes and women's clothing.

The **central column** extends to the top of the painting, separating Brutus from his family and emphasizing the great gulf between them.

The graceful curve that defines the back of the empty chair in front of the central column suggests the powers of human feeling, compassion, and love. The chair is surely Brutus' own, from which he has been exiled.

The relief portraying the legend of the founders of Rome, **Romulus and Remus**, suckled by a wolf suggests how, at its origin, the Roman republic was integrally connected to the importance of family, especially after the rise of Augustus.

Jacques-Louis David. Details from *The Lictors Returning to Brutus the Bodies of His Sons*. 1789. Oil on canvas, 10'7¼" × 13'10¼". Musée du Louvre, Paris. RMN Réunion des Musées Nationaux, France. Gerard Blot/C. Jean/Art Resource, NY. Brutus' emotional exile from his proper place at the table as patriarch is emphasized by the subtle analogy that David draws between Brutus' own toes and the scrolling decoration at the base of the table where once he sat.

Jacques-Louis David. *The Lictors Returning to Brutus the Bodies of His Sons*, 1789. Oil on canvas, 10'7¼" × 13'10¼". Musée du Louvre, Paris. RMN Réunion des Musées Nationaux, France. Gerard Blot/C. Jean/Art Resource, NY.

361

FOCUS Highly visual Focus features offer an in-depth look at a particular work from one of the disciplines of the humanities. These annotated discussions give students a personal tour of the work—with informative captions and labels—to help students understand its meaning.

THE WORKING CLASS AND THE BOURGEOISIE **CHAPTER 13**   389

One of the most important abolitionist texts of the day is the autobiography of Frederick Douglass (1817–1895), *Narrative of the Life of Frederick Douglass: An American Slave*, published in 1845. The book moves from Douglass's first clear memory, the whipping of his Aunt Hester, to the turning point, when as a young man Douglass resolves to stand up and fight his master. "From whence came the spirit I don't know," Douglass writes. "You have seen how a man was made a slave; you shall see how a slave was made a man," he says before summing up the fight's outcome (**Reading 13.3**):

to free territory with their little boy. Tom meets a different fate. Separated from his wife and children, he is sold by his first owner to a kind master, Augustine St. Clare, and then to the evil Simon Legree, who eventually kills him. Serialized in 1851 in the abolitionist newspaper *The National Era*, and published the year after, the book sold 300,000 copies in the first year after its publication. Stowe's depiction of the plight of slaves like Tom roused antislavery sentiment worldwide and it eventually became the bestselling novel of the nineteenth century.

The scene of Little Eva reading from the Bible to Tom (Fig. 13.3) as Stowe sets it up in chapter 22 of the novel is deeply romanticized (**Reading 13.4**):

READING 13.3   **from *Narrative of the Life of Frederick Douglass* (1845)**

This battle with Mr. Covey was the turning point in my career as a slave. It rekindled the few expiring embers of freedom, and revived within me a sense of my own manhood. It . . . inspired me again with a determination to be free. The gratification afforded by the triumph was a full compensation for whatever else might follow, even death itself. . . . I felt as I never felt before. It was a glorious resurrection, from the tomb of slavery, to the heaven of freedom. My long-crushed spirit rose, cowardice departed, bold defiance took its place; and I now resolved that, however long I might remain a slave in form, the day had passed forever when I could be a slave in fact. I did not hesitate to let it be known of me, that the white man who expected to succeed in whipping, must also succeed in killing me.

READING 13.4   **from Harriet Beecher Stowe, *Uncle Tom's Cabin* (1852)**

It is now one of those intensely golden sunsets which kindles the whole horizon into one blaze of glory, and makes the water another sky. The lake lay in rosy or golden streaks, save where white-winged vessels glided hither and thither, like so many spirits, and little golden stars twinkled through the glow, and looked down at themselves as they trembled in the water. . . .

At first, she read to please her humble friend; but soon her own earnest nature threw out its tendrils, and wound itself around the majestic book; and Eva loved it, because it woke in her strange yearnings, and strong, dim emotions, such as impassioned, imaginative children love to feel.

More than 100 book-length slave narratives were published in the 1850s and 1860s. Besides Douglass's, one of the other most important of these was the *Narrative of Sojourner Truth*, dictated by an illiterate former slave to her friend Olive Gilbert. Sojourner Truth (ca. 1797–1883) was born Isabella Baumfree to slave parents in Ulster County, New York, and was sold four times before she was 30 years old. In 1843,

This passage points to a central mission of the abolitionist movement. Abolitionists felt the duty to enlighten the darkened souls of slaves by asserting Christian beliefs. Notice how light is used as a metaphor in the passage. But the condescension apparent to the modern reader—both Tom and Eva are depicted as children—together with Tom's sentimental attachment to both Eva and her pious Christianity would eventually

PRIMARY SOURCE EXCERPTS Each chapter includes short excerpts from important works within the body of the text.

A **CD ICON** calls out musical selections discussed in the text that are found on the supplemental CDs available for use with the text.

sung. One such piece is his 1597 *Canzona Duodecimi Toni* [kan-ZOH-na doo-oh-DAY-chee-me TOH-nee] (*Canzona in C Major*), in which two brass ensembles create a musical dialogue (**CD-Track 10.2**). A **canzona** is a type of instrumental contrapuntal work, derived from Renaissance secular song, like the madrigal, which was increasingly performed in the seventeenth century in church settings. It is particularly notable for its dominant rhythm, LONG-shortshort, known as the "canzona rhythm." In Saint Mark's, the

chord, et
conceive
phonic e
voice an

The i
FAY-oh]
ater. Th
Monteve
[OR-fee-

An Extensive Teaching & Learning Resource Package

PEARSON

myhumanitieskit™

MyHumanitiesKit offers students and instructors a dynamic solution for humanities that can form the basis for an online course, featuring: robust quizzes, critical-thinking questions, image flashcards, Closer Look tours of key works of art, and much more!

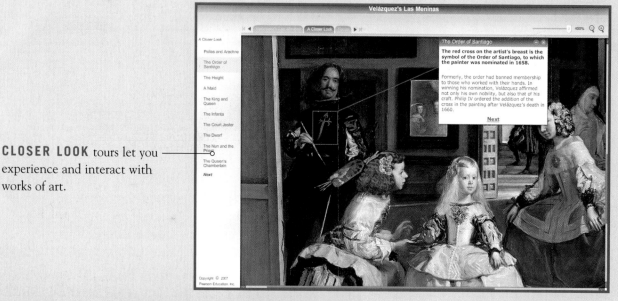

CLOSER LOOK tours let you experience and interact with works of art.

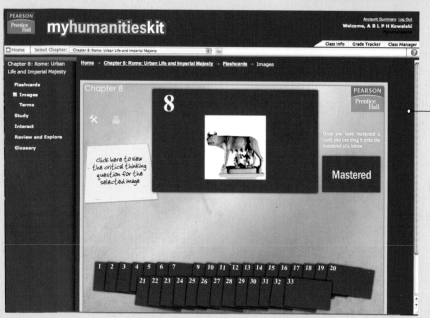

FLASHCARDS for every work of art in the book, with critical-thinking quizzes and print functionality.

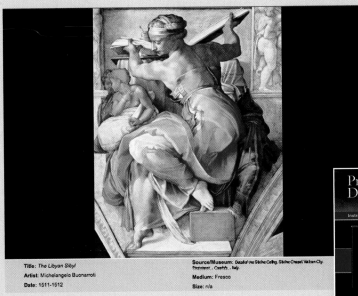

Title: *The Libyan Sibyl*
Artist: Michelangelo Buonarroti
Date: 1511-1512

Source/Museum: Detail of the Sistine Ceiling, Sistine Chapel, Vatican City, Photograph. Copyright. Italy.
Medium: Fresco
Size: n/a

THE PRENTICE HALL DIGITAL ARTS LIBRARY
contains every image in the book in the highest
resolution and pixellation possible for optimal
projections. Each image is available as a customizable
PowerPoint slide or in jpg format. Available to
instructors upon adoption of the book, the Digital Arts
Library also includes video clips for use in classroom
presentations. (ISBN: 978-0-205-67229-5)

Prentice Hall
Digital Arts Library
Instructor DVD Set

CourseSmart *Learn Smart. Choose Smart.* **COURSESMART
TEXTBOOKS ONLINE** is an
exciting new choice for students looking to save money. As
an alternative to purchasing the print textbook, students
can subscribe to the same content online and save up to
50% off the suggested list price of the print text. With a
CourseSmart eTextbook, students can search the text, make
notes online, print out reading assignments that incorporate
lecture notes, and bookmark important passages for later
review. For more information, or to subscribe to the
CourseSmart eTextbook, visit **www.coursesmart.com**

Instructor's Manual & Test Item File
(ISBN: 978-0-205-67235-6) by Nathan Poage,
Houston Community College

MyTest (ISBN: 978-0-205-67234-9) Instructors can
create an online test quickly and easily with MyTest.

Music CD (ISBN: 978-0-205-67232-5) Containing
many of the selections referenced in the text, this CD
is available for a nominal charge.

THE PRENTICE HALL ATLAS OF HUMANITIES
was produced in collaboration with Dorling
Kindersley, the leader in cartographic
publishing, and features the most modern and innovative
map-making techniques to present global history in all its
complexity and diversity. The Atlas can be bundled with
Discovering the Humanities for a nominal charge. Contact your
Pearson Arts and Sciences sales representative for details.
(ISBN: 978-0-13-238628-9)

Titles from the renowned Penguin
Classics series can be packaged at a
significant discount.

Please consult your Pearson representative for details on these and any other resources.

Developing *The Humanities*

The Humanities series is the result of an extensive development process involving the contributions of over one hundred reviewers and their students. We are grateful to all who participated in shaping this text. In particular, we thank the following people who provided input in the creation of *Discovering the Humanities:*

Mindi Bailey, *Collin County Community College*
Peggy Brown, *Collin County Community College*
Terre Burton, *Dixie College*
Elizabeth Cahaney, *Elizabethtown Community and Technical College*
Rick Davis, *Brigham Young University-Idaho*
Christa DiMaio Richie, *Salem Community College*
Tiffany Engel, *Tulsa Community College*
Gabrielle Fennmore, *St. Thomas University*
Michael Fremont Redfield, *Saddleback College*
Nat Hardy, *Savannah State University*

Thelma Ithier-Sterling, *Hostos Community College*
Stuart Kendall, *Eastern Kentucky University*
Maria Miranda, *Hostos Community College*
Nathan Poage, *Houston Community College*
Aditi Samarth, *Richland College*
Cheryl Smart, *Pima Community College*
Lynn Spencer, *Brevard Community College*
Alice Taylor, *West Los Angeles College*
Paul Van Heuklom, *Lincoln Land Community College*
Leila Wells, *Griffin Technical College*
Deborah J. Wickering, *Aquinas College*

Acknowledgments

Discovering the Humanities is a brief version of the larger text *The Humanities: Culture, Continuity and Change* and is inevitably indebted to all who contributed to that first, daunting project. No project of its scope could ever come into being without the hard work and perseverance of many more people than its author. In fact, this author has been humbled by a team at Pearson Prentice Hall that never wavered in its confidence in my ability to finish this enormous undertaking (or if they did, they had the good sense not to let me know); never hesitated to cajole, prod, and massage me to complete the project in something close to on time; and always gave me the freedom to explore new approaches to the materials at hand. At the down-and-dirty level, I am especially grateful to fact checker George Kosar; to Mary Ellen Wilson for the pronunciation guides, as well as the more specialized pronunciations offered by David Atwill (Chinese and Japanese), Jonathan Reynolds (African), Nayla Muntasser (Greek and Latin), and Mark Watson (Native American); to John Sisson for tracking down the readings; to Laurel Corona for her extraordinary help with Africa; and to Francelle Carapetyan and her assistant Rebecca Harris for their remarkable photo research. The maps and some of the line art are the work of cartographer and artist Peter Bull, with Precision Graphic drafting a large portion of the line art for the book. I find both in every way extraordinary.

I was extremely pleased with the look of the larger book, which was the work of Leslie Osher, Associate Director of Design, Nancy Wells, Senior Art Director, and Ximena Tamvakopoulos, designer. *Discovering the Humanities* follows their lead, adding innovative new touches, and I am grateful to Pat Smythe, Senior Art Director, and Laura Gardner, designer, for their inspired approach to keeping the same "look" while making *Discovering the Humanities* distinctive in its own right. The artistic layout of the book was created by Gail Cocker and Wanda España. Gail Cocker coordinated the map and line art program with the help of Mirella

Signoretto. The production of the book was the work of Lisa Iarkowski, Associate Director of Team-based Project Management; and Mary Rottino, Senior Managing Editor. Day-to-day coordination was overseen by the ever-thorough and good-humored Barbara Cappuccio. Brian Mackey, Operations Manager, ensured that this project progressed smoothly through its production route.

The marketing and editorial teams at Prentice Hall are beyond compare. On the marketing side, I have been working for months now marketing the 2-volume version of *The Humanities* with Brandy Dawson Director of Marketing, who has helped me understand what *Discovering the Humanities* should be. She is ably assisted by Kate Mitchell, Senior Marketing Manager, and Kyle VanNatter, Marketing Assistant. Marissa Feliberty, the book's original Executive Marketing Manager, would have jumped at the opportunity to market *Discovering the Humanities*, and I think we all would give anything if she were still with us to have done it. We miss her. On the editorial side, my thanks to Yolanda de Rooy, President of the Humanities and Social Science division; to Sarah Touborg, Editor in Chief; Amber Mackey, Senior Editor; Bud Therien, Special Projects Manager; Alex Huggins, Assistant Editor; and Editorial Assistants Carla Worner and Theresa Graziano. The combined human hours that this group has put into this project are staggering. Deserving of special mention is my development team: Rochelle Diogenes, Editor in Chief of Development; Roberta Meyer, Senior Development Editor; Karen Dubno and Elaine Silverstein; and, for *Discovering the Humanities*, Margaret Manos. Roberta may be the best in the business, and I feel extremely fortunate to have worked with her.

Finally, I want to thank my beautiful wife, Sandy Brooke, who has supported this project in every way. She continued to teach, paint, and write, while urging me on, listening to my struggles, humoring me when I didn't deserve it, and being a far better wife than I was the husband. Without you, Sandy, I couldn't do it. I love you very much.

Dear Reader,

You might be asking yourself, why should I be interested in the humanities? Why do I care about ancient Egypt, medieval France, or the Qing Dynasty of China?

I asked myself the same question when I was a sophomore in college. I was required to take a year-long survey of the humanities, and I soon realized that I was beginning an extraordinary journey. That course taught me where it was that I stood in the world, and why and how I had come to find myself there. My goal in this book is to help you take the same journey of discovery. Exploring the humanities will help you develop your abilities to look, listen, and read closely; and to analyze, connect, and question. In the end, this will help you navigate your world and come to a better understanding of your place in it.

What we see reflected in different cultures is something of ourselves, the objects of beauty and delight, the weapons and wars, the melodies and harmonies, the sometimes troubling but always penetrating thought from which we spring. To explore the humanities is to explore ourselves, to understand how and why we have changed over time, even as we have, in so many ways, remained the same.

About the Author

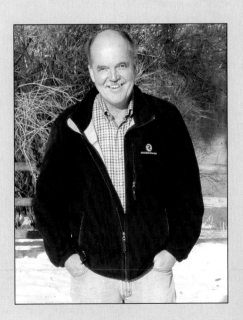

Henry M. Sayre is Distinguished Professor of Art History at Oregon State University–Cascades Campus in Bend, Oregon. He earned his Ph.D. in American Literature from the University of Washington. He is producer and creator of the 10-part television series, *A World of Art: Works in Progress*, aired on PBS in the fall of 1997; and author of seven books, including *A World of Art*, *The Visual Text of William Carlos Williams*, *The Object of Performance: The American Avant-Garde since 1970*; and an art history book for children, *Cave Paintings to Picasso*.

1 The Prehistoric Past

The River Cultures of the Ancient World

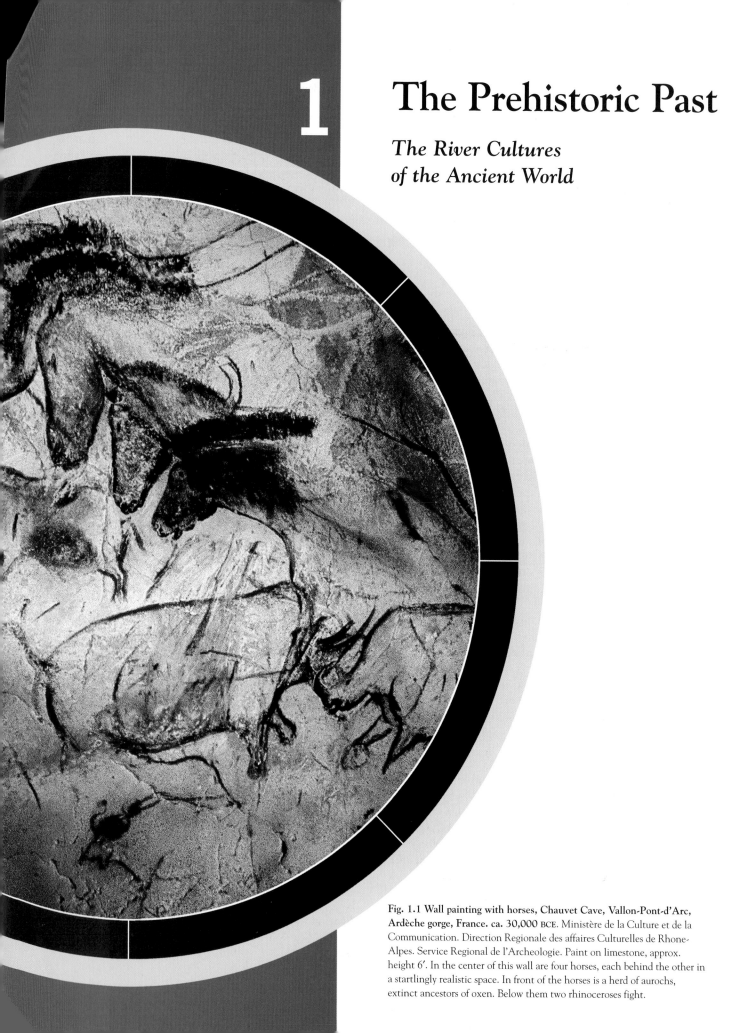

Fig. 1.1 Wall painting with horses, Chauvet Cave, Vallon-Pont-d'Arc, Ardèche gorge, France. ca. 30,000 BCE. Ministère de la Culture et de la Communication. Direction Regionale des affaires Culturelles de Rhone-Alpes. Service Regional de l'Archeologie. Paint on limestone, approx. height 6′. In the center of this wall are four horses, each behind the other in a startlingly realistic space. In front of the horses is a herd of aurochs, extinct ancestors of oxen. Below them two rhinoceroses fight.

> *Yes, indeed. In this world there was no one at all. Always the sun came up; always he went in. No one in the morning gave him sacred meal; no one gave him prayer sticks; it was very lonely.*
>
> *A Zuni Emergence Tale*

On a cold December afternoon in 1994, Jean-Marie Chauvet [shoh-veh] and two friends were exploring the caves in the steep cliffs along the Ardèche River gorge in southern France. After descending into a series of narrow passages, they entered a large chamber. There, beams from their headlamps lit up a group of drawings that would astonish the three explorers—and the world (Fig. 1.1).

Since the late nineteenth century we've known that prehistoric people drew on the walls of caves. Twenty-seven such caves had already been discovered in the cliffs along the 17 miles of the Ardèche gorge. But the cave found by Chauvet and his friends transformed our thinking about prehistoric peoples, peoples who lived before the time of writing and so of recorded history. This cave contains by far the most accomplished prehistoric cave drawings ever discovered. We can only speculate that other great artworks were produced in prehistoric times but have not survived, perhaps because they were made of wood or other perishable materials. It is even possible that art may have been made earlier than 30,000 years ago, perhaps as people began to inhabit the Near East, between 90,000 and 100,000 years ago.

At first, during the Paleolithic [PAY-lee-uh-LITH-ik] era, or "Old Stone Age," from the Greek *palaios*, "old," and *lithos*, "stone," the cultures of Europe sustained themselves on game and wild plants. The cultures themselves were small, scattered, and nomadic, though evidence suggests some interaction among the various groups. As the ice covering the Northern Hemisphere began to recede around 10,000 BCE, agriculture began to replace hunting and gathering, and with it, a nomadic lifestyle gave way to a more sedentary way of life. The consequences of this shift were enormous, and ushered in the Neolithic [nee-uh-LITH-ik] era, or "New Stone Age."

In the great river valleys of the Middle East and Asia (Map 1.1), distinct centers of people involved in a common pursuit began to form more and more sophisticated civilizations. A **civilization** is a social, economic, and political entity distinguished by the ability to express itself through images and written language. Civilizations develop when the environment of a region can support a large and productive population. An increasing population requires increased production of food and other goods, not only to support itself, but to trade for other commodities. Organizing this level of trade and production also requires an administrative elite to form and to establish priorities. The existence of such an elite is another characteristic of civilization. Finally, as the history of cultures around the world makes abundantly clear, one of the major ways that societies have acquired the goods they want and simultaneously organized themselves is by means of war.

We begin this book, then, with the first inklings of civilized cultures in prehistoric times, evidence of which survives in wall paintings in caves and small sculptures dating back more than 25,000 years. Before the invention of writing sometime after 10,000 BCE, these cultures created myths and legends that explained their origins and relation to the world. Then, beginning about 4000 BCE, across the ancient world, the science of metallurgy developed. As people learned to separate metals from their ores and then work or treat them to create objects, the stone and bone tools and weapons of the prehistoric world were replaced by metal ones, inaugurating the era archeologists have named the Bronze Age.

The Beginnings of Culture

A **culture** encompasses the values and behaviors shared by a group of people, developed over time, and passed down from one generation to the next. Culture manifests itself in the laws, customs, ritual behavior, and artistic production common to the group. The cave paintings at Chauvet suggest that, as early as 30,000 years ago, the Ardèche gorge was a center of culture, a focal point of group living in which the values of a community find expression. There were others like it: In northern Spain, the first decorated cave was discovered in 1879 at Altamira [al-tuh-MIR-uh]. In the Dordogne [dor-DOHN] region of southern France to the west of the Ardèche, schoolchildren discovered the famous Lascaux cave in 1940 when their dog disappeared down a hole (Fig. 1.2). And in 1991, along the French Mediterranean coast, a diver discovered the entrance to the beautifully decorated Cosquer [kos-KAIR] cave below the waterline near Marseille [mar-SAY].

1

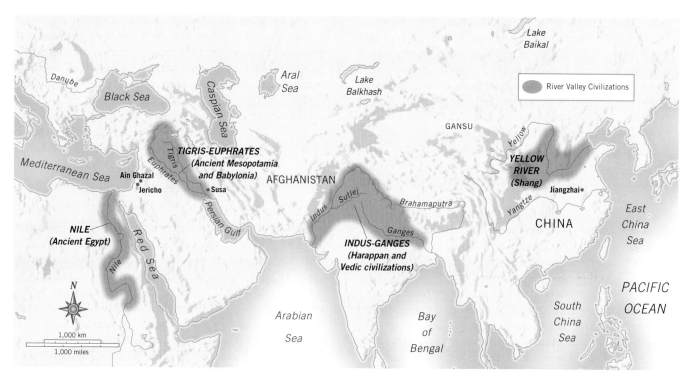

Map 1.1 The Great River Valley Civilizations, ca. 2000 BCE. Agriculture thrived in the great river valleys throughout the Neolithic era, but by the end of the period, urban life had developed there as well, and civilization as we know it had emerged.

Agency and Ritual: Cave Art

Ever since cave paintings were first discovered, scholars have been marveling at the skill of the people who produced them, but we have been equally fascinated by their very existence. Why were these paintings made? Until recently, it was generally accepted that such works were associated with the hunt. Perhaps the hunter, seeking game in times of scarcity, hoped to conjure it up by depicting it on cave walls. Or perhaps such drawings were magic charms meant to ensure a successful hunt. But at Chauvet, fully 60 percent of the animals painted on its walls were never, or rarely, hunted—such animals as lions, rhinoceroses, bears, panthers, and woolly mammoths. One drawing even depicts two rhinoceroses fighting horn to horn beneath four horses that appear to be looking on (See Fig. 1.1).

What role, then, did these drawings play in the daily lives of the people who created them? The caves may have been understood as gateways to the underworld and death, as symbols of the womb and birth, or as pathways to the world of dreams experienced in the dark of night. The general arrangement of the animals in the paintings by species or gender, often in distinct chambers of the caves, suggests to some that the paintings may have served as calendars for predicting the seasonal migration of the animals. Whatever the case, surviving human footprints indicate that these caves were ritual gathering places and in some way served the common good.

Fig. 1.2 Wall painting with bird-headed man, bison, and rhinoceros, Lascaux Cave, Dordogne, France. ca. 15,000–13,000 BCE. Paint on limestone, length approx. 9′. In 1963 Lascaux was closed to the public so that conservators could fight a fungus attacking the paintings. Most likely, the fungus was caused by carbon dioxide exhaled by visitors. An exact replica called Lascaux II was built and can be visited.

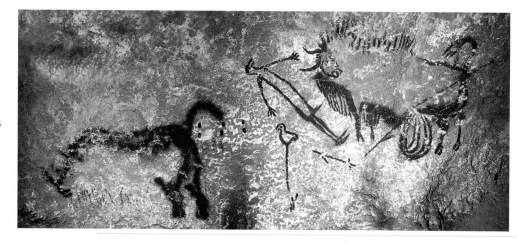

At Chauvet, the use of color suggests that the paintings served some sacred or symbolic function. For instance, almost all of the paintings near the entrance to the cave are painted with natural red pigments derived from ores rich in iron oxide. Deeper in the cave, in areas more difficult to reach, the vast majority of the animals are painted in black pigments derived from ores rich in manganese dioxide. This shift in color appears to be intentional, but we can only guess its meaning.

The skillfully drawn images at Chauvet raise even more important questions. The artists seem to have understood and practiced a kind of **perspectival drawing**—that is, they were able to convey a sense of three-dimensional space on a two-dimensional surface. In the painting reproduced on the opening page of this chapter, several horses appear to stand one behind the other (see Fig. 1.1). The head of the top horse overlaps a black line, as if peering over a branch or the back of another animal. In no other cave yet discovered do drawings show the use of shading, or **modeling**, so that the horses' heads seem to have volume and dimension. And yet these cave paintings, rendered over 30,000 years ago, predate other cave paintings by at least 10,000 years, and in some cases by as much as 20,000 years.

One of the few cave paintings that depict a human figure is found at Lascaux. What appears to be a male wearing a bird's-head mask lies in front of a disemboweled bison (Fig. 1.2). Below him is a bird-headed spear thrower, a device that enabled hunters to throw a spear farther and with greater force. (Several examples of spear throwers have survived.) In the Lascaux painting, the hunter's spear has pierced the bison's hindquarters, and a rhinoceros charges off to the left. We have no way of knowing whether this depicts an actual event or an imagined scene. One of the painting's most interesting and inexplicable features is the discrepancy between the relatively naturalistic representation of the animals and the highly stylized, almost abstract realization of the human figure. Was the sticklike man added later by a different, less talented artist? Or does this discrepancy suggest that man and beast are different orders of being?

It is unlikely that the work was meant to be purely decorative or ornamental. It almost certainly possessed some form of agency—that is, it was created to exert some power or authority over those who came into contact with it. Again, footprints indicate it was almost certainly part of some larger ritual activity that took place in the cave itself.

Before the discovery at Chauvet, historians divided the history of cave painting into a series of successive styles, each progressively more realistic. But Chauvet's paintings, by far the oldest known, are also the most advanced in their realism, and seem to result from a conscious quest for visual **naturalism**, that is, for representations that imitate the actual appearance of the animals. Not only were both red and black animals outlined, their shapes were also modeled by spreading paint, either with the hand or a tool, in gradual gradations of color. Such modeling is extremely rare elsewhere. In addition, the artists further defined many of the animals' contours by scraping the wall behind so that the beasts seem to stand out against a deeper white ground. Three handprints in the cave were evidently made by spitting paint at a hand placed on the cave wall, resulting in a stenciled image.

Art, the Chauvet drawings suggest, does not necessarily evolve in a linear progression from awkward beginnings to more sophisticated representations. On the contrary, already in the earliest artworks people obtained a very high degree of sophistication. Apparently, even in the earliest times, human beings could choose to represent the world naturalistically or not, and the choice not to represent the world in naturalistic terms should not necessarily be attributed to lack of skill or sophistication but to other, more culturally driven factors.

Paleolithic Culture and Its Artifacts

Footprints discovered in South Africa in 2000 and fossilized remains uncovered in the forest of Ethiopia in 2001 suggest that, about 5.7 million years ago, the earliest upright humans, or hominins (as distinct from the larger classification of hominids, which includes great apes and chimpanzees as well as humans), roamed the continent of Africa. Ethiopian excavations further indicate that some time around 2.5 or 2.6 million years ago hominid populations began to make rudimentary stone tools, though long before, between 14 million and 19 million years ago, the *Kenyapithecus* [ken-yuh-PITH-i-kus] ("Kenyan ape"), a hominin, made stone tools in east central Africa. Nevertheless, the earliest evidence of a culture coming into being are the stone artifacts of *Homo sapiens* [ho-moh SAY-pee-uhnz] (Latin for "one who knows"). *Homo sapiens* evolved about 100,000–120,000 years ago and can be distinguished from earlier hominids by the lighter build of their skeletal structure and larger brain. This species gradually spread out of Africa, across Asia, into Europe, and finally to Australia and the Americas.

Homo sapiens were **hunter-gatherers**, whose survival depended on the animals they could kill and the foods they could gather, primarily nuts, berries, and other edible plants. The tools they developed were far more sophisticated than those of their ancestors. They included cleavers, chisels, grinders, hand axes, and arrow- and spearheads made of flint, a material that also provided the spark to create an equally important tool—fire. In 2004, Israeli archeologists working at a site on the banks of the Jordan River reported the earliest evidence yet found of controlled fire created by hominids—cracked and blackened flint chips, presumably used to light a fire, and bits of charcoal dating from 790,000 years ago. Also at the campsite were the bones of elephant, rhino, hippo, and small species, demonstrating that these early hominids cut their meat with flint tools and ate steaks and marrow. Homo sapiens cooked with fire, wore animal skins as clothing, and used tools as a matter of course. They buried their dead in ritual ceremonies, often laying them to rest accompanied by stone tools and weapons.

The Paleolithic era is the period of *Homo sapiens'* ascendancy. These Paleolithic people carved stone tools and weapons that helped them survive in an inhospitable climate. They carved small sculptural objects as well, which, along with the cave paintings we have already seen, appear to be the first instances of what we have come to call "art." Among the most remarkable of these sculptural artifacts are a large number of female figures, found at various archeological sites across Europe. The most famous of these is the limestone statuette of a *Woman* found at Willendorf [VIL-un-dorf], in modern Austria (Fig. **1.3**), dating from about 22,000 to 21,000 BCE and often called the *Willendorf Venus*. Markings on the *Woman* and other similar figures indicate that they were originally colored, but what these small sculptures meant and what they were used for remains unclear. Most are 4 to 5 inches high and fit neatly into a person's hand. They may have had a ritual purpose. Their exaggerated breasts and bellies and their clearly delineated genitals suggest a connection to fertility and childbearing. We know, too, that the *Woman* from Willendorf was originally painted in red ochre, suggestive of menses. And, her navel is not carved; rather, it is a natural indentation in the stone. Whoever carved her seems to have perceived, in the raw stone, a connection to the origins of life. But such figures may have served other purposes as well. Perhaps they were dolls, guardian figures, or images of beauty and well-being in a cold, hostile world where having body fat might have made the difference between survival and death.

Female figurines vastly outnumber representations of males in the Paleolithic era, which suggests that women played a central role in Paleolithic culture. Most likely, they had considerable religious and spiritual influence, and their preponderance in the imagery of the era suggests that Paleolithic culture may have been *matrilineal* [mat-rih-LIN-ee-ul] (in which descent is determined through the female line) and matrilocal (in which residence is in the female's tribe or household). Such traditions exist in many primal societies today.

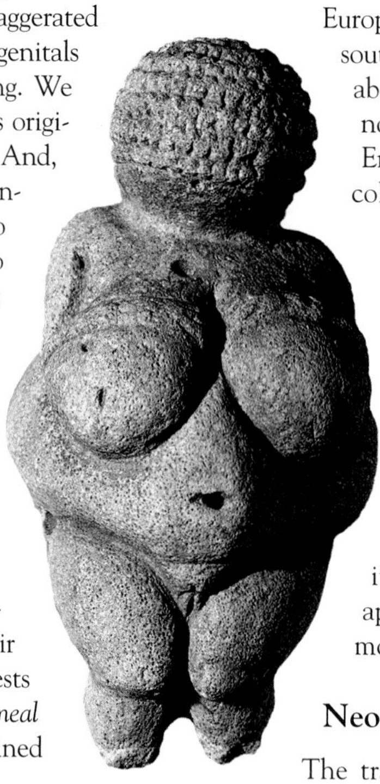

The Rise of Agriculture

For 2,000 years, from 10,000 to 8000 BCE, the ice covering the Northern Hemisphere receded farther and farther northward. As temperatures warmed, life gradually changed. During this period of transition, areas once covered by vast regions of ice and snow developed into grassy plains and abundant forests. As the ice melted, the seas rose, covering, for instance, the cave entrance at Cosquer, filling what is now the North Sea and English Channel with water, and inundating the land bridge that had connected Asia and North America. Hunters developed the bow and arrow, which were easier to use at longer range on the open plains. They fashioned dugout boats out of logs to facilitate fishing, which became a major food source. They domesticated dogs to help with the hunt as early as 11,000 BCE, and soon other animals as well—goats and cattle particularly. Perhaps most important, people began to cultivate the more edible grasses. Along the eastern shore of the Mediterranean they harvested wheat, in Asia they cultivated millet and rice, and in the Americas they grew

Fig. 1.3 *Woman (Venus of Willendorf)*, found at Willendorf, Austria. ca. 25,000–20,000 BCE. Limestone, height 4″. Naturhistorisches Museum, Vienna. For many years, modern scholars called this small statue the *Venus of Willendorf*. They assumed that its carvers attributed to it an ideal of female beauty comparable to the Roman ideal of beauty implied by the name Venus.

squash, beans, and corn. Gradually, farming replaced hunting as the primary means of sustaining life. A culture of the fields developed—an agri-culture, from the Latin *ager*, "farm," "field," or "productive land."

The rise of agricultural society defines the Neolithic era. Beginning in about 8000 BCE, Neolithic culture concentrated in the great river valleys of the Middle East and Asia; gradually, as the climate warmed, Neolithic culture spread across Europe. By about 5000 BCE, the valleys of Spain and southern France supported agriculture, but not until about 4000 BCE is there evidence of farming in the northern reaches of the European continent and England. The Neolithic era does not end in these colder climates until about 2000 BCE.

Meanwhile, the great rivers of the Middle East and Asia provided a consistent and predictable source of water, and people soon developed irrigation techniques that fostered organized agriculture and animal husbandry. As production outgrew necessity, members of the community were freed to occupy themselves in other endeavors—complex food preparation (bread, cheese, and so on), construction, religion, even military affairs. Soon permanent villages began to appear, and villages began to look more and more like cities.

Neolithic Pottery

The transition from cultures based on hunting and fishing to cultures based on agriculture led to the increased use of pottery vessels. Ceramic vessels are fragile, so hunter-gatherers would not have found them practical for carrying food, but people living in the more permanent Neolithic settlements could have used them to carry and store water and to prepare and store certain types of food.

Some of the most remarkable Neolithic painted pottery comes from Susa [soo-suh], on the Iranian plateau. The patterns on one particular beaker (Fig. **1.4**) from around 5000–4000 BCE are highly stylized animals. The largest of these is an ibex, a popular decorative feature of prehistoric ceramics from Iran. Associated with the hunt, the ibex may have been a symbol of plenty. The front and hind legs of the ibex are rendered by two triangles, the tail hangs behind it like a feather, the head is oddly disconnected from the body, and the horns rise in a large, exaggerated arc to encircle a decorative circular form. Hounds race around the band above the ibex, and wading birds form a decorative band across the beaker's top.

In Europe, the production of pottery apparently developed some time later, around 3000 BCE. By this time, the potter's wheel was in use in the Middle East as well as China. A machine

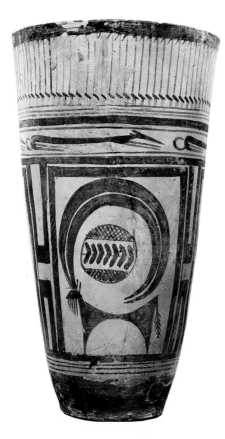

Fig. 1.4 Beaker with ibex, dogs, and long-necked birds, from Susa, southwest Iran. ca. 5000–4000 BCE. Baked clay with painted decoration, height 11¼″. Musée du Louvre, Paris. The ibex was the most widely hunted game in the ancient Middle East, which probably accounts for its centrality in this design.

created expressly to produce goods, the potter's wheel represents the first mechanical and technological breakthrough in history. As skilled individuals specialized in making and decorating pottery, and traded their wares for other goods and services, the characteristic elements of manufacturing began to emerge.

The Neolithic Megaliths of Northern Europe

A distinctive kind of monumental stone architecture appeared late in the Neolithic period, particularly in what is now Britain and France. Known as **megaliths** [MEG-uh-liths], or "big stones," these works were constructed without the use of mortar and represent the most basic form of architectural construction. Although scholars disagree about their significance, there can be no doubt that megaliths were designed to be permanent structures, where domestic architecture was not. Quite possibly the megaliths stood in tribute to the authority of the leaders responsible for assembling and maintaining the considerable labor force required to construct them.

Perhaps the most famous type of megalithic structure is the **cromlech** [krahm-lek], from the Celtic *crom*, "circle," and *lech*, "place." Without doubt the most famous megalithic structure in the world is the cromlech known as Stonehenge (Fig. **1.5**), on Salisbury Plain, about 100 miles west of modern London. A henge is a special type of cromlech, a circle surrounded by a ditch with built-up embankments, presumably for fortification.

The site at Stonehenge reflects four major building periods, extending from about 2750 to 1500 BCE. By about 2100 BCE, most of the elements visible today were in place. In the middle was a U-shaped arrangement of five post-and-lintel trilithons. The one

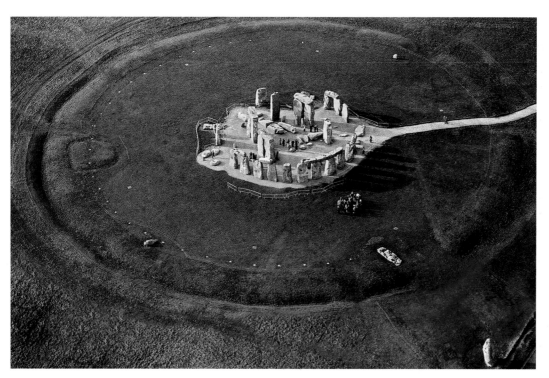

Fig. 1.5 Stonehenge, Salisbury Plain, Wiltshire, England. ca. 2750–1500 BCE. Like most Neolithic sites, Stonehenge invites speculation about its significance. Of this, however, we are certain: At the summer solstice, the longest day of the year, the sun rises directly over the Heel Stone, which stands just outside the outer banks of the site, near the bottom right hand corner of this photograph. This suggests that the site was intimately connected to the movement of the sun.

at the bottom of the U stands taller than the rest, rising to a height of 24 feet, with a 15-foot lintel 3 feet thick. A continuous circle of sandstone posts, each weighing up to 50 tons and all standing 20 feet high, surrounded the five trilithons. Across their top was a continuous lintel 106 feet in diameter. This is the Sarsen Circle. Just inside the Sarsen Circle was once another circle, made of bluestone—a bluish-colored dolorite—found only in the mountains of southern Wales, some 120 miles away.

Why Stonehenge was constructed remains a mystery, although its orientation toward the rising sun at the summer solstice connects it to planting and the harvest. Stonehenge reflects the growing importance of agricultural production in the northern reaches of Europe. Perhaps great rituals celebrating the earth's plenty took place here. Together with other megalithic structures of the era, it shows that the late Neolithic peoples were social beings, capable of great cooperation. They worked together not only to find the giant stones that rise at the site, but also to quarry, transport, and raise them. In other words, theirs was a culture of some magnitude and no small skill. It was a culture capable of both solving great problems and organizing itself in the name of creating a great social center. For Stonehenge is, above all, a center of culture. Its fascination for us today lies in the fact that we know so little of the culture that left it behind.

Neolithic Cultures of the Americas

Seventeen thousand years ago, about the time that the hunter-gatherers at Lascaux painted its caves, the Atlantic and Pacific oceans were more than 300 feet below modern levels, exposing a low-lying continental shelf that extended from northeastern Asia to North America. It was a landscape of grasslands and marshes, home to the woolly mammoth, the steppe bison, wild horses, caribou, and antelope. At some point around 15,000 BCE, bands of hunter-gatherers in northeastern Asia followed these animals across the grasslands land bridge into the Americas. By 12,000 BCE, prehistoric hunters had settled across North America and begun to move farther south, through Mesoamerica (the region extending from central Mexico to northern Central America), and on into South America, reaching the southern end of Chile no later than 11,000 BCE.

Around 9000 BCE, for reasons that are still hotly debated—perhaps a combination of over-hunting and climatic change—the peoples of the Americas developed agricultural societies. They domesticated animals—turkeys, guinea pigs, dogs, and llamas, though never a beast of burden as in the rest of the world—and they cultivated a whole new range of plants, including corn, beans, squash, tomatoes, avocados, potatoes, tobacco, and cacao, the source of chocolate. The wheel remained unknown to them, though they learned to adapt to almost every conceivable climate and landscape.

The Anasazi and the Role of Myth

A **myth** is a story that a culture assumes is true. It also embodies the culture's views and beliefs about its world, often serving to explain otherwise mysterious natural phenomena.

Myths stand apart from scientific explanations of the nature of reality, but as a mode of understanding and explanation, myth has been one of the most important forces driving the development of culture. Although myths are speculative, they are not pure fantasy. They are grounded in observed experience. They serve to rationalize the unknown and to explain to people the nature of the universe and their place within it.

Much of our understanding of the role of myth in prehistoric cultures comes from stories that have survived in cultures around the world that developed without writing—that is, **oral cultures**—such as the Oceanic [oh-shee-AN-ik] peoples of Tahiti in the South Pacific. These cultures have passed down their myths and histories over the centuries, from generation to generation, by word of mouth. Although, chronologically speaking, many of these cultures are contemporaneous with the medieval, Renaissance, and even modern cultures of the West, they are actually closer to the Neolithic cultures in terms of social practice and organization. Oceanic cultures are a case in point. Another is the Anasazi [ah-nuh-SAH-zee] culture of North America.

The Anasazi people thrived in the American Southwest from about 900 to 1300 CE, a time roughly contemporaneous with the late Middle Ages in Europe. They left us no written record of their culture, only ruins and artifacts. At Mesa Verde [may-suh vurd-ee], in what is today southwestern Colorado, their cliff dwellings (Fig. **1.6**) resemble many of the Neolithic cities of the Middle East, such as Ain Ghazal [ine gah-zahl] ("spring of the gazelles"), just outside what is now Amman, Jordan. Though Ain Ghazal flourished from about 7200 to 5000 BCE, thousands of years before the Mesa Verde community, both complexes were constructed with stone walls sealed with a layer of mud plaster. Their roofs were made of wooden beams cross-layered with smaller twigs and branches and sealed with mud. Like other Neolithic cultures, the Anasazi were accomplished in pottery making, decorating their creations with elaborately abstract, largely geometric shapes and patterns. As William M. Ferguson and Arthur H. Rohn, two prominent scholars of the Anasazi, have described them: "They were a Neolithic people without a beast of burden, the wheel, metal, or a written language, yet they constructed magnificent masonry housing and ceremonial structures, irrigation works, and water impoundments."

The Anasazi abandoned their communities in the late thirteenth century, perhaps because of a great drought that lasted from about 1276 to 1299. Their descendants are the Pueblo [PWEB-loh] peoples of the Southwest today, including the Hopi [HO-pee] and the Zuni [ZOO-nee]. (Anasazi is in fact a Navajo word meaning "enemy ancestors"—we do not know what the Anasazi called themselves.) What is remarkable about the Pueblo peoples, who despite the fact that they speak several different languages share a remarkably common culture, is that many aspects of their culture have survived and are practiced today much as they were in ancient times. For all Pueblo peoples, the village is not just the center of culture but the very center of the world. And at the center of the village is the **kiva** [KEE-vuh], a partly underground ceremonial enclosure that dates back to Anasazi times, with a hole in the floor that symbolizes the emergence of the people from the underworld.

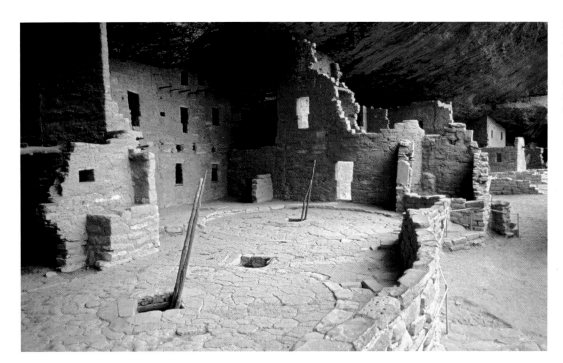

Fig. 1.6 **Spruce Tree House, Mesa Verde. Anasazi culture. ca. 1200–1300 CE.** The courtyard was formed by the restoration of the roofs over two underground kivas.

Zuni Pueblo Emergence Tales The Pueblos have maintained the active practice of their ancient Anasazi religious rites and ceremonies, which they have chosen not to share with outsiders. Most do not allow their ceremonial dances to be photographed. These dance performances tell stories that relate to the experiences of the Pueblo peoples, from planting, hunting, and fishing in daily life, to the larger experiences of birth, puberty, maturity, and death. Still other stories explain the origin of the world, the emergence of a particular Pueblo people into the world, and their history. Most Pueblo people believe that they originated in the womb of Mother Earth and, like seeds sprouting from the soil in the springtime, were called out into the daylight by their Sun Father. This belief about origins is embodied in a type of narrative known as an **emergence tale**, a form of creation myth (**Reading 1.1**).

READING 1.1   **Zuni Emergence Tale, *Talk Concerning the First Beginning***

Yes, indeed. In this world there was no one at all. Always the sun came up; always he went in. No one in the morning gave him sacred meal; no one gave him prayer sticks; it was very lonely. He said to his two children: "You will go into the fourth womb. Your fathers, your mothers, kä-eto·we, tcu-eto·we, mu-eto·we, le-eto·we, all the society priests, society pekwins, society bow priests, you will bring out yonder into the light of your sun father."

So begins this emergence tale, which embodies the fundamental principles of Zuni religious society. The Zuni, or "Sun People," are organized into groups, each responsible for a particular aspect of the community's well-being, and each group is represented by a particular *-eto·we*, or fetish, connecting it to its spiritual foundation in the Earth's womb. The pekwins alluded to here are sun priests who control the ritual calendar. Bow priests oversee warfare and social behavior. In return for corn and breath given them by the Sun Father, the Zuni offer him cornmeal and downy feathers attached to painted prayer sticks symbolizing both clouds—the source of rain—and breath itself. Later in the tale the two children of the Sun Father bring everyone out into the daylight for the first time:

Into the daylight of their sun father they came forth standing. Just as early dawn they came forth. After they came forth there they set down their sacred possessions in a row. The two said, "Now after a little while when your sun father comes forth standing to his sacred place you will see him face to face. Do not close your eyes." Thus he said to them. After a little while the sun came out. When he came out they looked at him. From their eyes the tears rolled down. After they had looked at him, in a little while their eyes became strong. "Alas!" Thus they said. They were covered all over with slime. With slimy tails and slimy horns, with webbed fingers, they saw one another. "Oh dear! is this what we look like? Thus they said.

Then they could not tell which was which of their sacred possessions.

From this point on in the tale, the people and priests, led by the two children, seek to find the sacred "middle place," where things are balanced and orderly. Halona-Itiwana [ha-LOH-nah it-ee-WAH-nah] it is called, the sacred name of the Zuni Pueblo, "the Middle Ant Hill of the World." In the process they are transformed from indeterminate, salamander-like creatures into their ultimate human form, and their world is transformed from chaos to order.

At the heart of the Zuni emergence tale is a moment when, to the dismay of their parents, many children are transformed into water-creatures—turtles, frogs, and the like—and the parents are instructed to throw these children back into the river. Here they become *katcinas* [kuh-CHEE-nuhs] or *katcinas*, deified spirits, who explain:

> "Do not worry." We have not perished. In order to remain thus forever we stay here. To Itiwana but one day's travel remains. Therefore we stay nearby.... Whenever the waters are exhausted and the seeds are exhausted you will send us prayer sticks. Yonder at the place of our first beginning with them we shall bend over to speak to them. Thus there will not fail to be waters. Therefore we shall stay quietly nearby.

The Pueblo believe that kachina spirits manifest themselves in performance and dance. Masked male dancers impersonate the kachinas, taking on their likeness as well as their supernatural character. Through these dance visits the kachinas, although always "nearby," can exercise their powers for the good of the people. The nearly 250 kachina personalities embody clouds, rain, crops, animals, and even ideas such as growth and fertility. Although kachina figurines (Fig. 1.7) are made for sale as art objects, particularly by the Hopi, the actual masks worn in ceremonies are not considered art objects by the Pueblo people. Rather, they are thought of as active agents in the transfer of power and knowledge between the gods and the men who wear them in dance, just like the African Baule mask. In fact, kachina dolls made for sale are considered empty of any ritual power or significance.

Pueblo emergence tales, and the ritual practices that accompany them, reflect the general beliefs of most Neolithic peoples. These include the following:

- belief that the forces of nature are inhabited by living spirits, which we call **animism**
- belief that nature's behavior can be compared to human behavior (we call the practice of investing plants, animals, and natural phenomena with human form or attributes **anthropomorphism**), thus explaining what otherwise would remain inexplicable
- belief that humans can communicate with the spirits of nature, and that, in return for a sacrificial offering or a prayer, the gods might intercede on their behalf.

A culture's religion—that is, its understanding of the divine—is thus closely tied to and penetrated by mythical elements. Its beliefs, as embodied in its religion, stories, and myths, were closely tied to seasonal celebrations and agricultural production—planting and harvest in particular, as well as

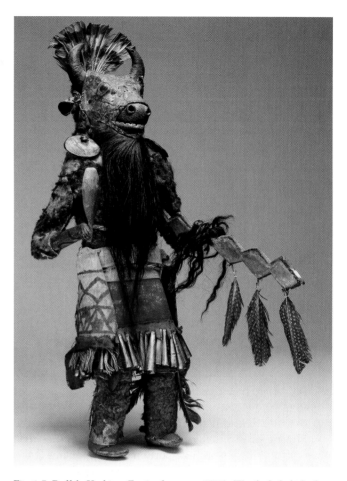

Fig. 1.7 Buffalo Kachina. Zuni culture. ca. 1875. Wood, cloth, hide, fur, shell, feathers, horsehair, tin cones. © Millicent Rogers Museum, Taos, New Mexico. The Buffalo Kachina is designed to increase the population of fur-bearing animals in the arid environment of the Southwest. Derived from a Plains Indian ritual dance, it was first danced by the Zuni near the end of the nineteenth century as the region's wildlife was becoming increasingly threatened.

rain—the success of which was understood to be inextricably linked to the well-being of the community. In a fundamental sense, myths reflect the community's ideals, its history (hence, the preponderance of creation myths among ancient societies), and its aspirations. Myths also tend to mirror the culture's moral and political systems, its social organization, and its most fundamental beliefs. They are not fanciful misconceptions about the nature of things; rather, they are reasonably accurate reflections of what a culture believes itself to be.

Mesopotamia: Power and Social Order in the Fertile Crescent

In September 1922, the British archeologist C. Leonard Woolley boarded a steamer, beginning a journey that would take him to Iraq. There, Woolley and his team would discover one of the richest treasure troves in the history of archeology in the ruins of the ancient city of Ur. Woolley concentrated his energies on the burial grounds surrounding the city's central ziggurat [ZIG-uh-rat], a pyramidal temple structure consisting of successive platforms with outside staircases and a shrine at the top (Figs. **1.8, 1.9**). Digging there in the winter of 1927, he unearthed a series of tombs with several rooms, many bodies, and spectacular objects. With the same sense of excitement that was felt by Jean-Marie Chauvet and her companions when they first saw the paintings on the wall of Chauvet cave, Woolley was careful to keep what he called the "royal tombs" secret. On January 4, 1928, he telegrammed his colleagues in Latin. Translated to English it read:

> I found the intact tomb, stone built, and vaulted over with bricks of queen Shubad [later known as Puabi] adorned with a dress in which gems, flower crowns and animal figures are woven. Tomb magnificent with jewels and golden cups.
>
> —Woolley

He had found masses of golden objects—vessels, crowns, necklaces, statues, and weapons—as well as jewelry and lyres made of electrum and the deep blue stone, lapis lazuli. The find was worldwide news for years.

Archeologists and historians were especially excited by Woolley's discoveries, because they opened a window onto the larger region we call Mesopotamia [mes-uh-po-TAY-mee-uh], the land between the Tigris [TIE-gris] and Euphrates [you-FRAY-teez] rivers. Ur was one of 30 or 40 cities that arose in Sumeria, the southern portion of Mesopotamia (Map **1.2**). Its people abandoned Ur more than 2,000 years ago, when the Euphrates changed its course away from the city.

Sumerian Ur

Ur is not the oldest city to occupy the southern plains of Mesopotamia, the region known as Sumer [SOO-mur]. That distinction belongs to Uruk [oo-RUK], just to the north, and Eridu [ER-uh-doo] to the south. Surviving literary fragments suggest that Eridu was defeated by Uruk sometime after 3400 BCE. By 3100 BCE, at any rate, the people of Uruk (modern Warka [wur-KA], Iraq) had erected two large temple complexes, one dedicated to Inanna [in-NAH-nah], the goddess of fertility and heaven, and another to Anu [AH-noo], the god of the sky. But the temple structure at Ur is of particular note because it is the most fully preserved and restored.

The Ziggurat at Ur The **ziggurat** at Ur (Figs. 1.8–1.9) was most likely designed to evoke the mountains surrounding the river valley, which were the source of the water that flowed through the two rivers and, so, the source of life. Topped by a sanctuary, the ziggurat might also have symbolized the bridge between heaven and earth. Woolley, who supervised the reconstruction of the first platform and stairway of the ziggurat at Ur, speculated that the platforms of the temple were originally not paved but covered with soil and planted with trees. The rainwater used to irrigate these trees would have flowed into the interior of the ziggurat and exited through a series of weeper-holes, venting ducts loosely filled with broken pottery, in the side of the ziggurat.

Visitors—almost certainly limited to members of the priesthood—would climb their way through a series of raised forests to arrive at the temple on top. They might bring an offering of food or an animal to be sacrificed to the resident god—at Ur, it was Nanna or Sin, god of the moon. Visitors often placed in the

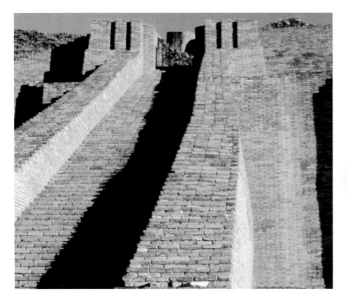

Fig. 1.8 The ziggurat at Ur (modern Muqaiyir, Iraq). ca. 2100 BCE. The best preserved and most fully restored of the ancient Sumerian temples, this ziggurat was the center of the city of Ur, in the lower plain between the Tigris and Euphrates rivers.

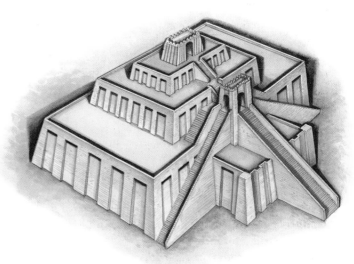

Fig. 1.9 Reconstruction drawing of the ziggurat at Ur (modern Muqaiyir, Iraq). ca. 2100 BCE. British archeologist Sir Leonard Woolley undertook reconstruction of the ziggurat in the 1930s. The temple on top, which was the home of the patron deity of the city, crowned a three-tiered platform, the base of which measures 140 by 200 feet. The entire structure rose to a height of 85 feet. Woolley's reconstruction was halted before the second and third platforms were completed.

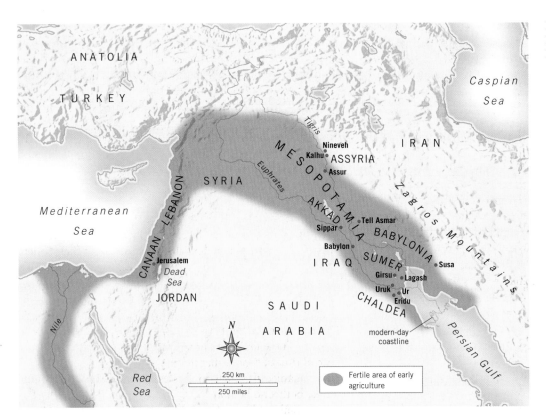

Map 1.2 Eastern Mediterranean basin and major Mesopotamian capitals, ca. 2600–2500 BCE.

temple a statue that represented themselves in an attitude of perpetual prayer. We know this from the inscriptions on many of the statues. One, dedicated to the goddess, protector of Girsu, a city-state across the Tigris and not far upstream from Ur, reads:

> To Bau, gracious lady, daughter of An, queen of the holy city, her mistress, for the life of Nammahani … has dedicated as an offering this statue of the protective goddess of Tarsirsir which she has introduced to the courtyard of Bau. May the statue, to which let my mistress turn her ear, speak my prayers.

A group of such statues, found in 1934 in the shrine room of the ziggurat at Tell Asmar, near modern Baghdad, includes ten men and two women (Fig. **1.10**). The men wear belted, fringed skirts. They have huge eyes, inlaid with lapis lazuli (a blue semiprecious stone) or shell set in bitumen. The single arching eyebrow and crimped beard (only the figure in the lower center is beardless) are typical of Sumerian sculpture. The two women wear robes, and the taller, in the middle, bares a small breast. Originally, a child stood beside her, inserted separately into the base. All figures clasp their hands in front of them, suggestive of prayer when empty and of

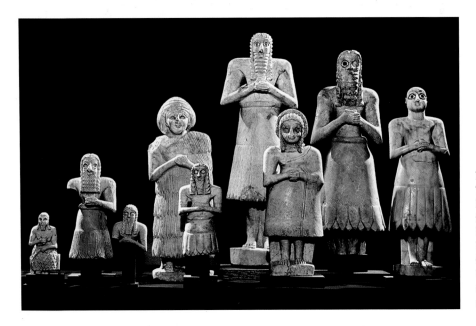

Fig. 1.10 Dedicatory statues, from the Abu Temple, Tell Asmar, Iraq. ca. 2950–2900 BCE. Marble, alabaster, and gypsum, height of tallest figure, approx. 30″. Excavated by the Iraq Expedition of the Oriental Institute of the University of Chicago, February 13, 1934. Courtesy of the Oriental Institute of the University of Chicago. The wide-eyed appearance of these figures is probably meant to suggest they are gazing in perpetual awe at the deity.

making an offering when holding a cup. Some scholars believe that the two tallest figures represent Abu, god of vegetation, and his consort, due to their especially large eyes, but all of the figures are probably worshipers.

Religion in Ancient Mesopotamia Although power struggles dominate Mesopotamian history, with one civilization succeeding another, and with each city-state or empire claiming its own particular divinity as chief among the Mesopotamian gods, the nature of Mesopotamian religion remained relatively constant across the centuries. With the exception of the Hebrews, the religion of the Mesopotamian peoples was polytheistic, consisting of multiple gods and goddesses connected to the forces of nature—sun and sky, water and storm, earth and its fertility. We know many of them by two names, one in Sumerian and the other in the Semitic language of the later, conquering Akkadians.

To the Mesopotamians, human society was merely part of the larger society of the universe governed by these gods and a reflection of it. Anu, father of the gods, represents the authority, which the ruler emulates as lawmaker and -giver. Enlil [EN-lil], god of the air—the calming breeze as well as the violent storm—is equally powerful, but he represents force, which the ruler emulates in his role as military leader. The active principles of fertility, birth, and agricultural plenty are those of the goddess Belitili [bell-eh-TEE-lee], while water, the life force itself, the creative element, is embodied in the god Ea, or Enki [EN-kee], who is also god of the arts. Both Belitili and Ea are subject to the authority of Anu. Ishtar is subject to Enlil, ruled by his breezes (in the case of love) and by his storm (in the case of war). A host of lesser gods represented natural phenomena, or, in some cases, abstract ideas, such as truth and justice.

The Mesopotamian ruler, often represented as a "priest-king," and often believed to possess divine attributes, acts as the intermediary between the gods and humankind. His ultimate responsibility is the behavior of the gods—whether Ea blesses the crop with rains, Ishtar his armies with victory, and so on.

Royal Tombs of Ur Religion was central to the people of Ur, and the cemetery at Ur, discovered by Sir Leonard Woolley in 1928, tells us a great deal about the nature of their beliefs. Woolley unearthed some 1,840 graves, most dating from between 2600 and 2000 BCE. The greatest number of graves were individual burials of rich and poor alike. However, some included a built burial chamber rather than just a coffin and contained more than one body, in some cases as many as eighty. These multiple burials, and the evidence of elaborate burial rituals, suggest that members of a king or queen's court accompanied the ruler to the grave. The two richest burial sites, built one behind the other, are now identified as the royal tombs of King Meskalamdug [mes-kah-LAM-doog] and Queen Puabi [poo-AH-bee].

One of Woolley's most important discoveries in the Royal Cemetery was the so-called *Royal Standard of Ur* (Fig. **1.11**). Music plays a large part here too. The main panels of this rectangular box of unknown function are called "War" and "Peace," because they illustrate, on one side, a military victory and, on the other, the subsequent banquet celebrating the event or perhaps a cult ritual. Each panel is

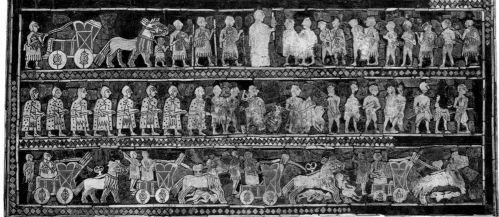

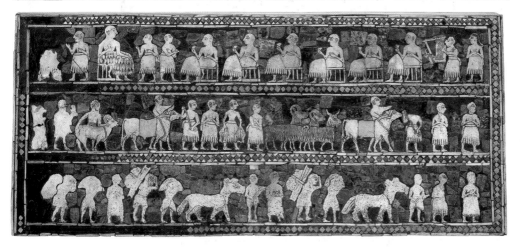

Fig. 1.11 *Royal Standard of Ur*, front ("War") and back ("Peace") sides, from tomb 779, cemetery at Ur (modern Muqaiyir, Iraq). ca. 2600 BCE. Shell, lapis lazuli, and red limestone, originally on a wooden framework, height 8″, length 19″. © The British Museum, London. For all its complexity of design, this object is not much bigger than a sheet of legal paper. Its function remains a mystery, though it may have served as a pillow or headrest. Sir Woolley's designation of it as a standard was purely conjectural.

composed of three registers, or self-contained horizontal bands within which the figures stand on a ground-line, or baseline.

At the right side of the top register of the "Peace" panel (the lower half of Fig. 1.11), a musician plays a lyre, and behind him another, apparently female, sings. The king, at the left end, is recognizable because he is taller than the others and wears a tufted skirt, his head breaking the register line on top. In this convention, known as **social perspective**, or **hierarchy of scale**, the most important figures are represented as larger than the others. In other registers on the "Peace" side of the *Standard*, servants bring cattle, goats, sheep, and fish to the celebration. These represent the bounty of the land and perhaps even delicacies from lands to the north. (Notice that the costumes and hairstyles of the figures carrying sacks in the lowest register are different from those in the other two.) This display of consumption and the distribution of food may have been intended to dramatize the power of the king by showing his ability to control trade routes.

On the "War" side of the *Standard*, the king stands in the middle of the top register. War chariots trample the enemy on the bottom register. (Note that the chariots have solid wheels; spoked wheels were not invented until approximately 1800 BCE.) In the middle register, soldiers wearing leather cloaks and bronze helmets lead naked, bound prisoners to the king in the top register, who will presumably decide their fate. Many of the bodies found in the royal tombs were wearing similar military garments. The importance of the *Royal Standard of Ur* is not simply as documentary evidence of Sumerian life but as one of the earliest examples we have of historical narrative.

Akkad

At the height of the Sumerians' power in southern Mesopotamia, a people known as the Akkadians arrived from the north and settled in the area around modern Baghdad. Their capital city, Akkad [AK-ad], has never been discovered and in all likelihood lies under Baghdad itself. Under Sargon [SAR-gun] I (r. ca. 2332–2279 BCE), the Akkadians conquered virtually all other cities in Mesopotamia, including those in Sumer, to become the region's most powerful city-state. Sargon named himself "King of the Four Quarters of the World" and equated himself with the gods, a status bestowed upon Akkadian rulers from Sargon's time forward. Legends about Sargon's might and power survived in the region for thousands of years. Indeed, the legend of his birth gave rise to what amounts to a **narrative genre** (a class or category of story with a universal theme) that survives to the present day: the boy from humble origins who rises to a position of might and power, the so-called "rags-to-riches" story.

As depicted on surviving clay tablets, Sargon was an illegitimate child whose mother deposited him in the Euphrates River in a basket. There a man named Akki [AK-kee] (after whom Akkad itself is named) found him while drawing water from the river and raised him as his own son. The story anticipates the biblical story of Moses in the bulrushes, as well as the legend of Romulus and Remus, the twin brothers who were discovered in the Tiber marshes by a she-wolf, then raised by a local farmer, and eventually founded the city of Rome.

The Akkadian language was very different from Sumerian. Nevertheless, the Akkadians adopted Sumerian culture and customs and the cuneiform writing style, if not their language. In fact, many bilingual dictionaries and Sumerian texts with Akkadian translations survive. The Akkadian language was Semitic in origin, having more in common with other languages of the region, particularly Hebrew, Phoenician, and Arabic. It quickly became the common language of Mesopotamia, and peoples of the region spoke Akkadian, or dialects of it, throughout the second millennium and well into the first.

Akkadian Sculpture Although Akkad was arguably the most influential of the Mesopotamian cultures, few Akkadian artifacts survive, perhaps because Akkad and other nearby Akkadian cities have disappeared under Baghdad and the alluvial soils of the Euphrates plain. An impressive bronze head of an Akkadian man (Fig. 1.12), found at Nineveh [NIN-eh-vuh], does survive. Once believed to be Sargon the Great himself, many modern scholars now think it was part of a statue of Sargon's grandson, Naramsin [nuh-RAHM-sin] (ca. 2254–2218 BCE). In either case, it is a highly realistic work, depicting a man who appears both powerful and majestic. In its damaged condition, the head is all that survives of a life-size statue that was destroyed in antiquity. Its original gemstone eyes were removed, perhaps by plundering soldiers, or possibly by a political enemy who recognized the sculpture as an emblem of absolute majesty. In the fine detail surrounding the face—in the beard and elaborate coiffure, with its braid circling the head—it testifies to the Akkadian mastery of the lost-wax casting technique, which originated in Mesopotamia as early as the third millennium BCE. It is the first existing monumental work made by that technique that we have.

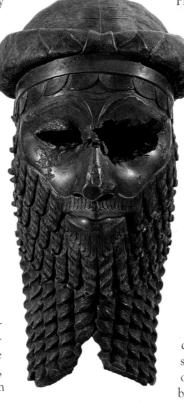

Fig. 1.12 *Head of an Akkadian Man*, from Nineveh (modern Kuyunjik, Iraq). ca. 2300–2200 BCE. Copper alloy, height 14 1/8". Iraq Museum, Baghdad. Many scholars believe this to be a likeness of Sargon I.

Babylon

The Akkadians dominated Mesopotamia for just 150 years, their rule collapsing not long after 2200 BCE. For the next 400 years, various city-states thrived locally. Still, no one in

Mesopotamia matched the Akkadians' power until the first decades of the eighteenth century BCE, when Hammurabi [ham-uh-RAH-bee] of Babylon [BAB-uh-lon] (r. 1792–1750 BCE) gained control of most of the region.

The Law Code of Hammurabi Hammurabi imposed order on Babylon where laxness and disorder, if not chaos, reigned. A giant stele, the so-called *Law Code of Hammurabi*, survives (Fig. **1.13**). By no means the first of its kind, though by far the most complete, the stele is a record of decisions and decrees made by Hammurabi over the course of some 40 years of his reign. Its purpose was to celebrate his sense of justice and the wisdom of his rule. Atop the stele, in sculptural relief, Hammurabi receives the blessing of Shamash, the sun god; notice the rays of light coming from his shoulders. The god is much larger than Hammurabi: In fact, he is to Hammurabi as Hammurabi, the patriarch, is to his people. If Hammurabi is divine, he is still subservient to the greater gods. At the same time, the phallic design of the stele asserts the masculine prowess of the king.

Below the relief, 282 separate "articles" cover both sides of the basalt monument. One of the great debates of legal history is the question of whether these articles actually constitute a code of law. If by code we mean a comprehensive, systematic, and methodical compilation of all aspects of Mesopotamian law, then it isn't. It is instead selective, even eccentric, in the issues it addresses. Many of its articles seem to be "reforms" of already existing law, and as such they define new principles of justice.

Chief among these is the principle of talion [TAL-ee-un]— an eye for an eye, a tooth for a tooth—which Hammurabi introduced to Mesopotamian law. (Sections of earlier codes from Ur compensate victims of crimes with money.) This principle punished the violence or injustice perpetuated by one free person upon another, but violence by an upper-class person on a lower-class person was penalized much less severely. Slaves (who might be either war captives or debtors) enjoyed no legal protection at all—only the protection of their owner.

The code tells us much about the daily lives of Mesopotamian peoples, including conflicts great and small. In rules governing family relations and class divisions in Mesopotamian society, inequalities are sharply drawn. Women are inferior to men, and wives, like slaves, are the personal property of their husbands (although protected from the abuse of neglectful or unjust husbands). Incest is strictly forbidden. Fathers cannot arbitrarily disinherit their sons—a son must have committed some "heavy crime" to justify such treatment. The code's strongest concern is the maintenance and protection of the family, though trade practices and property rights are also of major importance.

The code begins with Hammurabi's assertion of his descent from the gods and his status as their favorite (**Reading 1.2**).

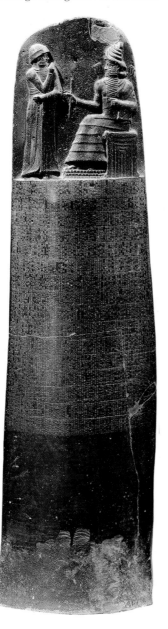

Fig. 1.13 *Stele of Hammurabi,* from Susa (modern Shush, Iran) ca. 1760 BCE. Basalt, height of stele, approx. 7′, height of relief, 28″. Musée du Louvre, Paris. This stele was stolen by invading Elamites and removed to Susa, where it was excavated by the French in 1898.

READING 1.2   **from the *Law Code of Hammurabi* (ca. 1792–1750 BCE)**

When Anu, the supreme, the king of the Aunnaki, and Be, the lord of heaven and earth, who fixes the destiny of the universe, had allotted the multitudes of mankind to Merodaeh, the first-born of Ea, the divine master of Law, they made him great among the Igigi; they proclaimed his august name in Babylon, exalted in the lands, they established for him within it an eternal kingdom whose foundations, like heaven and earth shall endure.

Then Anu and Bel delighted the flesh of mankind by calling me, the renowned prince, the god-fearing Hammurabi, to establish justice in the earth, to destroy the base and the wicked, and to hold back the strong from oppressing the feeble: to shine like the Sun-god upon the black-haired men, and to illuminate the land. . . .

Even if Hammurabi meant only to assert the idea of justice as the basis for his own divine rule, the stele established what amounts to a uniform code throughout Mesopotamia. It was repeatedly copied for over a thousand years, and it established the rule of law in Mesopotamia for a millennium. From this point on, the authority and power of the ruler could no longer be capricious, subject to the whim, fancy, and subjective interpretation of his singular personality. The law was now, at least ostensibly, more objective and impartial. The ruler was required to follow certain prescribed procedures. But the law, so prescribed in writing, was now also much less flexible, hard to change, and much more impersonal. Exceptions to the rule were few and difficult to justify. Eventually, written law would remove justice from the discretion of the ruler and replace it by a legal establishment of learned judges charged with enacting the king's statutes

Mesopotamian Literature and the *Epic of Gilgamesh*

Sumerian literature survives on nearly 100,000 clay tablets and fragments. Many deal with religious themes in the form of poems, blessings, and incantations to the gods. One of the great surviving manuscripts of Mesopotamian culture and the oldest story ever recorded is the *Epic of Gilgamesh*. An **epic** is a long, narrative poem in elevated language that follows characters of a high position through a series of adventures, often including a visit to the world of the dead. For many literary scholars, the epic is the most exalted poetic form. The central figure is a legendary or historical figure of heroic proportion, in this case the Sumerian king Gilgamesh. Homer's *Iliad* and *Odyssey* (see chapter 2) had been considered the earliest epic, until late in the nineteenth century, when *Gilgamesh* was discovered in the library of King Ashurbanipal at Nineveh.

The scope of an epic is large. The supernatural world of gods and goddesses usually plays a role in the story, as do battles in which the hero demonstrates his strength and courage. The poem's language is suitably dignified, often consisting of many long, formal speeches. Lists of various heroes or catalogs of their achievements are frequent.

Epics are often compilations of preexisting myths and tales handed down generation to generation, often orally, and finally unified into a whole by the epic poet. Indeed, the main outline of the story is usually known to its audience. The poet's contribution is the artistry brought to the subject, demonstrated through the use of epithets, metaphors, and similes. **Epithets** are words or phrases that characterize a person (for example, "Enkidu, the protector of herdsmen," or "Enkidu, the son of the mountain"). **Metaphors** are words or phrases used in place of another to suggest a similarity between the two, as when Gilgamesh is described as a "raging flood-wave who destroys even walls of stone." **Similes** compare two unlike things by the use of the word "like" or "as" (for example, "the land shattered like a pot").

Perhaps most important, the epic illuminates the development of a nation or race. It is a national poem, describing a people's common heritage and celebrating its cultural identi-

ty. It is hardly surprising, then, that Ashurbanipal preserved the *Epic of Gilgamesh*. which preserves the historical lineage of all Mesopotamian kings—Sumerian, Akkadian, Assyrian, and Babylonian. The tale embodies their own heroic grandeur, and thus the grandeur of their peoples.

Gilgamesh consists of some 2,900 lines written in Akkadian cuneiform script on eleven clay tablets, none of them completely whole. It was composed sometime before Ashurbanipal's reign, possibly as early as 1200 BCE, by Sinleqqiunninni [sin-lek-win-NEE-nee] a scholar-priest of Uruk. This would make Sinleqquinninni the oldest known author. We know that Gilgamesh was the fourth king of Uruk, ruling sometime between 2700 and 2500 BCE. (The dates of his rule were recorded on a clay tablet, the Sumerian King List.) Recovered fragments of his story date back nearly to his actual reign, and the story we have, known as the Standard Version, is a compilation of these earlier versions.

At the center of the poem, in Tablet VI, Ishtar, goddess of both love and war, offers to marry Gilgamesh. Gilgamesh refuses, which unleashes Ishtar's wrath. She sends the Bull of Heaven to destroy them, but Gilgamesh and and his close friend Enkidu slay it instead (**Reading 1.3**):

READING 1.3 **from the *Epic of Gilgamesh*, Tablet VI (ca. 1200 BCE)**

A Woman Scorned

...When Gilgamesh placed his crown on his head
Princess, Ishtar raised her eyes to the beauty of Gilgamesh.

"Come along, Gilgamesh, be you my husband,
to me grant your lusciousness.[1]
Be you my husband, and I will be your wife.
I will have harnessed for you a chariot of lapis lazuli and gold,
with wheels of gold . . .
Bowed down beneath you will be kings, lords, and princes.
The Lullubu people[2] will bring you the produce of the mountains and countryside as tribute.
Your she-goats will bear triplets, your ewes twins,
your donkey under burden will overtake the mule,
your steed at the chariot will be bristling to gallop,
your ox at the yoke will have no match."
Gilgamesh addressed Princess Ishtar saying:
. . . Where are your bridegrooms that you keep forever? . . .
You loved the supremely mighty lion,
yet you dug for him seven and again seven pits.

You loved the stallion, famed in battle,
yet you ordained for him the whip, the goad,
and the lash,
ordained for him to gallop for seven and seven
hours,
ordained for him drinking from muddied
waters,[3]
you ordained for his mother Silili to wail continually.
You loved the Shepherd, the Master Herder,
who continually presented you with bread baked
in embers,
and who daily slaughtered for you a kid.
Yet you struck him, and turned him into a wolf,
so his own shepherds now chase him
and his own dogs snap at his shins. . . .
And now me! It is me you love, and you will
ordain for me as for them!"

Her Fury

When Ishtar heard this
in a fury she went up to the heavens,
going to Anu, her father, and crying,
going to Antum, her mother, and weeping:

"Father, Gilgamesh has insulted me over and
over,
Gilgamesh has recounted despicable deeds
about me,
despicable deeds and curses!"

Anu addressed Princess Ishtar, saying:

"What is the matter? Was it not you who provoked King Gilgamesh?
So Gilgamesh recounted despicable deeds
about you,
despicable deeds and curses!"

Ishtar spoke to her father, Anu, saying:

"Father, give me the Bull of Heaven,
so he can kill Gilgamesh in his dwelling.
If you do not give me the Bull of Heaven,
I will knock down the Gates of the Nether-
world,
I will smash the door posts, and leave the doors
flat down,
and will let the dead go up to eat the living!
And the dead will outnumber the living!"

Anu addressed Princess Ishtar, saying:

"If you demand the Bull of Heaven from me,
there will be seven years of empty husks for the
land of Uruk.
Have you collected grain for the people?
Have you made grasses grow for the animals?"

Ishtar addressed Anu, her father, saying:

"I have heaped grain in the granaries for the
people,

I made grasses grow for the animals,
in order that they might eat in the seven years
of empty husks.
I have collected grain for the people,
I have made grasses grow for the animals. . . ."

When Anu heard her words,
he placed the nose-rope of the Bull of Heaven in her
hand.
Ishtar led the Bull of Heaven down to the earth.
When it reached Uruk…
It climbed down to the Euphrates…
At the snort of the Bull of Heaven a huge pit opened
up,
and 100 Young Men of Uruk fell in.
At his second snort a huge pit opened up,
and 200 Young Men of Uruk fell in.
At his third snort a huge pit opened up,
and Enkidu fell in up to his waist.
Then Enkidu jumped out and seized the Bull of Heaven
by its horns.
The Bull spewed his spittle in front of him,
with his thick tail he flung his dung behind him (?).
Enkidu addressed Gilgamesh, saying:

"My friend, we can be bold(?) …
Between the nape, the horns, and … thrust
your sword."

Enkidu stalked and hunted down the Bull of Heaven.
He grasped it by the thick of its tail
and held onto it with both his hands (?),
while Gilgamesh, like an expert butcher,
boldly and surely approached the Bull of Heaven.
Between the nape, the horns, and … he thrust his
sword. . . .
Ishtar went up onto the top of the Wall of Uruk-
Haven,
cast herself into the pose of mourning, and hurled her
woeful curse:

"Woe unto Gilgamesh who slandered me and
killed the Bull of Heaven!"

When Enkidu heard this pronouncement of Ishtar,
he wrenched off the Bull's hindquarter and flung it in her
face:

"If I could only get at you I would do the same
to you!
I would drape his innards over your arms!". . .

---

[1]Literally "fruit."

[2]The Lullubu were a wild mountain people living in the area of modern-day western Iran. The meaning is that even the wildest, least con-
trollable of peoples will recognize Gilgamesh's rule and bring tribute.

[3]Horses put their front feet in the water when drinking, churning up
mud.

Even as the passage describes the heroic comradeship of Enkidu and Gilgamesh, it also begins to address the main theme of the poem: the inevitability of death. In fact, the *Epic of Gilgamesh* is the first known literary work to confront the idea of death, which is, in many ways, the very embodiment of the unknown. Although the hero goes to the very ends of the Earth in his quest for immortality, he ultimately leaves with nothing to show for his efforts except an understanding of his own, very human, limitations. He is the first hero in Western literature to yearn for what he can never attain, to seek to understand what must always remain a mystery. And, of course, until the death of his friend Enkidu, ordered by the gods after their confrontation with Ishtar, Gilgamesh had seemed, in his self-confident confrontation with Ishtar and in the defeat of the Bull of Heaven, as near to a god as a mortal might be. In short, he embodied the Mesopotamian hero-king. Even as the poem asserts the hero-king's divinity—Gilgamesh is two parts god—it emphasizes his humanity and the mortality that accompanies it. By making literal the first words of the Sumerian King List—"After the kingship had descended from heaven"—the *Epic of Gilgamesh* acknowledges what many Mesopotamian kings were unwilling to admit, at least publicly: their own, very human, limitations, their own powerlessness in the face of the ultimate unknown—death.

The Hebrews

The Hebrews (from *Habiru*, "outcast" or "nomad") were a people forced out of their homeland in the Mesopotamian basin in about 2000 BCE. According to their tradition, it was in the delta of the Tigris and Euphrates rivers that God created Adam and Eve in the Garden of Eden. It was out of there that Abraham of Ur led his people into Canaan [KAY-nun], in order to escape the warlike Akkadians and the increasingly powerful Babylonians. We know these stories from the Hebrew Bible—a word that derives from the Greek, *biblia*, "books"—a compilation of hymns, prophecies, and laws transcribed by its authors between 800 and 400 BCE, some 1,000 years after the events the Hebrew Bible describes. Although the archeological record in the Near East confirms some of what these scribes and priests wrote, the stories themselves were edited and collated into the stories we know today. The recount conquest of Israel by the powerful Assyrians, who by the middle of the ninth century BCE dominated the entire Middle East from their capital at Kalhu (modern Nimrud, on the Tigris River, the Jews' later exile to Babylon after the destruction of Jerusalem by the Babylonian king Nebuchadnezzar [neb-uh-kud-NEZ-ur] in 587 BCE, and their eventual return to Jerusalem after the Persians conquered the Babylonians in 538 BCE. The stories represent the Hebrews' attempt to maintain their sense of their own history and destiny.

The Hebrews differed from other Fertile Crescent cultures in that their religion was monotheistic—they worshiped a single god, whereas others in the region tended to have gods for their clans and cities, among other things. According to Hebrew tradition, God made an agreement with the Hebrews, first with Noah after the flood, later renewed with Abraham and each of the subsequent **patriarchs** (scriptural fathers of the Hebrew people): "I am God Almighty; be fruitful and multiply; a nation and a company of nations shall come from you. The land which I gave to Abraham and Isaac I will give to you, and I will give the land to your descendants after you" (Genesis 35:11–12). In return for this promise, the Hebrews, the "chosen people," agreed to obey God's will. "Chosen people" means that the Jews were chosen to set an example of a higher moral standard (a light unto the nations), not chosen in the sense of favored, which is a common misunderstanding of the term.

Genesis, the first book of the Hebrew Bible, tells the story of the creation of the world out of a "formless void." It describes God's creation of the world and all its creatures and his continuing interest in the workings of the world, an interest that would lead, in the story of Noah, to God's near destruction of all things. It also posits humankind as easily tempted by evil. It documents the moment of the introduction of sin (and shame) into the cosmos, associating these with the single characteristic separating humans from animals—knowledge. And it shows, in the example of Noah, the reward for having "walked with God" as the basis of the covenant.

Moses and the Ten Commandments The biblical story of Moses and the Ten Commandments embodies the centrality of the written word to Jewish culture. For reasons we don't know, the Hebrew people left Canaan for Egypt in about 1600 BCE and had prospered there until the Egyptians enslaved them in about 1300 BCE. Defying the rule of the pharaohs, the Jewish patriarch Moses led his people out of Egypt. According to tradition, Moses led the Jews across the Red Sea (which miraculously parted to facilitate the escape) and into the desert of the Sinai [SYE-nye] peninsula. (The event became the basis for the book of Exodus.) Most likely, they crossed a large tidal flat called the Sea of Reeds; subsequently that body of water was misidentified as the Red Sea. Unable to return to Canaan, which was now occupied by local tribes of considerable military strength, the Jews settled in an arid region of the Sinai desert near the Dead Sea for a period of 40 years, which archeologists date to sometime between 1300 and 1150 BCE.

In the Sinai desert the Hebrews forged the principal tenets of a new religion based on worship of a single god. There, too, the Hebrew god supposedly revealed a new name for himself—YHWH, a name so sacred that it could neither be spoken nor written. The name is not known and YHWH is a cipher for it. (There are, however, many other names for God in the Hebrew Bible, among them Elohim [eh-loe-HEEM] (which is plural in Hebrew, meaning "gods, deities"), Adonai [ah-dun-EYE] ("Lord"), El Shaddai [shah-die] (literally "God of the fields" but usually translated "God Almighty.") Some scholars believe that this demonstrates the multiple authorship of the Bible. Others suggest that God has been

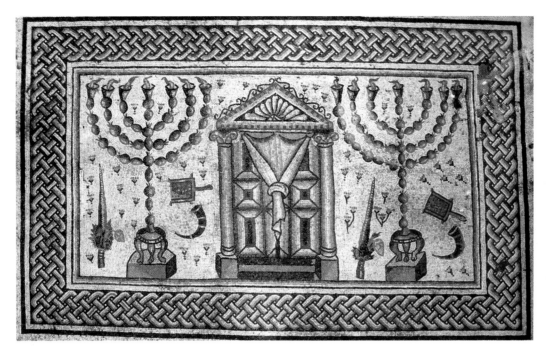

Fig. 1.14 The Ark of the Covenant and sanctuary implements, mosaic floor decorations from Hammath near Tiberias, Israel. Fourth century CE. Israel Antiquities Authority, Jerusalem. Two menorahs (seven-branched candelabras) flank each side of the Ark. The menorah is considered a symbol of the nation of Israel and its mission to be "a light unto the nations" (Isaiah 42:6). Instructions for making it are outlined in Exodus 25:31–40. Relatively little ancient Jewish art remains. Most of it was destroyed as the Jewish people were conquered, persecuted, and exiled.

Z. Radovan/www.BibleLandPictures.com

given different names to reflect different aspects of his divinity, or the different roles that he might assume—the guardian of the flocks in the fields, or the powerful master of all. Translated into Latin as "Jehovah" [ji-HOH-vuh] in the Middle Ages, the name is now rendered in English as "Yahweh." This God also gave Moses the Ten Commandments, carved onto stone tablets, as recorded in Deuteronomy 5:6–21. Subsequently, the Hebrews carried the commandments in a sacred chest, called the Ark of the Covenant (Fig. **1.14**), which was lit by seven-branched candelabras known as menorahs [men-OR-uhz]. The centrality to Hebrew culture of these written words is even more apparent in the words of God that follow the commandments (**Reading 1.4**).

READING 1.4   **from the Hebrew Bible (Deuteronomy 6:6–9)**

6 Keep these words that I am commanding you today in your heart.

7 Recite them to your children and talk about them when you are at home and when you are away, when you lie down and when you rise.

8 Bind them as a sign on your hand, fix them as an emblem on your forehead,

9 and write them on the doorposts of your house and on your gates.

Whenever the Hebrews talked, wherever they looked, wherever they went, they focused on the commandments of their God. Their monotheistic religion was thus also an eth-

ical and moral system derived from an omnipotent God. The Ten Commandments were the centerpiece of the Torah [tor-AH], or Law (literally "instructions"), consisting of the books of Genesis, Exodus, Leviticus, Numbers, and Deuteronomy. (Christians would later incorporate these books into their Bible as the first five books of the Old Testament.) The Hebrews considered these five books divinely inspired and attributed their original authorship to Moses himself, although the texts as we know them were written much later.

The body of laws outlined in the Torah is quite different from the code of Hammurabi. The code was essentially a list of punishments for offenses; it is not an ethical code (see Fig. 1.13 and Reading 1.2). Hebraic and Mesopotamian laws are distinctly different. Perhaps because the Hebrews were once themselves aliens and slaves, their law treats the lowest members of society as human beings. As Yahweh declares in Exodus 23:6: "You will not cheat the poor among you of their rights at law." At least under the law, class distinctions, with the exceptions of slaves, did not exist in Hebrew society, and punishment was levied equally. Above all else, rich and poor alike were united for the common good in a common enterprise, to follow the instructions for living as God provided.

After 40 years in the Sinai had passed, it is believed that the patriarch Joshua led the Jews back to Canaan, the Promised Land, as Yahweh had pledged in the covenant. Over the next 200 years, they gradually gained control of the region through a protracted series of wars described in the books of Joshua, Judges, and Samuel in the Bible. They named themselves the Israelites [IZ-ree-uh-lites], after Israel, the name that was given by God to Jacob. The nation consisted of 12 tribes, each descending from one of Jacob's 12 sons. By about 1000 BCE, Saul had established himself as king of Israel, followed by David, who as a boy had rescued the Israelites from the Philistines [FIL-uh-steenz] by killing the giant Goliath with a stone thrown from a sling, as described in First Samuel, and later united Israel and Judah into a single state.

Solomon undertook to complete the building campaign begun by his father, and by the end of his reign, Jerusalem was one of the most beautiful cities in the Middle East. A magnificent palace and, most especially, a splendid temple dominated the city. After Solomon's death, the United Monarchy of Israel split into two separate states. To the north was Israel, with its capital in Samaria [suh-MAR-ee-uh], and to the south, Judah, with its capital in Jerusalem. In this era of the two kingdoms, Hebrew culture was dominated by **prophets**, men who were prophetic not in the sense of foretelling the future, but rather in the sense of serving as mouthpieces and interpreters of Yahweh's purposes, which they claimed to understand through visions. The prophets instructed the people in the ways of living according to the laws of the Torah, and they more or less freely confronted anyone guilty of wrongful actions, even the Hebrew kings. They attacked, particularly, the wealthy Hebrews whose commercial ventures had brought them unprecedented material comfort and who were inclined to stray from monotheism and worship Canaanite [KAY-nuh-nite] fertility gods and goddesses. The moral laxity of these wealthy Hebrews troubled the prophets, who urged the Hebrew nation to reform spiritually.

In 722 BCE, Assyrians attacked the northern kingdom of Israel and scattered its people, who were thereafter known as the Lost Tribes of Israel. The southern kingdom of Judah survived another 140 years, until Nebuchadnezzar and the Babylonians overwhelmed it in 587 BCE, destroying the Temple of Solomon in Jerusalem and deporting the Hebrews to Babylon. Not only had the Hebrews lost their homeland and their temple, but the Ark of the Covenant itself disappeared. For nearly 60 years, the Hebrews endured what is known as the Babylonian Captivity. As recorded in Psalm 137: "By the rivers of Babylon, there we sat down, yea we wept, when we remembered Zion."

Finally, invading Persians, whom they believed had been sent by Yahweh, freed them from the Babylonians in 520 BCE. They returned to Judah, known now, for the first time, as the Jews (after the name of their homeland). They rebuilt a Second Temple of Jerusalem, with an empty chamber at its center, meant for the Ark of the Covenant should it ever return. And they welcomed back other Jews from around the Mediterranean, including many whose families had left the northern kingdom almost 200 years earlier. Many others, however, were by now permanently settled elsewhere, and they became known as the Jews of the Diaspora [die-AS-puh-ruh], or the "dispersion."

Hebrew culture would have a profound impact on Western civilization. The Jews provided the essential ethical and moral foundation for religion in the West, including Christianity and Islam, both of which incorporate Jewish teachings into their own thought and practice. In the Torah we find the basis of the law as we understand and practice it today. So moving and universal are the stories recorded in the Torah that over the centuries they have inspired—and continue to inspire—countless works of art, music, and literature. Most important, the Hebrews introduced to the world the concept of ethical monotheism, the idea that there is only one God, and that God demands that humans behave in a certain way, and rewards and punishes accordingly. Few, if any, concepts have had a more far-reaching effect on history and culture.

The Stability of Ancient Egypt: Flood and Sun

Civilization in Mesopotamia developed across the last three millennia BCE almost simultaneously with civilization in Egypt, another part of the Fertile Crescent to the south and east. The two civilizations have much in common. Both formed around river systems—the Tigris and Euphrates in Mesopotamia; the Nile in Egypt. Both were agrarian societies that depended on irrigation, and their economies were hostage to the sometimes fickle, sometimes violent flow of their respective river systems. As in Mesopotamia, Egyptians learned to control the river's flow by constructing dams and irrigation canals, and it was probably the need to cooperate with one another in such endeavors that helped Mesopotamia and Egypt to create the civilization that would eventually arise in the Nile Valley.

The Mesopotamians and the Egyptians built massive architectural structures dedicated to their gods—the ziggurat in Mesopotamia (see Figs. 1.8 and 1.9) and the pyramid in Egypt (Fig. **1.15**). Though the former appears to be dedicated, at least in part, to water and the latter to the sun, both unite earth and sky in a single architectural form. Indeed, the earliest Egyptian pyramids were stepped structures on the model of the Mesopotamian ziggurat. Both cultures developed forms of writing, although the cuneiform style of Mesopotamian culture and the hieroglyph style of Egyptian society were very different. There is ample evidence that the two civilizations traded with one another, and to a certain degree influenced one another.

What most distinguishes Egyptian from Mesopotamian culture, however, is the relative stability of the former. Mesopotamia was rarely, if ever, united as a single entity. Whenever it was united, it was through force, the power of an army, not the free will of a people striving for the common good. In contrast, political transition in Egypt was dynastic—that is, rule was inherited by members of the same family, sometimes for generations. As in Mesopotamia, however, the ruler's authority was cemented by his association with divine authority. He was, indeed, the manifestation of the gods on Earth. In fact there is clear reason to believe that the sculptural image of a ruler was believed to be, in some sense, the ruler himself.

The Nile and Its Culture

Like the Tigris and Euphrates in Mesopotamia, the Nile could be said to have made Egypt possible. The river begins in Africa, one tributary in the mountains of Ethiopia and another at Lake Victoria in Uganda, from which it flows north for over 4,000 miles. Egyptian civilization developed

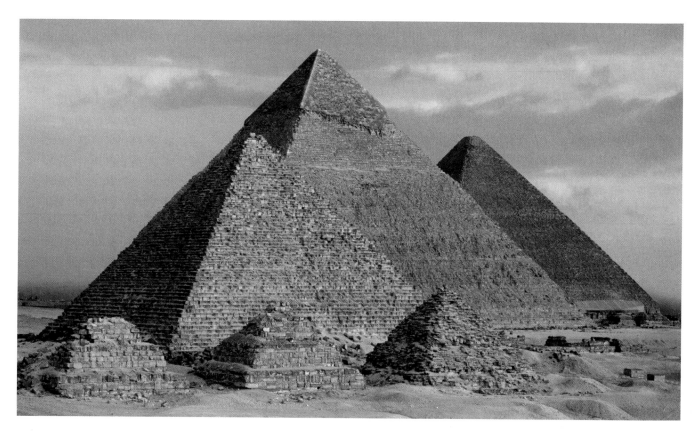

Fig.1.15 The Pyramids of Menkaure (ca. 2470 BCE), Khafre (ca. 2500 BCE), and Khufu (ca. 2530 BCE), Giza, Egypt. Though different in form, both the ziggurat and the pyramid emphasize the importance of monumentality to their respective cultures.

along the last 750 miles of the river's banks, extending from the granite cliffs at Aswan, north to the Mediterranean Sea (see **Map 1.3**).

Nearly every year, torrential rains caused the river to rise dramatically. Most years, from July to November, the Egyptians could count on the Nile flooding their land. When the river receded, deep deposits of fertile silt covered the valley floor. Crops would then be planted, fields tilled, plants tended. If no flood occurred for a period of years, famine could result. The cycle of flood and sun made Egypt one of the most productive cultures in the ancient world and one of the most stable. For 3,000 years, from 3100 BCE until the defeat of Mark Antony and Cleopatra by the Roman general Octavian in 31 BCE, Egypt's institutions and culture remained remarkably unchanged

As a result of the Nile's annual floods, Egypt called itself Kemet, meaning "Black Land." In Upper Egypt, from Aswan to the Delta, the black, fertile deposits of the river covered an extremely narrow strip of land. Surrounding the river's alluvial plain were the "Red Lands," the desert environment that could not support life, but where rich deposits of minerals and stone could be mined and quarried. Lower Egypt, consisting of the Delta itself, began some 13 miles north of Giza [GHEE-zuh], the site of the Great Pyramids, across the river from what is now modern Cairo.

In this land of plenty, great farms flourished, and wildlife abounded in the marshes. In fact, the Egyptians linked the marsh to the creation of the world and represented it that way in the famous hunting scene that decorates the tomb of Nebamun [NEB-ah-mun] at Thebes [theebz] (Fig. **1.16**). Nebamun is about to hurl a snake-shaped throwing stick into a flock of birds as his wife and daughter look on. The painting is a sort of visual pun, referring directly to sexual procreation. The verb "to launch a throwing stick" also means "to ejaculate," and the word "throwing stick" itself, to "create." The hieroglyphs written between Nebamun and his wife translate as "enjoying oneself, viewing the beautiful, … at the place of constant renewal of life."

Scholars divide Egyptian history into three main periods of achievement. Almost all of the conventions of Egyptian art were established during the first period, the *Old Kingdom*. During the *Middle Kingdom*, the "classical" literary language that would survive through the remainder of Egyptian history was first produced. The *New Kingdom* was a period of prosperity that saw a renewed interest in art and architecture. During each of these periods, successive dynasties—or royal houses—brought peace and stability to the country. Between them were "Intermediate Periods" of relative instability.

Egypt's continuous cultural tradition—lasting over three thousand years—is history's clearest example of how peace and prosperity go hand in hand with cultural stability. As opposed

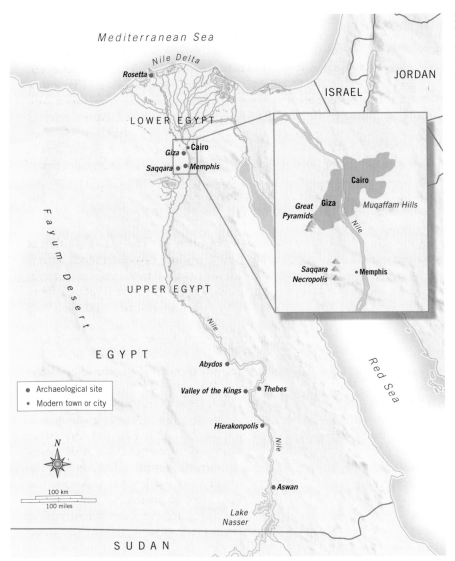

Map 1.3 **Nile River Basin with Predynastic and Old Kingdom sites in relation to modern Cairo.** The broad expanse of the Lower Nile Delta was crisscrossed by canals, allowing for easy transport of produce and supplies.

to the warring cultures of Mesopotamia, where city-state vied with city-state and empire with successive empire, Egyptian culture was predicated on unity. It was a **theocracy**, a state ruled by a god or by the god's representative—in this case a king (and very occasionally a queen), who ruled as the living representative of the sun god, Re [reh]. Egypt's government was indistinguishable from its religion, and its religion manifested itself in nature, in the flow of the Nile, the heat of the sun, and in the journey of the sun through the day and night and through the seasons. In the last judgment of the soul after death, Egyptians believed that the heart was weighed to determine whether it was "found true by trial of the Great Balance." Balance in all things— in nature, in social life, in art, and in rule— this was the constant aim of the individual, the state, and, Egyptians believed, the gods.

Whereas in Mesopotamia the flood was largely a destructive force, in Egypt it had a more complex meaning. It could, indeed, be destructive, sometimes rising so high that great devastation resulted. But without it, the Egyptians knew, their culture could not endure. So, in Egyptian art and culture, a more complex way of thinking about nature, and about life itself, developed. Every aspect of Egyptian life is countered by an opposite and equal force, which contradicts and negates it, and every act of negation gives rise to its opposite again. As a result, events are cyclical, as abundance is born of devastation and devastation closely follows abundance. Likewise, just as the floods brought the Nile Valley back to life each year, the Egyptians believed that rebirth necessarily followed death. So their religion, which played a large part in their lives, reflected the cycle of the river itself.

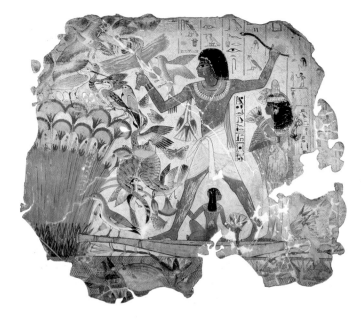

Fig. 1.16 *Nebamun Hunting Birds*, **from the tomb of Nebamun, Thebes. Dynasty 18, ca. 1400 BCE.** Fresco on dry plaster, approx. 2′ 8″ high. The British Museum, London. The fish and the birds, and the cat, are completely realistic, but this is not a realistic scene. It is a conventional representation of the deceased, in this case Nebamun, spearing fish or hunting fowl, almost obligatory for the decoration of a tomb. The pigments were applied directly to a dry wall, a technique that has come to be known as fresco secco [FRES-coh SEK-koh], dry fresco. Such paintings are extremely fragile and susceptible to moisture damage, but Egypt's arid climate has preserved them.

Egyptian Religion: Cyclical Harmony The religion of ancient Egypt, like that of Mesopotamia, was *polytheistic*, consisting of many gods and goddesses who were associated with natural forces and realms. When represented, gods and goddesses have human bodies and human or animal heads, and wear crowns or other headgear that identifies them by their attributes. The religion reflected an ordered universe in which the stars and planets, the various gods, and basic human activities were thought to be part of a grand and harmonious design. A person who did not disrupt this harmony did not fear death because his or her spirit would live on forever.

At the heart of this religion were creation stories that explained how the gods and the world came into being. Chief among the Egyptian gods was Re, god of the sun. According to these stories, at the beginning of time, the Nile created a great mound of silt, out of which Re was born. It was understood that Re had a close personal relationship with the king, who was considered the son of Re. But the king could also identify closely with other gods. The king was simultaneously believed to be the personification of the sky god, Horus [HOR-us], and deities associated with places like Thebes or Memphis were identified with the king when his power resided in those cities. Though not a full-fledged god, the king was *netjer nefer* [net-jer nef-er], literally, a "junior god." That made him the representative of the people to the gods, whom he contacted through statues of divine beings placed in all temples. Through these statues, Egyptians believed, the gods manifested themselves on earth. Not only did the orderly functioning of social and political events depend upon the king's successful communication with the gods, but so did events of nature—the ebb and flow of the river chief among them.

Like the king, all the other Egyptian gods descend from Re, as if part of a family. As we have said, many can be traced back to local deities of predynastic times who later assumed greater significance as a given place—Thebes, for instance, gained significance. Osiris [oh-SY-ris], ruler of the underworld and god of the dead, was at first a local deity in the eastern Delta. According to myth, he was murdered by his wicked brother Seth, god of storms and violence, who chopped his brother into pieces and threw them into the Nile. But Osiris's wife and sister, Isis [EYE-zis], the goddess of fertility, collected all these parts, put the god back together, and restored him to life. Osiris was therefore identified with the Nile itself, with its annual flood and renewal. The child of Osiris and Isis was Horus, who defeated Seth and became the mythical first king of Egypt. The actual king was not only considered the earthly manifestation of Horus (as well as the son of Re) but also closely identified with Osiris, in whose kingdom he continued his existence after death.

The cyclical movement through opposing forces, embodied in the story of Osiris and Isis, is one of the earliest instances of a system of religious and philosophic thought that survives even in contemporary thought. Life and death, flood and sun, even desert and oasis, were part of a larger harmony of nature, one that was predictable in both the diurnal cycle of day and night but also in its seasonal patterns of repetition. A good deity like Osiris was necessarily balanced by a bad deity like Seth. The fertile Nile Valley was balanced by the harsh desert surrounding it. The narrow reaches of the upper Nile were balanced by the broad marshes of the Delta. Even, at least from the Egyptian point of view, the orderly functioning of the Egyptian state was countered and balanced by the chaotic, warring factionalism of Mesopotamia. All things were predicated upon the return of their opposite, which negates them, but which in the process completes the whole and regenerates the cycle of being and becoming once again.

Pictorial Formulas in Egyptian Art This sense of duality, of opposites, informs even the earliest Egyptian artifacts, such as the *Palette of Narmer*, found at Hierakonpolis [hy-ruh-KAHN-puh-liss], in Upper Egypt. A palette is technically an everyday object used for grinding pigments and making body or eye paint.

The scenes on the *Palette of Narmer* are in low relief. Like the *Royal Standard of Ur* (see Fig. 1.11), they are arranged in

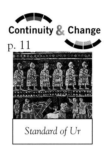

Continuity & Change
p. 11

Standard of Ur

registers that provide a ground-line upon which the figures stand (the two lion-tamers are an exception). The figures typically face to the right, though often, as is the case here, the design is **symmetrical**, balanced left and right. The artist represents the various parts of the human figure in what the Egyptians thought was their most characteristic view. So, the face, arms, legs, and feet are in profile, with the left foot advanced in front of the right. The eye and shoulders are in front view. The mouth, navel and hips, and knees are in three-quarter view. As a result the viewer sees each person in a **composite view**, the integration of multiple perspectives into a single unified image.

In Egyptian art, not only the figures but the scenes themselves unite two contradictory points of view into a single image. In the *Palette of Narmer*, the king approaches his dead enemies from the side, but they lie beheaded on the ground before him as seen from above. Egyptian art often represents architecture in the same terms. At the top middle of the Palette of Narmer, the external facade of the palace is depicted simultaneously from above, in a kind of ground plan, with its front columns at the bottom. The design contains Narmer's Horus-name, consisting of a catfish and a chisel (see *Focus*, pages 22–23). We now know it shows the two aspects of the king—his mortal self (the serpent or catfish) and his immortal self (his role as the gods' representative on earth), both of which are represented simultaneously. The dual role of the king—responsible to the gods for establishing order in the world and responsible to his people for maintaining the peace through force if necessary—is visually expressed as a composite view. Again we see the Egyptian tendency to regard the world as fundamentally dualistic.

Focus

Reading the *Palette of Narmer*

The Egyptians created a style of writing very different from that of their northern neighbors in Mesopotamia. It consists of **hieroglyphs**, "writing of the gods," from the Greek hieros, meaning "holy," and gluphein, "to engrave." Although the number of signs increased over the centuries from about 700 to nearly 5,000, the system of symbolic communication underwent almost no major changes from its advent in the third millennium BCE until 395 CE, when Egypt was conquered by the Byzantine Empire. It consists of three kinds of signs: pictograms, or stylized drawings that represent objects or beings, which can be combined to express ideas; **phonograms**, which are **pictograms** used to represent sounds; and **determinatives**, signs used to indicate which category of objects or beings is in question. The Palette of Narmer is an early example of the then developing hieroglyphic style. It consists largely of pictograms, though in the top center of each side, Narmer's name is represented as a phonogram.

The round circle formed by the two elongated lions' heads intertwined on the recto, or front, of the palette is a bowl for

Hathor, the sky mother, a goddess embodying all female qualities, flanks the top of each side of the palette. Here she appears wearing cow's horns; often, though not here, a sun disk rests between her horns. Such headdresses represent the divine attributes of the figure.

The **mace** was the chief weapon used by the king to strike down enemies, and the scene here is emblematic of his power.

As on the other side of the palette, the king is here accompanied by his sandal-bearer, who stands on his own ground-line. He carries the king's sandals to indicate that the king, who is barefoot, stands on **sacred ground**, and that his acts are themselves sacred.

Narmer, wearing the white crown of Upper Egypt, strikes down his enemy, probably the embodiment of **Lower Egypt** itself, especially since he is, in size, comparable to Narmer himself, suggesting he is likewise a leader.

Two more figures represent the defeated enemy. Behind the one on the left is a small aerial view of a **fortified city**; behind the one on the right, a **gazelle trap**. Perhaps together they represent Narmer's victory over both city and countryside.

The hawk is a symbolic representation of the god **Horus**. The king was regarded as the earthly embodiment of Horus. Here, Horus has a human hand with which he holds a rope tied to a symbolic representation of a conquered land and people.

A human head grows from the same ground as six **papyrus** blossoms, symbol of Lower Egypt. Each blossom represents 1,000 prisoners held captive by the Horus/king.

This hieroglyph identifies the man that Narmer is about to kill, a name otherwise unknown.

Palette of Narmer, **verso side, from Hierakonpolis. Dynasty 1, ca. 3000 BCE.** Schist, height 25 1/4". Egyptian Museum, Cairo.

mixing pigments. The palette celebrates the defeat by Narmer (ruled ca. 3000 BCE) of his enemies and his unification of both Upper and Lower Egypt, which before this time had been at odds. So on the recto side, Narmer wears the red cobra crown of Lower Egypt, and on the verso, or back, he wears the white crown of Upper Egypt—representing his ability (and duty) to harmonize antagonistic elements.

Narmer's palette was not meant for actual use. Rather, it is a **votive**, or ritual object, a gift to a god or goddess that was placed in a temple to ensure that the king, or perhaps some temple official, would have access to a palette throughout eternity. It may or may not register actual historical events, although, in fact, Egypt marks its beginnings with the unification of its Upper and Lower territories. Subsequent kings, at any rate, presented themselves in almost identical terms, as triumphing over their enemies, mace in hand, even though they had no role in a similar military campaign. It is even possible that by the time of Narmer such conventions were already in place, although our system of numbering Egyptian dynasties begins with him. Whether or not the scene depicted is real, the **pictorial formulas**, or conventions of representation, that Egyptian culture used for the rest of its history are fully developed in this piece.

These are two instances of the hieroglyphic sign for **Narmer**, consisting of a catfish above a chisel. Each individual hieroglyph is a pictogram but is utilized here for its phonetic sound. The word for "catfish" is *nar*, and the word for "chisel" is *mer*—hence "Narmer." In the lower instance, the hieroglyph identifies the king. In the instance at the top, the king's name is inside a depiction of his palace seen simultaneously from above, as a ground plan, and from the front, as a facade. This device, called a *serekh*, is traditionally used to hold the king's name.

We are able to identify **Narmer** not only from his hieroglyphic name, next to him, but by his relative size. As befits the king, he is larger than anyone else.

The hieroglyph next to this figure identifies him as the king's **vizier**, the highest official of royal administration.

The defeated **dead** lie in two rows, their decapitated heads between their feet. Narmer in sacred procession reviews them, while above them, a tiny Horus (the hawk) looks on.

Similarly positioned on the other side of the palette and identified by the accompanying hieroglyph, this is the king's **sandal-bearer**.

This is the **mixing bowl** of the palette. The lions may represent competing forces brought under control by the king. Each is held in check by one of the king's **lion-tamers**, figures that in some sense represent state authority.

The **bull** here strikes down his victim and is another representation of the king's might and power. Note that in the depictions of Narmer striking down his victim and in procession, a bull's tail hangs from his waistband.

This is a representation of a **fortified city** as seen both from above, as a floor plan, and from the front, as a facade. It is meant to represent the actual site of Narmer's victory.

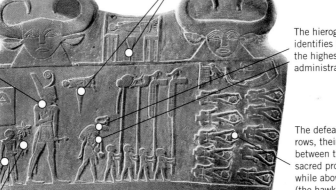

Palette of Narmer, recto side, from Hierakonpolis. Dynasty 1, ca. 3000 BCE. Schist, height 25 1/4". Egyptian Museum, Cairo.

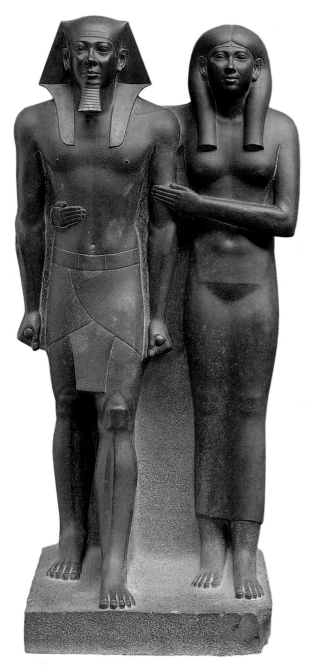

Fig. 1.17 Menkaure with a queen, probably Khamerernebty, from valley temple of Menkaure, Giza. Dynasty 4, ca. 2460 BCE. Schist, height 54½″. Reproduced with permission. © 2006 Museum of Fine Arts, Boston. Harvard University-Boston Museum of Fine Arts. All Rights Reserved. Note that the queen's close-fitting attire is nearly transparent, indicating a very fine weave of linen. Her left arm, circling her husband's waist, and her right hand on his arm is a conventional gesture indicating the couple's marital status.

The Old Kingdom

Although the *Palette of Narmer* probably commemorates an event in life, as a votive object it is devoted, like most surviving Egyptian art and architecture, to burial and the afterlife. The Egyptians buried their dead on the west side of the Nile, where the sun sets, a symbolic reference to death and rebirth since the sun always rises again. The pyramid was the first mon-

umental royal tomb. A massive physical manifestation of the reality of the king's death, it was also the symbolic embodiment of his eternal life. It would endure for generations as, Egyptians believed, would the king's *ka* [kah]. This idea is comparable to an enduring "soul" or "life force," a concept found in many other religions. The *ka*, which all persons possessed, was created at the same time as the physical body, itself essential for the person's existence since it provided the *ka* with an individual identity in which its personality, or *ba* [bah], might also manifest itself. This meant that it was necessary to preserve the body after death so that the *ba* and *ka* might still recognize it for eternity. All the necessities of the afterlife, from food to furniture to entertainment, were placed in the pyramid's burial chamber with the king's body.

Monumental Royal Sculpture: Perfection and Eternity
The word for sculpture in Egyptian is the same as for giving birth. Indeed, funerary sculpture served the same purpose as the pyramids themselves—to preserve and guarantee the king's existence after death, thereby providing a kind of rebirth. The stone materials used for funerary images had to be the hardest, most durable kind, as enduring as the *ka* itself. Sandstone or limestone would not do. The materials of choice were diorite, schist, and granite, stones that can also take on a high polish and, because they are not prone to fracture, they can be finely detailed when carved. Most Egyptian statues were monolithic, or carved out of a single piece of stone, even those depicting more than a single figure, such as the statue of Menkaure with a queen that was also found at his valley temple at Giza (Fig. **1.17**). Here, the deep space created by carving away the side of the stone to fully expose the king's right side seems to free him from the stone. He stands with one foot ahead of the other in the second traditional pose, the conventional depiction of a standing figure. He is not walking. Both feet are planted firmly on the ground (and so his left leg is, of necessity, slightly longer than his right). His back is firmly implanted in the stone panel behind him, but he seems to have emerged farther from it than his wife who accompanies him, as if to underscore his power and might. Although the queen is almost the same size as her husband, her stride is markedly shorter than his. She embraces him, her arm reaching round his back, in a gesture that reminds us of Horus's protective embrace of Khafre, but suggests also the simple marital affection of husband and wife. The ultimate effect of this sculpture—its solidity and unity, its sense of resolute purpose—testifies finally to its purpose, which is to endure for eternity.

The New Kingdom and Its Moment of Change

Throughout the Middle Kingdom and well into the New Kingdom, Egyptian artistic and religious traditions remained intact. But toward the end of the Eighteenth Dynasty, Egypt experienced one of the few real crises of its entire history when, in 1353 BCE, Amenhotep IV (r. 1353–1337 BCE) assumed the throne of his father Amenhotep III (r. 1391–1353 BCE).

Although previous Egyptian kings may have associated themselves with a single god whom they represented in human form, Egyptian religion supported a large number of gods. Even the Nile was worshiped as a god. Amenhotep IV abolished the pantheon of Egyptian gods and established a monotheistic religion in which the sun disk Aten was worshiped exclusively. Other gods were still acknowledged, but they were considered to be too inferior to Aten to be worth worshiping. This type of monotheism is known as *henotheism*. Amenhotep's new religion may have influenced the Hebrews, whose stay in Egypt was contemporaneous with Amenhotep's rule.

Amenhotep IV believed the sun was the creator of all life, and he was so dedicated to Aten that he changed his own name to Akhenaten [ah-ken-AH-ten] ("The Shining Spirit of Aten") and moved the capital of Egypt from Thebes to a site many miles north that he also named Akhetaten (modern Tell el-Amarna). This move transformed Egypt's political and cultural as well as religious life. At this new capital he presided over the worship of Aten as a divine priest and his queen as a divine priestess. Temples to Aten were open courtyards, where the altar received the sun's direct rays.

Why would Amenhotep IV/Akhenaten have substituted monotheism for Egypt's traditional polytheistic religion? Many Egyptologists argue that the switch had to do with enhancing the power of the pharaoh. With the pharaoh representing the one god that mattered, all religious justification for the power held by a priesthood dedicated to the traditional gods was gone. As we have seen, the pharaoh was traditionally associated with the sun god Re. Now in the form of the sun disk Aten, Re was the supreme deity, embodying the characteristics of all the other gods, therefore rendering them superfluous. By analogy, Amenhotep IV/Akhenaten was now supreme priest, rendering all other priests superfluous as well. Simultaneously, the temples dedicated to the other gods lost prestige and influence. These changes also converted the priests into dissidents.

A New Art: The Amarna Style Such significant changes had a powerful effect on the visual arts as well. Previously, Egyptian art had been remarkably stable because its principles were considered a gift of the gods—thus perfect and eternal. But now, the perfection of the gods was in question, and the principles of art were open to reexamination as well. A new art replaced the traditional canon of proportion—the familiar poses of king and queen—with realism, and a sense of immediacy, even intimacy. So Akhenaten allowed himself to be portrayed with startling realism, in what has become known, from the modern name for the new capital, as the Amarna style.

For example, in a small relief from his new capital, Akhenaten has a skinny, weak upper body, and his belly protrudes over his skirt; his skull is elongated behind an extremely long, narrow facial structure; and he sits in a slumped, almost casual position (Fig. **1.18**). (One theory holds that Akhenaten had Marfan's Syndrome, a genetic disorder that leads to skeletal abnormalities.) This depiction contrasts sharply with the idealized depictions of the pharaohs in earlier periods. Akhenaten holds one of his children in his arms and seems to have just kissed her. His two other children sit with the queen across from him, one turning to speak with her mother, the other touching the queen's cheek. The queen herself, Nefertiti [nef-er-TEE-tee], sits only slightly below her husband and appears to share his position and authority. In fact, one of the most striking features of the Amarna style is Nefertiti's prominence in the decoration of the king's temples. In one, for example, she is shown slaughtering prisoners, an image traditionally reserved for the king himself. It is likely that her prominence was part of Akhenaten's attempt to substitute the veneration of his own family (who, after all, represent Aten on earth) for the traditional Amun-Mut-Khonsu family group.

The Return to Thebes and to Tradition Akhenaten's revolution was short-lived. Upon his death, Tutankhaten (r. 1336–1327 BCE), probably Akhenaten's son, assumed the throne and changed his name to Tutankhamun (indicating a return to the more traditional gods, in this case Amun). The new king abandoned el-Amarna, moved the royal family to Memphis in the north, and reaffirmed Thebes as the nation's religious center. He died shortly after and was buried on the west bank of the Nile at Thebes, near the tomb of Hatshepsut.

Tutankhamun's is the only royal tomb in Egypt to have escaped the discovery of looters. When Howard Carter and Lord Carnarvon discovered it under the tomb of the Twentieth Dynasty king Ramses VI in the valley of the Kings near

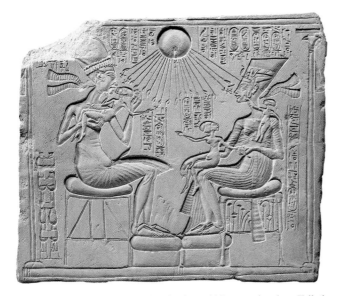

Fig. 1.18 *Akhenaten and His Family,* **from Akhetaten (modern Tell el-Amarna). Dynasty 18, ca. 1345 BCE.** Painted limestone relief, 12 ³/₄″ × 14 ⁷/₈″. Staatliche Museen su Berlin, Preussischer Kulturbesitz, Ägyptisches Museum. Between Akhenaten and his queen Nefertiti, the sun disk Aten shines down beneficently. Its rays end in small hands, which hold the ankh symbol for life before both the king and queen.

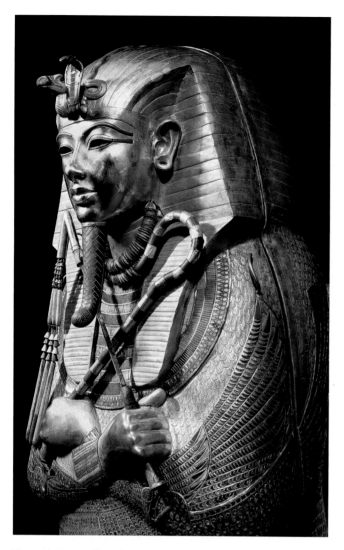

Fig. 1.19 Inner coffin of Tutankamun's sarcophagus, from his tomb, Valley of the Kings, Western Thebes. Dynasty 18, ca. 1335–1327 BCE. Gold, inlaid with glass and semiprecious stones, height 6′ ⁷/₈″. Egyptian Museum, Cairo. The king's mummified body was found inside this coffin, the last of three, consisting of approximately $1.5 million worth of gold.

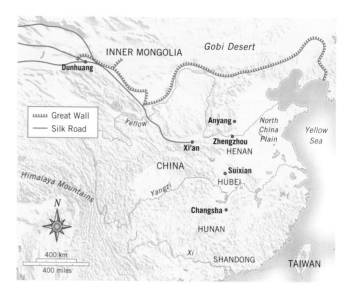

Map 1.4 Map of China, 1000–200 BCE.

goddess of truth, justice, and order. Egyptians believed the heart contained all the emotions, intellect, and character of the individual, and so represented both the good and bad aspects of a person's life. If the heart did not balance with the feather, then the dead person was condemned to nonexistence, to be eaten by a creature called Ammit [AH-mit], the vile "Eater of the Dead," part crocodile, part lion, and part hippopotamus. Osiris, wrapped in his mummy robes, oversaw this moment of judgment. Tut himself, depicted on his sarcophagus with his crossed arms holding crook and flail, was clearly identified with Osiris. From Tutankhamun's time through the Late Period (715–332 BCE) and until the fall of Egypt to the Romans in 30 BCE, the conventions of traditional representation that had begun centuries earlier remained in place.

The Early Civilizations of China and India

Around 4000 BCE, when the climate of the large, fertile valley of China's Yellow River, the North Central Plain, was much milder and the land more forested than it is today, the Neolithic tribal peoples inhabiting the area cultivated the land, growing primarily millet, and used stone tools. Although they domesticated animals, they maintained their hunter-gatherer heritage, until between about 800 BCE and 480 BCE, their culture began to evolve in ways that parallel developments in the Middle East during the same period. In this "Central Plain," so called because its inhabitants believed it to be the center of the country, China transformed itself from an agricultural society into a more urban-centered state (Map 1.4).

By the third century BCE, the government was sufficiently organized that it could build a giant wall across the hills north of the Central Plain to protect it from the menacing Central Asian Huns who lived beyond the northern borders. Some sec-

Dier el-Bahri, they found a coffin consisting of three separate coffins placed one inside the other (Fig. 1.19). These were in turn encased in a quartzite sarcophagus, a rectangular stone coffin that was encased in four gilded, boxlike wooden shrines, also placed one inside the other. In their rigid formality, the coffins within, each depicting the king, hark back to the traditional Egyptian art of the Middle Kingdom.

The elaborate burial process was not meant solely to guarantee survival of the king's *ka* and *ba*. It also prepared him for a "last judgment," a belief system that would find expression in the Hebrew faith as well. In this two-part ritual, deities first questioned the deceased about their behavior in life. Then their hearts, the seat of the *ka*, were weighed against an ostrich feather, symbol of Maat [mah-aht], the

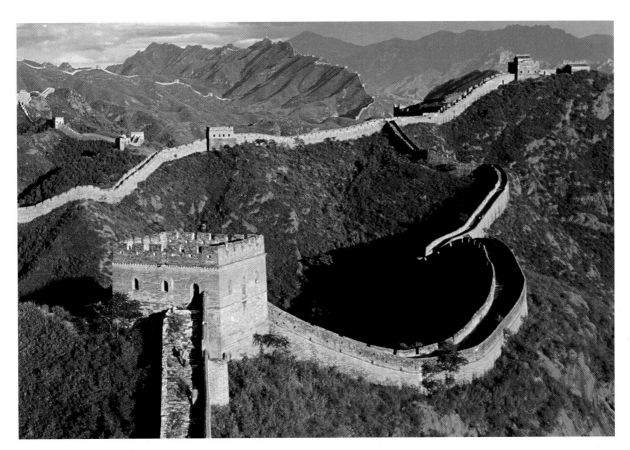

Fig. 1.20 The Great Wall, near Beijing, China. Begun late third century BCE. Length approx. 4,100 miles, average height 25′.
In the third century BCE, the Chinese Emperor Shihuangdi ordered his army to reconstruct, link, and augment walls on the
northern frontier of China in order to form a continuous barrier protecting his young country from northern Mongol "barbarians."

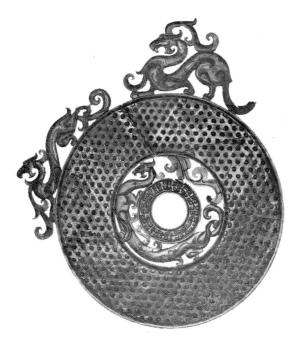

**Fig. 1.21 Ritual disc (Pi) with dragon and phoenix motif. Eastern Zhou
dynasty, Warring States period, 4th–3rd century** BCE. Jade, diameter 6½″.
The Nelson-Atkins Museum of Art, Kansas City, Missouri. Purchase: Nelson
Trust 33-81. This disc was discovered in a tomb, probably placed there
because the Chinese believed that jade preserved the body from decay.

tions of the wall were already in place, built in previous centuries to protect local areas. These were rebuilt and connected to form the Great Wall of China, stretching some 4,100 miles from northeast to northwest China (Fig. **1.20**). New roads and canal systems were built linking the entire nation.

The country had realized a dream of unification symbolized by a ritual jade disc, or *Pi* [pee], made sometime in the fourth or third century BCE (Fig. **1.21**). It is decorated with both a dragon and a phoenix, today commonly found in the context of Chinese wedding ceremonies, where they hang together over the table at the wedding feast. These mythological creatures represent the ancient peoples of China—those in the west and Central Plain who worshiped the dragon and those in the east along the coast who worshiped the phoenix. The union of the two cultures, east and west, was celebrated in the representation of the phoenix and dragon.

Early Chinese Culture

Little remains of the earliest Chinese civilizations. We know that by the middle of the second millennium BCE Chinese leaders ruled from large capitals, rivaling those in the West in their size and splendor. Beneath present-day Zhengzhou [juhng-joe], for instance, lies an early metropolitan center with massive earthen walls. Stone was scarce in this area, but abundant forests made wood plentiful, so it was used to build cities. As impressive as they were, cities built of wood were vulnerable to fire and military attack, and no sign of them remains. Yet we know a fair amount about early Chinese culture from the remains of its written language and the tombs of its rulers. Scholars examining fragments of written scrolls found that the ancient Chinese written language is closely related to modern Chinese. And archeologists discovered that royal Chinese tombs, like Egyptian burial sites, were filled with furnishings, implements, luxury goods, and clothing—anything that the deceased might need in the next world.

The Shang Dynasty (1700–1045 BCE) Chinese records tell of a King Tang who in 1700 BCE established the Shang dynasty. The Shang state was a linked collection of hilltop villages, each overlooking its fields in the river valleys below. It stretched across the plains of the lower Yellow River valley, but it was not a contiguous state with distinct borders; other villages separated some of the Shang villages from one another, and were frequently at war with the Shang. The royal family surrounded itself with priests, who soon developed into a kind of nobility and, in turn, created new walled urban centers focused around the nobles' palaces or temples. These were surrounded by workshop areas where bronze vessels, finely carved jades, and luxury goods were produced. The nobility organized itself into armies—surviving inscriptions describe forces as large as 13,000 men—that controlled and protected the countryside.

The first classic of Chinese literature, *The Book of Changes*, or *I Jing*, which originated in the Shang era, is a guide to interpreting the workings of the universe. A person seeking to understand some aspect of his or her life or situation poses a question and tosses a set of straws or coins. The arrangement they make when they fall leads to a specific text in the *I Jing*. The text describes the conditions of the specific moment, which is, as the title suggests, always a moment of transition, a movement from one set of circumstances to the next. The *I Jing* prescribes certain behaviors appropriate to the moment. Thus, it is a book of wisdom.

This wisdom is based on a simple principle—that order derives from balance, a concept that the Chinese share with the ancient Egyptians. The Chinese believe that over time, through a series of changes, all things work toward a condi-

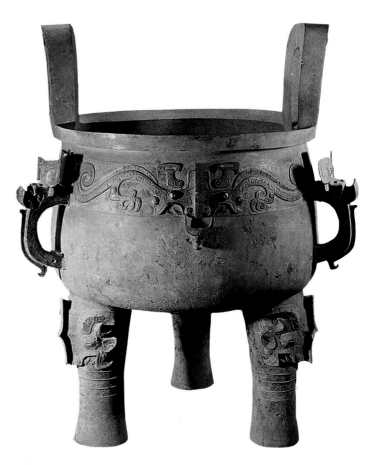

Fig. 1.23 Five-eared *ding* with dragon pattern. ca. 1200 BCE. Bronze, height 48″, diameter at mouth, 32 3/4″. Chinhua County Cultural Museum. One of the key features of Shang bronze decoration is the bilateral symmetry of the animal motifs, suggesting the importance of balance and order in ancient Chinese culture.

tion of balance. Thus, when things are out of balance, diviners might reliably predict the future by understanding that the universe tends to right itself. The image for *T'ai* [tie], or "Peace," for instance, is the unification of heaven and earth—"a time in nature when heaven seems to be on earth .... a sign of social harmony .... when the good elements of society occupy a central position and are in control, the evil elements coming under their influence and change for the better .... when the spirit of heaven rules in man."

In fact, according to the Shang rulers, "the foundation of the universe" is based on the marriage of Qian [chee-an] (at once heaven and the creative male principle) and Kun (the earth, or receptive female principle), symbolized by the Chinese symbol of *yin-yang* (Fig. 1.22). *Yin* is soft, dark, moist, and cool; *yang* is hard, bright, dry, and warm. The two combine to create the endless cycles of change, from night to day, across the four seasons of the year. They balance the five elements (wood, fire, earth, metal, and water) and the five powers of creation (cold, heat, dryness, moisture, and wind). The yin-yang sign, then, is a symbol of har-

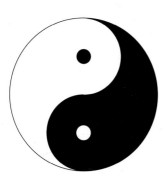

Fig. 1.22 Yin-yang symbol.

monious integration, the perpetual interplay and mutual relation among all things. And note that each side contains a circle of the same values as its opposite—neither side can exist without the other.

The symmetry of the yin-yang motif appears in almost all Shang bronze works. The Shang developed an extremely sophisticated bronze-casting technology, as advanced as any ever used. Many of their bronze vessels—or ding [dee-ung]—used for storage and for wine, had explicitly religious, political, and ceremonial functions (Fig. **1.23**). Most are decorated with fantastic, supernatural creatures, especially dragons, which, for the Shang, symbolized royal authority, strength, and fertility. Their symmetry in turn symbolized the balance the Shang leadership brought to the state. The Shang-ti (or "Lord on High") granted the Shang rulers their authority, and from the "dragon throne" they ruled China with great armies, consisting primarily of archers.

The Zhou Dynasty (1027–256 BCE) In 1027 BCE, a rebel tribe known as the Zhou [joe] overthrew the Shang dynasty, claiming that the Shang had lost the "mandate of heaven" by not ruling virtuously. It seems that the warrior culture of the Shang was incompatible with the more stable forces that drive an agricultural economy, where power resides less in military might and more in the production and trade of goods and foodstuffs. The principle of a natural order in the universe of the kind celebrated in the *Book of Changes* and embodied in the symbol of yin-yang is a manifestation of a society increasingly concerned with the agricultural cycle of planting, growing, and harvesting crops. In fact, both the *Book of Changes* and the yin-yang symbol were originated by the Shang but codified and written down by the Zhou. One of the oldest songs in the oldest collection of Chinese poetry, the "Shi jing" or *Book of Songs*, celebrates the harvest in particular (**Reading 1.5**):

READING 1.5   **from the *Book of Songs***

> Abundant is the year, with much millet, much rice;
> But we have tall granaries,
> To hold myriads, many myriads and millions of
>   grain.
> We make wine, make sweet liquor,
> We offer it to ancestor, to ancestress,
> We use it to fulfil all the rites,
> To bring down blessings upon each and all.

The harvest here is the sign of the family's harmony with nature, the symbol that the family's ancestors are part of the same natural cycle of life and death, planting and harvest, as the universe as a whole. It is communal in its expression, emphasizing less the importance of the individual so characteristic of Western thought, and more the good the harvest brings to the whole—a distinctly Asian worldview.

Daoism and Confucianism The songs in the *Shi jing* are contemporary with the poems that make up the *Dao de jing* [dow duh jee-ung] (*The Way and Its Power*), the primary philosophical treatise, written in verse, of Daoism, the Chinese mystical school of thought. The Dao ("the way") is deeply embedded in nature, and to experience it, the individual must let go of the self through contemplation and enter into the flow of life. Contemplation of the teachings in the 5,000-word *Dao de jing* aids this process. The book consists of 81 poems believed to have been composed by Lao Zi [lou zuh] ("the Old One") in the sixth century BCE. In essence, it argues for a unifying principle in all nature, what the Chinese call qi [chee]. The qi can be understood only by those who live in total simplicity, and the Dao is the path to such a life. The Daoist engages in strict dietary practices, breathing exercises, and meditation. In considering such images as the one expressed in the following poem, the first in the volume, the Daoist finds his or her way to enlightenment (**Reading 1.6**):

READING 1.6   **from the *Dao de jing***

> There are ways but the Way is uncharted;
> There are names but not nature in words:
> Nameless indeed is the source of creation
> But things have a mother and she has a name.
>
> The secret waits for the insight
> Of eyes unclouded by longing;
> Those who are bound by desire
> See only the outward container.
>
> These two come paired but distinct
> By their names.
> Of all things profound,
> Say that their pairing is deepest,
> The gate to the root of the world.

The final stanza seems to be a direct reference to the principle of yin-yang, itself a symbol of the qi. But the chief argument here, and the argument of the Dao as a whole, is that enlightenment lies neither in the visible world nor in language, although to find the "way" one must, paradoxically, pass through or utilize both. Daoism thus represents a spiritual desire to transcend the material world.

If Daoism seeks to leave the world behind, the second great canon of teachings developed during the Zhou dynasty, Confucianism, seeks to define the proper way to behave in the world. For 550 years, from about 771 BCE to the final collapse of the Zhou in 221 BCE, China was subjected to ever greater political turmoil as warring political factions struggled for power. Reacting to this state of affairs was the man many consider China's greatest philosopher and teacher, Kong Fu Zi, or, as he is known in the West, Confucius.

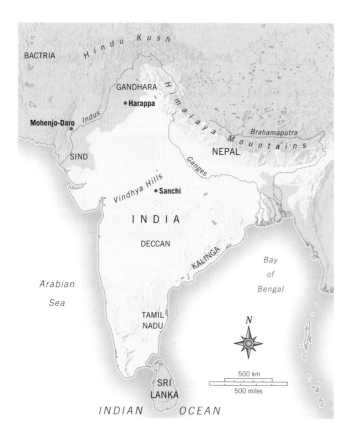

Map 1.5 India around 1500 BCE. Cut off from the rest of Asia by high mountains to the north, India was nevertheless a center of trade by virtue of its prominent maritime presence.

learn from it immediately to serve your parents and ultimately to serve your prince. It also provides wide acquaintance with the names of birds, beasts, and plants."

After his death, in 479 BCE, Confucius' followers wrote down his words in a book known in English as the *Analects*. Where the *Dao de jing* is a spiritual work, the *Analects* is a practical one. At the heart of Confucius' teaching is the principle of *li* [lee]—civility, propriety—in short, etiquette. Politeness and good manners lead to the second principle, *jen* [ren], or the ideal relationship that should exist between people. Based on respect for oneself, *jen* extends this respect to all others, manifesting itself as charity, courtesy, and above all, justice. *Te* [duh] is the power of moral example that an individual, especially a ruler, can exert through a life dedicated to the exercise of *li* and *jen*. Finally, in the ideal culture thus created, *wen*, or the arts of peace, will result. Poetry, music, painting, and the other arts will all reveal an inherent order and harmony reflecting the order and harmony of the state. Like the excellent leader, they provide a model of virtue. The Chinese moral order, like that of the Greeks (see chapter 2), did not depend upon divine decree or authority, but instead upon the people's own right actions.

Its emphasis on respect for age, authority, and morality made Confucianism extremely popular among Chinese leaders and the artists they patronized. It embraced the emperor, the state, and the family in a single ethical system with a hierarchy that was believed to mirror the structure of the cosmos. As a result, the Han [hahn] dynasty (first century BCE) adopted Confucianism as the Chinese state religion, and a thorough knowledge of the Confucian classics was subsequently required of any politically ambitious person.

Ancient India

Indian civilization was born along the Indus [IN-duhs] River in the northwest corner of the Indian subcontinent somewhere around 2700 BCE in an area known as Sind—from which the words India and Hindu originate (see Map **1.5**). The earliest Indian peoples lived in at least two great cities in the Indus valley, Mohenjo-daro [moh-HEN-joh-DAR-oh], on the banks of the Indus, and Harappa [huh-RAH-puh], on the river Ravi [RAH-vee], downstream from modern Lahore [luh-HORE]. By the early years of the second millennium they were adept at bronze casting, and they even had a written language, although it remains undeciphered.

Sometime around 1500 BCE the Aryans [AIR-ee-uhnz], nomads from the north, invaded the Indus River valley and conquered its inhabitants, making them slaves. Thus began the longest-lasting set of rigid, class-based societal divisions in world history, the Indian caste system. By the beginning of the first millennium BCE, these castes consisted of five principal groups, based on occupation: At the bottom of the ladder was a group considered "untouchable," people so scorned by society that they were not even considered a caste. Next in line were the Shudras [SHOO-druhz], unskilled workers. Then came the Vaishyas [VYSH-yuhz], artisans and mer-

Confucius was born to aristocratic parents in the province of Shandong in 551 BCE. By his early twenties, Confucius had begun to teach a way of life, Confucianism, based on self-discipline and proper relations among people. If each individual led a virtuous life, then the family would live in harmony. If the family lived in harmony, then the village would follow its moral leadership. If the village exercised proper behavior toward its neighbor villages, then the country would live in peace and thrive.

Traditional Chinese values—values that Confucius believed had once guided the Zhou, such as self-control, propriety, and respect for one's elders—lie at the core of this system. In order to capture these values, tradition has it that Confucius compiled and edited *The Book of Changes*, *The Book of Songs* (which he edited down to 305 verses), and four other "classic" Chinese texts: *The Book of History*, containing speeches and pronouncements of historical rulers; *The Book of Rites*, which is essentially a code of conduct; *The Spring and Autumn Annals*, a history of China up to the fifth century BCE; and a lost treatise on music.

Confucius particularly valued *The Book of Songs*. "My little ones," he told his followers, "why don't you study the Songs? Poetry will exalt you, make you observant, enable you to mix with others, provide an outlet for your vexations; you

chants. They were followed by the Kshatriyas [kuh-SHAHT-ree-uhz], rulers and warriors. At the highest level were the Brahmins [BRAH-minz], priests and scholars.

Hinduism and the Vedic Tradition The social castes were sanctioned by the religion the Aryans brought with them, a religion based on a set of sacred hymns to the Aryan gods. These hymns, called *Vedas* [VAY-duhz], were written in the Aryan language, Sanskrit, and they gave their name to an entire period of Indian civilization, the Vedic [VAY-dik] period (ca. 1500–322 BCE). From the *Vedas* in turn came the *Upanishads* [oo-PAHN-ih-shadz], a book of mystical and philosophical texts that date from sometime after 800 BCE. Taken together, the *Vedas* and the *Upanishads* form the basis of the Hindu religion, with Brahman, the universal soul, at its center. The religion has no single body of doctrine, nor any standard set of practices.

The *Upanishads* argue that all existence is a fabric of false appearances. What appears to the senses is entirely illusory. Only Brahman is real. Thus, in a famous story illustrating the point, a tiger, orphaned as a cub, is raised by goats. It learns, as a matter of course, to eat grass and make goat sounds. But one day it meets another tiger, who takes it to a pool to look at itself. There, in its reflection in the water, it discovers its true nature. The individual soul needs to discover the same truth, a truth that will free it from the endless cycle of birth, death, and rebirth and unite it with the Brahman in **nirvana** [nir-VAH-nuh], a place or state free from worry, pain, and the external world.

Brahman, Vishnu, and Shiva As Hinduism [HIN-doo-iz-um] developed, the functions of Brahman, the divine source of all being, were split among three gods: Brahma, the creator; Vishnu [VISH-noo], the preserver; and Shiva [SHEE-vuh], the destroyer. Vishnu was one of the most popular of the Hindu deities. In his role as preserver he is the god of benevolence, forgiveness, and love, and like the other two main Hindu gods, he was believed capable of assuming human form, which he did more often than the other gods due to his great love for humankind. Among Vishnu's most famous incarnations is his appearance as Rama [rah-mah] in the oldest of the Hindu epics, the *Ramayana* [rah-mah-yuh-nuh] (*Way of Rama*), written by Valmiki [vahl-MIH-kee] in about 550 BCE. Like Homer in ancient Greece, Valmiki gathered together many existing legends and myths into a single story, in this case narrating the lives of Prince Rama and his queen, Sita [SEE-tuh]. The two serve as models of Hindu life. Rama is the ideal son, brother, husband, warrior, and king, and Sita loves, honors, and serves her husband with absolute and unquestioning fidelity. These characters face moral dilemmas to which they must react according to **dharma** [DAHR-muh], good and righteous conduct reflecting the cosmic moral order that underlies all existence. For Hindus, correct actions can lead to cosmic harmony, and bad actions, violating dharma, can trigger cosmic tragedies such as floods and earthquakes.

An equally important incarnation of Vishnu is as the charioteer Krishna [KRISH-nuh] in the later Indian epic the Mahahbarata [muh-ha-BAHR-uh-tuh], composed between 400 BCE and 400 CE. In the sixth book of the *Mahahbarata*, titled the *Bhagavad Gita* [BUH-guh-vud GHEE-tuh], Krishna comes to the aid of Arjuna [ahr-JOO-nuh], a warrior who is tormented by the conflict between his duty to fight and kill his kinsmen in battle and the Hindu prohibition against killing. Krishna explains to Arjuna that as a member of the Kshatriya caste—that is, as a warrior—he is freed from the Hindu sanction against killing. In fact, by fighting well and doing his duty, he can free himself from the endless cycle of birth, death, and reincarnation, and move toward spiritual union with the Brahman (**Reading 1.7**):

READING 1.7 **from "The Second Teaching" in the *Bhagavad Gita: Krishna's Counsel in Time of War***

As the mountainous depths
of the ocean
are unmoved when waters
rush into it,
so the man unmoved
when desires enter him
attains a peace that eludes
the man of many desires.

When he renounces all desires
and acts without craving,
possessiveness,
or individuality, he finds peace.

This is the place of the infinite spirit;
achieving it, one is freed from delusion;
abiding in it even at the time of death,
one finds the pure calm of infinity.

But Vishnu's popularity is probably most attributable to his celebration of erotic love, which to Hindus symbolizes the mingling of the self and the absolute spirit of Brahman. In the *Vishnu Puranas* [poor-AH-nuhz] (the "old stories" of Vishnu), collected about 500 CE, Vishnu, in his incarnation as Krishna, is depicted as seducing one after another of his devotees. In one story, he seduces an entire band of milkmaids: "They considered every instant without him a myriad of years; and prohibited (in vain) by husbands, fathers, brothers, they went forth at night to sport with Krishna, the object of their affection." Allowing themselves to be seduced does not suggest that the milkmaids were immoral, but shows an almost inevitable manifestation of their souls' quest for union with divinity.

If Brahma is the creator of the world, Shiva takes what Brahma has made and embodies the world's cyclic rhythms.

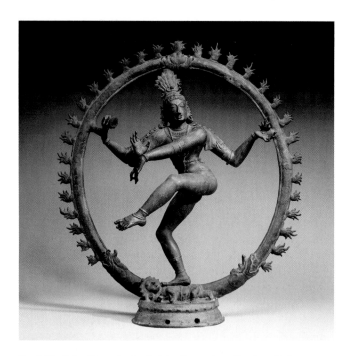

Fig. 1.24 *Shiva Nataraja, Lord of the Dance,* from Southern India. **Eleventh century CE.** Copper, height 43 ⅛". © The Cleveland Museum of Art. Purchase from the J. H. Wade Fund, 1930.331. Bronze and copper images of Shiva dancing were produced in large editions by tenth- and eleventh-century artists of Tamil Nadu, in South India.

Since in Hinduism, creation follows destruction, Shiva, though a god of destruction, is regarded as a reproductive power as well, one who restores what has been dissolved. In this reproduction mode, he is represented as the *linga* [LING-uh] (phallus), a symbol of regeneration. Shiva is also commonly portrayed as Shiva Nataraja [nah-tuh-RAH-juh], Lord of the Dance (Fig. **1.24**), framed in a circle of fire, symbolic of both creation and destruction, the endless cycle of birth, death, and reincarnation. Since Shiva embodies the rhythms of the universe, he is also a great dancer. All the gods were present when Shiva first danced, and they begged him to dance again. Shiva promised to do so in the hearts of his devotees as well as in a sacred grove in Tamil Nadu [TA-mul NAH-doo] in southern India. Artists there are responsible for many of the images of Shiva dancing, such as the one illustrated here.

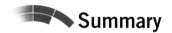 # Summary

■ **The Beginnings of Culture** Culture can be defined as a way of living practiced by a group of people and passed on from one generation to the next. It took thousands of years for cultures to develop into full-blown civilizations. A civilization is distinct from a culture in its ability to organize itself thoroughly as a social, economic, and political entity by means, especially, of written language, which did not come into being until about 3000 BCE, after human culture shifted from its hunter-gatherer origins to agriculture-based communities. As cultures became more stable and permanent, they became capable of producing not only pottery but metalwork, monumental architecture, and literature.

■ **Mesopotamia** In the Tigris and Euphrates valleys of the Fertile Crescent, a series of competing cultures arose beginning in the late fourth century BCE with the Sumerians, who built monumental ziggurats dedicated to the gods and developed a system of writing. They were succeeded by the Akkadians and Babylonians, the last of whom developed a code of law preserved in a carved stone monument. The first epic poem to survive, the *Epic of Gilgamesh,* originated in these cultures. While most cultures that arose in the Fertile Crescent were polytheistic, the Hebrew religion was monotheistic. The written word was central to their culure and lives on in their book of law, the Torah.

■ **Egypt** The predictable cycle of flood and sun, and with it the annual inundation of the Nile River valley, helped to create, in Egypt, a strong cultural belief in the stability and balance of all things. Each night the sun god Re, with whom the Egyptian kings were strongly identified, descends into darkness only to rise again, as does the Nile on a yearly basis. Each person's soul or life force (the *ka*) was believed to follow this same cycle, and as a result, most surviving Egyptian art and architecture is devoted to burial and the afterlife, the cycle of life, death, and rebirth.

■ **China and India** In the river valleys of China and India other civilizations arose. In China, the Qin dynasty unified the country and built a Great Wall to protect it. During the Shang dyansty, a philosophical and religious tradition arose that emphasized the balance of opposites embodied in the yin-yang symbol, leading to the development of the *Dao de jing* and Confucianism. In India, the Hindu religion developed, which also emphasizes the sacred rhythms of creation and destruction, birth, death, and rebirth.

Egyptian and Greek Sculpture

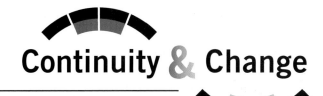

Continuity & Change

Freestanding Greek sculpture of the Archaic period—that is, sculpture dating from about 600–480 BCE—is notable for its stylistic connections to 2,000 years of Egyptian tradition. The Late Period statue of Mentuemhet [men-too-em-het] (Fig. **1.25**), from Thebes, dating from around 2500 BCE, differs hardly at all from Old Kingdom sculpture at Giza (see Fig. 1.17), and even though the *Anavysos* [ah-NAH-vee-sus] *Kouros* (Fig. **1.26**), from a cemetery near Athens, represents a significant advance in relative naturalism over the Greek sculpture of just a few years before, it still resembles its Egyptian ancestors. Remarkably, since it follows upon the Anavysos Kouros by only 75 years, the *Doryphoros* [dor-IF-uh-ros] (*Spear Bearer*) (Fig. **1.27**) is significantly more naturalistic. Although

this is a Roman copy of a lost fifth-century BCE bronze Greek statue, we can assume it reflects the original's naturalism, since the original's sculptor, Polyclitus [pol-ih-KLY-tus], was renowned for his ability to render the human body realistically. But this advance, characteristic of Golden Age Athens, represents more than just a cultural taste for naturalism. As we will see in the next chapter, it also represents a heightened cultural sensitivity to the worth of the individual, a belief that as much as we value what we have in common with one another—the bond that creates the city-state—our *individual* contributions are at least of equal value. By the fifth century BCE, the Greeks clearly understood that individual genius and achievement could be a matter of civic pride. ■

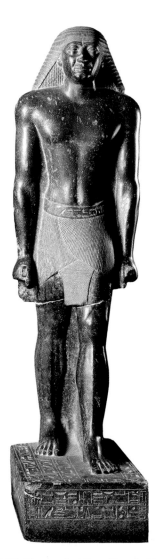

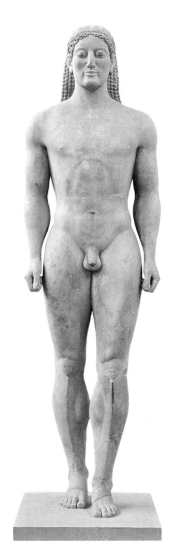

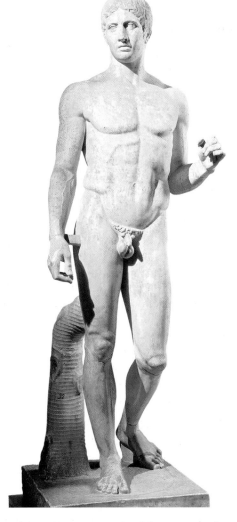

Fig. 1.25 *Mentuemhet*, **from Karnak, Thebes. ca. 660 BCE.** Granite, height 54″. Egyptian Museum, Cairo.

Fig.1.26 *Anavysos Kouros*, **perhaps young Kroisos, from a cemetery at Anavysos [ah-NAH-vee-sus], near Athens. ca. 525 BCE.** Marble with remnants of paint, height 6′ 4″. National Archaeological Museum, Athens; **Fig. 1.27** *Doryphoros (Spear Bearer)*, **Roman copy after the original bronze by Polyclitus of ca. 450–440 BCE.** Marble, height 6′ 6″. Museo Archeològico Nazionale, Naples.

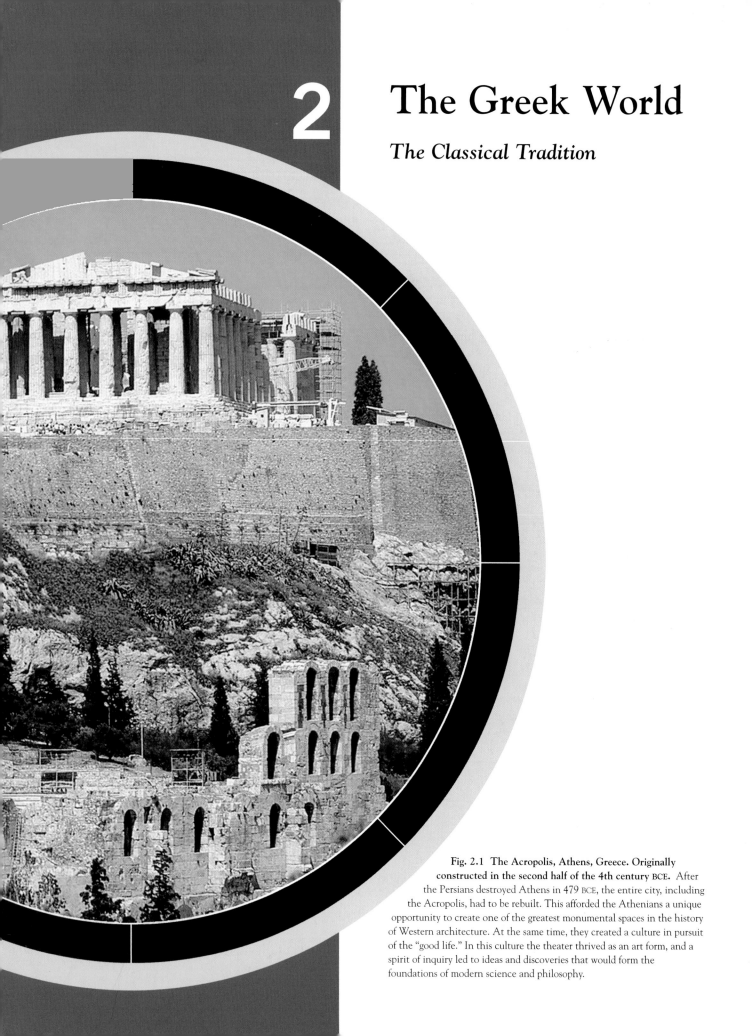

2 The Greek World

The Classical Tradition

Fig. 2.1 The Acropolis, Athens, Greece. Originally constructed in the second half of the 4th century BCE. After the Persians destroyed Athens in 479 BCE, the entire city, including the Acropolis, had to be rebuilt. This afforded the Athenians a unique opportunity to create one of the greatest monumental spaces in the history of Western architecture. At the same time, they created a culture in pursuit of the "good life." In this culture the theater thrived as an art form, and a spirit of inquiry led to ideas and discoveries that would form the foundations of modern science and philosophy.

> **❝** *Although they are only breath, words which I command are immortal* **❞**

Sappho

n the fifth and fourth centuries BCE, Athens was the center of the Greek world. Still predominantly rural and agricultural, it was one *polis* among some 800 other *poleis*—or city-states—that stretched across the Greek Peloponnese, the islands of the Aegean Sea, and even further around the Mediterranean to the Italian peninsula and the mainland of Asia Minor (see Map **2.1**). In fact, the Greek *poleis* are distinguished by their isolation from one another and their fierce sense of independence. The Greek mainland is a very rugged country of mountains separating small areas of arable land. The sea naturally separates each of the Greek islands from the mainland and each other. In this fractured geography, each polis came to think of itself less as a place and more as cultural center in its own right. Each citizen owed allegiance and loyalty to the *polis*. They depended upon and served in its military. And they asserted their iden-

tity, first of all, by participating in the affairs of their own particular city-state. And yet, curiously, they maintained an identity as Greeks.

Like most *poleis*, the *polis* of Athens consisted of an urban center, small by modern standards, surrounding a natural citadel which could serve as a fortification, but which usually functioned as the city-state's religious center (Fig. 2.1, Map **2.2**). The Greeks called this citadel an **acropolis** [uh-KROP-uh-liss]—literally, the "top of the city." On lower ground, at the foot of the acropolis, was the **agora** [AG-ur-ruh], a large open space that served as public meeting place, marketplace, and civic center. The principle architectural feature of the agora was the **stoa** (Fig. 2.2), a long open arcade supported by colonnades, rows of columns. While Athenians could shop for grapes, figs, flowers, and lambs in the agora, it was far more than just a shopping center. It was the place where citizens

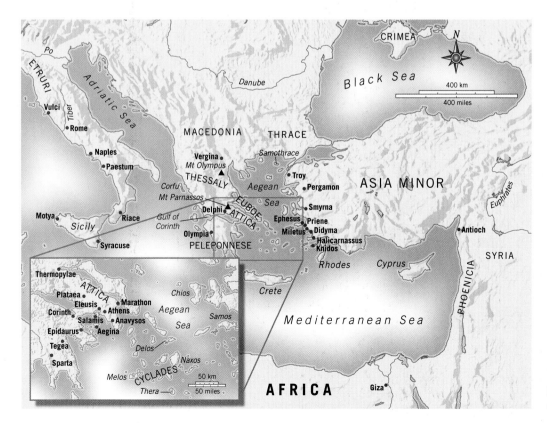

Map 2.1 The city-states of Ancient Greece.

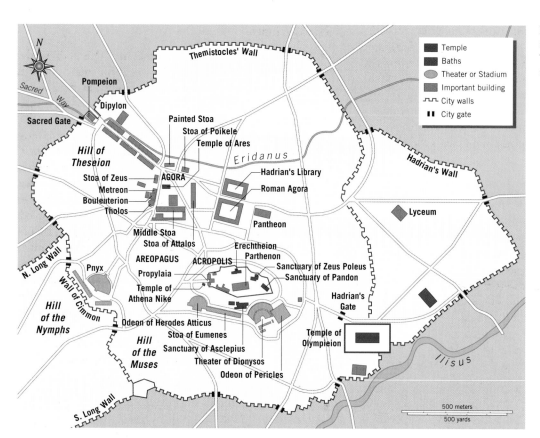

Map 2.2 **Athens as it appeared in the late 5th century** BCE. The map shows a modern artist's rendering of the city.

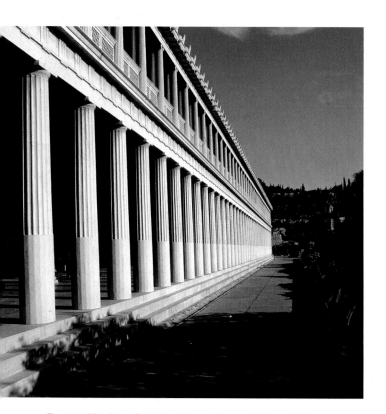

Fig. 2.2 The Stoa of Attalos, Athens, Greece. 150 BCE. This stoa, reconstructed at the eastern edge of the modern agora, retains traditional form. The broad causeway on the right was the Panathenaic Way, the route of the ritual processions to the Acropolis in the distance. The original agora buildings lie farther to the right and overlook the Panathenaic Way.

congregated, debated the issues of the day, argued points of law, settled disputes, and presented philosophical discourse. In short, it was the place where they practiced their politics.

The Greek philosopher Aristotle (384–322 BCE) described the Athenian *polis* in his *Politics* like this: "The partnership finally composed of several villages is the *polis*; it has at last attained the limit of virtually complete self-sufficiency, and thus while it comes into existence for the sake of mere life, it exists for the sake of the good life." For Aristotle, the essential purpose of the polis was to guarantee, barring catastrophe, that each of its citizens may flourish. Writing in the fourth century BCE, Aristotle is thinking back to the Athens of the fifth century BCE, the so-called Golden Age. During these years the pursuit of what Aristotle called *eudaimonia* [yoo-day-MOE-nee-uh], "the good or flourishing life," resulted in a culture of astonishing sophistication and diversity. For *eudaimonia* is not simply a happy or pleasurable existence; rather, the *polis* provides the conditions in which each individual may pursue an "activity of soul in accordance with complete excellence." For Aristotle, this striving to "complete excellence" defines Athens in the Golden Age. The *polis* produced a body of philosophical thought so penetrating and insightful that the questions it posed—the relationship between individual freedom and civic responsibility, the nature of the beautiful, the ideal harmony between the natural world and the intellectual or spiritual realm, to name a few—and the conclusions it reached dominated Western inquiry for centuries to come.

This chapter traces the rise of Greek culture from its earliest roots in the pre-literary cultures of the Aegean Sea, from whom the Greeks believed their own great culture sprang, through its Golden Age in the fifth century BCE, when Athens rose to a place of preeminence, and then finally tracing Greece's cultural domination of the Eastern Mediterranean world and beyond, until, in the first century BCE, Rome came to challenge Greek ascendancy across the Mediterranean basin.

Bronze Age Culture in the Aegean

The Aegean Sea, in the eastern Mediterranean, is filled with islands. Here, beginning in about 3000 BCE, seafaring cultures took hold. So many were the islands, and so close to one another, that navigators were always within sight of land. In the natural harbors where seafarers came ashore, port communities developed and trade began to flourish. A house from approximately 1650 BCE was excavated at Akrotiri on Thera, one of a group of islands known as the Cyclades.

The later Greeks thought of the Bronze Age Aegean peoples as their ancestors—particularly those who inhabited the islands Cyclades, the island of Crete, and Mycenae, on the Peloponnese [PEL-uh-poh-neez]—and considered their activities and culture as part of their own prehistory. They even had a word for the way they knew them—*archaiologia* [ar-kaee-oh-LOH-ghee-uh], "knowing the past." They did not practice archeology as we do today, excavating ancient sites and scientifically analyzing the artifacts discovered there. Rather, they learned of their past through legends passed down, at first orally and then in writing, from generation to generation. Interestingly, the modern practice of archeology has confirmed much of what was legendary to the Greeks.

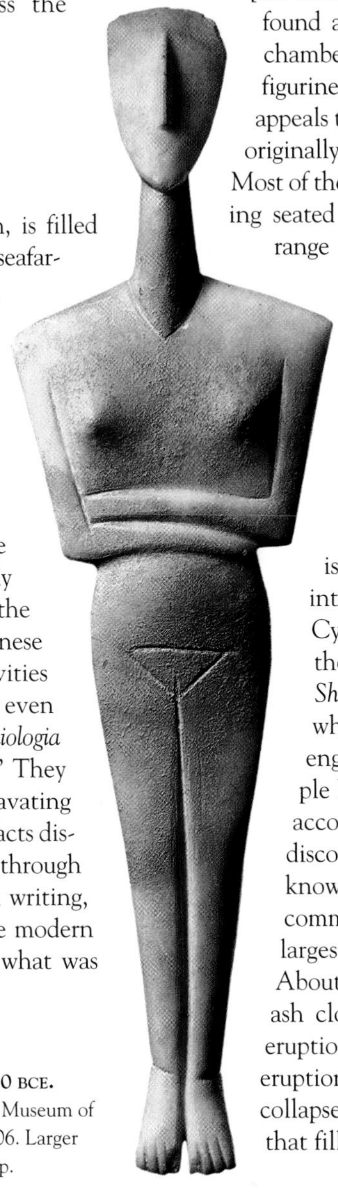

Fig. 2.3 Figurine of a woman from the Cyclades. ca. 2500 BCE. Marble, height 15³/₄″. Nicholas P. Goulandris Foundation. Museum of Cycladic Arts, Athens. N. P. Goulandris Collection, No. 206. Larger examples of such figurines may have been objects of worship.

The Cyclades

The Cyclades are a group of more than 100 islands in the Aegean Sea between mainland Greece and the island of Crete. They form a roughly circular shape, giving them their name, from the Greek word *kyklos* [kih-klos], "circle" (also the origin of our word "cycle"). No written records of the early Cycladic [sih-KLAD-ik] people remain, although archeologists have found a good deal of art in and around hillside burial chambers. The most famous of these artifacts are marble figurines in a highly simplified and abstract style that appeals to the modern eye (Fig. 2.3). The Cycladic figures originally looked quite different because they were painted. Most of the figurines depict females, but male figures, including seated harpists and acrobats, also exist. The figurines range in height from a few inches to life-size, but anatomical detail in all of them is reduced to essentials. With their toes pointed down, their heads tilted back, and their arms crossed across their chests, the fully extended figures are corpselike. Their function remains unknown, but some scholars suggest they were used for home worship and then buried with their owner.

By about 2200 BCE, trade with the larger island of Crete to the south brought the Cyclades into Crete's political orbit and radically altered late Cycladic life. Evidence of this influence survives in the form of wall paintings such as the *Miniature Ship Fresco*, a frieze at the top of at least three walls, which suggests a prosperous seafaring community engaged in a celebration of the sea (Fig. 2.4). People lounge on terraces and rooftops as boats glide by, accompanied by leaping dolphins. The painting was discovered in 1967 on the island of Thera (today known as Santorini [san-tor-EE-nee]), at Akrotiri, a community that had been buried beneath one of the largest volcanic eruptions in the last 10,000 years. About 7 cubic miles of magma spewed forth, and the ash cloud that resulted during the first phase of the eruption was about 23 miles high. The enormity of the eruption caused the volcano at the center of Thera to collapse, producing a caldera, a large basin or depression that filled with seawater. The present island of Thera is

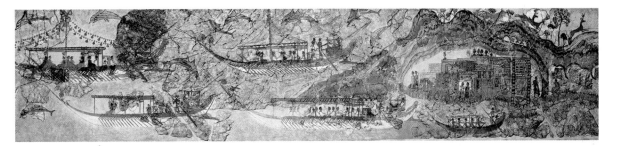

Fig. 2.4 *Miniature Ship Fresco* **(detail from the left section), from Room 5, West House, Akrotiri, Thera. Before 1623 BCE.** Height 15³/₄″. National Archaeological Museum, Athens. While oarsmen rowed these ships, they were also equipped with central masts for sailing.

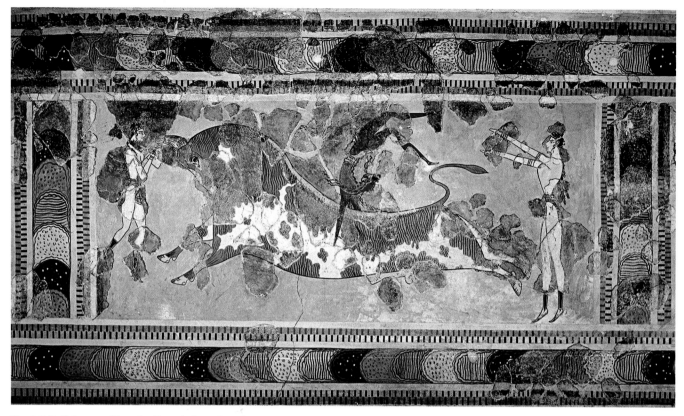

Fig. 2.5 *Bull Leaping (Toreador Fresco),* **from the palace complex at Knossos, Crete. ca. 1450–1375** BCE. Fresco, height approx. 24 $\frac{1}{2}$". Archaeological Museum, Iráklion, Crete. The darker patches of the fresco are original fragments. The lighter areas are modern restorations.

actually the eastern rim of the original volcano (small volcanoes are still active in the center of Thera's crescent sea).

The eruption was so great that it left evidence worldwide—in the stunted growth of tree rings as far away as Ireland and California and in ash taken from ice core samples in Greenland. With this evidence, scientists have dated the eruption to 1623 BCE. In burying the city, it also preserved the city of Akrotiri. Not only were their homes elaborately decorated—with mural paintings such as the *Miniature Ship Fresco,* made with water-based pigments on wet plaster—but they also enjoyed a level of personal hygiene unknown in Western culture until Roman times. Clay pipes led from interior toilets and baths to sewers built under winding, paved streets. Straw reinforced the walls of their homes, protecting them against earthquakes and insulating them from the heat of the Mediterranean sun.

Minoan Culture in Crete

Just to the south of the Cyclades lies Crete, the largest of the Aegean islands. Bronze Age civilization developed there as early as 3000 BCE. Trade routes from Crete established communication with such diverse areas as Turkey, Cyprus [SY-prus], Egypt, Afghanistan, and Scandinavia, from which the island imported copper, ivory, amethyst, lapis lazuli, carnelian, gold, and amber. From Britain, Crete imported the tin necessary to produce bronze. A distinctive culture called Minoan [mih-NO-un] flour-

ished on Crete from about 1900 to 1375 BCE. The name comes from the legendary king Minos [MY-nos], who was said to have ruled the island's ancient capital of Knossos [NOSS-us].

Many of the motifs in the frescoes at Akrotiri, in the Cyclades, also appear in the art decorating Minoan palaces on Crete, including the palace at Knossos. This suggests the mutual influence of Cycladic and Minoan cultures by the start of the second millennium BCE. Unique to Crete, however, is emphasis on the bull, the central element of one of the best-preserved frescoes at Knossos, the *Toreador Fresco* (Fig. **2.5**). Three almost-nude figures appear to toy with a charging bull. (As in Egyptian art, women are traditionally depicted with light skin, men with a darker complexion.) The woman on the left holds the bull by the horns, the man vaults over its back, and the woman on the right seems to have either just finished a vault or to have positioned herself to catch the man. It is unclear whether this is a ritual activity, perhaps part of a rite of passage. What we do know is that the Minoans regularly sacrificed bulls, as well as other animals, and that the bull was at least symbolically associated with male virility and strength.

Female Deities The people of Thera and Crete seem to have shared the same religion as well as similar artistic motifs. Ample archeological evidence tells us that the Minoans in Crete worshiped female deities. We do not know much more than that, but some students of ancient religions have proposed that the Minoan worship of one or more female deities is evidence that in very early cultures the principal deity was a goddess rather than a god.

It has long been believed that one of the Minoan female deities was a snake goddess, but recently, scholars have questioned the authenticity of most of the existing snake goddess figurines. Sir Arthur Evans (1851–1941), who first excavated at the Palace of Minos on Crete, identified images of the Cretan goddess as "Mountain Goddess," "Snake Goddess," "Dove Goddess," "Goddess of the Caves," "Goddess of the Double Axes," "Goddess of the Sports," and "Mother Goddess." Evans saw all of these as different aspects of a single deity, or Great Goddess. Arthur Evans was the archeologist responsible for the first major excavation on Crete in the early twentieth century. A century after he introduced the Snake Goddess (Fig. **2.6**) to the world, scholars are still debating its authenticity. In his book *Mysteries of the Snake Goddess* (2002), Kenneth Lapatin makes a convincing case that craftspeople employed by Evans manufactured artifacts for the antiquities market. He believes that the body of the statue is an authentic antiquity, but the form in which we see it is largely the imaginative fabrication of Evans's restorers. Many parts were missing when the figures were unearthed, and so an artist working for Evans fashioned new parts and attached them to the figure. The snake in the goddess's right hand lacked a head, leaving its identity as a snake open to question. Most of the goddess's left arm, including the snake in her hand, were absent and later fabricated. When the figure was discovered, it lacked a head, and this one is completely fabricated. The cat on the goddess's head is original, although it was not found with the statue. Lapatin believes that Sir Arthur, eager to advance his own theory that Minoan religion was dedicated to the worship of a Great Goddess, never doubted the manner in which the figures were restored. As interesting as the figure is, its identity as a snake goddess is at best dubious. We cannot even say with certainty that the principal deity of the Minoan culture was female, let alone that she was a snake goddess. There are no images of a snake goddess in surviving Minoan wall frescoes, engraved gems, or seals, and almost all of the statues depicting her are fakes or imaginative reconstructions.

The Palace of Minos The *Snake Goddess* was discovered along with other ritual objects in a storage pit in the Palace of Minos at Knossos. The palace as Evans found it is enormous, covering over six acres. There were originally two palaces at the site—an "old palace," dating from 1900 BCE, and a "new palace," built over the old one after an enormous earthquake in 1750 BCE. This "new palace" was the focus of Evans's attention.

As the reconstruction drawing of the palace makes clear, it was only loosely organized around a central, open courtyard (Fig. **2.7**). Leading from the courtyard were corridors, staircases, and passageways that connected living quarters, ritual spaces, baths,

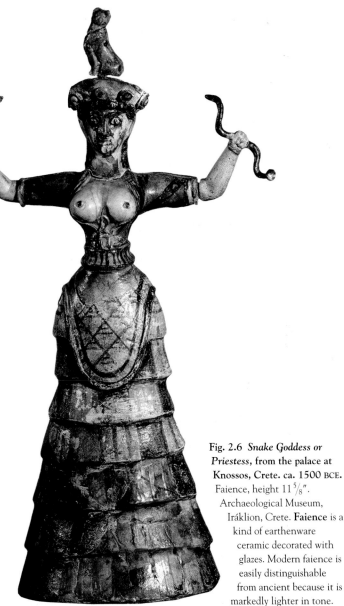

Fig. 2.6 *Snake Goddess or Priestess,* from the palace at Knossos, Crete. ca. 1500 BCE. Faience, height 11⅝". Archaeological Museum, Iráklion, Crete. **Faience** is a kind of earthenware ceramic decorated with glazes. Modern faience is easily distinguishable from ancient because it is markedly lighter in tone.

and administrative offices, in no discernable order or design. Workshops surrounded the complex, and vast storerooms could easily provide for the needs of both the palace population and the population of the surrounding countryside. In just one storeroom, excavators discovered enough ceramic jars to hold 20,000 gallons of olive oil. Hundreds of wooden columns decorated the palace. The columns were painted bright red with black **capitals,** the sculpted blocks that top them. The capitals are shaped like pillows or cushions. (In fact, they are very close to the shape of an evergreen's root ball, as if the original design were suggested by trees felled in a storm.) Over time, as the columns rotted or were destroyed by earthquakes or possibly burned by invaders, they must have become increasingly difficult to replace, for Minoan builders gradually deforested the island. This may be one reason why the palace complex was abandoned sometime around 1450 BCE. Representations of double axes decorated the

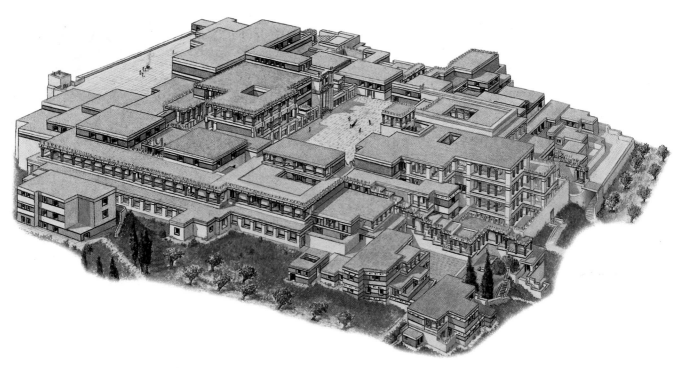

Fig. 2.7 Reconstruction drawing of the new palace complex at Knossos, Crete.
The complexity of the labyrinthine layout is obvious.

palace at every turn, and indeed the palace of Minos was known in Greek times as the House of the Double Axes. In fact, the Greek word for the palace was *labyrinth*, from *labrys*, "double ax." Over time, the Greeks came to associate the House of the Double Axes with its inordinately complex layout, and labyrinth came to mean "maze."

The Greeks solidified the meaning of the labyrinth in a powerful legend. King Minos boasted that the gods would grant him anything he wished, so he prayed that a bull might emerge from the sea that he might sacrifice to the god of the sea, Poseidon [puh-SY-dun]. A white bull did emerge from the sea, one so beautiful that Minos decided to keep it for himself and sacrifice a different one from his herd instead. This angered Poseidon, who took revenge by causing Minos's queen, Pasiphae [pah-sif-eye], to fall in love with the bull. To consummate her passion, she convinced Minos's chief craftsperson, Daedalus [DEE-duh-lus], to construct a hollow wooden cow into which she might place herself and attract the bull. The result of this union was a horrid creature, half man, half bull: the Minotaur. To appease the monster's appetite for human flesh, Minos ordered the city of Athens, which he also ruled, to send him 14 young men and women each year as sacrificial victims. Theseus, son of King Aegeus of Athens, vowed to kill the Minotaur. As he set sail for Crete with 13 others, he promised his father that he would return under white sails (instead of the black sails of the sacrificial ship) to announce his victory. At Crete, he seduced Ariadne [a-ree-AD-nee], daughter of Minos. Wishing to help Theseus, she gave him a sword with which to kill the Minotaur and a spindle of thread to lead himself out of the maze in which the Minotaur lived. Victorious, Theseus sailed home

with Ariadne but abandoned her on the island of Naxos, where she was discovered by the god of wine, Dionysus, who married her and made her his queen. Theseus, sailing into the harbor at Athens, neglected to raise the white sails, perhaps intentionally. When his father, King Aegeus, saw the ship still sailing under black sails, he threw himself into the sea, which from then on took his name, the Aegean. Theseus, of course, then became king. The story is a creation or **origin myth,** like the Zuni emergence tale (see Reading 1.1, page 7) or the Hebrew story of Adam and Eve in Genesis. But it differs from them on one important point: Rather than narrating the origin of humankind in general, it tells the story of the birth of one culture out of another. It is the Athenian Greeks' way of knowing their past, their *archaiologia*. The tale of the labyrinth explained to the later Greeks where and how their culture came to be. It correctly suggests a close link to Crete, but it also emphasizes Greek independence from that powerful island. It tells us, furthermore, much about the emerging Greek character, for Theseus would, by the fifth century BCE, achieve the status of a national hero. The great tragedies of Greek theater represent Theseus as wily, ambitious, and strong. He stops at nothing to achieve what he thinks he must. If he is not altogether admirable, he mirrors behavior the Greeks attributed to their gods. Nevertheless, he is anything but idealized or godlike. He is, almost to a fault, completely human. It was precisely this search for the origins of Greek culture that led Sir Arthur Evans to the discovery of the Palace of Minos in Crete. He confirmed "the truth" in the legend of the Minotaur. If there was no actual monster, there was indeed a labyrinth. And that labyrinth was the palace itself.

Mycenean Culture on the Peloponnese

When the Minoans abandoned the palace at Knossos in about 1450 BCE, warriors from the mainland culture of Mycenae, on the Greek Peloponnese, quickly occupied Crete. One reason for the collapse of Knossos was suggested earlier—the deforestation of the island. Another might be that Minoan culture was severely weakened in the aftermath of the volcanic eruption on Thera, and therefore susceptible to invasion. A third might be that the Mycenaean army simply overwhelmed the island. The Mycenaeans were certainly acquainted with the Minoan culture some 92 miles to their south, across the Aegean.

Minoan metalwork was prized on the mainland. Its fine quality is very evident in the *Vaphio Cup*, one of two golden cups found in the nineteenth century in a tomb at Vaphio [VAH-fee-oh], just south of Sparta, on the Peloponnese (Fig. 2.8). This cup was executed in **repoussé** [ruh-poo-SAY], a technique in which the artist hammers out the design from the inside. It depicts a man in an olive grove capturing a bull by tethering its hind legs. The bull motif is classically Minoan, and the setting suggests a religious meaning since the oil extracted from many olive groves was considered sacred. The Mycenaeans, however, could not have been more different from the Minoans. Whereas Minoan cities were unfortified, and battle scenes were virtually nonexistent in their art, the Mycenaeans lived in communities surrounding fortified hilltops, and battle and hunting scenes dominate their art. Minoan culture appears to have been peaceful, while the warlike Mycenaeans lived and died by the sword.

The ancient city of Mycenae, which gave its name to the larger Mycenaean culture, was discovered by the German

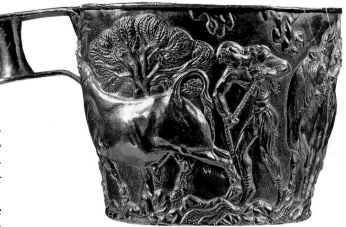

Fig. 2.8 *Vaphio Cup*, from a tomb at Vaphio, south of Sparta, Greece. ca. 1650–1450 BCE. Gold, height 3 1/2″. National Archaeological Museum, Iráklion, Crete. Mycenaean invaders used Crete as a base for operations for several centuries, and probably acquired the cup there.

archeologist Heinrich Schliemann (1822–1890) in the late nineteenth century, before Sir Arthur Evans discovered Knossos. Its citadel on the top of a hill looks down across a broad plain to the sea. Its walls—20 feet thick and 50 feet high—were built from huge blocks of rough-hewn stone, in a technique called **cyclopean** [sy-KLOPE-ee-un] **masonry** because it was believed by later Greeks that only a race of monsters known as the Cyclopes [sy-KLOH-peez] could have managed them. Visitors to the city entered through a massive Lion Gate at the top of a steep path that led from the valley below (Fig. 2.9). The lions that stood above the gate's lintel

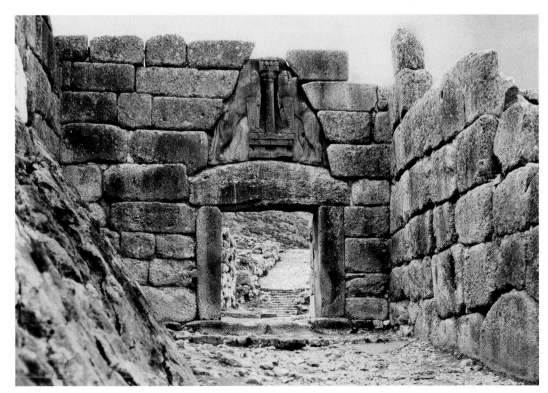

Fig. 2.9 Lion Gate, Mycenae, Greece. ca. 1300 BCE. Limestone relief, panel approx. 9′ 6″ high. The lions are carved on a triangle of stone that relieves the weight of the massive doorway from the lintel. The original heads, which have never been found, were attached to the bodies with dowels.

were themselves 9 feet high. It is likely that their missing heads originally turned in the direction of approaching visitors, and that they were intended to ward off evil. The heads were probably made of a different stone than the bodies and may have been plundered at a later time. From the gate, a long, stone street wound up the hill to the citadel itself. Here, overseeing all, was the king's palace. Mycenae was only one of several fortified cities on mainland Greece that were flourishing by 1500 BCE and that have come to be called Mycenaean. Mycenaean culture was the forerunner of ancient Greek culture and was essentially **feudal** in nature, that is, a system of political organization held together by ties of allegiance between a lord and those who relied on him for protection. Kings controlled not only their own cities but also the surrounding countryside. Merchants, farmers, and artisans owed their own prosperity to the king and paid high taxes for the privilege of living under his protection. More powerful kings, such as those at Mycenae itself, also expected the loyalty (and financial support) of other cities and nobles over whom they exercised authority. A large bureaucracy of tax collectors, civil servants, and military personnel ensured the state's continued prosperity. Like the Minoans, they engaged in trade, especially for the copper and tin required to make bronze.

The feudal system allowed Mycenae's kings to amass enormous wealth, as Schliemann's excavations confirmed. He discovered gold and silver death masks of fallen heroes (Fig. 2.10), as well as swords and daggers inlaid with imagery of events such as a royal lion hunt. He also found delicately carved ivory, from the tusks of hippopotamuses and elephants, suggesting if not the breadth of Mycenae's power,

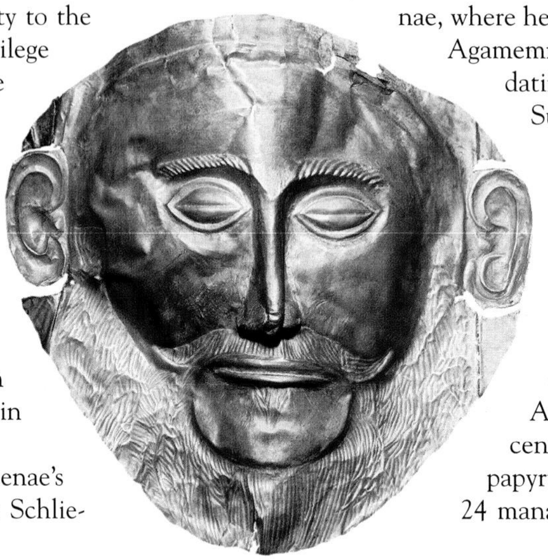

Fig. 2.10 Funerary mask (*Mask of Agamemnon*), from Grave Circle A, Mycenae, Greece. ca. 1600–1550 BCE. Gold, height approx. 12″. National Archaeological Museum, Athens. When Schliemann discovered this mask, he believed it was the death mask of King Agamemnon, but it predates the Trojan War by some 300 years. Recent scholarship suggests that Schliemann may have added the handlebar mustache and large ears, perhaps to make the mask appear more "heroic."

then the extent of its trade, which clearly included Africa. It seems likely, in fact, that the Mycenaean taste for war, and certainly its occupation of Crete, was motivated by the desire to control trade routes throughout the region.

The Homeric Epics

In about 800 BCE, the Greeks began to write down the stories from and about their past—their *archaiologia*—that had been passed down, generation to generation, by word of mouth. The most important of these stories were composed by an author whom history calls Homer. Homer was most likely a bard, a singer of songs about the deeds of heroes and the ways of the gods. His stories were part of a long-standing oral tradition that dated back to the time of the Trojan War, which we believe occurred sometime between 1800 and 1300 BCE. Out of the oral

materials he inherited, Homer composed two great epic poems, the *Iliad* and the *Odyssey*. The first narrates an episode in the 10-year Trojan War, which, according to Homer, began when the Greeks launched a large fleet of ships under King Agamemnon of Mycenae to bring back Helen, the wife of his brother King Menelaus of Sparta, who had eloped with Paris, son of King Priam [PRY-um] of Troy. The *Odyssey* narrates the adventures of one of the principal Greek leaders, Odysseus (also known as Ulysses), on his return home from the fighting.

Most scholars believed that these Homeric epics were pure fiction until the discovery by Heinrich Schliemann in the 1870s of the actual site of Troy, a multilayered site near modern-day Hissarlik [hih-sur-LIK], in northwestern Turkey. The Troy of Homer's epic was discovered at the sixth layer. (Schliemann also believed that the shaft graves at Mycenae, where he found so much treasure, were those of Agamemnon and his royal family, but modern dating techniques have ruled that out.) Suddenly, the *Iliad* assumed, if not the authority, then the aura of historical fact.

By the sixth century BCE, the *Iliad* was recited every four years in Athens (without omission, according to law), and many copies of it circulated around Greece in the fifth and fourth centuries BCE. Finally, in Alexandria, Egypt, in the late fourth century BCE, scribes wrote the poem on papyrus scrolls, perhaps dividing it into the 24 manageable units we refer to today as the poem's books.

The poem was so influential that it established certain epic conventions, standard ways of composing an epic that were followed for centuries to come. Examples include starting the poem *in medias res* [in MEH-dee-us rays], Latin for "in the middle of things," that is, in the middle of the story; invoking the muse at the poem's outset; and stating the poem's subject at the outset.

The *Iliad* tells but a small fraction of the story of the Trojan War, which was launched by Agamemnon of Mycenae and his allies to attack Troy around 1200 BCE. The tale begins after the war is under way and narrates what is commonly called "the wrath of Achilles" [uh-KIL-leez], a phrase drawn from the first line of the poem. Already encamped on the Trojan plain, Agamemnon has been forced to give up a girl that he has taken in one of his raids, but he takes the beautiful Briseis [bree-SAY-us] from Achilles as compensation. Achilles, by far the greatest of the Greek warriors, is outraged, suppresses his urge to kill Agamemnon, but withdraws from the war. He knows that the Greeks cannot succeed without him, and in his rage he believes they will deserve their fate. Indeed, Hector, the great Trojan prince, soon drives the Greeks back to their ships, and Agamemnon sends ambassadors to Achilles to offer him gifts and beg him to return to the battle. Achilles refuses: "His gifts, I loathe his gifts. . . . I wouldn't give you a splinter for that man! Not if he gave me ten times as much, twenty times over." When the battle resumes, things become desperate for the Greeks. Achilles partially relents, permitting Patroclus [puh-TROH-klus], his close friend and perhaps his lover, to wear his armor in order to put fear into the Trojans. Led by Patroclus, the Achaeans, as Homer calls the Greeks, drive the Trojans back.

A notable feature of the poem is the unflinching verbal picture Homer paints of the realities of war, not only its cowardice, panic, and brutality, but its compelling attraction as well. In this arena, the Greek warrior is able to demonstrate one of the most important values in Greek culture, his *areté* [ah-RAY-tay] often translated as "virtue," but actually meaning something closer to "being the best you can be" or "reaching your highest human potential." Homer uses the term to describe both Greek and Trojan heroes, and it refers not only to their bravery but their effectiveness in battle.

The sixth century BCE painting on the side of the *Botkin Class Amphora*—an **amphora** [am-FOR-uh] is a Greek jar with an egg-shaped body and two curved handles used for storing oil or wine—embodies the concept of *areté* (Fig. 2.11). Here two warriors, one armed with a sword, the other with a spear, confront one another with unwavering determination and purpose. At one point in the *Iliad*, Homer describes two such warriors, holding their own against one another, as "rejoicing in the joy of battle." They rejoice because they find themselves in a place where they can demonstrate their *areté*. The following passage, from Book 24, the final section of the *Iliad*, shows the other side of war and the other side of the poem, the compassion and humanity that distinguish Homer's narration (**Reading 2.1**). Hector, son of the king of Troy, has struck down Patroclus with the aid of the god Apollo. On hearing the news, Achilles is devastated and finally enters the fray. Until now, fuming over Agamemnon's insult, he has sat out the battle, refusing, in effect, to demonstrate his own *areté*. But now, he redirects his rage from Agamemnon to the Trojan warrior Hector, whom he meets and kills. He then ties Hector's body to his chariot and drags it to his tent. The act is pure sacrilege, a violation of the dignity due the great Trojan warrior and an insult to his memory. Late that night, Priam, the king of Troy, steals across enemy lines to Achilles' tent and begs for the body of his son:

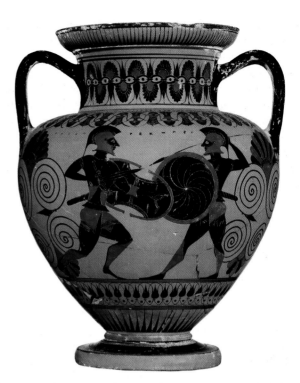

Fig. 2.11 *Botkin Class Amphora*, **Greek. ca. 540–530 BCE.** Black-figure decoration on ceramic, height 11 9/16", diameter 9 1/2". Museum of Fine Arts, Boston: Henry Lillie Pierce Fund 98.923. Photograph © 2008 Museum of Fine Arts, Boston. On the other side of this vase are two heavily armed warriors, one pursuing the other.

READING 2.1 **from Homer, *Iliad*, Book 24 (ca. 750 BCE)**

"Remember your own father, great godlike Achilles—
as old as I am, past the threshold of deadly old age!
No doubt the countrymen round about him plague him now,
with no one there to defend him, beat away disaster.
No one—but at least he hears you're still alive

and his old heart rejoices, hopes rising, day by day,
to see his beloved son come sailing home from Troy.
But I—dear god, my life so cursed by fate . . .
I fathered hero sons in the wide realm of Troy
and now not a single one is left, I tell you.
Fifty sons I had when the sons of Achaea came,
nineteen born to me from a single mother's womb
and the rest by other women in the palace. Many,
most of them violent Ares cut the knees from under.
But one, one was left me, to guard my wall, my people—
the one you killed the other day, defending his fatherland,
my Hector! It's all for him I've come to the ships now,
to win him back from you—I bring a priceless ransom.
Revere the gods, Achilles! Pity me in my own right,
remember your own father! I deserve more pity . . .
I have endured what no one on earth has ever done before—
I put to my lips the hands of the man who killed my son."

Those words stirred within Achilles a deep desire
to grieve for his own father. Taking the old man's hand
he gently moved him back. And overpowered by memory
both men gave way to grief. Priam wept freely
for man-killing Hector, throbbing, crouching
before Achilles' feet as Achilles wept himself,
now for his father, now for Patroclus once again,
and their sobbing rose and fell throughout the house. . . . .

Then Achilles called the serving-women out:
"Bathe and anoint the body—
bear it aside first. Priam must not see his son."
He feared that, overwhelmed by the sight of Hector,
wild with grief, Priam might let his anger flare
and Achilles might fly into fresh rage himself,
cut the old man down and break the laws of Zeus.
So when the maids had bathed and anointed the body
sleek with olive oil and wrapped it round and round
in a braided battle-shirt and handsome battle-cape,
then Achilles lifted Hector up in his own arms
and laid him down on a bier, and comrades helped him
raise the bier and body onto a sturdy wagon . . .
Then with a groan he called his dear friend by name:
"Feel no anger at me, Patroclus, if you learn—
ever there in the House of Death—I let his father
have Prince Hector back. He gave me worthy ransom
and you shall have your share from me, as always,
your fitting, lordly share."

Homer clearly recognizes the ability of these warriors to exceed their mere humanity, to raise themselves not only to a level of great military achievement, but to a state of compassion, nobility, and honor. It is this exploration of the "doubleness" of the human spirit, its cruelty and its humanity, its blindness and its insight, that defines the power and vision of the Homeric epic.

Homer's second epic, the *Odyssey*, narrates the adventures of Odysseus on his 20-year journey home from the war in Troy—his encounters with monsters, giants, and seductive enchantresses, a sojourn on a floating island and another in the underworld. But above all the poem's subject is Odysseus' passionate desire to once more see his wife, Penelope, and Penelope's fidelity to him. Where anger and lust drive the *Iliad*—from Achilles' angry sulk to Helen's fickleness—love and familial affection drive the *Odyssey*. Penelope is gifted with *areté* in her own right, since for the 20 years of her husband's absence she uses all the cunning in her power to ward off the suitors who flock to marry her, convinced that Odysseus is never coming home.

In later Greek culture, the *Iliad* and the *Odyssey* were the basis of Greek education. Every schoolchild learned the two poems by heart. They were the principal vehicles through which the Greeks came to know the past, and through the past they came to know themselves. The poems embodied what might be called the Greeks' own cultural, as opposed to purely personal *areté*, their desire to achieve a place of preeminence among all states. But in defining this larger cultural ambition, the *Iliad* and *Odyssey* laid out the individual values and responsibilities that all Greeks understood to be their personal obligations and duties if the state were ever to realize its goals.

The Rise of the Greek City-States

The Greek city-states, or *poleis*, arose during the ninth century BCE, just before the time of Homer. Colonists set sail from cities on the Greek mainland to establish new settlements. Eventually, there were as many as 1,500 Greek city-states scattered around the Mediterranean and the Black Sea from Spain to the Crimea, including large colonies in Italy (Fig. 2.12). Since the fall of Mycenae in about 1100 BCE, some 100 years after the Trojan War, Greece had endured a long period of cultural decline that many refer to as the Dark Ages. Greek legend has it that a tribe from the North, the Dorians, overran the Greek mainland and the Peloponnese. Historical evidence suggests that the Dorians possessed iron weapons and easily defeated the bronze-armored Greeks. Scattered and in disarray, the Greek people almost forgot the rudiments of culture, and reading and writing fell into disuse. For the most part, the Greeks lived in small rural communities that often warred with one another. But despite these conditions, which hardly favored the development of art and architecture, the Greeks managed to sustain a sense of identity and even, as the survival of the Trojan War legends suggests, some idea of their cultural heritage.

Gradually, across Greece, communities began to organize themselves and exercise authority over their own limited geographical regions, which were defined by natural boundaries—mountains, rivers, and plains. The population of even the largest communities was largely dedicated to agriculture, and agricultural values—a life of hard, honest work and self-reliance—predominated. The great pastoral poem of the poet Hesiod [HE-see-ud] (flourished ca. 800 BCE), *Works and Days*, testifies to this. *Works and Days* was written at about the same time as the Homeric epics in Boeotia [be-OH-she-uh], the region of Greece dominated by the city-state of Thebes. Hesiod gives us a clear insight not only into many of the details of Greek agricultural production, but into social conditions as well. He mentions that all landowners possessed slaves (taken in warfare), who comprised over half the population. He also speaks of the Greek gods Zeus [zoos], king of the gods and master of the sky, and Demeter, goddess of agriculture and grain, and of the necessity of working hard in order to please the gods. In fact, it was Hesiod, in his *Theogony* [the-OG-uh-nee] (*The Birth of the Gods*), who first detailed the Greek **pantheon** (literally, "all the gods").

The Greek Gods

The religion of the Greeks informed almost every aspect of daily life. The gods watched over the individual at birth, nurtured the family, and protected the city-state. They controlled the weather, the seasons, health, marriage, longevity, and the future, which they could foresee. Each polis traced its origins to a particular founding god—Athena for Athens, Zeus for Sparta. Sacred sanctuaries were dedicated to others.

The Greeks believed that the 12 major gods lived on Mount Olympus, in northeastern Greece. There they ruled over the Greeks; in a completely human fashion they quarreled and meddled, loved and lost, exercised justice or not—and they were depicted by the Greeks in human form. There was nothing special about them except their power, which was enormous, sometimes frighteningly so. But the Greeks believed that as long as they did not overstep their bounds

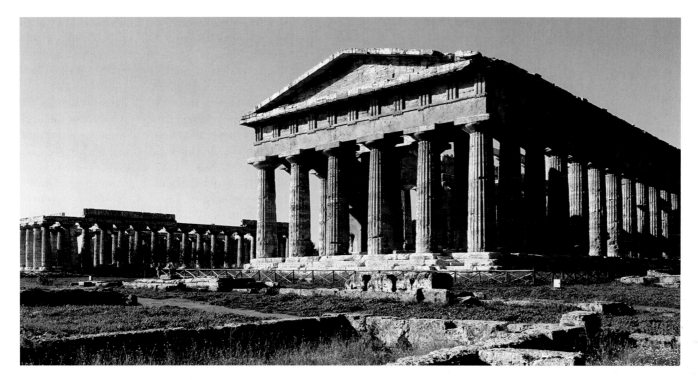

Fig. 2.12 The Temple of Hera I (background), ca. 560 BCE, and The Temple of Hera II (foreground), 460 BCE, Paestum, Italy.
Two of the best preserved Greek temples can be found in Italy, at Paestum, south of Naples, in a place the Greeks called Poseidonia after the god of the sea, Poseidon.

and try to compete with the gods—the sin of **hubris**, or pride—the gods would protect them.

Among the major gods (with their later Roman names in parentheses) are:

Zeus (Jupiter): King of the gods, usually bearded, and associated with the eagle and thunderbolt.

Hera (Juno [JOO-no]): Wife and sister to Zeus, the goddess of marriage and maternity.

Athena (Minerva): Goddess of war, but also, through her association with Athens, of civilization; the daughter of Zeus, born from his head; often helmeted, shield and spear in hand, the owl (wisdom) and the olive tree (peace) are sacred to her.

Ares (Mars): God of war, and son of Zeus and Hera, usually armored.

Aphrodite [af-ra-DIE-tee] (Venus): Goddess of love and beauty; Hesiod says she was born when the severed genitals of Uranus, the Greek personification of the sky, were cast into the sea and his sperm mingled with sea foam to create her. Eros is her son.

Apollo (Phoebus [FEE-bus]): God of the sun, light, truth, prophecy, music, and medicine; he carries a bow and arrow, sometimes a lyre; often depicted riding a chariot across the sky.

Artemis [AR-tuh-mis] (Diana): Goddess of the hunt and the moon; Apollo's sister, she carries bow and arrow, and is accompanied by hunting dogs.

Demeter [dem-EE-ter] (Ceres [SIR-eez]): Goddess of agriculture and grain.

Dionysus [dy-uh-NY-sus] (Bacchus [BAK-us]): God of wine and inspiration, closely aligned to myths of fertility and sexuality.

Hermes (Mercury): Messenger of the gods, but also god of fertility, theft, dreams, commerce, and the marketplace; usually adorned with winged sandals and a winged hat, he carries a wand with two snakes entwined around it.

Hades [HAY-deez] (Pluto): God of the underworld, accompanied by his monstrous dog Cerberus.

Hephaestus [hif-ES-tus] (Vulcan): God of the forge and fire; son of Zeus and Hera and husband of Aphrodite; wears a blacksmith's apron and carries a hammer.

Hestia [HES-te-uh] (Vesta): Goddess of the hearth and sister of Zeus.

Poseidon [po-SI-don] (Neptune): Brother of Zeus and god of the sea; carries a trident (a three-pronged spear); the horse is sacred to him.

Persephone [per-SEF-uh-nee] (Proserpina [pro-SUR-puh-nuh]): Goddess of fertility, Demeter's daughter, carted off each winter to the underworld by her husband Hades, but released each spring to restore the world to plenty.

Of particular interest here—as in Homer's *Iliad*—is that the gods are as susceptible to Eros [er-oss], or Desire, as is humankind. In fact, the Greek gods are sometimes more human than humans—susceptible to every human foible. Like many a couple on Earth, the husband, Zeus, is an all-powerful philanderer, whose wife, Hera [hi-ruh], is watchful, jealous, and capable of inflicting great pain upon rivals for her husband's affections. Their children are scheming and self-serving in their competition for their parents' attention. The gods think like humans, act like humans, and speak like humans. They sometimes seem to differ from humans only in the fact that they are immortal. Unlike the Hebrew God who requires obedience to his commandments, the Greek gods present humans with no clear principles of behavior, and the priests and priestesses who oversaw the rituals dedicated to them produced no scriptures or doctrines. The gods were capricious, capable of changing their minds, susceptible to argument and persuasion, alternately obstinate and malleable. If these qualities created a kind of cosmic uncertainty, they also embodied the intellectual freedom and the spirit of philosophical inquiry that would come to define the Greek state.

The Greek Architectural Tradition

The Greek *poleis* were distinguished by their physical isolation from one another and their fierce independence. In competition for the few really fertile lands on the mainland, they often warred with one another. And inevitably certain city-states became more powerful than others. Before the ninth century BCE, many Athenians had migrated to Ionia [eye-OH-nee-uh] in southwestern Anatolia [an-uh-TOE-lee-uh] (modern Turkey), and relations with the Near East helped Athens to flourish. Corinth, situated on the isthmus between the Greek mainland and the Peloponnese, controlled north–south trade routes from early times, but after it built a towpath to drag ships over the isthmus on rollers, it soon controlled the sea routes east and west as well. The Spartans, on the Peloponnese, traced their ancestry back to the legendary Dorians, whose legacy was military might. But despite their many differences, a common architectural tradition began to arise among the *poleis*, one which not only demonstrated their common cultural heritage, but which has also had a lasting influence on Western architecture as a whole.

As early as the eighth century BCE, various *poleis* began to establish sanctuaries where they could come together to share music, religion, poetry, and athletics. The sanctuary was a large-scale reflection of another Greek invention, the **symposium**, a "coming together" of men (originally of the same military unit) to share poetry, food, and wine. At the sanctuaries, people from different city-states came together to honor their gods and, by extension, to celebrate, in the presence of their rivals, their own accomplishments.

Delos and Delphi The sanctuaries were sacred religious sites. They inspired the city-states, which were always trying to outdo one another, to create the first monumental architecture since Mycenaean times. At Delphi [DEL-fie], high in the mountains above the Gulf of Corinth, and home to the Sanctuary of Apollo [uh-POLL-oh], the city-states, in their usual competitive spirit, built monuments and statues dedicated to the god, and elaborate treasuries to store offerings. Many built hostels so that pilgrims from home could gather. Delphi was an especially important site. Here, the Greeks believed, the Earth was attached to the sky by its navel. Here, too, through a deep crack in the ground, Apollo spoke, through the medium of a woman called the Pythia [PITH-ee-uh]. Priests interpreted the cryptic

omens and messages she delivered. The Greek author Plutarch [PLOO-tark], writing in the first century CE, said that the Pythia entered a small chamber beneath the temple, smelled sweet-smelling fumes, and went into a trance. This story was dismissed as fiction until recently, when geologists discovered that two faults intersect directly below the Delphic temple, allowing hallucinogenic gases to rise through the fissures, specifically ethylene, which has a sweet smell and produces a narcotic effect described as a floating or disembodied euphoria.

Greeks from the island of Siphnos [SIF-nus] built one of the most important of the treasuries at Delphi around 530 BCE in the Sanctuary of Apollo. The facade of the Treasury consisted of two columns here standing between two squared stone pillars. Behind them is the **pronaos** [pro-NAY-os], or enclosed vestibule, at the front of the building, with its doorway leading into the **cella** [SEL-uh] (or *naos* [NAY-os]), the principle interior space of the building (see the floor plan, Fig. 2.13). We can see the antecedents of this building type in a small ceramic model of an early Greek temple dating from the eighth century BCE and found at the Sanctuary of Hera near Argos [AR-gus] (Fig. 2.14). Its projecting porch supported by two columns anticipates the in antis columns and pronaos of the Siphnian [SIF-nee-un] Treasury. The triangular area over the porch created by the pitch of the roof is called the **pediment** and is filled with sculptural decoration in the Siphnian Treasury.

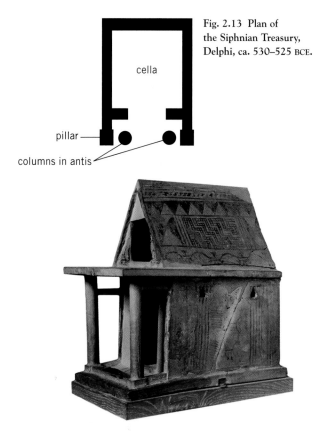

Fig. 2.13 Plan of the Siphnian Treasury, Delphi, ca. 530–525 BCE.

cella

pillar

columns in antis

Fig. 2.14 **Model of a temple, found in the Sanctuary of Hera, Argos, mid-eighth century BCE.** Terra cotta, length 4 1/2″. National Archaeological Museum, Athens. We do not know if later temples were painted like the model.

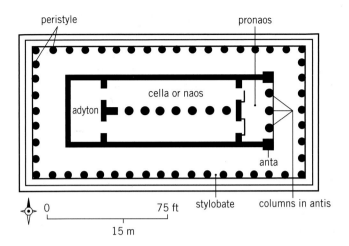

peristyle   pronaos

cella or naos

adyton

anta

0   75 ft
15 m

stylobate   columns in antis

Fig. 2.15 Plan of the Temple of Hera I, Paestum, ca. 560 BCE.

The Temples of Hera at Paestum From this basic form, surviving in the small treasuries at Delphi, the larger temples of the Greeks would develop. Two distinctive **elevations**—the arrangement, proportions, and appearance of the temple foundation, columns, and lintels—developed before 500 BCE, the **Doric order** and the **Ionic order** (see *Focus*, pages 48–49). Later, a third **Corinthian order** would emerge. The Siphnian Treasury is of the Ionic order, which most often employs columns with scrolled capitals. Among earliest surviving examples of a Greek temple of the Doric order are the Temples of Hera I and II in the Sanctuary of Hera at Paestum [PES-tum], a Greek colony established in the seventh century BCE in Italy, about 50 miles south of modern Naples (see Fig. 2.12). As

the plan of the Temple of Hera I makes clear (Fig. **2.15**), the earlier of the two temples was a large, rectangular structure, with a pronaos containing three (as opposed to two) columns and an elongated cella, behind which is an **adyton** [AD-ee-tun], the innermost sanctuary housing the place where, in a temple with an oracle, the oracle's message was delivered. Surrounding this inner structure was the **peristyle** [PER-uh-style], a row of columns that stands on the **stylobate** [STY-luh-bate], the raised platform of the temple. The columns swell about one-third of the way up and contract again at the top, a characteristic known as **entasis** [EN-tuh-sis], and are topped by the two-part capital of the Doric order with its rounded **enchinus** [EN-ki-nus] and tabletlike **abacus** [AB-uh-kus].

Olympia and the Olympic Games The Greeks date the beginning of their history to the first formal Panhellenic ("all-Greece") athletic competition, held in 776 BCE. These first Olympic Games were held at Olympia. There, a sanctuary dedicated to Hera and Zeus also housed an elaborate athletic facility. The first contest of the first games was a 200-yard dash the length of the Olympia stadium, a race called the *stadion* (Fig. **2.16**). Over time, other events of solo performance were added, including chariot racing, boxing, and the pentathlon (from Greek *penta*, "five," and *athlon*, "contest"), consisting of discus, javelin, long jump, sprinting, and wrestling. There were no second or third prizes. Winning was all. The contests were conducted every four years during the summer months and were open only to men (married women were forbidden to attend, and unmarried women probably did not attend). The Olympic Games were held for more than 1,000 years. They were revived in 1896 to promote understanding and friendship among nations.

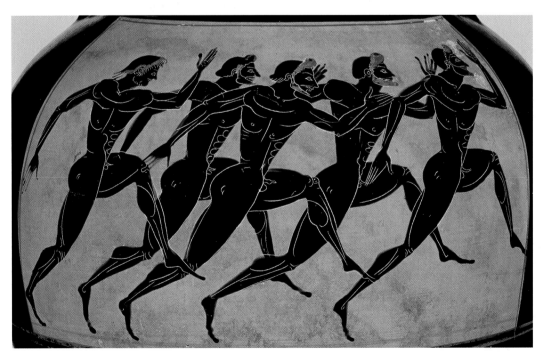

Fig. 2.16 Euphiletos Painter (?). Detail of a black-figure amphora showing a foot-race at the Panathenaic Games in Athens. ca. 530 BCE. Terra cotta, height 24½″. The Metropolitan Museum of Art, Rogers Fund, 1914 (14.130.12). Image © The Metropolitan Museum of Art. Greek athletes competed nude. In fact, our word *gymnasium* derives from the Greek word for "naked," *gymnos*.

Focus

The Classical Orders

Classical Greek architecture is composed of three vertical elements—the **platform**, the **column**, and the **entablature**—which comprise its elevation. The relationship of these three units is referred to as the elevation's **order**. There are three orders: Doric, Ionic, and Corinthian, each distinguished by its specific design.

The classical Greek orders became the basic design elements for architecture from ancient Greek times to the present day. A major source of their power is the sense of order, predictability, and proportion that they embody. Notice how the upper elements of each order—the elements comprising the entablature—change as the column supporting them becomes narrower and taller. In the Doric order, the **architrave**, the bottom layer of the entablature, and the frieze, the flat band just above the architrave decorated with sculpture, painting, or moldings, are comparatively massive. The Doric is the heaviest of the columns. The Ionic is lighter and noticeably smaller. The Corinthian is smaller yet, seemingly supported by mere leaves.

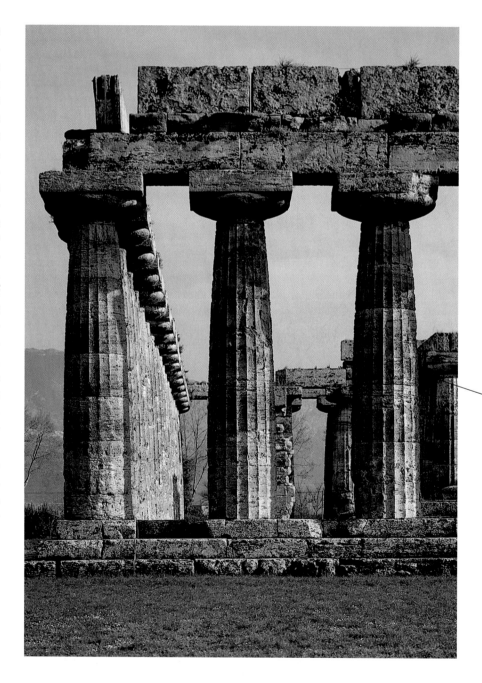

Doric columns at the Temple of Hera I, Pasteum, Italy, ca. 560.

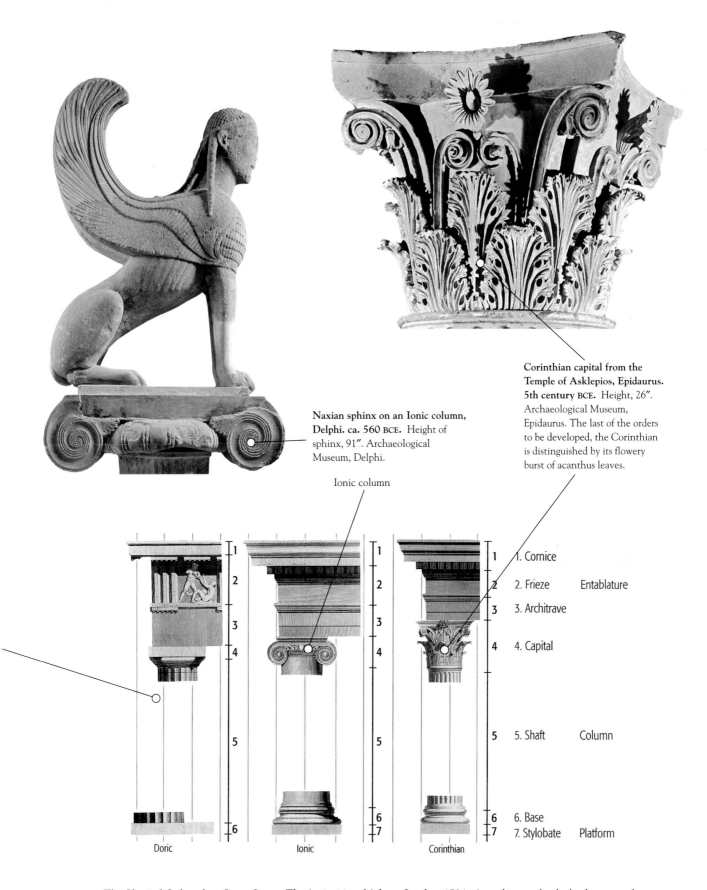

Naxian sphinx on an Ionic column, Delphi. ca. 560 BCE. Height of sphinx, 91″. Archaeological Museum, Delphi.

Corinthian capital from the Temple of Asklepios, Epidaurus. 5th century BCE. Height, 26″. Archaeological Museum, Epidaurus. The last of the orders to be developed, the Corinthian is distinguished by its flowery burst of acanthus leaves.

Ionic column

1. Cornice
2. Frieze — Entablature
3. Architrave
4. Capital
5. Shaft — Column
6. Base
7. Stylobate — Platform

Doric   Ionic   Corinthian

The Classical Orders, from James Stuart, *The Antiquities of Athens,* London, 1794. An architectural order lends a sense of unity and structural integrity to a building as a whole. By the 6th century BCE, the Greeks had developed the Doric and the Ionic orders. The former is sturdy and simple. The latter is lighter in proportion and more elegant in detail, its capital characterized by a scroll-like motif called a **volute**. The Corinthian order, which originated in the last half of the 5th century BCE, is the most elaborate of all. It would become a favorite of the Romans.

The Olympic Games were only one of numerous athletic festivals held in various locations. These games comprised a defining characteristic of the developing Greek national identity. As a people the Greeks believed in *agonizesthai*, [ahgon-ee-zus-TYE] a verb meaning "to contend for the prize." They were driven by competition. Potters bragged that their work was better than any other's. Playwrights competed for best play, poets for best recitation, athletes for best performance. As the city-states themselves competed for supremacy, they began to understand the spirit of competition as a trait shared by all.

Greek Sculpture and the Taste for Naturalism

Greek athletes performed nude, so it is not surprising that athletic contests gave rise to what may be called a "cult of the body." The physically fit male not only won accolades in athletic contests, he also represented the conditioning and strength of the military forces of a particular polis. The male body was also celebrated in a widespread genre of sculpture known as the **kouros** [KOOR-os], meaning "young man" (Fig. **2.17**). This celebration of the body was uniquely Greek. No other Mediterranean culture so emphasized depiction of the male nude. Over 20,000 *kouroi* [KOOR-oy] (plural of *kouros*) appear to have been carved in the sixth century BCE alone. They could be found in sanctuaries and cemeteries, most often serving as votive offerings to the gods or as commemorative grave markers. Their resolute features suggest their determination in their role as ever-watchful guardians.

Although we would never mistake this figure for the work of an Egyptian sculptor—its nudity and much more fully realized anatomical features are clear differences—still, its Egyptian influences are obvious, as can be seen in the comparison between a late Egyptian sculpture and a *kouros* dating from 525 BCE. In fact, as early as 650 BCE, the Greeks were in Egypt, and by the early sixth century BCE, 12 cooperating city-states had established a trading outpost in the Nile Delta. For

Continuity & Change
p. 24

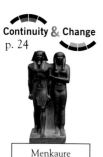

Menkaure with a queen

instance, the Greek *kouros* sculptures serve the same funerary function as their Egyptian ancestors. For instance, the inscription on the base of Fig. 1.26 reads, "Stop and grieve at the dead Kroisos [kroy-sos], slain by wild Ares [AR-eez] [the god of war] in the front rank of battle." This is a monument to a fallen hero, killed in the prime of youth.

During the course of the sixth century, *kouroi* became distinguished by **naturalism**. That is, they increasingly came to reflect the artist's desire to represent the human body as it appears in nature. This in turn probably reflects the growing role of the individual in Greek political life. We do not know why sculptors wanted to realize the human form more naturalistically, but we can surmise that the reason must be related to *agonizesthai*, the spirit of competition so dominant

Continuity & Change
p. 33

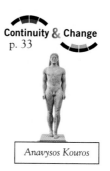

Anavysos Kouros

in Greek society. Sculptors must have competed against one another in their attempts to realize the human form. Furthermore, since it was believed that the god Apollo manifested himself as a well-endowed athlete, the more lifelike and natural the sculpture, the more nearly it could be understood to resemble the god himself.

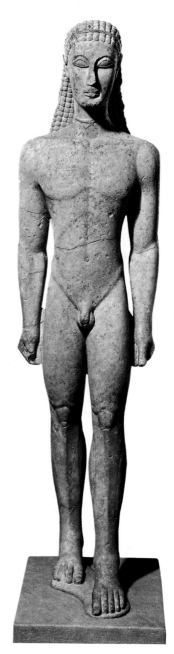

Fig. 2.17 *New York Kouros.* ca. 600 BCE. Height 6′ 4″. The Metropolitan Museum of Art, New York. Fletcher Fund, 1932 (32.11.1). Photograph © 1997 The Metropolitan Museum of Art. This sculpture is the earliest known life-size standing sculpture of a male in Greek art.

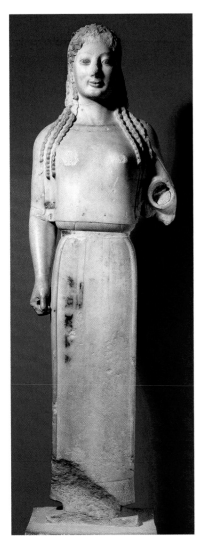
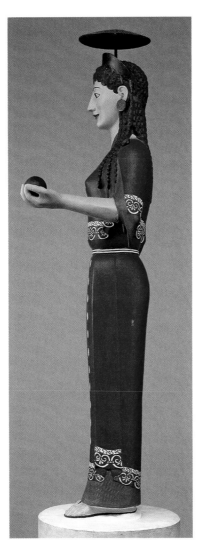
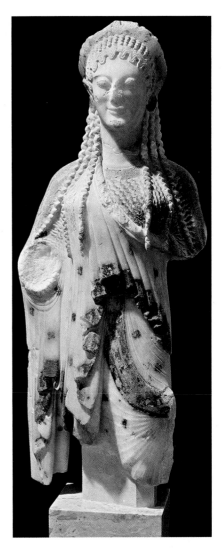

Fig. 2.18 *Peplos Kore* **and cast reconstruction of the original, from the Acropolis, Athens. Dedicated 530 BCE.** Polychromed marble, height 47 ½″. Acropolis Museum, Athens (original) and Museum of Classical Archaeology, Cambridge, England (cast). The extended arm, probably bearing a gift, was originally a separate piece, inserted in the round socket at her elbow. Note the small size of this sculpture, more than two feet shorter than the male *kouros* sculptures (Fig. 2.17).

Fig. 2.19 *Kore*, **from Chios (?). ca. 520 BCE.** Polychromed marble, height 21″. Acropolis Museum, Athens. Although missing half its height, the sculpture gives us a clear example of the elaborate dress of the last years of the sixth century BCE.

This same increasing naturalism is evident in the sculptural renderings of **korai** [KOR-eye], or "maidens." Just as the *kouros* statue seems related to Apollo, the *kore* [KOR-ee] statue appears to have been a votive offering to Athena and was apparently a gift to the goddess. Male citizens dedicated *korai* to her as a gesture of both piety and evident pleasure.

The trend toward an increasing naturalism is especially obvious in their dress. In the sculpture known as the *Peplos Kore* (Fig. 2.18), anatomical realism is suppressed by the straight lines of the sturdy garment known as a *peplos* [PEP-lus]. Usually made of wool, the *peplos* is essentially a rectangle of cloth folded down at the neck, pinned at the shoulders, and belted. Another *kore*, also remarkable for the amount of original paint on it, is the Kore dating from 520 BCE found on Chios [KY-os] (Fig. 2.19), an island off the western coast of Turkey.

This one wears a *chiton* [KY-ton], a garment that by the last decades of the century had become much more popular than the *peplos*. Made of linen, the *chiton* clings more closely to the body and is gathered to create pleats and folds that allow the artist to show off his virtuosity.

Athenian Pottery

The same trend toward increasing naturalism is also evident in the decorative painting on Greek pottery. By the middle of the sixth century BCE, Athens had become a major center of pottery making. Athenian potters were helped along by the extremely high quality of the clay available in Athens, which turned a deep orange color when fired.

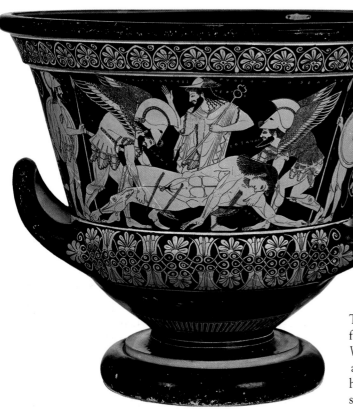

Fig. 2.20 Euphronius (painter) and Euxitheos (potter), *Death of Sarpedon,* **ca. 515 BCE.** Red-figure decoration on a calyx krater. Ceramic, height of krater 18″. The Metropolitan Museum of Art, New York. Purchase, Gift of Darius Ogden Mills, Gift of J. Pierpont Morgan, and Bequest of Joseph H. Durkee, by exchange, 1972 (1972.11.10). This type of krater is called a *calyx krater* because its handles curve up like the calyx flower.

reduced to the absolute minimum, turning the vessel black. At this point, as the temperature rose, the slip became vitrified, or glassy. Finally, oxygen entered the kiln again, turning the unslipped areas—in this case, the red figures—back into a shade of red. The areas painted with the vitrified slip were not exposed to oxygen, so that they remained black.

Black-figure vases are the reverse of the red-figure variety. The figures on these vases are painted with the slip, so that after firing they remain black against an unslipped red background. *Women at a Fountain House* (Fig. **2.21**) is an example. Here the artist, whom scholars have dubbed the Priam [PRY-um] painter, has added touches of white by mixing white pigment into the slip. By the second half of the sixth century, new motifs, showing scenes of everyday life, became increasingly popular. This hydria [HY-dree-uh], or water jug, shows women carrying similar

Many of their pots depict gods and heroes, including representations of the *Iliad* and *Odyssey* (see Fig. 2.11). An example of this tendency is a **krater** [KRAY-tur], or vessel in which wine and water are mixed, that shows the *Death of Sarpedon* [sar-PE-dun], painted by Euphronius [you-FRO-ne- us] and made by the potter Euxitheos [you-ZI-thee-us (soft th as in think)] by 515 BCE (Fig. **2.20**). Euphronius was praised especially for his ability to accurately render human anatomy. Here Sarpedon has just been killed by Patroclus. Blood pours from his leg, shoulder, and carefully drawn abdomen. The winged figures of Hypnos [HIP-nos] (Sleep) and Thanatos [THAN-uh-tohs] (Death) are about to carry off his body as Hermes [HER-meez], messenger of the gods who guides the dead to the underworld, looks on. But the naturalism of the scene is not the source of its appeal. Rather, its perfectly balanced composition transforms the tragedy into a rare depiction of death as an instance of dignity and order. The spears of the two warriors left and right mirror the edge of the vase, the design formed by Sarpedon's stomach muscles is echoed in the decorative bands both top and bottom, and the handles of the vase mirror the arching backs of Hypnos and Thanatos.

The Death of Sarpedon is an example of a **red-figure** vase. To decorate such vases, Greek artists used special "slips," mixtures of clay and water, which they painted over the background around the figures. Using the same slip, they also drew details on the figure (such as Sarpedon's abdomen) with a brush. The vase was then fired in three stages, each one varying the amount of oxygen allowed into the kiln. In the first stage, oxygen was allowed into the kiln, which "fixed" the whole vase in one overall shade of red. Then, oxygen in the kiln was

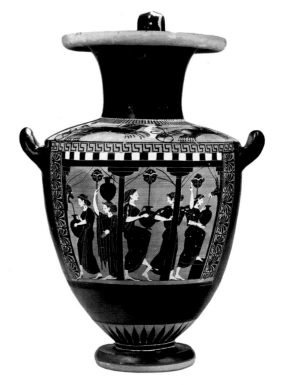

Fig. 2.21 The Priam Painter, *Women at a Fountain House,* **520–510 BCE.** Black-figure decoration on a hydria vase, height of hydria 20 7/8″. Courtesy, Museum of Fine Arts, Boston. Reproduced with permission. © 2005 Museum of Fine Arts, Boston. All Rights Reserved. The convention of depicting women's skin as white is also found in Egyptian and Minoan art.

jugs as they chat at a fountain house at the end of one of the aqueducts that brought water into Athens. Such fountain houses were extremely popular spots, offering women, who were for the most part confined to their homes a rare opportunity to gather socially. Water flows from animal-head spigots at both the sides and across the back of the scene. The composition's strong vertical and horizontal framework, with its Doric columns, is softened by the rounded contours of the women's bodies and the vases they carry. This vase underscores the growing Greek taste for realistic scenes and naturalistic representation.

The Poetry of Sappho

The poet Sappho (ca. 610–ca. 580 BCE) was hailed throughout antiquity as "the tenth Muse" and her poetry celebrated as a shining example of female creativity. We know little of Sappho's somewhat extraordinary life. She was the daughter of an aristocrat, married, had a daughter of her own, and then, apparently, left all behind to settle on the island of Lesbos. There she surrounded herself with a group of young women and engaged in the worship of Aphrodite—the Lesbian cult. Most of her circle shared their lives with one another only for a brief period before marriage.

Sappho produced nine books of **lyric poems**—poems to be sung to the accompaniment of a lyre—on themes of love and personal relationships, often with other women. Sappho's poetry was revered throughout the Classical world, but only fragments have survived. It is impossible to convey the subtlety and beauty of her poems in translation, but their astonishing economy of feeling does come across. In the following poem (**Reading 2.2a**) one of the longest surviving fragments, she expresses her love for a married woman:

READING 2.2a **Sappho, lyric poetry**

He is more than a hero
He is a god in my eyes
the man who is allowed
to sit beside you—he
who listens intimately
to the sweet murmur of
your voice, the enticing
laughter that makes my own
heart beat fast. If I meet
you suddenly, I can't
speak—my tongue is broken;
a thin flame runs under
my skin; seeing nothing
hearing only my ears
drumming, I drip with sweat;
trembling shakes my body
and I turn paler than
dry grass. At such times
death isn't far from me.

Sappho's talent is the ability to condense the intensity of her feelings into a single breath, a breath that, as the following poem suggests, lives on (**Reading 2.2b**):

READING 2.2b **Sappho, lyric poetry**

Although they are
only breath, words
which I command
are immortal

Even in so short a poem, Sappho realizes concretely the Greek belief that we can achieve immortality through our words and deeds.

The Rise of Democracy and the Threat of Persia

In 508 BCE, the Athenian aristocrat Kleisthenes [KLEYE-sthuh-neez] instituted the first Athenian political democracy—from the Greek *demokratia* [dem-oh-KRAY-te-uh], the rule (*kratia*) of the people (*demos*)—an innovation in self-government that might not have been possible had the Athenians not just endured over 50 years of tyranny.

Fifty years earlier, in 560 BCE, when Peisistratus [pie-SIS-truh-tus] assumed rule in Athens, the urban and rural regions of the Athenian polis were wracked by division. Wealthy landowners from the plains, poorer hill people living on the mountainsides, Athenian merchants and aristocracy all vied for power. Peisistratus had controlled this division with a heavy hand, ruling as a tyrant,—that is, as a dictator—without consulting the people. Although he succeeded in providing jobs for the entire population by commissioning large-scale public works, he exiled aristocrats who didn't support him, and he kept sons of noble families hostage to guarantee their families' loyalty. His son, Hippias [HIP-ee-us], who followed him to power in 527 BCE, was harsher still, exiling more nobles and executing many others. In 510 the exiled nobles revolted, with aid from Sparta, Hippias escaped to Persia, and Kleisthenes took over.

"Nothing is worse for a city than a tyrant," the Greek playwright Euripides would later write in his play, *The Suppliant Women*. "One man rules, and frames the law himself. Equality doesn't exist. But when laws are written down, both rich and poor have the same right to justice. This is freedom's rallying cry: 'What man has good advice to give the city? Make it public, and earn a reputation. . . . For the city's sake, what could be better than that? When the people are the pilots of the city, they control their own destiny.'" In other words, a politics—a dedication to the well-being of the *polis* through discussion, consensus, and united action—depends upon democracy. In a tyranny, there can be no politics because there can be no debate. Whatever their diverging views, the citizens of the *polis* were free to debate the issues, to speak their minds. They spoke as individuals, and they cherished the freedom to think as they pleased. But they spoke out of a concern for the common good, for the good of the *polis*, which, after all, gave them the freedom to speak in the first place. When Aristotle says, in his *Politics*, that "man is a political animal," he means that man is a creature of the polis, bound to it, dedicated to it, determined by it, and, somewhat paradoxically, liberated by it as well.

These principles were well understood by Kleisthenes, who reorganized the Athenian political system into **demes** [deemz], small local areas comparable to precincts or wards in a modern city. Because all citizens—remember, only males were citizens—registered in their given *deme*, landowners and merchants had equal political rights. Kleisthenes then grouped the demes into ten political "tribes," whose membership cut across all family, class, and regional lines, thus effectively diminishing the power and influence of the noble families. Each tribe appointed 50 of its members to a Council of Five Hundred, which served for 36 days. There were thus ten separate councils per year, and no citizen could serve on the council more than twice in his lifetime. With so many citizens serving on the council for such short times, it is likely that nearly every Athenian citizen participated in the government at some point during his lifetime.

The new Greek democracy was immediately threatened by the rise of the Persian Empire in the east. As early as 530 BCE, the Persians had taken control of the Greek cities in Ionia on the west coast of Anatolia. Under King Darius [duh-RY-us] (ruled 522–486 BCE), they soon ruled a vast empire that stretched from Egypt in the south, around Asia Minor, to the Ukraine [you-KRAIN] in the north. The capital of the empire was Parsa, which the Greeks called Persepolis [per-SEP-uh-lis], or city of the Persians, located in the Zagros [ZAG-rus] highlands of present-day Iran.

In 499 BCE, probably aware of the newfound political freedoms in Athens and certainly chafing at the tyrannical rule of the Persians, the Ionian cities rebelled, burning down the city of Sardis, the Persian headquarters in Asia Minor. In 495 BCE, Darius struck back. He burned down the most important Ionian city, Miletus [my-LEET-us], slaughtering the men and taking its women and children into slavery. Then, probably influenced by Hippias, who lived in exile in his court, Darius turned his sights on Athens, which had sent a force to Ionia to aid the rebellion.

In 490 BCE, a huge Persian army, estimated at 90,000, landed at Marathon, on the northern plains of Attica. They were met by a mere 10,000 Greeks, led by a professional soldier named Miltiades [mil-TIE-uh-deez] who had once served under Darius in Persia, and who understood the weakness of Darius' military strategy. Miltiades struck Darius' forces at dawn, killing 6,000 Persians and suffering minimal losses himself. The Persians were routed. The anxious citizens of Athens heard news of the victory from Phidippides [fih-DIP-uh-deez] who ran the 26 miles between Marathon and Athens, thus completing the original marathon, a run that the Greeks would soon incorporate into their Olympic Games. (Contrary to popular belief, Phidippides did not die in the effort.)

Darius may have been defeated, but the Persians were not done. Even as the Greeks basked in victory, Darius and his son Xerxes [ZURK-seez] were once again solidifying their power at Persepolis. The decorations at the palace during this time reflect their sense that all the peoples of the region owed them allegiance. The front steps rising up to the palace platform were covered with images of Darius' subjects bringing gifts to the palace—23 subject nations in all—Ionian, Babylonian, Syrian, Susian, and so on—each culture recognizable by its beards and costumes. On the wall of the audience hall, Darius receives tribute as Xerxes stands behind him (Fig. **2.22**), as if waiting to take his place as the Persian ruler.

In 486 BCE, Darius died fighting in Egypt, and Xerxes (r. 486–465 BCE) assumed the throne. By 481 BCE, it was apparent that Xerxes was preparing to attack Greece once again. Themistocles [thuh-MIS-tuh-kleez] (ca. 524–ca. 460 BCE), an Athenian statesman and general, had been anticipating the invasion for a decade. He convinced the Athenians to unite with the other Greek poleis under the direction of the Spartans, the strongest military power. When a large supply of silver was discovered in 483 BCE, Themistocles, convinced that the Persians could not be defeated on land, persuaded Athens to use its new-found wealth to build a fleet.

Finally, in 480 BCE, Xerxes led a huge army into Greece. In his nine-volume *Histories* (430 BCE), written 50 years after the events, Herodotus [hih-ROD-uh-tus], the first Greek historian, says that Xerxes' army numbered 5 million men and that whole rivers were dried when the army stopped to drink. These are doubtless exaggerations, but Xerxes' army was probably the largest ever assembled until that time. Modern estimates suggest it was composed of at least 150,000 men. Herodotus also tells us that the Delphic oracle had prophesied that Athens would be destroyed and advised the Athenians to put their trust in "wooden walls." Themistocles knew that the Persians had to be delayed so that the Athenians would have time to abandon the city and take to sea. At a narrow pass between the sea and the mountains called Thermopylae [ther-MOP-uh-lee], a band of 300 Spartans, led by their king, Leonidas [lee-ON-ih-dus], gave their lives so that the Athenians could escape. Herodotus tells the story (**Reading 2.3**):

READING 2.3 **from Book VII of Herodotus,
*The Histories***

The Lacedaemonians* fought a memorable battle; they made it quite clear that they were the experts, and that they were fighting against amateurs. This was particularly evident every time they turned tail and pretended to run away *en masse*; the Persians raised a great cry of triumph at the sight of the retreat and pressed forward after them, but the Lacedaemonians let them catch up and then suddenly turned and faced them—and cut the Persians down in untold numbers. However, a few Spartiates would be lost as well during this manoeuvre. Once their attempt on the pass had proved a complete failure and they had not gained the slightest foothold in it, whether they sent in regiment after regiment or whatever tactics they used for their attack, the Persians withdrew.

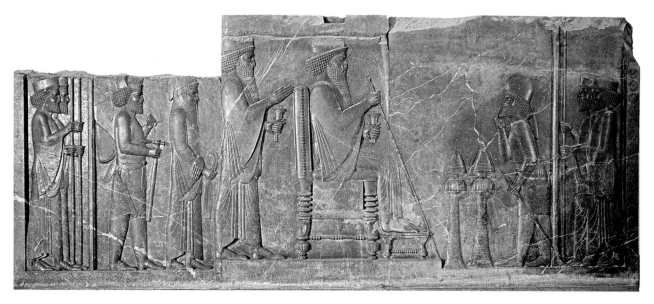

Fig. 2.22 *Darius and Xerxes Receiving Tribute,* detail of a relief from a stairway leading to the Apadana, ceremonial complex, Persepolis, Iran, 491–486 BCE. Limestone, height 8′ 4″. Iranbastan Museum, Teheran. This panel was originally painted in blue, scarlet, green, purple, and turquoise. Objects such as Darius' necklace and crown were covered in gold.

212 During this phase of the battle, as he watched his men attacking the Greek positions, it is said that fear for his army made the king leap up from his seat three times. The next day, after the first day of fighting had passed as described, the conflict went no better for the Persians. They went into battle in the expectation that the Greeks would no longer be capable of fighting back, given that there were so few of them and that they had already taken so many casualties. But the Greeks formed themselves into units based on nationality which took turns to fight, except for the Phocians who were posted on the heights above to guard the path. On finding that things had not changed from their experiences of the previous day, the Persians pulled back.

213 Xerxes did not know how to cope with the situation, but then a Malian called Ephialtes the son of Eurydemus arranged a meeting with him, with information for which he hoped the king would pay him handsomely. Ephialtes told him about the mountain path to Thermopylae, and so caused the deaths of the Greeks who had taken their stand there.

* Lacedaemon was the name of Sparta's city-state. Today, "Sparta" may refer to both the city and its broader city-state.

Ephialtes' treachery came too late, for by then the Athenians had abandoned Athens. At Salamis, off the Athenian coast, the Greeks won a stunning victory, led by Themistocles. The Persian fleet, numbering about 800 galleys, faced the Greek fleet of about 370 smaller and more maneuverable *triremes* [TRY-reemz], galleys with three tiers of oars on each side. Themistocles lured the Persian fleet into the narrow waters of the strait at Salamis.

The Greek *triremes* then attacked the crowded Persian fleet and used the great curved prows of their galleys to ram and sink about 300 Persian vessels. The Greeks lost only about 40 of their own fleet, and Xerxes was forced to retreat, never to threaten the Greek mainland again.

The Golden Age

After the Persian invasion of Greece in 480 BCE , the Athenians returned to a devastated city. They initially vowed to keep the Acropolis in a state of ruin as a reminder of the horrible price of war; however, the statesman Pericles (ca. 495–429 BCE) convinced them to rebuild it, ushering in a "Golden Age." No person dominated Athenian political life in the fifth century BCE more than Pericles. An aristocrat by birth, he was nonetheless democracy's strongest advocate. Late in his career, in 431 BCE he delivered a speech honoring soldiers who had fallen in early battles of the Peloponnesian War, a decades-long struggle for power between Sparta and Athens that would eventually result in Athens' defeat in 404 BCE, long after Pericles' own death. Pericles begins his speech by saying that, in order to properly honor the dead, he would like "to point out by what principles of action we rose to power, and under what institutions and through what manner of life our empire became great." First and foremost in his mind is Athenian democracy. But Pericles is not concerned with politics alone. He praises the Athenians' "many relaxations from toil." He acknowledges that life in Athens is as good as it is because "the fruits of the whole earth flow in upon us." And, he insists, Athenians are "lovers of the beautiful" who seek to "cultivate the mind." "To sum up," he concludes (**Reading 2.4**):

READING 2.4 Thucydides, *History of the Peloponnesian Wars*, Pericles' Funeral Speech

I say that Athens is the school of Hellas, and that the individual Athenian in his own person seems to have the power of adapting himself to the most varied forms of action with the utmost versatility and grace. This is no passing and idle word, but truth and fact; and the assertion is verified by the position to which these qualities have raised the state. . . . I have dwelt upon the greatness of Athens because I want to show you that we are contending for a higher prize than those who enjoy none of these privileges, and to establish by manifest proof the merit of these men whom I am now commemorating. Their loftiest praise has been already spoken. For in magnifying the city, I magnify them, and men like them whose virtues made her glorious.

When Pericles says that Athens is "the school of Hellas," he means that it teaches all of Greece by its example. He insists that the greatness of the state is a function of the greatness of its individuals. The quality of Athenian life depends upon this link between individual freedom and civic responsibility—which most of us in the Western world recognize as the foundation of our own political idealism (if, too often, not our political reality).

As for rebuilding the Acropolis, Pericles argued that, richly decorated with elaborate architecture and sculpture, the Acropolis could become a fitting memorial not only to the Persian war but especially to Athena's role in protecting the Athenian people. Furthermore, at Persepolis, the defeated Xerxes and then his son and successor Artaxerxes [ar-tuh-ZERK-seez] I (r. 465–424 BCE) were busy expanding their palace, and Athens was not about to be outdone. Pericles placed the sculptor, Phidias, in charge of the sculptural program for the new buildings on the Acropolis, and Phidias may have been responsible for the architectural project as well.

The Architectural Program at the Acropolis

The cost of rebuilding the Acropolis was enormous, but despite the reservations expressed by many over such an extravagant expenditure—financed mostly by tributes that Athens assessed upon its allies—the project (Fig. 2.23) had the virtue of employing thousands of Athenians—citizens, foreigners, and slaves alike—thus guaranteeing its general popularity. Writing a *Life of Pericles* five centuries later, the Greek-born biographer Plutarch (ca. 46–after 119 CE) gives us some idea of the scope of the rebuilding project and its effects (**Reading 2.5**):

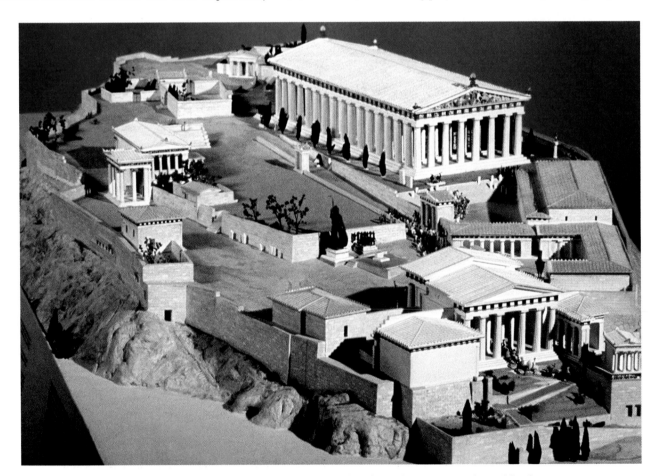

Fig. 2.23 Model of the Acropolis, ca. 400 BCE. American School of Classical Studies, Athens. Compare this model with the contemporary view of the site, Fig. 2.1.

READING 2.5   Plutarch, *Life of Pericles*

The raw materials were stone, bronze, ivory, gold, ebony, and cypress wood. To fashion them were a host of craftsmen: carpenters, moulders, coppersmiths, stonemasons, goldsmiths, ivory-specialists, painters, textile-designers, and sculptors in relief. Then there were the men detailed for transport and haulage: merchants, sailors, and helmsmen at sea; on land, cartwrights, drovers, and keepers of traction animals. There were also the rope-makers, the flax-workers, cobblers, roadmakers, and miners. Each craft, like a commander with his own army, had its own attachments of hired labourers and individual specialists organized like a machine for the service required. So it was that the various commissions spread a ripple of prosperity throughout the citizen body.

The Parthenon The centerpiece of the project was the Parthenon (Fig. **2.24**), which was completed in 432 BCE after 15 years of construction. As Pericles had argued, it was built to give thanks to Athena for the salvation of Athens and Greece in the Persian Wars, but it was also a tangible sign of the power and might of the Athenian state, designed to impress all who visited the city. It was built on the foundations and platform of an earlier structure, but the architects Ictinus and Callicrates clearly intended it to represent the Doric order in its most perfect form. It has eight columns at the ends and seventeen on the sides. Each column swells out about one-third of the way up, a device called entasis, to counter the eye's tendency to see the uninterrupted parallel columns as narrowing as they rise and to give a sense of "breath" or liveliness to the stone. The columns also slant slightly inward, so that they appear to the eye to rise straight up. And since horizontal lines appear to sink in the middle, the platform beneath them rises nearly five inches from each corner to the middle. There are no true verticals or horizontals in the building, a fact that lends its apparently rigid geometry a sense of liveliness and animation.

In the clarity of its parts, the harmony among them, and its overall sense of proportion and balance, the Parthenon represents the epitome of classical architecture. This classical sense of beauty manifests itself, particularly, in the architects' use of the **Golden Section** (Fig. **2.25**), believed by the Greeks to be the most beautiful of all proportions. It represents a ratio of (approx-

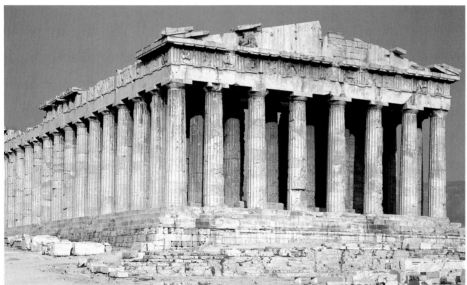

Fig. 2.24 **Ictinus, with contributions by Callicrates, the Parthenon, Acropolis, Athens. 447–438 BCE. Sculptural program completed 432 BCE.** The temple measures about 228′ × 101′ on the top step. The temple remained almost wholly intact (though it served variously as a church and then a mosque) until 1687, when the attacking Venetians exploded a Turkish powder magazine housed in it.

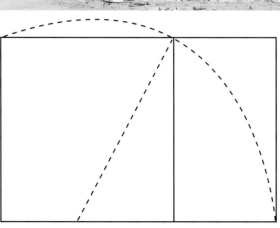

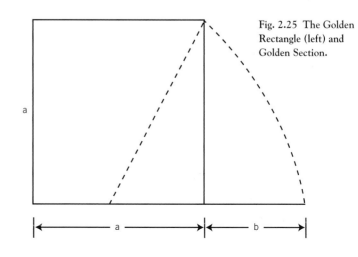

Fig. 2.25 **The Golden Rectangle (left) and Golden Section.**

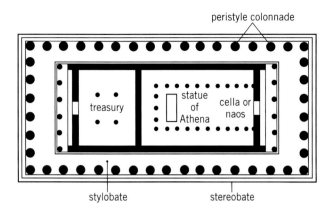

Fig. 2.26 Floorplan of the Parthenon. The giant 40-foot high sculpture of Athena Parthenos was located in the Parthenon's *cella* or *naos*, the central interior room of a temple in which the cult statue was traditionally housed.

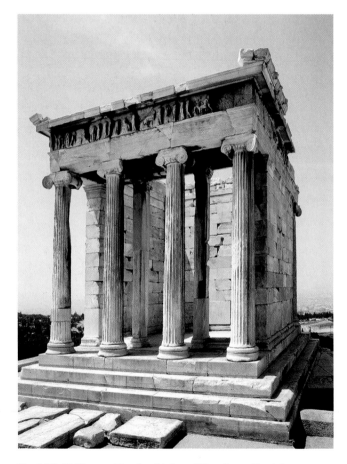

Fig. 2.27 Callicrates. Temple of Athena Nike, Acropolis, Athens. ca. 425 BCE. Overlooking the approach to the Propylaia, the lighter Ionic columns of the temple contrast dramatically with the heavier, more robust Doric columns of the gateway.

imately) 8:5, or, more precisely, 1.618:1. That is, any length may be divided into two parts *a* and *b* such that the whole length *a* + *b* is proportional to *a* as *a* is to *b*. The Greeks, with their great affinity for geometry, recognized that a rectangle based on these proportions could readily be divided and subdivided into identically proportioned sections, or Golden Rectangles. The east and west facades of the Parthenon are such rectangles—the width of the building is 1.618 times the height. Furthermore, the ground plan of the structure is laid out in similar proportions (Fig. **2.26**). The mathematical regularity of the temple is particularly suited to the worship of Athena, who is not only goddess of war but also goddess of wisdom, or rationality.

Other Architectural Projects on the Acropolis One of the architects employed in the project, Mnesicles [NES-ih-kleez], was charged with designing the **propylon**, or large entryway, where the Panathenaic Way approached the Acropolis from below. Instead of a single gate, he created five, an architectural tour de force named the Propylaia [prop-uh-LAY-uh] (the plural of *propylon*), flanked with porches and colonnades of Doric columns. The north wing included a picture gallery featuring paintings of Greek history and myth, none of which survive. Contrasting with the towering mass of the Propylaia was the far more delicate Temple of Athena Nike (Fig. **2.27**), situated on the promontory just to the west and overlooking the entranceway. Graced by slender Ionic columns, the diminutive structure (it measures a mere 27 by 19 feet) was designed by Callicrates and built in 425 BCE, not long after the death of Pericles. It was probably meant to celebrate what the Athenians hoped would be their victory in the Peloponnesian Wars, as *nike* is Greek for "victory." Before the end of the wars, between 410 and 407 BCE, it was surrounded by a **parapet**, or low wall, faced with panels depicting Athena together with her winged companions, the Victories.

The Sculpture Program at the Parthenon

If Phidias' hand is not directly involved in carving the sculpture decorating the Parthenon, most of the decoration is probably his design. He was, of course, heir to the ever-increasing interest in naturalistic representation that had developed at the end of the sixth century BCE in Athenian **kouros** sculpture (see Figs. 1.26 and 2.17). A sculpture attributed to Kritios (Fig. **2.28**), found in 1865 in a pile of debris on the Acropolis pushed aside by Athenians cleaning up after the Persian invasion (its head was found 25 years later in a separate location), demonstrates the increasing naturalism of Greek sculpture during the first 20 years of the fifth century BCE. The boy's head is turned slightly to the side. His weight rests on the left leg and the right leg extends forward, bent slightly at the knee. The figure seems to twist around its **axis**, or imaginary central line, the natural result of balancing the body over one supporting leg. The term for this stance, coined during the Italian Renaissance, is **contrapposto** ("counterpoise"), or weight-shift. The inspiration for this development seems to have been a growing desire by Greek sculptors to dramatize the stories narrated in the decorative programs of temples and

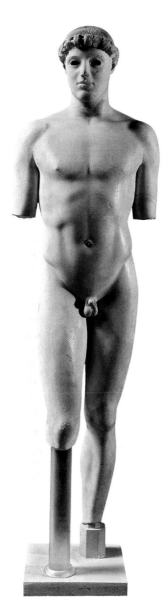

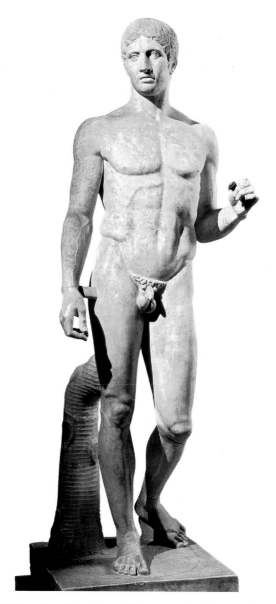

Fig. 2.28 *Kritios Boy,* **from Acropolis, Athens. ca. 480** BCE. Marble, height 46″. Acropolis Museum, Athens. The growing naturalism of Greek sculpture is clear when one compares the *Kritios Boy* to the earlier *kouros* figures. Sculptures such as this one mark a transition from the votive function of the *kouros* figures to the more decorative use of figurative sculpture in later Greek art.

Fig. 2.29 *Doryphoros (Spear Bearer),* **Roman copy after the original bronze by Polyclitus of ca. 450–440** BCE. Marble, height 6′ 6″. Museo Archeològico Nazionale, Naples. There is some debate about just what "measure" Polyclitus employed to achieve his ideal figure. Some argue that his system of proportions is based on the length of the figure's index finger or the width of the figure's hand across the knuckles. The idea that it is based on the distance between the chin and hairline derives from a much later discussion of proportion by the Roman writer Vitruvius, who lived in the first century CE. It is possible that Vitruvius had firsthand knowledge of Polyclitus's *Canon,* which was lost long ago.

sanctuaries. Liveliness of posture and gesture and a sense of capturing the body in action became their primary sculptural aim and the very definition of classical beauty.

An even more developed version of the *contrapposto* pose can be seen in the *Doryphoros,* or *Spear Bearer* (Fig. **2.29**), whose weight falls on the forward right leg. An idealized portrait of an athlete or warrior, originally done in bronze, the *Doryphoros* is a Roman copy of the work of Polyclitus, one of the great artists of the Golden Age. The sculpture was famous

throughout the ancient world as a demonstration of Polyclitus' treatise on proportion known as *The Canon* (from the Greek *kanon,* meaning "measure" or "rule"). In Polyclitus' system, the ideal human form was determined by the height of the head from the crown to the chin. The head was one-eighth the total height, the width of the shoulders was one-quarter the total height, and so on, each measurement reflecting these ideal proportions. For Polyclitus, these relations resulted in the work's *symmetria,* the origin of our word "symmetry," but meaning, in

Polyclitus' usage, "commensurability," or "having a common measure." Thus the figure, beautifully realized in great detail, right down to the veins on the back of the hand, reflects a higher mathematical order and embodies the ideal harmony between the natural world and the intellectual or spiritual realm.

Something of the quality of Phidias' work might be seen in a bronze sculpture recovered off the Italian coast near Riace (Fig. 2.30). There is some reason to believe that this piece was once part of an ensemble of thirteen bronzes commissioned by Kimon, son of the great general at Marathon, Miltiades, to honor his father. Sculpted by Phidias, they stood near the Athenian Treasury at Delphi. This particular bronze might represent Miltiades himself, since the figure wears a helmet pushed back on his head, the usual manner of depicting generals. Whatever the case, the bronze evidences an advanced *contrapposto* pose, a high degree of naturalism, and, at nearly six-and-a-half feet tall, an imposing monumentality. Bronze was, in fact, the material of choice for Greek sculptors. Marble was difficult to work with, susceptible to cracking during the sculpting process, and hard to fix if a mistake were made. But in sculpting the clay model for a bronze, artists could easily rework any part again and again. They could thus achieve a degree of perfection often unattainable in stone. Greek sculptors employed the lost-wax technique that had originated in the Middle East (see chapter 1), and they soon learned to create a variety of surface textures— for hair and skin, for instance. As here, they were able to embellish the works with copper-colored lips, ivory and glass-paste eyes, and teeth made of silver. Each eyelash on the Riace warrior is individually cast.

The decorative sculptures were in three main areas (Fig. 2.31)—in the pediments at each end of the building, on the **metopes**, or the square panels between the beam ends under the roof, and on the frieze that runs across the top of the outer wall of the cella. Brightly painted, these sculptures must have appeared strikingly lifelike. The three-foot-high frieze depicts a ceremonial procession (Fig. 2.32) and originally ran at a height of nearly 27 feet around the

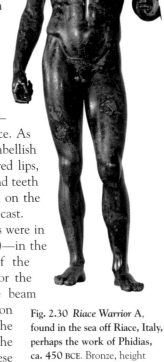

Fig. 2.30 *Riace Warrior* A, **found in the sea off Riace, Italy, perhaps the work of Phidias, ca. 450 BCE.** Bronze, height 6′ 8″. Reggio/ Museo Archeologico Nazionale di Napoli, Naples, Italy. This is one of two sculptures discovered in 1972 by scuba divers who saw an arm protruding out of the sand in about 25 feet of water.

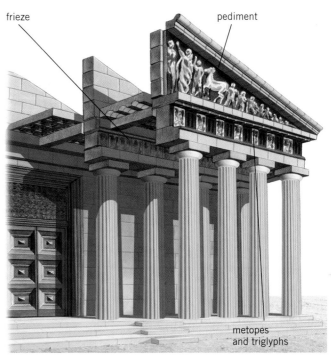

Fig. 2.31 **Cutaway drawing of the Parthenon porch showing friezes, metopes, and pediment.** Evident here is the architect Ictinus' juxtaposition of the Doric order, used for the columns with their capitals and the entablature on the outside, with the lighter Ionic order, with its continuous frieze, used for the entablature inside the colonnade.

central block of the building. Traditionally, the frieze has been interpreted as a depiction of the Panathenaic procession, an annual civic festival honoring Athena, but a recent interpretation suggests a mythological reading. The west pediment depicts Athena battling with Poseidon to determine who was to be patron saint of Athens. Scholars debate the identity of the figures in the east pediment, but it seems certain that overall it portrays the birth of Athena with gods and goddesses in attendance (Fig. 2.33). The 92 metopes on the four sides of the temple narrate battles between the Greeks and four enemies—the Trojans on one side, and on the other three, giants, Amazons (perhaps symbolizing the recently defeated Persians), and centaurs, mythological beasts with the legs and bodies of horses and the trunks and heads of humans. Executed in high relief (Fig. 2.34), these metopes represent the clash between the forces of civilization—the Greeks—and their barbarian, even bestial opponents. The male nude reflects not only physical but mental superiority, a theme particularly appropriate for a temple to Athena, goddess of both war and wisdom.

Philosophy and the *Polis*

The extraordinary architectural achievement of the Acropolis is matched by the philosophical achievement of the great Athenian philosopher Socrates, born in 469 BCE, a decade after the Greek defeat of the Persians. His death in 399 BCE

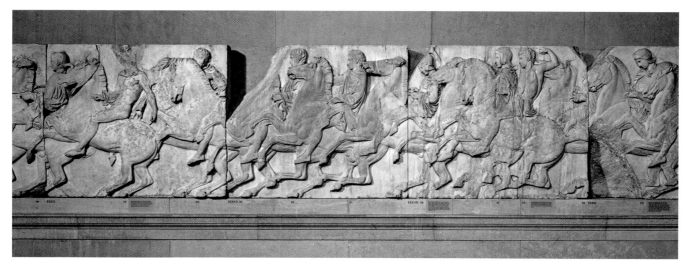

Fig. 2.32 *Young Men on Horseback,* segment of the north frieze, Parthenon. ca. 440 BCE. Marble, height 41″.
© The Trustees of the British Museum. This is just a small section of the entire procession, which extends completely
around the Parthenon.

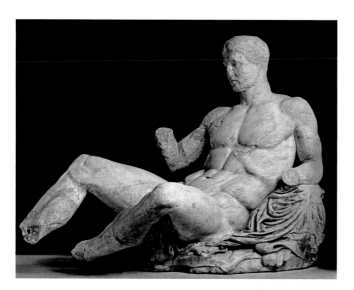

Fig. 2.33 **A recumbent god or hero, east pediment of the Parthenon, ca. 435 BCE.** © Copyright The British Museum. In 1801, Thomas Bruce, earl of Elgin and British ambassador to Constantinople, brought the marbles from the east pediment back to England to decorate his mansion—the source of their name, the *Elgin Marbles*. The identities of the figures are much disputed, but the greatness of their execution is not. Now exhibited in the round, in their original position on the pediment, they were carved in high relief. As the sun passed over the three-dimensional relief on the east and west pediments, the sculptures would have appeared almost animated by the changing light and the movement of their cast shadows.

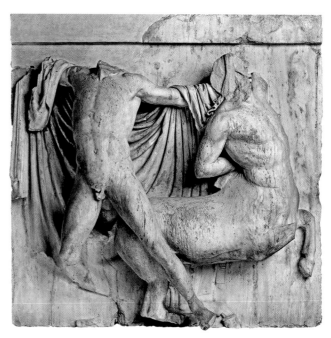

Fig. 2.34 **Lapith Overcoming a Centaur, south metope 27, Parthenon, Athens, 447–438 BCE.** Marble relief, height 4′ 5″. © Trustees of the British Museum, London. The Lapiths are a people in Greek myth who were defeated in a war provoked by drunken centaurs at the wedding of their king, Pirtihous. The Greeks identified themselves with the Lapiths after they were defeated by the Persians, whom they considered centaur-like.

arguably marks the end of Athens' Golden Age. Socrates' death was not a natural one. His execution was ordered by a polis in turmoil after its defeat by the Spartans in 404 BCE. The city had submitted to the rule of the oligarchic government installed by the victorious Spartans, the so-called Thirty Tyrants, whose power was ensured by a gang of "whip-bearers." They deprived the courts of their power and initiated a set of trials against rich men who opposed their

tyranny. Over 1,500 Athenians were subsequently executed. Socrates was brought to trial, accused of subversive behavior, corrupting young men, and introducing new gods, though these charges may have been politically motivated. He antagonized his jury of citizens by insisting that his life had been as good as anyone's and that far from committing any wrongs, he had greatly benefited Athens. He was convicted by a narrow majority and condemned to death by drinking poisonous hemlock. His refusal to flee and his willingness to submit to the will of the polis and drink the potion testify to his belief in the very polis that condemned him. His eloquent defense of his decision to submit is recorded in the *Crito* [KRIH-toh], a dialogue between Socrates and his friend Crito, actually written by Plato, Socrates' student and fellow philosopher. Although the Athenians would continue to enjoy relative freedom for many years to come, the death of Socrates marks the end of their great experiment with democracy. Socrates would become the model of good citizenship and right thinking for centuries to come.

The Philosophical Tradition in Athens To understand Socrates' position, it is important to recognize that the crisis confronting Athens in 404 BCE was not merely political, but deeply philosophical. And furthermore, a deep division existed between the philosophers and the polis. Plato, Socrates' student, through whose writings we know Socrates' teachings, believed good government was unattainable "unless either philosophers become kings in our cities or those whom we now call kings and rulers take to the pursuit of philosophy." He well understood that neither was likely to happen, and good government was, therefore, something of a dream. To further complicate matters, there were two distinct traditions of Greek *philosophia*—literally, "love of wisdom"—pre-Socratic and Sophist.

The oldest philosophical tradition, that of the **pre-Socratics**, referring to Greek philosophers who preceded Socrates, was chiefly concerned with describing the natural universe—the tradition inaugurated by Thales of Miletus. "What," the pre-Socratics asked, "lies behind the world of appearance? What is everything made of? How does it work? Is there an essential truth or core at the heart of the physical universe?" In some sense, then, they were scientists who investigated the nature of things, and they arrived at some extraordinary insights. Pythagoras [pie-THAG-uh-rus] (ca. 580–500 BCE), in studying the mathematical differences in the length of strings needed to produce various notes on the lyre, developed his famous mathematical theorem, which states that in a right triangle, the square of the hypotenuse is equal to the sum of the squares of the other two sides. Leucippus (fifth century BCE) was another pre-Socratic thinker. He conceived of an atomic theory in which everything is made up of small, indivisible particles and the empty space, or void, between them (the Greek word for "indivisible" is *atom*). Democritus of Thrace (ca. 460–ca. 370? BCE) furthered the theory by applying it to the mind. Democritus taught that everything from feelings and ideas to the physical sensations of taste, sight, and smell could be explained by the movements of atoms in the brain. Heraclitus of Ephesus (ca. 540–ca. 480 BCE) argued for the impermanence of all things. Change, or flux, he said, is the basis of reality, although an underlying Form or Guiding Force (*logos*) guides the process, a concept that later informs the Gospel of John in the Christian Bible, where *logos* is often mistranslated as "word."

Socrates was heir to the second tradition of Greek philosophy, that of the **Sophists**, literally "wise men." The Sophists no longer asked, "What do we know?" but, instead, "How do we know what we think we know?" and, crucially, "How can we trust what we think we know?" In other words, the Sophists concentrated not on the natural world but on the human mind, fully acknowledging the mind's many weaknesses. The Sophists were committed to what we have come to call **humanism**—that is, a focus on the actions of human beings, political action being one of the most important.

Protagoras (ca. 485–410 BCE), a leading Sophist, was responsible for one of the most famous of all Greek dictums: "Man is the measure of all things." By this he meant that each individual human, not the gods, not some divine or all-encompassing force, defines reality. All sensory appearances and all beliefs are true for the person whose appearance or belief they are. The Sophists believed that there were two sides to every argument. Protagoras' attitude about the gods is typical: "I do not know that they exist or that they do not exist."

The Sophists were teachers who traveled about, imparting their wisdom for pay. Pericles championed them, encouraging the best to come to Athens, where they enjoyed considerable prestige despite their status as foreigners. Their ultimate aim was to teach political virtue—*areté* [ah-RAY-tay]—emphasizing skills useful in political life, especially rhetorical persuasion, the art of speaking eloquently and persuasively. Their emphasis on rhetoric—their apparent willingness to assume either side of any argument merely for the sake of debate—as well as their critical examination of myths, traditions, and conventions, gave them a reputation for cynicism. Thus, their brand of argumentation came to be known as *sophistry*—subtle, tricky, superficially plausible, but ultimately false and deceitful reasoning.

Socrates and the Sophists Socrates despised everything the Sophists stood for, except their penchant for rhetorical debate, which was his chief occupation. He roamed the streets of Athens, engaging his fellow citizens in dialogue, wittily and often bitingly attacking them for the illogic of their positions. He employed the **dialectic method**—a process of inquiry and instruction characterized by continuous question-and-answer dialogue designed to elicit a clear statement of the knowledge supposed to be held implicitly by all reasonable beings. Unlike the Sophists, he refused to demand payment for his teaching, but like them, he urged his fellow men not to mistake their personal opinions for truth. Our beliefs, he knew, are built mostly on a foundation of prejudice and historical conditioning. He differed from the Sophists most crucially in his emphasis on virtuous behavior. For the Sophists, the true, the good, and the just were relative things. Depending on the situation or one's point of view, anything might be true, good, or just—the point, as will become evident in the next section, of many a Greek tragedy.

For Socrates, understanding the true meaning of the good, the true, and the just was prerequisite for acting virtuously, and the meaning of these things was not relative. Rather, true meaning resided in the **psyche**, the seat of both intelligence and character. Through **inductive reasoning**—moving from specific instances to general principles, and from particular to universal truths—it was possible, he believed, to understand the ideals to which human endeavor should aspire. Neither Socrates nor the Sophists could have existed without the democracy of the polis and the freedom of speech that accompanied it. Even during the reign of Pericles, Athenian conservatives had charged the Sophists with the crime of impiety. In questioning everything, from the authority of the gods to the rule of law, they challenged the stability of the very democracy that protected them. It is thus easy to understand how, when democracy ended, Athens condemned Socrates. He was democracy's greatest defender, and if he believed that the polis had forsaken its greatest invention, he himself could never betray it. Thus he chose to die.

Plato's *Republic* and Idealism So far as we know, Socrates himself never wrote a single word. We know his thinking only through the writings of his greatest student, Plato (ca. 428–347 BCE). Thus, it may be true that the Socrates we know is the one Plato wanted us to have, and that when we read Socrates' words, we are encountering Plato's thought more than Socrates'.

As Plato presents Socrates to us, the two philosophers, master and pupil, have much in common. They share the premise that the psyche is immortal and immutable. They also share the notion that we are all capable of remembering the psyche's pure state. But Plato advances Socrates' thought in several important ways. Plato's philosophy is a brand of **idealism**—it seeks the eternal perfection of pure ideas, untainted by material reality. He believes that there is an invisible world of eternal Forms, or Ideas, beyond everyday experience, and that the psyche, trapped in the material world and the physical body, can only catch glimpses of this higher order. Through a series of mental exercises, beginning with the study of mathematics and then moving on to the contemplation of the Forms of Justice, Beauty, and Love, the student can arrive at a level of understanding that amounts to superior knowledge.

Socrates' death deeply troubled Plato—not because he disagreed with Socrates' decision, but because of the injustice of his condemnation. The result of Plato's thinking is *The Republic*. In this treatise, Plato outlines his model of the ideal state. Only an elite cadre of the most highly educated men were to rule—those who had glimpsed Plato's ultimate Form, or Idea—the Good. In *The Republic*, in a section known as the "Allegory of the Cave" (Fig. **2.35**), Socrates addresses Plato's older brother, Glaucon [GLAW-kon], in an attempt to describe the difficulties the psyche encounters in its attempt to understand the higher Forms. Imagine, he says, a group of ordinary mortals chained in a cave, a fire lighting the interior behind them. Their whole lives they see only the shadows of forms cast upon the cave walls. These shadows are the only reality they know. Even when one is freed to turn around, he cannot believe his eyes. "Will he not," Plato asks, "fancy that the shadows which he formerly saw are truer than the objects which are now shown to him?" The higher Forms

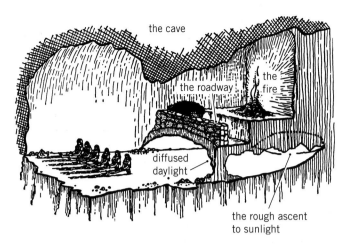

Fig. 2.35 "Allegory of the Cave," from *The Great Dialogues of Plato,* **trans. W.H.D. Rouse.** Translation © 1956, renewed 1984 by J.C.G. Rouse. Used by permission of Dutton Signet, a division of Penguin Books USA Inc.

are equally difficult to see. The Form of Goodness, Socrates says, is "the universal author of all things beautiful and right, parent of light and of the lord of light in this visible world, and the immediate source of reason and truth in the intellectual; and . . . this is the power upon which he who would act rationally, either in public or private life must have his eye fixed." The Form of Goodness, then, is something akin to God (though not God, from whom imperfect objects such as human beings descended, but more like an aspect of the Ideal, of which, one supposes, God must have some superior knowledge). The difficulty is that, once having attained an understanding of the Good, the wise individual will appear foolish to the people, who understand not at all. And yet, as Plato argues, it is precisely these individuals, blessed with wisdom, who must rule the commonwealth.

In many ways, Plato's ideal state is reactionary—it certainly opposes the individualistic and self-aggrandizing world of the Sophists. Plato is indifferent to the fact that his wise souls will find themselves ruling what amounts to a totalitarian regime. He believes their own sense of Goodness will prevail over their potentially despotic position. Moreover, rule by an intellectual philosopher king is superior to rule by any person whose chief desire is to satisfy his own material appetites.

To live in Plato's *Republic* would have been dreary indeed. Sex was to be permitted only for purposes of procreation. Everyone would undergo physical and mental training reminiscent of Sparta in the sixth century BCE. Although he believed in the intellectual pursuit of the Form or Idea of Beauty, Plato did not champion the arts. He condemned certain kinds of lively music because they affected not the reasonable mind of their audience but the emotional and sensory tendencies of the body. (But even for Plato, a man who did not know how to dance was uneducated—Plato simply preferred more restrained forms of music.) He also condemned sculptors and painters, whose works, he believed, were mere representations of representations—for if an actual bed is one remove from the Idea of Bed, a painting of a bed is twice removed, the faintest shadow. Furthermore, the images created by painters and sculptors appealed only to the senses. Thus he banished them from his ideal republic. Because they gave voice to tensions within the state, poets were banned as well.

The Theater of the People

Comparable to the sophistication of its achievements in art and architecture and philosophical discourse is the Greek contribution to—one might even say their invention of—the dramatic arts. The drama was originally a participatory ritual, tied to the cult of Dionysus. A chorus of people participating in the ritual would address and respond to another chorus or to a leader, such as a priest, perhaps representing (thus "acting the part" of) Dionysus. These dialogues usually occurred in the context of riotous dance and song—befitting revels dedicated to the god of wine.

This kind of behavior gave rise to one of the three major forms of Greek drama, the **satyr play**. Always the last event of the day-long performances, the satyr play was **farce**, that is, broadly satirical comedy, in which actors disguised themselves as satyrs, half-goat and half-man replete with extravagant genitalia. One whole satyr play survives, the *Cyclops* of Euripides, and half of another, Sophocles' *Trackers*. The spirit of these plays can perhaps be summed up best by the way in which Euripides spoofs or lampoons traditional Greek legend by setting it in a world turned topsy-turvy, a world in which Polyphemus the one-eyed giant in Homer's *Odyssey*, is stronger than Zeus because his farts are louder than Zeus' thunder.

Comedy Closely related to the satyr-plays was **comedy**, an amusing or lighthearted play designed to make its audience laugh. The word itself is derived from the *komos* [KO-mus], a phallic dance, and nothing is sacred to comedy. It freely slandered, buffooned, and ridiculed politicians, generals, public figures, and especially the gods. Foreigners, as always in Greek culture, are subject to particular abuse, as are women; in fact, by our standards, the plays are racist and sexist. Most of what we know about Greek comedies comes from two sources: vase painting and the plays of the playwright Aristophanes.

Comedic action was a favorite subject of vase painters working at Paestum in Italy in the fourth century BCE. They depict actors wearing masks and grotesque costumes distinguished by padded bellies, buttocks, and enlarged genitalia. These vases show a theater of burlesque and slapstick that relied heavily on visual gags (Fig. **2.36**).

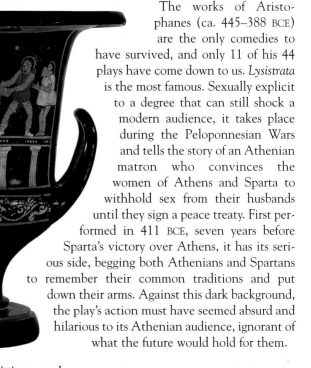

Fig. 2.36 Red-figure krater depicting a comedy by Assteas, from Paestum, Italy. ca. 350 BCE. Staatliche Museen, Berlin. On a stage supported by columns, with a scenic backdrop to the left, robbers try to separate a man from his strongbox.

The works of Aristophanes (ca. 445–388 BCE) are the only comedies to have survived, and only 11 of his 44 plays have come down to us. *Lysistrata* is the most famous. Sexually explicit to a degree that can still shock a modern audience, it takes place during the Peloponnesian Wars and tells the story of an Athenian matron who convinces the women of Athens and Sparta to withhold sex from their husbands until they sign a peace treaty. First performed in 411 BCE, seven years before Sparta's victory over Athens, it has its serious side, begging both Athenians and Spartans to remember their common traditions and put down their arms. Against this dark background, the play's action must have seemed absurd and hilarious to its Athenian audience, ignorant of what the future would hold for them.

Tragedy It was at **tragedy** that the Greek playwrights truly excelled. As with comedy, the basis for tragedy is conflict, but the tensions at work in tragedy—murder and revenge, crime and retribution, pride and humility, courage and cowardice—have far more serious consequences. Tragedies often explore the physical and moral depths to which human life can descend. The form also has it origins in the Dionysian rites—the name itself derives from *tragoidos* [trah-GOY-dus], the "goat song" of the half-goat, half-man satyrs, and tragedy's seriousness of purpose is not at odds with its origins. Dionysus was also the god of immortality, and an important aspect of his cult's influence is that he promised his followers life after death, just as the grapevine regenerates itself year after year. If tragedy can be said to have a subject, it is death—and the lessons the living can learn from the dead.

The original chorus structure of the Dionysian rites survives as an important element in tragedy. Thespis, a playwright from whom we derive the word *thespian*, "actor," first assumed the conscious role of an actor in the mid-sixth century BCE and apparently redefined the role of the **chorus**. At first, the actor asked questions of the chorus, perhaps of the "tell me what happened next" variety, but when two, three, and sometimes four actors were introduced to the stage, the chorus began to comment on their interaction. In this way the chorus assumed its classic function as an intermediary between actors and audience. Although the chorus's role diminished noticeably in the fourth century BCE, it remained the symbolic voice of the people, asserting the importance of the action to the community as a whole.

Greek tragedy often focused on the friction between the individual and his or her community, and, at a higher level, between the community and the will of the gods. This conflict manifests itself in the weakness or "tragic flaw" of the play's **protagonist**, or leading character, which brings the character into conflict with the community, the gods, or some **antagonist** who represents an opposing will. The action occurs in a single day, the result of a single incident that precipitates the unfolding crisis. Thus the audience feels that it is experiencing the action in real time, that it is directly involved in and affected by the play's action.

During the reign of the tyrant Peisistratus, the performance of all plays was regularized. An annual competitive festival for the performance of tragedies called the City Dionysia was celebrated for a week every March as the vines came back to life, and a separate festival for comedies occurred in January. At the City Dionysia, plays were performed in sets of four—**tetralogies**—all by the same author, three of which were tragedies, performed during the day, and the fourth a satyr play, performed in the evening. The audiences were as large as 14,000, and audience response determined which plays were awarded prizes. The entire citizenry, including slaves, women, and even those from outside the polis, judged the performances.

Although many Greek playwrights composed tragedies, only those of Aeschylus, Sophocles, and Euripides have come down to us. Three plays by Aeschylus (ca. 525–ca. 456 BCE), known as the *Oresteia* [oh-ray-STYE-ee-uh], form the only complete set of tragedies from a tetralogy that we have. The plays narrate the story of the Mycenaean king Agamemnon, murdered by his adulterous wife Clytemnestra and mourned and revenged by their children, Orestes and Electra. Playwright, treasurer for the Athenian *polis*, a general under Pericles, and advisor to Athens on financial matters during the Peloponnesian Wars, Sophocles (ca. 496–406 BCE) was an almost legendary figure in fifth century BCE Athens. He wrote over 125 plays, of which only seven survive, and he won the City Dionysia 18 times. In *Oedipus the King*, Sophocles dramatizes how the king of Thebes, a *polis* in east central Greece, mistakenly kills his father and marries his mother, then finally blinds himself to atone for his crimes of patricide and incest. In *Antigone*, he dramatizes the struggle of Oedipus' daughter Antigone with her uncle Creon, the tyrannical king who inherited Oedipus' throne. Antigone struggles for what amounts to her democratic rights as an individual to fulfill her familial duties, even when this opposes what Creon argues is the interest of the *polis*. Her predicament is doubly complicated by her status as a woman. The youngest of the three playwrights, Euripides (ca. 480–406 BCE), writing during the Peloponnesian Wars, brought a level of measured skepticism to the stage. Eighteen of his ninety works survive, but Euripides won the City Dionysia only four times. His plays probably angered more conservative Athenians, which may be why he moved from Athens to Macedonia in 408 BCE. In *The Trojan Women*, for instance, performed in 415 BCE, he describes, disapprovingly, the Greek enslavement of the women of Troy, drawing an unmistakable analogy to the contemporary Athenian victory at Melos, where women were subjected to Athenian abuse.

The Performance Space During the tyranny of Peisistratos, plays were performed in an open area of the agora called the **orchestra**, or "dancing space." Spectators sat on wooden planks laid on portable scaffolding. Sometime in the fifth century BCE, the scaffolding collapsed, and many people were injured. The Athenians built a new theater (*theatron*, meaning "viewing space"), dedicated to Dionysus, into the hillside on the side of the Acropolis away from the agora and below the Parthenon. Architecturally, it was very similar to the best preserved of all Greek theaters, the one at Epidaurus (Figs. 2.37, 2.38), built in the early third century BCE. The orchestra has been transformed into a circular performance space, approached on each side by an entryway called a *parados*, through which the chorus would enter the orchestra area. Behind this was an elevated platform, the **proscenium**, the stage on which the actors performed and where painted backdrops could be hung. Behind the proscenium was the **skene**, literally a "tent," and originally a changing room for the actors. Over time, it was transformed into a building, often two stories tall. Actors on the roof could portray the gods, looking down on the action below. By the time of Euripides, it housed a rolling or rotating platform that could suddenly reveal an interior space.

Music and dance Music and dance appear to have been central elements in the performance of plays. For the Greeks, music was divinely inspired by Euterpe, one of the nine **muses** (hence the word "music"), the nine sister goddesses who presided over song, poetry, and the arts and sciences. The only complete work of music to have survived from ancient Greece is a *skolion* [SKO-lee-un], or drinking song, by Seikolos [SYE-kuh-lus], found chiseled on the first-century BCE gravestone of his wife, Euterpe. We do, however, know something of the theory upon which Greek music was based. It was Pythagoras who, in seeking to understand the relationship of a string's length to the note it produced, created the Greek scale of eight notes, each one determined by its numerical ratio to the lowest tone. For Pythagoras, these ratios reflected the *cosmos*—meaning the harmonious and beautiful order of the universe. The movement of the planets, Pythagoras believed, produced a special harmony, called the *music of the spheres*.

Over time, musical **modes** evolved in which different pitches were believed to evoke different emotions. Each of the modes was thought to have a different emotional and ethical impact. The *Dorian mode*—favored by Plato for its restraint—was formal and dignified, and promoted virtue in its audience. The *Lydian mode* was sentimental and weak. And the *Phrygian mode*—condemned by Plato as irrational and overly emotional—was the mode of the satyrs—wild and frenzied.

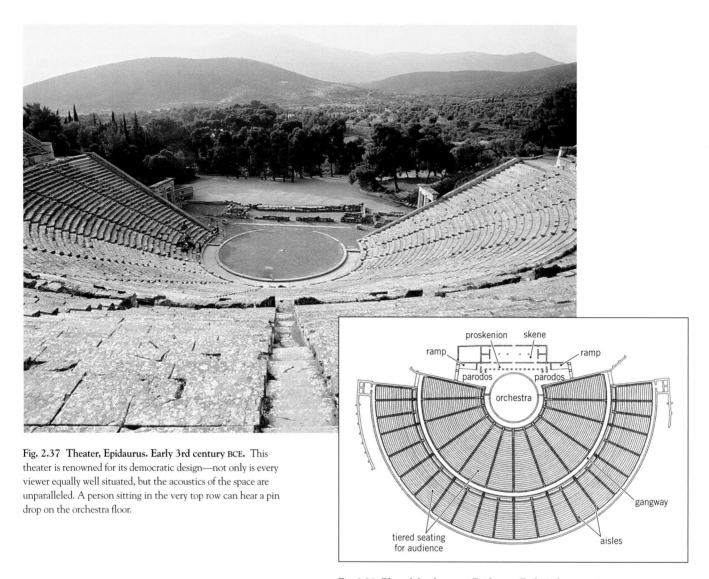

Fig. 2.37 **Theater, Epidaurus. Early 3rd century** BCE. This theater is renowned for its democratic design—not only is every viewer equally well situated, but the acoustics of the space are unparalleled. A person sitting in the very top row can hear a pin drop on the orchestra floor.

Fig. 2.38 **Plan of the theater at Epidaurus. Early 3rd century** BCE.

For the Greeks, music was a sensory reflection of the higher order that pervades all things. Its highest forms were believed to affect the moral character in a positive way, but, as Plato insisted, music of the wrong sort could be morally and socially destructive. Ultimately, all music had the power to mold people's souls in its own image. Ideally, Plato felt, it should reflect the Classicism that distinguished the art and architecture of fifth-century Athens. It should be balanced, harmonious, and dignified.

The Hellenistic World

Both the emotional drama of Greek theater and the sensory appeal of its music reveal a growing tendency in the culture to value emotional expression at least as much, and sometimes more, than the balanced harmonies of classical art. During the **Hellenistic** age in the fourth and third centuries BCE, the truths that the culture increasingly sought to understand were less idealistic and universal and more and more empirical and personal. This shift is especially evident in the new empirical philosophy of Aristotle (384–322 BCE), whose investigation into the workings of the real world supplanted, or at least challenged, Plato's idealism. In many ways, however, the ascendancy of this new aesthetic standard can be attributed to the daring, the audacity, and the sheer awe-inspiring power of a single figure, Alexander of Macedonia, known as Alexander the Great (356–323 BCE) (Fig. **2.39**). Alexander aroused the emotions and captured the imagination of not just a theatrical audience, but an entire people—perhaps even the entire Western world—and created a legacy that established Hellenic Greece as the model against which all cultures in the West had to measure themselves.

The Empire of Alexander the Great

Alexander was the son of Philip II (382–336 BCE) of Macedonia, a relatively undeveloped northern Greek state whose inhabitants spoke a Greek dialect unintelligible to Atheni-

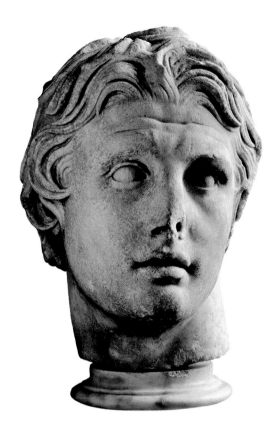

Fig. 2.39 *Alexander the Great*, **head from a Pergamene copy (ca. 200 BCE) of a statue, possibly after a 4th-century BCE original by Lysippus.** Marble, height 16 1/8". Archaeological Museum, Istanbul, Turkey. Alexander is traditionally portrayed as if looking beyond his present circumstances to greater things.

ans. Recognizing that after the Peloponnesian Wars the Greek poleis were in disarray, in 338 BCE Philip defeated the combined forces of Athens and Thebes and unified all of Greece, with the exception of Sparta. He then turned his attention to Persia, and when he was assassinated in 336 BCE, Alexander quickly took control.

Within two years Alexander had crossed the Hellespont into Asia and defeated Darius III of Persia. The victory realized Philip's plan to repay the Persians for their role in the Peloponnesian Wars and to conquer Asia as well. By 332 BCE, Alexander had conquered Egypt, founding the great city of Alexandria (named, of course, after himself) in the Nile Delta (Map **2.3**). Then he marched back into Mesopotamia, where he again defeated Darius III and then marched into both Babylon and Susa without resistance. After making the proper sacrifices to the Akkadian god Marduk—and thus gaining the admiration of the locals—he advanced on Persepolis, the Persian capital, which he burned after seizing its royal treasures. Then he entered present-day Pakistan.

Alexander's object was India, which he believed was relatively small. He thought if he crossed it, he would find what he called Ocean, and an easy sea route home. Finally, in 326 BCE his army reached the Indian Punjab. Under Alexander's leadership it had marched over 11,000 miles without a defeat. It had destroyed ancient empires, founded many cities (in the 320s BCE, Alexandrias proliferated across the world), and created the largest empire the world had ever known.

When Alexander and his army reached the banks of the Indus River in 326 BCE, he encountered a culture that had long

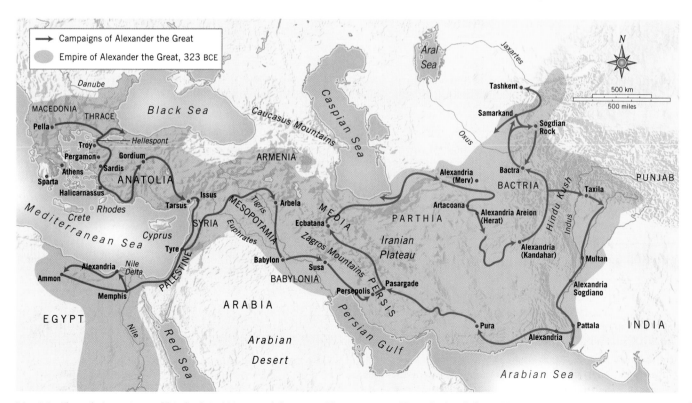

Map 2.3 Alexander's empire as of his death in 323 BCE and the route of his conquests. Alexander founded over 70 cities throughout his empire, naming many after himself.

fascinated him. His teacher Aristotle had described it, wholly on hearsay, as had Herodotus before him, as the farthest land mass to the east, beyond which lay an Endless Ocean that encircled the world. Alexander stopped first at Taxila (20 miles north of modern Islamabad, Pakistan), where King Omphis [OHM-fis] greeted him with a gift of 200 silver talents, 3,000 oxen, 10,000 sheep, 30 elephants, and bolstered Alexander's army by giving him 700 Indian cavalry and 5,000 infantry.

While Alexander was in Taxila, he became acquainted with the Hindu philosopher Calanus [kuh-LAY-nus]. Alexander recognized in Calanus and his fellow Hindu philosophers a level of wisdom and learning that he valued highly, one clearly reminiscent of Greek philosophy, and his encounters with them represent the first steps in a long history of the cross-fertilization of Eastern and Western cultures.

But in India the army encountered elephants, whose formidable size proved problematic. East of Taxila, Alexander's troops managed to defeat King Porus [PAW-rus], whose army was equipped with 200 elephants. Rumor had it that farther to the east, the kingdom of the Ganges, their next logical opponent, had a force of 5,000 elephants. Alexander pleaded with his troops: "Dionysus, divine from birth, faced terrible tasks—and we have outstripped him! . . . Onward, then: let us add to our empire the rest of Asia!" The army refused to budge. His conquests thus concluded, Alexander himself sailed down the Indus River, founding the city that would later become Karachi. As he returned home, he contracted fever in Babylon and died in 323 BCE. Alexander's life was brief, but his influence on the arts was long-lasting.

Toward Hellenistic Art: Sculpture in the Late Classical Period

During Alexander's time, sculpture flourished. Ever since the fall of Athens to Sparta in 404 BCE, Greek artists had continued to develop the Classical style of Phidias and Polyclitus, but they modified it in subtle yet innovative ways. Especially notable was a growing taste for images of men and women in quiet, sometimes dreamy and contemplative moods, which increasingly replaced the sense of nobility and detachment characteristic of fifth-century Classicism and found its way even into depictions of the gods. The most admired sculptors of the day were Lyssipus, Praxiteles, and Skopas. Very little of the latter's work has survived, though he was noted for high relief sculpture featuring highly energized and emotional scenes. The work of the first two is far better known.

The Heroic Sculpture of Lysippus Alexander hired the sculptor Lysippus (flourished fourth century BCE) to do all his portraits. Despite his cruel treatment of the Thebans early in his career, Alexander was widely admired by the Greeks. Even during his lifetime, but especially after his death, sculptures celebrating the youthful hero abounded, almost all of them modeled on Lyssipus' originals. Alexander is easily recognizable—his disheveled hair long and flowing, his gaze intense and melting, his mouth slightly open, his head alertly turned on a slightly tilted neck (see Fig. 2.39).

Lysippus dramatized his hero. That is, he did not merely represent Alexander as naturalistically as possible, he also animated him, showing him in the midst of action. In all likelihood, he idealized him as well. The creation of Alexander's likeness was a conscious act of propaganda. Early in his conquests the young hero referred to himself as "Alexander the Great," and Lysippus' job was to embody that greatness. Lysippus challenged the Classical *kanon* of proportion created by Polyclitus—smaller heads and slenderer bodies lent his heroic sculptures a sense of greater height. In fact, he transformed the Classical tradition in sculpture and began to explore new possibilities that, eventually, would define Hellenistic art, with its sense of animation, drama, and psychological complexity.

The Sensuous Sculpture of Praxiteles Competing with Lysippus for the title of greatest sculptor of the fourth century BCE was the Athenian Praxiteles (flourished 370–330 BCE). Praxiteles was one of the 300 wealthiest men in Athens, thanks to his skill, but he also had a reputation as a womanizer. The people of the port city of Knidos [ku-NEE-dus], a Spartan colony in Asia Minor, asked him to provide them with an image of their patron goddess, Aphrodite, in her role as the protectress of sailors and merchants. Praxiteles responded with a sculpture of Aphrodite as the goddess of love, here reproduced in a later Roman copy (Fig. **2.40**). She stands at her bath, holding her cloak in her left hand, and she was displayed in the middle of a large garden in a colonnaded, circular shrine, the remains of which have been discovered. The sculpture is a frank celebration of the body—reflecting in the female form the humanistic appreciation for the dignity of the human body in its own right. (Images of it on local coins suggest that her original pose was far less modest than that of the Roman copy, her right hand not shielding her genitals.) The statue made Knidos famous, and many people traveled there to see it. She was enshrined in a circular temple, easily viewed from every angle, the Roman scholar Pliny the Elder (23–79 CE) tells us, and she quickly became an object of religious attention—and openly sexual adoration. The reason for this is difficult to assess in the rather mechanical Roman copies of the lost original.

Praxiteles' *Aphrodite of Knidos* may be the first fully nude depiction of a woman in Greek sculpture, which may be why it caused such a sensation. Its fame elevated female nudity from a sign of low moral character to the embodiment of beauty, even truth itself. Paradoxically, it is also one of the earliest examples of artwork designed to appeal to what some art historians describe as the **male gaze** that regards woman as its sexual object. Praxiteles' canon for depicting the female nude—wide hips, small breasts, oval face, and centrally parted hair—remained the standard throughout antiquity.

Aristotle: Observing the Natural World

We can only guess what motivated Lysippus and Praxiteles to so dramatize and humanize their sculptures, but it is likely that the aesthetic philosophy of Aristotle (384–322 BCE) played a role. Aristotle was a student of Plato's. Recall that, for Plato, all reality is a mere reflection of a higher, spiritual

expression. Based on his observations of lunar eclipses, he concluded as early as 350 BCE that the earth was spherical, an observation that may have motivated Alexander to cross India in order to sail back to Greece. He described over 500 animals in his *Historia Animalium,* including many that he dissected himself. In fact, Aristotle's observations of marine biology were unequaled until the seventeenth century and were still much admired by Charles Darwin in the nineteenth.

He also understood the importance of formulating a reasonable hypothesis to explain phenomena. His *Physics* is an attempt to define the first principles governing the behavior of matter—the nature of weight, motion, physical existence, and variety in nature. At the heart of Aristotle's philosophy is a question about the relation of *identity* and *change* (not far removed, incidentally, from one of the governing principles of this text, the idea of continuity and change in the humanities). To discuss the world coherently, we must be able to say what it is about a thing that makes it the thing it is, that separates it from all the other things in the world. In other words, what is the attribute that we would call its material identity or *essence?* What it means to be human, for instance, does not depend on whether one's hair turns gray. Such "accidental" changes matter not at all. At the same time, our experience of the natural world suggests that any coherent account requires us to acknowledge process and change—the change of seasons, the changes in our understanding associated with gaining knowledge in the process of aging, and so on. For Aristotle, any account of a thing must accommodate both aspects: We must be able to say what changes a thing undergoes while still retaining its essential nature, and Aristotle thus approached all manner of things—from politics to the human condition—with an eye toward determining what constituted its essence.

Aristotle's *Poetics* What constitutes the essential nature of literary art, and the theater in particular, especially fascinated him. Like all Greeks, Aristotle was well acquainted with the theater of Aeschylus, Euripides, and Sophocles, and in his *Poetics* he defined their literary art as "the imitation of an action that is complete and whole." Including a whole action, or a series of events that ends with a crisis, gives the play a sense of unity. Furthermore, he argued (against Plato, who regarded imitation as inevitably degrading and diminishing) that such imitation elevates the mind ever closer to the universal.

One of the most important ideas that Aristotle expressed in the *Poetics* is **catharsis,** the cleansing, purification, or purgation of the soul. As applied to drama, it is not the tragic hero who undergoes catharsis, but the audience. The audience's experience of catharsis is an experience of change, just as change always accompanies understanding. In the theater, what moves the audience to change is its experience of the universality of the human condition—what it is that makes us human, our weaknesses as well as our strengths. At the sight of the action onstage viewers are struck with "fear and pity." Plato believed that both of these emotions were pernicious. But Aristotle argued that the audience's emotional response to the plight of the characters on stage clarified for

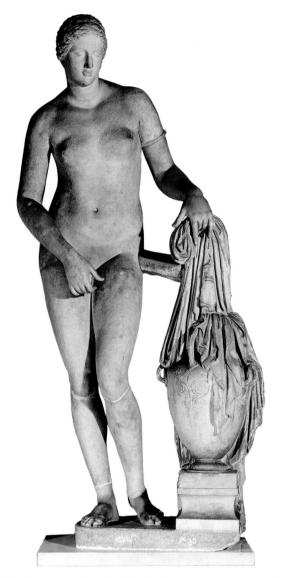

Fig. 2.40 Praxiteles, *Aphrodite of Knidos,* Roman copy of an original of ca. 350 BCE. P. Zigrossi/Vatican Museums, Rome, Italy. Marble, height 6′ 8″. The head of this figure is from one Roman copy, the body from another. The right forearm and hand, the left arm, and the lower legs of the *Aphrodite* are all seventeenth- and eighteenth-century restorations. There is reason to believe that her hand was not so modestly positioned in the original.

truth, a higher dimension of Ideal Forms that we glimpse only through philosophical contemplation (see Fig. 2.35).

Aristotle disagreed. Reality was not a reflection of an ideal form, but existed in the material world itself, and by observing the material world, one could come to know universal truths. So Aristotle observed and described all aspects of the world in order to arrive at the essence of things. His methods of observation came to be known as *empirical investigation.* And though he did not create a formal **scientific method,** he and other early empiricists did create procedures for testing their theories about the nature of the world that, over time, would lead to the great scientific discoveries of Bacon, Galileo, and Newton. Aristotle studied biology, zoology, physics, astronomy, politics, logic, ethics, and the various genres of literary

them the fragility and mutability of human life. What happens in tragedy is universal—the audience understands that the action could happen to anyone at any time.

The Golden Mean In Aristotle's philosophy, such Classical aesthetic elements as unity of action and time, orderly arrangement of the parts, and proper proportion all have ethical ramifications. He argued for them by means of a philosophical method based on the **syllogism**, two premises from which a conclusion can be drawn. The most famous of all syllogisms is this:

All men are mortal;
Socrates is a man;
Therefore, Socrates is mortal.

In the *Nicomachean Ethics*, written for and edited by his son Nicomachus [nee-koh-MAH-kus], Aristotle attempts to define, once and for all, what Greek society had striven for since the beginning of the polis—the good life. The operative syllogism goes something like this:

The way to happiness is through the pursuit of moral virtue;
The pursuit of the good life is the way to happiness;
Therefore, the good life consists in the pursuit of moral virtue.

The good life, Aristotle argued, is attainable only through balanced action. Tradition has come to call this the **Golden Mean**—not Aristotle's phrase but that of the Roman poet Horace—the middle ground between any two extremes of behavior. Thus, in a formulation that was particularly applicable to his student Alexander the Great, the Golden Mean between cowardice and recklessness is courage. And the state is a creation of this same sensibility. In his *Politics*, Aristotle collected over 150 state constitutions, compared and contrasted their virtues, and concluded that a constitutional regime ruled by the middle class was the perfect form of government. The middle class is a "mean" group, exciting neither the envy of the poor nor the contempt of the wealthy.

Despite the measure and moderation of Aristotle's thinking, Greek culture did not necessarily reflect the balanced approach of its leading philosopher. In his emphasis on catharsis—the value of experiencing "fear and pity," the emotions that move us to change—Aristotle introduced the values that would define the age of Hellenism, the period lasting from 323 to 31 BCE, that is, from the death of Alexander to the Battle of Actium in Egypt, the event that marks in the minds of many the beginning of the Roman Empire.

Pergamon: Capital of Hellenistic Greece

Upon his death, Alexander left no designated successor, and his three chief generals divided his empire into three successor states: the kingdom of Macedonia (including all of Greece), the kingdom of the Ptolemies (Egypt), and the kingdom of the Seleucids (Syria and what is now Iraq). But a fourth, smaller kingdom in western Anatolia, Pergamon (modern-day Bergama, Turkey), soon rose to prominence and became a center of

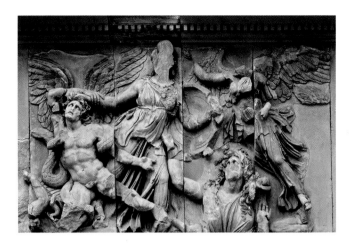

Fig. 2.41 Details of the east frieze of the Altar of Zeus, from Pergamon. ca. 165 BCE. In this image, Athena grabs the hair of a winged, serpent-tailed monster, who is identified on the base of the monument as Alkyoneos, son of the earth goddess Ge. Ge herself rises up from the ground on the right to avenge her son. Behind Ge, a winged Nike flies to Athena's rescue.

Hellenistic culture. Ruled by the Attalids [ATT-uh-lidz]—descendants of a Macedonian general named Attalus [ATT-uh-lus]—Pergamon was founded as a sort of treasury for the huge fortunes Alexander had accumulated in his conquests. It was technically under the control of the Seleucid kingdom. However, under the leadership of Eumenes [YOU-mee-neez] I (r. 263–241 BCE), Pergamon achieved virtual independence.

The Library at Pergamon The Attalids created a huge library filled with over 200,000 Classical Athenian texts. These were copied onto parchment, a word that derives from the Greek *pergamene*, meaning "from Pergamon," and refers to sheets of tanned leather. Pergamon's vast treasury allowed the Attalids the luxury of investing enormous sums of money in decorating their acropolis with art and architecture. Especially under the rule of Eumenes II (r. 197–160 BCE), the building program flourished. It was Eumenes II who built the library, as well as the theater and a gymnasium. And he was probably responsible for the Altar of Zeus which is today housed in Berlin.

A New Sculptural Style The altar is decorated with the most ambitious sculptural program since the Parthenon, but unlike the Parthenon, its frieze is at eye level and is $7\frac{1}{2}$ feet high. Its subject is the mythical battle of the gods and the giants for control of the world. The giants are depicted with snakelike bodies that coil beneath the feet of the triumphant gods (Fig. **2.41**). These figures represent one of the greatest examples of the Hellenized style of sculpture that depends for its effects on its **expressionism**, that is, the attempt to elicit an emotional response in the viewer. The theatrical effects of Lysippus (see Fig. 2.39) are magnified into a heightened sense of drama. Where Classical artists sought balance, order, and proportion, this frieze, with its figures twisting, thrusting, and striding in motion, stresses diagonal forces that seem to pull each other apart. Swirling bodies and draperies weave in and out of the sculpture's space, and the relief is so three-dimensional that contrasts of light and shade add to the dramatic effects. Above all, the frieze is an attempt to evoke the emotions of fear and pity that Aristotle argued led to catharsis in his *Poetics*, not the intellectual order of Classical tradition.

One other Hellenistic sculpture deserves particular attention: the *Nike of Samothrace*. Convincing arguments date the *Nike of Samothrace* (Fig. **2.42**) anywhere from 300 BCE to as late as 31 BCE, though most agree that it was probably commissioned to celebrate a naval victory before 190 BCE. It originally stood (with head and arms that have not survived, except for a single hand) upon the sculpted prow of a ship that was dramatically set in a pool of water at the top of a cliff on the island of Samothrace in the north Aegean. The dynamic forward movement of the striding figure is balanced dramatically by the open gesture of her extended wings and the powerful directional lines of her windblown gown across her body. When light rakes across the deeply sculpted forms of this figure, it emphasizes the contrasting textures of feathers, fabric, and flesh. Like the *Altar of Zeus*, this sculpture reflects a new direction in art. The calm and restraint of Classical art have disappeared, replaced by the freedom to explore the emotional extremes of the human experience.

Alexandria

If Pergamon was a spectacular Hellenistic city, it paled beside Alexandria in Egypt. Alexander had conceived of all the cities he founded as centers of culture. They would be hubs of trade and learning, and Greek culture would radiate out from them to the surrounding countryside. But Alexandria exceeded even Alexander's expectations.

The city's ruling family, the Ptolemies (heirs of Alexander's close friend and general, Ptolemy I), built the world's first museum—from the Greek *mouseion* [moo-ZAY-on], literally, "temple to the muses"—conceived as a meeting place for scholars and students. Nearby was the largest library in the world, exceeding even Pergamon's. It contained over 700,000 volumes when it was destroyed in 47 BCE, after Julius Caesar ordered his troops to set fire to the Ptolemaic fleet and winds spread the flames to warehouses and dockyards. Here were collected the great works of Greek civilization, the writings of Plato and Aristotle, the plays of the great tragedians Aeschylus, Sophocles, and Euripides, as well as the comedies of Aristophanes. Stimulated by the intellectual activity in the city, the great mathematician Euclid formulated the theorems of plane and solid geometry here.

The city was designed by Alexander's personal architect, Deinocrates [dye-NOK-rah-teez] of Rhodes (flourished fourth century BCE), laid out in a grid, enclosed by a wall, and accessible by four gates at the ends of major avenues. It was blessed by three extraordinary harbors, one connected to the Nile, allowing for the transfer of the Nile's enormous agricultural wealth. It was a cosmopolitan city, exceeding even Golden Age Athens in the diversity of its inhabitants. As its population approached 1 million at the end of the first century BCE, commerce was its primary activity. Peoples of different ethnic backgrounds—Jews, black Africans, Greeks, Egyptians, various races and tribes from Asia Minor—all came together with the single purpose of making money.

Gradually, Hellenistic and Egyptian cultures merged, a fact underscored by the Egyptian king Ptolemy I (r. 323–285 BCE) when he diverted the funeral train of Alexander the Great from its Macedonian destination to Egypt. Burying him either in Memphis or Alexandria (his tomb has never been found), Ptolomy guaranteed that the city would forever be associated with the cult of Alexander himself. Tomb decorations at Luxor depict Alexander in the traditional role and style of an Egyptian pharoah.

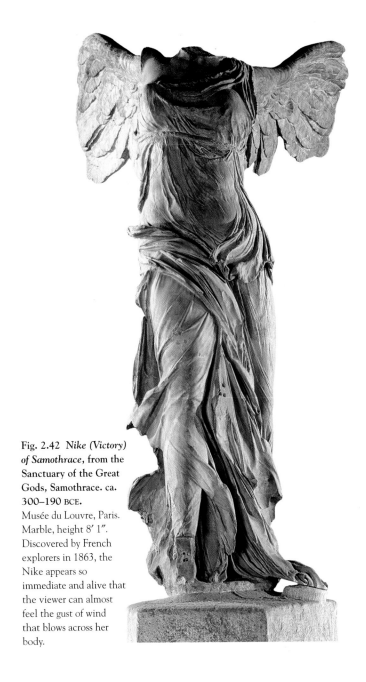

Fig. 2.42 *Nike (Victory) of Samothrace,* from the Sanctuary of the Great Gods, Samothrace. ca. 300–190 BCE.
Musée du Louvre, Paris. Marble, height 8′ 1″. Discovered by French explorers in 1863, the Nike appears so immediate and alive that the viewer can almost feel the gust of wind that blows across her body.

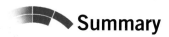**Summary**

■ **Bronze Age Culture in the Aegean** The later Greeks traced their ancestry to the cultures that arose in the islands of the Aegean Sea. The art of the Cyclades consisted of highly simplified Neolithic figurines, and later, under the influence of Minoan culture to the south on Crete, frescoes depicting everyday events. An enormous volcanic eruption on the island of Thera brought Cycladic culture to an end. Unique to Minoan culture on Crete is an emphasis on the bull, associated with the legend of King Minos and the Minotaur. The complex layout of Minos' palace at Knossos gave rise to the word *labyrinth*. Mycenaean warriors from the Greek mainland invaded Crete in about 450 BCE. From all appearances their two cultures could not have been more different. The Minoans were peace loving, building unfortified cities on the flat plains of the islands. The Mycenaeans were warlike, building walled cities surrounding fortified and highly defensible hilltops. Around 800 BCE, Homer's great epics, the *Iliad* and the *Odyssey*, were transcribed, recounting a war between Mycenae and Troy that occurred sometime between 1800 and 1300 BCE in the *Iliad*, and the Mycenaean warrior Odysseus' journey home after the conflict in the *Odyssey*.

■ **The Rise of the Greek City-States** Each of the rural areas of Greece, separated from one another by mountainous geography, gradually began to form into a community—the *polis*, or city-state—that exercised authority over its region. At Delos, Delphi, Olympia, and even in colonies such as Paestum on the Italian peninsula, the city-states came together to honor their gods and, by extension, to celebrate, in the presence of their rivals, their own accomplishments. As a people, the Greeks believed in *agonizesthai*, a verb meaning "to contend for the prize." In the Olympic Games, in the arts, in every endeavor, they were driven by a spirit of competition. The Greeks were unique among Mediterranean cultures in portraying the male nude, both on painted vases celebrating, for instance, athletic contests and in the widespread genre of *kouros* sculpture. These sculptures became increasingly naturalistic during the sixth century BCE. Coinciding with the increasing naturalism of Greek sculpture with its increasing sense of individualism was the rise of democratic institutions in Athens. Democracy was soon threatened by the invasion of the Persians, who were finally defeated by the Greek navy in the straits off Salamis.

■ **Golden Age Athens** In the fifth century BCE, the statesman Pericles dominated Athenian political life, claiming for Athenians "excellence" in all aspects of endeavor, from their sculpture and painted ceramics, to their architecture on the Acropolis and the perfection of Classical forms realized in the Parthenon, to their theater with the great tragedies of Aeschylus, Sophocles, and Euripides. Pericles also championed the practice of philosophy in Athens, giving rise to the great idealistic philosophies of Socrates and his pupil Plato.

■ **The Hellenistic World** Alexander the Great conquered most of the known world, extending Greek influence in the process. The empiricist philosophy of Aristotle challenged the idealism of Socrates and Plato. In sculpture, a new expressionist style arose, designed to evoke a strong emotional response in the viewer.

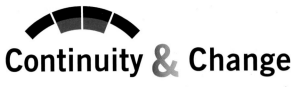

Continuity & Change

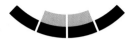

Rome traced its origins back to the Trojan warrior Aeneas, who at the end of the Trojan War sailed off to found a new homeland for his people. The Roman poet Virgil (70-19 BCE) would celebrate Aeneas' journey in his epic poem, the *Aeneid*, written in the last decade of his life. There he describes how the gods who supported the Greeks punished the Trojan priest Laocoön for warning his countrymen against accepting the "gift" of a wooden horse from the Greeks:

> I shudder even now,
> Recalling it—there came a pair of serpents
> With monstrous coils, breast the sea, and aiming
> Together for the shore. . . .
> Straight toward Laocoön, and first each serpent
> Seized in its coils his two young sons, and fastened
> The fangs in those poor bodies. And the priest
> Struggled to help them, weapons in his hand.
> They seized him, bound him with the mighty coils,
> Twice round his waist, twice round his neck, they squeezed
> With scaly pressure, and still towered above him
> Straining his hands to teach the knots apart,
> His chaplet's[1] stained with blood and the black poison,
> He uttered horrible cries, not even human,
> More like the bellowing of a bull when, wounded,
> It flees the altar, shaking from the shoulder
> The ill-aimed axe.

[1]chaplet: Garland for the head.

It is likely that as he wrote the *Aeneid*, Virgil had seen the original sculpture of *Laocoön and His Sons* (Fig. 2.43), carved in about 150 BCE, a remarkable copy of which was discovered in 1506 in the ruins of a palace belonging to the emperor Titus (r. 79–81 CE) in Rome. The drama and expressionism of the sculpture are pure Hellenism. So too are its complex interweaving of elements and diagonal movements reminiscent of Athena's struggle with the giants on the frieze of the Altar of Zeus at Pergamon (see Fig. 2.41).

In fact, even though Rome conquered Greece in 146 BCE (at about the time that the Laocoön was carved), Greece could be said to have "ruled" Rome, at least culturally. Rome was a fully Hellenized culture—it fashioned itself in the image of Greece almost from its beginnings. Indeed, many of the works of Greek art reproduced in this book are not Greek at all but later Roman copies of Greek originals. The emperor Augustus (r. 27 BCE -14 CE) sought to transform Rome into the image of Pericles' Athens. A sculpture by Lysippus was a favorite of the emperor Tiberius (r. 14–57 CE), who had it removed from public display and placed in his bedroom. So

outraged was the public, who considered the sculpture theirs and not the emperor's, that he was forced to return it to its public place. Later Roman emperors, notably Caligula and Nero, raided Delphi and Olympia for works of art.

It was not, in the end, its art in which Rome most prided itself. "Others," Virgil would write in his poem, "no doubt, will better mold the bronze." He concludes:

> . . . remember, Roman,
> To rule the people under law, to establish
> The way of peace, to battle down the haughty,
> To spare the meek. Our fine arts, these, forever. ■

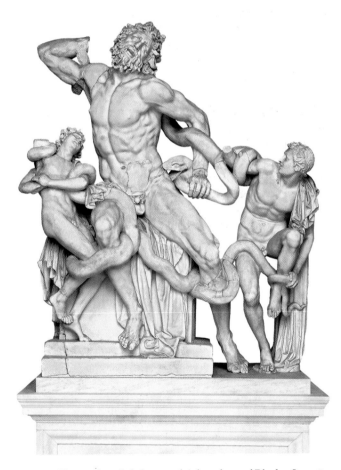

Fig. 2.43 Hagesandros, Polydoros, and Athanadoros of Rhodes. *Laocoön and His Sons*, marble copy of an original bronze probably made at Pergamon, ca. 150 BCE. Marble, height 95 ½". Museo Pio Clementino, Vatican Museums, Vatican State. Pliny the Elder attributes the sculpture to the three artists from Rhodes. It seems likely that the copy was inspired by the success of Virgil's poem.

3 Rome

Urban Life and Imperial Majesty

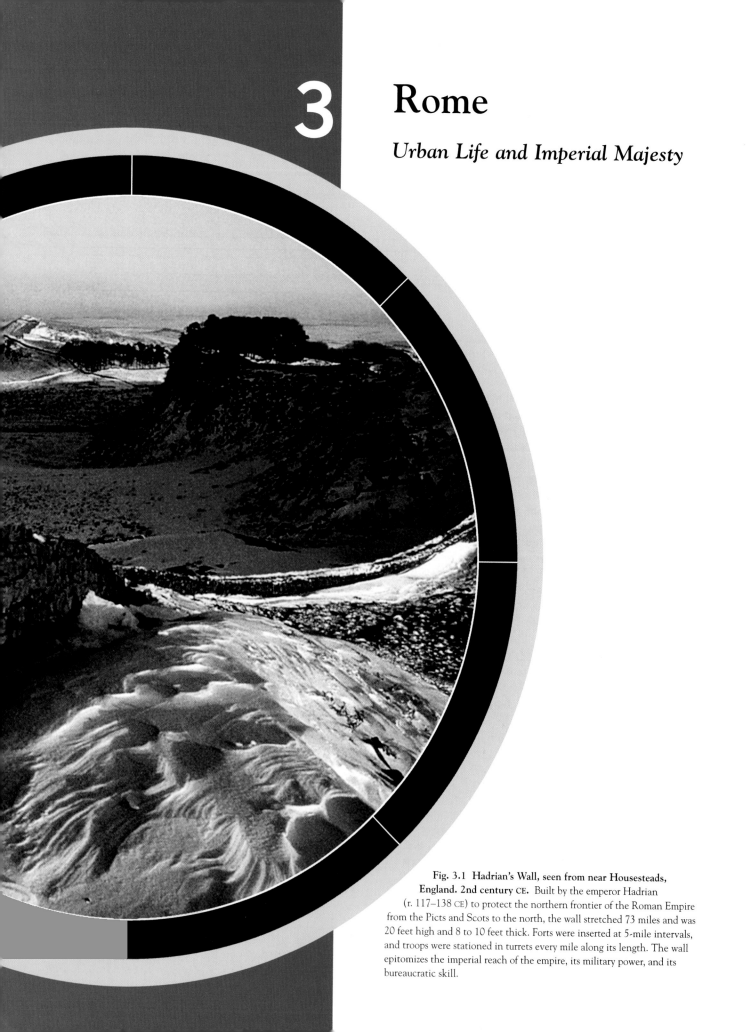

Fig. 3.1 Hadrian's Wall, seen from near Housesteads, England. 2nd century CE. Built by the emperor Hadrian (r. 117–138 CE) to protect the northern frontier of the Roman Empire from the Picts and Scots to the north, the wall stretched 73 miles and was 20 feet high and 8 to 10 feet thick. Forts were inserted at 5-mile intervals, and troops were stationed in turrets every mile along its length. The wall epitomizes the imperial reach of the empire, its military power, and its bureaucratic skill.

**" I found a city of brick,
and left it a city of marble. "**

Augustus

Rome, of all the cultures to arise in the Mediterranean, would become the most powerful, the political center of a vast empire. At the height of its power, the Roman Empire stretched from Scotland in the north (Fig. **3.1**) to the oases of the Sahara Desert in the south, from the Iberian Peninsula in the west to Asia Minor as far as the Tigris River in the east (Map **3.1**). Rome saw itself as the model for all other cities in its empire. The building program that distinguished the imperial city—its amphitheaters, theaters, racetracks, and baths, its forums, temples, triumphal arches, broad avenues, and aqueducts—all these amenities were replicated in the territories the Romans conquered. Whether in Gaul or North Africa, Anatolia or Spain, the Roman citizen deserved to live like a Roman. Rome admired Greece for its cultural achievements, from its philosophy to its sculpture, and, as we have seen, its own art developed from Hellenistic models. But Rome admired its own achievements as well, and its art differed from that of its Hellenic predecessors in certain key respects. Instead of depicting mythological events and heroes, Roman artists depicted current events and real people, from generals and their military exploits to portraits of their leaders and recently deceased citizens. They celebrated the achievements of a state that was their chief patron so that all the world might stand in awe of the state's accomplishments.

Nowhere was this identity more fully expressed than in Roman architecture. Though the structural principles of the arch had long been known, the Romans mastered the form, allowing for the construction of larger, more open spaces than ever before. They invented concrete, which provided the structural strength to support such expansive spaces. The Romans were great engineers, and public works were fundamental to the Roman sense of identity, propagandistic tools that symbolized Roman power.

This chapter traces the rise of Roman civilization from its Greek and Etruscan origins in the sixth century BCE to about 180 CE, when the empire began its slow decline. Based on values developed in Republican Rome and extended to the Imperial state, the Roman citizen owed the state dutiful respect. As the rhetorician and orator Marcus Tullius Cicero put it in his first-century BCE essay, *On Duty*, "It is our duty, then, to be more ready to endanger our own than the public welfare." This sense of duty was mirrored in family life, where reverence for one's ancestors was reflected in the profusion of portrait busts that decorated Roman households. One was obliged to honor one's father as one honored Rome itself. The family became one of the focuses of the first Roman emperor, Augustus, and his dedication to it was reflected in his public works and statuary, and in the work of the artists and writers he supported. But the lasting legacy of Augustus was his transformation of Rome into what he called "a city of marble." Subsequent emperors in the first two centuries CE would continue to transform Rome until it was arguably the most magnificent center of culture ever built.

Origins of Roman Culture

The origins of Roman culture are twofold. On the one hand, there were the Greeks, who as early as the eighth century BCE colonized the southern coastal regions of the Italian peninsula and Sicily and whose Hellenic culture the Romans adopted for their own. On the other hand, there were the Etruscans. Scholars continue to debate whether the Etruscans were indigenous to Italy or whether they migrated from the Near East. In the ninth and eighth centuries BCE, the Etruscans became known to the outside world for their mineral resources, and by the seventh and sixth centuries they were major exporters of fine painted pottery, a black ceramic ware known as *bucchero*, bronze-work, jewelry, oil, and wine. By the fifth century BCE, they were known throughout the Mediterranean for their skill as sculptors in both bronze and terra cotta.

Geographically, Rome developed between two cultures, with the Greek colonies to the south and the Etruscan settlements to the north. Its situation, in fact, is geographically improbable. Rome was built on a hilly site (seven hills to be precise) on the east bank of the Tiber. Its low-lying areas were swampy and subject to flooding, while the higher elevations of the hillsides did not easily lend themselves to building. The river Tiber itself provides a sensible explanation for the city's original siting, since it gave the city a trade route to the north and access to the sea at its port of Ostia to the south.

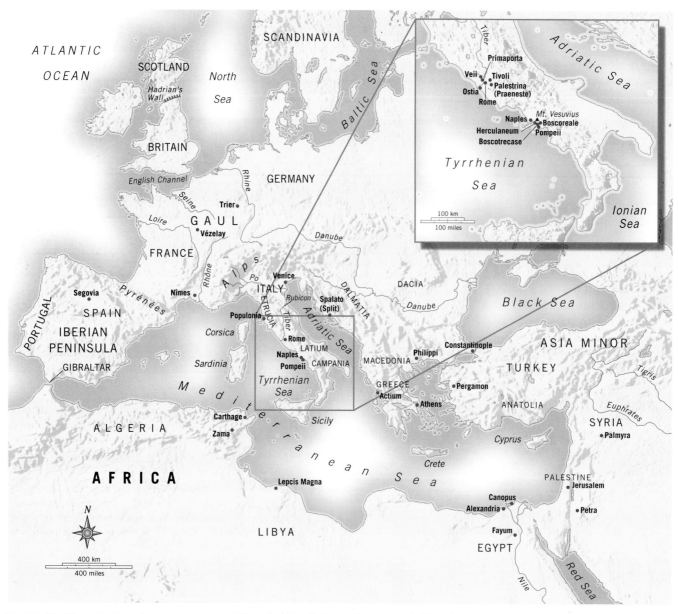

Map 3.1 The Roman Empire at its greatest extent, ca. 180 CE. By 180 CE the Roman Empire extended from the Atlantic Ocean in the west to Asia Minor, Syria, and Palestine in the east, and from Scotland in the north to the Sahara Desert in North Africa.

And so does Tiber Island, next to the Temple of Portunus, which was one of the river's primary crossings from the earliest times. Thus, Rome was physically and literally the crossing place of Etruscan and Greek cultures (see Map 3.1).

Etruscan Roots

The Etruscan homeland, Etruria, occupied the part of the Italian peninsula that is roughly the same as modern-day Tuscany (see Map 3.1). It was bordered by the Arno River to the north (which runs through Florence) and the Tiber River to the south (which runs through Rome). No Etruscan literature survives, although around 9,000 epigrammatic texts do, enough to make clear that even though the alphabet was related to Greek, the language itself was unrelated to any other in

Europe. Scholars know how to pronounce most of its words, although they do not understand the words themselves. Most of what we know about the Etruscans comes from their art, which has survived particularly in burial tombs decorated with vases, sculptures, and paintings, including large numbers of Attic vases that not only demonstrate the extent of Etruscan trade but contribute much to our understanding of Greek art.

Tombs: Clues to Etruscan Life The Etruscans buried their dead in cemeteries removed from their cities. The tombs were arranged in neat rows along a network of streets. They used a type of tomb called a **tumulus**, a round structure partially below and partially above ground and covered with earth. Inside, the burial chambers are rectangular and resemble domestic architecture. In fact, they may resemble actual Etruscan homes—only the foundations of their homes survive so we cannot be sure—since entire families were buried together. Plaster reliefs on the walls include kitchen implements, tools, and, in general, the necessities for everyday life, suggesting that the Etruscan sense of the afterlife was in some ways similar to that of the Egyptians, with whom, incidentally, they traded.

Most of what we know about the Etruscans comes from the sculptures and paintings that have survived in tombs. Women evidently played a far more important role in Etruscan culture than in Greece, and Roman culture would later reflect the Etruscan sense of women's equality. On Etruscan **sarcophagi**, or coffins, many of which are made of terra cotta, there are many examples of husbands and wives reclining together. One of the most famous examples comes from Cerveteri, on the coast north of Rome (Fig. **3.2**). Husband and wife are depicted reclining on a dining couch, and they are given equal status. Their hands are animated, their smiles full, and they seem engaged in a lively dinner conversation. Their smiles, in fact, are reminiscent of the Greek Archaic smiles found on sculptures such as the nearly contemporary *Anavysos Kouros* (see Fig. 1.26), suggesting that the Etruscans were acquainted with Greek art.

Continuity & Change
p. 33

Anavysos Kouros

The Etruscan Founding Myth
According to Etruscan legend, twin infants named Romulus and Remus were left to die on the banks of the Tiber but were rescued by a she-wolf who suckled them (Fig. **3.3**). Raised by a shepherd, the twins decided to build a city on the Palatine Hill above the spot where they had been saved (accounting, in the manner of foundation myths, for the unlikely location of the city). Soon, the two boys feuded over who would rule the new city. In his *History of Rome*, the Roman historian Livy (59 BCE–17 CE) briefly describes the ensuing conflict:

> Then followed an angry altercation; heated passions led to bloodshed; in the tumult Remus was killed. The more common report is that Remus contemptuously jumped over the newly raised walls and was forthwith killed by the enraged Romulus, who exclaimed, "So shall it be henceforth with every one who leaps over my walls." Romulus thus became sole ruler, and the city was called after him, its founder.

The date, legend has it, was 753 BCE.

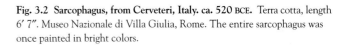

Fig. 3.2 Sarcophagus, from Cerveteri, Italy. ca. 520 BCE. Terra cotta, length 6′ 7″. Museo Nazionale di Villa Giulia, Rome. The entire sarcophagus was once painted in bright colors.

Fig. 3.3 *She-Wolf.* ca. 500–480 BCE. Bronze, with glass-paste eyes, height 33″. Museo Capitolino, Rome. The two suckling figures representing Romulus and Remus are Renaissance additions. This Etruscan bronze, which became a symbol of Rome, combines a ferocious realism with the stylized portrayal of, for instance, the wolf's geometrically regular mane.

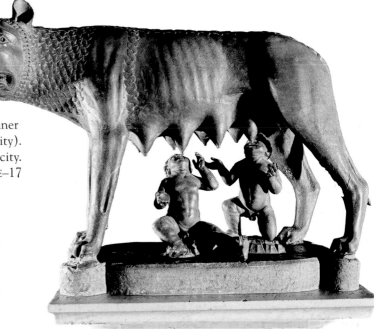

Republican Rome

By the time Virgil (70–19 BCE) wrote his epic poem *The Aeneid*, Greek and Etruscan myths had merged. According to Virgil, after Aeneas escaped the sack of Troy, his son founded the city of Alba Longa, just to the south of Rome, which was ruled by a succession of kings until Romulus brought it under Roman control.

According to legend, Romulus inaugurated the traditional Roman distinction between **patricians**, the land-owning aristocrats who served as priests, magistrates, lawyers, and judges, and **plebeians**, the poorer class who were craftspeople, merchants, and laborers. When, in 510 BCE, the Romans expelled the last of the Etruscan kings and decided to rule themselves without a monarch, the patrician/plebeian distinction became very similar to the situation in fifth-century BCE Athens, where aristocratic landowners shared citizenship with a much larger working class.

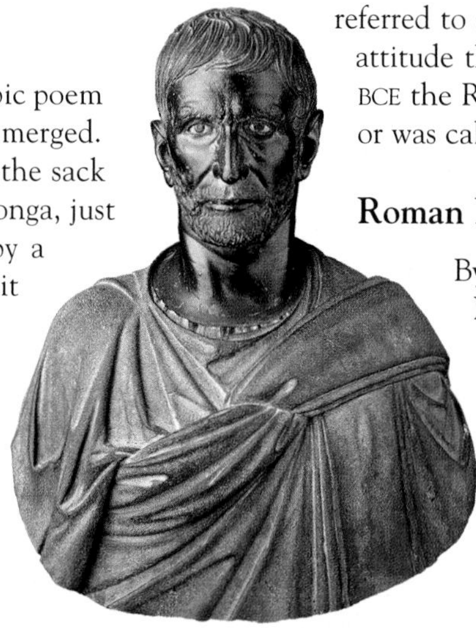

In Rome, as in the Greek model, every free male was a citizen, but in the Etruscan manner, not every citizen enjoyed equal privileges. The Senate, the political assembly in charge of creating law, was exclusively patrician. In reaction, the plebeians formed their own legislative assembly, the Consilium Plebis (Council of Plebeians), to protect themselves from the patricians, but the patricians were immune from any laws the plebeians passed, known as *plebiscites*. Finally, in 287 BCE, the plebiscite became binding law on all citizens, and something resembling equality of citizenship was assured.

The expulsion of the Etruscan kings and the dedication of the Temple of Jupiter on the Capitoline Hill in 509 BCE mark the beginning of actual historical records documenting the development of Rome. They also mark the beginning of the Roman Republic, a state whose political organization rested on the principle that the citizens were the ultimate source of legitimacy and sovereignty. Many people believe that the Etruscan bronze head of a man (Fig. **3.4**) is a portrait of Lucius Junius Brutus, the founder and first consul of the Roman Republic. However, it dates from approximately 100–200 years after Brutus' life, and it more likely represents a noble "type," an imaginary portrait of a Roman founding father, or *pater*, the root of the word *patrician*. This role is conveyed through the figure's strong character and strength of purpose.

In republican Rome every plebeian chose a patrician as his patron, whose duty it was to represent the plebeian in any matter of law. This paternalistic relationship—which we call *patronage*—reflected the family's central role in Roman culture. The *pater*, "father," protected not only his wife and family but also his clients, who submitted to his patronage. In return for the pater's protection, family and client equally owed the pater their total obedience—which the Romans

Fig. 3.4 Head of a Man (possibly a portrait of Lucius Junius Brutus). ca. 300 BCE. Bronze, height 27 1/2". Capitoline Museums, Palazzo dei Conservatori, Rome. The eyes, which look slightly past the viewer, and the intensely furrowed brow, give the figure an almost visionary force and suggest the influence of Lysippus (compare Fig. 2.39).

referred to as *pietas*, "dutifulness." So embedded was this attitude that when toward the end of the first century BCE the Republic declared itself an empire, the emperor was called *pater patriae*, "father of the fatherland."

Roman Rule

By the middle of the third century BCE, the Republic had embarked on a series of military exploits that recall Alexander's imperial adventuring of the century before. Whenever Rome conquered a region, it established permanent colonies of veteran soldiers who received allotments of land, virtually guaranteeing them a certain level of wealth and status. These soldiers were citizens. If the conquered people proved loyal to Rome, they could gain full Roman citizenship. Furthermore, when not involved in combat, the local Roman soldiery transformed themselves into engineers, building roads, bridges, and civic projects of all types, significantly improving the region. In this way, the Republic diminished the adversarial status of its colonies and gained their loyalty.

The prosperity brought about by Roman expansion soon created a new kind of citizen. They called themselves *equites* ("equestrians") to connect them to the cavalry, the elite part of the military, since only the wealthy could afford the necessary horses. The *equites* were wealthy businessmen, but not often landowners and therefore not patricians. The patricians considered the commercial exploits of the *equites* crass and their wealth ill-gotten. Soon the two groups were in open conflict, the *equites* joining ranks with the plebeians.

The Senate was the patrician stronghold, and it feared any loss of power and authority. When the general Pompey the Great (106–48 BCE) returned from a victorious campaign against rebels in Asia Minor in 62 BCE, the Senate refused to ratify the treaties he had made in the region and refused to grant the land allotments he had given his soldiers. Outraged, Pompey joined forces with two other successful military leaders. One had put down the slave revolt of Spartacus in 71 BCE. The other was Gaius Julius Caesar (100–44 BCE), a military leader from a prestigious patrician family that claimed descent from Aeneas and Venus. The union of the three leaders became known as the First Triumvirate.

A Divided Empire Wielding the threat of civil war, the First Triumvirate soon dominated the Republic's political life, but theirs was a fragile relationship. Caesar accepted a five-year appointment as governor of Gaul, present-day France. By 49 BCE, he had brought all of Gaul under his control. He summed up this conquest in his *Commentaries* in the famous phrase "*Veni, vidi, vinci*"—"I came, I saw, I conquered"—a statement that captures, perhaps better than any other, the militaristic nature of the Roman state as a whole. He was preparing to return home when Pompey changed sides and joined forces with the Senate. Together they reminded Caesar of a long-standing tradition that required a returning commander to leave his army behind, in this case on the Gallic side of the Rubicon River, but he refused. Pompey fled to Greece, where Caesar defeated him a year later. Again Pompey fled, this time to Egypt, where he was murdered. The third member of the Triumvirate had been captured and executed several years earlier.

Now unimpeded, Caesar assumed dictatorial control over Rome. Caesar treated the Senate with disdain, and most of its membership counted themselves as his enemies. On March 15, 44 BCE, the Ides of March, he was stabbed 23 times by a group of 60 senators at the foot of a sculpture honoring Pompey on the floor of the Senate. This scene was memorialized in English by Shakespeare's great play *Julius Caesar* and Caesar's famous line, as he sees his ally Marcus Junius Brutus (85–42 BCE) among the assassins, "Et tu, Brute?"—"You also, Brutus?" Brutus and the others believed they had freed Rome of a tyrant, but the people were outraged, the Senate disgraced, and Caesar martyred.

Cicero and the Politics of Rhetoric

In times of such political upheaval, it is not surprising that one of the most powerful figures of the day would be someone who specialized in the art of political persuasion. In pre-Augustan Rome that person was the **rhetorician** (writer and public speaker, or orator) Marcus Tullius Cicero (106–43 BCE). First and foremost, Cicero recognized the power of the Latin language to communicate with the people. Although originally used almost exclusively as the language of commerce, Latin, by the first century CE, was understood to be potentially a more powerful tool of persuasion than Greek, still the literary language of the upper classes. The clarity and eloquence of Cicero's style can be quickly discerned, even in translation, as an excerpt (**Reading 3.1**) from his essay *On Duty* demonstrates.

READING 3.1 **Cicero, *On Duty***

That moral goodness which we look for in a lofty, high-minded spirit is secured, of course, by moral, not physical strength. And yet the body must be trained and so disciplined that it can obey the dictates of judgment and reason in attending to business and in enduring toil. But that moral goodness which is our theme depends wholly upon the thought and attention given to it by the mind. And, in this way, the men who in a civil capacity direct the affairs of the nation render no less important service than they who conduct its wars: by their statesmanship oftentimes wars are either averted or terminated; sometimes also they are declared. Upon Marcus Cato's counsel, for example,

the Third Punic War was undertaken, and in its conduct his influence was dominant, even after he was dead. And so diplomacy in the friendly settlement of controversies is more desirable than courage in settling them on the battlefield; but we must be careful not to take that course merely for the sake of avoiding war rather than for the sake of public expediency. War, however, should be undertaken in such a way as to make it evident that it has no other object than to secure peace.

But it takes a brave and resolute spirit not to be disconcerted in times of difficulty or ruffled and thrown off one's feet, as the saying is, but to keep one's presence of mind and one's self-possession and not to swerve from the path of reason.

Now all this requires great personal courage; but it also calls for great intellectual ability by reflection to anticipate the future, to discover some time in advance what may happen whether for good or for ill, and what must be done in any possible event, and never to be reduced to having to say "I had not thought of that."

These are the activities that mark the spirit strong, high, and self-reliant in its prudence and wisdom. But to mix rashly in the fray and to fight hand to hand with the enemy is but a barbarous and brutish kind of business. Yet when the stress of circumstances demands it, we must gird on the sword and prefer death to slavery and disgrace. . . .

We must, of course, never be guilty of seeming cowardly and craven in our avoidance of danger; but we must also beware of exposing ourselves to danger needlessly. Nothing can be more foolhardy than that. . . .

The dangers attending great affairs of state fall sometimes on those who undertake them, sometimes upon the state. In carrying out such enterprises, some run the risk of losing their lives, others their reputation and the good-will of their fellow-citizens. It is our duty, then, to be more ready to endanger our own than the public welfare and to hazard honor and glory more readily than other advantages. . . .

Philosophically, Cicero's argument extends back to Plato and Aristotle, even Hesiod, but rhetorically—that is, in the structure of its argument—it is purely Roman. It is purposefully deliberative in tone—that is, its chief concern is to give sage advice rather than to engage in a Socratic dialogue to evolve that advice.

Portrait Busts, *Pietas*, and Politics

This historical context helps us understand a major Roman art form of the second and first centuries BCE, the portrait bust. These are generally portraits of patricians (and upper-middle-class citizens wishing to emulate them) rather than *equites*.

Roman portrait busts share with their Greek ancestors an affinity for naturalistic representation, but they are even more realistic, revealing their subjects' every wrinkle and wart (Fig. **3.5**). This form of realism is known as **verism** (from the Latin *veritas*, "truth"). Indeed, the high level of naturalism may have resulted from their original form, wax death masks, called *imagines*, which were then transferred to stone.

Compared to the Greek Hellenistic portrait bust—recall Lysippus's portrait of Alexander (see Fig. 2.39), copies of which proliferated throughout the Mediterranean in the third century BCE—the Roman portrait differs particularly in the age of the sitter. Both the Greek and Roman busts are essentially propagandistic in intent, designed to extol the virtues of the sitter, but where Alexander is portrayed as a young man at the height of his powers, the usual Roman portrait bust depicts its subject at or near the end of life. The Greek portrait bust, in other words, signifies youthful possibility and ambition, while the Roman version claims for its subject the wisdom and experience of age. These images celebrate *pietas*, the deep-seated Roman virtue of dutiful respect toward the gods, fatherland, and parents. To respect one's

parents was tantamount, for the Romans, to respecting one's moral obligations to the gods. The respect one owed one's parents was, in effect, a religious obligation.

If the connection to Alexander—especially the emphasis in both on the power of the gaze—is worth considering, the Roman portrait busts depict a class under attack, a class whose virtues and leadership were being threatened by upstart generals and *equites*. They are, in other words, the very picture of conservative politics. Their furrowed brows represent their wisdom, their wrinkles their experience, their extraordinarily naturalistic representation their character. They represent the Senate itself, which should be honored, not disdained.

Imperial Rome

On January 13, 27 BCE, Octavian came before the Senate and gave up all his powers and provinces. It was a rehearsed event. The Senate begged him to reconsider and take Syria, Gaul, and the Iberian Peninsula for his own (these provinces just happened to contain 20 of the 26 Roman legions, guaranteeing him military support). They also asked him to retain his title as consul of Rome, with the supreme authority of *imperium*, the power to give orders and exact obedience, over all of Italy and subsequently all Roman-controlled territory. He agreed "reluctantly" to these terms, and the Senate, in gratitude, granted him the semidivine title Augustus, "the revered one." Augustus (r. 27 BCE–14 CE) thereafter portrayed himself as a near-deity. The *Augustus of Primaporta* (Fig. **3.6**) is the slightly larger than life-size sculpture named for its location at the home of Augustus' wife, Livia, at Primaporta, on the outskirts of Rome. Augustus is represented as the embodiment of an admonition given to Aeneas by his dead father (*Aeneid*, Book 6):

> Others [namely Greeks], no doubt, will better mould the
> bronze
> To the semblance of soft breathing, draw, from marble
> The living countenance; . . .
> remember, Roman,
> To rule the people under law, to establish
> The way of peace, to battle down the haughty,
> To spare the meek. Our fine arts, these, forever.

Augustus, like Aeneas, is duty bound to exhibit *pietas*, the obligation to his ancestor "to rule earth's peoples."

The sculpture, though recognizably Augustus, is nevertheless idealized. It adopts the pose and ideal proportions of Polyclitus's *Doryphorus* (see Fig. 2.29). The gaze, reminiscent of the look of Alexander the Great, purposefully recalls the visionary hero of Greece who died 300 years earlier. The extended arm points toward an unknown, but presumably greater, future. The military garb announces his role as commander-in-chief. Riding a dolphin at his feet is a small Cupid, son of the goddess Venus, laying claim to the Julian family's divine descent from Venus and Aeneas. Though Augustus was over 70 years old when he died, he was always depicted as young and vigorous, choosing to

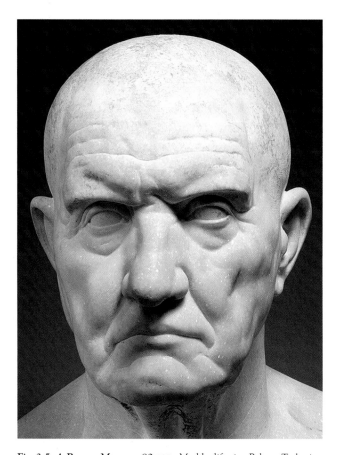

Fig. 3.5 *A Roman Man.* ca. 80 BCE. Marble, life-size. Palazzo Torlonia, Rome. The Metropolitan Museum of Art, Rogers Fund, 1912 (12.233). Image © The Metropolitan Museum of Art. His face creased by the wrinkles of age, this man is the very image of the *pater*, the man of *gravitas* (literally "weight," but also, "presence" or "influence"), *dignitas* ("dignity," "worth," and "character"), and *fides* ("honesty" and "conscientiousness").

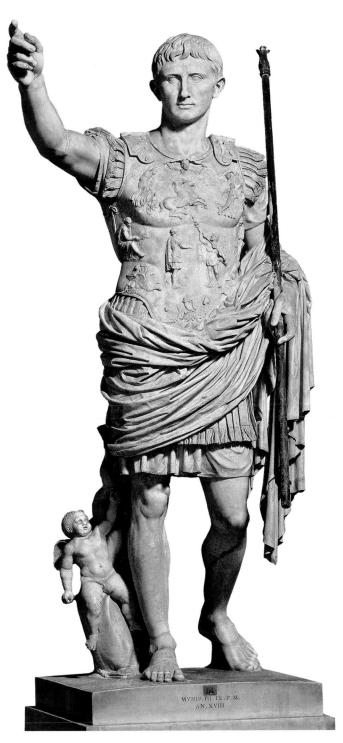

Fig. 3.6 *Augustus of Primaporta.* **ca. 20 BCE.** Marble, height 6′ 8″. Vatican Museums, Rome. On the breastplate a bearded Parthian from Asia Minor hands over Roman standards that had been lost in a battle of 53 BCE. In 20 BCE, when this statue was carved, Augustus had won them back.

portray himself, apparently, as the ideal leader rather than the wise, older *pater*.

Augustus was careful to maintain at least the trappings of the Republic. The Senate stayed in place, but Augustus soon eliminated the distinction between patricians and

equites and fostered the careers of all capable individuals, whatever their origin. Some he made provincial governors, others administrators in the city, and he encouraged still others to enter political life. Soon the Senate was populated with many men who had never dreamed of political power. All of them—governors, administrators, and politicians—owed everything to Augustus. Their loyalty further solidified his power.

Family Life

Augustus also quickly addressed what he considered to be another crisis in Roman society—the demise of family life. Adultery and divorce were commonplace. There were more slaves and freed slaves in the city than citizens, let alone aristocrats. And family size, given the cost of living in the city, was diminishing. He reacted by criminalizing adultery and passed several other laws to promote family life. Men between the ages of 20 and 60 and women between the ages of 20 and 50 were required to marry. A divorced woman was required to remarry within six months, a widow within a year. Childless adults were punished with high taxes or deprived of inheritance. The larger an aristocrat's family, the greater his political advantage. It is no coincidence that when Augustus commissioned a large monument to commemorate his triumphal return after establishing Roman rule in Gaul and restoring peace to Rome, the *Ara Pacis Augustae* (Altar of Augustan Peace), he had its exterior walls on the south decorated with a retinue of his own large family, a model for all Roman citizens, in a procession of lictors, priests, magistrates, senators, and other representatives of the Roman people (Figs. **3.7**, **3.8**).

Art historians believe that the *Ara Pacis Augustae* (Altar of Peace) represents a real event, perhaps a public rejoicing for Augustus' reign (it was begun in 13 BCE when he was 50), or the dedication of the altar itself, which occurred on Livia's fiftieth birthday in 9 BCE. The realism of the scene is typically Roman. A sense of spatial depth is created by depicting figures farther away from us in low relief and those closest to us in high relief, so high in fact that the feet of the nearest figures project over the architectural frame into our space (visible in the detail, Fig. 3.8). This technique would have encouraged viewers—the Roman public—to feel that they were part of the same space as the figures in the sculpture itself. The Augustan peace is the peace enjoyed by the average Roman citizen, the Augustan family a metaphor for the larger family of Roman citizens.

The *Ara Pacis Augustae* is preeminently a celebration of family. Three generations of Augustus' family are depicted in the relief. It also demonstrates the growing prominence of women in Roman society. Augustus' wife Livia is depicted holding Augustus' family together, standing between her stepson, Marcus Agrippa, and her own sons, Tiberius and Drusus.

Livia became a figure of idealized womanhood in Rome. She was the "female leader" of Augustus' programs of reform, a sponsor of architectural projects, and a trusted advisor to

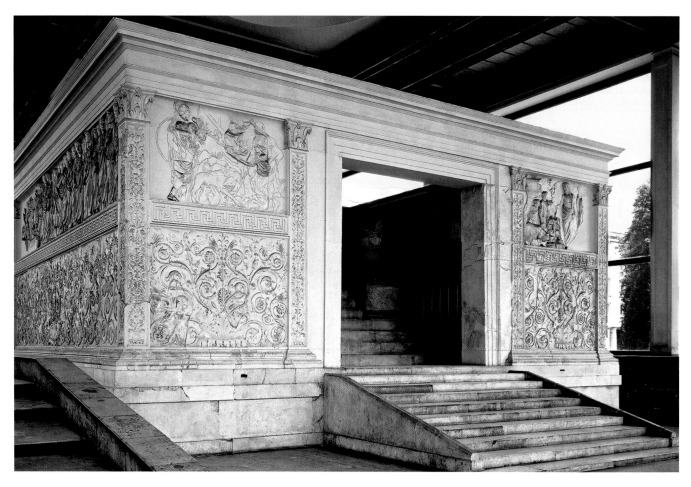

Fig. 3.7 *Ara Pacis Augustae*, west side.

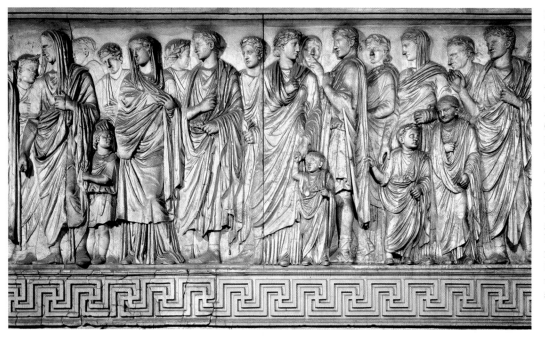

Fig. **3.8** *Ara Pacis Augustae*, **detail of Imperial Procession, south frieze, Rome. 13–9 BCE.** Marble, width approx. 35′. At the left is Marcus Agrippa, Augustus' son-in-law, married to his daughter Julia. Augustus' grandson, Gaius Caesar, who with his brother Lucius often traveled with their grandfather and whom Augustus taught to imitate his own handwriting, clings to his father's robe and looks backward and up at his grandmother, Augustus' wife, Livia, one of the most powerful people in Rome. Behind Livia is her son by an earlier marriage, Tiberius, who would succeed Augustus as emperor.

both her husband and son. While Livia enjoyed greater power and influence than most, Roman women possessed the rights of citizenship, although they could not vote or hold public office. Still, married women retained their legal identity. They controlled their own property and managed their own legal affairs. Elite women modeled themselves after Livia, wielding power through their husbands and sons.

Literary Rome: Virgil, Horace, and Ovid

When Augustus took control of Rome, he arranged for all artistic patronage to pass through his office. During the civil wars, the two major poets of the day, Virgil and Horace, had lost all their property, but Augustus' patronage allowed them to keep on with their writings. Because the themes they pursued were subject to Augustus' approval, they tended to glorify both the emperor and his causes. He was far less supportive of the poet Ovid, whom he permanently banished from Rome.

Virgil and the *Aeneid* After Augustus' triumph over Antony and Cleopatra at the battle of Actium in 31 BCE, Virgil retired to Naples, where he began work on an epic poem designed to rival Homer's *Iliad* and to provide the Roman state—and Augustus in particular—with a suitably grand founding myth. Previously he had been engaged with two series of pastoral idylls, the *Eclogues* (or *Bucolics*) and the *Georgics*. The latter poems (**Reading 3.2**) are modeled after Hesiod's *Works and Days* (see chapter 4). They extol the importance of hard work, the necessity of forging order in the face of a hostile natural world, and, perhaps above all, the virtues of agrarian life.

READING 3.2   **from Virgil, *Georgics***

In early spring-tide, when the icy drip
Melts from the mountains hoar, and Zephyr's breath
Unbinds the crumbling clod, even then 'tis time;
Press deep your plough behind the groaning ox,
And teach the furrow-burnished share to shine.
That land the craving farmer's prayer fulfils,
Which twice the sunshine, twice the frost has felt;
Ay, that's the land whose boundless harvest-crops
Burst, see! the barns.

The political point of the *Georgics* was to celebrate Augustus' gift of farmlands to veterans of the civil wars, but in its exaltation of the myths and traditions of Italy, it served as a precursor to the *Aeneid*. It was written in **dactylic hexameter**, the verse form that Homer had used in the *Iliad* and *Odyssey* (the metrical form of the translation above, however, is iambic pentameter—five rhythmic units, each short long, as in *dee-dum*—a meter much more natural to English than the Latin dactylic hexameter). In dactylic hexameter each line

consists of six rhythmic units, or **feet**, and each foot is either a **dactyl** (long, short, short, as in *dum-diddy*) or a **spondee** (long, long, as in *dum-dum*).

Virgil reportedly wrote the *Georgics* at a pace of less than one line a day, perfecting his understanding of the metrical scheme in preparation for the longer poem.

The *Aeneid* opens in Carthage, where, after the Trojan War, Aeneas and his men have been driven by a storm, and where they are hosted by the Phoenician Queen Dido. During a rainstorm Aeneas and Dido take refuge in a cave, where the queen, having fallen in love with the Trojan hero, gives herself willingly to him. She now assumes that she is married, but Aeneas, reminded by his father's ghost of his duty to accomplish what the gods have predetermined—a classic instance of *pietas*—knows he must resume his destined journey. An angry and accusing Dido begs him to stay. When Aeneas rejects her pleas, Dido vows to haunt him after her death and to bring enmity between Carthage and his descendants forever (a direct reference on Virgil's part to the Punic Wars). As his boat sails away, she commits suicide by climbing a funeral pyre and falling upon a sword. The goddesses of the underworld are surprised to see her. Her death, in their eyes, is neither deserved nor destined, but simply tragic. Virgil's point is almost coldly hard-hearted: All personal feelings and desires must be sacrificed to one's responsibilities to the state. Civic duty takes precedence over private life.

The poem is, on one level, an account of Rome's founding by Aeneas, but it is also a profoundly moving essay on human destiny and the great cost involved in achieving and sustaining the values and principles upon which culture—Roman culture in particular, but all cultures by extension—must be based. Augustus, as Virgil well knew, claimed direct descent from Aeneas, and it is particularly important that the poem presents war, at which Augustus excelled, as a moral tragedy, however necessary.

In Book 7, Venus gives Aeneas a shield made by the god Vulcan. The shield displays the important events in the future history of Rome, including Augustus at the Battle of Actium. Aeneas is, Virgil writes, "without understanding. . . proud and happy . . . [at] the fame and glory of his children's children." But in the senseless slaughter that ends the poem, as Aeneas and the Trojans battle Turnus and the Italians, Virgil demonstrates that the only thing worse than not avenging the death of one's friends and family is, perhaps, avenging them. In this sense the poem is a profound plea for peace, a peace that Augustus would dedicate himself to pursuing.

The Horatian *Odes* Quintus Horatius Flaccus [KWIN-tus hor-AY-she-us FLAK-us], known as Horace (65–8 BCE), was a close friend of Virgil. Impressed by Augustus' reforms, and probably moved by his patronage, Horace was won over to the emperor's cause, which he celebrated directly in two of his many **odes**, lyric poems of elaborate and irregular meter. Horace's odes imitated Greek precedents. The following lines open the fifth ode of Book Three of the collected poems, known simply as the *Odes*:

Jove [the Roman Zeus, also called Jupiter] rules in heav-
en, his thunder shows;
Henceforth Augustus earth shall own
Her present god, now Briton foes
And Persians bow before his throne.

The subject matter of the *Odes* ranges from these patriotic pronouncements to private incidents in the poet's own life, the joys
of the countryside (Fig. 3.9), the pleasures of wine, and so on.
His villa offered him an escape from the trials of daily life in
Rome itself. But no Roman poet more gracefully harmonized
the Greek reverence for beauty with the Roman concern with
duty and obligation.

Ovid's *Art of Love* and *Metamorphoses* Augustus' support
for poets did not extend to Publius Ovidius Naso [POO-ble-
us ov-ID-ee-us NAY-so], known as Ovid (43 BCE–17 CE).
Ovid's talent was for love songs designed to satisfy the notoriously loose sexual mores of the Roman aristocrats, who
lived in somewhat open disregard of Augustus and Livia's
family-centered lifestyle. His *Ars Amatoria* [ahrs ah-mah-
TOR-ee-uh] (Art of Love) angered Augustus, as did some
indiscretion by Ovid. As punishment, Augustus permanently

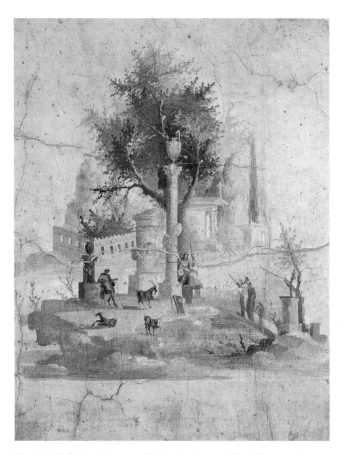

Fig. 3.9 *Idyllic Landscape,* **wall painting from a villa at Boscotrecase,
near Pompeii. 1st century BCE.** Museo Nazionale, Naples. This landscape
depicts the love of country life and the idealizing of nature that is
characteristic of the Horatian *Odes.* It contrasts dramatically with urban life
in Rome.

exiled him to the town of Tomis [TOE-mus] on the Black
Sea, the remotest part of the empire, famous for its wretched
weather. The *Metamorphoses,* composed in the years just
before his exile, is a collection of stories describing or revolving around one sort of supernatural change of shape or another, from the divine to the human, the animate to the
inanimate, from the human to the vegetal.

In the *Ars Amatoria* the poet describes his desire for the
fictional Corinna. Ovid outlines the kinds of places in Rome
where one can meet women, from porticoes to gaming houses, from horse races to parties, and especially anywhere wine,
that great banisher of inhibition, can be had. Women, he
says, love clandestine affairs as much as men; they simply
don't chase after men, "as a mousetrap does not chase after
mice." Become friends with the husband of a woman you
desire, he advises. Lie to her—tell her that you only want to
be her friend. Nevertheless, he says, "If you want a woman to
love you, be a lovable man."

Ovid probably aspired to Virgil's fame, though he could
admit, "My life is respectable, but my Muse is full of jesting." His
earliest major work, the *Amores* [ah-MOHR-eez] (Loves), begins
with many self-deprecating references to Virgil's epic, which
begins with the famous phrase, "Arms and the man I sing":

Arms, warfare, violence—I was winding up to produce
A regular epic, with verse-form to match—
Hexameters, naturally. But Cupid (they say) with a snicker
Lopped off one foot from each alternate line.
"Nasty young brat," I told him, "who made *you* Inspector
of Metres?"

Nevertheless, Ovid uses dactylic hexameter for the
Metamorphoses and stakes out an epic scope for the poem in
its opening lines:

My intention is to tell of bodies changed
To different forms; the gods, who made the changes,
Will help me—or I hope so—with a poem
That runs from the world's beginning to our own days!

If the *Metamorphoses* is superficially more a collection of
stories than an epic, few poems in any language have contributed so importantly to later literature. It is so complete in
its survey of the best-known classical myths, plus stories from
Egypt, Persia, and Italy, that it remains a standard reference
work. At the same time, it tells its stories in an utterly moving and memorable way. The story of Actaeon, for instance,
is a cautionary tale about the power of the gods. Actaeon
happens to see the virgin goddess Diana bathing one day
when he is out hunting with his dogs. She turns him into a
stag to prevent him from ever telling what he has seen. As his
own dogs turn on him and savagely tear him apart, his friends
call out for him, lamenting his absence from the kill. But he
is all too present:

Well might he wish not to be there, but he was there,
and well might he wish to see
And not to feel the cruel deeds of his dogs.

In the story of Narcissus, Echo falls in love with the beautiful youth Narcissus, but when Narcissus spurns her, she fades away. He in turn is doomed to fall in love with his own image reflected in a pool, according to Ovid, the spring at Clitumnus [clye-TOOM-nus]. So consumed, he finally dies beside the pool, his body transformed into the narcissus flower. In such stories, the duality of identity and change, Aristotle's definition of the essence of a thing, becomes deeply problematic. Ovid seems to deny that any human characteristic is essential, that all is susceptible to change. To subsequent generations of readers, from Shakespeare to Freud, Ovid's versions of myths would raise the fundamental questions that lie at the heart of human identity and psychology.

Augustus and the City of Marble

Of all the problems facing Augustus when he assumed power, the most overwhelming was the infrastructure of Rome. The city was, quite simply, a mess. Seneca reacted by preaching Stoicism. He argued that it was what it was, and one should move on as best one can. Augustus reacted by calling for a series of public works, which would serve the people of Rome and, he well understood, himself. The grand civic improvements Augustus planned would be a kind of imperial propaganda, underscoring not only his power but also his care for the people in his role as *pater patriae*. Public works could—and indeed did—elicit the public's loyalty.

Rome had developed haphazardly, without any central plan, spilling down the seven hills it originally occupied into the valleys along the Tiber. By contrast, all of the empire's provincial capitals were conceived on a strict grid plan, with colonnaded main roads leading to an administrative center, and adorned with public works like baths, theaters, and triumphal arches. In comparison, Rome was pitiable. Housing conditions were dreadful, water was scarce, food was in short supply. Because the city was confined by geography to a small area, space was at a premium.

Urban Housing: The Apartment At least as early as the third century BCE, the ancient Romans created a new type of living space in response to overcrowding—the multistoried apartment block, or *insula* [IN-soo-luh] (Fig. **3.10**). In Augustus' time, the city was increasingly composed of such *insulae* [IN-soo-lye], in which 90 percent of the population of Rome lived.

The typical apartment consisted of two private rooms—a bedroom and a living room—that opened onto a shared central space. The poor lived in kitchenless apartments, cooking and eating in the shared space.

The *insulae* were essentially tenements, with shops on the ground floor and living quarters above. They rose to a height of 60 or 70 feet (five or six stories), were built with inadequate wood frames, and often collapsed. Fire was an even greater danger. Richer apartment dwellers—and there were many, buildable land being scarce—often employed slaves as their own private fire brigades. In 6 CE, Augustus introduced

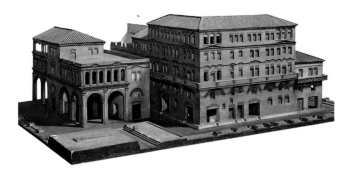

Fig. 3.10 **Reconstruction model of a Roman apartment, or *insula*, ruins of which survive at Ostia, Rome's port. ca. 150 CE.** The ground floor of this *insula* contained shops. Above these were many apartments. There were also single-room living quarters behind the shops.

vigils [VI-juls] to the city, professional firefighters (and policemen) who patrolled the city at night.

In the *insulae*, noise was a constant problem, and hygiene an even worse issue. Occupants of the upper stories typically dumped the contents of their chamber pots into the streets rather than carry them down to the cesspool. As the satirist Juvenal described the situation: "You can suffer as many deaths as there are open windows to pass under. So offer up a prayer that people will be content with just emptying out their slop bowls."

Augustus could not do much about the housing situation, although he did build aqueducts to bring more water into the city. He created a far larger administrative bureaucracy than before and oversaw it closely, guaranteeing its efficiency. But most of all he implemented an ambitious building program designed to provide elegant public spaces where city dwellers could escape from their cramped apartments. He once claimed that he had restored 82 temples in one year. But if he could boast, "I found a city of brick, and left it a city of marble," that was largely because he had put a lot of marble veneer over brick wall. By the second century CE, the city would be one of the most beautiful in the world, but the beauty was only skin deep. The housing situation that Augustus inherited had barely improved.

Public Works and Monuments Augustus inaugurated what amounted to an ongoing competition among the emperors to outdo their predecessors in the construction of public works and monuments. His ambitions are reflected in the work of the architect Vitruvius (flourished late first century BCE to early first century CE). A military engineer for Julius Caesar, under Augustus' patronage, Vitruvius wrote the ten-volume *On Architecture*. The only work of its kind to have survived from antiquity, it would become extremely influential over 1,000 years later, when Renaissance artists became interested in classical design. In its large scale, the work matches its patron's architectural ambitions, dealing with town planning, building materials and construction methods, the construction of temples, the classical orders, and the rules of proportion. Vitruvius also wrote extensively about one of Rome's most pressing needs—how to satisfy the city's needs for water. In fact, one of the most significant contributions of the Julio-Claudian dynasty, which extends from Augustus through Nero (r. 54–68 CE), was an enormous aqueduct, the Aqua Claudia. These aqueducts depended on Roman ingenuity in perfecting the arch and vault so that river gorges could be successfully spanned to carry the pipes bringing water to a city miles away. The Aqua Claudia delivered water from 40 miles away into the very heart of the city, not so much for private use as for the fountains, pools, and public baths.

The Colosseum Nero was succeeded by one of his own generals, Vespasian (r. 69–79 CE), the former commander in Palestine. Vespasian built the Colosseum (Fig. **3.11**) across from Nero's Golden House. He named it after the Colossus, a 120-foot high statue of Nero as sun god that stood in front of it. A giant oval, 615 feet long, 510 feet wide, and 159 feet high, audiences estimated at 50,000 entered and exited through its 76 vaulted arcades in a matter of a few minutes.

These vaults were made possible by the invention of concrete, which the Romans had increasingly utilized in their buildings since the second century BCE. Mixed with vol-

canic aggregate from nearby Naples and Pompeii, it set faster and was stronger than any building material yet known. The Colosseum's wooden floor, laid over a maze of rooms and tunnels that housed gladiators, athletes, and wild animals that entertained the masses, was sturdy enough that the *arena* (Latin for "sand," which covered the floor) could be flooded for mock sea battles. The top story of the building housed an awning system that could be extended on a system of pulleys and ropes to shield part of the audience from the hot Roman sun. Each level employed a different architectural order: on the ground floor the Tuscan order, a native Etruscan order similar to the Doric, but smooth-shafted and rising from a pedestal, the Ionic on the second, and the Corinthian, the Romans' favorite, on the third. All of the columns are engaged and purely decorative, serving no structural purpose. The facade—originally covered with marble, most of which was removed for use in later buildings—thus moves from the heaviest and sturdiest elements at the base to the lightest, most decorative at the top, a logic that seems both structurally and visually satisfying.

Arches, Triumphal Arches, and Columns While the arch was known to cultures such as the Mesopotamians, the Egyptians, and the Greeks, it was the Romans who perfected it,

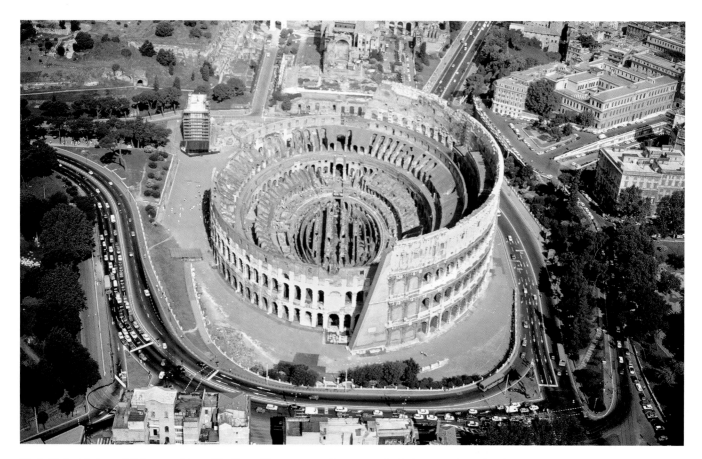

Fig. 3.11 Aerial view of Colosseum, Rome. 72–80 CE. The opening performance at the Colosseum in 80 CE lasted 100 days. During that time, 9,000 wild animals—lions, bears, snakes, boars, even elephants, imported from all over the empire—were killed, and so were 2,000 gladiators.

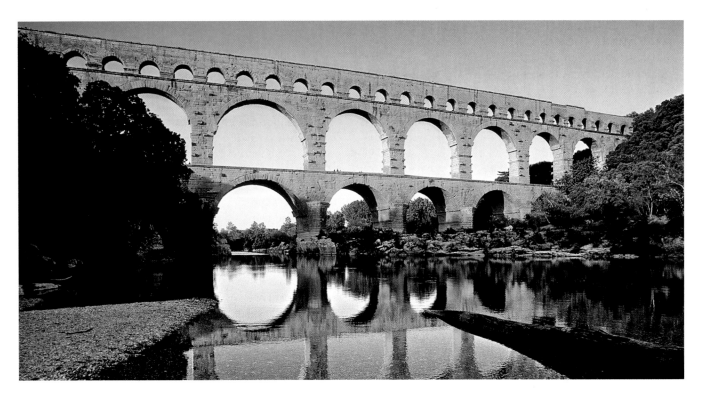

Fig. 3.12 **Pont du Gard, near Nîmes, France, late 1st century BCE–early 1st century CE.** Height 180'. The Roman city of Nîmes received 8,000–12,000 gallons of water a day from this aqueduct.

evidently learning its principles from the Etruscans but developing those principles further. The Pont du Gard, a beautiful Roman aqueduct in southern France near the city of Nîmes (Fig. **3.12**), is a good example.

The Romans understood that much wider spans than the Etruscans had bridged could be achieved with the **round arch** (left, Fig. **3.13**) than with post-and-lintel construction. The weight of the masonry above the arch is displaced to the supporting upright elements (**piers** or **jambs**). The arch is constructed on a temporary support (called centering) and is composed of wedge-shaped blocks, called **voussoirs** [voo-swarrs], and capped with a large, wedge-shaped stone, called the **keystone**, the last element put in place, after which the centering can be removed. The space inside the arch is called

a **bay**. And the wall areas between the arches of an **arcade** (a succession of arches, such as seen on the Pont du Gard) are called **spandrels**.

When a round arch is extended, it forms a **barrel vault** (middle, Fig. **3.13**). To ensure that the downward pressure from the arches does not collapse the walls, a **buttress** support is often added. When two barrel vaults meet one another at a right angle, they form a **groin vault** (right, Fig. **3.13**). The interior corridors of the Colosseum in Rome utilize both barrel and groin vaulting. Since all the stones in a vault must be in place to support the arched structure, the vault cannot be penetrated by windows.

During Vespasian's reign, his son Titus (r. 79–81 CE) defeated the Jews in Palestine, who were rebelling against Roman

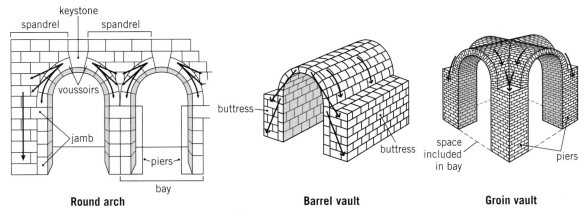

Fig. 3.13 **Arches**

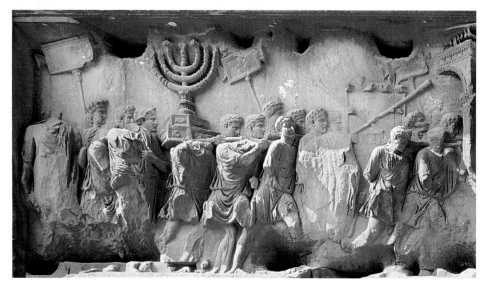

Figs. 3.14 and 3.15 Arch of Titus, Rome, ca. 81 CE and *Spoils from the Temple in Jerusalem*, **a detail of the interior relief of the arch.** Height of relief, approx. 7′ 10″. The figures in the relief are nearly life-size. The relief has been badly damaged, largely because in the Middle Ages, a Roman family used the arch as a fortress, constructing a second story in the vault. Holes for the floor beams appear at the top of the relief.

interference with their religious practices. Titus' army sacked the Second Temple of Jerusalem in 70 CE. To honor this victory and the death of Titus 11 years later, a memorial arch was constructed on the Sacred Way. Originally the Arch of Titus was topped by a statue of a four-horse chariot and driver. Such arches, known as *triumphal arches* because triumphant armies marched through them, were composed of a simple barrel vault enclosed within a rectangle, and enlivened with sculpture and decorative engaged columns (Fig. **3.14**). They would deeply influence later architecture, especially the facades of Renaissance cathedrals. Hundreds of triumphal arches were built throughout the Roman Empire. Like all Roman monumental architecture, they were intended to symbolize Rome's political power and military might.

The Arch of Titus was constructed of concrete and faced with marble, its inside walls decorated with narrative reliefs. One of them shows Titus' soldiers marching with the treasures of the Second Temple in Jerusalem (Fig. **3.15**). In the foreground the soldiers carry the golden Ark of the Covenant, and behind that a *menorah,* the sacred Jewish candelabrum, also made of gold. They bend under the weight of the gold and stride forward convincingly. The carving is extremely deep, with nearer figures and elements rendered with undercutting and in higher relief than more distant ones. This creates a sense of real space and, when light and shadow play over the sculptural relief, even a sense of real movement.

Another type of monument favored by the Romans and with similar symbolic meaning—suggestive not only of power but also of male virility—is the ceremonial column. Like the triumphal arch it was a masonry and concrete platform for narrative reliefs. Two of the so-called Five Good Emperors who ruled Rome after the Flavian dynasty—Trajan and Marcus Aurelius—built columns to celebrate their military victories. Trajan's Column, perhaps the most complete artistic statement of Rome's militaristic character, consists of a spiral of 150 separate scenes from his military campaign in Dacia, across the Danube River in what is now Hungary and Romania. If laid

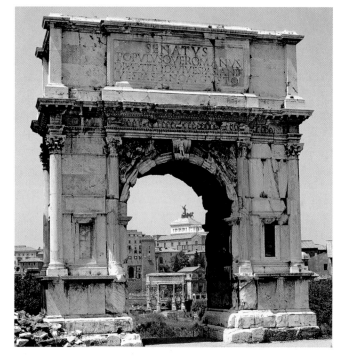

out end to end, the complete narrative would be 625 feet long (Fig. **3.16**). At the bottom of the column the band is 36 inches wide, at the top 50 inches, so that the higher elements might be more readily visible. In order to eliminate shadow and increase the legibility of the whole, the carving is very low relief. At the bottom of the column, the story begins with Roman troops crossing the Danube on a pontoon bridge (Fig. **3.17**). A river god looks on with some interest. To the left of the second band and at the right side of the fourth band, Trajan addresses his troops. Battle scenes constitute less than a quarter of the entire narrative. Instead, we witness the Romans building fortifications, harvesting crops, participating in religious rituals. All in all, the column's 2,500 figures are carrying out what Romans believed to be their destiny—they are bringing the fruits of civilization to the world.

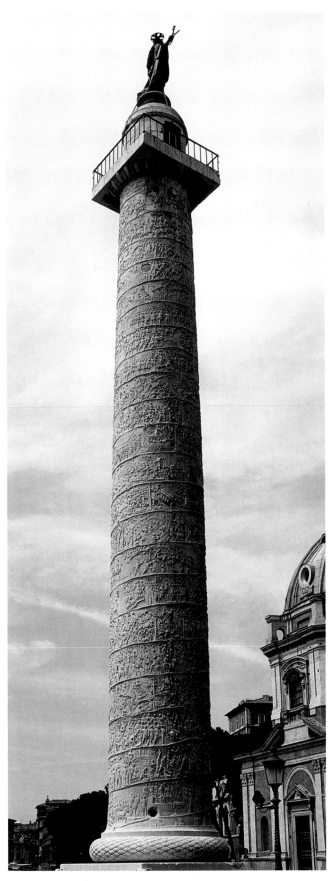

Fig. 3.16 **Column of Trajan, Rome, 106–113 CE.** Marble, overall height with base, 125′.

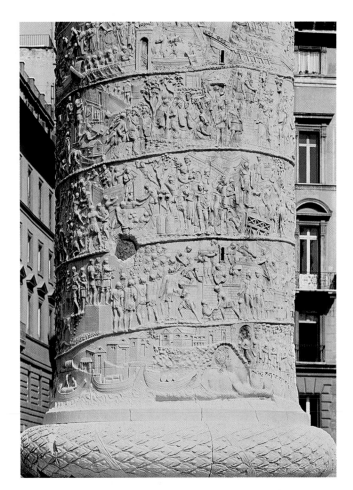

Fig. 3.17 Lower portion of the Column of Trajan, Forum of Trajan, Rome. 106–113 CE.

The Imperial Roman Forum Trajan's Column stands in what was once the Forum of Trajan. This vast building project was among the most ambitious undertaken in Rome by the Five Good Emperors. (See *Focus*, pages 90–91.)

Rome thrived under the rule of the Five Good Emperors: Nerva (r. 96–98 CE), Trajan (r. 98–117 CE), Hadrian (r. 117–138 CE), Antonius Pius (r. 138–161 CE), and Marcus Aurelius (r. 161–180 CE). The stability and prosperity of the city was due, at least in part, to the fact that none of these men except Marcus Aurelius had a son to whom he could pass on the empire. Thus, each was handpicked by his predecessor from among the ablest men in the Senate. When, in 180 CE, Marcus Aurelius' decadent and probably insane son, Commodus (r. 180–192 CE), took control, the empire quickly learned that the transfer of power from father to son was not necessarily a good thing.

The Pantheon Hadrian's Pantheon ranks with the Forum of Trajan as one of the most ambitious building projects undertaken by the Good Emperors. The Pantheon (from the Greek *pan*, "all," and *theos*, "gods") is a temple to "all the gods," and sculptures representing all the Roman gods were set in recesses around its interior. The facade imitates a

Focus

The *Forum Romanum* and Imperial Forums

The *Forum Romanum*, or Roman Forum, was the chief public square of Rome, the center of Roman religious, ceremonial, political, and commercial life. Originally, a Roman forum was comparable to a Greek *agora,* a meeting place in the heart of the city. But gradually the forum took on a symbolic function as well, becoming a symbol of imperial power that testified to the prosperity—and peace—that the emperor bestowed upon Rome's citizenry. Julius Caesar was the first to build a forum of his own in 46 BCE, just to the north of the *Forum Romanum.* Augustus subsequently paved it over, restored its Temple of Venus, and proceeded to build his own forum with its Temple of Mars the Avenger. Thus began what amounted to a competition among successive emperors to outdo their predecessors by creating their own more spectacular forums. These imperial forums lined up north of and parallel to the great Roman Forum, which over the years was itself subjected to new construction. Stretched out along the Via dei Fori Imperiali (Street of Imperial Forums) were Vespasian's Forum of Peace (laid out after the Jewish War in 70 CE), the Forum of Nerva (completed in 97 CE), the Forum of Augustus, the Forum of Caesar, and the Forum of Trajan (completed by Hadrian, ca. 117 CE). The result was an extremely densely built city center. Trajan's was the last, largest, and most splendid forum. It sheltered the Column of Trajan, Trajan's Market, and the Basilica Ulpia—the largest basilica in the empire.

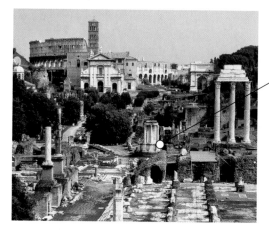

Contemporary view of the *Forum Romanum.* Little remains of the Roman forums but a field of ruins in the heart of the city. The rounded white columns are the ruins of the Temple of Vesta, one of the earliest buildings erected there.

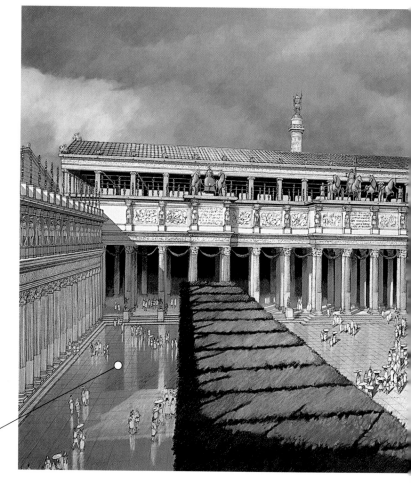

Forum of Trajan, Rome. 110–112 CE. Restored view by Gilbert Gorski. To make up for the destruction of a major commercial district that was required to construct his forum, Trajan commissioned a large marketplace. Like a contemporary mall, the market had 150 different shops on several levels.

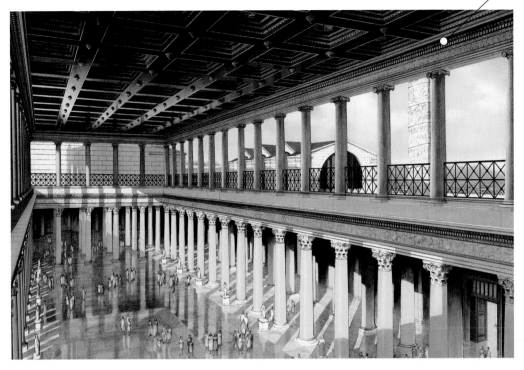

Reconstruction drawing of the central hall, Basilica Ulpia, Forum of Trajan, Rome. 113 CE. A **basilica** is a large rectangular building with a rounded extension, called an **apse**, at one or both ends, and easy access in and out. It was a general-purpose building that could be adapted to many uses. Designed by Trajan's favorite architect, the Greek Apollodorus of Damascus, the Basilica Ulpia was 200 feet wide and 400 feet long. In a courtyard outside a door in the middle of the colonnade to the right stood the Column of Trajan. Relatively plain and massive on the outside, the basilica is distinguished by its vast interior space, which would later serve as the model for some Christian churches.

Model of the Roman Forum and the Imperial Forums, Rome. ca. 46 CE–117 BCE. This model emphasizes the dense building plan of ancient Rome.

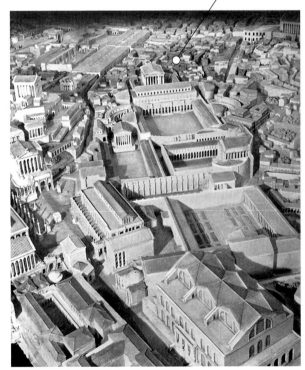

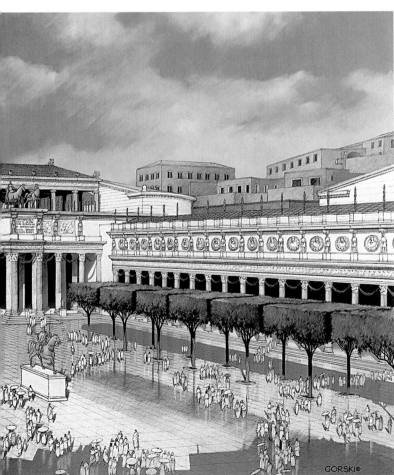

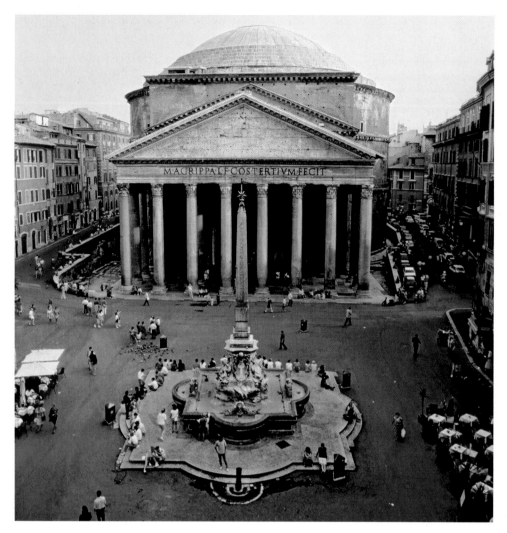

Fig. 3.18 The Pantheon, Rome. 118–125 CE. The Pantheon is an impressive feat of architectural engineering, and it would inspire architects for centuries to come. However, Hadrian humbly (and politically) refused to accept credit for it. He passed off the building as a "restoration" of a temple constructed on the same site by Augustus' original heir, Marcus Agrippa, in 27–25 BCE. Across the architrave (the bottom element in an entablature above the columns) of the facade is an inscription that serves both propagandistic and decorative purposes: "Marcus Agrippa, son of Lucius, three times consul, made this."

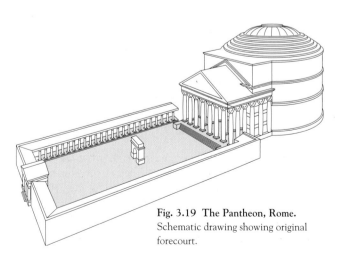

Fig. 3.19 The Pantheon, Rome. Schematic drawing showing original forecourt.

Greek temple, with its eight massive Corinthian columns and deep portico, behind which are massive bronze doors (Fig. **3.18**). Contemporary photographs give little evidence of its monumental presence, elevated above its long forecourt (Fig. **3.19**). Today both the forecourt and the elevation have disappeared beneath the streets of modern Rome. Figure 3.18 shows the Pantheon as it looks today.

The facade gives no hint of what lies beyond the doors. The interior of the Pantheon consists of a cylindrical space topped by a dome, the largest built in Europe before the twentieth century (Fig. **3.20**). The whole is a perfect hemisphere—the diameter of the rotunda is 144 feet, as is the height from floor to ceiling. The weight of the dome rests on eight massive supports, each more than 20 feet thick. The dome itself is 20 feet thick at the bottom but narrows to only 6 feet thick at the **oculus**, the circular opening at the top, which Hadrian conceived of as the "Eye of Jupiter." The *oculus* is 30 feet in diameter. Recessed panels, called **coffers**, further lighten the weight of the roof. The *oculus*, or "eye," admits light, which forms a round spotlight that moves around the building during the course of a day (it admits rain as well, which is drained out by small openings in the floor). For the Romans, this light symbolized Jupiter's ever-watchful eye cast over the affairs of state, illuminating the way.

In the vast openness of its interior, the Pantheon mirrors the cosmos, the vault of the heavens. Mesopotamian and Egyptian architecture had created monuments with exterior mass. Greek architecture was a kind of sculptural event, built up of parts that harmonized. But the Romans concentrated on sheer size, including the vastness of interior space. Like the Basilica Ulpia (see *Focus*, pages 90–91) in the Forum of Trajan, the Pantheon is concerned primarily with realizing a single, whole, uninterrupted interior space.

In this sense, the Pantheon mirrors the empire. It too was a single, uninterrupted space, stretching from Hadrian's Wall in the north of England (see Fig. 3.1 and Map 3.1) to the Rocks of Gibraltar in the south, across north Africa and Asia Minor, and encompassing all of Europe except what is now northern Germany and Scandinavia. Like Roman architecture, the empire was built up of parts that were meant to har-

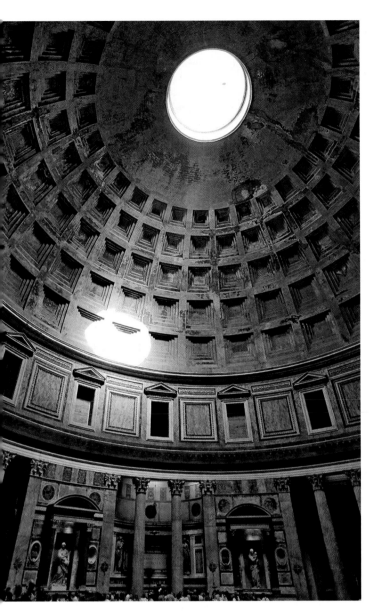

Fig. 3.20 The Pantheon, Rome. Interior. The sun's rays entering through the *oculus* form a spotlight on the Pantheon's interior, moving and changing intensity with the time of day.

monize in a unified whole, governed by rules of proportion and order. And if the monuments the empire built to celebrate itself were grand, the empire was grander still.

Pompeii

In 79 CE, during the rule of the Emperor Titus, the volcano Vesuvius erupted southeast of Naples, burying the seaside town of Pompeii in 13 feet of volcanic ash and rock. Its neighbor city Herculaneum was covered in 75 feet of a ground-hugging avalanche of hot ash that later solidified. Stationed nearby was Pliny the Elder, a commander in the Roman navy and the author of *The Natural History*, an encyclopedia of all contemporary knowledge. At the time of the eruption, his nephew, Pliny the Younger (ca. 61–ca.

113 CE), was staying with him. This is his eyewitness account (**Reading 3.3**):

READING 3.3 from *Letters of Pliny the Younger*

On 24 August, in the early afternoon, my mother drew his attention to a cloud of unusual size and appearance. He had been out in the sun, had taken a cold bath, and lunched while lying down, and was then working at his books. He called for his shoes and climbed up to a place which would give him the best view of the phenomenon. It was not clear at that distance from which mountain the cloud was rising (it was afterwards known to be Vesuvius); its general appearance can best be expressed as being like an umbrella pine, for it rose to a great height on a sort of trunk and then split off into branches, I imagine because it was thrust upwards by the first blast and then left unsupported as the pressure subsided, or else it was borne down by its own weight so that it spread out and gradually dispersed. . . .

They debated whether to stay indoors or take their chance in the open, for the buildings were now shaking with violent shocks, and seemed to be swaying to and fro as if they were torn from their foundations. Outside on the other hand, there was the danger of falling pumice-stones, even though these were light and porous; however, after comparing the risks they chose the latter. In my uncle's case one reason outweighed the other, but for the others it was a choice of fears. As a protection against falling objects they put pillows on their heads tied down with cloths. . . .

We also saw the sea sucked away and apparently forced back by the earthquake: at any rate it receded from the shore so that quantities of sea creatures were left stranded on dry sand. On the landward side a fearful black cloud was rent by forked and quivering bursts of flame, and parted to reveal great tongues of fire, like flashes of lightning magnified in size. . . .

You could hear the shrieks of women, the wailing of infants, and the shouting of men; some were calling their parents, others their children or their wives, trying to recognize them by their voices. People bewailed their own fate or that of their relatives, and there were some who prayed for death in their terror of dying. Many besought the aid of the gods, but still more imagined there were no gods left, and that the universe was plunged into eternal darkness for evermore. . . .

Pliny's uncle, Pliny the Elder, interested in what was happening, made his way toward Vesuvius, where he died, suffocated by the poisonous fumes. Pliny the Younger, together with his mother, survived. Of the 20,000 inhabitants of Pompeii, 2,000 died, mostly slaves and the poor left behind by the rich who escaped the city after early warning shocks.

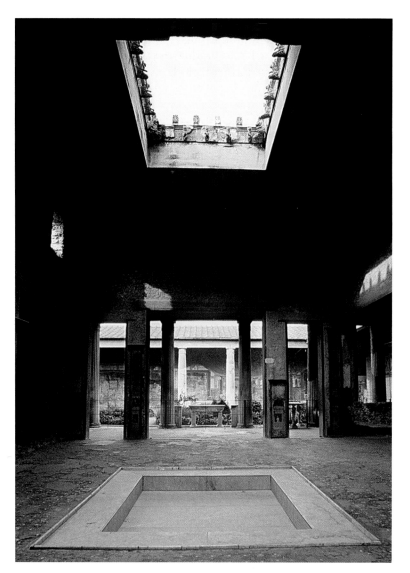

Fig. 3.21 Atrium, House of the Silver Wedding, Pompeii. 1st century BCE. This view looks through the atrium to the main reception area and the peristyle court. The house gets its name from the silver wedding anniversary of Italy's King Humbert and his queen, Margaret of Savoy, in 1893, the year it was excavated. They actively supported archeological fieldwork at Pompeii, which began in the mid-eighteenth century.

Much of what we know today about everyday Roman life is the direct result of the Vesuvius eruption. Those who survived left their homes in a hurry, and were unable to recover anything they left behind. Buried under the ashes were not only homes and buildings but also food and paintings, furniture and garden statuary, even pornography and graffiti. The latter include the expected—"Successus was here," "Marcus loves Spendusa"—but also the unexpected and perceptive—"I am amazed, O wall, that you have not collapsed and fallen, since you must bear the tedious stupidities of so many scrawlers." When Pompeii was excavated, beginning in the eighteenth century, many of the homes and artifacts were found to be relatively well preserved. The hardened lava and ash had protected them from the ravages of time. But eighteenth-century excavators also discovered something unexpected. By filling the hollows where the bodies of those caught in the eruption had decomposed, they captured images of horrific death.

Domestic Architecture: The *Domus* Although by no means the most prosperous town in Roman Italy, Pompeii was something of a resort, and, together with villas from other nearby towns, the surviving architecture gives us a good sense of the Roman ***domus***—the townhouse of the wealthier class of citizen. The *domus* was oriented to the street along a central axis that extended from the front entrance to the rear of the house. The *domus* was a measure of a Roman's social standing, as the vast majority lived in an apartment block or *insulae*. The house itself was designed to underscore the owner's reputation. Each morning, the front door was opened and left open. Gradually, the house would fill with clients—remember, the head of a Roman household was patron to many—who came to show their respect in a ritual known as the *salutatio* [sah-loo-TAH-tee-oh]. Passersby could look in to see the crowded atrium, and the patron himself was generally seated in the reception area, silhouetted by the light from the peristyle court behind. Surrounded by the busts of his ancestors, the symbol of his social position and prestige, he watched over all who entrusted themselves to his patronage.

The House of the Silver Wedding at Pompeii is typical in its design (Figs. **3.21**, **3.22**). An **atrium**, a large space with a shallow pool for catching rainwater below its open roof, extends directly behind the vestibule. Behind the atrium and opening onto it is a reception area, often decorated with por-

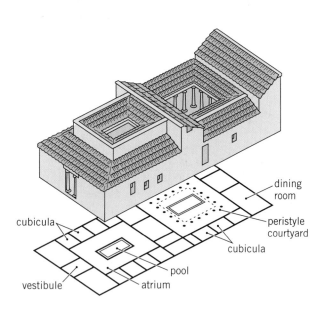

cubicula

dining room

peristyle courtyard

cubicula

pool

vestibule   atrium

Fig. 3.22 Plan of the House of the Silver Wedding, Pompeii. 1st century CE.

trait busts of the family's ancestors. These busts were also housed in the reception rooms just off the main one, which in turn opens onto a central **peristyle courtyard**, surrounded by a colonnaded walkway. The dining room faces into the courtyard, as do a number of *cubicula*, small general-purpose rooms often used for sleeping quarters. At the back of the house, facing into the courtyard, is a hall furnished with seats for discussion. Servants probably lived upstairs at the rear of the house.

At the center of the Roman *domus* was the garden of the peristyle courtyard, with a fountain or pond in the middle (Fig. **3.23**). Thanks to the long-term research of the archeologist Wilhelmina Jashemski, we know a great deal about these courtyard gardens. At the House of G. Polybius [poe-LEE-bee-us] in Pompeii, excavators carefully removed ash down to the level of the soil on the summer day of the eruption in 79 CE, when the garden would have been in full bloom. They were able to collect pollen, seeds, and other evidence, including root systems (obtained by pouring plaster into the surviving cavities) and thus determine what plants and trees were cultivated in it. Polybius's garden was lined, at one end, with lemon trees in pots, which were apparently trained and pruned to cover the wall in an *espalier*—a geo-

metric trellis. Cherry, pear, and fig trees filled the rest of the space. Gardens at other villas suggest that most were planted with nut- and fruit-bearing trees, including olive, which would provide the family with a summer harvest. Vegetable gardens are often found at the rear of the *domus*, a source of more fresh produce.

The garden also provided visual pleasure for the family. In the relatively temperate Roman climate the garden was in bloom for almost three-quarters of the year. It was the focus of many rooms in the *domus*, which opened onto the garden. And it was evidently a symbol for the fertility, fecundity, and plenty of the household itself, for many a Roman garden was decorated with statuary referencing the cult of Dionysus.

Wall Painting Mosaics decorated many floors of the *domus*, and paintings adorned the walls of the atrium, the hall, the dining room, and other reception rooms throughout the villa. Artists worked with pigments in a solution of lime and soap, sometimes mixed with a little wax, polished with a special metal or glass, and then buffed with a cloth. Even the *cubicula* bedrooms were richly painted.

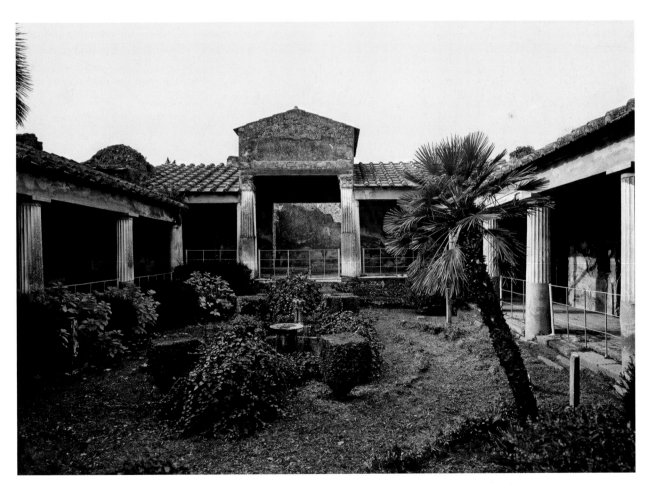

Fig. 3.23 Peristyle garden, House of the Golden Cupids, Pompeii. 62–79 CE. Built just before the eruption of Vesuvius, this house dispensed with the atrium; all its rooms are built around the peristyle garden. The dining room was entered through the pedimented portal at the rear of the garden, a dramatic setting for the *domus*'s primary social space.

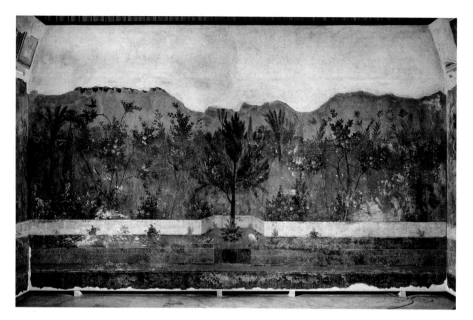

Fig. 3.24 *Garden Scene*, **detail of a wall painting from the Villa Livia at Primaporta, near Rome. Late 1st century** BCE. Museo Nazionale Romano, Rome. The artist created a sense of depth by setting a wall behind a fence with its open gate.

The . . . decoration—the frescoes on the walls, the beauty of their colors, and the beauty, exactitude and truth of each detail—might well be compared with the face of spring and with a flowery field, except that those things fade and wither and change and cast their beauty, while this is spring eternal, field unfading, bloom undying.

In Rome, at the villa of Livia and Augustus at the Primaporta, a wall painting depicting a garden full of fresh fruit, songbirds, and flowers reflects this sensibility (Fig. **3.24**). It is rendered as if it were an extension of the room itself, as if Livia and Augustus and their visitors could, at any time, step through the wall into their "undying" garden. Thus, although naturalistically rendered, it is an idealistic representation. As we shall discuss in chapter 4, Jesus was born in Palestine during Augustus' reign and Christianity was just beginning to take hold during Lucian's career. Lucian's essay and this painting suggest that the desire for enduring life promised by the Christian faith was already a central tenet of Roman culture.

Writing in the second century CE, the satirist and rhetorician Lucian (ca. 120–after 180 CE) describes what he takes to be the perfect house—"lavish, but only in such degree as would suffice a modest and beautiful woman to set off her beauty." He continues, describing the wall paintings:

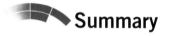

Summary

■ **Origins of Roman Culture** Roman culture developed out of both Greek and indigenous Etruscan roots. Most of what we know of the Etruscans comes from sculptures and paintings that survive in tombs. The Etruscans also provided the Greeks with one of their founding myths, the legend of Romulus and Remus (Virgil's *Aeneid* was the other). According to legend, it was Romulus who inaugurated the traditional Roman distinction between patricians and plebeians with its system of patronage and *pietas*.

■ **Republican Rome** During the Republic, Rome embarked on a series of military exploits. Whenever Rome conquered a region, it established permanent colonies and gave land to the victorious citizen-soldiers. In the first century BCE, power swayed back and forth between the *equites*, Rome's military elite, and the Senate, dominated by patricians, and between the generals themselves. Julius Caesar eventually assumed dictatorial control of Rome until his assassination in 44 BCE. During the first century, the powerfully eloquent and persuasive writing of the rhetorician Cicero helped to make Latin the chief language of the empire. His essay *On Duty* helped to define *pietas* as a Roman value, a value evidenced in the portrait busts of the era with their veristic realism.

■ **Imperial Rome** In 27 BCE, the Senate granted Octavian the imperial name Augustus and the authority of *imperium* over all the empire. Augustus idealized himself in the monumental statues dedicated to him and presented his family as the ideal Roman family in the sculptural program of the *Ara Pacis Augustae*. His wife, Livia, became the ideal figure for womanhood. Virgil's epic poem the *Aeneid* is consciously inspired by the example of Homer, but it leaves its Greek sources behind in its profound examination of the values on which the Roman state was founded. Horace's *Odes* blended the Greek love of beauty with a distinctly Roman sense of duty. Ovid's *Metamorphoses* constitutes one of the most moving works of the era in its exploration of human identity and transformation.

But Augustus' greatest achievement, and that of the emperors to follow him, was the transformation of Rome into, in Augustus' words, "a city of marble." In Rome itself citizens lived in the crowded conditions of the apartment block, or *insula*, but the more spacious Roman *domus* was more common in rural areas. In Rome itself, life was largely lived in the open spaces of the avenues, in its wide forums and spacious basilicas. In the seemingly endless spaces of the Imperial Forums, in the throngs that filled the Colosseum, in the vast interior of the Pantheon, Roman architecture mirrored the empire, each a vast unified whole, governed by rules of proportion and order.

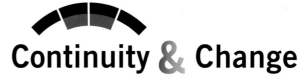

Continuity & Change

During the period we call the Middle Ages, the naturalism in art that we associate with the classical traditions of Greece and Rome faded away. Christianity began, like both Judaism and Islam, as a religion not of images but of scriptures. Even as images came to play a role in the Christian tradition—in Byzantium, for instance, where the Virgin and Child became a standard motif—they served to tell sacred stories that Christians understood and appreciated emotionally for the events they symbolized. Not until the Renaissance, nearly a thousand years later, would the individual portrait, so commonplace in Rome, gain popular favor once again.

It would be a mistake to see a decline of artistic ability or sensitivity in the abandonment of naturalism. The forces in the Middle Ages that resulted in flat surfaces, schematic or diagramlike figuration, and an almost total disregard for depicting real space were, rather, manifestations of a desire to reveal truths higher than those readily visible to the naked eye. Such truths were to be understood through the mind and heart instead, as expressions of faith.

For nearly a millennium after Rome's official acceptance of Christianity under the emperor Constantine in 313 CE, sight served a role of secondary importance to faith. Insofar as sight served the Christian faith, inspiring the faithful in the light of a stained glass window or the illuminated image in a manuscript, it was deemed acceptable, even desirable, by the clergy. But one could never see—at least not in this lifetime—the God in which they believed, and, as the faithful were constantly reminded, that ultimate vision is what mattered most of all.

Nevertheless, Roman traditions did live on in the Middle Ages, particularly in architecture. The Roman basilica would become the model for the Christian basilica-plan church, and certain aspects of Roman villa architecture would also come to inform Christian designs for the "house of God." Both the Romans and the Christians understood the power of grand architectural space to enthrall visitors and capture their imaginations. By the first years of the second millennium, even the Roman triumphal arch would find its way into the architecture of Christian churches—compare, for instance, the Arch of Constantine (Fig. 3.25) with the portal of the Church of Sainte-Marie-Madeleine in Vézeley, France (Fig. 3.26). This similarity is one of many that account for the designation "Romanesque," or "Roman-like," to

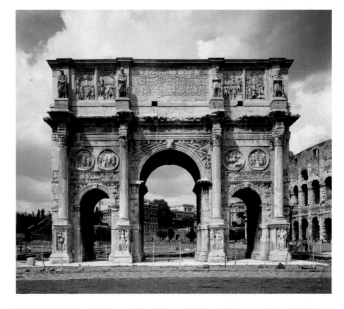

Fig. 3.25 Arch of Constantine, Rome. 315 CE. The monumental effects produced by this triumphal arch would find their way to the portals of Christian churches, such as Old St. Peter's Basilica, built in Rome shortly after this arch in 320–327 CE.

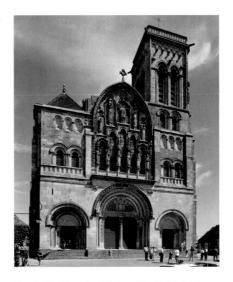

Fig. 3.26 Church of Sainte-Marie-Madeleine, Vézeley, France. ca. 1089–1206 CE. As we shall see in Chapter 5, the architectural style of this facade is so clearly indebted to Roman precedents that it has been labeled Romanesque.

describe the style of early medieval architecture. Features that had once celebrated the glory of the emperor now celebrated the glory of God.

Later, during the Renaissance, individual genius would once again be valued, and classical naturalism would be restored. Architects like Brunelleschi, Alberti, and Michelangelo would visit Rome to study and learn from its ruins. Playwrights like Shakespeare would study Roman history and retell it on the stage. Long-lost manuscripts by Tacitus, Cicero, Propertius, and Petronius would all be unearthed as Rome was excavated, and these would influence writers and teachers. By the eighteenth century, when Pompeii and Herculaneum were excavated, a kind of Roman fever gripped the West. In America, John Adams and Thomas Jefferson, both well read in classical literature, would model their new nation on the Roman Republic, remembering, among other things, their Cicero: "The people's good is the highest law." Napoleon, in France, would model his new civil code on Roman law (and his imperial aspirations on Roman history). These are stories that subsequent chapters will tell, all Roman in inspiration. ■

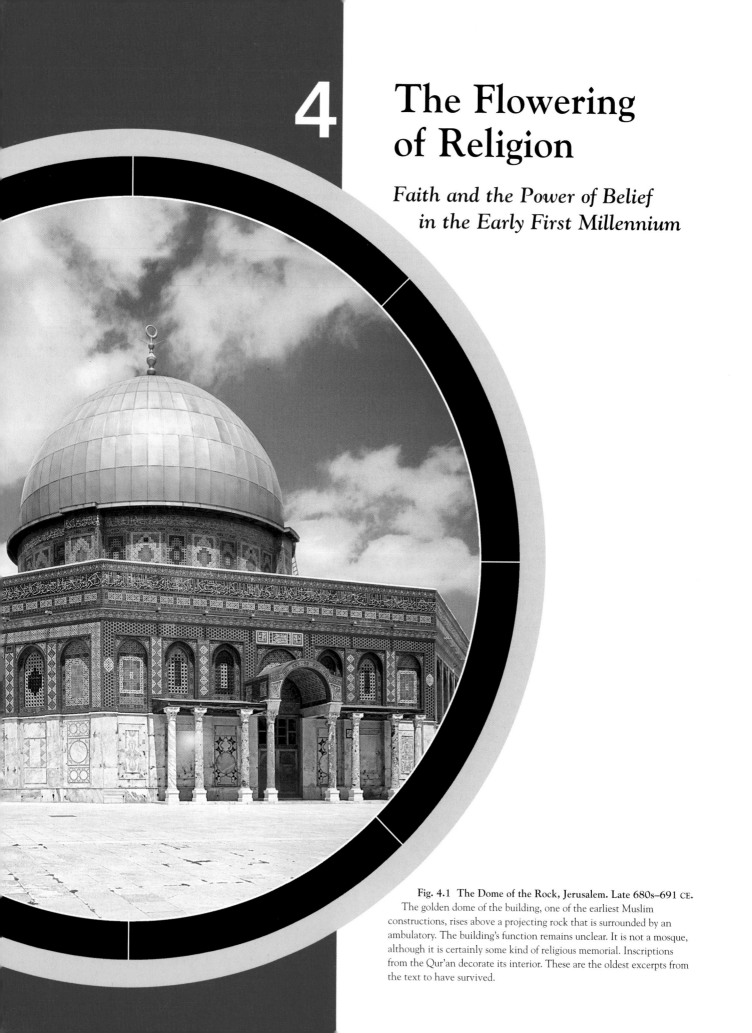

4

The Flowering of Religion

Faith and the Power of Belief in the Early First Millennium

Fig. 4.1 The Dome of the Rock, Jerusalem. Late 680s–691 CE. The golden dome of the building, one of the earliest Muslim constructions, rises above a projecting rock that is surrounded by an ambulatory. The building's function remains unclear. It is not a mosque, although it is certainly some kind of religious memorial. Inscriptions from the Qur'an decorate its interior. These are the oldest excerpts from the text to have survived.

((*So the church has made a spectacle of great beauty, stupendous to those who see it and altogether incredible to those who hear of it.*))

Procopius, *On Justinian's Buildings*

The Dome of the Rock (Fig. 4.1) stands atop the Temple Mount in Jerusalem, on the site where, in Jewish tradition, Abraham prepared to sacrifice his son Isaac. The Jewish Temple of Solomon originally stood here, and the site is further associated—by Jews, Christians, and Muslims alike—with God's creation of Adam. The Second Temple of Jerusalem also stood on this spot until it was destroyed by Roman soldiers when they sacked the city in 70 CE, to put down a Jewish revolt (see Fig. 3.14). Only the Wailing Wall remains, part of the original retaining wall for the platform supporting the Temple Mount and for Jews the most sacred site in Jerusalem. To this day, the plaza in front of the wall functions as an open-air synagogue where daily prayers are recited and other Jewish rituals are performed. On Tisha B'Av, the ninth day of the month of Av, which occurs either in July or August, a fast is held commemorating the destruction of the successive temples on this site, and people sit on the ground before the wall reciting the Book of Lamentations.

One of the earliest examples of Muslim architecture, built in the 680s CE, the Dome's **ambulatory**, its circular, colonnaded walkway, encloses a projecting rock that lies directly beneath its golden dome. By the sixteenth century, Islamic faithful claimed that the Prophet Muhammad ascended to heaven from this spot, on a winged horse named Buraq, but there is no evidence that this story was in circulation when the Dome was originally built. Others thought that it represents the ascendancy of Islam over Christianity in the Holy Land. Still others believed the rock is the center of the world, or that it could refer to the Temple of Solomon, the importance of which is fully acknowledged by Muslims, who considered Solomon a founding father of their own faith. All of this suggests that the Dome was meant to proselytize, or convert, Jews and Christians both to the Muslim faith.

The sanctity of this spot, then, at the heart of Jerusalem, is recognized equally by the three great faiths of the Western world—Judaism, Christianity, and Islam—and the intersection of these religions is the subject of this chapter. As Christianity came to differentiate itself from its Judaic heritage, it came into increasing conflict with imperial Rome: Both Rome and the Church demanded absolute allegiance and loyalty of the citizen/believer. Until the Emperor Constantine granted religious freedom to all Romans in 313 CE, the power of the state was at odds with the power of Christian faith. And when, in 325 CE, Constantine moved the imperial capital of the Roman Empire to Constantinople, named after himself, on the shores of the Bosporus, the straits linking the Black Sea with the Aegean, Christianity found itself divided in a contest of belief and doctrine between the Western (Catholic) Church, centered in Rome, and the Eastern (Orthodox) Church, centered in Constantine's new capital. When, in the seventh century CE, Islam arose as a religious force on the Arabic peninsula, the Christian world as a whole was quickly challenged. One need only compare two maps, the first showing the spread of Christianity to the year 600 CE (Map 4.1), and the second showing the expansion of Islam to 850 CE (Map 4.2), to recognize the points of conflict, stretching from the Caspian Sea, south around the eastern Mediterranean, including Palestine and Jerusalem, across Egypt and North Africa, all the way to Spain in the west, as the two religions vied for followers. Meanwhile, in India, China, and Japan, a fourth religion had established itself, based on the teachings of Siddhartha Gautama, known as the Buddha (or "Enlightened One").

Developments in Judaic Culture

After the Babylonian Captivity of 587–520 BCE, the Jewish religion became increasingly **messianic**—that is, it prophesied that the world would end in **apocalypse**, the coming of God on the day of judgment, and that the post-apocalyptic world would be led by a **Messiah**, or Anointed One, in everlasting peace. By the early first century CE, large numbers of people claiming to be the Messiah and larger numbers of apocalyptic preachers roamed Judea (modern Israel). This situation was complicated by the growing sectarianism of Judaism itself. Much of what we know about this time comes from the writings of Josephus [joe-SEE-fus], a Jewish historian (ca. 37–ca. 100 CE). In a history completed in the early 80s CE, he writes,. "There are three philosophical sects among the Jews, the followers of the first of which are the Pharisees [FAIR-uh-sees], a scribal group associated with the masses; of the second, the Sadducees [SAD-juh-seez] priests and high priests associated with the aristocracy; and the third sect, which pretends to a severer discipline, are called Essenes [ESS-eenz]."

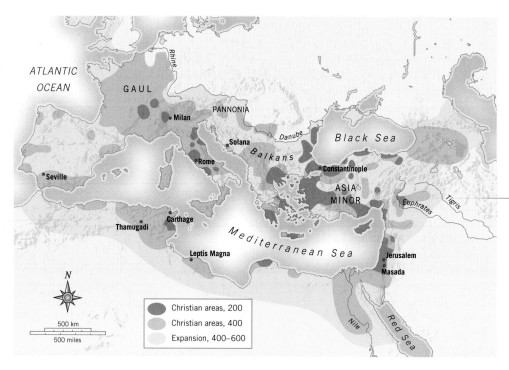

Map 4.1 The spread of Christianity by 600 CE.

strongly enforced social boundaries between its members and all others. Finally, members of a sect view themselves as good and all others as evil. Of the three sects Josephus described, the Essenes were the most conservative, going so far as to ban women from their community so that they might live in celibacy and purity. The Essenes are generally identified with the group of Jews who lived at Qumran [kum-RAHN], on the Dead Sea southeast of Jerusalem, where in 1947 a Bedouin [BED-uh-wun] shepherd discovered the oldest extant version of the Hebrew Scriptures, dating from around the time of Jesus—the so-called Dead Sea Scrolls. These documents are the richest source of our knowledge of Jewish sectarianism, for they include the Hebrew Scriptures—the *Torah* [TOH-ruh] (the five books of Moses), *Nevi'im* [neh-fee-EEM] (the Prophets), and *Ketubim* [kuh-tuh-BEEM] (the Writings), what Christians call the "Old

A **sect** is a small, organized group that separates itself from the larger religious movement because it asserts that it alone understands God's will and therefore it alone embodies the ideals of the religion. As a result, a sect generally creates

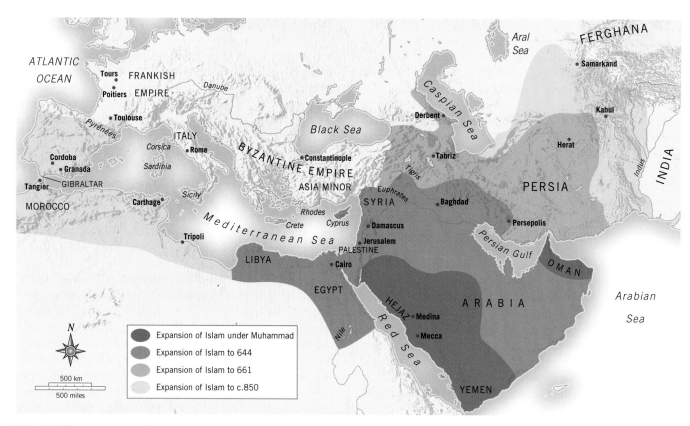

Map 4.2 The expansion of Islam to 850 CE.

Testament"—as well as other works originating in sectarian circles within and outside the Qumran community.

The Jewish purity laws were a point of special contention with far-reaching implications for the temple. According to Leviticus [luh-VIT-ih-kus] and Numbers (two books of the Torah), the house of God (the temple) must be pure, and that which is impure must be expelled. In practice, the laws of purity prevented normal social relations between those who observed them and those who did not, to the point that even routine physical contact (a handshake, for instance) with a non-observer was forbidden. Since all the sects developed their own purity laws, they were in essence forbidding contact with one another. The Qumran Essenes withdrew completely from Jewish society. Furthermore, the sectarian communities, especially the Pharisees, considered the Jerusalem Temple, the traditional center of Jewish worship, to be polluted, its priests—particularly the Sadducees—corrupt, and its rituals debased. The Pharisees, and perhaps the Sadducees as well, considered the house of God to be the larger state of Judea rather than just the temple in Jerusalem, and they felt compelled to expel the "impure" Romans from their midst.

The Romans, for their part, installed a client king, Herod (the Great), who claimed to be Jewish but was not according to Jewish law. Herod tried to reconcile Jews and Romans, primarily through religious tolerance and a massive building program. During his reign (37–4 BCE), he rebuilt the city of Jerusalem, constructing a large palace and enlarging the Second Temple (Fig. **4.2**). We can see the Hellenistic influence in its tall, engaged Corinthian columns and its decorative frieze, and its Roman roots in its triple-arched gateway. Herod also engaged in other massive building programs, including a port at Caesarea and a mountain fortress above the Dead Sea at Masada. Though Herod's three sons ruled briefly after their father's death, Rome became less and less tolerant of the Jewish faith—the laws of Rome often coming into conflict with the Law of the Book—and direct Roman rule was soon imposed.

Finally, in 66 CE, the Jews revolted. In 68 CE, the Romans destroyed Qumran. In 70 CE, they sacked the temple in Jerusalem, as depicted on the Arch of Titus in Rome (see Figs. 3.14 and 3.15). At Masada, a band of zealots held out until 73 CE. The Roman general Flavius Silva surrounded the mountain with a wall and eight encampments, then built a huge earthen ramp up the mountainside. Rather than submit to the Romans, the Jews inside the fortress committed mass suicide, each man responsible for killing his own family and then himself. The Romans renamed the land Palestine, "land of the Philistines" [FIL-ih-steenz], instead of Judea, "land of the Jews." Finally, in 135 CE, after yet another Jewish revolt, the Emperor Hadrian rebuilt Jerusalem as a Roman city, which Jews were forbidden to enter. Hundreds of thousands of Jews were killed or sold into slavery, their land and property was confiscated, and the survivors fled throughout the Mediterranean and Middle East. The diaspora that had begun with the Assyrian

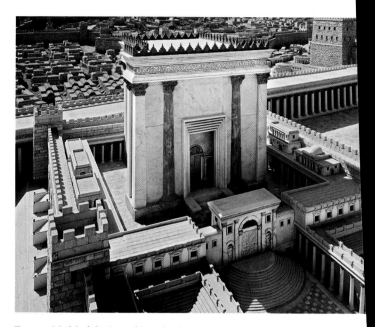

Fig. 4.2 Model of the Second Temple of Jerusalem, ca. 20 BCE. Only the Western Wall of Herod's temple survives today, and for Jews it remains the most sacred site in Jerusalem, symbolizing the sense of loss felt by the Jewish people.

invasion of Israel in 722 BCE was now complete. Not until 1948, when the state of Israel was established by the United Nations, would Jews regain their homeland.

The Rise of Christianity

The development of Christianity, the religion that would have such a profound effect upon the history of the Western world, can only be understood in the context of Jewish history. It developed as one among many other minor sects of Judaism, at first so inconsequential that Josephus does not even mention it. Later theological writings, as opposed to actual historical accounts written at the time, tell us that in Judea's sectarian climate, Jesus of Nazareth was born to Mary and Joseph of Judea in about 4 BCE. At about the age of 30, Jesus began to lead the life of an itinerant rabbi. He preached repentance, compassion for the poor and meek, love of God and neighbor, and the imminence of the apocalypse, which he called the coming of the kingdom of God.

Although his teachings were steeped in the wisdom of the Jewish tradition, they antagonized both Jewish and Roman leaders. Jesus, in the spirit of reform, had challenged the commercialization of the Jewish Temple in Jerusalem, especially the practice of money-changing within its sacred precincts, alienating the Sadducee sect that managed it. After his followers identified him as the Messiah, or Savior—he did not make the claim for himself—both conservative Jewish leaders and Roman rulers were threatened. The proclamation by his followers that he was the son of God amounted to a crime against the Roman state, since the emperor was considered to

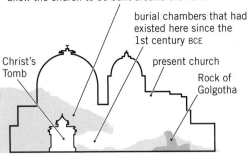

the hillside dug away in the 4th century to allow the church to be built around the Tomb

burial chambers that had existed here since the 1st century BCE

Christ's Tomb

present church

Rock of Golgotha

Fig. 4.3 Cutaway drawing of the Church of the Holy Sepulchre, Jerusalem, showing site of Christ's Tomb. This site was originally a small rocky hill, Golgotha, upon which Jesus was crucified, and an unused stone quarry in which tombs had been cut. The first basilica on the site was built by the Emperor Constantine between 326 and 335 CE.

be the only divine human on earth. In fact, since Jews were monotheistic and refused to worship other gods, including the emperor, their beliefs were a political threat to the Romans. The Christian sect's belief in the divinity of Jesus posed a special problem.

An enemy of the state, denounced by the other Jews that he had antagonized, betrayed by his disciple Judas (a betrayal now called into question with the publication of the Gospel of Judas), Jesus was crucified in about 30 CE, a degrading fate reserved for criminals and non-Roman citizens. Christian tradition has it—we possess no actual historical account—that the crucifixion occurred outside the city walls on a hillside known as Golgotha, now the site of the Church of the Holy Sepulchre (Fig. **4.3**), and that Jesus was buried in a rock tomb just behind the site. Three days later, his followers reported that he rose from the dead and reappeared among them. The promise of resurrection, already a fundamental tenet of the Pharisee and Essene sects, became the foundation of Christian faith.

The Evangelists

Upon his death, Jesus' reputation grew as his **evangelists** spread the word of his life and resurrection (the word "evangelist" comes from the Greek *evangelos* [eh-van-GEH-los], meaning "bearer of good"—and note the root *angel* in the word as well). Preeminent among these was Paul, who had persecuted Jews in Judea before converting to the new faith in Damascus (in modern Syria) in 35 CE. Paul's epistles, or letters, are the earliest writings of the new Christian faith. In letters written to churches he founded or visited in Asia Minor, Greece, Macedonia, and Rome, which comprise 14 books of the Christian Scriptures, he argues the nature of religious truth and interprets the life of Christ—his preferred name for Jesus, one that he coined. "Christ" means, literally, "the Anointed One." It refers to the Jewish tradition of anointing priests, kings, and prophets with oil, and

the fact is that by Jesus' time Jews had come to expect a savior who embodied all the qualities of priest, king, and prophet. In true sectarian tradition, for Paul the only correct expression of Judaism included faith in Christ. Paul conflated Jewish tradition, then, with his belief that Jesus' crucifixion was the act of his salvation of humankind. He argued that Christ was blameless and suffered on the cross to pay for the sins of humanity. Resurrection, he believed, was at the heart of the Christian faith, but redemption was by no means automatic—sinners had to show their faith in Christ and his salvation.

Not long after Paul's death, as the religion spread rapidly through Asia Minor and Greece, other evangelists began to write gospels, or "good news," specifically narrating the story of Jesus' life. What would become the first three books of the Christian New Testament, the gospels of Matthew, Mark, and Luke, are believed by scholars to have been written between 70 and 90 CE. Each emphasizes slightly different aspects of Jesus' life, though all focus particularly on his last days. Particularly important to the normative view of Jesus' life is the recording in the Gospel of Matthew of the so-called Sermon on the Mount. The Gospel was probably written in the last decades of the first century CE. So many of the principles of Jesus' message are included in this sermon that some scholars believe it is more an anthology of many sermons than a single address. In fact, it incorporates many traditional Jewish teachings, and Jesus' primary source is his Judaism. The sermon contains Jesus' most famous sayings, and his most famous metaphors. It includes the famous Lord's Prayer—itself a kind of collage of passages from the Hebrew Scriptures—and it differentiates, particularly, between accepted wisdom ("You have heard that it was said, 'You shall love your neighbor and hate your enemy . . .'") and the compassionate wisdom of the new faith ("But I say to you, Love your enemies and pray for those who persecute you, so that you may be children of your Father in heaven"). It is, furthermore, a masterpiece of rhetorical persuasion, as the section known as "the Beatitudes" demonstrates (**Reading 4.1**):

READING 4.1   **The Sermon on the Mount, from the Bible, (Matthew 5:1-12)**

And seeing the multitudes, he went up into a mountain: and when he was set, his disciples came unto him: and he opened his mouth, and taught them, saying,
Blessed are the poor in spirit: for theirs is the kingdom of heaven.
Blessed are they that mourn: for they shall be comforted.
Blessed are the meek: for they shall inherit the earth.
Blessed are they which do hunger and thirst after righteousness: for they shall be filled.
Blessed are the merciful: for they shall obtain mercy.
Blessed are the pure in heart: for they shall see God.

Blessed are the peacemakers: for they shall be called the children of God.

Blessed are they which are persecuted for righteousness' sake: for theirs is the kingdom of heaven.

Blessed are ye, when men shall revile you, and persecute you, and shall say all manner of evil against you falsely, for my sake. Rejoice, and be exceeding glad: for great is your reward in heaven: for so persecuted they the prophets which were before you.

Symbols and Iconography in Christian Thinking and Art

The new Christian faith did not immediately abandon its traditions as a Jewish sect. Jesus, for instance, never thought of himself as anything other than a Jew. All of his associates and disciples were Jews. He regularly worshiped in Jewish communal worship and he preached from the Torah, the authority of which he never denied. The major distinction was that Christian Jews believed in Jesus' resurrection and status as Messiah, while non-Christian Jews did not. Christian Jews regarded the failure of the larger Jewish community to recognize the importance of Jesus as reason to separate themselves from that community to pursue what they believed to be the true will of God. Not until sometime in the early second century CE did Christianity cease to be a Jewish sect. By then, Christians had abandoned Jewish rituals, including circumcision, but even as it slowly distinguished itself from its Jewish roots, Christianity had to come to terms with those roots. In doing so, it found a distinctive way to accept the Hebrew Scriptures.

Christians believed the stories in the Hebrew Scriptures prefigured the life of Jesus. For example, Adam and Eve's fall from grace in the Garden of Eden—the original sin that was believed to doom all of humanity—was seen as anticipating the necessity of God's sacrifice of his son, Jesus, to atone for the sins of humankind. As Paul put it in his Epistle to the Church in Rome (Romans 5:12–14):

12 Therefore, just as sin came into the world through one man, and death came through sin, and so death spread to all because all have sinned—13 sin was indeed in the world before the law, but sin is not reckoned when there is no law. 14 Yet death exercised dominion from Adam to Moses, even over those whose sins were not like the transgression of Adam, who is a type of the one who was to come. . . .

Similarly, Christians interpreted Abraham's willingness to sacrifice his son, Isaac, as prefiguring God's sacrifice of his son. This view of history is called **typology**, from the Greek *tupos* [TOO-pus], meaning "example" or "figure." Thus Solomon, in his wisdom, is a *type* for Christ.

Very little early Christian art survives, and most of what we have dates from the third and fourth centuries. In paintings decorating catacombs, underground cemeteries, and a few sculptures, certain themes and elements are so prevalent that we can assume they reflect relatively long-standing representational traditions. In almost all of these works it is not so much the literal meaning of the image that matters, but rather its symbolic significance. Likewise, the aesthetic dimension of the work is clearly less important than its message. A very common image is that of Christ as the Good Shepherd, which derives from Jesus' promise, "I am the good shepherd. A good shepherd lays down his life for the sheep" (John 10:11). As the Lamb of God, a reference to the age-old role of the lamb in sacrificial offerings, Jesus is, of course, both shepherd and sheep—guardian of his flock and God the Father's sacrificial lamb. In fact, it is unclear whether images such as the free-standing representation of *The Good Shepherd* (Fig. **4.4**) represent Christ or symbolize a more general concept of God caring for his flock, perhaps even capturing a sheep for sacrifice. The naturalism of the sculpture echoes Classical and Hellenistic traditions. We

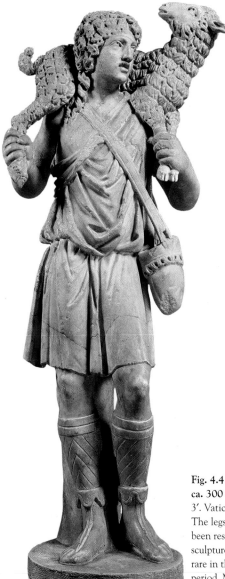

Fig. 4.4 *The Good Shepherd*, ca. 300 CE. Marble, height 3′. Vatican Museums, Rome. The legs of this figure have been restored. Free-standing sculptures such as this one are rare in the early Christian period. Much more common are wall paintings.

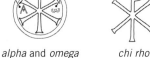

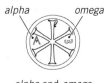

alpha and omega
I and X

chi rho

Fig. 4.5 Traditional Christian symbols.

see this too in monumental funerary sculpture, such as the *Sarcophagus of Junius Bassus* (see *Focus*, pages 106–107). The shepherd adopts a contrapposto pose, reminiscent of Polyclitus' *Doryphoros*. His body is confidently modeled beneath the drapery of his clothing. He turns as if engaged with some other person or object outside the scope of the sculpture itself, animating the space around him. And the sheep he carries on his back seems to struggle to set itself free.

Continuity & Change
p. 59

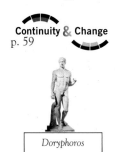

Doryphoros

These examples make clear the importance of symbolism to Christian thinking. Over the course of the first 200 years of Christianity, before freedom of worship was legalized, Christians developed many symbols that served to identify them to each other and to mark the articles of their faith. Their symbols allowed them to represent their faith in full view of a general populace that largely rejected it. They adopted the symbol of the fish, for instance, because the Greek word for fish, *ichthys* [IK-tis], is a form of acronym, a combination of the first letters of the Greek words for "Jesus Christ, Son of God, Savior." The first and last letters of the Greek alphabet, *alpha* and *omega* [oh-MEG-uh], symbolize Christ's presence from the beginning to the end of time. The *alpha* and *omega* often flank the initials *I* and *X*, the first letters of Jesus and Christ in Greek, and the initials *XP* were the first two letters of the word *Christos* [KRIH-stohs] (Fig. **4.5**).

Over the years, Christians developed a consistent **iconography**—the subject matter of a work, both literal (factual) and figurative (symbolic)—in their art and literature. A story or person might be a type for some other story or person. A figure might symbolize something else, as particular figures symbolized each of the four evangelists—an angel for Matthew; a lion for Mark; an ox for Luke; an eagle for John. And the stories surrounding Jesus' life coalesced into distinct story "cycles," each part in some sense signifying the whole, and all of them becoming standard themes in the arts throughout the history of the West.

Christian Rome

Throughout its history, the Roman Empire had been a polytheistic state in which literally dozens of religions were tolerated. But as Christianity became a more and more dominant force in the Empire, it threatened the political and cultural identity of the Roman citizen. No longer was a Roman Christian first and foremost Roman. Increasingly, that citizen was first and foremost Christian.

In reaction to this threat to imperial authority, during the chaotic years after the fall of the Severan emperors in 235 CE, Christians were blamed, as their religion spread across the Empire (see Map 4.1), for most of Rome's troubles. By the end of the third century, there were about 5 million Christians in the Roman Empire, nearly a tenth of the population. Rome had a particularly large Christian congregation with considerable influence, since its leadership was believed to have descended from Jesus' original disciples, Peter and Paul. In 303, the emperor Diocletian [di-o-CLEE-shun] (r. 284–305) unleashed a furious persecution of Christians that lasted for eight years. Diocletian had risen to power after a long period of virtual anarchy in the Roman Empire by implementing a scheme of government known as the **tetrarchy**, a four-part monarchy ruling the Empire from capitals in Solana—a city on the Adriatic near modern-day Split, Croatia—Milan, the Balkans, and Gaul.

Constantine, the Church, and Change

In 305, Diocletian retired due to bad health, ushering in a period of instability, as the other members of the tetrarchy competed for control of the Empire. Finally, Constantine I, known as "Constantine the Great" (r. 306–337), won a decisive battle against Maxentius (son of one of the tetrarchy monarchs), at the Milvian [MIL-vee-un] Bridge, at the entrance to Rome, on October 28, 312. Under the tetrarchy, Constantine had ruled Gaul, the Iberian Peninsula, and Britannia. Two years earlier, as Constantine was advancing on Rome from Gaul, the story had circulated that he had seen a vision of the sun god Apollo accompanied by Victory (Nike) and the Roman numeral XXX symbolizing the 30 years he would reign. By the end of his life he claimed to have seen, instead, above the sun, a single cross, by then an increasingly common symbol of Christ, together with the legend, "In this sign you shall conquer." At any rate, it seems certain that at the Battle of the Milvian Bridge, Constantine ordered that his troops decorate their shield with crosses, and perhaps the Greek letters *chi* [ky] and *rho* [roh] as well. As we have seen, these letters stood for *Christos*, although *chi* and *rho* had long meant *chrestos* [KREH-stohs], "auspicious," and Constantine probably meant only this and not Jesus Christ. While Constantine himself reasserted his devotion to the Roman state religion, within a year, in 313, he issued the Edict of Milan, which granted religious freedom to all, ending religious persecution in the Empire.

Constantine recognized that Diocletian's scheme for controlling the Empire was, in most respects, sound. Particularly important was an imperial presence near the eastern and Danubian frontiers of the Empire. To provide this imperial presence in the East, in 324 Constantine founded the city of Constantinople, modern Istanbul, on the site of the Greek city of Byzantium [bih-ZAN-tee-um]. The city was dedicated with both pagan rites and Christian ceremonies on May 11, 330. Constantine's own Christianity became more and more pronounced in his new eastern capital. Though he did not persecute pagans, he officially rejected pagan practices, openly favored Christians as officials, and admitted Church clergy to his court. Perhaps his most important act was to convene the first **ecumenical**, or worldwide, **council** of Church leaders in 325 at Nicaea [nye-SEE-uh] (modern Iznik), a site just southeast of Constantinople. The council produced a document, the Nicene [NYE-seen] Creed, that unified the Church behind a prescribed doctrine, or **dogma**, creating, in effect, an orthodox faith. Church leaders believed that by memorizing the Creed, laypeople would be able to easily identify deviations from orthodox Christianity.

The Creed was revised and extended in 381 by a Second Ecumenical Council in Constantinople, quoted here (**Reading 4.2**):

READING 4.2   The Nicene Creed

We believe in one God the Father All-Sovereign, maker of heaven and earth, and of all things visible and invisible;

And in one Lord Jesus Christ, the only-begotten Son of God, Begotten of the Father before all the ages, Light of Light, true God of true God, begotten not made, of one essence with the Father, through whom all things were made; who for us men and for our salvation came down from the heavens, and was made flesh of the Holy Spirit and the Virgin Mary, and became man, and was crucified for us under Pontius Pilate [PON-chus PYE-lut], and suffered and was buried, and rose again on the third day according to the Scriptures, and ascended into the heavens, and sitteth on the right hand of the Father, and cometh again with glory to judge living and dead, of whose kingdom there shall be no end;

And [we believe] in the Holy Spirit, the Lord and the Life-giver, that proceedeth from the Father, who with Father and Son is worshiped together and glorified together, who spake through the prophets;

In one holy catholic and apostolic Church: We acknowledge one baptism unto remission of sins. We look for a resurrection of the dead, and the life of the age to come.

The Creed is an article of mystical faith, not a doctrine of rational or empirical observation. In its very first line, it states its belief in the invisible. It argues for the virgin birth of Jesus, for a holy "spirit," for the resurrection of the dead. It imagines what cannot be rationally known: Jesus in heaven at the right hand of God (perhaps not coincidentally an image evocative of Diocletian modeling himself as *dominus*, "lord," ruling at the will of and beside God).

Nothing could be further from the Aristotelian drive to describe the knowable world and to represent it in naturalistic terms. (See chapter 2.)

But perhaps most important, the Nicene Creed establishes "the one holy catholic and apostolic Church," that is, a united church that is universal ("catholic") and based on the teachings of the apostles ("apostolic"). The Church was organized around the administrative divisions of the Roman state—archbishops oversaw the provinces, bishops the dioceses, and priests the parishes—an organization that provided Constantine with the means to impose the Creed throughout the Empire, eliminate rivalries within the Empire, and rule over both church and state. Finally, the Church's **liturgy**, the rites prescribed for public worship, was established. In Rome, Saint Jerome (ca. 342–420) translated the Hebrew Bible and the Greek books of the New Testament into Latin. The resulting **Vulgate**, meaning "common" or "popular," became the official Bible of the Roman Catholic Church. As the version of the Bible known by the faithful for over a thousand years, from about 400 CE to 1530, it would exert an influence over Western culture, which came to consider it virtually infallible.

Music in the Liturgy   The Roman prelate Ambrose (339–397), bishop of Milan, wrote hymns to be sung by the congregation, an important part of the new liturgy. Recognizing that common people, with no musical training, were to sing along with the clergy, Ambrose composed simple, melodic songs or psalms, generally characterized by one syllable for each note of the hymn. "The psalm is our armor by night," he wrote, "our instructor by day. The dawn of the day resounds with the psalm, and with the psalm re-echoes at sunset." St. Augustine, whose writings are discussed later in this chapter, tells us in his *Confessions* that "the practice and singing of hymns and psalms . . . was established so that the people [of Milan] would not become weak as a result of boredom or sorrow. It has been retained from that day to this; many, in fact, nearly all of God's flocks now do likewise throughout the rest of the world." These hymns and songs, Augustine says, represented a "kind of consolation and exhortation, in which the voice and the hearts of the brethren joined in zealous harmony."

Ambrose's authorship is certain for only four hymns, all attributed to him by Augustine. The melodies survive only in tenth- and eleventh-century versions, and their authenticity is disputed. Each hymn is composed of eight four-line stanzas, each written in a strict **iambic tetrameter** (short-long, short-long, short-long, short-long). Ambrose also seems to have introduced an **antiphonal** method of chanting, where one side of the choir responds to the other.

Roman and Greek Influences on Christian Churches and Rituals   The community that developed around the new liturgy required a physical church, and Constantine obliged with a building that became a model for many subsequent churches: Saint Peter's Basilica, begun in 320 on the site of

Focus

The *Sarcophagus of Junius Bassus*

The stone coffin known as the *Sarcophagus of Junius Bassus* is one of the most extraordinary pieces of sculpture of the late Roman Empire. It consists of ten individual scenes on two tiers, each separated from the next by a column (in fact, the two top right-hand scenes are one, representing Christ's confrontation with Pontius Pilate). The columns framing the central two scenes are decorated with *putti* [POO-tee], plump, naked boys who in Classical art are usually cupids and in Christian art are called *cherubs*. They can be seen here harvesting grapes, symbolic of the blood of Christ and his sacrifice. This element underscores the importance of these two central panels, which depict Christ in his glory. The bottom panel represents Christ's triumphal entry into Jerusalem on Palm Sunday, the top his presentation of the Christian law to Peter and Paul after his resurrection. Note, in the top panel, how Christ's feet rest on what is generally taken to be a symbolic representation of the world as a whole, but the figure is unmistakably the Roman god Neptune (the Greek Poseidon) and represents Christ's triumph over the Roman gods as well.

Across the top of the sarcophagus these words are written: "Junius Bassus, a man of highest rank, who lived 42 years, 2 months, in his own prefecture of the city, went to God, the 8th day from the Kalends of September, Eusebius [yoo-SEE-bee-us] and Hypatius [hie-PAY-shus] being consuls [25 August 359]." Thus, the sarcophagus collapses the "present" time of Junius Bassus' death into historical time. Four scenes from the Old Testament prophesy the story of Christ, itself represented in four panels, as well as the arrest and persecution of two Roman martyrs, Paul and Daniel, who represent the fate of all Roman Christians up until the Edict of Milan, which Constantine endorsed just four years before Junius Bassus' birth. In his sarcophagus, Bassius assumes his place in Christian history.

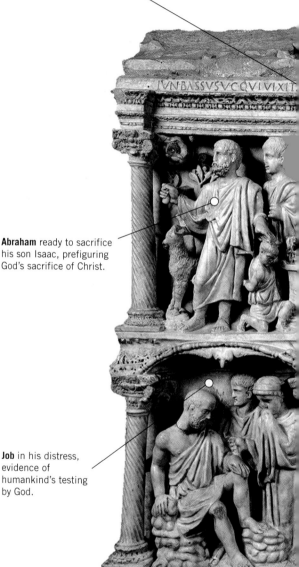

The arrest of **St. Peter**, who would be crucified in Rome in imitation of Christ. At his own insistence, Peter was crucified upside down, to emphasize his status as lesser than his Savior's.

Abraham ready to sacrifice his son Isaac, prefiguring God's sacrifice of Christ.

Job in his distress, evidence of humankind's testing by God.

Adam and Eve in the Garden of Eden, at the moment when they succumbed to the Temptation of Satan, who is shown wrapped around the Tree of the Knowledge of Good and Evil in his guise as a serpent.

Sarcophagus of Junius Bassus. 359 CE. Marble, Museo Storico del Tesoro della Basilica di San Pietro, Vatican City.

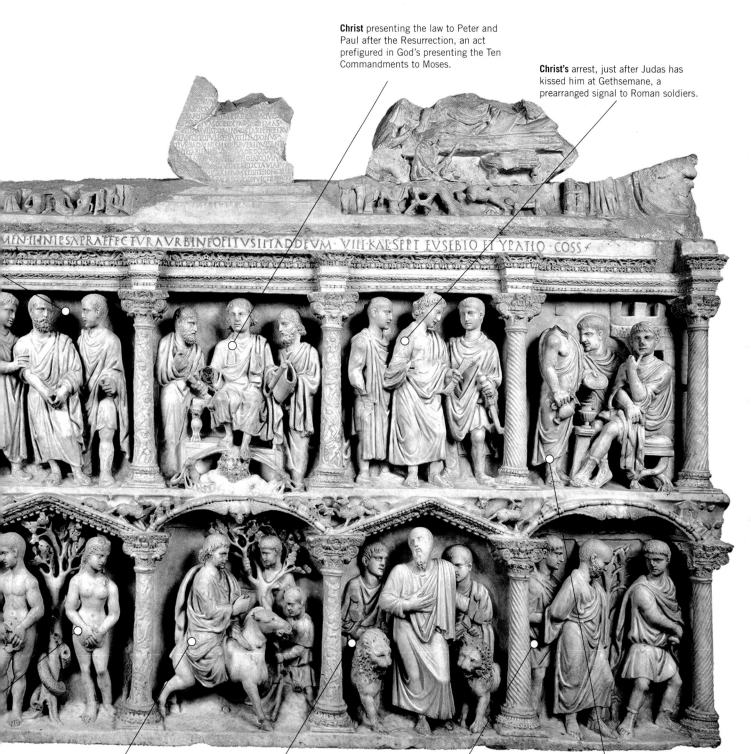

Christ presenting the law to Peter and Paul after the Resurrection, an act prefigured in God's presenting the Ten Commandments to Moses.

Christ's arrest, just after Judas has kissed him at Gethsemane, a prearranged signal to Roman soldiers.

Christ's triumphant entry into Jerusalem on Palm Sunday, a week before the Crucifixion.

Daniel in the lion's den where, because of his faithfulness to God, he was spared.

The arrest of **St. Paul**, who was later martyred for his beliefs in Rome.

Christ's trial before Pontius Pilate, charged with treason for calling himself King of the Jews. Pilate is shown here about to wash his hands, symbolizing his denial of responsibility for Jesus's death.

Peter's crucifixion and tomb in Rome (Figs. **4.6**, **4.7**). The church was as long, as high, and as wide as the Roman basilicas upon which it was modeled. It was approached up a set of stairs to a podium. Entering through a triple-arched gateway (reminiscent of Roman triumphal arches), visitors found themselves in a colonnaded atrium with a fountain in the center (reminiscent of the Roman *domus*, Fig. 3.21—perhaps suggesting the "House of God").

The church proper consisted of a **narthex**, or entrance hall, and a **nave**, with two aisles on each side. At the eastern end was an apse, housing the altar framed by a giant triumphal arch, where the sacrament of Holy Communion was performed. A transverse aisle, or **transept**, crossed between the nave and the apse; in other church plans it could be extended north and south to form a **Latin cross** (a long arm, the nave, with three shorter arms—the apse and the arms of the transept). The nave was two stories high, the aisles one story, allowing for a **clerestory**, a zone with windows that lit the length of the church. Open timber work tresses supported the roof (making the structure particularly susceptible to fire).

All in all, the basilica church was far more than an assembly hall. It was a richly decorated spiritual performance space, designed to elicit awe and wonder in its worshipers. As the liturgy was performed, as the congregation—consisting of lit-erally thousands—raised their voices together in song and then fell silent in prayer, the effect would have been stunning. No one, it was hoped, could leave without their faith re-energized.

A second type of Christian church also first developed in Rome, although it was initially conceived as a mausoleum for the daughter of Constantine, a devout Christian who died in 354. Santa Costanza [koh-STAN-zuh] is a **central plan church**, so called because of its circular structure, topped by a dome (Figs. **4.8**, **4.9**), reminiscent, actually, of the later Islamic shrine, the Dome of the Rock (see Fig. 4.1). The ambulatory is elaborately decorated with mosaics (Fig. **4.10**), consisting of an overall vine pattern interspersed with small scenes, such as laborers picking grapes and putting them into carts, transporting them to a press, and then crushing them underfoot. One of the Christian references here is to the use of wine in the Eucharist, symbolizing the blood of Christ. But the Dionysian implications of the scene, with its unruly swirls of undulating line—the very opposite of the Roman (and Classical) sense of order and proportion—are unmistakable. Used to decorate a church, these lines imply the very nature of faith—that is, the abandonment by faith of reason and logic, the very principles of Classical balance and proportion.

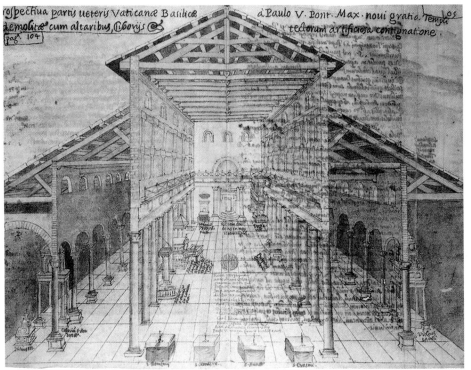

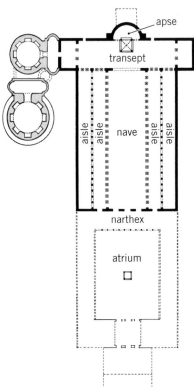

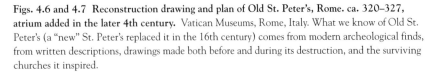

Figs. 4.6 and 4.7 Reconstruction drawing and plan of Old St. Peter's, Rome. ca. 320–327, atrium added in the later 4th century. Vatican Museums, Rome, Italy. What we know of Old St. Peter's (a "new" St. Peter's replaced it in the 16th century) comes from modern archeological finds, from written descriptions, drawings made both before and during its destruction, and the surviving churches it inspired.

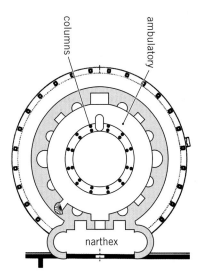

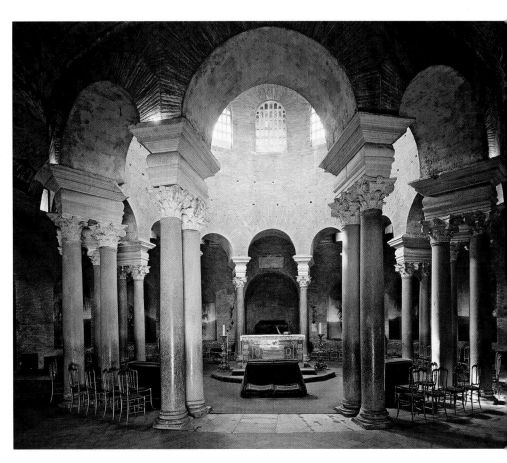

Figs. 4.8 and 4.9 Interior view and plan of the Church of Santa Costanza, Rome. ca. 350 CE. The view above is from the ambulatory into the central space. This is the earliest surviving central plan building in the world. Originally the central plan was used for mausoleums or shrines. Another central plan church very much like this one originally covered Christ's tomb in Jerusalem, but it was later incorporated into the basilica. The Church of Santa Costanza was originally attached to the now destroyed basilica of Saint Agnes Outside the Walls.

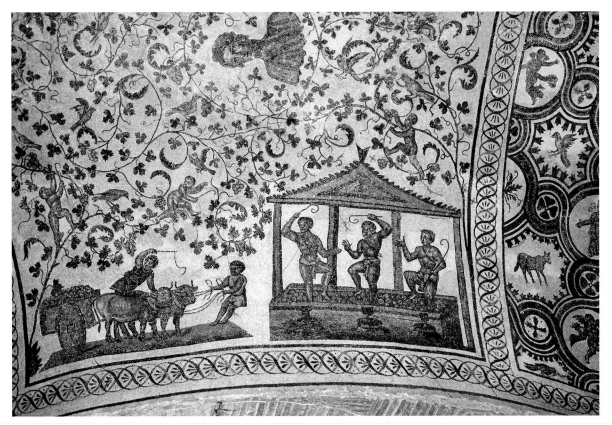

Fig. 4.10 Ambulatory vault mosaic, Church of Santa Costanza, Rome. ca. 350 CE. The figure at the top of this reproduction (which is actually positioned in the center of the volute motif) is probably Constantine's daughter Constantia herself.

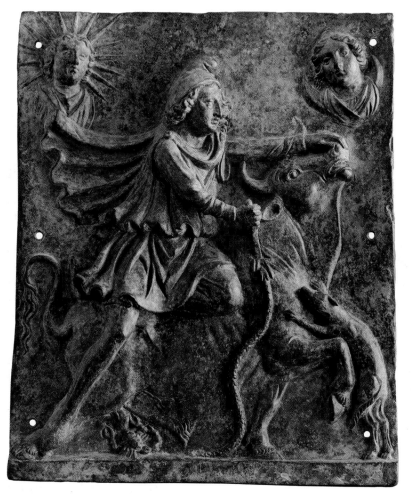

Fig. 4.11 Mithraic relief, early 3rd century. The Metropolitan Museum of Art. Gift of Mr. and Mrs. Klaus G. Peris, 1997 (1997.145.3). Image © The Metropolitan Museum of Art. Similar versions of this image have been found throughout the Roman Empire.

were secret, were also popular among the Romans, and Christianity borrowed freely from these as well. In a remarkable process of cross-fertilization, each cult adapted elements from the others.

The secret cult of Mithras [MITH-rus], which originated in Persia perhaps as far back as Neolithic times, became very popular among the Roman troops stationed in Palestine at the time of Christ. In the second through fourth centuries it spread across the Empire, and examples of its iconography can be found in Mithraic temples from Syria to Britain. Almost no texts explaining the cult survive; its rites and traditions were likely passed down orally among initiates. What we know of it comes from wall paintings and relief sculptures in its sanctuaries. In the most widespread of his representations, Mithras is depicted killing a bull by stabbing him in the neck, as a snake and dog lap up the bull's blood and a scorpion clutches the bull's testicles (Fig. **4.11**). The end of the bull's tail is metamorphosed into an ear of wheat. At the top left and right are busts of the sun and moon. Zoroastrian sources suggest that Mithras was sent to earth by a divine bull, and all living things sprang from the bull's blood. The story can be read as a reverse version of God's sacrifice of Jesus. Mithras sacrifices his "father"—or, at least, his divine ruler, the bull—in order to create life itself. The cult had seven stages of initiation, one of which was baptism. We also know that the birthday of Mithras was celebrated each year on December 25. When this date was adopted in about 350 CE as the traditional birth date of Jesus, the choice was most likely an attempt to appropriate the rites of Mithraic cults, then still active throughout the Roman Empire, to Christianity.

Augustine and Early Christian Philosophy: There is one other aspect of Mithras' cult that we also know—he was the god of truth and light. How much the Mithras cult influenced the Church Fathers is unclear, but light played an important role in their writing, and images of light appear often in the writings of early Christians. The Roman prelate Ambrose's "Ancient Morning Hymn," for instance, refers to God as the "Light of light, light's living spring." Perhaps the most important of the early Church Fathers, Augustine of Hippo (modern Annaba, Algeria), describes the moment of his conversion to Christianity as one in which he was infused with "the light of full certainty."

Augustine, who lived from 354 to 430 CE, was in his forties and had recently been made bishop of Hippo when he felt the need to come to terms with his past. He did this in the form of a prose work, the *Confessions*, the first Western autobiography. Augustine's storytelling is so compelling that the *Confessions* became one of the most influential books of the Middle Ages.

The design makes clear, in fact, the ways in which Christianity incorporated into itself many Greek and Roman mythic traditions—a practice known as **syncretism** [SIN-kruh-tiz-um], the reconciliation of different rites and practices into a single philosophy or religion. This occurred not only in the design of Christian churches but also in the symbolism of its art and literature—and it makes perfect sense. How better to convert pagan peoples than to present your religious program in their own terms? After all, the Greek wine god Dionysus had, like Christ, promised human immortality in the manner of the grapevine itself, which appears to die each autumn only to be reborn in the spring. Just as Christians had found prefigurings of Christ in the Hebrew Bible, it was possible to argue that Dionysus was a pagan type of Christ.

The cult of Bacchus, as the Romans referred to Dionysus, was extremely popular in Rome. So high-spirited were the drunken orgies engaged in by the cult of Dionysus that the Roman Senate had restricted its activities in 186 BCE. Other cults, known as **mystery cults** because their initiation rites

The frankness of Augustine's autobiographical self-assessment—for instance, he is not proud of the follies of his youth though he is clearly still fascinated by them—would also make it influential later, in the context of the general rediscovery of the self that defines the great awakening to awareness of the human body known as the Renaissance.

But the *Confessions* is also a profoundly religious treatise that became influential on the merits of its religious arguments as well as its narrative power. For Augustine, humankind is capable of understanding true ideas only when they are illuminated by the soul of God. He adds to the Platonic emphasis on pure ideas a Christian belief in the sacred word of God, in which God's "light" is understood to shine. In the *Confessions*, too, Augustine codified the idea of typological readings of the Bible, proposing, for example, Eve, the biological mother of humanity, as a type for Mary, the spiritual mother. Similarly, he saw the deliverance of the Israelites from Egypt as a prefiguration of the redemption of Jesus.

Augustine was a prolific writer and thinker and a renowned teacher. One of his most important works is *The City of God*, written between 413 and 425 (**Reading 4.3**). It is a reinterpretation of history from a theological point of view. In many ways, the book was a response to the sack of Rome by the Visigoths in 410. What had happened to the once powerful empire that had controlled the world, in a common phrase, "to its very edge"? How had such a disaster come to pass? Augustine attempts to answer these questions.

Many Romans blamed the Christians for the city's downfall, but Augustine argued, to the contrary, that pagan religion and philosophy, and particularly the hubris, or arrogance, of the emperors in assuming to be divine had doomed Rome from the beginning. Even more to the point, Augustine argued that the fall of Rome was inevitable, since the city was a product of humankind, and thus corrupt and mortal. Even a Christian Rome was inevitably doomed. History was a forward movement—at least in a spiritual sense—to the Day of Judgment, a movement from the earthly city, with its secular ways, to the heavenly city, untouched by worldly concerns:

READING 4.3   **from Augustine, *The City of God***

The two cities were created by two kinds of love: the earthly city by a love of self even to the point of contempt for God, the heavenly city by a love of God carried even to the point of contempt for self. Consequently, the earthly city glories in itself while the heavenly city glories in the Lord. . . . In the one, the lust for dominion has dominion over its princes as well as over the nations it subdues; in the other, both those put in charge and those placed under them serve one another in love, the former by their counsel, the latter by their obedience. . . .

Augustine's worldview is essentially dualistic, composed of two parts. In his writings the movement of history (and of life itself) follows a linear progression from darkness to light, from body to soul, from evil to goodness, from doubt to faith, and from blindness to understanding. His own life story, as described in *Confessions*, revealed him as the sinner saved. He saw himself, in fact, as a *type* for all Christians, whose ultimate place, he believed, would one day be the City of God.

The Byzantine Empire and Its Church

Constantine had built his new capital at Constantinople in 325 CE in no small part because Rome was too vulnerable to attack from Germanic tribes. Located on a highly defensible peninsula, Constantinople was far less susceptible to threat, and indeed, while Rome finally collapsed after successive Germanic invasions in 476, Constantinople would serve as the center of Christian culture throughout the early Middle Ages, surviving until 1453 when Ottoman Turks finally succeeded in overrunning it.

In Constantine's Constantinople, Christian basilicas stood next to Roman baths, across from a Roman palace and senate, the former connected to a Roman hippodrome, an entertainment complex for horse and chariot races. All but the basilicas were elaborately decorated with pagan art gathered from across the Empire. Christians soon developed an important new understanding of these pagan works: They could ignore their pagan elements and think of them simply as *art*. This was the argument of Basil the Great (ca. 329–379), the major theologian of the day. In his twenties he had studied the classics of Greek literature in Athens and had fallen in love with them. He believed it was possible to understand them as literature, not theology, as great works of art, not as arguments for the existence of pagan gods.

Pagan practices gave way to Christian doctrine. Constantine himself outlawed pagan sacrifices, and though the emperor Julian the Apostate (r. 361–363) briefly attempted to reinstate paganism, by the time of Theodosius [the-uh-DOE-she-us] I's rule (379–395), all pagan temples were closed throughout the Empire, and Christianity was the official religion. However, Roman law, not Biblical law, remained the norm in Byzantine culture; schools taught Classical Greek texts, especially Homer's *Iliad*; and important writers still modeled their work on Classical precedents. Nevertheless, by the middle of the sixth century, the emperor Justinian closed the Academy of Athens, the last pagan school of philosophy in the Empire, and over 100 churches and monasteries stood in Constantinople alone.

Justinian's Empire

After Rome collapsed in 476, Odoacer, a Germanic leader, named himself king of Italy (r. 476–493), which he governed from the northern Italian city of Ravenna. Finally, the Ostrogothic ("Eastern Gothic") king Theodoric the Great overthrew Odoacer in 493 and ruled Italy until 526. The Byzantine emperors tolerated Theodoric's rule in Italy largely because he was

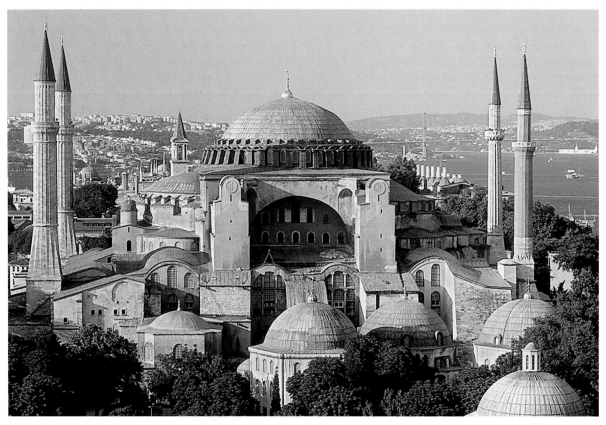

Fig. 4.12 Hagia Sophia, Istanbul (formerly Constantinople). 532–537. Originally dedicated to Christ as the personification of Holy (*hagia*) Wisdom (*sophia*), Muslim conquerors transformed the cathedral into a mosque in 1453. Today, it serves as a museum, although it remains one of the oldest religious sanctuaries in the world.

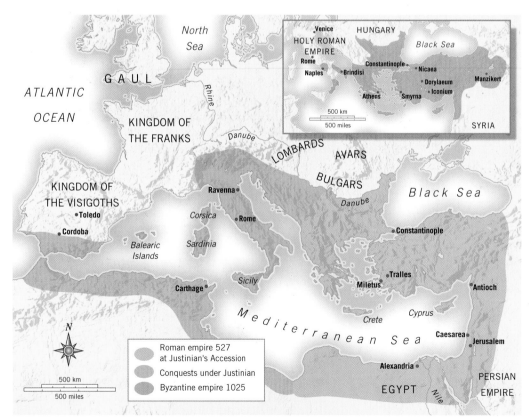

Map 4.3 The Byzantine Empire at the death of Justinian in 565 and in 1025. The insert shows the Empire nearly 500 years after Justinian's reign, in 1025. Although it had shrunk in size, the Byzantine Empire remained a powerful force in the Eastern Mediterranean throughout the Middle Ages.

Christian and had been raised in the imperial palace in Constantinople. But after a new young emperor, Justinian (r. 527–565), assumed the Byzantine throne, things quickly changed. Justinian launched a massive campaign to rebuild Constantinople, including the construction of a giant new Hagia Sophia (Fig. **4.12**) at the site of the old one when the latter was burned to the ground in 532 by rioting civic "clubs"—that probably were more like modern "gangs." The riots briefly caused Justinian to consider abandoning Constantinople, but his queen, Theodora [the-oh-DOR-uh], persuaded him to stay: "If you wish to save yourself, O Emperor," she is reported to have counseled, "that is easy. For we have much money, there is the sea, here are the boats. But think whether after you have been saved you may not come to feel that you would have preferred to die." Justinian may well have begun construction of the new Hagia Sophia to divert attention from the domestic turmoil stirred up by the warring gangs. And he may have conceived his imperial adventuring to serve the same end (Map **4.3**). In 535, he retook North Africa from the Visigoths, and a year later he launched a campaign, headed by his general Belisarius, to retake Italy from the successors of Theodoric. But through his massive building program, especially, Justinian aimed to assert not only his political leadership but his spiritual authority as well. His rule was divine, as his divine works underscored.

Hagia Sophia Procopius [pruh-KOH-pee-us] of Caesarea (ca. 490–ca. 560), Justinian's official court historian, wrote a treatise, *On Justinian's Buildings*, celebrating the emperor's building campaign. Book I is dedicated to the new Hagia Sophia (Fig. **4.13**) that Justinian erected on the site of the one that had burned down. As a result of Procopius's writings, we know a great deal about the building itself, including the identity of its architects, two mathematicians named Isidorus of Miletus and Anthemius of Tralles. Isidorus had edited the works of Archimedes, the third-century BCE geometrician who established the theory of the lever in mechanics, and both he and Anthemius had made studies of parabolas and curved surfaces. Their deep understanding of mathematics and physics is evident in their plan for Hagia Sophia.

Their completely original design (Fig. **4.14**) consisted of a giant dome on a square base, the thrust of the dome carried on four giant arches that make up each side of the

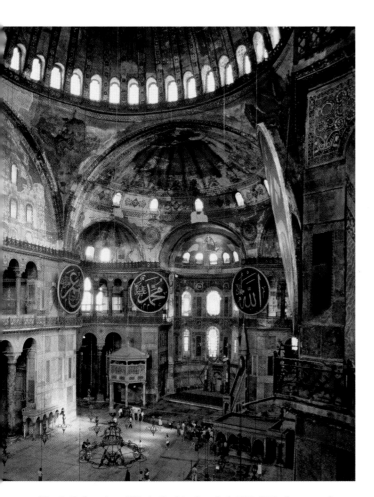

Fig. 4.13 Interior of Hagia Sophia, Istanbul. 532–537. So vast is the central dome of the church that it was likened, in its own time, to the dome of heaven. It was said that to look up at the dome from below was akin to experiencing the divine order of the cosmos.

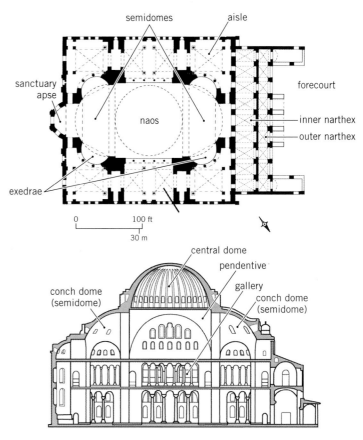

Fig. 4.14 Anthemius of Tralles and Isidorus of Miletus. Plan and section of Hagia Sophia, Istanbul. 532–537.

square. Between these arches are triangular curving vault sections, called **pendentives**, that spring from the corners of the base. The dome that rises from these pendentives has around its base 40 windows, creating a circle of light that makes the dome appear to float above the naos, underscoring its symbolic function as the dome of heaven. The sheer height of the dome adds to this effect—it is 184 feet high (41 feet higher than the Pantheon), and 112 feet in diameter. In his treatise *Justinian's Buildings*, Procopius describes the central domed section of the church (**Reading 4.4**):

READING 4.4   **from Procopius, *On Justinian's Buildings* (ca. 537)**

So the church has been made a spectacle of great beauty, stupendous to those who see it and altogether incredible to those who hear of it. . . . It abounds exceedingly in gleaming sunlight. You might say that the [interior] space is not illuminated by the sun from the outside, but that the radiance is generated within, so great an abundance of light bathes this shrine all round. In the middle of the church there rise four man-made eminences which are called piers, two on the north and two on the south, each pair having between them exactly four columns. The eminences are built to a great height. As you see them, you could suppose them to be precipitous mountain peaks. Upon these are placed four arches so as to form a square, their ends coming together in pairs and made fast at the summit of those piers, while the rest of them rise to an immense height. Two of the arches, namely those facing the rising and setting sun, are suspended over empty air, while the others have beneath them some kind of structure and rather tall columns. Above the arches the construction rises in a circle. Rising above this circle is an enormous spherical dome which makes the building exceptionally beautiful. It seems not to be founded on solid masonry, but to be suspended from heaven by that golden chain and so covers the space.

Procopius does not mention that to the east and west, beneath the arches, are conch domes, or half domes, semicircular structures that spread out from a central dome, extending the space, and that these in turn are punctuated by yet smaller conch domes. Thus, a succession of curving spaces draw the visitor's eyes both upward to the symbolically heavenly space of the dome and forward to the sanctuary apse, seat of the altar and the liturgy. The intricate and lacy carving on the lower levels lends the stonework an almost immaterial lightness. The domes above are believed to have been covered with mosaics, probably consisting in the sixth century of plain gold grounds ornamented with crosses. Light from the windows around the base of the dome and conch domes would have ricocheted around the gold-covered interior, creating the magical, even celestial light that Procopius describes.

St. Catherine's Monastery Justinian was not content merely to rebuild Constantinople. Bridges, roads, aqueducts, monuments, churches, and monasteries sprang up around the Empire. Not the least important of these sixth-century works was the fortress and monastery known as St. Catherine's, at the foot of Mount Sinai [SY-nye], in the desert near the tip of the Sinai Peninsula, in modern Egypt. It was at Mount Sinai that, according to the Old Testament, God gave Moses the Ten Commandments. The monastery was sited on the spot of the burning bush, where tradition held that God had first addressed Moses and instructed him to go to Egypt and lead the Jews to the Promised Land. Thus, the monastery had great symbolic significance.

Especially important to Justinian's architectural program were the decorative embellishments—**icons**, or images— that his artists added to Church interiors. Among the earliest examples of icons are a set of paintings on wooden panels from St. Catherine's, among them a *Theotokos* [the-OT-uh-kus] *and*

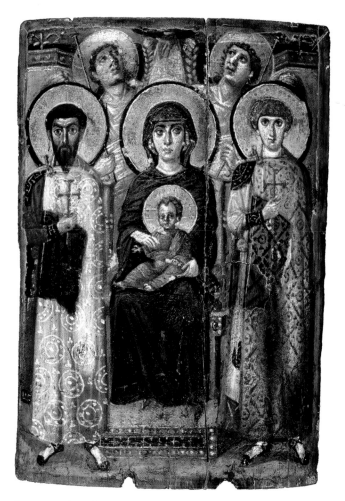

Fig. 4.15 *Theotokos and Child with Saint Theodore and Saint George.* **6th century.** Encaustic on board, 27″ × 19³/₄″. Monastery of St. Catherine, Mount Sinai. Byzantine culture rarely, if ever, referred to Mary as "the Virgin." Instead she was rather the *Theotokos,* the "Mother of God."

Child (Fig. **4.15**). *Theotokos* means "God-bearing," an epithet defining Mary as the Mother of God, an official Byzantine Church view after 431. If Mary is the mother of Jesus, the Church argued, and if Jesus is God, then Mary is the Mother of God. Such images, and the doctrine associated with them, were expected to stir the viewer to prayer. Mary's eyes are averted from the viewer's, but the Christ Child, like the two military saints, Theodore (left) and George, who flank the central pair, looks straight out. The two angels behind raise their eyes to the sky, down from which God's hand descends in blessing. The words of the sixth-century Byzantine poet Agathias (ca. 536–582) are useful here: "The mortal man who beholds the image directs his mind to a higher contemplation. . . . The eyes encourage deep thoughts, and art is able by means of colors to ferry over the prayer of the mind." Thus the icon was in some sense a vessel of prayer directed to the saint and, given her military escort, must have offered the viewer her protection.

But such imagery soon became the focus of controversy. The sudden rise of Islam as a powerful military force had a chilling effect on Byzantine art. The Byzantine emperor Leo III (r. 717–741), who came to power during the second Muslim siege of Constantinople, began to formulate a position opposing the use of holy images. He understood that the Muslims, who were still regarded as Christian heretics, had barred images from their mosques, and, so the logic went, their military successes against the Byzantine Empire were a sign both of God's approval of their religious practice and disapproval of Byzantium's. Like the Muslims, Leo argued that God had prohibited religious images in the Ten Commandments—"Thou shalt not make any graven image, or any likeness of any thing that is in heaven above, or that is in the earth beneath, or that is in the water under the earth: Thou shalt not bow down thyself to them nor serve them" (Exodus 20:4–5). Therefore, anyone worshiping such images was an idolater and was offending God. The solution was to ban images.

Thus was inaugurated a program of **iconoclasm**, from the Greek *eikon* ("icon" or "image") and *klao* (to "break" or "destroy"), the practice of destroying religious images. While iconoclasts like Leo III set out to destroy religious images, iconophiles ("lovers of images") defended their use, usually in terms very similar to those expressed by the poet Agathias quoted above. But whatever position one assumed, the artistic style of the icons was employed in almost every form of artistic endeavor.

Byzantine icons employed a standardized shorthand. It is as if their artistic vocabulary consisted of a limited repertoire of feet, hands, robes, and faces, all of which could be used over and over again in any context, the most important figure being the largest. We call this style, which is at once formally abstract and priestly, **hieratic**.

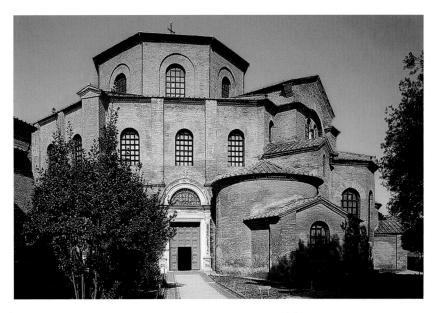

Fig. 4.16 Exterior of San Vitale, Ravenna. Dedicated 547. Like most Byzantine churches, San Vitale is a study in contrasts. The exterior is exceedingly plain. (The decorated doorway is a later addition.) But inside, the elaborate decoration symbolizes the richness of the spiritual world.

The Art of Ravenna The most extensive examples of Byzantine art and this hieratic style survive in Ravenna [ruh-VEN-uh], a relatively small city in northern Italy near the Adriatic [ay-dree-AT-ik] Sea. There Justinian's new Orthodox clergy oversaw the construction of the church of San Vitale [ve-TAHL-eh], a unique central plan building, similar to Santa Costanza [koh-STAHN-zuh] in Rome (see Figs. 4.8, 4.9), but octagonal in design rather than circular (Fig. **4.16**). On seven of its eight sides, the central space opens out into semicircular bays or niches called **exedrae** [EK-suh-dree], which themselves open, through a triple arcade, to the ambulatory. On the eighth side, the bay extends into a rectangular sanctuary and apse. The narthex (entrance hall), which has long since disappeared, was a lozenge-shaped space set at an angle to the church itself. Entering from the double doors, the visitor has two options. One is to wander through into the exedrae spaces, seeing a complex pattern of curves, niches, columns, and mosaics. The other is to go directly across the central space to the sanctuary and apse, which rose two stories to a conch dome, gorgeously decorated with intricately interwoven vines and animals in a predominantly gold and green mosaic.

On the side walls of the apse, level with the windows, are two mosaics, one featuring the emperor Justinian (Fig. **4.17**) and the other the empress Theodora (Fig. **4.18**). The emperor and empress lead retinues of courtiers toward the back of the apse. Possibly they proceeded toward reunion with Christ in paradise, as depicted in the conch-dome mosaic of the apse. A haloed Justinian carries a paten, the plate on which the bread is placed in

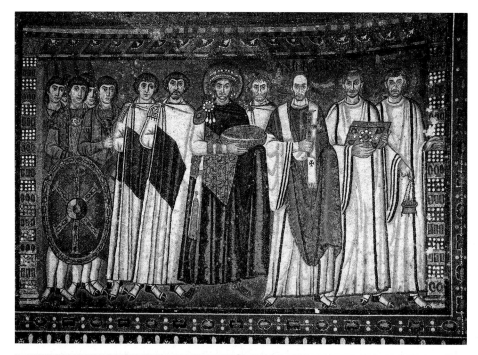

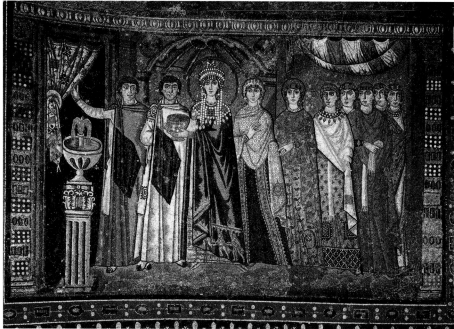

Figs. 4.17 and 4.18 (top) *Emperor Justinian with Maximian, Clergy, Courtiers, and Soldiers*; and (bottom) *Empress Theodora with Courtiers and Ladies of Her Court*; both wall mosaics, San Vitale, Ravenna. ca. 547. Standing between and behind Justinian and Maximian is Julianus Argentarius, the benefactor of the church.

The most intriguing aspect of the two mosaics, however, is their composition. Even though Theodora, for instance, stands before a scalloped half-dome niche and the attendant to her right pulls back a curtain as if to reveal the space beyond, these mosaics do not represent a view into a natural world extending back toward a distant horizon (compare Fig. 3.24). Rather, Byzantine artists conceived of space as extending forward from the picture plane, with parallel lines converging on the eye of the beholder. This technique, known as **reverse perspective**, makes objects appear to tip upward—note the top of the fountain to Theodora's right—and elongates and heightens figures. Human eyesight, Byzantine artists believed, is imperfect and untrustworthy, a fact demonstrated by the apparent decrease in the size of objects as they recede in the distance. By depicting objects in reverse perspective and in shallow space, Byzantine artists rejected earthly illusion, privileging the sacred space of the image over the mundane space of the viewer.

The Rise and Spread of Islam

The iconoclastic controversy that swept the Byzantine Empire in the seventh and eighth centuries was a direct result of the increasing influence of Islam on the Mediterranean world. Mecca, the holiest city of Islam, is located about 50 miles inland from the Red Sea on the Arabian peninsula in modern Saudi Arabia (see Map 4.2). There, in about 570, the prophet Muhammad was born to a prominent family that traced its ancestry back to Ishmael,

the celebration of the Eucharist [YOO-kuh-rist]. On the other side of the apse, the empress holds a chalice of wine for the Eucharist, and on the bottom of her robe are the Three Magi, who like her come bearing gifts to the Virgin and Child. These mosaics possess a distinct political agenda, serving as propaganda to remind the faithful of the emperor's divine authority—the union of the political and spiritual spheres.

son of Abraham. Orphaned at age six and receiving little formal education, Muhammad worked in the desert caravan trade, first as a camel driver for his uncle, and then, after marrying a wealthy widow 15 years his senior, as head of his wife's flourishing caravan firm. At the age of 40, in 610, he heard a voice in Arabic—the Archangel Gabriel's, as the story goes—urging him, "Recite!" He responded "What shall I recite?" And for the next 22 years, he claimed to receive messages, or "recitations," from God through the agency of Gabriel. These he memorized and dictated to scribes, who collected them to form the scriptures of Islam, the **Qur'an** [kuh-RAN] (or Koran), which means "recitations." Muhammad also claimed that Gabriel commanded him to declare himself the "Seal of the Prophets," that is, the messenger of the one and only Allah (the Arab word for God) and the final prophet in a series of prophets extending from Abraham and Moses to Jesus.

At the core of Muhammad's revelations is the concept of submission to God—the word *Islam*, in fact, means "submission" or "surrender." God, or Allah, is all—all-powerful, all-seeing, all-merciful. Because the universe is his creation, it is necessarily good and beautiful, and the natural world reflects Allah's own goodness and beauty. To immerse oneself in nature is thus to be at one with God. But the most beautiful creation of Allah is humankind, which God made in his own image. Like Christians, Muslims believe that human beings possess immortal souls and that they can live eternally in heaven if they surrender to Allah and accept him as the one and only God.

Muslims, or practitioners of Islam, dedicate themselves to the "five pillars" of the religion:

1. **Shahadah:** The repetition of the *shahadah* [sha-HAH-dah], or "creed," which consists of a single sentence, "There is no God but Allah; Muhammad is the messenger of Allah."
2. **Prayer:** The practice of daily prayer, recited facing Mecca, five times each day, at dawn, midday, mid-afternoon, sunset, and nightfall, and the additional requirement for all men to gather for a noon prayer and sermon on Fridays.
3. **Alms:** The habit of giving alms to the poor and needy, consisting of at least one-fortieth of a Muslim's assets and income.
4. **Fasting:** During the lunar month of Ramadan (which, over a 33-year period, will occur in every season of the year), the ritual obligation to fast by abstaining from food, drink, medicine, tobacco, and sexual intercourse from sunrise to sundown each day.
5. **Hajj:** At least once in every Muslim's life, in the twelfth month of the Muslim calendar, the undertaking of a pilgrimage (called the **hajj**) to Mecca.

The five pillars are supported by the teachings of the Qur'an, which, slightly shorter than the New Testament, consists of 114 *surahs* [SOO-rahs], or chapters, each numbered but more commonly referred to by their titles. Each begins, as do most Muslim texts, with the **bismillah** [bees-MEEL-lah], a sacred invocation that can be translated "In the name of Allah, the Beneficent, Ever-Merciful." When, after Muhammad's death in 632, the Qur'an's text was established in its definitive form, the 114 *surahs* were arranged from the longest to the shortest. Thus, the first *surah* contains 287 *ayas* [ay-YAS], or verses, while the last consists of only three. The mandatory ritual prayer (*salat*) [sah-LAAT] that is performed five times a day consists of verses from *surahs* 2, 4, and 17.

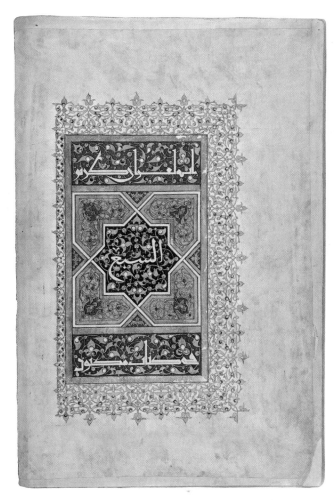

Fig. 4.19 Left page of double frontispiece to volume VII of the Qur'an of Baybars Jashnagir, from Egypt. 1304–1306. Illuminated manuscript, 18½" × 12½". British Library, London. The most elaborate Qur'ans, such as this one, were financed by endowments created by wealthy individuals in support of a mosque and attendant buildings.

The Qur'an

The Qur'an is a work of poetry, and in pre-Islamic Arabia, poetry was the highest form of art. Poets recited their own works, or professional reciters performed the works of others. The beauty of the poetry inspired the creation of many beautiful editions of the work (Fig. **4.19**) and, as we shall see, the art of calligraphy. But unfortunately, the beautiful, melodic qualities of the Arabic language are completely lost in translation, a fact that has helped to inspire generations of non–Arabic-speaking Muslims to learn the language. Almost all Muslims regularly read the Qur'an in Arabic, and many have memorized it completely. Translations of the Qur'an are problematic on another, more important level. Since the Qur'an is believed to be the direct word of God, it cannot be modified, let alone translated—a translation of the Qur'an is no longer the Qur'an. Nevertheless, something of the power of the poem's imagery can be understood in translation. Consider a passage describing paradise from the seventy-sixth *surah*, known as "Time" (**Reading 4.5**):

READING 4.5 **from the Qur'an, *Surah* 76**

76.11 Therefore Allah will guard them from the evil of that day and cause them to meet with ease and happiness;

76.12 And reward them, because they were patient, with garden and silk,

76.13 Reclining therein on raised couches, they shall find therein neither (the severe heat of) the sun nor intense cold.

76.14 And close down upon them (shall be) its shadows, and its fruits shall be made near (to them), being easy to reach.

76.15 And there shall be made to go round about them vessels of silver and goblets which are of glass,

76.16 (Transparent as) glass, made of silver; they have measured them according to a measure.

76.17 And they shall be made to drink therein a cup the admixture of which shall be ginger,

76.18 (Of) a fountain therein which is named Salsabil [sal-sa-BEEL].

76.19 And round about them shall go youths never altering in age; when you see them you will think them to be scattered pearls.

76.20 And when you see there, you shall see blessings and a great kingdom.

76.21 Upon them shall be garments of fine green silk and thick silk interwoven with gold, and they shall be adorned with bracelets of silver, and their Lord shall make them drink a pure drink.

76.22 Surely this is a reward for you, and your striving shall be recompensed.

This vision of paradise addresses all the senses—touch, taste, and smell (the fruit so "easy to reach," the drink of ginger), sight ("when you see there, you shall see blessings"), and sound (in the very melody of the verse itself). All is transformed into riches. Even the young people in attendance will appear to be "scattered pearls."

The *Hadith*

In addition to the Qur'an, another important source of Islamic tradition is the **hadith** [ha-DEET], meaning "narrative" or "report," which consists of sayings of Muhammad and anecdotes about his life. The *hadith* literature was handed down orally, as was common in Arab society until about 100 years

after Muhammad's death, when followers began to write the sayings down (**Reading 4.6**).

READING 4.6 **from the *Hadith***

"Actions are but by intention and every man shall have but that which he intended."

"None of you [truly] believes until he wishes for his brother what he wishes for himself."

"Get to know Allah in prosperity and He will know you in adversity. Know that what has passed you by was not going to befall you; and that what has befallen you was not going to pass you by. And know that victory comes with patience, relief with affliction, and ease with hardship."

"If you feel no shame, then do as you wish."

"Everyone starts his day and is a vendor of his soul, either freeing it or bringing about its ruin."

"O My servants, it is but your deeds that I reckon up for you and then recompense you for, so let him who finds good [i.e., in the hereafter] praise Allah, and let him who finds other than that blame no one but himself."

"Renounce the world and Allah will love you, and renounce what people possess and people will love you."

The *Hijra* and Muslim Practice

In 622, Muhammad was forced to flee Mecca when its polytheistic leadership became irritated at his insistence on the worship of only one God. In a journey known as the **hijra** [HIJ-rah] (or *hegira*, "emigration"), he and his followers fled to the oasis of Yathrib [YA-trub], 200 miles north, which they renamed al-Medina, meaning "the city of the Prophet." Here Muhammad created a community based not on kinship, the traditional basis of Arab society, but on common submission to the will of God. Such submission did not need to be entirely voluntary. Muslims were obligated to pursue the spread of their religion, and they did so by means of the **jihad** [jee-HAAD], the impassioned religious struggle that could take either of two forms: a lesser form, holy war; or a greater form, self-control over the baser human appetites. In order to enforce submission, Muhammad raised an army of some 10,000 men and returned to Mecca, conquering the city.

It was especially important for Mohammad to return to Mecca because it was the site of the Kaaba [KAAH-buh], literally "cube" (Fig. **4.20**). Built with a bluish gray stone from the hills surrounding Mecca, it is now usually covered with a black curtain. The Kaaba also held a sacred Black Stone, probably a meteorite, which reportedly "fell from heaven." To this day, practitioners of the Muslim faith from all over the world face toward the Kaaba when they pray. They believe it is their place of origin, the site of the first "house of God," built at God's command by the biblical Abraham and his son

Ishmael, the ancestors of all Muslims, on the spot where Abraham, in Islamic tradition, prepared to sacrifice his son Ishmael (not Isaac, as in the Christian tradition). Thus, walking around the Kaaba is a key ritual in the Muslim pilgrimage to Mecca, the *hajj*, for the cube represents the physical center of the planet and the universe. It is the physical center of Muslim life, around which all things turn and to which all things in the universe are connected, symbolic of the cosmos itself.

Muhammad's new community, known as the *Umma* [OOM-mah], was such a departure from tradition that its creation required a new calendar. Based on lunar cycles, the Muslim year is about 11 days shorter than the Christian year, resulting in a difference of about three years per century. The calendar began in 622 CE. Thus, in the year 2007, the Muslims celebrated the start of their year 1428.

The Mosque At Medina, Muhammad built a house that surrounded a large, open courtyard, which served as a community gathering place, on the model of the Roman forum. There the men of the community would gather on Fridays to pray and listen to a sermon delivered by Muhammad. It thus became known as the *masjid* [mahs-JEED], the Arabic word for **mosque**, or "place of prostration." On the north and south ends of the courtyard, covered porches supported by palm tree trunks and roofed by thatched palm fronds protected the community from the hot Arabian sun. This many-columned covered area, known as a **hypostyle** space (from the Greek *hupostulos* [hye-pos-TOO-lus], "resting upon pillars"), would later become a required feature of all Muslim mosques. Another required feature was the *qibla* [KIB-lah], a wall that indicated the direction of Mecca. On this wall were both the *minbar* [MIN-bur], or stepped pulpit for the preacher, and the *mihrab* [meeh-RAAB], a niche commemorating the spot at Medina where Muhammad planted his lance to indicate the direction in which people should pray.

Women in Islam Although Muslim practice today varies widely, in Muhammad's time women were welcome in the mosque. In the Qur'an, Muhammad teaches that women and men are equal partners: "The faithful men and the faithful women are protecting friends for each other" (*Surah* 9:7). The husband's honor becomes an integral part of his wife's honor, and vice versa. They share equally in each other's prosperity and adversity. But Muhammad further allowed for Muslim men to have up to four wives, provided that they treated all justly and gave each equal attention. (Polygamy was widely practiced in the Arab world at the time, and marrying the widow of a deceased comrade, for instance, was understood to be an act of protective charity.) Muhammad himself—and subsequently other prophets as well—was exempt from the four-wife limitation. Although he had only one wife for 28 years, after she died when he was 53, he

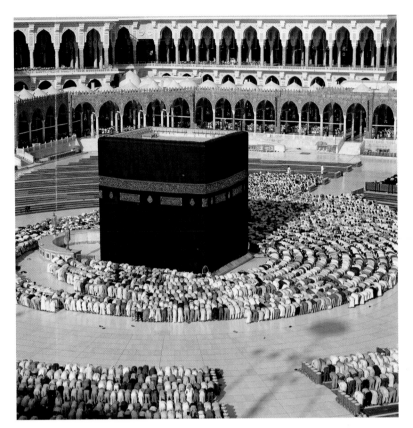

Fig. 4.20 The *Kaaba*, center of the Haram Mosque, Mecca. Scholars believe that the original Kaaba was linked to the astronomical year, containing an array of 360 idols, representing various Arab gods, each associated with seasonal rituals and the passing of the days and months. Muhammad destroyed these idols when he conquered Mecca.

married at least 10 other women. The Qur'an describes the wives of Muhammad—and by extension, the wives of all Muslim men—as "Mothers of the Faithful" whose duty was the education of the *umma*'s children. They helped them along their spiritual path, transmitting and explaining the teaching of Muhammad in all spheres of life.

One of the most discussed and most controversial aspects of Muslim faith (even among Muslims) is the **hajib** [hih-JUHB], literally "curtain," the requirement that women be covered or veiled. Its origins can be traced to Islam's Jewish heritage and the principle of *tzenuit* [dzen-WEET], which in Hebrew means "modesty" in both dress and behavior and which requires, among other strictures, that all married women cover their hair whenever non–family members are present. Islamic covering ranges from a simple scarf covering the hair to the **chador** [sha-DOHR], which covers the wearer from head to toe, leaving only her hands and her face (or part of her face) exposed. This full covering is currently popular, especially in Iran. Interestingly, the Qur'an is not explicit about the covering. Women are advised to dress in a way that enables them to avoid harassment by not drawing attention to their beauty, or *zinat* [ZEE-nat], a word that means both physical beauty and material adornment in Arabic. The basic instruction expressed in the Qur'an is for Muslims to act modestly and dress modestly, a rule that applies to men and women.

The Art of Calligraphy The Arabic language has 28 distinctive sounds, but only 18 letterforms. As a result, the same letter has to be used to represent a variety of sounds—for instance, the same letterform is used to represent the sounds *ba, ta, tha, nun,* and *ya* [baa, taa, thaa, noon, and yaa]. And the letterforms themselves are variable, changing according to whether they stand alone or occur at the beginning, middle, or end of a word. This can cause confusion for readers, who must decide what is being said from context. Confusion is not acceptable for the word of God as transmitted in the Qur'an. Thus, when the Umayyad caliph Abd al-Malik took control of the Islamic world, he introduced a series of marks to help distinguish between the different sounds that share the same letterform. For instance, *ba* consisted of the letterform with two lines above it, *ya* by two strokes under it, and so on. (Over time, these strokes would become shortened into dots.)

Written from right to left, like Hebrew, Arabic script is entirely cursive—that is, "flowing," often with the strokes of successive characters joined and the angles rounded. As a result, it is highly susceptible to artful treatment. The art of producing artistic, stylized writing is called **calligraphy**. The beauty of Islamic calligraphy depends on how the letters are shaped and connected and on the unity of the composition as a whole. Unlike most Western art, which presumes a single focal point, every part of a work of Islamic calligraphy should have equal value. The decoration should harmonize with the text. Consider the page showing the heading for chapter 18 of the Qur'an, "The Cave" (Fig. **4.21**). The chapter heading is written in richly bordered gold, beginning with a fanciful leaf form that extends into the margin. The first lines of the chapter follow in black. The distinction between chapter heading and text indicates that the former is not part of the "received" message of God, but a conventional name for the verse. The flow of the calligraphy, the rhythmic pattern of horizontal and vertical elements, creates a sense of abstract design that is independent of the meaning of the words.

Because Arabic, as the language of divine revelation, was believed to have a sacred nature, writing, too, was thought to have a divinely inspired power. Thus, in Islamic culture, writing—especially calligraphy—developed into the preeminent form of visual art. It is a form that required knowledge of different scripts and took years of training, with instruction passing from master to student through the practice of imitating the work of the master.

The Spread of Islam

Following the death of the Prophet in 632, the **caliphs** [KAY-lifs], or successors to Muhammad, assumed political and religious authority, and Islam spread with a rapidity that is almost unimaginable (see Map 4.2). Damascus fell to the caliphs in 634, Persia in 636, Jerusalem in 638, and Egypt in 640. By 710, all of North Africa and Spain were under Muslim rule.

The speed of the conquest can be partially accounted for by the fact that the Byzantine and Persian empires were exhausted by a long war. Most of the peoples in these territories, although Christian, were of the same linguistic and ethnic background as their new Muslim conquerors. Furthermore, the brand of Greek Orthodox Christianity that the Byzantine rulers had imposed on them was far too conservative for many. From Persia to Egypt, many peoples accepted their Muslim conquerors as preferable to the Byzantine rulers who had preceded them.

The successes of Islam must also be attributed to its appeal both as a religion and as a form of social organization. It denied neither Judaism nor Christianity, but merely superseded them. As opposed to the Jewish faith, which was founded on a common ethnic identity, Islam opened its arms to any and all comers—a feature it shared with Christianity. But unlike Christianity, it did not draw any special distinction between the clergy and the laity. It brought people together in the mosque, which served as a community meetinghouse, courthouse, council chamber, military complex, and administrative center. Traders naturally migrated to it, as did poets, artists, and scholars. In fact, the mosque was closer in function to the Classical agora than to the Christian tabernacle. The sense of community that the mosque inspired played a central role in the spread of Islam.

By the eleventh century, *madrasas* [MAD-ra-sas], or teaching colleges, were attached to the mosques, and mosques became centers of learning as well. Here students studied the Qur'an, the *hadith*, and Islamic law, as well as mathematics, poetry, and astronomy. The *madrasas* eventually contributed to the rise of an intellectual elite, the *ulama* [OO-la-mah] (people possessing "correct knowledge"), a group that functioned more or less in the manner of Christian priests or Jewish rabbis. Yet

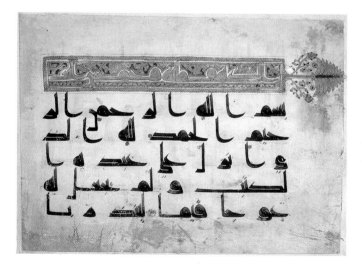

Fig. 4.21 Page from the Qur'an, with six lines of text showing heading from *Surah 18, Surat al-Kahf* ("The Cave"), from Syria. Ninth or tenth century. Ink and gold on parchment, $7\frac{1}{4}" \times 10\frac{1}{4}"$. © The Trustees of the Chester Beatty Library, Dublin. Parchment manuscripts of the Qur'an were sometimes bound together in leather covers or stored as loose leaves in boxes.

any man of great religious learning could serve as an *alim* [AA-lum] (the singular form of *ulama*), and *ulama* had the singular role of overseeing the rulers of Islam, guaranteeing that they followed the letter of the law as stated in the Qur'an.

Islamic Africa The Muslim impact on the culture of North Africa cannot be overstated. Beginning in about 750, not long after Muslim armies had conquered most of North Africa, Muslim traders, following the trade routes created by the Saharan Berber peoples, began trading for salt, copper, dates, and especially gold with the sub-Saharan peoples of the Niger [NY-jur] River drainage. Gradually they came to dominate the trans-Saharan trade routes, and Islam became the dominant faith of West Africa. By the ninth century, a number of African states existed in the broad savanna south of the Sahara Desert known as the Sudan [soo-DAN] (which literally means "land of the blacks"). These states seemed to have formed in response to the prospects of trade with the Muslim and Arab world.

Ghana [GAHN-uh], which means "war chief," is an early example, and its name suggests that a single chieftain, and later his family, exerted control over the material goods of the region, including gold, salt, ivory, iron, and particularly slaves. Muhammad, who considered slaves the just spoils of war, explicitly authorized slavery. Between the ninth and twelfth centuries the slave trade grew from 300,000 to over a million, and it was so lucrative that the peoples of the Sudan, all eager to enslave each other for profit, fought each other. (There is some reason to believe that many African converts to Islam were initially attracted to the religion as a way to avoid becoming slaves, since the faithful were exempt from servitude.) Finally, the empire of the Mali [MAH-lee] people subsumed Ghana under the leadership of the warrior-king Sunjata [soon-JAH-tuh] (r. 1230–1255), and gained control of the great trade routes north out of the savanna, through Timbuktu, the leading trading center of the era.

In 1312, Mansa Moussa [MAHN-sah MOO-sah] (*mansa* is the equivalent of the term "emperor") came to the Malian throne. A devout Muslim, he built magnificent mosques throughout his empire, including the Djingareyber [jin-gah-REY-bur] Mosque in Timbuktu [tim-BUK-too] (Fig. **4.22**). Still standing today and made of burnt brick and mud, it dominates the city. Under Moussa's patronage, Timbuktu grew in wealth and prestige and became a cultural focal point for the finest poets, scholars, and artists of Africa and the Middle East. To draw further attention to Timbuktu, and to attract more scholars and poets to it, Mansa Moussa embarked on a pilgrimage to Mecca in 1334. He arrived in Cairo at the head of a huge caravan of 60,000 people, including 12,000 servants, with 80 camels carrying more than two tons of gold to be distributed among the poor. Five hundred of the servants carried staffs of pure gold. In fact, Moussa distributed so much gold in Egypt that the value of the precious metal fell dramatically and did not recover for a number of years. When Moussa returned from the holy cities of Mecca and Medina, he built mosques, libraries, and *madrasas* throughout his kingdom.

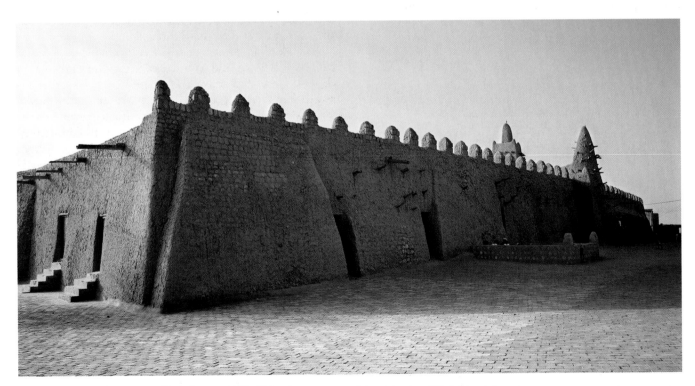

Fig. 4.22 Djingareyber Mosque, Timbuktu. ca. 1312. Today the mosque—and the entire city of Timbuktu—is in danger of becoming a desert, as the sands from the Sahara overtake what once was the Mali savanna.

Islamic Spain Like Islamic Africa, Islamic Spain maintained its own indigenous traditions while it absorbed Muslim ones, thus creating a distinctive cultural and political life. In 750, the Abbasids [AB-ass-eed], a large family that claimed descent from Abbas [AB-bass], an uncle of Muhammad, overthrew the Umayyad caliphs. The Abbasids shifted the center of Islamic power from Mecca to a magnificent new capital in Iraq popularly known as Baghdad. Meanwhile Spain remained under Umayyad control, initially under the leadership of Abd ar-Rahman (r. 756–788) [abd-ur-rahh-MAN], who had escaped the Abbasid massacre of Umayyads in Syria in 750 by fleeing to Córdoba [KOR-doh-buh]. The Spain he encountered had been controlled by a Germanic tribe from the north, the Visigoths, for over three centuries, but gradually he solidified Muslim control of the region, first in Córdoba, then in Seville, Toledo (the former Visigothic capital), and Granada.

The Great Mosque of Córdoba In the last years of his reign, secure in his position, Abd ar-Rahman built a magnificent new mosque in Córdoba, converting an existing Visigothic church into an Islamic institution, for which the Christian church was handsomely reimbursed. Abd ar-Rahman's original design included a double-tiered system of columns and arches topped by a wooden roof (Fig. **4.23**). The double arches have a practical function. The Visigoths tended to build with relatively short, stubby columns. To create the loftier space required by the mosque, the architects superimposed another set of columns on top, creating two tiers of arches, using a distinctive alternation of stone and red brick voussoirs, the wedge-shaped stones used to build an arch. The use of two different materials is functional as well, combining the flexibility of brick with the strength of stone. The hypostyle plan of the mosque was infinitely expandable, and subsequent Umayyad caliphs enlarged the mosque in 852, 950, 961–976, and 987, until it was more than four times the size of the Abd ar-Rahman's original and incorporated 1,200 columns.

Under the Umayyad caliphs, Muslim Spain thrived intellectually. Religious tolerance was extended to all. (It is worth noting that Muslims were exempt from taxes, while Christians and Jews were not—a practice that encouraged

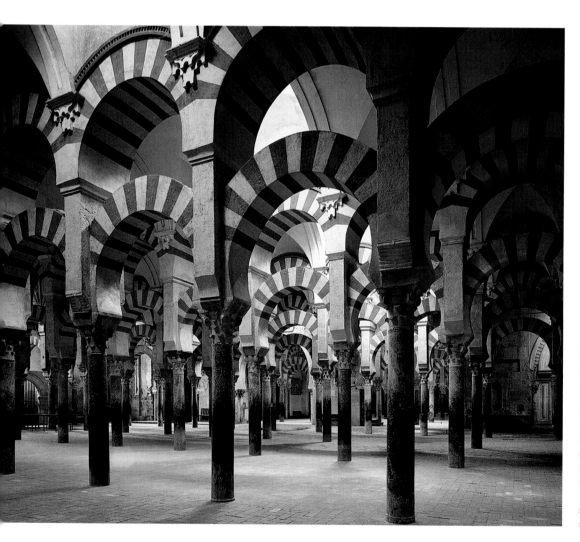

Fig. 4.23 Great Mosque of Córdoba. Begun 785, extensions 852, 950, 961–76, and 987. The caliphs of Spain intended their mosque to rival those in Jerusalem, Damascus, and Iraq. The forestlike expanse of the interior is a result of these aspirations. Even though only 80 of the original 1,200 columns survive, the space appears infinite, like some giant hall of mirrors.

conversion.) Spanish Jews, who had been persecuted under the Visigoths, welcomed the Muslim invasion and served as scientists, scholars, and even administrators in the caliphate [KAY-lih-fate]. Classical Greek literature and philosophy had already been translated into Arabic in Abbasid Baghdad. The new School of Translation established by the Umayyads in Toledo [toh-LEH-doh] soon was responsible for spreading the nearly forgotten texts throughout the West. Muslim mathematicians in Spain invented algebra and introduced the concept of zero to the West, and soon their Arabic numerals replaced the unwieldy Roman system. By the time of Abd ar-Rahman III (r. 912–961), Córdoba was renowned for its medicine, science, literature, and commercial wealth, and it became the most important center of learning in Europe. The elegance of Abd ar-Rahman III's court was unmatched, and his tolerance and benevolence extended to all, as Muslim students from across the Mediterranean soon found their way to the mosque-affiliated *madrasa* that he founded—the earliest example of an institution of higher learning in the Western world.

Buddhism: "The Path of Truth"

Buddhism originated in India, where the freedom of thought and practice that mark the Hindu religion actually encouraged other religious movements to develop from it. Its founder, Shakyamuni [SHAHK-yuh-moo-nee] Buddha, lived from about 563 to 483 BCE. He was born Prince Siddhartha Gautama [sid-DAR-thuh gau-tah-muh], child of a ruler of the Shakya [SHAK-yuh] clan—Skakyamuni means "sage of the Shakyas"—and was raised to be a ruler himself. Troubled by what he perceived to be the suffering of all human beings, he abandoned the luxurious lifestyle of his father's palace to live in the wilderness. For six years he meditated, finally attaining complete enlightenment while sitting under a bo, or fig, tree at Bodh Gaya [bod GUY-ah]. Shortly thereafter he gave his first teaching, at the Deer Park at Sarnath, expounding the Four Noble Truths:

1. Life is suffering.
2. This suffering has a cause, which is ignorance.
3. Ignorance can be overcome and eliminated.
4. The way to overcome this ignorance is by following the Eightfold Path of right view, right resolve, right speech, right action, right livelihood, right effort, right mindfulness, and right concentration.

Living with these truths in mind, one might overcome what Buddha believed to be the source of all human suffering—the desire for material things, which he considered the primary form of ignorance. In doing so, one would find release from the illusions of the world, from the cycle of birth, death, and rebirth, and ultimately reach nirvana. These principles are summed up in the *Dhammapada* [dah-muh-PAH-duh], the most popular canonical text of Buddhism,

compiled by followers and consisting of 423 aphorisms, or sayings, attributed to Buddha. Its name is a compound consisting of *dhamma*, the vernacular form of the formal Sanskit word *dharma*, mortal truth, and *pada*, meaning "foot" or "step"—hence it is "the path of truth." The aphorisms are widely admired for their wisdom and their sometimes stunning beauty of expression.

The Buddha (which means "Enlightened One") taught for 40 years until his death at age 80. His followers preached that anyone could achieve buddhahood, the ability to see the ultimate nature of the world. Persons of very near total enlightenment, but who have vowed to help others achieve buddhahood before crossing over to nirvana, came to be known as **bodhisattvas** [boh-dih-SUT-vuhz], meaning "those whose essence is wisdom." In art, bodhisattvas wear the princely garb of India, while buddhas wear a monk's robe.

Buddhism, which aims to end suffering, became the official state religion of India as a reaction to warfare. On a battlefield in 261 BCE, the emperor Ashoka [uh-SHOH-kuh] (r. ca. 273–232 BCE) was appalled by the carnage he had inflicted in his role as a warrior king. As he watched a monk walking slowly among the dead, Ashoka was moved to decry violence and force of arms and to spread the teachings of Buddha. From that point Ashoka, who had been described as "the cruel Ashoka," began to be known as "the pious Ashoka." He pursued an official policy of nonviolence. The unnecessary slaughter or mutilation of animals was forbidden. Sport hunting was banned, and although the limited hunting of game for the purpose of consumption was tolerated, Ashoka promoted vegetarianism. He built hospitals for people and animals alike, preached the humane treatment of all living things, and regarded all his subjects as equals, regardless of politics, religion, or caste.

Ashoka also embarked on a massive Buddhist architectural campaign, erecting as many as 8,400 shrines and monuments to Buddha throughout the empire, including a series of pillars spread across the empire engraved with proclamations reflecting Buddhist teachings. Among the most famous of the Buddhist monuments that Ashoka erected is the Great Stupa [STOO-puh] at Sanchi [SAHN-chee] (Fig. **4.24**), which was enlarged in the second century BCE. A **stupa** is a kind of burial mound. The earliest eight of them were built around 483 BCE as reliquaries for Buddha's remains, which were themselves divided into eight parts. In the third century, Ashoka opened the original eight stupas and further divided Buddha's relics, scattering them among a great many other stupas, probably including Sanchi.

The stupa as a form is deeply symbolic, consisting first and foremost of a hemispheric dome, built of rubble and dirt and faced with stone, evoking the Dome of Heaven. Perched on top of the dome is a small square platform, in the center of which is a mast supporting three circular discs or "umbrellas," called chatras [CHAH-truz]. These signify both the bo tree beneath which Buddha achieved enlightenment and the three levels of Buddhist consciousness—

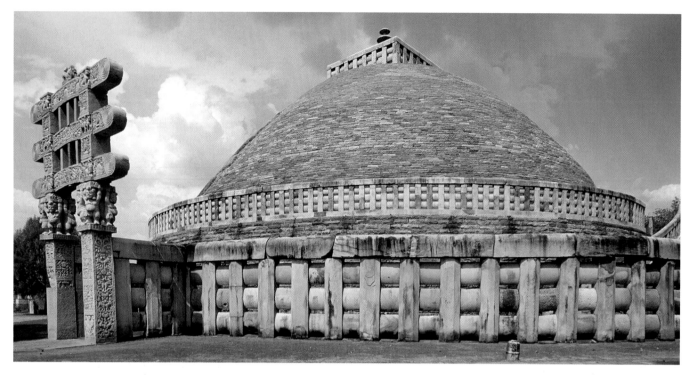

Fig. 4.24 The Great Stupa, Sanchi, Madhya Pradesh, India, view of the West Gateway, founded 3rd century BCE, enlarged ca. 150–50 BCE. Shrine height 50′, diameter 105′. In India, the stupa is the principal monument to Buddha. The stupa symbolizes, at once, the World Mountain, the Dome of Heaven, and the Womb of the Universe.

desire, form, formlessness—through which the soul ascends to enlightenment. The dome is set on a raised base, around the top of which is a circumambulatory walkway. As pilgrims to the stupa circle the walkway, they symbolically follow Buddha's path, awakening to enlightenment. The whole is a **mandala** [MUN-duh-luh] (literally "circle"), the Buddhist diagram of the cosmos.

Soon, Buddhism would spread beyond India as Buddhist monks from China traveled to India to observe Buddhist practices and carry his teachings back to their homeland. After the fall of the Han dynasty in 220 CE, China had entered an uneasy period. Warring factions vied for control of greater or lesser territories, governments rose to power and fell again, civil wars erupted, and tribes from Central Asia continuously invaded. The Confucian ethical system (see chapter 1) seemed to have resulted in civil and cultural dysfunction. In contrast, Buddhism offered an ethical system based less on social and civic duty and more on each person's duty to his or her own soul. Especially in its emphasis on meditation and enlightenment, Buddhism was compatible with Daoism (also discussed in chapter 1). By the last half of the fifth century, Chinese rulers habitually ordered images of the Buddha. And by the seventh century CE, Chinese leaders had learned to take the best from all three—Confucianism, Buddhism, and Daoism.

In early Buddhist art, the Buddha was never shown in figural form. It was believed to be impossible to represent the Buddha, since he had already passed to nirvana. Instead, his presence was symbolized by such things as his footprints, the bo tree, the wheel (representing *dharma*, or the Wheel of Law), or elephants. But by the fourth century, in India, the Buddha was commonly represented in human form. Typically his head is oval, framed by a halo. Atop his head is a mound, symbolizing his spiritual wisdom, and on his forehead is a "third eye," symbolizing his spiritual vision. His demeanor is gentle, reposed, and meditative. His elongated ears refer to his royal origins, and his hands are set in one of several symbolic gestures, called **mudra**. The seated Buddha carved from the solid rock of cliffs that line the Silk Road (see *Continuity and Change*, page 127) (Fig. **4.25**) exhibits the *Dhyana mudra* [Duh-YAH-nuh mood-rah], a gesture of meditation and balance. The lower hand represents the physical world of illusion, the upper, nirvana. Together they symbolize the path to enlightenment. The *bodhisattva*—a person of near total enlightenment who has vowed to help others achieve it— standing next to him is exhibiting the *Abhaya mudra* [Uh-BAH-yah mood-rah], a gesture of reassurance, blessing, and protection.

The Tang Dynasty (618–907 CE) reestablished a period of peace and prosperity in China that, except for a brief

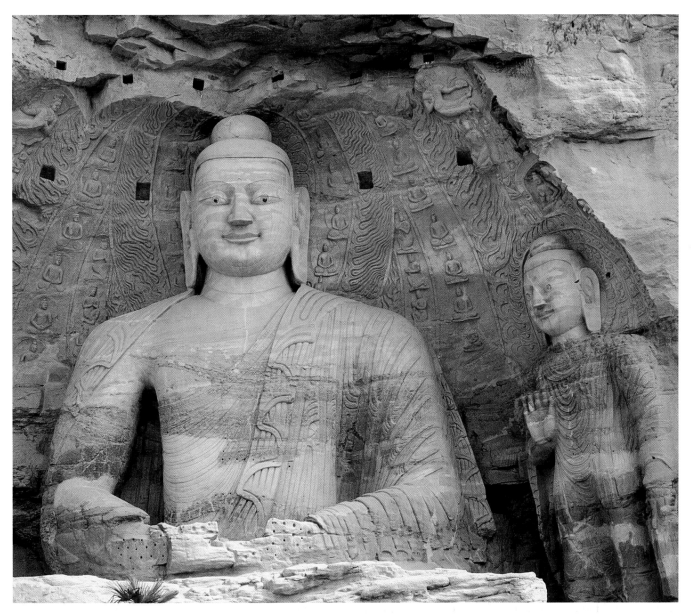

Fig. 4.25 *Large Seated Buddha with Standing Bodhisattva,* **from cave 20, Ungang, Shaanxi, China, Northern Wei dynasty. ca. 460–470 CE.** Stone, height 44'. Smaller caves, high on the cliffs above, served as retreats for Buddhist monks.

period of turmoil in the tenth century, would last for 660 years. The Tang dynasty was the product of by far the largest and most organized government in the world in the last half of the first millennium. Its capital was the eastern end of the Silk Road, Chang'an, "City of Enduring Peace" (present-day Xi'an, which is about one-seventh the size of the Tang capital). The city had served as the capital of the Han dynasty as well, but as the Tang restored trade along the Silk Road, they created elaborate plans to restore the city, too. By the eighth century, its population was well over 1 million, living inside a walled perimeter nearly 26 miles in length and enclosing almost 42 square miles. Out-

side the walls lived perhaps as many as another million people. Among its inhabitants were Korean, Japanese, Jewish, and Christian communities, and its emperors maintained diplomatic relations with Persia.

Chang'an was the largest city in the world, laid out in a carefully conceived grid that dramatized the Tang commitment to social order and mirrored, they believed, the order of the cosmos (Fig. **4.26**). Each of the city's 108 blocks was itself a miniature walled city, with its own interior streets and gates that locked at night. Astronomers laid out the streets by aligning them with the shadow of the sun at noon and the position of the North Star at night, thereby orienting the city to the four cardinal directions. The imperial palace was located at the north end, facing south, thus symbolizing the emperor looking out over his city and, by extension, his empire. Traditionally, Chinese emperors turned their backs to the north, from where, it was believed, evil spirits (not to mention Huns) came. Government buildings occupied the space in front of the imperial palace. A 500-foot-wide avenue led from these directly to the southern gate.

The Tang valued education above all. The imperial college at Chang'an trained all civil servants (women were excluded), and intellectual achievement was held in high esteem. They were trained to read and write poetry, paint, and essentially memorize the Chinese literary tradition handed down since the time of Confucius. In fact, the scholars that graduated from the imperial college made up China's highest social class, an aristocracy of the learned, unequaled anywhere in the world.

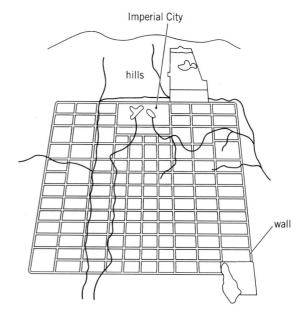

Fig. 4.26 Plan of the Tang capital of Chang'an, China. ca. 600. The location of the capital had been determined, in Han times, by the practice of *feng shui*, literally "wind and water," which assesses the primal energy that flows through a particular landscape. In this case, the hills to the north of the city and the streams running through it were understood to protect the precinct. *Feng shui* is still practiced to this day.

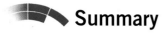 **Summary**

■ Developments in Judaic Culture By the first century CE, Judaism had become increasingly sectarian in nature, each sect believing that it possessed the one true understanding of God's will. It had also become increasingly messianic, apocalyptic, and sectarian.

■ The Rise of Christianity Christianity developed as a sect of Judaism. Jesus preached a sectarian doctrine based on his understanding of the Hebrew Scriptures. His life and teachings, as described in the Gospels, written 40 to 80 years after his death, are the foundation of Christian faith. The religion was spread by evangelists, chief among them Paul, whose epistles comprise 14 books of the New Testament. To incorporate its Jewish heritage, early Christianity viewed its history as a typology, seeing the stories and figures of the Hebrew Scriptures as prefiguring the life of Jesus. In 313, Constantine I ("Constantine the Great"), who had assumed total authority of the Roman Empire the year before, granted religious freedom to all Romans in the Edict of Milan. Constantine became increasingly supportive of Christianity, convening the first ecumenical council of Church leaders in 325 at Nicea, near his new capital at Constantinople. The resulting Nicene Creed established a uniform liturgy.

■ The Byzantine Empire and Its Church Under Justinian and his empress, Theodora, a mammoth new church Hagia Sophia was built in Constantinople, along with other

massive building projects. In Byzantine art, the naturalism that dominated Classical Greek and Roman art disappeared. Artists evidently had less interest in depicting the visual appearance of the material world because they focused their attention on the spiritual truth that they believed manifested itself in their icons.

■ The Rise and Spread of Islam According to tradition, beginning in 610 the Muslim prophet Muhammad began to recite messages from God, which he dictated to scribes who collected them to form the scriptures of Islam, the Qur'an. The rapid spread of Islam can be attributed to its appeal as both a religion and form of social organization. The mosque was the community's focal point, and as Islam spread, mosques appeared across North Africa and Spain, and with them, in their attendant *madrasas*, cultures dedicated to learning.

■ Buddhism: "The Path of Truth" Buddhism, the teachings of Shakyamuni Buddha, who lived in India from about 563 to 483 BCE, became the official state religion of India when the emperor Ashoka adopted it on a battlefield in 261 BCE. Ashoka built thousands of monuments celebrating Buddha's life across India, including the Great Stupa at Sanchi. As Buddhism spread north to China, where it was understood to be compatible with Confucianism and Daoism, figurative representations of the Buddha became increasingly common.

The Silk Road

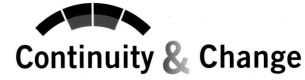

Continuity & Change

Under the Han (206 BCE–220 CE), Chinese trade flourished. Western linen, wool, glass, and gold, Persian pistachios, and mustard originating in the Mediterranean, were imported in exchange for the silk, ceramics, fur, lacquered goods, and spices that made their way west along the "Silk Road" that stretched from the Yellow River across Asia to the Mediterranean (see Map **4.4**). The road followed the westernmost spur of the Great Wall to the oasis town of Dunhuang [doon-hwahng], where it split into northern and southern routes, passing through smaller oasis towns until converging again at Kashgar [KAHSH-gahr] on the western edge of the western Chinese deserts. From there traders could proceed into present-day Afghanistan, south into India, or westward through present-day Uzbekistan, Iran, and Iraq, into Syria and the port city of Antioch [AN-tee-ahk]. Goods passed through many hands, trader to trader, before reaching the Mediterranean, and according to an official history of the Han dynasty compiled in the fifth century CE, it was not until 97 CE that one Gan Ying went "all the way to the Western sea and back." According to Gan Ying, there he encountered an empire with "over four hundred walled cities" to which "tens of small states are subject"—probably all outposts of the Roman Empire.

Goods and ideas spread along the Silk Road, as trade spurred the cultural interchange between East and West, India and China. As early as the first century BCE, silk from China reached Rome, where it captured the Western imagination, but the secret of its manufacture remained a mystery in the West until the sixth century CE when Justinian directed his ambassadors to China to smuggle silkworm eggs back to Constantinople. Between the first and third centuries CE, Buddhist missionaries from India carried their religion over the Silk Road into Southeast Asia and north into China and Korea, where it quickly became the dominant religion.

Finally, the Venetian merchant Marco Polo (ca. 1254–1324), bearing a letter of introduction from Pope Gregory X, crossed the Asian continent on the Silk Road in 1274. He arrived at the new Chinese capital of Beijing, and served in the imperial court for nearly two decades. His *Travels*, written after his return to Italy in 1292, constitute the first eyewitness account of China available in Europe. Polo was most impressed by the city of Hangzhou, a city in the Yangzi river delta, connected to the river itself by a massive Grand Canal. Its lakes and parks were so beautiful, filled with floating teahouses from which passengers could view the palaces, pagodas, and temples that dotted the shore, that the city was known as Kinsai [KEEN-sa-hee], or the "City of Heaven." The entire city, some 200 square miles, was protected by a 30-foot-high wall, with even higher watchtowers rising above it. Inside the walls, a system of canals, which must have reminded Marco of his native Venice, was crisscrossed by some 12,000 bridges. "The houses of the citizens are well built and elaborately finished," Polo claims, "and the delight they take in decoration, in painting and in architecture, leads them to spend in this way sums of money that would astonish you." In other words, Hangzhou was a center of Asian culture that no one in the West, save Marco Polo, could even dream existed, in many ways exceeding anything the West had yet realized. ■

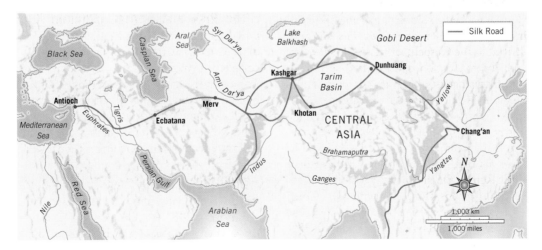

Map 4.4 The Silk Road, the trading route between the East and West and between Southeast Asia and China.

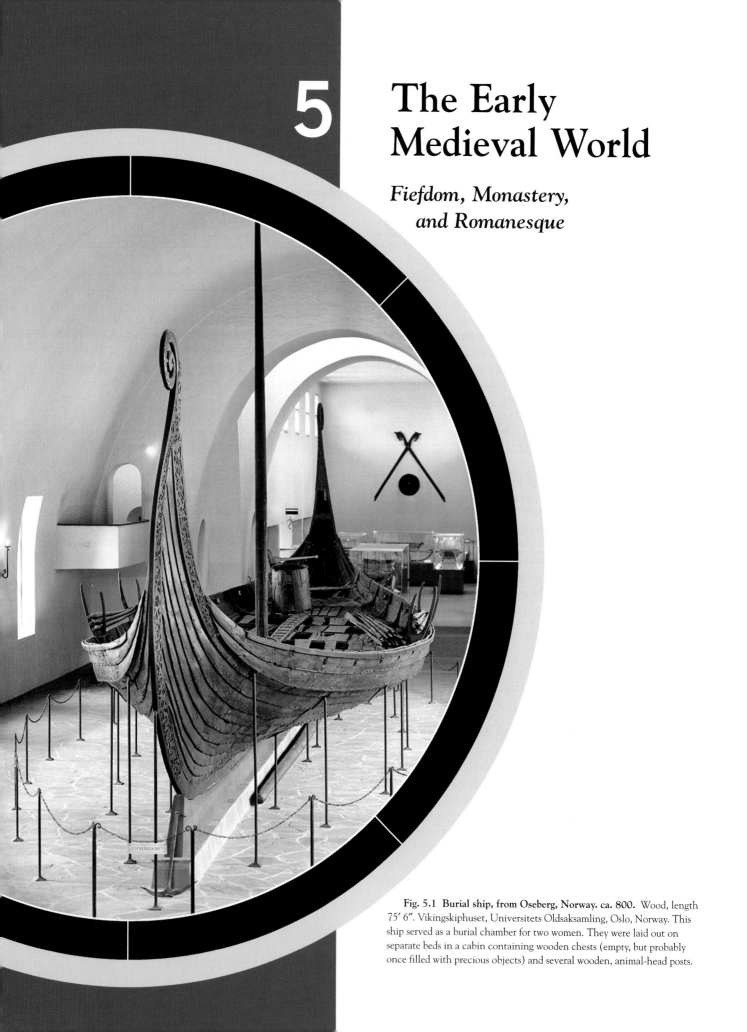

5 The Early Medieval World

Fiefdom, Monastery, and Romanesque

Fig. 5.1 Burial ship, from Oseberg, Norway. ca. 800. Wood, length 75′ 6″. Vikingskiphuset, Universitets Oldsaksamling, Oslo, Norway. This ship served as a burial chamber for two women. They were laid out on separate beds in a cabin containing wooden chests (empty, but probably once filled with precious objects) and several wooden, animal-head posts.

❝ In his lord's service, a man must suffer pain,
Bitterest cold and burning heat endure
He must be willing to lose his flesh and blood. ❞

The Song of Roland

Sutton Hoo lies near the modern city of Ipswich, England, in the county of Suffolk, East Anglia (Map **5.1**). There, a burial mound contains the remains of a wealthy and powerful Anglo-Saxon man, probably a seventh-century king. (Coins found at the site date to the late 630s.) The burial mound concealed a ship, 90 feet long and 14 feet wide, a little larger than a similar burial ship excavated in 1904 from Oseberg, just outside Oslo, Norway (Fig. **5.1**). A thick layer of blue clay, nearly impenetrable by water or air and topped with turf, preserved the ship at Oseberg. The burial ship at Sutton Hoo had been dragged up a 100-foot hill—or "hoo"—above the river Deben and laid in a trench. Midway between the ship's bow and stern, a house had been constructed. Inside the house was the coffin, accompanied by a treasure horde of richly decorative ornaments and armor, gold coins from France, silver spoons and bowls from the Eastern Mediterranean, and a wooden harp. The trench was filled in and a mound was raised over it. For 1,300 years it remained untouched, high above the Deben estuary, as if the dead warrior were standing perpetual guard over East Anglia, looking eternally out to sea.

First excavated in 1939, only two objects discovered at the site show any evidence of Christian culture—two silver spoons inscribed with the names Saulos and Paulos in Greek lettering. The names might refer to the biblical King Saul of the Hebrew Bible and St. Paul of the New Testament. Christianity had, in fact, almost completely disappeared in England shortly after the Romans left in 406. Over the next 200 years, Germanic and Norse tribes—Angles, Saxons, Jutes, and Frisians—invited in as mercenaries by Romanized British leaders, began to operate on their own. Their Anglo-Saxon culture, steeped in Germanic and Norse values and traditions, soon came to dominate cultural life in Britain. Nevertheless, at the time of the Sutton Hoo burial, the late 630s, Christianity had begun to reassert itself in England. There is some speculation that the elaborate Sutton Hoo burial ceremony, which included cremation—forbidden by Christianity—and apparent human and animal sacrifice, represented an open defiance of Christian practices.

At the time of its seventh-century burials, Sutton Hoo was, at best, a remote outpost of Anglo-Saxon culture, but no other archeological site has revealed more about the Anglo-Saxons. Whoever was buried there was a lord or chief to whom his followers owed absolute loyalty, the basis of the feudal societies that would later dominate European life in the Middle Ages. **Feudalism** is related to the Roman custom of patronage (see chapter 3), under which a patron, usually a lord or nobleman, provided protection to a person working his land in exchange for his loyalty. In the Middle Ages, this relationship developed into an economic system, based on the landholder's rights to the land, as determined by his lord, and the relationship between the tenant and the landholder. In exchange for use of a piece of land—called a **fief**

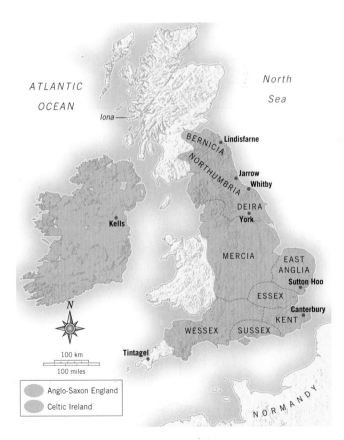

Map 5.1 Anglo-Saxon England and Celtic Ireland.

[feef]—and the protection of the lord or noble who owned the fief, the tenant was obligated to serve the nobleman (often militarily) and pay him with goods or produce.

The rudiments of this system were in place in sixth-century England. The Anglo-Saxons comprised only about one-tenth of a total population of roughly 1 million; the remainder were Britons. The Anglo-Saxons controlled the land while the Britons largely worked it, and the wealth the Anglo-Saxons extracted from this relationship is everywhere apparent in the treasures discovered at Sutton Hoo. The nobles in control of their various fiefdoms in turn owed allegiance to their king, who was overlord of all the fiefdoms in his kingdom. In return for their loyalty, the king rewarded his nobles with gold, weaponry, and elaborately decorated items of personal adornment, like the artifacts buried at Sutton Hoo.

When Christianity was reintroduced to Anglo-Saxon England in the seventh century, the Church adapted the principles of feudalism. Instead of the tenant owing allegiance to his nobleman and the nobleman to his king, all owed allegiance to the Christian God. Briton and Anglo-Saxon alike might make gifts to the Church, and in return the Church offered them not protection, but salvation. As a result, the Church quickly became wealthy. To decorate its sanctuaries, the Church promoted the same refined and elaborate handiwork as the feudal lords had commissioned for their personal use, incorporating Christian themes and imagery into the animal and interlace styles of Germanic and Norse culture. And it acquired large parcels of property overseen by a clergy who were feudal lords themselves. These properties soon developed into large working monasteries, where like-minded individuals gathered in the pursuit of religious perfection. The monasteries in turn became great centers of learning.

Monasteries soon began to promote the idea of doing penance for one's sins by embarking on religious pilgrimages. Part of the reason seems to have been the increasing urbanization of Europe, and with it, worsening hygienic conditions that spread disease. Believing that disease was related to sinfulness, pilgrims sought to atone for their sins, saving themselves from sickness and contagion on earth and perpetual damnation in the afterlife. Political and religious motives also played a role. The pilgrimage to Mecca had played an important role in Islamic tradition, and the economic benefits realized by that relatively remote city on the Arabian peninsula were not lost on Rome. But more important, the religious value of a Christian pilgrimage to Jerusalem—the most difficult and hence potentially most rewarding of Christian pilgrimages—demanded that the Western church eliminate Muslim control of the region, a prospect the Church frankly relished. By 1100, thousands of pilgrims annually were making their way to Jerusalem—which Christian forces retook in 1099 in the First Crusade and to Rome, where the remains of Saints Peter and Paul were housed. Large numbers of pilgrims traveled across Europe to Santiago de Compostela [san-tee-AH-go day kom-poh-STEL-uh], in the northwest corner of modern Spain, where the body of the apostle Saint James the Greater lay at rest, and in England pilgrims would soon journey to Canterbury to worship at the shrine of Saint Thomas à Becket, the Archbishop of Canterbury, who had staunchly defended the authority of the Church over that of the English throne, resulting, in 1170, in his assassination.

This chapter outlines the rise to power of feudal society and the adaptation of feudal practices by the medieval kings and emperors and by the Christian Church. Perhaps the most important ruler to codify and adopt these practices was Charlemagne [SHAR-luh-mane], who dreamed not only of unifying Europe under his rule, but also of unifying church and state in a single administrative and political bureaucracy. Although Charlemagne's empire dissolved with his death in 843, subsequent rulers, such as the Ottonian kings in Germany, followed his example by building a tightly knit political bureaucracy and championing the arts. But the Church competed with the kings for the loyalty of the people, and in their architecture, in the art that decorated them, and in the music of their liturgy, they sought to appeal to the emotions of the people, calling on them to reject the worldly aspirations of the court and seek the rewards of heaven.

Anglo-Saxon Artistic Style and Culture

A purse cover from the Sutton Hoo site (Fig. **5.2**) is a fine example of the artistic style of the non-Christian Germanic culture of the Anglo-Saxons. It is a work of **cloisonné** [kloy-zun-AY], a technique in which strips of gold are set on edge to form small cells. The cells are then filled with a colored enamel glass paste and fitted with thin slices of semiprecious stones (in this case, garnet). At the top of the purse cover shown here, two hexagons flank a central motif of **animal interlace**. In this design two pairs of animals and birds, facing each other, are elongated into serpentine ribbons of decoration, a common Scandinavian motif. Below this, two Swedish hawks with curved beaks attack a pair of ducks. On each side of this design, a male figure stands between two animals. This **animal style** was used in jewelry design throughout the Germanic and Scandinavian world in the era before Christianity. Notice its symmetrical design, its combination of interlaced organic and geometric shapes, and, of course, its animal motifs. Throughout the early Middle Ages this style was imitated in manuscripts, stone sculpture, church masonry, and wood sculpture.

In many ways, the English language was shaped by Anglo-Saxon traditions. Our days of the week are derived from the names of Saxon gods: Tuesday and Wednesday are named after two Saxon gods of war, Tiw and Woden. Thursday is named after Thor, the god of thunder, and Friday after Frigg, Woden's wife. Similarly, most English placenames have Saxon origins. *Bury* means fort, and Canterbury means

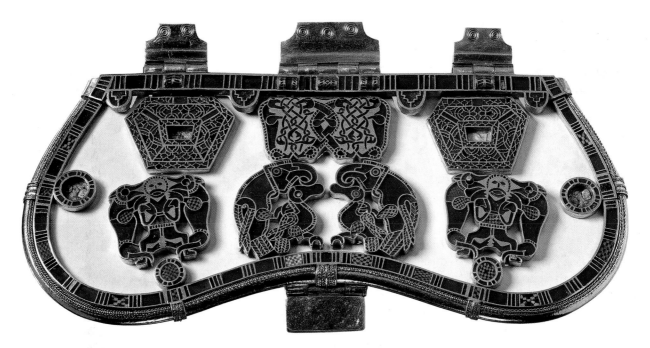

Fig. 5.2 Purse cover, from Sutton Hoo burial ship. ca. 625. Gold with Indian garnets and cloisonné enamels, originally on an ivory or bone background (now lost), length 8″. © The Trustees of the British Museum, London. This elaborate purse lid would have been attached to the owner's belt by hinges. In the Sutton Hoo burial mound, the purse contained gold coins and ingots.

the fort of the Cantii tribe. *Ings* means tribe or family; Hastings is where the family of chief Haesta lived. *Strat* refers to a Roman road; Stratford-on-Avon designates the place where the Roman road fords the river Avon. *Chester* means Roman camp, as in Dorchester; *minster* means monastery, as in Westminster; and *ham* means home, as in Nottingham.

Anglo-Saxon culture revolved around the king and his thanes (lords). The king possessed his own large estate, as did each of his thanes, and the king and his retinue moved continually among the estates of the thanes, who owed hospitality and loyalty to the throne. Aside from these few powerful persons, feudal society was composed of peasants. Some were *ceorls*, or churls, free men who owned farms of 90–100 acres. Others rented land from the thanes, usually in lots of 20 acres. They paid their lords in goods—sheep or grain—and worked his fields two or three days per week. All employed serfs (day laborers) and thralls (slaves), often captives of wars. (Evidence suggests that by the eighth century, the Anglo-Saxons were routinely marketing slaves abroad, in France and Rome particularly.) Runaway slaves were punished by death, as were those convicted of disloyalty to their thanes.

Anglo-Saxon law was based on the idea of the *wergeld*, or "life-price" of an individual. A thane's value was roughly six times that of a churl, and a thrall had no value at all. If a thane were killed (or injured), his family (or in the case of injury, he himself) was entitled to be compensated at the

highest fixed rate. But a thane could kill or injure a thrall with no *wergeld* due at all. The *wergeld* for men and women was identical, although a pregnant woman was worth as much as three times the usual rate, and a woman's potential as a bearer of children could raise her value even if she were not pregnant.

Beowulf, the Oldest English Epic Poem

The rigidly hierarchical nature of feudal society is probably nowhere better demonstrated than in the oldest English epic poem, *Beowulf*. In the poem, a young hero, Beowulf [BAY-uh-wolf], comes from afar to rid a community of monsters, headed by the horrific Grendel, who have been ravaging it. He returns home to his native Sweden and rules well for 50 years, until he meets up with a dragon who is menacing his people. Beowulf demonstrates his fierce courage and true loyalty to his vassals by taking the dragon on, but it kills him. The lesson drawn from his fate is a simple one: "So every man must yield / the leasehold of his days."

Beowulf concludes with the hero's warriors burning his body along with his treasures on a funeral byre, thus rounding out a story that opens with a burial as well. A treasure very much like that found in the Sutton Hoo ship burial is described just 26 lines into the poem, when the death of Danish king Shield Sheafson is described (**Reading 5.1**).

READING 5.1 *Beowulf*, trans. Seamus Heaney

Shield was still thriving when his time came
and he crossed over into the Lord's keeping.
His warrior band did what he bade them
when he laid down the law among the Danes:
they shouldered him out to the sea's flood,
the chief they revered who had long ruled them.
A ring-whorled prow rode in the harbour,
ice-clad, outbound, a craft for a prince.
They stretched their beloved lord in his boat,
laid out by the mast, amidships,
the great ring-giver. Far-fetched treasures
were piled upon him, and precious gear.
I never heard before of a ship so well furbished
with battle tackle, bladed weapons
and coats of mail. The massed treasure
was loaded on top of him: it would travel far
on out into the ocean's sway.
They decked his body no less bountifully
with offerings than those first ones did
who cast him away when he was a child
and launched him alone out over the waves.
And they set a gold standard up
high above his head and let him drift
to wind and tide, bewailing him
and mourning their loss. No man can tell,
no wise man in hall or weathered veteran
knows for certain who salvaged that load.

The findings at Sutton Hoo, as well as the ship discovered at Oseberg (see Fig. 5.1), suggest that *Beowulf* accurately reflects many aspects of life in the northern climates of Europe in the Middle Ages. The poem was composed in Anglo-Saxon, or Old English, sometime between 700 and 1000 CE, handed down first as an oral narrative and later transcribed. Its 3,000 lines represent a language that predates the merging of French and English tongues after 1066, when William the Conqueror, a Norman duke, invaded England. The poem survived in a unique tenth-century manuscript, copied from an earlier manuscript and itself badly damaged by fire in the eighteenth century. It owes its current reputation largely to J.R.R. Tolkien, author of *The Lord of the Rings*, who in the 1930s argued for the poem's literary value. The source of Tolkien's attraction to the poem will be obvious to anyone who knows his own great trilogy.

Beowulf is an English poem, but the events it describes take place in Scandinavia. One of its most notable literary features, common to Old English literature, is its reliance on compound phrases, or **kennings**, substituted for the usual name of a person or thing. Consider, for instance, the following line:

Hwæt we Gar-Dena in gear-dagum
So. The Spear-Danes in days gone by

Instead of saying "the past," the poem says *gear-dagum*, which literally means "year-days." Instead of "the Danes," it says *Spear-Danes*, implying their warrior attributes. The poet calls the sea the *fifelstréam*, literally the "sea-monster stream," or "whale-path," and the king, the "ring-giver." A particularly poetic example is *beado-leoma*, "battle-light," referring to a flashing sword. In a sense, then, these compound phrases are metaphoric riddles that context helps to explain. *Beowulf* contains many such compounds that occur only once in all Anglo-Saxon literature—*hapax legomena*, as they are called, literally, "said or counted once"—and context is our only clue to their meaning.

Some have interpreted phrases such as Shield Sheaf-son's crossing "over into the Lord's keeping" as evidence that the poem is a Christian allegory. And although Beowulf does indeed give "thanks to Almighty God," and admit that his victory over the monster Grendel would not have been possible "if God had not protected me," there is nothing in the poem to suggest that this is the Christian God. There are no overtly Christian references in the work. The poem teaches its audience that power, strength, fame, and life itself are fleeting—a theme consonant with Christian values, but by no means necessarily Christian. And although Beowulf, in his arguably foolhardy courage at the end of the poem, displays a Christ like willingness to sacrifice himself for the greater good, the honor and courage he exhibits are fully in keeping with the values of feudal warrior culture.

The Merging of Pagan and Christian Styles

Whatever *Beowulf*'s relation to Christian tradition, it is easy to see how the poem might have been read, even in its own time, in Christian terms. But after the Romans withdrew from Britain in 406, Christianity had survived only in the westernmost reaches of the British Isles—in Cornwall, in Wales, and in Ireland, where St. Patrick had converted the population between his arrival in 432 and his death in 461. Around 563, an Irish monk, Columba, founded a monastery on the Scottish island of Iona. He traveled widely through Scotland and converted many northern Picts, a Scottish tribe, to Christianity. In about 635, almost simultaneous with the pagan burial at Sutton Hoo, in which only a few if any Christian artifacts were discovered, a monk from Iona built another monastery at Lindisfarne [LIN-dis-farn], an island off the coast of Northumbria [north-UM-bree-uh] in northeast England. The "re-Christianization" of Britain was underway.

The Celtic [KELL-tik] Christian Church differed from Roman Christianity in several important ways. It celebrated Easter on the Vernal equinox and believed that Mary, mother of Jesus, was exempt from original sin. It invented private confession. The office of bishop was a ceremonial position, and authority rested instead with abbots and abbesses, giving women an important role in the Church. And the Celtic cross is itself unique, symmetrical and superimposed upon a circle.

These differences would later cause considerable difficulty, but meanwhile, in 597, Pope Gregory I (pope 590–604) sent a mission to England of 40 monks, headed by the Benedictine [ben-uh-DIK-teen] prior Augustine (d. 604)—not the same Augustine who had written *The Confessions* and *The City of God*—to convert the pagan Anglo-Saxons. Augustine met with the Anglo-Saxon king, Aethelberht [ETH-el-bert] (r. 560–616), on the island of Thanet, in Kent. The encounter is described by the eighth-century historian Bede [beed] (ca. 672–735), in his *History of the English Church and People*, written in 731:

> After some days, the king came to the island and, sitting down in the open air, summoned Augustine and his companions to an audience. But he took precautions that they should not approach him in a house; for he held an ancient superstition that, if they were practicers of magic, they might have opportunity to deceive and master him. But the monks were endowed with power from God, not from the devil, and approached the king carrying a silver cross as their standard and the likeness of our Lord and Savior painted on a board.

The story narrates the confrontation, in other words, of two distinct styles of thought and art—the animal style, with which Aethelberht was at home, and the Christian icon; pagan superstition and Christian faith; an oral, illiterate culture and a text-based one. Although Aethelberht was slow to convert, he allowed Augustine to build a cathedral at Canterbury on the site of an old Roman church and, soon after, a church in London dedicated to St. Paul.

Manuscript Illustration: Blending of Anglo-Saxon and Christian Traditions

In 601, Gregory sent Augustine a letter urging him not to eliminate pagan traditions overnight, but to incorporate them into Christian practice: "For it is certainly impossible to eradicate all errors from obstinate minds at one stroke, and whoever wishes to climb a mountain top climbs gradually step by step, and not in one leap." This is one reason that the basic elements of the animal style, evident in the purse cover from Sutton Hoo (see Fig. 5.2), appear in a manuscript page from the *Lindisfarne Gospels*, designed by Bishop Eadfrith of Lindisfarne in 698 (Fig. **5.3**). Notice particularly how the geometric grids in the border decoration of the purse cover are elaborated in the central circle of the Lindisfarne **carpet page** (a descriptive term, not used in the Middle Ages, that refers to the resemblance between such pages and Turkish or Islamic carpets). The animal interlace of the purse cover reappears in the corner designs that frame the central circle of the carpet page, where two birds face outward and two inward. And the beasts that turn to face one another in the middle of the cover are echoed in the border figures of the carpet page, top and bottom, left and right. The pre-Christian decorative vocabulary of the Sutton Hoo treasure, created to honor a pagan king, has been transformed to honor the Christian conception of God.

This carpet page is an example of a Celtic cross. Legend has it that while preaching to a group of the soon-to-be-converted, St. Patrick had been shown an ancient standing stone monument with a circle carved onto it, symbolic, he was told, of the moon goddess. Patrick reportedly made the mark of a Latin cross through the circle and blessed the stone, thereby making the first Celtic cross. The story is probably only a legend—the circle with a cross through it antedates Patrick's arrival in Ireland, where it probably symbolized, in pagan culture, the sun and moon, male and female, unity and balance in all things—but the legend speaks to the *syncretism* [SIN-krih-tiz-um] (the combining of different practices and principles) of the age.

The syncretic [sin-KRET-ik] style of art that flourished in England and Ireland during the early Middle Ages is called *Hiberno-Saxon* (*Hibernia* [hy-BUR-nee-uh] is the Latin name for Ireland). Hiberno-Saxon manuscript illustration is notable particularly for its unification of Anglo-Saxon visual

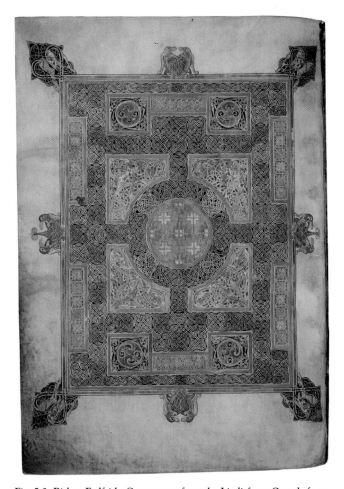

Fig. 5.3 Bishop Eadfrith, Carpet page, from the *Lindisfarne Gospels* from Northumbria, England. ca. 698. Tempera on vellum, 13 1/2″ × 9 3/4″. British Library, London. An inscription on the manuscript identifies Eadfrith as its scribe and decorator, Ethelwald as its binder, Billfrith as the monk who adorned it with gems, and Aldred as its translator into Anglo-Saxon: "Thou living God be mindful of Eadfrith, Ethelwald, Billfrith, and Alfred a sinner; these four have, with God's help, been engaged upon this book."

culture with the textual tradition of Christianity. In the monastic *scriptoria* (sing. **scriptorium**)—the halls in which monks worked to copy and decorate biblical texts—artists soon began to decorate the letterforms themselves, creating elaborate capitals at the beginning of important sections of a document. One of the most beautiful capitals is a page from the *Book of Kells*, made at Iona in the late eighth century (Fig. **5.4**). The basis of the design consists of the Greek letters *chi* [ky], *rho* [roe], and *iota* [eye-OH-tuh] (*X*, *P*, and *I*, or *chri*), an abbreviation of *Christi*. In this instance, the text begins *Christi autem generatio*, "Now this is how the birth of

Jesus Christ came about," quoting Matthew 1:18. The dominant letterform is *chi*, a giant unbalanced *X* much larger on the left than on the right. Below the right side of the *chi* is *rho*, which curves around and ends with the head of a red-haired youth, possibly a depiction of Christ, which also dots the *I*. Not long after Ionan monks completed this manuscript, Vikings began to threaten the Scottish coast, and the monks retreated to Kells in the interior of Ireland. So great was the renown of the book they had created that in 1006 it was referred to as "the chief relic of the Western world."

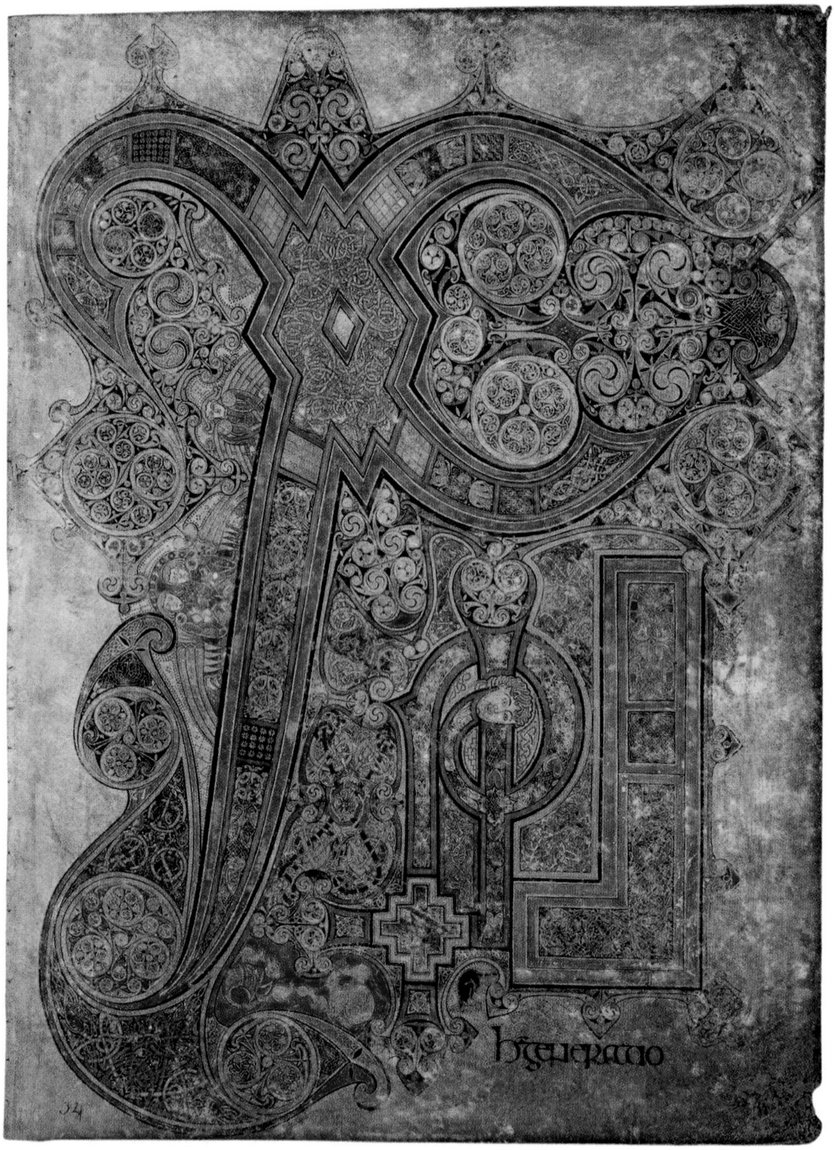

The task of Christian missionaries in England was to transfer the allegiance of the people from their king, or thane, to God. They could not offer gold, or material wealth, but only salvation, or spiritual fulfillment. They had to substitute for the great treasure at Sutton Hoo the more subtle treasures of faith and hope. The missionaries' tactic was simple—they bathed the spiritual in material splendor. They illuminated their manuscripts with a rich decorative vocabulary. They adorned Christianity in gold and silver, jewels and enamel, and placed it within an architecture of the most magnificent kind. And they transplanted pagan celebrations to the context of the Christian worship service.

A manuscript page probably created at Canterbury in the first half of the eighth century is revealing on this last point (Fig. **5.5**). It depicts an enthroned David, author of the Psalms, surrounded by court musicians. The scene could as easily illustrate an episode in *Beowulf* when a great celebration takes place in Hrothgar's hall after Beowulf defeats the monster Grendel:

> They sang then and played to
>   please the hero,
> words and music for their warrior
>   prince,
> harp tunes and tales of adventure:
> there were high times on the hall
>   benches
> and the king's poet performed his
>   part. . . .

Beowulf, ll. 1062–66

David, indeed, is a Judeo-Christian version of "the king's poet," only his king is the Christian God. More to the point, the harp that David plays in the manuscript illustration is very like the six-stringed wooden harp discovered at Sutton Hoo. As the animal-style frames and borders of the scene suggest, this is a celebration any Anglo-

Fig. 5.4 *Chi Rho Iota* page, *Book of Matthew, Book of Kells*, **probably made at Iona, Scotland, late 8th or early 9th century.** Tempera on vellum, 13″ × 9½″. The Board of Trinity College, Dublin, MS 58 (A.1.6.), fol. 34v. While the abbreviation for *Christi—XPI* or *Chri*—dominates the page, the remainder of the verse from Matthew is at the bottom right. *Autem* appears as an abbreviation resembling the letter *h*, followed by *generatio*, which is fully written out. So common were abbreviations in manuscript illumination, saving both time and space, that the scribes were often given the title of official court "abbreviator."

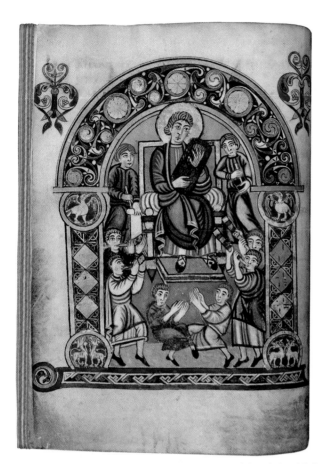

Fig. 5.5 Page with *David and Court Musicians*, now fol. 30b, but likely once the frontispiece of the *Vespasian Psalter*, Canterbury, England, first half of 8th century. British Library, MS Cotton Vespasian A.i. A psalter is a book of psalms. One of the most interesting aspects of this illustration is that it suggests that instrumental music may have played a role in Christian liturgy long before the twelfth century, when instrumentation is usually thought to have been introduced.

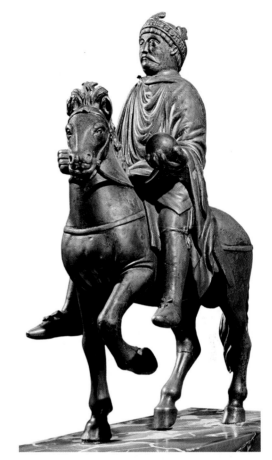

Fig. 5.6 Equestrian statue of Charlemagne, early 9th century. Bronze with traces of gilt, height 9 1/2″. Musée du Louvre, Paris. In person, Charlemagne stood 6′ 3 1/2″ tall, remarkably tall for the time.

Saxon noble would have recognized. In the centuries to come, Christianity would create its own treasure trove, its own celebratory music, its own great halls (the cathedrals), its own armored warriors fighting their own heroic battles (the Crusades). Beowulf's Grendel would become the infidel Muslim, and his king, his Lord God.

Carolingian Culture

Although England was slow to Christianize, the European continent was not. Christianity was firmly established in 732, at Poitiers [PWAH-tee-ay], France, just south of Tours [toor] in the Loire Valley. There Charles Martel [sharl MAR-tel], king of the Franks, defeated the advancing Muslim army, which had entered Spain in 711 and had been pushing northward ever since. The Arabs retreated south, beyond the Pyrenees, and settled into Spain. The Franks were one of many Germanic tribes—like the Angles and Saxons in England—that had moved westward beginning in the fourth century CE.

Most of these tribes adopted most of the Christian beliefs of the Roman culture they conquered, most notably the Ostrogoths in Italy, the Visigoths in southern Gaul (France) and Spain, the Vandals in North Africa, and the Franks, who controlled most of modern France.

Within a hundred years the Franks would come to control most of Western Europe under the leadership of Charlemagne, "Charles the Great" (r. 768–814) (Fig. **5.6**). (It is for him that historians have labeled this the Carolingian era, from *Carolus*, Latin for Charles.) Charlemagne brought one after another pagan tribe to submission, forcing them to give up their brand of Christianity and submit to Rome's Nicene Creed. Charlemagne's kingdom grew to include all of modern-day France, Holland, Belgium, Switzerland, almost all of Germany, Northern Italy and Corsica, and Navarre, in Northern Spain (Map **5.2**). Even larger areas paid him tribute. In return for his Christianization of this vast area, Pope Leo III crowned him emperor on Christmas Day, 800, creating what would later be known as the Holy Roman Empire.

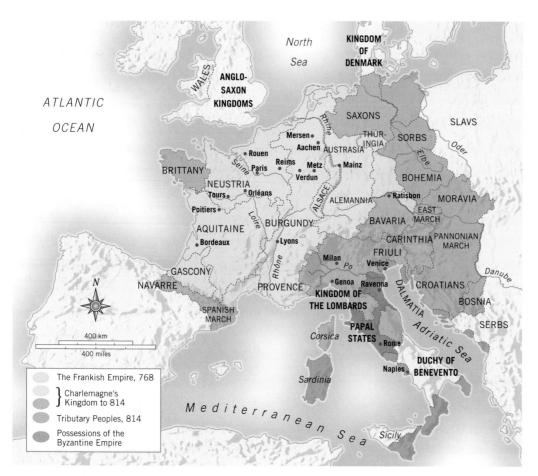

Map 5.2 The Empire of Charlemagne to 814.

The *Song of Roland*: Feudal and Chivalric Values

Charlemagne's military might was the stuff of legend. For centuries after his rule, tales of his exploits circulated throughout Europe in cycles of poems sung by *jongleurs* [zhohn-GLER], professional entertainers or minstrels who moved from court to court and performed *chansons de geste* [shahn-SOHN deh zhest] ("songs of deeds"). The oldest of these, and the most famous, is the *Song of Roland*, a poem built around a kernel of historical truth transformed into legend and eventually embellished into an epic. Four thousand lines long, composed of ten-syllable lines grouped in stanzas, it was transmitted orally for three centuries and finally written down in about 1100, by which time the story of a military defeat of little consequence had become an epic drama of ideological importance. The *jongleurs* sang the poem accompanied by a lyre. The only surviving musical notations to the poem are the letters *AOI* that end some verses. The exact meaning of this phrase is unclear, but it probably indicates a musical refrain, repeated throughout the performance. Most likely, the poem was sung in a **syllabic** setting, one note per syllable, in the manner of most folk songs even today. Its melody was probably also **strophic**—that is, the same music repeated for each stanza of the poem.

The *Song of Roland* tells the story of an event that occurred in 778, when Charlemagne's rear guard, led by his nephew

Roland, Roland's friend Oliver, and other peers, was ambushed by Muslim forces as Charlemagne's army returned from his invasion of Spain. (In fact, it was Basque [bask] Christians who ambushed Charlemagne, and he had actually been invited into Spain by Muslim Saracens [SAR-uh-senz] to help them fight other Muslims. However, over time, the story's villains were transformed from Basque Christians into Muslims for political and propagandistic purposes, as armies were organized to fight in the Middle East for the liberation of Jerusalem from Islam.)

The story is a simple one: The heroic Roland's army is betrayed by Ganelon, who tells the Saracen Muslim army of Roland's route through Roncevaux [ROHNS-voh], where his 20,000 soldiers are attacked by 400,000 Muslims. Roland sounds his ivory horn, alerting Charlemagne to the Saracen presence, but by then the Frankish guard has been defeated. Discovering Roland and his army dead, Charlemagne executes the treacherous Ganelon, and an epic battle between Charlemagne and the Muslims ensues. Charlemagne is victorious—but not without divine intervention. Charlemagne's prayer keeps the sun from setting, allowing his army time to defeat the Saracens.

Roland as the Ideal Feudal Hero The poem embodies the values of feudalism, celebrating courage and loyalty to one's ruler above all else, in this case Roland's loyalty to Charlemagne. Although the feudal obligation of the vassal to his lord had long been established in Germanic culture—among the Anglo-Saxons, for instance—its purest form was probably Carolingian. Roland is an ideal feudal hero, courageous and loyal, but he possesses—or is possessed by—a sense of pride that inevitably leads to his demise, just as Beowulf's self-confidence leads to his. In the following reading (**Reading 5.2**), Roland's companion, Oliver, counsels Roland that the Muslim (Saracen) army is so great that he ought to use his horn, Oliphant, to call Charlemagne to help him, but Roland's pride prevails.

READING 5.2   *Song of Roland*

85 "Roland, my friend, I pray you, sound your horn!
King Charlemagne, crossing the mountain pass,
Won't fail, I swear it, to bring back all his Franks."
"May God forbid!" Count Roland answers then.
"No man on earth shall have the right to say
That I for pagans sounded the Oliphant!
I will not bring my family to shame.
I'll fight this battle; my Durendal shall strike
A thousand blows and seven hundred more.
You'll see bright blood flow from the blade's keen steel,
We have good men; their prowess will prevail,
And not one Saracen shall live to tell the tale."

86 Oliver says, "Never would you be blamed;
I've seen the pagans, the Saracens of Spain.
They fill the valleys, cover the mountain peaks;
On every hill, and every wide spread plain,
Vast hosts assemble from that alien race;
Our company numbers but a few."
Roland replies, "The better, then, we'll fight!
If it please God and His angelic host,
I won't betray the glory of sweet France!
Better to die than learn to live with shame—
Charles loves us more as our keen swords win fame."

87 Roland is brave, and Oliver is wise;
Both are so brave men marvel at their deeds.
When they mount chargers, take up their swords and shields,
Not death itself could drive them from the field.
They are good men; their words are fierce and proud.

The loyalty of the Franks—and of Roland and Oliver in particular—to Charlemagne is expressed in these words, uttered by Roland a moment later:

"In his lord's service, a man must suffer pain,
Bitterest cold and burning heat endure;
He must be willing to lose his flesh and blood. . . .
And if I die, whoever takes my sword
Can say its master has nobly served his lord."

It is out of a sense of duty that Roland turns to face the Saracens—duty to Charlemagne, his lord, and by extension,

duty to the Christian God in the battle against Islam. Roland's insistence that he "will strike great blows with Durendal" (his sword is itself a gift from Charlemagne) expresses the Christian nature of the combat. Durendal's golden hilt conceals four relics (venerated objects associated with saints or martyrs), including hairs of St. Denis, the patron saint of France whose name the Franks shout as a battle cry. Thus, each blow is a blow for Christendom. The reward for such dutiful combat is, as he says, the love of his king. But it is also the love of the whole Christian world. Indeed, Roland ultimately sacrifices all for his king and his God. Mortally wounded in combat, he "knows that death is very near / His ears give way, he feels his brain gush out." Explicit and vivid language heightens the intensity of the moment, and the directness lends credence to characters who are otherwise reduced to stereotypes ("Roland is brave, and Oliver is wise"). But, finally, in his slow and painful death— "Count Roland feels the very grip of death / Which from his head is reaching for his heart"—he becomes a type for Jesus, sacrificing himself for all of Christendom.

The Chivalric Code The *Song of Roland* is one of the earliest expressions of feudalism's **chivalric code**. The term *chivalry* (from the French *chevalier* [shuh-VAHL-ee-ay], "horseman") expressed the qualities of an ideal knight, and may in fact more nearly reflect the values of the eleventh century (when the poem was written down) than the eighth-century practices of Charlemagne's day. Nevertheless, something very like this set of values already exists in *Beowulf*. The chevalier was a **knight** (from the German *knecht*, "young soldier"), and he was guided by a strict, though unwritten, code of conduct: courage in battle, loyalty to his lord and peers, and a courtesy verging on reverence toward women. Although in practice these values often broke down, feudalism and chivalry were powerful mechanisms for maintaining social order and political harmony throughout medieval Europe.

Promoting Literacy

Across Europe, the Church had traditionally served as the chief guardian of culture. In its monastic centers, the Roman love of learning had been maintained, especially in the manuscripts transcribed by monastic copyists. But literacy was anything but widespread. Charlemagne sought to remedy this situation at his court at Aachen, which soon attracted leading scholars and artists, whose efforts Charlemagne rewarded handsomely. Chief among these was an Englishman, perhaps even of Anglo-Saxon origin, Alcuin [AL-kwin] of York (735–804), who in 782 became head of Charlemagne's court school. One of the foremost grammarians and theologians of the period, Alcuin served as Charlemagne's personal tutor.

Alcuin's main purpose in Aachen was to create a curriculum to promote literacy that could be disseminated throughout the Carolingian Empire. Schools designed to teach children basic skills in reading and writing and some further study in the liberal arts and theology were established in Lyon [lee-OH], Orléans [or-lay-AH], Mainz [mynts], Tours, Laon [lan], and Metz [mes], which was a center for singing and liturgy (see Map 5.2). By 798, a decree from Aachen ordered prelates and country clergy throughout the empire to start schools for children. The emphasis was on educating males. The work of the state bureaucracy would fall to them, and by receiving a Christian education, they would lead in accordance with Church principles. But there is evidence that girls, especially those of noble birth, were also admitted to the local schools created by Alcuin.

There was also a religious purpose in educating the people. Charlemagne believed that to spread the gospel, people should be able to read aloud and sing in church, to say nothing of grasping the fundamental truth believed to be revealed in the Bible. Education thus furthered the traditional role of the Church. It provided a means for the Church—and Charlemagne's state as agent of the Church—to insert itself into the lives of every individual. Alcuin published a book of Old and New Testament passages to be read during Mass, as well as a book of prayers and rites that was made obligatory for all churches in the empire in 785. The last eight years of Alcuin's life were dedicated to producing a corrected version of the Latin Vulgate Bible that would become the standard text throughout the Middle Ages.

The Medieval Monastery

The monastery was a central part of Carolingian culture, arguably its most important institution. Before the Carolingian era, monastic life varied widely across Europe. In Italy, the rule of solitude (the Greek word *monos*, from which *monasticism* derives, means "alone") was barely enforced, and life in a monastery could be positively entertaining. If, in Ireland, more austere conditions prevailed, still the lively intellectual climate of the monastery attracted men and women seeking a vocation. Even from monastery to monastery, different conditions and rules prevailed.

Charlemagne imposed on all monasteries in the Frankish kingdom the rule of Benedict of Nursia [NOOR-she-uh], an Italian monk who had lived two centuries earlier (ca. 480–547). The Rule of St. Benedict defined monastic life as a community of like-minded individuals, all seeking religious perfection, under the direction of an abbot elected by the monks. Monks were to live a family life in the pursuit of religious perfection. They were to possess nothing of their own, accepting worldly poverty. They were to live in one place and not wander, guaranteeing the community's stability. And they were never to marry, acknowledging their chastity. Each day was divided into eight parts, the *horarium* [hor-AR-ee-um] (from the Latin *hora*, "hour"). The *horarium* is the daily prayer schedule of liturgical praise called the **Divine Office** (the word "Office" comes from the Latin *officium*, meaning "duty"), marked by recitations of the psalms and the chanting of hymns and prayers at eight specific times of the day, from early morning until bedtime. Between services, the monks studied, worked, and ate a light breakfast and heartier dinner. They lived by the motto of their order: "Pray and work."

The Ideal Monastery: St. Gall   The Swiss monastery of St. Gall, near Lake Constance, was Charlemagne's ideal monastery (Figs. **5.7**, **5.8**); its functional, orderly plan was used in many Benedictine monasteries. As medieval historian Walter Horn pointed out in the 1970s, the original plan was laid out in modules, or standard units, of $2\frac{1}{2}$ feet, and the entire complex was composed of multiples or parts of this standard unit. The nave and the transept of the church, each 40 feet wide, are composed of 16 modules. The area where they cross is a perfect square with 16 modules on a side. Each arm of the transept is equal to the crossing square—that is, 16 modules square. The area between the transept and the apse is also one crossing square. And the nave is $4\frac{1}{2}$ crossing squares long—or 56 modules. The rest of the monastery is built on this rational and orderly plan. The length of each monk's bed was to be $2\frac{1}{2}$ modules, the width of each garden path $1\frac{1}{4}$ modules, and so on. This systematic arrangement reflects an increasing tendency in medieval thinking to regard Christianity as a logical and rational philosophy of life, based on carefully constructed arguments and precise definitions of parts as orderly as the "rule" of the day in the *horarium*.

A **cloister**, or rectangular courtyard, typically arcaded and dedicated to contemplation and reflection, lies adjacent to the church, which is dominated by its imposing **westwork**—an innovation of Carolingian architecture, consisting of two tall towers surrounded by a multi-storied narthex on the west side of the church. Beside it, on the east side, are the monks' dormitories, latrines, and baths, and on the west, storage cellars. To the south of the cloister is the **refectory**, or dining hall. Farther to the south, and to the west and east, behind and adjacent to the refectory are outbuildings housing all the facilities necessary to support a community of approximately 100 monks—a kitchen, a brewery, a bakery, a mill, workshops for artisans, barns for various animals, a vegetable garden (with its own gardener), and an orchard that doubles as a cemetery. Surrounding the entire complex were fields in which the brothers worked. This side of the monastery was reserved for the members of the community.

The general public could enter the north side of the monastery. Here, beside the entrance to the church, we find a hostel, or inn, for housing less-well-to-do visitors, as well as a guesthouse for nobility, and between them a special kitchen (St. Benedict had directed that monasteries extend hospitality to all visitors). Directly to the north of the church is the monastery school, dedicated, by imperial decree, to educating the youth of local nobility. Another school, the novitiate, to the east of the church, was dedicated to the education and housing of young novices—those hoping to take vows and become brothers. In the northeast corner of the monastery was a public hospital, including an herb garden for remedies, the physician's quarters, and a facility for bloodletting—in the Middle Ages and until the nineteenth century the most common means of curing severe illness.

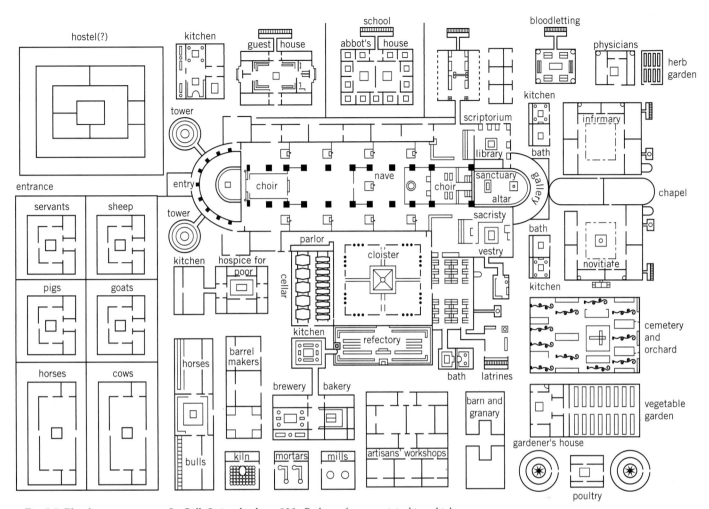

Fig. 5.7 Plan for a monastery at St. Gall, Switzerland. ca. 820. Redrawn from an original in red ink on parchment (inscriptions translated into English from Latin). 28″ × 44⅛″. Stiftsbibliothek, St. Gall, Switzerland.

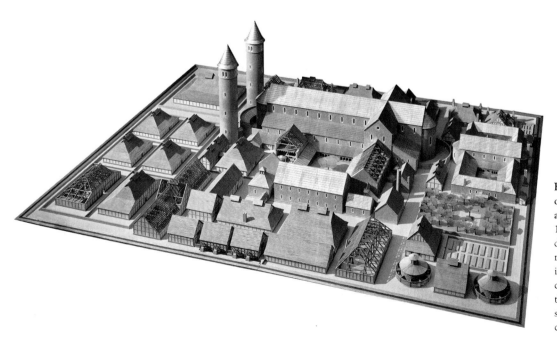

Fig. 5.8 Reconstruction model of the monastery of St. Gall, after the plan, by Walter Horn. 1965. The monastery builders did not follow this plan exactly; nevertheless, the plan was widely influential. Many of the surviving cathedrals of Europe discussed in the next chapters were originally surrounded by monasteries constructed on this model.

Women in Monastic Life Although the religious life offered women an alternative to life as housewife or worker, life in the convent or nunnery was generally available only to the daughters of aristocrats. Within the monastic system, women could achieve significant prestige. St. Benedict himself had a sister, Scholastica (d. ca. 543), who headed a monastery not far from his own. Hilda, abbess of Whitby (614–680), ran one of the most prominent Anglo-Saxon monasteries, a community of both monks and nuns. One of her most important acts was to host a Council at Whitby in an attempt to reconcile Celtic and Latin factions of the Church in England. She is one of the first women who rose to a prominent position within the largely male medieval Church.

Roswitha [ros-VEE-tah] of Gandersheim [GAHN-durs-hime] (ca. 935–975) never achieved Hilda's political prominence, but she was one of the notable playwrights of her day. Forgotten until the late fifteenth century, her plays concentrate on women heroines whose personal strength and sense of self-worth allow them to persevere in the face of adversity and challenges to their modesty and chastity.

One of the foremost women of the age was Hildegard [HIL-duh-garth] of Bingen [BING-un] (1098–1179), who ran the monastery at Bingen, near Frankfurt, Germany. She entered the convent at the age of eight and eventually became its abbess. Extraordinarily accomplished—she wrote tracts on natural science, medicine, and the treatment of disease, an allegorical dialogue between the vices and virtues, as well as a significant body of devotional songs (see the next section on Monastic Music)—she is best known as the first in a long line of female Christian visionaries and mystics, a role anticipated in Western culture by the Delphic priestesses (see chapter 2). Her visions are recorded in the *Scivias*, a work whose title derives from the Latin *Scite vias domini*, "Know the ways of the Lord" (**Reading 5.3**). The *Scivias* was officially designated by the pope as divinely inspired. A zealous advocate for Church reform, she understood that this recognition lent her the authority to criticize her secular and Church superiors, including the pope himself, and she did not hesitate to do so.

READING 5.3 **Hildegard of Bingen, *Scite vias domini***

In the year 1141 of the incarnation of Jesus Christ the Son of God, when I was forty-two years and seven months of age, a fiery light, flashing intensely, came from the open vault of heaven and poured through my whole brain. . . . And suddenly I could understand what such books as the psalter, the gospel and the other catholic volumes of the Old and New Testament actually set forth.

Indeed, from the age of girlhood, from the time that I was fifteen until the present, I had perceived in myself, just as until this moment, a power of mysteri-

ous, secret, and marvelous visions of a miraculous sort. . . . I have not perceived these visions in dreams, or asleep, or in a delirium, or with my bodily eyes, or with my external mortal ears, or in secreted places, but I received them awake and looking attentively about me with an unclouded mind, in open places, according to God's will.

The page from the *Scivias* reproduced here (Fig. **5.9**) illustrates this passage. Hildegard is shown recording her divine revelation, as her copyist waits to transcribe her words. Such images were directly supervised by Hildegard herself.

Later in the *Scivias*, Hildegard has a vision of the devil, embodied as a monstrous worm who oversees a marketplace full of material goods. After describing her vision, she interprets some of the key images. Hildegard's impulse to interpret her own words is typical of religious literature in the Middle Ages: Its primary purpose was to teach and instruct. But, more than that, Hildegard's *Scivias* shares with other visionary and mystical writing of the period an impulse to make the unknowable vividly present in the mind's eye of her audi-

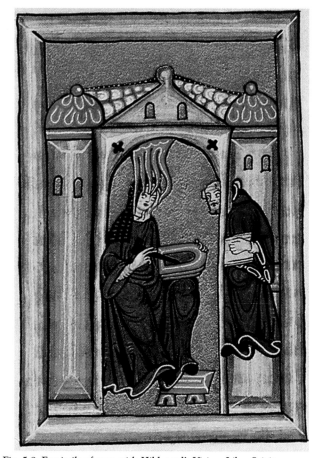

Fig. 5.9 Facsimile of page with *Hildegard's Vision, Liber Scivias*. ca. 1150–1200. Hildegard wrote 33 visionary tracts, collected in *Liber Scivias*, which were acknowledged by the Church as divine. The original manuscript was lost during World War II.

ence. Like the Delphic priestess, she directly encounters the divine through revelation and vision.

Monastic Music Hildegard is responsible for more surviving compositions than any other musician, male or female, who worked before the early fourteenth century. Her *Ordo virtutum* (Play of the Virtues) is a composition of texts and 82 melodies that dramatizes the conflict between good and evil. In it the devil, who never sings but shouts all his lines, confronts a personification of each of the 16 Virtues. Hildegard collected all of her liturgical works in a *Symphonia armonie electium revelationum* (Symphony of the Harmony of Celestial Revelations). Like her *Scivias*, Hildegard's music is designed to illuminate spiritual truths. She believed that in singing and playing music, the mind, heart, and body become one, that discord among celebrants is healed, and the harmony of the heavens is realized on earth.

By the time that Hildegard was composing, the liturgy, and particularly its music, had become remarkably unified. This had been accomplished at Charlemagne's insistence. Although we have no written melodies from Charlemagne's time, most scholars agree that he adopted a form that later became known as **Gregorian chant**—named after Pope Gregory the Great, the same pope who sent Augustine to England in 597. Called *cantus planus*, plainsong or **plainchant**, it consisted of **monophonic** songs (that is, songs for one or many voices singing a single melodic line with no harmony). The style of Gregorian chant probably originated in the way that ancient Jews sang the Psalms. In its simplest form, the chant is sung **a capella** (that is, without musical accompaniment) and performed in a syllabic style (a single note for each syllable). Often the final word of each phrase is emphasized by the addition of one or two other notes:

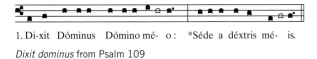

1. Di-xit Dóminus Dómino mé- o :   *Séde a déxtris mé- is.

Dixit dominus from Psalm 109

This is the opening line of Psalm 109 ("The Lord said to my Lord: sit on my right hand"). Its four-line staff would become the traditional Gregorian notation, with each note, or **neume** [noom], indicated by a small square. **Neumatic** [noo-MAT-ik] chant derives its name from these notes. In neumatic chant, the syllabic style gives way to a form in which each syllable is sung to two or three notes **(CD-Track 5.1)**. In later medieval chant, a single syllable is sung to many notes, a practice known as **melismatic** [mel-uz-MAT-ik] chant **(CD-Track 5.2):**

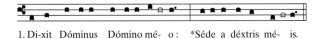

1. Di-xit Dóminus Dómino mé- o :   *Séde a déxtris mé- is.

Kyrie Eleison from opening of mass

The Mass Since the earliest times, the celebration of the mass was a central rite of the Christian Church. It is a celebration of the Eucharist, the fulfillment of Jesus's instruction (recorded in 1 Corinthians 11:24–25) to do in memory of him what he did for his disciples at the Last Supper—that is, Jesus gave his disciples bread, saying, "This is my body," and wine, saying "This is my blood." Christians generally recognized, in its celebration, the presence of Christ. In the medieval Mass, the *Kyrie* [KIR-ee-ay], which is either the first or second element in every Mass, consists of three phrases: *Kyrie eleison* [ih-LAY-ih-son] ("Lord, have mercy") is sung three times, followed by *Christe* [KRIS-tay] *eleison* ("Christ, have mercy"), likewise sung three times, and then another *Kyrie eleison*, set to different music, repeated three times again. The repetition of three phrases three times each is deeply symbolic, the number three referring to the Trinity, and the three squared (three times three) signifying absolute perfection.

The plainchant composed by Hildegard of Bingen is unique in the range of musical effects it employs. In contrast to the rather narrow scope of most chants of her day, she uses extremes of register to create "soaring arches" which, she believed, brought heaven and earth together. Although traditional plainchant rarely employed intervals greater than a second or third (one or two notes apart on a keyboard), Hildegard regularly used wider intervals such as fourths and fifths, again to create a sense of moving between the divine and mundane. Her melodies ascend rapidly upward as if toward the heavens. She combines neumatic and melismatic passages: The former seem grounded in the everyday, while the latter suggest the joy of salvation. Her unique style can be more readily appreciated by comparing **CD-Track 5.3** to the more traditional approaches to plainchant represented in CD tracks 5.1 and 5.2.

The most important single element in determining the nature of a given plainchant melody is its function in the liturgy, which remained consistent from the time of Charlemagne through the sixteenth century. Certain chants, focusing on the Psalms, were composed specifically for the eight *horarium* (hours) of the Divine Office and sung exclusively by cloistered monks and nuns. The Rule of St. Benedict required that the entire 150 Psalms be recited each week.

The Mass had its own repertoire of plainchant. It was celebrated once each day, between 6 AM and 9 AM in every church, convent, and monastery, and was open to any baptized member of the community or congregation. Some elements were performed at every Mass, including the Credo, a musical setting of the Nicene Creed (see chapter 4), while others were sung only on special Sundays or feast days of the liturgical year. The liturgical year revolves around two major feast days, Christmas and Easter; each is preceded by a season of penitence.

Charlemagne standardized the liturgy by creating several singing schools, including one at St. Gall, where plainchant was taught to choirmasters from throughout the empire. "In every bishop's see," he ordered in the Law of 789, "instruction shall be given in the psalms, musical notation, chant, the computation of the years and seasons, and grammar."

Capetian France and the Norman Conquest

In the middle of the ninth century, France was invaded by Normans—that is, "Northmen"—Viking warriors from Scandinavia. The Viking onslaught was devastating, as they plundered and looted across the north European seas, targeting especially isolated but wealthy monasteries such as Lindisfarne, which they attacked even earlier, in 793. The Viking invasions fragmented the former empire and caused nobility, commoners, and peasants alike to attach themselves to anyone who might provide military protection—thus cementing the feudal system. By the tenth century, they had raided, explored, and settled territories from North America, which the explorer Leif [leef] Eriksson reached about the year 1000, to Iceland, Greenland, the British Isles, and France. In France, they besieged Paris in 845 and gained control of the lower Seine [sen] valley. In 915, the Frankish king Charles III (r. 893–923) was forced to grant the Norse leader Rolf, or Rollo, permanent control of the region. Rollo became the first duke of Normandy.

The rest of the western Carolingian Empire, now called France, remained fragmented, with various counts and dukes competing for power. Finally, in 987, Hugh Capet [KAY-pit], lord of the Ile de France [eel deh-frahns], a relatively small domain stretching from Paris and its environs south to Orléans in the Loire [lwahr] Valley, was selected to serve as king. Hugh began a dynasty of Capetian [kuh-PEE-shun] kings that ruled for the next 350 years. From the beginning, the Capetians concentrated their energies on building a tightly knit administrative bureaucracy. Their most contentious relationship was with the dukes of Normandy, who were fiercely independent, going so far as to claim England for themselves, independent of Capetian influence.

The Normans invaded England in 1066, a story narrated in the famous *Bayeux* [BY-yuh] *Tapestry* (see *Focus* on pages 144–145).

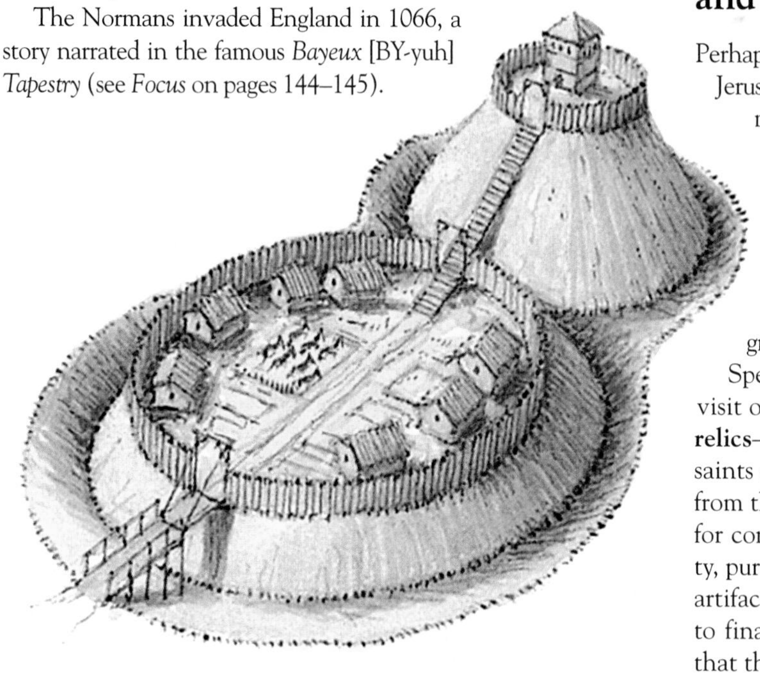

Fig. 5.10 Motte and bailey castle. When Normans first landed in England they constructed mounds, called mottes, upon which they built a square wooden tower called a keep. First used as a lookout tower and elevated fighting point, the keep later became an accommodation for the lord of the castle. At the foot of the motte was a flat area called a bailey, surrounded by a wooden stockade. Domestic buildings, including stables, kitchens, and servants' quarters, were located in the bailey. A moat, or trench filled with water, often surrounded the castle—a natural result of digging dirt for the motte.

England and northern France thus became one country, with one king, William I, the Conqueror, and a small group of barons who owned estates on both sides of the English Channel. To both pacify and defend themselves against the Saxons, the Normans constructed **motte and bailey** castles (Fig. **5.10**). A motte is a raised earth mound, and a bailey is the enclosed courtyard at its base. Archeologists estimate that the Normans built about 500 of them between 1066 and 1086, or one every two weeks. Such fortifications could be built in as little as eight days.

Fearing an invasion from Denmark, William I ordered a complete survey of the country so that he could more accurately determine how much tax he could raise to provide a new army. Known as the *Domesday* [DOOMZ-day] (or "Judgment") *Book*, it measured the population of England at about 1 million, with fully three-quarters of the country's wealth resting in the hands of the king and 300 landowners. Two hundred of these were French nobles, and only two were English. The other hundred were archbishops, bishops, and the heads of monasteries. The rest of the land was in the hands of small farmers, and 90 percent of the population worked on the land. Some were freemen, but most owed at least partial allegiance to a local lord. Ten percent of the people were serfs, who owned no land at all. The *Domesday Book* gives us a remarkable view of medieval society and of the great gulf between rich and poor upon which it was based.

Pilgrimage Churches and the Romanesque

Perhaps because it was closer to Northern Europeans than either Jerusalem or Rome, Santiago de Compostela was by far the most popular site of pilgrimages in the eleventh through thirteenth centuries. It had also developed a reputation for repeated miracles, and by the mid-twelfth century, a *Pilgrim's Guide to Santiago de Compostela* had appeared. A widely circulated manuscript probably written in Latin by monks in southern France, it describes and illustrates the towns and monuments on the major pilgrimage routes through France and Spain (Map. **5.3**).

Specific routes soon developed that allowed pilgrims to visit other sacred sites along the way. These sites housed the **relics**—bones, clothing, or other possessions—of Christian saints and martyrs. Relics arrived, virtually by the boatload, from the Middle East, where Crusaders, fighting the Muslims for control of Jerusalem and other sites sacred to Christianity, purchased them for resale in the West. The resale of these artifacts, whose authenticity was often questionable, helped to finance the Crusades. What was reputed to be the tunic that the Virgin Mary wore when she gave birth to Christ was housed at Chartres [shart]. At Vézelay [VAYZ-lay], the starting point of one of the three routes to Santiago de Compostela, pilgrims could pray to what were asserted to be the bones of Mary Magdalene. Pilgrims believed that the saints would perform miracles and cure diseases.

The Abbey Church of Sainte-Foy [sant fwah] at Conques [cohnk], the oldest of the pilgrimage churches (Fig. **5.11**),

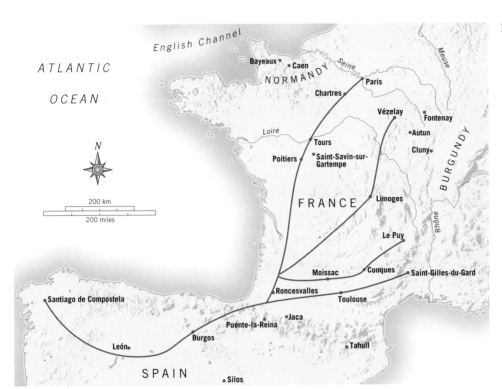

Map 5.3 The Pilgrimage Routes.

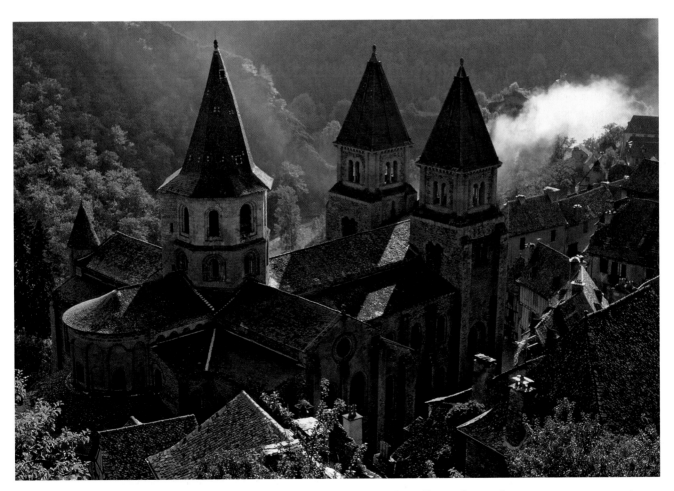

Fig. 5.11 Abbey Church of Sainte-Foy, Conques, Auvergne, France. ca. 1050–1120. Sainte-Foy was the second church on the route to Santiago de Compostela that began at Le Puy.

Focus

The Bayeux Tapestry

The *Bayeux Tapestry*—actually a 231-foot embroidery—was sewn between 1070 and 1080, almost certainly by women at the School of Embroidery at Canterbury, in Kent, England—one of the few surviving works by women we have from the period. The embroiderers of the *Bayeux Tapestry* worked with twisted wool, dyed in eight colors, and used only two basic stitches. It was commissioned by Bishop Odo of Bayeux, half-brother of William, duke of Normandy, whose conquest of England in 1066 it narrates in both pictures and words (in Latin). Like the Column of Trajan (see fig. 3.16), its story is both historical and biased. The tapestry was designed to be hung around the choir of Odo's Bayeux Cathedral—an unabashed act of self-promoting propaganda on the part of the Normans.

When the English king Edward the Confessor died on January 5, 1066, without an heir, William, duke of Normandy, claimed the throne, swearing that Edward had promised William the English throne when Edward died. But on his deathbed, Edward named Harold of Wessex king, while two other contenders, Harold Hardrada of Norway and Tostig, earl of Northumbria, also laid their claims. Battle was inevitable.

William was particularly unhappy with Harold of Wessex's claim to the throne. Harold had visited Normandy, sometime between 1064 and the end of 1065, at the insistence of King Edward. In fact, the *Bayeux Tapestry* begins at this point. The tapestry narrates the Norman point of view, so its reliability is uncertain, but according to both the tapestry and other Norman sources, during his stay, Harold recognized William as Edward's heir. Whether Harold did so willingly is debatable—even the tapestry shows Harold being taken prisoner by a vassal of William.

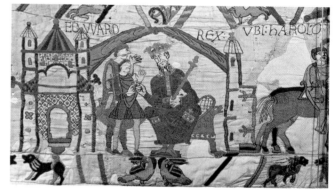

The *Bayeux Tapestry*. 1070–80. Embroidered wool on linen, height 20″. Entire length of fabric, 231′. With special authorization of the city of Bayeux, Musée de la Tapisserie, Bayeux, France/The Bridgeman Art Library. This, the first section of the tapestry depicts King Edward the Confessor talking to Harold, earl of Wessex, his wife's brother. He is sending Harold on a mission to France, ostensibly to tell William, duke of Normandy, that he will be Edward's successor.

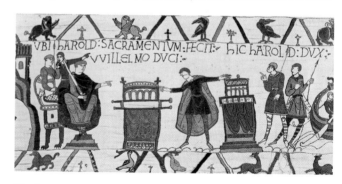

The *Bayeux Tapestry*. 1070–80. With special authorization of the city of Bayeux, Musée de la Tapisserie, Bayeux, France/The Bridgeman Art Library. Harold swears allegiance to William, his right hand on the altar between them, and his left on a chest presumably housing sacred objects from the Cathedral at Bayeux.

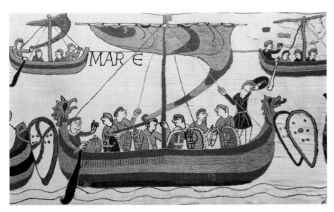

The *Bayeux Tapestry.* 1070–1080. With special authorization of the city of Bayeux, Musée de la Tapisserie, Bayeux, France/The Bridgeman Art Library. The Normans sail for England. Note the animal-head prow of the ship, which underscores the Norse origins of the Normans.

Harold was back in England before Edward died on January 5, 1066, and he became king, abrogating whatever oath he may have sworn to William. The tapestry shows him in February with Halley's Comet in the sky—interpreted by the Anglo-Saxons as a portent of disaster and resulting, the tapestry implies, from his having broken his oath. Ghost ships, perhaps from a dream, decorate the border below the troubled king, foreshadowing the invasion to come.

As William prepared to invade England from the south, Harold Hardrada and the Norwegians prepared to press their own claims from the north. The weather determined the course of battle. Strong northerly winds kept William docked in Normandy, but the same winds favored the Norwegians, who soon landed on the north coast. Harold met them at Stamford Bridge, near York, on September 25, 1066, and defeated them. By then, the winds had changed, and William sailed from the south, landing in Sussex. Harold turned his troops southward, but exhausted from both battle and the hurried march, they were defeated by William's army at Hastings on October 14, 1066. Harold died in the battle. The embroidery ends with a simple statement—"and the English turned and fled"—as if there is nothing more to say.

For seven centuries, the tapestry was cared for at Bayeux Cathedral, where it was hung round the nave on feast days and special occasions. It escaped destruction in the French Revolution in 1789, and was taken to Paris in the early eighteenth century when Napoleon exhibited it in his own propaganda campaign as he prepared to invade England.

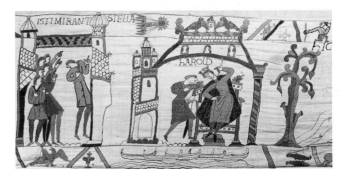

The *Bayeux Tapestry.* 1070–1080. With special authorization of the city of Bayeux, Musée de la Tapisserie, Bayeux, France/The Bridgeman Art Library. Having returned to England just before Edward's death and having assumed the throne, Harold is disturbed by the arrival of a comet with a fiery tail, visible in the top border.

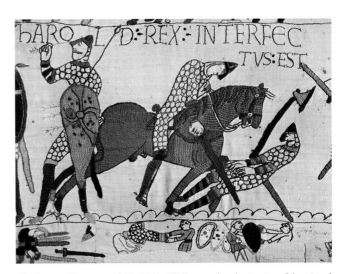

The *Bayeux Tapestry.* 1070–1080. With special authorization of the city of Bayeux, Musée de la Tapisserie, Bayeux, France/The Bridgeman Art Library. Harold, with the green shield, receives an arrow to the eye at the Battle of Hastings. Immediately to the right, a Norman soldier slays him. Note the soldiers stripping armor from the dead in the bottom border.

housed the relics of Saint Foy ("Saint Faith" in English), a child who was martyred in 303 for refusing to worship pagan gods. Her skull was contained in an elaborate jeweled **reliquary** (Fig. **5.12**), a container used to protect and display sacred relics. It stood in the choir of the church, where pilgrims could view it from the ambulatory. The head of the reliquary, which is disproportionately large, was salvaged from a late Roman wooden mask and covered with gold foil. Many of the precious stones that decorate the reliquary were gifts from pilgrims. The actual skull of the saint was housed in a recess carved into the back of the reliquary, and below it, on the back of her throne, was an engraving of the Crucifixion, indicating the connection between Saint Foy's martyrdom and Christ's.

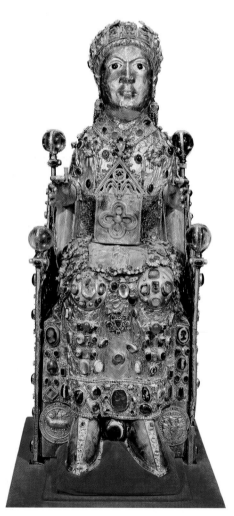

Fig. 5.12 Reliquary effigy of Sainte-Foy, made in the Auvergne region, France, for the Abbey Church of Sainte-Foy, Conques, mostly 983–1013 with later additions. Gold and silver over a wooden core, studded with precious stones and cameos, height 34". Church Treasury, Conques. This jewel-encrusted reliquary survived because monks hid it in the wall of the church when Protestants burned the abbey in 1568. It was not discovered until restoration of the church in the 1860s.

The Abbey Church is one of the earliest examples of a style that art historians have come to call the **Romanesque** [roh-mun-ESK], "in the manner of the Romans," because it incorporates elements of Roman architectural tradition. The basilica tradition that extends back to the Roman basilica (see *Focus*, Chapter 3) became the model for the Romanesque church floor plan, although the wooden ceilings of churches like Old Saint Peter's (see Figs. 4.6, 4.7) were replaced by much more fire-resistant barrel vaults.

The portals of the new pilgrimage churches were modeled after the triumphal arches of Rome, but they celebrate the triumph of the Christian God, not a worldly leader. Such architectural continuity, spanning an entire millennium, represents in part a lack of technological innovation rather than a philosophical return to Roman traditions. However, the Christian adoption of Roman architectural styles also suggests the Christian rejection of its Judaic heritage—the temple and the synagogue—as well as a growing identification with the Greco-Roman West. As this identification took hold, religious fervor came to define the age.

Like other pilgrimage churches, Sainte-Foy was constructed to accommodate large numbers of visitors. Its west portal was large and opened directly into the nave (Figs. **5.13, 5.14**). Wide aisles skirted the nave and continued around the transept, choir, and apse, creating the ambulatory. A second-story gallery was built over the side aisles; it both accommodated still more people and served structurally to support the extra weight of the arched stone ceilings.

The **barrel vault** that rises above the nave of Sainte-Foy is one of the distinctive features of Romanesque architecture. As we saw in Chapter 3, barrel vaults are elongated arched masonry structures spanning an interior space and shaped like a half cylinder. In Romanesque churches, the space created by such vaults was designed to raise the worshiping pilgrims' eyes and thus direct their thoughts to heaven.

The pilgrimage churches evidently competed with one another in decorating their basilicas, all with an eye on appealing to the viewer's emotions. Writing in the eleventh century, the French Benedictine monk Raoul Glaber [rah-ool glay-bur] noted, "throughout the world, especially in Italy and Gaul, a rebuilding of church basilicas [is occurring], . . . each Christian people striving against the others to erect nobler ones." The portals to the churches were of special importance. Not only was the portal the first thing the visitor would see; it also marked the boundary between secular and sacred space. The space created under the portal arch, called the **tympanum** [TIM-puh-num], was filled with sculptural relief.

All of the elements of Romanesque portals were equally subject to decorative relief (see diagram, Fig. **5.15**): the lintel, **jambs** (the vertical elements on both sides of door supporting the lintel or arch), **trumeau** [troo-MOH] (the column or post in the middle of a large door supporting the lintel), and the **archivolt** [AR-ki-volt] (the curved molding formed by the voussoirs making up the arch). The tympa-

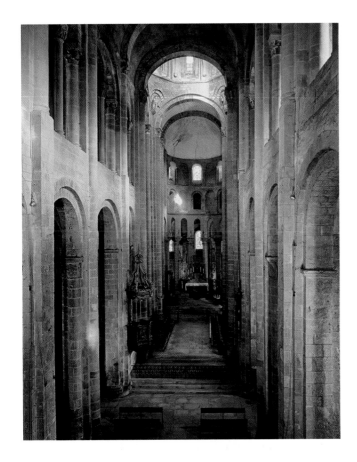

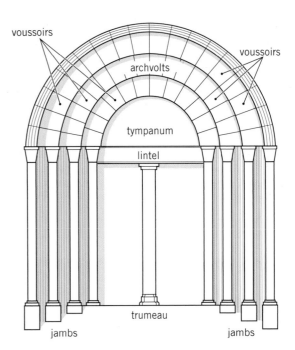

Fig. 5.15 Diagram of a Romanesque portal.

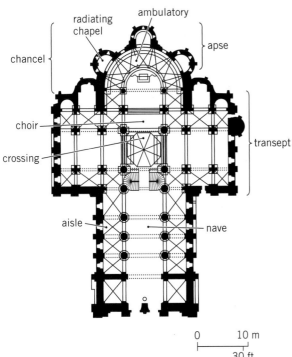

Figs. 5.13 and 5.14 Interior and floor plan of the nave, Sainte-Foy, Conques. ca. 1050–1120. Some of the innovations of the Romanesque cathedral can be explained, at least in part, by the need to allow pilgrims to pass through the church—around the ambulatory, for instance—without disturbing the monks as they attended to their affairs at the main altar in the choir.

num of Sainte-Foy at Conques depicts *The Last Judgment* (Figs. **5.16**, **5.17**). At the center of the tympanum, Christ raises his right arm to welcome those who are saved. His lowered left hand points to hell, the destination of the damned. He sits enthroned in a **mandorla**, an almond-shaped oval of light signifying divinity, a motif imported to the Western world from the Far East, through Byzantium, and one widely used by Romanesque artists. Below Christ's feet, the weighing of souls is depicted as a contest between the archangel Michael and a desperate demon who cheats by pressing his forefinger onto the pan, nevertheless failing to overcome the goodness of the soul in question.

The lintel is divided into two parts: on the left, heaven, and on the right, hell. The two are divided by a partition: An angel welcomes the saved, while on the other side, a demon armed with a bludgeon shoves the damned into hell's monstrous jaws. Situated frontally under the arches of heaven, the saved give the appearance of order and serenity, while all is confusion and chaos on hell's side. Satan stands in the center of the right lintel, presiding over an astonishing array of tortures. On Satan's left, a figure symbolizing Pride is thrown from his high horse, stabbed through with a pitchfork. Next to them, a bare-breasted adulteress and her lover await Satan's wrath. A figure symbolizing Greed is hung from on high with his purse round the neck and a toad at his feet. A demon tears the tongue out of Slander. In the small triangular space at the right above Satan, two fiendish-looking rabbits roast a poacher on a spit. In the corresponding triangular space to the left,

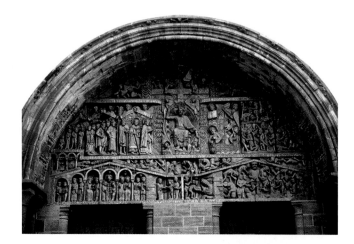

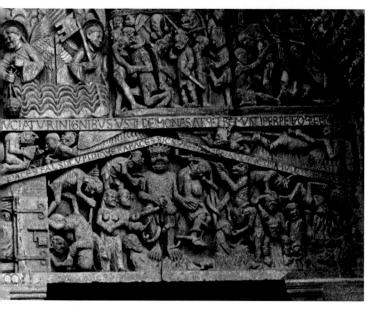

Figs. 5.16 and 5.17 *Last Judgment,* tympanum and detail of west portal, Sainte-Foy, Conques. ca. 1065. This depiction of the Last Judgment uses composition subtly and effectively to distinguish the saved from the damned. To Christ's left, the action is chaotic—figures twist and turn in often unpredictable directions. To his right, on the other hand, everyone stands upright under orderly arrangements of arches.

a devil devours the brain of a damned soul who commits suicide by plunging a knife into his throat. Close by, another hunchbacked devil has just grabbed the harp of a damned soul and tears his tongue with a hook. Such images were designed to move the pilgrim to the right hand of Christ, not the left.

These themes are the focus of perhaps the most famous sermon of the Middle Ages, *On the Misery of the Human Condition.* Pope Innocent III (pope 1198–1216) wrote this tract before his ascension to the papacy; on his election, the Church cardinals unanimously approved it as official Church doctrine. In the sermon, Innocent rails at length on the wretchedness and worthlessness of human beings, their weak-

nesses, folly, selfishness, vileness, their crimes, and their sins. He describes the human body as putrid in both life and death: "In life, [man] produced dung and vomit; in death he produces rottenness and stench." But perhaps most dramatically, he catalogues the fate that awaits them in hell (**Reading 5.4**):

READING 5.4　from Pope Innocent III, *On the Misery of the Human Condition*

There shall be weeping and gnashing of teeth, there shall be groaning, wailing, shrieking and flailing of arms and screaming, screeching, and shouting; there shall be fear and trembling, toil and trouble, holocaust and dreadful stench, and everywhere darkness and anguish; there shall be asperity, cruelty, calamity, poverty, distress, and utter wretchedness; they will feel an oblivion of loneliness and namelessness; there shall be twistings and piercings, bitterness, terror, hunger and thirst, cold and hot, brimstone and fire burning, forever and ever world without end. . . .

Such imagery is meant to strike terror into the soul of listeners by serving as a *memento mori* [mi-MENT-oh MORE-ee], a "reminder of death." Faced with such prospects, pilgrims were willing to endure the physical hardship and considerable danger their journeys entailed. Some brought great sums of money with them—gold, silver, jewelry, at least enough money to pay for their lodging and meals. If they inaugurated a new economy of hospitality in their travels, they also invited larceny, even murder, and bandits plagued the pilgrimage routes.

Cluny and the Monastic Tradition

Most of the Romanesque pilgrimage churches were controlled by the Abbey of Cluny. Like Charlemagne's Saint-Gall (see Figs. 5.7, 5.8), Cluny, founded in about 910, was a reformed Benedictine monastery. The Cluniac order enjoyed a special status in the Church hierarchy, reporting directly to the pope and bypassing all feudal or ecclesiastic control. No secular ruler could exercise any control over the monastery (the origin of our modern insistence on the separation of Church and State). Furthermore, the Cluniac order insisted on the celibacy of its monks and nuns—the Church was to be their only lord and spouse. Celibacy was not the rule elsewhere, and was not officially imposed on Catholic priests until 1139. Even then, Cluny's abbot was among the most powerful men in Europe; Abbot Hugh de Semur, who ruled the abbey from 1049 to 1109, was the most influential of these. In 1088, Hugh began work on a new church for the abbey, supported financially by King Alfonso VI of León [lay-

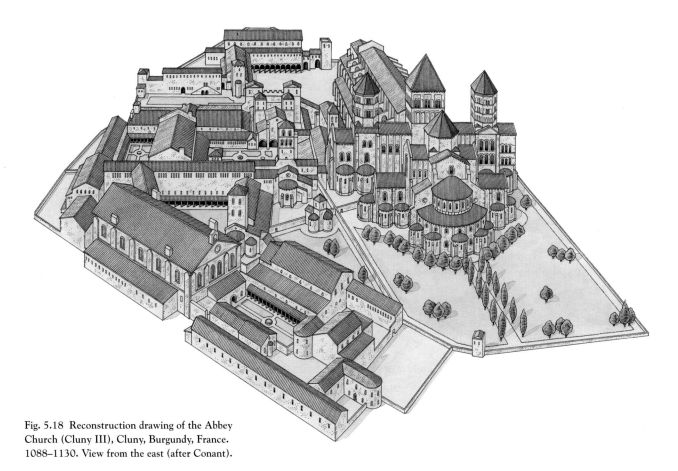

Fig. 5.18 Reconstruction drawing of the Abbey Church (Cluny III), Cluny, Burgundy, France. 1088–1130. View from the east (after Conant).

OHN] and Castile [kah-STEEL], in northern Spain. Known as Cluny III (Fig. **5.18**) because it was the third church built on the site, it was described by a contemporary as "shining on the earth like a second sun." Today only a portion of its south transept and tower remain—the rest was destroyed in the late eighteenth century by French revolutionaries.

Choral Music Benedictine monks at Cluny introduced choral music into the liturgy sometime in the first half of the tenth century. Odo of Cluny (879–942), the monastery's second abbot, was an important musical theorist. He is often credited with developing one of the first effective systems of musical notation, used to teach choral music to other monasteries in the Cluniac fold. The method used the letters A through G to name the seven notes of the Western scale. Working from Odo's example, 100 years later Guido [GWEE-doh] of Arezzo [ah-RET-soh] (ca. 990–ca. 1050) introduced the idea of depicting notes on a staff of lines so that the same note always appears on the same line. With this innovation, modern musical notation was born.

Choral music introduces the possibility of **polyphony** [puh-LIF-uh-nee]—two or more lines of melody—as opposed to the monophonic quality of Gregorian chant. The earliest form of this new polyphonic music was called **organum**. It simply consists of voices singing note-to-note in parallel. Probably the first instance of this would have been adult monks singing a monophonic chant in parallel with boys' voices singing the same melody at a higher pitch. Soon the second voice began to move in contrary motion to the bass chant **(free organun)**, or to add numerous notes to individual syllables above the bass chant **(melismatic organum)**. An excellent example of melismatic organum is the "Alleluia, dies sanctificatus" by the composer Léonin, who worked from 1163 to 1190 at Notre-Dame [noh-truh-dahm] Cathedral in Paris (**CD-Track5.4**). The movement of the two voices could be diagrammed as shown in Figure **5.19**. The lower voices hold unusually long notes, while the upper voices move faster and more freely, creating two independent musi-

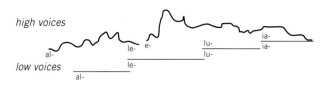

Fig. 5.19 Diagram of melismatic organum from Léonin's "Alleluia, dies sanctificatus."

cal lines. One can only imagine how music like this, performed by as many as 100 voices, might have sounded in Cluny III, which was famous for its acoustics.

The Crusades and the Culture of Romance

On November 25, 1095, at the Council of Clermont [KLER-mohn] (modern Clermont-Ferrand [fuh-RAHND]), Pope Urban II (pope 1088–1099) preached the First Crusade. The pope had received his training as a monk at Cluny, under the direct tutelage of Hugh de Semur. What motivated the First Crusade is difficult to say. We know that throughout Christendom there was a widespread desire to regain free access to Jerusalem, which had been captured by the Arabs in 638. In part, however, the aim was to bring peace to Europe. Because of the feudal **primogeniture** system, by which the eldest son in a family inherited all of its property, large numbers of aristocratic younger brothers were disinherited and left to their own devices. They had taken to feuding with one another (and with their elder brothers) and raiding other people's land. The Crusades organized these disenfranchised men with the promise of reward, both monetary and spiritual: "Jerusalem," Urban preached, "is the navel of the world; the land is fruitful above all others, like another paradise of delights. . . . Undertake the journey [also] for the remission of your sins, with the assurance of the imperishable glory of the kingdom of heaven." The pope also presented the Crusades as a Holy War.

> A race from the kingdom of the Persians, an accursed race, a race utterly alienated from God . . . has invaded the lands of the Christians and has depopulated them by the sword, pillage and fire. . . . They destroy the altars, after having defiled them with their uncleanness. . . . When they wish to torture people by a base death, they perforate their navels, and dragging forth the extremity of the intestines, bind it to a stake; then with flogging they lead the victim around until the viscera having gushed forth the victim falls prostrate upon the ground. . . . What shall I say of the abominable rape of the women? . . . On whom therefore is the labor of avenging these wrongs and of recovering this territory, if not upon you?

It was convincing rhetoric. Nearly 100,000 young men signed on.

The First Crusade was thus motivated by several forces: religious zeal, the desire to reduce conflict at home by sending off Europe's feuding aristocrats, defending Christendom from barbarity, the promise of monetary reward otherwise unavailable to the disenfranchised young nobility, and, not least of all, that nobility's own hot blood and sense of adventure. The First Crusade was a low point in Christian culture. Late in the year 1098, having destroyed the city of Antioch, the Frankish army (called the *Franj* by the Muslims) attacked the city of Ma'arra (modern Ma'arrat an Nu'man in Syria). "For three days they put people to the sword," the Arab historian Ibn al-Athïr wrote, "killing more than a hundred thousand people and taking many prisoners." This is undoubtedly an exaggeration, since the city's population was then something under 10,000, but the horror of what happened next somewhat justifies Ibn al-Athïr's numbers. As reported by Frankish chronicler Radulph of Caen, "In Ma'arra our troops boiled pagan adults in cooking pots; they impaled children on spits and devoured them grilled." In an official letter to the pope, the commanders explained: "A terrible famine racked the army in Ma'arra, and placed it in the cruel necessity of feeding itself upon the bodies of the Saracens." An anonymous poet of Ma'arra lamented: "I know not whether my native land be a grazing ground for wild beasts or yet my home!" Descriptions of the slaughter of the citizens of Jerusalem, when the Crusaders finally took that city on July 15, 1099, are no less gruesome.

The Muslim peoples of the Middle East were not the only victims of the Crusades. During the early days of the First Crusade in 1096, Count Emicho of Leiningen, in present-day Germany, making his way down the Rhine to embark for Jerusalem, robbed and murdered all the Jews he could find, killing 800 in Worms and wiping out the entire Jewish population of both Mainz and Cologne. Emicho seems to have been motivated by the need for funds to support his army, but his was a religious war as well. In his eyes, the Jews, like the Muslims, were the enemies of Christ. Local bishops, to their credit, attempted to stop the carnage, and Bernard of Clairvaux would later preach against the persecution of Jews, but in the Middle East, once Jerusalem was taken, Jews were burned alive or sold into slavery. The small number who survived did so by converting to Christianity.

The First Crusade was militarily successful. But by the middle of the eleventh century Islamic armies had recaptured much of the Middle East, prompting a Second Crusade from 1147 to 1149, and then a Third in 1189. Politically and religiously, the first three Crusades were failures. Rather than freeing the Holy Land from Muslim influence, they cemented it more firmly than ever. But they did succeed in stimulating Western trade with the East. Merchants from Venice, Genoa, and Pisa followed the Crusaders into the region, and soon new wealth, generated by these new markets, flowed into Europe. The Fourth Crusade in 1202 was motivated almost entirely by profit as Venice agreed to transport some 30,000 Crusaders in return for their destroying its commercial rivals in the Adriatic and Aegean, particularly Constantinople.

Krak des Chevaliers and the Medieval Castle Krak des Chevaliers [krahk day shuh-VAHL-yay] (Fig. **5.20**), in northern Syria, was first occupied by Crusaders in 1109, and, beginning in 1142, it was occupied by the Knights Hospitaller, whose mission was to care for the sick and wounded. During the Crusades, it was besieged 12 times, finally falling to Berber invaders in 1271.

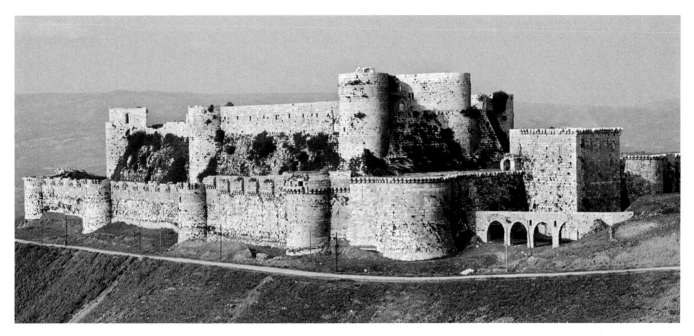

Fig. 5.20 Krak des Chevaliers, Syria. First occupied 1109. Two lines of defense made the castle virtually impenetrable. An aqueduct brought water to the castle. Water was stored in huge cisterns beneath the outer ward. If during siege the water supply was cut off, the knights could hold out for several months.

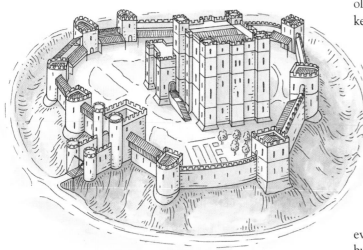

Fig. 5.21 Stone castle. Surrounded by a moat, the stone castles that replaced motte and bailey castles were eminently defensible, comparatively immune from fire, and rising as high as 100 feet, imposing symbols of Norman power.

Krak des Chevaliers was modeled on the castle-fortresses built by the Normans in England and northern France (see Fig. 5.10). Beginning in 1078, stone castles gradually replaced these wooden fortifications (Fig. **5.21**). The sheer weight of the stone keep required that it be built on solid ground. So, unless a natural hill presented itself, the motte (the mound on which the older wooden towers had been built) was eliminated. Now the keep served as the main residence of the lord and included a main hall, a chapel, and a dungeon. Workshops, kitchens, and storehouses surrounded the bailey. Most stone castles had a well for fresh water in case of siege, a great advantage over the aqueduct supplying Krak des Chevaliers.

Eleanor of Aquitaine and the Art of Courtly Love
In the Second Crusade, Eleanor of Aquitaine [ak-wuh-TAIN] (ca. 1122–1204) accompanied her husband, King Louis [LOO-ee] VII, into battle in the Middle East, along with 300 ladies of similar mind, all dressed in armor and carrying lances. Her intent was to help the sick and wounded. The women, most of whom eventually returned safely to Europe, never engaged in battle, but theirs was an act of uncommon personal and social bravery. They were widely chided by contemporary commentators, but their actions underscore the changing role of women in medieval society.

Perhaps most notably, women, especially women of noble birth, were becoming increasingly literate. This was the time in which the great oral poems of the first millennium—poems like *Beowulf* and *Song of Roland*—were first written down. Furthermore, over 2,600 poems survive as texts composed by the **troubadour** poets of Eleanor's own day. In the decade that she lived at Poitiers, from 1170 to 1179, Eleanor and her daughter by Louis VII, Marie, countess of Champagne, established that city as the center of a secular culture and literary movement that celebrated the art of courtly love.

The troubadour poets, most of them men, though a few were women, usually accompanied themselves on a lyre or lute, and in their poems they can be said to have "invented" romantic love as we know it today—not the feelings and emotions associated with love, but the conventions and vocabulary that we use to describe it. The primary feeling is one of longing, of a knight or nobleman for a woman (usually unattainable because married or of a higher status), or, when the troubadour was a woman—a **trobairitz**—the reverse. Thus, to love is to suffer, to wander aimlessly, unable to concentrate on anything but the mental image of the beloved, to lose one's appetite, to lie sleepless at night—in short, to give up life for a dream. There was, in addition, a quasi-religious aspect to courtly love. Recognizing that he is beset by earthly desires, the lover sees his ability to resist these temptations and rise above his own base humanity as evidence of his spiritual purity. Finally, in the courtly love tradition, the smitten knight or nobleman must be willing to perform any deed to win his lady's favor. In fact, the loyalty that he once conferred upon his lord in the feudal system is, in courtly love, transferred to his lady (who is often, in fact, his lord's wife), as the scenes on a jeweled twelfth-century casket make clear (Fig. 5.22). If the courtly love tradition reduced women to little more than objects of male desire, in some measure it also allowed them to share in the power enjoyed by their husbands.

We know of 12 or so *trobairitz*, or woman troubadour poets. Of these, one of the best is Beatriz de Dia, wife of William, count of Poitiers. While married, Beatriz fell in love with a knight and, according to a contemporary chronicler, wrote "many good songs" dedicated to him. Four of these late twelfth or early thirteenth century songs survive. Beatriz's "Cruel Are the Pains I've Suffered" is an example of the remarkable freedom of expression that a *trobairitz* could enjoy. She clearly regrets her choice to remain true to her husband, and in fact the poem reads as a frank invitation to adultery (**Reading 5.5**):

READING 5.5 Contessa de Dia's "Cruel Are the Pains I've Suffered," from *Lark in the Morning: The Verses of the Troubadors*

Cruel are the pains I've suffered
For a certain cavalier
Whom I have had. I declare
I love him—let it be known forever.
But now I see that I was deceived:
When I'm dressed or when I languish
In bed, I suffer a great anguish—
I should have given him my love.

One night I'd like to take my swain
To bed and hug him, wearing no clothes—
I'd give him reason to suppose
He was in heaven, if I deigned
To be his pillow! For I've been more
In love with him than Floris was
With Blanchefleur: my mind, my eyes
I give to him; my life, *mon cor.**

When will I have you in my power,
Dearest friend, charming and good?
Lying with you one night I would
Kiss you so you could feel my ardor.
I want to have you in my husband's
Place, of that you can rest assured—
Provided you give your solemn word
That you'll obey my every command.

* *Mon cor* means "my heart" and alludes to a popular French romance, *Floris et Blanchefleur.*

That poems such as this survived, let alone that they became well known, underscores the remarkable personal freedom of court women of the age.

The Romance: Chrétien de Troyes's *Lancelot* Because the poetry of the courtly love tradition was written in the vernacular—the common language of everyday life—and not in the Latin of the highly educated, a broader audience was able

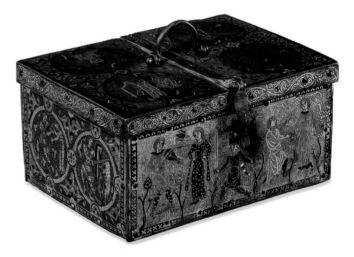

Fig. 5.22 Casket with scenes of courtly love, from Limoges. ca. 1180. Champlevé enamel, $3\frac{5}{8} \times 8\frac{1}{2} \times 6\frac{3}{8}$". © The Trustees of the British Museum/Art Resource, NY. At the left, a lady listens, rather sternly, as a troubadour poet expresses his love for her. In the center is a knight, sword in one hand and key to the lady's heart in the other. On the right, the knight kneels before the lady, his hands shaped in a heart; a rope around his neck, held by the lady, signifies his fidelity to her.

to enjoy it. And longer forms, like the *Song of Roland*, also began to circulate widely, some of them in prose.

One of the most popular works of the day, Chrétien de Troyes's [kray-tee-EN duh trwah] *Lancelot*, appeared around 1170. Centered on the adventures of Lancelot, a knight in the court of the legendary King Arthur of Britain, and focusing particularly on his courtly-love-inspired relationship with Guinevere, Arthur's wife, the poem is an example of the **medieval romance**. The term "romance" derives from the Old French term *romans*, which referred to the vernacular, everyday language of the people as opposed to Latin. The medieval romance was designed to entertain a broad audience with stories of adventure and love, while it pretended to be an actual historical account of Charlemagne, King Arthur, or Roman legend.

The love of woman celebrated in medieval romance and troubadour poetry was equated in the Christian mind with love for the Virgin Mary. As Mother of Heaven and of Christ, as the all-compassionate mediator between the Judgment seat and the horrors of hell, Mary was increasingly recognized as the spiritual equivalent of the lady of chivalry, crowned the Queen of Heaven, overseeing her heavenly court. Songs were sung to her, cathedrals built in her honor (all cathedrals named Notre Dame, "Our Lady," are dedicated to her), and a Cult of the Virgin developed around her.

Indeed, *Lancelot* was written at the request of Eleanor of Aquitaine's daughter, Marie—herself named after the Virgin—as its laudatory prologue, a standard feature of the form, attests (**Reading 5.6**):

Chrétien presents himself as the servant of Marie who devotes his writer's skill to doing her bidding, just as the knight Lancelot serves Queen Guinevere with his knightly skill, and as the Christian serves the Virgin Mary. Similarly, Chrétien's story transforms the heroism of the *Song of Roland*, which is motivated by feudal loyalty to king and country, to a form of chivalry based on the allegiance of the knight to his lady. In a medieval romance, the knight is driven to heroic action not so much by the lure of greater glory as by his own desire for his lady. To the knight, the lady is a prize to be won, an object to be possessed. Beyond the drama of his exploits and his lady's distress, the conflict between the sexual desires of both knight and lady and the hypothetical purity of their "spiritual" love gives the story its narrative power. In a medieval romance, as well as in the troubadour poem, perhaps the greatest test the lovers face is their own sexuality—an almost sure fire guarantor of the form's popularity.

READING 5.6   **from Chrétien de Troyes, *Lancelot***

Since my lady of Champagne wishes me to undertake to write a romance, I shall very gladly do so, being so devoted to her service as to do anything in the world for her, without any intention of flattery. But if one were to introduce any flattery upon such an occasion, he might say, and I would subscribe to it, that this lady surpasses all others who are alive, just as the south wind which blows in May or April is more lovely than any other wind. But upon my word, I am not one to wish to flatter my lady. I will simply say: "The Countess is worth as many queens as a gem is worth of pearls and sards." Nay I shall make no comparison, and yet it is true in spite of me; I will say, however, that her command has more to do with this work than any thought or pains that I may expend upon it. Here Chrétien begins his book. . . . The material and the treatment of it are given and furnished to him by the Countess, and he is simply trying to carry out her concern and intention.

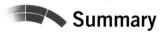 **Summary**

■ **Anglo-Saxon Artistic Style and Culture** The burial mound at Sutton Hoo has revealed more about the art and culture of Anglo-Saxon England than any other archeological site. The treasures discovered in the Sutton Hoo burial mound possess the distinctive animal-style designs of Anglo-Saxon culture. Buried in the mound was a lord or chief to whom his followers owed absolute loyalty. The Anglo-Saxon ruler exchanged a tenant's use of a fief for his protection and payment in goods or produce, a feudal relationship that also characterizes the epic poem *Beowulf*, written in Old English. The poem teaches its audience that power, strength, fame, and life itself are transitory—a theme consonant with Christian values, but by no means necessarily Christian.

Christianity survived the end of Rome's control of Britain only in the farthest reaches of the British islands—in Cornwall, Wales, and Ireland. In 597, Pope Gregory I sent the Benedictine prior Augustine on a mission to convert the pagan Anglo-Saxons. The pope urged Augustine not to try to eliminate pagan traditions but to incorporate them into Christian practice. Thus, in the Christian manuscripts produced in the region's monasteries, the visual tradition of Anglo-Saxon animal style merged with the Christian textual tradition.

■ **Carolingian Culture** Charlemagne converted even those who were Aryan to Roman Catholicism as he gained control of most of the continent, creating what would later be known as the Holy Roman Empire. Charlemagne's exploits were celebrated in many poems, chief among them the *Song of Roland*, which embodies the values of feudalism, celebrating courage and loyalty to one's ruler above all else. The poem is one of the earliest manifestations of feudalism's chivalric code.

Arguably the most important institution of the Carolingian era was the monastery. Charlemagne imposed the Rule of St. Benedict on all monasteries and created what he believed to be the ideal monastery at St. Gall. Music played an important role in monastic life, where plainsong or plainchant, later known as Gregorian chant, was sung daily in the Mass. Women had a significant role in monastic life. Foremost among them was Hildegard of Bingen, a theologian, philosopher, medical authority, painter, poet, playwright, and musician.

■ **Pilgrimage Churches and the Romanesque** Churches such as the Abbey Church of Sainte-Foy in Conques, France, became the focus of Western culture in the Middle Ages as Christians began to do penance for their sins by undertaking pilgrimages to churches housing the relics of venerated saints. The churches were Romanesque—that is, certain elements of Roman architectural tradition were incorporated into their design, particularly the basilica tradition and the barrel vaults that arched above the church naves. Most of the pilgrimage churches were controlled by the Abbey of Cluny. Cluny's abbot was among the most powerful men in Europe, and the church at Cluny was a model for all pilgrimage churches. Music was central to the Cluniac liturgy. The choral music sung there was polyphonic, and increasingly complex varieties of organum developed.

■ **The Crusades and the Culture of Romance** On November 25, 1095, Pope Urban II, who had been trained at Cluny, preached the First Crusade, pleading with Christians to retake Jerusalem from the Muslims. Nearly 100,000 young men signed on. Although the First Crusade was successful in recapturing Jerusalem, Muslim armies retook the city, requiring three subsequent Crusades that became increasingly mercenary in character. Eleanor of Aquitaine, who accompanied her husband, King Louis VII of France, on the Second Crusade, championed the art of courtly love as exemplified in the poetry of the troubadours and in medieval romances such as *Lancelot*.

Toward a New Urban Style: The Gothic

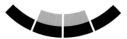
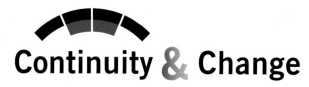

Romanesque art and architecture thrived, especially along the pilgrimage routes in the south of France, from roughly 1050 to 1200. But in the 1140s a new style began to emerge in the north that today we call Gothic. New cathedrals—at Saint-Denis, just outside Paris, and at Chartres—were dominated by soaring spires and stained-glass windows. Decorative sculpture proliferated. Pointed arches, as opposed to the rounded arches of the Romanesque barrel vault, lifted interior spaces to new heights. All of these new elements were anticipated in the Romanesque, in the magnificent stained glass at Poitiers, in the sculpture of the pilgrimage route church portals, and in the pointed arches of Fontenay Abbey. And like their Romanesque forebears, most of the new Gothic cathedrals were built to house precious relics and to accommodate large crowds of pilgrims.

The Romanesque style was a product of rural monastic life, separated from worldly events and interactions, but the Gothic style was a creation of the emerging city—of the craft guilds and artisans, merchants, lawyers, and bankers who gathered there. It represents the first step in a gradual shift in the West from a spiritually centered culture to one with a more secular focus. No longer was religion—worshiping at a

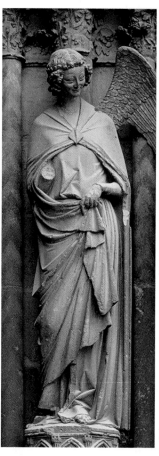

Fig. 5.24 *The Angel of the Annunciation*, west front portal, Reims Cathedral, Reims, France. ca. 1245–1255 (detail of Fig. 6.16).

pilgrimage church or fighting a Crusade—the dominant motive for travel. Instead, trade was. Merchants and bankers grew in importance. Craftsmen flourished. Secular rulers became more ambitious. In fact, personal ambition and success would increasingly be defined in worldly, rather than spiritual, terms.

The Gothic does not give up its interest in the spiritual. Although the architecture was intended to invoke intensely spiritual feelings, we also see the beginning of a renewed interest in worldly things. This shift is evident in two images of angels. The flattened, distorted features of the angel on the Romanesque capital from Vézelay (Fig. **5.23**) contrast dramatically with the heightened naturalism of the angel from the portal at Reims (Fig. **5.24**). Freed from the stone backdrop of relief sculpture, the Gothic angel steps forward with an amazingly lifelike gesture. So lifelike is the Reims sculpture that it seems to have been modeled on a real person—nothing of the formulaic vocabulary of Romanesque sculpture remains. Its winsome smile and delicate figure are, finally, more worldly than angelic. ■

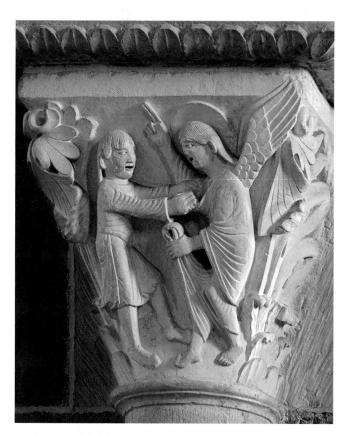

Fig. 5.23 *Angel Subduing Demon*, decorated column capital, Church of Sainte-Madeleine, Vézelay, France. ca. 1089–1206.

6

The Gothic and the Rebirth of Naturalism

Civic and Religious Life in an Age of Inquiry

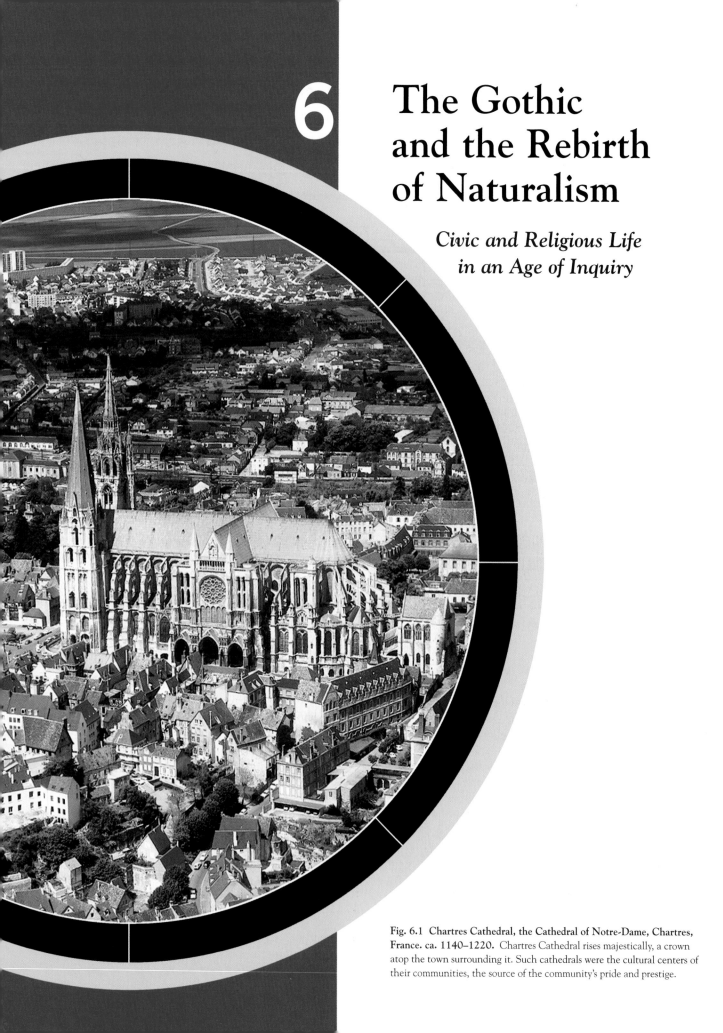

Fig. 6.1 Chartres Cathedral, the Cathedral of Notre-Dame, Chartres, France. ca. 1140–1220. Chartres Cathedral rises majestically, a crown atop the town surrounding it. Such cathedrals were the cultural centers of their communities, the source of the community's pride and prestige.

> **“** *I find no peace, and yet I am not warlike;*
> *I fear and hope, I burn and turn to ice;*
> *I fly beyond the sky, stretch out on earth;*
> *my hands are empty, yet I hold the world.* **”**

Petrarch, Sonnet 134

On June 11, 1144, King Louis VII, his queen, Eleanor of Aquitaine, and a host of dignitaries traveled a few miles north of Paris to the royal Abbey of Saint-Denis, where they dedicated a new choir for the royal church. It would be the crowning achievement of the king's personal domain, the Île-de-France [eel duh frahns], the area comprising Paris and its environs. Designed by Abbot Suger [soo-ZHER] of Saint-Denis, the choir would quickly inspire a new style of architecture and decoration that came to be known as **Gothic**.

"Gothic" was originally a derogatory term, adopted in sixteenth-century Italy to describe the art of northern Europe, where, it was believed, classical traditions had been destroyed by Germanic invaders—that is, by the Goths. In its own time, this style was known as *opus modernum* (modern work) or *opus francigenum* (French work). These terms highlight the style's decidedly new and contemporary flavor as well as its place of origin.

By the end of the twelfth century and the beginning of the thirteenth, town after town across northern France would imitate Suger's design at Saint-Denis. At Chartres, just to the west of the Île-de-France on the Eure [ur] River (Fig. **6.1**), to the north at Rouen [roo-ON], Amiens [ah-mee-EN], and Beauvais [boh-VAY], to the east at Laon and Reims, to the south at Bourges [boorzh], and in Paris itself, Gothic cathedrals sprang up with amazing rapidity. Much of the rest of Europe would soon follow suit.

With the rise of this new Gothic style came a new standard of beauty in Western architecture and decoration. A new masonry architecture developed, eventually resulting in intricate stonework that was almost skeletal in its lightness and soaring ever higher to create lofty interior spaces. Gothic architecture matched the decorative richness of stained glass with sculptural programs that were increasingly inspired by classical models of naturalistic representation. A new, richer liturgy developed as well, and with it, polyphonic music that by the thirteenth century was accompanied by a new instrument—the organ. The Île-de-France was the center of all these developments. It was there, as well, at the University of Paris, founded in 1200, that a young Dominican monk named Thomas Aquinas initiated the most important theological debates of the age, inaugurating a style of intellectual inquiry that we associate with higher learning to this day.

Even as an elaborate and flamboyant new style of Gothic architecture developed in the north, closely associated with the court of King Louis IX (r. 1226-1270) in Paris, the Gothic arrived in Italy where it was adopted in Florence and Siena particularly, as the two cities competed for preeminence during the thirteenth and fourteenth centuries. Out of this competition, the modern Western city as we know it—a more or less self-governing center of political, economic, and social activity, with public spaces, government buildings, and urban neighborhoods—was born. Republican Rome (see chapter 3) and Golden Age Athens (see chapter 2) were both models, but what distinguished Florence and Siena from these earlier republics was the role that the citizenry played in expressing their civic pride. The churches, monuments, and buildings of these late medieval cities were the work not of enlightened rulers but of the people themselves. Perhaps because the people were the great artistic patrons of the era, a new type of literature developed, written in Italian, not Latin, and often focusing on the more ordinary aspects of everyday life as lived by common people. The citizenry was genuinely thankful to God for its well-being and gave thanks by building, maintaining, and embellishing cathedrals. They built churches for the new monastic orders that served the cities' common folk. As in France, the cult of the Virgin inspired artists in both cities, and both cities placed themselves under her protection.

Until 1348, despite the ups and downs each city experienced, the Virgin seemed to bless both with good fortune. But that year, as many as half the populations of both cities died of the plague. To many people, the Black Death represented the vengeance of an angry God punishing the people for their sins. But, in its wake, artists, writers, merchants, and scholars discovered greater personal freedom and opportunity. Perhaps inspired by the harsh realities they confronted during the plague, artists created works of ever-greater realism and candor.

The Gothic Cathedral

Even as a pupil at the monastery school, Abbot Suger (1085-1151) had dreamed of transforming the Abbey of Saint-Denis into the most beautiful church in France. The dream was partly inspired by his desire to lay claim to the larger territories surrounding the Île-de-France. Suger's design placed the royal domain at the center of French culture, defined by an architecture surpassing all others in beauty and grandeur.

After careful planning, Suger began work on the Abbey in 1137, painting the walls, already almost 300 years old, with gold and precious colors. Then he added a new facade with twin towers and a triple portal. Around the back of the ambulatory he added a circular string of chapels (Figs. **6.2, 6.3**), all lit with large stained-glass windows (Fig. **6.4**), "by virtue of which," Suger wrote, "the whole would shine with the miraculous and uninterrupted light."

This light proclaimed the new Gothic style. In preparing his plans, Suger had read what he believed to be the writings of the original Saint Denis. (We now know that he was reading the mystical tracts of a first-century Athenian follower of Saint Paul.) According to these writings, light is the physical and material manifestation of the Divine Spirit. Suger would later survey the accomplishments of his administration and explain his religious rationale for the beautification of Saint-Denis:

> Marvel not at the gold and the expense but at the craftsmanship of the work.
> Bright is the noble work; but being nobly bright, the work
> Should brighten the minds, so that they may travel, through the true lights,
> To the True Light where Christ is the true door.

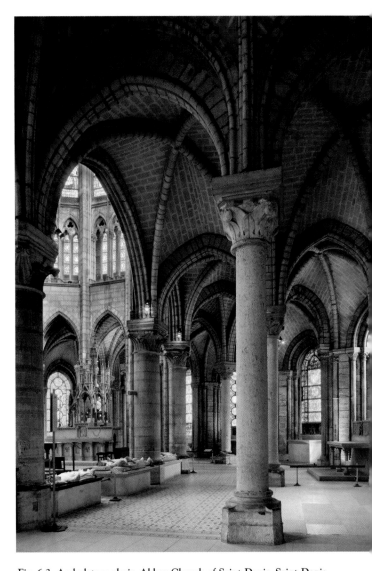

Fig. 6.3 Ambulatory choir, Abbey Church of Saint-Denis, Saint-Denis, France. 1140–1144. In Abbot Suger's design, the ambulatory and radiating chapels around the apse were combined, so that the stained-glass windows—two in each chapel—fill the entire choir with light.

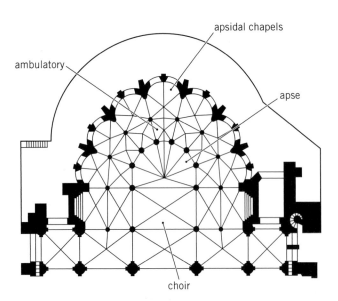

Fig. 6.2 Plan of the ambulatory choir, Abbey Church of Saint-Denis, Saint-Denis, France. 1140–1144. By supporting the arches over the choir with columns instead of walls, Suger created a unified space reminiscent of the hypostyle space of the Mosque of Córdoba.

The church's beauty, therefore, was designed to elevate the soul to the realm of God.

When Louis VII and Eleanor left France for the Second Crusade in 1147 (see chapter 5), just three years after Suger's dedication of his choir, they also left the abbot without the funds necessary to finish his church. It was finally completed a century later. Much of its original sculptural and stained-glass decoration was destroyed in the late eighteenth century during the French Revolution. Although partially restored in the nineteenth and twentieth centuries, only five of its original stained-glass windows remain, and we must turn to other churches modeled on its design to comprehend its full effect. Chief among these is the Cathedral of Notre-Dame [noh-truh dahm] at Chartres [SHAR-truh], which, like the other Gothic cathedrals both in the Île-de-France and its surrounding territories, drew its inspiration from Paris.

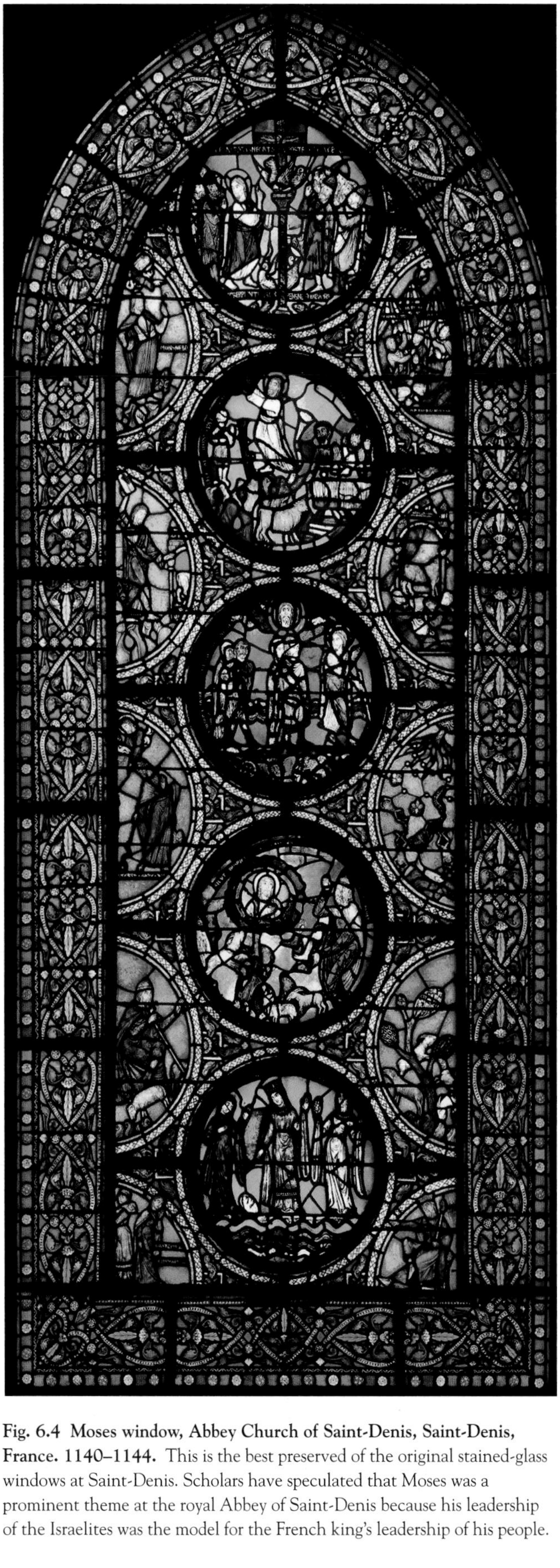

The cathedral's spires can be seen for miles in every direction, lording over town and countryside as if it were the very center of its world (Fig. **6.5**). Chartres was, in fact, located in the heart of France's grain belt, and its economy thrived as France exported grain throughout the Mediterranean basin. But more important, Chartres was the spiritual center of the cult of the Virgin, which throughout the twelfth and thirteenth centuries assumed an increasingly important role in the religious life of Western Europe. The popularity of this cult contributed, perhaps more than any other factor, to the ever-increasing size of the era's churches. Christians worshiped the Virgin as the Bride of Christ, Personification of the Church, Queen of Heaven, and prime Intercessor with God for the salvation of humankind. This last role was especially important, for in it the Virgin could intervene to save sinners from eternal damnation. The cult of the Virgin manifested itself especially in the French cathedrals, which are often dedicated to *Notre Dame*, "Our Lady."

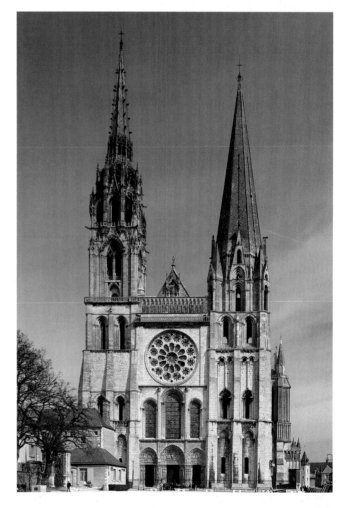

Fig. 6.4 Moses window, Abbey Church of Saint-Denis, Saint-Denis, France. 1140–1144. This is the best preserved of the original stained-glass windows at Saint-Denis. Scholars have speculated that Moses was a prominent theme at the royal Abbey of Saint-Denis because his leadership of the Israelites was the model for the French king's leadership of his people.

Fig. 6.5 West facade, Chartres Cathedral. ca. 1134–1220; south spire ca. 1160; north spire, 1507–1513. The different designs of the two towers reflect the Gothic dismissal of Romanesque absolute balance and symmetry as well as the growing refinements of the Gothic style. The later, north tower (left) was much more elaborately decorated and, in the more open framework of its stonework, more technically advanced.

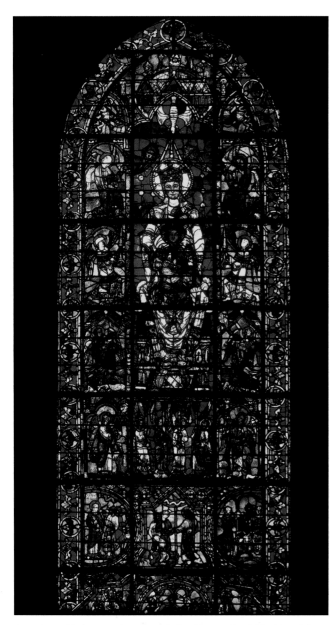

Fig. 6.6 *Notre-Dame de la Belle Verrière* (Our Lady of the Beautiful Window) window, Chartres Cathedral. Central portion, 12th century; surrounding angels, 13th century. This window is renowned for its stunning combination of red and blue stained glass.

Soon after the first building phase was completed at Chartres, between about 1140 and 1150, pilgrims thronged to the cathedral to pay homage to what the Church claimed was the Virgin's tunic, worn at Jesus' birth. This relic was housed in the cathedral and was believed to possess extraordinary healing powers. But in 1194, the original structure was destroyed by fire, except for the west facade, a few stained-glass windows, including one of the most beautiful, known as *Notre-Dame de la Belle Verrière* [noh-truh dahm duh la bel vair-ee-AIR] ("Our Lady of the Beautiful Window") (Fig.

6.6), and the tunic of the Virgin. The survival of the window and the tunic was taken as a sign of divine providence, and a massive reconstruction project was begun in gratitude. Royalty and local nobility contributed their financial support, and the local guilds gave both money and work.

Stained Glass

Behind the more or less Romanesque west facade of Chartres, with its round-arch windows, rose what many consider the most magnificent of all Gothic cathedrals, its stained glass unrivaled in Europe. The stained-glass program is immensely complex. The innovative engineering that marks Gothic architecture (to be discussed later in this chapter) freed the walls of the need to bear the weight of the structure. It also freed the walls to contain glass.

The purpose of the stained-glass programs in all Gothic cathedrals was to tell the stories of the Bible in a compelling way to an audience that was largely illiterate. The art allowed them to read the scriptural stories for themselves. At Chartres, 175 glass panels, containing more than 4,000 figures, are carefully designed, in Abbot Suger's words, "to show simple folk . . . what they ought to believe." *Notre-Dame de la Belle Verrière*,

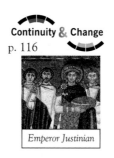

Continuity & Change
p. 116

Emperor Justinian

whose central panel survived the fire of 1194, embodies the shift in style that occurred in the twelfth century as the Gothic supplanted the Romanesque. The Virgin and Child in the middle are almost Byzantine in their stiffness, their feet pointed downward, their pose fully frontal, the drapery of their clothing almost flat (see Figure 4.17, *Emperor Justinian*). But the angels on the side, which are thirteenth-century additions, are both less stiff and more animated. The swirls and folds of their gowns flow across their limbs, revealing the anatomy beneath them.

A second window depicts the so-called Tree of Jesse (Fig. 6.7). Jesse trees are a common motif in twelfth- and thirteenth-century manuscripts, murals, sculpture, and stained glass, and their associated traditions are still celebrated by Christians during the season of Advent. They were thought to represent the genealogy of Christ, since they depict the Virgin Mary as descended from Jesse, the father of King David, thus fulfilling a prophecy in the book of Isaiah (11:1): "And there shall come forth a rod out of the stem of Jesse and a Branch shall grow out of his roots." Most Jesse trees have at their base a recumbent Jesse with a tree growing from his side or navel. On higher branches of the tree are various kings and prophets of Judah. At the top are Christ and Mary. Sometimes the Virgin holds the infant Jesus, but here, as in a similar window at Saint-Denis, Mary appears in the register below Jesus. Since Jesse trees portray Mary as descending from royal lineage, they played an important role in the cult of the Virgin.

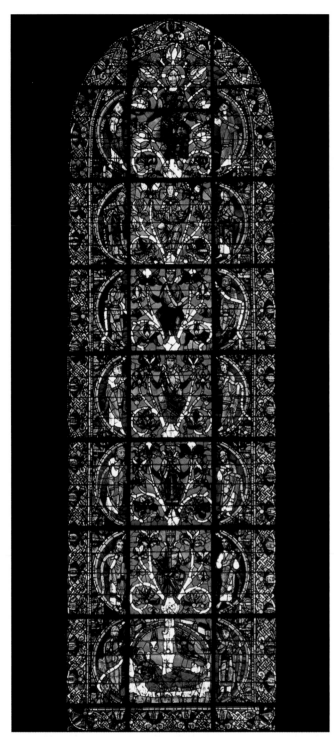

Fig. 6.7 *The Tree of Jesse* window, Chartres. ca. 1150–1170. Jesse was the father of King David, who, according to the Gospels, was an ancestor of Mary. At the base of the window lies the body of Jesse, a tree growing out of him. The tree branches into the four kings of Judea, one on each row. Mary is just below Christ. Seven doves, representing the seven gifts of the Holy Spirit, encircle Christ. In half-moons flanking each section of the tree stand the fourteen prophets.

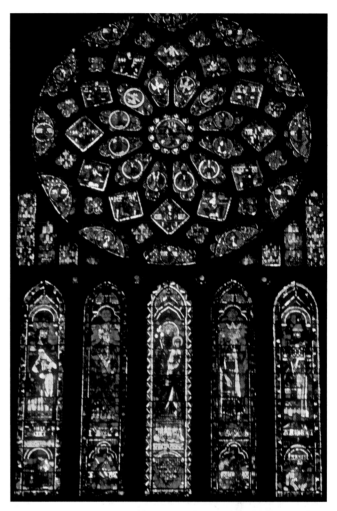

Fig. 6.8 Rose window and lancets, north transept, Chartres. ca. 1150–1180. The rich blue colors of this rose window were especially treasured because legend had it that Abbot Suger had produced the blues by grinding up sapphires. The richness of the blues, however, derives from a cobalt oxide.

A third window in the north transept of the Cathedral also evokes the Virgin (Fig. **6.8**). A **rose window**—a round window with mullions (framing elements) and traceries extending outward from its center in the manner of the petals of a rose—it is symbolic of the Virgin Mary in her role as the Mystic Rose—the root plant, it was believed, of the Jesse tree. It measures 42 feet in diameter.

The stained glass at Chartres covers more than 32,000 square feet of surface area, and the overall effect of so many windows can hardly be imagined. The windows were donated by the royal family, by noblemen, and by merchant guilds. On an average day, the light outside the cathedral is approximately 1,000 times greater than the light inside. Thus the windows, backlit and shining in the relative darkness of the nave, seem to radiate with an ethereal and immaterial glow, suggesting a spiritual beauty beyond the here and now.

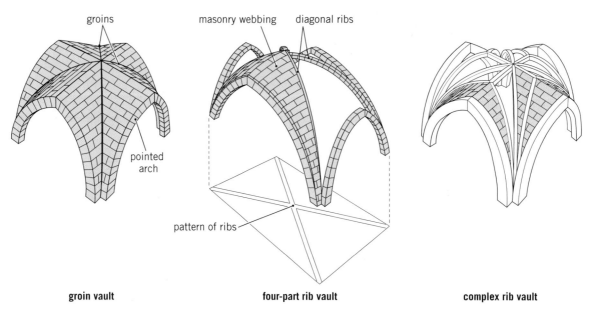

groins

masonry webbing   diagonal ribs

pointed
arch

pattern of ribs

groin vault   **four-part rib vault**   **complex rib vault**

Fig. 6.9 Rib vaulting.

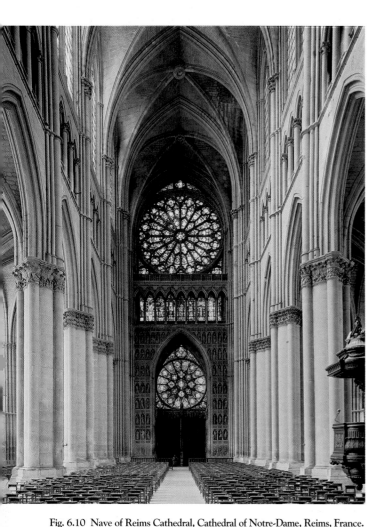

Fig. 6.10 Nave of Reims Cathedral, Cathedral of Notre-Dame, Reims, France. 1211–1290. The nave is almost three times higher than it is wide, creating a dramatic vertical space. This view looks west toward the central portal.

Gothic Architecture

As the Gothic style developed, important architectural innovations contributed to the goal of elevating the soul of worshipers to the spiritual realm. Key among these innovations was rib vaulting. The principles of rib vaulting (Fig. **6.9**) were known to Romanesque architects, but Gothic architects used these techniques with increasing sophistication. Rib vaults are a form of groin vault (see Fig. 3.13). They are based on the pointed arch, which can reach to a greater height than a rounded arch. At the groins, structural moldings called ribs channel the vault's thrust outward and downward. These ribs were constructed first and supported the scaffolding upon which masonry webbing was built. These ribs were essentially a "skeleton" filled with a lightweight masonry "skin." Rib vaulting allowed for the massive stonework of the Romanesque style to be replaced, inside and out, by an almost lacy play of thin columns and patterns of ribs and windows, all pointing upward in a gravity-defying crescendo that carries the viewer's gaze toward the heavens. Extremely high naves—Chartres's nave is 120 feet high, Reims's nave is 125, and the highest of all, Beauvais's, is 157, the equivalent of a 15-story building—add to this emphasis on verticality, contributing a sense of elevation that is both physical and spiritual.

The preponderance of pointed rather than rounded arches in the nave of Reims Cathedral (Fig. **6.10**) creates a similar feeling. The pointed arch, in fact, possesses structural properties that contribute significantly to the Gothic style—the flatter or rounder an arch is, the greater outward thrust or pressure it puts on the supporting walls. By reducing outward thrust, the pointed arch allows for larger windows and lighter **buttresses**, pillars traditionally built against exterior walls to brace them and strengthen the

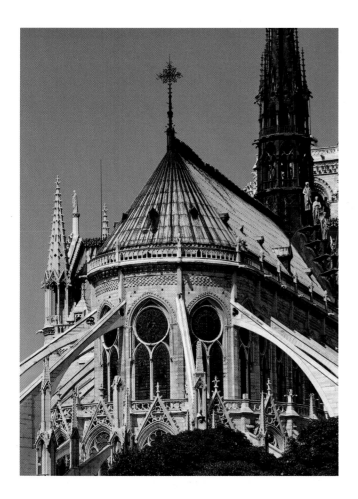

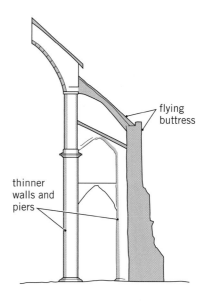

Figs. 6.11 and 6.12 Flying buttresses, Cathedral of Notre-Dame, Paris. 1211–1290. Romanesque architects used buttressing, but enclosed it under the aisle roofs. Revealing the buttresses on the outside of the structure created an impression of vigor that contributed to the aesthetic appeal of the building as much as to its structural integrity. A flying buttress is basically a huge stone prop that pushes in against the walls with the same force that the vaults push out. The thrust of the vaulted ceilings still come down the piers and walls, but also move down the arms of the flying buttresses, down the buttresses themselves, and into the ground. The flying buttresses help spread the weight of the vaults over more supporting stone, allowing the walls to be thinner while still supporting as much weight as earlier, thicker walls.

vault. **Flying buttresses** (Figs. **6.11**, **6.12**) allow for even lighter buttressing and more windows. They extend away from the wall, employing an arch to focus the strength of the buttress's support at the top of the wall, the section most prone to collapse from the outward pressure of the vaulted ceiling. As the magnificent flying buttresses at Notre-Dame Cathedral in Paris demonstrate, they also create a stunning visual spectacle, arching winglike from the building's side as if defying gravity.

The Gothic style spread rapidly across Europe. It was especially well received in England, which, after all, was dominated by French Normans, and in Germany, where a fragmented conglomeration of independent cities, principalities, and bishoprics all sought to imitate what they conceived as the style of the French court. Wells Cathedral is one of the finest Gothic cathedrals built in England in the thirteenth century (Fig. **6.13**).

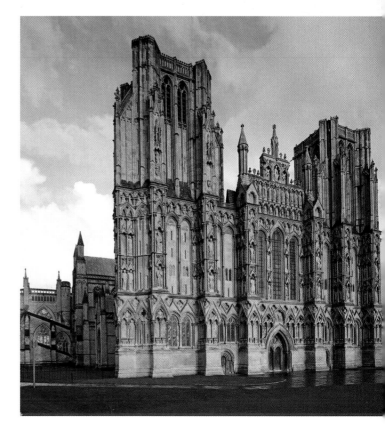

Fig. 6.13 West facade, Wells Cathedral, Wells, England. 1230–1250. This cathedral exemplifies the preference for pattern and decoration in English Gothic architecture. The portal has become less important, and the rhythmic structure of the wide facade takes precedence. Life-size sculptures occupy each of the niches—originally 384 of them—representing the Last Judgment.

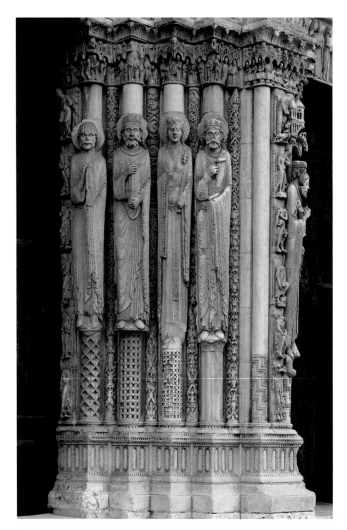

Fig. 6.14 Jamb statues, west portal, Chartres Cathedral. 1145–1170.
The decorative patterns at the bottom of these jamb columns are,
interestingly, reminiscent of Islamic designs in Spain.

Gothic Sculpture

If we look at developments in architectural sculpture from
the time of the decoration of the west portal of Chartres
Cathedral (1145–1170) to the time of the sculptural plan of
the south transept portal (1215–1220), and, finally, to the
sculptures decorating the west front of Reims Cathedral
(1225–1255), we can see that, in a little over 100 years,
Gothic sculptors had begun to reintroduce classical principles
of sculptural composition into Western art.

Although they seem almost Byzantine in their long, narrow verticality, feet pointing downward, the jamb sculptures
on the west portal of Chartres mark a distinct advance in the
sculptural realization of the human body (Fig. 6.14). These,
and five more sets, flank the three doorways of the cathedral's
Royal Portal. The center tympanum of the Portal depicts
Christ Enthroned in Royal Majesty, the north tympanum the
Ascension of Christ, and the south the Virgin and Child
Enthroned. The jamb sculptures represent figures from the

Hebrew Bible considered to be precursors of Christ. These
works have little in common with Romanesque relief sculpture, typified by the *Last Judgment* tympanum on the Cathedral of Sainte-Foy in Conques (see Fig. 5.16). While the
Chartres figures remain contained by the form of the colonnade behind them, they are fully rounded and occupy a space
in front of the column itself.

When Chartres was rebuilt after the fire of 1195, a new
sculptural plan was realized for the transept doors. The figures
stand before a colonnade, as do the jamb figures on the west
portal, but their form is hardly determined by it (Fig. 6.15).
Now they stand flat-footed. Their faces seem animated, as if
they see us. The monk just to the right of the dividing column
seems quite concerned for us. The portrait of the knight Saint
Theodore, to the left of the column, is particularly remarkable.
For the first time since antiquity, the figure is posed at ease, his
hip thrusts slightly to the right, his weight falling on his right
foot. He stands, in other words, in a *contrapposto* position. The
weight of his sword belt seems to have pulled his cloak off to
the right. Then, below the belt, the cloak falls back to the left.
The strict verticality of the west portal is a thing of the past.

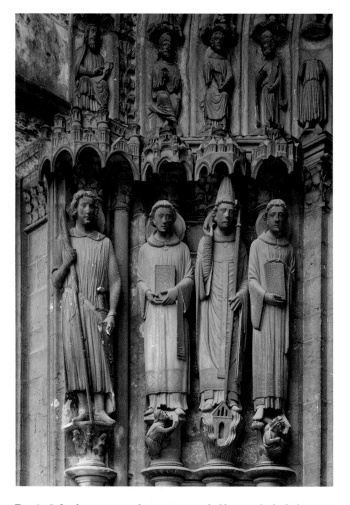

**Fig. 6.15 Jamb statues, south transept portal, Chartres Cathedral. ca.
1215–1220.** The statue of Saint Theodore, on the left, is meant to evoke
the spirit of the Crusades.

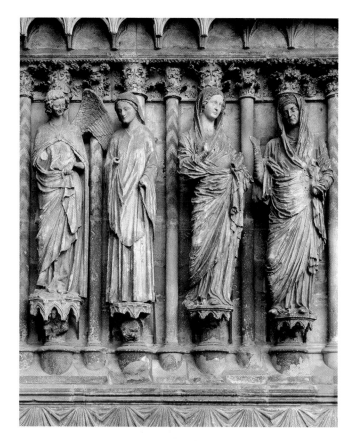

Fig. 6.16 *Annunciation* and *Visitation*, central portal, west facade, Reims Cathedral. Angel of the Annunciation, ca. 1245–1255; Virgin of the Annunciation, 1245; Visitation group, ca. 1230–1233. If these sculptures seem more naturalistic than any for nearly a thousand years, it is partly because they engage one another. It is as if, looking at them, we can overhear their conversation. Note that the most naturalistic sculpture, the Angel of the Annunciation, dates from 15 or 20 years after the Visitation group, suggesting an extraordinary advance, and preference for, naturalism in a very short span of years.

The sculptures at Reims break even further from Romanesque tradition. They are freed of their backdrop (Fig. **6.16**). The Angel of the Annunciation tells Mary (the figure next to the angel on the right) that she is with child. The next two figures, to the right, represent the Visitation, when Mary tells her cousin Elizabeth that she is with child and Elizabeth in turn announces the divinity of the baby in Mary's womb. Note how the drapery adorning the pair on the left, with its simple, soft folds, differs profoundly from the drapery of the pair on the right, whose robes are Roman in their complexity. The earlier Mary bears little, if any, resemblance to the other Mary, the first probably carved by a sculptor trained in Romanesque traditions, the latter by one acquainted with Classical models.

The two pairs are as different, in fact, as the two towers of Chartres Cathedral (see Fig. 6.5), which reflect both a weakening of the Romanesque insistence on balance and symmetry as well as the fact that both were done at different times. And yet the two pairs of sculptures share a certain emotional attitude—the good-humored smile of the angel, the stern but wise concern of Elizabeth. Even the relative ages of the per-

sons depicted are apparent, where age would have been of no concern to a sculptor working in the Romanesque tradition. These are, in short, the most fully human, most natural sculptures since Roman times. During the Gothic period artists developed a new visual language. The traditional narratives of biblical tradition could no longer speak through abstracted and symbolic types, but instead required believable, individual bodies to tell their stories. This new language invests the figures of Jesus, Mary, the saints, and even the Angel of the Annunciation with personality.

Music in the Gothic Cathedral: Growing Complexity

With its vast spaces and stone walls, the Gothic cathedral could be as animated by its acoustics as by its light, or, as at Reims, the liveliness of its sculpture. Ecclesiastical leaders were quick to take advantage of this quality in constructing their liturgy. At the School of Notre-Dame, in Paris, the first collection of music in two parts, the *Magnus Liber Organi* [MAG-nus LEE-bur or-GAN-ee] (The Great Book of Polyphony), was widely distributed in manuscript by about 1160. Among its many anonymous composers was Léonin [lay-OH-nen] (see CD–Track 5.4). The *Magnus Liber Organi* was arranged in song cycles to provide music for all the feast days of the Church calendar. The *Magnus Liber* was created at a time when most polyphony was produced and transmitted only orally. What makes it so significant is that it represents the beginning of the modern sense of "composition"—that is, works attributable to a single composer.

At the end of the century, Léonin's successor, Pérotin [pay-roh-TEN], revised and renotated the *Magnus Liber*. One of his most famous works is *Viderunt Omnes* (All Have Seen), a four-part polyphonic composition based on the traditional plainchant of the same name, meant to be sung in the middle of the Christmas Mass at Notre-Dame Cathedral in Paris (**CD-Track 6.1**). Throughout the piece, the choir sings a smooth monophonic plainchant, while three soloists sing the second, third, and fourth melodic lines in **counterpoint**, that is, in opposition, to the plainchant. The clear but intertwined rhythms of the soloists build to a crescendo of sustained harmony and balance that must have inspired awe in the congregation. The music seems to soar upward, imitating the architecture of the cathedral and elevating the faithful to new heights of belief.

The words are simple, but because each syllable is sung across a range of notes and rhythms, the music takes almost 12 minutes to perform. What follows is the Latin and translation:

Viderunt omnes fines terrae salutare Dei nostri. Jubilate Deo omnis terra.	All the ends of the earth have seen the salvation of our God. Praise God all the earth.
Notum fecit Dominus salutare suam. Ante conspectum gentium revelavit justitiam suam	The Lord has made known his salvation. Before the face of the people he has revealed his justice.

The complexity of such rhythmic invention mirrors the growing textural complexity of the facade of Gothic cathedrals, with their spires, gables, crockets, and finials. Developing from this polyphony was an even more complex musical form, the **motet** [moh-TET], consisting of three (sometimes four) voices. The tenor—from the Latin *tenere*, "to hold"—generally maintained a traditional line based on ecclesiastical chant. The tenor line might be sung or played instrumentally, perhaps by the organ, an invention of the period, which began to replace the choir in the performance of many of these songs. In some ways, this was a practical gesture, since large choirs of the caliber needed to perform the liturgical songs were not easy to organize. But the rich tones of the organ, resonating through the nave of the cathedral, soon gained favor, and the organ became necessary to every large cathedral. In the motet, above the tenor line, two or three voices sang interweaving melodies.

By the late thirteenth century a motet might be sung in either Latin or vernacular French, and either or both parts might be hymns or troubadour love songs. All these competing lines were held together like the complex elements of the Gothic facade—balanced but competing, harmonious but at odds. They reflected, in short, the great debates—between church and state, faith and reason—that defined the age.

These debates raged at centers of higher learning, where music was part of the regular liberal arts curriculum. It was studied as a branch of the **quadrivium** [kwah-DRIV-ee-um] (the mathematical arts), alongside arithmetic, geometry, and astronomy, all fields dependent upon proportion and universal harmony. (The other liberal arts constituted the **trivium** [TRIV-ee-um], the language arts, which included grammar, rhetoric, and dialectic.) At the cathedral School of Notre-Dame in Paris, whose purpose was to train clergy, music was emphasized as an all-important liturgical tool. But by the middle of the twelfth century, cathedral schools began allowing nonclerical students to attend lectures. In 1179, a papal degree ordered the schools to provide for the teaching of the *laity* [LAY-ih-tee] (nonclerics), the decree that would eventually give rise to the university as an institution.

The Rise of the University

The first university was founded in Bologna [buh-LOHN-yuh], Italy, in 1148. Two hundred years earlier, in Spain, Islamic institutions of higher learning were generally attached to mosques since learning was considered sacred. At first, the term *university* meant simply a *union* of students and the instructors they contracted with to teach them.

Universitas was an umbrella term for *collegia*, the groups of students who shared a common interest or, as at Bologna, hailed from the same geographic area. The University of Bologna quickly established itself as a center for the study of law (Fig. **6.17**), an advanced area of study that students prepared for by mastering the seven liberal arts.

Proficiency in Latin was mandatory, and students studied Latin in all courses of their first four years of study. They read the writings of the ancient Greeks—Aristotle, Ptolemy, Euclid—in Latin translation. Augustine of Hippo's *On Christian Doctrine* was required reading. To obtain their bachelor of arts (BA) degree, students took oral exams after three to five years of study. Further study to acquire mastery of a special field led to the master of arts (MA) degree and might qualify a student to teach theology or practice medicine or law. Four more years of study were required to acquire the title of *doctor* (from the Latin, *doctus* [DOK-tus], learned), culminating in a defense of a thesis before a board of learned examiners.

The University of Paris was chartered in 1200, and soon after came Oxford and Cambridge universities in England. These northern universities emphasized the study of theology. In Paris, a house or college system was organized, at first to provide students with housing and then to help them focus

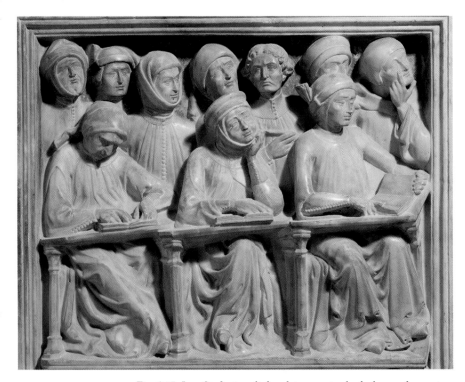

Fig. 6.17 *Law Students,* relief sculpture on tomb of a law professor at the University of Bologna. ca. 1200. Marble. Masegne, Jacobello & Pier Paolo dalle (fl. 1383–1409). Giraudon, Museo Civico, Bologna, Italy. The Bridgeman Art Library. Although women were generally excluded from the professions of medicine and law, there were exceptions. In this group of law students, the central figure in the front row appears to be a woman, Novella d'Andrea (1312–1366). She lectured at the university on both philosophy and law, although it is said that she was required to speak from behind a curtain so as not to distract the male students.

their education. The most famous of these was organized by Robert de Sorbon in 1257 for theology students. The Sorbonne, named after him, remains today the center of Parisian student life.

Abelard and the Dialectical Method

The quality of its teaching most distinguished the University of Paris. Because books were available only in handwritten manuscripts, they were extremely expensive, so students relied on lectures and copious note-taking for their instruction. Peter Abelard [AB-uh-lahr] (1079–ca. 1144), a brilliant logician and author of the treatise *Sic et Non* ("Yes and No"), was one of the most popular lecturers of his day. Crowds of students routinely gathered to hear him. He taught by the **dialectical method**—that is, by presenting different points of view and seeking to reconcile them. This method of teaching originates in the Socratic method, but whereas Socratic dialogue consisted of a wise teacher who was questioned by students, or even fools, Abelard's dialectical method presumed no such hierarchical relationships. Everything, to him, was open to question. "By doubting," he famously argued, "we come to inquire, and by inquiring we arrive at truth."

Heloise and Abelard The Church found it difficult to deal with Abelard, who demonstrated time and again that various Church Fathers—and the Bible itself—held hopelessly opposing views on many issues. Furthermore, the dialectical method itself challenged the unquestioning faith in God and the authority of the Church. Abelard was particularly opposed by Bernard of Clairvaux, who in 1140 successfully prosecuted him for heresy. By then, Abelard's reputation as a teacher had not faded, but his moral position had long been suspect. In 1119, he had pursued a love affair with his private student, Heloise [HEL-oh-eez]. Ablelard not only felt that he had betrayed a trust by falling in love with her and subsequently impregnating her, but he was further humiliated by Heloise's angry uncle, in whose home he had tutored and seduced the girl. Learning of the pregnancy, the uncle hired thugs to castrate Abelard in his bed. Abelard retreated to the monastery at Saint-Denis, accepting the protection of the powerful Abbot Suger. Heloise joined a convent and later served as abbess of Paraclete [PAR-uh-kleet], a chapel and oratory founded by Abelard.

The Education of Women Heloise's story reveals much about the education of women in the Middle Ages. Intellectually brilliant, she became Abelard's private student because women were not allowed to study at the university. There were some exceptions, particularly in Italy. At Bologna, Novella d'Andrea (1312–1366) lectured on philosophy and law. At Salerno, in southern Italy, the chair of medicine was held by Trotula (d. 1097), one of the most famous physicians of her time, although some scholars debate whether she was actually a woman, and convincing evidence suggests that her works are actually compendiums of works by three different authors. Concerned chiefly with

alleviating the suffering of women, the major work attributed to her is *On the Diseases of Women*, commonly known throughout the Middle Ages as the *Trotula*. As the author says at the beginning of the treatise:

> Because women are by nature weaker than men and because they are most frequently afflicted in childbirth, diseases very often abound in them. . . . Women, from the condition of their fragility, out of shame and embarrassment do not dare reveal their anguish over their diseases (which happen in such a private place) to a physician. Therefore, their misfortune, which ought to be pitied, and especially the influence of a certain woman stirring my heart, have impelled me to give a clear explanation regarding their diseases in caring for their health.

In 63 chapters, the book addresses issues surrounding menstruation, conception, pregnancy, and childbirth, along with general ailments and diseases. The book champions good diet, warns of the dangers of emotional stress, and prescribes the use of opiates during childbirth, a practice otherwise condemned for centuries to come. It even explains how an experienced woman might pretend to be a virgin. The standard reference work in gynecology and obstetrics for midwives and physicians throughout the Middle Ages, the *Trotula* was translated from Latin into almost all vernacular languages and was widely disseminated.

Thomas Aquinas and Scholasticism

In 1245, Thomas Aquinas [uh-KWY-nus] (1225–1274), a 20-year-old Dominican monk from Italy, arrived at the University of Paris to study theology, walking into a theological debate that had been raging for nearly 100 years, ever since the conflict between Abelard and Bernard: How does the believer come to know God? With the heart? With the mind? Or with both? Do we come to know the truth intuitively or rationally? Aquinas took on these questions directly and soon became the most distinguished student and lecturer at the university.

Aquinas was accompanied to Paris by another Dominican, his teacher Albertus Magnus (ca. 1200–1280), a German who taught at both Paris and Cologne and who later produced a biological classification of plants based on Aristotle. The Dominicans had been founded in 1216 by the Spanish priest Dominic (ca. 1170–1221) as an order dedicated to the study of theology. Aquinas and Magnus, and others like them, increasingly trained by Dominicans, were soon labeled *scholastics*. Their brand of theological inquiry, which was based on Abelard's dialectical method, was called **Scholasticism**.

Most theologians understood that there was a seeming conflict between faith and reason, but, they argued, since both proceeded from God, this conflict must, by definition, be a misapprehension. In the universities, rational inquiry and Aristotle's objective descriptions of physical reality were all the rage (see chapter 2), so much so that theologians worried that students were more enthralled with logical argumentation than right outcomes. Instead of studying heavenly truths and Scriptures, they were studying pagan philosophy, dating from the fourth century BCE. Scholasticism sought to reconcile the two. One of the greatest efforts in this direction is Aquinas's *Summa Theologica*, begun in 1265 when he was 40 years old. At Albertus Magnus' request, Aquinas set out to write a theology based entirely on the work of ancient philosophers, demonstrating the compatibility of classical philosophy and Christian religion. The *Summa Theologica* takes on virtually every theological issue of the age, from the place of women in society and the Church, to the cause of evil, the question of free choice, and whether it is lawful to sell a thing for more than it is worth. The medieval *summa* was an authoritative summary of all that was known on a traditional subject, and it was the ultimate aim of every highly educated man to produce one.

In a famous passage Aquinas takes on the largest issue of all—the *summa* of *summas*—attempting to prove the existence of God once and for all. Notice particularly the Aristotelian reliance on observation and logically drawn conclusions (**Reading 6.1**):

Continuity & Change

READING 6.1　**Thomas Aquinas, from *Summa Theologica***

Is there a God?

REPLY: There are five ways in which one can prove there is a God.

The FIRST . . . is based on change. Some things. . . are certainly in the process of change: this we plainly see. Now anything in the process of change is being changed by something else. . . . Hence one is bound to arrive at some first cause of change not itself being changed by anything, and this is what everybody understands by God.

The SECOND is based on the nature of causation. In the observable world causes are found to be ordered in series. . . . Such a series must however stop somewhere. . . . One is therefore forced to suppose some first cause, to which everyone gives the name "God."

The THIRD way is based on what need not be and on what must be. . . . Some . . . things can be, but need not be for we find them springing up and dying away. . . . Now everything cannot be like this [for then we must conclude that] once upon a time there was nothing. But if that were true there would be nothing even now, because something that does not exist can only be brought into being by something already existing. . . . One is forced therefore to suppose something which must be . . . [and] is itself the cause that other things must be.

The FOURTH way is based on the gradation observed in things. Some things are found to be more

good, more true, more noble. . . and other things less [so]. But such comparative terms describe varying degrees of approximation to a superlative . . . [something that is] the truest and best and most noble of things. . . . There is something, therefore, which causes in all other things their being, their goodness, and whatever other perfection they have. And this we call "God."

The FIFTH way is based on the guidedness of nature. An orderedness of actions to an end is observed in all bodies obeying natural laws. . .; they truly tend to a goal and do not merely hit it by accident. . . . Everything in nature, therefore, is directed to its goal by someone with intelligence, and this we call "God."

Such a rational demonstration of the existence of God is, for Aquinas, what he called a "preamble of faith." What he calls the "articles of faith" necessarily follow upon and build on such rational demonstrations. So, although Christians cannot rationally know the essence of God, they can, through faith, know its divinity. Faith, in sum, begins with what Christians can know through what God has revealed to them in the Bible and through Christian tradition. Aquinas maintains, however, that some objects of faith, including the Incarnation, lie entirely beyond our capacity to understand them rationally in this life. Still, since we arrive at truth by means of both faith and reason—and, crucially, since all truths are equally valid—there should be no conflict between those arrived at through either faith or reason.

Although conservative Christians never quite accepted Aquinas' writings, arguing, for instance, that reason can never know God directly, his influence on Christian theology was profound and lasting. In the scope of its argument, the intellectual heights to which it soars, the *Summa Theologica* is at one with the Gothic cathedral. Like the cathedral, it is an architecture, built of logic rather than of stone, dedicated to the Christian God.

The Radiant Style and the Court of Louis IX

By the middle of the thirteenth century, the Gothic style in France had been elaborated into increasingly flamboyant patterns of repeated traceries and ornament that we have come to refer to as the *Rayonnant* [RAY-oh-nahnt] or **radiant style**. This style was associated closely with the court of Louis IX (r. 1226–1270), in Paris, which was considered throughout Europe to be the model of perfect rule. Louis was a born reformer, as much a man of the people as any medieval king could be. Under his rule the scholastics and Aquinas argued theology openly in the streets of Paris, just across the river from the royal palace. Louis believed in a certain freedom of thought, but even more in the rule of law. He dispatched royal commissioners into all of the provinces to check up on the Crown's representatives and ensure that they were treating the people fairly. He abolished serfdom and made private wars—which many believe to have been the ultimate motivation for the First Crusade—illegal. He reformed the tax structure and gave his subjects the right to appeal decisions in court. He was, in short, something of a saint. Indeed, the Church later beatified him as Saint Louis.

The Church especially valued Louis's dedication to its well-being. One of his most important contributions to the Church, and to the history of Gothic architecture, is the royal chapel of Sainte-Chapelle [sant-shah-PELL] (Fig. **6.18**), constructed in the center of the royal palace on the Île de la Cité not far from Notre-Dame de Paris. Louis had the chapel designed so that the royal family could enter directly from the palace, at the level of the stained glass, thus symbolizing his own eminence, while others—court officials and the like—entered through a smaller, ground-level chapel below. He created for himself, in other words, a **palatine chapel**—a palace chapel—on the model of Charlemagne, thus connecting himself to his great predecessor.

The chapel was nothing short of a reliquary built large. While on Crusade, Louis purchased what was believed to be the crown of thorns that Christ wore at the Crucifixion, as well as other precious objects, from the emperor of Constantinople. These precious pieces were destined to be housed in Sainte-Chapelle. No other structure in the Gothic era so completely epitomized the Radiant style even as it embodied the original vision of the Abbot Suger:

> Thus, when—out of my delight in the beauty of the house of God—the loveliness of the many-colored gems [of stained glass] has called me away from external cares, and worthy meditation has induced me to reflect, transferring that which is material to that which is immaterial, on the diversity of the sacred virtues: then it seems to me that I see myself dwelling, as it were, in some strange region of the universe which neither exists entirely in the slime of the earth nor entirely in the purity of heaven; and that, by the grace of God, I can be transported from this interior to that higher world in an analogical manner.

Bathing the viewer in the light of its stained glass—light so bright, in fact, that the viewer can hardly distinguish the details of its biblical narrative—Sainte-Chapelle is designed to relieve the faithful of any external cares and transport them into a realm of heavenly beauty. It is spiritual space, the immateriality of its

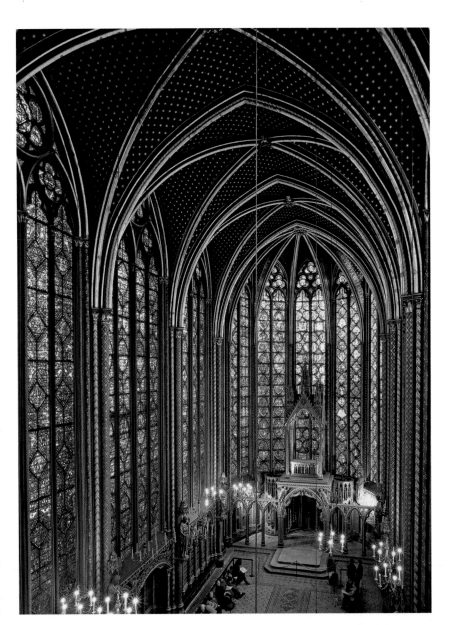

Fig. 6.18 Interior, upper chapel, Sainte-Chapelle, Paris. 1243–1248. Although the chapel was originally surrounded by the royal castle—today it is surrounded by the Ministry of Justice—it remains more or less intact, save for a 19th-century repainting. Its acoustics were originally among the best in Paris and remain so today.

light comparable, in Suger's perspective, to the immateriality of the immortal soul. The ratio of glass to stone is higher than in any other Gothic structure, the windows separated by the slenderest of columns. The lower parts of the walls, beneath the windows, are richly decorated in red, blue, and gilt, so that stone and glass seem one and the same. Golden stars shine down from the deep blue of the delicately vaulted ceiling. Louis's greatest wish was to make Paris a New Jerusalem, a city as close to paradise as could be found on earth. For many visitors, he came as close as may be humanly possible in Sainte-Chapelle.

Civic and Religious Life in Siena and Florence

By the thirteenth century, Italian life and politics were dominated by two prominent city-states, Siena and Florence. So weakened was the Church that, despite the fact that it controlled considerable territory, it exercised little real influence. Siena lies in the mountainous southern region of Tuscany, at the center of a rich agricultural zone famous for its olive oil and wine. Florence is located in the Arno river valley, the region's richest agricultural district (Map **6.1**).

The two cities were fierce rivals, their division dating back to the contest for supremacy between the pope and the Holy Roman Emperor during the time of Charlemagne. The Guelphs sided with the pope, while the Ghibellines sided with the emperor. Siena was generally considered a Ghibelline city, and Florence a Guelph stronghold, although factions of both parties competed for leadership within each city, especially in Florence. By the end of the thirteenth century, the pope retaliated against Siena for its Ghibelline leanings by revoking the city's papal banking privileges and conferring them instead on Florence. As a result, by the fourteenth century, Florence had become the principal economic and political power in Tuscany.

Both Siena and Florence were republics; the nobility did not rule them. Out of their competition with one another, the modern Western city was born. What distinguished Florence and Siena was the role that the citizenry played in expressing their civic pride.

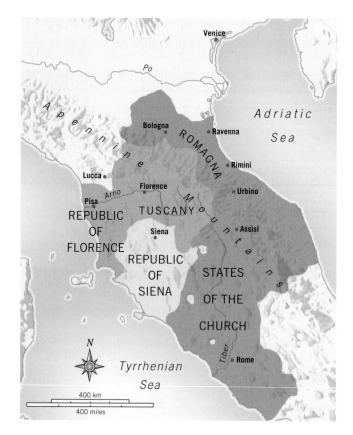

Map 6.1 Central Italy in about 1494, showing the Republics of Florence and Siena and the Papal States.

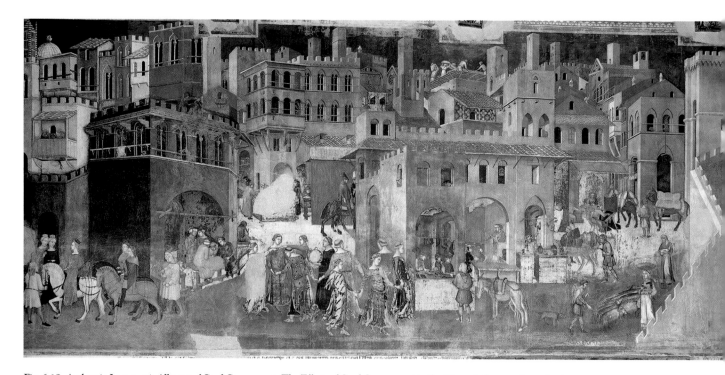

Fig. 6.19 Ambrogio Lorenzetti, *Allegory of Good Government: The Effects of Good Government in the City and Country*, fresco in the Sala della Pace, Palazzo Pubblico, Siena. 1338–1339. Across from this painting Lorenzetti also painted an *Allegory of Bad Government*, in which there is no commerce, no dancing, only man killing man, destruction and darkness all around.

The governments of both cities were controlled by *arti*, or **guilds**, associations of people with likeminded, often occupation-based interests, exercising power over their membership. Leading the way in Siena was the merchants' guild, organized as early as 1192. The richest merchant families lent money (charging interest on their loans, despite a papal ban on the practice) and dealt in wax, pepper, and spices, as well as Flemish cloth, shoes, stockings, and belts. Other guilds, such as masons, carpenters, innkeepers, barbers, butchers, and millers, soon established themselves as well. By the end of the twelfth century in Florence there were seven major guilds and fourteen minor ones. The most prestigious was the lawyers' guild (the Arte dei Giudici), followed closely by the wool guild (the Arte della Lana), the silk guild (the Arte di Seta), and the cloth merchants' guild (the Arte di Calimala). Also among the major guilds were the bankers, the doctors, and other merchant classes. Butchers, bakers, carpenters, and masons composed the bulk of the minor guilds.

Siena: A Free Commune

When Siena established itself, in 1125, as a free **commune** (a collective of people gathered together for the common good), it achieved an immense advantage over its feudal neighbors. "Town air brings freedom" was a common saying in the late Middle Ages. As the prospect of such freedom attracted an increasing number of people to Siena, its prosperity was soon unrivaled.

Crucial to the growing town's success was a new model of government, celebrated in 1338 by the painter Ambrogio Lorenzetti (active 1319–1347) in a fresco called *Allegory of Good Government* (Fig. **6.19**), commissioned for the council chamber of Siena's city hall, the Palazzo Pubblico. The fresco depicts Siena as it actually appeared. Richly dressed merchants dance in the street, one couple passing beneath the arching arms of another, followed by a chain of revelers dancing hand in hand. To the left, in an arched portico, three men play a board game. To their right is a shoe shop, behind that a schoolroom where a teacher expounds to a row of students, and beside the schoolroom, a wine shop. At the very top, masons construct a new building. Outside the city gate, to the right, the surrounding countryside is lush. Farmers bring livestock and produce to market, workers till the fields and labor in the vineyards. Above them all, floating in the sky, is the nearly nude figure of *Securitas* [she-koo-ree-TASS] ("Security"), carrying a gallows in one hand and a scroll in the other, to remind citizens that peace depends upon justice. At the horizon, the sky is ominously dark, suggesting perhaps that Siena's citizens thought of themselves as living in a uniquely enlightened place.

Florence: Archrival of Siena

Like Siena, Florence was extremely wealthy, and that wealth was based on trade. By the twelfth century, Florence was the center of textile production in the Western world and played a central role in European trade markets. The Arno River provided ample water for washing and rinsing sorted wool and finished cloth. The city's dyeing techniques were unsurpassed—to this day the formulas for the highly prized Florentine reds remain a mystery. Dyestuffs were imported from throughout the Mediterranean and even the Orient, and each

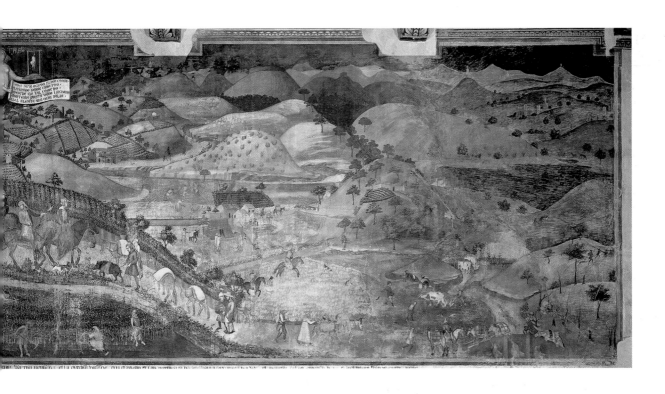

year Florentine merchants traveled to England, Portugal, Spain, and Flanders to purchase raw wool for their factories.

As in Siena, it was the city's bankers and moneylenders who made Florence a vital player in world trade. Florentine bankers invented checks, credit, even life insurance. Most important, in 1252 they introduced Europe's first single currency, the gold *florin*. By 1422, over 2 million florins were in circulation throughout Europe. This was a staggering number considering that a family could live comfortably on about 150 florins a year, and the finest palace cost about 1,000 florins. Florence was Europe's bank, and its bankers were Europe's true nobility.

Tuscan Religious Life

Although the guilds exercised considerable influence over day-to-day life in fourteenth-century Tuscany, nothing influenced the people more than the Church. It is natural, therefore, that in addition to building new city halls and public plazas, civic leaders turned their attention to the cathedrals. Siena took the lead, commissioning a new facade for its cathedral in 1284. A decade later, in 1294, Florence responded to Siena's initiative when the Arte della Lana formed the Opera del Duomo, or Department of Works of the Duomo ("duomo" comes from *domus dei*, or "house of God"), a committee in charge of building a new cathedral.

Construction began in 1296, although the building would not be completed until the first half of the fifteenth century (see chapter 7). The guild claimed that the Duomo would be "the most beautiful and honorable church in Tuscany," an assertion that everyone understood to mean it would compete with Siena's cathedral.

The New Mendicant Orders Aside from cathedrals, civic leaders also engaged in building projects for the new urban religious orders: the Dominicans, founded by the Spanish monk Dominic de Guzman (ca. 1170–1221), whose most famous theologian was Thomas Aquinas (see Reading 6.1); and the Franciscans, founded by Francis of Assisi (ca. 1181–1226). Unlike the traditional Benedictine monastic order, which functioned apart from the world, the Dominicans and the Franciscans were reformist orders, dedicated to active service in the cities, especially among the common people. Their growing popularity reflects the growing crisis facing the mainstream Church, as isolation and apparent disregard for laypeople plagued it well into the sixteenth century.

The mainstream Church held property and engaged in business—sources, many felt, of the Church's corruption. The Dominicans and Franciscans were both **mendicant orders**: that is, they neither held property nor engaged in business, relying for their support on contributions from their communities. The Dominicans and the Franciscans were rivals, and they often established themselves on opposite sides of a city. The Dominicans' priority was preaching. The Franciscans committed themselves to a severe regimen of prayer, meditation, fasting, and mortification of the flesh, based on Francis's conviction that one could come closer to God by rejecting worldly goods. But both orders borrowed freely from one another. The Franciscans adopted the more efficient organizing principles of the Dominicans as well as their love of learning and emphasis on preaching, while the Dominicans accepted the Franciscan repudiation of worldly goods.

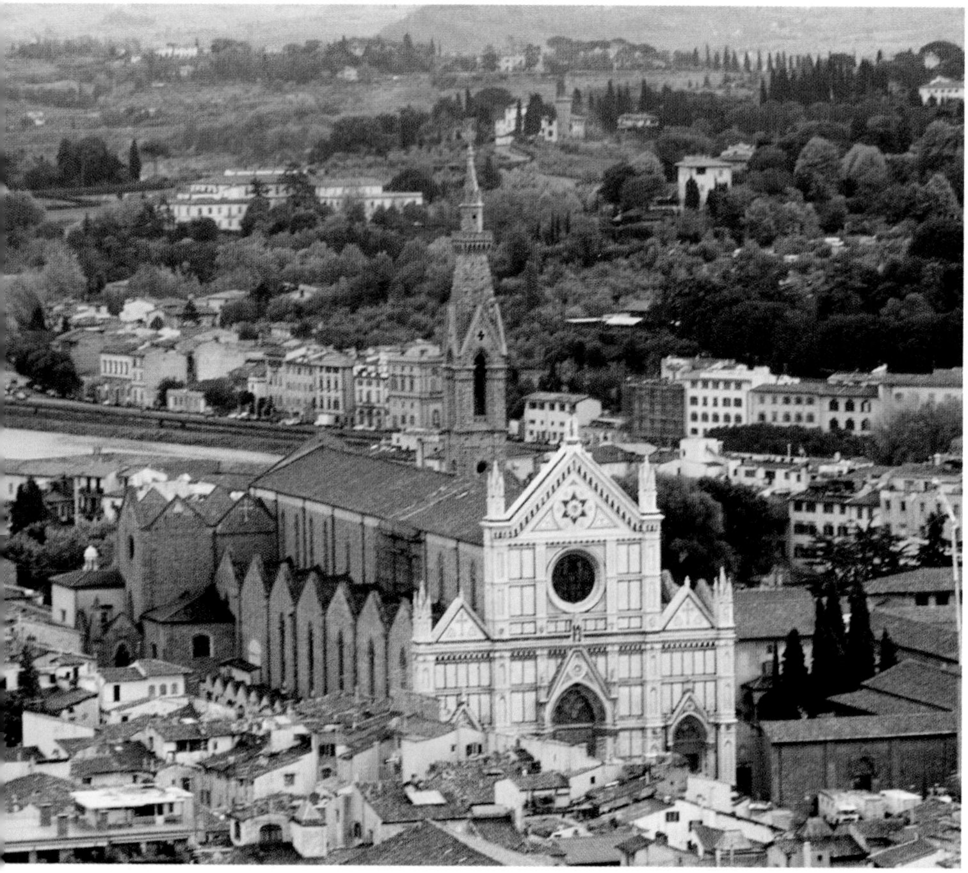

Franciscan and Dominican Churches In Florence, the civic government and private citizens worked with the Franciscans to build the church of Santa Croce (Fig. **6.20**). Construction began in 1294 and continued even as the city began constructing its main cathedral. Santa Croce was on the eastern side of the city, and the Dominican church of Santa Maria Novella (Fig. **6.21**) was built on the western side, underscoring the rivalry between the two orders.

A Franciscan church and a Dominican church were also built in Siena.

Fig. 6.20 **Santa Croce, Florence. Begun 1294.** Santa Croce was commissioned by the Franciscans with the support of the Florentine government and private citizens.

Compared to Gothic churches of the period, the mendicant churches are austere in their decoration. Nothing like the dramatic gables, finials, and sculpture program that decorate Giovanni Pisano's Siena Cathedral distinguish their plain facades, and their interiors are likewise unembellished. The ceiling of Santa Croce consists of an open wooden truss, a far cry from the rising vaults of the Gothic interior. At Santa Maria Novella, the marble striping that defines the rich surfaces of Siena's cathedral is used only on the arches, leaving the rest of the interior surface bare. Families supported the construction of both Florentine churches by donating chapels, held as family property, and built on either side. Private family masses could be celebrated in these chapels, and, as opposed to the more public spaces in the churches, they were often richly decorated and their walls painted with frescoes. Thus, a rich family expected to guarantee its salvation by contributing to the church, and the order could accept the church and its chapels as a form of alms, consistent with its vow of poverty.

The Appeal of Saint Francis Francis was not canonized until 1218, two years after his death. By then his reputation as a man of the people, capable of the most remarkable miracles and cures, was well established. His love of the natural world was profound; in his mystical poem *Canticle of the Sun*, his language suggests an intimate bond with the universe. Addressing "brother sun" and "sister moon," "brother wind" and "sister water," this poem may be the first work of literature in the vernacular, or the language spoken by the people in everyday usage, as opposed to Latin. Toward the end of his life, as he fasted in isolation, legend had it that he received the signs of the *stigmata*—the physical signs of the Crucifixion—confirming his spiritual connection to Christ.

His own Franciscan order and the Dominican order were sanctioned by Pope Innocent III (papacy 1198–1216). Innocent exercised papal authority as no pope had before him. He went so far as to claim that the pope was to the emperor as the sun was to the moon, a reference to the fact that the emperor received his "brilliance" (that is, his crown) from the hand of the pope. Innocent established the papacy as a self-sustaining financial and bureaucratic institution. He formalized the Church hierarchy, from pope to parish priest, and gave full sanction to the doctrine of *transubstantiation* (the belief that the bread and wine of sacrament become the true body and blood of Christ when consecrated by a priest), and made annual confession and Easter communion mandatory for all adult Christians.

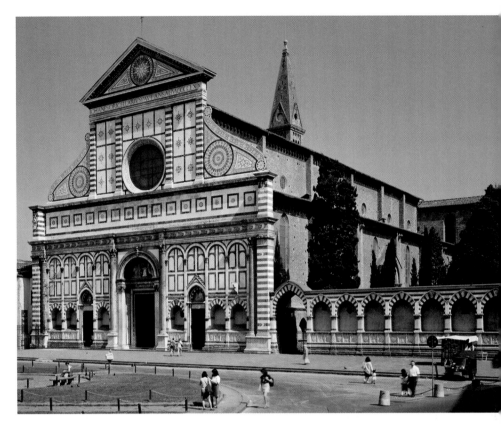

Fig. 6.21 Santa Maria Novella, Florence. Founded before 1246, nave begun after 1279. Santa Maria Novella was commissioned by the Dominicans and, like Santa Croce, its construction was supported by the Florentine government and private citizens.

Innocent was also a remarkably gifted preacher—his sermon *On the Misery of the Human Condition* was one of the most famous of its day (see Reading 5.4)—and the power of his words, if not the fierceness of his rhetoric, served as a model for both the Dominicans and the Franciscans. But, where Innocent appealed to the fear of death and damnation, mendicant orders appealed to the promise of life and salvation. Nevertheless, Innocent clearly understood the popular appeal of preaching and the influence that preaching gave to the new mendicant orders. He especially understood the attraction offered by the example of Francis of Assisi and his affirmation of a life led in service to all God's creatures.

Painting: A Growing Naturalism

Even though Saint John the Baptist was the patron saint of Florence, the city, like Siena, relied on the Virgin Mary to protect it. Her image appeared frequently in the mendicant churches and elsewhere, and these images were said to perform miracles. Pilgrims from Tuscany and beyond flocked to Florence to receive the Madonna's good graces. As in Siena, whenever the city was threatened—by war, by flood, by plague—the Madonna's image was carried through the city in ceremonial procession. The two cities put themselves under the protection of the Virgin, and it was not long before they were competing to prove who could paint her the most magnificently. In the process, they began to represent her less in the stiff, abstracted manner of the Byzantine icon and more as a real person of flesh and blood.

Duccio and Simone Martini

After the Venetian rout of Constantinople in the Fourth Crusade in 1204, Byzantine imagery flooded Europe. One of the first artists to break from the Byzantine tradition was the Sienese native Duccio di Buoninsegna (active 1278–1318). In 1308, the *commune* commissioned Duccio to paint a *Maestà,* or *Virgin and Child in Majesty* (Fig. **6.22**), to be set under the dome of Siena's cathedral.

The finished work was greeted with a great celebration:

> "On the day that it was carried to the [cathedral]," a contemporary chronicler reports, "the shops were shut, and the bishop conducted a great and devout company of priests and friars in solemn procession, accompanied by . . . all the officers of the commune, and all the people, and one after another the worthiest with lighted candles in their hands took places near the picture, and behind came the women and children with great devotion . . . making the procession around the Campo, as is the custom, all the bells ringing joyously, trumpets and bagpipes playing, out of reverence for so noble a picture as is this."

Duccio was well aware of the greatness of his achievement. Along the base of the Virgin's throne he wrote these words: "Holy Mother of God, give Siena peace and Duccio life because he painted Thee thus," announcing both the

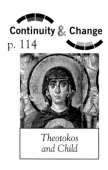

Continuity & Change
p. 114

Theotokos and Child

artist's piety and pride in his work and the growing prominence of artists in Italian society as a whole.

Duccio's *Maestà* begins to leave the conventions of the Byzantine icon behind and incorporates the Gothic tendency to naturalism. (Compare the Byzantine Fig. 4.15.) Duccio's Christ Child seems to be an actual baby, and a slightly chubby one at that. Similarly, beneath the Madonna's robes, we can sense a real body. Her knee especially asserts itself, and the drapery falling from it drops in long, gentle curves, much more natural-looking than the rigid, angular drapery of earlier Byzantine works. Four angels peer over the top of the Madonna's throne, gazing on the child like proud relations. The saints who kneel in the front row appear to be individuals rather than types. Notice especially the aging and bearded cleric at the left. All are patron saints of the city, underscoring the fact that Duccio's painting is both an ecclesiastical and civic commission.

If Duccio's *Maestà* reflects the growing realism of Sienese art, the *Maestà* of Simone Martini, in the Hall of the Mappamondo in Siena's Palazzo Pubblico, is even more naturalistic (Fig. **6.23**). Simone had worked on the cathedral *Maestà* as Duccio's apprentice from 1308 to 1311, and he probably modeled his own work on it. Situated in a public building, overlooking the workings of civic administration, Simone's painting announces, even more dramatically than Duccio's, the blending of the sacred and secular in Tuscan culture.

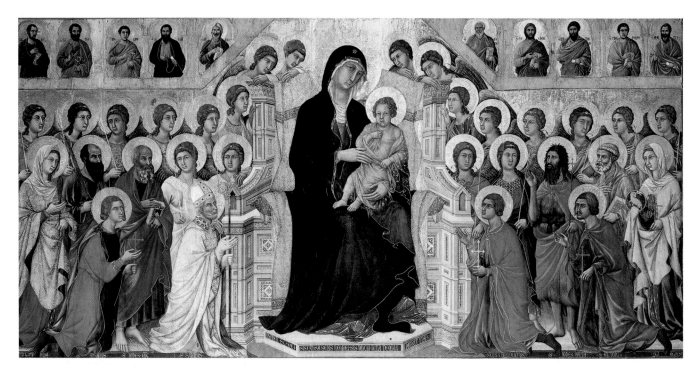

Fig. 6.22 Duccio di Buoninsegna. *Maestà,* main panel of *Maestà Altarpiece,* from Siena Cathedral. 1308–1311. Tempera and gold on wood, 7′ × 13′ 6¼″. Museo dell'Opera del Duomo, Siena. The Madonna's throne imitates the stone facade of the Siena cathedral.

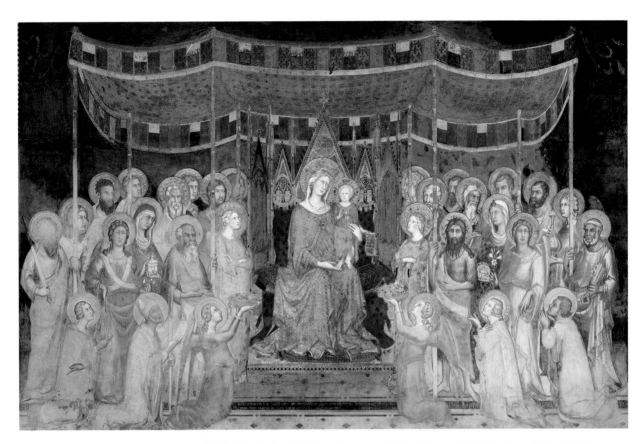

Fig. 6.23 Simone Martini, *Maestà,* **Council Chamber, Palazzo Pubblico, Siena. ca. 1311–1317, repaired 1321.** Fresco, 25′ × 31′ 9″.
Martini's fresco covers the end wall of the Council Chamber, symbolically submitting that civic body's deliberations to the Madonna's watchful gaze and care.

One of the great innovations of Simone's fresco is the Virgin's crown, which signifies her status as Queen of Heaven. Surrounded by her celestial "court," she reveals the growing influence of French courtly poetry (see chapter 5) in Italy. She becomes a model for human behavior, an emblem in the spiritual realm for the most noble types of secular love and devotion, including devotion to the right conduct of government. Highlighting the secular message, Jesus holds a parchment, adhered to the surface of the fresco, that reads, "Love Justice you who judge the earth." Like Duccio's painting, Simone's fresco carries a propagandistic message to the city fathers. Inscribed at the base of the throne are these words: "The angelic little flowers, roses and lilies, Which adorn the heavenly meadow, do not please me more than good counsel." The painting suggests that the Virgin is as interested in worldly affairs as divine ones. Because of the realistic way Simone has represented her, she is as human as she is divine.

Stylistic differences separate the two works as well. As in the Byzantine icon from which she derives, Duccio's Madonna wears no crown, her brows turn without interruption down into the length of her nose, she is draped in blue, with an orange undergarment, and her rounded hood echoes the halo behind her head. She is much larger than those attending her, conforming to the hierarchies of Byzantine art. In Simone's version of the theme, the Virgin and surrounding figures are depicted almost in the same scale. As opposed to Duccio's painting, with its stacked receding space, Simone's Virgin sits in a deep space of the canopy with its delicate Gothic arches behind the throne. Both of the Virgin's knees are visible, with the Christ Child standing firmly on one of them. Her head and neck, rather than being shrouded behind an all-embracing hood, are rounded and full beneath the crown and its softly folded train, which is itself fully rounded in shadow behind her neck. Her robe, neglecting convention, is composed of rich, transparent silks, beneath which we can see her right arm. Above all, her porcelain-white skin, tinged with pink, gives her complexion a realistic tone. Blood flows through her body, rouging her cheeks, and her flesh breathes with life. She embodies, in fact, a standard of beauty absent in Western art since Classical times—the physical beauty of the flesh as opposed to the divine beauty of the spirit.

Cimabue and Giotto

Florence, too, had its master painters of the Virgin. Even before Duccio became active in Siena, a painter known as Cimabue had produced a large-scale Virgin for the altarpiece of the Church of Santa Trinità in Florence (Fig. **6.24**). Cimabue's *Madonna Enthroned with Angels and Prophets* solidified his posi-

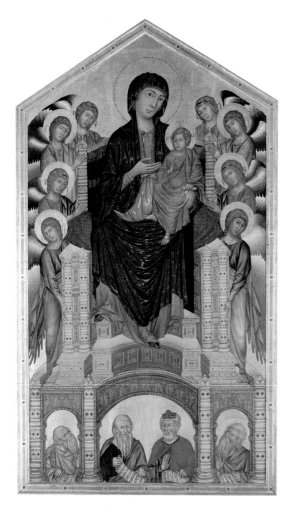

Fig. 6.24 Cimabue, *Madonna Enthroned with Angels and Prophets*, from high altar of Santa Trinità, Florence. ca. 1285. Tempera and gold on wood, 11′ 7½″ × 7′ 4″. Galleria degli Uffizi, Florence. The later Renaissance historian Giorgio Vasari would claim that Cimabue had been apprenticed to a Greek painter from whom he learned the fundamentals of Byzantine icon painting.

individual likenesses also tell us that Italian artists were becoming more skillful in painting with **tempera**, which allowed them to portray the world in ever-increasing detail. Perhaps most interesting of all is the position of the Virgin's feet, the right one propped upon the throne in an almost casual position.

According to an old story, one day Cimabue discovered a talented shepherd boy by the name of Giotto di Bondone and tutored him in the art of painting. The pupil soon surpassed the teacher. The sixteenth-century historian Giorgio Vasari would later say that Giotto set "art upon the path that may be called the true one, learned to draw accurately from life and thus put an end to the crude Greek [i.e., Byzantine] manner."

Giotto's 1310 *Madonna Enthroned with Angel and Saints* (Fig. **6.25**), painted just a quarter century after Cimabue's, is as remarkable a shift toward naturalism as Simone's *Maestà* is over Duccio's. While it retains a Byzantine hierarchy of figures—the Christ Child is almost as big as the angels and the

tion as the leading painter in Florence. Although its Byzantine roots are clear—following closely, for instance, a Byzantine hierarchy of figures, with the Madonna larger than the figures that surround her—the painting is remarkable on several fronts. First, it is enormous. Standing almost 12 feet high, it seems to have begun a tradition of large-scale altarpieces, helping to affirm the altar as the focal point of the church. But most important are Cimabue's concern for spatial volume and his treatment of human figures with naturalistic expressions. The throne is especially interesting, creating as it does a spatial setting for the scene, and the angels seem to be standing on the architectural frame; the front two clearly are. If the Virgin and Child are stock Byzantine figures, the four prophets at the base of the throne are surprisingly individualized, suggesting the increasing prominence of the individual personality in the era, an especially important characteristic, as we will see later in the chapter, of the literature of the period. These remarkably

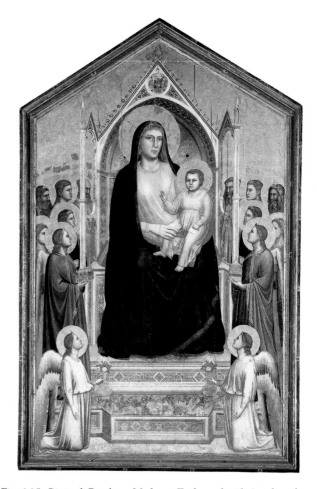

Fig. 6.25 Giotto di Bondone, *Madonna Enthroned with Angels and Saints*, from Church of the Ognissanti, Florence. ca. 1310. Tempera and gold on wood, 10′ 8″ × 6′ 8¼″. Galleria degli Uffizi, Florence. Giotto was a notoriously ugly but witty man. Legend has it that when the Florentine poet Dante Alighieri (discussed later on page 177) asked him how his children could be so ugly when his paintings were so beautiful, Giotto replied that he painted by daylight but procreated in the dark.

Virgin three or four times their size—it is spatially convincing in a way that Cimabue's painting is not. Giotto apparently learned to draw accurately from life, and his figures reveal his skill. The paintings in the Chapel were done in **buon fresco**. In this technique, the artist applies pigments onto wet rather than dry plaster. Light plays across their forms—note the folds and pleats of the angels' gowns in the foreground—and substantial bodies seem to press outward from beneath the material. Giotto's colors gradually and continuously blend from light to dark around the contours of his figures and their draperies, re-creating the realistic appearance of shadows. Giotto was also a master of the human face, capable of revealing a wide range of emotion and character. This skill is particularly evident in the frescoes of the Arena Chapel (pages 178-179). (The chapel is also known as the Scrovegni Chapel, after the family that commissioned it in Padua.) The total effect is to humanize Christ, the Virgin, and the saints, to portray them as real people.

The Spread of Vernacular Literature in Europe

Until the early twelfth century, the language of almost all educated circles in Europe, and certainly in literature, was Latin. Gradually, however, writers began to address their works to a wider lay audience and to write in the **vernacular**, the language spoken in the streets. The French led the way, in twelfth-century works such as the *Song of Roland* and Chrétien de Troyes's *Lancelot* (see chapter 5), but early in the fourteenth century vernacular works began to appear throughout Italy as well, spreading to the rest of Europe.

Dante's *Divine Comedy*

One of the greatest medieval Italian writers working in the vernacular was the poet Dante Alighieri (1265–1321). In Florence, in about 1308, he began one of the greatest works of the literary imagination, the *Divine Comedy* (Fig. **6.26**). This poem records the travels of the Christian soul from Hell to Purgatory and finally to Salvation in three books—the *Inferno*, *Purgatorio*, and *Paradiso*. It is by no means an easy journey. Dante, who is the leading character in his own poem, is led by

the Roman poet Virgil, author of the *Aeneid* (see chapter 3). (Virgil, too, visits the underworld in the sixth book of his poem.)

Virgil cannot lead Dante into Heaven in the *Paradiso*, since he is a pagan who is barred from salvation. He is thus condemned to Limbo, the first level of Hell, a place of sorrow without torment, populated by virtuous pagans, the great philosophers and authors, unbaptized children, and others unfit to enter the kingdom of heaven. Among those who inhabit the realm with Virgil are Caesar, Homer, Socrates, and Aristotle. There is no punishment here, and the atmosphere is peaceful, yet sad. Virgil is, in fact, the model of human rationality, and in the *Inferno*, he and Dante study the varieties of human sin. Many of the characters who inhabit Dante's Hell are his contemporaries—the lovers Paolo and Francesca from Ravenna and Rimini, the usurer Reginaldo Scrovegni (patron of the chapel painted by Giotto; see *Focus*, pages 178–179), and so on. Dante also makes much of the Guelph/Ghibelline rivalries in his native Florence. He was himself a Guelph, but so divided were the Guelphs among themselves—into factions called the Blacks and the Whites, papal versus imperial bankers—that his efforts to heal their schism as one of the *Priori*, one of the nine leaders of the Florentine commune, resulted in a two-year exile beginning in 1302. Embittered, he never returned to Florence.

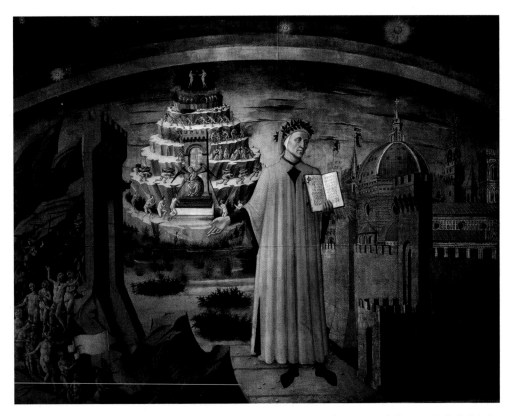

Fig. 6.26 Domenico di Michelino, *Dante and His Poem*. 1465. Fresco, 10′ 6″ × 9′ 7″. Florence Cathedral, Italy. To Dante's right is the Inferno, and behind him the seven-stepped hill of Purgatory. To his left is Paradise, imaged as Florence Cathedral, here topped by Brunelleschi's dome (discussed in chapter 7). Dante himself would never live to see or even imagine the dome.

Focus

Giotto's Arena Chapel

Giotto's greatest paintings are surely those in the Arena Chapel in Padua, painted around 1305. Giotto covered virtually every space of the barrel-vaulted family chapel of the Scrovegni family with buon fresco, the technique of painting on wet plaster. The top of the vault is a starry blue sky, painted with lapis lazuli. Lapis lazuli does not properly combine with wet plaster, so it was applied on a dry wall. As a result, the blues of the ceiling and other blues in the frescoes have faded far more than the other colors, most of which still look fresh. On the side walls are scenes from the life of the Virgin and the life of Christ.

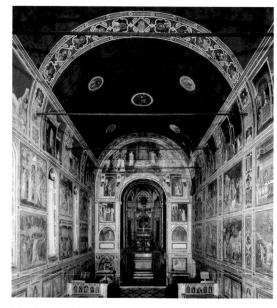

The Arena Chapel, Padua. The Life of Christ and the Virgin frescoes by Giotto. 1305–1306. A view of the Arena (Scrovegni) Chapel. In the bottom layer of images, closest to the floor, figures of the Virtues and Vices appear as painted, black-and-white simulations of sculpture, a technique known as *grisaille*. On the back wall above the door is a Last Judgment, figured as the final episode in the life of Christ.

Even the angels are wracked with grief.

John the Evangelist flings his arms back in a gesture that echoes that of the angels, almost as if his arms were wings.

The blue void at the center of the painting is a metaphor for the emptiness felt by the mourners.

The single leafless tree is a traditional symbol of death. It sits on a barren ridge that plunges in a stark diagonal toward the dead Christ.

The direction of the Virgin Mary's grief-stricken gaze continues down the diagonal line created by the barren ridge, reinforcing its emptiness.

Mary Magdalene, recognizable by her long hair, is traditionally represented at the Crucifixion kissing Christ's feet. Here, the Crucifixion over, she holds his feet in her hands, in an act of consummate tenderness and affection.

Giotto was the first artist since antiquity to depict figures from behind, contributing to the sense that we are viewing a real drama.

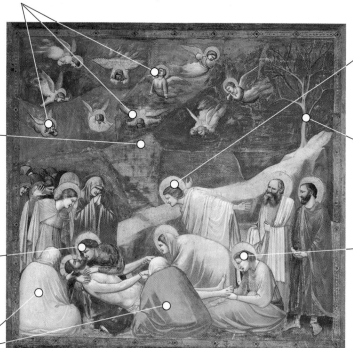

Giotto, *The Lamentation*, Arena Chapel, Padua. 1305–1306. Fresco, $78\frac{1}{2}'' \times 73''$. Among the most moving scenes in the chapel is Giotto's depiction of human suffering. The painter focused on the real pain felt by Jesus' followers upon his death, rather than the promise of salvation that it symbolized.

Halley's Comet made one of its regular appearances in 1301, just a few years before this painting was made. (We saw it depicted in the Bayeux Tapestry of 1066 [see chapter 5, *Focus*, page 144]). Giotto apparently modeled the star that guides the Magi on that phenomenon.

The boy looks up at the Magi's camels in astonishment. This expression of emotion is typical of Giotto's frescoes. Giotto had probably never seen a camel: These have blue eyes and cows' feet.

Note Giotto's attempt to render the wooden shed in perspective. If he does not quite "get it," he is coming close.

Giotto has abandoned the Byzantine hierarchy of figures. The angels, the Magi, the Virgin, and the Child are all drawn to the same scale. (For a comparison, see Duccio's *Maestà Altarpiece*, Fig. 6.22.)

The king, Caspar, has removed his crown and placed it at the foot of the angel receiving gifts. The gesture signifies his understanding that Christ is the "King of Kings."

The blue of Mary's skirt has almost completely flaked off. Lapis lazuli, the stone used to make blue pigment, does not combine with wet plaster, so the blue had to be painted on after the plaster had dried, leaving it far more susceptible to heat and humidity, which eventually cause flaking.

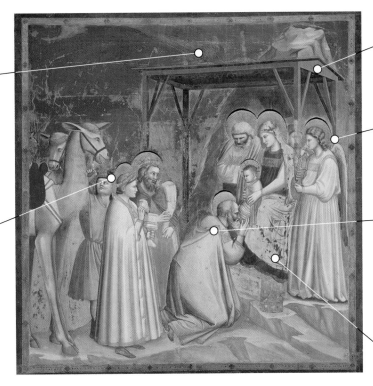

Giotto, *Adoration of the Magi*, Arena Chapel, Padua. 1305–1306. Fresco, 78½″ × 73″. Boccaccio, author of the extraordinarily realistic story-cycle the *Decameron*, admired Giotto's painterly realism: "There is nothing in the whole creation he cannot depict," Boccaccio wrote.

Above the door is a depiction of the Last Judgment, in which the patron, Enrico Scrovegni, offers a model of the chapel to the Virgin. The purpose of the chapel seems clear: It was meant as penance on Enrico's part for his own and his father's sins—notably their flagrant usury.

The paintings depicting the life of Christ and the Virgin deliberately abandon the balance and symmetry that distinguish Byzantine painting (and, for that matter, the *Maestàs* of the period) in order to create a heightened sense of reality. In *The Lamentation*, for instance, Giotto places Christ in the lower left-hand corner of the work, at the bottom of a stark diagonal. Throughout the cycle, the action takes place on a narrow platform at the front of the painting. The architecture in the paintings is small in comparison to the figures, as in *The Adoration of the Magi*. Giotto may have been influenced by the stage sets made for the contemporary revival in Padua of Roman theater. Whatever the case, the drama of Giotto's paintings is undeniable. They possess a psychological intensity and emotional immediacy that involve the viewer directly in the scene.

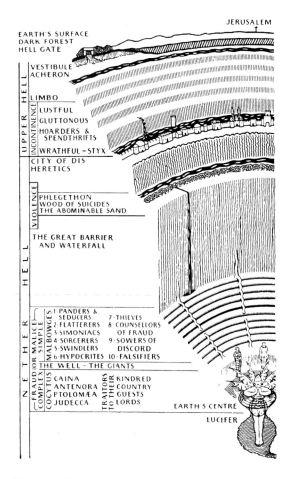

Fig. 6.27 Plan of Dante's Inferno.

Dante's *Inferno* is composed of nine descending rings of sinners undergoing punishment, each more gruesome than the one before it (Fig. **6.27**). In the poem's first Canto the poet is lost in a Dark Wood of Error, where Virgil comes to his rescue, promising to lead him "forth to an eternal place." In Hell, the two first encounter sinners whose passion has condemned them to Hell—Paolo and Francesca, whose illicit love was motivated, they tell Dante, by reading Chrétien de Troyes' *Lancelot*. The lovers are forever condemned to unreconciled love, to touch each other but never consummate their feelings. In the next ring are the gluttonous, condemned to wallow like pigs in their own excrement. Sinners, in other words, are punished not *for* their sins but *by* their sins. Dante finds intellectual dishonesty more sinful than any sin of passion, and thus flatterers, hypocrites, and liars occupy the next lower rings of hell. The violent are further down, immersed for eternity in boiling blood. And finally, at the very bottom of the pit, imprisoned in ice "like straws in glass," are the traitors. Among the lowest of the low are Guelphs and Ghibellines from all over Tuscany who betrayed their cities' well-being. Finally, in Canto 34, Dante once again integrates the pagan and Christian worlds as Satan himself chews on the worst of all traitors—Judas (thought to have betrayed Jesus) and Brutus and Cassius (assassins of Julius Caesar) (**Reading 6.2**):

READING 6.2   from Dante, *Inferno*, Canto 34

...With what a sense of awe I saw his head
towering above me! for it had three faces:[1]
one was in front, and it was fiery red;

the other two, as weirdly wonderful,
merged with it from the middle of each shoulder
to the point where all converged at the top of the skull;

the right was something between white and bile;
the left was about the color one observes
on those who live along the banks of the Nile.

Under each head two wings rose terribly,
their span proportioned to so gross a bird:
I never saw such sails upon the sea.

They were not feathers—their texture and their form
were like a bat's wings—and he beat them so
that three winds blew from him in one great storm:

it is these winds that freeze all Cocytus.
He wept from his six eyes, and down three chins
the tears ran mixed with bloody froth and pus.[2]

In every mouth he worked a broken sinner
between his rake-like teeth. Thus he kept three
in eternal pain at his eternal dinner.

For the one in front the biting seemed to play
no part at all compared to the ripping: at times
the whole skin of his back was flayed away.

"That soul that suffers most," explained my Guide,
"is Judas[3] Iscariot, he who kicks his legs
on the fiery chin and has his head inside.

Of the other two, who have their heads thrust forward,
the one who dangles down from the black face
is Brutus: note how he writhes without a word.

And there, with the huge and sinewy arms,[4] is the soul
of Cassius. But the night is coming on
and we must go, for we have seen the whole."...

Notes
[1] **three faces:** Numerous interpretations of these three faces exist. What is essential to all explanations is that they be seen as perversions of the qualities of the Trinity.
[2] **bloody froth and pus:** The gore of the sinners he chews which is mixed with his slaver (saliva).
[3] **Judas:** Note how closely his punishment is patterned on that of the Simoniacs (Canto XIX).
[4] **huge and sinewy arms:** The Cassius who betrayed Caesar was more generally described in terms of Shakespeare's "lean and hungry look." Another Cassius is described by Cicero (*Catiline* III) as huge and sinewy. Dante probably confused the two.

In the universe of the *Divine Comedy*, Virgil, as the embodiment of rationality, can take Dante no further than Hell and Purgatory, since in order to enter Paradise faith must triumph over reason, something impossible for the pagan Roman. Dante's guide through Paradise is Beatrice, the love of his life. Beatrice was the daughter of the Florentine nobleman Folco Potinari, and Dante first saw her when she was nine years old and he was eight. He describes meeting her in his first major work, *La Vita Nuova*: "love ruled my soul . . . and began to hold such sway over me . . . that it was necessary for me to do completely all his pleasure. He commanded me often that I should endeavor to see this youthful angel, and I saw her in such noble and praiseworthy deportment that truly of her might be said these words of the poet Homer— *She appeared to be born not of mortal man but of God.*"

Dante wrote these words in 1293. Ten years earlier, when she was 18, Beatrice had entered into a marriage, arranged when she was eight, with Simone di Bardi. It lasted only seven years, ending in her death at age 25. Dante's love for her was, then, the classic love of the courtier for his lady, marked by an unconsummated physical desire necessarily transformed into a spiritual longing that leads him, at the end of the *Divine Comedy*, to a comprehension of God's love, as he contemplates "in a great flash of light" a vision so powerful that he can barely find words to express it.

The Black Death and Its Aftermath

In 1316 and 1317, not long before Dante's death, crop failures across Europe resulted in the greatest famine the continent had ever known. For two summers, the sun rarely shone (no one knew that huge volcanic eruptions thousands of miles away in Indonesia had sent vast clouds of ash into the atmosphere). Furthermore, between 1000 and 1300, the continent's population had doubled to a point where it probably exceeded its ability to feed itself even in the best of times. In these dark years, which were followed by a century-long cooling period marked by too much rain to allow for good grain harvests, common people were lucky to eat, let alone eat well. Then, in December 1347, rats infested with fleas carrying bubonic plague arrived on the island of Sicily. They were carried on four Genoese ships that had set sail from Kaffa, a Genoese trading center on the Black Sea.

The disease began in the lymph glands of the groin or armpits, which slowly filled with pus and turned black. The inflammations were called buboes—hence the name bubonic plague—and their black color lent the plague its other name, the Black Death. Since it was carried by rodents, which were commonplace even in wealthy homes, hardly anyone was spared. It was an egalitarian disease—archbishops, dukes, lords of the manor, merchants, laborers, and peasants fell equally before it. For those who survived the pandemic, life seemed little more than an ongoing burial service. In many towns, traditional funeral services were abandoned, and the dead were buried in mass graves. By 1350, all of Europe, with the exception of a few territories far from traditional trade routes, was devastated by the disease. In Tuscany, the death rate in the cities was near 60 percent. In Florence, on June 24, 1348, the feast day of the city's patron saint, John the Baptist, 1,800 people reportedly died, and another 1,800 the next day—about 4 percent of the city's population in two days' time. Severe outbreaks of the plague erupted again in 1363, 1388–1390, and 1400.

Literature after the Black Death: Boccaccio's *Decameron*

The frank treatment of reality found in the visual arts carried over into literature, where the direct language of the vernacular proved an especially appropriate vehicle for rendering truth. The *Decameron*, or "Work of Ten Days," is a collection of framed prose tales (a **framing tale** is narrative device that allows a writer to unite different tales under an overarching narrative umbrella). The Florentine writer Giovanni Boccaccio (1313–1375), who lived through the plague, sets the stage for the 100 prose stories of the collection with a startlingly direct description of Florence in the ravages of the disease (**Reading 6.3**):

READING 6.3   from Boccaccio, *Decameron*

The virulence of the plague was all the greater in that it was communicated by the sick to the well by contact, not unlike fire when dry or fatty things are brought near it. But the evil was still worse. Not only did conversation and familiarity with the diseased spread the malady and even cause death, but the mere touch of the clothes or any other object the sick had touched or used, seemed to spread the pestilence. . . .

It used to be common, as it is still, for women, friends and neighbors of a dead man, to gather in his house and mourn there with his people. . . . Now, as the plague gained in violence, these customs were either modified or laid aside altogether. . . . It was a rare occasion for a corpse to be followed to church by more than ten or twelve mourners—not the usual respectable citizens, but a class of vulgar grave-diggers who called themselves "sextons" and did these services for a price. . . .

More wretched still were the circumstances of the common people and, for a great part, of the middle class, for, confined to their homes either by hope of safety or by poverty, and restricted to their own sections, they fell sick daily by thousands. There, devoid of help or care, they died almost without redemption. A great many breathed their last in the public streets, day and night; a large number perished in their homes, and it was only by the stench of their decaying bodies that they proclaimed their death to their neighbors. Everywhere the city was teeming with corpses. A general course was now adopted by the people, more out of fear of contagion than of any charity they felt toward the dead. Alone, or with the assistance of whatever bearers they could muster, they would drag the corpses out of their homes and pile them in front of the doors, where often, of a morning, countless bodies might be seen. Biers were sent for. When none was to be had, the dead were laid upon ordinary boards, two or three at once. It was not infrequent to see a single bier carrying husband and wife, two or three brothers, father and son, and others besides. . . .

So many bodies were brought to the churches everyday that the consecrated ground did not suffice to hold them, particularly according to the ancient custom of giving each corpse its individual place. Huge trenches were dug in the crowded churchyards and the new dead were piled in them, layer upon layer, like merchandise in the hold of a ship. . . .

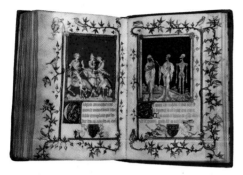

Fig. 6.28 Jean Le Noir, pages with *The Three Living* (left) and *The Three Dead* (right), from the Psalter and Book of Hours of Bonne of Luxembourg. **Before 1349.** Grisaille, color, gilt and brown ink on vellum, 5″ × 3 1/2″. The Metropolitan Museum of Art, The Cloisters Collection. 1969 (69.86). Image © The Metropolitan Museum of Art/Art Resource, NY. On the left page, three horsemen contemplate three cadavers in increasing states of decay on the right page. One horseman brings a handkerchief to his nose to fight off the stench. The cadavers address the horsemen: "What you are we were and what we are you will be!"

Boccaccio describes a world in virtual collapse (Fig. **6.28**). The social breakdown caused by the plague is especially evident in the widespread death of the ruling class and the rise of the class of men who called themselves "sextons," technically guardians of the church edifice, treasures, and vestments, but now a vile band of mercenary gravediggers. All tradition has been abandoned.

In the midst of this, seven young women and three young men of Florence retreat to the country together. As one of the young women explains: "There we shall hear the chant of birds, have sight of verdant hills and plains, of cornfields undulating like the sea . . . things far fairer for eyes to rest on than the desolates walls of our city." And there they entertain each other by telling tales, some of them quite ribald—that is, vulgar and indecent, often involving people of the lower and middle classes. Their characters, in their shrewdness and wit, ingenuity and resourcefulness, unscrupulous behavior and bawdy desires, introduce into Western literature a kind of social realism previously unexplored. Perhaps reflecting the reality of death that surrounds them, the stories depict daily life as it is truly lived. Boccaccio's world is of flesh and blood, not knights in shining armor. If the world of the *Decameron* is a fictitious one, in its penetrating revelation of workings of human psychology, it also represents an unprecedented brand of literary realism.

Petrarch's Sonnets

One of Boccaccio's best friends was the itinerant scholar and poet Francesco Petrarca (1304–1374), known as Petrarch. Raised near Avignon, in France, where the papacy had established itself in 1309 and where it remained through most of Petrarch's lifetime, Petrarch studied at Montpellier and Bologna and traveled throughout northern France, Germany, and Italy. He was always in search of manuscripts that preserved the priceless literary works of antiquity—copying those he could not pry loose from monastic libraries.

It was Petrarch who rediscovered the forgotten works of the Roman orator and statesman Cicero, and his own private library consisted of over 200 classical texts. He persuaded Boc-

caccio to bring the Greek scholar Leo Pilatus to Venice to teach them to read Greek. Boccaccio learned the language, but, put off by Pilatus' bad manners, Petrarch did not. Both, however, benefited from Pilatus' translation of Homer into Latin prose, as well as from his genealogy of the Greek gods.

Perhaps Petrarch' greatest work was his book of over 300 poems, the *Canzoniere* (Songbook), inspired by his love for a woman named Laura, whom he first met in 1327 in Avignon, where he was working for an influential cardinal. She is generally believed to have been the 19-year-old wife of Hugues de Sade. Whether Petrarch ever revealed his love to Laura, or simply poured it into his verses, remains a matter of speculation.

The majority of Petrarch's verses to Laura take the form of the **Italian sonnet**, known also as the **Petrarchan sonnet** because he perfected the form. The Petrarchan sonnet is composed of 14 lines divided into two parts: an *octave* of eight lines that presents a problem, and a *sestet* of six lines that either attempts to solve the problem or accepts it as unsolvable. The octave is further divided into two four-line *quatrains*. The first presents the problem and the second develops the idea. Many of Petrarch's verses to Laura were composed after her death from the bubonic plague in 1348, and it seems likely that her death motivated Petrarch to circulate them.

Especially influential were his pure love poems. One of the most famous of these is Sonnet 134, in which Petrarch explores the complexities of his feelings—all the ambivalence, contradiction, and paradox—in the face of his love for Laura (**Reading 6.4**):

READING 6.4 **Petrarch, Sonnet 134**

I find no peace, and yet I am not warlike;
I fear and hope, I burn and turn to ice;
I fly beyond the sky, stretch out on earth;
my hands are empty, yet I hold the world.

One holds me prisoner, not locked up, not free;
won't keep me for her own but won't release me;
Love does not kill me, does not loose my chains,
he'd like me dead, he'd like me still ensnared.

I see without my eyes, cry with no tongue,
I want to die and yet I call for help,
hating myself but loving someone else.

I feed on pain, I laugh while shedding tears,
both death and life displease me equally;
and this state, Lady, is because of you.

Such poems would have a lasting influence, because they seemed to capture all the emotional turbulence of love.

Chaucer's *Canterbury Tales*

The first Englishman to translate Petrarch was Geoffrey Chaucer (ca. 1342–1400). Well-educated, able to read both Ovid and Virgil in the original Latin, Chaucer was a middle-class civil servant and diplomat. In 1368, both he and Petrarch were guests at a wedding in Milan Cathedral, and four years later he was in Florence, where he probably met Boccaccio.

Chaucer's masterwork, *The Canterbury Tales*, is modeled roughly on Boccaccio's *Decameron*, but it is written in verse, not prose, and is composed in **heroic couplets**. Like the *Decameron*, it is a framed collection of stories, this time told by a group of pilgrims traveling from London to the shrine of Saint Thomas à Becket, Archbishop of Canterbury. In 1170, Becket had been murdered in Canterbury Cathedral by followers of King Henry II in a dispute over the rights and privileges of the Church.

Chaucer had planned to write 120 tales. Before his death, he completed only 22 tales and fragments of two others, but they are extraordinary in the range of characters and social types that they portray. Not only are the characters in the stories fully developed, but so are their narrators, and as a result the stories reflect perhaps the most fully developed realism of the era. Consider Chaucer's description of the Wife of Bath from the Prologue to the work (**Reading 6.5**):

READING 6.5   **from Chaucer, *The Canterbury Tales*, Prologue**

A worthy woman there was from near the city
Of Bath, but somewhat deaf, and more's the pity.
For weaving she possessed so great a bent
She outdid the people of Ypres and Ghent.[1]
No other woman dreamed of such a thing
As to precede her at the offering.
Or if any did, she fell in such a wrath
She dried up all the charity in Bath.
She wore fine kerchiefs of old-fashioned air,
And on a Sunday morning, I could swear,
She had ten pounds of linen on her head.
Her stockings were the finest scarlet-red,
Laced tightly, and her shoes were soft and new.
Bold was her face, and fair, and red in hue.
She had been an excellent woman all of her life.
Five men in turn had taken her to wife,
Not counting other youthful company—
But let that pass for now! Over the sea
She'd traveled freely; many a distant stream
She crossed, and visited Jerusalem
Three times. She had been at Rome and at Boulogne,
At Compostella's shrine, and at Cologne.
She'd wandered by the way through many a scene.
Her teeth were set with little gaps between.[2]
Easily on her ambling horse she sat.
She was well wimpled, and she wore a hat
As wide in circuit as a shield or targe,[3]
A skirt swathed up her hips, and they were large.
Upon her feet she wore sharp-roweled spurs.
She was a good fellow; a ready tongue was hers.
All remedies of love she knew by name,
For she had all the tricks of that old game.

[1] **Ypres and Ghent:** Centers of the weaving industry in Flanders.
[2] **teeth . . . gaps between:** For a woman to be gap-toothed was considered a sign of being highly sexed.
[3] **targe:** A type of shield.

Chaucer accomplishes what few writers before him had—he creates character and personality through vivid detail and description. This elaborately dressed, gap-toothed, large- hipped, easy-riding survivor of five husbands comes off as a real person. The tales themselves sometimes rival Boccaccio's in their bawdy realism, but the variety of the pilgrims and the range of their moral characters creates at least as profound a moral world as Boccaccio's, one whose scope even rivals that of Dante. The integrity of the Knight plays against the depravity of the Pardoner, just as the sanctity of the Parson plays against the questionable morals of the Wife of Bath. Chaucer's characters come from all three **estates**, or social ranks—the nobility, the clergy, and the common people—a fact that has led some to refer to his work as an "estates satire," a critique of social relations in his day.

Christine de Pizan: An Early Feminist

As the example of Eleanor of Aquitaine makes clear, women were beginning to play an increasingly active role in the courts of Europe. In 1404, Philip the Bold, duke of Burgundy, commissioned Christine de Pizan (1364–ca. 1430) to write a biography of his deceased brother, titled *The Book of the Deeds and Good Manners of the Wise King Charles V*. Christine had been educated at the French court, apparently against her mother's wishes, by her father, a prominent Venetian physician, who had been appointed court astrologer to King Charles V. Her husband, secretary and notary to the king, further promoted her education. But when her father and husband died, she needed to support three children, a niece, and her mother. To do so she became the first female professional writer in European history.

As she gradually established her reputation as a writer, she worked as a copyist and illustrator, and her first successes were books of poems and ballads. In 1402, she made her reputation by attacking as misogynistic and demeaning to women the popular thirteenth-century poem the *Roman de la Rose* (*Romance of the Rose*). Two years later, in her *Book of the City of Ladies*, she again attacked male misogyny by recounting the accomplishments of women throughout the ages in an allegorical debate between herself and Lady Reason, Lady Rectitude, and Lady Justice (Fig. **6.29**). Her most immediate source was Boccaccio's

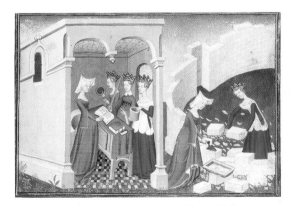

Fig. 6.29 Anonymous, *La Cité des Dames de Christine de Pizan.* ca. 1410. Illumination on parchment, page size 4 3/4″ × 7″. Bibliothèque Nationale, Paris. On the left stands Christine de Pizan, engaged in composition while receiving the visit of Reason, Honesty, and Justice. On the right, Christine and one of the royal ladies build the Ideal City.

Concerning Famous Women, but her treatment is completely different, treating only good women and freely mixing pagan and Christian examples. Her city's queen is the Virgin Mary herself, a figure whose importance confirms the centrality of women to Christianity. Thus, she opens the book by wondering why men are so inclined to demean women (**Reading 6.6**):

READING 6.6   **from Christine de Pizan,**
Book of the City of Ladies

[I wondered] how it happened that so many different men—and learned men among them—have been and are so inclined to express both in speaking and in their treatises and writings so many wicked insults about women and their behavior. Not only one or two ... but, more generally, from the treatises of all philosophers and poets and from all the orators—it would take too long to mention their names—it seems that they all speak from one and the same mouth. Thinking deeply about these matters, I began to examine my character and conduct as a nat-

ural woman and, similarly, I considered other women whose company I frequently kept, princesses, great ladies, women of the middle and lower classes, who had graciously told me of their most private and intimate thoughts, hoping that I could judge impartially and in good conscience whether the testimony of so many notable men could be true. To the best of my knowledge, no matter how long I confronted or dissected the problem, I could not see or realize how their claims could be true when compared to the natural behavior and character of women.

She then turns to God for guidance and is granted a dream vision in which the three allegorical ladies encourage her to build an Ideal City, peopled with a variety of women, from Sappho to her own name-saint, all of whom help her to redefine what it means to be female.

Near the end of her life Christine wrote a poem glorifying Joan of Arc, the French peasant girl who drove the English out of France in 1429. For Christine, Joan's achievement was as much a victory for women as for France.

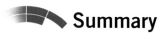

Summary

■ **The Gothic Cathedral** The architectural style that came to be known as Gothic originated at the Abbey Church of Saint-Denis just north of Paris, the most prominent feature of which was its stained glass. Chartres Cathedral, to the southwest, soon followed suit. Freed of load-bearing necessity by the innovative engineering that marks Gothic construction, its walls were thus also free to contain glass. Soon extremely high naves were made possible by rib vaulting and flying buttresses. During the thirteenth century, architects began to embellish the exteriors of their cathedrals with increasingly elaborate decoration, including ambitious sculptural programs that culminated, during the thirteenth century, in the re-Classicizing of Western art. With its vast spaces and stone walls, the Gothic cathedral could easily be as animated by its acoustics as it was by its light, and the *Magnus Liber Organi*, chiefly the work of the composers Léonin and Pérotin, was widely distributed in manuscript by about 1160.

■ **The Rise of the University** The quality of the teaching at the University of Paris distinguished it from the others. Peter Abelard, who taught by the dialectical method, was the school's most renowned lecturer. But probably the most important scholar at the University of Paris was Thomas Aquinas, whose *Summa Theologica* is an ambitious attempt to sum up all that was known about theology.

■ **The Radiant Style and the Court of Louis IX** By the middle of the thirteenth century, the Gothic style in France had been elaborated into increasingly flamboyant patterns of repeated traceries and ornament that we refer to as the Radiant style, the grandest example of which is the royal chapel of Sainte-Chapelle in Paris.

■ **Civic and Religious Life in Siena and Florence** Siena and Florence were both free *communes*, watched over, they believed, by the Virgin Mary. Both communes were controlled by their guilds, and in both civic leaders engaged in massive religious building projects, uniting Church and state. In Florence, the civic government and private citizens constructed new churches for the new mendicant orders, the Franciscans and the Dominicans.

■ **Painting: A Growing Naturalism** In both Siena and Florence, artists began to break from the Byzantine style, especially Giotto, who brought an expressiveness and emotional symbolism to his work not seen in Western art since Hellenism.

■ **The Spread of Vernacular Literature in Europe** In the early twelfth century, writers across Europe began to address their works to a wider lay audience and to write in the vernacular, the language spoken in the streets. One of the greatest medieval Italian vernacular writers was the poet Dante Alighieri, whose *Divine Comedy* records the travels of the Christian soul from Hell to Purgatory and finally to Salvation.

■ **The Black Death and Its Aftermath** In December 1347, bubonic plague arrived in Sicily. Within months, the disease spread northward, through Europe. Boccaccio's *Decameron* reflects the reality of death in his narrative, and his stories represent life as it is truly lived. Other innovative forms of vernacular literature followed the plague, including Petrarch's sonnets, Chaucer's *Canterbury Tales*, and the work of Christine de Pizan, the first female professional writer in European history.

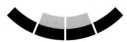
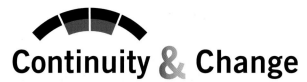

In 1351, the poet Petrarch (Fig. **6.30**) wrote to a friend describing his culture's neglect of the great works of the past. These manuscripts, written in a classical Latin and hard for monks to decipher, were, he feared, in danger of being lost forever:

> It is a state of affairs that has resulted in an incredible loss to scholarship. Books that by their nature are a little hard to understand are no longer multiplied [i.e., copied and distributed], and have ceased to be generally intelligible, and so have sunk into utter neglect, and in the end have perished. This age of ours consequently has let fall, bit by bit, some of the richest and sweetest fruits that the tree of knowledge has yielded; has thrown away the results of the vigils and labors of the most illustrious men of genius, things of more value, I am almost tempted to say, than anything else in the whole world.

So great was Petrarch's zeal for the classics that he would become known as the Father of Humanism, the revival of Greco-Roman culture that would come to define the Renaissance in the two centuries to follow.

Humanism can be defined as the recovery, study, and spread of the art and literature of Greece and Rome, and the application of their principles to education, politics, social life, and the arts in general. In turn, humanism stimulated a new appreciation for the value of the individual. Each person, it was understood, possesses the capacity for self-determination in the search for truth and morality. Faith, sacred texts, or religious tradition were no longer the only guides available to the inquiring mind.

One of the most important humanists to emerge in the fifteenth century was the Florentine banker, Cosimo de' Medici (1389–1464), who, as banker to the papacy, secured Florence's domination over rival Siena, putting the city at the very center of Italian politics. But Cosimo was no mere civic leader. He and his family supported a blossoming of cultural life in fifteenth-century Florence that redefined everything from the nature of political rule to the standards of beauty and intellectual achievement.

Cosimo surrounded himself with humanists. He collected ancient Greek and Roman art, bringing to Florence the finest examples of sculpture he could find. He also sought the humanists' guidance about what books and manuscripts of the ancients he ought to collect. Especially after the fall of Constantinople in 1453, Greek texts and Greek scholars arrived in large numbers from the East, and he commissioned translations of Greek philosophy and literature, since he himself could not master the language. (The translations were from the Greek to Latin, which all educated people knew and read.) Inspired by new translations of the

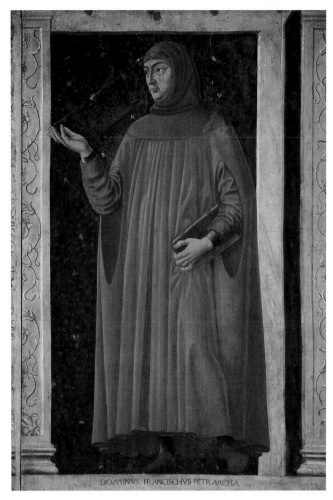

Fig. 6.30 Andrea del Castagno, *Francesco Petrarca*. ca. 1450. Fresco transferred to wood, 97$\frac{1}{4}$″ × 60$\frac{1}{4}$″. Galleria degli Uffizi, Florence.

works of Plato, Cosimo founded the Platonic Academy in Florence, a group which often gathered at a suburban villa, with Cosimo in attendance, to discuss Plato and other Classical authors.

Humanist scholarship, in fact, encouraged Cosimo's politics as well. Cicero, the noted Roman orator whose works had been recovered by Petrarch, insisted that civic responsibility was the chief duty of citizens (see Reading 3.1, *On Duty*, page 79). Cosimo believed that it was a citizen's duty to contribute to the common good of the community, a brand of civic humanism that he thought all citizens should emulate. He saw his patronage—especially insofar as church and state were inextricably linked in Renaissance Florence as they had been in the late Middle Ages—as activity for the good of God that would in turn benefit his city. ■

185

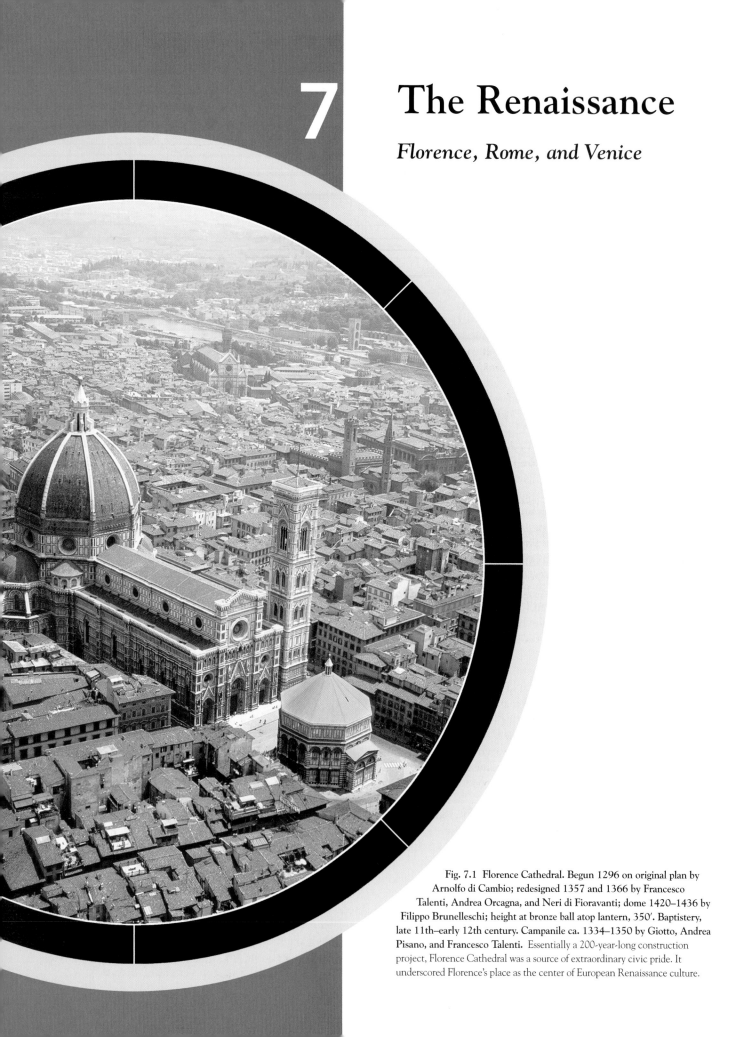

7 The Renaissance

Florence, Rome, and Venice

Fig. 7.1 Florence Cathedral. Begun 1296 on original plan by
Arnolfo di Cambio; redesigned 1357 and 1366 by Francesco
Talenti, Andrea Orcagna, and Neri di Fioravanti; dome 1420–1436 by
Filippo Brunelleschi; height at bronze ball atop lantern, 350'. Baptistery,
late 11th–early 12th century. Campanile ca. 1334–1350 by Giotto, Andrea
Pisano, and Francesco Talenti. Essentially a 200-year-long construction
project, Florence Cathedral was a source of extraordinary civic pride. It
underscored Florence's place as the center of European Renaissance culture.

Florence, Italy, was the center of a more than 150-year-long cultural revival in Europe that we have come to call the Renaissance. It lasted from the time of the Black Death in the mid-fourteenth century (see chapter 6) until the early years of the sixteenth century. The word Renaissance, from the Italian *rinascita* [ree-nah-shee-TAH], "rebirth," became widely used in the nineteenth century as historians began to assert that the beliefs and values of the medieval world were transformed in Italy, and in Florence particularly. Where the Middle Ages had been an age of faith, in which the salvation of the soul was an individual's chief preoccupation, the Renaissance was an age of intellectual exploration, in which the **humanist** strove to understand in ever more precise and scientific terms the nature of humanity and its relationship to the natural world.

This chapter traces the rise of the humanist Renaissance city-state as a center of culture in Italy in the fifteenth century, concentrating on Florence, Rome, and Venice (Map **7.1**). In Florence the Medici [MED-uh-chee] family, whose wealth derived from their considerable banking interests, did much to position the city as a model that others felt compelled to imitate. In Rome, the wealth at the disposal of the papacy, and the willingness of the Church to bestow that wealth in the form of commissions to artists and architects in an effort to restore that city to the greatness it enjoyed over a thousand years earlier at the height of the Roman Empire, essentially guaranteed its rebirth as a new and vital center of culture. And the citizenry of Venice, where goods from Northern Europe flowed into the Mediterranean, and goods from the Mediterranean and points east flowed into Europe, thought of themselves as the most cosmopolitan and the most democratic people in the world. In this environment of enlightened leadership, the arts flourished.

The State as a Work of Art: Florence and the Medici

The most preeminent Italian city-state in the fifteenth century was Florence. It was so thoughtfully and carefully constructed by the ruling Medici family that later scholars would come to view it as a work of art in its own right. The Medici were the most powerful family in Florentine affairs from 1418, when they became banker to the papacy, until 1494, when irate citizens removed them from power. A family of bankers with offices in Pisa, Rome, Bologna, Naples, Venice, Avignon, Lyon, Geneva, Basel, Cologne, Antwerp, Bruges, and London during the fifteenth century, the Medici never ruled Florence outright, but managed its affairs from behind the scenes.

No event better exemplifies the nature of the Italian Renaissance and anticipates the character of Florence under the Medici than a competition held in 1401 to choose a designer for a pair of bronze doors for the north entrance to the city's **baptistery** (Fig. **7.1**), a building standing in front of the cathedral and used for the Christian rite of baptism.

By the thirteenth century, a legend had developed that the baptistery stood on the site of a Roman temple to Mars, subsequently rededicated to Saint John the Baptist. The octagonal building was thus the principal civic monument connecting Florence to its Roman roots, and it stood at the very heart of the city, in front of the cathedral, which was still under construction in 1401. The original doors, at the south entrance, had been designed before the advent of the Black Death, and had fallen into disrepair. The Cloth Merchants' Guild, or "Arte della Lana," which was in charge of the Opera del Duomo—literally, the "Works of the Cathedral"—was determined to create a new set of doors for the north entrance.

In many ways it is remarkable that the competition to find the best design for the baptistery doors could even take place. As much as four-fifths of the city-state's population had died in the Black Death of 1348, and the plague had returned, though less severely, in 1363, 1374, 1383, and 1390. Finally, in the summer of 1400, it came again, this time killing 12,000 Florentines, about one-fifth of the population. Perhaps the guild hoped that a facelift for the baptistery might appease an evidently wrathful God. Furthermore, civic pride and patriotism were also at stake. Milan, the powerful city-state to the north, had laid siege to Florence, blocking trade to and from the seaport at Pisa and creating the prospect of famine. The fate of the Florentine Republic seemed to be in the balance.

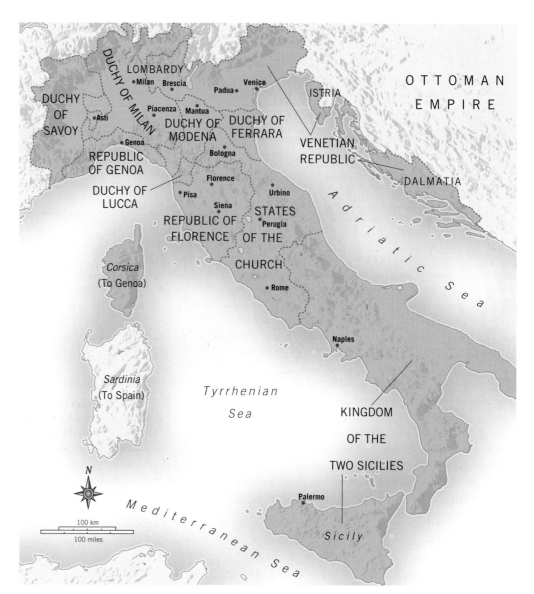

Map 7.1 Major Italian City-States during the Renaissance.

So the competition was not merely about artistic talent. The general feeling was that if God looked with favor on the enterprise, the winner's work might well be the city's salvation. In fact, during the summer of 1402, as the competition was concluding, the duke of Milan died in his encampment outside the walls of Florence. The siege was over, and Florence was spared. If the Cloth Merchants Guild could not take credit for these events, no one could deny the coincidence.

Thirty-four judges—artists, sculptors, and prominent citizens, including a Medici—chose the winner from among the seven entrants. Each artist was asked to create a bronze relief panel depicting the Hebrew Bible's story of the Sacrifice of Isaac (Genesis 22) in a 21 by 17½-inch *quatrefoil* (a four-leaf clover shape set on a diamond). All but two designs were eliminated, both by little-known 24-year-old goldsmiths: Filippo Brunelleschi [broo-nel-ESS-kee] (1377–1446) and Lorenzo Ghiberti [ghee-BEHR-tee] (1378–1455).

The Sacrifice of Isaac is the story of how God tested the faith of the patriarch Abraham by commanding him to sacrifice Isaac, his only son. Abraham took Isaac into the wilderness to perform the deed but at the last moment, an angel stopped him, implying that God was convinced of Abraham's faith and would be satisfied with the sacrifice of a ram instead. Brunelleschi and Ghiberti both depicted the same aspect of the story, the moment when the angel intervenes. Brunelleschi placed Isaac in the center of the panel and the other figures, whose number and type were probably prescribed by the judges, all around (Fig. **7.2**). The opposition between Abraham and the Angel, as the Angel grabs Abraham's arm to stop him from plunging his knife into his son's breast, is highly dramatic and realistic, an effect achieved by the figures' jagged movements. Ghiberti, in contrast, set the sacrifice to one side of the panel (Fig. **7.3**). He replaced a sense of physical strain with graceful rhythms, so that Isaac and Abraham are unified by the bowed curves of their bodies, Isaac's nude body turning on

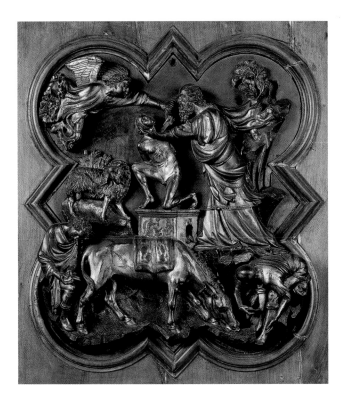

Fig. 7.2 Filippo Brunelleschi, *Sacrifice of Isaac,* competition relief commissioned for the doors of the baptistery. **1401–1402.** Parcel-gilt bronze, 21″ × 17½″. Museo Nazionale del Bargello, Florence. Brunelleschi's background seems to be little more than a flat surface against which his forms are set.

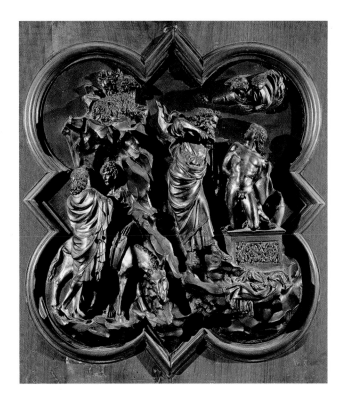

Fig. 7.3 Lorenzo Ghiberti, *Sacrifice of Isaac,* competition relief commissioned for the doors of the baptistery. **1401–1402.** Parcel-gilt bronze, 21″ × 17½″. Museo Nazionale del Bargello, Florence. As opposed to Brunelleschi's, Ghiberti's background seems to be real, deep space, as if containing the air itself.

its axis to face Abraham. The angel in the upper right corner is represented in a more dynamic manner than in Brunelleschi's panel. This heavenly visitor seems to have rushed in from deep space. The effect is achieved by **foreshortening**, a technique used to suggest that forms are sharply receding. In addition, the strong diagonal of the landscape, which extends from beneath the sacrificial altar and rises up into a large rocky outcrop behind the other figures, creates a more vivid sense of real space than Brunelleschi's scene.

Despite the artistic differences in the two works, the contest might have been decided by economics. Brunelleschi cast each of his figures separately and then assembled them on the background. Ghiberti cast separately just the body of Isaac, which required only two-thirds of the bronze used by his rival. The process also resulted in a more unified panel, and this may have given Ghiberti the edge. Disappointed, Brunelleschi left Florence for Rome and gave up sculpture forever. Their competition highlights the growing emphasis on individual achievement in the young Italian Renaissance: The work of the individual craftsperson was replacing the collective efforts of the guild or workshop in decorating public space. The judges valued the originality of Brunelleschi's and Ghiberti's conceptions. Rather than placing their figures on a shallow platform, as one might

expect in the shallow space available in a relief sculpture, both sought to create a sense of a deep, receding space, enhancing the appearance of reality.

As humanists, Ghiberti and Brunelleschi valued the artistic models of antiquity and looked to classical sculpture for inspiration. Notice Ghiberti's nude Isaac posed in classical contrapposto (see Fig. 2.29), and Brunelleschi's servant at the lower left of the relief, a direct quotation of an ancient Roman bronze known as the *Thorn Puller.* Finally, the artworks they created captured human beings in the midst of a crisis of faith with which every viewer might identify. In all this, their competition looks forward to the art that defines the Italian Renaissance itself.

The *Gates of Paradise*

Ghiberti worked on the north-side doors for the next 22 years, designing 28 panels in four vertical rows illustrating the New Testament (originally the subject had been the Hebrew Bible, but the guild changed the program). Immediately upon their completion in 1424, the Cloth Merchants' Guild commissioned a second set of doors from Ghiberti for the east side of the baptistery. These would take him another 27 years. Known as the *Gates of Paradise* because they open onto the *paradiso,* Italian for the area between a baptistery and the entrance to its cathedral, these doors depict scenes from the Hebrew Bible in ten square panels. The borders surrounding them contain other biblical figures, as well as a self-portrait (Fig. **7.4**). The artist's head is slightly bowed, perhaps in humility, but perhaps, situated as it is just above the average viewer's head, so that he might look out upon his audience. The proud image functions as both a signature and a bold assertion of Ghiberti's own worth as an artist and individual.

Each of the panels in the east doors depicts one or more events from the same story. For instance, the first panel, at the upper left of the doors (Fig. **7.5**), contains four episodes from the book of Genesis: the Creation of Adam, at the bottom left; the Creation of Eve, in the center; the Temptation, in the distance behind the Creation of Adam; and the Expulsion, at the bottom right. This portrayal of sequential events in the same frame harkens back to medieval art. But if the content of the space is episodic, the landscape is coherent and realistic, stretching in a single continuity from the foreground into the far distance. The figures themselves hark back to classical Greek and Roman sculpture. Adam, in the lower left-hand corner, resembles the recumbent god

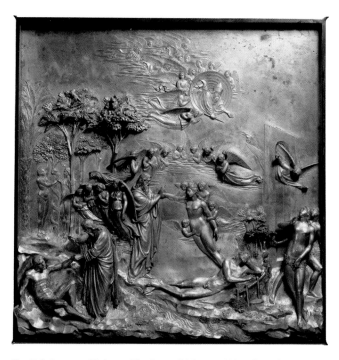

Fig. 7.5 Lorenzo Ghiberti, *The Story of Adam and Eve,* from the *Gates of Paradise,* east doors of the baptistery, Florence. ca. 1425–1437. Gilt bronze, 31 ¼″ × 31 ¼″. The influence of classical antiquity is clear in the portrayal of Eve, whose pose, at the center, derives from birth of Venus sculptures, and, on the right, from images of the Venus Pudica, or "modest" Venus.

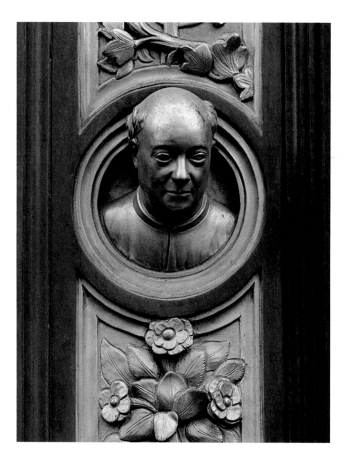

Fig. 7.4 Lorenzo Ghiberti, Self-portrait from the *Gates of Paradise,* east doors of the baptistery, Florence. ca. 1445–1448. Gilt bronze. Ghiberti included his self-portrait among the prophets and other biblical figures framing the panels as he had earlier on the north doors. The extreme naturalism of this self-portrait underscores the spirit of individualism that characterizes the Renaissance.

from the east pediment of the Parthenon (see Fig. 2.33), and Eve, in the right-hand corner, is a Venus of recognizably Hellenistic origin (see Fig. 2.40).

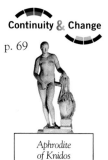

Continuity & Change

p. 69

Aphrodite of Knidos

Ghiberti meant to follow the lead of the ancients in creating realistic figures in realistic space. As he wrote in his memoirs: "I strove to observe with all the scale and proportion, and to endeavor to imitate Nature . . . on the planes one sees the figures which are near appear larger, and those that are far off smaller, as reality shows." Not only do the figures farther off appear smaller, they also decrease in their projection from the panel, so that the most remote ones are in very shallow relief, hardly raised above the gilded bronze surface.

Whereas medieval artists regarded the natural world as an imperfect reflection of the divine, and hardly worth attention, Renaissance artists understood the physical universe as an expression of the divine and thus worth copying in the greatest detail. To understand nature was, in some sense, to understand God. Ghiberti's panel embodies this growing desire in the Renaissance to reflect nature as accurately as possible. It is a major motivation for the development of perspective in painting and drawing.

The work had political significance as well. The only panel to represent a single event in its space is the *Meeting of Solomon and Sheba* (Fig. 7.6). Here, the carefully realized symmetry of the architecture, with Solomon and Sheba framed in the middle

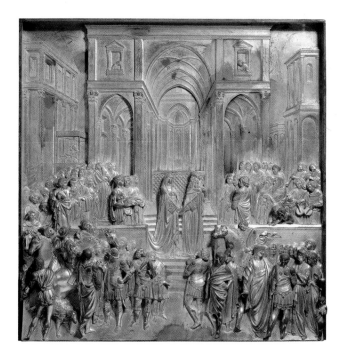

Fig. 7.6 Lorenzo Ghiberti. *Meeting of Solomon and Sheba,* from the *Gates of Paradise,* east doors of the baptistery, Florence. ca. 1425–1437. Gilt bronze, 31 $\frac{1}{4}$″ × 31 $\frac{1}{4}$″. The reunification of the Eastern and Western churches, symbolically represented here, was announced on the steps of Florence Cathedral on July 9, 1439, with the Emperor of Byzantium present. The agreement was short-lived, and by 1472 the Eastern church had formally rejected the Florence accords.

of its space, was probably designed to represent the reunification of the eastern Orthodox and western Catholic branches of the Church. Solomon was traditionally associated with the Western Church, while the figure of Sheba, queen of the Arabian state of Sheba, was meant to symbolize the Eastern. In 1438, Cosimo de' Medici had financed a Council of Churches that had convened in Florence, and, for a time, it had seemed possible, even likely, that reunification might become a reality. This would have restored symmetry and balance to a divided church just as Ghiberti had achieved balance and symmetry in his art. But above all, especially in the context of the other nine panels, all of which possess multiple events with multiple focal points, this composition's focus on a single event reflects the very image of the unity sought by the Church.

Florence Cathedral

Construction of the Duomo (Fig. 7.1), as Florence Cathedral is known, began in 1296 under the auspices of the Opera del Duomo, which was controlled by the Cloth Merchants' Guild. The cathedral was planned as the most beautiful and grandest in all of Tuscany. It was not consecrated until 140 years later, and even then, was hardly finished. Over the years, its design and construction became a group activity as an ever-changing panel of architects prepared model after model of the church and its details were submitted to the Opera and either accepted or rejected.

Brunelleschi's Dome During visits to Rome, Brunelleschi had carefully measured the proportions of ancient buildings, including the Colosseum, the Pantheon, the remains of the Baths of Caracalla, and the Domus Aurea (Golden Palace) of Nero. Using these studies, Brunelleschi produced the winning design for the dome of Florence Cathedral (Fig. 7.7). The design guaranteed his reputation as one of the geniuses of Renaissance Florence, even in his own day.

Brunelleschi's design for the dome solved a number of technical problems. For one thing it eliminated the need for the temporary wooden scaffolding normally used to support the dome vaulting as it was raised. Though critics disagreed, Brunelleschi argued that a skeleton of eight large ribs, visible on the outside of the dome, alternating with eight pairs of thinner ribs beneath the roof, all tied together by only nine sets of horizontal ties, would be able to support themselves as the dome took form. The thinner ribs would lie between two shells—the outer roof and the interior ceiling—again creating a dome much lighter in weight than a solid structure (Fig. 7.8). Scaffolding would be cantilevered out from the base of the drum and moved up, horizontal band by horizontal band, as the dome rose up. Additional support could be achieved through the use of lightweight bricks set in an interlocking herringbone pattern.

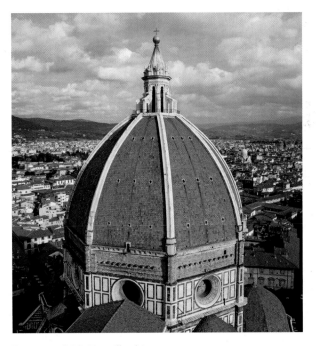

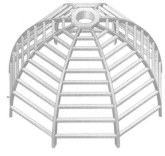

Figs. 7.7 and 7.8 Brunelleschi, dome and lantern of Florence Cathedral, and diagram of ribs and horizontal bands within the dome. **Dome 1420–1436; lantern, after 1446.** Despite its enormous scale, the cathedral's dome is a model of visual simplicity and clarity.

Brunelleschi completed the dome in 1436. In yet another competition, he then designed a **lantern** (a windowed turret at the top of a dome and visible in Fig. 7.7) to cover the **oculus** (hole) and thus put the finishing touch on the dome. Made of over 20 tons of stone—Brunelleschi designed a special hoist to raise the stone to the top of the dome—construction had barely begun when Brunelleschi died in 1446.

"Songs of Angels": Music for Church and State For the consecration of Florence Cathedral, rededicated as Santa Maria del Fiore [FYOR-eh] (Saint Mary of the Flower) on March 25, 1436, Brunelleschi constructed a 1,000-foot walkway, 6 feet high and decorated with flowers and herbs, on which to guide celebrated guests into the cathedral proper. These included Pope Eugenius IV and his entourage of seven cardinals, thirty-seven bishops, and nine Florentine officials (including Cosimo de' Medici), all of whom were observed by the gathered throng. Once inside, the guests heard a new musical work, picking up the floral theme of the day, called *Nuper rosarum flores* [NOO-pur roh-ZAH-room FLOH-rehs] ("The Rose Blossoms") **(CD-Track 7.1)**.

It was composed especially for the consecration by French composer Guillaume Dufay [ghee-YOHM doo-FAY] (ca. 1400–1474), who worked in both France and Italy. The piece is a **motet** [moh-TET], the form of polyphonic vocal work that had gained increasing popularity since the mid-thirteenth century. Dufay's motet introduced a richer and fuller sonority to the form. The **cantus firmus** [CAN-tus FIR-mus]—or "fixed melody"—on which the composition is based is stated in not one but two voices, both moving at different speeds.

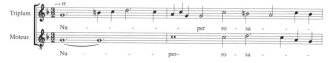

Cantus firmus melody from Dufay's *Nuper rosarum flores*

The melody derives from a chant traditionally used for the dedication of new churches, *Terribilis est locus iste* [teh-REE-bee-lis EH-st LOH-kus EE-steh] ("Awesome Is This Place").

Dufay's motet also reflects the ideal proportions of the Temple of Solomon in Jerusalem, which, according to I Kings, was laid out in the proportions 6:4:2:3, with 6 being the length of the building, 4 the length of the nave, 2 the width, and 3 the height. Florence Cathedral followed these same proportions, and Dufay mirrors them in his composition by repeating the cantus firmus four times, successively based on 6, 4, 2, and 3 units per *breve* [brev] (equivalent to two whole notes in modern notation). Hearing the entire work, one witness wrote, "it seemed as though the symphonies and songs of the angels and divine paradise had been set forth from Heaven to whisper in our ears an unbelievable celestial

sweetness." It is not surprising, given this reaction, that Dufay was regarded as the greatest composer of the fifteenth century. It is even less surprising that the Florentines selected him to celebrate the consecration of their new cathedral and its dome by creating an original work. In performing this service he announced the preeminence of both the cathedral and the city that had built it.

Scientific Perspective and Naturalistic Representation

No aspect of the Renaissance better embodies the spirit of invention evidenced by both Brunelleschi's dome and Dufay's music than **scientific**, or **linear, perspective**, which allowed artists to translate three-dimensional space onto a two-dimensional surface, thereby satisfying the age's increasing taste for naturalistic representations of the physical world. It was the basis of what would later come to be called *buon disegno* [bwon dee-ZEN-yoh], literally "good design" or "drawing," but the term refers more to the intellectual conception of the work than to literal drawing. Giorgio Vasari [JOR-joh vuh-SAHR-ee] (1511–1574), whose *Lives of the Most Excellent Painters, Architects, and Sculptors* is one of our most important sources of information about Italian Renaissance art in the fourteenth, fifteenth, and sixteenth centuries, defined it as follows: "Design (*disegno*) is the imitation of the most beautiful things of nature in all figures whether painted or chiseled, and this requires a hand and genius to transfer everything which the eye sees, exactly and correctly, whether it be in drawings, on paper panel, or other surface, both in relief and sculpture." It distinguished, in his mind, the art of Florence above all others.

Brunelleschi, Alberti, and the Invention of Scientific Perspective

It was Brunelleschi who first mastered the art of scientific perspective sometime in the first decade of the fifteenth century. The ancient Greeks and Romans had at least partially understood its principles, but their methods had been lost. Brunelleschi almost certainly turned to them for the authority, at least, to "reinvent" it. His investigation of optics in Arab science also contributed to his understanding, particularly Alhazen's [al-HAH-zens] *Perspectiva* [pehr-spehk-TEE-vah] (ca. 1000 CE), which integrated the classical works of Euclid, Ptolemy, and Galen. Their understanding of the principles of geometry, and the sense of balance and proportion that geometry inspired, affected every aspect of Brunelleschi's architectural work.

But it was geometry's revelation of the rules of perspective that most fascinated Brunelleschi. As he surveyed the Roman ruins, plotting three-dimensional architectural forms on flat paper, he mastered its finer points. Back in Florence, he would demonstrate the principles of perspective in his own architectural work. Brunelleschi's findings were codified in 1435 by the architect Leon Battista Alberti [all-BAYR-tee]

(1404–1474) in his treatise *On Painting*. Painting, Alberti says, is an intellectual pursuit, dedicated to replicating nature as accurately as possible. A painting's composition should be based on the orderly arrangement of parts, which relies on rendering space in **one-point perspective**. He provides step-by-step instructions for the creation of such space, and diagrams it as well (Fig. **7.9**). The basic principles of the system are these: (1) All parallel lines in a visual field appear to converge at a single **vanishing point** on the horizon (think of train tracks merging in the distance); (2) These parallel lines are realized on the **picture plane**—the two-dimensional surface of the panel or canvas, conceived as a window through which the viewer perceives the three-dimensional world—as diagonal lines called **orthogonals**; (3) Forms diminish in scale as they approach the vanishing point along these orthogonals; and (4) The vanishing point is directly opposite the eye of the beholder, who stands at the **vantage point**, thus, metaphorically at least, placing the individual (both painter and viewer) at the center of the visual field.

Perspective and Naturalism in Painting: Masaccio

Although Alberti dedicated *On Painting* first and foremost to Brunelleschi, he also singled out several other Florentine artists. One of these was Masaccio, whoses masterpiece of naturalistic representation is *The Tribute Money* (Fig. **7.10**). Commissioned by a member of the Brancacci [bran-KAH-chee] family in the 1420s as part of a program to decorate the family's chapel in the church of Santa Maria del Carmine [KAR-mee-neh] in Florence, it illustrates an event in the Gospel of Matthew (17:24–27). Christ responds to the

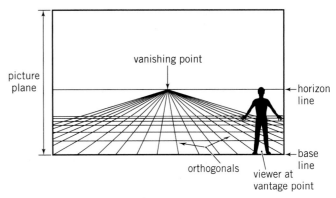

Fig. **7.9** Alberti's perspective diagram.

demand of a Roman tax collector for money by telling Saint Peter to catch a fish in the Sea of Galilee, where he will find, in its mouth, the required amount. This moment occurs in the center of the painting. Behind the central group, to the left, Saint Peter finds the money, and to the right he pays the tax. The vanishing point of the painting is behind the head of Christ, where the orthogonals of the architecture on the right converge. In fact, the function of the architecture appears to be to lead the viewer's eyes to Christ, identifying him as the most important figure in the work.

Another device, known as **atmospheric perspective**, also gives the painting the feeling of naturalism. This system depends on the observation that the haze in the atmosphere makes distant elements appear less distinct and bluish in color, even as the sky becomes paler as it approaches the horizon. As

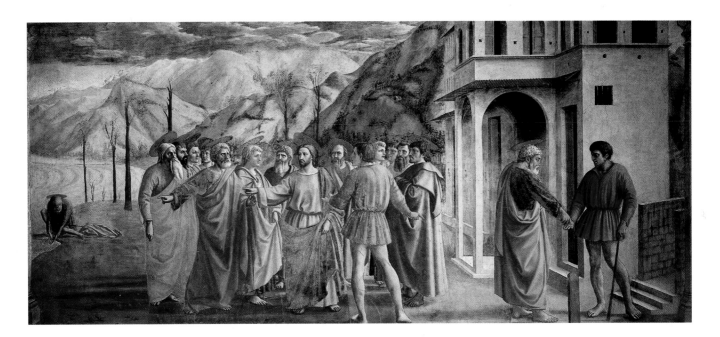

Fig. **7.10 Masaccio, *The Tribute Money*, Brancacci Chapel, Santa Maria del Carmine, Florence. 1420s.** Fresco, 8′1¼″ × 19′7″. Studio Mario Quattrone. When this fresco was restored between 1981 and 1991, cleaning revealed that every character in this scene originally had a gold-leaf halo, except the tax collector, probably not a Christian. Masaccio drew these halos according to the laws of scientific perspective.

a result, the house and trees on the distant hills in this fresco are loosely sketched, as if we see them through a hazy filter of air. The diminishing size of the barren trees at the left also underscores the fact that, in a perspectival rendering of space, far-off figures seem smaller (as does the diminished size of Saint Peter at the edge of the sea).

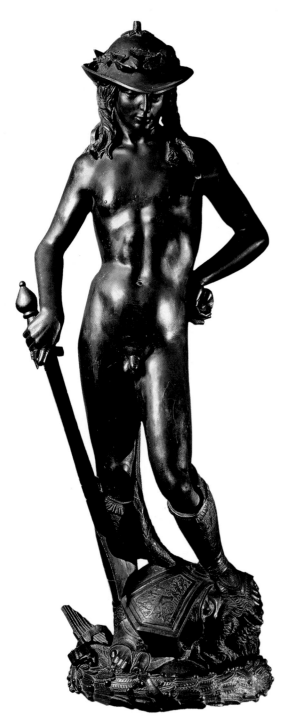

Fig. 7.11 Donatello, *David*. 1440s. Bronze, height 62 ¼″. Museo Nazionale del Bargello, Florence, Italy. By 1469, this sculpture stood in the courtyard of the Medici palace as a symbol of the Florentine state.

Perhaps the greatest source of naturalism in the scene comes from the figures themselves, who provide a good imitation of life through their dynamic gestures and poses, their individuality, and their emotional engagement in the events. Here the human figure is fully alive and active. This is especially evident in the contrapposto pose of the Roman tax collector, whom we see both with his back to us in the central group of figures and at the far right, where Saint Peter is paying him. Christ, too, throws all of his weight to his right foot. This is a naturalistic device that Masaccio borrowed from antiquity. Indeed, the blond head of Saint John is almost surely a copy of a Roman bust.

The Classical Tradition in Freestanding Sculpture: Donatello

Masaccio probably learned about the classical disposition of the body's weight from Donatello [doh-nah-TELL-oh], who had accompanied Brunelleschi to Rome years before. Many of Donatello's own works seem to have been inspired by antique Roman sculpture.

Although it dates from nearly 15 years after Masaccio's *Tribute Money*, Donatello's *David* (Fig. **7.11**), which celebrates this Hebrew Bible hero's victory over the giant Goliath, indicates how completely the sculptor had absorbed classical tradition. The first life-size freestanding male nude sculpted since antiquity, it is revolutionary in other ways as well. The contrapposto pose is quite feminine, especially the positioning of the back of the hand against the hip. The young adolescent's self-absorbed gaze accentuates his self-delight. The figure's eroticism is amplified by the way David's left foot plays with the mustache on Goliath's severed head.

It is difficult to imagine that such a slight, adolescent figure could have slain a giant. It is as if Donatello portrayed David as an unconvincing hero in order to underscore the ability of virtue, in whatever form, to overcome tyranny. And so this soft, elegant, and refined young man might represent the virtue of the Florentine republic as a whole and the city's persistent resistance to domination. In fact, when in 1469 the statue stood in the courtyard of the Medici palace, it bore the following inscription: "The victor is whoever defends the fatherland. All-powerful God crushes the angry enemy. Behold a boy overcame the great tyrant. Conquer, O citizens." The Medici thus secularized the religious image even as they implicitly affirmed their right to rule as granted by an all-powerful God whose might they shared.

The Medici Family and Humanism

The Medici family had been prominent in Florentine civic politics since the early fourteenth century. The family had amassed a fortune by skill in trade—especially the banker's trade in money—and became strong supporters of many of the city's smaller guilds. But their power was only fully cemented by Cosimo de' Medici (*Continuity & Change*, chapter 6).

Cosimo inherited great wealth from his father and secured the family's hold on the political fortunes of the city. Without upsetting the appearance of republican government, he mastered the art of behind-the-scenes power by controlling appointments to chief offices. But he also exerted considerable influence through his patronage of the arts. His father had headed the drive to rebuild the church of San Lorenzo, which stood over the site of an early Christian basilica dedicated in 393. San Lorenzo thus represented the entire Christian history of Florence, and after his father's death, Cosimo himself paid to complete its construction and decorate it. In return, it was agreed that no family crest other than the Medici's would appear in the church. Cosimo also rebuilt the old monastery of San Marco for the Dominican Order, adding a library, cloister, chapter room, bell tower, and altarpiece. In effect, Cosimo had made the entire religious history of Florence the family's own.

Marsilio Ficino and Neoplatonism Humanist that he was, Cosimo was particularly impressed by one scholar, the young priest Marsilio Ficino [fee-CHEE-noh] (1433–1499). Beginning in about 1453, Cosimo supported Ficino in his translations and interpretations of the works of Plato and later philosophers of Platonic thought. As described in chapter 2, Platonic thought distinguished between a sphere of being that is eternal and unchanging and the world in which we actually live, in which nothing is fixed forever. Following Plato's lead, Ficino argued that human reason belonged to the eternal dimension, as human achievement in mathematics and moral philosophy demonstrated, and that through human reason we can commune with the eternal sphere of being.

Ficino coined the term **Platonic love** to describe the ideal spiritual (never physical) relationship between two people, based on Plato's insistence on striving for and seeking out the good, the true, and the beautiful. The source of Ficino's thought is his study of the writings of Plotinus [ploh-TIE-nus] (ca. 205–270 CE), a Greek scholar of Platonic thought who had studied Indian philosophy (both Hinduism and Buddhism) and who believed in the existence of an ineffable and transcendent One, from which emanated the rest of the universe as a series of lesser beings. For Plotinus, human perfection (and, therefore, absolute happiness) was attainable in this world through philosophical meditation. This **Neoplatonist** [nee-oh-PLAY-tuh-nist] philosophy (a modern usage) recast Platonic thought in contemporary terms. It appealed immensely to Cosimo. He could see everywhere in the great art and literature of antiquity the good, the true, and the beautiful he sought, and so he surrounded himself with art and literature, both contemporary and classical, and lavished them upon his city.

Domestic Architecture for Merchant Princes In 1444, Cosimo commissioned for the family a new **palazzo** [pah-LAH-tsoh] ("palace") that would redefine domestic architecture in the Renaissance. He first rejected a plan by Brunelleschi, considering it too grand, and built instead a

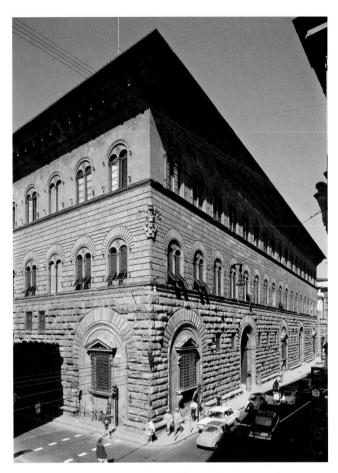

Fig. 7.12 Michelozzo di Bartolommeo. Palazzo Medici-Ricardi, Florence. Begun 1444. If it seems odd to think of such a structure as a palace, it is worth remembering that the Italian word *palazzo* refers to any reasonably large urban house.

palace designed by Michelozzo di Bartolommeo [mee-ku-LO-tso bar-toh-loh-MAY-oh] (1396–1472), now known as the Palazzo Medici-Riccardi [ree-CAR-dee] (Fig. **7.12**). He filled it with the art of the day (including Donatello's *David*, Fig. 7.11). The bottom story is 20 feet high and made of rough-cut stone meant to imitate the walls of ancient Roman ruins. It housed the family's commercial interests, including their bank. The outside of the second story, which housed the living quarters, is cut into smooth stones, with visible joints between them. The outside of the third story, reserved for servants, is entirely smooth, thus giving the facade the appearance of decreasing mass and even airiness.

The Palazzo Medici became the standard for townhouses of wealthy Florentine merchants. Two years later, Leon Battista Alberti, author of *On Painting* and a close friend and adviser to Cosimo, designed a home for the Florentine patrician Giovanni Rucellai [roo-chel-LIE] that brought the more or less subtle classical references of Michelozzo's design for

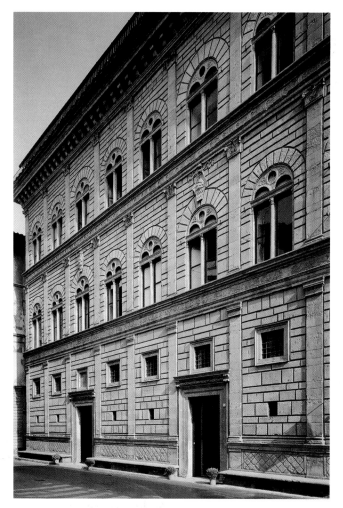

Fig. 7.13 Leon Battista Alberti, Palazzo Rucellai, Florence. 1446–1451. In Alberti's time, the Rucellai's house extended to the right by four more bays and one more doorway, or portal.

Cosimo to full light. The Palazzo Rucellai (Fig. **7.13**) reflects on a domestic level many of the ideas that Alberti would publish in about 1450 in his *On the Art of Building*.

For Alberti, architecture is the highest art and all buildings need to reflect properly their social "place." Thus the Duomo, which Alberti believed to be the most important building in Florence, is at the heart of the city and rises high above it, the very center of Florentine culture. It follows that leading families should live in houses that reflect those families' stability and strength.

The Palazzo Rucellai does that and more. In direct imitation of the Roman Colosseum (see Fig. 3.11), Alberti uses three classical orders, one for each of the three stories: the Tuscan (substituting for the Doric) at the bottom, the Ionic at the second story, and the Corinthian at the top. As at the Colosseum, the columns are engaged (that is, decorative rather than functional), and an arch is set between them. Many people thought Alberti's plan too grand because, in its reference to the Colosseum, it embodies not Republican but Imperial Rome. However, Alberti's design reflects the real

state of affairs in Florence at that time. For the city was ruled by what was in fact hereditary monarchy—the Medici—supported by a wealthy, albeit mercantile, "nobility," consisting of families such as the Rucellai.

Lorenzo the Magnificent: "... I find a relaxation in learning."

After Cosimo's death in 1464, his son Piero [pee-YER-oh] (1416–1469) followed in his father's footsteps, championing the arts, supporting the Platonic Academy, and otherwise working to make Florence the cultural center of Europe. But when Piero died only five years after his father, his 20-year-old son Lorenzo (1449–1492) assumed responsibility for leading the family and the city. So great and varied were his accomplishments that in his own time he was known as *il Magnifico*— "the Magnificent."

As a young man, Lorenzo had been tutored by Ficino, and among his favorite pastimes was spending the evening talking with Ficino and other friends. "When my mind is disturbed with the tumults of public business," he wrote Ficino in 1480, "and my ears are stunned with the clamors of turbulent citizens, how would it be possible for me to support such contentions unless I found a relaxation in learning?" In support of learning, he rebuilt the University of Pisa and continued to support the study of Greek philosophy and literature in Florence at the Platonic Academy.

Lorenzo's own circle of acquaintances included many of the greatest minds of the day. Delighted by a copy of an ancient Greek or Roman faun's head made by an unknown adolescent named Michelangelo Buonarroti [mee-kuh-LAN-juh-loh bwoh-nah-ROT-tee], Lorenzo invited the sculptor to live in the Medici palace, and the young man was soon a regular in the philosophical discussions that occupied Lorenzo for so many evenings. Besides Ficino, other frequent guests included the painter Botticelli, the composer Heinrich Isaac, and the philosopher Pico della Mirandola [PEE-koh DEL-lah mee-RAN-doh-lah].

Sandro Botticelli: Humanist Painter It seems very likely that these discussions inspired Sandro Botticelli to paint his *Primavera* [pree-mah-VAIR-ah] (*Spring*) on commission from Lorenzo (Fig. **7.14**). In Botticelli's *Primavera* the nymph stands in the center, depicted as Venus, goddess of Love, surrounded by other mythological characters, who appear to move through the garden setting from right to left. To the humanists in Lorenzo's court, Venus was an allegorical figure who represented the highest moral qualities. According to Ficino, she was the very embodiment of "Humanitas . . . her Soul and mind are Love and Charity, her eyes Dignity and Magnanimity, the hands Liberality and Magnificence, the feet Comeliness and Modesty. The whole, then, is Temperance and Honesty, Charm and Splendor." On the far right of the embodiment of the humanities, Zephyrus [ZEF-uh-rus], god of the west wind, attempts to capture Chloris [KLOR-us], the nymph of spring, in his cold, blue grasp. But Flora, goddess of

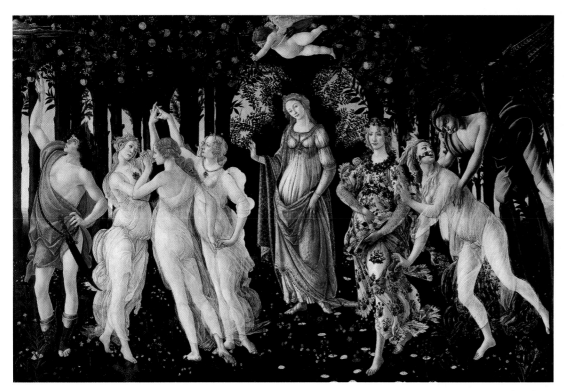

Fig. 7.14 Sandro Botticelli, *Primavera*. Early 1480s. Tempera on panel, 6'8" × 10'4". Galleria degli Uffizi, Florence. *Primavera* means both "spring" and "first truth" in Italian. Though the title is strongly allegorical, its exact meaning is still debated.

flowers, who stands beside the nymph, ignores the west wind's threat, and distributes blossoms across the path. To the left of Venus, the three Graces, daughters of Zeus and personifications of beauty, engage in a dance that recalls a specific one created for three people by Lorenzo in the 1460s. Lorenzo called the dance "Venus" and described it as based on the movement of two figures around a third one:

> First they do a slow side-step, and then together they move with two pairs of forward steps, beginning with the left foot; then the middle dancer turns round and across with two reprises, one on the foot sideways and the other on the right foot, also across; and during the time that the middle dancer is carrying out these reprises the other two go forward with two triplet steps and then give half a turn on the right foot in such a way as to face each other.

Finally, to the left, Mercury, messenger of the gods, holds up his staff as if to brush away the remnants of a straying cloud. Over the whole scene and positioned just above the head of Venus, Cupid reigns.

Primavera captures the spirit of the Medici court. It celebrates love, not only in a Neoplatonic sense, as a spiritual, humanist endeavor, but also in a more direct, physical way. For Lorenzo hardly shied from physical pleasure. A prolific poet himself, his most famous poem, the 1490 "Song of Bacchus," deliberately invites the kind of carefree behavior we associate with carnivals, lavish festivities that Lorenzo regularly sponsored, complete with floats, processions through mythological settings, dance, and song (**Reading 7.1**):

READING 7.1 **Song of Bacchus, or "Triumph of Bacchus and Ariadne" from *Lorenzo de' Medici: Selected Poems and Prose***

How lovely is youth in its allure,
Which ever swiftly flies away!
Let all who want to, now be gay:
About tomorrow no one's sure.

Here are Bacchus, Ariadne,
For one another all afire:
Because time flies and plays us false,
They always yield to their desire.
These nymphs of theirs and other folk
Are merry every single day.
Let all who want to, now be gay:
About tomorrow no one's sure.

Those who love these pretty nymphs
Are little satyrs, free of cares,
Who in the grottoes and the glades
Have laid for them a hundred snares.
By Bacchus warmed and now aroused
They skip and dance the time away.

Let all who want to, now be gay:
About tomorrow no one's sure.

In fact, it seems likely that Botticelli's painting decorated Lorenzo's wedding chamber. Clearly, a lighthearted spirit of play tempered Lorenzo's thirst for knowledge. As Machiavelli [mah-kee-uh-VEL-lee] would later say of him: "If one examines the light and serious side of his life, one sees in him two different persons joined in an almost impossible conjunction."

Heinrich Isaac: Humanist Composer Lorenzo's love of music equaled his love of painting and poetry. Music was an important part of Florentine life, so much so that in 1433 the Opera del Duomo commissioned a series of eight reliefs from Luca della Robbia [DEL-lah ROE-bee-ah] celebrating music. The reliefs were to be displayed in a gallery above the north door of the sacristy (Fig. **7.15**). They were conceived to illustrate Psalm 150, which calls for worshipers to praise God "with sound of the trumpet . . . with psaltry and harp . . . with timbrels and dance . . . with stringed instruments and organs . . . upon the high-sounding cymbals." Luca's youthful figures are the very embodiment of the joy and harmony that made music such an ideal manifestation of the humanist spirit.

Lorenzo's household employed its own private music master, and in 1475 Lorenzo appointed the Flemish composer Heinrich Isaac (1450–1517) to the position. Isaac oversaw the Medici's five household organs, taught music to Lorenzo's sons, served as organist and choirmaster at Florence Cathedral, and, before he knew it, found himself collaborating with Lorenzo writing songs for popular festivals.

The scores for many of the songs produced by this collaboration survive. They are examples of a musical form known as the *frottola* [FROT-toh-lah], from the Italian for "nonsense" or "fib," and are extremely lighthearted. These *frottole* [FROT-toh-leh] offer evidence of a strongly Italian movement away from the complex polyphony and counterpoint of church music in favor of simple harmonies and dancelike rhythms. Most *frottole* consist of three musical parts, with the melody in the highest register. The melodic line is generally taken by a soprano voice, accompanied in the two lower parts by either a lute and viol, two viols, other instruments, or two other voices.

From Lorenzo's point of view, such songs, sung in his native Italian, not Greek or Latin, demonstrated once and for all that Italian was the most harmonious and beautiful of languages when set to music. This sentiment would have lasting impact, especially on the development in the sixteenth and seventeenth centuries of the musical form known as opera.

Pico della Mirandola: Humanity "at the . . . center of the world . . . ." Cultural life in Lorenzo's court was grounded on moral philosophy. The young humanist philosopher, Pico della Mirandola (1463–1494), shared Lorenzo's deep interest in the search for divine truth. By age 23, in 1486, Pico had compiled a volume of some 900 theological and philosophical

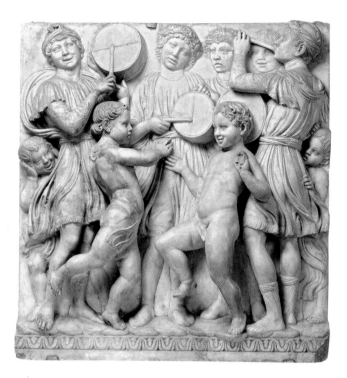

Fig. 7.15 Luca della Robbia. *Drummers* (detail of the *Cantoria*). 1433–1440. Marble, 42 ⅛″ × 41″. Museo dell'Opera del Duomo, Florence. The 17-foot length of the gallery containing the *Cantoria* would have accommodated small choirs and portable organs.

theses, 13 of which Pope Innocent VIII (papacy 1484–1492) considered heretical. When Pico refused to recant the 13, Innocent condemned all 900.

Pico's thinking was based on wide reading in Hebrew, Arabic, Latin, and Greek, and he believed that all intellectual endeavors shared the same purpose—to reveal divine truth. Pico proposed defending his work, in public debate in Rome, against any scholar who might dare to confront him, but the pope banned the debate and even imprisoned him for a brief time in France, where he had fled. Lorenzo offered Pico protection in Florence, defying the pontiff in a daring assertion of secular versus papal authority. As a result, Pico became an important contributor to Lorenzo's humanist court.

In his 1486 *Oration on the Dignity of Man*—the introduction to his proposed debate and one of the great manifestos of humanism—Pico argued that humanity was part of the "great chain of being" that stretches from God to angels, humans, animals, plants, minerals, and the most primal matter. This idea can be traced to the Idea of the Good developed by Plato in Book 7 of the *Republic*, an idea of perfection to which all creation tends. Plotinus' brand of Neoplatonic thought took it a step further in proposing that the material world, including humanity, is but the shadowy reflection of the celestial, a condition that the pursuit of knowledge allows humanity, if it chooses, to at least begin to overcome. According to Pico, humanity finds itself in a middle position in the great chain of being—not by natural law but by the exercise of its own free will. Humans, then, are not fixed in the middle position. They are, in fact, pure potential, able to make of themselves what they wish. Humanity, it follows, is God's greatest miracle: "There is nothing to be seen more wonderful than man," Pico wrote. In his *Oration*, he has God explain to Adam that he has placed him "at the very center of the world" and given him the gift of pure potential to shape himself (**Reading 7.2**):

READING 7.2   **from Pico della Mirandola,** ***Oration on the Dignity of Man* (1486)**

We have given you, Oh Adam, no visage proper to yourself, nor any endowment properly your own, in order that whatever place, whatever form, whatever gifts you may, with premeditation, select, these same you may have and possess through your own judgment and decision. The nature of all other creatures is defined and restricted within laws which We have laid down; you, by contrast, impeded by no such restrictions, may, by your own free will, to whose custody We have assigned you, trace for yourself the lineaments of your own nature. I have placed you at the very center of the world, so that from that vantage point you may with greater ease glance round about you on all that the world contains. . . . You may, as the free and proud shaper of your own being, fashion yourself in the form you prefer. It will be in your power to descend to the lower, brutish forms of life; [or] you will be able, through your own decision, to rise again to the superior orders whose life is divine.

For Pico, the role of the philosopher in this anthropocentric ("human-centered") world is as "a creature of heaven and not of earth." This is because "unmindful of the body, withdrawn into the inner chambers of mind," the philosopher is part of "some higher divinity, clothed with human flesh." It is imperative, therefore, in Pico's view, for individuals to seek out virtue and knowledge, even while knowing their capability of choosing a path of vice and ignorance. Pico argues that humanity is completely free to exercise its free will. And this gift of free will makes humans "the most fortunate of living things."

Such thinking reflects what may be the most important transformation wrought by Renaissance thinkers on medieval ideas. Art, literature, and philosophy, as the free expression of the individual's creative power, can, if they aim high enough, express not only the whole of earthly creation but the whole

of the divine. The human being is a *parvus mundus* [PAHR-wus MOON-dus], a "small universe."

Beyond Florence: The Ducal Courts and the Arts

Pico's message of individual free will and of humanity's ability to choose a path of virtue and knowledge inspired Lorenzo's court and the courts of other Italian city-states as well. These leaders were almost all nobility, not merchants like the Medici (who it must be said had transformed themselves into nobility in all but name), and each court reflected the values of its respective duke—and, very often, his wife. But if they were not about to adopt the republican form of government of Florence, they all shared the humanistic values that were so thoroughly developed there.

The Montefeltro Court in Urbino and Castiglione

One of the most prominent of these city-states was Urbino, some 70 miles east of Florence across the Apennines (see Map 17.1), where the military strategist and learned duke Federigo da Montefeltro [mohn-tay-FEL-troh] (1422–1482) ruled. Federigo surrounded himself with humanists, scholars, poets, and artists, from whom he learned and from whom he commissioned works to embellish Urbino. He financed these expenditures through his talents as a *condottiero* [cohn-doht-TYER-oh], a mercenary soldier who was a valuable and highly paid ally to whoever could afford both him and his army. His court was also a magnet for young men who wanted to learn the principles of noble behavior.

Castiglione's *Book of the Courtier* One of the most important books of the age, written between 1513 and 1518, recalled conversations, probably imaginary, that took place in 1507 among a group of aristocrats at the Urbino court of Guidobaldo da Montefeltro (1472–1508), the son of Federigo. *The Book of the Courtier* by Baldassare Castiglione [kah-still-YOH-neh] (1478–1529) takes the form of a dialogue in which the eloquent courtiers at Urbino compete with each other to describe the perfect courtier—the man (or woman) whose education and deportment is best fashioned to serve the prince. It was not published until 1528, but by 1600 it had been translated into five languages and reprinted in 57 editions.

The Book of the Courtier is, in essence, a nostalgic recreation of Castiglione's nine years (1504–1512) in the Urbino court, which he labeled "the very abode of joyfulness." It takes place on four successive evenings in the spring of 1507. The dialogue is in the form of a dialectic, as the viewpoints of some speakers are challenged and ridiculed by others. The first two books debate the qualities of an ideal gentleman. The goal is to be a completely well-rounded person, *l'uomo universale*. Above all, a courtier must be an accomplished soldier (like Federigo), not only mastering the martial arts but demonstrating absolute bravery and total loyalty in war. His liberal education must include Latin and Greek, other modern languages such as French and Spanish (necessary for diplomacy), and study of the great Italian poets and writers, such as Petrarch and Boccaccio, so that he might imitate their skill in his own verse and prose, both in Latin and in the vernacular. The courtier must also be able to draw, appreciate the arts, and excel in dance and music (though one must avoid the wind instruments since they deform the face). Above all, the courtier must demonstrate a certain *grazia* [GRAH-tsee-ah] ("gracefulness") (**Reading 7.3a**):

READING 7.3a **from Baldassare Castiglione, *The Courtier*, Book 1 (1513–1518; published 1528)**

I wish then, that this Courtier of ours should be nobly born and of gentle race; . . . for noble birth is like a bright lamp that manifests and makes visible good and evil deeds, and kindles and stimulates to virtue both by fear of shame and by hope of praise. . . .

Besides this noble birth, then, I would have the Courtier favored in this regard also, and endowed by nature not only with talent and beauty of person and feature, but with a certain grace and (as we say) air that shall make him at first sight pleasing and agreeable to all who see him; and I would have this an ornament that should dispose and unite all his actions, and in his outward aspect give promise of whatever is worthy the society and favor of every great lord.

Grazia must be tempered by *gravitas* [GRAH-vee-tahs] ("dignity") in all things. This balanced character trait is obtained, Castiglione explains in *The Book of the Courtier*, by means of "one universal rule":

Flee as much as possible . . . affectation; and, perhaps to coin a word . . . make use in all things of a certain *sprezzatura*, which conceals art and presents everything said and done as something brought about without laboriousness and almost without giving it any thought.

Sprezzatura [spray-tsah-TOOR-ah] means, literally, "undervaluing" or "setting a small price" on something. For the courtier it means simply doing difficult things as if effortlessly and with an attitude of nonchalance. The ideal gentleman, in other words, is a construction of absolute artifice, a work of art in his own right who cuts *una bella figura* [OO-nah BEL-lah fee-GOOR-ah], "a fine figure," that all will seek to emulate.

Ultimately, Castiglione suggests, a state led by such perfect gentlemen would itself reflect their perfection, and thus the state does not create great individuals so much as great individuals create the perfect state, in the kind of exercise of free will that Pico discussed.

Much of what we know about what was accepted as the proper behavior of ladies of the court derives from Castiglione's *Book of the Courtier* since, as part of its concern with the conduct of the aristocratic gentleman, it details the gentleman's expectations of his lady. It was generally agreed, for instance, by the conversationalists at the Urbino court that a courtier's lady should profit from most of the rules that serve the courtier. Thus, her accomplishments should demonstrate the casual effortlessness of *sprezzatura.* In one of the book's conversations, for instance, Giuliano de' Medici addresses a gathering of ladies and gentlemen, intent on pointing out what the lady needs *beyond* the accomplishments of her husband (**Reading 7.3b**):

READING 7.3b **from Baldassare Castiglione, *The Courtier*, Book 3**

[The court lady] must have not only the good sense to discern the quality of him with whom she is speaking, but knowledge of many things, in order to entertain him graciously; and in her talk she should know how to choose those things that are adapted to the quality of him with whom she is speaking, and should be cautious lest occasionally, without intending it, she utter words that may offend him. . . . Let her not stupidly pretend to know that which she does not know, but modestly seek to do herself credit in that which she does know. . . . I wish this Lady to have knowledge of letters, music, painting, and to know how to dance and make merry; accompanying the other precepts that have been taught the Courtier with discreet modesty and with the giving of a good impression of herself. And thus, in her talk, her laughter, her play, her jesting, in short, in everything, she will be very graceful, and will entertain appropriately, and with witticisms and pleasantries befitting her, everyone who shall come before her. . . .

Whereas, for Castiglione, the courtier must strive to exemplify the perfectly well-rounded *l'uomo universale*, the court lady must use her breeding and education to further the perfection of the home.

Laura Cereta: Renaissance Feminist Many fifteenth-century women strove for a level of education beyond the mere "knowledge of letters, music, painting" called for by Castiglione. One of the most interesting is Laura Cereta

[LOUGH-rah (as in "bough") cheh-REH-tah] (1469–1499). She was the eldest child of a prominent family from the city of Brescia [BRAY-shuh]. Until she was 11, she was educated by nuns at a convent school. There, she studied reading, writing, embroidery, and Latin until her father called her home to help raise her siblings. But he encouraged her to continue her studies, and in his library she read deeply in Latin, Greek, and mathematics. At 15, however, Cereta chose motherhood over the pursuit of her studies and married a local merchant. When he died, two years later, she returned to her studies. In 1488, at just 19 years of age, she published *Family Letters*, a Latin manuscript containing 82 letters addressed to friends and family, an unusually large number of them women, as well as a mock funeral oration in the classical style.

Cereta's letter, known as the *Defense of Liberal Instruction for Women*, is one of the most remarkable fifteenth-century Italian documents. It is a response to a critic who had praised her as a prodigy, implying that true woman humanist scholars were rare and that, perhaps, her father had authored her letters. In the *Defense*, Cereta explains why so few women were scholars and then defends her own learning (**Reading 7.4**):

READING 7.4 | **from Laura Cereta, *Defense of Liberal Instruction for Women* (1488)**

Only the question of the rarity of outstanding women remains to be addressed. The explanation is clear: women have been able by nature to be exceptional, but have chosen lesser goals. For some women are concerned with parting their hair correctly, adorning themselves with lovely dresses, or decorating their fingers with pearls and other gems. Others delight in mouthing carefully composed phrases, indulging in dancing, or managing spoiled puppies. Still others wish to gaze at lavish banquet tables, to rest in sleep, or, standing at mirrors, to smear their lovely faces. But those in whom a deeper integrity yearns for virtue, restrain from the start their youthful souls, reflect on higher things, harden the body with sobriety and trials, and curb their tongues, open their ears, compose their thoughts in wakeful hours, their minds in contemplation, to letters bonded to righteousness. For knowledge is not given as a gift, but [is gained] with diligence. The free mind, not shirking effort, always soars zealously toward the good, and the desire to know grows ever more wide and deep. It is because of no special holiness, therefore, that we [women] are rewarded by God the Giver with the gift of exceptional talent. Nature has generously lavished its gifts upon all people, opening to all the doors of choice through which reason sends envoys to the will, from which they learn and convey its desires. The will must choose to exercise the gift of reason.

Cereta's argument parallels Pico della Mirandola's in the *Oration on the Dignity of Man*. Women, like men, can choose to exercise their free will in the pursuit of learning. If Adam could choose to fashion himself in whatever form he might prefer, so could Eve.

The Sforza Court in Milan and Leonardo da Vinci

The Sforza family's control over the court of Milan was somewhat less legitimate than most other ducal city-states in Italy. Francesco Sforza (1401–1466) became ruler of Milan by marrying the illegitimate daughter, but sole heir, of the duke of Milan. His own illegitimate son, Ludovico (1451–1508), called *il Moro*, "the Moor," because of his dark complexion, wrested control of the city from the family of Francesco's legitimate brother and proclaimed himself duke of Milan in 1494. Both Francesco and Ludovico understood the tenuousness of their claims to rule, and they actively sought to win the support of the people through the arts. They welcomed artists from throughout central Italy to their city and embraced humanism.

The most important of these artists was Leonardo da Vinci (1452–1519), who first arrived in Milan in 1482 as the emissary of Lorenzo de' Medici to present a silver lyre, perhaps made by Leonardo himself, to Ludovico Sforza. Ludovico was embroiled in military matters, and Leonardo pronounced himself a military engineer, capable of constructing great "machines of war," including designs for a catapult and covered vehicles that resemble modern-day armored cars.

Leonardo's restless imagination, in fact, led him to the study of almost everything: natural phenomena like wind, storms, and the movement of water; anatomy and physiology; physics and mechanics; music; mathematics; plants and animals; geology; and astronomy, to say nothing of painting and drawing. Leonardo was a humanist, and as such was deeply swayed by Neoplatonic thought. He saw connections among all spheres of existence and wrote of them:

> If man has in himself bones, the supports and armature for the flesh, the world has the rocks, the supports of the earth; if man has in himself the lake of blood, in which the lungs increase and decrease in breathing, the body of the earth has its oceanic sea, which likewise increases and decreases every six hours with the breathing of the world; if from the said lake veins arise, which proceed to ramify throughout the human body, the oceanic sea fills the body of the earth with infinite veins of water.

Thus, the miracle of the fetus in the womb, which Leonardo depicts in a famous anatomical study from his notebooks (Fig. **7.16**), is analogous in his mind to the mysteries that lie deep within the body of earth. "I came to the entrance of a great cavern," he writes in one note. "There immediately arose in me two feelings—fear and desire—fear of the menacing, dark cavity, and desire to see if there was anything miraculous within." Leonardo's fascination with the human body—an image, for him, of both attraction and repulsion—led him to produce this and his other precisely drawn dissections of the human body in 1510–1512, probably working under the direction of a young professor of anatomy.

Leonardo was already known for his skill as a portrait painter when he arrived in Milan, and his fascination with revealing the human personality in portraiture is nowhere more evident than in his *Mona Lisa* (Fig. **7.17**). Leonardo fuses his subject with the landscape behind her by means of light. He called this technique ***sfumato*** [sfoo-MAH-toh] ("smoki-ness"). Its hazy effects, which create a half-waking, dreamlike quality reminiscent of dusk, could only be achieved by build-ing up color with many layers of transparent oil paint—a process called **glazing**. But it is the mysterious personality of Leonardo's sitter that most occupies the viewer's imagination. For generations, viewers have asked, Who is this woman? What is she thinking about? What is her relation to the artist? Leonardo presents us with a particular personality, whose

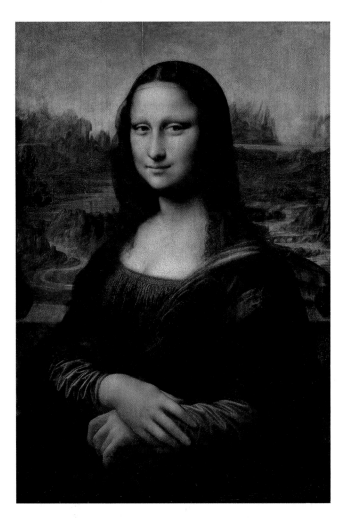

Fig. 7.17 Leonardo da Vinci, *Mona Lisa*. 1503–1515. Oil on wood, 30$\frac{1}{4}$″ × 21″. Musée du Louvre, Paris, France. The woman in this picture is believed to be the wife of the Florentine patrician Francesco del Giocondo. She is seated on a balcony, originally between two columns that have been cut off (the base of the left column is just visible).

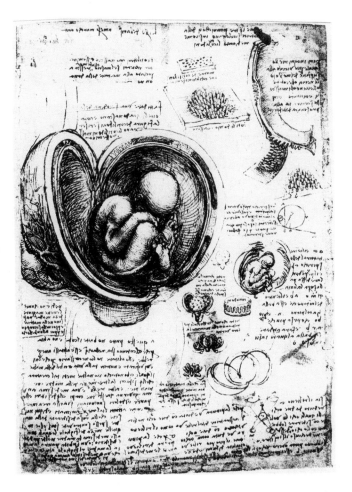

Fig. 7.16 Leonardo da Vinci, *Embryo in the Womb*. ca. 1510. Pen and brown ink, 11$\frac{3}{4}$″ × 8$\frac{1}{2}$″. The Royal Collection, Windsor Castle, Royal Library. © 2007 Her Majesty Queen Elizabeth II. Leonardo's notes on this page from one of his notebooks relate not only to standard questions of anatomy and physiology, including the nourishment of the fetus, but also to the relationship of the fetus's soul to that of its mother.

half-smile suggests that he has captured her in a particular, if enigmatic, mood. And the painting's hazy light reinforces the mystery of her personality. Apparently, whatever he captured in her look he could not give up. The *Mona Lisa* occupied Leonardo for years, and it followed him to Rome and then to France in 1513, where King Louis XII offered him the Château [shah-TOH] of Cloux [kloo] near Amboise [ahm-BWAHZ] as a residence. Leonardo died there on May 2, 1519.

In 1495, Ludovico commissioned Leonardo to paint a monumental fresco of the *Last Supper* for the north wall of the refectory of the Dominican monastery of Santa Maria delle Grazie [GRATZ-ee-ay] (Fig. **7.18**). The intent was that at every meal the monks would contemplate Christ's last meal in a wall-sized painting. The *Last Supper* illusionistical-ly extends the refectory walls in perfect one-point perspec-tive, carrying the present of architectural space into the past of the painting's space.

The moment Leonardo chose to depict is just after Christ has announced to the apostles that one of them will betray him. Each apostle reacts in his characteristic way. Saint Peter grabs a knife in anger, while Judas turns away and Saint John appears to faint. The vanishing point of the painting is directly behind Christ's head, focusing the viewer's attention and establishing Christ as the most important figure in the work. He extends his arms, forming a perfect equilateral triangle at the center of the painting, an image of balance and a symbolic reference to the Trinity. What is unique about this painting of an otherwise completely traditional subject for a refectory is its psychological realism. We see this in the sense of agitated doubt and confusion among the apostles, their intertwined bodies twisting and turning as if drawn toward the self-contained and peaceful image of Christ. The apostles, even Judas, are revealed in all their humanity, while Christ is composed in his compassion for them.

In 1499, the French, under Charles VIII, deposed Ludovico and imprisoned him in France, where he died in 1508. Leonardo abandoned Milan, eventually returning to Florence in about 1503. Both of Ludovico's sons would briefly rule as duke of Milan in the early sixteenth century, but both were soon deposed and the male line of the Sforza family died out.

From Florence to Rome: The High Renaissance

When Brunelleschi arrived in Rome in 1402, shortly after the competition for the baptistery doors in Florence, the city must have seemed a pitiful place. Its population had shrunk from around 1 million in 100 CE to around 20,000. It was located in a relatively tiny enclave across the Tiber from the Vatican and Saint Peter's Basilica and was surrounded by the ruins of a once great city. Even 150 years later, in the sixteenth century, the city occupied only a small fraction of the territory enclosed by its third-century CE walls (see Fig. **7.19**). The ancient Colosseum was now in the countryside, the Forum a pasture for goats and cattle. The ancient aqueducts that had once brought fresh water to the city had collapsed. The popes had even abandoned the city when, in 1309, under pressure from the king of France, who sought to assert secular authority over the clergy, they left Italy and established Avignon [ah-veen-YOHN] as the seat of the Church. When Rome finally reestablished itself as the titular seat of the Church in 1378, succeeding popes rarely chose to visit the city, let alone live in it. The city held little appeal, except perhaps for the ruins themselves, and, as we have already seen, it was to the ruins of Rome that Brunelleschi was most attracted.

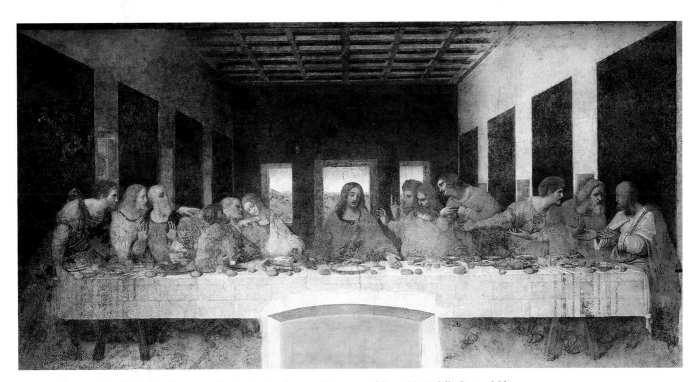

Fig. 7.18 Leonardo da Vinci, *Last Supper*, wall painting in refectory, Monastery of Santa Maria delle Grazie, Milan. ca. 1495–1498. Fresco, oil, and tempera on plaster, 15′1 1/8″ × 28′10 1/2″. Santa Maria delle Grazie, Milan. Today, even after "restoration," Leonardo's original painting remains in very bad shape. The fault is almost entirely Leonardo's—or maybe Ludovico Sforza's, who rushed him to complete it. Instead of using the established fresco technique of painting tempera into wet plaster, Leonardo applied oil and tempera to dry plaster. As early as 1517, the paint began to flake off, unable to adhere to the wall.

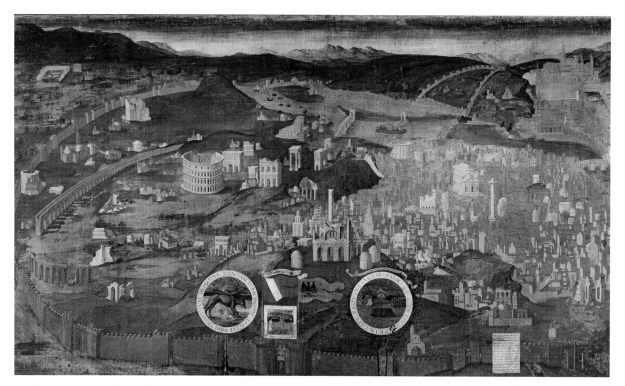

Fig. 7.19 Anonymous, *View of Rome*. ca. 1550. Oil on canvas. Palazzo Ducale, Mantua. Renaissance Rome occupied a fragment of the territory inside the walls of the ancient city. The Colosseum, left of center, though within the walls, was virtually in the countryside, and had long since fallen into ruin. The Pantheon was the largest building visible in the city proper. It was in good repair because it had been converted to a Christian church.

After 1420, when Pope Martin V (papacy 1417–1431) brought the papacy back to Rome for good, it became something of a papal duty to restore the city to its former greatness. Because as many as 100,000 visitors might swarm into Rome during religious holidays, it was important that they be "moved by its extraordinary sights," as one pope put it, and thus find their "belief continually confirmed and daily corroborated by great buildings . . . seemingly made by the hand of God." In other words, the popes were charged with the sacred duty of becoming great patrons of the arts and architecture of Rome.

By and large, Rome imported its artists from Florence. In 1481, Botticelli and a group of his fellow Florentine painters arrived to decorate the walls of the Vatican's Sistine [SIS-teen] Chapel. When Pope Julius II (papacy 1503–1513) began a massive campaign to rebuild Saint Peter's Basilica and the Vatican, he commanded Michelangelo to leave Florence for Rome in 1505 and commissioned major paintings and monuments from the then 30-year-old artist. In 1508, Michelangelo was followed by Raphael (Raffaello Santi or Sanzio, 1483–1520), a young painter from Urbino who had arrived in Florence in 1505. Julius set him the task of decorating the papal apartments. Rome must have seemed something of a Florentine place. In November 1494, the domination of Florence by the Medici family had come to an end. But when the Medici returned to power in Florence in 1512, they did so

under the sway of two great Medici popes: Leo X (papacy 1513–1521), who was Lorenzo the Magnificent's son, Giovanni de' Medici; and Clement VII (papacy 1523–1534), who was Lorenzo's nephew, Giulio [JOO-lyoh] de' Medici. Whether in the church or the republic, Rome or Florence, the males of this patrician family were the dominant force in the Renaissance political world.

Bramante and the New Saint Peter's Basilica

Shortly after he was elected pope in 1503, Julius II made what may have been the most important commission of the day. He asked the architect Donato Bramante [brah-MAHN-teh] (1444–1514) to renovate the Vatican Palace and serve as chief architect of a plan to replace Saint Peter's Basilica with a new church. The pope's chosen architect, Bramante, had worked with Leonardo da Vinci in Milan, and Julius was deeply impressed by Leonardo's understanding of the writings of the ancient Roman architectural historian Vitruvius. For Vitruvius, the circle and square were the ideal shapes. Not only did these perfect shapes originate from the ideal human figure, they also mirrored the symmetry of the body and the proportional coherence of all its parts. (Vitruvius' enumeration of human proportions is usually taken to recount the lost *Canon* of the fifth century BCE Greek sculptor Polyclitus; see Fig. 2.29). The ratio of these proportions was the figurative equivalent of Pythagoras' **music of the spheres**, the theory that each planet produced a musical sound, fixed mathematically by its velocity and distance from earth, which harmonized with those produced by other planets and was audible but not recognized on earth. Thus, according to Vitruvius, if the human head is one-eighth the total height of an idealized figure, then the human body itself fits into the ideal musical interval of the **octave**, the interval that gives the impression of duplicating the original note at a higher or lower pitch. In his *Vitruvian Man*, Leonardo illustrated how the ideal human figure generates both the circle and the square (Fig. **7.20**).

In Rome, Bramante applied these ideas of geometrical perfection to one of his earliest commissions, a small free-standing circular chapel in the courtyard of a Spanish church in Rome, San Pietro in Montorio, directly over what was revered as the site of Saint Peter's martyrdom. Because of its small size and the fact that it was modeled on a classical temple that was excavated in Rome during the reign of Sixtus IV, this structure is known as the Tempietto [tem-PYET-toh] (Little Temple) (Fig. **7.21**). The 16 exterior columns are Doric—in fact, their shafts are original ancient Roman granite columns—and the frieze above them is decorated with objects of the Christian liturgy in sculptural relief. The diameter of the shafts defines the entire plan. Each shaft is spaced four diameters from the next, and the colonnade they form is two diameters from the circular walls. In its classical reference, its incorporation of original classical Roman columns into its architectural scheme, and, above all, in the proportional coherence of its parts, the Tempietto is the very embodiment of Italian humanist architecture in the High Renaissance.

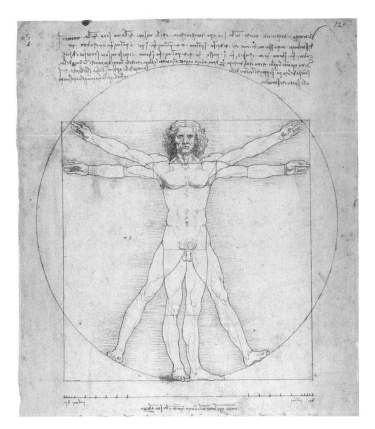

Fig. 7.20 Leonardo da Vinci. *Vitruvian Man*. ca. 1485–1490. Pen and ink, 13½″ × 9⅝″. Gallerie dell'Accademia, Venice. Vitruvius specifically related the harmonious physical proportions of man to those of architecture, which reflect their divine creator.

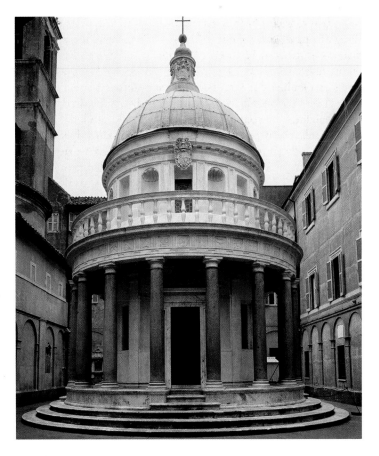

Fig. 7.21 Donato Bramante, Tempietto. 1502. San Pietro in Montorio, Rome. This chapel was certainly modeled after a classical temple. It was commissioned by King Ferdinand and Queen Isabella of Spain, financiers of Christopher Columbus's voyages to America. It was undertaken in support of Pope Alexander VI, who was himself Spanish.

The task of replacing Old Saint Peter's was a much larger project and Bramante's most important one. Old Saint Peter's was a **basilica**, a type of ancient Roman building with a long central nave, double side aisles set off by colonnades (see Fig. 4.6), an apse in the wall opposite the main door, and a transept near the apse so that large numbers of visitors could approach the shrine to Saint Peter. In his plan for a new Saint Peter's (Fig. **7.22a**), Bramante adopted the Vitruvian square, as illustrated in Leonardo's drawing, placing inside it a **Greek cross** (a cross in which the upright and transverse shafts are of equal length and intersect at their middles) topped by a central dome purposely reminiscent of the giant dome of the Pantheon (see Fig. 3.18). The resultant central plan is essentially a circle inscribed within a square. In Renaissance thinking, the central plan and dome symbolized the perfection of God. Construction began in 1506.

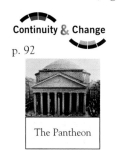

Continuity & Change
p. 92

The Pantheon

Julius II financed the project through the sale of **indulgences**, dispensations granted by the Church to shorten an individual's stay in purgatory. This was the place where, in Catholic belief, individuals temporarily reside after death as punishment for their sins. Those wanting to enter heaven faster than they otherwise might could shorten their stay in purgatory by purchasing an indulgence. The Church had been selling these documents since the twelfth century, and Julius's building campaign intensified the practice. (In protest against the sale of indulgences, Martin Luther would launch the Protestant Reformation in Germany in 1517; see chapter 8.) The New Saint Peter's would be a very expensive project, but there were also very many sinners willing to help pay for it. With the deaths of both pope and architect, in 1513 and 1514 respectively, the project came to a temporary halt. Its final plan would be developed in 1546 by Michelangelo (Fig. **7.22b**).

Michelangelo and the Sistine Chapel

After the fall of the Medici in 1494, a young Michelangelo, not yet twenty years old, had left Florence for Rome. There must have seemed little prospect for him in Florence, where a Dominican friar, Girolamo Savonarola [jee-ROH-lah-moh sav-oh-nah-ROH-lah] (1452–1498), abbot of the monastery of San Marco, wielded tremendous political influence. Savonarola appealed, first and foremost, to a moralistic faction of the populace that saw, in the behavior of the city's upper classes, and in their humanistic attraction to classical Greek and Roman culture, clear evidence of moral decadence. Savonarola railed against the Florentine nobility—the Medici in particular—going so far as to organize troops of children to collect the city's "vanities"—everything from cosmetics to books and paintings—and burn them in giant bonfires. Finally, in June 1497, an angry Pope Alexander VI excommunicated him for his antipapal preachings and for disobeying his directives for the administration of the monastery of San Marco. Savonarola was commanded not to preach, an order he chose to ignore. On May 28, 1498, he was forcibly removed from San Marco, tortured as a heretic along with two fellow friars, hanged until nearly dead, and then burned at the stake. His ashes were subsequently thrown into the Arno River. Florence felt itself freed from tyranny.

With the fall of Savonarola, the Signoria, Florence's governing body, quickly moved to assert the republic's survival in visual terms. It moved Donatello's *David* (see Fig. 7.11) from the Medici palace to the Palazzo della Signoria, where the governing body met to conduct business. It also asked Michelangelo to return to Florence in 1501 to work on a huge cracked block of marble that all other sculptors had abandoned in dismay. It was to be another freestanding statue of the biblical hero David, but colossal in scale. Michelangelo rose to the challenge.

The completed figure (Fig. **7.23**), over 17 feet high—even higher on its pedestal—intentionally references Donatello's boyish predecessor but then challenges it. Michelangelo represents David before, not after, his triumph, sublimely confident, ready to take on whatever challenge faces him, just as the republic itself felt ready to take on all comers. The nudity of the figure and the contrapposto stance are directly indebted to the Medici celebration of all things ancient Greek. Its sense of self-contained, even heroic individualism captures perfectly the humanist spirit. Michelangelo's triumph over the complexity of the stone transformed it into an artwork that his contemporaries lauded for its almost unparalleled beauty. It was an achievement that Michelangelo

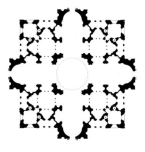
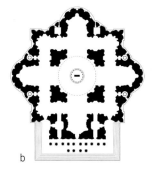

a   b

Fig. 7.22 Plans for Saint Peter's, Rome by (a) Donato Bramante, and (b) Michelangelo. Bramante's original plan (a), in the form of a Greek cross, was sporadically worked on after Julius II's death in 1513. The project came to a complete halt for a decade after the Sack of Rome by the troops of the Habsburg Emperor, Charles V, in 1527. In 1547, Pope Paul III appointed Michelangelo as architect, and he revived Bramante's original plan but added more support for the dome and thickened the walls. He also added a portico consisting of ten columns in the second row and four in the front, which created the feeling of a Latin cross, especially when extended by his other addition to Bramante's scheme, the massive flight of steps rising to the main portal (b).

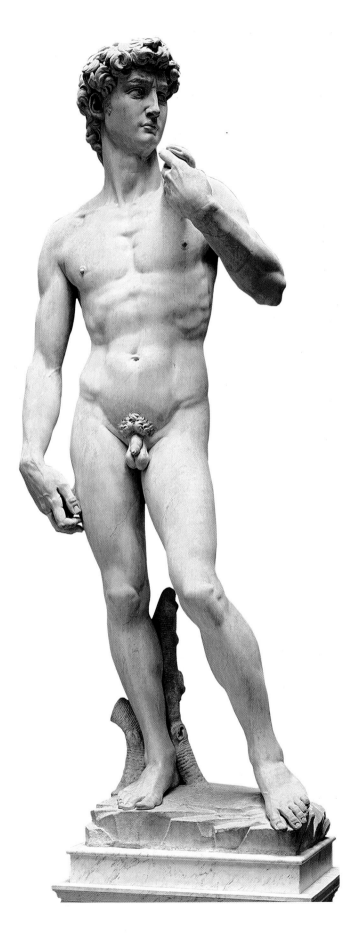

would soon equal, in another medium, in his work on the Sistine Chapel ceiling at the Vatican, in Rome.

The fate of the *David* underscores the political and moral turbulence of the times. Each night, as workers installed the statue in the Piazza della Signoria, supporters of the exiled Medici hurled stones at it, understanding, correctly, that the statue was a symbol of the city's will to stand up to any and all tyrannical rule, including that of the Medici themselves. Another group of citizens soon objected to the statue's nudity, and before it was even installed in place, a skirt of copper leaves was prepared to spare the general public any possible offense. The skirt is long gone, but it symbolizes the conflicts of the era, even as the sculpture itself can be thought of as truly inaugurating the High Renaissance.

But it is Michelangelo's work on the Sistine Chapel in Rome that remains one of the era's crowning achievements. Just as the construction of the New Saint Peter's was about to get under way, Julius II commissioned Michelangelo to design his tomb. It would be a three-storied monument, over 23 feet wide and 35 feet high, and it represents Michelangelo's first foray into architecture. For the next 40 years, Michelangelo would work sporadically on the tomb, but from the beginning he was continually interrupted, most notably in 1506 when Julius himself commanded the artist to paint the 45- by 128-foot ceiling of the Sistine Chapel, named after Sixtus IV, Julius's uncle, who had commissioned its construction in 1473. Ever since its completion, the chapel has served as the meeting place of the conclave of cardinals during the election of new popes. Michelangelo at first refused Julius's commission, but by 1508 he reconsidered, signed the contract, and began the task.

Julius first proposed filling the spandrels between the windows with paintings of the twelve apostles and then decorating the ceiling proper with ornamental designs. But when Michelangelo objected to the limitations of this plan, the pope freed him to paint whatever he liked, and Michelangelo undertook for himself a far more ambitious task—nine scenes from Genesis, the first book of the Hebrew Bible, on the ceiling proper surrounded by prophets, Sibyls, the ancestors of Christ, and other scenes (Figs. **7.24**, **7.25**). Thus, the ceiling would narrate events before the coming of the law of Moses, and would complement the narrative cycles on the walls below.

Fig. 7.23 Michelangelo, *David*. 1501–1504.
Marble, height 17′ 3″. Accademia, Florence. The *David* was originally conceived to be placed high on the facade of Florence Cathedral. It was probably situated in the Piazza della Signoria because it could not be lifted into place.

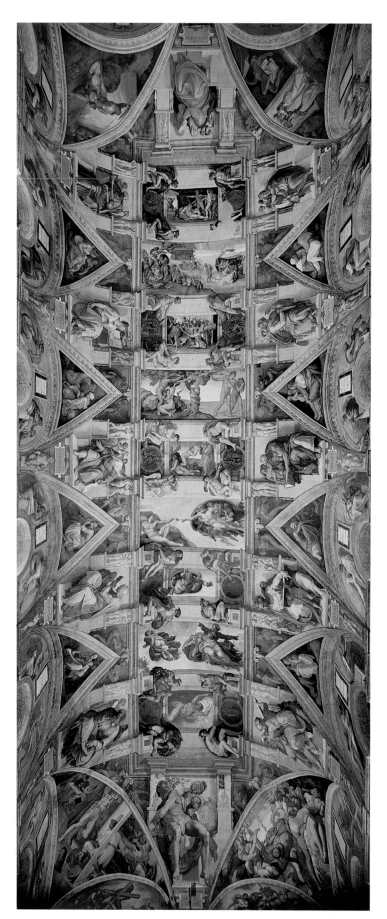

Figs. 7.24 and Fig. 7.25 Michelangelo, Sistine Chapel ceiling and plan of its narrative program, Vatican, Rome. 1508–1512. Fresco, 45′ × 128′. The intense and vibrant colors of the ceiling were revealed after a thorough cleaning, completed in 1990. Centuries of smoke and grime were removed by a process that involved the application of a solvent, containing both a fungicide and an antibacterial agent, mixed with a cellulose gel that would not drip from the ceiling. This mixture was applied in small sections with a bristle brush, allowed to dry for three minutes, and then removed with sponge and water. Until the cleaning, no one for centuries had fully appreciated Michelangelo's daring, even sensual, sense of color.

David and Goliath	Zacharias	Judith and Holofernes
Joel	Drunkenness of Noah	Delphic Sibyl
Zorobabel	The Flood	Josiah
Eritrean Sibyl	Sacrifice of Noah	Isaiah
Ozias	Temptation and Expulsion	Ezekias
Ezekiel	Creation of Eve	Cumaean Sibyl
Roboam	Creation of Adam	Asa
Persian Sibyl	Separation of Land from Water	Daniel
Salmon	Creation of Sun, Moon, and Planets	Jesse
Jeremiah	Separation of Light from Darkness	Libyan Sibyl
Death of Haman	Jonah	Moses and the Serpent of Brass

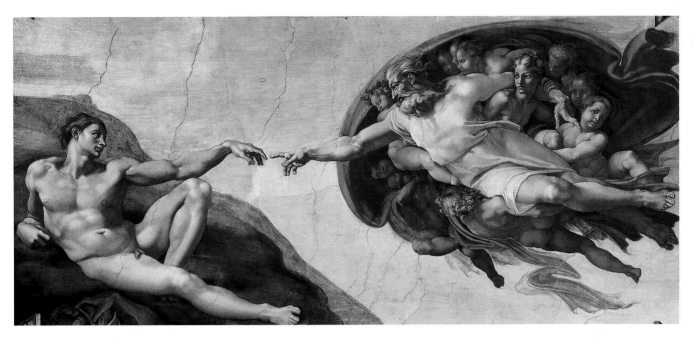

Fig. 7.26 Michelangelo, *Creation of Adam,* Sistine Chapel, Vatican, Rome. 1510. Fresco. Note the analogy Michelangelo creates between Adam and God, between the father of humankind and God the Father. Although they face one another, Adam and God are posed along parallel diagonals, and their right legs are in nearly identical positions. The connection is further highlighted by the fluttering green ribbon in God's space that echoes the colors of the earth upon which Adam lies.

Throughout the ceiling Michelangelo includes the della Rovere heraldic symbols of oak (*rovere*) and acorn to symbolize the pope's patronage, usually in the hands of **ignudi** [ee-NYOO-dee], nude youths who sit at the four corners of alternate central panels. These same panels are framed by bronze shields that underscore the patron's military prowess. The whole is contained in an entirely illusionistic architecture that appears to open at each end to the sky outside. Only the spandrels over the windows and the **pendentives** (concave triangular sections that form a transition between a rectilinear and a dome shape) at each corner are real.

The nine central panels tell the story, in three panels each, of Creation, Adam and Eve, and Noah. The series begins over the chapel altar with the Separation of Light from Darkness, a moment associated with the eternal struggle between good and evil, truth and falsehood. In fact, this pairing of opposites characterizes the entire program. At the center of the ceiling is the *Creation of Eve.* Life and death, good and evil, the heavenly and the earthly, the spiritual and the material, pivot around this central scene. Everything between here and the altar represents Creation before the knowledge of good and evil was introduced to the world by the temptation of Eve in the Garden of Eden, a scene represented, together with the Expulsion, in the panel just to the right. From here to the panel over the door to the chapel we witness the early history of fallen humankind, for viewers entering the chapel look up to see directly above them the Drunkenness of Noah, an image symbolic of their own

frailty. They see the goodness and truth of God's creation only at the greatest remove from them, far away at the chapel's other end.

The tension between the spiritual and the material worlds is nowhere better represented on the ceiling than in the *Creation of Adam* (Fig. **7.26**). Adam is earthbound. He seems lethargic, passive, barely interested, while a much more animated God flies through the skies carrying behind him a bulging red drapery that suggests both the womb and the brain, creativity and reason. Under his arm is a young woman, who may be Eve, who prefigures the Virgin, while God's left hand touches the shoulder of an infant, who may symbolize the future Christ. The implication of the scene is that in just one moment, God's finger will touch Adam's and infuse him with not just energy but soul, not just life but the future of humankind.

To paint the ceiling, Michelangelo had to construct a scaffold that moved down the chapel from the entrance to the altar. Thus, the first frescoes painted were the Noah group, and the last, the Creation. He painted the ceiling standing, not lying down, his eyes focused on the work above him. As the work progressed, it appears that he grew more comfortable, for his style became increasingly energetic and bold. This is especially apparent in his depiction of the *ignudi,* Sibyls [SIB-ulz], and prophets, which he presented with increasing skill in more poses exhibiting greater physical movement as he progressed down the ceiling from entrance to altar.

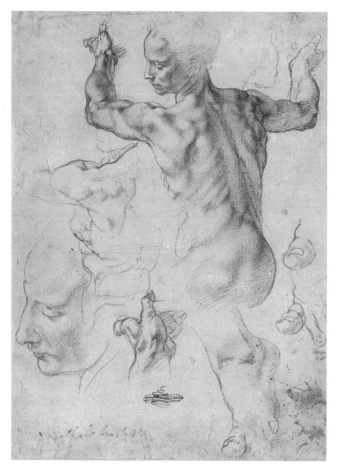

Fig. 7.27 Michelangelo, *Studies for the Libyan Sibyl*. ca. 1510. Red chalk, 11⅜″ × 8⁷/₁₆″. The Metropolitan Museum of Art, New York, Joseph Pulitzer Bequest, 1924 (24.197.2). Photograph © 1995. The Metropolitan Museum of Art, New York. Very few of Michelangelo's drawings for the Sistine Chapel survive, even though he prepared hundreds as he planned the ceiling.

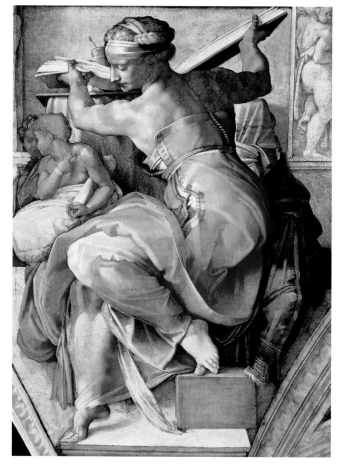

Fig. 7.28 Michelangelo, *Libyan Sibyl*, Sistine Chapel, Vatican, Rome. 1512. Fresco. In Michelangelo's program for the ceiling, the Sibyls alternate with Hebrew Bible prophets around the room. One of the most striking characteristics of these figures is the way they seem to project in front of the decoration and enter into the real space of the chapel, creating a stunning illusionistic effect.

Michelangelo worked on the ceiling from May 1508 until 1512. His accomplishment becomes even clearer when we compare the final painting to the preparatory studies. In a drawing of one of the later figures painted, the *Libyan Sibyl* (Fig. 7.27), the figure's hands are balanced evenly, at the same level, but by the time he painted her (Fig. 7.28), the left hand had dropped below the right to emphasize her downward turn, emphasizing the fact that she is bringing knowledge down to the viewer. The artist has paid special attention to the left foot, seeing the need to splay the four smaller toes backward. And finally, his model in the drawing was apparently male. In his reworking of the face at the lower left of the drawing, he softens the figure's cheekbones and fills out her lips. In the final painting, he reduces the model's prominent brow, hides the musculature of the model's back, and exaggerates the buttocks and hips, feminizing the original masculine sketch. As graceful as it is powerful and majestic, the *Libyan Sibyl* is a virtuoso display of technical mastery.

The *Stanza della Segnatura*

The young painter Raphael arrived in Rome as Michelangelo was beginning work on the Sistine ceiling and quickly secured a commission from Julius II to paint the pope's private rooms in the Vatican Palace. The first of these rooms was the so-called *Stanza della Segnatura* [STAHN-zah DEL-lah Sayn-yah-TOOR-ah], Room of the Signature, where subsequent popes signed official documents, but which Julius used as a library. Julius had determined the subjects. On each of the four walls Raphael was to paint one of the four major areas of humanist learning: Law and Justice, to be represented by the *Cardinal Virtues*; the Arts, to be represented by *Mount Parnassus*; Theology, to be represented by the *Disputà* [dees-poo-TAH], or *Dispute over the Sacrament*; and Philosophy, to be represented by the *School of Athens* (see *Focus*, pages 212–213). In an apparent attempt to balance classical paganism and Christian faith, a gesture completely in keeping with

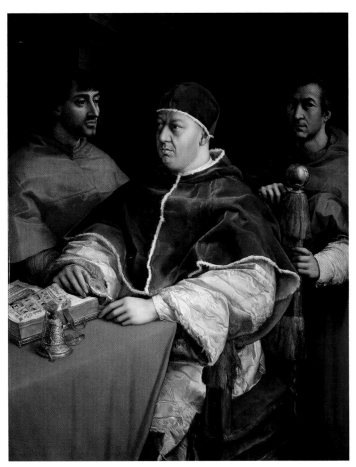

Fig. 7.29 Raphael, *Pope Leo X with Cardinals Giulio de' Medici and Luigi de' Rossi*. **1517.** Panel, 60½″ × 47″. Galleria degli Uffizi, Florence. The illuminated manuscript on the table in front of the pope is from his private collection. It contributes significantly to the highly naturalistic feeling of the scene, even as it symbolizes his humanism.

Julius' humanist philosophy, two of these scenes—*Mount Parnassus* and the *School of Athens*—had classical themes, the other two Christian.

The Medici Popes

Pope Julius II died in 1513, not long after Michelangelo had completed the Sistine Chapel ceiling and Raphael the Stanza della Segnatura. He was succeeded by Leo X, born Giovanni de' Medici, son of Lorenzo the Magnificent. Leo's papacy began a nearly 21-year period of dominance from Rome by the Medici popes, which ended with the death of Clement VII in 1534. The patronage of these Medici popes had a significant effect on art.

Leo X and Raphael After his work in the Stanza, Leo was quick to hire Raphael for other commissions. When Bramante died in 1514, Leo appointed the young painter as papal architect, though Raphael had never worked on any substantial building project. It was not long before Leo asked Raphael to paint his portrait.

Pope Leo X with Cardinals Giulio de' Medici and Luigi de' Rossi (Fig. **7.29**), painted in 1517, suggests a new direction in Raphael's art. The lighting is more somber than in the vibrantly lit paintings of the Stanza della Segnatura. Architectural detail is barely visible as the figures are silhouetted, seated against an intensely black ground. Although posed as a group, the three figures look in different directions, each preoccupied with his own concerns. It is as if they have just heard something familiar but ominous in the distance, something that has given them all pause. There is, furthermore, a much greater emphasis on the material reality of the scene. One can almost feel the slight stubble of Leo's beard, and the beards of the two cardinals are similarly palpable. The velvet of Leo's ermine-trimmed robe contrasts dramatically with the silk of the cardinals' cloaks. And the brass knob on the pope's chair reflects the rest of the room like a mirror, including a brightly lit window that stands in total opposition to the darkness of the rest of the scene. All in all, the painting creates a sense of drama, as if we are witness to an important historical moment.

In fact, in 1517, the papacy faced some very real problems. To the north, in Germany, Martin Luther had published his *Ninety-Five Theses*, attacking the practice of papal indulgences and calling into question the authority of the pope (see chapter 8). Back in Florence, where the Medici had resumed power in 1512, the family maintained control largely through its connections to Rome, and its control was constantly threatened. Despite these difficulties, as Leo tried to rule the Church in Rome and Florence from the *stanze* of the Vatican, he continued his patronage of the arts unabated. He commissioned Raphael to decorate more rooms in the papal apartments and to develop a series of **cartoons** (full-scale drawings used to transfer a design onto another surface) for tapestries to cover the lower walls of the Sistine Chapel. Leo also celebrated his papacy with a series of commissions at San Lorenzo, the neighborhood church in Florence that had served as the Medici family mausoleum for nearly 100 years. He hired Michelangelo to design a new funerary chapel there, the so-called New Sacristy, for recently deceased members of the family.

Clement VII and the Laurentian Library When Leo X died in 1521, he was briefly succeeded by a Dutch cardinal who deplored the artistic patronage of the Medici popes as both extravagant and inappropriate. He died only a year into his reign, and when Giulio de' Medici succeeded him as Clement VII (papacy 1523–1534), artists and humanists reacted enthusiastically. As cardinal, he had commissioned major works from Raphael and others, and he had worked closely with Leo on Michelangelo's New Sacristy at San Lorenzo in Florence. But Clement was never able to sustain the scale of patronage in Rome that his uncle had managed. This failure resulted in part from the Sack of Rome by the German mercenary troops of Holy Roman Emperor Charles V in 1527. During this crisis, many of the artists' workshops in the city were destroyed, and many artists abandoned the city altogether.

Focus

Raphael's *School of Athens*

The *School of Athens*, also known as *Philosophy*, is generally acknowledged as the most important of Raphael's four paintings for the Stanza della Segnatura of the Vatican Palace in Rome. Its classicism is clearly indicated in several ways: by its illusionistic architectural setting, based on ancient Roman baths; by its emphatic one-point perspective, which directs viewer attention to the two central figures, Plato and Aristotle, fathers of philosophy; and by its subject matter, the philosophical foundation of the Renaissance humanistic enterprise. All of the figures here—the Platonists on the left, the Aristotelians on the right, though not all have been identified—were regarded by Renaissance humanists as embodying the ideal of continual pursuit of learning and truth. The clarity, balance, and symmetry that distinguish this Raphael composition became a touchstone for painters in centuries to come.

The gestures of the central figures indicate heavenly and earthly duality. Plato points toward the heavens, the realm of ideal forms that so informs his work, while Aristotle stretches out his hand palm down toward the earth, from where, in his view, all knowledge originates in empirical observation. Other philosophers spread out across the room, those ranked on Plato's side beneath a niche containing a statue of Apollo, the god of sunlight, rationality, poetry, music, and the fine arts; those on Aristotle's side beneath a statue of Minerva, goddess of wisdom and the mechanical arts. But for Raphael and many other humanists, Plato and Aristotle were more alike than dissimilar. They believed that the greatest difference between the two was more a matter of style than substance. Plato's poetic images and Aristotle's rational analysis were actually arguing for the same things but from different directions. The painting is, after all, entitled *School of Athens*, not *Schools of Athens*. This unified humanist philosophical tradition is mirrored, then, in the balanced clarity of the painting's composition.

Plato (ca. 428–348 BCE) resembles a self-portrait of Leonardo da Vinci. He points upward to the realm of ideas. (Note the resemblance of this gesture to that of Doubting Thomas in Leonardo's *Last Supper*, Fig. 7.18.) He carries the *Timaeus*, the dialogue on the origin of the universe in which he argued that the circle is the image of cosmic perfection.

Apollo, holding a lyre, is god of reason, patron of music, and symbol of philosophical enlightenment.

Epicurus (341–270 BCE) reads a text and wears a crown of grape leaves, symbolic of his philosophy that happiness could be attained through the pursuit of pleasures of the mind and body.

Pythagoras (ca. 580–500 BCE), the Greek mathematician, illustrates the theory of proportions to interested students—among them, wearing a turban, the Arabic scholar, **Averroës** (1126–1198).

Raphael. *School of Athens*. 1510–1511. Stanza della Segnatura, Vatican, Rome. Fresco, 19′ × 27′.

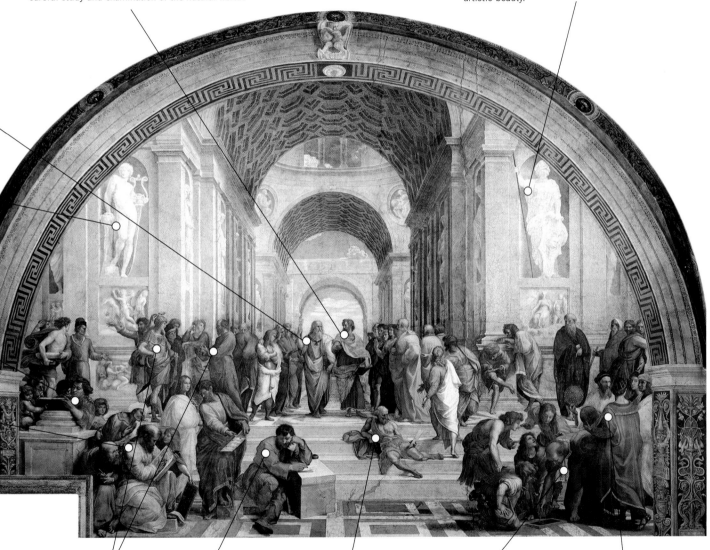

Aristotle (384–322 BCE) carries his *Nicomachean Ethics* and gestures outward toward the earthly world of the viewer, emphasizing his belief in empiricism— that we can only understand the universe through the careful study and examination of the natural world.

Minerva, the goddess of wisdom, is the traditional patron of those devoted to the pursuit of truth and artistic beauty.

Alexander the Great (356–323 BCE) debates with **Socrates** (ca. 470–399 BCE), who makes his points by enumerating them on his fingers.

Heraclitus (ca. 535–475 BCE), the brooding Greek philosopher who despaired at human folly, wears stonecutter's boots and is actually a portrait of **Michelangelo.**

Diogenes the Cynic (ca. 412–323 BCE), who roamed the streets of Athens looking for an honest man, hated worldly possessions, and lived in a barrel.

Euclid (3rd century BCE), whose *Elements* remained the standard geometry text down to modern times, is actually a portrait of **Bramante**.

Ptolemy, the second-century astronomer and philosopher, holds a terrestrial globe, while **Zoroaster** (ca. 628–551 BCE) faces him holding a celestial globe. Both turn toward a young man who looks directly out at us. This is a self-portrait of **Raphael**.

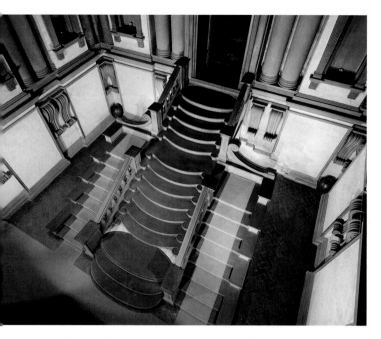

Fig. 7.30 Michelangelo, Laurentian Library staircase. Designed beginning 1524, completed 1559. San Lorenzo, Florence. In *On Architecture*, Alberti advised that interior staircases occupy as little room as possible. Michelangelo ignored his recommendation, asserting his independence from the strictures of tradition.

In Florence, Clement was more successful in his patronage efforts, especially at San Lorenzo. In 1523, he commissioned Michelangelo to build a library complex over the preexisting cloister, even as he was at work on the New Sacristy. The Laurentian [law-REN-chen] Library was designed to house the enormous book collection of the Medici family and serve as a place of quiet refuge and study. Michelangelo's most original contribution to the library is the large triple stairway leading from the vestibule to the library reading room a story above (Fig. **7.30**). The central flight is composed of three oval steps at the bottom and one at the top, with segments of ovals ending in scrolls in between. Two rectangular flights flank the central staircase and separate it from them by wide banisters. These side flights have no outside banister and end at a square that turns into the central stairs about two-thirds of the way up, a turning emphasized by broad scrolls that rise up to the central banisters. The trapezoidal form of the staircase creates a perspective rise to the doorway into the library, which is flanked by pairs of heavy Tuscan columns. These columns continue around the room, placed in niches as if they were sculptures in their own right.

The overall effect is more sculptural than architectural, and in its combination of classical and nonclassical forms— for instance, Tuscan columns juxtaposed with oval stairs, and rigid horizontals and verticals juxtaposed with sensuous scrolls—it announces a new architectural freedom undoubtedly related to the freedom of movement in paintings such as the *Libyan Sibyl* (see Fig. 7.28) in the Sistine Chapel.

Michelangelo once described this project as "a certain stair that comes back to my mind as in a dream," and its cascading waterfall effect, filling the space of the vestibule as no other stair had done before, certainly suggests that Michelangelo was becoming increasingly interested in exploring realms of the imagination beyond the humanist vision of a rational world governed by structural logic.

Josquin des Prez and the Sistine Chapel Choir

The inventiveness that marks the patronage of Isabella d'Este and the Medici popes and cardinals as well as the work of Raphael, Leonardo, and Michelangelo was a quality shared by Renaissance musicians, especially in the virtuosity of their performances. Such originality was the hallmark of the Sistine Chapel Choir, founded in 1473 by Sixtus IV. It performed only on occasions when the pope was present and typically consisted of between 16 and 24 male singers. The choir's repertory was limited to the polyphonic forms common to the liturgy: motets, masses, and psalm settings. These were arranged in four parts (voices), for boy sopranos, male altos, tenors, and basses. The choir usually sang without instrumental accompaniment, *a cappella*, "in the manner of the chapel," an unusual practice at the time, since most chapel choirs relied on at least organ accompaniment.

Composers from all over Europe were attracted to the Sistine Chapel Choir. Between 1489 and 1495, one of the principal members of the choir was the Franco-Flemish composer Josquin des Prez [JOSS-kin day PRAY] (ca. 1450–1521). Afterward, beginning in about 1503, he served as musical director of the chapel at the court of Ferrara. During his lifetime, he wrote some 18 masses, almost 100 motets (see chapter 6 and the discussion of Guillaume Dufay earlier in this chapter), and some 70 songs, including three Italian *frottole*.

Josquin's last mass, the *Pange lingua* [PAN-geh LIN-gwah] ("Sing, my tongue"), written some time after 1513, is structured by means of **paraphrase**. In paraphrase structure, all voices elaborate on an existing melody. One voice introduces a musical idea that is subsequently repeated with some variation in sequence by each of the other voices throughout the entire work or section of a work, so that all the parts are rhythmically and melodically balanced. This creates the richly polyphonic texture of the whole. This contrasts with *cantus firmus*, which, as we saw in chapter 5, is the plainchant (monophonic), "fixed melody" on which the composition is based. The source of Josquin's melody in *Pange lingua* is a very well-known plainchant hymn written in the sixth century by Venantius Fortunatus [wen-AN-see-us for-too-NAH-tus] (ca. 530–609), one of the earliest medieval poets and composers. Josquin transforms the original into a completely new composition, even as he leaves the melody entirely recognizable.

The opening *Kyrie* (Fig. **7.31**) **(CD-Track 7.2)** is based on the opening of the Fortunatus plainchant. In a technique known as **point of imitation**, this musical theme is taken up by all the voices of Josquin's polyphonic composition in succession so that all four voices weave round one another in imitation. This kind of innovative play upon a more or less standard theme is testimony to Josquin's ingenuity and humanist individualism. And it brings a level of expressiveness to the liturgy that far exceeds the more or less unemotional character of the plainchant. Largely because of this expressiveness, his compositions were among the first polyphonic works to be widely performed long after the death of their composer.

Niccolò Machiavelli and the Perfect Prince

If Josquin des Prez represents the inventiveness of the Renaissance individual to remake musical tradition, the political philosopher Niccolò Machiavelli (1469–1527) represents the individual's capacity to ignore tradition altogether and follow the dictates of pragmatic self-interest. Machiavelli's treatise *The Prince* (1513) is part of a long tradition of literature giving advice to rulers that stretches back to the Middle Ages. But Machiavelli's revolutionary political pragmatism sets the work apart. Humanist education had been founded on the principle that it alone prepared people for a life of virtuous action. Machiavelli's *Prince* challenged that assumption.

Machiavelli had served the Florentine city-state for years, assuming the post of second chancellor of the Republic in 1498. He had studied the behavior of ancient Roman rulers and citizens at great length, and he admired particularly their willingness to act in defense of their country. On the other hand, he disdained the squabbling and feuding that marked Italian internal relations in his own day. Assessing the situation in the Italian politics of his day, he concluded that only the strongest, most ruthless leader could impose order on the Italian people.

From Machiavelli's point of view, the chief virtue any leader should display is that of ethical pragmatism. For the statesman's first duty, he believed, was to preserve his country and its institutions, regardless of the means he used. Thus, a prince's chief preoccupation, and his primary duty, says Machiavelli, is to wage war (**Reading 7.5a**):

READING 7.5a **from Niccolò Machiavelli, *The Prince*, Chapter 14 (1513)**

A Prince . . . should have no care or thought but for war, and for the regulations and training it requires, and should apply himself exclusively to this as his peculiar province; for war is the sole art looked for in one who rules and is of such efficacy that it not merely maintains those who are born Princes, but often enables men to rise to that eminence from a private station; while, on the other hand, we often see that when Princes devote themselves rather to pleasure than to arms, they lose their dominions.

His attention turned to war, the prince must be willing to sacrifice moral right for practical gain, for "the manner in which we live, and that in which we ought to live, are things so wide asunder, that he who quits the one to betake himself to the other is more likely to destroy than to save himself." Therefore, "it is essential . . . for a Prince who desires to maintain his position, to have learned how to be other than good." Goodness, from Machiavelli's point of view, is a relative quality anyway. A prince, he says, "need never hesitate . . . to incur the reproach of those vices without which his authority can hardly be preserved; for if he well consider the whole matter, he will find that there may be a line of conduct having the appearance of virtue, to follow which would be his ruin, and that there may be another course having the appearance of vice, by following which his safety and well-being are secured." The well-being of the prince, in other words, is of the utmost importance because upon it rests the well-being of the state.

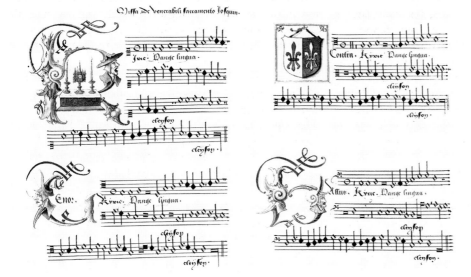

Fig. 7.31 Score for the opening bars of Josquin des Prez's *Pange Lingua* Mass.
16th century. The four voices of the mass are represented here, each one indicated by the decorative capital at the beginning of the line.

Machiavelli further argues that the prince, once engaged in war, has three alternatives for controlling a state once he has conquered it: He can devastate it, live in it, or allow it to keep its own laws. Machiavelli recommends the first of these choices, especially if the prince defeats a republic (**Reading 7.5b**):

READING 7.5b **from Niccolò Machiavelli,** ***The Prince*, Chapter 5 (1513)**

In republics there is a stronger vitality, a fiercer hatred, a keener thirst for revenge. The memory of their former freedom will not let them rest; so that the safest course is either to destroy them, or to go and live in them.

This is probably a warning directed at the absentee Medici popes, far away in Rome and not tending to business in Florence, for Machiavelli originally planned to dedicate the book to Giuliano de' Medici, by then Pope Leo X. (He eventually dedicated it to Lorenzo de' Medici, then Duke of Florence, hoping to secure political favor.) Its lessons, drawn from Roman history, were intended as a guide to aid Italy in rebuffing the French invasions.

Finally, according to Machiavelli, the prince should be feared, not loved, for "Men are less careful how they offend him who makes himself loved than him who makes himself feared." This is because "love is held by the tie of obligation, which, because men are a sorry breed, is broken on every whisper of private interest; but fear is bound by the apprehension of punishment which never relaxes."

From Machiavelli's point of view, humans are "fickle," "dishonest," "simple," and, as he says here, all in all a "sorry breed." The state must be governed, therefore, by a morality different than that governing the individual. Such moral and

ethical pragmatism was wholly at odds with the teachings of the Church. In 1512, Pope Julius II's troops overran the Florentine republic, restored the Medici to power in Florence, and dismissed Machiavelli from his post as second chancellor. Machiavelli was then (wrongfully) accused of involvement in a plot to overthrow the new heads of state, imprisoned, tortured, and finally exiled permanently to a country home in the hills above Florence. It is here, beginning in 1513, that he wrote *The Prince*.

Although widely circulated, *The Prince* was too much at odds with the norms of Christian morality to be well received in the sixteenth century. Throughout the seventeenth and eighteenth centuries, it was more often condemned than praised, particularly because it appeared to be a defense of absolute monarchy. Today we value *The Prince* as a pioneering text in political science. As an essay on political power, it provides a rationalization for political expediency and duplicity that society has all too often witnessed in modern political history.

The High Renaissance in Venice

In a mid-fifteenth-century painting by Vittore Carpaccio [vee-TOR-eh car-PAH-choh] (1450–1525) of Saint Mark's lion (Fig. **7.32**), symbol of the Venetian Republic, the lion stands with its front paws on land and its rear paws on the sea, symbolizing the importance of both elements to the city. In the sixth or seventh century, invading Lombards from the north had forced the local populations of the Po river delta to flee to the swampy lagoon islands that would later become the city of Venice. Ever since, trade had been the lifeblood of Venice.

Not only did the city possess the natural fortification of being surrounded on all sides by water, but, as a larger city-state, it also controlled the entire floodplain north of the Po

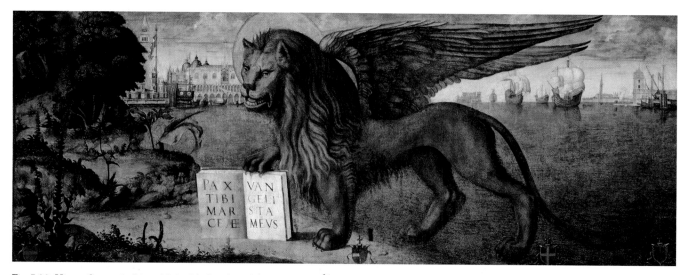

Fig. 7.32 Vittore Carpaccio, ***Lion of Saint Mark*. 1516.** Oil on canvas, 4′6¾″ × 12′1″. Doge's Apartments, Doge's Palace, Venice. Venetians believed that an angel visited Saint Mark and prophesied that he would be buried in Venice, on the very spot where Saint Mark's Cathedral stands. So they felt justified in removing his relics from Egypt and bringing them to Venice.

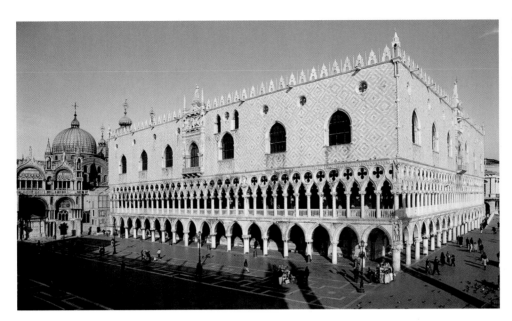

Fig. 7.33 View of the Doge's Palace, Venice, with Saint Mark's Cathedral to the left. Elaborating on the Gothic style, Venetian art was possessed by a fascination with texture that developed with a love of all the sensuous possibilities of expression.

River, including the cities of Padua and Verona and extending eastward nearly to Milan (Map **7.2**). This larger territory was called *Terraferma* (from the Latin *terra firma*, "firm ground"), to distinguish it from the watery canals and islands of the city proper. From *Terraferma*, the Venetians established trade routes across the Alps to the north, and eastward across Asia Minor, Persia, and the Caucasus. As one Venetian historian put it in a thirteenth-century history of the city: "Merchandise passes through this noble city as water flows through fountains." By the fifteenth century, the city had become a center of fashion. In 1423 the doge observed, "Now we have invested in our silk industry a capital of 10 million ducats [roughly $39 million today] and we make 2 million [roughly $7.8 million] annually in export trade; 16,000 weavers live in our city." These weavers produced satins, velvets, and brocades that were in demand across the continent. On this tide of merchandise flowed even greater wealth. As a result, the city became a great naval power and a preeminent center of shipbuilding, able to protect and contribute to its maritime resources as no other European city (except possibly Genoa) could even imagine.

Venice considered itself blessed by Saint Mark, whose relics resided in the cathedral of Saint Mark's. Protected by its patron saint, the city could prosper in peace. "Peace unto you, Mark my evangelist," reads the Latin inscription in the book the lion holds with its right paw in Carpaccio's painting. Behind the lion, visible across the lagoon, is the Piazza San Marco (Saint Mark's Square), with its tall campanile, or bell tower, the domes of Saint Mark's, and the Palace of the Doge [dohj], the Venetian Republic's leader, whom they elected for life. In almost every other Italian city, church and state were physically separated, but in Venice the political and religious centers of the city stood side by side. Peace, prosperity, and unity of purpose were the city's greatest assets—and the citizens of Venice believed, above all, in those principles.

Venetian Architecture

During the Renaissance, an elaborate, sensuous style of architecture would develop in Venice, influenced by the elaborate Gothic style of the facades of buildings such as the Doge's Palace, which was begun in 1340 (Fig. **7.33**). There is no hint, in this building, of any need to create a defensible space to protect the state. Two stories of open arcades, rising in pointed arches and topped by open quatrefoils, provide covered walkways aound the outside, as if to invite the citizenry into its halls. The diamond pattern of the stonework in the upper stories creates a sense of lightness to what might otherwise seem a massive facade. And the colors of the ornament and stone—white and pink—seem calculated to reflect light

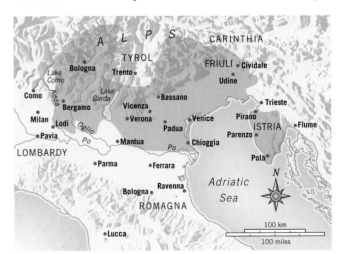

Map 7.2 Venice and the Venetian *Terraferma*, the Venetian-controlled mainland, at the end of the fifteenth century. Venice controlled all the land in the rose-colored areas. Its territories extend almost to Milan in the west, northward into the Alps, and almost as far as Ferrara and Mantua to the south. The causeway connecting Venice to the mainland was constructed in the middle of the nineteenth century. Until then, the city was approachable only by water.

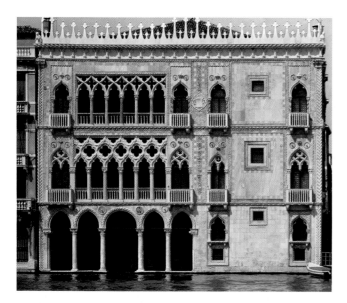

Fig. 7.34 Giovanni and Bartolomeo Bon, the Ca' d'Oro ("House of Gold"), Contarini Palace, Venice. 1421–1437. The Ca' d'Oro, built for one of Venice's most prominent families, is still spectacular today. We can only imagine how it must have looked with its original gilded ornamental detail. The attic, where servants lived, is not visible in this view.

painted with very expensive ultramarine blue, made of ground lapis lazuli, an imported semiprecious stone.

The Contarini finished the Ca' d'Oro just seven years before Cosimo de' Medici began the Medici Palace in Florence (see Fig. 7.12), but nothing could be more distant in feeling and taste. Contarini's palace, with its airy traceries and ornamentation, is light and refined; Cosimo's palace, with its monumental facade, is massive—a wall of stone. One opens to the canal; the other turns inward away from the street. The Ca' d'Oro is an ostentatious celebration of personal wealth and social status; the Medici palace projects state authority and power.

Masters of the Venetian High Renaissance: Giorgione and Titian

The two great masters of painting in the Venetian High Renaissance were Giorgione da Castelfranco, known simply as Giorgione [jor-JOH-neh] (ca. 1478–1510), and Tiziano Vecelli, known as Titian [TISH-un] (ca. 1489–1576). Giorgione had been especially inspired when Leonardo visited the city in 1500. In the first decade of the sixteenth century, they worked sometimes side by side, gaining increased control of their surfaces, building up color by means of glazing, as Leonardo did in his soft, luminous landscapes. Their paintings, like the great palaces of Venice whose reflections shimmered on the Grand Canal, demonstrate an exquisite sensitivity to the play of light and shadow, to the luxurious display of detail and design, and to an opulent variety of pattern and texture.

Giorgione The mysterious qualities of Leonardo's highly charged atmospheric paintings like the *Mona Lisa* (see Fig. 7.17) are fully realized in Giorgione's *Tempest* (Fig. **7.35**). The first known mention of the painting dates from 1530, when the painting surfaced in the collection of a Venetian patrician. We know almost nothing else about it, which contributes to its mystery. At the right, an almost nude young woman nurses her child. At the left, a somewhat disheveled young man, wearing the costume of a German mercenary soldier, gazes at the woman and child with evident pride. Between them, in the foreground, stands a pediment topped by two broken columns. A creaky wooden bridge crosses the estuary in the middle ground, and lightning flashes in the distance, illuminating a densely built cityscape.

Giorgione evidently began work on his paintings without preliminary drawings, and X-ray examination of this one reveals that in the young man's place there originally stood a second young woman stepping into the pool between the two figures. At the time that the work surfaced in a wealthy Venetian's collection in 1530, it was described simply as a small landscape with a soldier and a gypsy. It seems to have satisfied the Venetian taste for depictions of the affairs of everyday life, and even though its subject remains obscure, the painting continues to fascinate us.

Giorgione did not make preliminary drawings for his paintings, which led Vasari, in his *Lives of the Most Excellent Painters, Architects, and Sculptors,* to charge that he was simply hiding his inability to draw well beneath a virtuoso display of surface color and

itself, so that the building might shine like a gemstone set in the public square, literally a reflection of the city's wealth and well-being. The building's emphasis on texture and the play of light and shadow across richly elaborated surfaces would become one of the hallmarks of Venetian art and architecture.

The wealth and general well-being of Venice were evident along the city's main, curving thoroughfare, the Grand Canal, where its most important families built their homes. One of the most magnificent of these is the Ca' d'Oro (Fig. **7.34**), built by the head of the Contarini family. (*Ca'* is a Venetian abbreviation of *casa,* "house," and Ca' d'Oro means "House of Gold.") Although built in the Renaissance, the house, like the Doge's Palace, is distinctly Gothic in character. Venetian palazzi and civic architecture retained Gothic elements for so long probably because the citizens regarded their continued use as a sign of the stability of the city's culture.

The asymmetry of the Ca' d'Oro facade, with its three distinct loggias, or arcades, is characteristic of the design of other moderate-sized Venetian palazzi. Originally, Contarini ordered that the stone carved for the tracery work be painted with white lead and oil to make it shine like marble. The red Verona marble used in the detailing was oiled and varnished to bring out its deepest and richest hues. The balls atop the facade's parapet, the rosettes at the bottom of the arches, the leaves on the capitals at the corners, the architectural moldings, window finials, and the roundels over the windows and the portico arches, were all gilded—giving the house its name. Finally, the backgrounds of the capitals, and other details, were

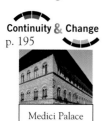

Continuity & Change
p. 195

Medici Palace

light. The shortcoming of all Venetian artists, Vasari claimed, was their sensuous painterly technique, as opposed to the intellectual pursuits of the Florentines, epitomized by their careful use of scientific perspective and linear clarity.

In a certain sense, Vasari was right. Sensuality, even outright sexuality, would become a primary subject of Venetian art. Giorgione's *Pastoral Concert* (Fig. **7.36**), sometimes attributed to Titian, who early in his career often collaborated with Giorgione, offers a different picture of love. Here men and women sit together in a countryside setting. The men are fully clothed, one in the costume of a Venetian nobleman, the other barefoot and in peasant garb; the women are nude. A shepherd passes by in the near distance with his flock. In the far distance is a country estate. The nobleman plays a lute while the seated nude woman with her back to us plays a flute. If we take these instruments as metaphors for parts of male and female anatomy, a usage common in both the art and literature of the period, the sexual implications become clear. However, the meaning of the activity of the woman at the left, pouring water into rather than drawing water out of the well, is somewhat enigmatic. Perhaps it has to do with the life-giving essence of water.

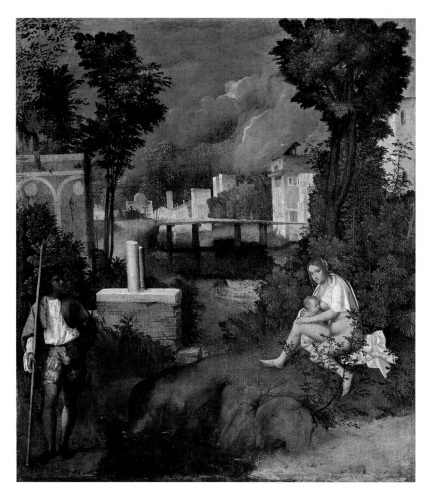

Fig. 7.35 Giorgione, *Tempest.* ca. 1509. Oil on canvas, 31 1/4″ × 28 3/4″. Gallerie dell'Accademia, Venice. There is nothing about this painting that could be called controlled. The landscape is overgrown and weedy—just as the man and woman are disheveled and disrobed. It is as if, for a moment, the lightning has revealed to the viewer a scene not meant to be witnessed.

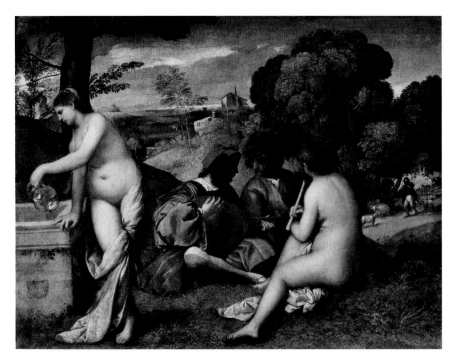

Fig. 7.36 Giorgione, *Pastoral Concert (Fête Champêtre).* ca. 1510. Oil on canvas, 43 1/4″ × 54 3/8″. Musée du Louvre, Paris. The narrative of the image is purposefully mysterious, giving the viewer's imagination the freedom to play.

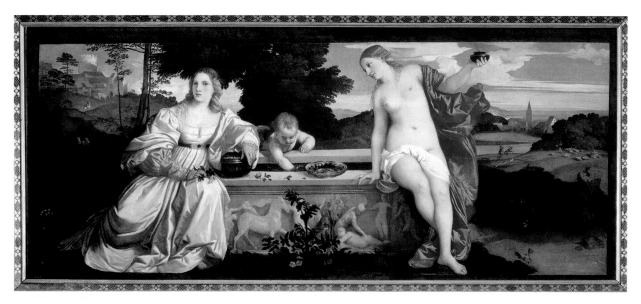

Fig. 7.37 Titian, *Sacred and Profane Love*. ca. 1514. Oil on canvas, $46\frac{1}{2}'' \times 109\frac{7}{8}''$. Galleria Borghese, Rome. The painting was commissioned by Niccolò Aurelio, a Venetian, to celebrate his marriage to Laura Bagarotto and was probably intended for the couple's sleeping chamber. The husband's coat of arms is carved on the fountain; the wife's is inside the silver bowl on the fountain's ledge.

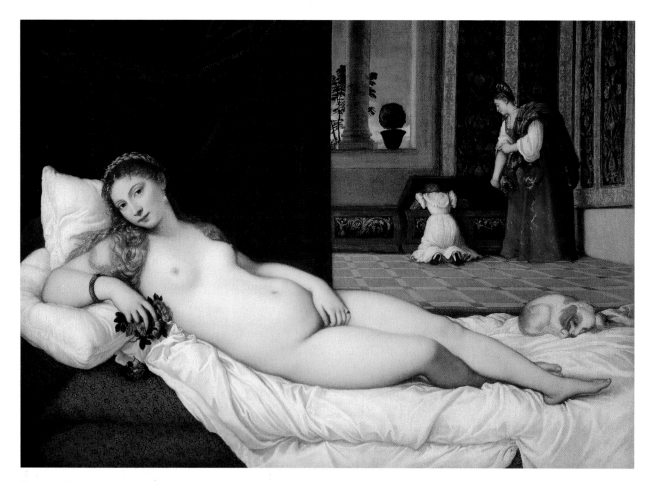

Fig. 7.38 Titian, *Reclining Nude (Venus of Urbino)*. ca. 1538. Oil on canvas, $47'' \times 65''$. Galleria degli Uffizi, Florence. Titian's technique contributes significantly to the power of the painting. Although not visible in reproduction, the nude's skin is built up of layers of semitransparent yellow-whites and pinks that contrast to the cooler bluish whites of the bedsheets. Behind her, the almost black panel and curtain further contrast with the luminous light on her body. She seems literally "alight."

The *Pastoral Concert* is a harmony of oppositions: not just male and female, but the clothed and the nude, the nobleman and the peasant, court music and folk song, city and country, and so on. What unites the diverse figures is the natural setting in which they find themselves and the uniform glow of light that bathes them all. There is nothing documentary about this scene—except perhaps the realistic portrayal of the women's bodies, which are voluptuously rounded and fleshy. Rather, Giorgione presents us with a dream world, a representation destined for the study of a humanist nobleman who could contemplate the possibilities offered up by the scene as if it were an erotic poem by Ovid.

Titian Giorgione died of the plague in 1510, at only 32 years of age. It seems likely that his friend Titian, 10 years younger, finished several of Giorgione's paintings. Certainly they share the same sensibility.

In Titian's *Sacred and Profane Love* (Fig. **7.37**), the nude figure at the right and the well at the center clearly echo Giorgione's *Pastoral Concert*. The nude holds a lamp, perhaps symbolizing divine light and connecting her to the Neoplatonic ideal of the celestial Venus and thus sacred love. The luxuriously clothed, fully dressed figure on the left, whom we might think of as the "*earthly* lady," or profane love, holds a bouquet of flowers, a symbol of her fecundity. Between the two, Cupid reaches into the fountain.

The painting was a commission from Niccolò Aurelio [oh-RAY-lee-oh] on the occasion of his marriage to Laura Bagarotto in 1514. Behind the clothed figure on the left, two rabbits cavort in the grass, underscoring the conjugal theme of the image. It seems probable that the two female figures represent two aspects of the same woman, and thus embody the limited range of roles that the Renaissance woman filled for her humanist husband, combining classical learning and intelligence with a candid celebration of sexual love in marriage.

Titian's *Venus of Urbino* (Fig. **7.38**), painted for Duke Guidobaldo della Rovere of Urbino in 1538, more fully acknowledges the sexual obligations of most Renaissance women. This "Venus"—more a real woman than an ethereal goddess, and referred to by Guidobaldo as merely a "nude woman"—is frankly available. She stares out at the viewer, Guidobaldo himself, with matter-of-factness suggesting she is totally comfortable with her nudity. (Apparently the lady-in-waiting and maid at the rear of the palatial rooms are searching for suitably fine clothing in which to dress her.) Her hand both covers and draws attention to her genitals. Her dog, a traditional symbol of both fidelity and lust, sleeps lazily on the white sheets at her feet. She may be, ambiguously, either a courtesan or a bride. (The chest from which the servant is removing clothes is a traditional reference to marriage.) In either case she is, primarily, an object of desire.

As Titian's work continued to develop through the 1550s, 1560s, and 1570s, his brushwork became increasingly loose and gestural. The frank sensuality conveyed by crisp contours in *Sacred and Profane Love* and the *Venus of Urbino* found expression, instead, in the artist's handling of paint itself. In *The Rape of Europa*, Jupiter has assumed the form of a bull to abduct the nymph Europa as she adorns its horns with flowers (Fig. **7.39**). It is as if Titian's brushwork is designed to convey the sensuality of his own touch. Indeed, the viewer can feel Titian's very hand in these later works, for he would actually paint with his fingers and the stick end of his brush too. But Titian's mastery of color—the rich varieties of warm reds, the luminosity of his glazes—so evident in all his paintings, never altered. In fact, his color came to define the art of Venice itself. When people speak of "Venetian" color, they have Titian in mind.

The Literary Courtesan in Venice

Among the city's most educated citizens were its courtesans. "Thou wilt find the Venetian Courtezan a good Rhetorician and an elegant discourser," wrote one early seventeenth-century visitor to the city. These intellectual women were labeled "honest courtesans," and although subject to the usual public ridicule—and often blamed, together with the city's Jews, for any troubles that might befall the republic—they were known for their ability to be both sexual and intellectual. This group of courtesans dominated the Venetian literary scene. Many of their poems transform the clichés of courtly love poetry into frankly erotic metaphors.

Among the most remarkable Venetian courtesans was Veronica Franco (1546–1591), who published two volumes of poetry: *Terze rime* [TER-tseh REE-meh] (1575), named after the plural of the Italian poetic form first introduced by Dante (see chapter 6), and *Homely Letters to Diverse People* (1580). She also collected the works of other leading writers in respected anthologies and founded and funded a charity for courtesans and their children.

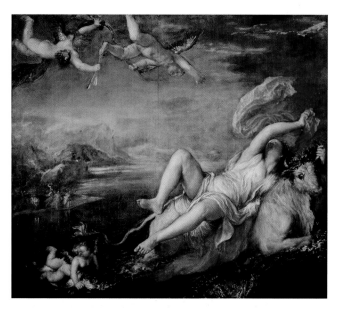

Fig. 7.39 Titian, *The Rape of Europa*. 1559–1562. Oil on canvas, 5' 9¼" × 7' 8¼". © Isabella Stewart Gardner Museum, Boston, MA.
On the distant shore, Europa's maidservants gesture in vain at her abduction.

Franco first gained notoriety in the 1570s at a renowned Venetian literary salon where male and female poets read and exchanged their works. Her poetry celebrates her sexual expertise as a courtesan and, in the slightly veiled imagery of the courtly tradition, promises to satisfy her interlocutor's desires. Consider *Capitolo* 13, in which she playfully challenges a lover to a "duel" (**Reading 7.6**):

READING 7.6 **from Veronica Franco,** ***Terze Rime, Capitolo* 13**

No more words! To deeds, to the battlefield, to arms!
For, resolved to die, I want to free myself
from such merciless mistreatment.
Should I call this a challenge? I do not know,
since I am responding to a provocation;
but why should we duel over words?
If you like, I will say that you challenged me;
if not, I challenge you; I'll take any route,
and any opportunity suits me equally well.
Yours be the choice of place or of arms,
and I will make whatever choice remains;
rather, let both be your decision. . . .

Come here, and, full of most wicked desire,
braced stiff for your sinister task,
bring with daring hand a piercing blade.
Whatever weapon you hand over to me,
I will gladly take, especially if it is sharp
and sturdy and also quick to wound.
Let all armor be stripped from your naked breast,
so that, unshielded and exposed to blows,
it may reveal the valor it harbors within.
Let no one else intervene in this match,
let it be limited to the two of us alone,
behind closed doors, with all seconds sent away. . . .

To take revenge for your unfair attack,
I'd fall upon you, and in daring combat,
as you too caught fire defending yourself,
I would die with you, felled by the same blow.
O empty hopes, over which cruel fate
forces me to weep forever!
But hold firm, my strong, undaunted heart,
and with that felon's final destruction,
avenge your thousand deaths with his one.
Then end your agony with the same blade. . . .

Here Franco transforms the language of chivalric knighthood into the banter of the bedroom in a masterful use of **double entendre** [ahn-TAHN-druh], a figure of speech in which a phrase can be understood in either of two ways. This duality, the simultaneous expression of intellectual wit and

erotic sensuality, is fundamental to the Venetian style. (Recall the multiple meanings of the instruments in Giorgione's *Pastoral Concert*.)

Music in the Venetian High Renaissance

Almost without exception, women of literary accomplishment in the Renaissance were musically accomplished as well. Isabella d'Este [DES-teh] (1474–1539), duchess of Mantua, a ducal city-state in the Po river valley between Venice and Milan, played both the lute and the *lira da braccio*, the precursor to the modern violin (Fig. **7.40**). Through her patronage, she and her sister-in-law Lucrezia Borgia, duchess of Ferrara, competed for musicians and encouraged the cultivation of the *frottola*, discussed earlier. Courtesans such as Veronica Franco could both sing and play. And both Isabella and Elisabetta Gonzaga, duchess of Urbino, were well known for their ability to improvise songs. By the last decades of the sixteenth century, we know that women were composing music as well. The most famous of these was the Venetian Madalena Casulana [mah-dah-LAY-nah kah-soo-LAH-nah].

Madalena Casulana's Madrigals Madalena Casulana was the first professional woman composer to see her own compositions in print. In 1566, her anthology entitled *The Desire* was published in Venice. Two years later, she dedicated her first book of songs to Isabella de' Medici Orsina with these words: "I would like . . . to show the world . . . the vain error of men, who so much believe themselves to be the masters of the highest gifts of the intellect, that they think those gifts cannot be shared equally by a woman."

Casulana's known work consists almost entirely of madrigals. The **madrigal** [MAD-rih-gul] is a secular vocal composition for three or more voices. It became popular throughout Italy in the sixteenth century, where it dominated secular music. Whereas the *frottola* uses the same music for each successive stanza, the madrigal is **through-composed**—that is, each line of text is set to new music. This allows for **word painting**, where the musical elements imitate the meaning of the text in mood or action. Anguish, for example, is conveyed with an unusually low pitch, as in Casulana's *Morir non può il mio cuore* [moh-REER nohn pwo eel MEE-oh KWOR-eh] ("My Heart Cannot Die") (**CD-Track 7.3**). The song laments a relationship gone bad, and the narrator contemplates driving a stake through her heart because it is in so much pain. When she says that her suicide might kill her beloved—*so che morreste voi* [so keh mor-EH-stay VOY] ("I know that you would die")—the word painting by rising progression of the melody suggests that, for her, his death might not be such a bad thing.

The ladies of the courts of Mantua and Ferrara were especially well known for their vocal accomplishments. At Ferrara, the "Ensemble of Ladies" attracted many of the most prominent madrigal composers of the day. But even when such ensembles were not available, madrigals and other songs could be performed by a single voice, accompanied by, perhaps, a flute and a lute. The words themselves were of paramount importance, however the music was performed.

Adrian Willaert's Innovations for Polyphonic Form

Without question, the figure most responsible for the popularity of the madrigal form in sixteenth-century Venice was Adrian Willaert [VIL-ahrt] (1490–1562), a Netherlander who was appointed to the highest musical position in Venice in 1527, choirmaster of Saint Mark's. By the time he accepted the position, he had already been a leading figure at the court of Ferrara for over a decade. He brought to his new position a deeply felt humanist spirit, one dedicated to innovation and originality even as it acknowledged the great achievements of the past. Willaert's chief interest was polyphonic music such as the motet and the madrigal. To both of these forms he brought radical new ideas, as exemplified in the corpus of 27 motets and 25 madrigals for between four and seven voices called *New Music*, published in 1559, but probably written for the most part between the late 1530s and mid-1540s.

The madrigals of the *New Music* departed from all

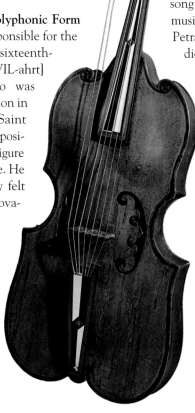

Fig. 7.40 *Lira da braccio.* Like the violin, the five strings over the fingerboard of the lira da braccio were played with a bow, but, unlike the violin, the two strings on the instrument's bass side were plucked by the player's left thumb.

previous ones by consistently setting complete sonnets—all but one of them by Petrarch (see chapter 6)—in the form of the motet and by adapting a dense counterpoint formerly reserved for sacred music. Willaert's chief aim was to present Petrarch's words with as much clarity and restraint as possible. His choice of the Petrarchan sonnet, with its sense of *gravitas*, as the source of his lyrics was most likely driven by a desire to raise secular song to the level of the religious motet. Both were, at least musically, of equal weight and importance. And although Petrarch's sonnets spoke of worldly love, they most often did so as metaphor for spiritual love.

Willaert's love of polyphonic forms led to other innovations as well. At Saint Mark's he regularly used two choirs—sometimes more—to create a **polychoral style** in which choirs on either side of the church sang to and against each other in increasingly complicated forms that anticipate by over four centuries the effects of stereophonic music. This arrangement drew notice after the publication in 1550 of his *Salmi spezzati* [SAHL-mee spayt-TSAH-tee] (literally "broken psalms," but a reference to alternating choirs). He also added new instrumental forms to the liturgy, including an organ **intonazione** [een-toh-naht-tsee-OH-nay] (short prelude) and a virtuoso prelude, also for organ, called the **toccata** [toh-KAH-tah] (from the Italian *toccare*, "to touch"), designed to feature both the range of the instrument and the manual dexterity of the performer. Both were soon widely emulated across Europe. The richness of musical experience in Willaert's Venice, then, was not unlike the richness of its painting—full of light and emotion, as words found their emotional equivalent in sound.

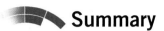

Summary

■ **The State as a Work of Art** Florence was the center of a more than 150-year-long cultural revival in Europe that we have come to call the Renaissance, a "rebirth" of classical values that amounted to a revolution in human consciousness. From 1418 to 1494, the Medici family ruled Florence. They built upon a tradition of civic patronage that is exemplified in the Baptistery Doors competition of 1401, the two finalists of which were Filippo Brunelleschi and Lorenzo Ghiberti. Brunelleschi was the first Renaissance artist to master the art of scientific perspective. His findings were codified in 1435 by the architect Leon Battista Alberti in his treatise *Della pittura* [DEL-lah pee-TOO-rah] (On Painting). Scientific perspective informs Ghiberti's panels for the *Gates of Paradise*, as well as works by the painter Masaccio. Both Masaccio and Donatello turned to classical sources to create highly realistic human figures, and Donatello's *David* is the first life-size freestanding male nude sculpted since antiquity.

Medici control of Florentine politics was secured by Cosimo de' Medici, who surrounded himself with humanists, championing especially the translations and interpretations of the works of Plato by Marsilio Ficino. Ficino's Neoplatonist philosophy recast Platonic thought in contemporary terms. Cosimo's grandson, Lorenzo, "the Magnificent," continued the Medici tradition. His own circle of acquaintances included many of the greatest minds of the day, including Michelangelo, the painter Botticelli, the composer Heinrich Isaac, and the philosopher Pico della Mirandola.

■ **Beyond Florence: The Ducal Courts and the Arts** Lorenzo's court inspired the courts of the leaders of other Italian city-states, the leaders of which were almost all nobility. At Urbino, Baldassare Castiglione wrote *The Book of the Courtier*, his treatise on the nature of courtly life and what it takes to become a well-rounded person, *l'uomo universale*. In Milan, Ludovico Sforza commissioned Leonardo da Vinci to paint the *Last Supper* for the Dominican monastery of Santa Maria delle Grazie.

■ **From Florence to Rome: The High Renaissance** Until 1527, when German mercenaries in the employ of the Holy Roman Emperor Charles V sacked the city, the patronage of the popes and their cardinals transformed Rome. Pope Julius II commissioned Michelangelo's ceiling for the Sistine Chapel, Bramante's Tempietto and his new basilica for Saint Peter's, and Raphael's frescoes for the Stanza della Segnatura. Composer Josquin des Prez shared the inventiveness of the humanist artists in the papal court, composing many polyphonic works for the Sistine Chapel Choir. Florentine statesman Niccolò Machiavelli argued, in *The Prince*, that the ideal ruler should follow the dictates of pragmatic self-interest.

■ **The High Renaissance in Venice** In Venice, the religious and political centers of the city—Saint Mark's Cathedral and the Doge's Palace—stood side by side, symbolizing peace, prosperity, and, above all, unity of purpose. The wealth and general well-being of Venice was displayed in its Gothic-inspired architecture. The painters Giorgione and Titian painted in a manner that lent their works an almost physical immediacy, helping to establish a sense of touch, sensuality, and even outright sexuality as primary subjects of Venetian art. The Venetian literary scene was dominated by a group of courtesans whose reputations were built upon the ability to combine sexual and intellectual pursuits. Chief among these was Veronica Franco, who in many poems transforms the clichés of courtly love poetry into frankly erotic metaphor. Madalena Casulana, the first professional woman composer to see her own compositions in print, composed madrigals, a form mastered by the choirmaster of Saint Mark's, Adrian Willaerts.

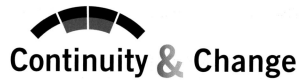
The settings of Giorgione's *Pastoral Concert* and Titian's *Sacred and Profane Love* represent an escapist tendency that we first saw in Boccaccio's *Decameron* (chapter 6). In Boccaccio's stories, a group of young men and women flee the onset of the plague in Florence, escape to the country, and for 10 days entertain each other with a series of tales, many of which are alternately ribald and erotic, moral and exemplary. Renaissance humanists considered retreats to the country to be an honored ancient Roman tradition, the pleasures of which were richly documented by such Roman poets as Horace in his *Odes* (chapter 3):

How in the country do I pass the time?
The answer to the question's brief:
I lunch and drink, I sing and play,
I wash and dine, I rest.

By the High Renaissance, wealthy Venetian families, following classical precedent, routinely escaped the heat and humidity of the city to private villas in the countryside. Andrea Palladio's [pah-LAH-dee-oh] Villa La Rotunda (Fig. **7.41**), located just outside the city of Vicenza, set the standard for the country villa. As in so much Venetian architecture, the house looks outward, toward the light of the countryside, rather than inward to the shadow of a courtyard. It is situated on the crest of a hill. On each of its four sides Palladio has placed a pedimented loggia, approached by a broad staircase, designed to take advantage of the view.

Built in the 1560s for a humanist churchman, the centralized plan of Villa Rotonda recalls Leonardo's *Vitruvian Man* (see Fig. 7.20). Palladio was, in fact, a careful student of Vitruvius, as was

Leonardo. It is not surprising, then, that the central dome of La Rotunda is modeled after the Pantheon (see Fig. 3.18), which was itself known in the sixteenth century as La Rotunda, as was any large, domed circular room. Although lacking the Pantheon's coffered ceiling and size, Palladio's villa was originally distinguished by a seven-foot diameter oculus, like that at the Pantheon open to the sky, but today covered by a small cupola. Directly below the oculus, a stone drain in the shape of a faun's face allowed rainwater to fall into the basement. Although Venice depended on the agricultural economy of the *Terraferma*, the Villa Rotunda was not designed to be a working farm. The house was designed for family life and entertaining.

Palladio built many villas in the vicinity of Venice. Each of them is interesting in a different way, and they constitute an important body of High Renaissance architecture that influenced architects in many countries and later centuries down to our own day. Over three hundred years after Palladio's death, Thomas Jefferson would model his own country estate at Monticello (Fig. **7.42**) after Palladio's example. Set atop a hill outside Charlottesville, Virginia, its vistas were in every way comparable to those of the Villa Rotunda. As opposed to La Rotunda, Monticello was the centerpiece of a working farm, where Jefferson continually experimented with agricultural techniques and methods. But Jefferson recognized in Palladio's use of elemental geometric forms—circle, cube, and sphere—a sense of order and harmony that seemed, from his point of view, ideal for the architecture of his new American republic. ∎

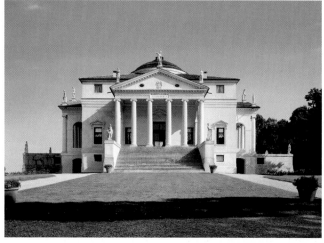

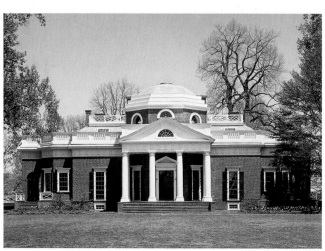

Figs. 7.41 and 7.42 (top) Andrea Palladio, Villa La Rotunda. Begun 1560s. (bottom) Thomas Jefferson, Monticello, Charlottesville, VA. 1770–1784, 1796–1806.

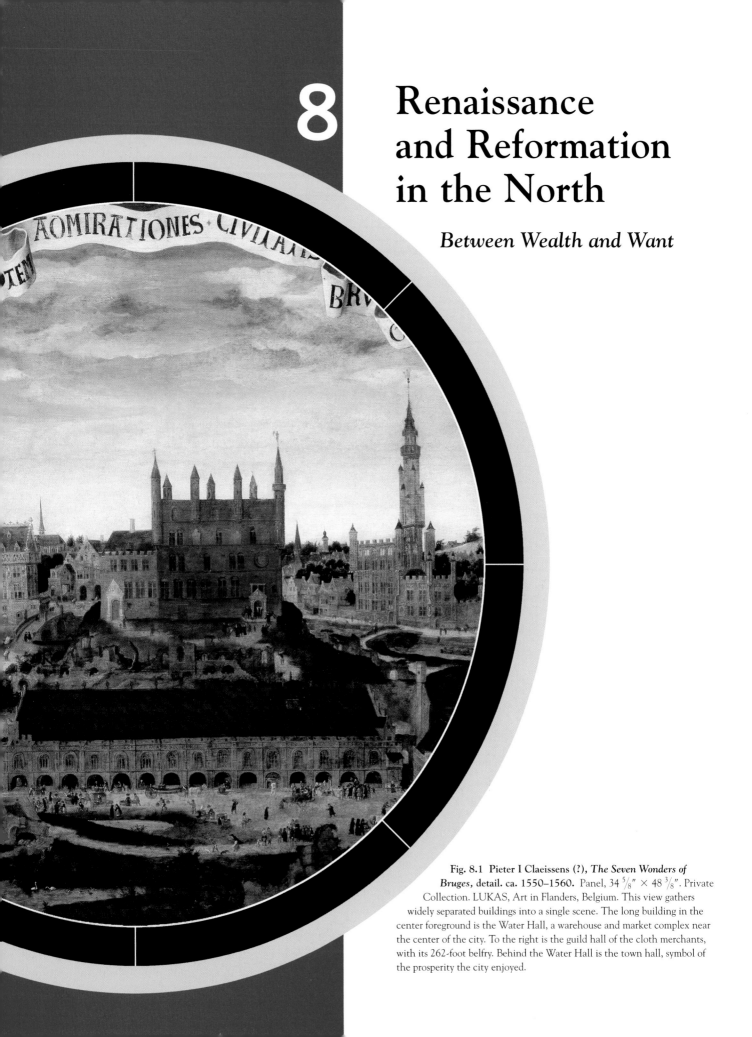

8 Renaissance and Reformation in the North

Between Wealth and Want

Fig. 8.1 Pieter I Claeissens (?), ***The Seven Wonders of Bruges,*** **detail. ca. 1550–1560.** Panel, 34 $^5/_8$″ × 48 $^3/_8$″. Private Collection. LUKAS, Art in Flanders, Belgium. This view gathers widely separated buildings into a single scene. The long building in the center foreground is the Water Hall, a warehouse and market complex near the center of the city. To the right is the guild hall of the cloth merchants, with its 262-foot belfry. Behind the Water Hall is the town hall, symbol of the prosperity the city enjoyed.

*ΚΚ Between the absolute denial of all worldly
joys and a frantic yearning for wealth and
pleasure, between dark hatred and merry
conviviality, they live in extremes.* **,,**

Johan Huizinga, *The Autumn of the Middle Ages*

Fifteenth- and sixteenth-century Italy did not hold a monopoly on the arts in Europe. To the north, the city of Bruges [broozh] was a major center of culture, rivaling the Italian city-states in both art and commerce. The financial capital of the north, the city was home to the Medici banking interests in the region and had a strong merchant class of its own. Today, Bruges is in Belgium, but in the sixteenth century it was part of Flanders. Controlled by the dukes of Burgundy, the region of Flanders encompassed modern Holland, Belgium, and Luxembourg (Map **8.1**). Although inland, its link to the North Sea gave Bruges access to other mercantile centers by a waterway, closed off at the mouth of the sea by a lock, where, in the words of one sixteenth-century report, "it is a pleasure and a marvel to behold the wild sea let in and out, as it were, through a wooden door, with artfulness and human ingenuity." The waterway terminated in the heart of the city at the Water Hall, a long warehouse where ships could load and unload goods (see Fig. **8.1**).

The city's prosperous merchant class, like the nobility, actively supported the arts. This chapter outlines the development of a commercial art market in several Northern European centers of culture like Bruges—Antwerp, Paris, and London especially—that would permanently change the nature of artistic culture in the West. A spirit of innovation dominated the arts, spurred on largely by competition in the marketplace. Civic and merchant patronage would rival that of the nobility and Church, and artistic workshops increasingly functioned as businesses. In London, audiences of all classes flocked to the south bank of the Thames River to see plays performed by theatrical companies competing for profits sufficient to support them.

But there was a darker side to the North's growing prosperity. In his classic text on the rise of the Renaissance in the North, *The Autumn of the Middle Ages*, Johan Huizinga describes the tensions that informed life in the north:

There was less relief available for misfortune and for sickness; they came in a more fearful and more painful way. Sickness contrasted more strongly with health. The cutting cold and the dreaded darkness of winter were more concrete evils. Honor and wealth were enjoyed more fervently and greedily because they contrasted still more than now with lamentable poverty. A fur-lined robe of

office, a bright fire in the oven, drink and jest, and a soft bed still possessed . . . high value for enjoyment. . . .

So intense and colorful was life that it could stand the mingling of the smell of blood and roses. Between hellish fears and the more childish jokes, between cruel harshness and sentimental sympathy the people stagger—like the giant with the head of a child, hither and thither. Between the absolute denial of all worldly joys and a frantic yearning for wealth and pleasure, between dark hatred and merry conviviality, they live in extremes.

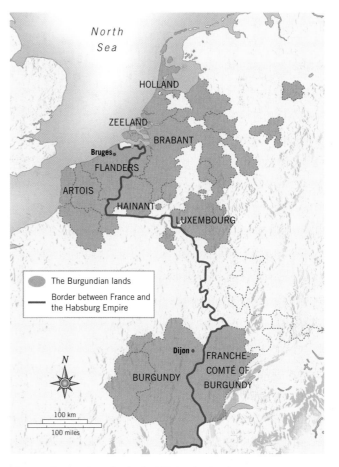

Map 8.1 Burgundy at the death of Philip the Good in 1467.

The Church itself offered little solace since it seemed to many the very center of sin and corruption. In the magnificence of the art it commissioned to glorify God, a Northerner would likely be reminded of the poverty and darkness that surrounded him. The northern imagination was, in fact, pervaded by a sense of pessimism. From a pessimist's point of view, Christ's crucifixion represented the inevitability of pain and suffering, not the promise of the glory of the afterlife. In art, this pessimism was reflected in the painstakingly rendered depictions of suffering, realized particularly in Germany. In the English theater, it manifested itself in the profound self-doubt of Shakespearean tragedy. In religion, it gave rise to so serious a questioning that the practices and doctrines of the Catholic Church were called into question, unleashing a period of social and political conflict that would last for three centuries.

Art, Commerce, and Merchant Patronage

Through the fifteenth century, the population of Bruges ranged between 40,000 and 50,000, quite large by Northern European standards. (Most cities averaged just 2,000–3,000 inhabitants, and across Northern Europe 70 percent of the population still lived in the countryside.) Wages in Bruges were the highest in Northern Europe, especially for crafts-

people, and the city took pride in providing one of the most extensive social-care networks anywhere—including 11 hospitals and hospices. Desiderius Erasmus (ca. 1466–1536), the humanist scholar from Rotterdam (now part of Holland), would compare the population of Bruges to the people of Golden Age Athens. Rome, Florence, and Venice may have been larger cities, but the richness of daily life they offered their citizens paled by comparison.

Selling Art: Bruges and Antwerp

In Bruges, painting was a major commodity, second only to cloth. The Corporation of Imagemakers produced for sale many small devotional panels, private prayer books, portraits, and town views. Each May the city of Bruges sponsored a great fair, where painters, goldsmiths, booksellers, and jewelers displayed their wares in over 180 rented stalls on the grounds of a Franciscan cloister. Especially popular, because they were relatively inexpensive, were oil paintings. The medium of oil painting had been known for several centuries, and medieval painters had used oils to decorate stone, metal, and occasionally plaster walls. As we will see, oil painting enabled artists such as Jan van Eyck [van ike] to add the kind of detail and subtle color and value gradations to their paintings that resulted in a remarkable realism. For many art historians this detailed naturalism is the most distinctive feature of Northern European art. By the sixteenth century, at any rate, Bruges printmaker Johannes Stradanus [STRAH-dah-nus] popularized the idea of van Eyck's mastery of the medium with the publication of his print, *Jan van Eyck's Studio* (Fig. **8.2**). This print shows van Eyck's Bruges studio as a factory where paintings are made as goods for consumption by a rising middle class.

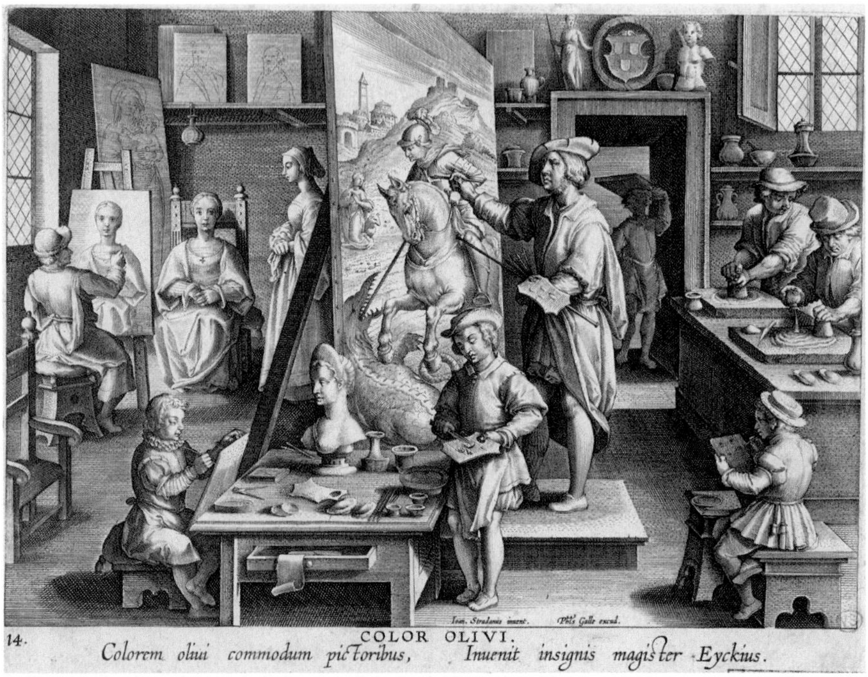

By the middle of the fifteenth century, the Flanders city of Antwerp, on the river Scheldt [skelt], had supplanted Bruges in importance. In a quirky instance of geography influencing history, silt built up in Bruges's canal system, making its harbor inaccessible to large vessels. Antwerp did not hesitate to take advantage. All artwork in Antwerp was sold at its fair. By the middle of the sixteenth century, huge quantities of art were bought and sold at the building where the fair was held, and nearly 300 painters lived nearby. In 1553 alone, Spanish and Portuguese ships left the Antwerp docks with more than 4 tons of paintings and 70,000 yards of tapestries—all purchased at the fair. And the trade in art went both ways. Art and commerce were now inextricably linked.

COLOR OLIVI.

Colorem olivi commodum pictoribus,   Inuenit insignis magister Eyckius.

Fig. 8.2 Johannes Stradanus, *Oil Painting*, or *Jan van Eyck's Studio*. Late 16th century.
8″ × 10 ½″. Stedelijke Museum, Bruges. LUKAS, Art in Flanders, Belgium. In his *Lives of the Painters*, Giorgio Vasari wrote that van Eyck had discovered oil painting. Vasari had met Stradanus, from whom he learned of van Eyck's work.

Merchant Patrons and Oil Painting in Flanders

One of the greatest differences between the Renaissance cultures of the north and south is the nature of patronage that developed in each. In the south of Europe, the most important patrons were the politically powerful families. The Medici, the Gonzagas, and the Montefeltros—and the papacy (often members of these same families)—all used their patronage to further their political prestige. In the north, trade had created a wealthy and relatively large class of merchants, who soon rivaled the French and Burgundian courts as the most important patrons of the day. Wealthy nobles, like Philip the Good of Burgundy, certainly influenced artistic developments, but gradually, the taste of the new business class came to dominate the production and distribution of works of art. This new business class represented a new audience for artists, in both the north and south. Motivated by the marketplace, artists sought to please this new class. In turn, members of the business class fostered the careers of several artists who were highly skilled in the use of oil paint. These artists, Robert Campin, Jan van Eyck, and Hieronymus Bosch, are associated with particular Northern centers of culture.

Robert Campin in Tournai The growing influence of the merchant class pervades the *Mérode [may-ROHD] Altarpiece* (Fig. 8.3), painted by the so-called Master of Flémalle

[flay-MAHL]. His real name, say many scholars, was Robert Campin (ca. 1375–1444). Campin was a member of the painters' guild and the city council in Tournai. Since the Middle Ages, this city near the southern border of Flanders was known for metalwork, jewelry, and architectural sculpture. We know little about Campin's life, but we do know that the Tournai city fathers condemned him for leading a dissolute life with his mistress. His punishment was reduced, but the story shows the moral seriousness of Northern European culture in the fifteenth century, a seriousness that would grow even greater during the later Protestant Reformation.

The *Mérode Altarpiece* is a three-part work, or **triptych** [TRIP-tik]. The left-hand panel depicts the altarpiece's patrons, Ingelbrecht of Mechlin and his wife, kneeling. They are ordinary people, though a little wealthier than most, and their family coats-of-arms decorate the top windows in the center panel. Here, in the living room of a middle-class Flemish home, the magic of the Annunciation takes place. Mary sits on the footrest of a wooden settee before the fireplace, intently reading a book. Another book, richly illustrated, lies on the table beside her. **Finials**, or ornamental tops, at each corner of the settee depict dogs, symbols of fidelity and domesticity, and lions, symbols of Jesus and his resurrection. The archangel Gabriel approaches Mary from the left, almost blocking the view of the two patrons, who peer in through the

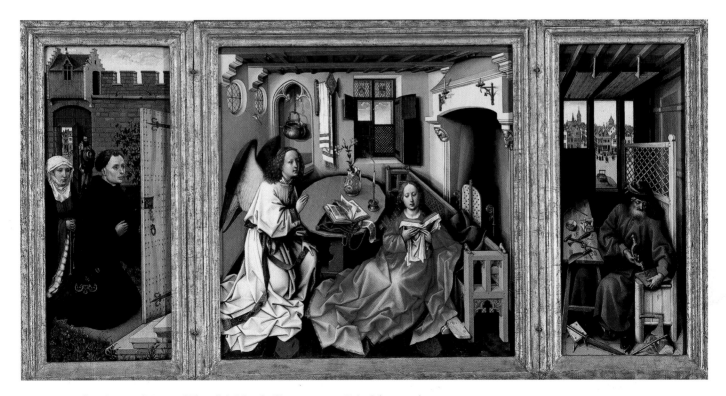

Fig. 8.3 Robert Campin (Master of Flémalle), *Mérode Altarpiece.* **ca. 1426.** Oil on panel, center
$25\frac{5}{16}$″ × $24\frac{7}{8}$″, each wing $25\frac{3}{8}$″ × $10\frac{7}{8}$″. The Metropolitan Museum of Art, New York. 1956. (56.70).

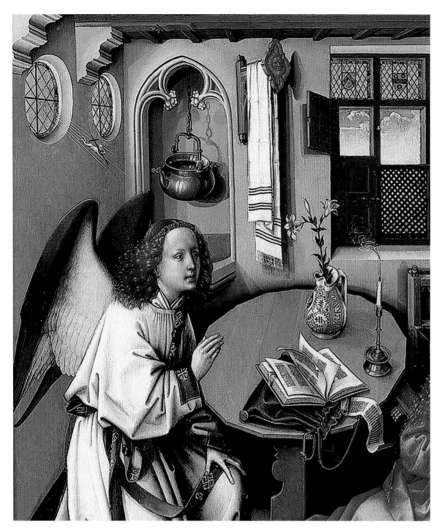

Fig. 8.4 Robert Campin (Master of Flémalle), *Mérode Altarpiece*, detail. ca. 1426.
The Metropolitan Museum of Art, New York. The Cloisters Collection. 1956. (56.70).
The extraordinarily fine detail of Campin's painting was made possible by his use of oil paint.

In the next room, behind the fireplace and settee next to which Mary reads and in the right-hand panel, Joseph works as a carpenter. On the table in front of him is a recently completed mousetrap, probably a reference to a metaphor created by Saint Augustine to the effect that the Passion of Christ is a trap baited by Christ's own blood to catch Satan. Another mousetrap sits outside on the window ledge, apparently for sale. Joseph is in the act of boring holes in a piece of wood, perhaps a grape press and thus another reference to the blood of Christ—Christ's declaration of wine as his own blood in the Eucharist. Through the window, its shutters latched to the ceiling above, we can see the main square of a typical Flemish town, perhaps Tournai itself.

This Annunciation is clearly an entirely local and bourgeois affair. Mary is a Flemish housewife, Joseph a Flemish carpenter and owner of the house, even though the two were not yet married at the time of Annunciation. Time has collapsed—the New Testament becomes a current event. Every element seems a necessary and real part of everyday Flemish life. Each common object in this middle-class home serves a real, material purpose as well as a religiously symbolic one.

Another noteworthy aspect of Campin's triptych is its astonishingly small size for an altarpiece. If its two side panels were closed over the central panel, as they are designed to work, the altarpiece is just over two feet square—making it easily portable. This little altarpiece is itself a material object, so intimate and detailed that it functions more like the book that lies open on the table within its frame than a painting. It is very different from the altarpieces being made in Italy during the first half of the fifteenth century. Most were monumental in scale and painted in fresco, permanently embedded in the wall, and therefore not portable. Campin's altarpiece is made to be held up close, in the hands, not surveyed from afar, suggesting its function as a private, rather than public, devotional object.

As an exploration of the private nature of religious experience, the painting's subtext is *touch*. Working with oil paint, Campin and other contemporary northern painters were able to blend, shade, and bleed colors so skillfully that textures—Gabriel's exquisitely curly hair, Mary's soft skin and velvet dress, Joseph's wool robe, the brass pot hanging in the back alcove, even the transparent smoke rising from

doorway. Seven rays of sunlight illuminate the room and fall directly on Mary's abdomen. On one of the rays, a miniature Christ carrying the Cross flies into the room (Fig. **8.4**). Campin is telling the viewers that the entire life of Christ, including the Passion itself, enters Mary's body at the moment of conception. The candle on the table beside her, symbolic of the "old faith" (that is, Judaism), is extinguished by the "true light" of Christ entering the room. This potent theological proposition kindled the anti-Jewish sentiment that erupted during the Crusades (see chapter 5). It would also underlie anti-Semitic feelings from the later Renaissance Inquisitions, in which Jews were required to convert to Christianity or face exile or death, down to the Holocaust in the twentieth century. The lilies in the vase on the table are a traditional symbol of Mary's purity, though, since there are three of them, they may also represent the Trinity.

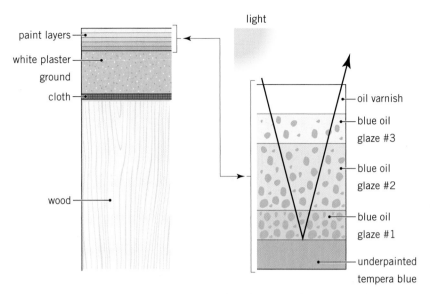

Fig. 8.5 Diagram of a section of a 15th-century Flemish painting, demonstrating the luminosity of the oil medium. The large arrow suggests how light penetrates the translucent glazes of the medium and is reflected back to the viewer.

the candle—become nearly palpable. They understood that working with oils, they could create layers of paint with greater or lesser translucency, depending on the density of the pigment suspended in the oil. As light penetrates the paint layers (Fig. **8.5**), it is reflected back at the viewer, creating a gemlike brilliance of color. This sense of seeing colored light in the painting is the distinguishing characteristic of Flemish oil painting.

Oil offers other advantages as a painting medium. It dries much more slowly than tempera, and the drying process can be further slowed by adding turpentine. Slow-drying paint allows artists to blend the colors in minute amounts, creating subtle modulations of tone that suggest a sense of light falling across an object. Furthermore, using oil paint, the artist can work with extremely soft, fine brushes, eliminating any hint of brushstrokes. The smooth finish that results heightens the illusion that the viewer is looking at the object itself. Implicit in the Flemish artist's sensitivity to the light-enhancing qualities of the oil medium is the understanding that light suggests spiritual truth. So, as light falls across an object and is literally reflected back at the viewer, the object assumes, at least potentially, a deeper symbolic resonance or meaning. From this point of view, the world and its objects become "alight" with the Creator, and painters can find in their task a profound spiritual importance.

Light seems to emanate from within Campin's canvas. Gabriel's wings glow, an effect created by layering very thin, almost transparent coats of oil paint on the surface of the painting—a process known as **glazing**. The wings literally contain light, lending the archangel a physical presence and material reality. The spiritual is made real. In fact, the archangel appears no less (and no more) "real" than the brass pot above his head.

Because of its intimacy and portability, its realism and emphasis on physical things, the *Mérode Altarpiece* and other Northern Renaissance paintings like it introduce a new set of possibilities for painting. Patrons in the south gained personal satisfaction and even honor from their patronage—recall the Medici patronage in Florence—but such acts were intended to enhance the glory of the city-state, the guild, or the Church. But here, the motive of Ingelbrecht of Mechlin and his wife seems wholly personal. Under the patronage of the merchant class of the north, painting begins to function something like the mousetrap Joseph has set outside his window for sale; that is, as a commodity. And in fact, the patrons of the *Mérode Altarpiece* have conceived of it as a kind of object of barter. Its commission is a form of indulgence, or payment, which spares them from purgatory and paves their way into heaven. One of the most distinctive features of Campin's painting is the everyday appearance of the scene. This ordinariness lends the image of Christian miracle a reality never before seen in European painting. The reality was heightened by the depiction of objects through the medium of oil paint.

Jan van Eyck in Bruges

The celebration of individual identity marks Renaissance art in both the North and South. It is especially apparent in van Eyck's double portrait of Giovanni Arnolfini, an Italian merchant representing Medici interests in Bruges, and his wife, Giovanna Cenami (Fig. **8.6**). Scholars continue to

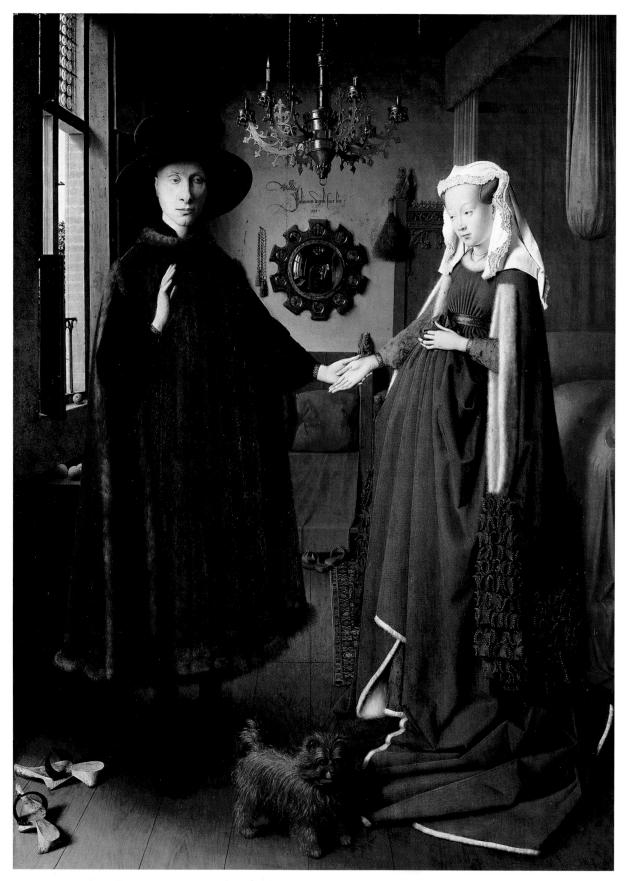

Fig. 8.6 Jan van Eyck, *Giovanni Arnolfini and His Wife Giovanna Cenami.* **ca. 1434.** Oil on panel, $32\frac{1}{4}$″ × $23\frac{1}{2}$″.
© National Gallery, London. Giovanna may look pregnant but she is probably not. However, she has pulled her robe up
before her abdomen and dressed in green to suggest her fertility.

debate the meaning and purpose of the work, but most have agreed that the couple are exchanging marriage vows in a bedroom before two witnesses. One of them is van Eyck himself, who is reflected in the mirror at the back of the room (Fig. **8.7**). (Above the mirror he inscribed in Latin "*Johannes de Eyck fuit hic. 1434*" [deh IKE FOO-it hik] ["Jan van Eyck was here, 1434"]). Recently a persuasive argument has been made that this scene represents an engagement rather than a marriage—a touching of the hands was the traditional sign of an agreement to wed—and that the scene takes place in the front parlor of a Dutch home, a room that was commonly decorated with a canopied bed as a symbol of hospitality.

The painting abounds with other symbolic elements, transforming what is at first glance a wholly secular image into one filled with religious significance, a characteristic feature of northern art. Many scholars speculate that the little dog at the feet of the couple represents fidelity, and the two pair of shoes, at the left front of the painting and at the back of the room, suggest that the couple stand on ground hallowed by the sacred character of the ceremony that engages them. The chandelier, with its single burning candle, is traditionally thought to represent the presence of Christ. The fruits on the window ledge and table behind Arnolfini suggest abundance. Atop the high chairback at the back of the room is a sculptural finial representing either Saint Margaret, the patron saint of

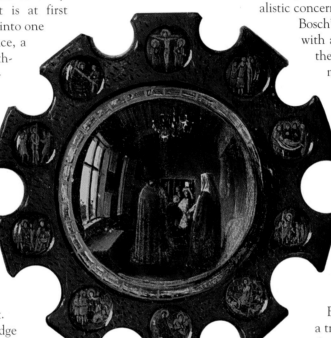

Fig. 8.7 Jan van Eyck, *Giovanni Arnolfini and His Wife Giovanna Cenami*, detail. ca. 1434. Each of the ten small circles around the mirror contains a scene of Christ's Passion.

childbirth, or Saint Martha, the patron saint of housewives. The dusting brush beside it probably symbolizes the wife's household duties. Above all, the painting seems to celebrate the couple's spiritual and material well-being. Its many textures, from Arnolfini's fur robe to the rich red velvet of the bed, symbolize what we might call "the good life," a phrase with a long classical history.

In his paintings van Eyck expresses his love of detail through his ability to render in oil paint the texture of things and the way light plays across their surfaces. This skill is apparent in the green wool of Giovanna Cenami's dress or the ermine of Giovanni Arnolfini's robe. This love of detail, presented through a smooth surface that does not show brushstrokes, is the hallmark of Northern Renaissance painting, the characteristic that distinguishes it most from painting in the South.

Hieronymus Bosch in 's-Hertogenbosch

Hieronymus Bosch (1450–1516) was born, lived, and worked in the town of 's-Hertogenbosch [SER-toh-gun-boss] (now in southern Holland). The town owed its prosperity to wool and cloth. Bosch is a contemporary of the painters in Southern Europe who worked in the so-called High Renaissance. Such a distinction seems inappropriate in the North, where there was greater continuity between fifteenth- and sixteenth-century art. (Only Albrecht Dürer, a German, discussed later in the chapter, fits comfortably into the High Renaissance cult of the individual creative genius.) Bosch's paintings are at once minutely detailed and brutally imaginative, casting a dark, satiric shadow over the materialistic concerns of his northern predecessors.

Bosch's work is, furthermore, permeated with a sense of doom characteristic of the North. It continues from the medieval sermon tradition exemplified by Pope Innocent III's *On the Misery of the Human Condition* (see Reading 5.4) through the devastation of the Bubonic Plague. From the 1340s well into the sixteenth century the plague periodically ravaged northern cities due to the colder climate and harsher conditions that defined day-to-day life in the North.

Northern pessimism manifests itself most dramatically in Bosch's most ambitious painting, a triptych with closing doors known as the *Garden of Earthly Delights*, painted around 1505–1510 (see *Focus*, pages 234–235). Although the painting takes the form of a triptych altarpiece, it was never intended for a religious setting. The *Garden of Earthly Delights* hung in a palace in Brussels, where invading Spanish troops seized it in 1568 and took it to Madrid, where it remains.

The painting is really a **conversation piece**, a work designed to invite discussion of its meaning. Bosch has given us an enigmatic essay on what the world might be like if the fall of Adam and Eve had never happened. It presents, in other words, a world technically without sin, yet rampant with behavior that its viewers, the fallen sons and daughters of Adam and Eve, could only identify as sinful. Other parts of the painting, the right panel in particular, seem to suggest life after the fall, life in which Adam and Eve's sin has made humankind aware of good and evil. These are the painting's paradoxes and its source of endless fascination. Equally intriguing is its meticulous detail, which gives the most grotesquely imaginative landscapes a sense of reality.

Focus

Bosch's *Garden of Earthly Delights*

ieronymus Bosch's *Garden of Earthly Delights* is full of strange hybrid organisms, part animal or bird, part human, part plant, sometimes part mechanical contraption. In the left panel of the triptych we see the Garden of Eden, populated with such strange creatures as albino giraffes and elephants, unicorns, and flying fish. In the right panel we see Bosch's deeply disturbing vision of Hell, in which fire spits from the skyline and tortured souls are impaled on musical instruments or eaten alive by monsters. The central panel presents an image of life on earth, with hundreds of naked young men and women frolicking in a garden full

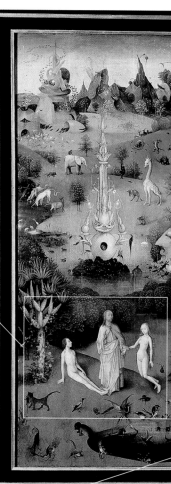

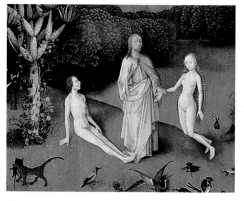

Even as God commands Adam and Eve to "be fruitful and multiply and fill the earth and subdue it" (Gen. 1:26), death is imminent: A cat walks off to the left with a mouse in its teeth, and ravens perch above on the Fountain of Life.

of giant berries and other fruits. Lovers are variously contained in transparent columns or globes of glass—a reference to the proverb "Happiness and glass, how soon they pass." This landscape is a parody. The world here has gone awry. Illicit lust replaces love of God, wanton seduction replaces beauty, and Bosch's own wild imagination replaces reason.

Hieronymus Bosch, *Garden of Earthly Delights*, closed. ca. 1505–1510. Oil on panel, each wing 7′2 1/2″ × 38″. Museo del Prado, Madrid. When closed, the triptych reveals the world at the moment of creation. At the top left-hand corner, God floats on a cloud and looks down at the earthly orb. The landscape has no people. Inscribed across the top are these words from Psalms 33:9: "*Ipse dixit et facta su[nt]. Ipse ma[n]davit et creata su[n]t*"—"He himself spoke, and they were made; he himself commanded, and they were created." The irony of what is hidden inside these exterior panels could not be greater.

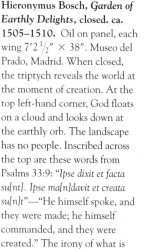

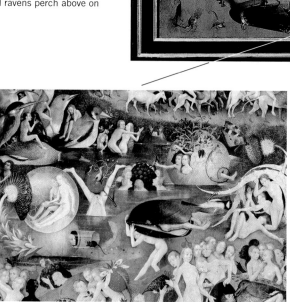

Here are the results of God's command to Adam and Eve to "be fruitful and multiply." Recall that it was eating the forbidden fruit of the Garden of Eden that was the Original Sin. Swimmers suck at the blackberry in the middle of the pool or float upside down, with fruit atop their genitals, or peek out of a floating orange, an image of gluttony. In fact, all of the Seven Deadly Sins are here—Pride, Envy, Greed, Gluttony, Anger, Sloth, and, above all, Lust.

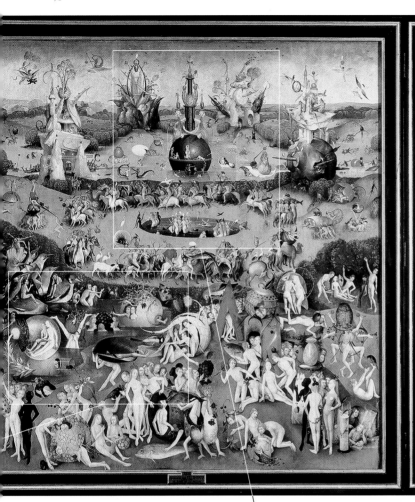

Hieronymus Bosch, *Garden of Earthly Delights*, open. ca. 1505–1510. Oil on panel, center $7'2\frac{1}{2}'' \times 6'4\frac{3}{4}''$; each wing $7'2\frac{1}{2}'' \times 38''$. Derechos reservados © Museo Nacional Del Prado—Madrid.

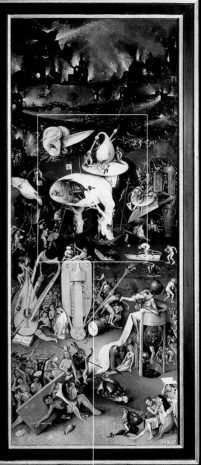

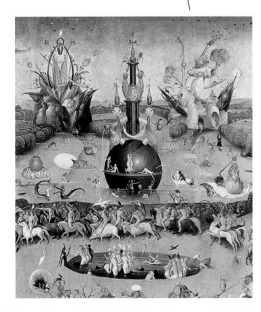

The focus of the central panel is this pool surrounded by the four so-called Castles of Vanity (this detail shows two of them). Horns, a symbol of cuckoldry, decorate the central fountain, known as the Tower of Adulteresses. Circling around the lower pool of bathing women, called the Bath of Venus, young men ride pigs, horses, goats, griffins, and other animals, apparently intent on "riding" the young women as well.

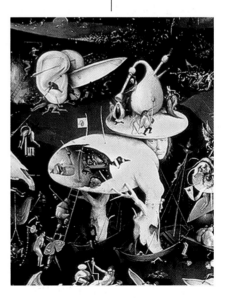

This strange creature presides over hell. Its legs are supported by tree trunks, each standing in a boat; its eggshell stomach is cracked open; and its head, with an astonishingly realistic face, is topped by a disk with bagpipe (a traditional symbol of lust). Behind it, two ears, pierced by arrows, flank a knife blade, like some monstrous cannon or hellish phallus.

The German Tradition

By 1500, cities in the German-speaking regions to the southeast of Flanders and in the Netherlands to the northeast had begun to grow rapidly. Many of the larger cities had doubled in size in the century after 1400. The population of Cologne, the largest city in Germany, was about 40,000, and Nuremberg, Strasbourg, Vienna, Prague, and Lübeck could all claim between 20,000 and 30,000 residents, which made them substantial centers of culture though smaller than Florence, Paris, and London at about 100,000 inhabitants. In all these cities, an increasingly wealthy, self-made mercantile class supported the production of art. Caught between North and South, between the richly detailed and luminous oil painting of a van Eyck and the more linear, scientific, and classically idealized style of a Raphael, German painters at the dawn of the sixteenth century exhibited instances of each.

Emotion and Christian Miracle: The Art of Matthias Grünewald

The intensity of feeling and seriousness that we saw in the painting of Bosch also appear in the work of Matthias Grünewald [GROO-nuh-wold] (ca. 1470–1528). Multi-talented, Grünewald served as architect, engineer, and painter to the court of the archbishops of Mainz. His most famous work is the so-called *Isenheim Altarpiece*, a monumentally large polyptych painted around 1510–1515 for the hospital of the Abbey of Saint Anthony, a facility in Isenheim [IZE-en-hime], near Strasbourg, dedicated to the treatment of people with skin diseases. These included syphilis, leprosy, and ergotism, a gangrenous condition caused by eating grain contaminated with the ergot fungus. Physical illness was viewed as a function of spiritual illness, and so Grünewald's altarpiece, like Pope Innocent III's sermon *On the Misery of the Human Condition* of nearly 300 years earlier, is designed to move these sinners to repentance. But it also reminded the patients at the Abbey that they were not alone in their suffering, that Christ had suffered like them.

The Crucifixion in the *Isenheim Altarpiece* is among the grimmest ever painted (Fig. 8.8); Christ's flesh is ripped and torn by thorns, more startlingly realistic in its detail than any Crucifixion ever painted in the South. His body seems emaciated, his ashen skin drawn tightly across his abdomen and rib cage. He hangs limply from the cross, which seems to bend under his weight, his hands splayed open, contorted by pain. His lips are blue, and, as if to emphasize Christ's morbidity, Grünewald's palette of purple-green and yellow-brown almost reeks of rotten flesh. All is darkness, echoing the account of the Crucifixion in the Gospel of Mark (15:33): "And when the sixth hour was come, there was darkness over the whole land until the ninth hour." Below, in the **predella** [pruh-DEL-ah], or

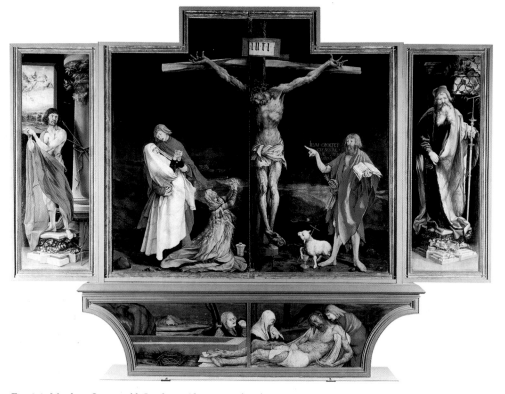

Fig. 8.8 Matthias Grünewald, *Isenheim Altarpiece*, closed. ca. 1510–1515. Main body, *Crucifixion*; base, *Lamentation*; side panels, *Saint Sebastian* (left) and *Saint Anthony* (right). Oil on wood, center: 9′9$\frac{1}{2}$″ × 10′9″; each wing 8′2$\frac{1}{2}$″ × 3$\frac{1}{2}$″; base: 2′5$\frac{1}{2}$″ × 11′2″. Musée d'Unterlinden, Colmar, France. Saint Sebastian appears in his role as protector from the plague. Saint Anthony, patron saint of the Isenheim hospital, stands before a window through which a demon, representing the plague, blows its evil breath.

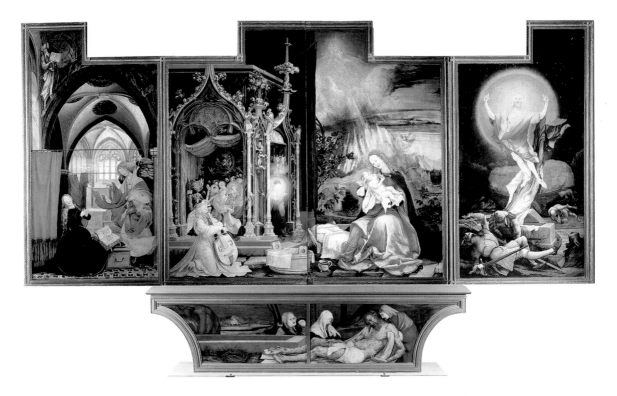

Fig. 8.9 Matthias Grünewald, *Isenheim Altarpiece,* **first opening. ca. 1510–1515. Left,** *Annunciation;* **middle,** *Virgin and Child with Angels;* **right,** *Resurrection.* **Oil on panel, center:** 9′9$\frac{1}{2}$″ × 10′9″; **each wing:** 9′9$\frac{1}{2}$″ × 5′4$\frac{1}{2}$″. Musée d'Unterlinden, Colmar, France. In the left-hand panel, the gesture of the angel of the Annunciation as he points to Mary echoes the gesture of Saint John pointing to the crucified Christ in the closed altarpiece, underscoring the transformation of spirit between the closed and the open doors.

supporting base, of the altarpiece, a Lamentation shows Christ's body, stiff in rigor mortis, as it is settled into the tomb.

The altarpiece is composed of one set of fixed wings, two movable sets, and one set of sliding panels to cover the predella, the base, so that the altarpiece could be exhibited in different configurations. Hospital patients saw the horrifying realism of Grünewald's Crucifixion and Lamentation on the closed wings throughout the week, but on holy days and possibly Sundays, the altarpiece was opened to reveal, inside, brightly lit scenes of the Annunciation, the Virgin and Child with Angels, and the Resurrection (Fig. 8.9). In the Annunciation panel, the angel appears to Mary in a Gothic church. The Bible on her lap is open to Isaiah 11:1: "And there shall come forth a rod out of the stem of Jesse, and a Branch shall grow out of his roots." Above her, the dove of the Holy Spirit hovers on suspended wing and is bathed in a luminous light. In the central panel, Mary cares for the Christ Child in an array of detail that a patient at the hospital of the Abbey of Saint Anthony would recognize—torn linen rags for cleansing the skin, a bed, a tub, a towel, and even a chamberpot. In the Resurrection panel on the right, Christ soars up in an aureole of translucent light, the Roman soldiers blown to the ground as he explodes from the tomb. Christ's skin is now white and pure in contrast to the gangrenous green of the closed panel. So the promise of salvation—the Christian miracle—was always at least latent in the patient's

mind, the glory and joy of the hereafter always imaginable behind the pain and suffering of the moment.

Grünewald's altarpiece underscores the Northern European preoccupation with death. In the face of recurring plagues ever since the Black Death of 1348, the fragility of life and the ultimate horror of death were constant thematic concerns. It is hardly surprising that among the most popular texts in Northern Europe was the *Art of Dying Well.* Although its origins are unclear, over 100 different versions appeared in several different languages between the 1460s and 1500. Grünewald's altarpiece is typical of Northern European art in its unswerving attention to the reality of death, represented in the minutest detail, but it is also uniquely German in its intense emotionalism and almost mystical sense of transcendence.

Northern Detail Meets Southern Humanism: The Art of Albrecht Dürer

Born in 1471 in the city of Nuremberg, Albrecht Dürer [AL-brekt Doo-ruhr] represents a trend in German culture distinct from the emotionalism and mysticism of Grünewald, one based on humanism. By his death in 1528, he had become one of the leading painters of the Renaissance, successfully wedding his German-Netherlandish Gothic heritage with the Renaissance interest in perspective, empirical observation, and rules of ideal beauty for representing the human figure.

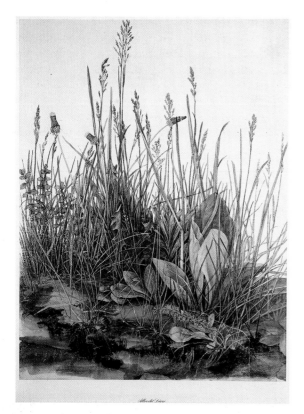

Fig. 8.10 Albrecht Dürer, *The Large Turf*. 1503. Watercolor, 16 ¼″ × 12 ⅛″. Albertina, Vienna. Dürer's interest in nature reached a scientific dimension, demonstrated here.

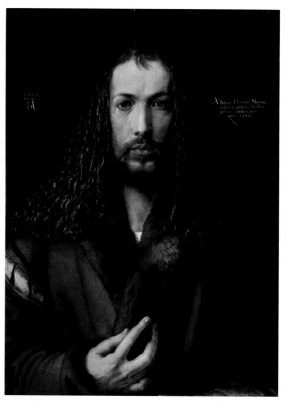

Fig. 8.12 Albrecht Dürer, *Self-Portrait*. 1500. Oil on panel, 26 ¼″ × 19 ¼″. Alte Pinakothek, Munich. Dürer's skill as a portraitist is embodied in the story that his dog once barked and wagged its tail at one of his self-portraits. We cannot vouch for the accuracy of the story.

Dürer's landscape studies, such as *The Large Turf* (Fig. **8.10**), display his northern interest in the minutest details of nature but also his scientific mind, his humanist interest in the phenomena of the natural world. This he shared with Leonardo da Vinci. In fact, after visiting Italy in 1505–1506 to learn the laws of scientific perspective from the Italian masters, Dürer was determined to introduce a more scientific approach to painting to Germany. To do so he published the-

oretical treatises on drawing, perspective, proportion, measurement, and the techniques of painting.

The *Draftsman Drawing a Reclining Nude* (Fig. **8.11**), from one of these treatises, is an example of Dürer's attempt to marry the detailed textural vision of the northern tradition with the scientific humanism of the south. The artist's model here is frankly, even shockingly nude—especially given the artist's point of view—and yet he subjects her to an intensely mathematical and rational regime. Functioning as a metaphor for the ability of the artist to subject nature to the discipline of his gaze is a series of tensions: between the grid of the screen and the paper; between the curvilinear folds of the model's body and the drapery; and between "measuring" the world and submitting to the feelings that the world might provoke. Dürer presents the artist as a disinterested observer. His imagination is moved by the objective recording of reality, not by the subjective feelings the model might inspire in him. And, like Johannes Stradanus's vision of *Jan van Eyck's Studio* (see Fig. 8.2), this print is a look into the artist's private world, a revelation of his technical means. These feelings— his love for his craft and his passion for his art—may actually be the real subject of the illustration.

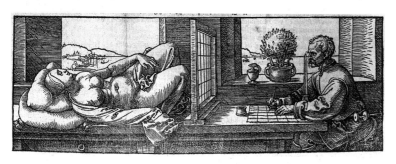

Fig. 8.11 Albrecht Dürer, *Draftsman Drawing a Reclining Nude*. ca. 1525. Woodcut, second edition, 3″ × 8½″. One of 138 woodcuts and diagrams in *Teaching of Measurement with Compass and Ruler*. Horatio Greenough Curtis Fund, Museum of Fine Arts, Boston. The artist looks at his foreshortened model through a grid and then transfers what he sees to a similarly gridded paper. This gives him an accurate representation of the figure in foreshortened perspective.

Like other Northern artists, Dürer was a master of oil painting. *Self-Portrait* of 1500 (Fig. **8.12**) takes full advantage of its oil medium to create a highly textured surface that glows with a light that seems to emanate from within the artist himself. Acknowledging his own skill with oil colors, Dürer inscribed the painting as follows: "Thus I, Albrecht Dürer from Nuremburg, painted myself with undying colors at the age of 28 years." The intimation of artistic immortality embodied in the word "undying" is underscored in the way that Dürer self-consciously paints himself as a sort of icon. His frontal pose, bearded face, and intense gaze recall traditional images of Christ. At the very least, he means for us to see in his face evidence of divine inspiration. "Art," he would write, "derives from God; it is God who has created all art; it is not easy to paint artistically. Therefore, those without aptitude should not attempt it, for it is an inspiration from above." For Dürer, creating art was a sacred act; it made manifest God's work, from the Creation to Christ's Passion.

Humanism and Reformation in the North

Dürer's piety should not be mistaken for a lack of interest or belief in the humanist values of the Renaissance. To the contrary, his was a deeply humanist sensibility. *Melancholia I* (Fig. **8.13**), of 1514, is a fully humanist image, a complex depiction of failed inspiration and genius, informed by a wealth of classical allusion. Dürer himself suffered from melancholy, or depression, and this can be understood as an image of his own muse. She is at once divinely inspired (note her wings) and incapable of action. Note the way she carelessly holds the compass. With head resting on hand, she strikes the traditional pose of a melancholic personality. (Raphael had portrayed Michelangelo as Heraclitus in a similar position just a few years earlier in his *School of Athens*; see *Focus*, pages 212–213.) Tools lie idly beneath her feet. Time passes (indicated by the hourglass on the wall behind her). Even a pudgy cupid, almost always busy at work, sits dejected and uninspired beside her.

But within three years of creating this image, the events of history would overtake Dürer and his art. In fact, they would overtake all artistic and cultural production in Europe, changing the course of the arts forever. The person responsible for this extraordinary change was Martin Luther (1483–1546), a German monk and humanist scholar bent on religious reform. The technology responsible was the printing press, which gave Luther the means to transmit his radical ideas across Europe.

Luther's Protestant Reformation, as it came to be called, was the result of a century-long reexamination of the role of the Church in daily life. Throughout the fifteenth century in Northern Europe, a new religious movement, known as the "modern devotion," had taken hold in city after city. Lay citizens gathered in houses organized to promote a lifestyle similar to that of monks and nuns, though they stopped short of taking monastic vows. These Brothers and Sisters of the Common Life, as they came to be known, tried to bring the message of Jesus into daily practice. But the life of austerity and simplicity that such popular religious movements promoted clashed sharply with the prosperity and material pleasures of the northern mercantile class.

The Satire of Desiderius Erasmus

The values of the modern devotion clashed even more dramatically with the extravagance and corruption of the Church in Rome. One of the most vigorous opponents of Church excesses was Desiderius Erasmus [ih-RAZ-mus] (ca. 1466–1536). Like Luther, Erasmus was a monk and humanist scholar, but he had been raised in Rotterdam among the Brothers of the Common Life. By his mid-thirties he had become one of Europe's most sought-after educators, and he was the first humanist scholar to take advantage of the printing press to disseminate his work.

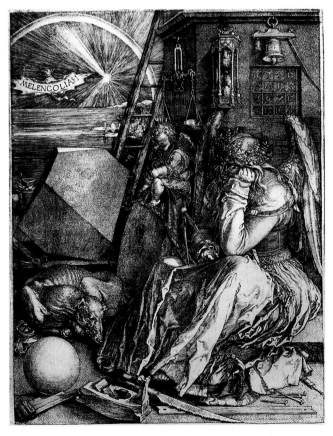

Fig. 8.13 Albrecht Dürer, *Melancholia I*. 1514. Engraving, 9 7/8″ × 7 3/8″. Victoria & Albert Picture Library. In the background, a bat carries a sign bearing the print's title. A creature of the night, the bat symbolizes darkness, as behind it the sun (the light of inspiration) sets below the western horizon.

Luther's own antipapal feelings were inspired, at least in part, by his reading of Erasmus's works, including his 1516 translation of the Greek New Testament into Latin. He was also impressed by Erasmus's satiric attack on the corruption of the clergy in *In Praise of Folly* (1509) and by Erasmus's anonymously published attack on Pope Julius II in *Julius Excluded from Heaven* (1513). In this satiric dialogue, Saint Peter and the pope encounter each other at the doors to paradise (**Reading 8.1**):

READING 8.1   **from Desiderius Erasmus,**
Julius Excluded from Heaven
(1513)

PETER: Immortal God, what a sewer I smell here! Who are you?
JULIUS: . . . so you'll know what sort of prince you insult, listen up. . . . Even though I supported such a great army, celebrated so many splendid triumphs, erected buildings in so many places, still, when I died I left five million ducats. . . .
PETER: Madman! . . . all I hear about is a leader not of the church but of this world. . . .
JULIUS: Perhaps you are still dreaming of that old church. . . . What if you could see today so many sacred buildings erected by kingly wealth, so many thousands of priests everywhere (many of them very rich), so many bishops equal to the greatest kings in military power and in wealth, so many splendid palaces belonging to priests. . . . What would you say?
PETER: That I was looking at a tyrant worse than worldly, an enemy of Christ, the bane of the church.

Julius believes that his "good works"—his military victories, his public projects, even the wealth he has brought to the Church—are all it takes to get himself admitted to paradise. Saint Peter—and, of course, Erasmus and Luther—believed otherwise. (Although extremely critical of the Church, Erasmus would remain a Catholic to the end of his life.)

In 1509, Erasmus wrote *In Praise of Folly* while living in the home of his friend the English humanist, philosopher, and statesman Thomas More (1478–1535) in London (the work's Latin title, *Encomium Moriae*, is a pun that can also be translated "In Praise of More"). Like the later tract, *Julius Excluded from Heaven*, the work, a satiric attack upon the vices and follies of contemporary society, went through more than two dozen editions in Erasmus's lifetime. **Satire**, the literary genre that conveys the contradictions between real and ideal situations, had lain dormant in Western culture since Greek and Roman times when such writers as Aristophanes, in his comedies, and Horace and Juvenal, in their poems and essays, used it to critique the cultures of their own day. Humanist scholars like Erasmus and More, thoroughly acquainted with these classical sources, reinvigorated the genre.

In Praise of Folly helped to secure Erasmus's reputation as the preeminent humanist in Europe and was his most influential work. It is written in the voice, or **persona**, of an allegorical figure named Folly (*Moria*). She is a fool, and plays the fool. Thus, in the work's opening pages, she addresses her readers as follows, pleading for her reputation by noting how pervasive in human behavior is her rule (**Reading 8.2a**):

READING 8.2a   **from Desiderius Erasmus,**
In Praise of Folly **(1509)**

[T]ell me whether fools . . . are not infinitely more free and happy than yourselves? Add to this, that fools do not barely laugh, and sing, and play the good-fellow alone to themselves: but . . . impart their mirth to others, by making sport for the whole company they are at any time engaged in, as if providence purposely designed them for an antidote to melancholy: whereby they make all persons so fond of their society, that they are welcomed to all places, hugged, caressed, and defended, a liberty given them of saying or doing anything; so well beloved, that none dares to offer them the least injury; nay, the most ravenous beasts of prey will pass them by untouched, as if by instinct they were warned that such innocence ought to receive no hurt.

Through the device of Folly, therefore, Erasmus is free to say anything he pleases, and, as Folly reminds us, "It is one further very commendable property of fools, that they always speak the truth." Erasmus spares virtually no one among Folly's "regiment of fools," least of all theologians and Church officials. He attacks, especially, those who "maintain the cheat of pardons and indulgences"—a sentiment that would deeply influence Martin Luther (**Reading 8.2b**):

READING 8.2b   **from Desiderius Erasmus,**
In Praise of Folly **(1509)**

By this easy way of purchasing pardons, any notorious highwayman, any plundering soldier, or any bribe-taking judge, shall disburse some part of their unjust gains, and so think all their grossest impieties sufficiently atoned for; so many perjuries, lusts, drunkenness, quarrels, blood-sheds, cheats, treacheries, and all sorts of debaucheries, shall all be, as it were, struck a bargain for, and such a contract made, as if they had paid off all arrears, and might now begin upon a new score.

The rhetorical power of such verbal abuse accounts for much of the appeal of Erasmus's prose. So too does his sense of **irony**, his ability to say one thing explicitly but implicitly mean another—to speak with "tongue in cheek." Irony is, in fact, one of the chief tools of satire, and is embodied in the very title of Erasmus's work. *In Praise of Folly* is, of course, a *condemnation* of human folly.

Martin Luther's Reformation

Martin Luther (Fig. **8.14**) entered the Order of the Hermits of Saint Augustine in Erfurt, in 1505, at the age of 22. This decision was apparently motivated by an oath he had taken when, in a severe lightning storm, he had promised to become a monk if he survived the storm. By 1511, he had moved to the Augustinian monastery in Wittenberg, a small town of about 2,500 people on the Elbe [elb] River, almost halfway between Hamburg and Berlin, earning a doctorate in theology in 1512. In the winter semester of 1513–1514, he began lecturing at the university there. His primary subject was the Bible.

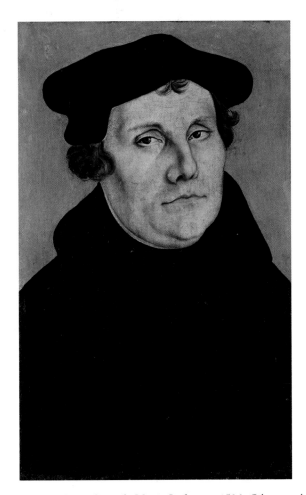

Fig. 8.14 Lucas Cranach, *Martin Luther*. ca. 1526. Oil on panel, 15″ × 9″. Uffizi Gallery, Florence. A remarkable aspect of this painting is Luther's sideways glance, which suggests a personality capable of concentrating on more than one thing at once.

In the Preface to the complete edition of his writings, published just a year before his death, Luther recalled the crisis in belief that preoccupied him between 1513 and 1517 (**Reading 8.3**):

READING 8.3 **from Martin Luther, Preface to *Works* (1545)**

Though I lived as a monk without reproach, I felt that I was a sinner before God with an extremely disturbed conscience. . . . I was angry with God, and said, "As if, indeed, it is not enough, that miserable sinners, eternally lost through original sin, are crushed by every kind of calamity . . . without having God by the gospel threatening us with his righteousness and wrath!" Thus I raged with a fierce and troubled conscience. . . .

At last, by the mercy of God, meditating day and night, I gave heed to the context of the words, namely, "In it the righteousness of God is revealed, as it is written, 'He who through faith is righteous shall live'" [Romans 1:17]. There I began to understand that the righteousness of God is that by which the righteous [person] lives by a gift of God, namely by faith. . . . Here I felt that I was altogether born again and had entered paradise itself through open gates.

Luther's thinking amounts to an almost total rejection of traditional Church doctrine. He argued that the moral virtue that God commands of humanity does not exhibit itself in good deeds or works—in commissioning an altarpiece, for instance—for if this were true, people could never know if they had done enough good works to merit salvation. This was the source of Luther's frustration, even anger. God, Luther was certain, accepts all believers *in spite of*, not because of, what they do. The Bible, he argued, rejects "the wicked idea of the entire kingdom of the pope, the teaching that a Christian man must be uncertain of the grace of God toward him. If this opinion stands, then Christ is completely useless. . . . Therefore the papacy is a veritable torture chamber of consciences and the very kingdom of the devil." From Luther's point of view, Christ had already atoned for humankind's sins—what was the point of his sacrifice?—and he provided the faithful with the certainty of their salvation. So Luther began to preach the doctrine of salvation by faith rather than by works.

Like Dante, Chaucer, and Erasmus before him, Luther was particularly bothered by the concept of **indulgences**, remissions of penalties to be suffered in purgatory. Theoretically, then, indulgences paved the way to heaven for any sinner. Luther's specific target was Johannes Tetzel [TET-sul], a Dominican monk notorious as a traveling seller of indulgences (Fig. **8.15**). Tetzel had been jointly hired by

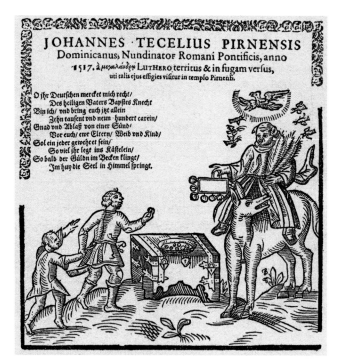

Fig. 8.15 Anonymous, *Johannes Tetzel, Dominican Monk.* ca. 1517. Staatliche Lutherhalle, Wittenberg. The last lines of the poem at the top of this contemporary caricature read: "As soon as the coin in the basin rings, Hurray the soul into heaven springs."

Archbishop Albrecht of Mainz and Pope Leo X to raise money to cover the archbishop's debts and to fund Leo's rebuilding of Saint Peter's in Rome. The sale of indulgences supported these projects.

In general terms, Luther detested both the secular or materialist spirit evident in Church patronage of lavish decorative programs and the moral laxity of its cardinals in Rome. He longed for the Church to return to the spiritual ways of the early Church and to back away from the power and wealth that were corrupting it. In particular, Luther found the practice of selling indulgences to be contradictory to scripture. In the *Ninety-Five Theses*, which he nailed to the church door at Wittenberg on October 31, 1517, he wrote: "Those who believe that, through letters of pardon, they are made sure of their own salvation will be eternally damned along with their teachers," he wrote in the 32nd thesis. More to the point, he wrote in the 86th: "Why does not the Pope, whose riches are at this day more ample than those of the wealthiest of the wealthy, build the single Basilica of Saint Peter with his own money rather than with that of poor believers?"

At the heart of his opposition, in fact, was class division. Only the rich could afford to pay for the remission of their sins and those of their families. If the poor did buy them, they did so at great sacrifice to the well-being of their families. Then they had to watch the proceeds from the practice build the most extravagant, even profligate of projects in Rome. Such injustice and inequity fueled Luther's rage.

On August 7, 1518, Luther was summoned to appear in Rome within 60 days to answer a charge of heresy. As Erasmus

declared: "He has committed a great sin—he has hit the monks in their belly and the Pope in his crown!" It was thus inevitable that on January 3, 1521, the Church excommunicated Luther. All his writings were declared heretical and ordered burned. By 1526, menaced by threats from France and Turkey, and in order to keep peace at home, the German emperor granted each German territory and city discretion in choosing whether or not to follow Luther's example. However, three years later, he rescinded the order, resulting in 18 German states signing a *protestatio* [proh-tes-TAH-tsee-oh], the act of protest that actually gave rise to the term "Protestant."

The Spread of the Reformation

Even as Luther led the Reformation in Germany, other reformists initiated similar movements in France and Switzerland, and still others radicalized his thinking. The appeal of Luther's Reformation was as much due to its political as its religious implications. His defense of the individual conscience against the authority of the pope was understood to free the German princes—and King Henry VII in England—of the same papal tyranny that plagued the Church. And to many townspeople and peasants, freedom from the pope's authority seemed to justify their own independence from authoritarian rule, whether of a peasant from his feudal lord, a guild from local government, or a city from its prince.

Thomas Müntzer and the Peasant War By 1524, peasant leaders across Germany, many of whom were Lutherans, were openly requesting Luther's support in their struggle for political and economic freedom, especially release from serfdom. Luther was hesitant to endorse the aims of the peasants, but Thomas Müntzer (ca. 1489–1525), a German cleric who had studied at Wittenberg, was not. Müntzer thoroughly believed that reform of the Church required the absolute abolition of the vestiges of feudalism, the rule of what he called the "Godless princes" and the self-serving scholars and priests who worked for them. He numbered Luther among these.

Luther was actually sympathetic to the peasants' plight, but he lacked the militancy of Müntzer, who quickly raised an army. Within days, the troops of the German princes encircled Müntzer's army, but certain that God was on his side, Müntzer led the peasants against the princes in the so-called Peasant War. In the ensuing battle, the princes lost six men, Müntzer 6,000. Ten days later, Müntzer was executed.

The Peasant War was not an isolated incident. The feelings that erupted so violently in Germany were the result of long-standing socioeconomic discontent across Europe. As rising expectations for increased economic prosperity and a moderate degree of social freedom energized the general population—especially the rural peasants—the thought that anyone might thwart those expectations met increasing opposition.

Ulrich Zwingli in Zurich In 1519, Ulrich Zwingli [ZWING-lee] (1484–1531), strongly influenced by Erasmus, entered the contest to be chosen as people's priest of the Great Minster Church in Zurich [ZOOR-ik], Switzerland. Zwingli's candidacy was compromised by the fact that he lived openly with a woman with whom he had fathered six children. The open rejection of celibacy galvanized the electorate, who believed celibacy to be an entirely unfair demand on the clergy. Zwingli was elected, and from that position of power, he soon challenged not only the practice of clerical celibacy, but also such practices as fasting, the veneration of saints, the value of pilgrimages, and the ideas of purgatory and transubstantiation.

By the late 1520s, civil war between Protestant and Catholic cantons, or states, broke out in Switzerland. The Protestants won the first major battle, but during the second battle, Zwingli was wounded by his Catholic adversaries, then summarily executed, and his remains scattered so that no relics would survive his death. The compromise that resulted was that each Swiss canton was now free to choose its own religion.

John Calvin in Geneva In the late 1520s, local residents of the Swiss canton of Geneva had successfully revolted against their local prince (who also happened to be the bishop) and bestowed power on a city council. By May 1536, Protestants in the city had succeeded in persuading the city to vote to adopt the Reformation and "to live according to the Gospel and Word of God . . . [without] any more masses, statues, idols, or other papal abuses." Two months later John Calvin (1509–1564) arrived in the city. Calvin was a French religious reformer who had undergone a religious conversion of extreme intensity.

Calvin believed that men were "elected" by God to salvation, and that anyone so elected must live in a way that pleased God. In fact, later Calvinists would come to believe that living a pure and pious life—often coupled with business success—made one's election manifest to one's neighbors. As Calvin explained election in his *Institutes of the Christian Religion* (1536): "God divinely predestines some to eternal salvation—the Elect—and others to eternal perdition—the Damned; and since no one knows with absolute certainty whether he or she is one of the Elect, all must live as if they were obeying God's commands." In effect, one could only intuit one's election, but never know it with certainty.

To this end, Calvinist Geneva—a city where all lived by God's commands—prohibited dancing and singing ("If any one sing immoral, dissolute, or outrageous songs, or dance the virollet or other dance, he shall be put in prison for three days. . . ."), drunkenness ("If any one be found intoxicated he shall pay for the first offense 3 sous . . . for the second offense he shall be held to pay the sum of 6 sous, and for the third 10 sous and be put in prison"), and blasphemy. Women were prohibited from wearing rouge, lace, and jewelry; men from gambling and playing cards. Men who beat their wives were severely punished, quickly giving the city a reputation as "a paradise for women." So vigilant—and intolerant—was Calvin's Consistory, the ecclesiastical court that supervised the morals of the city and that was made up of 12 city elders and the pastors of its churches, that in some ways Geneva came to resemble a religious police state.

Nevertheless, by the time he was done instituting his reforms, Calvin was extremely popular. Before his death in 1564, nearly 7,000 religious refugees had arrived in Geneva seeking protection for their own religious practice. Many of these carried his teachings back to their homelands—to France, the Netherlands, England, Scotland, Poland, and even the fledgling Americas. So austere was the life they had learned in Geneva that, in England, they soon became known by the name of "Puritans." The intolerance of Calvin's Geneva migrated with them, especially to the Puritan colonies in North America.

King Henry VIII and the Anglican Church The English crown's decision to align itself with Protestant reformers was driven much more by political expediency than religious doctrine. King Henry VIII (r. 1509–1547) was, in the first place, a devout Catholic who had attacked Luther in a tract delivered to Pope Leo X in 1521, earning him the title "Defender of the Faith." But in 1527, desperately wanting a male heir, he sought to divorce his first wife, Katherine of Aragon, who had delivered only two children, only one of whom had survived, Mary. When his request that the pope annul his marriage was denied—the two had been married, after all, for eighteen years—Henry convened what became known as the Protestant Parliament, which promptly recognized Henry, not the pope, as head of the Church of England. England was now in open defiance of the papacy, and Henry no longer its "Defender of the Faith," although he continued to claim the title for the English crown. What might be called the *de facto* Protestantization of the Catholic Church, now known as the Anglican Church, quickly followed. In order to assert his kingship, Henry was forced to defy Rome, and in doing so he legitimized English Protestantism.

Relations between Henry and Rome were further exacerbated by the Dissolution Act of 1536 dissolving the monasteries and selling off Church holdings. Henry's high-handed decree was motivated primarily by a need for money, though Henry's quarrel with the Roman Church and his desire to assert authority as head of the Church in England may have played a part. Considerable wealth was required to support his numerous estates and the palaces he was in the habit of building—as well as the enormous court that followed him everywhere. One day in 1532, for instance, as the king and his traveling household were headed to Calais, they reportedly consumed 6 oxen, 8 calves, 40 sheep, 12 pigs, 132 capons, 7 swans, 20 storks, 34 pheasant, 192 partridges, 192 cocks, 56 herons, 84 young hens, 720 larks, 240 pigeons, 24 peacocks, and 192 plovers and teals. Feeding the court alone cost Henry the equivalent of approximately $9 million per year.

Even though the vast revenues of the monasteries flowed directly into the king's coffers after the Dissolution, it was the sale of the monastic lands that contributed most to his wealth, transforming London in the process. Before the Dissolution, as much as 60 percent of the property in some parts of the city was in ecclesiastical hands, and the Church had vast holdings outside the city as well. Henry sold these properties to wealthy gentry, who used the rural parcels for country estates, the urban ones for townhouses.

The Dissolution of the Monasteries affected not only the growth of London and the wealth of the Crown but also Henry's political power. This is because those who received properties from him tended to support his split with Rome, and because Parliament was able to raise money without raising taxes. Politically, the city was unique in Renaissance Europe, both self-governing and under royal rule. Its Lord Mayor was the city's voice in dealing with the king as well as the king's agent in the city. A group of aldermen served as justices of the peace and presided over the city's courts and jails. They controlled the city's charities, assisted in levying its taxes, and often served as members of Parliament. Thus, in the city, they exercised something like democratic rule within the overarching rule of the monarch. Henry VIII and his successors, particularly Queen Elizabeth I (r. 1558–1603), rarely meddled in city politics, and in return the city bestowed upon its monarch almost undivided loyalty.

The Printing Press: A Force for Ideas and Art

It is debatable whether the Reformation would have occurred without the invention, a half-century earlier, of the printing press. Sometime between 1435 and 1455, in the German city of Mainz, Johannes Gutenberg [GOOT-en-burg] (ca. 1390–1468) discovered a process for casting individual letterforms by using an alloy of lead and antimony. These letterforms could be composed into pages of type and then printed on a wooden standing press using ink made of lampblack and oil varnish. Although the Chinese alchemist Pi Sheng [pee shung] had invented **moveable type** in 1045 CE, now, for the first time, the technology was available in the West, and identical copies of written works could be reproduced over and over again.

In 1455, Gutenberg published his first major work, the *Forty-Two Line Bible* (Fig. **8.16**)—so named because each column of type contains 42 lines, the first substantial book to be published from moveable type in Europe. The text is Saint Jerome's translation into Latin of the original Hebrew and Greek. The book's typeface is heavily influenced by the Gothic manuscript tradition, probably because the printer wanted it to look as if it were hand-copied. The publication of another Bible, the so-called *Thirty-Six Line Bible*, quickly followed in 1458–1461. By the end of the century, printing presses were churning out a wide variety of books in at least 60 German cities and in 200 others throughout Europe. Publishers were quick to print the great humanist texts. Gutenberg's press published the writings of Augustine of Hippo in the early 1460s, the writings of Cicero in 1465, and Dante's *Divine Comedy* in 1472. Even an Arabic edition of the Qur'an was printed in Italy in 1500.

More popular than the humanist texts, however, was the Bible, which was the Continent's best seller. Up to this time the Bible had been an item of some rarity, available only in churches and monasteries. A vellum edition required 170 calfskins or 300 sheepskins, and therefore was prohibitively expensive. Now the less costly, printed Bible found its way into the homes of individual citizens. The excommunicated Martin Luther occupied himself with translating Erasmus's New Testament Bible from Latin into vernacular German, "not word for word but sense for sense," as he put it. His object was to make the Bible available to ordinary people, in the language they spoke on the street, so that they could meditate for themselves on its meanings without the intervention of a priest. No longer would the Catholic Church be the sole authority of biblical interpretation.

Luther's vernacular New Testament was published in 1522. The entire printing of 3,000 copies sold out within three months, and a second printing quickly followed. Considering that the entire population of Wittenberg was only 2,500, the sellout of the first printing was an incredible achievement.

By the time of Luther's death in 1546, 3,830 separate editions of the Bible—altogether about one million copies—had been published, many in vernacular German. Although there were still a large number of variant texts, there were many fewer than before, and something close to the standardization of Scripture was beginning to take place. In England, William Tyndale (ca. 1494–1536) translated the Bible into English,

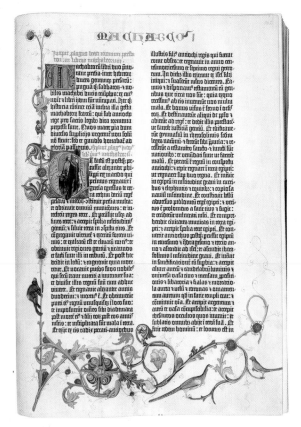

Fig. 8.16 **Page from the Gutenberg Bible, text printed with moveable letters and hand-painted initials and marginalia: page 162 recto with initials "M" and "E" and depiction of Alexander the Great. Johannes Gutenberg: Mainz, 1455–1456.** Staatsbibliothek zu Berlin, Berlin, Germany. An artist added the colors of the still Gothic decorative designs by hand after the page was printed to lend the book the feeling of a medieval manuscript. The appearance of Alexander the Great in the design further contributes to the effect.

and the works of Luther as well. The bishop of London, Cuthbert Tunstall (1474–1559), was mortified at the prospect of the people being able to interpret the Bible for themselves. "We must root out printing," he warned, "or printing will root out us." In Antwerp in 1535, imperial authorities arrested the "dangerous" Tyndale, strangled him, and then burned him at the stake. Ironically, when King James I of England instructed translators to create what has come to be known as the King James Version of the Bible in 1604, it was a lightly edited version of Tyndale's translation that provided the basis for the work: As much as 80 percent of the text is Tyndale's. The King James Version would have a profound impact on all subsequent Bible translations and on English literature as a whole.

Luther's fame protected him from such hostile acts. He was the Continent's best-selling author. It is estimated that between 1518 and 1525, one-third of all texts published in Germany were by him—roughly 300,000 a year. His *Address to the Christian Nobility of the German Nation* sold 4,000 copies in three weeks in Wittenberg alone. In the next two years, it went through 13 editions. For Luther, the printing press was a true gift from God, and he understood how to use it. Not only did the literate few, about 30 percent of the urban population, heed his words, but so did those to whom Luther's texts were read aloud. "Faith," Luther wrote, "comes by hearing." His writings, he knew, were well heard.

Music in Print

A trained musician, Luther understood the power of a hymn sung in the vernacular by the entire congregation, a form known as the **chorale** [koh-RAL], rather than in Latin by a chorus of monks separated from the worshipers. While he did not invent the chorale form, between 1524 and 1545 he composed and compiled nine hymnals, consisting of Latin hymns, popular religious songs, and secular tunes recast with religious lyrics. The most famous of Luther's chorales is *Ein feste Burg ist unser Gott* [ine FES-teh boorg ist UN-zer got] ("A Mighty Fortress Is Our God") (**CD-Track 8.1**), still widely sung today. Luther probably wrote the melody, and he adopted the text from Psalm 46 ("God is our refuge and our strength . . ."). When sung in unison by all the voices in the congregation, it embodies Luther's sense that "next to the Word of God, music deserves the highest praise."

In England, Thomas Morley, the organist at Saint Paul's Cathedral and owner of the monopoly on publishing music in England, wrote and published more madrigals than any other English composer, many of them inspired by printed Italian sources. Morley's compositions sometimes employ very short texts and, as a result, repeat each phrase many times. The text of *Fyre and Lightning*, a madrigal for two tenor voices, reads:

> Fyre and lightning from heaven fall
> And sweetly enflame that hart with love arightfull,
> O Flora my delightfull,
> So faire but yet so spightfull.

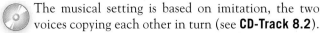
The musical setting is based on imitation, the two voices copying each other in turn (see **CD-Track 8.2**).

At times, the imitation is very close, the second voice following so closely on the heels of the first that a feeling of emotional intensity or agitation develops. The song ends with both voices singing in **homophonic harmony**, a unison movement of the voices in chords that employs a dissonant chord to underscore in word-painting the last stinging word, "spitefull."

Writing for Print and Play: The New Humanists

The sudden availability of books in large numbers transformed not only the spread of knowledge but its production as well. Suddenly, scholars could work in their own personal libraries and write knowing that their thinking could quickly find its way into print. Similarly, composers could see their music in print and expect it to be performed across the Continent. In short, the printing press created a new economy that transformed the speed at which information traveled.

Thomas More One of the most popular books of the era was Thomas More's *Utopia*, published in Latin in 1516, but soon translated into virtually all European languages, including English. Places like John Calvin's Geneva can usefully be thought of as attempts to fashion, in their own terms, communities modeled after More's ideal society. But the book was widely understood to be more than just a description of an unrealized, ideal state—in Greek, *eu* means "good" and *topos* "place," hence "Good place," but also, the root might be, *ou* meaning "not," hence "No place"—and thus a profound critique of the English political system. At the heart of the critique is More's implicit comparison between his own corrupt Christian society and the ideal society he imagines. This ideal society was inspired, at least in part, by the accounts of explorers returning from the Americas. Its fictional narrator is himself an explorer who has discovered an island culture in which people share goods and property, where war is held in contempt, personal vanity despised, education available to all (except, notably, slaves—a blind spot in More's cultural critique), and freedom of religion a given. Each individual works (six hours a day) for the common good, assuming personal responsibility for social justice rather than entrusting it to some higher authority. Equality, kindness, and charity are the virtues most esteemed by all. In short, Utopia seemed the very antithesis of More's England.

By the time *Utopia* was published, More was Henry VIII's unofficial secretary. As if to endorse More's point of view, Henry promoted him within the year to a position on his advisory council. This was the first of many advancements, culminating in More's appointment as Lord Chancellor, the presiding officer of the House of Lords, in 1529. In *Utopia*, More dedicated considerable discussion to matters of religion, in many ways anticipating the Reformation politics that would begin in the following year. Utopus, king of Utopia, enforces a practice of religion (**Reading 8.4**):

READING 8.4 **from Thomas More, *Utopia*, Book II (1516)**

By those among them [the Utopians] that have not received our religion [Christianity], do not fright any from it, and use none ill that goes over to it; so that all the while I was there, one man was only punished on this occasion. He being newly baptized, did, notwithstanding all that we could say to the contrary, dispute publicly concerning the Christian religion with more zeal than discretion; and with so much heat, that he not only preferred our worship to theirs, but condemned all their rites as profane; and cried out against all that adhered to them, as impious and sacrilegious persons, that were to be damned to everlasting burnings. Upon his having frequently preached in this manner, he was seized, and after trial he was condemned to banishment, not for having disparaged their religion, but for his inflaming the people to sedition: for this is one of their most ancient laws, that no man ought to be punished for his religion. At the first constitution of their government, Utopus having understood that before his coming among them the old inhabitants had been engaged in great quarrels concerning religion . . . he made a law that every man might be of what religion he pleased, and might endeavor to draw others to it by force of argument, and . . . . that he ought to use no other force but that of persuasion, and was neither to mix with it reproaches nor violence. . . .This law was made by Utopus, not only for preserving the public peace, which he saw suffered much by daily contentions and irreconcilable heats, but because he thought the interest of religion itself required it.

Eventually More fell victim to the politics of the day himself. He was himself an ardent Catholic, but when he argued in 1535 that Mary, daughter of Katharine of Aragon, was the rightful heir to the English throne, Henry had him executed, not for his religious beliefs, but for treason.

Michel de Montaigne A generation younger than More, Michel de Montaigne [deh mon-TAYN] (1533–1592) was nevertheless equally affected by the conflicts between Catholics and Protestants. He was the son of a wealthy merchant and mayor of Bordeaux [bor-DOH], who sent him away at birth to be nursed by a peasant woman so that he might develop a love and respect for the common folk. A resident German tutor taught him Latin as he learned to speak, so that, in fact, Latin was his native tongue. By the age of six he was enrolled in the prestigious Collège de Guienne [koll-EZH deh ghee-EN], in Bordeaux, and by the age of 21 he had finished law school. At 24 he became one of 60 magistrates charged with enforcing the king's law in Bordeaux. In that capacity, watching the sometimes vicious persecution of the Protestant "heretics," he developed a lifelong distaste for brutality and cruelty.

In 1570, after 13 years of service as a magistrate, Montaigne retired from public life to the Montaigne estate and the sanctuary of his library: "It is on the third story of a tower," he later wrote. "The first contains my chapel; the second a bed-chamber with a dressing-room. . . . My library is round in shape, squared off only for the needs of my table and chair and, as it curves around, it offers me a single glance at all my books." Before the printing press, such private libraries were virtually nonexistent, but in the privileged surroundings of his books, Montaigne invented a new style of writing, the **personal essay**. *Essai*, in French, means "try out," or "attempt," and the form is a vehicle for trying out ideas, testing them even as they are written. In his essays, Montaigne revealed his own mind at work, often contradicting himself, openly challenging his own assumptions, and, in short, approaching the workings of his own mind with a significant measure of skepticism. In his essays Montaigne often posed more questions than he answered, and any answer was, almost by definition, tentative. Among his most famous essays is "Of Cannibals," a work that reflects his fascination with reports from the New World. The essay delights in the captivating details of cannibal life, but it also, tellingly, draws analogy to the writer's own world and the religious conflicts

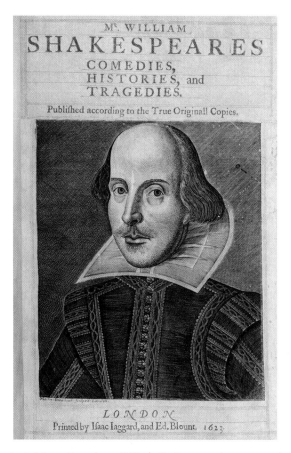

Fig. 8.17 Martin Droeshout, *William Shakespeare*, frontispiece of the first folio edition of his works, published in London. 1623. British Library, London, UK. The first edition of the collected plays of Shakespeare was prepared by John Heminges and Henry Condell, both fellow actors at the Globe.

that were, in his view, tearing French society apart. "So we may call these people barbarians," he writes, "in respect to the rules of reason, but not in respect to ourselves, who surpass them in every type of barbarity."

William Shakespeare: "The play's the thing!" There were many great playwrights in Elizabethan England, during the reign, that is, of Elizabeth I (r. 1558–1603), daughter of Henry VIII and Anne Boleyn, including Christopher Marlowe (1564–1593) and Thomas Kyd (1558–1594). But William Shakespeare (1564–1616) even in his own time was the acknowledged master of the medium. He wrote 37 plays: great cycles narrating English history; romantic comedies that deal with popular themes such as mistaken identity, the battle of the sexes, lovers' errors in judgment, and so on; romances that treat serious themes but in unrealistic, almost magical settings; and 11 tragedies. Fellow actors prepared the first edition of his collected plays and published them in 1623, after his death (Fig. **8.17**).

Until 1576, no permanent theater existed in England. Amphitheaters in Southwark [SUTH-urk], on the south bank of the Thames, were used for bear-baiting, and many inns made for natural playhouses, as they were designed around inner courtyards with upstairs rooms looking in. Companies of actors were officially adopted by noblemen, wore their patron's feudal livery, and were officially his servants. James Burbage [BUR-bij] belonged to a troop adopted by the Earl of Leicester [LES-ter], known as Leicester's Men. In the spring of 1576, Burbage opened the Theatre of Shoreditch, just outside the walls of London, and the relationship between actors and patrons changed. Troops of actors no longer depended completely on their masters; now they could also rely on the popularity of their plays to bring in profits and support themselves.

The basic price of admission to Burbage's Theatre was one penny, which in 1600 could buy one chicken or two tankards of ale. A laborer's wage was three or four pence, or pennies, a day. Burbage's Theatre was thus affordable, which partly accounts for its success; one penny soon became the standard base price of admission for all London theaters. In 1598, the company, now headed by James's son Richard, tore down the Shoreditch theater, in a dispute over the lease, and rebuilt it across the river in Southwark at Bankside, in the neighbor-

hood previously associated with bear-baiting. He renamed it "The Globe" (Fig. **8.18**). It could seat 3,000 people. The Swan and the Rose, large theaters that were already established at Bankside, could seat about the same. Watermen who transported London audiences across the river to the theaters claimed to carry 3,000–4,000 theatergoers to Bankside every afternoon. Including those arriving by foot across London Bridge, as many as 9,000 Londoners descended on the playhouses each day.

Although public playhouses varied, in general they were open-air structures consisting of three tiers of covered galleries (in which seats cost between three and six pence). In front of the stage, an open courtyard area held the **groundlings**. These theatergoers paid the one-penny base price of admission, stood throughout the performance, and wandered in and out at will, eating and drinking as they enjoyed the play. A rectangular stage, about 40 feet wide, projected into the courtyard. Behind it were exits to dressing rooms and balconies where players might look out on the action beneath them on the stage proper. Out of a trap door, in center stage, a ghost might rise.

Women were prohibited from appearing on stage, and so males—generally boys—played all female roles, which, in turn, required elaborate costuming. Stage props were sometimes minimal, consisting of no more than a chair or two, a chest, or the like, but some companies possessed elaborate sets. Lighting was nonexistent. Thus, under the light of an afternoon sky, the playwright might evoke night or storm by having one of the lesser actors carry a torch or lantern, and the audience would have to suspend its disbelief and imagine the scene (just as they had to accept boys as women). As a result, Elizabethan drama often focuses on the relation between illusion and reality, questioning what is "real" and what is not.

Shakespeare's company was Burbage's newly renamed Lord Chamberlain's players at the Globe, and he earned 10 percent of its profits. He wrote his plays with specific actors in the company in mind and played only minor roles himself. Richard Burbage was the leading man, playing the title role in Shakespeare's major tragedies, *Richard II*, *Romeo and Juliet*, *Hamlet*, *Othello*, and *King Lear*. Though many of Shakespeare's characters sing—and music plays an important role in the plays—none of the characters played by Burbage ever sing a note, because Burbage himself was tone deaf.

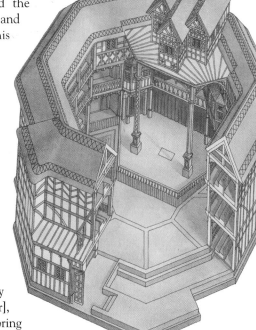

Fig. 8.18 Reconstruction and cross-section of the Globe Theater. 1599–1613. The stage was surrounded on three sides by three stories of tiered seating. Groundlings, those who paid one penny, stood in the open area in front of the stage. Admission to the lower gallery was another penny, to the middle galleries yet another.

Hamlet is arguably Shakespeare's greatest achievement. It is a **revenge play**, constructed around a murder that must be avenged by the victim's relative, usually at the request of the murdered person's ghost. An Elizabethan audience would have recognized the plot as formulaic, but nothing about the play is standard fare. Hamlet himself, the Danish prince who must avenge the murder of his royal father, is one of the most complex and ambiguous personalities in the history of the theater. Early in the play, his father's ghost reveals to Hamlet that his uncle, Claudius, murdered his father to replace him as king and as husband to Hamlet's mother. The ghost orders Hamlet to avenge his murder, setting the play in motion. Hamlet alternately behaves like a raving madman and an intellectual of the most refined sensibility, at once deeply perceptive and blind to the most obvious truths. Even in the company of friends, he is alone with himself, an intensely self-reflective soul tormented by the very act of self-reflection.

Consider Hamlet's famous soliloquy at the end of Act II. A band of traveling actors has just performed for him some lines concerning the death of King Priam [PRY-am] of Troy and the grief borne by his wife, Hecuba [HEK-yoo-buh]. Hamlet marvels at the players' ability to so emotionally identify with their roles (**Reading 8.5**):

READING 8.5   **from William Shakespeare, *Hamlet*, Act II, scene II (1623)**

O, what a rogue and peasant slave am I!
Is it not monstrous that this player here,
But in a fiction, in a dream of passion,
Could force his soul so to his own conceit
That from her working all his visage wann'd
Tears in his eyes, distraction in's aspect,
A broken voice, and his whole function suiting
With forms to his conceit? and all for nothing!
For Hecuba!
What's Hecuba to him, or he to Hecuba,
That he should weep for her? . . .

The players are moved by their fiction, while he, Hamlet, burdened by the responsibility of avenging his father but unable to act, seems not moved at all:

Yet I,
A dull and muddy-mettled[1] rascal, peak[2]
Like John-a-dreams, unpregnant of[3] my cause
And can say nothing—no, not for a king,
Upon whose property and most dear life
A damn'd defeat was made. . . .

But even as Hamlet damns himself for procrastinating, he devises a plan of action to "catch the conscience of the king"—he will have a play performed before his uncle the king:

. . . I'll have these players

Play something like the murder of my father
Before mine uncle: I'll observe his looks;
I'll tent him to the quick: if he but blench,
I know my course. The spirit that I have seen
May be the devil: and the devil hath power
To assume a pleasing shape; yea, and perhaps
Out of my weakness and my melancholy,
As he is very potent with such spirits,
Abuses me to damn me: I'll have grounds
More relative than this: the play's the thing
Wherein I'll catch the conscience of the king.

[1] **muddy-mettled:** dull-spirited
[2] **peak:** mope
[3] **unpregnant:** not quickened to action

This is Shakespeare at his most dramatic. Written almost entirely in blank verse (unrhymed iambic pentameter)—a form that Marlowe first introduced in his tragedies and that became known as "Marlowe's mighty line"—the soliloquy is alternately fast or slow, smooth or rough, the rhythm changing at almost every line with Hamlet's emotional twists and turns. By the time Hamlet finishes this soliloquy, with a rhymed couplet to round off the passage, Shakespeare has himself captured the conscience of his audience. Is it not a miracle, we ask ourselves, that this actor playing Hamlet "in a fiction, in a dream of passion, / Could force his soul so to his own conceit" that we are moved to complete identification with his plight?

In the next act, Shakespeare furthers the audience's identification with his play. In scene 1, Hamlet rejects the love of Ophelia, but, like the players in Act II, he is playacting, feigning madness in order to achieve his ends. However, the audience understands that Hamlet's feigned madness—believed by all—is potentially more destructive than productive. Then, in scene 2, the players perform what has become known as "the play within the play." As Hamlet planned in the soliloquy at the end of Act II, he means the play to move his uncle to such identification with the scene that he will reveal his own involvement in the murder of Hamlet's father. But the audience members recognize that they too must identify with the play they are watching. This is, after all, as Hamlet says at the beginning of the scene, "the purpose of playing, whose end, both at the first and now, was and is, to hold, as 'twere, the mirror up to nature. . . ." The audience members understand, therefore, that they are looking at a reflection of themselves.

In all his contradiction and ambiguity, Hamlet is the most desired role and the most often performed character in the history of the English stage, because he lays himself so bare before us, like some open wound that refuses to heal. He demands our understanding, even as he resists it. In fact, Hamlet represents a new idea of character—no longer a unified and coherent being, but rather a conflicted and driven personality, as mysterious to itself as to others, and as unpredictable as its very dreams. Hamlet is, in this sense, the first modern person. He inaugurates a type who will become in future centuries increasingly recognizable as a version of ourselves.

Above all, Hamlet is an individual. But the questions he poses in his soliloquies—the famous "To be or not to be" speech, for instance, in Act III, scene 1—reveal a first-person "I" new to the Western tradition in 1600, but totally recognizable to us today. Just as Montaigne, Shakespeare's contemporary, became increasingly convinced that he could never wholly know himself, creating for himself the motto "*Que sais-je?*" [KUH sezh] ("What do I know?"), Shakespeare's Hamlet recognizes that knowing anything fully and truly is at best difficult, and that knowing one's self is even more so. You can only take stabs at it—*essais* [es-SAY], as Montaigne called them. From 1600 onward, the human personality increasingly becomes the obsessive object of human study. In Shakespeare's Hamlet and Montaigne's first-person "I," Western culture inaugurates its tradition of self-examination and self-absorption.

The English Portrait Tradition

Hamlet represents the logical outcome of the English taste for portraiture, the dramatic embodiment of the nation's humanist emphasis on individualism. One of the most important portraitists of wealthy society in Europe was Hans Holbein [hahnz HOLE-bine] the Younger (ca. 1497–1543). He painted hundreds of works during his two extended visits to England (1526–1528, 1532–1543), including many of Henry VIII (Fig. **8.19**), four of Henry's six wives, scores of portraits of English courtiers and humanists, and just as many of the London German merchant community. Each portrait conveyed the sitter's status and captured something of the sitter's identity, in the case of Henry nothing less than his imposing self-confidence—he was, for his time, physically imposing as well, his six-foot-two-inch frame supporting a 54-inch waistline.

Like her father, Elizabeth was also the subject of many portraits. But few later English painters could match Holbein's skill in depicting volume, texture, and light. Most portraits of Elizabeth, such as the so-called *Darnley Portrait of Elizabeth I* (Fig. **8.20**), tend to concentrate on elaborate decorative effects. Set behind the flat patterning of her lace collar, pearl necklaces, and jewel-encrusted dress, Elizabeth appears almost bodiless—the exact opposite of Holbein's emphatically embodied portrait of Henry VIII. And yet, no other portrait of Elizabeth better conveys her steadfast determination, even toughness, while still capturing something of her beauty. By all accounts, she could alternately swear like a common prostitute and charm like the most refined diplomat, the very embodiment of the tensions that dominated her age.

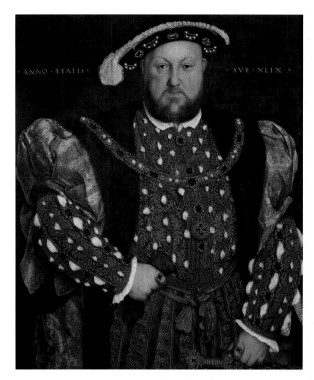

Fig. 8.19 Hans Holbein the Younger, *Henry VIII in Wedding Dress*. 1540. Oil on panel, 32 1/2″ × 29″. Galleria Barberini, Rome. Henry is in the clothes that he wore when he married the 25-year-old Anne of Cleves in 1540. He was 49.

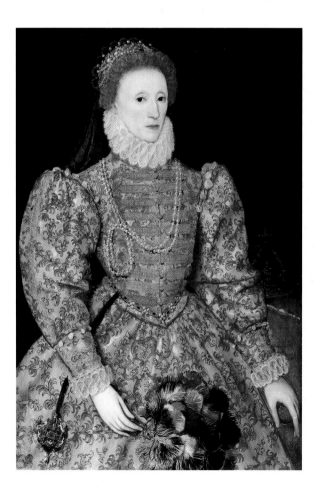

Fig. 8.20 Attributed to Federigo Zuccaro, *The Darnley Portrait of Elizabeth I*. ca. 1575. Oil on panel, 44 1/2″ × 31″. National Portrait Gallery, London. Behind Elizabeth, on the table at the right, lies her crown.

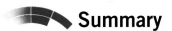 **Summary**

■ **Art, Commerce, and Merchant Patronage** The center of commercial activity in Flanders by the beginning of the fifteenth century was Bruges. Each year it sponsored a great fair where luxury art goods, especially tapestries and paintings, were sold to a rising merchant class, for both local consumption and export. Flemish painters took oil painting to new heights, using it to render the material world in meticulous detail. Oil paintings on panel were portable—therefore commercially viable—but the medium was also widely used for altarpieces, many commissioned by middle-class merchants. Often, the objects depicted in these paintings were imbued with a sense of reality never before realized in European painting.

■ **The German Tradition** The Flemish attention to representational detail in painting is reflected in German painting as well, but German artists such as Matthias Grünewald often used this realism to intensify the emotional, even mystical impact of their work. Perhaps the most interesting development in Germany is Nuremberg artist Albrecht Dürer's attempt to synthesize the Northern interest in detailed representation with the traditions of Italian humanism he had assimilated on his visit there in 1505–1506.

■ **Humanism and Reformation in the North** The papal practice of granting indulgences irritated both the humanist philosopher Desiderius Erasmus, who broadly satirized his contemporaries, and the humanist theologian Martin Luther, who attacked Church practices on many other grounds as well in his *Ninety-Five Theses* of 1517. At the heart of Luther's call for a reformation was, in fact, class division. Only the rich could afford to pay for the remission of their sins and those of their families. If the poor did buy them, they did so at great sacrifice to the well-being of their families.

Luther's Reformation quickly spread. Led by Thomas Müntzer, peasants throughout Germany revolted. Led by Ulrich Zwengli of Zurich, Protestant armies fought with Catholics in Switzerland. John Calvin sought to create an ideal moral community in Geneva. And in England, King Henry VIII split with Rome in order to annul his marriage, assert his own authority, and reap vast profits for the crown by dissolving the monasteries.

The Reformation's quick success can probably be attributed to the printing press, introduced to European culture by Johannes Gutenberg sometime between 1435 and 1455. The press made the publication of Luther's tracts possible, to say nothing of his translation into German of the Latin Bible. Musical scores could now be disseminated widely. And the works of other writers became popular as well, especially Thomas More's *Utopia*, Michel de Montaigne's *Essais*, and the plays of William Shakespeare, whose tragic hero Hamlet embodies the growing individualism of humanist culture in the North.

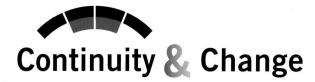

No movement as radical as the Reformation could take place without a strong reaction from the Roman Catholic Church. The challenge of Protestantism to the moral authority of the pope threatened the Church with downfall, and Rome soon recognized this. Yet the Roman Catholic Church had come to some of the same conclusions about its shortcomings as its northern critics. In self-defense, therefore, it launched a Counter-Reformation, both to strike back against the fundamental ideas advanced by reformists like Luther and to implement reforms of its own.

The Counter-Reformation, which is the subject of chapter 10, had the support of clergy and lay people through newly organized groups such as the Modern Devotion and the Oratory of Divine Love. These groups encouraged a return to the principles of simplicity, ethical living, and piety that Erasmus had championed. The Society of Jesus, known more familiarly as the Jesuits, took a tougher approach. Founded by Ignatius of Loyola in the 1530s, it advocated a return to strict and uncompromising obedience to the authority of the Church and its ecclesiastical hierarchy. The society's Rule 13 sums up its notion of obedience: "I will believe that the white that I see is black if the hierarchical Church so defines it." Then, in 1545, Pope Paul III convened the Council of Trent in order to define Church doctrine and recommend far-reaching reforms in the practices of the Church, particularly the selling of indulgences.

The Council of Trent, which convened in two more sessions between 1545 and 1563, also decided to counter the Protestant threat "by means of the stories of the mysteries of our Redemption portrayed by paintings or other representations, [so that] the people be instructed and confirmed in the habit of remembering and continually revolving in mind the articles of faith." The arts should be directed, the Council said, toward clarity and realism, in order to increase understanding, and toward emotion, in order to arouse piety and religious fervor. While the Council of Trent generally preached restraint in design, its desire to appeal to the emotions of its audience resulted in increasingly elaborate church architecture, so that the severe simplicity of the Calvinist church (Fig. 8.21), devoid of any art, would seem emotionally empty beside the grand expanse of the Catholic interior (Fig. 8.22). Yet the basic configuration would remain the same. For the next two centuries both churches would vie for the souls of Christians in Europe and the Americas. ■

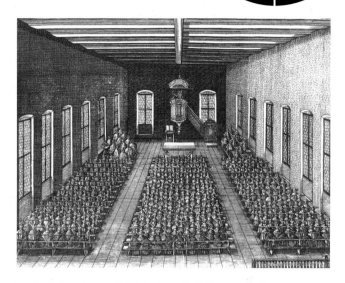

Fig. 8.21 Interior of a Calvinist Church. 17th century. German National Museum, Nuremberg.

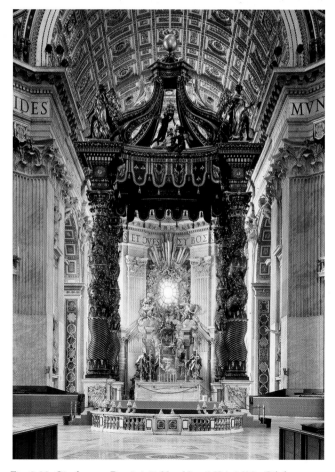

Fig. 8.22 Gianlorenzo Bernini, *Baldacchino.* 1624–1633. Gilt bronze, marble, stucco, and glass, height approx. 100′. Saint Peter's Basilica, Vatican, Rome.

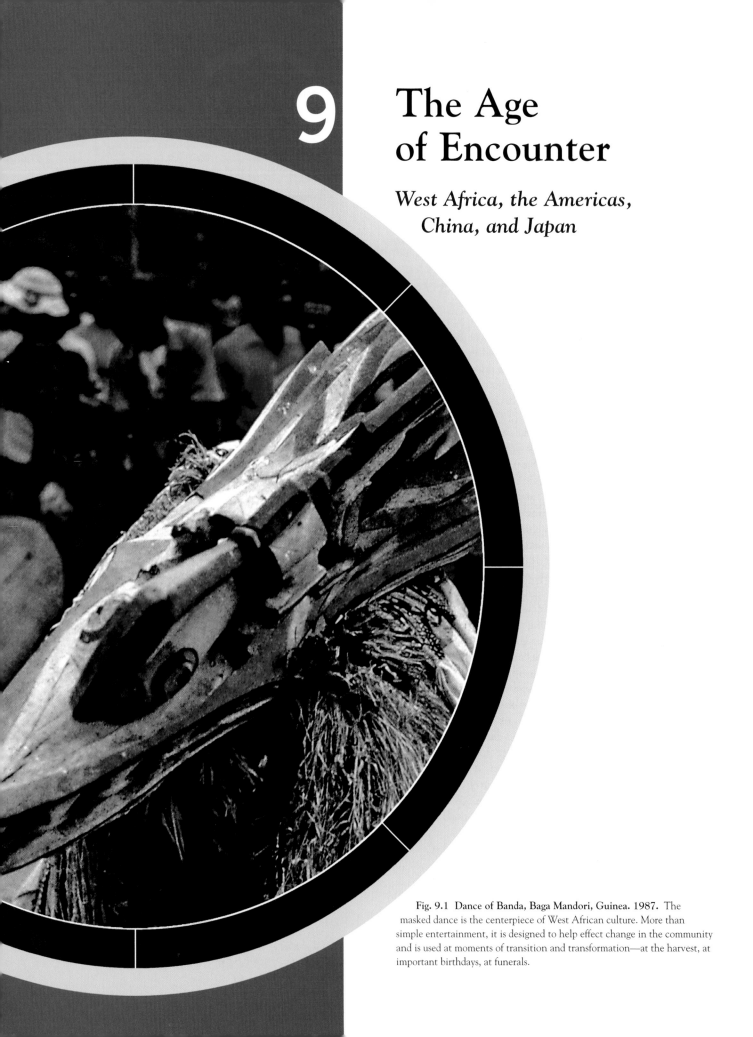

9 The Age of Encounter

West Africa, the Americas, China, and Japan

Fig. 9.1 Dance of Banda, Baga Mandori, Guinea. 1987. The masked dance is the centerpiece of West African culture. More than simple entertainment, it is designed to help effect change in the community and is used at moments of transition and transformation—at the harvest, at important birthdays, at funerals.

(We were astounded. . . . These buildings rising from the water, all made of stone, seemed like an enchanted vision. . . . Indeed some of our soldiers asked whether it was not all a dream.)

Bernal Diaz, *True History of the Conquest of New Spain*

Long before anyone in Europe knew they existed, richly diverse cultures flourished in Sub-Saharan Africa (Map **9.1**). People in the region spoke nearly 800 distinct but related languages of the Niger-Congo family. When European explorers finally encountered these cultures in the latter half of the fifteenth century, they were interested in them for commercial reasons—chiefly the trade in slaves. The Church, however, was also interested in converting what they considered Africa's pagan populations to Christianity, as they would in the Americas. Sub-Saharan African cultures consisted largely of villages united by kinship ties and generally ruled by chieftains. Almost all of these cultures emphasized the well-being of the group over the individual, a conviction invoked, guaranteed, and celebrated by the masked dance. The masked dance is, in fact, a ritual activity so universally practiced from one culture to the next across West Africa that it could be called the center of the region's culture. It unites the creative efforts of sculptors, dancers, musicians, and others. Originally performed as part of larger rituals connected with stages in human development, the passing of the seasons, or stages of the agricultural year, the masked dance in recent years has become increasingly disconnected from its original social context. A modern photograph of the *banda* [BAHN-dah] mask performed by the Baga Mandori [BAH-guh man-DOR-ee] people who live on the Atlantic coastline of Guinea was taken during an actual *banda* dance (Fig. **9.1**). Usually, the *banda* mask is danced at night, with only torches for illumination. However, for the sake of photography, villagers agreed to begin the performance at dusk, and the photographs taken that evening by Fred Lamp, Curator of African Art at the Yale University Art Gallery, are the only extant photographs of an actual *banda* performance.

The *banda* mask is a sort of amalgam of different creatures, combining the jaws of a crocodile, the face of a human, the elaborate hairstyle of a woman, the body of a serpent, the horns of an antelope, the alert ears of a deer, and, rising between the horns, the tail of a chameleon. The *banda* mask is generally danced at initiations, harvest ceremonies, and funerals, and is renowned for its spectacular acrobatics, with the wearer spinning high in the air and low to the ground in

defiance of the enormous weight of the mask itself. Like Native American kachina dolls discussed in chapter 1 (see Fig. 1.7), the *banda* mask is believed to possess **agency**. That is, it helps to effect change—the transformation (as symbolized by the chameleon's tail) from adolescence to adulthood, from fall to winter, from life to death. And it embodies the collective consciousness of the group by incorporating into its single visage the diversity of the natural world.

Traditionally, the head is of supreme importance in African cultures. In Ife culture, to which the later Yoruba people trace their ancestry, the head was the home of the spirit, the symbol of the king's capacity to organize the world and to prosper. The Ife culture is one of the oldest in West Africa. It developed beginning around the eighth century along the Niger [nee-ZHER] River, in what is now Nigeria. It was centered in the city of Ife. The Ife people believed that they depended on

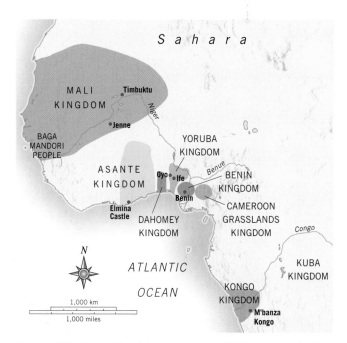

Map 9.1 Sub-Saharan West Africa, 1200–1700. While Muslim traders had extensive knowledge of North Africa, little was known of Sub-Saharan Africa before the Portuguese explorations of the fifteenth and sixteenth centuries.

their kings' heads for their own welfare. By 1100, they were producing highly naturalistic, sculptural, commemorative portraits in clay and stone, probably depicting their rulers, and not long after, cast brass sculptures as well.

An example of Ife brasswork is the *Head of a King* (or *Oni* [OH-nee]) (Fig. **9.2**). The parallel lines that run down the face represent decorative effects made by scarring—**scarification**. A hole in the lower neck suggests that the head may have been attached to a wooden mannequin, and in memorial services the mannequin may have worn the royal robes of the Ife court. Small holes along the scalp line suggest that hair, or perhaps a veil of some sort, also adorned the head.

Sometime around 1170, the city-state of Benin [bay-NEEN], some 150 miles southeast of Ife, also in the Niger basin, asked the *oni* of Ife to provide a new ruler for their territory, which was, legend has it, plagued by misrule and disorder. The *oni* sent Prince Oranmiyan [Oh-RHAN-mee-yan], who founded a new dynasty and named it *ibini*, "land of vexation," from which the name Benin derives. Some two centuries later, the fourth king, or *oba*, as the Benin culture called their leader, declared the value of creating lifelike images of their ancestor rulers, as the Ife were doing. He

asked the Ife if they would send a master metalworker south, and that artist, Iguegha [Eh-GUAY-gah], whose name has come down through legend, taught the artists of Benin the method of lost-wax casting.

The artists, members of the royal casters' guild, lived in their own quarters just outside the palace in Benin, where they are located to this day. Only the *oba* could order brasswork from them. These commissions were usually memorial heads, commemorating the king's royal ancestors in royal costume (Fig. **9.3**). (The head shown in figure 9.3 was made in the mid-sixteenth century, but heads like it were made in the earliest years of bronze production in the culture.) As in Ife culture, the *oba*'s head was the home of the spirit and the symbol of the *oba*'s capacity to organize the world and to prosper.

Interestingly, African languages do not have a word for "mask," the image of the head and its power. Rather, each mask has a particular name that is generally the word for the ancestor or supernatural being that the mask helps to make manifest. The mask, then, is not so much an object in its own right as it is a thing to be performed. Thus the helmet mask *elefon* [eh-leh-FOHN], from Yoruba [YOR-uh-buh] culture at the eastern end of the West Atlantic forests, near the Niger River, evokes

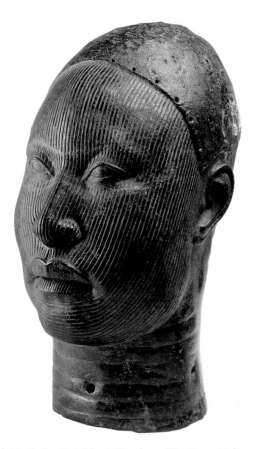

Fig. 9.2 Head of an *Oni* (King). Ife culture, Nigeria. ca. 13th century. Brass, height, 11 7/16". Museum of Ife Antiquities, Ife, Nigeria. The metal used to cast this head is an alloy of copper and zinc, and therefore not technically bronze, but brass.

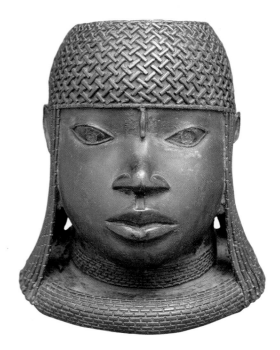

Fig. 9.3 Head of an *Oba*. Nigeria; Edo, Court of Benin ca. 1550. Image © The Metropolitan Museum of Art / Art Resource, NY. Such heads were usually commissioned upon the death of an *oba* by his successor, so that the deceased leader might continue to influence his community.

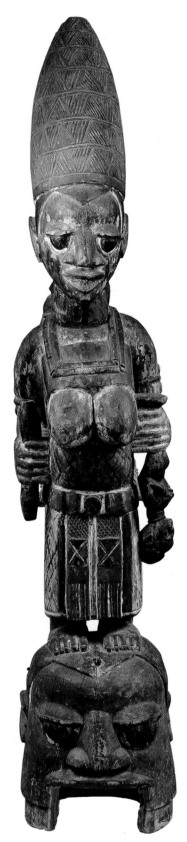

Fig. 9.4 Helmut mask *elefon*, Yoruba, Nigeria. After 1900.
Wood, height 51 ¹/₂″. University of Iowa Museum of Art. The Stanley
Collection. When not in use in a ritual dance, such masks were kept in the
shrine of the family patriarch where they were worshiped.

the spirit of the ancestral emperors of the Yoruba city of Oyo
[OI-yoh], who were called *Elefon* (Fig. **9.4**). Like most African
masks, this one was worn by a male, and the mask proper—its
bottom half—is male. But the top half is the representation of
a female. She carries a fly whisk in one hand and wears a tall
conical crown and a necklace of large coral beads—all symbols
of a Yoruba chief. And, indeed, though rare, there are instances
of Yoruba women serving as chief. The highest-ranking woman
was called *Iyalode* [EE-ah-LOH-day], or "mother of all." The
female figure on the *elefon* mask holds the upside-down figure
of another woman in her left hand. This gesture represents the
power of the *Iyalode* to exercise discipline over women who
have erred. The *Iyalode* also represented the collective interests
of women before the king.

The ritual practices of West Africa, especially the central
role in their culture of what we think of as their "art objects"
(dance masks, for instance), underscore the difference
between Western and non-Western ways of thinking. These
differences became increasingly apparent in the sixteenth
century, the Age of Encounter. Under the impetus of trade
and subsequent colonization, the West and the rest of the
world began to meet and, inevitably, confront each other's
ways of being and understanding.

This chapter surveys the cultures of the Americas, Africa,
China, and Japan in this period, and explores ways in which
Europe transformed these cultures and was itself transformed
by contact with them. From a Western perspective, these cultures represented a wider world of which Europe was the center. But from the point of view of these cultures, Europe
represented a force invading their own centers of culture
from the outside. European incursion threatened the social
integrity and cultural identity of the peoples in each of these
regions. In the Americas, encounter with Europe was devastating. In Africa, the results were barely better. Only in far-
away China and Japan were the cultures sufficiently resilient
to withstand foreign interference, and to continue to flourish
relatively unimpeded.

The Spanish Empire

When Christopher Columbus (1451–1506), an explorer from
Genoa, Italy, made landfall in the Americas on October 12,
1492, his mission was to find a more direct trade route to the
East, source of such valued goods as silks and spices. He was
sponsored by King Ferdinand II (1452–1516) and Queen
Isabella I (1451–1504) of Spain. Like most other Europeans,
the royal couple did not quite recognize the significance of
the great navigator's discoveries. But in all events, Columbus
was a man of his age. Like the artists and intellectuals of the
era, he was driven by a spirit of inquiry.

To reach the East, Columbus sailed west. He believed he
had landed on an island off the coast of Asia, possibly near the
great island of Cipango [chee-PAWN-go], as Japan was then
known. In his copy of *The Image of the World* by French theologian and astrologer Pierre d'Ailly [pyer die-YEE]

(1350–1420), he had underscored a few key phrases: "Between the end of Spain and the beginning of India is no great width," and "This Sea is navigable in a few days with a fair wind." As it turned out, the world was bigger than Columbus had imagined. Two great continents, north and south, lay between him and what he believed to be his destiny.

Columbus's landfall was most probably on one of the 700 islands that make up the Bahamas. Like other explorers of the time, he immediately recognized the exploitative value of the land and its natural resources—including gold, for which they all continually quested. He understood the "value" of the island's native people—Tainos [tah-EE-nos] of the Lucayo tribe who spoke the Arawak language. This is his own account of his first meeting with them (**Reading 9.1**):

READING 9.1   from Christopher Columbus, *Diaries* (1492)

In order that they would be friendly to us—because I recognized that they were people who would be better freed from their error and converted to our Holy Faith by love than by force—to some of them I gave red caps and glass beads they put on their chests, and many other things of small value, in which they took so much pleasure and became so much our friends that it was a marvel. . . . It seemed to me that they were a people very poor in everything. All of them go around as naked as their mothers bore them; and the women also. . . . They are very well formed, with handsome bodies and good faces. Their hair coarse—almost like the tail of a horse—and short. They wear their hair down over their eyebrows except for a little in the back which they wear long and never cut. Some of them paint themselves with black, and they are of the color of the Canarians, neither black nor white; and some of them paint themselves with white, and some of them with red, and some of them with whatever they find. And some of them paint their faces, and some of them the whole body, and some of them only the eyes, and some of them only the nose. They do not carry arms nor are they acquainted with them, because I showed them swords and they took them by the edge and through ignorance cut themselves. They have no iron. . . . They should be good and intelligent servants, for I see that they say very quickly everything that is said to them; and I believe that they would become Christians very easily, for it seemed to me that they had no religion. Our Lord pleasing, at the time of my departure I will take six of them from here to Your Highnesses in order that they may learn to speak. No animal of any kind did I see on this island except parrots.

This passage reveals Columbus's zeal to convert the native people to Catholicism, his sense of superiority, and his presumption that the Tainos would make good slaves, from which

he and his king might profit. (On his second voyage, in 1493, he would capture nearly 1,000 Tainos and transport them back to Spain for sale in the Seville slave market.) History would leave an even darker legacy. Although today a few Bahamians speak of their Taino descent, the claim is hard to prove. Of the original Taino population in the Bahamas, whose number has been estimated to be 300,000, about one-third were killed or died of disease brought to the islands by their European visitors before 1496. By 1508, the population had dwindled to 60,000, by 1512 to 20,000, and by the middle of the sixteenth century, no more than 500 Taino survived. The devastation was even greater in the rest of the West Indies, where Arawak-speaking peoples who had numbered around 2 to 3 million before the encounter with Europeans dwindled to a few thousand by the early sixteenth century. By the end of the century they were extinct. The scenario occurred repeatedly in the following three centuries throughout the Americas and Africa as European explorers crossed the globe in search of precious metals and other goods (see Map **9.2**).

The Pre-Columbian Era

Great cultures had existed in the Americas in Pre-Columbian times—that is, in the era before the arrival of Columbus in 1492. In the arid north of present-day Mexico a mysterious but enormously influential civilization centered at Teotihuacán [tay-oh-tee-wah-KHAN] flourished. By the fourth century CE, it was a center of culture comparable in size and influence to Constantinople. In Mesoamerica, comprising modern-day Honduras, Guatemala, Belize, and southern Mexico, between 250 and 900 CE the Maya established vast palace complexes that were both the administrative and religious centers of their culture.

These cultures were themselves preceded by others. As early as 1300 BCE, a preliterate group known as the Olmec [OHL-mek] came to inhabit the area between Veracruz and Tabasco on the southern coast of the Gulf of Mexico, where they built huge ceremonial precincts in the middle of their communities. In these precincts, they erected giant pyramidal mounds, where an elite group of ruler-priests lived. These pyramids may have been an architectural reference to the volcanoes that dominate Mexico, or they may have been tombs. Excavations may eventually tell us. At La Venta [luh VEN-tuh], very near the present-day city of Villahermosa [vee-yuh-er-MOH-suh], three colossal stone heads stood guard over the ceremonial center on the south end of the platform (Fig. **9.5**), and a fourth guarded the north end by itself. Each head weighs between 11 and 24 tons, and each bears a unique emblem on its headgear, which is similar to old-style American leather football helmets. They are carved of basalt, although the nearest basalt quarry is 50 miles to the south in the Tuxtla [toost-luh] Mountains. They were evidently at least partially carved at the quarry, then loaded onto rafts and floated downriver to the Gulf of Mexico before going back upriver to their final resting places. Many of the characteristic features of later Mesoamerican culture, such as pyramids, ball courts, mirror-making, and the calendar system, probably originated with the Olmec.

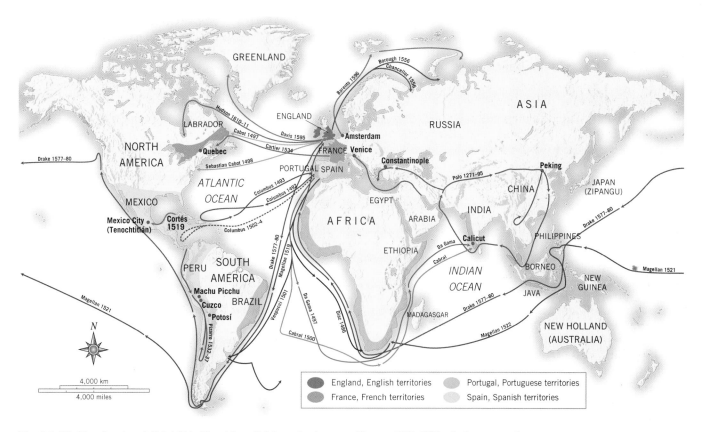

Map 9.2 World exploration, 1486–1611. Note Marco Polo's overland route to China in 1271–1295, which anticipated the great sea explorations by 200 years.

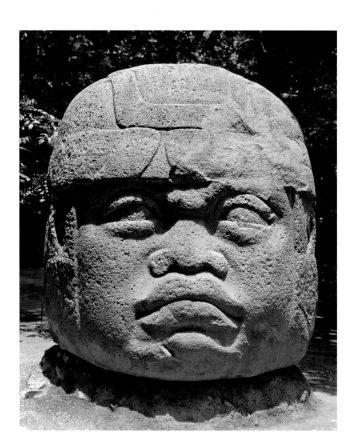

Teotihuacán The sense of colossal scale is found again and again throughout Pre-Columbian culture in Mesoamerica. The city of Teotihuacán, for instance, is laid out in a grid system, the basic unit of which is 614 square feet, and every detail is subjected to this scheme, conveying a sense of power and mastery. A great broad avenue, known as the Avenue of the Dead, runs through the city (Figs. **9.6**, **9.7**). It links two great pyramids, the Pyramids of the Moon and the Sun, each surrounded by about 600 smaller pyramids, 500 workshops, numerous plazas, 2,000 apartment complexes, and a giant market area. The Pyramid of the Sun is oriented to mark the passage of the sun from east to west and the rising of the stellar constellation, the Pleiades, on the days of the equinox. Each of its two staircases contains 182 steps, which, when the platform at its apex is added, together total 365. The pyramid is thus an image of time. This representation of the solar calendar is echoed in another pyramid at Teotihuacán, the Temple of Quetzalcoatl [ket-zahl-co-AH-tull], which is decorated with 364 serpent fangs.

Fig. 9.5 Colossal head, from La Venta, Mexico. Olmec culture. ca. 900–500 BCE. Basalt, height 7'5". La Venta Park, Villahermosa, Tabasco, Mexico. The stone heads are generally believed to be portraits of Olmec rulers, and they all share the same facial features, including wide, flat noses and thick lips. They suggest that the ruler was the culture's principal mediator with the gods, literally larger than life.

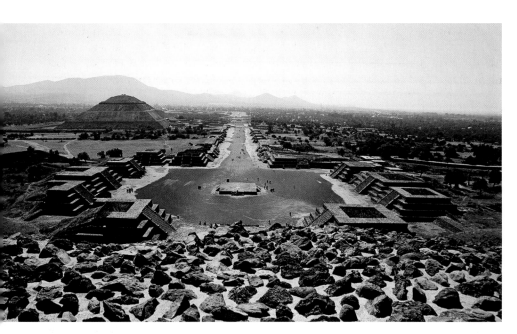

Fig. 9.6 Teotihuacán, Mexico, as seen from the Pyramid of the Moon, looking south down the Avenue of the Dead, the Pyramid of the Sun at the left. ca. 350–650 CE. One of the largest cities in the world by the middle of the first millennium, Teotihuacán covered an area of nearly nine square miles.

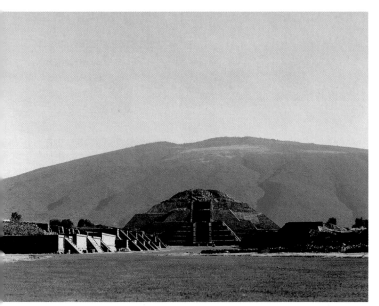

Fig. 9.7 The Pyramid of the Moon, looking north up the Avenue of the Dead. Beginning at the southern end of the city, and culminating at the Pyramid of the Moon, the Avenue of the Dead is 2 1/2 miles long.

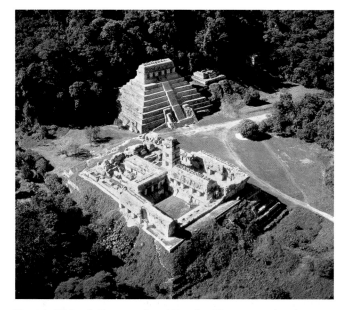

Fig. 9.8 "Palace" (foreground) and Temple of Inscriptions (tomb pyramid of Lord Pacal), Palenque, Mexico. Maya culture. 600–900 CE. The Museum of Modern Art. These two buildings, along with two other temples not seen in this view, formed the central complex of Palenque. Another complex to the north is composed of five temples and a ball court, and a third group of temples lies to the south. Palenque was the center of a territory that may have been populated by as many as 100,000 people.

At its height, in about 500 CE, about 200,000 people lived in Teotihuacán, making it one of the largest cities in the world. Scholars believe that a female deity, associated with the moon, as well as cave and mountain rituals, played an important role in Teotihuacán culture. The placement of the Pyramid of the Moon, in front of the dead volcano Cerro Gordo (see Fig. 9.7), supports this theory. It is as if the mountain, seen from a vantage point looking north up the Avenue of the Dead, embraces the pyramid in its flanks. And the pyramid, in turn, seems to channel the forces of nature—the water abundant on the mountain in particular—into the heart of the city.

For the Aztecs, a thousand years later, Teotihuacán remained the mythic center of Mesoamerican civilization, a site of pilgrimage for even the most exalted Aztec ruler.

Mayan Culture To the south of Teotihuacán a competing culture, that of the Maya, held sway for the better part of the first millennium CE. An elaborate calendar system enabled them to keep track of their history—and, evidence suggests, to predict the future. It consisted of two interlocking ways of recording time, a 260-day calendar and a 365-day calendar. The 260-day calendar probably derives from the length of human gestation, from a pregnant woman's first missed menstrual period to birth. When both calendars were synchronized, it took exactly 52 years of 365 days for a given day to repeat itself—the so-called *calendar round*—and the end of each cycle was widely celebrated.

Among the most important Mayan cities is Palenque, one of the best preserved of all Mayan sites. Lost in the jungle for centuries following its decline, which occurred around the year 850, Palenque was rediscovered in 1746 by a Spanish priest who had heard rumors of its existence. The Temple of Inscriptions, facing into the main courtyard of the so-called Palace, which may have been an administrative center rather than a royal residence, rises in nine steps, representing the nine levels of the Mayan Underworld (Fig. **9.8**). It is inscribed with the history of the Palenque kings, who were associated with the jaguar. The first recorded king is Bahlum Kuk [Bahlum Koohk], "Jaguar Quetzal," who, so the inscriptions say, founded the city on March 11, 431. Palenque's most powerful king was Pacal (603–683), who ruled for 67 years, and the Temple of Inscriptions was erected over his grave.

In 1952, Alberto Ruz, a Mexican archeologist, discovered the entrance to the tomb of Lord Pacal, under the pyramid. It was hidden under large stone slabs in the floor of the temple at the top of the pyramid. Ruz had to clear the passage down to Pacal's tomb, at the very base of the structure, which had been back-filled with stone debris. When he reached the tomb, he found that Pacal's face was covered with a jade death mask. A small tube connected the tomb with the upper level, thus providing the dead king with an eternal source of fresh air. He was buried in a large uterus-shaped stone sarcophagus weighing over five tons and covered with jade and cinnabar. The sarcophagus lid was decorated with a relief image of Pacal falling off the Wacah Chan [Wah-kah Chahn], the Tree of Life (Fig. **9.9**), which connects the Upperworld, the Middleworld, and the Underworld. At the top of the tree sits the feathered serpent, Quetzalcoatl. A double-headed serpent, signifying Pacal's royal lineage, encircles the tree. The Maya believed the king embodied the Wacah Chan, and when he stood at the top of a pyramid in a ritual ceremo-

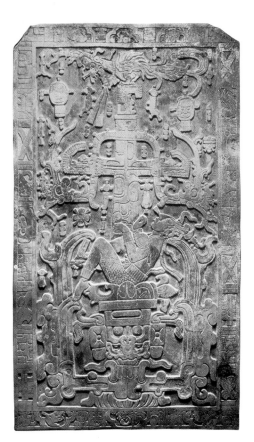

Fig. 9.9 Funerary lid of the sarcophagus of Pacal. 683 CE. Limestone, 12′ 6″ × 7′. National Museum of Archeology, Mexico City. Since the sarcophagus weighs over five tons, it was surely put in place before the Pyramid of Inscriptions was built above it, though it may well not have contained the body of Pacal when it was constructed.

ny, he linked the three layers of the universe in his own person. During such rituals, the king would let his own blood to give sustenance to the spiritual world. Some now believe that the Wacah Chan can actually be read astronomically as the Milky Way, along which the spirits of the dead travel before being reborn into a new life.

By 900 CE, Mayan culture had collapsed as a result of a wide variety of events, including overpopulation and accompanying ecological degradation, political competition, and war. Its peoples, who survive in large numbers to this day, returned to simple farming around the ruins of their once-great cities.

The Aztec In the north, after the decline of Teotihuacán, warring tribes struggled for control until one of them, the Mexica, later known as the Aztecs, wandered into the Valley of Mexico in about 1325 and built a village on the shores of Lake Texcoco. There they saw an eagle perching on a prickly pear cactus (*tenochtli*) [teh-nok-tlee], a sign that their wandering was over. They dug canals and drained the shallow areas of the lake, converting them into fertile fields, and there, as well, they built the city of Tenochtitlán on an island in the lake's center.

Blood sacrifice, a practice inherited from the Maya, was central to Aztec culture, merging perfectly with their warrior traditions. The Aztecs believed that the sun, moon, and earth all depended upon human blood for their sustenance. Their chief activity, as a result, was war, and the chief goal of war was to capture sacrificial victims. At puberty, boys were placed under jurisdiction of a local warrior house and trained for war, where they learned that success in life equaled the number of enemies captured alive for later ritual killing. Death itself, when realized in the pursuit of such honor, was the greatest honor an Aztec male could achieve.

Cortés in Mexico

Centered at Tenochtitlán, Aztec culture would survive until the arrival of the Spanish, led by Hernán Cortés [cor-TES] (1485–1547), in 1519. The Spaniards called the adventurers, soldiers, and administrators (some were all three) such as Cortés *conquistadores*, "conquerors." In 1519–1521, Cortés conquered the Aztec empire of Mexico with 600 men through a combination of military technology (gunpowder, cannon, and muskets), disease inadvertently introduced by his troops, and a series of lies and violations of trust. When Cortés entered the Aztec island capital of Tenochtitlán (Fig. **9.10**), present-day Mexico City, more than 200,000 people lived there. Gold-laden temples towered above the city. Gardens rich in flowers and fruit, and markets with every available commodity dominated the city itself as Bernal Díaz (1492–1584), one of Cortés's conquistadores, would later recall the sight (**Reading 9.2**):

READING 9.2   **from Bernal Diaz, *True History of the Conquest of New Spain* (ca. 1568; published 1632)**

We were astounded. . . . These buildings rising from the water, all made of stone, seemed like an enchanted vision. . . . Indeed some of our soldiers asked whether it was not all a dream. . . . It was all so wonderful that I do not know how to describe this first glimpse of things never heard of, seen, or dreamed of before. . . .

Let us begin with the dealers in gold, silver, and precious stones, feathers, cloaks, and embroidered goods, and male and female slaves who are also sold there. . . .Next there were those who sold coarser cloth, and cotton goods and fabrics made of twisted threads, and there were chocolate merchants with their chocolate. In this way you could see every kind of merchandise to be found anywhere in New Spain. . . . We were astounded at the great number of people and the quantities of merchandise, and at the orderliness and good arrangements that prevailed.

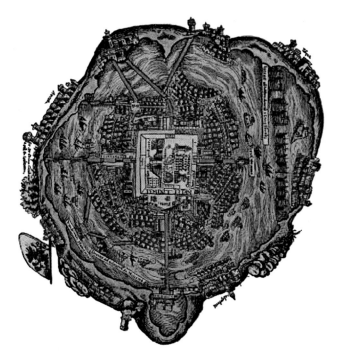

Fig. 9.10 Plan of Tenochtitlán, from Cortés's first letter to the king of Spain. 1521. Bernal Díaz, one of Cortés's conquistadores, compared the plan of Tenochtitlán to Venice. Set in the middle of Lake Texcoco, it was crisscrossed by canals.

What most astonished Cortés himself, as it had Díaz, was that Aztec civilization was as sophisticated as his own and unlike the civilization Columbus had encountered, with its naked, seemingly innocent natives. "So as not to tire Your Highness with the description of things of this city," Cortés wrote Queen Isabella of Spain, "I will say only that these people live almost like those in Spain, and in as much harmony and order as there, and considering that they are barbarous and so far from the knowledge of God and cut off from all civilized nations, it is truly remarkable to see what they have achieved in all things." This willingness to see a thriving civilization as uncivilized because it is unlike one's own is typical of the attitude of Westerners toward the peoples with whom they came into contact in the Age of Encounter. Other peoples were exactly that—the "Other"—a separate category of being that freed Western colonizers from any obligation to identify these peoples as equal, or even similar, to themselves.

In fact, the Aztecs possessed neither guns nor horses, nor much in the way of clothing or armor, all of which made them appear if not uncivilized, then completely vulnerable. They were also vulnerable because other native populations in Mexico deeply resented the fact that the

Aztecs regularly raided their villages to obtain victims for blood sacrifice. In fact, anthropological evidence suggests that just before Cortés's arrival, in about 1450, the Aztecs had wiped out the entire population of Casas Grandes, near present-day Chihuahua in northern Mexico, a trading center containing over 2000 pueblo apartments. Given such Aztec behavior, other tribes were willing to cooperate with Cortés. Cortés exploited these circumstances to great military advantage.

Cortés was also able to take advantage of Aztec myth. The Spanish conquistador had learned of an Aztec myth concerning Quetzalcóatl, the Feathered Serpent, who was widely worshiped throughout Mexico. In this myth, Quetzalcóatl was dethroned by his evil brother, Tezcatlipoca [tets-cat-li-POH-cah], god of war, and fled to the Gulf of Mexico, where he burst into flames and ascended to the heavens, becoming the Morning Star, Venus. In yet another version, he sailed away across the sea on a raft of serpents, promising one day to return. It was reputed that Quetzalcóatl was fair-skinned and bearded. Evidently, the Aztec king Motecuhzoma [mo-tek-koo-ZOH-mah] (formerly spelled Montezuma) believed that Cortés was the returning Quetzalcóatl and welcomed him without resistance. Cortés in turn imprisoned him, and within two years, Cortés's army had crushed Motecuhzoma's people in the name of Spain. Of the 20 to 25 million inhabitants of Mexico at that time, only about two million survived—the remainder were wiped out by war and disease.

Pizarro in Peru

Spain conquered Peru in 1533 through the exploits of Francisco Pizarro [pee-ZAH-roh] (1474–1541) with an army of only 180 men. The Inca Empire Pizarro found in Peru was one of the largest empires in the world and included, in addition to Peru itself, most of what is now modern Ecuador, Bolivia, northern Chile, and part of Argentina. Around 1300, in South America, Inca culture had emerged in the southern Peruvian highlands, where the Inca took advantage of the Andean camelids—llamas, alpacas, vicuñas, and guanacos, beasts of burden unknown to the cultures of Mesoamerica— to forge trading networks that eventually united the southern highlands and northern coastal lowlands under their rule. Large irrigation projects transformed both the river valleys and the desert between them into rich agricultural regions.

The Inca were, above all, masterful masons. Working with stone tools and without mortar, they crafted adjoining granite blocks that fit so snugly together that their walls have, for centuries, withstood earthquakes that have destroyed many later structures. Few of the blocks are the same size, and some have as many as 30 faces. Still, the joints are so tight that even the thinnest knife blade cannot be forced between the stones. Cuzco (meaning "navel of the earth"), the capital of the Inca Empire, was laid out to resemble a giant puma, and its masonry, much of which still survives, is unmatched anywhere in the world. At Machu Picchu (Fig. **9.11**), stone buildings, whose thatched and gabled roofs have long since collapsed, are set on stone terraces in a setting that was a religious retreat or refuge for the Inca ruler, Pachacuti Inka Yupanqui [Pah-chah-coo-tee Ink-ah Yoo-pahn-kee], who built the complex between 1460 and 1470.

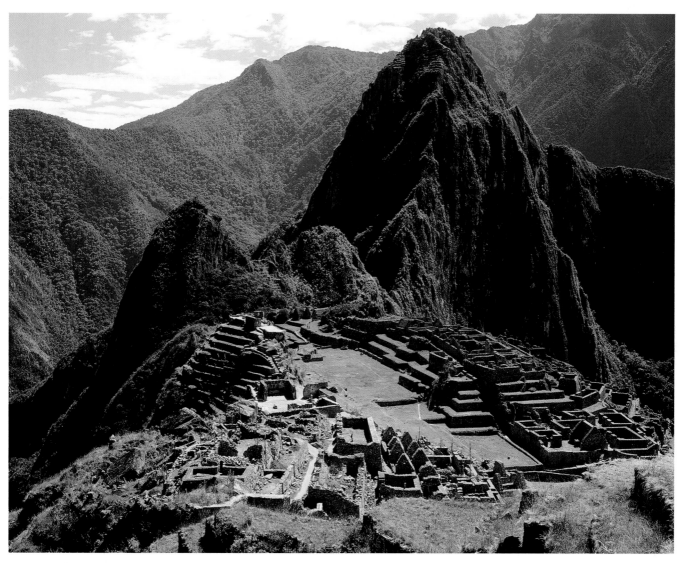

Fig. 9.11 Machu Picchu, Inca culture, Peru. ca. 1450. Machu Picchu survived destruction by the Spanish when they invaded in 1532, partly because of its remote location, high in the Andes, and partly because, compared to the Inca capital of Cuzco, it probably seemed small and comparatively insignificant. Nevertheless, by about 1537 it was abandoned as Inca civilization collapsed, victim not only of the Spanish conquistadores, but also of disease, especially smallpox.

About 1,200 people lived in Machu Picchu's approximately 170 residences, most of them women, children, and priests. The Inca also created an extraordinary network of roads, ranging from as wide as 50 feet to as narrow as 3 feet, and extending from desert to Andes peaks for some 15,000 miles. Nearly a thousand lodgings were built along the routes, and relay runners could carry news across the region in less than a week.

The Inca were especially attracted to textiles, which apparently they valued even more than gold or other minerals, at least in part because of the extremely high, and cold, elevations at which they lived. The exact meaning of the design of an Inca weaving that survives from the time of the Spanish conquest is unclear, but scholars believe it is largely symbolic (Fig. 9.12).

But Pizarro cared little for Inca textiles. Like Cortés, his primary motive for conquering the Inca was the acquisition of gold, silver, and precious stones. According to Spanish commentators, a white llama was paraded through the streets of the city during celebrations of the coming plant ing season each April, dressed in a red tunic and wearing gold jewelry. These processions also included life-size gold and silver images of llamas, people, and gods. Small objects of gold and silver, which symbolized to the Inca the sun and the moon, were scattered through the central plaza of Cuzco. The plaza—in Incan times twice as large as it is today—was excavated to a depth of between six and twelve inches, its sacred soil carried away to each of the four quadrants of Tahuantinsuyu [Ta-WAHN-tin-SOO-yah], as the Inca called their homeland, "Land of the Four Quadrants." The plaza was then refilled with sand brought from the ocean, in which offerings of gold and silver llamas and human figures were distributed. The plaza thus symbolized a great body of water, at once the Pacific Ocean and Lake Titicaca, from which the Inca creator deity, Ticsivirachocha [TIC-see-VEER-ah-COH-cha], had emerged after the great flood to repopulate the world.

More elaborately decorated was the Coricancha [KORE-eh-KAHN-cha] (literally, "the corral of gold"), the Inca Temple of the Sun facing the plaza. (The Coricancha was converted by the Spaniards to a Dominican church and monastery.) Dedicated to Inti [In-tee], the sun god, the original temple was decorated with 700 sheets of gold studded with emeralds and turquoise and designed to reflect the sunlight admitted through its windows. Its courtyard was filled with golden statuary—"stalks of corn that were of gold—stalks, leaves and ears," the Spanish chronicler Pedro de Cieza de León reported in the mid-sixteenth century. "Aside from this," he continued, there were "more than twenty sheep [llamas] of gold with their lambs and the shepherds who guarded them, all of this metal."

Great masses of such treasure were sent home from both Mexico and Peru. When the first Royal Fifth (that is, one-fifth of the treasures collected by Cortés and earmarked by contract for the king) arrived in Brussels, the German artist Albrecht Dürer was present:

I saw the things which were brought to the King from the New Golden Land: a sun entirely of gold, a whole fathom [six feet] broad; likewise, a moon, entirely of silver, just as big; likewise, sundry curiosities from their weapons, armor, and missiles; very odd clothing, bedding, and all sorts of strange articles for human use, all of which is fairer to see than marvels. These things were all so precious that they were valued at a hundred thousand guilders. But I have never seen in all my days that which so rejoiced my heart, as these things. For I saw among them amazing artistic objects, and I marveled over the subtle ingenuity of the men in these distant lands. Indeed I cannot say enough about the things which were there before me.

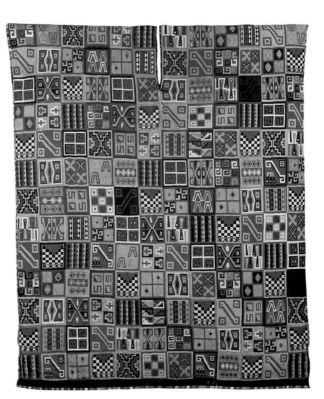

Fig. 9.12 Tapestry weave Inca tunic, south coast of Peru. ca. 1440–1540. Camelid fiber and cotton, 35 1/8″ × 30″. Dunbarton Oaks Research Library and Collections, Washington, DC. Each square represents a specific group, or an individual's identity, and functions much like a heraldic device or a logo.

Accounts like this helped give rise to the belief in an entire city of gold, El Dorado, which continued to elude the grasp of the conquistadores under royal order who followed in Pizarro's footsteps in Peru, often with unhappy results. The treasures of gold and silver that were brought back would be melted down for currency, far more important than their artistic value to the warring Spanish monarchy. In fact, almost no gold or silver objects survive from the conquest.

Pizarro's military strategy in Peru was aided by simple deceit. He captured the Inca emperor, Atahuallpa [ah-tah-

HWAHL-pah], who offered Pizarro a ransom of 13,420 pounds of gold and 26,000 pounds of silver. Pizarro accepted the ransom and then executed the unsuspecting emperor. He then proceeded to plunder Peru as a whole.

West African Culture and the Portuguese

Portugal was as active as Spain in seeking trading opportunities through navigation, but focused on Africa and the East instead of the Americas. In 1488, Bartholomeu Dias [DEE-az] (ca. 1450–1500), investigating the coast of West Africa, was blown far south by a sudden storm, and turning northeast, found that he had rounded what would later be called the Cape of Good Hope and entered the Indian Ocean. Following Dias, Vasco da Gama [VAHZ-koh da GAH-mah] (ca. 1460–1524) sailed around the cape with four ships in 1497 and reached Calicut, India, 10 months 14 days after leaving Lisbon. Then, in 1500, Pedro Cabral [kah-BRAHL] (ca. 1467–ca. 1520), seeking to repeat da Gama's voyage to India, set out from the bulge of Africa. Sailing too far westward, he landed in what is now Brazil, where he claimed the territory for Portugal.

After Bartholomeu Dias's exploration of the west coast of Africa, it did not take long for the Portuguese to join an already thriving slave market among the African kingdoms themselves and in the Muslim markets of North Africa (see chapter 4). They were financed principally by a Florentine banker together with a group of other financiers from Genoa. Over the course of four centuries, the Portuguese transported millions of Africans across the Atlantic (Map **9.3**) on the **Middle Passage**, so named because it formed the base of a triangular trade system: Europe to Africa, Africa to the Americas (the Middle Passage), and the Americas to Europe. No one can say with certainty just how many slaves made the crossing, although estimates range between fifteen and twenty million. Part of the problem is the unknown numbers who died of disease and harsh conditions during the voyage. For instance, in 1717, a ship reached Buenos Aires with only 98 survivors of an original 594 slaves. Such figures were probably not unusual.

For a while, at least, the Portuguese enjoyed a certain status as divine visitors from the watery world, the realm of Olokun [OH-loh-koon], god of the sea. They were considered to be the equivalent of the mudfish, because they could both "swim" (in their boats) and walk on land. The mudfish was sacred to the people of Benin, who saw it as a symbol of both transformation and power. (It lies dormant all summer on dry mudflats until fall when the rains come and it is "reborn.") (The fish is a symbol of power because it can deliver strong electric shocks and possesses lethal spines.) Likewise, the Portuguese seemed to be born of the sea and possessed "spines" of their own—rifles and musketry.

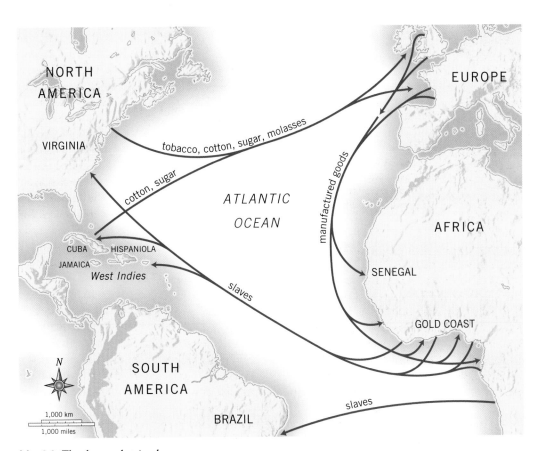

Map 9.3 The slave trade triangle.

An example of this association of the mudfish with the Portuguese is a decorative design that forms the tiara of an ivory mask worn as a hip pendant by the *oba* Esigie [OH-bah ay-SEE-gee-yay] (r. 1504–1550) (Figs. **9.13, 9.14**). (An *oba* is the traditional supreme leader of a Yoruba town.) The pendant probably depicts the queen mother (that is, the *oba*'s mother), or *iyoba* [ee-YOH-bah]. Esigie's mother was named Idia [ih-dee-YAH], and she is the first woman to officially hold the position of *iyoba*. Apparently, when the neighboring Igala [ee-GAH-lah] people of lower Niger threatened to conquer the Benin, Idia raised an army and by using magical powers helped Esigie defeat the Igala army. Part of her magic may have been the enlistment of Portuguese help. In acknowledgment of the Portuguese aid, the *iyoba*'s collar bears decorative images of bearded Portuguese sailors and alternating sailors and mudfish at the top of her tiara.

The impact of the Portuguese merchants, and of the Catholic missionaries who followed them, was not transforming though it was undeniable and at times devastating. The Benin culture has remained more or less intact since the time of encounter. Today, for instance, during rituals and ceremonies the *oba* wears at his waist five or six replicas of masks such as the *iyoba*'s, as well as the traditional coral-bead headdress. Oral traditions, like the praise poem, remain in place, despite attempts by Western priests to suppress them. If anything, it has been the last 50 years that have most dramatically transformed the cultures of Africa. But it was the institution of slavery, long practiced in Africa by the Yoruba and Benin peoples, that most dramatically impacted Portuguese and Western culture.

At first Benin had traded gold, ivory, rubber, and other forest products for beads and, particularly, brass. The standard medium of exchange was a horseshoe-shaped copper or brass object called a *manilla* [mah-NEEL-lah], five of which appear in an early sixteenth-century Benin plaque portraying a Portuguese warrior (Fig. **9.15**). Such metal plaques decorated the palace and royal altar area particularly, and here the soldier brings with him the very material out of which the plaque is made. If his weapons—trident and sword—suggest his power, it is a power in the service of the Benin king, at least from the Benin point of view.

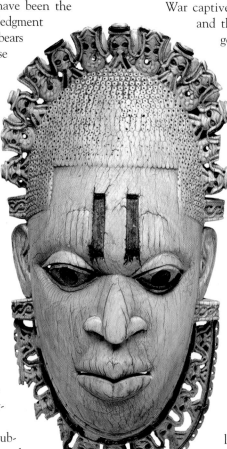

Fig. 9.13 Mask of an *iyoba* (queen mother), probably Idia, Court of Benin, Nigeria. ca. 1550. Ivory, iron, and copper, height 9 3/8″. The Metropolitan Museum of Art, New York. The Michael C. Rockefeller Memorial Collection, Gift of Nelson A. Rockefeller, 1972. (1978.412.323). The scarification lines on the forehead were originally inlaid with iron, and so were its pupils, both symbols of strength.

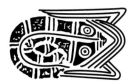

Fig. 9.14 Symbol of a coiled mudfish. Found throughout the art of Benin and in the tiara worn by the *iyoba* in Fig. 9.13.

The Portuguese picked up thousands of small objects—amulets, trinkets, and so on—that they termed *fetisso* [feh-TEE-sah], a sixteenth-century Afro-Portuguese pidgin word from which derives our word **fetish**, an object believed to have magical powers. But eventually the trade turned to slaves. Africans had long been selling captives from neighboring territories as slaves to Muslim traders. But with the Portuguese the practice expanded dramatically. At the start of the era, around 1492, there were an estimated 140,000–170,000 African slaves in Europe. But in about 1551, the Portuguese began shipping thousands of slaves to Brazil to work in the sugar plantations.

War captives proved an insufficient source of bodies, and the Portuguese took whomever they could get their hands on. They treated these slaves much more harshly than the Muslims had. They chained them, branded them, and often literally worked them to death. In short, the Portuguese inaugurated a practice of **cultural hegemony** (cultural domination) that set the stage for the racist exploitation that has haunted the West ever since.

Kingdom of the Kongo

A thousand miles south of Benin, in the basin of the Congo River, comprising parts of present-day Angola, Gabon, the Democratic Republic of Congo, and the Republic of Congo, the kingdom of the Kongo rose to prominence sometime around 1400. Like many of the West African cultures to the north, its resources derived from the equatorial forest. Its capital city, Mbanza Kongo [um-BAHN-zah KON-go], was home to from two to three million people. *Mbanza* means "residence of the king," and its king lived in a royal residence on the top of a hill overlooking the Lulunda River.

One of the king's titles was *Matombola* [mah-tom-BOH-lah], "the one who summons spirits from the land of the dead." This land, the Kongolese believed, lay across the sea, beneath the waters of the earth. Thus, when the Portuguese arrived by sea, they were believed to be visitors from that other world, and it was assumed that their king was the Kongo ruler's counterpart among the dead. As a result, one of the first gifts that the Kongolese king sent to the king of Portugal was an ivory horn carved from an elephant tusk (Fig. **9.16**), associated in the Kongolese mind

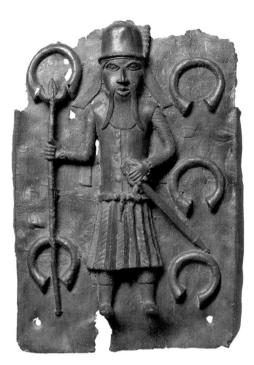

Fig. 9.15 *Portuguese Warrior Surrounded by Manillas*, Court of Benin, **Nigeria. Sixteenth century.** Bronze. Kunsthistorisches Museum, Vienna, Austria. Notice the background of the bronze incised with jungle floral images.

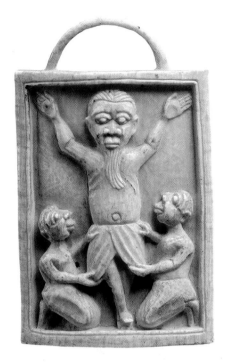

Fig. 9.17 **Crucifixion Plaque, from Loango area of Pointe Noire (Democratic Republic of the Congo), Vili culture. Collected in 1874.** Ivory, $3\frac{1}{4}" \times 2\frac{1}{4}"$. Museum für Völkerkunde, Berlin. The Portuguese claimed to have converted the Kingdom of the Kongo to Christianity as early as the 1490s.

with all royalty. An account of a visit to Mbanza Kongo by Portuguese missionaries in 1491 describes how horn players, who were painted in white in memory of their ancestors, met them. They played their song 12 times, a deep resonating melody that the missionaries found wholly melancholy. In fact, the Kongolese believed that the dead understood these notes, and that at their sound the ancestors of the royal line rose up to aid the ruler in governing his people.

The Kongolese were attracted to Christianity. As early as 1491 the Kongo King Nzinga a Nkuwa [un-ZING-ah ah-un-KOO-ah] converted and was baptized as Joao I. Not long after, his son and heir ordered that Christianity become the state religion. The susceptibility of the African peoples to the message of the Christian missionaries (as well as earlier, in the sub-Sahara, to Islamic missionaries) can be explained by the fact that they, too, traditionally accepted the duality of the universe and the existence of an afterlife. And yet the Africans showed an amazing capacity to adapt the outward forms of Christianity to their own cultural practices. For instance, across almost all of West Africa, the cross traditionally stood for the order of the cosmos, and was a talisman of extraordinary power usually associated with royal authority. Furthermore, in the Kongo in particular, the cross shape echoed the shape of the iron swords that served as the symbol of Kongo political authority. It is hardly surprising, then, that Christian crosses were soon adapted to the traditional ritual practices of the Kongo royal court. They could help the ruler in his role as healer, judge, or even rainmaker—any time it might be necessary to make contact with ancestral spirits.

Such Africanization of the Christian tradition is especially apparent in an ivory crucifixion plaque from the Vili [VEE-lee] culture (a subset of the Kongo kingdom) on the Atlantic coast north of the Congo River (Fig. **9.17**). The Vili artist depicted Christ with African facial features, as well as the beard (symbol of wisdom) and hairstyle of the Kongo nobility. Attendants kneel beside Christ in the traditional posture of respect, touching his loincloth, which he wears in the Vili royal manner, in

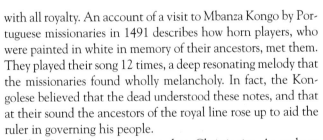

Fig. 9.16 *Mpungi*, **an ivory horn, from Kongo. Collected before 1553.** Length $32\frac{1}{2}"$. Museo degli Argenti, Florence. Ivory horns are found throughout equatorial Africa, almost always associated with the royal court. They are used today to announce the arrival of a king, among other things.

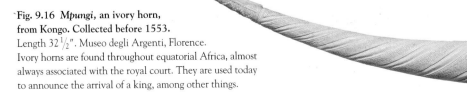

admiration for the material itself. It is not so clear, in other words, whether the Vili artist who made this plaque was representing Christian doctrine or adapting it to African tradition by equating Christ with Kongolese royalty. What this and other images like it demonstrate is the complex exchange between cultures that the Age of Encounter inaugurated. We must read these images, simultaneously, as emblems of the forcible transformation of other cultures into the likeness of the West and as adaptive strategies for cultural survival.

China and Its Influence

The **cultural syncretism**, or intermingling of cultural traditions, that marks the Americas and Africa, was largely resisted by Asia and Indian populations when Europeans arrived on their shores. The reasons are many, but of great importance was the inherent belief of these cultures in their own superiority. This was especially true of the Chinese, who for centuries had resisted Mongolian influence, for instance, and at the same time had come to prefer isolation.

The Song Dynasty (960–1279 CE)

This is not to say that the Chinese totally removed themselves from the world stage. The Song dynasty enjoyed tremendous prosperity. It was the world's greatest producer of iron. It was the Song port of Hangzhou that Marco Polo visited in 1274 and described as "the most splendid city in the world," and its flourishing merchant class traded not only along the Silk Road (see *Continuity & Change*, chapter 4) but also throughout the Southeast Asian seas by boat.

The government was increasingly controlled by this wealthy merchant class. Crucial to their rise was the development of movable type, which allowed the Song to begin printing books on paper. The printing press revolutionized the transmission of knowledge in China. (Gutenberg's movable-type printing press, which, in the West, we commonly credit with revolutionizing the transmission of knowledge, was 400 years in the future.) The children of the thriving merchant class attended public, private, and religious schools, where they could study the newly printed books—including *The Book of Songs*, required reading for all Chinese civil servants, and various encyclopedias—as they prepared for government examinations. This new class of cultured intellectuals (called **literati**) restored Confucianism to dominance and strengthened it with relevant additions from Daoism and Buddhism. Buddhism was officially rejected as foreign, but its explanation of the universe provided an invaluable metaphysical element to Confucianism. As a result, highly educated officials brought to government a deep belief, based on neo-Confucian teaching, that the well-run society mirrored the unchanging moral order of the cosmos.

Chan Buddhism Especially important to artists and literati in the Song era was the development of Chan Buddhism. "Chan" (better known in the West as "Zen," as it is pronounced in Japanese) derives from the Sanskrit word *dhyana*,

meaning "meditation." Like Daoism, Chan Buddhism teaches that one can find happiness by achieving harmony with nature. By using yoga techniques and sitting meditation, the Chan Buddhist strives for oneness with the Dao ("the Way") and the Confucian *li*, the principle or inner structure of nature. The Chan Buddhists thought that the traditional scriptures, rituals, and monastic rules of classical Buddhism were essentially beside the point, because Buddha's spirit was innate in everyone, waiting to be discovered through meditation. Thus, the poets and artists who practiced Chan Buddhism considered themselves instruments through which the spirit of nature expressed itself.

Song Painting This essential "rightness" of the Song world is manifested especially in Chinese painting of the Song era, when landscape painting became the principal and most esteemed means of personal and philosophic expression in the arts. The landscape was believed to embody the underlying principle behind all things, made manifest in the world through its material presence. Closely akin to the spiritual quest of the Dao, the task of the artist was to reveal the unifying principle of the natural world, the eternal essence of mountain, waterfall, pine tree, rock, reeds, clouds, and sky. Human figures are dwarfed by the landscape, insignificant in the face of nature. Over and over again, the paintings of the period rise from foreground valleys to high mountaintops, the eye following paths, cascading waterfalls, rocky crags, and tall pines pointing ever higher in imitation of "the Way," the path by which one leaves behind the human world and attains the great unifying principle (see *Focus*, pages 268–269).

The Yuan Dynasty (1279–1368)

Throughout the period known as the medieval era in the West, China was threatened from the north by nomadic tribes. The Northern Song capital of Bianjing [Beeehn-geeng] had fallen to tribes from Manchuria in 1126, forcing the Song to retreat south to Hangzhou. Finally, the Song dynasty succumbed to the Mongol leader Kublai Khan in 1279. Kublai Khan ruled from a new capital at present-day Beijing, transforming it into a walled city constructed on a grid plan and extending the Grand Canal to provision the city.

Calling themselves the Yuan dynasty, the Mongols under Kublai Khan and his descendants controlled the highest posts in the government, but they depended on Chinese officials to collect taxes and maintain order. The Chinese understood the need to cooperate with the Mongols, but they viewed the Mongols as foreigners occupying their homeland.

At the time of Marco Polo's arrival in China, the scholar-painters of the Chinese court, unwilling to serve under foreign domination, were retreating from public life. But while in exile they created an art symbolic of their resistance. Paintings of bamboo, for instance, abound, because bamboo is a plant that might bend, like the Chinese themselves, but never break. Painted in 1306, Cheng Sixiao's [Chehng-sih-she-how] *Ink Orchids* (Fig. **9.18**), according to its inscription, is meant to protest the "theft of Chinese soil by the invaders."

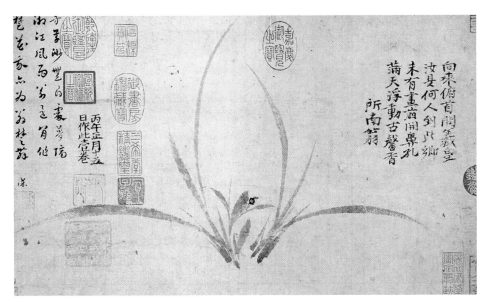

Fig. 9.18 Cheng Sixiao, *Ink Orchids.* **Yuan dynasty, 1306.** Ink on paper, $10\frac{1}{8}'' \times 16\frac{3}{4}''$. Municipal Museum of Fine Art, Osaka, Japan. Artists of the Yuan dynasty such as Cheng Sixiao painted for their fellow artists and friends, not for the public. Thus, Cheng Sixiao could feel comfortable describing his political intentions in the text accompanying this painting.

Orchids, in fact, can live without soil, in rocks or in trees, sustained by the moisture in the air around them, even as Sixiao the painter thrives.

The Ming Dynasty (1368–1644)

The Mongols were finally overthrown in 1368, when Zhu Yuanzhang [joo-wan-jang] (r. 1368–1398) drove the last Yuan emperor north into the Gobi desert and declared himself first emperor of the the dynasty known as Ming ("bright" or "brilliant"). China was once again ruled by the Chinese.

The Ming emperors were consumed by fear of Mongol reinvasion and in defense created what was arguably the most despotic government in Chinese history. Zhu Yuanzhang enlisted thousands of workers to reinforce the Great Wall of China (see Fig. 1.20) against invasion from the north, and untold numbers of them perished in the process. He equipped huge armies and assembled a navy to defend against invasion from the sea. Artists whose freedoms had been severely restricted under the Mongols were even less free under the Ming. But in a bow to scholarship and the arts, Zhu Yuanzhang's son, Zhu Di [joo dee] (r. 1402–1424), commissioned the compilation of an authoritative 11,095-volume encyclopedia of Chinese learning. He also undertook the construction of an Imperial Palace compound in Beijing on the site of Kublai Khan's ruined capital (Fig. 9.19). The palace complex, known as the Forbidden City, was, among other things, the architectural symbol of his rule.

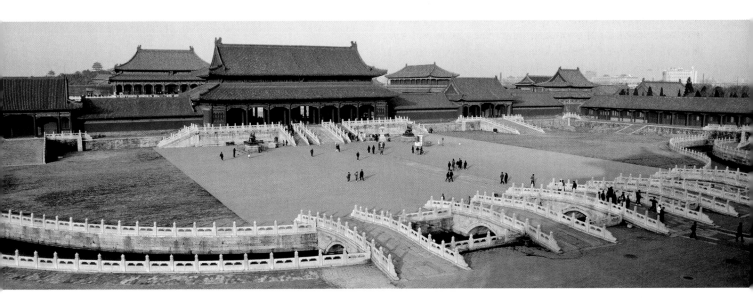

Fig. 9.19 **The Forbidden City, now the Palace Museum, Beijing. Mostly Ming dynasty (1368–1644).** The view is of the Hall of Supreme Being, as seen from across the square beyond the Gate of Supreme Harmony. Height 115′. Elevated on three tiers of marble platforms, the hall is the largest building in the complex.

Focus

Guo Xi's *Early Spring*

The human presence in nature goes almost unnoticed in Guo Xi's [Gwoh hsee] hanging scroll, *Early Spring*. Nature, embodied by the mountain, is all-embracing, a powerful and imposing symbol of eternity. The composition of Guo Xi's painting is based on the Chinese written character for mountain. The fluid gestures of the calligrapher's hand are mirrored in Guo Xi's painting, both in the organization of the whole and in the individual brush-and-ink strokes that render this ideal landscape. Like the calligrapher, Guo Xi is interested in the balance, rhythm, and movement of his line.

A court painter during the reign of the Emperor Shenzong [Shehn-tsohng] (r. 1068–1085), Guo Xi was given the task of painting all the murals in the Forbidden City, the imperial compound in Beijing that foreigners were prohibited from entering. His ideas about landscape painting were recorded by his son, Guo Si [Gwoh-seh], in a book entitled *The Lofty Message of the Forests and Streams*. According to this book, the central peak here symbolizes the emperor himself, its tall pines the gentlemanly ideals of the court. Around the emperor the masses assume their natural place, as around this mountain the trees and hills fall into the order and rhythms of nature.

The central mountain is painted so that we gaze up to it in the "high distance," as we would gaze up at the emperor.

Chinese character for "mountain."

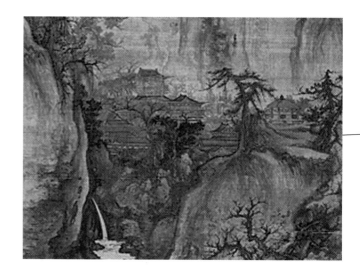

Barely noticeable, two figures get out of their boat at the bottom left, and another figure stands on the shoreline at the right. Two waterfalls cascade down the hillside behind this second figure, and a small village can be seen nestled on the mountainside above the falls.

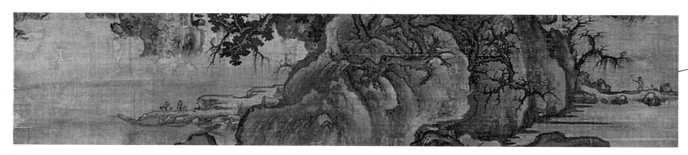

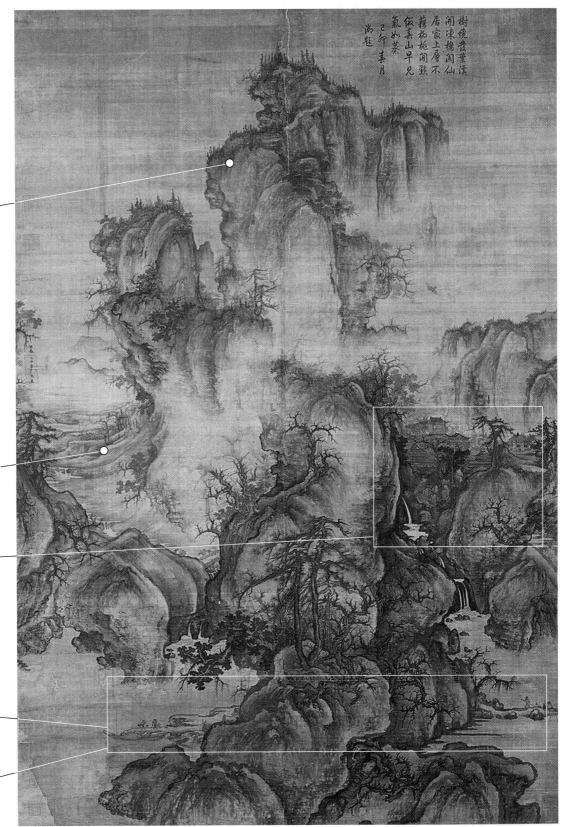

On the left side of the painting, we gaze far off into a "level distance," creating a sense of limitless, eternal space.

In the humbling "deep distance" of the foreground, far below our point of view, we see images that reflect our own insignificance in nature.

Guo Xi, *Early Spring*. Song dynasty, 1072. Hanging scroll, ink and slight color on silk, length 5′. Collection of the National Palace Museum, Taipei, Taiwan, Republic of China. Everything has its proper place in the Chinese universe, and thus the painting possesses multiple points of view. Accordingly, each part of this painting is constructed at the appropriate "distance."

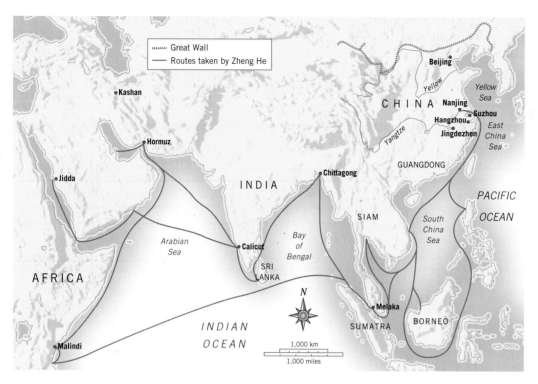

Map 9.4 Ming China, 1368–1644. This map also shows the routes taken by Zheng He and the Chinese Treasure Fleet. In 30 years, Zheng He traveled more than 186,000 miles, the equivalent of 7 $\frac{1}{2}$ circumnavigations of the world.

The Forbidden City The Forbidden City's name refers to the fact that only those on official imperial business could enter its gates. Although largely rebuilt in the eighteenth century during the Qing [ching] dynasty (1644–1911), the general plan is Ming but based on Mongol precedents. In fact, the Mongols had reserved the entire northern side of Beijing for themselves, and the resident Chinese had lived only in the southern third of the city. Ming emperors preserved this division, allowing ministers and officials to live in the northern or Inner City and commoners in the southern or Outer City.

Like the Tang capital of Chang'an (see Fig. 4.26), Beijing is laid out on a grid, and the Forbidden City is laid out on a grid within the grid along a north–south axis according to the principles of *feng shui* [fung shway] ("wind and water"). Following traditional practice, the Forbidden City covers about 240 acres and is walled by 15 miles of fortifications. It is composed of 9,999 buildings and rooms, each constructed with nails, nine nails per row. The number nine in Chinese sounds like the word for "everlasting," and because nine was believed to be the extreme of positive numbers, the maximum of the singular, it was thus reserved for use only by the emperor. The buildings in the complex follow traditional patterns of post-and-lintel construction that date back to the Shang and Zhou periods.

The emperors and their families rarely left the Forbidden City's confines. Visitors entered through a monumental U-shaped Meridian Gate, and then crossed the Golden Water River spanned by five arched marble bridges (see Fig. 9.19). Across the courtyard stands the Gate of Supreme Harmony,

on the other side of which is another giant courtyard leading to the Hall of Supreme Harmony. Here, on the most important state occasions, the emperor sat on his throne, facing south, his back to the evil forces of the north. Behind the Hall of Supreme Harmony are increasingly private spaces, devoted to day-to-day routine and living quarters. The balance and symmetry of the compound were believed to mirror the harmony of the universe. Situated, as it was believed, in the middle of the world, the Forbidden City was the architectural symbol of the emperor's rule and of his duty as the Son of Heaven to maintain order, balance, and harmony in his land.

The Treasure Fleet: Extending China's Influence Zhu Di called himself the Yongle [yohng-leh] emperor, meaning "lasting joy," a propagandistic name designed to deflect attention from the tyranny of his court. His massive construction projects served to establish the grandeur of his authority. Among the largest of these was his "treasure fleet" of 317 ships, crewed by 27,000 men, and headed by one of the largest wooden ships ever built. Under the command of Zheng He [jehng heh] (1371–1435), a Muslim eunuch who had served Zhu Di since childhood, the fleet sailed in seven expeditions between 1404 and 1435 throughout the oceans of Southeast Asia to India, Saudi Arabia, and down the African coast (see Map **9.4**).

China, like many cultures, saw itself through ethnocentric eyes. It viewed itself as the great Middle Kingdom, believed to be at the center of the four seas and at the heart of the four cardinal directions. Zhu Di conceived of the treasure fleet as his chief means to extend Chinese influence throughout the "four corners" of the world. To that end, all the provinces of China had to provide goods for the fleet to trade—from Suzhou [soo-joh] and Hangzhou [hahng joh], fine silks and brocades; from the imperial porcelain works at Jingdezhen, fine white porcelain; from Jiaxing [ja-hseeng], lacquerware; and from Guangdong [gwah-dohng], iron, required not only for trade but for construction of the fleet itself.

Zheng He's first voyage was to Calicut, the center of the spice trade. Here he obtained cardamom, cinnamon, ginger, turmeric, and, above all, pepper, literally worth its weight in gold. (The small cargo of pepper that Vasco da Gama eventually brought back from Calicut paid for his voyage several times over.) Calicut became a regular port of call for the fleet, as did Malacca, on the Malay peninsula, where cloves, nutmeg, sambal oelek [SAM-bal OH-lek] (a red hot pepper), and other Indonesian spices were available. He also traded for precious tree resins, such as camphor and frankincense, used for making incense. In Siam (now Thailand), he discovered mahogany, a hard wood, excellent for making ship rudders, and he paid the Siamese in gold for the trees. But

the Middle East and Africa yielded some of the most precious treasures. Hormuz [HOR-muz], on the Persian Gulf, was famous for its pearls from the banks off what is now Bahrain, but it was also a center of trade in precious stones. In return for porcelains and silks, Zheng He acquired sapphires, rubies, topaz, and amber, as well as Middle Eastern woolens and carpets.

Luxury Arts The lavish lifestyle of the Ming court ensured the production of vast quantities of decorative luxury goods. In addition, as trade flourished, many Chinese merchants became increasingly wealthy and began to collect paintings, antiques, finely made furniture, and other quality objects for themselves. **Lacquerware** was extremely popular. Made from the sap of the Chinese *Rhus vernicifera* (roos ver-ni-SI-fer-ah) tree (a variety of sumac), lacquer is a clear, natural varnish that, when applied to wood, textiles, or other perishable materials, makes them airtight, waterproof, and resistant to both heat and acid. A surface coated with many thin layers of lacquer can be carved through into all manner of designs. Lacquerware furniture, bowls, dishes, and other small articles were very desirable.

One of the commodities most prized by the Chinese themselves and by those who traded with China was **porcelain** ceramic ware. The Chinese had invented the process for making porcelain around 1004 CE at Jingdezhen, which by the beginning of the Ming dynasty boasted 20 kilns. At Zhu Di's death in 1424, it had almost tripled in size to 58 kilns.

Ming painters decorated the unfired surfaces of their porcelain ware with blue cobalt glazes, covered everything with a layer of white glaze, and then fired their works. During the reign of Zhu Di, the look of Chinese porcelain improved dramatically. This was due largely to the fact that Zheng He had traded Chinese produce for a cobalt ore, probably from Kashan [kah-SHAHN], Persia, high in iron and low in manganese (just the opposite of Chinese ore), which allowed for a new richness of color. Among the Ming artists' favorite motifs were fish, waves, and sea monsters, but particularly dragons, because they symbolized the emperor. His veins were said to flow with the dragon's blood (Fig. **9.20**). The dragon was everywhere on Ming

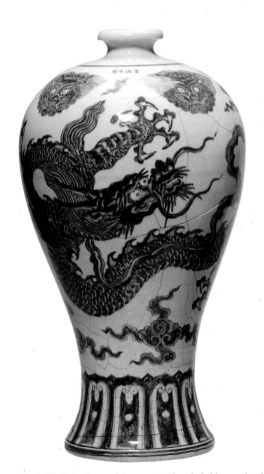
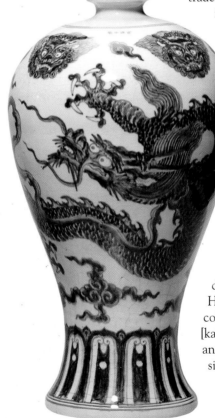

Fig. 9.20 Pair of porcelain vases with cobalt blue underglaze. Ming dynasty, Xuande period (1426–1435). Height 21 3/4". The Nelson-Atkins Museum of Art, Kansas City, Missouri. As early as the Bronze Age, the Chinese associated the dragon with sudden manifestations of nature, such as wind, rain, and lightning. By the Song and Tang dynasties (5th–10th centuries), painting pictures of dragons was a method of praying for rain. For Chan Buddhists, the dragon symbolized sudden enlightenment.

art, from textiles to lacquerware and jade carvings. Note that the two vases in figure 9.20 are mirror images, the finely outlined forms of the dragons seemingly mimicking each other's flight. Their gestures, in fact, suggest the graceful movements of **T'ai Chi Ch'uan** [ty chee chwahn], the Chinese martial art that includes solo forms, or routines, and two-person forms, known as "pushing hands." These two dragons, their bony claws reaching toward one another, particularly evoke the "pushing hands" form. The two vases create a sense of balance, like the balance of *yin* and *yang*, the symbol for which is, in fact, the symbol for *T'ai Chi* itself.

Painting and Poetry: Competing Schools The imperial court and the newly rich merchant class also acquired paintings, considered luxury goods in their own right. As in the Tang dynasty, a class of highly educated literati—artists equally expert in poetry, calligraphy, and painting—executed the works. Many paintings combine image and poem, the latter written in a calligraphy distinctly the artist's own.

Late in the Ming dynasty, an artist, calligrapher, theorist, and high official in the government bureaucracy named Dong Qichang [dahng chee-chang] (1555–1636) wrote an essay that has affected the way we look at the history of Chinese painting ever since, although many scholars, even in Dong Qichang's time, viewed it as oversimplified. He divided the history of Chinese painting into two schools, northern and southern, although geography had little to do with it. It was not place but the spirit in which the artist approached the painting that determined its school. A painter was "southern" if unorthodox, radical, and inventive, like the southern brand of Chan (Zen) Buddhism; a painter was "northern" if conservative and traditional in approach, like the northern brand of Chan Buddhism.

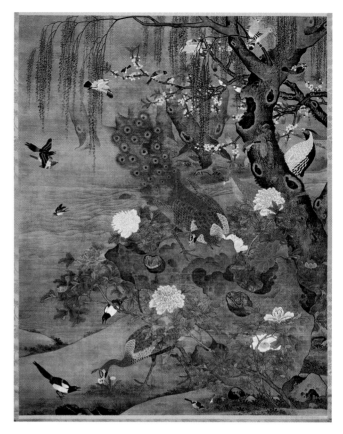

Fig. 9.21 Yin Hong, *Hundreds of Birds Admiring the Peacocks*. Ming dynasty, ca. late 15th century–early 16th century. Hanging scroll, ink and color on silk, 7′ 10½″ × 6′5″. © The Cleveland Museum of Art. Purchase from the J. H. Wade Fund, 74.31. The Chinese traded in the Middle East for peacocks, considered the most supreme of all ornamental birds, in exchange for silk.

Fig. 9.22 Shen Zhou. *Poet on a Mountaintop*, leaf from an album of landscapes; painting mounted as part of a handscroll. Ming dynasty, ca. 1500. Ink and color on paper, 15¼″ × 23¾″. The Nelson-Atkins Museum of Art, Kansas City, Missouri. Shen Zhou places himself at the center of this composition in a relaxed and casual manner that reflects Chan Buddhism, which is more intuitive than intellectual. Note the informal simplicity of his brushwork and calligraphy.

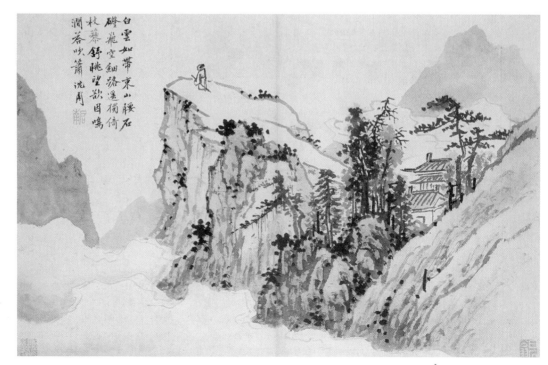

Hundreds of Birds Admiring the Peacocks by Yin Hong, a court artist active in the late fifteenth and early sixteenth centuries, is an example of the northern style (Fig. **9.21**). It has a highly refined decorative style, which emphasizes the technical skill of the painter. It also has a rich use of color and reliance on traditional Chinese painting, in this case the birds-and-flowers genre that had been extremely popular in the Song dynasty, which flourished contemporaneously with the Early Middle Ages in the West. Like Guo Xi's Song dynasty painting *Early Spring* (see *Focus*, pages 268–269), the Yin Hong painting also has a symbolic meaning that refers directly to the emperor. Just as the central peak in *Early Spring* symbolizes the emperor himself, with the lower peaks and trees subservient to him, here a peacock symbolizes the emperor, and around it "hundreds of birds"—that is, the court officials—gather in respect and submission.

The southern style is much more understated than the northern school, preferring ink to color and free brushwork (emphasizing the abstract nature of painting) to meticulously detailed linear representation. For the southern artist, reality rested in the mind, not the physical world, and so self-expression is the ultimate aim. Furthermore, in the southern school the work of art more systematically synthesized the three areas of endeavor that any member of the literati should have mastered: poetry, calligraphy, and painting.

So, a southern-school painting like *Poet on a Mountaintop* by Shen Zhou [joh] (1427–1509) radicalizes traditional Chinese landscape (Fig. **9.22**). In the earlier Song dynasty landscapes, the unifying embrace of the natural world dwarfs human figures (see *Focus*, pages 268–269). But in Shen Zhou's Ming-dynasty painting, the poet is the central figure. He faces out over an airy void in which hangs the very image of his mind, the following poem:

> White clouds like a belt encircle the
> mountain's waist
> A stone ledge flying in space and the far
> thin road.
> I lean alone on my bramble staff and gazing contented into
> space
> Wish the sounding torrent would answer to your flute.

An artist capable of putting himself at the center of both painting and poem would have had no desire to enter the government bureaucracy. Shen Zhou lived out his life in the district of Suzhou, far from court. But, interestingly, it was Shen Zhou's style of work, and the style of other literati painters in the southern school, that the Ming theorist Dong Qichang most preferred and that would become the dominant, orthodox style of painting in the Qing dynasty to follow.

The Flowering of Japan

Of all the great Asian civilizations, the latest to develop was that of Japan. Before 300 CE, Japan was fragmented; its various regions were separated by sea and mountain and ruled by more than 100 competing and often warring states. These states did, however, share a mythology—finally collected in about 700 CE in the *Kojiki* [Koh-JEE-kee] or *Chronicles of Ancient Events*. According to the *Kojiki*, the islands that constitute Japan were formed by two **kami** [KAH-mee], or gods—Izanagi [izah-NAH-gee] and his consort Izanami [izah-NAH-mee]. Among their offspring was the sun goddess, Amaterasu Omikami [AH-mah-tay-rah-soo OH-mee-kah-mee], from whom all Japanese emperors are believed to descend. In other words, the Japanese emperor was not merely put in position by the gods, as in China; he was a direct descendant of the gods, and hence divine.

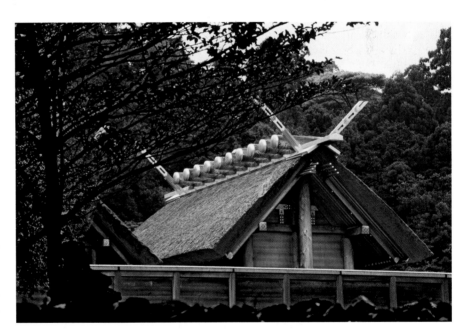

Fig. 9.23 Naiku (Inner) Shrine housing Amaterasu, Ise, Japan. Late 5th–early 6th century. Beginning in the reign of the emperor Temmu (r. 673–686), the Shinto shrine at Ise has been rebuilt by the Japanese ruling family, with some inevitable lapses, every 20 years—the natural cycle of growth and decay in nature. The most recent reconstruction occurred in 1993. Shinto is today the official state religion of Japan.

Shinto: Reverence for the Natural World

When Buddhism arrived in Japan in about 600 CE, the dominant religion was Shinto, an indigenous Japanese faith whose principal goddess was Amaterasu. She was housed in a shrine complex at Ise, a sacred site from prehistoric times. The main sanctuary, or **shoden** [SHOH-dehn] (Fig. **9.23**), consists of undecorated wooden beams and a thatched roof. These plain and simple materials embody the basic tenet of Shinto—reverence for the natural world—and are typical of Shinto architecture. The shrine at Ise houses the three sacred symbols of Shinto: a sword, a mirror, and a jewel.

Millions of Japanese pilgrims visit it each year. The shrine is ritually rebuilt at 20-year intervals in exactly the same style. Like Japanese culture, it is both traditional and continuously new.

In Shinto, trees, rocks, water, mountains—especially Mount Fuji, the volcano just outside Tokyo, which is said to look over the country as its protector—are all manifestations of the *kami*, the spirits that are embodied in them. Even the natural materials with which artists work, such as clay, wood, and stone, are imbued with the *kami* and are to be treated with the respect and reverence due to a god.

Buddhism Arrives in Japan

Buddhism arrived in Japan, by way of Korea and China, in the middle of the sixth century (the first known image of Buddha arrived in Japan about 564). Chinese calligraphy was already the basis of the Japanese written language, and to some, Buddhism seemed equally amenable to Japanese adaptation. In its reverence for nature, it mirrored Shinto, but it had the advantage of codifying and organizing Shinto's diffuse set of practices into a coherent program. During the rule of Prince Shotoku [SHOH-toh-koo] (r. 593–622), whose name means "Wise and Virtuous," Buddhism became the religion of the Japanese aristocracy.

Raised in the pro-Buddhist Soga clan, Shotoku emphasized the importance of the Chinese model of civil administration, and when he built a new palace at Ikaruga [ee-KAH-roo-gah], he constructed a Buddhist temple next to it. Others were built during his administration, and over 1,300 Buddhist monks and nuns were ordained. When Shotoku died, Shinto factions destroyed both his palace and his temple. Shinto's popularity probably stems, at least partly, from its position as a "native" religion as opposed to the "imported" Buddhism. Nevertheless, Shotoku so instilled Buddhist thought in the Japanese aristocracy that by 670 his ruined temple was rebuilt; it remains the oldest surviving Buddhist temple in Japan and the oldest wooden temple in the world.

The Heian Period: Courtly Refinement

Between 784 and 794, the capital of Japan was moved to Heiankyo—modern-day Kyoto—which quickly became the most densely populated city in the world. Between the late eleventh and the middle of the twelfth century at Heiankyo, scholars estimate that the royal family dedicated a new Shinto shrine every year and founded a new Buddhist temple every five years. But distinctions between Buddhism and Shinto began to blur. The *kami* and Buddhist deities were conflated, Shinto temples were used by Buddhist priests for meditation, and Shinto temples even assumed Buddhist architectural features, forgoing, to a degree, the rigorous plain style of Ise.

Literature and Calligraphy Although many court gatherings took place for the purpose of poetry competitions, poems were generally composed for a single recipient—a friend or lover—and a reply was expected. In her *Diaries*—or *Nikki* in Japanese—Murasaki Shikibu (973/8–aft. 1014), one of the most accomplished women of the Heian court, a lady-in-waiting to the Empress Shoshi [SHOH-shee] (988–1074), describes just such an exchange (**Reading 9.3**):

READING 9.3 **from Murasaki Shikibu,** *Diaries*

I can see the garden from my room beside the entrance to the gallery. The air is misty, the dew is still on the leaves. The Lord Prime Minister is walking there; he orders his men to cleanse the brook. He breaks off a stalk of omenaishi[1] [Oh-MEH-nah-ee-shee] which is in full bloom by the south end of the bridge. He peeps in over my screen! His noble appearance embarrasses us, and I am ashamed of my morning face.[2] He says, "Your poem on this! If you delay so much the fun is gone!" and I seize the chance to run away to the writing-box, hiding my face:

> Flower-maiden in bloom—
> Even more beautiful for the bright dew,
> Which is partial, and never favors me.

"So prompt!" said he, smiling, and ordered a writing-box to be brought [for himself].
His answer:

> The silver dew is never partial.
> From her heart
> The flower-maiden's beauty.

[1] **omenaishi:** a flowering plant.
[2] **morning face:** a face without powder or makeup.

Something of the flavor of court life is captured in this brief passage, in the private space of the gentlewoman's world, her relation to the gentlemen of the court, the attention of the two poets to natural beauty, and the expression of that beauty as a means of capturing personal feeling.

Diaries, or *nikki*, comprised an important literary form that tells us much about court life in the Heian period. Murasaki's poems—indeed her entire text—are written in a new purely Japanese writing system, known as **hiragana** [HEER-ah-gah-nah]. Beginning in the early ninth century, *hiragana* gradually replaced the use of Chinese characters and enabled writers to spell out the Japanese language phonetically. The university curriculum remained based on Chinese classics and history, and the formal workings of state and government still required the use of Chinese. But women, who could not attend the university and were actively discouraged from studying the Chinese classics, were taught the *hiragana* script.

The popularity of *hiragana*, even among men, who recognized its convenience, encouraged the development of new Japanese forms of poetry, especially the **waka** [WAH-kah] (literally the "poetry of Wa," or Japan). A *waka* consists of thirty-one syllables in five lines on a theme drawn from nature and the changing of seasons. Here is a *waka* by one of the great poets of the Heian period, Ki no Tomonori [KEE noh TOH-moh-noh-ree] (act. 850–904) (**Reading 9.4**):

READING 9.4 **from Ki no Tomonori, "This Perfectly Still"**

This perfectly still
Spring day bathed in the soft light
From the spread-out sky.
Why do the cherry blossoms
So restlessly scatter down?

The tension here, between the calm of the day and the restlessness of the cherry blossoms, is meant to mirror a similar tension in the poet's mind, suggesting a certain sense of anticipation or premonition. *Waka* serves as a model for other Japanese poetic forms, particularly the famous **haiku**, the three-line, seventeen-syllable form that developed out of the first three lines of the *waka*.

The First Novel: *The Tale of Genji* In addition to her *Diaries*, Murasaki Shikibu is the author of a long book of prose (over 1,000 pages in English translation) that many consider the world's first novel—certainly no fiction in the Western world matches its scope until the eighteenth century. Called *The Tale of Genji*, it tells the story of Genji, an imperial prince, born to the favorite wife of the emperor, though she is too low in rank for her son to be an heir to the throne. Much of the action takes place in the homes and gardens of Heiankyo, and besides being a moving romantic story covering 75 years of the hero's life, from his birth to his death, the novel presents us with a vivid picture of life in Japanese society at the turn of the millennium.

The Kamakura Period (ca. 1185–1392): Samurai and Shogunate

During the Heian period, the emperors began to see their authority challenged by regional warrior clans from outside Heiankyo known as **samurai** (literally, "those who serve"). The absence of tax revenues from temples and nobles' valuable properties, and subsequent economic difficulties, contributed to a weak central government and a general state of unrest. While the samurai paid lip service to the sovereign, they increasingly exercised complete authority over all aspects of Japanese society.

The samurai dressed in elaborate iron armor and were master archers and swordsmen. Their essentially feudal code of conduct, the **bushido** ("way of the warrior"), was based on fidelity to one's superior, contempt for death, and total selflessness. The code demanded ritual suicide, usually by self-disembowelment, of any samurai who was dishonored. In 1192, Minamoto no Yoritomo, the greatest samurai of the day, gave himself the title of **shogun**, general-in-chief of the samurai, inaugurating the first shogunate at Kamakura, which gives its name to the period. He established the military-based *bakufu* [BAH-koo-foo], or "tent government" (because his soldiers lived in tents), which functioned as a government separate from the emperor's government in Kyoto. While the emperor still appointed civil governors, collected taxes, and controlled the area surrounding the titular capital of Heian, the real power of the state came to the shogunate, to whom local lords all swore allegiance.

Realism defined the art of the Kamakura period. Yoritomo is pictured in a masterful blend of realism and a powerful compositional abstraction (Fig. **9.24**). The painting shows his sword, the hallmark of his class, protruding from his robe.

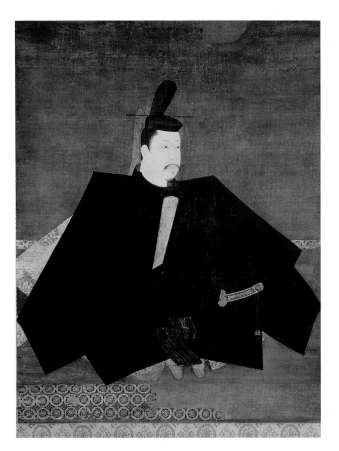

Fig. 9.24 Attributed to Fujiwara Takanobu, *Minamoto no Yoritomo*. Sentoin (Hall of the Retired Emperor). Kamakura period, second half of the 12th century. Hanging scroll, ink and color on silk, height 4′ 6½″. Jingoii Temple, Kyoto, Kyoto, Japan. The shogun's authority is underscored by his life-size portrait.

His face, with its determined eyes, is absolutely realistic, while his robe is a flat geometry of black angles without detail. Almost pyramidal in form, the figure of Yoritomo is above all a symbol of authority and self-assurance.

The Muromachi Period (1392–1573): Cultural Patronage

Long before Ming rulers finally overthrew the Mongol Yuan dynasty in China in 1368, the rulers of the Kamakura period had repelled the Mongol Kublai Khan's attempts to conquer their island country in both 1274 and 1281. The cost was high, and the islands, left impoverished, collapsed in political disarray. Competing provincial *daimyo* [DY-mee-oh], or "sudden lords," largely uncultured samurai swordsmen, ruled the country independently of the shoguns. They had little interest in the traditional Japanese art and literature of the earlier Heian court. However, the principles and ethics of Daoist philosophy, especially as manifested in Zen Buddhism, the Japanese version of Chinese Chan Buddhism, did appeal to them. This was because of its emphasis on self-discipline and self-denial and its reliance on intuitive understanding, unmediated by intellectual reasoning.

By 1392, one shogun family, the Ashikaga [ah-she-KAH-gah], had begun to exercise more authority over Japanese society than any of the *daimyo*. They had their headquarters in the Muromachi [MOO-roh-mah-chee] district of Kyoto. Although Kyoto remained in a state of near-total devastation—starvation was not uncommon—the Ashikaga shoguns built elaborate palaces around Kyoto as refuges from the chaos outside their walls. One of the most elaborate of these, now known as Kinkakuji [KIN-kah-koo-jee], the Golden Pavilion (Fig. **9.25**), was built as a setting for the retirement of the Ashikaga shogun Yoshimitsu [yoh-shi-MEE-tsoo] (1358–1408). Begun in 1399, its central pavilion is modeled on Chinese precedents. Its first floor was intended for relax-

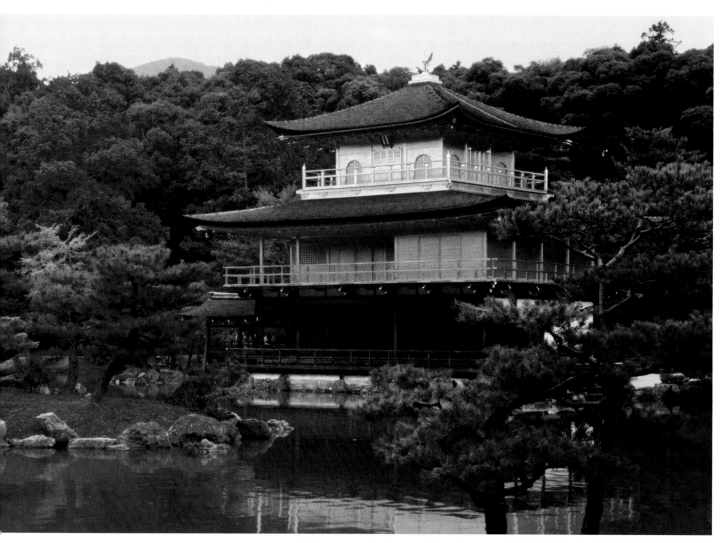

Fig. 9.25 Kinkakuji (Temple of the Golden Pavilion), Rokuonji, Kyoto. Rebuilt in 1964 after the original of the 1390s.
The original Kinkakuji was set ablaze and completely destroyed in 1950 by a young monk protesting the commercialization of Buddhism after World War II. The restoration closely approximates its original appearance.

ation and contemplation of the lake and gardens. A wide veranda for viewing the moon, a popular pastime, fronted its second floor. And the top floor was designed as a small Buddhist temple. The gardens surrounding the pavilions at Kinkakuji provided the casual stroller with an ever-changing variety of views, thus creating a tension between the multiplicity of scenes and the unity of the whole. This was attractive to Zen Buddhist sensibilities. As a matter of policy, Yoshimitsu associated himself with the arts in order to lend his shogunate authority and legitimacy. Therefore, he and later Ashikaga shoguns encouraged some of the most important artistic developments of the era in painting and garden design. They also championed important new forms of expression, including the tea ceremony and Noh drama.

Painting in the New Zen Manner The popularity of Zen Buddhism in Japan led to a renewed interest in Chinese painting, particularly landscapes of the so-called southern school variety, which expressed intuitive and personal feelings in the context of the natural world (see Fig. 9.22). In order to acquaint himself more fully with Chinese traditions, Sesshu Toyo [ses-shoo toh-yoh] (1420–1506), a Zen priest-painter, traveled to China in 1468–1469, copying the Song dynasty masters and becoming adept at the more abstract forms of representation practiced by the Chan Buddhist literati. *Haboku Landscape for Soen* represents an extreme example of this new Zen Buddhist manner (Fig. **9.26**). *Haboku* [HAH-boh-koo] means "broken ink," which refers to the technique that gives ink the appearance of having been casually splashed onto the surface. No mark on this painting could actually be thought of as representational. Rather, the denser ink suggests trees and rocks, while the softer washes evoke tall mountains in the distance, water, and mist. Sesshu executed the work as a farewell gift for his pupil, Josui Soen [JOH-soo-ee soh-ehn] (active 1495–1499), a monk painter who subsequently took the painting to Kyoto. It was so admired there that six leading Zen Buddhist monks added expressions of praise for the work above Sesshu's own inscription. Perhaps a phrase from Sesshu's inscription most fully captures the spirit of the piece: "My eyes are misty," he writes, "and my spirit exhausted"—the very essence of a heartfelt farewell.

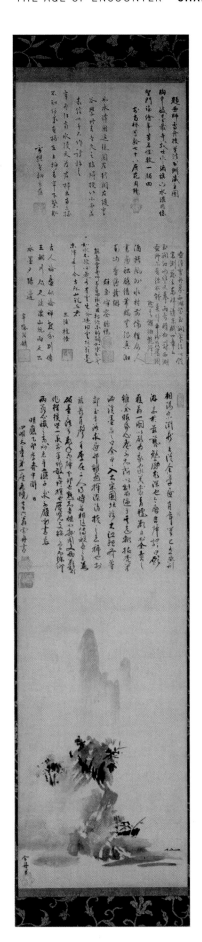

Fig. 9.26 Sesshu Toyo, *Haboku Landscape for Soen*. Muromachi period, 1495. Hanging scroll, ink on two joined sheets of paper, total height 58¼″. Tokyo National Museum. At the top of this scroll is Sesshu's long inscription to Soen and the expressions of praise for the work later added by Zen monks in Kyoto.

The Tea Ceremony More than any other, the court of Yoshimasa lent its support to the development of the tea ceremony, the **Way of the Tea**, *cha no yu* [CHAH noh-yoo]. In small rooms specifically designed for the purpose and often decorated with calligraphy on hanging scrolls or screens, the guest was to leave the concerns of the daily world behind and enter a timeless world of ease, harmony, and mutual respect. The master of the ceremony would assemble a few examples of painting and calligraphy together with a variety of different objects and utensils for making tea—the kettle, the water pot, the whisk, the tea caddy, and above all the tea bowl, each prized for its aesthetic shape and texture. In a quiet muted light, and on a floor covered with *tatami* [tah-TAH-mee], woven straw mats, the master and his guest would contemplate the tea, its preparation, and the objects accompanying the ensemble, which, it was understood, expressed the master's artistic sensibility. Together, guest and master would collaborate in a ritual of meditation to transform the drinking of tea into a work of highly refined art. The entire ceremony was imbued with a Zen sensibility.

The tea bowl, usually of the utmost simplicity, became a prized element in the tea ceremony, and the most beautiful tea bowls had their own special names. A bowl by the tea master Hon'ami Koetsu [hon-AH-mee ko-EH-tsoo], named *Amagumo* [ah-mah-GOO-moh] (*Rain Clouds*), is an example (Fig. **9.27**). Perfectly shaped to fit the hand, this tea bowl was made in the early seventeenth century at one of the so-called Six Ancient Kilns, the traditional centers of wood-fired ceramics in Japan. These early kilns, known as *anagama* [ah-nah-GAH-mah], were in the form of narrow underground tunnels that followed the contour of a hillside. The potter filled the pit with pottery, and heat moved through the tunnel from the firebox at the lower end to the chimney at the upper end. The firing would take an average of seven days. The coloration that distinguished these pieces results from wood ash in the kiln melting and fusing into glass on the pottery. Because the pots were removed from the kiln while still hot, unpredictable chance designs often resulted, an aesthetic of sudden change that appealed to the Zen philosopher. The most prized effect is a scorch, or *koge* [KO-gay], when the firing has completely oxidized the natural glaze leaving only a gray-black area. Such a *koge* forms the "rain clouds" on Koetsu's tea bowl.

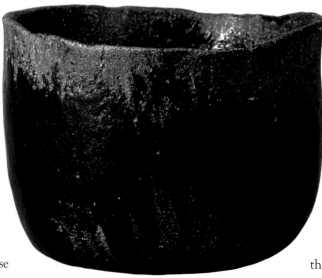

Fig. 9.27 Hon'ami Koetsu. *Tea Bowl Named Amagumo.* **Momoyama or early Edo period, late 16th or early 17th century.** Ceramic, 3 1/2" × 4 9/10". Mitsui Bunko, Museum, Tokyo. This is a *raku* bowl, which literally means "pleasure," but came to refer to the slow firing process.

Noh Drama The Ashikaga shoguns, including Yoshimitsu and Yoshimasa, also enthusiastically supported the development of the important literary genre of Noh drama. The Noh drama was primarily the result of the efforts of Kan'ami Kiyotsugu [KAHN-ah-mee KEE-yoh-tsoo-goo] (1333–1384) and his son Zeami Motokiyo [SHE-ah-mee MOH-toh-kee-yoh] (1363–1443). They conceived of a theater incorporating music, chanting, dance, poetry, prose, mime, and masks to create a world of sublime beauty based on the Zen ideal of *yugen* [YOO-gehn], which referred to that which lies beneath the surface of things, intimations of another hidden and more profound world.

The word **noh** means "accomplishment," and it refers to the virtuoso performance of the drama's main character, whose inner conflicts must be resolved before his or her soul can find peace. The Noh play *Semimaru* [she-MEE-mah-roo], written by Zeami in the early fifteenth century, recreates the medieval Japanese legend of Semimaru, a blind prince who lived as a beggar in a bamboo hut on Mount Osaka. His blindness was attributed to laxity in the performance of his religious duties in a former life for which his emperor father exiled him from court, as Semimaru explains to his attendant, Kiyotsura [KEE-yoh-tsoo-rah], so that his ascetic lifestyle might "purge in this world my burden from the past,/And spare me suffering in the world to come." In the play, Semimaru meets up with his deranged sister, who was apparently similarly lacking in her performance of religious duties and is thus condemned to wander the countryside. She hears him playing the biwa [bee-wah], a short-necked lute. In fact, traditionally Semimaru was considered the greatest master of the biwa and flute, the music of which apparently brought his soul to a state of peace.

Noh is very different from Western drama. Semimaru wears a beautifully crafted mask with shut eyes that signify his blindness. He is accompanied by a chorus, which narrates events to the sound of wind instruments and drums, and by secondary characters, who help him accomplish his goals. The plot, which the audience would know quite well, is almost irrelevant—certainly it does not drive the action of the drama forward. The characters speak their lines in a stylized manner, and make no attempt at realistic tonal inflections. Three drums and a flute accompany their lines, their movements turn into dance, and the

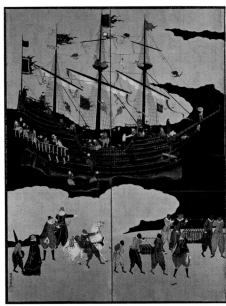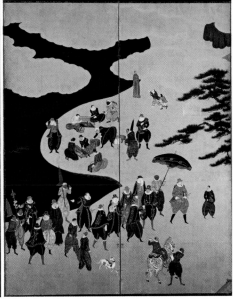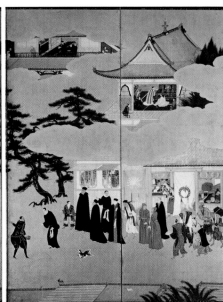

Fig. 9.28 **School of Kano. *Namban* six-panel screen. 1593–1600.** Kobe City Museum of Namban Art, Japan.
Across the bottom left of the screen, African slaves, dressed in Portuguese costume, carry goods.

performance lasts for a much longer time than it takes simply to read it. In fact, although Noh plays often read well on the page, the total effect is lost without the nonverbal elements.

The Momoyama Period (1573–1615): Foreign Influences

Even as Japanese culture flowered under the patronage of the Ashikaga shoguns, the country simultaneously endured many years of near-total political and social disorder. By the middle of the sixteenth century, the Ashikaga family had lost all semblance of power and various *daimyo* controlled the provinces once again. Finally, one of their number, Oda Nobunaga [OH-dah NOH-boo-nah-gah] (1534–1582), son of a minor vassal, forged enough alliances to unify the country under a single administration. By 1573, together with his two principal generals, Nobunaga had driven what remained of the Ashikaga out of Kyoto, burning the city behind them. He inaugurated a period now known as the Momoyama, literally "Peach Hill," after an orchard of peach trees later planted on the ruins of the castle of his successor Toyotomi Hideyoshi (1536–1598), south of Kyoto.

Nobunaga's victory was aided by the gunpowder and firearms introduced to Japan by Portuguese traders after they arrived in 1543. During the reign of Nobunaga, the West greatly expanded trade throughout Japan. By the 1580s, the Church had converted as many as 150,000 Japanese to Catholicism, encouraged by Nobunaga, who hoped Christianity might help him curtail the power of the Buddhists and warring *daimyo*.

The presence of foreign traders in Japan, principally Portuguese and Dutch, soon influenced Japanese imagery, particularly in a new genre of screen painting known as **namban** [NAHM-bahn]. *Namban* literally means "southern barbarian," referring to the "barbarian" Westerners who arrived from the south by ship. In the most popular theme of this genre, a foreign galleon arrives in Kyoto harbor (Fig. **9.28**). The ship's crew unloads goods, and the captain and his men proceed through the streets of the city to Nambanji, the Jesuit church in Kyoto. The priests themselves are Japanese converts to Christianity. The *namban* screens are unique in Japanese art in that they depict action from left to right in deference to Western habits of reading.

The Closing of Japan

Although Nobunaga encouraged the Christianization of Japan, his successor, Hideyoshi, was deeply suspicious of the Western religion. By 1587 he had prohibited the Japanese from practicing it and, in 1597, went so far as to execute 26 Spanish and Japanese Jesuits and Franciscans in Nagasaki. Succeeding rulers pursued an increasingly isolationist foreign policy. Christianity, even as practiced by foreigners, was banned altogether in 1614. They forbade the Japanese to travel abroad in 1635, and limited foreign trade in 1641 to the Dutch, whom they confined to a small area in Nagasaki harbor, and the Chinese, whom they confined to a quarter within the city of Nagasaki itself.

Japan would remain sealed from foreign influence until 1853, when the American commodore Matthew Perry sailed into Edo [ED-oh] Bay, today known as Tokyo Bay, with four warships and a letter from the President of the United States urging the Japanese to receive the American sailors. The following year, Japan formally reopened its ports to the world.

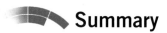

Summary

■ **The Spanish Empire** The Pre-Columbian cultures of the Americas produced extraordinarily accurate calendars and magnificent cities, such as Teotihuacán and the Mayan city of Palenque. In South America, the Inca built cities notable for their stone masonry.

When Christopher Columbus arrived in the Americas in 1492 believing he had discovered a western route to Asia, he was intent on converting the natives to Christianity and assumed they would make good slaves, but he was even more intent on discovering gold. The acquisition of gold and other treasure was the primary motivation for European colonization of the Americas. Columbus's voyages inaugurated 125 years of nautical exploration by Europeans. Spain focused on the Americas. In 1519–1521, the conquistador Hernán Cortés conquered the Aztec Empire of Mexico, and in 1533 Francisco Pizarro accomplished the Spanish conquest of Peru.

■ **West African Culture and the Portuguese** By 1100, the Yoruba civilization, centered in the West African city of Ife, was producing highly naturalistic commemorative portraits in clay and stone, probably depicting their rulers, and not long after elegant brass sculptures as well, which the people of Benin soon adopted. In the sixteenth century, the Portuguese slave trade transported many millions of Africans across the Atlantic on the Middle Passage and devastated the cultures of West Africa, but it did not transform them. The presence of the Portuguese is evident in much of the art produced in West Africa, including bronze objects from Benin that depict Portuguese soldiers and images of Christ as Kongolese royalty from the Kongo, where the people were strongly attracted to Christianity.

■ **China and Its Influence** During the Song dynasty, poets and artists, who practiced the neo-Confucian Chan Buddhism, believed that the spirit of nature expressed itself directly through them. Painting, then, might represent the Daoist Way or portray a mountain's dominance of the natural world as a metaphor for the emperor's rule over the court.

In 1279, the Song fell to the Mongol leader Kublai Khan, who ruled China from Beijing as founder of the Yuan dynasty. The scholar-painters of the Chinese court, unwilling to serve under foreign domination, retreated into exile, but they created an art symbolic of their resistance. With the advent of the Ming dynasty, China conducted trade expeditions throughout the area. Chinese porcelain was in great demand. One of the most important undertakings of the emperor Zhu Di's reign was the construction of the royal compound in Beijing, known as the Forbidden City. In the Ming court, the history of Chinese painting was divided into two schools, northern and southern, each with different aesthetic priorities.

■ **The Flowering of Japan** When Buddhism arrived in China around 600, it encountered the indigenous religion of Shinto, which preached a reverence for the natural world that reflected the belief that all things were imbued with the spirits of nature, or *kami*. Buddhism was essentially compatible with this system of belief. The Heian court was one of extreme elegance and refinement. Women led a highly protected and isolated existence, but they were expected to be educated, and many participated in the literary life of the court, where poetry was held in especially high esteem. When economic difficulties led to the downfall of the Heian dynasty, warriors known as samurai took over the country. Their code of conduct, the *bushido*, was based on fidelity to one's superior, contempt for death, and total selflessness.

During the Muromachi period (1392–1573), the popularity of Zen Buddhism led to a renewed interest in Chinese painting. The tea ceremony was ritualized as a highly refined art of Zen meditation. The court also supported the development of Noh drama.

After the introduction of gunpowder, firearms, and cannon by Portuguese traders in the Momoyama period (1573–1615), screen painting became especially popular and depicted a wide variety of subjects, including the Portuguese traders (*namban* painting). However, by 1641, Japan essentially closed its doors to foreign trade and influence.

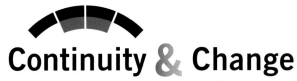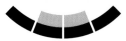

The Influence of Zen Buddhism

Once Japan reopened its doors to world trade in 1854, the culture that it had developed over the 11 preceding centuries had an almost immediate impact on the West. Western artists of the nineteenth century, including Claude Monet [moh-NAY], Vincent van Gogh [go], and Mary Cassatt [kuh-SAHT], were fascinated by Japanese prints, which flooded European and New York markets in what amounted to an avalanche of images. Noh theater generated considerable excitement among Western writers. German playwright Bertolt Brecht and Irish poet William Butler Yeats would each write Noh plays of their own, and the American poet Ezra Pound freely adapted a number of traditional Noh plays. Especially appealing to Western sensibilities was Zen Buddhist philosophy.

The most influential disseminator of Zen Buddhist philosophy in the West was the Japanese scholar D. T. Suzuki (1870–1966). In 1921, he and his wife began publishing *The Eastern Buddhist,* an English-language quarterly intended mostly for Westerners. His *Essays in Zen Buddhism,* published in London in 1927 and expanded upon in both 1933 and 1934, firmly established Suzuki's reputation. When, in April 1936, Suzuki was invited to London to speak at the World Congress of Faiths, he

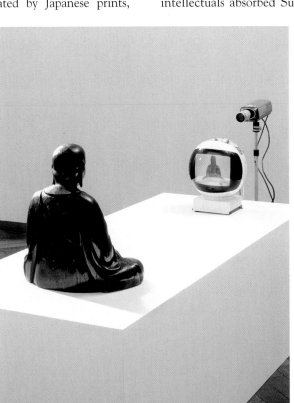

Fig. 9.29 Nam June Paik, *TV Buddha.* 1974. Video installation with statue. Collection Stedelijk Museum, Amsterdam. Paik was deeply influenced by D. T. Suzuki through his close friendship with composer John Cage.

met the 20-year-old Alan Watts, who later the same year would publish his own very influential book, *The Spirit of Zen.*

After spending World War II in seclusion at Enkakuji [ehn-KAH-koo-jee], an important Zen temple in Kamakura,

Suzuki moved to California in 1949, then to New York City, where from 1952 to 1957 he taught seminars on Zen at Columbia University. Composer John Cage attended these seminars for two years, and they deeply influenced his musical direction. A number of other twentieth-century Western intellectuals absorbed Suzuki's teachings as well, including psychoanalyst Carl Jung; poets Thomas Merton, Gary Snyder, and Allen Ginsberg; novelist Jack Kerouac; and potter Bernard Leach.

The many Asian members of the international Fluxus movement of artists, composers, and designers in the 1960s and 1970s, including Yoko Ono, popularized the Zen philosophical practice of posing riddles as a way to lead students to enlightenment. Ono's Fluxus compatriot, the Korean-born Nam June Paik [nahn joon pike] (1932–2006), one of the great innovators of video art, poses just such a riddle in his *TV Buddha* of 1974 (Fig. **9.29**). If he were alive today, would Buddha withdraw from the culture around him in order to meditate in pursuit of enlightenment? In meditating upon his own image reflected back to him on a TV screen, could he escape the charge of self-indulgent narcissism? What does it really mean to reflect upon oneself? These are the kind of questions that a Zen master might ask of Paik's work, just as they are the kind of questions a contemporary viewer might ask as well, which begins to suggest just how much Eastern philosophy has come to influence Western thought. ∎

10

The Counter-Reformation and the Baroque

Emotion, Inquiry,
and Absolute Power

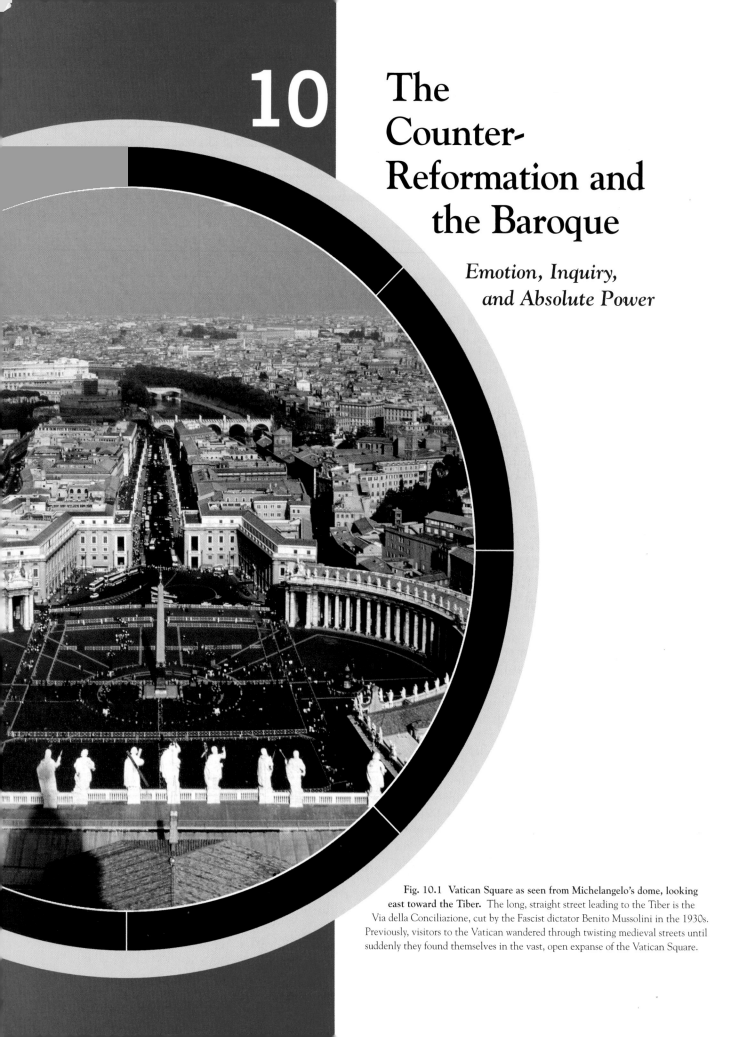

Fig. 10.1 **Vatican Square as seen from Michelangelo's dome, looking east toward the Tiber.** The long, straight street leading to the Tiber is the Via della Conciliazione, cut by the Fascist dictator Benito Mussolini in the 1930s. Previously, visitors to the Vatican wandered through twisting medieval streets until suddenly they found themselves in the vast, open expanse of the Vatican Square.

> ❝ *I would see beside me, on my left hand, an angel in bodily form. . . . In his hands I saw a long golden spear and at the end of the iron tip I seemed to see a point of fire. With this he seemed to pierce my heart. . .*❞
>
> Teresa of Ávila, "Visions"

As the seventeenth century began, the Catholic church was struggling to win back those who had been drawn away by the Protestant Reformation. To wage its campaign, the Church undertook a Counter-Reformation, a conscious attempt on the Church's part to reform itself. But the Church also felt that it needed to attract people back into its fold by more direct means, and the arts took what can best be described as a sensual turn, an appeal not just to the intellect but to the range of human emotion and feeling. This appeal was embodied in an increasingly ornate and grandiose form of expression that came to be known as the Baroque [bah-ROAK] style. Its focal point was the Vatican City, in Rome.

Just as in the sixteenth century, when Pope Julius II (r. 1503–1513) had attempted to revitalize Rome as the center of the Christian world by constructing a new Saint Peter's Basilica, so in the first half of the seventeenth century a series of popes began to impose their own monumental changes to Saint Peter's. The visual impact of the church was underscored by Gian Lorenzo Bernini [JAHN lor-EN-zoh bair-NEE-nee] (1598–1680) in his design for a colonnade to enclose Saint Peter's Square (Fig. **10.1**), the space in front of the main facade of the basilica. Bernini's curved porticoes, composed of 284 huge Doric columns placed in rows of four, create a vast open space—nearly 800 feet across—designed specifically for its dramatic effect. Bernini considered the colonnade enclosing the square to symbolize "the motherly arms of the church" embracing its flock. Here, as crowds gathered to receive the blessing of the pope, the architecture dramatized the blessing itself.

Even before Bernini began his colonnade in 1656, Paul V had hired the leading architect of the day, Carlo Maderno [mah-DAIR-noh] (1556–1629), to design a new facade for the building. The facade, extending across the front of the church to the entire width of Michelangelo's original Greek-cross plan (see Fig. 7.22), was carefully conceived to leave viewers in a state of awe. As one writer described the effect in 1652, "Anyone contemplating the new church's majesty and grandeur has to admit . . . that its beauty must be the work of angels or its immensity the work of giants. Because its magnificent proportions are such that . . . neither the Greeks,

the Egyptians nor the Jews, nor even the mighty Romans ever produced a building as excellent and vast as this one." It was, in short, an embodiment—and an announcement—of the Church's own triumph over the Protestant threat, and Bernini's colonnade only heightened its impact.

Attention to the way viewers would emotionally experience a work of art is a defining characteristic of the Baroque, a term many believe takes its name from the Portuguese *barroco* [bah-roh-koh], literally a large, irregularly shaped pearl. It was originally used in a derogatory way to imply a style so heavily ornate and strange that it verges on bad taste. The rise of the Baroque is the subject of this chapter. We look at it first as it developed in Rome, and at the Vatican in particular, as a conscious style of art and architecture dedicated to furthering the aims of the Counter-Reformation, then in Venice, which in the seventeenth century was the center of musical activity in Europe.

Mannerism and the Early Counter-Reformation

As Bernini conceived it, the Baroque was a compromise between, on the one hand, religious propriety and, on the other, an especially exuberant style of art that had arisen in Italy in the last half of the sixteenth century that has come to be known as **Mannerism**. Although seemingly at odds, from the point of view of creating works of art that might move an audience to belief, Bernini understood that exuberance and propriety might go hand in hand.

The Council of Trent and Catholic Reform of the Arts

The movement toward a greater sense of propriety had been instigated by the Church just a decade before Bernini began work on his colonnade at the Vatican. The Church recognized that its own excesses had fueled the Reformation, but a feud between two Catholic monarchs—the Holy Roman Emperor Charles V (r. 1519–1558), head of the far-flung Spanish Empire, and Francis I of France (r. 1515–1547)—

stymied its efforts to respond politically. But despite their ongoing conflict, financed, on the Spanish side, by gold and silver from the newly discovered Americas, both monarchs understood the necessity of addressing the threat posed by the Protestant Reformation. They convinced the pope to convene the so-called Council of Trent in 1545. Its charge was to outline a path of reform for the Church itself.

Spanning the careers of four different popes over 18 years— 1545–1547, 1551–1552, and 1562–1563—the Council concentrated on restoring internal Church discipline. It called a halt to the selling of Church offices and religious goods, a common practice used by clergy to pad their coffers. It required bishops, many of whom lived in Rome, to return to their dioceses, where, they were told, they needed to preach regularly, exert discipline over local religious practice, and be active among their parishioners. They were warned not to live ostentatiously:

> It is to be desired that those who undertake the office of bishop shall understand . . . that they are called, not to their own convenience, not to riches or luxury, but to labors and cares, for the glory of God. . . . Wherefore . . . this Council not only orders that bishops be content with modest furniture and a frugal table and diet, but that they also give heed that in the rest of their manner of living and in their whole house there be nothing seen which is alien to this holy institution, and which does not manifest simplicity, zeal toward God, and a contempt of vanities.

The bishops were to maintain strict celibacy, which they had not been required to do before. And they were to construct a seminary in every diocese.

The Council of Trent's injunction against luxury and its assertion of the principle of simple piety were directly translated to the arts. Contrary to many Protestant sects, the Council of Trent insisted on the use of religious imagery:

> The images of Christ, of the Virgin Mother of God, and of other saints are to be placed and retained especially in churches . . . [and] set before the eyes of the faithful so that they . . . may fashion their own life and conduct in imitation of the saints and be moved to adore and love God and cultivate piety.

Subsequent treatises on art, written by clergy, called explicitly for direct treatment of subjects, unencumbered by anything "sensuous," from brushwork to light effects.

The Council of Trent's order for a visual art that would directly affect the souls of the people influenced the direction in which church music developed as well. The function of music in the liturgy, the Council insisted, was to serve the text, and so the text should be clear and intelligible to the congregation:

> The whole plan of singing should be constituted not to give empty pleasure to the ear, but in such a way that the words be clearly understood by all, and thus the hearts of the listeners be drawn to the desire of heavenly har-

monies. . . . They shall also banish from church all music that contains, whether in the singing or in the organ playing, things that are lascivious or impure.

For some, polyphony (two or more voices of equal importance) constituted "lascivious or impure" music, and they argued that only the single line of monophonic plainchant should be performed in the church. The Council rejected this idea.

Legend has it that the Council's support of polyphony was the result of a particular **Missa**, or polyphonic mass, composed in 1567 by Giovanni Pierluigi da Palestrina [pyer-loo-EE-gee da pah-less-TREE-nah] (ca. 1525–1594): *Missa Papae Marcelli* [MISS-ah pah-PYE mar-CHEL-lee], or *Mass for Pope Marcellus*. The story is not true, but that it was widely believed for centuries testifies to the power of Palestrina's choral work. In his career, which included serving as choirmaster at the Capella Giulia [kah-PEL-lah JOO-lee-ah] in the Vatican for many years, Palestrina wrote 104 settings for the Mass, 375 motets, 80 hymns, and about 140 songs, both sacred and secular. He was the first composer of the sixteenth century to have his complete works published and was one of the most influential composers of his day.

The *Missa Papae Marcelli* is notable for the way it carries out the requirements of the Council of Trent. Its music is restrained so that the words, when sung by the choir, stand out in utter clarity, especially at the beginning of phrases. Although the voices generally enunciate each syllable of the text in chordal unison (usually thirds and sixths, or what we have come to recognize as consonant intervals), a constant interplay between counterpoint, in which voices imitate the main melody in succession, and **homophony**, in which the subordinate voices simply accompany the melody in unison, enlivens the music. Likewise, Palestrina often plays one voice sustaining a single note per syllable against a voice engaged in **melisma**, or many notes per syllable. Above all, however, the intelligibility of the text is of paramount concern.

This quality is also audible in Palestrina's setting for *Super Flumina Babylonis*, or *By the Rivers of Babylon*, one of his most famous motets (**CD-Track 10.1**). The motet, as has been noted earlier, was the most important form of polyphonic vocal music in the Middle Ages and Renaissance. From the Renaissance onward it normally had a Latin sacred text and, like a *Missa*, was sung during Catholic service. The text of *Super Flumina Babylonis* is from Psalm 137 of the Bible and expresses the lamentation of the Jewish people:

> By the rivers of Babylon, there we sat down and wept,
> When we remembered you, O Zion.
> On the willows, in the midst of everything, we hung up
>   our harps.

The rhythm of each word matches up directly to the musical cadence. The accented syllable of each word is also usually set to a higher note, thus blending text and music with absolute clarity. In Palestrina's own words, the intention is to draw out "the vital impulse given to its words, according to their meaning." In keeping with the thinking of the Council of Trent, Palestrina's music serves to enliven, even glorify the

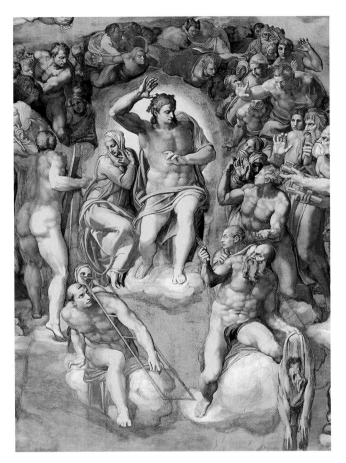

Fig. 10.2 Michelangelo, *Last Judgment*. 1534–1541. Detail. Fresco, 48′ × 44′. Sistine Chapel, Vatican, Rome. Foto Musei Vaticani. Nudity such as Michelangelo paints here was virtually unheard of in church decorative programs.

often, elongated proportions. It is marked by the rejection of the classicizing tendencies of the High Renaissance and by the artist's display of virtuosity through manipulations and distortions of the conventional figure.

In his first commission in Rome after returning in 1534, a *Last Judgment* fresco for the altar wall of the Sistine Chapel (Fig. **10.2**), Michelangelo took enormous liberties with the figure. Saint Bartholomew, for instance, who was martyred by being skinned alive, sits just below Christ's feet, holding in his right hand a knife, the instrument of his torture, and in his left hand his own flayed skin. Many scholars believe that the face on the flayed skin is a self-portrait of Michelangelo, suggesting his sense of his own martyrdom under the unrelenting papal commissions of Pope Paul III. But it is the nudity of his figures that drew the most attention. In 1545, the poet Pietro Aretino wrote a letter to the painter, objecting to the fresco (**Reading 10.1**):

READING 10.1   **from Pietro Aretino, Letter to Michelangelo (1545)**

The pagans when they made statues I do not say of Diana who is clothed, but of naked Venus, made them cover with their hand the parts which should not be seen. And here there comes a Christian who, because he rates art higher than faith, deems a royal spectacle martyrs and virgins in improper attitudes, men dragged down by their genitals, things in front of which brothels would shut their eyes in order not to see them. Your art would be at home in some voluptuous *bagnio* [bathhouse], certainly not in the highest chapel in the world. . . . Restore it to good repute by turning the indecent parts of the damned to flames, and those of the blessed to sunbeams, or imitate the modesty of Florence, who hides your David's shame beneath some gilded leaves. And yet that statue is exposed upon a public square, not in a consecrated chapel.

When Michelangelo did not respond to this letter, Aretino published it. The letter underscores the growing tension between the developing Mannerist style and the aims of the Counter-Reformation, especially in the context of the Council of Trent, which was then in session. In fact, as long as Paul III remained pope, the *Last Judgment* stayed as Michelangelo had painted it. But with the election of Paul IV in 1555, the first new pope after Paul III had convened the Council of Trent in 1545, the painting fell into ever-increasing disfavor. Shortly after Michelangelo's death in 1564, Daniele da Volterra [dan-YEH-lay da vol-TER-rah] and others painted draperies over the genital areas of the fresco's nude figures, a feat for which they ignominiously earned the name *braghettoni* [brah-get-TOH-nee], "breeches-painters." Even when the painting was cleaned and restored in 1994, the Vatican chose to leave the draperies in place.

words, words that the Council believed every member of the congregation must be moved to understand and believe.

The Rise of Mannerism

The demand for clarity and directness that marks the art and music of the Counter-Reformation did not constrain so original an artist as Michelangelo, who introduced a different, more inventive direction in sixteenth-century art. Raphael had already arrived at a new style in the last paintings he executed for the Vatican before his death in 1520. He replaced the clarity, restraint, and order of his *School of Athens* (see *Focus*, pages 212–213) with a more active, dynamic, even physically distorted realization of the human figure, probably in response to Michelangelo's own innovations in the same direction in the later frescoes for the Sistine Chapel ceiling—in the *Libyan Sibyl*, for instance (see Fig. 7.28). This new Mannerist style, reflecting the virtuosity and sophistication of its practitioners, manifests itself in architecture in Michelangelo's stairway for the Laurentian Library (see Fig. 7.30), which some believe to be among the style's earliest examples. In painting and sculpture, it resulted in distorted, artificial poses, mysterious or obscure settings, and, very

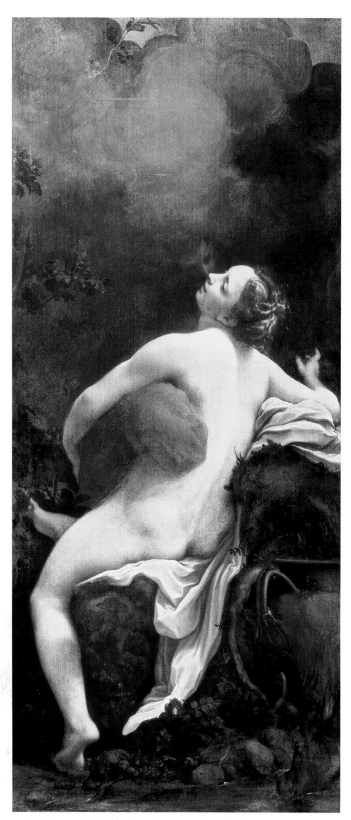

Fig. 10.3 Correggio, *Jupiter and Io*. Early 1530s. Oil on canvas, 69″ × 29½″. Kunsthistoriches Museum, Vienna, Austria. In the myth, Jupiter (Zeus) appears in a dream to Io, daughter of the king of Argos, and takes her to Lerna, a marsh and stream in the eastern Peloponnese, where he seduces her disguised as a cloud. The painting was created for the pleasure chamber of Federico Gonzaga in the Palazzo Ducale, Mantua.

As long as painting confined itself to depicting nonreligious subjects for nonreligious venues, it was more or less free to do as it pleased. Even the nudity of Michelangelo's Sistine Chapel figures would have been tolerable if painted in some less holy place. The Roman cardinal Cirillo Franco summed up the general attitude in a letter: "I hold the painting and sculpture of Michelangelo to be a miracle of nature; but I would praise it so much more if, when he wants to show the supremacy of his art in all that posturing of naked limbs, and all those nudes . . . he did not paint it on the vault of the Pope's Chapel, but in a gallery, or some garden loggia." It was a matter of decorum, or propriety. What might be decorous and appropriate in a gallery or garden loggia was absolutely indecorous in a church.

In the private galleries of the princely courts throughout Europe this more indecorous but highly inventive imagery thrived. In the early 1530s, for instance, Federico Gonzaga of Mantua commissioned a set of erotic paintings that seem almost intentionally the embodiment of what the Council of Trent would label "the lascivious or impure. " They were the work of the northern Italian artist Correggio [kor-REJ-ee-oh] (given name Antonio Allegri [ah-LEH-gree]; ca. 1494–1534) and depicted the loves of Jupiter, or Zeus.

Jupiter and Io, painted in the early 1530s, is one of these (Fig. **10.3**). The painting illustrates Jupiter consummating his love for Io [EYE-oh], a priestess of Hera (Jupiter's wife). Jupiter appears to Io in the guise of a cloud, his face barely visible behind her, kissing her lightly on the cheek. His bear-like arm embraces her as she abandons herself, quite visibly, to sensual pleasure. In addition to the unabashed sensuality of the presentation, the somewhat bizarre juxtaposition of Io's fully lit and well-defined body with Jupiter's dark and amorphous form is fully Mannerist in spirit.

The liberty to invent in such unprecedented ways is the defining characteristic of Mannerist art. But if invention led to the kind of indecorous images produced in the courts of Europe, the Church could not tolerate it. Artists working on religious subjects had to discover ways to blend their Mannerist style with properly decorous religious imagery. Nor could the Church tolerate religious beliefs that did not strictly follow Church doctrine. Catholics inspired by a different kind of spirituality than the Church recognized were deemed a special threat and suffered greatly under repression or worse.

Veronese and the Italian Inquisition A clear example of the need to use invention decorously in art is provided by the fate of a *Last Supper*, now known as the *Feast in the House of Levi*, by the Venetian artist Veronese [vay-roh-NAH-say] (1528–1588). Veronese was born Paolo Cagliari [POW-loh kah-LYAR-ee] and nicknamed after the city of his birth, Verona (Fig. **10.4**). As early as 1542, Pope Paul III had initiated a Roman **Inquisition**—an official inquiry into possible heresy—and in 1573, Veronese was called before the Inquisition to answer charges that his *Last Supper*, painted with life-size figures for a Dominican monastery in Venice, was heretical in its inappropriate treatment of the subject matter.

His testimony before the tribunal illuminates the aesthetic and religious concerns of the era (**Reading 10.2**):

READING 10.2   from The Trial of Veronese (1573)

VERONESE: This is a picture of the Last Supper that Jesus Christ took with His Apostles in the house of Simon.

INQUISITOR: At this Supper of Our Lord have you painted other figures?

VERONESE: Yes, milords.

INQUISITOR: Tell us how many people and describe the gestures of each.

VERONESE: There is the owner of the inn, Simon; beside this figure I have made a steward, who, I imagined, had come there for his own pleasure to see how the things were going at the table. There are many figures there which I cannot recall, as I painted the picture some time ago . . .

INQUISITOR: In this Supper which you made for SS. Giovanni e Paolo, what is the significance of the man whose nose is bleeding?

VERONESE: I intended to represent a servant whose nose was bleeding because of some accident.

INQUISITOR: What is the significance of those armed men dressed as Germans, each with a halberd in his hand?

VERONESE: We painters take the same license the poets and the jesters take and I have represented these two halberdiers, one drinking and the other eating nearby on the stairs. They are

placed there so that they might be of service because it seemed to me fitting, according to what I have been told, that the master of the house, who was great and rich, should have such servants.

INQUISITOR: And that man dressed as a buffoon with a parrot on his wrist, for what purpose did you paint him on that canvas?

VERONESE: For ornament, as is customary . . .

INQUISITOR: Are not the decorations which you painters are accustomed to add to paintings or pictures supposed to be suitable and proper to the subject and the principal figures or are they for pleasure—simply what comes to your imagination without any discretion or judiciousness?

VERONESE: I paint pictures as I see fit and as well as my talent permits.

INQUISITOR: Does it seem fitting at the Last Supper of the Lord to paint buffoons, drunkards, Germans, dwarfs and similar vulgarities?

VERONESE: No, milords.

The tribunal concluded that Veronese should "improve and correct" the painting in three months' time or face penalties. But rather than change the painting, Veronese simply changed the painting's title to *Feast in the House of Levi*. This title refers to a biblical passage: "Levi gave a great banquet for him [Jesus] in his house, and a large crowd of tax collectors and others were at table with them" (Luke 5:29). Through this strategy Veronese could justify the artistic invention in his crowded scene.

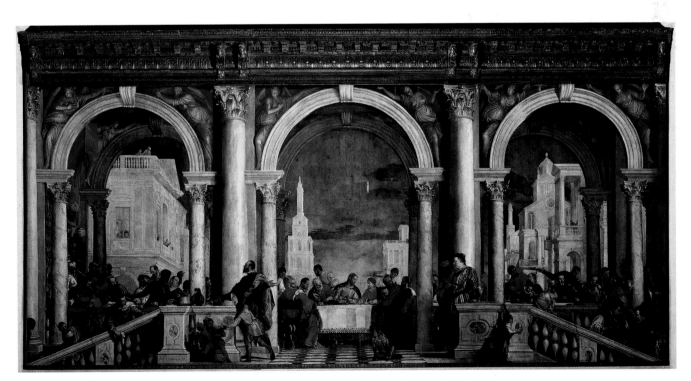

Fig. 10.4 Veronese, *Feast in the House of Levi*. 1573. Oil on canvas, 18′3″ × 42′. Galleria dell'Accademia, Venice. After his testimony before the Inquisition, Veronese made it clear that his "new" source for the painting was the feast in the house of Levi by citing the biblical reference on the balustrade.

The Spanish Inquisition In sixteenth century Spain, a brand of religious mysticism threatened the Church from within. The *alumbrados* [ah-loom-BRAH-dohs], or "illuminated ones," nuns, monks, and priests lit by the Holy Spirit, practiced an extremely individualistic and private brand of faith which led to accusations that they also claimed to have no need of the sacraments of the Church. The *alumbrados* were therefore susceptible to charges of heresy. Chief among them were the Carmelite nun Teresa of Ávila [AH-vih-lah] (1515–1582) and the Carmelite friar Juan de la Cruz (1542–1591), known as John of the Cross. Teresa was from a *converso* family—converted Jews—that lived in Ávila, the medieval center of Jewish mystical thought. Dissatisfied with the worldliness that had crept into her Carmelite order, Teresa campaigned to reform it, founding the Discalced [dis-KALST] (or shoeless) Carmelites, dedicated to absolute poverty and the renunciation of all property. Between 1567 and 1576 she traveled across Spain, founding Discalced convents and a reform convent for Carmelite men. Juan de la Cruz was one of the first two members, and the two would become close friends. Juan's powers as a teacher, preacher, and poet served to strengthen the movement. Teresa's writings, including an autobiography and *The Way to Perfection*, both written before 1567, and *The Interior Castle*, written in 1577, all describe the ascent of the soul to union with the Holy Spirit in four basic stages. In the final of these stages, "devotion of ecstasy or rapture," consciousness of being in the body disappears and the spirit finds itself alternating between the ecstatic throes of a sweet, happy pain and a fearful, glowing fire.

In 1574, Teresa was denounced to the Inquisition as a restless wanderer who under the pretext of religion lived a life of dissipation. As a result, in 1576, she was confined in a convent. Juan de la Cruz suffered an even worse fate. Calced Carmelites arrested him in Toledo on the night of December 3, 1577. They held him in solitary confinement and lashed him before the community on a weekly basis until he escaped eight months later. Among the great works written following his escape is *The Dark Night of the Soul*, a book-length account of the author's mystical union with God.

The moral strictures of the Inquisition and the mysticism of the *alumbrados* are recognizable in the art of one of the most original sixteenth-century painters, El Greco [GREK-oh], "The Greek" (born Domenico Theotokopulos [the-oh-tok-OP-uh-lus] 1541–1614). He trained as an icon painter in his native Crete, in those days a Venetian possession. In 1567 he went to Venice, then three years later to Rome, and in 1576 to Spain, where he soon developed a style that wedded Mannerism with the elongated, iconic figures of his Byzantine training. He used painting to convey an intensely expressive spirituality.

Painted at the turn of the sixteenth century, El Greco's *Resurrection* is decorous to the extent that draperies carefully conceal all inappropriate nudity (Fig. **10.5**). The poses of the writhing Roman soldiers who surround the vision of the triumphant Christ are as artificial and contrived as any in Mannerist art. The verticality of the composition, popular since

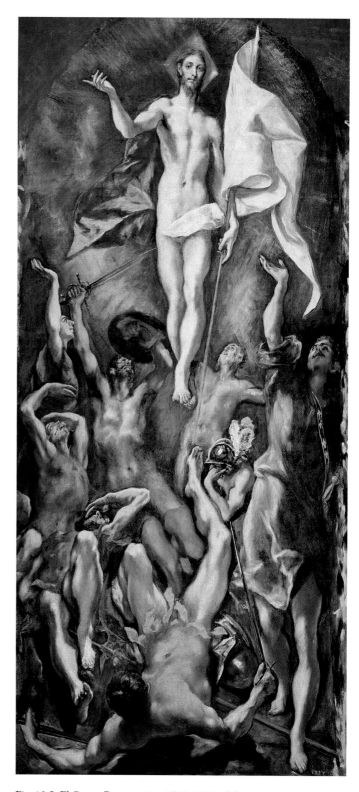

Fig. 10.5 El Greco, *Resurrection*. 1597–1604. Oil on canvas, 9′ 1/4″ × 4′ 2″. Museo del Prado, Madrid. The image was probably painted for the Colegio de Doña Maria, Madrid, and paired with a depiction of the Pentecost, the descent of the Holy Spirit upon the apostles on the seventh Sunday after Easter.

the time of Correggio, mirrors the elongated anatomies of El Greco's figures. And yet, El Greco's style is unique, singular in the angularity of its draperies, in the drama of the representation, and in its overall composition. The Roman soldiers rise and fall in elongated, serpentine poses, twisting around Christ like petals on a blossom, with Christ himself as the flower's stamen. If Christ's sexuality has been repressed, the effect of his presence on the soldiers, who swoon in near-hysterical ecstasy, is unmistakable. Above all, this painting celebrates raw physicality, even as it presents the greatest spiritual mystery of the Christian faith. Here the aspirations of the Counter-Reformation and the inventiveness of the Mannerist style are fully united, as they would come to be in the Baroque art of the seventeenth century.

Cervantes and the Picaresque Tradition

In the last half of the sixteenth century, a literary genre originated in Spain that celebrated inventiveness, particularly suited to Spanish taste, and had a strong effect on literary events in the seventeenth century. This was the **picaresque novel**, a genre of prose that narrates, in a realistic way, the adventures of a *picaro* [PEE-kah-roh], a roguish hero of low social rank living by his wits in a corrupt society. The first book to introduce the picaresque tradition in Spain was *Lazarillo de Tormes* [la-zah-REEL-lyoh day TOR-mays], published anonymously in 1554. Raised by beggars and thieves, Lazarillo is a frankly common man, particularly bent on ridiculing and satirizing the Catholic Church and its officials. For that reason and probably because its hero was not highborn, the Spanish crown banned the book and listed it in the Index of Forbidden Books of the Inquisition. A much more complex *picaro* and undoubtedly the greatest hero of the picaresque tradition in Spanish literature is Don Quixote [don kee-HOH-tay], the creation of novelist, poet, and playwright Miguel de Cervantes [ser-VAHN-tes] (1547–1616).

Cervantes was himself a hero in the army of Philip II at the Battle of Lepanto in 1569 (where Spain defeated the Turks, gaining control of the Mediterranean), a captive of Barbary pirates for five years (1575–1580), a supplier of provisions for the ill-fated Spanish Armada, and several times imprisoned for debt. In 1605, when he was 58 years of age, he published *The Ingenious Hidalgo Don Quixote de la Mancha*. (A *hidalgo* is a member of the lower Spanish nobility, generally exempt from paying taxes but not necessarily owning any real property.) A second part followed a decade later, a year before his death. The novel is more familiarly known today simply as *Don Quixote*.

Don Quixote is often considered the first great modern novel. It is set in La Mancha, a great arid plain southeast of Madrid. Into this landscape Cervantes places his two principal characters, Don Quixote and his servant Sancho Panza [SAHN-cho PAHN-zah]. Don Quixote is obsessed with the old stories of romance literature about questing knights and decides to become one himself. Cervantes presents him as a highly satiric recreation of the conquistadors, whose exploits in the Americas were, Cervantes understood, similarly inspired by a thirst for romantic adventuring. Don Quixote's

enthusiasm and self-deception unintentionally produce comic results. Sancho Panza, on the other hand, is a down-to-earth realist who believes the Don to be a bit crazy but plays along and accompanies him as squire on his adventures, hoping to get rich. The two search for the Don's ideal—and imaginary—lady, Dulcinea [dul-sin-AY-ah]. Sancho convinces the Don that she is a plain, poorly dressed peasant riding a donkey and that he cannot recognize her for the beauty he knows Dulcinea to be because his vision has been bewitched by an enchantress. In other scenes, the Don mistakes a common country inn for a castle, a herd of sheep for a pagan army at battle with Christian forces, and two windmills for battling giants sent by an evil enchanter. This last is his most famous adventure, and in it Don Quixote, ever the noble conquistador, proceeds to tilt at the two windmills with his lance.

All of these episodes are parables of the relation between illusion and reality, art and life. They anticipate the psychological complexities that will come to define the novel as a form. Don Quixote cannot reconcile his dreams with the realities of life itself, and his comic adventuring becomes his tragic fate. Above all, Don Quixote's adventures underscore both the marvelous possibilities that come from unleashing the imagination and the dangers of leaving the world behind.

Because in most of his adventures the Don attempts to apply the simple morality of a knight to situations in which more complex issues are at hand, the novel satirizes chivalric romances, a literary genre that had been popular for more than a century in both written and oral form. But in the prologue to his novel Cervantes states other, related goals. He says that he wanted to give a picture of real life and manners, and to do so in clear language. This was a departure from chivalric fiction. *Don Quixote* is innovative in using everyday speech in dialogue (for which Cervantes was acclaimed by his contemporaries), creating vivid and complex portraits of both his main and subordinate characters, and presenting the narrative in a solemn style free from affectation and in delicate juxtaposition with the comic scenes. The extent of Cervantes's achievement can be gauged, in part, by the fact that his picaresque hero so captured the imagination of his time and of future generations that he gave his name to the adjective *quixotic*, meaning "idealistic and impractical," and inspired the expression "tilting at windmills" to describe fighting illusory battle.

The Baroque in Italy

By the middle of the seventeenth century, artists were increasingly comfortable working in the inventive and exuberant Baroque style that had been inaugurated by Mannerism, while, at the same time, they still followed the edicts of the Council of Trent. The Church's point of view was embodied in the teachings of the Society of Jesus founded by the Spanish nobleman Ignatius [ig-NAY-shuhs] of Loyola [loy-OH-luh] (1491–1556). From their headquarters at the Church of Il Gesù [eel jay-ZOO] in Rome, the Jesuits [JEZ-uh-wits], as they were known, led the Counter-Reformation in the seventeenth century and the revival of the Catholic

Church worldwide. All agreed that the purpose of religious art was to teach and inspire the faithful, that it should always be intelligible and realistic, and that it should be an emotional stimulus to piety.

In his *Spiritual Exercises,* published in 1548, Loyola had called on Jesuits to develop all of their senses—an idea that surely influenced the many and richly diverse elements of the Baroque style. For instance, in the Fifth Exercise, a meditation on the meaning of Hell, Loyola invokes all five senses (**Reading 10.3**):

READING 10.3   **from Ignatius Loyola, *Spiritual Exercises,* Fifth Exercise (1548)**

FIRST POINT: This will be to see in imagination the vast fires, and the souls enclosed, as it were, in bodies of fire.
SECOND POINT: To hear the wailing, the howling, cries, and blasphemies against Christ our Lord and against His saints.
THIRD POINT: With the sense of smell to perceive the smoke, the sulphur, the filth, and corruption.
FOURTH POINT: To taste the bitterness of tears, sadness, and remorse of conscience.
FIFTH POINT: With the sense of touch to feel the flames which envelop and burn the souls.

Loyola's invocation of the senses helps explain a remarkable ceiling by a Jesuit lay brother, Fra Andrea Pozzo [POH-tzoh] (1642–1709), for the Church of Sant'Ignazio [sahnt-ig-NAH-tzee-oh] in Rome. Its subject is the *Triumph of Saint Ignatius of Loyola* (Fig. **10.6**).

By the middle of the seventeenth century, the technique of foreshortening was widely used on the ceilings of many Roman churches and palaces. Foreshortening allowed artists to make the ceiling appear larger than it actually was. To create the illusion of greater space, the artist would paint representations of architectural elements—such as vaults or arches or niches—and then fill the remaining space with foreshortened figures that seem to fly out of the top of the building into the heavens above. Because of Pozzo's masterful use of foreshortening, it is difficult for a visitor to Sant'Ignazio to tell that the space above the nave is a barrel vault. Pozzo painted it over with a rising architecture that seems to extend the interior walls an extra story. A white marble square in the pavement below indicates to the viewer just where to stand to appreciate the perspective properly. On each side of the space overhead are allegorical figures representing the four continents. America is at the upper left, crowned by a feathered headdress of red, white, and blue. At the lower right, in black robes, Ignatius Loyola, founder of the Jesuit order, is transported on a cloud toward the waiting Christ, in the center of the composition. Other Jesuit saints rise to meet them. In Pozzo's ceiling, the faithful are invited to see not Hell, as

Loyola outlines in his *Spiritual Exercises,* but Heaven. They are invited to hear "in imagination" not wailing but hosannas, smell not smoke but perfume, taste not bitter tears but sweet tears of joy, and touch not flames but the glorious light of God.

Baroque Sculpture: Bernini

Probably no image sums up the Baroque movement better than Bernini's sculptural program for the Cornaro [kor-NAH-roh] Chapel. Located in Carlo Maderno's Church of Santa Maria della Vittoria in Rome, the work was a commission from the Cornaro family and executed by Bernini in the middle of the century, at about the same time he was working on the colonnade for Saint Peter's Square. Bernini's theme is a pivotal moment in the life of Teresa of Ávila. Teresa was steeped in the mystical tradition of the Jewish Kabbalah [kuh-BAH-luh], the brand of mystical Jewish thought that seeks to attain the perfection of Heaven while still living in this world by transcending the boundaries of time and space. Bernini illustrates the vision she describes in the following passage (**Reading 10.4**):

READING 10.4   **from Teresa of Ávila, "Visions," Chapter 29 of *The Life of Teresa of Ávila* (before 1567)**

It pleased the Lord that I should sometimes see the following vision. I would see beside me, on my left hand, an angel in bodily form. . . . He was not tall, but short, and very beautiful, his face so aflame that he appeared to be one of the highest types of angel who seem to be all afire. They must be those who are called cherubim; they do not tell me their names but I am well aware that there is a great difference between certain angels and others, and between these and others still, of a kind that I could not possibly explain. In his hands I saw a long golden spear and at the end of the iron tip I seemed to see a point of fire. With this he seemed to pierce my heart several times so that it penetrated to my entrails. When he drew it out, I thought he was drawing them out with it and he left me completely afire with a great love for God. The pain was so sharp that it made me utter several moans; and so excessive was the sweetness caused me by this intense pain that one can never wish to lose it, nor will one's soul be content with anything less than God. It is not bodily pain, but spiritual, though the body has a share in it—indeed, a great share. So sweet are the colloquies of love which pass between the soul and god that if anyone thinks I am lying I beseech God, in His goodness, to give him the same experience.

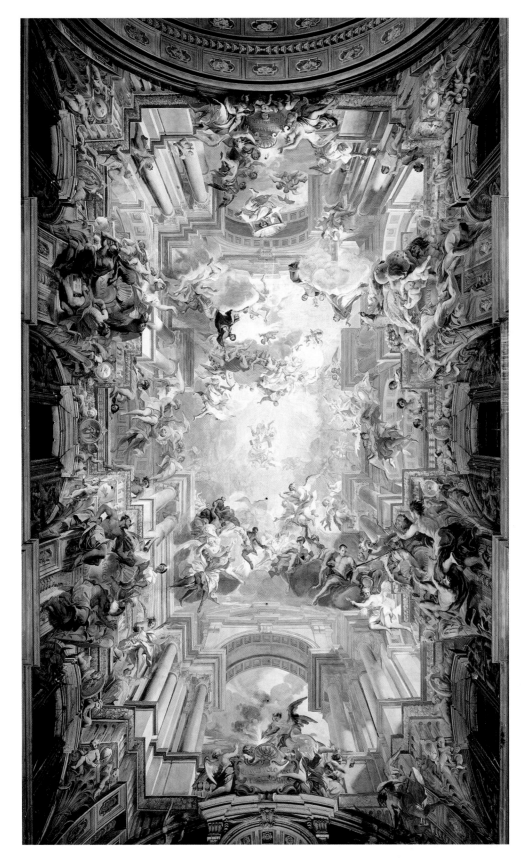

Fig. 10.6 Fra Andrea Pozzo. *Triumph of Saint Ignatius of Loyola.* **1691–1694.** Ceiling fresco, Sant'Ignazio, Rome. Allegorical works in each corner represent the four continents—Europe, Asia, Africa, and America—where the Society of Jesus carried out its missionary work.

Bernini recognized in Teresa's words a thinly veiled description of sexual orgasm. And he recognized as well that the sexuality that Protestantism and the Catholic Counter-Reformation had deemed inappropriate to religious art, but which had survived in Mannerism, had found, in Saint Teresa's vision, a properly religious context, uniting the physical and the spiritual. Thus, the sculptural centerpiece of his chapel decoration is Teresa's implicitly erotic swoon, the angel standing over her, having just withdrawn his penetrating arrow from her "entrails," as Teresa throws her head back in ecstasy (Fig. 10.7).

Bernini's program is far more elaborate than just its sculptural centerpiece (Fig. 10.8). The angel and Teresa are positioned beneath a marble canopy from which gilded rays of light radiate, following the path of the real light entering the chapel from the glazed yellow panes of a window hidden from view behind the canopy pediment. Painted angels, sculpted in stucco relief, descend across the ceiling, bathed in a similarly yellow light that appears to emanate from the dove of Christ at the top center of the composition. On each side of the chapel, life-size marble recreations of the Cornaro family lean out of what appear to be theater boxes into the chapel proper, as if witnessing the vision of Saint Teresa for themselves. Indeed, Bernini's chapel is nothing less than high drama, the stage space of not merely religious vision, but visionary spectacle. Here is an art designed to appeal to the feelings and emotions of its audience and draw them emotionally into the theatrical space of the work.

The Drama of Painting: Caravaggio and the Caravaggisti

Ever since the Middle Ages, when Abbot Suger [soo-ZHAY] of Saint-Denis [san duh-NEE], Paris, had insisted on the power of light to heighten spiritual feeling in the congregation, particularly through the use of stained glass, light had played an important role in church architecture. Bernini used it to great effect in his *Ecstasy of Saint Theresa* (see Fig. 10.7), and Baroque painters, seeking to intensify the viewer's experience of their paintings, sought to manipulate light and dark to great advantage as well. The acknowledged master of light and dark, and perhaps the most influential painter of his day, was Michelangelo Merisi, known as Caravaggio [kah-rah-VAH-gee-oh] (1571–1610), after the town in northern Italy where he was born. His work inspired many followers, who were called the Caravaggisti [kah-rah-vah-GEE-stee].

Master of Light and Dark: Caravaggio Caravaggio arrived in Rome in about 1593 and began a career of revolutionary painting and public scandal. His first major commission in Rome was *The Calling of Saint Matthew* (Fig. 10.9), arranged for by his influential patron Cardinal del Monte and painted about 1599–1600 for the Contarelli [con-tah-RAY-lee] Chapel in the Church of San Luigi dei Francesi [sahn LWEE-gee day frahn-CHAY-zee], the church of the French community (dei Francesi) in Rome. The most dramatic element in this work is light. This light that streams in from an unseen window at the upper right of the painting is almost palpable. It falls onto the table where the tax collector Levi (Saint Matthew's name before becoming one of Jesus' apostles) and his four assistants count the day's take, highlighting their faces and gestures.

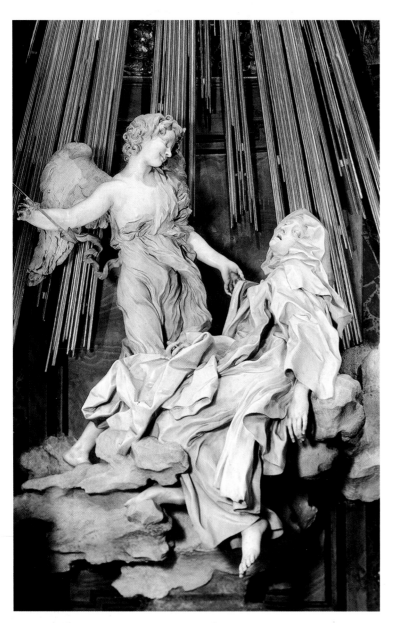

Fig. 10.7 Gian Lorenzo Bernini. *The Ecstasy of Saint Teresa*, Cornaro Chapel, Santa Maria della Vittoria, Rome. 1645–1652. Marble, height of group, 11′ 6″.

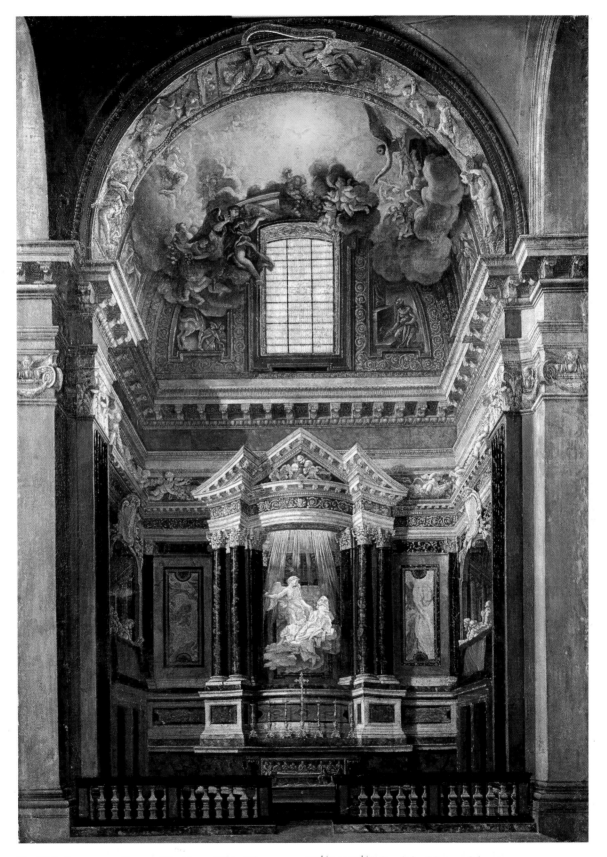

Fig. 10.8 Anonymous. Cornaro Chapel. ca. 1654. Oil on canvas, 5′6¼″ × 3′¼″. Staatliches Museum, Schwerin, Germany. This seventeenth-century painting reproduces the relatively shallow and narrow space of the actual chapel and reveals the Cornaro family portraits at each side of the space.

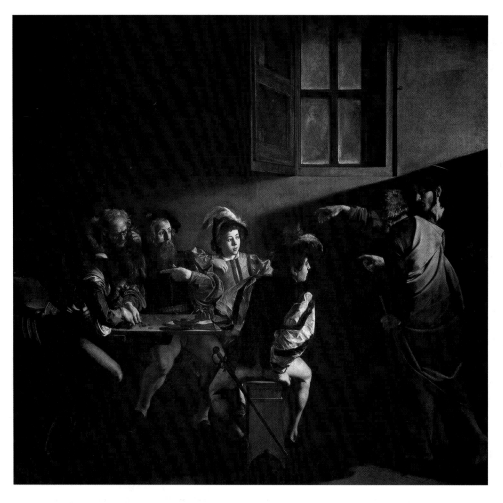

Fig. 10.9 Caravaggio. *The Calling of Saint Matthew.* ca. 1599–1600. Oil on canvas, 11′ 1″ × 11′ 5″. Contarelli Chapel, San Luigi dei Francesi, Rome. The window at the top of the painting is covered by parchment, often used by painters to diffuse light in their studios. This makes the intensity of light entering the room from the right especially remarkable.

ment, specifically John 8:12, where Christ says: "I am the light of the world; he that followeth me shall not walk in darkness, but shall have the light of life."

Caravaggio's insistence on the reality of his scene is thus twofold: He only depicts real people of his own day engaged in real tasks (by implication Christ himself assumes a human reality as well), but he also insists on the reality of its psychological drama. The revelatory power of light—its ability to reveal the world in all its detail—is analogous, in Caravaggio's painting, to the transformative power of faith. Faith, for Caravaggio, fundamentally changes the way we *see* the world, and the way we *act* in it. Time and again his paintings dramatize this moment of conversion through use of the technique known as **tenebrism** [TEN-uh-briz-um]. As opposed to **chiaroscuro** [key-AH-roh-SKYOOR-oh], which many artists employ to create spatial depth and volumetric forms through slight gradations of light and dark, a tenebrist style is not necessarily connected to modeling at all. Tenebrism makes use of large areas of dark contrasting sharply with smaller brightly illuminated areas. In *The Calling of Saint Matthew*, Christ's hand and face rise up out of the darkness, as if his very gesture creates light itself—and by extension Matthew's salvation.

They are dressed not of Jesus' time, but of Caravaggio's, making it more possible for his audience to identify with them. With Saint Peter at his side, Christ enters from the right, a halo barely visible above his head. He reaches out with his index finger extended in a gesture derived from Adam's gesture toward God in the Sistine Chapel ceiling *Creation*—an homage, doubtless, by the painter to his namesake (see Fig. 7.26). One of the figures at the table—it is surely Levi, given his central place in the composition—points with his left hand, perhaps at himself, as if to say, "Who, me?" or perhaps at the young man bent over at the corner of the table intently counting money, as if to say, "You mean him?" All in all, he seems to find the arrival of Jesus uninteresting. In fact, the assembled group is so ordinary—reminiscent of gamblers seated around a table—that the transformation of Levi into Saint Matthew, which is imminent, takes on the aspect of a miracle, just as the light flooding the scene is reminiscent of the original miracle of creation: "And God said, 'Let there be light: and there was light'" (Gen. 1:3). The scene also echoes the New Testa-

One of the clearest instances of Caravaggio's use of light to dramatize moments of conversion is the *Conversion of Saint Paul*, painted around 1601 (Fig. 10.10). Though painted nearly 50 years before Bernini's *The Ecstasy of Saint Teresa* (see Fig. 10.7), its theme is essentially the same, as is its implied sexuality. Here, Caravaggio portrays the moment when the Roman legionnaire Saul (who will become Saint Paul) has fallen off his horse and hears the words, "Saul, Saul, why persecutest thou me?" (Acts 9:4). Neither Saul's servant nor his horse hears a thing. Light, the visible manifestation of Christ's words, falls on the foreshortened soldier. Saul reaches into the air in both a shock of recognition and a gesture of embrace. A sonnet, "Batter My Heart," by the English metaphysical poet John Donne [dun] (1572–1631), published in 1618 in his *Holy Sonnets*, captures Saul's experience in words (**Reading 10.5**):

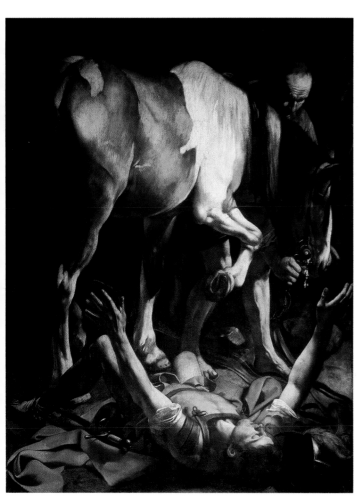

Fig. 10.10 Caravaggio. *Conversion of Saint Paul.* ca. 1601. Oil on canvas, 90$\frac{1}{2}$″ × 68$\frac{7}{8}$″. Santa Maria del Popolo, Rome. This painting was designed to fill the right wall of the narrow Carasi family chapel in Santa Maria del Popolo. Caravaggio had to paint it to be seen at an angle of about 45 degrees, a viewpoint that can be replicated by turning this page about half open to an angle of 45 degrees to the reader's face. The resulting space is even more dramatic and dynamic.

READING 10.5   John Donne, "Batter My Heart" (1618)

Batter my heart, three-person'd God, for you
As yet but knock, breathe, shine, and seek to mend;
That I may rise and stand, o'erthrow me, and bend
Your force to break, blow, burn, and make me new.
I, like an usurp'd town to'another due,
Labor to'admit you, but oh, to no end;
Reason, your viceroy in me, me should defend,
But is captiv'd, and proves weak or untrue.
Yet dearly' I love you, and would be lov'd fain,
But am betroth'd unto your enemy;
Divorce me,'untie or break that knot again,
Take me to you, imprison me, for I,
Except you'enthrall me, never shall be free,
Nor ever chaste, except you ravish me.

There is no reason to believe the English poet knew the Italian's painting, but the fact that the two men share so completely in the ecstasy of the moment of conversion, imaged as physical ravishment, suggests how widespread such conceits were in the seventeenth century. Both share with Teresa of Ávila a profound mysticism, the pursuit of achieving communion or identity with the divine through direct experience, intuition, or insight. All three believe that such experience is the ultimate source of knowledge or understanding, and they seek to convey that in their art. Such mystical experience, in its extreme physicality and naturalistic representation, also suggests how deeply the Baroque as a style was committed to sensual experience.

Artemisia Gentileschi and Caravaggisti Painting One of Caravaggio's most important followers, and one of the first female artists to achieve an international reputation, was Artemisia Gentileschi [jen-tee-LESS-key] (1593–1652/53). Born in Rome, she was raised by her father, Orazio, himself a painter and Caravaggisto. Orazio was among Caravaggio's closest friends. As a young girl, Artemisia could not have helped but hear of Caravaggio's frequent run-ins with the law—for throwing a plate of artichokes at a waiter, for street brawling, for carrying weapons illegally, and, ultimately, in 1606, for murdering a referee in a tennis match. Artemisia's own scandal would follow. It and much of her painting must be understood within the context of this social milieu—the loosely renegade world of Roman artists at the start of the seventeenth century. In 1612, when she was 19, she was raped by Agostino Tassi, a Florentine artist who worked in her father's studio and served as her teacher. Orazio filed suit against Tassi for injury and damage to his daughter. The transcript of the seven-month trial survives. Artemisia accused Tassi of repeatedly trying to meet with her alone in her bedroom and, when he finally succeeded, of raping her. When he subsequently promised to marry her, she freely accepted his continued advances, naïvely assuming marriage would follow. When he refused to marry her, the lawsuit followed.

At trial, Tassi accused her of having slept with many others before him. Gentileschi was tortured with thumbscrews to "prove" the validity of her testimony, and was examined by midwives to ascertain how recently she had lost her virginity. Tassi further humiliated her by claiming that Artemisia was an unskilled artist who did not even understand the laws of perspective. Finally, a former friend of Tassi's testified that Tassi had boasted about his exploits with Artemisia. Ultimately, he was convicted of rape and served only a year in prison. Soon after the long trial ended, Artemesia married an artist and moved with him to Florence. In 1616, she was admitted to the Florentine Academy of Design.

Beginning in 1612, Artemisia painted five separate versions of the biblical story of Judith and Holofernes [hol-uh-FUR-neez]. The subject was especially popular in Florence, which identified with both the Jewish hero David and the Jewish heroine Judith (both of whom had been celebrated in sculptures by Donatello and Michelangelo). When Artemisia

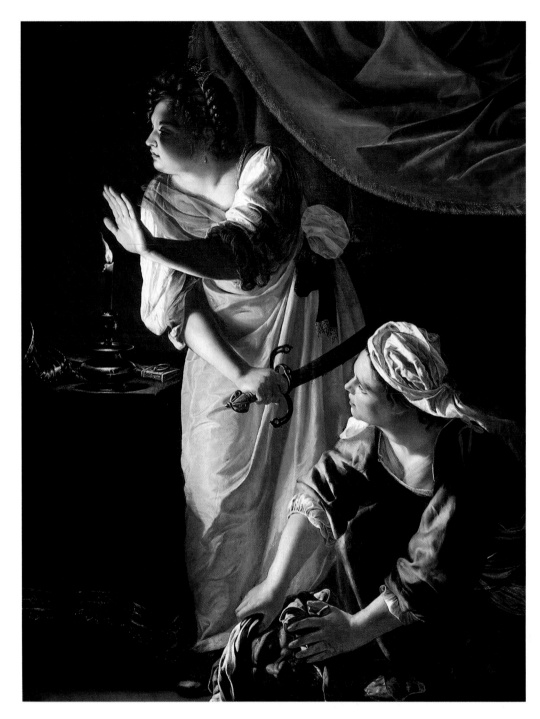

Fig. 10.11 Artemisia Gentileschi. *Judith and Maidservant with Head of Holofernes.* **ca. 1625.** Oil on canvas, $72\frac{1}{2}$" × $55\frac{3}{4}$". The Detroit Institute of Arts. Gift of Leslie H. Green. 52.253. Photo © 1984 Detroit Institute of Art. Judith is a traditional symbol of fortitude, a virtue with which Artemisia surely identified.

moved there, her personal investment in the subject found ready patronage in the city. Nevertheless, it is nearly impossible to see the paintings outside the context of her biography. She painted her first version of the theme during and just after the trial itself, and the last, *Judith and Maidservant with Head of Holofernes,* in about 1625 (Fig. **10.11**), suggesting that in this series she transforms her personal tragedy in her painting. In all of them, Judith is a self-portrait of the artist. In the Hebrew Bible's Book of Judith, the Jewish heroine enters the enemy Assyrian camp intending to seduce their lustful leader, Holofernes, who has laid siege to her people. When Holofernes

falls asleep, she beheads him with his own sword and carries her trophy back to her people in a bag. The Jews then go on to defeat the leaderless Assyrians.

Gentileschi lights the scene by a single candle, dramatically accentuating the Caravaggesque [kah-rah-vah-JESK] tenebrism of the presentation. Judith shades her eyes from its light, presumably in order to look out into the darkness that surrounds her. Her hand also invokes our silence, as if danger lurks nearby. The maid stops wrapping Holofernes's head in a towel, looking on alertly herself. Together, mistress and maid, larger than life-size and heroic, have taken their revenge on not only the Assyrians, but on lust-driven men in general. As is so often the case in Baroque painting, the space of the drama is larger than the space of the frame.

Gentileschi was not attracted to traditional subjects like the Annunciation. She preferred biblical and mythological heroines and women who played major roles. In addition to Judith, she dramatized the stories of Susannah, Bathsheba, Lucretia, Cleopatra, Esther, Diana, and Potiphar. A good business woman, Gentileschi also knew how to exploit the taste for paintings of female nudes.

Venice and Baroque Music

In the sixteenth century, the Council of Trent rejected the use of secular music, which by definition it deemed lascivious and impure, as a model for sacred compositions. Renaissance composers such as Guillaume Dufay and Josquin des Prez (see chapter 7) had routinely used secular music in composing their masses, and Protestants had adapted the chorales of their liturgy from existing melodies, both religious and secular.

The division between secular and religious music was far less pronounced in Venice, a city that had traditionally chafed at papal authority. As a result, Venetian composers felt freer to experiment and work in a variety of forms, so much so that in the seventeenth century the city became the center of musical innovation and practice in Europe.

Giovanni Gabrieli and the Drama of Harmony Venice earned its place at the center of the musical world largely through the efforts of Giovanni Gabrieli [gah-bree-AY-lee] (1556–1612), the principal organist at Saint Mark's Cathe-

dral. Gabrieli composed many secular madrigals, but he also responded to the Counter-Reformation's edict to make church music more emotionally engaging. To do this, he expanded on the polychoral style that Adrian Willaert had developed at Saint Marks in the mid-1500s (see chapter 7). Gabrieli located contrasting bodies of sound in different areas of the cathedral's interior, which already had two organs, one on each side of the chancel (the space containing the altar and seats for the clergy and choir). Playing them off against one another, he was able to produce effects of stunning sonority. Four choirs—perhaps a boy's choir, a women's ensemble, basses and baritones, and tenors in another group—sang from separate balconies above the nave. Positioned in the alcoves were brass instruments, including trombones and cornetts. (A cornett was a hybrid wind instrument, combining a brass mouthpiece with woodwind finger technique. The nineteenth-century band instrument has a similar name but is spelled with a single "t.") Both the trombone and the cornett were staples of Venetian street processions, which are in many ways responsible for the development of instrumental music in Venice. By 1570 there were approximately 40 street processions a year, in which participants were accompanied by singers, bagpipes, shawms (a double-reed instrument similar to a bagpipe, but without the bag), drums, recorders, viols, flutes, and *pifarri*, or ensembles of wind instruments often composed of cornetts and trombones (two or three of each) (Fig. **10.12**). The Venetian love for these ensembles led to their adaptation from secular ceremonies to religious ones (many of these processions were associated with religious feast days in the first place).

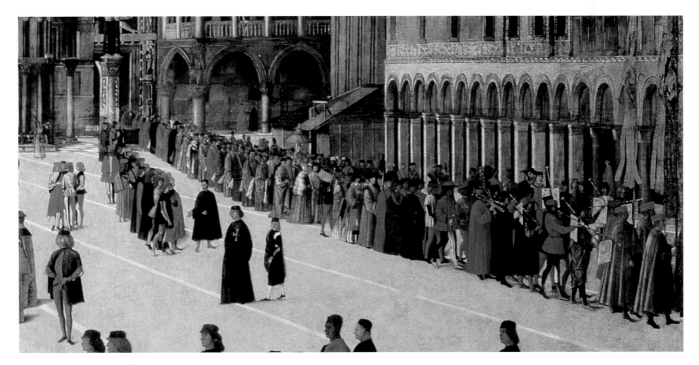

Fig. 10.12 Detail of Gentile Bellini. *Procession of the Reliquary of the True Cross in Piazza San Marco.* **1496.**
Oil on canvas, 12′1½″ × 24′5¼″. Gallerie dell'Accademia, Venice. The procession here includes six *trombe lunghe*, or long silver trumpets, followed by three shawms, and two trombonists.

Gabrieli was among the first to write religious music intended specifically for wind ensemble—music that was independent of song and that could not, in fact, be easily sung. One such piece is his 1597 *Canzona Duodecimi Toni* [kan-ZOH-na doo-oh-DAY-chee-me TOH-nee] (*Canzona in C Major*), in which two brass ensembles create a musical dialogue (**CD-Track 10.2**). A **canzona** is a type of instrumental contrapuntal work, derived from Renaissance secular song, like the madrigral, which was increasingly performed in the seventeenth century in church settings. It is particularly notable for its dominant rhythm, LONG-short-short, known as the "canzona rhythm." In Saint Mark's, the two ensembles would have been placed across from one another in separate lofts. The alternating sounds of cornett and trombone or, in other compositions, brass ensemble, choir, and organ coming from various parts of the cathedral at different degrees of loudness and softness create a total effect similar to stereophonic "surround sound."

For each part of his composition Gabrieli chose to designate a specific voice or instrument, a practice we have come to call **orchestration**. Furthermore, he controlled the **dynamics** (variations and contrast in force or intensity) of the composition by indicating, at least occasionally, the words *piano* ("soft") or *forte* ("loud"). In fact, he is the first known composer to specify dynamics. The dynamic contrasts of loud and soft in the *Canzona Duodecimi Toni*, mirroring the taste for tenebristic contrasts of light and dark in Baroque painting, is a perfect example of Gabrieli's use of dynamic variety. As composers from across Europe came to Venice to study, they took these terms back with them, and Italian became the international language of music.

Finally, and perhaps most important, Gabrieli organized his compositions around a central note, called the **tonic note** (usually referred to as the **tonality** or **key** of the composition). This tonic note provides a focus for the composition. The ultimate resolution of the composition into the tonic, as in the *Canzona Duodecimi Toni*, where the tonic note is C, provides the heightened sense of harmonic drama that typifies the Baroque.

Claudio Monteverdi and the Birth of Opera A year after Gabrieli's death, Claudio Monteverdi [KLAU-dee-oh mohn-tay-VAIR-dee] (1567–1643) was appointed musical director at Saint Mark's in Venice. Monteverdi introduced a new, text-based musical form, the **opera**, a term that is the plural of *opus*, or "work." Operas are works consisting of many smaller works. (The term *opus* is used, incidentally, to catalogue the musical compositions of a given composer, usually abbreviated *op.*, so that "*op.* 8" would mean the eighth work in the composer's repertoire.)

The form itself was first suggested by a group known as the Camerata of Florence (*camerata* means "club " or "society"), a group dedicated to discovering the style of singing used by the ancient Greeks in their drama, which had united poetry and music but was known only through written accounts. The group's discussions stimulated the composer Giulio Caccini to write works that placed a solo vocal line above an instrumental line, known as the **basso continuo**, or "continuous bass," usually composed of a keyboard instrument (organ, harpsichord, etc.) and melody instrument (usually a cello), that was conceived as a supporting accompaniment, not as the polyphonic equivalent, to the vocal line. This combination of solo voice and basso continuo came to be known as **monody**.

The inspiration for Monteverdi's first opera, *Orfeo* [or-FAY-oh] (1607), was the musical drama of ancient Greek theater. The **libretto** [lih-BRET-toh] (or "little book") for Monteverdi's opera was based on the Greek myth of Orpheus [OR-fee-us] and Eurydice [yoor-ID-ih-see]. Although *Orfeo* is by no means the first opera, it is generally accepted as the first to successfully integrate music and drama. Monteverdi tells the story through a variety of musical forms—choruses, dances, and instrumental interludes. Two particular forms stand out—the **recitativo** [ray-chee-tah-TEE-voh] and the **aria** [AH-ree-uh]. *Recitativo* is a style of singing that imitates very closely the rhythms of speech. Used for dialogue, it allows for a more rapid telling of the story than might be possible otherwise. The *aria* would eventually develop into an elaborate solo or duet song that expresses the singer's emotions and feelings, expanding on the dialogue of the recitative (in Monteverdi's hands, the aria could still be sung in recitative style).

Orfeo required an orchestra of three dozen instruments—including ten viols, three trombones, and four trumpets—to perform the overture, interludes, and dance sequences, but generally only a harpsichord or lute accompanied the arias and recitatives so that the voice would remain predominant. For the age, this was an astonishingly large orchestra, financed together with elaborate staging by the Mantuan court where it was composed and first performed, and it provided Monteverdi with a distinct advantage over previous opera composers. He could achieve what his operatic predecessors could only imagine—a work that was both musically and dramatically satisfying, one that could explore the full range of sound and, with it, the full range of psychological complexity.

Antonio Vivaldi and the Concerto Venice's most important composer of the early eighteenth century was Antonio Vivaldi [vee-VAHL-dee] (1678–1741). Vivaldi, son of the leading violinist at Saint Mark's, assumed the post of musical director at the Ospedale della Pietà [oh-spay-DAH-lay DAY-lah pee-ay-TAH] in 1703, one of four orphanages in Venice that specialized in music instruction for girls. (Boys at the orphanages were not trained in music since it was assumed they would enter the labor force.) As a result, many of the most talented harpsichordists, lutists, and other musicians in Venice were female, and many of Vivaldi's works were written specifically for performance by Ospedali [oh-spay-DAH-lee] girl choirs and instrumental ensembles. By and large, the Ospedali musicians were young girls who would subsequently go on to either a religious life or marriage, but several were middle-aged women who remained in the Ospedali, often as teachers, for their entire lives. The directors of the Ospedali hoped that wealthy members of the audience would be so dazzled by the performances that they would donate money to the orphanages. Audiences from across Europe attended these concerts, which were among the first in the history of Western music that took place outside a church or theater and were open to the public. And they were, in fact, dazzled by the talent of these female musicians; by all accounts, they were as skilled and professional as any of their male counterparts in Europe.

Vivaldi specialized in composing **concertos** [kun-CHAIR-tohs], a three-movement secular form of instrumental music popular at court. Vivaldi systematized its form. The first movement of a concerto is usually *allegro* (quick and cheerful), the second slower and more expressive, like the pace of an opera aria, and the third a little livelier and faster than the first. Concertos usually feature one or more solo instruments that, in the first and third movements particularly, perform passages of material, called episodes, that contrast back and forth with the orchestral score—a form known as **ritornello** [re-tor-NEL-loh], "something that returns" (i.e., returning thematic material). At the outset, the entire orchestra performs the ritornello in the tonic—the specific home pitch around which the composition is organized. Solo episodes interrupt alternating with the ritornello, performed in partial form and in different keys, back and forth, until the ritornello returns again in its entirety in the tonic in the concluding section.

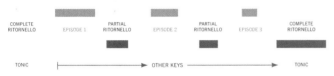

Ritornello

In the course of his career, Vivaldi composed nearly 600 concertos—for violin, cello, flute, piccolo, oboe, bassoon, trumpet, guitar, and even recorder. Most of these were performed by the Ospedale ensemble. The most famous is a group of four violin concertos, one for each season of the year, called *The Four Seasons*. It is an example of what would later come to be known as **program music**, or purely instrumental music in some way connected to a story or idea. The program of the first of these concertos, *Spring* (**CD-Track 10.3**), is supplied by a sonnet, written by Vivaldi himself, at the top of the score. The first eight lines suggest the text for the first movement, and the last six lines, divided into two groups of three, the text for its second and third movements:

Spring has arrived, and full of joy
The birds greet it with their happy song.
The streams, swept by gentle breezes,
Flow along with a sweet murmur.
Covering the sky with a black cloak,
Thunder and lightning come to announce the season.
When all is quiet again, the little birds
Return to their lovely song.

The ritornello in this concerto is an exuberant melody played by the whole ensemble. It opens the movement, and corresponds to the poem's first line. Three solo violins respond in their first episode—"the birds greet it with their happy song"—imitating the song of birds. In the second episode, they imitate "streams swept by gentle breezes," then, in the third, "thunder and lightning," and finally the birds again, which "Return to their lovely song." The whole culminates with the ritornello, once again resolved in the tonic.

In its great rhythmic freedom (the virtuoso passages given to the solo violin) and the polarity between orchestra and solo instruments (the contrasts of high and low timbres, or sounds, such as happy bird song and clashing thunder), Vivaldi's concerto captures much of what differentiates Baroque music from its Renaissance predecessors. Gone are the balanced and flowing rhythms of the *prima prattica* and the polyphonic composition in which all voices are of equal importance. Perhaps most of all, the drama of beginning a composition in a tonic key, moving to different keys and then returning to the tonic—a pattern known as **modulation**—could be said to distinguish Baroque composition from what had come earlier. The dramatic effect of this modulation, together with the rich texture of the composition's chord clusters, parallels the dramatic lighting of Baroque painting, just as the embellishment of the solo voice finds its equivalent in the ornamentation of Baroque architecture.

The Secular Baroque in the North

A more austere Baroque style dominated northern Europe in the seventeenth century. Amsterdam was at its center. The city's economy thrived, sometimes too hotly, as in 1636 when mad speculation sent the market in tulip bulbs skyrocketing (a single bulb in Amsterdam sold for 4,600 florins, fifteen or twenty times the annual income of a skilled craftsman). But this tendency to excess was balanced by the conservatism of the Dutch Reformed Church. The Calvinist fathers of the Dutch Reformed Church found no place for art in the Calvinist liturgy, by and large banning art from its churches.

But the prosperous Dutch populace avidly collected pictures. A visiting Englishman, John Evelyn, explained their passion for art this way, in 1641: "The reason of this store of pictures and their cheapness proceeds from want of land to employ their stock [wealth], so that it is an ordinary thing to find a common farmer lay out two or three thousand pounds in this commodity. Their houses are full of them and they vend them at their fairs to very great gains." If Evelyn exaggerates the sums invested in art—a typical landscape painting sold for only three or four guilders, still the equivalent of two or three days' wages for a Delft cloth-worker—he was accurate in his sense that almost everyone owned at least a few prints and a painting or two.

New Imagery: Still Life, Landscape, and Genre Painting

Despite Dutch Reformed distaste for religious history painting—commissions from the Church had dried up almost completely by 1620—about a third of privately owned paintings in the city of Leiden (one of the most iconoclastic in Holland) during the first 30 years of the seventeenth century represented religious themes. But other, more secular forms of painting thrived. Most Calvinists did not object to sitting for their portraits, as long as the resulting image reflected their Protestant faith. And most institutions wanted visual documentation of their activities, resulting in a thriving industry in group portraiture. Painting also came to reflect the matter-of-fact materialism of the Dutch character—its interest in all manner of things, from carpets, to furnishings, to clothing, collectibles, foodstuffs, and everyday activities. And the Dutch artists themselves were particularly interested in technical developments in the arts, particularly Caravaggio's dramatic lighting. To accommodate the taste of the buying public, Dutch artists developed a new visual vocabulary that was largely vernacular, reflecting the actual time and place in which they lived.

Still Lifes Among the most popular subjects were **still lifes**, paintings dedicated to the representation of common household objects and food. At first glance, they seem nothing more than a celebration of abundance and pleasure. But their subject is also the foolishness of believing in such apparent ease of life. Johannes Goedaert's *Flowers in a Wan-li Vase with Blue-Tit* (Fig. **10.13**) is, on the one hand, an image of pure floral exuberance. The arrangement contains four varieties of tulip—somewhat ominously, given the memories of tulipomania—and a wide variety of other flowers, including a Spanish iris, nasturtiums from Peru, fritalleries [FRIT-ul-er-eez] from Persia, a stripped York and Lancaster Rose—a whole empire's worth of blossoms. The worldliness of the blooms is underscored by the Wan-li vase in which they are placed, a type of Ming dynasty porcelain (see Fig. 9.20) that became popular with Dutch traders around the turn of the century. The short life of the blooms is suggested by the yellowing leaves; the impermanence of the scene by the fly perched on one of the tulips. But perhaps the most telling detail is the bird at the bottom left of the painting, a blue-tit depicted in the act of consuming a moth. Dutch artists of this period used such details to remind the viewer of the frivolous quality of human existence, our vanity in thinking only of the pleasures of the everyday. Such *vanitas* [VAN-ih-tahss] **paintings**, as they are called, remind us that pleasurable things in life inevitably fade, that the material world is not as long-lived as the spiritual, and that the spiritual should command our attention. They are, in short, examples of the *momento mori*— reminders that we will die. Paintings such as Goedaert's were extremely popular. Displayed in the owner's home, they were both decorative and imbued with a moral sensibility that announced to a visitor the owner's upright Protestant sensibility.

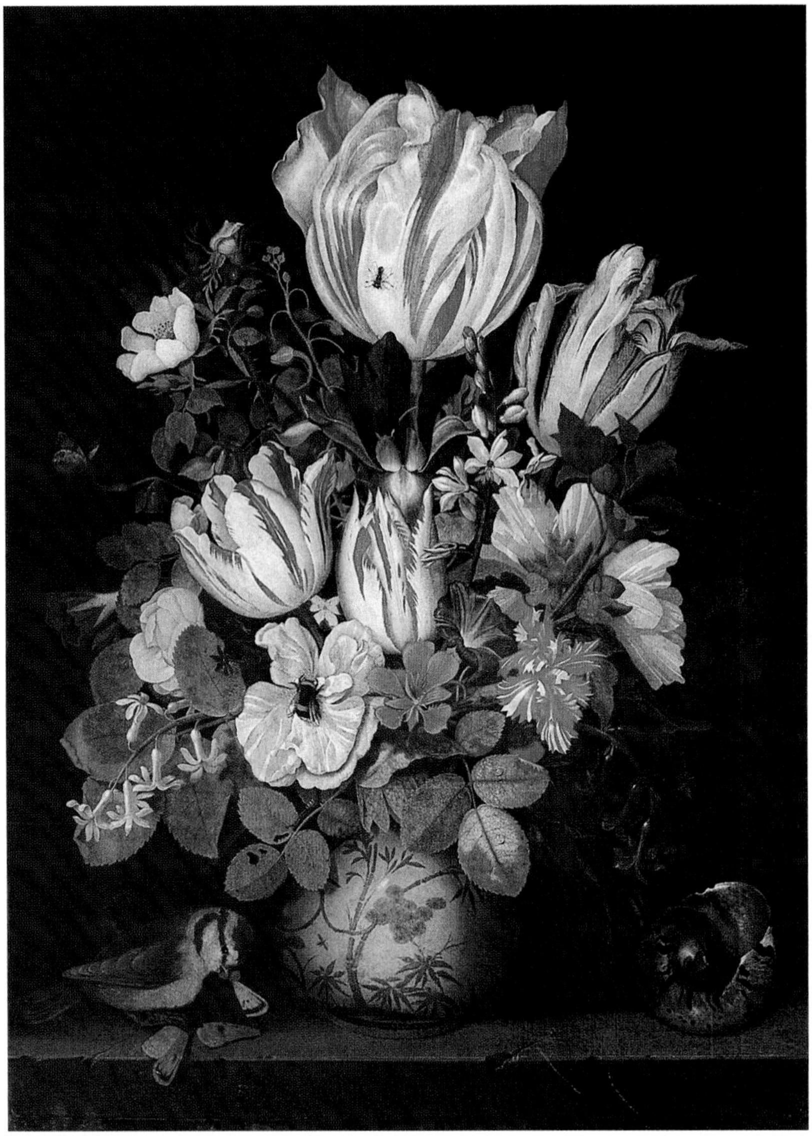

Fig. 10.13 Johannes Goedaert. *Flowers in a Wan-li Vase with Blue-Tit.* ca. 1660. Private collection, Middleburg, Germany. The shell in the lower right corner is a symbol of worldly wealth, but as it is broken and empty, it is also a reminder of our vanity and mortality.

Landscapes Another popular subject was landscape. Landscape paintings such as Jacob van Ruisdael's [vahn ROYS-dahl] *View of Haarlem*

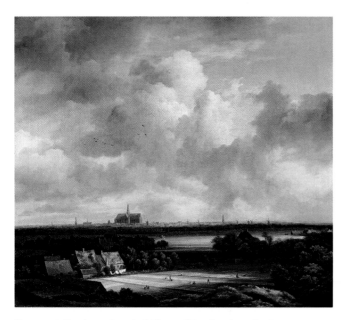

Fig. 10.14 Jacob van Ruisdael. *View of Haarlem from the Dunes at Overveen.* ca. 1670. Oil on canvas, 22″ × 24³⁄₈″. Mauritshuis, The Hague. The play of light and dark across the landscape can be understood in terms of the rhythms of life itself.

mate genre scenes that reveal a moment in the domestic world of women.

The example here is *Woman with a Pearl Necklace* (Fig. **10.15**). Light floods the room from a window at the left, where a yellow curtain has been drawn back, allowing the young woman to see herself better in a small mirror beside the window. She is richly dressed, wearing an ermine-trimmed yellow satin jacket. On the table before her are a basin and a powder brush; she has evidently completed the process of putting on makeup and arranging her hair as she draws the ribbons of her pearl necklace together and admires herself in the mirror. From her ear hangs a pearl earring, glistening in the light. The woman brims with self-confidence, and nothing in the painting suggests that Vermeer intends a moralistic message of some sort. While the woman's pearls might suggest her vanity—to say nothing of pride because of the way she gazes at them—they also traditionally symbolize truth, purity, even virginity. This latter reading is supported by the great, empty, and white stretch of wall that extends between her and the mirror. It is as if this young woman is a *tabula rasa* [TAB-yuh-luh RAHZ-uh], a blank slate, whose moral history remains to be written.

from the Dunes at Overveen reflect national pride in the country's reclamation of its land from the sea (Fig. **10.14**). The English referred to the United Provinces as the "united bogs," and the French constantly poked fun at the baseness of what they called the *Pays-Bas* [PAY-ee bah] (the "Low Countries"). But the Dutch themselves considered their transformation of the landscape from hostile sea to tame farmland, in the century from 1550 to 1650, as analogous to God's recreation of the world after the Great Flood.

In Ruisdael's landscape painting, this religious undertone is symbolized by the great Gothic church of Saint Bavo at Haarlem, which rises over a flat, reclaimed landscape where figures toil in a field lit by an almost celestial light. It is no accident that two-thirds of Ruisdael's landscape is devoted to sky, the infinite heavens. In flatlands, the sky and horizon are simply more evident, but more symbolically, the Dutch thought of themselves as *Nederkindren*, the "children below," looked after by an almighty God with whom they had made an eternal covenant.

Genre Scenes Paintings that depict events from everyday life—or **genre scenes**—were another favorite of the Dutch public. One of the masters of this type of painting was Jan Vermeer (1632–1675). His paintings illuminate—and celebrate—the material reality of Dutch life. We know very little of Vermeer's life, and his painting was largely forgotten until the middle of the nineteenth century. But today he is recognized as one of the great masters of the Dutch seventeenth century. Vermeer painted only 34 works that modern scholars accept as authentic, and most depict inti-

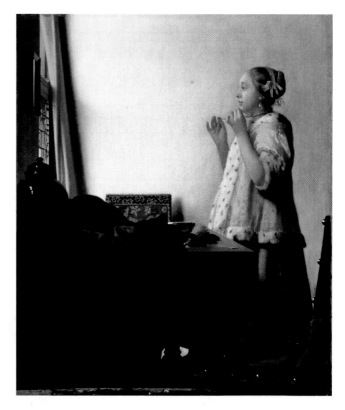

Fig. 10.15 Jan Vermeer. *Woman with a Pearl Necklace.* ca. 1664. Oil on canvas, 22⁵⁄₃₂″ × 17³⁄₄″. Post-restoration. Inv.: 912 B. Photo: Joerg P. Anders. Gemäeldegalerie, Staatliche Museen zu Berlin, Berlin, Germany. Bildarchiv Preussischer Kulturbesitz/Art Resource, NY. The mirror can symbolize both vanity—self-love—and truth, the accurate reflection of the world.

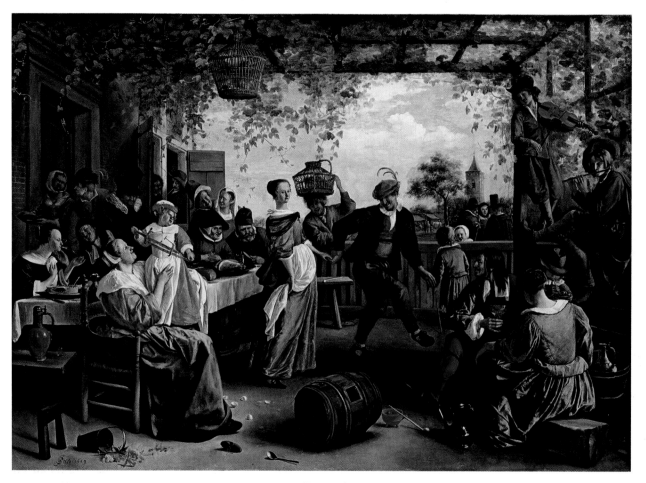

Fig. 10.16 Jan Steen. *The Dancing Couple.* 1663. Oil on canvas, $40\,^3/_8$″ × $56\,^1/_8$″. Widener Collection. 1942.9.81.
Photograph © 2007 Board of Trustees, National Gallery of Art, Washington, D.C. Steen's paintings, whatever their
moralizing undercurrents, remind us that the Dutch were a people of great humor and happiness. They enjoyed life.

Vermeer's paintings of interiors are, for many art historians, a celebration of Dutch domestic culture. As much as
anything else they extol the comforts of home. In fact, the
home is the chief form of Dutch architecture. Decorated with
paintings and maps, furnished with comfortable furniture and
carpets, its larder filled with foodstuffs from around the world,
the home was the center of Dutch life.

A genre scene of a completely different character is *The
Dancing Couple* (Fig. **10.16**) by Jan Steen (1626–1679). Like
many of Steen's paintings, it depicts festivities surrounding
some sort of holiday or celebration. Steen was both a painter
and a tavern keeper, and the scene here is most likely a tavern patio in midsummer. An erotic flavor permeates the
scene, an atmosphere of flirtation and licentiousness. To the
right, musicians play as a seated couple drunkenly watch the
dancers. To the left, two men enjoy food at the table, a
woman lifts a glass of wine to her lips, and a gentleman—a
self-portrait of the artist—gently touches her chin. Steen
thus portrays his own—and, by extension, the Dutch—penchant for merrymaking, but in typical Dutch fashion he also
admonishes himself for taking such license. On the tavern
floor lie an overturned pitcher of cut flowers and a pile of

broken eggshells, both *vanitas* symbols. Together with the
church spire in the distance, they remind us of the fleeting
nature of human life as well as the hellfire that awaits those
who have fallen into the vices so openly displayed in the rest
of the painting.

Rembrandt van Rijn and the Drama of Light

In the seventeenth century, Rembrandt van Rijn (1606–1669)
was the leading painter in Amsterdam and by far its most
sought-after portrait painter. And he was himself the subject
of over 60 self-portraits. His work was distinguished by his
ability to build up the figure with short dashes of paint or, alternately, long fluid lines of loose, gestural brushwork. The result,
paradoxically, is an image of extreme clarity. Consider Rembrandt's portrait of Amsterdam fur trader Nicolaes Ruts, commissioned by the merchant in 1631 (Fig. **10.17**).

Ruts is dressed in the stuff of his trade, sable fur, the most
sought-after and finest of all materials. In one hand he holds
a note—perhaps a letter of credit—while the other rests firmly on the corner of a table or chair. His eyes gaze out of the
picture—not at the viewer, but as if inward—with an almost
ferocious intensity of thought. The picture is a piece of self-

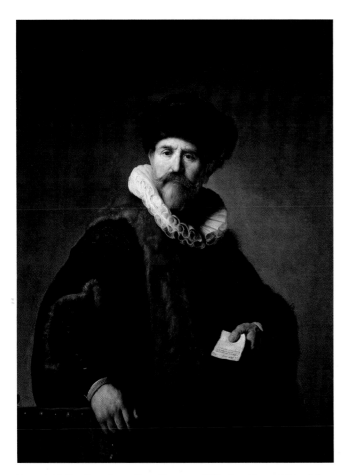

Fig. 10.17 Rembrandt van Rijn. *Portrait of Nicolaes Ruts*. 1631. Oil on mahogany, 46″ × 34⅜″. Frick Collection, NY. That Rembrandt painted this work on mahogany, instead of the usual oak, speaks to the sitter's wealth and taste for fine objects.

propaganda, commissioned to evoke the sitter's business acumen and success, the reliability and soundness of his enterprise. It accomplishes this by juxtaposing his wealth—captured in Rembrandt's rendering of the fur, each hair on the right sleeve realized with a single, minute stroke of oil paint—with the plainness and austerity of the painting's brown colors and setting. Devoid of the red, blue, and green draperies that mark Italian painting (see Fig. 10.6 for example), and purged of all architectural ornament, this painting announces the *economy* of its means in both senses of the word: the prosperity and wealth of the man and the thrift and frugality of their management. What Rembrandt brought to his portrait paintings, beyond the requirement that they look like their sitters, is what Simon Schama in his biography *Rembrandt's Eyes* terms "the urgency and energy of characters caught in a personal drama—their own."

The painting also reveals one of Rembrandt's important contributions to the art of portraiture—his use of light to animate the figure. Where light falls through the windows of Vermeer's paintings onto his figures, it seems to emanate from the figures themselves in Rembrandt's. It is as if light is a symbol for life itself. In one of his most famous group portraits, *The Anatomy Lesson of Dr. Tulp* (see *Focus*, pages 304-305), Rembrandt would use this symbolic light for ironic effect. But in his religious works, especially, it would come to stand for the redemption offered to humankind by the example of Christ.

Rembrandt's love of the play of light and dark drew him to printmaking, a medium where the contrast between rich darks and brilliant lights could be exploited to great effect. Among the greatest of his many prints is *Christ Preaching* (Fig. **10.18**), also known as the "Hundred-Guilder Print" because it sold for 100 guilders at a seventeenth-century auction, at that time an unheard-of price for a print. The image illustrates the Gospel of Matthew, showing Christ addressing the

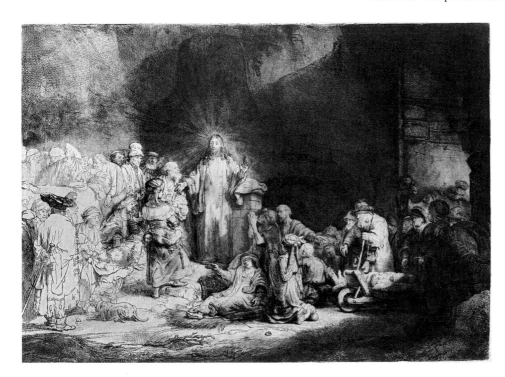

Fig. 10.18 Rembrandt van Rijn. *Christ Preaching* (the "Hundred-Guilder Print"). ca. 1648–1650. Etching, 11″ × 15½″. Rijksmuseum, Amsterdam. Many of the figures in this etching were suggested by Spanish and Jewish refugees who crowded the streets of Amsterdam and whom Rembrandt regularly sketched.

Focus

Rembrandt's *The Anatomy Lesson of Dr. Tulp*

The Anatomy Lesson of Dr. Tulp was commissioned by Dr. Tulp to celebrate his second public anatomy demonstration performed in Amsterdam on January 31, 1632. Public dissections were always performed in the winter months in order to better preserve the cadaver from deterioration. The body generally was that of a recently executed prisoner. The object of these demonstrations was purely educational—how better to understand the human body than to inspect its innermost workings? By understanding the human body, the Dutch believed, one could come to understand God. As the Dutch poet Barlaeus put it in 1639, in a poem dedicated to Rembrandt's painting:

> Listener, learn yourself! And while you proceed through the parts,
> believe that, even in the smallest, God lies hid.

Public anatomies, or dissections, were extremely popular events. Town dignitaries would generally attend, and a ticket-paying public filled the amphitheater. As sobering as the lessons of an anatomy might be, the event was also an entertaining spectacle. An example of the Dutch group portrait, this one was designed to celebrate Tulp's medical knowledge as well as his following. He is surrounded by his students, all of whom are identified on the sheet of paper held by the figure standing behind the doctor. Their curiosity underscores Tulp's prestige and the scientific inquisitiveness of the age.

The figures are arranged in a triangle. Dr. Tulp, in the bottom right corner, holds a scalpel that is the focus of almost everyone's attention. As is characteristic of Rembrandt's work, light plays a highly symbolic role. It shines across the room, from left to right, directly lighting the faces of the three most inquisitive students, suggesting the light of revelation and learning. And it terminates at Tulp's face, almost as if he himself is the source of their light. Ironically, the best-lit figure in the scene is the corpse. Whereas light in Rembrandt's work almost always suggests the kind of lively animation we see on the students' brightly lit faces, here it illuminates death.

Dr. Frans van Loenen points at the corpse with his index finger as he engages the viewer's eyes. The gesture is meant to remind us that we are all mortal.

The pale, almost bluish skin tone of the cadaver contrasts dramatically with the rosy complexions of the surgeons. Typically, the cadaver's face was covered during the anatomy, but Rembrandt unmasked the cadaver's face for his painting. In fact, we know the identity of the cadaver. He is Adriaen Adriaenszoon, also known as "Aris Kindt"—"the Kid"—a criminal with a long history of thievery and assault who was hanged for beating an Amsterdam merchant while trying to steal his cape. Dr. Tulp and his colleagues retrieved the body from the gallows. In another context, a partly draped nude body so well lit would immediately evoke the entombment of Christ with its promise of Resurrection. It is the very impossibility of that fate for Adriaen Adriaenszoon that the lighting seems to underscore here.

Dr. Tulp is displaying the flexor muscles of the arm and hand and demonstrating their action by activating various muscles and tendons. It is the manual dexterity enabled by these muscles that physically distinguishes man from beast.

Dr. Hartman Hartmanszoon holds in his hand a drawing of a flayed body upon which someone later added the names of all the figures in the scene.

Dr. Tulp was born Claes Pieterszoon but took the name *Tulp*—Dutch for "tulip"—sometime between 1611 and 1614 when still a medical student in Leiden, where he encountered the flower in the botanical gardens of the university. Throughout his career, a signboard painted with a single golden yellow tulip on an azure ground hung outside his house.

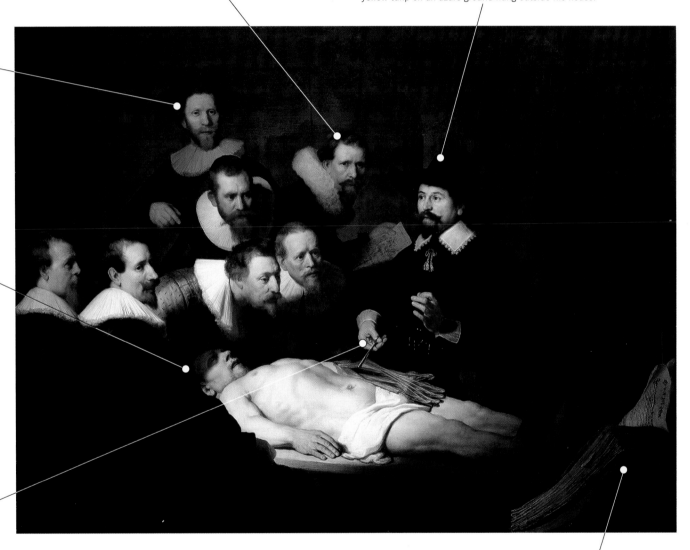

This large book may be the *De humani corporis fabrica,* the first thorough anatomy, published in 1543 by the Dutch scientist Andreis van Wesel (1514–1564), known as Vesalius, who had taught anatomy at the University of Padua. Tulp thought of himself as *Vesalius redivivus,* "Vesalius revived."

Rembrandt van Rijn. *The Anatomy Lesson of Dr. Tulp.* **1632.** Oil on canvas, $66^3/_4"\times85^1/_4"$. Royal Cabinet of Paintings Maurithsuis Foundation, The Hague, Netherlands.

sick and the lame, grouped at his feet and at his left, and the Pharisees, at his right. Always aware of Albrecht Dürer's great achievements in the medium (see Fig. 8.13), Rembrandt here constructs a triangle of light that seems to emanate from the figure of Christ himself, which seems to burst from the deep black gloom of the night. What the light is meant to offer, of course, is hope—and life.

Baroque Music in the North

In the late eighteenth century, the philosopher and some-times composer Jean-Jacques Rousseau [roo-SOH] (whose work will be discussed in chapter 11) described Baroque music in the most unflattering terms: "A baroque music is that in which the harmony is confused, charged with modulation and dissonances, the melody is harsh and little natural, the intonation difficult, and the movement constrained." In many ways, the description is accurate, although Rousseau's negative reaction to these characteristics reveals more about the musical taste of his own later age than it does the quality of music in the Baroque era itself. Stylistically, the music of the Baroque era is as varied as the Baroque art of Rome and Amsterdam. Like the art created in both centers, it is purposefully dramatic and committed to arousing emotion in the listener. Religious music, particularly, was devoted to evoking the passion of Christ. Also like Baroque art in both cities, Baroque music sought to be new and original, as Catholic and Protestant churches, north and south, constantly demanded new music for their services. At the same time, Baroque musicians created new secular forms of music as well. Perhaps most significant of all, the Baroque era produced more new instruments than any other. Additionally, even traditional instruments were almost totally transformed. This was the golden age of the organ. The deep intonations of this very ancient instrument, dating from the third century BCE, reached new heights as it commanded the emotions of both Catholic and Protestant churchgoers alike. By the first half of the eighteenth century, the piano began to emerge as a vital instrument even as the harpsichord was perfected technically. And for the first time in the history of music, instrumental virtuosos, especially on violin and keyboard, began to rival vocalists in popularity.

The North German School: Johann Sebastian Bach Perhaps the greatest northern composer of the day was Johann Sebastian Bach [bakh] (1685–1750). Bach was very much a master of the keyboard, and he sought to convey the devotional piety of the Protestant tradition through his religious music. He was an organist, first in the churches of small German towns, then in the courts of the Duke of Weimar [VY-mahr] and the Prince of Cöthen, and finally at Saint Thomas's Lutheran Church in Leipzig [LIPE-zig]. There he wrote most of the music for the Lutheran church services, which were much more elaborate than the Calvinist services in Amsterdam.

For each Sunday service, Bach also composed a **cantata**, a multimovement musical commentary on the chosen text of

the day sung by soloists and chorus accompanied by one or more instruments, usually the organ. The first half of the cantata was performed after the scriptural lesson and the second half after the sermon, concluding with a chorale, a hymn sung in the vernacular by the entire congregation. Like operas, cantatas include both recitative parts and arias.

Bach's cantatas are usually based on the simple melodies of Lutheran chorales, but are transformed by his genius for counterpoint, the addition of one or more independent melodies above or below the main melody, in this case the line of the Lutheran chorale. The result is an ornate musical texture that is characteristically Baroque. *Jesu, der du meine Seele* ("Jesus, It Is By You That My Soul") provides a perfect example, and it reveals the extraordinary productivity of Bach as a composer, driven as he was by the Baroque demand for the new and the original. He wrote it in 1724, a week after writing another entirely new cantata, and a week before writing yet another. (Bach was compelled to write them in time for his choir and orchestra to rehearse.) The opening chorus (**CD-Track 10.4**) is based on the words and melody of a chorale that would have been familiar to all parishioners. That melody is always presented by the soprano, and is first heard 21 measures into the composition after an extended passage for the orchestra. Even the untrained ear can appreciate the play between this melody and the others introduced in counterpoint to it.

Over the course of his career Bach composed more than 300 cantatas, or five complete sets, one for each Sunday and feast day of the church calendar. In addition, he composed large-scale **oratorios**. These are lengthy choral works, either sacred or secular, but without action or scenery, performed by a narrator, soloists, chorus, and orchestra for Christmas and Easter. Bach's *Christmas Oratorio* is a unique example of the form. It consists of six cantatas, written to be sung on six separate days over the course of the Christmas season in 1734–1735, beginning on Christmas Day and ending on Epiphany (January 6). Based on the gospels of Saint Luke and Saint Matthew, the story is narrated by a tenor soloist in the role of an Evangelist. Other soloists include an Angel, in the second cantata, and Herod, in the sixth. The chorus itself assumes several roles: the heavenly host singing "Glory to God" in the second cantata; the shepherds singing "Let us, even now, go to Bethlehem" in the third; and, in the fifth, the Wise Men, singing "Where is this new-born child; the king of the Jews?" Solo arias interrupt the narrative in order to reflect upon the meanings of the story.

One of Bach's greatest achievements in vocal music is the *The Passion According to Saint Matthew*, written for the Good Friday service in Leipzig in 1727. A **passion** is similar to an oratorio in form but tells the story from the Gospels of the death and resurrection of Jesus. Based on the sung texts of chapters 26 and 27 of the Gospel of Matthew, it narrates the events between the Last Supper and the Resurrection. It is a huge work, over three hours long. A double chorus assisted by a boys' choir alternates with soloists (representing Matthew, Jesus, Judas, and others) who sing arias and recitatives, all accompanied by a double orchestra and two organs. As in the *Christmas Oratorio*, the story is narrated by a tenor Evangelist. The words of Jesus are surrounded by a lush string accompaniment, Bach's way of creating a musical halo around them. All told, in *The Passion of Saint Matthew* Bach seems to have captured the entire range of human emotion, from terror and grief to the highest joy.

Bach wrote instrumental music for almost all occasions, including funerals, marriages, and civic celebrations. Among his most famous instrumental works are the six *Brandenburg* concertos, dedicated to the Margrave of Brandenburg in 1721. (A margrave was a German title, of lesser rank than a duke.) Each of the six is scored differently, and in fact Bach seems to have been intent on exploring the widest possible range of orchestral instruments in often daring combinations.

One of Bach's great contributions to secular instrumental musical history, however, is his *The Well-Tempered Clavier*. It is an attempt to popularize the idea of **equal temperament** in musical tuning, especially the tuning of keyboard instruments like the harpsichord, the virginal (a smaller harpsichord), and the clavichord. The harpsichord is a piano-like instrument whose strings are plucked rather than struck as with a piano. A clavichord's brass or metal strings are struck by metal blades (Fig. 10.19). Equal temperament consists in dividing the octave into twelve half-steps of equal size. *The Well-Tempered Clavier* is a two-part collection of musical compositions, the first part completed in 1722, and the second around 1740. Each part consists of 24 preludes and fugues, one prelude and one fugue in each of the 12 major and minor keys.

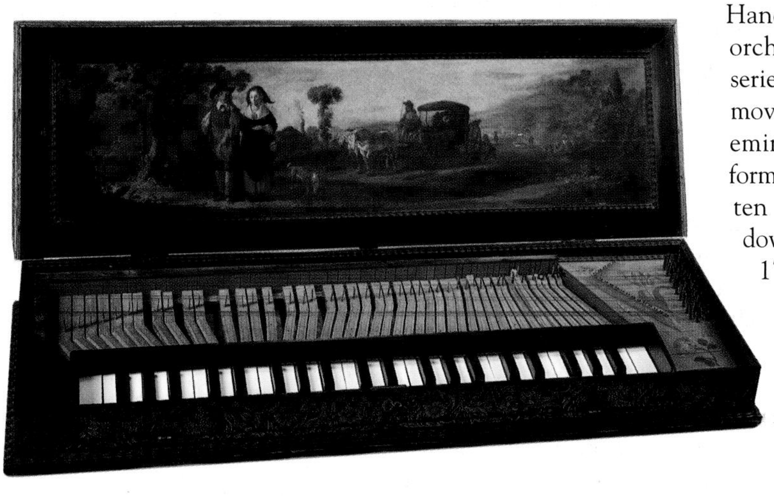

The **fugue** is a genre that carries a single thematic idea for the entire length of the work. As Bach wrote on the title page to the first part, the pieces were intended "for the profit and use of musical youth desirous of learning and especially for the pastime of those already skilled in this study." Bach's fugues, of which the *Fugue in D major* from Part II of *The Well-Tempered Clavier* is a remarkable example, consist of four independent parts (or occasionally three), one part, or *voice*, of which states a theme or melody—called a *subject*—and is then imitated by a succession of the other voices. The parts constantly overlap as the first voice continues playing in counterpoint, using material other than the main subject, while the second takes up the subject, and so on. The trick is

Fig. 10.19 **Clavichord with painted images, Dirk Stoop (painter). ca. 1660–1680.**
Painted musical instrument, $4'' \times 32\frac{1}{2}'' \times 10\frac{3}{4}''$. Collection Rijksmuseum, Amsterdam. Item # NM -9487. Clavichords were built as early as the fifteenth century, perhaps even earlier. It was at once the most personal and quietest of European keyboard instruments, perfect for the household chamber.

to give each voice a distinctly independent line and to play all four voices simultaneously with two hands on a single instrument (**CD-Track 10.5**). In the end, the fugues in *The Well-Tempered Clavier* are almost sublime examples of a new-born rationalism, laying out a range of feeling with a virtually mathematical clarity.

Handel and the English Oratorio In England, the music of German-born George Frederick Handel (1685–1759) defined the Baroque style. Handel had studied opera in Italy for several years, and was serving as Master of the Chapel in the Hanover court when George I was named king of England. He followed the king to London in the autumn of 1712. He was appointed composer to the Chapel Royal in 1723, became a British citizen in 1727, and when George II was crowned in 1728, he composed four anthems for the ceremony.

Over the course of his career Handel composed several orchestral suites (musical series of thematically related movements) that remain preeminent examples of the form. *Water Music* was written for a royal procession down the River Thames in 1717, and *Music for the Royal Fireworks* (1749) celebrated the end of a war with Austria. He wrote concertos for the oboe and the organ, performing the latter himself between acts of his operas and oratorios at London theaters. Opera was, in fact, his chief preoccupation— he composed 50 in his lifetime, 46 in Italian and 4 in German—but it was the oratorio, the same form that so attracted Johann Sebastian Bach, that made his reputation.

Handel composed his oratorios in English rather than Italian, the preferred opera language at that time. It is not clear just why he wrote oratorios, but a displeased bishop of London may have had something to do with it. The bishop banned Handel's biblical opera, *Esther*, in 1732, asserting that a stage production of the Bible was inappropriate. By using the oratorio form, Handel could treat biblical themes decorously.

Handel's greatest achievement is the oratorio *Messiah*. Written in 24 days, the work premiered in Dublin, Ireland, in 1742, as a benefit for Irish charities. It is probably the best known of all oratorios, although it is thoroughly atypical of the genre: The *Messiah* has no narrator, no characters, and no plot. Instead, Handel collected loosely related verses from the Old and New Testaments. It was an immediate success. Many Englishmen thought of their country as enjoying

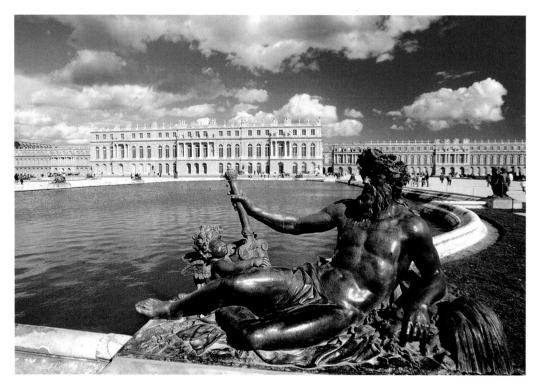

Fig. 10.20 Grand façade, Palace of Versailles, France. 1669–1685. Louis XIV planned Versailles as the grandest royal palace in Europe. It could house over 10,000 people—servants, members of the court, and ambitious aristocrats on the rise. Like Baroque architecture in other royal courts of Europe, it is a giant stage upon which the drama of the aristocratic sensibilities of the seventeenth century could be played out.

God's favor as biblical Israel had in the Old Testament, and Handel tapped into this growing sense of national pride. It recounts, in three parts, the biblical prophecies of the coming of a Savior, the suffering and death of Jesus, and the resurrection and redemption of humankind. *Messiah* is sometimes remarkable in its inventiveness. When, for instance, Handel scored the text "All we, like sheep, have gone astray," he made the last words scatter in separate melodies across the different voices, mimicking the scattering referred to in the text. This technique, known as *word painting*, had been used during the Renaissance—the mood of the musical elements imitated the meaning of the text. Tradition has it that in 1743 when George II first heard the now famous "Hallelujah Chorus" (**CD-Track 10.6**), which concludes the second part of the composition, he rose from his seat—whether in awe or simply because he was tired of sitting, no one knows—a gesture that has since become standard practice for all English-speaking audiences. For the rest of Handel's life, he performed *Messiah* regularly, usually with a chorus of 16 voices and an orchestra of 40, both relatively large for the time.

Absolutism and the Baroque Court

By the start of the eighteenth century, almost every royal court in Europe modeled itself on the court of King Louis XIV of France (r. 1643–1715). Louis detested the Louvre, the royal palace in Paris that had been the seat of French government and home to French kings since the Middle Ages. In 1661 he began construction of a new residence in the small town of Versailles [vair-SIGH], 12 miles southeast of Paris. For twenty years, some 36,000 workers labored to make Versailles the most magnificent royal residence in the world (Fig. **10.20**). When Louis permanently moved his court and governmental offices there in 1682, Versailles became the unofficial capital of France and symbol of Louis's absolute power and authority.

By the start of the eighteenth century, almost every royal court in Europe modeled itself on Louis XIV's court at Versailles. Louis so successfully asserted his authority over the French people, the aristocracy, and the Church that the era in which he ruled has become known as the Age of Absolutism. **Absolutism** is a term applied to strong centralized monarchies that exert royal power over their dominions, usually on the grounds of divine right. The principle had its roots in the Middle Ages, when the pope crowned Europe's kings, and went back even further to the man/god kings of ancient Mesopotamia and Egypt. But by the seventeenth century, the divine right of kings was assumed to exist even without papal acknowledgment. The most famous description of the nature of absolutism is by Bishop Jacques-Bénigne Bossuet [BOS-sway] (1627–1704), Louis's court preacher and tutor to his son. While training the young dauphin for a future role as king, Bossuet wrote *Politics Drawn from the Very Words of Holy*

Scripture, a book dedicated to describing the source and proper exercise of political power. In it he says the following:

> God is infinite, God is all. The prince, as prince, is not regarded as a private person: he is a public personage, all the state is in him; the will of all the people is included in his. As all perfection and all strength are united in God, so all the power of individuals is united in the person of the prince. What grandeur that a single man should embody so much! . . .
>
> Behold an immense people united in a single person; behold this holy power, paternal and absolute; behold the secret cause which governs the whole body of the state, contained in a single head: you see the image of God in the king, and you have the idea of royal majesty. God is holiness itself, goodness itself, and power itself. In these things lies the majesty of God. In the image of these things lies the majesty of the prince.

At court, Louis fully regulated the lives of the nobility. He thought of himself as *Le Roi Soleil* [leh wah so-LAY], "the Sun King," because like the sun (associated with Apollo, god of peace and the arts) he saw himself dispensing bounty across the land. His ritual risings and retirings (the *levée du roi* [leh-VAY dew wah] and the *couchée du roi* [koo-SHAY]) symbolized the actual rising and setting of the sun. They were essentially state occasions, attended by either the entire court or a select group of fawning aristocrats who eagerly entered their names on waiting lists. Louis encouraged the noblewomen at court to consider it something of an honor to sleep with him; he had many mistresses and many illegitimate children. Life in his court was entirely formal, governed by custom and rule, so etiquette became a way of social advancement. He required the use of a fork at meal times instead of using one's fingers. Where one sat at dinner was determined by rank. In fact, rank determined whether footmen opened one or two of Versailles's glass-paneled "French doors" for each guest passing through the palace. Louis's control over the lives of his courtiers had the political benefit of making them financially dependent on him. According to the memoirs of the duc de Saint Simon, Louis de Rouvroy (1675–1755):

> He loved splendour, magnificence, and profusion in all things, and encouraged similar tastes in his Court; to spend money freely on equipages and buildings, on feasting and at cards, was a sure way to gain his favour, perhaps to obtain the honour of a word from him. Motives of policy had something to do with this; by making expensive habits the fashion, and, for people in a certain position, a necessity, he compelled his courtiers to live beyond their income, and gradually reduced them to depend on his bounty for the means of subsistence.

Louis's sense of his own authority—to say nothing of his notorious vanity—is wonderfully captured in Hyacinthe Rigaud's [ree-GOH] official state portrait of 1701 (Fig. **10.21**). The king has flung his robes over his shoulder in order to reveal his white stockings and red high-heeled shoes. He designed the shoes himself to compensate for his five-foot-four-inch height. He is 63 years old in this portrait, but he means to make it clear that he is still a dashing courtier.

The Arts of the French Court

Louis was the absolute judge of taste at the French court and a great patron of the arts. He inherited some 200 paintings from his father but increased the royal collection tenfold during his reign. Over the course of his career he established the national academies of painting and sculpture, dance, music, and architecture. His motives were simple enough: Championing the greatest in art would establish him as the greatest of kings. "Gentlemen," he is reputed to have said to a group of academicians, "I entrust to you the most precious thing on earth—my fame."

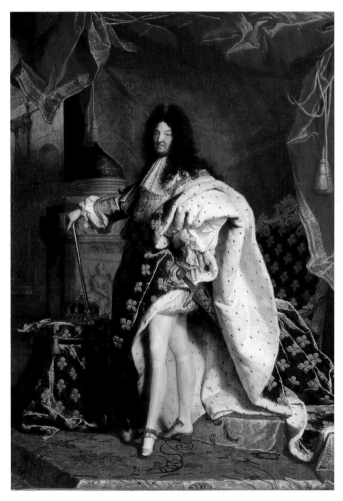

Fig. 10.21 Hyacinthe Rigaud. *Louis XIV, King of France.* **(1638–1715). 1701.** Oil on canvas, 9′1″ × 6′4⅜″. Musée du Louvre/RMN Réunion des Musées Nationaux, France. Herve Lewandowski/Art Resource, NY. In his ermine coronation robes, his feet adorned in red high-heeled shoes, Louis both literally and figuratively looks down his nose at the viewer, his sense of superiority fully captured by Rigaud.

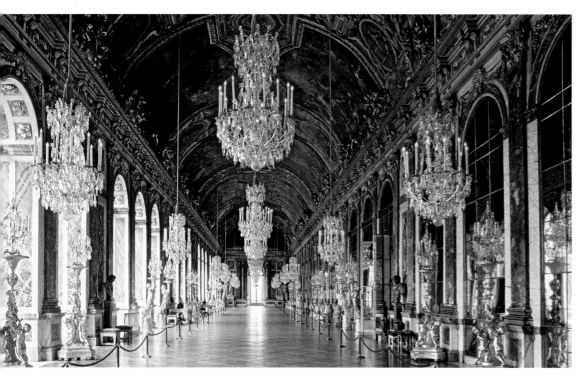

Fig. 10.22 Jules Hardouin-Mansart and Charles Le Brun. Galerie des Glaces (Hall of Mirrors), Palace of Versailles. Versailles. Begun 1678. The Galerie des Glaces is 233 feet long and served as a reception space for state occasions. It gets its name from the Venetian mirrors—extraordinarily expensive at the time—that line the wall opposite windows of the same shape and size, creating by their reflection a sense of space even vaster than it actually is.

Versailles More than any other art, French architecture was designed to convey the absolute power of the monarchy. From the moment that Louis XIV initiated the project at Versailles, it was understood that the new palace must be unequaled in grandeur, unparalleled in scale and size, and unsurpassed in lavish decoration and ornament. It would be the very image of the king, in whose majesty, according to the bishop, "lies the majesty of God."

The elaborate design of the palace was intended to leave the attending nobility in awe. Charles Le Brun served as chief painter to the king, and directed the team of artists who decorated the palace's interior. The Hall of Mirrors (Fig. **10.22**) was begun in 1678 to celebrate the high point of Louis XIV's political career, the end of six years of war with Holland. Louis asked Le Brun to depict his government's accomplishments on the ceiling of the hall in 30 paintings, framed by stuccowork, showing the monarch as a Roman emperor, astute administrator, and military genius. Le Brun balanced the 17 windows that stretch the length of the hall and overlook the garden with 17 arcaded mirrors along the interior wall, all made in a Paris workshop founded to compete with Venice's famous glass factories. Originally, solid silver tables, lamp holders, and orange-tree pots adorned the gallery. Louis later had them all melted down to finance his ongoing war efforts.

Landscape architect André Le Nôtre [leh NOHT] was in charge of the grounds at Versailles. He believed in the formal garden, and his methodical, geometrical design has come to be known as the **French garden**. The grounds were laid out around a main axis, emphasized by the giant cross-shaped Grand Canal, which stretched to the west of the palace (Figs. **10.23, 10.24**). Pathways radiated from this central

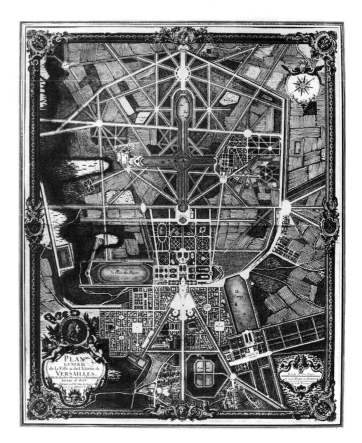

Fig. 10.23 André Le Nôtre. Plan of the gardens and park, Versailles. Designed 1661–1668, executed 1662–1690. Drawing by Leland Roth after Delagive's engraving of 1746. To the right are the main streets of the town of Versailles. Three grand boulevards cut through it to converge on the palace itself.

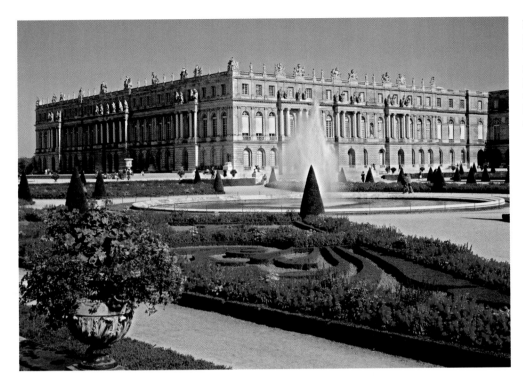

Fig. 10.24 André Le Nôtre. North flower bed, formal French gardens, Versailles. 1669–1685. The gardens are most formal near the palace and become increasingly less elaborate farther out in the park. Louis's gardener had more than 2 million flowerpots at his disposal.

axis, circular pools and basins surrounded it, and both trees and shrubbery were groomed into abstract shapes to match the geometry of the overall site. The king himself took great interest in Le Nôtre's work, even writing a guide to the grounds for visitors. Neat boxwood hedges lined the flower beds near the chateau, and a greenhouse provided fresh flowers to be planted in the gardens as the seasons changed. Over 4 million tulip bulbs, imported from Holland, bloomed each spring.

The Painting of Peter Paul Rubens: Color and Sensuality

One of Louis's favorite artists was the Flemish painter Peter Paul Rubens (1577–1640). Louis's grandmother, Marie de' Medici [deh-MED-ih-chee], had commissioned Rubens in 1621 to celebrate her life in a series of 21 monumental paintings. The cycle took four years (1621–1625) to complete with the help of studio assistants.

Rubens's pictorial approach to such self-promoting biographical commissions was through lifelike allegory. *The Arrival and Reception of Marie de' Medici at Marseilles* depicts the day Marie arrived in France from her native Italy on route to her marriage to King Henry IV (Fig. **10.25**). The figure of Fame flies above her, blowing a trumpet, while Neptune, god of the sea, and his son Triton, accompanied by three water nymphs, rise from the waves to welcome her. A helmeted allegorical figure of France, wearing a *fleur-de-lis* robe like that worn by Louis XIV in his 1701 portrait, bows before her. Marie herself, not known for her beauty, is so enveloped by rich textures, extraordinary colors, and sensuous brushwork that she seems transformed into a vision as extraordinary as the scene itself.

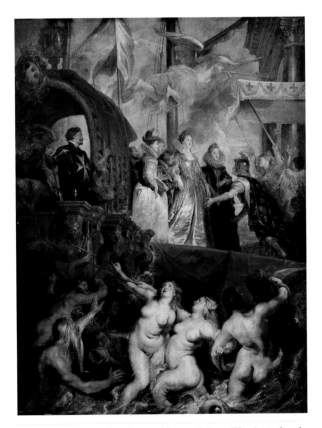

Fig. 10.25 Peter Paul Rubens and his workshop. *The Arrival and Reception of Marie de' Medici at Marseilles.* **1621–1625.** Oil on canvas, 13' × 10'. Musée du Louvre/ RMN Réunion des Musées Nationaux, France. Erich Lessing/Art Resource, NY. The point of view here is daringly low, perhaps even in the water, beside the nymphs. This creates a completely novel relationship between viewer and painting.

The fleshy bodies of the nymphs in this painting are a signature stylistic component of Rubens's work. In fact, Rubens's style is almost literally a "fleshing out" of the late Italian Renaissance tradition. It is so distinctive that it came be known as "Rubenesque." His nudes, which often startle contemporary viewers because we have developed almost entirely different standards of beauty, are notable for the way in which their flesh folds and drapes across their bodies. Their beauty rests in the sensuality of this flesh, which in some measure symbolizes the sensual life of self-indulgence and excess. Rubens pushed to new extremes the Mannerist sensibilities of Michelangelo's *Last Judgment* (see Fig. 10.2), the color and textures of the Venetian school as embodied in Titian's *The Rape of Europa* (see Fig. 7.39), and the play of light and dark of the Caravaggisti [kah-rah-vah-GEE-stee] (see Fig. 10.9). He brought to the Italian tradition a northern appreciation for observed nature—in particular, the realities of human flesh—and an altogether inventive and innovative sense of space and scale. Only rarely are Rubens's paintings what might be called frontal, where the viewer's position parallels the depicted action. Rather, the action moves diagonally back into space from either the front left or right corner of the composition.

In a painting like *The Kermis* [ker-miss], or *Peasant Wedding*, Rubens transforms a simple tavern gathering—a genre common to northern painting (see Fig. 10.16)—into a mon-

umental celebration (Fig. **10.26**). *The Kermis* is over 8 feet wide. Its wedding celebration spills in a diagonal out of the confines of the tavern into the panoramic space of the Flemish countryside. At the pinnacle of this sideways pyramid of entwined flesh a young man and a disheveled woman, her blouse fallen fully from her shoulders, run off across the bridge, presumably to indulge their appetites behind some hedge. Like the Hall of Mirrors at Versailles, with its mathematical regularity overlaid with sumptuously rich ornamentation, Rubens's painting seems at once moralistic and libertine. Arms and legs interlace in a swirling, twirling riot that can be interpreted as either a descent into debauchery or a celebration of sensual pleasure, readings that Rubens seems to have believed were not mutually exclusive.

Such frank sensuality is a celebration of the simple joy of living in a world where prosperity and peace extend even to the lowest rungs of society. Yet in keeping with his northern roots, Rubens gave the painting moralistic overtones. The posture of the dog with its nose in the cloth-draped tub at the bottom center of the canvas echoes the form of the kissing couple directly behind it and the dancing couples above it and, once more, represents the base, animal instincts that dominate the scene. The nursing babes at breast throughout the painting do not so much imply abundance as animal hunger, the desire to be fulfilled. Rubens knew full well that

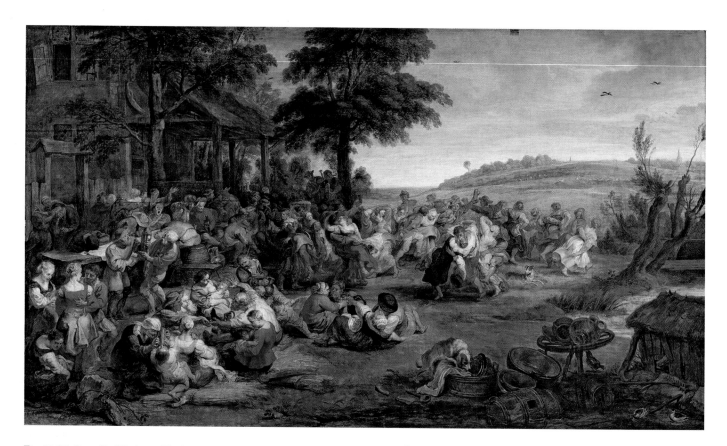

Fig. 10.26 Peter Paul Rubens. *The Kermis (La Kermesse)*. ca. 1635. Oil on canvas, 56 ⁵⁄₈" × 102 ³⁄₄". Musée du Louvre/RMN Réunion des Musées Nationaux, France. Erich Lessing/Art Resource, NY. In this painting Rubens reveals his Flemish heritage, taking up the traditional subject matter of Bruegel and others, a genre scene of everyday life.

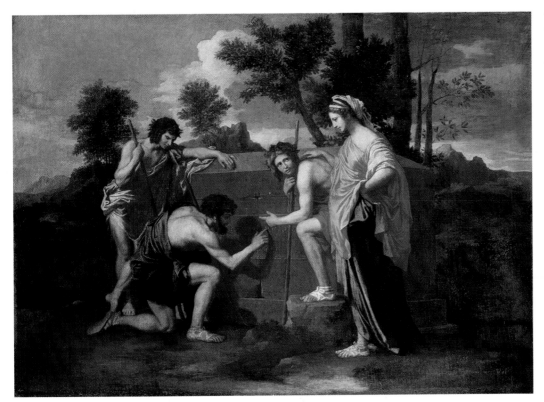

Fig. 10.27 Nicolas Poussin. *The Shepherds of Arcadia* (also called *Et in Arcadia Ego*). 1638–1639. Oil on canvas, 33 1/2″ × 47 5/8″. INV7300. Photo: René-Gabriel Ojéda. Musée du Louvre/RMN Reunion des Musees Nationaux, France. Art Resource, NY. Note how even the bands on the shepherds' sandals parallel other lines in the painting.

the bacchanal was not merely an image of prosperity but also of excess. In his later years, excess enthralled him, and *The Kermis* is a product of this sensibility.

Some 50 years later, in April 1685, Louis XIV purchased *The Kermis* for Versailles. What did the monarch see in this painting? For one thing, it was probably important to the man who considered himself Europe's greatest king to possess the work of the artist widely considered to be Europe's greatest painter. For another, Louis must have appreciated the painting's frank sexuality, which the artist emphasized by his sensual brushwork and color. It recalled the king's own sexual exploits.

The Painting of Nicolas Poussin: Classical Decorum By the beginning of the eighteenth century, 14 other Rubens paintings had found their way to the court of Louis XIV. Armand-Jean du Plessis [dew play-SEE], duc de Richelieu [duh REESH-uh-lee-yuh] (1629–1715), the great-nephew of Cardinal Richelieu (1585–1642), who had served as artistic advisor to Marie de' Medici and Louis XIII, purchased 14 other paintings that had remained in Rubens's personal collection after his death in 1640. Before he acquired his own collection of Rubens's work, Richelieu had wagered and lost his entire collection of paintings by Nicolas Poussin [poo-SEHN] (1594–1665) against Louis's own collection of works by Rubens in a tennis match between the two. A debate had long raged at court as to who was the better painter—Poussin or Rubens. Charles Le Brun had gone so far as to declare Poussin the greatest painter of the seventeenth century. Although a Frenchman, Poussin had spent most of his life in

Rome. He particularly admired the work of Raphael and, following Raphael's example, advocated a classical approach to painting. A painting's subject matter, he believed, should be drawn from classical mythology or Christian tradition, not everyday life. There was no place in his theory of painting for a genre scene like Rubens's *Kermis*, even if portrayed on a monumental scale. Painting technique itself should be controlled and refined. There could be no loose brushwork, no "rough style." Restraint and decorum had to govern all aspects of pictorial composition.

This *poussiniste* [poo-sehn-EEST] style is clearly evident in *The Shepherds of Arcadia* of 1638–1639 (Fig. **10.27**). Three shepherds trace out the inscription on a tomb, *Et ego in Arcadia*, "I too once dwelled in Arcadia," suggesting that death comes to us all. The Muse of History, standing to the right, affirms this message. Compared to the often exaggerated physiques of figures in Rubens's paintings, the muscular shepherds seem positively understated. Color, while sometimes brilliant, as in the yellow mantle robe of History, is muted by the evening light. But it is the compositional geometry of horizontals and verticals that is most typically *poussiniste*. Note how the arms of the two central figures form right angles and how they all fit within the cubical space suggested by the tomb itself. This cubic geometry finds its counterpoint in the way the lighted blue fold of History's dress parallels both the red-draped shepherd's lower leg and the leftmost shepherd's staff. These lines suggest a diagonal parallelogram working both against and with the central cube.

Louis XIV was delighted when he defeated the duc de Richelieu at tennis and acquired his Poussins. But to Louis's surprise, Richelieu quickly rebuilt his collection by purchasing 14 Rubens paintings and then commissioning Roger de Piles [deh peel] to write a catalogue describing his acquisitions. De Piles was a *rubeniste* [roo-bayn-EEST]. He argued that color was the essence of painting. Color is to painting as reason is to man, as he put it. The *poussinistes,* by contrast, were dedicated to drawing, and to the art of Raphael.

Poussin's paintings addressed the intellect, Rubens's the senses. For Poussin, subject matter, the connection of the picture to a classical narrative tradition, was paramount; for Rubens, the expressive capabilities of paint itself were primary. In 1708, de Piles scored each painter on his relative merits. Rubens received 18 points for composition, 13 for design, 17 for color, and 17 for expression. Poussin earned 15 points for composition, 17 for design, 6 for color, and 15 for expression. By de Piles's count, Rubens won 65 to 53. In essence, Rubens represented Baroque decorative expressionism and Poussin, Classical restraint. Both would have their supporters in the Academy over the course of the following decades.

Music and Dance at the Court of Louis XIV Louis XIV loved the pomp and ceremony of his court and the art forms that allowed him to most thoroughly engage this taste: dance and music. The man largely responsible for entertaining the king at court was Jean-Baptiste Lully [lew-LEE] (1632–1687), who was born in Florence but moved to France in 1646 to pursue his musical education.

Lully composed a number of popular songs, including the famous "Au Clair de la lune." By the 1660s he had become a favorite of the king, who admired in particular his **comédie-ballets** [koh-may-DEE bah-LAY], performances that were part opera and part ballet and that often featured Louis's own considerable talents as a dancer (Fig. **10.28**). Louis commissioned many ballets that required increasingly difficult movements of the dancers. As a result, his Royal Academy of Dance soon established the rules for the five positions of ballet that became the basis of classical dance. They valued, above all, clarity of line in the dancer's movement, balance, and, in the performance of the troop as a whole, symmetry. But in true Baroque fashion, the individual soloist was encouraged to elaborate upon the classical foundations of the ballet in exuberant, even surprising expressions of virtuosity.

Lully used his connections to the king to become head of the newly established Royal Academy of Music, a position that gave him exclusive rights to produce all sung dramas in France. In this role he created yet another new operatic genre, the **tragédie en musique** [trah-zhay-DEE on moo-ZEEK], also known as the *tragédie lyrique* [leer-EEK]. Lully's *tragédies* seamlessly blended words and music. The meter of the music constantly shifts, but the rhythms closely follow the natural rhythms of the French language. Supported and financed by the court, Lully composed and staged one of these *tragédies* each year from 1673 until 1687, when he died of gangrene after hitting his foot with the cane he used to pound out the beat while conducting.

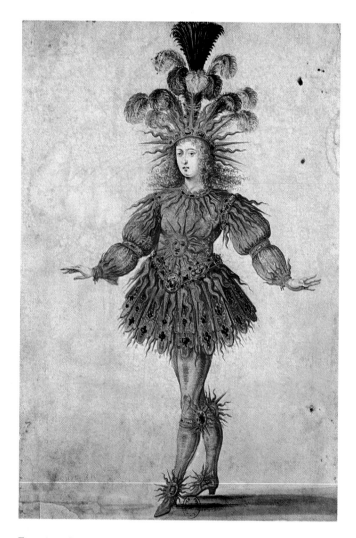

Fig. 10.28 Louis XIV as the sun in the *Ballet de la Nuit*. 1653. Bibliothèque Nationale, Paris. Louis, who was 15 years old at the time, appeared as himself wearing this costume during the ballet's intermezzo, a short musical entertainment between the main acts.

Louis's love of the dance promoted another new musical form at his court, the **suite**, a series of dances, or dance-inspired movements, usually all in the same key, though varying between major and minor modes. Most suites consist of four to six dances of different tempos and meters. These might include the following:

- Allemande [ah-luh-MAHND], a dance of continuous motion in double meter (marked by two or a multiple of two beats per measure) and moderate tempo
- Bourrée [boo-RAY], a dance of short, distinct phrasing, in double meter and moderate to fast in tempo
- Courante [koo-RAHNT], a dance often in running scales, in triple meter, and moderate to fast in tempo
- Gavotte [gah-VOT], a "bouncy" dance, in double meter, and moderate to fast in tempo
- Gigue [zheeg], a very lively dance, fast in tempo, and usually employing a 6/8 meter

- Sarabande [sah-rah-BAHND], a slow and stately dance, with accent on the second beat, in triple meter

In a suite, two moderately fast dances—say, an allemande and a courante—might precede a slower, more elegant dance—perhaps a sarabande—and then conclude with an exuberant gigue. Although it did not commonly occur in the dance suites themselves, the most important of the new dance forms was the **minuet**, an elegant triple-time dance of moderate tempo. It quickly became the most popular dance form of the age.

Theater at the French Court When, in 1629, Louis XIII appointed Cardinal Richelieu as his minister of state, he coincidentally inaugurated a great tradition of French theater. This tradition would culminate in 1680 with the establishment of the *Comédie Française* [koh-may-DEE frahn-SEZ], the French national theater. It was created as a cooperative under a charter granted by Louis XIV to merge three existing companies, including the troupe of the playwright Molière [moh-lee-AIR].

The son of a court upholsterer, Molière had been touring France for 13 years with a troupe of actors when he was asked, in 1658, to perform a tragedy before the young king Louis XIV. The performance was a miserable failure, but Molière asked if he might perform a farce of his own, *Le Docteur Amoureux* [leh DOK-ter ah-moo-REH] ("The Amorous Doctor"). The king was delighted with this comedy, and Molière's company was given what was intended to be a permanent home.

Molière's first play to be performed was *Les Précieuses Ridicules* [lay PRAY-see-erz ree-dee-KEWL] ("The Pretentious Ladies"), in 1659. It satirized a member of the French court named Madame de Rambouillet [deh RAHM-boo-yeh], who fancied herself the chief guardian of good taste and manners in Parisian society. The success of the play soon led Molière to double the admission price, and the king himself was so delighted that he honored the playwright with a large monetary reward. But not so, Madame de Rambouillet. Outraged, she tried to drive Molière from the city but succeeded only in having the company's theater demolished. The king struck back by immediately granting Molière the right to perform in the Théâtre du Palais Royal [tay-AT-ruh dew pah-LAY roy-AHL], in Richelieu's former palace, and there he staged his productions for the rest of his life.

Molière spared no one his ridicule, attacking religious hypocrisy, misers, hypochondriacs, pretentious doctors, aging men who marry younger women, the gullible, and all social parasites. (Ironically, he himself was capable of the most audacious flattery.) His play *Tartuffe* [tar-TEWF], or *The Hypocrite* (1664), concludes, for instance, with an officer praising the ability of the king to recognize hypocrisy of the kind displayed by Tartuffe in earlier scenes from the play (**Reading 10.6**):

READING 10.6   **from Molière, *Tartuffe*, Act V (1664)**

We serve a Prince to whom all sham is hateful,
A Prince who sees into our inmost hearts,
And can't be fooled by any trickster's arts.
His royal soul, though generous and human,
Views all things with discernment and acumen;
His sovereign reason is not lightly swayed,
And all his judgments are discreetly weighed.
He honors righteous men of every kind,
And yet his zeal for virtue is not blind,
Nor does his love of piety numb his wits   10
And make him tolerant of hypocrites.
'Twas hardly likely that this man could cozen
A King who's foiled such liars by the dozen.

These words undoubtedly warmed the heart of the king, described here as if he were a god. But until Molière's sudden death of an aneurysm during a coughing fit onstage, the playwright remained in disfavor with many in Louis's court who felt threatened by his considerable insight and piercing wit. They recognized what perhaps the king could not—the irony of flattering the king by saying he is above flattery.

The Court Arts of England and Spain

Although the monarchs of Europe were often at war with one another, they were united in their belief in the power of the throne and the role of the arts in sustaining their authority. In England the arts were dramatically affected by tensions between the absolutist monarchy of the English Stuarts and the much more conservative Protestant population. As in France, throughout the seventeenth century the English monarchy sought to assert its absolute authority, although it did not ultimately manage to do so. The first Stuart monarch, James I (1566–1625), succeeded Queen Elizabeth I in 1603. "There are no privileges and immunities which can stand against a divinely appointed King," he quickly insisted.

His son, Charles I (1600–1649), shared these absolutist convictions, but Charles's reign was beset by religious controversy. Although technically head of the Church of England, he married a Catholic, Henrietta Maria, sister of the French king Louis XIII. Charles proposed changes in the Church's liturgy that brought it, in the opinion of many, dangerously close to Roman Catholicism. Puritans (English Calvinists) increasingly dominated the English Parliament and strongly opposed any government that even remotely appeared to accept Catholic doctrine.

Parliament raised an army to oppose Charles, and civil war resulted, lasting from 1642 to 1648. The key political question was, Who should rule the country—the king or the Parliament? Led by Oliver Cromwell (1599–1658), the Puritans

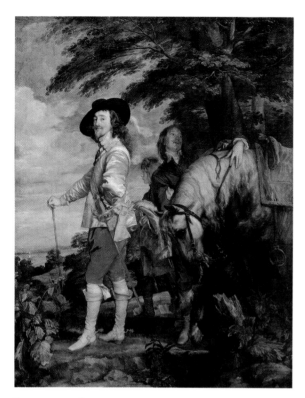

Fig. 10.29 Anthony van Dyck. *Portrait of Charles I Hunting.*
1635. Oil on canvas, 8′11″ × 6′11″. Inv 1236. Musée du
Louvre/RMN Réunion des Musées Nationaux, France. SCALA/Art
Resource, NY. Charles's posture, his left hand on his hip, and his
right extended outward where it is supported by a cane, adopts the
positions of the arms in court dance.

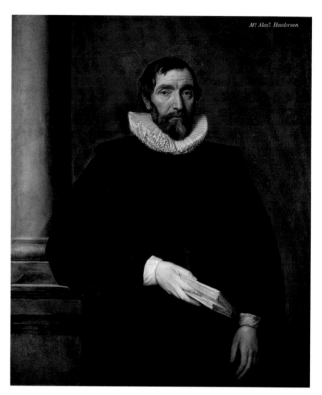

Fig. 10.30 Anthony van Dyck. *Alexander Henderson, Presbyterian
divine and diplomatist.* **ca. 1641.** Oil on canvas, 50″ × 41½″.
National Galleries of Scotland. PG 2227. Van Dyck probably came to
paint this portrait because Charles I admired Henderson for his
forthrightness and honesty in their troubled negotiations over the
liturgy.

defeated the king in 1645, and executed him for treason on
January 30, 1649, a severe blow to the divine right of kings.
Meanwhile, Cromwell tried to lead a commonwealth—a
republic dedicated to the common well-being of the people—
but he soon dissolved the Parliament and assumed the role of
Lord Protector. His protectorate occasionally called the Parliament into session, but only to ratify his own decisions.
Cromwell's greatest difficulty was requiring the people to
obey "godly" laws—in other words, Puritan doctrine. He forbade swearing, drunkenness, and cockfighting. No shops or
inns could do business on Sunday. The country, used to the
idea of a freely elected parliamentary government, could not
tolerate such restriction, and when, in September 1658,
Cromwell died, his system of government died with him.

The monarchy was restored, but the threat of the monarchy
adopting Catholicism continued to cause dissension among
Puritans. Finally, in September 1688, William of Orange, married to the Protestant daughter of James II who had become
king in 1685, invaded Britain from Holland at the invitation
of the Puritan population. James II fled, and what has come to
be called the Glorious Revolution ensued. Parliament enacted
a Bill of Rights endorsing religious tolerance and prohibiting
the king from annulling parliamentary law. Constitutional
monarchy was reestablished once and for all in Britain, and the
divine right of kings permanently suspended.

Anthony van Dyck in England The tension between the
Catholic-leaning English monarchy and the more Puritan-ori-
ented Parliament is clearly visible in two portraits by Flemish
artist Anthony van Dyck [dike] (1599–1641), court painter to
Charles I. Sometime in his teens, van Dyck went to work in
Rubens's workshop in Antwerp and led the studio by the time
he was 17. Van Dyck's great talent was portraiture. After working in Italy in the 1620s, in 1632 he accepted the invitation of
Charles I of England to come to London as court painter. He was
knighted there in 1633. Van Dyck's *Portrait of Charles I Hunting*
is typical of the work that occupied him (Fig. **10.29**). He often
flattered his subjects by elongating their features and portraying
them from below to increase their stature. In the case of the
painting shown here, van Dyck positioned Charles so that he
stands a full head higher than the grooms behind him, lit in a
brilliant light that glimmers off his silvery doublet. The angle of
his jauntily cocked cavalier's hat is echoed in the trees above his
head and the neck of his horse, which seems to bow to him in
respect. He is, in fact, the very embodiment of the **Cavalier** [kav-
uh-LEER] (from the French *chevalier* [shuh-vahl-YAY], meaning
"knight"), as his royalist supporters were known. Like the king
here, Cavaliers were famous for their style of dress—long, flowing hair, elaborate clothing, and large, sometimes feathered hats.

Cavaliers are the very opposite in style and demeanor from
the so-called **Roundheads**, supporters of the Puritan Parlia-

ment who cropped their hair short and dressed as plainly as possible. Just before his death in 1641, van Dyck painted one such Roundhead, Alexander Henderson, one of the most important figures in the Church of Scotland in the early seventeenth century (Fig. 10.30). Henderson was one of the authors of the National Covenant, a document that pledged to maintain the "true reformed religion" against the policies of Charles I. This portrait was probably painted when Henderson was in London negotiating with Charles I. Henderson's short-cropped hair and dark, simple clothing contrast dramatically with van Dyck's portrait of Charles I, as does the shadowy interior of the setting. Henderson's finger holds his place in his Bible, seeming to announce that here is a man of the Book, little interested in things of this world.

Diego Velázquez in Spain The Spanish court understood that in order to assert its absolutist authority it needed to impress the people through its patronage of the arts. So when Philip IV (r. 1621–1665), great grandson of the Holy Roman Emperor Charles IV, assumed the Spanish throne at the age of 16, his principal advisor suggested that his court should strive to rival all the others of Europe by employing the greatest painters of the day. The king agreed, hiring Rubens in the 1630s to paint a cycle of 112 mythologies for his hunting lodge. But when the 24-year-old Diego Rodríguez de Silva y Velázquez [vah-LASS-kez] (1599– 1660) was summoned to paint a portrait of the king in the spring of 1623, both the king and his advisor recognized that one of the great painters of seventeenth-century Europe was homegrown. An appointment as court painter quickly followed, and Velázquez became the only artist permitted to paint the king.

In 1628, when Rubens visited the Spanish court, Velázquez alone among artists in Madrid was permitted to visit with the master at work. And Velázquez guided Rubens through the royal collection, which included Bosch's *Garden of Earthly Delights* (see *Focus*, chapter 8) and, most especially, Titian's *The Rape of Europa* (see Fig. 7.39), which had been painted expressly for Philip II. Rubens copied both. He also persuaded Velázquez to go to Italy in 1629–1630, where he studied the work of Titian in Venice. In Florence and Rome, Velázquez disliked the paintings of Raphael, whose linear style he found cold and inexpressive.

Velázquez's chief occupation as painter to Philip IV was painting court portraits and supervising the decoration of rooms in the various royal palaces and retreats. Most were portraits of individuals, but *Las Meninas* [las may-NEE-nahss] (*The Maids of Honor*) is a life-size group portrait and his last great royal commission (Fig. 10.31). It elevates the portrait to a level of complexity almost unmatched in the history of art. The source of this complexity is the competing focal points of the composition. At the very center of the painting, bathed in light, is the Infanta Margarita, beloved daughter of King Philip IV and Queen Mariana. In one sense, the painting is the Infanta's portrait, as she seems the primary focus. Yet the title *Las Meninas*, "The Maids of Honor," implies that

her attendants are the painting's real subject. However, Velázquez has painted himself into the composition at work on a canvas, so the painting is, at least partly, also a self-portrait. The artist's gaze, as well as the gaze of the Infanta and her dwarf lady-in-waiting, and perhaps also of the courtier who has turned around in the doorway at the back of the painting, is focused on a spot outside the painting, in front of it, where we as viewers stand. The mirror at the back of the room, in which Philip and Mariana are reflected, suggests that the king and queen also occupy this position, acknowledging their role as Velázquez's patrons. This work continues to inspire later artists.

The Spanish Baroque in the Americas The Americas were Spain's greatest source of wealth, and Spanish culture quickly took hold in both North and South America. This was a politically important enterprise, because it underscored that the absolute authority in the Americas was the Spanish monarchy. Over time, Spanish leaders and missionaries believed, the distinction between worshiping the Inca gods and worshiping the sacred in general would become increasingly less clear, and Christianization of the native population would occur naturally.

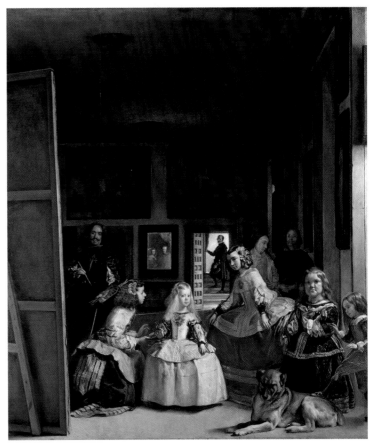

Fi.g 10.31 Diego Velázquez. *Las Meninas (The Maids of Honor)*. 1656. Oil on canvas, 10'3/4" × 9'3/4". Museo del Prado, Madrid. No other Velázquez painting is as tall as *Las Meninas*, which suggests that the back of the canvas in the foreground is, in fact, *Las Meninas* itself. Velázquez thus paints himself painting this painting.

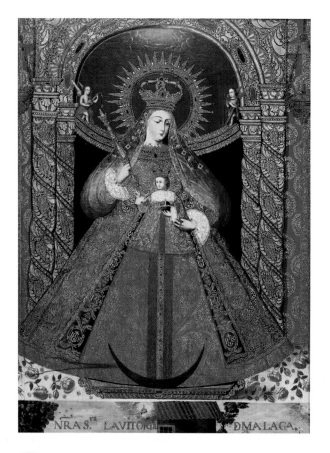

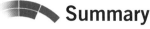

In truth, the indigenous native populations Indianized the Christian art imposed upon them, creating a unique visual culture, part Baroque, part Indian. *Our Lady of the Victory of Málaga* (Fig. **10.32**) by Luis Niño (active 1730–1760) employs a technique extremely popular among the painters of Cuzco, Peru, **brocateado** [broh-kah-tay-AH-doh], the application of gold leaf to canvas, used especially for creating elaborate brocadelike effects on saints' garments. Here the Virgin stands on a silver crescent moon above the tiled roofs and trees of the Cuzco countryside, recalling the Inca association of silver with religious worship of the moon, while the flat symmetry of the *brocateado* evokes the flat patterns of Inca textile design (see Fig. 9.12) and the Inca association of gold with worship of the sun. In fact, some scholars argue that the crescent at the virgin's feet, together with the two vertical red lines that rise straight up from its center, take the shape of the curved blade and handle of the Inca ceremonial knife used in traditional sacrifices, a shape also worn as a pin by Inca princesses as a symbol of good luck. Thus Catholic and native traditions are compounded in a single Baroque image.

Fig. 10.32 Luis Niño. *Our Lady of the Victory of Málaga.* **Southern Cuzco school, Potosí, Bolivia. ca. 1737.** Oil on canvas overlaid with gold and silver, 59 1/2″ × 43 3/4″. Gift of John C. Freyer for the Frank Barrows Freyer Collection. Denver Art Museum, CO. Despite Spain's program to convert indigenous populations in the Americas to Christianity, Native American cultures never completely assimilated Western religion.

Summary

■ Mannerism and the Early Counter-Reformation

The Counter-Reformation was the Roman Catholic Church's conscious attempt to reform itself in reaction to the Protestant Reformation. To that end, Pope Paul III convened the Council of Trent in 1545 to restore Church discipline. The Council also called for clarity and directness in the arts, a call that did not constrain Michelangelo, who declared his own virtuosity as an artist through manipulations and distortions of the conventional figure. Many found the nudity of his *Last Judgment*, painted for the back wall of the Sistine Chapel, offensive, but its lack of decorum was acceptable outside a religious context, and it spawned, in the private galleries of the princely courts throughout Europe, the more inventive—and often lascivious—imagery that we have come to call Mannerism.

■ The Baroque in Italy
Baroque art addressed the aim of the Counter-Reformation to appeal to the masses by balancing religious propriety and the exuberance and inventiveness of Mannerism. Bernini's majestic new colonnade for the square in front of Saint Peter's in Rome created the dramatic effect of the Church embracing its flock. His sculptural program for the Cornaro Chapel in Rome, with its celebration of the mystical revelations of Teresa of Ávila, epitomizes the Baroque. Caravaggio and his fellow Caravaggisti utilized the play of light and dark to create paintings of stunning drama and energy that reveal a new Baroque taste for vividly realistic detail and the creation of dramatic space. Venice was the center of Baroque music. There composers began to explore the dramatic possibilities of the madrigal, the opera, and the concerto.

■ The Secular Baroque in the North
In still lifes, landscapes, and genre paintings, Baroque painting in northern Europe reflects an interest in everyday objects and activities. Most popular of all, however, were portrait paintings, of which Rembrandt van Rijn's were unsurpassed, a result of his ability to imbue his sitters with a dramatic sense of life, an effect achieved in no small part by his mastery of light and dark.

■ Absolutism and the Baroque Court
All European courts modeled themselves on that of Louis XIV in France, whose palace at Versailles embodied his own status as absolute ruler. Various members of the court favored one or the other of two competing styles of art, represented by the lush color, loose brushwork, and diagonal compositions of Peter Paul Rubens and by the classical, linear style of Nicolas Poussin. Louis indulged his taste for pomp and ceremony in music, dance, and theater. The premier artist of the English court was portrait painter Anthony van Dyck, while in Spain, Diego Velázquez filled the same role.

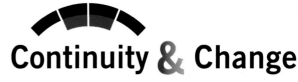
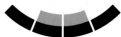
An underlying characteristic of the Baroque age is its ultimate trust in the powers of reason. Major breakthroughs in mathematics, astronomy, geology, physics, chemistry, biology, and medical science dominate the history of the age. These products of empirical reasoning constituted a so-called **Scientific Revolution** that transformed the way the Western mind came to understand its place in the universe.

It may seem odd that painters like Caravaggio, Rubens, and Rembrandt, who appealed to the emotional and dramatic, the sensual and the spectacular, should be products of the same age as the Scientific Revolution. It would seem more reasonable to say that the scientific energies of the age found their painterly expression more in the likes of Poussin than Rubens, in Poussin's emphasis on design rather than Rubens's on expression. And yet Rembrandt's *Anatomy Lesson of Dr. Tulp* (see the *Focus*, pages 304–305) clearly engages the scientific mind, and Rubens's swirling, flowing lines are the product of a mind confident that order and wholeness are the basic underpinnings of experience. In a very real sense, then, Caravaggio and Gentileschi, Rubens and Rembrandt, Molière and Cervantes can best be understood in terms of their ability to look beneath the surface of experience for the human truths that motivate us all. Their work—like the autobiographical writings of Montaigne in the sixteenth century—announces the dawn of modern psychology.

Still, the Baroque age does embody a certain tension between reason and emotion, decorum and excess, clearly defined in the contest between the *poussinistes* and the *rubenistes* for ascendancy in the arts. This tension is evident in a painting that shows Louis XIV visiting the Académie des Sciences in 1671 (Fig. **10.33**). Following the lead of King Charles II of England, who had chartered the Royal Society in 1662, Louis created the French Academy of Sciences in 1666. He stands surrounded by astronomical and scientific instruments, charts and maps, skeletal and botanical specimens. Out the window, the ordered geometry of a classical French garden dominates the view. At the same time, Louis seems alien to his surroundings. Decked out in all his ruffles, lace, ribbons, and bows, he is the very image of ostentatious excess. The tension he embodies will become a defining characteristic of the following century. In the eighteenth century the demands of reason, the value that defines the so-called Enlightenment, and the limits of excess, the aristocratic style that has come to be known as the Rococo, would come to compete, both equally the product of the Baroque age that precedes them. ■

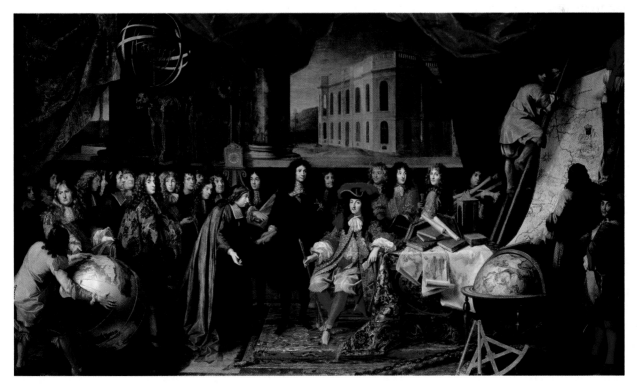

Fig. 10.33 Henri Testelin. *Jean-Baptiste Colbert Presenting the Members of the Royal Academy of Science to Louis XIV*. ca. 1667. Oil on canvas. © Chateau de Versailles, France/Lauros/Giraudon/The Bridgeman Art Library.

11

Enlightenment and Rococo

The Claims of Reason and the Excesses of Privilege

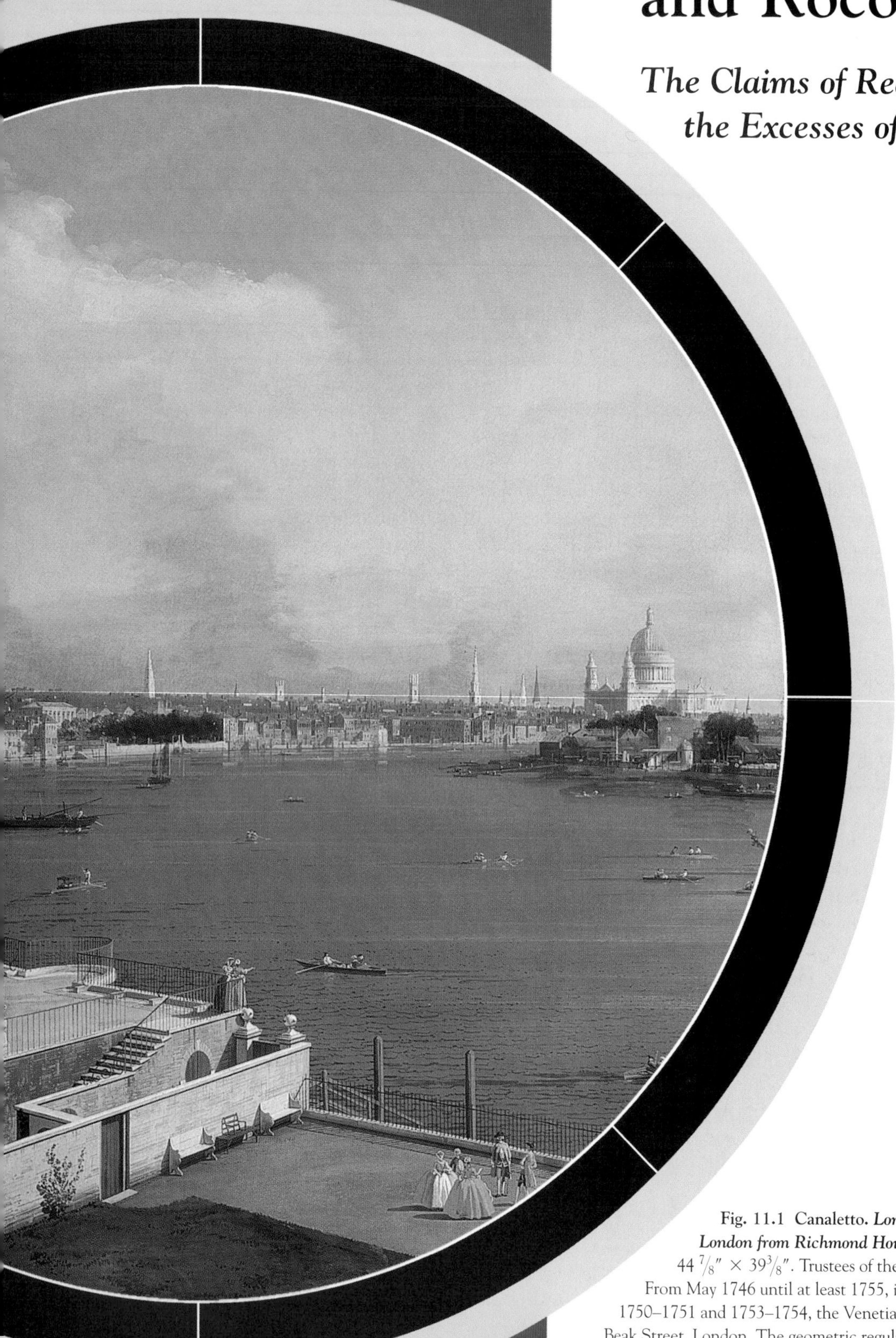

Fig. 11.1 Canaletto. *London: The Thames and the City of London from Richmond House* (detail). **1747.** Oil on canvas, 44 ⁷⁄₈″ × 39 ³⁄₈″. Trustees of the Goodwood House, West Sussex, UK. From May 1746 until at least 1755, interrupted by only two visits to Venice in 1750–1751 and 1753–1754, the Venetian painter Canaletto occupied a studio in Beak Street, London. The geometric regularity and perspectival inventiveness of his paintings reflect the Enlightenment's taste for rationality. But his sense of grandeur and scale is, like Louis XIV's Versailles, purely aristocratic.

> *Know then thyself, presume not God to scan;*
> *The proper study of Mankind is Man.* **"**
>
> Alexander Pope, *An Essay on Man*

London, the city of elegance and refinement painted in 1747 by Venetian master of cityscapes Canaletto (Giovanni Antonio Canal; 1697–1768), was rivaled only by Paris, across the Channel, as the center of European intellectual culture in the eighteenth century (Fig. **11.1**). The painting offers no hint that the city had been devastated by fire 80 years earlier. Before dawn on the morning of September 2, 1666, a baker's oven exploded on Pudding Lane in London. A strong east wind hastened the fire's spread until, by morning, some 300 houses were burning. In his private diaries, Samuel Pepys [peeps] (1633–1703) recorded what he saw on that fateful day:

> I rode down to the waterside, . . . and there saw a lamentable fire. . . . Everybody endeavoring to remove their goods, and flinging into the river or bringing them into lighters that lay off; poor people staying in their houses as long as till the very fire touched them, and then running into boats, or clambering from one pair of stairs by the waterside to another. . . .
>
> [I hurried] to [Saint] Paul's; and there walked along Watling Street, as well as I could, every creature coming away laden with goods to save and, here and there, sick people carried away in beds. Extraordinary goods carried in carts and on backs. At last [I] met my Lord Mayor in Cannon Street, like a man spent, with a [handkerchief] about his neck. . . . "Lord, what can I do? [he cried] I am spent: people will not obey me. I have been pulling down houses, but the fire overtakes us faster than we can do it." . . . So . . . I . . . walked home; seeing people all distracted, and no manner of means used to quench the fire. The houses, too, so very thick thereabouts, and full of matter for burning, as pitch and tar, in Thames Street; and warehouses of oil and wines and brandy and other things.

From Samuel Pepys, *Diary* (September 2, 1666)

The fire in these warehouses so fueled the blaze that over the course of the next two days it engulfed virtually the entire medieval city and beyond. Almost nothing was spared. About 100,000 Londoners were left homeless. Eighty-seven churches had burned. Businesses, particularly along the busy wharves on the north side of the Thames, were bankrupted. Taken together with the Great Plague that had killed some 70,000 Londoners just the year before, John Evelyn, one of the other great chroniclers of the age, summed up the situation in what amounts to typical British understatement: "London was, but is no more."

Such devastation was both a curse and a blessing. While the task of rebuilding London was almost overwhelming, the fire gave the city the opportunity to modernize its center in a way that no other city in the world could even imagine. By 1670, almost all the private houses destroyed by the fire had been rebuilt, and businesses were once again thriving. Over the course of the next century, the city would prosper as much or more than any other city in the world, so that by the middle of the eighteenth century it would come to look so beautiful that Canaletto had to muster every bit of his skill to capture its grandeur. "London," as one writer put it, "is the centre to which almost all the individuals who fill the upper and middle ranks of society are successively attracted. The country pays its tribute to the supreme city."

This chapter surveys developments in London and Paris, the literary centers of what would come to be known as the Age of Enlightenment. Across Europe intellectuals began to advocate rational thinking as the means to achieving a comprehensive system of ethics, aesthetics, and knowledge. The rationalist approach owed much to scientist Isaac Newton (1642–1727), who in 1687 demonstrated to the satisfaction of just about everyone that the universe was an intelligible system, well ordered in its operations and guiding principles. The workings of human society—the production and consumption of manufactured goods, the social organization of families and towns, the functions of national governments, even the arts—were believed to be governed by analogous universal laws. The intellectuals of Enlightenment England and France thought of themselves as the guiding lights of a new era of progress that would leave behind, once and for all, the irrationality, superstition, and tyranny that had defined Western culture, particularly before the Renaissance. Still, recognizing that society was deeply flawed, they also satirized it, attacking especially an aristocracy whose taste for elaborate ornamentation and frivolous pleasure seemed not just decadent but depraved. At the same time, an expanding publishing industry and an increasingly literate public offered Enlightenment writers the opportunity to instruct their readers in moral behavior, even as they described vice in often prurient detail. And in music, the intricate and sometimes confusing compositions of the Baroque gave way to a more rational, and Classical, form and structure.

The English Enlightenment

After the Great Fire, architect Christopher Wren (1632–1723) proposed a grand redesign scheme that would have replaced the old city with wide boulevards and great squares. But the need to quickly rebuild the city's commercial infrastructure made his plan impractical, and each property owner was essentially left to his own devices.

Nevertheless, certain real improvements were made. Wood construction was largely banned; brick and stone were required. New sewage systems were introduced, and streets had to be at least 14 feet wide. Just a year after the fire, in a poem celebrating the devastation and reconstruction, "Annus Mirabilis" ("year of wonders"), the poet John Dryden (1631–1700) would equate London to the mythological Phoenix rising from its own ashes, reborn: "a wonder to all years and Ages . . . a *Phoenix* in her ashes." Moved by the speed of the city's rebuilding, Dryden is sublimely confident in London's future—the city would become even greater than before (**Reading 11.1**):

READING 11.1   **from John Dryden, "Annus Mirabilis," 1667**

More great than human, now, and more august,[1]
New-deified she from her fires does rise:
Her widening streets on new foundations trust,
And, opening, into larger parts she flies. . . .

Now like the maiden queen, she will behold
From her high turrets, hourly suitors come:
The East with incense, and the West with gold,
Will stand like suppliants, to receive her doom.

[1] Augusta was the old name of London.

For Dryden, the Great Fire was not so much a disaster as a gift from God. And Charles II must have thought so as well, for as a way of thanking Dryden for the poem, the king named him poet laureate of the nation in 1668.

Although Christopher Wren's plans to redesign the entire London city center after the Great Fire proved impractical, he did receive the commission to rebuild 52 of the churches destroyed in the blaze. Rising above them all was Saint Paul's Cathedral (Fig. **11.2**), a complex yet orderly synthesis of the major architectural styles of the previous 150 years. In its design, Wren drew on Classical, Gothic, Renaissance, and

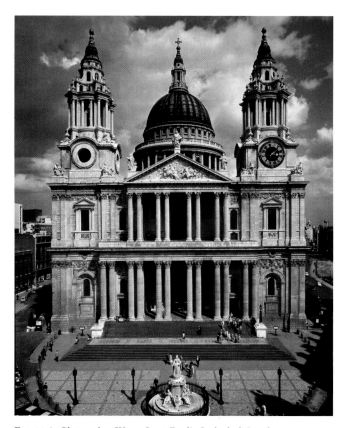

Fig. 11.2 Christopher Wren. Saint Paul's Cathedral, London, western façade. 1675–1710. A statue of Saint Paul stands on top of the central portico, flanked by statues of Saint John (*right*) and Saint Peter (*left*). The sculptural detail in the portico pediment depicts the conversion of Paul following his vision on the road to Damascus.

Baroque elements. Its imposing two-story facade is crowned by symmetrical twin clock towers and a massive dome. The floor plan—an elongated, cruciform (crosslike) design—is Gothic. The dome is Renaissance, purposefully echoing Bramante's Tempietto (see Fig. 7.21) but maintaining the monumental presence of Michelangelo's dome for Saint Peter's (see Fig. 7.22). The facade, with its two tiers of paired Corinthian columns, recalls the French Baroque Louvre in Paris. And the two towers are inspired by a Baroque church in Rome. Wren manages to bring all these elements together into a coherent whole.

According to Wren's son, "a memorable omen" occurred on the occasion of his father's laying the first stone on the ruins of the old cathedral in 1675:

When the SURVEYOR in Person [Wren himself, in his role as King's Surveyor of Works] had set out, upon the Place, the Dimensions of the great Dome and fixed upon the centre; a common Labourer was ordered to bring a flat stone from the Heaps of Rubbish . . . to be laid for a Mark and Direction to the Masons; the Stone happened to be a piece of Grave-stone, with nothing remaining on the Inscription but the simple word in large capitals,

RESURGAM [the Latin for "REBORN"].

"RESURGAM" still decorates the south transept of the cathedral above a figure of a phoenix rising from the ashes.

Something of the power of Wren's conception can be felt in Canaletto's view of *The Thames and the City of London from Richmond House* (see Fig. 11.1). The cathedral does indeed rise above the rest of the city, not least because, in rebuilding, private houses had been limited to four stories. Only other church towers, almost all built by Wren as well, rise above the roof lines, as if approaching the giant central structure in homage.

The New Rationalism and the Scientific Revolution

The new London was, in part, the result of the empirical thinking that came to dominate the Western imagination in the late seventeenth century. Newly invented instruments allowed scientists to observe and measure natural phenomena with increasing accuracy, and new methods of scientific, philosophical, and mathematical investigation provided a theoretical framework to exploit the capabilities of these instruments. According to these new ways of reasoning, *Scientia*, the Latin word for "knowledge," was to be found in the world, not in religious belief.

Francis Bacon and the Empirical Method One of the most fundamental principles guiding the new science was the proposition that, through the direct and careful observation of natural phenomena, one could draw general conclusions from particular examples. This process is known as **inductive reasoning**, and with it, scientists believed they could predict the workings of nature as a whole. When inductive reasoning was combined with scientific experimentation, it produced a manner of inquiry that we call the **empirical method**. The leading advocate of the empirical method in the seventeenth century was the English scientist Francis Bacon (1561–1626). His *Novum Organum Scientiarum* (*New Method of Science*), published in 1620, is the most passionate plea for its use. "One method of delivery alone remains to us," he wrote, "which is simply this: we must lead men to the particulars themselves, and their series and order; while men on their side must force themselves for a while to lay their notions by and begin to familiarize themselves with facts." The greatest obstacle to human understanding, Bacon believed, was "superstition, and the blind and immoderate zeal of religion." For Bacon, Aristotle represented a perfect example (see chapter 2). While he valued Aristotle's emphasis on the study of natural phenomena, he rejected as false doctrine Aristotle's belief that the experience coming to us by means of our senses (things as they *appear*) automatically presents to our understanding things as they *are*. Indeed, he felt that reliance on the senses frequently led to fundamental errors.

A proper understanding of the world could only be achieved, Bacon believed, if we eliminate the errors in rea-

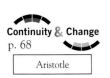

Continuity **&** Change
p. 68

Aristotle

soning developed through our unwitting adherence to the false notions that every age has worshiped. He identified four major categories of false notion, which he termed Idols, all described in his *Novum Organum Scientiarum*. The first of these, the Idols of the Tribe, are the common fallacies of all human nature, derived from the fact that we trust, wrongly, in our senses. The second, the Idols of the Cave, derive from our particular education, upbringing, and environment—an individual's religious faith or sense of his or her ethnic or gender superiority or inferiority would be examples. The third, the Idols of the Market Place, are errors that occur as a result of miscommunication, words that cause confusion by containing, as it were, hidden assumptions. For instance, the contemporary use of "man" or "mankind" to refer to people in general (common well into the twentieth century), connotes a worldview in which hierarchical structures of gender are already assumed. Finally, there are the Idols of the Theater, the false dogmas of philosophy—not only those of the ancients but those that "may yet be composed." The object of the empirical method is the destruction of these four Idols through intellectual objectivity. Bacon argued that rather than falling back on the preconceived notions and opinions produced by the four Idols, "Man, being the servant and interpreter of Nature, can do and understand so much and so much only as he has observed in fact or in thought of the course of Nature; beyond this he neither knows anything nor can do anything."

Bacon's insistence on the scientific observation of natural phenomena led, in the mid-1640s, to the formation in England of a group of men who met regularly to discuss his new philosophy. After a lecture on November 28, 1660, by Christopher Wren, then Gresham College Professor of Astronomy, they officially founded "a College for the Promoting of Physico-Mathematicall Experimentall Learning." It met weekly to witness experiments and discuss scientific topics. Within a couple of years, the group became known as "The Royal Society of London for Improving Natural Knowledge," an organization that continues to the present day as the Royal Society. It remains one of the leading forces in international science, dedicated to the recognition of excellence in science and the support of leading-edge scientific research and its applications.

René Descartes and the Deductive Method Bacon's works circulated widely in Holland, where they were received with enthusiasm. But equally influential were the writings of the French-born René Descartes [day-CART] (1596–1650). Descartes, in fact, lived in Holland for over 20 years, from 1628 to 1649, moving between 13 different cities, including Amsterdam, and 24 different residences. It was in Holland that he wrote and published his *Discourse on the Method of Rightly Conducting the Reason and Seeking for Truth in the Sciences* (1637). As opposed to Bacon's inductive reasoning, Descartes proceeded to his conclusions by the opposite method of **deductive reasoning**. He began with clearly established general principles and moved from those to the establishment of particular truths.

Like Bacon, Descartes distrusted almost everything, believing that both our thought and our observational senses can and do deceive us. In his *Meditations on the First Philosophy*, he draws an analogy between his own method and that of an architect (**Reading 11.2**):

Throughout my writings I have made it clear that my method imitates that of the architect. When an architect wants to build a house which is stable on ground where there is a sandy topsoil over underlying rock, or clay, or some other firm base, he begins by digging out a set of trenches from which he removes the sand, and anything resting on or mixed in with the sand, so that he can lay his foundations on firm soil. In the same way, I began by taking everything that was doubtful and throwing it out, like sand.

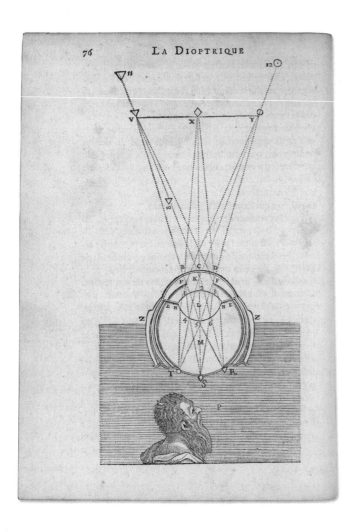

He wants, he says, "to reach certainty—to cast aside the loose earth and sand so as to come upon rock and clay." The first thing, in fact, that he could not doubt was that he was thinking, which led him to the inevitable conclusion that he must actually exist in order to generate thoughts about his own existence as a thinking individual, which he famously expressed in *Discourse on Method* in the Latin phrase "*Cogito, ergo sum*" [KOH-guh-toh er-goh sum] ("I think, therefore I am").

The remarkable result of this approach is that, beginning with this one "first principle" in his *Discourse on Method*, Descartes comes to prove, at least to his own satisfaction, the existence of God. As a result, he is one of the most important founders of **deism** (from the Latin *deus* [DAY-us], "god"), the brand of faith that argues that the basis of belief in God is reason and logic rather than revelation or tradition. Descartes did not believe that God was at all interested in interfering in human affairs. Nor was God endowed, particularly, with human character. He was, in Descartes's words, "the mathematical order of nature." Descartes was himself a mathematician of considerable inventiveness, founding analytic geometry, the bridge between algebra and geometry crucial to the invention of calculus.

Johannes Kepler, Galileo Galilei, and the Telescope The same year that he published *Discourse on Method*, Descartes also published a treatise entitled *Optics*. There, among other things, he used geometry to calculate the angular radius of a rainbow (42 degrees). But his entire project was built upon the earlier discoveries in optics of the German mathematician Johannes Kepler [KEP-lur] (1571–1630). Descartes was so taken with Kepler's insights that he included Kepler's illustration of the working of the human eye in his *Optics* (Fig. **11.3**).

Kepler had made detailed records of the movements of the planets, substantiating Copernicus's theory that the planets orbited the sun, not the earth. The long-standing tradition of a **geocentric** (earth-centered) cosmos was definitively replaced with a **heliocentric** (sun-centered) theory. Kepler also challenged the traditional belief that the orbits of the planets were spherical, showing that the five known planets moved around the sun in elliptical paths determined by the magnetic force of the sun and their relative distance from it.

Fig. 11.3 Illustration of the theory of the retinal image as described by Johannes Kepler. From René Descartes, *Optics (La Dioptrique)* (Leiden, 1637). Bancroft Library, Berkeley, CA. Descartes was more interested in what happened to the image in the brain after it registered itself on the retina, while Kepler was interested in the physical optics of the process itself.

Wright illustrated the crueler demonstration, and the outcome is uncertain. Perhaps, if the bird's lungs have not yet collapsed, the scientist can bring it back from the brink of death. Whatever the experiment's conclusion, life or death, Wright not only painted the more horrific version of the experiment but drew on the devices of Baroque painting—dramatic, nocturnal lighting and chiaroscuro—to heighten the emotional impact of the scene. The painting underscores the power of science to affect us all.

The Industrial Revolution Among Wright's closest friends were members of a group known as the Lunar Society. The Society met in and around Birmingham each month on the night of the full moon (providing both light to travel home by and the name of the society). Its members included prominent manufacturers, inventors, and naturalists. Among them were Matthew Boulton (1728–1809), whose world-famous Soho Manufactory produced a variety of metal objects, from buttons and buckles to silverware; James Watt (1736–1819), inventor of the steam engine, who would team with Boulton to produce it; Erasmus Darwin (1731–1802), whose writings on botany and evolution anticipate by nearly a century his grandson Charles Darwin's famous conclusions; William Murdock (1754–1839), inventor of gas lighting; Benjamin Franklin (1706–1790), who was a corresponding member; and Josiah Wedgwood (1730–1795), Charles Darwin's other grandfather and the inventor of mass manufacturing at his Wedgwood ceramics factories. From 1765 until 1815, the group discussed chemistry, medicine, electricity, gases, and any and every topic that might prove fruitful for industry. It is fair to say that the Lunar Society's members inaugurated what we think of today as the **Industrial Revolution**. The term itself was invented in the nineteenth century to describe the radical changes in production and consumption that had transformed the world.

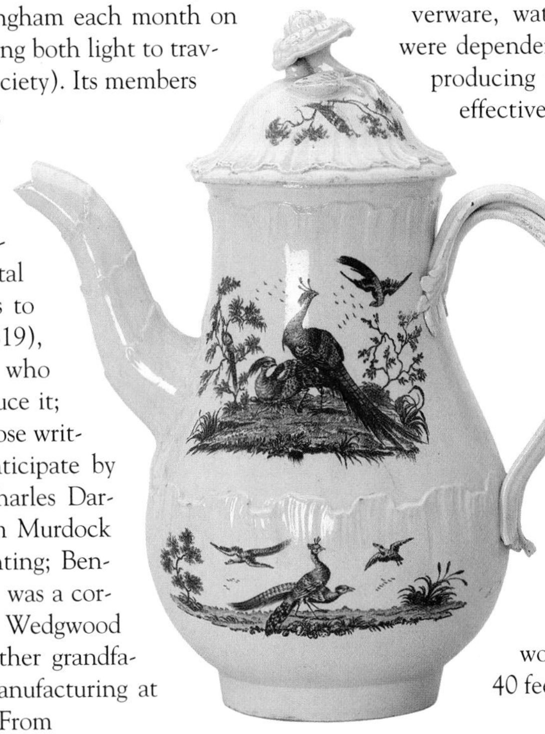

Wedgwood opened his first factory in Burslem, Staffordshire, on May 1, 1759, where he began to produce a highly durable cream-colored earthenware (Fig. **11.6**). Queen Charlotte, wife of King George III, was so fond of these pieces that Wedgwood was appointed royal supplier of dinnerware. Wedgwood's production process was unique. Instead of shaping individual pieces by hand on the potter's wheel—the only way ceramic ware had been produced—he cast liquid clay in molds and then fired it. This greatly increased the speed of production, as did mechanically

Fig. 11.6 Transfer-printed Queen's Ware. ca. 1770. The Wedgwood Museum, Barlaston, England. Decorations such as the one on this coffee pot were mechanically printed on ceramic tableware at Wedgwood's factory. Queen's Ware became so popular that pattern books, showing the available designs, were available across Europe by the turn of the century.

printing decorative patterns on the finished china rather than painting them. The catalog described Queen's Ware, as it came to be known, as "a species of earthenware for the table, quite new in appearance . . . manufactured with ease and expedition, and consequently cheap." It was soon available to mass markets in both Europe and America, and Wedgwood's business flourished.

Wedgwood's Queen's Ware is an exemplary product of the Industrial Revolution. New machinery in new factories created a supply of consumer goods unprecedented in history, answering an ever-increasing demand for everyday items, from toys, furniture, kitchen utensils, and china, to silverware, watches, and candlesticks. These factories were dependent upon the discovery of techniques for producing iron of unprecedented quality in a cost-effective manner. Early in the century, Abraham Darby (1678–1717) discovered that it was possible to fire cast iron with coke—a carbon-based fuel made from coal. Darby's grandson, Abraham Darby III (1750–1791), inherited the patent rights to the process; to demonstrate the structural strength of the cast iron he was able to manufacture, he proposed to build a single-arch cast-iron bridge across the River Severn, high enough to accommodate barge traffic on the river. The bridge at Coalbrookdale (Fig. **11.7**) was designed by a local architect, while its 70-foot ribs were cast at Darby's ironworks. The bridge's 100-foot span, arching 40 feet above the river, demonstrated once and for all the structural potential of iron. A century later, such bridges would carry railroad cars, as the need for transporting new mass-produced goods exploded.

Textiles were in particular demand, and in many ways, advances in textile manufacture could be called the driving force of the Industrial Revolution. At the beginning of the eighteenth century, textiles were made of wool from sheep raised in the English Midlands. A thriving cottage industry, in which weavers used handlooms and spinning wheels, textile manufacture changed dramatically in 1733 when John Kay in Lancashire invented the flying shuttle. Using this device, a weaver could propel the shuttle, which carries the yarn that forms the weft through the fibers of the warp, beyond the weaver's reach. Cloth could be made both wider and faster. Invention after invention followed, culminating in 1769 when Richard Arkwright patented the water frame, a waterwheel used to power looms. With their increased power, looms

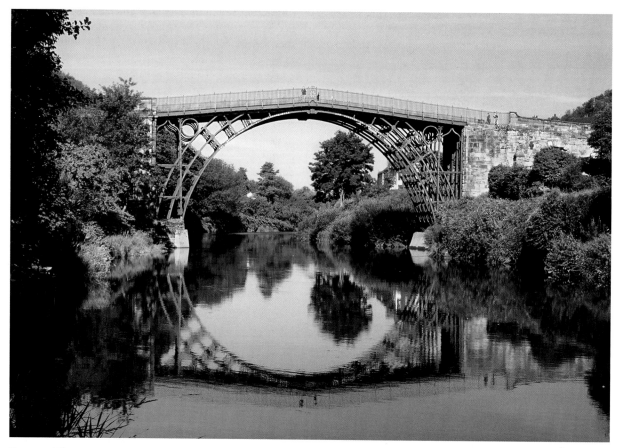

Fig. 11.7 Thomas Farnolls Pritchard. Iron Bridge, Coalbrookdale, England. 1779. Cast iron. Pritchard was keenly aware that the reflection of the bridge would form a visual circle, a form repeated in the ironwork at the corners of the bridge.

could operate at much higher speeds. Arkwright had duped the actual inventors out of their design, and in 1771 installed the water frame in a cotton mill in Derbyshire, on the river Derwent. These first textile mills, needing water power to drive their machinery, were built on fast-moving streams like the Derwent. But after the 1780s, with the application of Watts's steam power, mills soon sprang up in urban centers. In the last 20 years of the eighteenth century, English cotton output increased 800 percent, accounting for 40 percent of the nation's exports.

Absolutism Versus Liberalism: Thomas Hobbes and John Locke

Following the Civil War led by Oliver Cromwell and the subsequent restoration, with a greatly disempowered monarchy, one of the most pressing issues of the day was how best to govern the nation, and one of the most important points of view had been published by Thomas Hobbes [hobz] (1588–1679) in 1651, in *Leviathan; or The Matter, Forme, and Power of a Commonwealth, Ecclesiasticall and Civil.* His classical training had convinced Hobbes that the reasoning upon which Euclid's geometry was based could be

extended to political and social systems. A visit to Galileo in Italy in 1636 reaffirmed that Galileo's description of the movement of the solar system—planets orbiting the central sun—could be extended to human relations—a people orbiting their ruler. Hobbes argued that people are driven by two things—the fear of death at someone else's hands and the desire for power—and that the government's role is to check both of these instincts, which if uncontrolled would lead to anarchy. Given the context in which *Leviathan* was written—the English Civil War had raged throughout the previous decade—Hobbes's position is hardly surprising. Most humans, Hobbes believed, recognize their own essential depravity and therefore willingly submit to governance. They accept the **social contract**, which means giving up sovereignty over themselves and bestowing it on a ruler. They carry out the ruler's demands, and the ruler, in return, agrees to keep the peace. Humankind's only hope, Hobbes argued, is to submit to a higher authority, the "Leviathan" [luh-VY-uh-thun], the biblical sea monster who is the absolutist "king over all the sons of pride" (Job 41:34).

John Locke (1632–1704) disagreed. In his 1690 *Essay on Human Understanding*, Locke repudiated Hobbes, arguing that people are perfectly capable of governing themselves. The human mind at birth, he claimed, is a *tabula rasa*, a "blank slate," and our environment—what we learn and how we learn it—fills this slate (**Reading 11.3**):

READING 11.3 **from Locke's *Essay on Human Understanding* (1690)**

1. Idea is the object of thinking. Every man being conscious to himself that he thinks; and that which his mind is applied about whilst thinking being the ideas that are there, it is past doubt that men have in their minds several ideas—such as are those expressed by the words whiteness, hardness, sweetness, thinking, motion, man, elephant, army, drunkenness, and others: it is in the first place then to be inquired, How he comes by them? . . .

2. All ideas come from sensation or reflection. Let us then suppose the mind to be, as we say, white paper, void of all characters, without any ideas—How comes it to be furnished? Whence comes it by that vast store which the busy and boundless fancy of man has painted on it with an almost endless variety? Whence has it all the materials of reason and knowledge? To this I answer, in one word, from EXPERIENCE. In that all our knowledge is founded; and from that it ultimately derives itself. Our observation employed either, about external sensible objects, or about the internal operations of our minds perceived and reflected on by ourselves, is that which supplies our understandings with all the materials of thinking. These two are the fountains of knowledge, from whence all the ideas we have, or can naturally have, do spring.

3. The objects of sensation one source of ideas. First, our Senses, conversant about particular sensible objects, do convey into the mind several distinct perceptions of things . . . [and] thus we come by those ideas we have of yellow, white, heat, cold, soft, hard, bitter, sweet, and all those which we call sensible qualities. . . .

4. The operations of our minds, the other source of them. Secondly, the other fountain from which experience furnisheth the understanding with ideas, is the perception of the operations of our own mind within us, as it is employed about the ideas it has got; which operations, when the soul comes to reflect on and consider, do furnish the understanding with another set of ideas, which could not be had from things without. And such are perception, thinking, doubting, believing, reasoning, knowing, willing, and all the different actings of our own minds. . . .

Given this sense that we understand the world through experience, if we live in a reasonable society, it should follow, according to Locke's notion of the *tabula rasa*, that we will grow into reasonable people. In his *Second Treatise of Government*, also published in 1690, Locke went further. He refuted the divine rights of kings and argued that humans are "by nature free, equal, and independent." They agree to government in order to protect themselves, but the social contract they admit to does not require them to surrender their own sovereignty to their ruler. The ruler has only limited authority that must be held in check by a governmental system balanced by a separation of powers. Finally, they expect the ruler to protect their rights, and if the ruler fails, they have the right to revolt in order to reclaim their natural freedom. This form of **liberalism**—from the Latin, *liberare*, "to free"—set the stage for the political revolutions that dominated the eighteenth and nineteenth centuries.

John Milton's *Paradise Lost*

The debate between absolutism and liberalism also informs what is arguably the greatest poem of the English seventeenth century, *Paradise Lost* by John Milton (1608–1674). Milton had served in Oliver Cromwell's government during the Commonwealth. (He had studied the great epics of classical literature, and he was determined to write his own, one which would, as he puts it in the opening verse of the poem, "justifie the wayes of God to men.") In 12 books, Milton composed a densely plotted poem with complex character development, rich theological reasoning, and long wavelike sentences of blank verse. The subject of the epic is the Judeo-Christian story of the loss of Paradise by Adam and Eve and their descendents. As described in the Bible, the couple, enticed by Satan, disobey God's injunction that they not eat the fruit of the Tree of Knowledge. Satan had revolted against God and then sought to destroy humanity.

While occasionally virulently anti-Catholic, the poem is, among other things, an essay on the possibilities of liberty and justice. In many ways, God assumes the position of royal authority that Hobbes argues for in his *Leviathan*. In Book 5 of Milton's poem, God sends the angel Raphael to Adam to warn him of the nearness of Lucifer (Satan) and to explain how Lucifer became God's enemy. Raphael recounts how God had addressed the angels to announce that he now had a son, Christ, whom all should obey as if he were God, in keeping with the traditions of hereditary kingship (**Reading 11.4a**):

READING 11.4a **from John Milton, *Paradise Lost*, Book 5 (1667)**

"Hear all ye angels, Progeny of Light,
Thrones, Dominations, Princedoms, Virtues, Powers,
Hear my Decree, which unrevoked shall stand.
This day I have begot whom I declare
My only Son, and on this holy hill
Him have anointed, whom ye now behold
At my right hand; your head I him appoint;
And by my Self have sworn to him shall bow
All knees in heav'n, and shall confess him Lord."

Lucifer, formerly God's principal angel, is not happy about the news of this new favorite. Motivated by his own desire for power, he gathers the angels loyal to him, and addresses them in terms more in the spirit of Locke than Hobbes. He begins his speech as God had begun his, invoking the imperial titles of those present; he reminds them, "which assert / Our being ordain'd to govern, not to serve" (**Reading 11.4b**):

READING 11.4b   **from John Milton,**
Paradise Lost, Book 5 (1667)

Thrones, Dominations, Princedoms, Virtues, Powers,
If these magnific titles yet remain
Not merely titular, since by decree
Another now hath to himself engrossed
All power, and us eclipsed under the name
Of King anointed. . . .

Will ye submit your necks, and choose to bend
The supple knee? ye will not, if I trust
To know ye right, or if ye know yourselves
Natives and sons of heav'n possessed before
By none, and if not equal all, yet free,
Equally free; for orders and degrees
Jar not with liberty. . . .

Who can in reason then or right assume
Monarchy over such as live by right
His equals, if in power and splendor less,
In freedom equal?

Lucifer's is a "reasonable" argument. Like Locke, he thinks of himself and the other angels as "by nature free, equal, and independent." The battle that ensues between God and Lucifer is reminiscent of the English Civil War, with its complex protagonists, its councils, and its bids for leadership on both sides. It results in Lucifer's expulsion from Heaven to Hell, where he is henceforth known as Satan. While many readers understood God as a figure for the Stuart monarchy, and Satan as Cromwell, it is not necessary to do so in order to understand the basic tensions that inform the poem. The issues that separate God from Satan are clearly the issues dividing England in the seventeenth century: the tension between absolute rule and the civil liberty of the individual.

Satire: Enlightenment Wit

Not every Englishman was convinced that the direction England was heading in the eighteenth century was for the better. London was a city teaming with activity; Canaletto's painting (see Fig. 11.1) was an idealized view of city life. Over the course of the eighteenth century, the rich and the middle class largely abandoned the city proper, moving west into present-day Mayfair and Marylebone, and even to outlying villages such as Islington and Paddington. At the start of the century these villages were surrounded by meadows and market gardens, but by century's end they had been absorbed into an ever-growing suburbia.

In the heart of London, a surging population of immigrants newly arrived from the countryside filled the houses abandoned by the middle class and subdivided into tenements. The very poor lived in what came to be called the East End, a semicircle of districts surrounding the area that extended from Saint Paul's in the west to the Tower of London in the East (the area contained by the old London Wall). Here, in the neighborhoods of Saint Giles, Clerkenwall, Spitalfields, Whitechapel, Bethnal Green, and Wapping, the streets were narrow and badly paved, the houses old and in disrepair, and drunkenness, prostitution, pickpocketing, assault, and robbery were the norm. On the outer edges, pig keepers and dairymen labored in a landscape of gravel pits, garbage dumps, ash heaps, and manure piles.

Meanwhile, Parliament's two factions, the Whigs and the Tories, were at odds. The Whig faction opposed absolutism and tended to support constitutional monarchy and non-Anglican Protestants, such as the Presbyterians. The Tories tended to support the English gentry and the Anglican church. Naturally, they preferred a strong monarchy, while the Whigs favored Parliament retaining final sovereignty. Nevertheless, the Whigs gained favor with King George I (r. 1714–1727), and so, when he assumed the throne, George was predisposed to the Whigs and to their leading the government. For the next 40 years, the Whigs had access to public office and enjoyed royal patronage, and the Tories were effectively eliminated from public life. The end result was that Whig leadership, chiefly that of Robert Walpole (1676–1745), who can be regarded as the first English prime minister and who dominated the English political scene from 1721 to 1742, was consistent and predictable. Nothing could have fostered the Enlightenment more. Above all else, England's transformation from a state in near chaos to one in comparative harmony demonstrated what is probably the fundamental principle of Enlightenment thought—that social change and political reform are not only desirable but possible.

Whatever the promise of the social order established by Walpole and the Georgian government, thoughtful commentators who looked beneath the surface detected a cauldron of social ferment and moral bankruptcy. By uncovering what might be called the "dark side" of the Enlightenment, satirists like William Hogarth (1697–1764), Jonathan Swift (1667–1745), and Alexander Pope (1688–1744) sought, by means of irony and humor to return England to its proper path.

Hogarth and the Popular Print   By 1743, thousands of Londoners were addicted to gin, their sole means of escape from the misery of poverty. In 1751, just four years after Canaletto painted his view of _The Thames and the City of London from Richmond House_ (see Fig. 11.1), William Hogarth published _Gin Lane_, a print illustrating life in the gin shops (Fig. **11.8**).

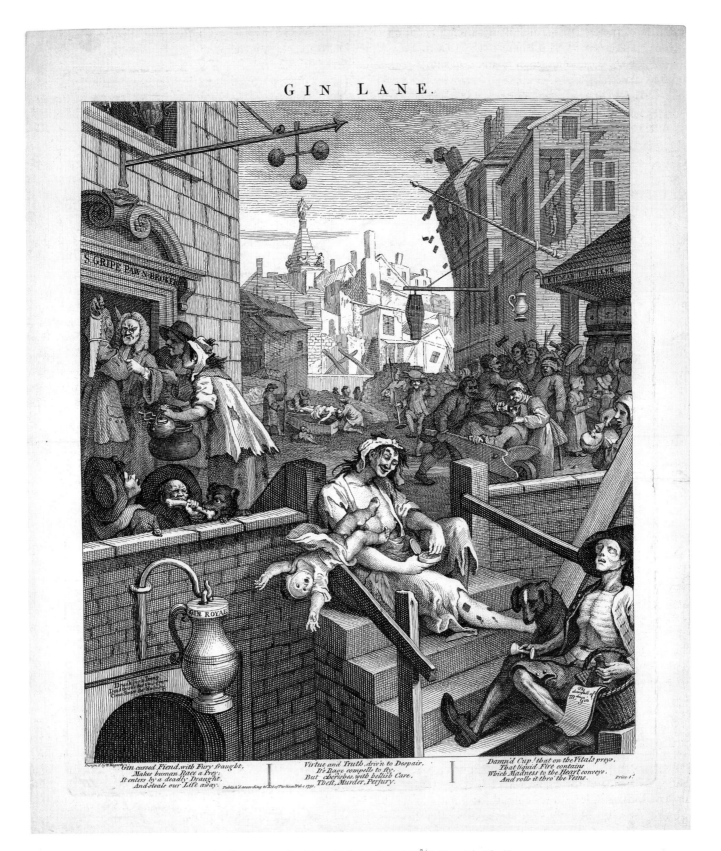

Fig. 11.8 William Hogarth. *Gin Lane.* **1751.** Engraving and etching, third state, 14″ × 11⅞″. Copyright The Trustees of the British Museum, London/Art Resource, NY. In his *Autobiographical Notes,* Hogarth wrote: "In gin lane every circumstance of its [gin's] horrid effects are brought to view; nothing but Idleness, Poverty, misery, and ruin are to be seen . . . not a house in tolerable condition but Pawnbrokers and the Gin shop."

In the foreground a man so emaciated by drink that he seems a virtual skeleton lies dying, half-naked, presumably having pawned the rest of his clothes. A woman takes snuff on the stairs as her child falls over the railing beside her. At the door to the thriving pawnshop behind her, a carpenter sells his tools, the means of his livelihood, as a woman waits to sell her kitchen utensils, the means of her nourishment. In the background, a young woman is laid out in a coffin, as her child weeps beside her. A building comes tumbling down, a man parades down the street with a bellows on his head and a child skewered on his staff—an allegorical if not realistic detail. In the top story of the building on the right, another man has hanged himself. At the lower left, above the door to the Gin Royal, one of the only buildings in good condition, are these words: "Drunk for a penny/ Dead drunk for two pence/ Clean Straw for Nothing."

In *Gin Lane*, Hogarth turned his attention not to the promise of the Enlightenment, but to the reality of London at its worst. He did so with the savage wit and broad humor that marks the best social satire. And he did so with the conviction that his images of what he called "modern moral subjects" might not only amuse a wide audience, but would influence that audience's behavior as well. Hogarth usually painted his subjects first, but recognizing the limited audience of a painting, he produced engraved versions as well for wider distribution. "As the Subjects of these Prints are calculated to reform some reigning Vices peculiar to the lower Class of People, in hopes to render them of the most extensive use," wrote Hogarth in his advertisement for them, "the Author has publish'd them in the cheapest Manner possible." In other words, Hogarth recognized that his work appealed to a large popular audience, and that by distributing engravings of his works he might make a comfortable living entertaining it.

The Satires of Jonathan Swift Perhaps the most biting satirist of the English Enlightenment was Jonathan Swift. In a letter to fellow satirist and friend Alexander Pope, Swift confided that he hated the human race for having misused its capacity for reason simply to further its own corrupt self-interest. After a modestly successful career as a satirist in the first decade of the eighteenth century, Swift was named dean of Saint Patrick's Cathedral in Dublin in 1713, and it was there that he wrote his most famous works, *Gulliver's Travels*, published in 1726, and the brief, almost fanatically savage *A Modest Proposal* in 1729. There, reacting to the terrible poverty he saw in Ireland, Swift proposed that Irish families who could not afford to feed their children breed them to be butchered and served to the English.

In *Gulliver's Travels*, Swift's satire is less direct. Europeans were familiar with the accounts of travelers' adventures in far-off lands at least since the time of Marco Polo, and after the exploration of the Americas, the form had become quite common. Swift played off the travel-adventure narrative to describe the adventures of one Lemuel Gulliver as he moves among lands peopled by miniature people, giants, and other fabulous creatures. But Swift employs his imaginary peoples and creatures to comment on real human behavior. In Book I, the Lilliputians, a people that average 6 inches in height, are "little people" not just physically but ethically. In fact, their politics and religion are very much those of England, and they are engaged in a war with a neighboring island that very closely resembles France. Swift's strategy is to reduce the politics of his day to a level of triviality. In Book IV, Gulliver visits Houyhnhnms, a country of noble horses whose name sounds like a whinnying horse and is probably pronounced *hwinnum*. Gulliver explains that "the word *Houyhnhnm*, in their tongue, signifies a *horse*, and, in its etymology, *the perfection of nature*." Their ostensible nobility contrasts with the bestial and degenerate behavior of their human-looking slaves, the Yahoos. Of course, Gulliver resembles a Yahoo as well. At one point, Gulliver's Houyhnhnm host compliments him, saying "that he was sure I must have been born of some noble family, because I far exceeded in shape, colour, and cleanliness, all the yahoos of his nation." Gulliver's response is a model of Swift's satiric invective (**Reading 11.5**):

<hr>

READING 11.5   **from Jonathan Swift, *Gulliver's Travels*, Book IV, Chapter VI (1726)**

I made his Honour my most humble acknowledgments for the good opinion he was pleased to conceive of me, but assured him at the same time, "that my birth was of the lower sort, having been born of plain honest parents, who were just able to give me a tolerable education; that nobility, among us, was altogether a different thing from the idea he had of it; that our young noblemen are bred from their childhood in idleness and luxury; that, as soon as years will permit, they consume their vigor, and contract odious diseases among lewd females; and when their fortunes are almost ruined, they marry some woman of mean birth, disagreeable person, and unsound constitution (merely for the sake of money), whom they hate and despise. That the productions of such marriages are generally scrofulous, rickety, or deformed children; by which means the family seldom continues above three generations, unless the wife takes care to provide a healthy father, among her neighbours or domestics, in order to improve and continue the breed. That a weak diseased body, a meager countenance, and sallow complexion, are the true marks of noble blood; and a healthy robust appearance is so disgraceful in a man of quality, that the world concludes his real father to have been a groom or a coachman. The imperfections of his mind run parallel with those of his body, being a composition of spleen, dullness, ignorance, caprice, sensuality, and pride.

Gulliver's Travels was an immediate best seller, selling out its first printing in less than a week. "It is universally read," said his friend, Alexander Pope, "from the cabinet council to the nursery." So enduring is Swift's wit that names of his characters and types have entered the language as descriptive terms—"yahoo" for a coarse or uncouth person, "Lilliputian" for anything small and delicate.

The Classical Wit of Alexander Pope The English poet Alexander Pope shared Swift's assessment of the English nobility. For 12 years, from 1715 until 1727, Pope spent the majority of his time translating Homer's *Iliad* and *Odyssey*, and producing a six-volume edition of Shakespeare, projects of such popularity that he became a wealthy man. But in 1727, his literary career changed directions and, as he wrote, he "stooped to truth, and moralized his song"—he turned, in short, to satire. His first effort was the mock epic *Dunciad* [DUN-see-ad], published in 1728 and dedicated to Jonathan Swift. The poem opens with a direct attack on the king, George II (r. 1727–1760), who had recently succeeded his father, George I, to the throne. For Pope, this suggested the goddess Dullness reigned over an England where "Dunce the second rules like Dunce the first." Pope's dunces are the very nobility that Swift attacks in the fourth book of Gulliver—men of "dullness, ignorance, caprice, sensuality, and pride"—and the writers of the day whom Pope perceived to be supporting the policies of Walpole and the king.

Against what he believed to be the debased English court, Pope argues for honesty, charity, selflessness, and the order, harmony, and balance of the classics, values set forth in *An Essay on Man*, published between 1732 and 1734. Pope intended the poem to be the cornerstone of a complete system of ethics that he never completed. His purpose is to show that despite the apparent imperfection, complexity, and rampant evil of the universe, it nevertheless functions in a rational way, according to natural laws. The world appears imperfect to us only because our perceptions are limited by our feeble moral and intellectual capacity. In reality, as he puts it at the end of the poem's first section (**Reading 11.6**):

READING 11.6 **from Alexander Pope,**
An Essay on Man (1732)

All Nature is but Art, unknown to thee;
All Chance, Direction, which thou canst not see;
All Discord, Harmony not understood;
All partial Evil, universal good;
And, spite of Pride in erring Reason's spite,
One truth is clear: WHATEVER IS, IS RIGHT.

Pope does not mean to condone evil in this last line. Rather, he implies that God has chosen to grant humankind a certain imperfection, a freedom of choice that reflects its position in the universe. At the start of the second section of the poem, immediately after this passage, Pope outlines humankind's place:

> Know then thyself, presume not God to scan;
> The proper study of Mankind is Man.
> Placed on this isthmus of a middle state,
> A Being darkly wise, and rudely great;
> With too much knowledge for the Sceptic side,
> With too much weakness for the Stoic's pride.
> He hangs between, in doubt to act, or rest;
> In doubt to deem himself a God, or Beast;
> In doubt his Mind or Body to prefer;
> Born but to die, and reas'ning but to err;
> Alike in ignorance, his reason such,
> Whether he thinks too little, or too much:
> Chaos of Thought and Passion, all confused;
> Still by himself abused, or disabused;
> Created half to rise, and half to fall;
> Great lord of all things, yet a prey to all;
> Sole judge of Truth, in endless Error hurled:
> The glory, jest, and riddle of the world!

In the end, for Pope, humankind must strive for good, even if in its frailty it is doomed to fail. But the possibility of success also looms large. Pope suggests this through the very form of his poem—**heroic couplets**, rhyming pairs of iambic pentameter lines (the meter of Shakespeare, consisting of five short-long syllabic units)—that reflect the balance and harmony of classical art and thought.

Literacy and the New Print Culture

Since the seventeenth century, literacy had risen sharply in England, and by 1750 at least 60 percent of adult men and between 40 and 50 percent of adult women could read. Not surprisingly, literacy was connected to class. Merchant-class men and women were more likely to read than those in the working class. And among the latter, city dwellers had higher literacy rates than those in rural areas. But even the literate poor were often priced out of the literary marketplace. Few had enough disposable income to purchase even a cheap edition of Milton, which cost about 2 shillings at midcentury. (At Cambridge University, a student could purchase a week's meals for 5 shillings.) And even though, by the 1740s, circulating libraries existed in towns and cities across Britain, the poor generally could not afford the annual subscription fees. Nevertheless, libraries broadened considerably the periodicals and books—particularly, that new, increasingly popular form of fiction, the novel—available to the middle class. Priced out of most books and libraries, the literate poor depended on an informal network of trading books and newspapers. Sharing reading materials was so common, in fact, that the publisher of one popular daily periodical estimated "twenty readers to every paper."

The Rise of the English Novel The novel as we know it was not invented in eighteenth-century England—Cervantes's

Don Quixote, written a century earlier, is often considered the first example of the form in Western literature (see chapter 10). But the century abounded in experiments in fiction writing that anticipate many of the forms that novelists have employed down to the present day. Works that today are called novels (from the French *nouvelle* and Italian *novella*, meaning "new") were rarely called "novels" in the eighteenth century itself. That term did not catch on until the very end of the century. Typically, they were referred to as "histories," "adventures," "expeditions," "tales," or—Hogarth's term—"progresses." They were read by people of every social class. What the novel claimed to be, and what appealed to its ever-growing audience, was a realistic portrayal of contemporary life. It concentrated almost always on the trials of a single individual, offering insight into the complexities of his or her personality. It also offered the promise, more often than not, of upward social mobility through participation in the expanding British economy and the prospect of prosperity that accompanied it. As London's population swelled with laborers, artisans, and especially young people seeking fame and fortune, and as the Industrial Revolution created the possibility of sudden financial success for the inventive and imaginative, the novel endorsed a set of ethics and a morality that were practical, not idealized. Above all, the novel was entertaining. Reading novels offered some respite from the drudgery of everyday life and, besides, was certainly a healthier addiction than drinking gin.

One of the most innovative experiments in the new novelistic form was devised by Samuel Richardson (1689–1761). He fell into novel writing as the result of his work on a "how-to" project commissioned by two London booksellers. Aware that "Country Readers" could use some help with their writing, the booksellers hired Richardson to write a book of "sample letters" that could be copied whenever necessary. Richardson was both a printer and the author of a history based on the letters of a seventeenth-century British ambassador to Constantinople and India. He had never written fiction before, but two letters in his new project suggested the possibility of writing a novel— "A Father to a Daughter in Service, on hearing of her Master's attempting her Virtue," and "The Daughter's Answer." In just over two months, Richardson wrote *Pamela, or Virtue Rewarded*, the first example of what we have come to call the **epistolary novel**—that is, a novel made up of a series of "epistles," or letters. It was published in two volumes in 1740.

The morality of Richardson's *Pamela* was praised from church pulpits, recommended to parents skeptical of the novel as a form, and generally celebrated by the more Puritan elements of British society, who responded favorably to the heroine's virtue. Pamela herself asked a question that women readers found particularly important: "How came I to be his Property?" But the novel's smug morality (and the upward mobility exhibited by the novel's heroine) offended many, most notably Richardson's contemporary Henry Fielding (1707–1754), who responded, a year after the appearance of *Pamela*, with *Shamela*. Fielding's title tips the reader off that his work is a **parody**, a form of satire in which the style of an author or work is closely imitated for comic effect or ridicule. In Fielding's parody, his lower-class heroine's sexual appetite is every bit a match for her Squire Booby's—and from Fielding's point of view, much more realistic. Fielding presents Pamela's ardent defense of her chastity against her upper-class seducer as a sham; it is simply a calculated strategy, an ambitious hussy's plot to achieve financial security.

One of the first great novels written in English is *Robinson Crusoe* by Daniel Defoe [dih-FOH] (1660–1731). Published in 1719, the full title of this sprawling work is *The Life and Strange Surprising Adventures of Robinson Crusoe of York, Mariner; Who lived Eight and Twenty Years, all alone in an uninhabited Island on the coast of America, near the Mouth of the Great River of Oronoque; Having been cast on Shore by Shipwreck, wherein all the Men perished but himself. With An Account how he was at last as strangely deliver'd by Pirates. Written by Himself.* The last three words are crucial, for they establish Defoe's claim that this novel is actually an autobiography.

Defoe's audience was used to reading accounts of real-life castaways that constituted a form of voyage literature. But far from falling into the primitive degradation and apathy of the average castaway, he rises above his situation, realizing, in his very ability to sustain himself, his God-given human potential. So many of Defoe's readers felt isolated and alone, like castaways, in the sea of London. For them, Crusoe represented hope and possibility.

This theme of the power of the average person to survive and flourish is what assured the novel's popularity and accounted for four editions by the end of the year. Defoe followed *Robinson Crusoe* with a series of other fictitious autobiographies of adventurers and rogues—*Captain Singleton* (1720), *Moll Flanders* (1722), *Colonel Jack* (1722), and *Roxanna* (1724). In all of them, his characters are in one way or another "shipwrecked" by society and as determined as Crusoe to overcome their situations through whatever means—not always the most virtuous—at their disposal.

Not all readers were charmed and entertained by the sometime lavish portraits of vice found in the novels of Fielding and Defoe. These readers found an antidote to Fielding in the writings of Jane Austen (1775–1817). Although Austen's best-known novels were published in the first quarter of the nineteenth century, she was more in tune with the sensibilities of the late eighteenth century, especially with Enlightenment values of sense, reason, and self-improvement.

None of Austen's heroines better embodies these values than the heroine of *Pride and Prejudice* (1813), Elizabeth Bennett, one of five daughters of a country gentlemen whose wife is intent on marrying the daughters off. The novel famously opens (**Reading 11.7**):

READING 11.7   **from Jane Austen,**
Pride and Prejudice,
Chapter 1 (1813)

It is a truth universally acknowledged, that a single man in possession of a good fortune, must be in want of a wife.

However little known the feelings or views of such a man may be on his first entering a neighbourhood, this truth is so well fixed in the minds of the surrounding families, that he is considered the rightful property of some one or other of their daughters.

The level of Austen's irony in these opening sentences cannot be overstated, for while she describes the fate that awaits any single, well-heeled male entering a new neighborhood, these lines are a less direct, but devastating reflection upon the possibilities for women in English society. Their prospect in life is to be married. And if they are not themselves well-heeled and attractive—that is, marriageable—their prospects are less than that.

Austen first told this story in _First Impressions_ (1796–1797), in the form of an exchange of letters between Elizabeth and Fitzwilliam Darcy, an English gentleman. When we first meet him in _Pride and Prejudice_, Austen describes him as follows: "He was looked at with great admiration for about half the evening, till his manners gave a disgust which turned the tide of his popularity; for he was discovered to be proud, to be above his company, and above being pleased; and not all his large estate in Derbyshire could then save him from having a most forbidding, disagreeable countenance...." The novel's plot revolves around the two words of its title, "pride" and "prejudice." Where Elizabeth at first can only see Darcy's pride, she comes to realize that her view is tainted by her prejudice. Darcy's disdain for country people and manners is a prejudice that Elizabeth's evident pride helps him to overcome. Together, they come to understand not only their own shortcomings but their society's.

The Enlightenment in France

Until his death in 1715, Louis XIV had opened his private apartments in Versailles three days a week to his courtiers, where they entertained themselves by playing games. After his death such entertainments continued, only not at Versailles but in the hôtels—or Paris townhouses—of the French nobility, where the same crowd who had visited the king's apartments now entertained on their own. The new king, Louis XV, was only 5 years old, and so there was no point in staying so far out of town in the rural palace where the Sun King had reigned supreme.

The _hôtels_ all had a **salon**, a room designed especially for social gatherings. Very soon the term _salon_ came to refer to the social gathering itself. A number of these rooms still survive, including the Salon de la Princesse, which was designed by Germain Boffrand to commemorate the 1737 marriage of the 80-year-old prince of Soubise to the 19-year-old Marie-Sophie de Courcillon (Fig. **11.9**). Decorated around the top of the room with eight large paintings by Charles-Joseph Natoire [nah-TWAHR] (1700–1777) depicting the story of Cupid and Psyche from Ovid's _Metamorphoses_ (Fig. **11.10**), the room embodies the eroticism that dominated the art of the French aristocracy in the eighteenth century.

These salons became the center of French culture in the eighteenth century, and by 1850 they were emulated across Europe. The new princess de Soubise was perhaps too young to be herself an active **salonnière** [sah-lohn-YAIR], one of the hostesses who presided over the weekly gatherings that soon dominated Parisian social life. Among the most popular salons were those of Jeanne-Julie-Eleonore de Lespinasse [deh less-peen-AHSS] (1732–1776). In his memoirs, Friederick Melchior, baron von Grimm (1723–1807), a frequent guest, recalls the ambiance:

> Her circle met daily from five o'clock until nine in the evening. There we were sure to find choice men of all orders in the State, the Church, the Court—military men, foreigners, and the most distinguished men of letters. Every one agrees that though the name of M. d'Alembert [an intellectual who lived with Julie de Lespinasse, and who is discussed later in the chapter] may have drawn them thither, it was she alone who kept them there. Devoted wholly to the care of preserving that society, of which she was the soul and the charm, she subordinated to this purpose all her tastes and all her personal intimacies. She seldom went to the theatre or into the country, and when she did make an exception to this rule it was an event of which all Paris was notified in advance.... Politics, religion, philosophy, anecdotes, news, nothing was excluded from the conversation, and, thanks to her care, the most trivial little narrative gained, as naturally as possible, the place and notice it deserved. News of all kinds was gathered there in its first freshness.

The baron numbered among his friends many of the most influential Parisian thinkers of the day, the so-called **philosophes** [FILL-loh-sof], "philosophers," who frequented the salons and dominated the intellectual life of the French Enlightenment. Not philosophers in the strict sense of the word because they did not concentrate on matters metaphysical, but turned their attention to secular and social concerns, the _philosophes_ were almost uniformly alienated from the Church, despising its hierarchy and ritual. They were also committed to the abolition of the monarchy, which they saw as intolerant, unjust, and decadent.

The _philosophes_, who aspired to establish a new social order of superior moral and ethical quality, and the French courtiers,

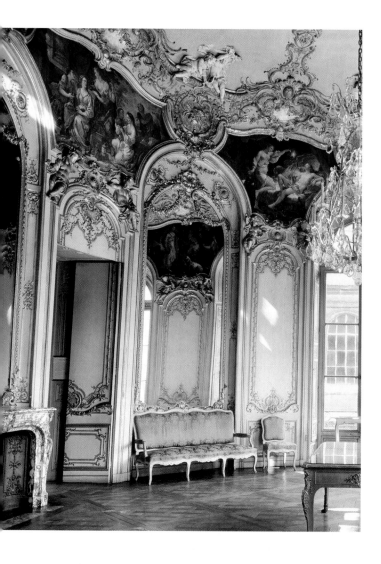

whose taste favored a decorative and erotic excess that the *philosophes* abhorred, often collided at the salons. Consider, for instance, the salons of Madame de Pompadour [mah-DAHM deh pohm-pah-DOOR] (1721–1764), born into a middle-class family involved in Parisian financial circles. She was a great defender of the *philosophes*, but she was also mistress to Louis XV after he assumed full power in 1743. She blocked efforts to have the works of the *philosophes* suppressed by censors and was successful in keeping works attacking the *philosophes* out of circulation. And yet, she was also the king's trusted advisor and the subject of many erotic paintings done at court depicting her as Venus. The competing styles of Louis XIV's Baroque court survived into the eighteenth century, but now were no longer united or comfortable together. Whereas at Versailles essentially Classical architecture was embellished with Baroque ornamentation, the nobility now appreciated only an ever more elaborate decoration and ornament, while the *philosophes* shunned ornamentation altogether, preferring the order, regularity, and balance of the Classical tradition.

Fig. 11.9 Germain Boffrand. *Salon de la Princesse de Soubise (Salon oval)*, **Hôtel de Soubise, Paris. ca. 1740.** Oval shape, 33′ × 26′. Photo: Bulloz. Reunion des Musées Nationaux/Art Resource, NY. In his 1745 *Livre d'architecture* (*Book on Architecture*), Boffrand compared architecture to theater, arguing that it had both a tragic and pastoral mode. In the lightness of its ornament and the eroticism of its paintings, the Salon de la Princesse is an example of the pastoral mode.

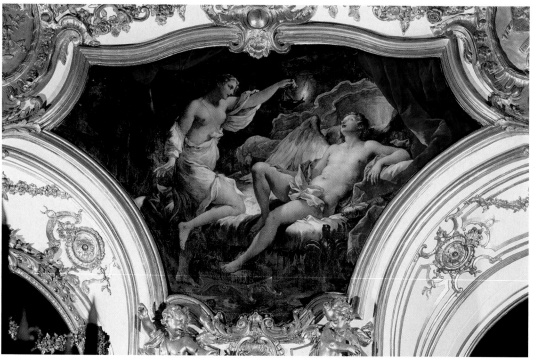

Fig. 11.10 Charles-Joseph Natoire. *Cupid and Psyche*, **Salon de la Princesse, Hôtel de Soubise, Paris. 1738.** Oil on canvas, 5′7 3/4″ × 8′6 3/8″. Peter Willi/The Bridgeman Art Library. Here Psyche has been brought to the palace of Love where Cupid, under cover of darkness, has consummated their union. Psyche had promised never to seek to know his identity but she breaks her oath by lighting her lamp to reveal Cupid's face.

The Rococo

The decorative style fostered by the French court in the eighteenth century and quickly emulated by royal courts across Europe was known as the **Rococo** [ruh-KOH-koh]. The term is thought to derive from the French word *rocaille* [roh-KYE], a type of decorative rockwork made from round pebbles and curvilinear shells. But it also derives from *barocco*, the Italian word for "baroque." In fact, the Rococo style is probably best understood as the culmination of developments in art and architecture that began in the late work of Michelangelo and progressed through Mannerism and the Baroque into the eighteenth century. Along the way, the style became increasingly elaborate, with architectural interiors employing a vocabulary of S- and C-curves, shell, wing, scroll, and plant tendril forms, and rounded, convex, often asymmetrical surfaces.

Most eighteenth-century French painters still relied on the court for commissions. But once the courtiers had moved back from Versailles to the comfort of their Paris townhouses and country estates, they were less interested in commissioning paintings that glorified them than those that entertained. The new Rococo style as applied to French painting suited this domestic goal perfectly. Its subject matter is often frivolous, emphasizing the pursuit of pleasure, particularly love. Its compositions were generally asymmetrical, and its color range was light, emphasizing gold, silver, and pastels.

Jean-Antoine Watteau The Rococo found its most eloquent expression in France in the paintings of Jean-Antoine Watteau [wah-TOH] (1684–1721). This is ironic because he did not have aristocratic patrons and was little known during his lifetime beyond a small group of bourgeois buyers, such as bankers and dealers. Watteau was best known for his paintings of ***fêtes galantes*** [fet gah-LAHNT]—gallant, and by extension amorous, celebrations or parties enjoyed by an elite group in a pastoral or garden setting.

The erotic overtones of these *fêtes galantes* are immediately apparent in *The Embarkation from Cythera* in the pedestal statue of Venus at the right side of the painting and the flock of winged cupids darting about among the revelers (Fig. **11.11**). The scene is the island of Cythera, the mythical birthplace of the goddess. Below her statue, which the pilgrims have decked with garlands of roses, a woman leans across her companion's lap as three cupids try to push the two closer together. Behind them, a gentleman leans toward his lady to say words that will be overheard by another woman behind them, who gathers

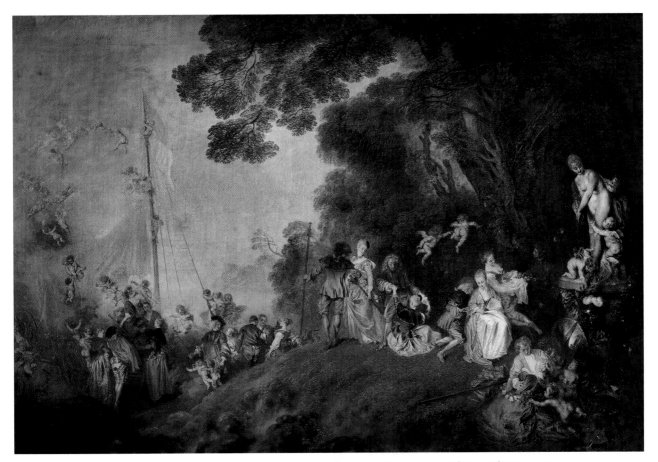

Fig. 11.11 Jean-Antoine Watteau. *The Embarkation from Cythera.* ca. 1718–1719. Oil on canvas, 50¾″ × 76⅜″. Staatliche Museen, Schloss Charlottenburg, Berlin. This painting was purchased by Frederick the Great of Prussia for his own collection. Frederick often staged *fêtes galantes* at Sanssouci, his luxurious summer palace.

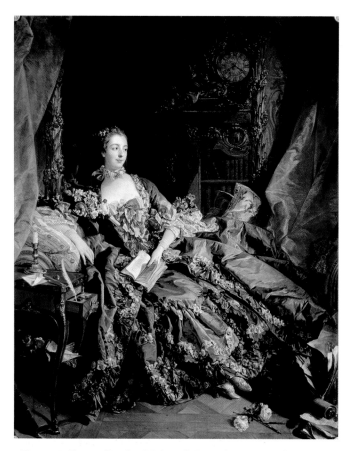

Fig. 11.12 **François Boucher.** *Madame de Pompadour.* 1756. Oil on canvas, $79\frac{1}{8}''$ × $61\frac{7}{8}''$. The Bridgeman Art Library. Bayerische Hypo und Vereinsbank, Alte Pinakothek, Bayerische Staatsgemäldesammlungen, Munich. Boucher's playful and fragile imagery, evident here in the elaborate frills decorating Madame's dress and in the decorative details on the column behind her, reflects the surfaces of the vases and urns of the Royal Porcelain Manufactory at Sevres, Madame de Pompadour's pet project.

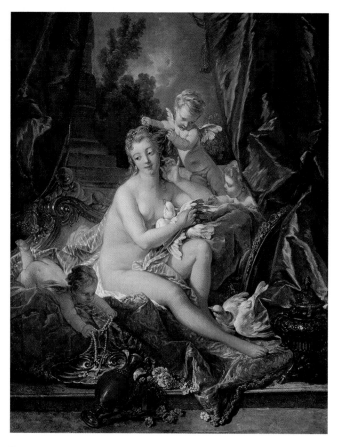

Fig. 11.13 **François Boucher.** *The Toilet of Venus.* 1751. Oil on canvas, $42\frac{5}{8}''$ × $33\frac{1}{8}''$. Signed and dated (lower right): f-Boucher-1751. Bequest of William K. Vanderbilt, 1920 (20.155.9). Photograph © 1993. The Metropolitan Museum of Art, New York. Boucher's contemporaries likened his palette, which favored pinks, blues, and soft whites, to "rose petals floating in milk."

roses with her lover as she leans over them both. Further back in the scene a gentleman helps his lady to her feet while another couple turns to leave, the woman looking back in regret that they must depart the garden island.

François Boucher Madame de Pompadour's favorite painter was François Boucher [BOO-shay] (1703–1770), who began his career, in the mid-1720s, copying the paintings of Watteau owned by Jean de Jullienne, the principal collector of Watteau's works in France. Jullienne, a manufacturer of dyes and fine fabrics, had conceived the idea of engraving Watteau's work so that a wider public could enjoy it, and Boucher was easily the best of Jullienne's copyists. Boucher himself felt he needed more training, so he set off for Rome with his profits from Jullienne. Once there, he found the work of Raphael "trite" and that of Michelangelo "hunchbacked," perhaps a reference to the well-developed musculature of his figures. By the time Madame de Pompadour established herself as Louis XV's mistress, Boucher had returned from Rome and was firmly established as Watteau's heir, the new master of *fêtes galantes*.

In the 33 years since the death of Louis XIV, court life had been relatively relaxed, and the younger king, Louis XV, essentially adapted himself to its carefree ways. He felt free to take a mistress. Madame de Pompadour was by no means the first, though by 1750 the king had apparently left her bed because, so the story went, her health was frail. But she remained his closest and probably most trusted advisor, and she happily arranged for other women to take her place in the king's bed. Given this context, it is hardly surprising that many of Boucher's portraits of Madame de Pompadour are like the portrait of 1756, which portrays her as an intellectual supporter of the French Enlightenment, reading a book, her writing table nearby with her quill inserted in the inkwell (Fig. **11.12**). What *is* somewhat surprising are his many paintings of nude goddesses in which the nude bears a striking resemblance to the king's mistress. (Boucher was notorious for such nudes.) *The Toilet of Venus*, for instance, was commissioned by Madame de Pompadour for the bathing suites of the château of Bellevue, one of six residences just outside Paris that Louis built for her (Fig. **11.13**). She had played the title role in a production called *La Toilette de Vénus* staged at Versailles a year earlier, and evidently

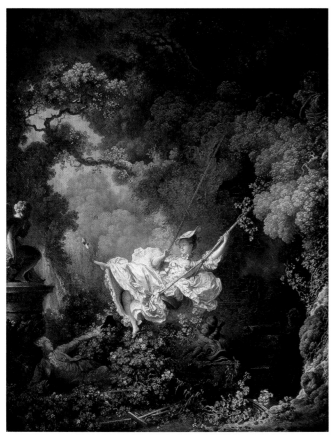

Fig. 11.14 Jean-Honoré Fragonard. *The Swing.* **1767.** Oil on canvas, $32\frac{5}{8}''$ × 26″. Wallace Collection, London. Contributing to the erotic overtones of the composition is the lush foliage of the overgrown garden into which the male lover has inserted himself.

this is a scene—or more likely an idealized version of one — from that production. The importance of the work is that it openly acknowledges both Madame de Pompadour's sexual role in the court and the erotic underpinnings of the Rococo as a whole.

Jean-Honoré Fragonard Boucher's student Jean-Honoré Fragonard [frah-goh-NAHR] (1732–1806) carried his master's tradition into the next generation. Fragonard's most important commission was a series of four paintings for Marie-Jeanne Bécu, comtesse du Barry [kohn-TESS dew bah-REE], the last mistress of Louis XV. Entitled *The Progress of Love*, it was to portray the relationship between Madame du Barry and the king, but in the guise of young people whose romance occurs in the garden park of the countess's château at Louveciennes, itself a gift from Louis.

The most famous painting in the series, *The Swing*, suggests an erotic intrigue (Fig. **11.14**) between two lovers. It implies as well the aesthetic intrigue between the artist and the patron, a conspiracy emphasized by the sculpture of Cupid to the left, holding his finger to his mouth as if to affirm the secrecy of the affair. The painting's subject matter was in fact

suggested by another artist, Gabriel-François Doyen, who was approached by the baron de Saint-Julien to paint his mistress "on a swing which a bishop is setting in motion. You will place me in a position in which I can see the legs of the lovely child and even more if you wish to enliven the picture." Doyen declined the commission but suggested it to Fragonard.

Much of the power of the composition lies in the fact that the viewer shares, to a degree, the voyeuristic pleasures of the reclining lover. The entire image is charged with an erotic symbolism that would have been commonly understood at the time. For instance, the lady on the swing lets fly her shoe—the lost shoe and naked foot being a well-known symbol of lost virginity. The young man reaches toward her, hat in hand—the hat that in eighteenth-century erotic imagery was often used to cover the genitals of a discovered lover. Even more subtly, and ironically, the composition echoes the central panel of Michelangelo's Sistine Ceiling, the *Creation of Adam* (see Fig. 7.26). The male lover assumes Adam's posture, and the female lover God's, although she reaches toward Adam—to bring him to life, as it were—with her foot, not her hand.

The English Garden

The landscapes of Watteau's *fêtes galantes* and Fragonard's *The Swing* were inspired by a new kind of garden that first became popular in England beginning in about 1720 and that aspired to imitate rural nature. Instead of the straight, geometrical layout of the French garden, the walkways of the **English garden** are, in the words of one garden writer of the day, "serpentine meanders . . . with many twinings and windings." The English found precedent for this new garden in the Roman author Pliny's descriptions of the gardens of his Roman contemporaries, translated in 1728 by Robert Castell in *Villas of the Ancients Illustrated*. According to Castell, Pliny described three styles of Roman garden: the plain and unadorned; the "regular," laid out "by the Rule and Line"; and the *Imitatio Ruris*, or the imitation of rural landscapes. This last consisted of "wiggly" paths opening on "vast amphitheaters such as could only be the work of nature." But Castell understood that such landscapes were wholly artificial. For him, the *Imitatio Ruris* was

> . . . a close Imitation of Nature; where, tho' the Parts are
> disposed with the greatest Art, the Irregularity is still pre-
> served; so that their Manner may not improperly be said
> to be an artful Confusion, where there is no Appearance
> of that Skill which is made use of, their Rocks, Cascades,
> and Trees, bearing their natural Forms.

The ideal estate was to be "thrown open" in its entirety to become a vast garden, its woods, gardens, lakes, and marshes all partaking of a carefully controlled "artificial rudeness" (in the sense of raw, primitive, and undeveloped).

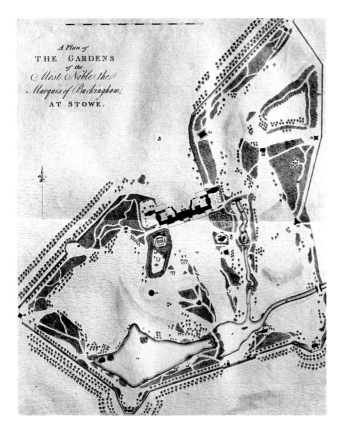

Fig. 11.15 Charles Bridgeman and Lancelot "Capability" Brown. Plan of the Gardens of the Most Noble Marquis of Buckingham at Stowe, from the *Visitor's Guide Book*. 1797. Lithograph. English School (18th century). Private Collection. The Bridgeman Art Library. This reflects the site plan of Stowe as it has appeared since the mid-eighteenth century. Although the landscape looks completely natural, it is as thoroughly designed as a modern-day golf course.

The gardens at Stowe, in Buckinghamshire, are exemplary. Prior to about 1730, they were composed of straight pathways bordering geometrically shaped woods and by lakes with clearly defined linear forms, including, at the bottom of the hill below the house, an octagonal pool. These more regular gardens were adorned by artificial Greek temples. But by the early 1750s the edges of the lakes at Stowe, once neatly regular, were completely naturalized, and the landscape had been reformed into an almost entirely pastoral setting, with wide vistas and broad views. The site plan for the garden, redesigned by Lancelot "Capability" Brown (1716–1783)—nicknamed "Capability" because, he argued, any landscape is capable of improvement—shows this more natural-looking arrangement (Fig. **11.15**).

Aristocratic visitors to Stowe would, on the one hand, have admired the Classical facade of the manor house itself. On the other, they would have discovered, in the grounds, a space in which they might escape emotionally from the very civilization that Classical architecture symbolized. The English garden, in other words, embodied many of the same contradictions as the Parisian salon, where the demands of reason championed by the *philosophes* confronted the excesses of the French court.

Art Criticism and Theory

One of the "gardens" most carefully cultivated by the French intellectuals (and those with intellectual pretensions) was art. By the last half of the eighteenth century, it was becoming increasingly fashionable for educated upper-class people to experience what the English called the "Grand Tour" and the French and Germans referred to as the "Italian Journey." Art and architecture were the focal points of these travels, along with picturesque landscapes and gardens. A new word was coined to describe the travelers themselves—"tourist."

Tourists then, as they do today, wanted to understand what they were seeing. Among the objects of their travel were art exhibitions, particularly the Paris Salon—the official exhibition of the French Royal Academy of Painting and Sculpture. It took place in the Salon Carré [kah-ray] of the Louvre, which lent the exhibition its name. It ran from August 25 until the end of September almost every year from 1737 until 1751, and every other year from 1751 to 1791. But few visitors were well equipped to appreciate or understand what they were seeing, so a new brand of writing soon developed in response: art criticism.

The *philosophe* Denis Diderot [deh-NEES deed-ROH] began reviewing the official exhibitions of the Paris Salon in 1759 for a private newsletter circulated to a number of royal houses outside France. Many consider these essays (there are nine of them) the first art criticism. Boucher and his fellow Rococo artists were the object of his wrath. In 1763 Diderot asked, "Haven't painters used their brushes in the service of vice and debauchery long enough, too long indeed?" Painting, he argued, ought to be "moral." It should seek "to move, to educate, to improve us, and to induce us to virtue." And in his *Salon of 1765*, Diderot would complain about Boucher:

> I don't know what to say about this man. Degradation of taste, color, composition, character, expression, and drawing have kept pace with moral depravity. . . . And then there's such a confusion of objects piled one on top of the other, so poorly disposed, so motley, that we're dealing not so much with the pictures of a rational being as with the dreams of a madman.

An artist who did capture his imagination was the still-life and genre painter Jean-Baptiste-Siméon Chardin [shar-DEHN] (1699–1779). Considering the small Chardin still life *The Brioche* (Fig. **11.16**), a painting of the famous French bread or cake eaten at the breakfast table, Diderot in the *Salon of 1767* wrote: "One stops in front of a Chardin as if by instinct, as a traveler tired of his journey sits down almost without being aware of it in a spot that offers him a bit of greenery, silence, water, shade, and coolness." What impressed Diderot most was Chardin's use of paint: "Such magic leaves one amazed. There are thick layers of superimposed color and their effect rises from below to the surface. . . . Come closer, and everything becomes flat, confused, and indistinct; stand back again, and everything springs back into life and shape." What Diderot valued especially in Chardin's work was its detail, what amounts to an almost

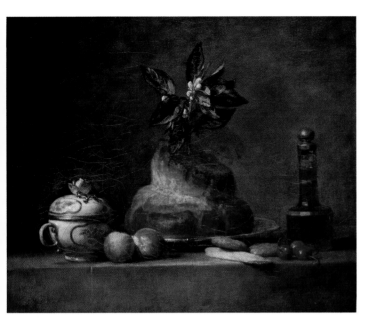

Fig. 11.16 Jean-Baptiste-Siméon Chardin. *The Brioche (The Dessert).*
1763. Oil on canvas, 18½″ × 22″. Photo: Hervè Lewandowski. Musée du
Louvre/RMN Reunion des Musèes Nationaux, France. SCALA/Art
Resource, NY. Chardin painted from dark to light, the brightest parts of the
canvas coming last.

humans had to take control of their own destinies. Deists
viewed the Bible as a work of mythology and superstition, not
the revealed truth of God. They scoffed at the idea of the
divine right of kings. The logic of their position led the
philosophes to a simple proposition, stated plainly by Diderot:
"Men will not be free until the last king is strangled with the
entrails of the last priest."

Denis Diderot and the *Encyclopédie* The crowning achievement of the *philosophes* was the *Encyclopédie* [on-see-kloh-
pay-dee], begun in 1751 and completed in 1772. Its editors
were Denis Diderot and Jean le Rond d'Alembert [DAHL-
ohm-behr] (1717–1783), a mathematician who was in charge
of the articles on mathematics and science. Both were active
participants in salon society, and d'Alembert in fact lived
with the great hostess Julie de Lespinasse. The work was
unpopular in the French court: Louis XV claimed that the
Encyclopédie was doing "irreparable damage to morality and
religion" and twice banned its printing. But despite the opposition, the court's salons proved useful to the Encyclopedists.
In his memoirs, d'Alembert would recall a conversation with
Madame Geoffrin [zhoh-fren] (1699–1777), the hostess who
was Julie de Lespinasse's mentor:

encyclopedic attention to the everyday facts of the world. As
opposed to the Rococo artists of the court, whose *fêtes
galantes*, he complained, conveyed only the affected and
therefore false manners and conventions of polite society,
Chardin was able to convey the truth of things. "I prefer rus-
ticity to prettiness," Diderot proclaimed.

The *Philosophes*

When in 1753 Chardin exhibited his *A Philosopher Occupied
with His Reading* in Paris, one French commentator described
the painting (Fig. **11.17**) as follows:

> This character is rendered with much truth. A man wear-
> ing a robe and a fur-lined cap is seen leaning on a table
> and reading very attentively a large volume in bound
> parchment. The painter has given him an air of intelli-
> gence, reverie, and obliviousness that is infinitely pleas-
> ing. This is a truly philosophical reader who is not content
> merely to read, but who meditates and ponders, and who
> appears so deeply absorbed in his meditation that it seems
> one would have a hard time distracting him.

In short, this is the very image of the French *philosophe*.

Most *philosophes* were **Deists** [DEE-ists], who believed that
God created the universe but did not have much, if anything,
to do with its day-to-day workings. Rather, the universe proceeded according to what they termed **natural law**, law derived
from nature and binding upon human society. In Newtonian
terms, God had created a great clock, and it ran like clock-
work, except for the interference of inept humanity. So

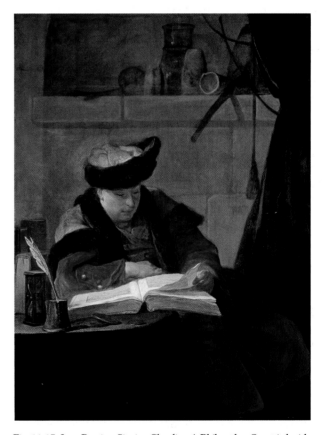

Fig. 11.17 Jean-Baptiste-Siméon Chardin. *A Philosopher Occupied with
His Reading.* **1734.** Oil on canvas, 54⅜″ × 41⅜″. Photo: Hervé
Lewandowski/ Musée du Louvre/RMN Reunion des Musées Nationaux,
France. SCALA/Art Resource, NY. This is actually a portrait of Joseph
Aved, a painter who was a friend of Chardin's.

As she had always among the circle of her society persons of the highest rank and birth, as she appeared even to seek an acquaintance with them, it was supposed that this flattered her vanity. But here a very erroneous opinion was formed of her; she was in no respect the dupe of such prejudices, but she thought that by managing the humours of these people, she could render them useful to her friends. "You think," said she, to one of the latter, for whom she had a particular regard, "that it is for my own sake I frequent ministers and great people. Undeceive yourself,—it is for the sake of you, and those like you who may have occasion for them."

It is very likely that d'Alembert was the "friend" to whom she addressed these words.

Although the *Encyclopédie* was rather innocently subtitled a *Classified Dictionary of the Sciences, Arts, and Trades*, the stated intention of the massive 35-volume text, which employed more than 180 writers, was "to change the general way of thinking." Something of the danger that the *Encyclopédie* presented to the monarchy is evident in the entry on natural law written by French lawyer Antoine-Gaspart Boucher d'Argis [boo-SHAY dar-ZHEES] (1708–1791) (**Reading 11.8**):

READING 11.8

from "Law of Nature or Natural Law," from the *Encyclopédie* (1751–1772)

LAW OF NATURE, OR NATURAL LAW, in its most extended sense, refers to certain principles inspired only by nature that are common to men and to animals: on this *law* are based the union of male and female, the procreation of children and concern for their education, the love of liberty, the conservations of one's own person, and the effort each man makes to defend himself when attacked by others.

But it is an abuse of the term *natural* law to use it to refer to the impulses that govern the behavior of animals; for they have not the use of reason and are therefore incapable of perceiving any law or justice.

More frequently, we mean by *natural* law certain rules of justice and equity, which natural reason alone has established among men, or to put it better, which god has engraved in our hearts.

Such are the fundamental precepts of *law* and of all justice: to live honestly, to offend no one, and to render unto every man what belongs to him. From these general precepts are derived many other particular rules, which nature alone, that is to say reason and equity, suggests to men.

Such thinking was fundamental to the Enlightenment's emphasis on human liberty and would fuel revolutions in both America and France. Similar thinking could be found in the sections of the *Encyclopédie* on political science written by the baron de Montesquieu (1689–1755), a deep believer in the writings of John Locke and England's parliamentary democracy. In his 1748 treatise *The Spirit of the Laws*, he had argued for the separation of powers, dividing government into executive, legislative, and judicial branches—an argument that would provide one of the foundations for the American Constitution in the 1780s. Freedom of thought was, in fact, fundamental to the transmission of knowledge, and any state that suppressed it was considered an obstacle to progress. So when Louis XV's censors halted publication of the *Encyclopédie* in 1759, the *philosophes* affirmed the despotism of the French state, even if other government officials, prompted by the salon hostesses, secretly worked to ensure the work's continued viability.

Funded by its 4,000 subscribers, the *Encyclopédie* was read by perhaps 100 times that many people, as private circulating libraries rented it to customers throughout the country. In its comprehensiveness, it represents a fundamental principle of the Enlightenment to accumulate, codify, and preserve human knowledge. Like the *Histoire Naturelle* (*Natural History*) of Georges-Louis Leclerc [leh-kler], published in 36 volumes from 1749 to 1788, which claimed to include everything known about the natural world up to the moment of publication, the *Encyclopédie* claimed to be a collection of "all the knowledge scattered over the face of the earth." The principle guiding this encyclopedic impulse is **rational humanism**, the belief that through logical, careful thought, progress is inevitable. In other words, the more people knew, the more likely they would invent new ways of doing things. Thus, the *Encyclopédie* illustrated manufacturing processes in the most careful detail, imagining that astute readers might recognize better, more efficient methods of manufacturing even as the processes were demystified.

Jean-Jacques Rousseau and the Cost of the Social Contract
Another contributor to the *Encyclopédie* was Jean-Jacques Rousseau [roo-SOH] (1712–1778), an accomplished composer originally hired by Diderot to contribute sections on music. Rousseau had been born Protestant, in Geneva, was orphaned early in life, and converted to Catholicism while wandering in Italy. He eventually arrived in Paris. Published after his death, the *Confessions* is an astonishingly frank account of his troubles, from sexual inadequacy to a bizarre marriage, including his decision to place each of his five children in an orphanage soon after birth. More forthcoming and revealing than any autobiography previously written, it explains in large part the origins of Rousseau's tendency to outbursts of temper and erratic behavior, and makes it very clear why he eventually fell out with the other *philosophes*. Rousseau was not a social being, even though his writings on social issues were among the most influential of the age.

Rousseau believed in the natural goodness of humankind, a goodness corrupted by society and the growth of civilization. Virtues like unselfishness and kindness were inherent—a belief that gives rise to what he termed the "noble savage"—but he strongly believed that a new social order was required to foster them. In *The Social Contract*, published in 1762, Rousseau describes an ideal state governed by a somewhat mystical "General Will" of the people that delegates authority to the organs of government as it deems necessary. In Chapter 4, "Slavery," Rousseau addresses the subjugation of a people by their monarch (**Reading 11.9**):

READING 11.9   from Jean-Jacques Rousseau, *The Social Contract*, Book 1, Chapter 4 ("Slavery") (1762)

No man has a natural authority over his fellow, and force creates no right. . . .

If an individual . . . can alienate his liberty and make himself the slave of a master, why could not a whole people do the same and make itself subject to a king? . . .

It will be said that the despot assures his subjects civil tranquility. Granted; but what do they gain, if the wars his ambition brings down upon them, his insatiable avidity, and the vexatious conduct of his ministers press harder on them than their own dissensions would have done? What do they gain, if the very tranquility they enjoy is one of their miseries? Tranquility is found also in dungeons; but is that enough to make them desirable places to live in? . . .

To say that a man gives himself gratuitously, is to say what is absurd and inconceivable; such an act is null and illegitimate, from the mere fact that he who does it is out of his mind. To say the same of a whole people is to suppose a people of madmen; and madness creates no right.

Even if each man could alienate himself, he could not alienate his children: they are born men and free; their liberty belongs to them, and no one but they has the right to dispose of it. Before they come to years of discretion, the father can, in their name, lay down conditions for their preservation and well-being, but he cannot give them irrevocably and without conditions: such a gift is contrary to the ends of nature, and exceeds the rights of paternity. It would therefore be necessary, in order to legitimize an arbitrary government, that in every generation the people should be in a position to accept or reject it; but were this so, the government would be no longer arbitrary.

To renounce liberty is to renounce being a man, to surrender the rights of humanity and even its duties.

This passage explains the famous opening line of *The Social Contract*: "Man is born free, and everywhere he is in chains." What Rousseau means is that humans have enslaved themselves, and in so doing have renounced their humanity. He is arguing here, in many ways, against the precepts of the Enlightenment, for it is their very rationality that has enslaved humans.

Even though he was a contributor to it, Rousseau came to reject the aims of the *Encyclopédie*, especially its celebration of manufacturing and invention. In his 1755 *Discourse on the Origin of Inequality among Men*, he argues that so long as men tried to do what they could do alone, by themselves, without the help of others, "they lived as free, healthy, good and happy men." But when men found themselves in need of working with others (**Reading 11.10**):

READING 11.10   from Jean-Jacques Rousseau, *Discourse on the Origin of Inequality among Men* (1755)

. . . equality disappeared, property was introduced, work became necessary, and vast forests were transformed into pleasant fields which had to be watered with the sweat of men, and where slavery and misery were soon seen to germinate and flourish with the crops.

Given such thinking, it is hardly surprising that Rousseau ultimately withdrew from society altogether, suffering increasingly acute attacks of paranoia, and died insane.

Voltaire and French Satire The third great figure among the Parisian *philosophes* was François-Marie Arouet, known by his pen name, Voltaire (1694–1778). So well-schooled, so witty, and so distinguished was Voltaire that to many minds he embodies all the facets of a very complex age. He wrote voluminously—plays, novels, poems, and history. More than any other *philosophe*, he saw the value of other, non-Western cultures and traditions and encouraged his fellow *philosophes* to follow his lead. He was a man of science and an advisor to both Louis XV and Frederick the Great of Prussia. He believed in an enlightened monarchy, but even as he served these rulers, he satirized them. This earned him a year in the Bastille prison in 1717–1718, and later, in 1726, another year in exile in London.

Voltaire's year in England convinced him that life under the British system of government was far preferable to life under what he saw as a tyrannical French monarchy. He published these feelings in his 1734 *Philosophical Letters*. Not surprisingly, the court was scandalized by his frankness, so in order to avoid another stint in prison, Voltaire removed himself to the country town of Cirey, home of his patroness the Marquise du Châtelet [dew SHAHT-lay], a woman of learning who exerted an important intellectual influence on him. In 1744 he returned once again to court, which proved tedious and artificial, but in 1750 he discovered in the court of Frederick the Great what he believed to be a more congenial atmosphere. While there he published his greatest historical work, *Le Siècle de Louis XIV* (*The Century of Louis XIV*) (1751). In four brief years he wore out his welcome in Prussia and had to remove himself to the countryside once again. From 1758 to 1778, he lived in the village of Freney in the French Alps. Here he was the center of what amounted to an intellectual court of artists and intellectuals who made regular pilgrimages to sit at his feet and talk.

Voltaire did not believe in the Bible as the inspired word of God. "The only book that needs to be read is the great book of nature," he wrote. He was, more or less, a Deist. What he championed most was freedom of thought, including the freedom to be absolutely pessimistic. This pessimism dominates his most famous work, *Candide* [kahn-DEED], or *Optimism* (1758). It is a prose satire, based in part on the philosophical optimism of Alexander Pope's *Essay on Man*. Voltaire's work tells the tale of Candide, a simple and good-natured but star-crossed youth, as he travels the world struggling to be reunited with his love, Cunegonde. Although Candide survives his adventures—a testament to human resilience—and eventually finds his Cunegonde, the book concludes with the famous sentiment: "We must cultivate our garden." We must, in other words, give up our naïve belief that we live in "the best of all possible worlds," tend to the small things that we can do well—thus keeping total pessimism at bay—and leave the world at large to keep on its incompetent, evil, and even horrific way.

Cross-Cultural Contact

The impact of the Enlightenment's encounters with other cultures should not be underestimated. As the exploration of the South Sea islands by Captain James Cook (1728–1779) suggested, Europeans had much to learn from the peoples of the world. Cook returned from the Pacific with sketches of peoples and societies as well as specimens of plants and beasts unknown in Europe. During the eighteenth century, China was still the largest empire in the world. In many respects, it was more advanced than any society in the West. Its people were better educated, with over a million graduates of its highly sophisticated educational system, and its industry and commerce more highly developed. It was also a more egalitarian society (at least for males) than any in the West, for, although a wealthy, landed nobility did exist, it was subject to a government of scholar-bureaucrats drawn from every level of society. As a result, China's was a society widely admired, especially by the *philosophes*, and its porcelains, lacquers, and textiles—even its garden design—deeply influenced European taste. And although the Chinese themselves continued to regard Westerners as barbarians, they began to create works of art, especially export wares, that incorporated Western pictorial traditions. In India, where Muslim leaders ruled over a people that were largely Hindu, religious tolerance supported a society in which Christians, Jews, Hindus, Buddhists, and others were invited to debate with Muslim scholars. Influenced by the presence of the British East India Company, founded in 1599

to promote trade, Indian rulers developed a taste for Western art, although their architecture remained distinctly Muslim in inspiration.

The South Pacific

By the eighteenth century, both Chinese and Indian culture were relatively well known in Europe, but the South Seas remained unexplored. This was a place, it was generally believed, from which the industrialized world might take some valuable lessons. And so, when, on August 26, 1768, Captain Cook set sail on the *Endeavor* from Plymouth, England, for the uncharted waters of the South Pacific, both he and his sponsors, the Royal Society and the British Admiralty, believed the enterprise to be consistent with the aims of the Enlightenment. While Cook would claim new territories for the British crown, his primary mission was to extend human knowledge: to map the South Seas, record his observations, and otherwise classify a vast area of the world then unknown to European civilization. Although he was careful to document the lives of the people he encountered, his primary mission was to visit Tahiti in order to chart the transit of Venus, the moment when the planet Venus crosses directly between the sun and the earth. This phenomenon occurs twice, eight years apart, in a pattern that repeats every 243 years; in the eighteenth century that was in 1761 and 1769. (Astronomers around the world watched in fascination when it occurred in June 2004, and will study it again in June 2012.) The measurement of the transit of Venus was understood to be useful in calculating the size of the solar system.

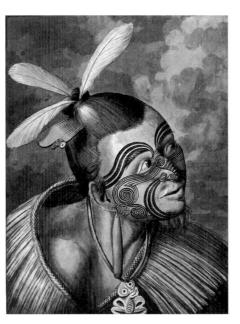

Fig. 11.18 Sydney Parkinson. *Portrait of a Maori.* **1769.** Wash drawing, 15 1/2″ × 11 5/8″, later engraved and published as Plate XVI in Parkinson's *Journal*, 1773. The British Library, London. Add. 23920 f.55. Parkinson's drawings provide some of the earliest records of Polynesian life.

The Royal Society knew of Tahiti because one of its members, the Frenchman Louis-Antoine de Bougainville [deh boo-gahn-VEEL] (1729–1811), had landed on its shores just months before, in April 1768. Bougainville's descriptions of Tahitian life, published in 1771 as *Voyage around the World*, captured the Enlightenment's imagination. Denis Diderot quickly penned a *Supplement* to Bougainville's text, arguing that the natives of Tahiti were truly Rousseau's "noble savages." They were free from the tyrannical clutches of social hierarchy and private property—in Diderot's words, "no king, no magistrate, no priest, no laws, no 'mine' and 'thine.'" All things were held for the common good, including the island's women, who enjoyed, in Diderot's eyes, the pleasures of free love. By following their natural instincts, these people had not fallen into a state of degradation and depravity, as Christian thinkers would have predicted, but rather formed themselves into a nation of gentleness, general well-being, and harmonious tranquility.

Cook, upon his return, took exception to Diderot's picture of Tahitian life. The careful observer would have noticed, he pointed out, a highly stratified social hierarchy of chiefs and local nobility, that virtually every tree on the island was the private property of one of the natives, and that the sexual lives of the Tahitians were in general as morally strict as those of the English (although women in port were as likely in Tahiti as in Plymouth to sell their sexual favors to visiting sailors). But if Cook's position seems at odds with that of the Enlightenment, it was, in its way, also consistent. The *philosophes* had argued that human nature and behavior were the same all over the world, and in his view the Tahitians proved that point. In addition, Enlightenment economists had argued that private property and social stratification were the basic features of a complex and flourishing society. Cook found both in Tahitian society, and this accounted for the general well-being of their society, he believed.

One of the most distinctive art forms that Cook and his crew encountered in Polynesia was tattooing, a word derived from *tatau* [ta-ta-OO], the Tahitian term for the practice. One of Cook's crew, Sydney Parkinson, a young draftsman on board to record botanical species, captured the tattooed face of a Maori warrior during the first voyage (Fig. **11.18**). The Maori had imported the practice from the Polynesian islands to the north.

Tattooing is an aspect of complex sacred and ritual traditions found throughout the Pacific Islands. The islanders believed that individuals, many places, and a great many objects are imbued with **mana** [MAH-nah], a spiritual substance that is the manifestation of the gods on earth. Chiefs, considered descendants of the gods, were supposedly born with considerable quantities of *mana*, nobility with less, and commoners with almost none. Anything or anyone possessing *mana* was protected by *tapu*, a strict state of restriction indicating that an object or person cannot be touched or a place entered. A chief's food might be protected by *tapu*. A person might increase his or her *mana* by skillful or courageous acts, or by wearing certain items of dress, including tattoos. Thus, the warrior depicted by Parkinson possesses considerable *mana*. This derives from the elegance of his tattoo, from his headdress and comb, his long earring, probably made of greenstone (a form of jade), and his necklace. From it hangs a *hei-tiki*, a stylized carving of a human figure, a legendary hero or ancestor figure whose *mana* the warrior carries with him.

Cook's exploration led him to Easter Island, where he discovered the remnants of a culture that had erected *moai*, monumental heads with torsos, since about 1000 CE. In the western half of New Guinea, he encountered the Asmat, headhunters who believed that in displaying the head of an enemy warrior on *bis* poles, they could possess that warrior's strength. Finally, in Australia, Cook was the first to encounter Australian Aborigines, whose rock art represents the longest continuously practiced artistic tradition in the world. Finally, in Hawaii, Cook found himself in conflict with King Kamehameha I, the first Hawaiian king to consolidate the islands under one rule, and in 1779 Cook was killed.

The Arts of the Qing Dynasty (1644–1911)

The first Portuguese trading vessels had arrived in China in 1514, and by 1715 every major European trading nation had an office in Canton. Chinese goods—porcelains, wallpapers, carved ivory fans, boxes, lacquerware, and patterned silks—flooded the European markets, creating a widespread taste for what quickly became known as **chinoiserie** [sheen-WAHZ-ree] (meaning "all things Chinese"). The craze for *chinoiserie* even reached the English garden (see *Focus*, pages 346–347). Blue-on-white porcelain ware—"china" as it came to be known in the West—was especially desirable (see Fig. 9.20) and before long ceramists at Meissen [MY-sen], near Dresden [DREZ-den], Germany, had learned how to make their own porcelain. This allowed for almost unbounded imitation and sale of Chinese designs on European-manufactured ceramic wares. Even the Rococo court painter François Boucher imitated the blue-on-white Chinese style in oil paint (Fig. **11.19**). The scene is simply a *fête galante* in Chinese costume. A balding Chinese man bends to kiss the hand of his lady, who sits with her parasol beneath a statue, not of Venus (as might be appropriate in a European setting), but of Buddha [BOO-duh]. A blue-on-white Chinese vase of the kind Boucher is imitating rests on a small platform behind the lady, and the whole scene is set in a Rococo-like cartouche.

European thinkers were equally impressed by Chinese government. In his *Discourse on Political Economy*, 1755, Jean-Jacques Rousseau praised the Chinese fiscal system, noting that in China "taxes are great and yet better paid than in any other part of the world." That was because, as Rousseau explained, food was not taxed, and only those who could afford to pay for other commodities were taxed. It was, for Rousseau, a question of tax equity: "The necessaries of life, such as rice and corn, are absolutely exempt from taxation, the common people are not oppressed, and the duty falls only on those who are well-to-do." And he believed the Chinese emperor to be an exemplary

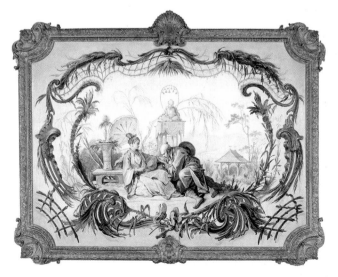

Fig. 11.19 François Boucher. *Le Chinois galant.* **1742.** Oil on canvas, 41″ × 57″. The David Collection, inv.B275. Photo: Pernille Klemp. Boucher also created a suite of tapestries on Chinese themes for the king. The style of both this painting and the tapestries is decidedly Rococo.

Focus

Europe's *Chinoiserie* Craze

Although as early as the Renaissance, Chinese silks and blue-and-white porcelains were imitated in Italy and France, the term *chinoiserie* refers to objects in "the Chinese style" either imported from China or made in Europe in the late seventeenth and eighteenth centuries. *Chinoiserie* furniture was especially popular. European furniture makers lacked the ingredients for making true lacquer, but methods of imitating Oriental lacquer (known as "Japanning") were widespread. European imitations, such as that by the German furniture maker David Roentgen, were made of gum resin and shellac, dissolved in spirits. Although usually decorated in Western motifs, the best of Roentgen's works are remarkably like true Oriental lacquer.

An important source for the irregularity of the English garden was the Chinese garden. In the 1740s, the influential English landscape architect William Chambers (1723–1796) visited China, and by the 1760s he was including Chinese architectural features in English garden architecture. His most famous design is for the Chinese Pagoda in London's Kew Gardens. Kew, in fact, became the model for a whole new kind of garden architecture that swept France in the last half of the eighteenth century, the *jardin anglo-chinois*, the English-Chinese garden.

Not everyone was enamored of the "Chinese Style," however. In 1756, J. Shebbeare complained that "the simple and sublime have lost all influence almost everywhere, all is Chinese or Gothic. Every chair in an apartment, the frames of glasses and tables must be Chinese: the walls covered with Chinese paper fill'd with figures which resemble nothing in God's creation, and which a prudent nation would prohibit for the sake of pregnant women."

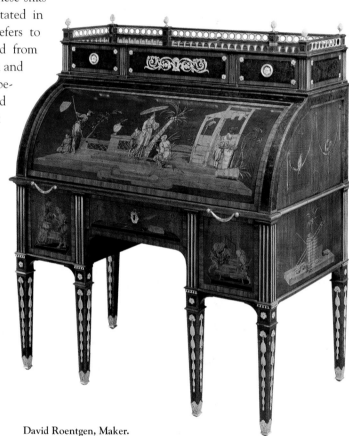

David Roentgen, Maker.
Cylinder-fall Desk with Cabinet Top. ca. 1776–1778.
Made in Neuwied, Germany. Various woods, brass, bronze-gilt, mother-of-pearl; height 53 1/2", width 43 1/2", depth 26 1/2". The Metropolitan Museum of Art, Rogers Fund, 1941 (41.82). Image copyright © The Metropolitan Museum of Art. Roentgen's desk, with its remarkably detailed inlay made of tiny pieces of various exotic woods, depicts, in its main panel, a man kneeling before his lady, but the costumes of Roentgen's characters are an odd amalgam of Chinese and Western fashions.

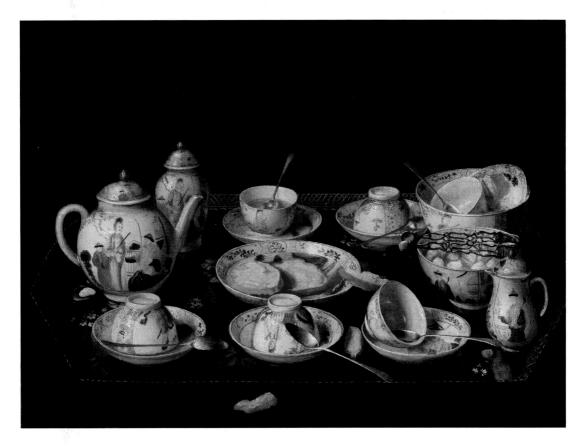

Jean-Étienne Liotard. *Still Life: Tea Set.* ca. 1781–1783. Oil on canvas mounted on board, 14⁷/₈″ × 20⁵/₁₆″. The J. Paul Getty Museum, Los Angeles, CA. Liotard represents three varieties of chinoiserie objects here. Perhaps the most important is tea, the trade in which was dominated by the Dutch. Across Europe, tea consumption rose from 40,000 pounds in 1699 to an annual average of 240,000 pounds by 1708. Liotard's still life also depicts a Chinese tea service made in China for export to Europe, and a lacquer tray, probably made in Europe in imitation of Chinese lacquerware.

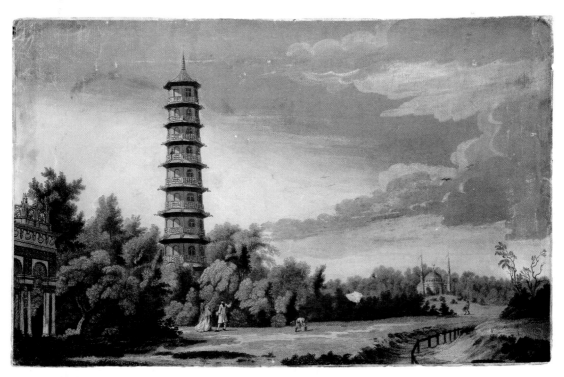

William Marlow. View of the *Wilderness at Kew.* 1763. Watercolor; sheet: 11¹/₁₆″ × 17¹⁷/₁₆″. Metropolitan Museum of Art, New York. The Chinese Pagoda was designed by Sir William Chambers (1726–1796). Chambers visited China in the 1740s, and his work on garden architecture, published in 1762 as *Dissertation on Oriental Gardening*, was widely influential.

ruler, resolving disputes between officials and the people according to the dictates of the "general will"—decidedly different from the practices of the French monarchy.

Likewise, in his 1756 *Essay on the Morals and Customs of Nations*, Voltaire praised the Chinese emperors for using government to protect civilization, creating a social stability unmatched in Europe and built upon Confucian principles of respect and service. He somewhat naively believed that the Chinese ruling class, in cultivating virtue, refined manners, and an elevated lifestyle, set an example that the rest of its people not only followed but revered. Others praised China's civil service examination system as one of the country's highest achievements, far more significant than their invention of the compass, gunpowder, or printing.

The China that the West so idealized was ruled by Qing [ching] ("clear" or "pure") Manchus, or Manchurians, who had invaded China from the north, capturing Beijing in 1644. They made Beijing their capital and ruled China continuously until 1911, but they solidified their power especially during the very long reign of the Qianlong emperor (r. 1736–1795). By 1680, the Qing rulers had summoned many Chinese artists and literati to the Beijing court, and under the Qianlong, the imperial collections of art grew to enormous size, acquired as gifts or by confiscating large quantities of earlier art. (Today the collection is divided between the National Palace Museum in Taipei and the Palace Museum in Beijing.) The collection was housed in the Forbidden City (see Fig. 9.19), which the Qing emperors largely rebuilt.

While many court artists modeled their work on the earlier masterpieces collected by the emperor, others turned to the study of Western techniques introduced by the Jesuits. The most famous of these Jesuits was Giuseppe Castiglione [kah-steel-YOH-nay] (1688–1766), who had been trained as a painter of religious subjects before being sent to China in 1715. Once there, he virtually abandoned his religious training and worked in the court, where he was known as Lang Shi'ning. He painted imperial portraits, still lifes, horses, dogs, architectural scenes, and even designed French-style gardens on the model of Versailles. A series of prints made for the Qianlong emperor celebrated the suppression of rebellions in the Western provinces (present-day Xinjiang). The print illustrated here, *The Presentation of Uigar Captives*, from the series *Battle Scenes of the Quelling of Rebellions in the Western Regions, with Imperial Poems*, is a fine example of the representation of space through careful scientific perspective, a practice virtually unknown in Chinese painting before 1700 (Fig. **11.20**). It is the kind of work that made Castiglione extremely popular in the Qianlong court, for it combines an Eastern appreciation for the order of the political state with the Western use of perspective.

But it was not at court that Western conventions were most fully expressed. In the port cities such as Yangzhou and Guangzhou, throughout the eighteenth century, Chinese artists created images for export to both the West and Japan. At the same time, Westernized ceramics became very popular with the increasingly wealthy Chinese mercantile class. Local commercial artists decorated ceramic wares with images provided by European traders, as Western trad-

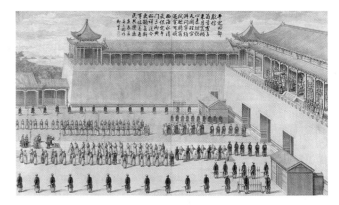

Fig. 11.20　Jean Denis Attiret, *The Presentation of Uigur Captives*. From *Battle Scenes of the Quelling of Rebellions in the Western Regions, with Imperial Poems*. ca. 1765–1774; poem dated 1760. Etching, mounted in album form, 16 leaves plus two additional leaves of inscriptions; 20″ × 34¼″. © The Cleveland Museum of Art, John L. Severanc Fund. 1998.103.14. In order to indicate his pride in the Qing military, the Qianlong emperor wrote a poem to accompany each etching.

ing companies placed large orders to meet the European demand for ceramics.

Islamic India: The Taste for Western Art

The synthesis of indigenous art traditions with Western conventions so evident in eighteenth-century Chinese art is also apparent in the art of India during the same period. In fact, in India, the synthesis is even more complex. The reason has much to do with the tolerance practiced by India's leaders in the seventeenth and eighteenth centuries.

India's leaders in the seventeenth and eighteenth centuries were Muslim. Islamic groups had moved into India through the northern passes of the Hindu Kush by 1000 and had established a foothold for themselves in Delhi by 1200. In the early sixteenth century a group of Turko-Mongol Sunni Muslims known as Moguls (a variation on the word *Mongol*) established a strong empire in northern India, with capitals at Agra and Delhi, although the Hindus temporarily expelled them from India between 1540 and 1555.

Their exile, in Tabriz, Persia, proved critical. Shah Tamasp Safavi [SAH-fah-vee] (r. 1524–1576), a great patron of the arts who especially supported miniature painting, received them into his court. The Moguls reconquered India with the aid of the shah in 1556. The young new Mogul ruler, Akbar [AK-bar] (r. 1556–1605), was just 14 years of age when he took the throne, but he had been raised in Tabriz and he valued its arts. He soon established a school of painting in India, open to both Hindu and Islamic artists, taught by Persian masters brought from Tabriz. He also urged his artists to study the Western paintings and prints that Portuguese traders began to bring into the country in the 1570s. By the end of Akbar's reign, a state studio of more than 1,000 artists had created a library of over 24,000 illuminated manuscripts.

Akbar ruled over a court of thousands of bureaucrats, courtiers, servants, wives, and concubines. Fully aware that the population was largely Hindu, Akbar practiced an official policy of religious toleration. He believed that a synthesis of the world's faiths would surpass the teachings of any one of them. Thus he invited Christians, Jews, Hindus, Buddhists, and others to his court to debate with Muslim scholars. Despite taxing the peasantry heavily to support his luxurious lifestyle, he also instituted a number of reforms, particularly banning the practice of immolating surviving wives on the funeral pyres of their husbands.

Under the rule of Akbar's son, Jahangir [juh-HAHN-geer] (r. 1605–1627), the English taste for portraiture found favor in India. The painting *Jahangir in Darbar* is a good example (Fig. **11.21**). It shows Jahangir, whose name means "World Seizer," seated between the two pillars at the top of the painting, holding an audience, or *darbar*, at court. His son, the future emperor Shah Jahan [shah juh-HAHN], stands just behind him. The figures in the street are a medley of portraits, composed in all likelihood from albums of portraits kept by court artists. Among them is a Jesuit priest from Europe dressed in his black robes (although nothing in the painting shows a familiarity with Western scientific perspective). The stiff formality of the figures, depicted in profile facing left and right toward a central

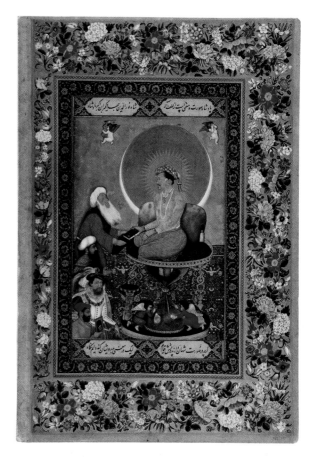

Fig. 11.22 Bichitr. *Jahangir Seated on an Allegorical Throne,* from the *Leningrad Album of Bichitr.* ca. 1625. Opaque watercolor, gold, and ink on paper, 10″ × 7⅛″. Freer Gallery of Art, Smithsonian Institution, Washington, D.C. (42.15V). Behind the shah is a giant halo or nimbus consisting of the sun and a crescent moon. It recalls those behind earlier images of Buddha.

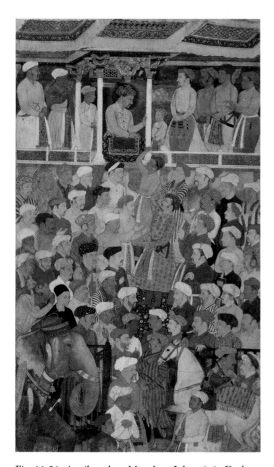

Fig. 11.21 Attributed to: Manohar, *Jahangir in Darbar,* Indian. Mughal period. About 1620. Northern India. Opaque watercolor and gold on paper, 13¾″ × 7⅞″. Francis Bartlett Donation of 1912 and Picture Fund 14.654. Courtesy, Museum of Fine Arts, Boston. Nothing underscores the Mogul lack of interest in Western perspective more than the way in which the figure in the middle of the street seems to stand on the head of the figure below him.

axis, makes a sharp contrast to the variety of faces with different racial and ethnic features that fill the scene.

The force behind this growing interest in portraiture was the British East India Company, founded by a group of enterprising and influential London businessmen in 1599. King James I awarded the Company exclusive trading rights in the East Indies. A few years later, James sent a representative to Jahangir to arrange a commercial treaty that would give the East India company exclusive rights to reside and build factories in India. In return, the company offered to provide the emperor with goods and rarities for his palace from the European market.

Jahangir's interest in all things English is visible in a miniature, *Jahangir Seated on an Allegorical Throne,* by an artist named Bichitr (Fig. **11.22**). The miniaturist depicts Jahangir on an hourglass throne, a reference to the brevity of life. The shah hands a book to a sufi teacher, evidently preferring the mystic's company to that of the two kings who stand below, an Ottoman [OT-tuh-mun] Turkish ruler who had been conquered by Jahangir's ancient ancestor Tamerlane and, interestingly, King James I of England. The English monarch's pose is a three-quarter view, typical of Western portraiture but in clear contrast to the preferred profile pose of the Mogul court, which

Jahangir assumes. The figure holding a picture at the bottom left-hand corner of the composition may be the artist Bichitr himself. Two Western-style putti [POO-tee] (cherubs) fly across the top of the composition: The one at the left is a Cupid figure, about to shoot an arrow, suggesting the importance of worldly love. The one at the right apparently laments the impermanence of worldly power (as the inscription above reads). At the bottom of the hourglass, two Western-style angels inscribe the base of the throne with the prayer, "Oh Shah, may the span of your life be a thousand years." The throne itself is depicted in terms of scientific perspective, but the carpet it rests upon is not. Framing the entire image is a border of Western-style flowers, which stand in marked contrast to the Turkish design of the interior frame. All told, the image is a remarkable blend of stylistic and cultural traditions, bridging the gap between East and West in a single page.

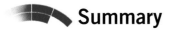

Summary

■ **The English Enlightenment** When on September 2, 1666, the better part of London was destroyed by fire, the devastation was in many ways a blessing in disguise. The city rebuilt in a way that no other European capital could imagine. Simultaneously, English intellectuals—among them Christopher Wren, whose Saint Paul's Cathedral symbolizes London's rebirth—began to advocate rational thinking as the means to achieve a comprehensive system of ethics, aesthetics, and knowledge. New developments in philosophy and science supported this thinking. In England, Francis Bacon developed the empirical method, a process of inductive reasoning, while in Holland René Descartes developed his own brand of philosophy based on deductive reasoning. From his "first principle"—"I think, therefore I am"—Descartes was able to deduce, at least to his own satisfaction, the existence of God. Scientific discoveries by Johannes Kepler, Galileo Galilei, and Antoni van Leeuwenhoek supported the philosophies of Bacon and Descartes. Isaac Newton's demonstration that the universe was an intelligible system led many to believe the state's political problems could be solved through rational thinking and the careful observation of the world. Rational thinking as a solution to commercial problems also inspired the many inventions of the Lunar Society that launched what we think of today as the Industrial Revolution.

Political strife in England inevitably raised the question of who should govern and how. In *Leviathan*, Thomas Hobbes argued that ordinary people were incapable of governing themselves and should willingly submit to the sovereignty of a supreme ruler. John Locke argued in opposition that humans are "by nature free, equal, and independent." The ruler in this case should have only limited authority. The debate between Hobbes's absolutism and Locke's liberalism underlies one of the greatest poems of the English seventeenth century, John Milton's epic *Paradise Lost*.

Deeply conscious of the fact that English society fell far short of its ideals, artists and writers like William Hogarth and Jonathan Swift turned to satire. In a more serious vein, Alexander Pope's *Essay on Man* attempts to define a complete ethical system in classical terms of balance and harmony. As the English population grew increasingly literate, the novel began to take shape as a form.

■ **The Enlightenment in France** Parisian court life was conducted in the Rococo *salons* of the city's hostesses, where *philosophes*, artists, and intellectuals gathered, and where there was a continuing tension between the aims and values of the French monarchy and the Enlightenment views of the *philosophes*. On the one hand, artists, such as Jean-Antoine Watteau, François Boucher, and Jean-Honoré Fragonard, captured the court's Rococo style in paintings of *fêtes galantes* and other erotic subjects. On the other, the *philosophes* carried the ideals of the Enlightenment forward. They rejected the rule of a monarchy and championed what they believed to be humanity's inherent love of liberty. The guiding principle of Denis Diderot's *Encyclopédie* was rational humanism, the belief that through logical, careful thought, progress is inevitable. In his social commentary *The Social Contract*, Jean-Jacques Rousseau validated virtues like unselfishness and kindness, which he believed were inherent human virtues. Finally, the satirist Voltaire challenged all the forms of absolutism and fanaticism that he saw in the world.

■ **Cross-Cultural Contact** Denis Diderot saw the peoples of the South Seas as unfettered by social hierarchy and private property, and therefore free to follow their natural instincts, which by definition were inherently good. But Captain Cook found things otherwise. He saw in South Seas societies a well-developed social hierarchy and a well-established sense of private property. European thinkers such as Rousseau and Voltaire thought that China offered a model of exemplary government. Trade with China brought luxury goods from Asia to European markets in vast quantities, creating a widespread taste in Europe for "things Chinese"—*chinoiserie*—even as the Jesuit priest Giuseppe Castiglione introduced scientific perspective to the court of the Qianlong emperor. In India, Mogul rulers in India, Akbar and Jahangir in particular, opened the doors of the country to English traders from the British East India Company. A synthetic style of representation developed, incorporating elements of Eastern and Western art in a single image.

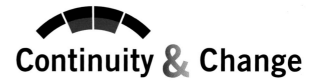
A major talent of the Rococo era was the painter Marie-Louise-Elisabeth Vigée-Lebrun [vee-ZHAY le-BRUN] (1755–1842), whose career spanned two centuries. By 1775, when she was only 20 years old, her paintings were commanding the highest prices in Paris. Vigée-Lebrun painted virtually all the famous members of the French aristocracy, including on many occasions Marie-Antoinette, Louis XVI's queen, for whom she served as official portraitist.

Vigée-Lebrun was an ardent royalist, deeply committed to the monarchy. When she submitted *Marie-Antoinette en chemise* (Fig. **11.23**) to the Salon of 1783, she was asked to withdraw it, because many on the committee thought the very expensive gown the queen wore in the painting was lingerie—*chemise*, in French usage, refers to undergarments. But the queen herself adored the painting, with its soft curves and petal-like textures. It presents her as the ideal Rococo female, the *fête galante*'s very object of desire.

Within six years the French nation was convulsed by revolution and Marie-Antoinette had fallen completely from grace. When Jacques-Louis David [da-VEED] (1748–1825) sketched her from a second-story window as she was transported by cart to the guillotine on October 16, 1793, she was dressed in a much humbler chemise and cap (Fig. **11.24**). Her chin is thrust forward in defiance and perhaps a touch of disdain, and her erect posture hints at the royal preeminence she once enjoyed. David was one of the great painters of the period, and his career, like Vigée-Lebrun's, spanned two centuries. In fact, and as we shall soon see, his large-scale paintings with their classical structure and balance explicitly reject the Rococo values of the French monarchy. Instead, they embrace the moral authority of the French people who overthrew so corrupt a court.

Meanwhile, Marie-Antoinette's favorite painter, Vigée-Lebrun, escaped from Paris, traveling first to Italy, then Vienna, and finally Saint Petersburg. In all of these places she continued to paint for royal patrons and in the Rococo style she had used in France. Finally, in 1802, after 255 fellow artists petitioned the government, she was allowed to return to France, where, ever the ardent royalist, she lived in obscurity for the next 40 years. ■

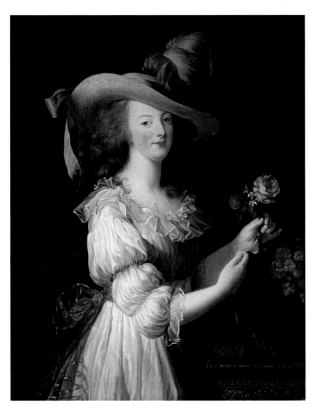

Fig. 11.23 **Elisabeth-Louise Vigée-Lebrun.** *Marie-Antoinette en chemise.* **1783.** Oil on canvas, 35½″ × 28¼″. Hessische Hausstiftung (Hessian House Foundation) Museum Schloss Fasanerie. Schloßmuseum, Darmstadt.

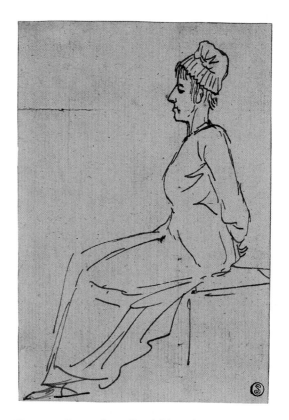

Fig. 11.24 **Jacques-Louis David.** *Marie-Antoinette conduite au supplice.* **(Queen Marie-Antoinette on the way to the guillotine) 1793.** Ink drawing. DR 3599 Coll. Rothschild. Musee du Louvre/RMN Reunion des Musées Nationaux, France. SCALA/Art Resource, NY.

12

The Age
of Revolution

From Neoclassicism to Romanticism

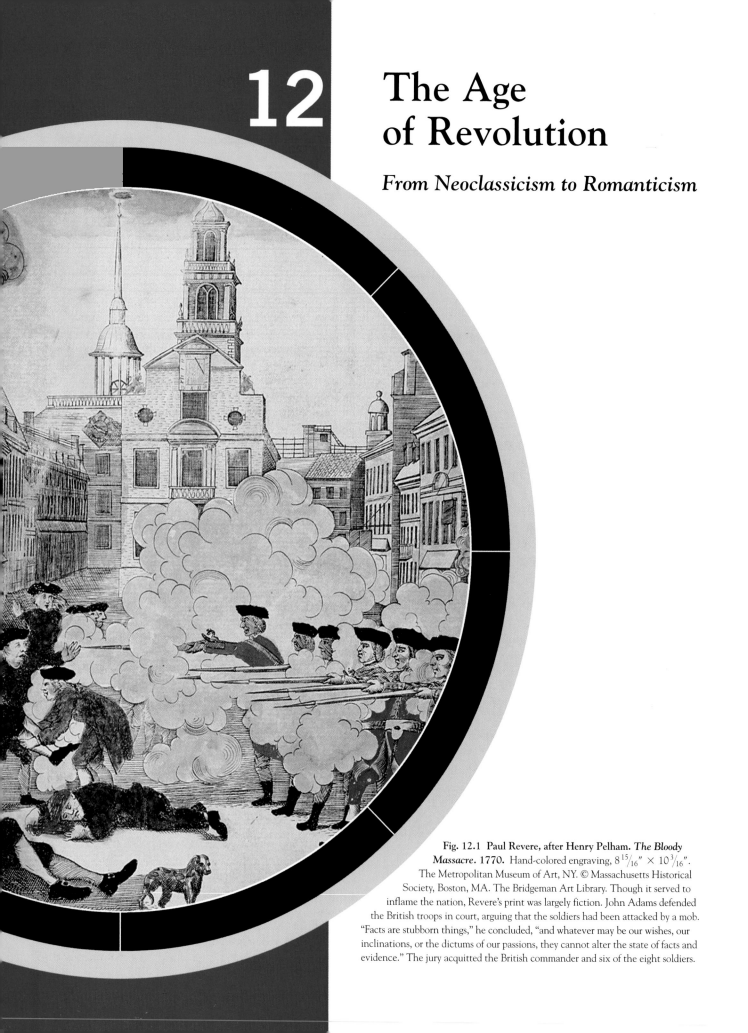

Fig. 12.1 Paul Revere, after Henry Pelham. *The Bloody Massacre.* 1770. Hand-colored engraving, $8\,^{15}/_{16}''\times 10\,^{3}/_{16}''$. The Metropolitan Museum of Art, NY. © Massachusetts Historical Society, Boston, MA. The Bridgeman Art Library. Though it served to inflame the nation, Revere's print was largely fiction. John Adams defended the British troops in court, arguing that the soldiers had been attacked by a mob. "Facts are stubborn things," he concluded, "and whatever may be our wishes, our inclinations, or the dictums of our passions, they cannot alter the state of facts and evidence." The jury acquitted the British commander and six of the eight soldiers.

"We hold these truths to be self-evident, that all men are created equal, that they are endowed by their Creator with certain unalienable Rights, that among these are Life, Liberty and the pursuit of Happiness."

The Declaration of Independence

The American and French Revolutions

The Neoclassical Spirit

The Romantic Imagination

From Classical to Romantic Music

By the last decades of the eighteenth century, the idea of freedom had become a rallying cry around which both European and American cultures organized themselves. In Philadelphia in 1785, the word "freedom" was on everybody's lips. Freedom, it was understood, would be the driving force of the new American culture, and the importance of the concept was understood throughout Europe.

In Germany, the philosopher Immanuel Kant (1724–1804) argued in his essay "What Is Enlightenment?" (1784) that the precondition of the Enlightenment was freedom:

Dare to know! "Have the courage to use your own understanding"—that is the motto of Enlightenment. . . .

[T]hat the public should enlighten itself is more possible; indeed, if only freedom is granted enlightenment is almost sure to follow. For there will always be some independent thinkers, even among the established guardians of the great masses, who, after throwing off the yoke of tutelage from their own shoulders, will disseminate the spirit of the rational appreciation of both their own worth and every man's vocation for thinking for himself. It is more nearly possible, however, for the public to enlighten itself; indeed, if it is only given freedom, enlightenment is almost inevitable. . . .

For this enlightenment, however, nothing is required but freedom, and indeed the most harmless among all the things to which this term can properly be applied. It is the freedom to make public use of one's reason at every point.

Enlightenment historian Peter Gay sums up the driving forces of the era as "freedom from arbitrary power, freedom of speech, freedom of trade, freedom to realize one's talents, freedom of aesthetic response, freedom, in a word, of moral man to make his way in the world."

Both the American colonists and the people of France chafed under the denial of the freedoms. The British had challenged the American colonies' sense of freedom since the imposition of the Stamp Act of 1765, which taxed all sorts of items, from legal documents to playing cards, calendars,

liquor licenses, newspapers, and academic degrees. The colonists were infuriated, calling it a "manifest" example of the British desire "to subvert the rights and liberties of the colonies." Tensions rose. To protect its customs agents and tax collectors, the British sent troops to Boston in 1768, and on the evening of March 5, 1770, a mob attacked a small band of British troops stationed at the Custom House, yelling "Kill them! Kill them!" The troops fired on the mob, killing five, including Crispus Attucks, an African who had escaped slavery 20 years earlier. A print of the event by silversmith and engraver Paul Revere (1735–1818) called *The Bloody Massacre* was soon widely distributed, arousing the colonists to even greater resistance, though its depiction of the troops' brutal attack on a defenseless crowd misrepresented the facts (Fig. **12.1**).

In May 1773, another law, allowing direct importation of tea into the American colonies without the usual colonial tax, was met with opposition because it represented one more instance of English interference in tax matters without the colonists' consent, and because it also removed colonial middlemen from participation in the tea trade. The following December, Massachusetts Bay colonists gathered at the Boston waterfront and cheered as a group of men dressed as Native Americans, almost all of them with a financial stake in the tea market, emptied three ships of thousands of pounds of tea, dumping it into the harbor. The so-called Boston Tea Party outraged the British, and they retaliated. Revolutionary war had begun

In Paris, sixteen years later, on July 14, 1789, a mob gathered outside the Bastille, a prison on the eastern edge of the city, upset by rumors, probably true, that King Louis XVI (r. 1774–1792) was about to overthrow the National Assembly. The prison governor panicked and ordered his guard to fire on the crowd. In retaliation, the mob stormed the Bastille, decapitating the prison governor and slaughtering six of the guards. The only practical effect of the battle was to free a few prisoners, but the next day Louis XVI asked if the incident had been a riot. "No, your majesty," was the reply, "it was a revolution."

The social changes produced by these two revolutions strongly influenced world history, and would spur the nineteenth-century revolutions in South America, again in France, and, in 1848, at the end of the Age of Revolution, all across Europe. Both the French and the Americans looked to classical antiquity for models upon which to build their new societies. When their revolution appeared to be descending into chaos, the French appealed to the Neoclassical values of a young commander of their army, Napoleon Bonaparte (1769–1821), to rescue themselves. As a style of art reflecting these values, Neoclassicism would hold sway in Europe well into the middle of the nineteenth century, but even in the last years of the eighteenth century, a new style was beginning to arise that seemed to many the very opposite of the Neoclassical. This style, which we have come to call Romanticism, is anticipated in the emotional turbulence that underlies many otherwise Neoclassical works. It values the personal and the individual—with all its psychological complexity—over the social and orderly. It praises the individual's relationship to the myriad forms of nature—from the beautiful to the most wild—over the individual's relation to the state. It distrusts the "checks and balances" that the authors of the American constitution believed would control government, and worries that its institutions would not so much free humankind as imprison it. Above all, where Neoclassicists considered human passion a threat to the stability and health of society, the Romantics developed what might best be described as a cult of feeling. To dive into the depths of the emotional world and discover whatever one might was the Romantics' goal. And much of what was found was beyond the bounds of reason, including passions like love, hatred, and the wellsprings of creativity itself.

The American and French Revolutions

The American Declaration of Independence was signed at Independence Hall in Philadelphia on July 4, 1776 (Fig. 12.2), and the French Declaration of the Rights of Man and Citizen in Paris on August 26, 1789. The American Revolution was essentially the revolt of an upper class that felt disenfranchised by its distant king, while the French Revolution was a revolt against an absolute monarch whose abuse of power had disenfranchised his own people. But both were inspired by the age's somewhat idealized view of the classical cultures of Rome and Athens, and both represent major turning points in the history of Western democracy.

The Declaration of Independence

The chairman of the committee that prepared the American Declaration of Independence, and its chief drafter, was Thomas Jefferson (1743–1826) of Virginia. Jefferson's argument came from his reading of English philosopher John Locke's vigorous denial of the divine rights of kings (see chapter 11). In *Two Treatises on Government* (1689), Locke asserted that humans are "by nature free, equal, and independent." Jefferson's denunciation of the monarchy was further stimulated by Rousseau's *Social Contract* (1763) and its principal point: "No man has a natural authority over his fellow," wrote Rousseau, "and force creates no right" (see chapter 11).

Jefferson was influenced as well by the writings of many of his colleagues in the Continental Congress, who were themselves familiar with the writings of Locke and Rousseau. George Mason had written: "All men are born equally free

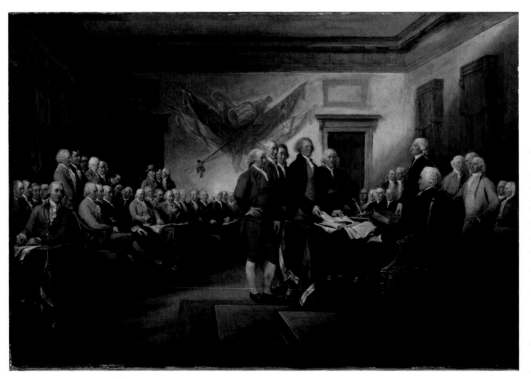

Fig. 12.2 John Trumbull. *The Declaration of Independence, 4 July 1776.* 1786–1797. Oil on canvas, 21⅛" × 31⅛". Trumbull Collection. 1832.3, Yale University Art Gallery, New Haven, CT/Art Resource, NY. The canvas portrays 47 of the 56 delegates who signed the Declaration of Independence, and Trumbull painted 36 of them from life. Standing in front of John Hancock are, from left to right, John Adams, Roger Sherman, Robert R. Livingston, Thomas Jefferson, and Benjamin Franklin.

and independent and have certain inherent natural rights . . . among which are the enjoyment of life and liberty." An even greater source of inspiration came from the writings of Jefferson's friend John Adams (1735–1826), whose Preamble to the Massachusetts State Constitution (1779) reflects their common way of thinking:

> The end of the institution, maintenance, and administration of government is to secure the existence of the body politic; to protect it; and to furnish the individuals who compose it with the power of enjoying, in safety and tranquility, their natural rights and the blessings of life; and whenever these great objects are not obtained, the people have a right to alter the government, and to take measures necessary for their safety, happiness, and prosperity.

But as powerful as the thinking of Mason and Adams might be, neither man could rise to the level of Jefferson's eloquence **(Reading 12.1)**:

READING 12.1   **from The Declaration of Independence (1776)**

When in the Course of human events, it becomes necessary for one people to dissolve the political bands which have connected them with another, and to assume among the powers of the earth, the separate and equal station to which the Laws of Nature and of Nature's God entitle them, a decent respect to the opinions of mankind requires that they should declare the causes which impel them to the separation.

We hold these truths to be self-evident, that all men are created equal, that they are endowed by their Creator with certain unalienable Rights, that among these are Life, Liberty and the pursuit of Happiness.— That to secure these rights, Governments are instituted among Men, deriving their just powers from the consent of the governed,—That whenever any Form of Government becomes destructive of these ends, it is the Right of the People to alter or to abolish it, and to institute new Government, laying its foundation on such principles and organizing its powers in such form, as to them shall seem most likely to effect their Safety and Happiness.

As indebted as it is to John Locke's *Two Treatises of Government*, Jefferson's Declaration extends and modifies Locke's arguments in important ways. While Locke's writings supported a government *for* the people, he did not reject the idea of a monarchy per se. The people would tell the king what he should do, and the king was obligated to respect their rights and needs. But Jefferson rejected the idea of a monarchy altogether and argued that the people were themselves sovereign, that theirs was a government not *for* the people but *of* and *by* the people. Where Locke, in his *Two Treatises*, had argued for

"life, liberty, and property," Jefferson argued for "Life, Liberty, and the pursuit of Happiness." Locke's basic rights are designed to guarantee justice. Jefferson's are aimed at achieving human fulfillment, a fulfillment possible only if the people control their own destiny.

A year after the colonists signed the Declaration of Independence, they adopted the Articles of Confederation, combining the 13 colonies into a loose confederation of sovereign states. The war itself continued into the 1780s and developed an international scope. France, Spain, and the Netherlands supported the revolutionaries with money and naval forces in order to dilute British power. This alliance was critical in helping the Americans defeat the British at Yorktown, Virginia, in 1781. This victory convinced the British that the war was lost and paved the way for the Treaty of Paris, signed on September 3, 1783. The war was over.

The Declaration of the Rights of Man and Citizen

In France, the situation leading to the signing of the Declaration of the Rights of Man and Citizen was somewhat more complicated. It was, in fact, the national debt that abruptly brought about the events leading to revolution, the overthrow of the royal government, and the country becoming a republic. In the 15 years after Louis XVI ascended to the throne in 1774, the debt tripled. In 1788, fully one-half of state revenues were dedicated to paying interest on debt already in place, despite the fact that two years earlier bankers had refused to make new loans to the government. The cost of maintaining Louis XVI's court was enormous, so the desperate king attempted to levy a uniform tax on all landed property. Riots, led by aristocrat and bourgeois alike, forced the king to bring the issue before an Estates General, an institution little used and indeed half-forgotten (it had not met since 1614).

The Estates General convened on May 5, 1789, at Versailles. It was composed of the three traditional French **estates**. The First Estate was the clergy, which comprised a mere 0.5 percent of the population (130,000 people) but controlled nearly 15 percent of French lands. The Second Estate was the nobility, consisting of only 2 percent of the population (about 500,000 people) but controlling about 30 percent of the land. The Third Estate was the rest of the population, composed of the bourgeoisie (around 2.3 million people), who controlled about 20 percent of the land, and the peasants (nearly 21 million people), who controlled the rest of the land, although many owned no land at all.

Traditionally, each estate deliberated separately and each was entitled to a single vote. Any issue before the Estates General thus required a vote of at least 2:1—and the consent of the crown—for passage. The clergy and nobility usually voted together, thus silencing the opinion of the Third Estate. But from the outset, the Third Estate demanded more clout, and the king was in no position to deny it. The winter of 1788–1789 had been the most severe in memory. In December, the temperature had dropped to −19° Celsius (or −2° Fahrenheit), freezing the Seine over to a considerable

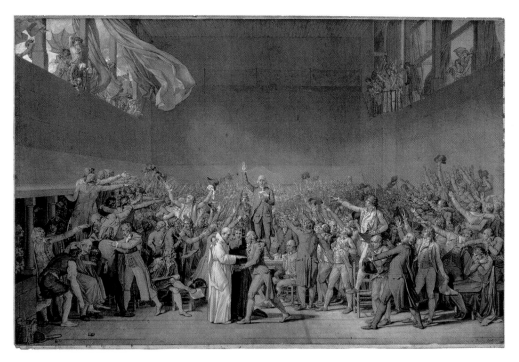

Fig. 12.3 Jacques-Louis David. *The Tennis Court Oath.* 1789–1791. Pen and brown ink and brown wash on paper, 26″ × 42″. Musée National du Château, Versailles. MV 8409: INV Dessins. Photo: Gerard Blot. RMN Reunion des Musées Nationaux/Art Resource, NY. Note how the figures in this painting, all taking an oath, stretch out their hands in the manner of David's earlier Neoclassical masterpiece, *The Oath of the Horatii* (see Fig. 12.5).

depth. The ice blockaded barges that normally delivered grain and flour to a city already filled by unemployed peasants seeking work. With flour already in short supply after a violent hailstorm had virtually destroyed the crop the previous summer, the price of bread almost doubled. As the Estates General opened, Louis was forced to appease the Third Estate in any way he could. First he "doubled the third," giving the Third Estate as many deputies as the other two estates combined. Then he was pressured to bring the three estates together to debate and "vote by head," each deputy having a single vote. Louis vacillated on this demand, but on June 17, 1789, the Third Estate withdrew from the Estates General, declared itself a National Assembly, and invited the other two estates to join them.

A number of the First Estate, particularly parish priests who worked closely with the common people, accepted the Third Estate's offer, but the nobility refused. When the king banned the commoners from their usual meeting place, they gathered nearby at the Jeu de Paume [zhurd pohm], an indoor tennis court at Versailles that still stands, and there, on June 20, 1789, swore an oath never to disband until they had given France a constitution. Jacques-Louis David recreated the scene a year later in a detailed sketch for a painting that he would never finish, as events overtook its subjects (Fig. 12.3). David's plan, like Trumbull's celebration of the signing of the Declaration of Independence, was to combine exact observation (he drew the major protagonists from life) with monumentality on a canvas where everyone would be life-size (many of his subjects would soon fall out of favor with the revolution itself and be executed). The "winds of freedom" blow

in through the windows as commoners look on. At the top left, these same winds turn an umbrella inside out, signaling the change to come. In the middle of the room, the man who would soon become mayor of Paris reads the proclamation aloud. Below him a trio of figures, representing each of the three estates, clasp hands as equals in a gesture of unity. At the actual event, all of the members of the National Assembly marched in alphabetical order and signed the Tennis Court Oath, except for one. He signed, but wrote after his name the word "opposed." David depicts him, an object of ridicule, seated at the far right, his arms folded despairingly across his chest. Faced with such unanimity, Louis gave in, and on June 27 ordered the noble and clerical deputies to join the National Assembly.

But the troubles were hardly over. While the harvest was good, drought had severely curtailed the ability of watermills to grind flour from wheat. Just as citizens were lining up for what bread was available, a false rumor spread through the Paris press that the queen, Marie Antoinette, had flippantly remarked, on hearing that the people lacked bread, "Let them eat cake!" The antiroyalists so despised the queen that they were always willing to believe anything negative said about her. Peasant and working-class women, responsible for putting bread on the table, had traditionally engaged in political activism during times of famine or inflation, when bread became too expensive, and would march on the civic center to demand help from the local magistrates. But now, on October 5, 1789, about 7,000 Parisian women, many of them armed with pikes, guns, swords, and even cannon, marched on the palace at Versailles demanding bread (Fig. 12.4). The next day, they marched back to the city with the king and queen in tow. The now essentially powerless royal couple lived as virtual prisoners of the people in their Paris palace at the Tuileries.

The National Assembly, which also relocated to Paris after the women's march on Versailles, had passed, on August 26, 1789, the Declaration of the Rights of Man and Citizen. It was a document deeply influenced by Jefferson's Declaration of Independence, as well as the writings of John Locke. It listed 17 "rights of man and citizen," among them these first three, which echo the opening of the American document (**Reading 12.2**):

READING 12.2 **from The Declaration of the Rights of Man and Citizen (1789)**

1. Men are born and remain free and equal in rights. . . .
2. The aim of every political association is the preservation of the natural and imprescriptible [inherent or inalienable] rights of man. These rights are liberty, property, security, and resistance to oppression.
3. The principle of all sovereignty resides essentially in the nation. No body nor individual may exercise authority which does not proceed from the nation.

Due process of law was guaranteed, freedom of religion was affirmed, and taxation based on the capacity to pay was announced.

For a time, the king managed to appear as if he were cooperating with the National Assembly, which was busy drafting a constitution declaring a constitutional monarchy on the model of England. Then, in June 1791, just a couple of months before the new constitution was completed, Louis tried to flee France with his family, an act that seemed treasonous to most Frenchmen. The royals were evidently planning to join a large number of French nobility who had removed themselves to Germany, where they were actively seeking the support of Austria and Russia in a counterrevolution. A radical minority of the National Assembly, the **Jacobins** [zhak-oh-behns], had been lobbying for the elimination of the monarchy and the institution of egalitarian democracy for months. Louis's actions strengthened their position. When the Constitutional Convention convened, it immediately declared France a Republic, the only question being just what kind. Moderates favored executive and leg-

islative branches independent of one another and laws that would be submitted to the people for approval. But Jacobin extremists, led by Maximilien Robespierre [rohbz-pee-YAIR] (1758–1794), argued for what he called a "Republic of Virtue," a dictatorship led by a 12-person Committee for Public Safety, of which he was one of the members. A second Committee for General Security sought out enemies of the republic and turned them over to the new Revolutionary Tribunal, which over the course of the next three years executed as many as 25,000 citizens of France. These included not only royalists and aristocrats, but also good republicans whose moderate positions were in opposition to Robespierre. Louis XVI himself was tried and convicted as "Citizen Louis Capet" (the last of the Capetian dynasty) on January 21, 1793, and his queen, Marie Antoinette, referred to as "the widow Capet," was executed ten months later (see Fig. 11.24). As Robespierre explained, defending his Reign of Terror:

> If virtue be the spring of popular government in times of peace, the spring of that government during a revolution is virtue combined with terror. . . . Terror is only justice prompt, severe and inflexible; it is then an emanation of virtue. . . .
>
> It has been said that terror is the spring of despotic government. . . . The government in revolution is the despotism of liberty against tyranny.

The Constitutional Convention instituted many other reforms as well. Some bordered on the silly—expunging the king and queen from the deck of cards and eliminating use of the formal *vous* ("thou") in discourse, substituting the informal *tu* ("you") in its place. Others were of greater import. The delegates banned slavery in all the French colonies. They de-Christianized the country, requiring that all churches become "Temples of Reason." The calendar was no longer to be based on the year of the birth of Christ, but on the first day of the Republic. Year one began, then, on September 21, 1792. New names, associated with the seasons and the climate, were given to the months. "Thermidor," for instance, was the month of Heat, roughly late July through early August. Finally, the idea of the Sunday Sabbath was eliminated, and every tenth day was a holiday.

The Reign of Terror ended suddenly in the summer of 1794. Robespierre pushed through a law speeding up the work of the Tribunal, with the result that in six weeks some 1,300 people were sent to death. Finally, he was hounded out of the Convention to shouts of "Down with the tyrant!" and chased to city hall. Here he tried to shoot himself but succeeded only in shattering his lower jaw. He was executed the next day with 21 others.

The last act of the convention was to pass a constitution on August 17, 1795. It established France's first bicameral (two-body)

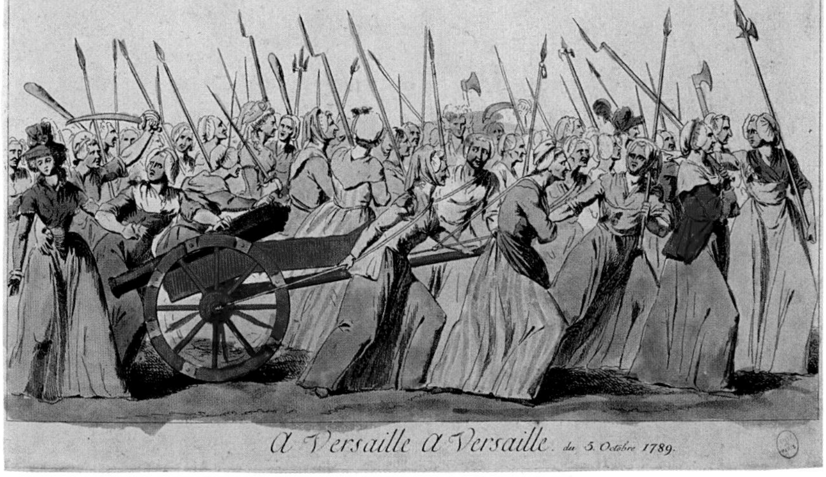

Fig. 12.4 *To Versailles, To Versailles, October 5, 1789.* Engraving. Musée de la Ville de Paris, Musée Carnavalet, Paris. The despair on the face of the aristocratic woman at the left contrasts sharply with the determined working-class women heading for Versailles.

legislature, led by a five-person executive Directory. Over the next four years, the Directory improved the lot of French citizens, but its relative instability worried moderates. So, in 1799, the successful young commander of the army, Napoleon Bonaparte (1769–1821), conspired with two of the five directors in the *coup d'état* [coo day-tah] that ended the Directory's experiment with republican government. This *coup* would put Napoleon in position to assume control of the country. He dreamed that he might lead a new classical empire—a Neoclassical empire—modeled on Rome.

The Neoclassical Spirit

The rise of the Neoclassical in France, with its regularity, balance, and proportion, can be attributed to the same ideals that would lead to the overthrow of the aristocracy in the French Revolution. The civilizations of Greece and Rome were considered as close to a Golden Age as the Western world had ever

come, and the aim of any revolution was to restore the intellectual and artistic values that those classical civilizations embodied. But France had more recent examples of order and balance as well in, for instance, the formal symmetries of the gardens at Versailles (see Fig. 10.23). The Neoclassical could also claim descent from Poussin (see Fig. 10.27) and Palladio, not coincidentally Jefferson's favorite architect (see Figs. 7.41, 7.42). But it was in the painting of Jacques-Louis David that the Neoclassical found its first full expression.

Jacques-Louis David and the Neoclassical Style

No artist more fully exemplifies the values of Neoclassicism in France than the painter Jacques-Louis David (1748–1825). His career stretches from pre-Revolutionary Paris, through the turmoil of the Revolution and its aftermath, and across the reign of Napoleon Bonaparte. He was, without doubt, the most influential artist of his day. "I do not feel an interest in any pencil but that of David," Thomas Jef-

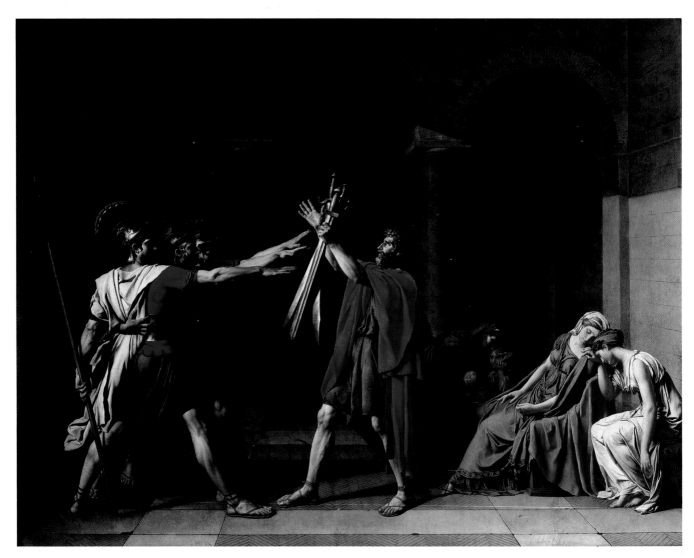

Fig. 12.5 Jacques-Louis David. *The Oath of the Horatii*. 1784–1785. Oil on canvas, 10'10" × 13' 11½". Musée du Louvre, Paris. RMN Reunion des Musées Nationaux, France/Art Resource, NY. Corneille's play *Horace* inspired the painting.

ferson wrote in a flush of enthusiasm from Paris during his service as minister to the court of Louis XVI from 1785 to 1789. And artists flocked to David's studio for the privilege of studying with him. In fact, many of the major artists of the following century were his students.

David abandoned the traditional complexities of composition that had defined French academic history painting for decades and substituted a formal balance and simplicity that is fully Neoclassical. His works had a frozen quality to emphasize rationality, and the brushstrokes were invisible to create a clear focus and to highlight details. At the same time, his works had considerable emotional complexity. A case in point is his painting *The Oath of the Horatii* (Fig. **12.5**), commissioned by the royal government in 1784–1785. The story derives from a play by French playwright Corneille, and is a sort of parable or example of loyal devotion to the state. It concerns the conflict between early Rome, ruled by Horatius [hor-AY-shus], and neighboring Alba, ruled by Curatius [kyoor-AY-shus]. In order to spare a war that would be more generally destructive, the two leaders agreed to send their three sons—the Horatii [hor-AY-shee-eye] and the Curatii [kyoor-AY-shee-eye]—to battle each other. David was contemplating painting the battle's aftermath, when Horatius's youngest son, the sole survivor of the conflict, murders his sister Camilla, whom he discovered mourning the loss of her husband, one of the Curatii.

But David chose instead to present the moment *before* the battle when the three sons of Horatius swear an oath to their father, promising to fight to the death. The sons on the left, the father in the middle, and the sisters to the right are each clearly and simply contained within the frame of one of three arches behind them. Except for Horatius's robe, the colors are muted and spare, the textures plain, and the paint itself almost flat. The male figures stand rigidly in profile, their legs extending forward tensely, as straight as the spear held by the foremost brother, which they parallel. Their orderly Neoclassical arrangement contrasts with that of the women, who are disposed in a more conventional, Baroque grouping. Seated, even collapsing, while the men stand erect, the women's soft curves and emotional despair contrast with the male realm of the painting. David's message here is that civic responsibility must eclipse the joys of domestic life, just as reason supplants emotion and classical order supplants Baroque complexity. Sacrifice is the price of citizenship (a message that Louis XVI would have been wise to heed).

David's next major canvas, *The Lictors Returning to Brutus the Bodies of his Sons*, was painted in 1789, the year of the Revolution but before it had begun. It is a more complex response to the issues of sacrifice for the state. The painting shares with the *Oath of the Horatii* the theme of a stoic father's sacrifice of his sons for the good of the state, as Brutus' lictors (the officers in his service as ruler) return the sons' bodies to him after their execution. Although received by the public in 1789 as another assertion of the priority of the republic over the demands of personal life, the painting is emotionally far more complex. That is, it seems to question the wisdom of such acts of heroism (see *Focus*, pages 360–361). Although David

would serve the new French Republic with verve and loyalty as its chief painter after the Revolution, his paintings are rarely as straighforward as they at first appear. In David's work, it would seem, the austerity of the Neoclassical style is something of a mask for an emotional turbulence within, a turbulence that the style holds in check.

Napoleon's Neoclassical Tastes

Napoleon adopted the Neoclassical style quite intentionally for propagandistic purposes—as the image of the state. Amid the threat of economic and international chaos, order was the call of the day, and Napoleon was bent on restoring it.

Seeking to lend Paris a sense of order and reason, he commissioned the construction of Roman arches of triumph and other classically inspired monuments to commemorate his victories and convey the political message of the glory of his rule. One of the most impressive works was the redesign of a church that had been started under Louis XVI but that Napoleon wanted to see reinterpreted as a new Temple of the Glory of the Grand Army. This work, commissioned in 1806 from Pierre-Alexandre Vignon (1763–1828), was to have been identified by the following dedicatory inscription: "From the Emperor to the soldiers of the Great Army." It was another of the many Parisian churches that were converted to secular temples during the revolution. Ironically, Napoleon reversed his decision to honor the army in 1813 after the unfortunate Battle of Leipzig and the loss of Spain. Although work continued on the building, its original name, the church of La Madeleine, was restored.

Not completed until after Napoleon's downfall, but nevertheless to Vignon's original design, La Madeleine is imperially Roman in scale and an extraordinary example of Neoclassical architecture (Fig. **12.6**). Eight 63-foot-high Corinthian columns dominate its portico, and 18 more rise to

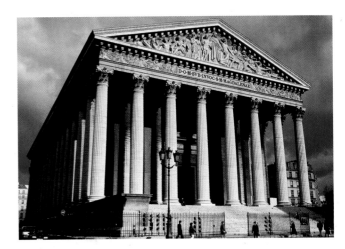

Fig. 12.6 Pierre-Alexandre Vignon. La Madeleine, Paris. 1806–1842. Length, 350', width 147', height of podium 23', height of columns 63'. The church of La Madeleine was built to culminate a north–south axis that began on the left bank of the Seine at the Chamber of Deputies (newly refurbished with a facade of Corinthian columns), crossing a new bridge northward into the Place de la Concorde.

Focus

David's *The Lictors Returning to Brutus the Bodies of His Sons*

The French monarchy commissioned Jacques-Louis David to create *The Lictors Returning to Brutus the Bodies of His Sons*, and it was exhibited in 1789, just six weeks after the storming of the Bastille. As a result, the public closely identified it with the cause of the French republic. The hero of the historical tale that is the subject of this painting is the founder of the Roman republic, Lucius Junius Brutus (6th century BCE; not to be confused with the Brutus who would later assassinate Julius Caesar). He had become head of Rome and inaugurated the republic by eliminating the former monarch, Tarquinius, who had assumed the throne by conspiring with the wife of the former king. She murdered her husband, and he his own wife, and the two married. Brutus' sons had conspired to restore the monarchy—their mother was related to Tarquinius—and under Roman law Brutus was required not only to sentence them to death, but to witness the execution.

In David's painting, Brutus sits in shadow at the left, his freshly beheaded sons passing behind him on stretchers carried by his lictors (officers who served rulers). Brutus points at his own head, as if affirming his responsibility for the deed, the sacrifice of family to the patriotic demands of the state. In contrast to the darkened shadows in which Brutus sits, the boys' mother, nurse, and sisters await the bodies in a fully lighted stage space framed by a draperied colonnade. The mother reaches out in a gesture reminiscent of Horatius' in the *Oath of the Horatii*. The nurse turns and buries her head in the mother's robe. One of the sisters appears to faint in her mother's arms, while the other shields her eyes from the terrible sight. Their spotlit anguish emphasizes the human cost of patriotic sacrifice, whereas the *Oath of the Horatii* more clearly celebrates the patriotic sacrifice itself.

This shift in David's emphasis can be at least partly explained by his own biography. Early in 1888, his favorite apprentice, Jean-Germain Drouais, died of smallpox at the age of 25. David was devastated by this loss of one of the best young painters in France. (Drouais was a winner of the Prize of Rome, which sent him to study in that city for five years.) *The Lictors* probably reflects the strength of David's feelings for his young companion.

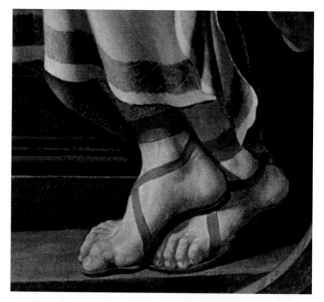

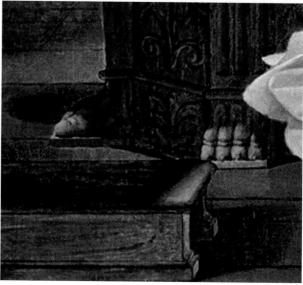

Jacques-Louis David. Details from ***The Lictors Returning to Brutus the Bodies of His Sons***. 1789. Oil on canvas, 10'7 1/4" × 13'10 1/4". Musée du Louvre, Paris. RMN Reunion des Musées Nationaux, France. Gerard Blot/C. Jean/Art Resource, NY. Brutus' emotional exile from his proper place at the table as patriarch is emphasized by the subtle analogy that David draws between Brutus' own toes and the scrolling decoration at the base of the table where once he sat.

The **statue of Roma** represents the state and is darkened to suggest the turmoil that Rome is enduring.

The **Doric order** of the architecture underscores the severity of the scene and represents the reasonable and rational order of the Roman republic—the very model of the new French republic about to be born.

David reverses the structure of the *Horatii* by having Brutus' wife extend her hand as Horatius does in the earlier painting. Now the women stand, and the males sit (or lie dead). Female emotion stands triumphant over the demands of reason.

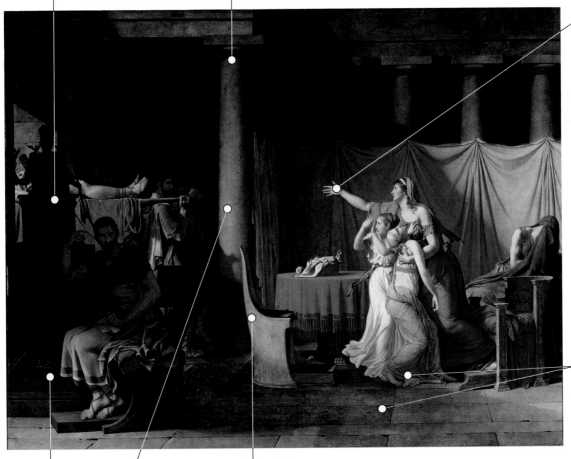

Much of the emotional tension of the painting derives from the contrast between the rigorous scientific perspective of the composition, most explicit in the floor tiles, and the soft, falling curves of the drapes and women's clothing.

The **central column** extends to the top of the painting, separating Brutus from his family and emphasizing the great gulf between them.

The graceful curve that defines the back of the empty chair in front of the central column suggests the powers of human feeling, compassion, and love. The chair is surely Brutus' own, from which he has been exiled.

The relief portraying the legend of the founders of Rome, **Romulus and Remus**, suckled by a wolf suggests how, at its origin, the Roman republic was integrally connected to the importance of family, especially after the rise of Augustus.

Jacques-Louis David. *The Lictors Returning to Brutus the Bodies of His Sons.* 1789. Oil on canvas, 10′ 7$\frac{1}{4}$″ × 13′10$\frac{1}{4}$″. Musée du Louvre, Paris. RMN Reunion des Musees Nationaux, France. Gerard Blot/C. Jean/Art Resource, NY.

the same height on each side. Beneath the classical roofline of its exterior, Vignon created three shallow interior domes that admit light through oculi at their tops that are hidden by the roofline. They light a long nave without aisles that culminates in a semicircular apse roofed by a semidome. This interior evokes traditional Christian architecture, even as the exterior announces its classicism through the Roman temple features.

Napoleon also modeled his government on ancient Roman precedents. By 1802, he had convinced the legislators to declare him First Consul of the French Republic for life, with the power to amend the constitution as he saw fit. In 1804, he instigated the Senate to go a step further and declare that "the government of the republic is entrusted to an emperor." This created the somewhat paradoxical situation of a "free" people ruled by the will of a single individual. But Napoleon was careful to seek the consent of the electorate in all of these moves. When he submitted his constitution and other changes to the voters in a plebiscite, they ratified them by an overwhelming majority.

Napoleon justified voter confidence by moving to establish stability across Europe by force. To this end, in 1800 he crossed into Italy and took firm control of Piedmont and Lombardy.   Although Napoleon never defeated the British, his principal enemy, from 1805 to 1807 he launched a succession of campaigns against Britain's allies, Austria and Prussia. He defeated both, and by 1807 the only European countries outside Napoleon's sphere of influence were Britain, Portugal, and Sweden. Through ten years of war and short periods of armed truce, Napoleon changed the map of Europe (see Map **12.1**). Everywhere he was victorious, he brought the reforms that he had established in France and overturned much of the old political and social order.

David, who had survived the revolutionary era and painted many of its events, went on to portray many of the major moments of Napoleon's career. He celebrated the Italian campaign in *Napoleon Crossing the Saint-Bernard* (Fig. **12.7**). Here he depicts Napoleon on horseback leading his troops across the pass at Saint-Bernard in the Alps. In its clearly drawn central image and its emphasis on right angles (consider Napoleon's leg, the angle of his pointing arm to his body, the relation of the horse's head and neck, and the angle of its rear legs), the painting is fully Neoclassical. In the background, as is typical of David, is a more turbulent scene as Napoleon's troops drag a cannon up the pass. In the foreground, inscribed on the rocks, are the names of the only generals

who crossed the Alps into Italy: Hannibal, whose brilliance in defeating the Romans in the third century BCE Napoleon sought to emulate; Karolus Magnus (Charlemagne); and Napoleon.

Actually, Napoleon did not lead the crossing of the pass but crossed it with his rear guard, mounted on a mule led by a peasant. So the work is pure propaganda, designed to create a proper myth for the aspiring leader. Though still four years from crowning himself emperor, the First Consul's aspirations to unite Europe and rule it are made clear in his identification with the great Frankish emperor of the Holy Roman Empire, Charlemagne. Napoleon was boldly creating a myth that is probably nowhere better expressed than by the great German philosopher Georg Wilhelm Friedrich Hegel [HAY-gul] (1770–1831) in a letter of October 13, 1806: "I have seen the emperor, that world soul, pass through the streets of the town on horseback. It is a prodigious sensation to see an individual like him who, concentrated at one point, seated on a horse, spreads over the world and dominates it."

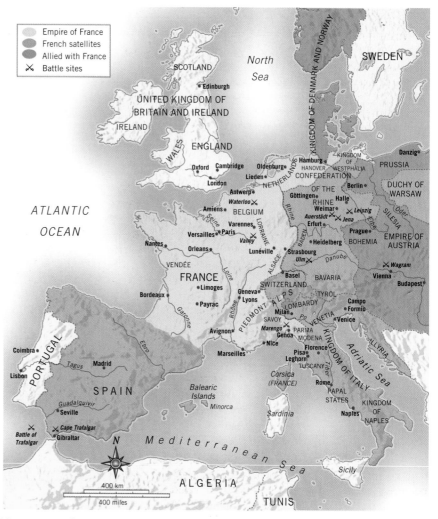

Map 12.1 Napoleonic Europe in 1807. Only Portugal, Britain, and Sweden were free of Napoleonic domination. Sicily and Sardinia, in the Mediterranean, were protected by the British fleet.

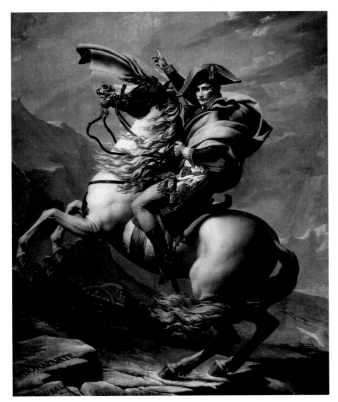

Fig. 12.7 Jacques-Louis David. *Napoleon Crossing the Saint-Bernard.* **1800–1801.** Oil on canvas, 8′11″ × 7′7″. Musée National du Château de la Malmaison, Rueil-Malmaison, France. RMN Reunion des Musées Nationaux/Art Resource, NY. David would claim to everyone, "Bonaparte is my hero!" This is one of five versions of the painting, which differ significantly in color, painted by David and his workshop. There are also many copies in French museums and elsewhere done by others.

Neoclassicism in America

Like Napoleon in France, the founders of the newly created United States of America modeled their new republic on classical precedents. Theirs would be a Neoclassical society—a stable, balanced, and rational culture that might imitate their admittedly idealized view of Rome and Athens. On October 27, 1787, a Federal Convention presented the states with a new constitution. James Madison (1751–1836) had been responsible for drafting the constitution itself, and his inspiration came from ancient Greece and Rome. (Among his papers was a list of books he thought were essential for understanding the American political system, among them Edward Gibbon's *On the Decline of the Roman Empire*, Basil Kennett's *Antiquities of Rome*, Plutarch's *Lives*, Plato's *Republic*, and Aristotle's *A Treatise on Government*.)

The Neoclassical style of architecture dominated the architecture of the new American republic, where it became known as the **Federal style**. Its foremost champion was, of course, Jefferson. Like almost all leaders of the American colonies, Jefferson was well educated in the classics and knew works such as Stuart and Revett's *Antiquities of Athens* (1758) and Adam's *Works of Architecture* well. His taste for the classical would affect the design, the furniture, and even the gar-

dens at his home, Monticello, outside Charlottesville, Virginia (see Fig. 7.42).

Jefferson's Neoclassical tastes were not limited to his private life. He designed the Virginia State Capitol (the very name derived from Rome's Capitoline Hill), in Richmond, Virginia, as a literal copy of the Maison Carrée [may-ZOHN kah-RAY] in Nîmes [neem], France, a Roman temple built in the first century BCE. To ensure that the country grew in an orderly manner, Jefferson proposed in 1785 that Congress pass a land ordinance requiring all new communities to be organized according to a grid. The measure resulted in a regular system of land survey across the American continent. It effectively installed a Neoclassical pattern on the American landscape.

The nation's new capitol in Washington, D.C., would, however, modify Jefferson's rectilinear scheme. President Washington believed that the swampy, humid site along the Potomac River required something more magnificent, so he hired Major Pierre Charles L'Enfant [lahn-FAHN] (1754–1825) to create a more ambitious design. The son of a court painter at Versailles, L'Enfant had emigrated to America from Paris in 1776 to serve in the Continental army. His plan (Fig. **12.8**) is a conscious echo of the diagonal approaches and garden pathways at Versailles (see Fig. 10.23), superimposed upon Jefferson's grid. The result is a mixture of angles and straightaways that mirrored, though unintentionally, the complex workings of the new American state. Visiting in 1842, a half century later, English novelist Charles Dickens

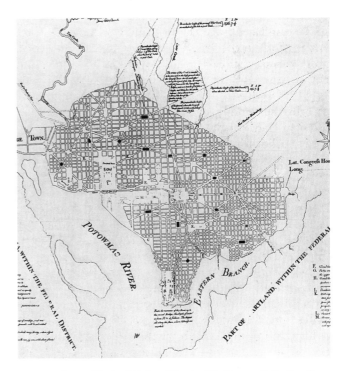

Fig. 12.8 Pierre Charles L'Enfant. Plan for Washington, D.C. (detail). 1791. Published in the *Gazette of the United States*, Philadelphia, January 4th 1792. The Bridgeman Art Library. Engraving after the original drawing, Library of Congress, Washington, DC. The architect, L'Enfant, had served as a volunteer in the Revolutionary War. He also designed Federal Hall in New York City, which hosted the first Continental Congress.

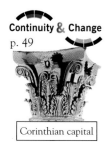

Continuity & Change
p. 49

Corinthian capital

would be struck by the city's absurdity: "Spacious avenues . . . begin in nothing, and lead nowhere; streets, mile-long, that only want houses, roads, and inhabitants; public buildings that need but a public to be complete." It was, he wrote, a city of "Magnificent Intentions," as yet unrealized. The city somewhat oddly combined Neoclassical cultivation with what might be called rural charm. When Jefferson's disciple, architect Benjamin Henry Latrobe [lah-TROHB] (1764–1820), was hired to rebuild the Capitol Building after the British burned it during the War of 1812, he invented a new design for the capitals of the Corinthian columns in the vestibule and rotunda of the Senate wing, substituting corncobs and tobacco for the Corinthian's acanthus leaves (Fig. **12.9**).

The Issue of Slavery

The high-minded idealism reflected in the American adoption of Neoclassicism in its art and architecture was clouded, from the outset, by the issue of slavery. In the debates leading up to the revolution, slavery had been lumped into the debate over free trade. Americans had protested not only the tax on everyday goods shipped to the colonies from Britain, including glass, paint, lead, paper, and tea, but the English monarchy's refusal to allow the colonies to trade freely with other parts of the world, and that included trade in enslaved Africans.

The Atlantic slave trade followed an essentially triangular pattern (see Map 9.3, p.263). Europe exported goods to Africa, where they were traded for African slaves (see chapter 9), who were then taken to the West Indies and traded for sugar, cotton, and tobacco; these goods were then shipped either back to Europe or north to New England for sale. Since the slaves provided essentially free labor for the plantation owners, these goods, when sold, resulted in enormous profits. Although a port like Boston might seem relatively free of the slave trade, Boston's prosperity and the prosperity of virtually every other port on the Atlantic depended on slavery as an institution. And the American taste for Neoclassical art, epitomized by Wedgwood's assertion that for "North America we cannot make anything too rich and costly," was in very large part made possible by the slave trade.

The conditions on board slave ships were appalling. Food was bad, space so cramped that movement was virtually impossible, and disease devastating. Olaudah Equiano [ay-kee-AH-noh], a native of Benin [ben-EEN], in West Africa, who was kidnapped and enslaved in 1756 at age 11, described the passage in one of the first bestselling slave narratives of the era. Freed in 1766, he traveled widely, educated himself, and mastered the English language. In his autobiography, published in England in 1789, he describes the transatlantic journey (**Reading 12.3**):

READING 12.3

from Olaudah Equiano,
***The Interesting Narrative of the Life of Olaudah Equiano, or Gustavus Vassa the African* (1789)**

The stench of the hold while we were on the coast [of Africa] was so intolerably loathsome that it was dangerous to remain there for any time, and some of us had been permitted to stay on the deck for the fresh air, but now that the whole ship's cargo were confined together it became absolutely pestilential. The closeness of the place and the heat of the climate, added to the number in the ship, which was so crowded that each had scarcely room to turn himself, almost suffocated us. This produced copious perspirations, so that the air soon became unfit for respiration from a variety of loathsome smells, and brought on a sickness among the slaves, of which many died, thus falling victims to the improvident avarice, as I may call it, of their purchasers. This wretched situation was again aggravated by the galling of the chains, now become insupportable; and the filth of the necessary tubs, into which the children often fell and were almost suffocated. The shrieks of the women and the groans of the dying soon rendered the whole a scene of horror almost inconceivable.

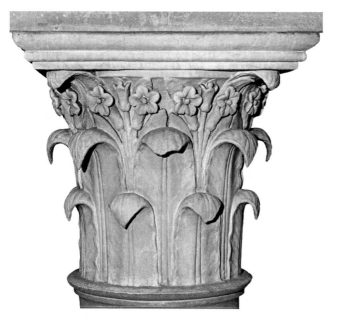

Fig. 12.9 Benjamin Henry Latrobe. Tobacco Leaf Capital for the U.S. Capitol, Washington, DC. ca. 1815. Despite this unique design, Latrobe used more traditional capitals elsewhere in the Capitol. For the Supreme Court area of the building, he designed Doric capitals in proportions similar to those at Paestum (see *Focus*, chapter 2, p.48–49).

Recent biographical discoveries cast doubt on Equiano's claim that he was born and raised in Africa and that he endured the Middle Passage (the name given to the slave ships' journey across the Atlantic Ocean) as he describes. Baptismal and naval records suggest, instead, that he was born around 1747 in South Carolina. Still, if Equiano did fabricate his early life, it appears that he did so based on the firsthand accounts of his fellow slaves, for the story he tells, when compared to other sources, is highly accurate. Whatever the case, Equiano's book was widely read, one of over 100 volumes on the subject of slavery published the same year, and it became essential reading for a growing abolitionist movement in England and the Americas.

The lot of the slaves, once they were delivered to their final destination, hardly improved. One of the most interesting accounts is *Narrative of a Five Years' Expedition against the Revolted Negroes of Surinam, in Guiana, on the Wild Coast of South America, from the Year 1772 to 1777*, written by John Gabriel Stedman (1747–1797) and illustrated by William Blake (1757–1827) (Fig. **12.10**). Blake was already an established engraver and one of England's leading poets. Stedman had been hired by the Dutch to suppress rebel slaves in Guiana, but once there, he was shocked to see the conditions the slaves were forced to endure. Their housing was deplorable, but worse, they were routinely whipped, beaten, and otherwise tortured for the nonperformance of impossible tasks, as a means of instilling a more general discipline. Female slaves endured sexual abuses that were coarse beyond belief. The planters maintained what amounted to harems on their estates and freely indulged their sexual appetites.

Slavery pitted abolitionist sentiments against freethinking economic theory. Free-trade economists, such as Adam Smith (1723–1790), argued that people should be free to do whatever they might to enrich themselves. Thus Smith would claim that a **laissez-faire** [lay-say-FAIR], "let it happen as it will," economic policy was the best. "It is the maxim of every prudent master of a family," Smith wrote in *The Wealth of Nations*, published in 1776, "never to make at home what it will cost him more to make than to buy. . . . What is prudence in the conduct of every private family, can scarce be folly in that of a great kingdom. If a foreign country can supply us with a commodity cheaper than we ourselves can make it, better buy it of them." Labor, it could be argued, was just such a commodity and slavery its natural extension.

In 1776, arguments for and against slavery seemed, to many people, to balance each other out. Economics and practicality favored the practice of slavery, while human sentiment and, above all, the idea of freedom, denied it. Jefferson himself owned about 200 slaves; Southerners generally viewed slavery as necessary for the survival of their agricultural economy. Although his first draft of the Declaration of Independence forcefully repudiated the practice, the final version failed to include this assertion. Abigail Adams (1744–1818), who, like her husband John, knew and respected Jefferson, but unlike him owned no slaves, was unequivocal on the subject: "I wish most sincerely," she wrote her husband in 1774, as he was attending the First Continental Congress in Philadelphia, "that there was not

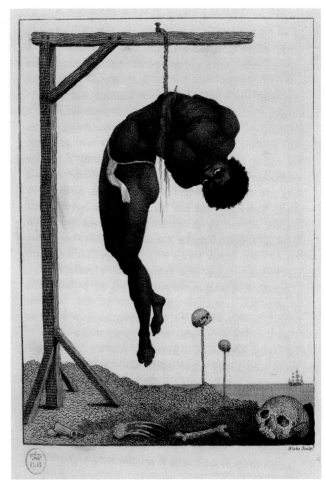

Fig. 12.10 William Blake. *Negro Hung Alive by the Ribs to a Gallows*, engraved illustration to John Gabriel Stedman's *Narrative of a Five Years' Expedition against the Revolted Slaves of Surinam. . .* **1796.** Library of Congress, Catalog no. 1835. Private Collection, Archives Charmet/The Bridgeman Art Library. Blake executed the etchings for Stedman's volume after original drawings by Stedman himself. Stedman was impressed that the young man being tortured here stoically endured the punishment in total silence.

a slave in the province. It always seemed a most iniquitous scheme to me—fight for ourselves what we are daily robbing and plundering from those who have as good a right to freedom as we have."

Many Britons, looking from across the Atlantic at the American Revolution, shared Abigail Adams's sentiments. As long as the colonies tolerated slavery, their demand for their own liberty seemed hypocritical. The English poet Thomas Day (1748–1789) described the typical American as "signing resolutions of independence with one hand, and with the other brandishing a whip over his affrighted slaves."

Abolitionist opposition to slavery in both England and the American colonies began to gain strength in 1771 when Granville Sharp pled the case of an escaped American slave, James Somerset, before the Lord Chief Justice, Lord Mansfield. Somerset's American owner had recaptured him in England, but the Lord Chief Justice set Somerset free, ruling that the laws governing another country carried no weight in England. Leading the fight against slavery were the Quakers as well as the members of the Lunar Society (see chapter 11). In 1787, Josiah Wedgwood made hundreds of ceramic cameos of a slave in chains, on bent knee, pleading, "Am I Not a Man and a Brother?" (Fig. **12.11**). He distributed them widely, and the image became the emblem for the abolitionist movement as a whole. In Philadelphia, Benjamin Franklin, president of the Philadelphia Abolitionist Society, received a set.

The Romantic Imagination

Originally coined in 1798 by the German writer and poet Friedrich von Schlegel [SHLAY-gul] (1772–1829), "Romanticism" was an overt reaction against the Enlightenment and classical culture of the eighteenth century. For Schlegel, Romanticism refers mainly to his sense that the common cultural ground of Europe—the Classical past from which it had descended, and the values of which it shared—was disintegrating, as Europeans formed new nation-states based on individual cultural identities.

Schlegel's own thinking was deeply influenced by the philosopher Immanuel Kant [kahnt] (1724–1804). In his *Critique of Judgment* (1790), Kant defined the pleasure we derive from art as "disinterested satisfaction." By this he meant that contemplating beauty, whether in nature or in a work of art, put the mind into a state of free play in which things that seemed to oppose each other—subject and object, reason and imagination—are united. Schlegel was equally influenced by the perspective on Greek art offered by Johann Winckelmann (1717–1768) in his *History of Ancient Art* (1764)—the first book to include the words "history" and "art" in its title. What the Greeks offered were not works of art to be slavishly imitated, in the manner of Neoclassical artists. For Winckelmann, and for Schlegel, the Greeks provided a new way for the Romantic artist to approach nature: The Greeks studied nature in order to discover its essence. Nature only occasionally rises to moments of pure beauty. The lesson taught by the Greeks, Winckelmann argued, was that art might capture and hold those rare moments.

As a way of approaching the world, the Romantic movement amounts to a revolution in human consciousness. Dedicated to the discovery of beauty in nature, the Romantics discounted the truth of empirical observation, which John Locke and other Enlightenment thinkers had championed. The objective world mattered far less to them than their subjective experience of it. The poet Samuel Taylor Coleridge [KOLE-rij] (1772–1834), one of the founders of the Roman-

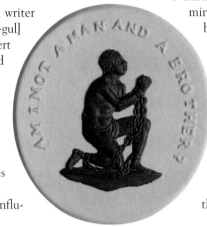

Fig. 12.11 William Hackwood, for Josiah Wedgwood. *"Am I Not a Man and a Brother?"* 1787. Black-and-white jasperware, $1\frac{3}{8}$" × $1\frac{3}{8}$". The Wedgwood Museum, Barlaston, Staffordshire, England. The image illustrated Erasmus Darwin's poem, "The Botanic Garden," which celebrates not only the natural world, but also the rise of British manufacturing at the dawn of the Industrial Revolution. The poem nevertheless severely criticized British involvement in the slave trade, which it deemed highly "unnatural."

tic movement, offered a pithy summary in a letter to a friend: "My opinion is this—that deep Thinking is attainable only by a man of deep Feeling, and that all Truth is a species of Revelation." Knowing the exact distance between the earth and the moon mattered far less than how it *felt* to look at the moon in the dark sky. And it must be remembered that for Romantics, the night was incomparably more appealing, because it was more mysterious and unknowable, than the daylight world.

Nor did they believe that the human mind was necessarily a thinking thing, as Descartes had argued, when he wrote, "I think, therefore I am." For the Romantics, the mind was a feeling thing, not distinct from the body as Descartes had it, but intimately connected to it. Feelings, they believed, led to truth, and most of the major writers and artists of the early nineteenth century used their emotions as a primary way of expressing their imagination and creativity. Indeed, since nature stimulated the emotions as it did the imagination, the natural world became the primary subject of Romantic poetry, and landscape the primary genre of Romantic painting. In nature the Romantics discovered not just the wellspring of their own creativity, but the very presence of God, the manifestation of the divine on earth.

The Romantic Poem

The Romantic imagination found its first—and certainly its most articulate — expression in poetry. By its nature poetry is inherently intuitive and personal. It is a medium capable of expressing the most deeply felt emotions. And in the beauty of its expression—the eloquence of its sounds and cadences—it might capture, even mirror, the beauty of nature itself.

William Wordsworth's "Tintern Abbey" Perhaps the most eloquent expression of the Romantic imagination is a poem by William Wordsworth (1770–1850) generally known by the shortened title "Tintern Abbey." Its complete title is "Lines Composed a Few Miles above Tintern Abbey, on Revisiting the Banks of the Wye during a Tour, July 13, 1798." Tintern Abbey is a ruined medieval monastery on the banks of the Wye River north of Bristol in South Wales, England. Its roofless buildings were open to the air and its skeletal Gothic arches overgrown with weeds and saplings (Fig. **12.12**). In the late eighteenth century, it was common for British travelers to tour the beautiful Wye River, and the final destination of the journey was the Abbey itself.

Wordsworth had visited the valley of the Wye five years before he wrote the poem, and he begins his poem by thinking back to that earlier trip (**Reading 12.4**):

READING 12.4   **from William Wordsworth, "Tintern Abbey" (1798)**

Five years have passed; five summers, with the length
Of five long winters! and again I hear
These waters, rolling from their mountain-springs
With a soft inland murmur. —Once again
Do I behold these steep and lofty cliffs,
That on a wild secluded scene impress
Thoughts of more deep seclusion; and connect
The landscape with the quiet of the sky.

The implication is that the scene evokes thoughts "more deep" than mere appearance, thoughts in which landscape and sky—and perhaps the poet himself—are all connected, united together as one.

After describing the scene before him at greater length, the poet then recalls the solace that his memories of the place had brought him in the five intervening years as he had lived "in lonely rooms, and 'mid the din / Of towns and cities." His memories of the place, he says, brought him "tranquil restoration," but even more important "another gift," in which "the weary weight / Of all this unintelligible world, / Is lightened" by allowing the poet to "see into the life of things." Wordsworth does not completely comprehend the power of the human mind here. What the mind achieves at such moments remains to him something of a "mystery." But it seems to him as if his breath and blood, his very body—that "corporeal frame"—is suspended in a "power / Of harmony" that informs all things.

Wordsworth next describes how he reacted to the scene as a boy. The scene, he says, was merely "an appetite." But now, as an adult, he looks on the natural world differently. He finds in nature a connection between landscape, sky, and thought that is intimated in the opening lines of the poem. Humankind and Nature are united in total harmony:

A motion and a spirit, that impels
All thinking things, all objects of all thought,
And rolls through all things.

In this perception of the unity of all things, Wordsworth is able to define nature as his "anchor" and "nurse," "The guide, the guardian of my heart, and soul / Of all my mortal being." Wordsworth's vision is informed not just by the scene itself, but by his memory of it, and by his imagination's understanding of its power. As the poem moves toward conclusion, Wordsworth turns to his sister beside him, praying that she too will know, as he does, that "Nature never did betray / The heart that loved her." Indeed, Wordsworth's prayer for his sister Dorothy is really intended as a prayer for us all. We should each of us become, as he is himself, "a worshiper of Nature."

"Tintern Abbey" can be taken as one of the fullest statements of the Romantic imagination. In the course of its 159 lines, it argues that in experiencing the beauty of

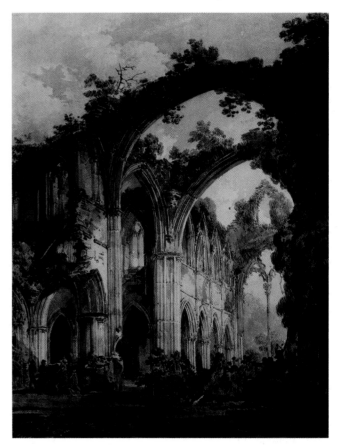

Fig. 12.12 J. M. W. Turner. *Interior of Tintern Abbey.* 1794. Watercolor, 12⅝″ × 9⅞″. The Trustees of the Victoria and Albert Museum, London, Art Resource, NY. Turner toured South Wales and the Wye Valley in 1792, when he was 19 years old. This watercolor is based on a sketch made on that trip.

nature, the imagination dissolves all opposition. Wordsworth suggests that the mind is an active participant in the process of human perception rather than a passive vessel. There is an ethical dimension to aesthetic experience, a way to stand above, or beyond, the "dreary intercourse of daily life," both literally and figuratively on higher ground. Perhaps most of all, the poem provides Wordsworth with the opportunity for communion, not merely with the natural world, but with his sister beside him, and by extension his readers as well. In individual experience, Wordsworth makes contact with the whole.

The publication history of the poem reveals something more of his intentions. On his way to Tintern Abbey in 1798, Wordsworth had stopped in Bristol to drop off a book of poems at Joseph Cottle's publishing house. He had co-written the book, *Lyrical Ballads*, with his friend, Samuel Taylor Coleridge. Coleridge had published with Cottle already, but *Lyrical Ballads* was published anonymously. As Coleridge put it, "Wordsworth's name is nothing—[and] to a large number of persons mine stinks." At the last moment, on his way back from South Wales, Wordsworth added "Tintern Abbey" to the volume.

For its next editions, in 1800 and 1802, the book was significantly revised and augmented, and Wordsworth included an important preface that discussed why poetry should attempt to reflect what he called "the language of conversation" (**Reading 12.5**):

---

from William Wordsworth, "Preface" to *Lyrical Ballads* (1800)

The principal object ... proposed in these Poems was to choose incidents and situations from common life, and to relate or describe them, throughout, as far as was possible, in a selection of language really used by men.... Humble and rustic life was generally chosen, because, in that condition, the essential passions of the heart find a better soil in which they can attain their maturity, are less under restraint, and speak a plainer and more emphatic language; because in that condition of life our elementary feelings co-exist in a state of greater simplicity, and, consequently, may be more accurately contemplated, and more forcibly communicated; because the manners of rural life germinate from those elementary feelings; and, from the necessary character of rural occupations, are more easily comprehended, and are more durable; and lastly, because in that condition the passions of men are incorporated with the beautiful and permanent forms of nature. The language, too, of these men is adopted ... because such men hourly communicate with the best objects from which the best part of language is originally derived; and because ... they convey their feelings and notions in simple and unelaborated expressions.

Although the Wordsworth of "Tintern Abbey" is no humble rustic, the aim of the poem is precisely that of the *Lyrical Ballads* as a whole, to discover that moment when "the passions of men are incorporated with the beautiful and permanent form of nature." Wordsworth further defines poetry as "the spontaneous overflow of powerful feelings" resulting from "emotion recollected in tranquility," emotions like those he recollected overlooking Tintern Abbey. The poet, Wordsworth writes, "considers man and nature as essentially adapted to each other, and the mind of man as naturally the mirror of the fairest and most interesting qualities of nature."

In 1799 Wordsworth and his sister moved to the northern Lake District, where they had grown up. Over the course of the next seven years, he wrote some of his greatest short poems, although much of the remainder of his life was dedicated to completing two long poems, *The Recluse*, a meditation on the relationship between humanity, nature, and society that he never completed, and a book-length autobiographical poem,

tracing, as he says, "the growth of a poet's mind," and published after his death in 1850 under the title of *The Prelude*.

Classical versus Romantic: The Odes of John Keats The odes of John Keats (1795–1821) represent the essence of Romantic poetry. An **ode** is a poem of exaltation, exhibiting deep feeling. Keats's life was tragically short. Most of his greatest poems were written in one year (September 1818 to September 1819) when he was deeply in love with a young woman and was simultaneously diagnosed with tuberculosis, the disease that had killed his mother. All of his great odes were written during this period.

Faced with death, in his poems, Keats strives to arrive at an awareness of its opposite—eternal beauty. This is nowhere more clear than in his "Ode on a Grecian Urn"—the beauty of art, he argues, lives on. In the poem, Keats contemplates a Greek vase covered with figures whose joy in the fleeting pleasures of life is, paradoxically, permanently immortalized in the design of the vase (**Reading 12.6**):

John Keats, "Ode on a Grecian Urn" (1819)

Thou still unravish'd bride of quietness,
Thou foster-child of silence and slow time,
Sylvan historian, who canst thou express
A flowery tale more sweetly than our rhyme:
What leaf-fring'd legend haunt about thy shape
Of deities or mortals, or of both,
In Tempe or the dales of Arcady?
What men or gods are these? What maidens loth?
What mad pursuit? What struggle to escape?
What pipes and timbrels? What wild ecstasy?

Heard melodies are sweet, but those unheard
Are sweeter: therefore, ye soft pipes, play on;
Not to the sensual ear, but, more endear'd,
Pipe to the spirit ditties of no tone:
Fair youth, beneath the trees, thou canst not leave
Thy song, nor ever can those trees be bare;
Bold lover, never, never canst thou kiss,
Though winning near the goal—yet, do not grieve;
She cannot fade, though thou hast not thy bliss,
For ever wilt thou love, and she be fair!

Ah, happy, happy boughs! that cannot shed
Your leaves, nor ever bid the spring adieu;
And, happy melodist, unwearied,
For ever piping songs for ever new;
More happy love! more happy, happy love!
For ever warm and still to be enjoy'd,
For ever panting, and for ever young;
All breathing human passion far above,
That leaves a heart high-sorrowful and cloy'd,
A burning forehead, and a parching tongue.

Who are these coming to the sacrifice?
To what green altar, O mysterious priest,
Lead'st thou that heifer lowing at the skies,
And all her silken flanks with garlands drest?
What little town by river or sea shore,
Or mountain-built with peaceful citadel,
Is emptied of this folk, this pious morn?
And, little town, thy streets for evermore
Will silent be; and not a soul to tell
Why thou art desolate, can e'er return.

O Attic shape! Fair attitude! with brede
Of marble men and maidens overwrought,
With forest branches and the trodden weed;
Thou, silent form, dost tease us out of thought
As doth eternity: Cold Pastoral!
When old age shall this generation waste,
Thou shalt remain, in midst of other woe
Than ours, a friend to man, to whom thou say'st,
"Beauty is truth, truth beauty,"—that is all
Ye know on earth, and all ye need to know.

Contemplating a Greek vase—probably a composite "ideal" vase made up of scenes derived from those in the collection of the British Museum—Keats admits ignorance about the symbolism of the decorative motifs and what "deities or mortals, or both" are painted on it. Yet the vase's scenes come alive in his imagination and are all the more poignant for being eternal, unchangeable, and silent. The melodies being played by the musicians illustrated on the vase, if anyone were to hear them, would, of course, be beautiful, "but those unheard / Are sweeter." The trees can never lose their leaves. And though the lover will never succeed in kissing his love, thus painted, he can take solace in the fact that she "cannot fade" and will be forever fair. He imagines that the people who populate the vase have been drawn out of some "little town," the streets of which are now forever silent. Then, to conclude, the poet addresses the vase directly: "O Attic shape," he says, when we are dead, you shall remain a "friend to man." The vase imparts an important message to humankind:

"Beauty is truth, truth beauty,"—that is all
Ye know on earth, and all ye need to know.

These last two lines are possibly the most discussed and debated in English poetry. They suggest that the vase, and by extension the poem itself, is a higher form of nature than mortal life. This is, of course, a traditional theme of poetry, but in the context of Keats's own tragic struggle with tuberculosis and his imminent death, it takes on a stunningly poignant and deeply Romantic tone. Rather than being terrified by the prospect of mortality, the individual contests death and exalts in the confrontation. Perhaps the poem's greatest achievement is that it dissolves the greatest opposition of them all, uniting life and death in the circularity of the "leaf-fring'd legend" that draws the viewers' eyes around

the vase's shape. In February 1821, a few months after his twenty-fifth birthday, Keats died in Rome, survived only by his posthumously published poems.

The Romantic Landscape

The most notable landscape painting in Europe had developed in Italy and the Netherlands 200 years earlier. Even the term "landscape" derives from the Dutch word "landschap," meaning a patch of cultivated ground. Although influenced by Italian artists' use of light and color, the great seventeenth-century Dutch landscape painters, including Jacob van Ruisdael (see Fig. 10.14), were also inspired by a dramatically changing physical geography sparked by the reclamation of hundreds of thousands of acres of land along the coasts. The Dutch landscape painters in turn influenced later English landscape painters.

John Constable: Painter of the English Countryside Tension between the timeless and the more fleeting aspects of nature deeply informs the paintings of John Constable (1776–1837). Constable focused most of his efforts on the area around the valley of the Stour River in his native East Bergholt, Suffolk. Like Wordsworth, he felt his talents depended on "faithful adherence to the truth of nature." "Nature," he wrote, "is the fountain's head, the source from which all originally must spring."

Like Wordsworth, Constable believed that his art could be traced back to his childhood on the Stour, to places that he had known his whole life. "I should paint my own places best," he wrote to a friend in 1821, "I associate my 'careless boyhood' to all that lies on the banks of the Stour. They made me a painter (& I am grateful)." Like Wordsworth, Constable also wished to depict incidents and situations from common life, including villages, churches, farmhouses, and cottages. But most of all, Constable was, like Wordsworth, "a worshipper of Nature." As Constable wrote in a letter of May 1819, "Every tree seems full of blossom of some kind & the surface of the ground seems quite living—every step I take & on whatever object I turn my Eye that sublime expression of the Scripture 'I am the resurrection and the life' &c, seems verified about me." In fact, the cathedral at the center of so many Constable landscapes symbolizes the permanence of God in nature.

From 1819 to 1825, Constable worked on a series of what he referred to as his "six-footers," all large canvases depicting scenes on the Stour painted in his London studio from sketches and drawings done earlier, of which *The Hay Wain* (Fig. **12.13**) is one. The painting contains more than one state of mind—the passing storm, indicated by the darkened clouds on the left, contrasts with the brightly lit field below the billowing clouds at the right, the longevity of the tree behind the house with its massive trunk contrasts with the freshly cut hay at the right, the gentleman fisherman contrasts with the hard-working cart drivers. The house is Willy Lott's. Lott lived in the house his entire 80 years, spending only four nights of his life away from it. For Constable, the

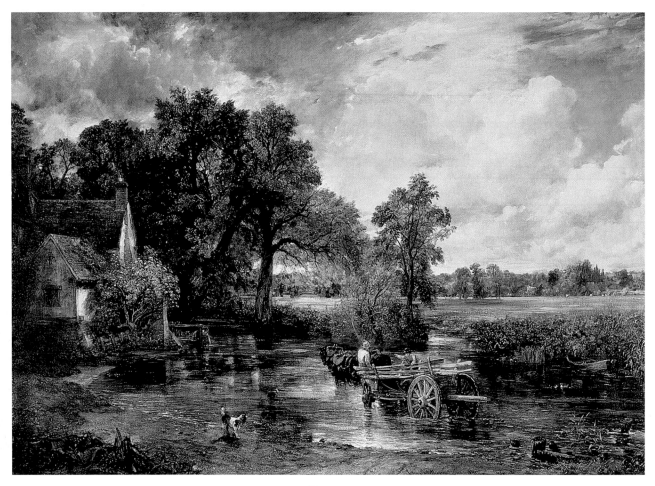

Fig. 12.13 John Constable. *The Hay Wain.* **1821.** Oil on canvas, 51 3/8″ × 73″. The National Gallery, London.
Constable failed to sell *The Hay Wain* when it was exhibited at the Royal Academy in 1821, though he turned down an
offer of £70 for it.

house symbolized a stability and permanence that contrasts dramatically with the impermanence of the weather, the constant flux of light and shadow, sun and cloud.

When the painting was first exhibited at the Royal Academy in 1821, Londoners could not accept that this was a "finished" painting because it had been painted in economic, almost abstract terms. Constable used short, broken strokes of color in a variety of shades and tints to produce a given hue (the green of foliage, for example). Nor did they understand how such a common theme deserved such a monumental canvas. Constable subsequently complained to a friend, "Londoners with all their ingenuity as artists know nothing of the feeling of a country life (the essence of Landscape)—any more than a hackney coach horse knows of pasture."

Joseph Mallord William Turner: Colorist of the Imagination The other great English landscape painter of the day, Joseph Mallord William Turner (1775–1851), freely explored what he called "the colors of the imagination." Even his contemporaries recognized, in the words of the critic William Hazlitt (1778–1830), that Turner was interested less in "the

objects of nature than . . . the medium through which they are seen." In Turner's paintings earth and vegetation seem to dissolve into light and water, into the very medium—gleaming oil or translucent watercolor—with which he paints them. In *The Upper Falls of the Reichenbach* [RY-khun-bahk], for instance, Turner's depiction of the falls, among the highest in the Swiss Alps, seems to animate the rocky precipice (Fig. **12.14**). Turner draws our attention not to the rock, cliff, and mountain, but to the mist and light through which we see them.

Perhaps the best way to understand the difference between Constable and Turner is to consider the *scale* of their respective visions. Constable's work is "close," nearby and familiar, with an abundance of human associations. Turner's is exotic, remote, and even alienating. The human figure in Constable's paintings is an essential and elemental presence, uniting man and nature. The human figure in Turner's paintings is minuscule, almost irrelevant to the painting except insofar as its minuteness underscores nature's very indifference. Not only is *The Upper Falls of the Reichenbach* removed from the close-at-hand world of

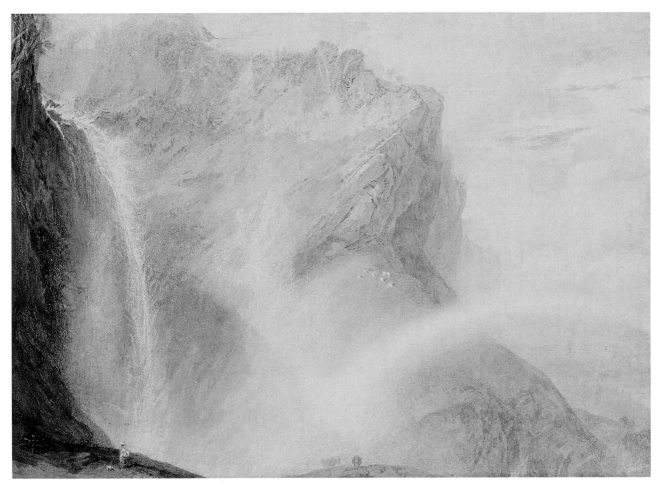

Fig. 12.14 J. M. W. Turner. *The Upper Falls of the Reichenbach.* ca. 1810–1815. Watercolor, $10^7/_8'' \times 15^7/_{16}''$.
Yale Center for British Art, Paul Mellon Collection. The Bridgeman Art Library. Turner achieved the transparent effect
of the rainbow and the spray rising from the falls by scraping away the watercolor down to the white paper beneath.

Constable's paintings, but the cowherd and his dog, barely visible at the lower left of the painting, are dwarfed by the immensity of the scene. Cattle graze on the rise at the bottom middle, and another herd is on the ridge across the gorge. The effect is similar to that described by Wordsworth in "Tintern Abbey":

And I have felt
A presence that disturbs me with the joy
Of elevated thought; a sense sublime
Of something far more deeply interfused,
Whose dwelling is the light of setting suns,
And the round ocean and the living air
And the blue sky, and in the mind of man:
A motion and a spirit, that impels
All thinking things, all objects of all thought,
And rolls through all things.

We must keep in mind, though, nature is never altogether benign or kind. The viewer has nowhere to stand, except in the path of nature's force. A painting like *Snow Storm—Steam-Boat off a Harbour's Mouth* (Fig. **12.15**) suggests the "extinction" of the very "hope of man"—a sentiment far removed from Constable's pastoral landscapes or Wordsworth's "natural piety." Originally subtitled *The author was in this storm on the night the Ariel left Harwich,* the painting is the record of the immersion of the self (and the viewer) into the primal forces of nature. "I wished to show," Turner said, "what such a scene was like. I got the sailors to lash me to the mast to observe it . . . and I did not expect to escape: but I felt bound to record it if I did." We have no evidence confirming a ship named *Ariel.* Most likely, Turner imagined this scene of a maelstrom of steam and storm that deposits us at its very heart. We descend into Turner's chaos of light and dark, the very opposite of the Enlightenment ideal of the natural world characterized by clarity, order, and harmony. The feeling of terror at the chaotic vastness of nature is termed the **sublime**.

The Romantic in Germany: Friedrich and Kant Although Constable and Turner's approaches are very different, both believed that nature provoked their imaginations. In the German Romantic tradition, the imagination is also the

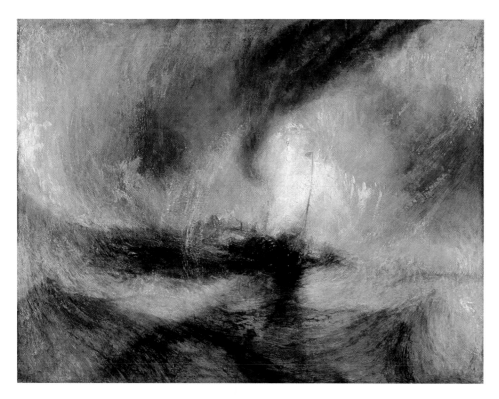

Fig. 12.15 J. M. W. Turner. *Snow Storm—Steam-Boat off a Harbour's Mouth.* **1842.** Oil on canvas, 36″ × 48″. Clore Collection, Tate Gallery, London/Art Resource, NY. Turner bequeathed 19,049 drawings and watercolors to the British nation. Many of these works anticipate the gestural freedom of this painting, with its sweeping linear rhythms.

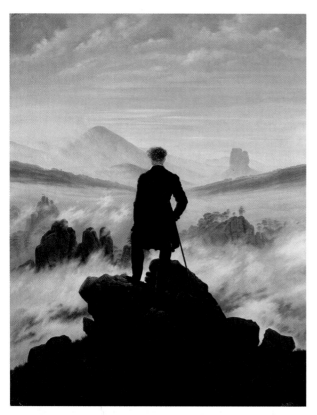

Fig. 12.16 Caspar David Friedrich. *Wanderer above the Mists.* **ca. 1817–1818.** Oil on canvas, 37 1/4″ × 29 1/2″. Inv.: 5161. On permanent loan from the Foundation for the Promotion of the Hamburg Art Collections. Photo: Elke Walford. Hamburger Kunsthalle, Hamburg, Germany. Bildarchiv Preussischer Kulturbesitz/Art Resource, NY. The artist's identification with nature is underscored by the analogy Friedrich establishes between the figure's head and the distant rock at the right.

fundamental starting point. The painter Caspar David Friedrich [FREED-rikh] (1774–1840) represents the imaginative capacities of the Romantic mind by placing figures, often solitary ones, in sublime landscapes. In his *Wanderer above the Mists*, Friedrich pictures a lone man with windblown hair on a precipice (Fig. **12.16**). We can view him as a projection of ourselves. His view is interrupted by the vast expanse of mist just as ours is cut off by the outcropping of rock. The full magnificence of the scene is only hinted at, a vague promise of eventual revelation. Friedrich, in fact, had this to say about the value of uncertainty:

> If your imagination is poor, and in fog you see nothing but gray, then an aversion to vagueness is understandable. All the same, a landscape enveloped in mist seems vaster, more sublime, and it animates the imagination while also heightening suspense—like a veiled woman. The eye and the imagination are generally more intrigued by vaporous distances than by a nearby object available to the eye.

The viewer's imagination is further stimulated by the contrast between near and far, between the rock in the foreground and the ethereal atmosphere stretching into the distance—that is, between the earthly and spiritual realms.

The theme of doubt is a constant in Friedrich's paintings, but more as a stimulant to the imagination than a source of anxiety and tension. These sentiments echo the philosopher Immanuel Kant's *Critique of Pure Reason* (1781), in which Kant had argued that the mind is not a passive recipient of information—not, that is, the "blank slate" that Locke had claimed. For Kant, the mind is an active agent in the creation of knowledge. He believed that the ways we understand concepts like space, time, quantity, the relations among things, and, especially, quality, are innate from birth. We come to understand the world through the operation of these innate mental abilities as they perceive the various aspects of experience. Each of our experiences is various as well, and so each mind creates its own body of knowledge, its own world. No longer was the nature of reality the most important question. Instead, the mind confronting reality was paramount. Kant shifted the basic question of philosophy, in other words, from What do we know? to How do we know?—even to How do we know that we know?

The Romantic Hero

So stunningly successful were Napoleon's military campaigns, so fierce was his dedication to the principles of liberty, fraternity, and equality (abolishing serfdom throughout much of Europe), and so brilliant was his reorganization of the government, the educational system, and civil law, that in the first years of the nineteenth century, he seemed to many a savior. As well as being a national icon, Napoleon was the very personification of the Romantic hero, a man of common origin who had risen, through sheer wit and tenacity, to dominate the world stage.

But the promise of Napoleon—his ability to impose classical values of order, control, and rationality upon a French society that had been wracked with revolution and turmoil—was undermined by a darker reality. The Romantics, whose fascination with the powers of individual intuition and creativity had led them to lionize Napoleon, would react to his ultimate defeat and to the ensuing disorder that marked the first half of the nineteenth century with a profound pessimism about the course of human events.

To the Romantic imagination, Napoleon was something of a Promethean figure. In Greek myth, Prometheus [pro-MEE-thee-us] is a member of the race of deities known as Titans. Prometheus stole fire from the sun and gave it to humankind, to whom Zeus, ruler of the Gods, had denied it. For this crime Zeus chained him to a rock, where an eagle fed daily on his liver, which was restored each night, so that he might suffer the same punishment day after day. On the one hand, the Romantics revered him as the all-suffering but ever noble champion of human freedom. But on the other, in his reckless ambition to achieve his goals by breaking the laws imposed by supreme authority, as well as in his endless suffering, they also recognized in Prometheus a certain futility and despair.

The Promethean Idea in England: Lord Byron and the Shelleys For poet George Gordon, Lord Byron (1788–1824), Prometheus was the embodiment of his own emphatic spirit of individualism. Byron was a prodigious traveler to foreign countries, a sexual experimenter, and a champion of oppressed nations. In his 1816 ode "Prometheus," Byron rehearses the myth as described in

Aeschylus' play *Prometheus Bound*, and then addresses his mythical hero (**Reading 12.7**):

READING 12.7 **from George Gordon, Lord Byron, "Prometheus" (1816)**

Thou art a symbol and a sign
To Mortals of their fate and force;
Like thee, Man is in part divine,
A troubled stream from a pure source;
And Man in portions can foresee

His own funereal destiny;
His wretchedness, and his resistance,
And his sad unallied existence:
To which his Spirit may oppose
Itself—an equal to all woes,

And a firm will, and a deep sense,
Which even in torture can descry
Its own concentred recompense,
Triumphant where it dares defy,
And making Death a Victory.

Prometheus' daring to oppose the Olympian gods was, for Byron, the same daring that he saw in Napoleon, and he balances the poem's sense of almost hopeless resignation by his defiant insistence on the power of the human spirit to overcome any and all troubles it encounters—even death.

Byron was close friends with the English poet Percy Bysshe Shelley (1792–1822) and his wife Mary Godwin Shelley (1797–1851). Shelley's Prometheus project, a four-act play entitled *Prometheus Unbound*, concerns Prometheus' final release from captivity following the overthrow of Zeus, his tyrannical oppressor. A revolutionary text that champions free will, goodness, and idealism in the face of oppression, *Prometheus Unbound* is Shelley's answer to the mistakes of the French Revolution and its cycle of replacing one tyrant with another. Mary Shelley was as galvanized by the Prometheus myth as her husband and Byron, but her attitude toward it was more ambivalent. When Byron arrived in Italy, she had already begun her novel *Frankenstein; or the Modern Prometheus*. The novel is narrated by an English explorer in the Arctic, whose ice-bound ship takes on a man in terrible condition named Victor Frankenstein, and reports the passenger's story. Dr. Frankenstein had learned the secret of endowing inanimate material with life.

Dr. Frankenstein subsequently created a monster of giant proportion and supernatural strength from assembled body parts taken from graveyards, slaughterhouses, and dissecting rooms. But as soon as the creature opened his eyes, the scientist realized that he had not so much created a miracle as a horror, a creature doomed to a miserable existence of exile from normal society. Dr. Frankenstein flees his laboratory, leaving the creature to fend for himself. What follows is the story of the monster's revenge—a series of murders that adversely affect Frankenstein and his family. So, like Prometheus, Dr. Frankenstein is punished for the acquisition of powerful knowledge. Promethean ambition and power, Mary Shelley tells us, can step beyond the bounds of reason and the human capacity to manage the consequences—as Napoleon had demonstrated.

In July 1823, Byron sailed to Greece to aid the Greeks in their War of Independence from the Ottoman Turks. Greece was for Byron a Promethean country, longing to be "unbound." Now he would come to its aid himself. But he never did face any action. Instead, he died in 1824 of fever and excessive bleeding, the result of his doctor's mistaken belief that bleeding would cure him. He was buried in his family vault in England, except for his heart and lungs, which were interred at Missolonghi, where he had perished. Keats had died of tuberculosis in 1821, Shelley had drowned in a boating accident in 1822. Of all the great English Romantic poets, only Wordsworth and Coleridge were still alive by the mid-1820s.

Goethe's _Faust_ and the Desire for Infinite Knowledge
One of the great ironies in the development of Romanticism is that one of its greatest heroes, Faust (rhymes with "oust"), was the creation of an imagination that defined itself as Classical. The creator of this hero, Johann Wolfgang von Goethe [GUH-tuh] (1749–1832), had strong classical tastes and is often categorized as a "classical" author. He had moved to Weimar [VY-mar], one of the great cultural centers of Europe, in 1775, and later filled his house there with Greek and Roman statuary. Indeed he found Romanticism abhorrent. In a famous letter of 1829, Goethe wrote a friend, "The classical I call healthy, the Romantic sick . . . [the Romantic] is weak, sickly, ill, and the [classical] is strong, fresh, cheerful . . ."

Goethe's Faust, embodies something of this same ambiguity. _Faust_ is a 12,000-line verse play based on a sixteenth-century German legend about an actual traveling physician named Johann or Georg Faust, who was reputed to have sold his soul to the devil in return for infinite knowledge. To Goethe, he seemed an ideal figure for the Romantic hero—driven to master the world, with dire consequences.

Faust is a man of great learning and breadth of knowledge—like Goethe himself—but bored with his station in life and longing for some greater experience. In essence, Faust is profoundly bored, suffering from one of the great afflictions of the Romantic hero, _ennui_ [ahn-wee], a French term that denotes both listlessness and a profound melancholy. He longs for something that will challenge the limits of his enormous intellect. That challenge appears in the form of Mephistopheles [mef-ih-STOFF-uh-leez]—the devil—who arrives in Faust's study dressed as a dandy, a nineteenth-century man of elegant taste and appearance.

Mephistopheles makes a pact with Faust: He promises Faust "ravishing samples of my arts" which will satisfy his greatest yearnings, but in return, if Faust agrees that he is satisfied, Mephistopheles will win Faust's soul. As Faust leaves

to prepare to accompany Mephistopheles, the fiend contemplates the doctor's future (**Reading 12.8**):

READING 12.8　　**from Johann Wolfgang von Goethe, _Faust_, Part I (1808)**

MEPHISTOPHELES . . . We just say go—and skip.
But please get ready for this pleasure trip.
[_Exit Faust_]
　　Only look down on knowledge and reason,
The highest gifts that men can prize,
Only allow the spirit of lies
To confirm you in magic and illusion,
And then I have you body and soul.
Fate has given this man a spirit
Which is always pressing onwards, beyond control,
And whose mad striving overleaps
All joys of the earth between pole and pole.
Him I shall drag through the wilds of life
And through the flats of meaninglessness,
I shall make him flounder and gape and stick
And to tease his insatiableness
Hang meat and drink in the air before his watering lips;
In vain he will pray to slake his inner thirst,
And even had he not sold himself to the devil
He would be equally accursed.

Mephistopheles recognizes Faust as the ultimate Promethean hero, a man "always pressing onwards, beyond control," whose insatiable ambition will inevitably lead him to "overleap" his limitations. After a tumultuous love affair with a young woman named Gretchen—"Feeling is all!" he proclaims—he abandons her, which causes her to lose her mind and murder their illegitimate child. For this she is condemned to death, but the purity of her love wins her salvation in the afterlife.

In Book Two, Faust follows Mephistopheles into the "other dark worlds" of the Romantic imagination, a nightmare world filled with witches, sirens, monsters, and heroes from the distant past, including Helen of Troy, with whom he has a love affair. But, in Goethe's ultimately redemptive story, Faust is unsatisfied with this unending variety of experiences. What begins to quench his thirst, ironically, is good works, namely putting knowledge to work in a vast land-reclamation project designed to provide good land for millions of people. (This reminds us of Prometheus' desire to benefit humanity through the gift of fire.) Before achieving his dream, Faust dies, but without ever having actually declared his satisfaction.

In the end, Goethe's Faust is an extremely ambiguous figure, a man of enormous ambition and hence enormous possibility, and yet, like Frankenstein, his will to power is self-destructive. We see these ambiguities in the poem's high seriousness countered by ribald comedy, and in Faust's great goodness countered by deep moral depravity.

Goya's Tragic Vision The impact of Napoleon's Promethean ambition, and the human tragedy associated with it, extended also to Spain. The Spanish painter Francisco Goya [GOY-ah] (1746–1828) was, at first, enthusiastic about Napoleon's accession to power in France and his ostensible desire to establish a fair and efficient government in Spain. But Goya came to simply hate Napoleon, as most Spaniards did.

When Napoleon decided to send a French army across the Iberian Peninsula to force Portugal to abandon its alliance with Britain, he did not foresee a problem since Spain had been his ally since 1796. At first, Napoleon's army was unopposed, but by the time the troops reached Saragossa, the Spanish population rose up in nationalistic fervor. For the next five years, the Spanish conducted a new kind of warfare, engaging the French in innumerable *guerrillas* [gay-REEL-yah], or "little wars," from which derives the concept of guerrilla warfare.

In March 1808, Napoleon made a fatal error. Maneuvering the Spanish royal family out of the way through bribery, he named his brother, Joseph Bonaparte (r. 1808–1814), to the Spanish throne. This gesture infuriated the Spanish people. The crown was *their* crown, after all, not Napoleon's.

Even as the royal family was negotiating with Napoleon, rumors had spread that Napoleon was planning to execute them. On May 2, 1808, the citizens of Madrid rose up against Napoleon's troops, resulting in hundreds of deaths in battle, with hundreds more executed the next day on a hill outside Madrid. Six years later, in 1814, after Napoleon had been deposed and Ferdinand reinstated as king, Goya commemorated the events of May 2 and 3 in two paintings, the first depicting the battle and the second the executions of the following day.

The Third of May, 1808 is one of the greatest testaments to the horrors of war ever painted (Fig. **12.17**). The night after the events of May 2, Napoleon's troops set a firing squad and executed hundreds of Madrileños—anyone caught bearing weapons of any kind. The only illumination comes from a square stable lantern that casts a bright light on a prisoner with his arms raised wide above his head in a gesture that seems at once a plea for mercy and an act of heroic defiance. Below him the outstretched arms of a bloody corpse mirror his gesture. To his left, in the very center of the painting, another soon-to-be casualty of the firing squad hides his eyes in terror, and behind him stretches a line of victims to follow.

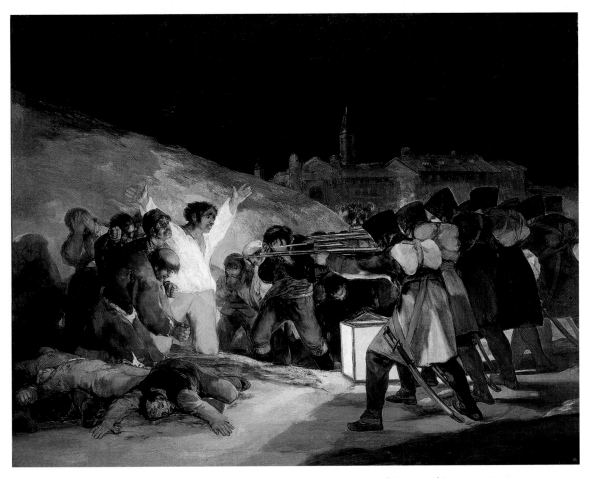

Fig. 12.17 Francisco Goya. *The Third of May, 1808*. 1814–1815. Oil on canvas, 8'9½" × 13'4½". Museo del Prado, Madrid. Goya was later asked why he had painted the scene with such graphic reality. His reply was simple: "To warn men never to do it again."

Above them, barely visible in the night sky, rises a solitary, darkened church steeple. Much of the power of the painting lies in its almost Baroque contrast of light and dark and its evocation of Christ's agony on the cross, especially through the cruciform pose of the prisoner. The faceless executioners represent the grim reality of following orders, as opposed to following one's conscience.

The Politics of Paint: Géricault and Delacroix After the fall of Napoleon, the battle between Classicism and Romanticism raged within France, fueled by political factionalism. Bourbon rule had been restored when Louis XVIII (r. 1814–1824), the deposed Louis XVI's brother, assumed the throne. Royalists, who favored this return of the monarchy, championed the more conservative Neoclassical style. Liberals identified with the new Romantic style, which from the beginning had allied itself with the French Revolution's radical spirit of freedom and independence.

Against this political backdrop, Théodore Géricault [ZHAY-ree-koh] (1791–1824), trained in Paris in a Neoclas-

sical style, inaugurated his career. In fact, Géricault joined the Royal Musketeers, assigned to protect the future Louis XVIII from Napoleon. But events quickly overcame Géricault's brief royalist career. On July 2, 1816, a government frigate named the *Medusa*, carrying soldiers and settlers to Senegal, was shipwrecked on a reef 50 miles off the coast of West Africa. The captain and crew saved themselves, leaving 150 people, including a woman, adrift on a makeshift raft. Only 15 survived the days that followed, days marked by insanity, mutilation, famine, thirst, and finally, cannibalism. An inexperienced captain, commissioned on the basis of his noble birth and connections to the monarchy, saved himself, providing a profound indictment of aristocratic privilege. Géricault was outraged.

Géricault set himself the task of rendering the events. He interviewed survivors, and painted mutilated bodies in the Paris morgue. The enormous composition of *The Raft of the "Medusa"* is organized as a double triangle (Fig. **12.18**). The mast and the two ropes supporting it form the apex of one triangle, and the torso of the figure waving in the direction

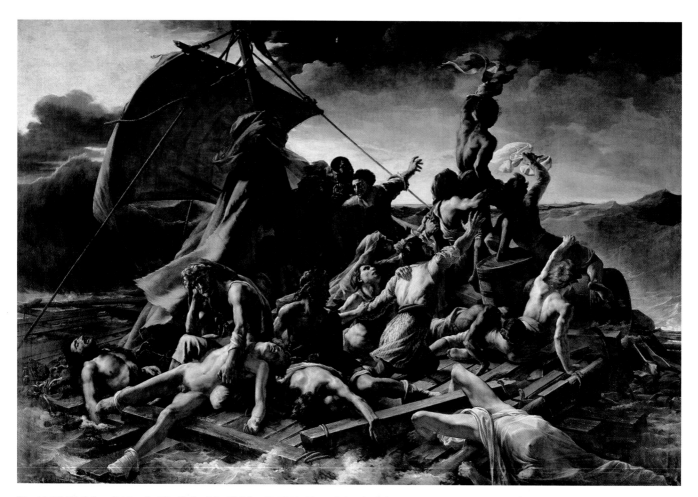

Fig. 12.18 Théodore Géricault. *The Raft of the "Medusa"*. 1818. First oil sketch. Oil on canvas, 16′1″ × 23′6″.
Musée du Louvre, Paris. Photo: Hervé Lewandowski. Inv.: RF 2229. © Réunion des Musées Nationaux/Art Resource, NY.
The painting today is much darker than it was originally because Géricault used bitumin, an organic carbon-based
material, in his pigment.

of the barely visible *Argus*, the ship that would eventually rescue the castaways, the apex of the other. The opposing diagonals form a dramatic "X" centered on the kneeling figure whose arm reaches upward in the hope of salvation. Ultimately, however, the painting makes mockery of the idea of deliverance, just as its rigid geometric structure parodies the ideal order of Neoclassicism. Géricault's Romanticism assumed a political dimension through his art. He had himself become a Promethean hero, challenging the authority of the establishment.

When Géricault's painting was exhibited at the French Academy of Fine Arts Salon of 1819, it was titled simply *A Shipwreck Scene*, in no small part to avoid direct confrontation with the Bourbon government. Royalist critics dismissed it. The conservative press wrote that the painting was "not fit for moral society. The work could have been done for the pleasure of vultures." But its sense of immediacy, its insistence on depicting current events (but not how the castaways actually looked after 13 days adrift), made an enormous impression on another young painter, Eugène Delacroix (1798–1863), who actually had served as the model for the facedown nude in the bottom center of the *Raft*. Soon after Géricault's accidental death, Delacroix exhibited his *Scenes from the Massacres at Chios* at the Salon of 1824 (Fig. **12.19**).

The full title of the painting—*Scenes from the Massacres at Chios; Greek Families Awaiting Death or Slavery, etc.—See Various Accounts and Contemporary Newspapers*—reveals its close association with journalistic themes. It depicts events of April 1822, after the Greeks had initiated a War of Independence from Turkey, a cause championed by all of liberal Europe. In retaliation, the sultan sent an army of 10,000 to the Greek island of Chios [KY-oss], just several miles off the west coast of Turkey. The troops killed 20,000 and took thousands of women and children into captivity, selling them into slavery across North Africa. In the left foreground, defeated Greek families await their fate. To the right a grandmother sits dejectedly by what is perhaps her dead daughter, even as her grandchild tries to suckle at its dead mother's breast. A prisoner vainly tries to defend a Greek woman tied to a triumphant Turk's horse. The vast space between the near fore-

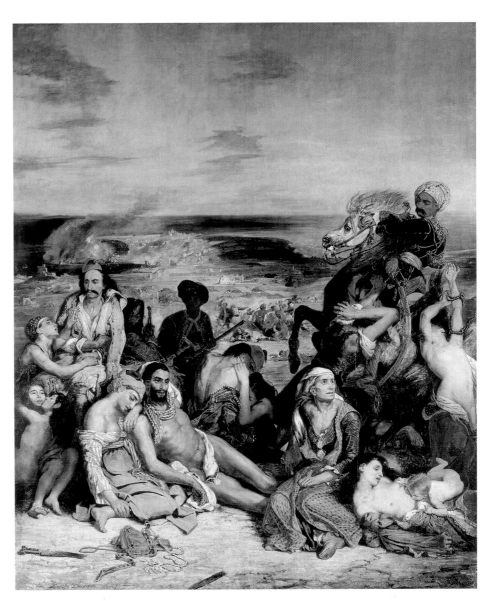

Fig. 12.19 Eugène Delacroix. *Scenes from the Massacres at Chios.* 1824. Oil on canvas, 165″ × 139¼″. Musée du Louvre, Paris. Photo: Le Mage. © Réunion des Musées Nationaux/Art Resource, NY. Delacroix relied on the testimony of a French volunteer in the Greek cause for the authenticity of his depiction.

ground and the far distance is startling, almost as if the scene transpires before a painted tableau. Even more disconcerting is the void that seems to sit in the painting's center, at the shadowed point of the Turk's gun. This is a painting without a center, around which swirls the chaos of modern life.

From Classical to Romantic Music

Fascination with the Promethean hero was not limited to literature. It was reflected in music, and especially that of Ludwig van Beethoven (1770–1827), the key figure in the transition from the Classical to the Romantic era in music. His Third Symphony, which came to be known as the *Eroica* [eh-ROH-ee-kah]—Italian for the "Heroic"—was originally dedicated to Napoleon because of the composer's admiration for the French leader as a champion of freedom. But when, on December 2, 1804, Napoleon had himself crowned as emperor, Beethoven changed his mind, saying to a friend: "Is he then, too, nothing more than an ordinary human being? Now he, too, will trample on all the rights of man and indulge only his ambition. He will exalt himself above all others, become a tyrant!" Thus, on the title page of the symphony he crossed out the words "*Intitulata* [in-tee-too-LAH-tah] *Bonaparte*," "Entitled Bonaparte."

The Classical Tradition

As Beethoven began his career as a young pianist in Vienna in 1792, he was steeped in the tradition we have come to call **Classical music**, which reflects the growing distaste for the Rococo and the decadence associated with it. Developing first in Vienna about 1760, the "Classical" style shares with Greek and Roman art the essential features of symmetry, proportion, balance, formal unity, and, perhaps above all, clarity. This clarity was a direct result of the rise of a new musical audience, a burgeoning middle class that demanded from composers a more accessible and recognizable musical language than found in the ornate and complex structures of the Baroque.

The most important development of the age, designed specifically to address the new middle-class audience, was the **symphonic orchestra**. This musical ensemble was much larger than the ensemble used by Baroque composers. The Classical orchestra was divided into separate sections according to type of instrument: the *strings*, made up of violins, violas, cellos, and double basses; *woodwinds*, consisting of flutes, oboes, clarinets, and bassoons; a *brass* section of trumpets and French horns (by the end of the century, trombones were added); and a *percussion* section, featuring the kettledrums and other rhythm instruments. The composer himself usually led the orchestra and often played part of the composition on the piano or clavier in the space now reserved for the conductor. The modern symphony orchestra (Fig. **12.20**) is a dramatically enlarged version of this new Classical ensemble.

In order to organize such a large group, an overall **score**, which indicated what music was to be played by each instrument, was required. This let the composer view the composition as a whole, while each instrument section was given its own individual part. The **time signature** (number of beats per measure), **key signature** (showing which notes should be played as a sharp or flat whenever they appear), **dynamics** (*forte*, for instance, for loud, *piano* for soft), **pace** (*allegro* [uh-LEG-roh], for fast; *lente* [LEN-tay], for slow), and interpretative directions (*affettuoso* [ah-fet-too-OH-soh] for "with feeling") were indicated both in the score as a whole and the individual parts. These devices have remained part of the vocabulary of Western musical composition ever since.

The music most often played by the symphonic orchestra was the **symphony**. The term derives from the Italian *sinfonia*—the three-movement, fast–slow–fast, introduction or overture to Italian operas. A Fourth movement might be added after the first two, usually based on the stately rhythms of the minuet. The predictability of the form is the source of its drama, since audiences anticipated the composer's inventiveness as the composition proceeded through three or four movements. The first *allegro* movement (and occasionally the fourth) possessed its own distinct **sonata form**, a kind of small form within the larger symphonic form.

Each movement in the sonata form was divided into three parts: exposition, development, and recapitulation. In the *exposition*, the composer "exposes" the main theme in the composition's "home" key and then contrasts it with a second theme in a different key. In the *development*, the composer further develops the two themes in contrasting keys, and then, in the *recapitulation*, restates the two themes, but both now in the home key. Use of the home key in the restatement resolves the tension between the two themes. A short *coda* (or "tail") is often added to bring the piece to a definitive end.

Haydn and Mozart One of the most important contributors to the development of the symphonic form was the composer Joseph Haydn [HY-din] (1732–1809). In 1761, at the age of 29, he was appointed musical director to the court of the Hungarian nobleman Prince Paul Anton Esterházy. Haydn worked for Esterházy for nearly 30 years, isolated at Esterháza Palace in Eisenstadt, about 30 miles south of Vienna. The palace, modeled on Versailles, included two theaters (one for opera) and two concert halls. In these surroundings Haydn composed an extraordinary amount of music: operas, oratorios, concertos, sonatas, overtures, liturgical music, and above all, the two genres that he was instrumental in developing—the classical symphony and the string quartet. (He composed 106 of the former and 67 of the latter.) He also oversaw the repair of instruments, trained a chorus, and rehearsed and performed with a symphony of about 25 musicians.

The **string quartet**, the first of the new Classical genres that Haydn played such a large role in developing, features four string instruments: two violins, a viola, and a cello. Since all the instruments are from the same family, the music has a distinctly uniform sound. Its form closely followed that of the symphony. The string quartet was a product of the Classical age of music, performed almost exclusively in private settings, such as salons, for small audiences that understood the form to be a musical variation of their own conversations, an intimate exchange among friends.

When Esterházy died in 1790, his son disbanded the orchestra and a London promoter, Johann Peter Salomon, invited Haydn to England. There he composed his last 12 symphonies for an orchestra of some 60 musicians. Among the greatest of the London symphonies is *Symphony No. 94*, the so-called "*Surprise*" Symphony. It was so named for a completely unanticipated *fortissimo* [for-TIS-uh-mo] ("very loud") percussive stroke that occurs on a weak beat in the second movement of the piece (see **CD-Track 12.1**). This moment was calculated, so the story goes, to awaken Haydn's dozing audience, since concerts usually lasted well past midnight.

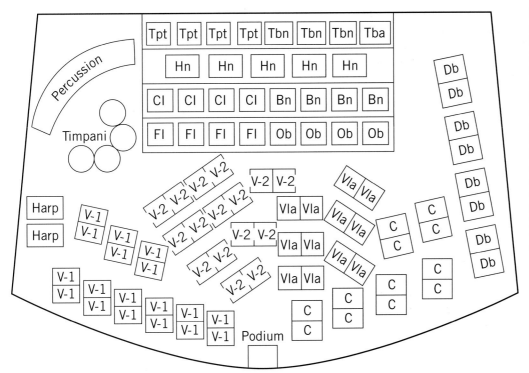

Fig. 12.20 The Classical symphonic orchestra today. From Jay Zorn, *Listening to Music*, 2nd edition. Used by permission of Prentice Hall, Inc. Over the years, the symphonic orchestra has added new instruments as composers increasingly experimented with them, and larger numbers of traditional instruments as they sought a fuller and richer sound. V-1: first violin; V-2: second violin; Vla: viola; C: cello; Db: double bass; Ob: oboe; Fl: flute; Cl: clarinet; Bn: bassoon; Hn: French horn; Tpt: trumpet; Tbn: trombone; Tba: tuba.

The greatest musical genius of the Classical era was Haydn's younger contemporary and colleague, Wolfgang Amadeus Mozart [MOHT-sart] (1756–1791). Mozart wrote his first original composition at age six, in 1762, the year after Haydn assumed his post with Prince Esterházy. When he was just eight, the prodigy penned his first symphony. Over the course of his short, 35-year life, he would write 40 more, plus 70 string quartets, 20 operas, 60 sonatas, and 23 piano concertos. Haydn told Mozart's father that the boy was simply "the greatest composer I know in person or by name," and in 1785 Mozart dedicated six string quartets to the older composer. On several occasions the two met at parties, where they performed string quartets together—Haydn on the violin, Mozart on the viola.

Mozart's music was generally regarded as overly complicated, too demanding emotionally and intellectually for a popular audience to absorb. When the Habsburg Emperor Joseph II commented that the opera *Don Giovanni* was beautiful "but no food for the teeth of my Viennese"—meaning too refined for their taste—Mozart reportedly replied, "Then give them time to chew it." Indeed, his work often took time to absorb. Mozart could pack more distinct melodies into a single movement than most composers could write for an entire symphony, and each line would arise and grow naturally from the beginning to the end of the piece. But the reaction of Joseph II to another of his operas is typical: "Too many notes!" Ironically, it is exactly this richness that we value today.

An example of Mozart's complexity is his *Symphony No. 40*, composed in the course of eight weeks in the summer of 1788. In the first movement, Mozart utilizes the sonata form in a way that is very easy for the listener to hear, and yet the movement is full of small—and sometimes larger—surprises (**CD-Track 12.2**). The composition shifts dramatically between loud and soft passages, woodwinds and strings, rising and falling phrasings, and major and minor keys. Particularly dramatic is the way Mozart leads the listener to anticipate the beginning of the recapitulation, only to withhold it.

Among Mozart's greatest works are his last four operas—*The Marriage of Figaro, Don Giovanni, Cosi fan tutte*, and *The Magic Flute*. The first three bring together nobles and commoners in stories that are at the same time comic and serious. What distinguishes them most, however—and the Italian librettist Lorenzo da Ponte (1749–1838) must be given some credit for this—is the depth of their characters. From the lowest to the highest class and rank, all are believable as they sort out their stormy relationships and love lives.

Beethoven: From Classicism to Romanticism

Beethoven's music is a direct reflection of his life's journey, his joys and sorrows, and, in turn, an indication of the shift from the formal structural emphases of Classical music to the expression of more personal, emotional feelings in Romantic music. Other, earlier composers had expressed emotion in their works, but not in the personal, autobiographical way that Beethoven did.

Completed in 1802, a decade after Beethoven arrived in Vienna from Bonn, Germany, his First and Second Symphonies suggest a sense that he is consciously taking on the Classical tradition, recapitulating it, summarizing it, and preparing to move on to more exciting breakthroughs. Over the next decade a personal crisis, brought on by his increasing deafness, instigated an extraordinary period of creativity for Beethoven in which he produced six symphonies, four concertos, and five string quartets, leaving the Classical tradition behind.

In April 1802, Beethoven left Vienna for the small village of Heiligenstadt [HY-lig-en-shtaht], just north of the city. Though his hearing had been deteriorating for some time, what had started as humming and buzzing was becoming much worse. Moody and temperamental by nature, his deafness deeply depressed him. His frustrations reached a peak in early October as he contemplated ending his life. His feelings are revealed in a remarkable document found among his papers after his death, a letter to his brothers today known as the *Heiligenstadt Testament* (**Reading 12.9**):

READING 12.9 from Ludwig van Beethoven, *Heiligenstadt Testament* (1802)

From childhood on, my heart and soul have been full of the tender feeling of goodwill, and I was ever inclined to accomplish great things. But, think that for six years now I have been hopelessly afflicted, made worse by senseless physicians, from year to year deceived with hopes of improvement, finally compelled to face the prospect of a lasting malady . . . Though born with a fiery, active temperament, even susceptible to the diversions of society, I was soon compelled to withdraw myself, to live life alone . . . It was impossible for me to say to people, "Speak louder, shout, for I am deaf." Ah, how could I possibly admit an infirmity in the one sense which ought to be more perfect in me than in others. . . . I must live almost alone, like one who has been banished . . . If I approach near to people a hot terror seizes upon me, and I fear being exposed to the danger that my condition might be noticed. . . . What a humiliation for me when someone standing next to me heard a flute in the distance and I heard nothing, or someone heard a shepherd singing and again I heard nothing. Such incidents drove me almost to despair; a little more of that and I would have ended my life—it was only my art that held me back. . . .

Beethoven reconciled himself to his situation, recognizing that his isolation was, perhaps, the necessary condition to his creativity. His sense of self-sufficiency, of an imagination turned inward, guided by an almost pure state of subjective feeling, lies at the very heart of Romanticism.

Beethoven's post-Heiligenstadt works, often called "heroic" because they so thoroughly evoke feelings of struggle and triumph, mark the first expression of a genuinely Romantic musical style. When composer and author E. T. A. Hoffmann said, in 1810, that Beethoven's music evokes "the machinery of awe, of fear, of terror, of pain," he meant that it evokes the sublime. To this end, it is much more emotionally expressive than its Classical predecessors. In Beethoven's ground-breaking compositions, this expression of emotion manifests itself in three distinct ways: long, sustained *crescendos* that drive the music inexorably forward; sudden and surprising key changes that always make harmonic sense; and both loud and soft repetitions of the same theme that are equally, if differently, poignant.

Beethoven's Third Symphony, the *Eroica*, is the first major expression of this new style in his work. Much longer than any previous symphony, the 691 measures of the first movement alone take approximately 19 minutes to play compared to 8 minutes for the first movement of Mozart's Symphony No. 40 in G minor. In fact, the first movement is almost as long as an entire Mozart symphony! Dramatically introducing the main theme and recapitulating it after elongated melodies, this movement ends in a monumental climax, establishing the Romantic, Promethean mood of the piece. The finale brings together the themes and variations of the first movement in a broad, triumphant conclusion featuring a majestic horn. Ultimately, this symphony dramatizes Beethoven's own descent into despair at Heiligenstadt (figured in the second movement), his inward struggle, and his ultimate triumph through art.

Beethoven's Fifth Symphony, like the *Eroica*, brings musical form to the triumph of art over death, terror, fear, and pain. Premiering on December 22, 1808, the symphony's opening four-note motif, with its short-short-short-long rhythm, is in fact the basis for the entire symphony (for the first movement see **CD-Track 12.3**):

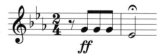

Throughout the symphony's four movements, this rhythmic unit is used again and again, but never in a simple repetition. Rather, the rhythm seems to grow from its minimal opening phrasings into an expansive and monumental theme by the symphony's end.

A number of startling innovations emerge as a counterpoint to this theme: an interruption of the opening motif by a sudden oboe solo; the addition of piccolo and double bassoons to the woodwind sections and of trombones in the finale; the lack of a pause between the last two movements; and the ending of the piece in a different key than it began—a majestic C major rather than the original C minor. In fact, the Fifth Symphony ends with one of the longest, most thrilling conclusions Beethoven ever wrote. Over and over again it seems as if the symphony is about to end, but instead it only gets faster and faster, until it finally comes to a rest on the single note C, played *fortissimo* [for-TISS-eh-moh] by the entire orchestra.

Romantic Music after Beethoven

Beethoven's musical explorations of individual feelings were immensely influential on the Romantic composers who succeeded him. They strove to find new ways to express their own emotions. Some focused on the symphony as the vehicle for their most important statements. Others found a rich vehicle in piano music and song.

Hector Berlioz and Program Music French composer Hector Berlioz [BER-lee-ohz] (1803–1869) was the most startlingly original of Beethoven's successors, both musically and personally. His compositions were frankly autobiographical; Berlioz attracted attention with new approaches to symphonic music and instrumentation. He wrote three symphonies: the *Symphonie fantastique* [SAM-foh-nee FAHN-tahss-teek] (1830); *Harold en Italie* [AH-rold ahn EE-tah-lee] (1834), based on a poem by Lord Byron; and *Roméo et Juliette* [ROH-may-oh ay joo-lee-ET] (1839). All are notable for their inventiveness and novelty, and especially for the size of the orchestras Berlioz enlisted to play them. The enormity of the sound could be deafening. The symphonies are also instances of program music, which suggests a sequence of images or incidents and may be prefaced with a text identifying these themes. As large as the orchestras were and as intricate as their narrative structure was, Berlioz was able to unify his symphonies by introducing recurring themes that provided continuity through the various movements.

Felix Mendelssohn and the Meaning of Music Program music was an important part of the work of another Romantic composer after Beethoven. As a young man, Felix Mendelssohn [MEN-dul-zohn] (1809–1847) was befriended by Goethe, and their great friendship convinced the composer, who was recognized as a prodigy, to travel widely across Europe from 1829 to 1831. These travels inspired many of his orchestral compositions. These include the *Italian* Symphony (1833), which with its program has become his most popular work; the *Scottish* Symphony (1842), which is the only symphony he allowed to be published in his lifetime; and the *Hebrides* (1832), also known as *Fingal's Cave*. The last is a concert overture, a form that grew out of the eighteenth-century tradition of performing opera overtures in the concert hall. It consists of a single movement and is usually connected in some way with a narrative plot known to the audience, and in this sense is programmatic. The *Hebrides* overture, however, does not tell a story. Rather, it sets a scene—one of the first such compositions in Western music—the rocky landscape and swell of the sea that inspired Mendelssohn when he visited the giant cave carved into basalt columns on an island off the Scottish coast.

Mendelssohn himself played both piano and violin. For the piano he composed 48 "Songs without Words," published in eight separate books that proved enormously popular. The works challenge the listener to imagine the words that the compositions evoke. When asked by a friend to provide descriptive titles to the music, he replied:

> I believe that words are not at all up to it [the music], and if I should find that they were adequate I would stop making music altogether. . . . So if you ask me what I was thinking of, I will say: just the song as it stands there. And if I happen to have had a specific word or specific words in mind for one or another of these songs, I can never divulge them to anyone, because the same word means one thing to one person and something else to another, because only the song can say the same thing, can arouse the same feelings in one person as in another—a feeling that is not, however, expressed by the same words.

The meaning of music, in other words, lies for Mendelssohn in the music itself. It cannot be expressed in language. The music creates a feeling that all listeners share, even if no two listeners would interpret it in the same terms.

Song: Franz Schubert and the Schumanns Not all Romantic composers followed Beethoven in concentrating on the symphonic form to realize their most important innovations and to communicate most fully their personal emotions. Beginning in about 1815, German composers became intrigued with the idea of setting poetry to music, especially the works of Schiller and Goethe. Called **lieder** [LEE-der] (singular *lied* [leet]), these songs were generally written for solo voice and piano. Their popularity reflected the growing availability and affordability of the piano in middle-class households and the composers' willingness to write compositions that were within the technical grasp of amateur musicians. This early expansion of the market for music freed composers from total reliance on the patronage of the wealthy.

The *lieder* of Franz Schubert [SHOO-burt] (1797–1828) and Robert (1810–1856) and Clara Schumann [SHOO-mahn] (1819–1896) were especially popular. Schubert's life was a continual struggle against illness and poverty, and he worked feverishly. In his brief career, he composed nearly 1,000 works, 600 of which were *lieder*, as well as nine symphonies and 22 piano sonatas. Schubert failed to win international recognition in his lifetime, for which his early death by typhoid was partially to blame. But his melodies, for which he had an uncanny talent, seemed to capture, in the minds of the many who discovered him after his death, the emotional feeling and depth of the Romantic spirit.

By the age of 20, Clara Schumann was so well known as a piano virtuoso that the Viennese court had given her the title Royal and Imperial Virtuosa. She was one of the most famous and respected concert pianists and composers of her day, despite her difficult marriage to Robert Schumann. She specialized in performing piano works known as **character pieces**, works of relatively small dimension that explore the mood or "character" of a person, emotion, or situation, including her husband's 1835 *Carnaval*. After Robert's death she supported her family by performing lengthy concert tours and was among the first artists to do this on a regular basis.

Piano Music: Frédéric Chopin Performance of character pieces often occurred at **salon concerts**, in the homes of wealthy music enthusiasts. Among the most sought-after composer/performer pianists of the day was the Polish-born Frédéric Chopin [SHOH-pan] (1810–1849). He composed almost exclusively for the piano. Among his most impressive works are his *études* [ay-TOOD], or "studies," which address particular technical challenges on the piano; *polonaises* [poh-loh-NEZ], stylized versions of the Polish dance; **nocturnes** [NOK-turns], character pieces related to the tradition of the serenade performed outside a loved one's window; and larger-scale works, particularly the four **ballades**

[bah-LAHD], dramatic narrative forms that are among his most famous works. Focusing on melodramatic romance, supernatural events, and stormy emotion, Chopin's ballades are rich and complex, synthesizing contemporary poetry and diverse moods.

The *Fantasie impromptu* [fahn-tah-ZEE em-prohm-TOO] showcases the expressive range Chopin was capable of even in a brief composition (see **CD-Track 12.4**). Like other pianists of the day, Chopin enhanced the emotional mood of the piece by using *tempo rubato* [TEM-poh roo-BAH-toh] (literally "robbed time"), in which the tempo of the piece accelerates or decelerates in a manner "akin to passionate speech" as described by one of his students. While the word *fantasie* connotes creativity, imagination, magic, and the supernatural, the word *impromptu* suggests spontaneous improvisation, though, of course, the piece was written down. Combining impulsive, spur-of-the-moment creativity and imaginary and fantastical effects, Chopin's work is the very definition of Romanticism.

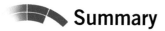

Summary

■ **The American and French Revolutions** The idea of human freedom was fundamental to the Enlightenment, finding political expression in the American Declaration of Independence and the French Declaration of the Rights of Man and Citizen. The American Revolution was essentially the revolt of an upper class that felt disenfranchised by its distant king, while the French Revolution was a revolt against an absolute monarch whose abuse of power had disenfranchised his own people.

■ **The Neoclassical Spirit** The founders of the newly created United States modeled their republic on classical precedents, seeking to establish an orderly society. The French revolutionaries dreamed of the same outcome, but when their revolution appeared to be descending into chaos, the French appealed to a young commander of their army, Napoleon Bonaparte, to rescue them. Both Napoleon and the fledgling United States embraced Neoclassicism as an architectural style, signifying stability, balance, and rational government, and Napoleon employed Neoclassical painter Jacques-Louis David, the undisputed master of the Neoclassical style, to enhance the emperor's own Neoclassical image. But the issue of slavery dogged the new American republic, obscured as it was by the debate over free trade, of which it was generally considered a form.

■ **The Romantic Imagination** The Romantics were dedicated to the discovery of beauty in nature through their subjective experience of it. In poetry, William Wordsworth's poem

"Tintern Abbey" embodies the growing belief in the natural world as the source of inspiration and creativity. For John Keats, the essence of beauty, a form of nature higher than mortal life itself, can be discovered in great works of art, such as a Grecian urn or, for that matter, his own poetry. Landscape painters saw the natural world around them as the emotional focal point or center of their own artistic imaginations—John Constable in the constant variety of the everyday, J. M. W. Turner in light, and Caspar David Friedrich in the sublime. For many, Napoleon personified the Romantic hero, a modern Prometheus, but he also possessed a darker side. In Johann Wolfgang von Goethe's *Faust*, Mary Shelley's *Frankenstein*, and many other works, the Promethean figure's almost insatiable drive for knowledge and experience leads inevitably to failure, even self-destruction. Indeed, in the paintings of Goya, Géricault, and Delacroix, the very possibility of heroism is questioned.

■ **From Classical to Romantic Music** Classical music shares with Greek and Roman art the essential features of symmetry, proportion, balance, formal unity, and clarity. The symphony orchestra is its primary vehicle. Two of the greatest Classical composers were Joseph Haydn and Wolfgang Amadeus Mozart. Beethoven's ground-breaking new Romantic music is much more emotionally expressive than its Classical predecessors. Great symphonies like the *Eroica* and the Fifth revealed an innovative and original temperament of extraordinary emotional range, and succeeding generations of composers followed his lead in their own virtuoso compositions and performances.

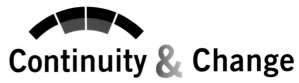
The Romantic imagination as embodied in the works of Beethoven, Goethe, and Goya is profoundly subjective, the product of an interior world that was intent, like Faust, on developing itself to the fullest. Beethoven spoke regretfully on his deathbed of his failure to set Goethe's *Faust* to music not because he approved of Faust as a man, but because he recognized in the sweep of the character's ambition something of his own expansive spirit.

However, it was not to the subjective imagination alone that the nineteenth-century imagination turned. In paintings like Géricault's *Raft of the "Medusa"* or Delacroix's *Scenes from the Massacres at Chios*, we are witness to the reality of contemporary events. In such works, the painter accepts the role of a newspaper reporter and attempts to convey, if not the actuality, then the emotional reality of events.

Such realism in art gained new prominence after the summer of 1830. Three years earlier, after liberals won a majority in the Chamber of Deputies, King Charles X (r. 1824–1830), who had assumed the throne after the death of Louis XVIII, responded by relaxing censorship of the press and government control of education. But these concessions irked him, and in the spring of 1830 he called for new elections. The liberals won a large majority, but Charles was not to be thwarted. On July 25, he dissolved the new Chamber, reinstituted censorship of the press, and restricted the right to vote to the wealthiest French men. The next day, rioting erupted as workers took to the streets, erected barricades, and confronted royalist troops. In the following days, 1,800 people died. Soon after, Charles abdicated the throne and left France for England. In his place, the Chamber of Deputies named the duke of Orléans, Louis-Philippe [loo-EE-fee-LEEP] (r. 1830–1848), king of their new constitutional government that came to be known as the July Monarchy.

Eugène Delacroix's version of the events of July 1830, *Liberty Leading the People* (Fig. **12.21**), is an allegorical representation with realistic details, an emotional call to political action depicting the July Monarchy as a creation of all the classes of Parisian society joining together in common cause. A bare-breasted Lady Liberty, symbolic of freedom's nurturing power, strides over a barricade, the tricolor flag of the revolution in hand, accompanied by a street urchin waving a pair of pistols. Behind him, to the right, rise the towers of Notre Dame Cathedral, across the Seine. On the other side of Lady Liberty is a middle-class gentleman in his top hat and frock coat, a self-portrait of Delacroix, and beside him a man wielding a saber. A worker, dressed in the colors of the revolution, rises from below the barricade. But the whole triangular structure of the composition rises from the bodies of two French royalist guards, both stripped of their shoes and one of his clothing by the rioting workers. These figures purposefully recall the dead at the base of Géricault's *Raft of the "Medusa"* (see Fig. 12.18), and they suggest the reality upon which the events of July 1830 were based.

To the middle-class liberals who had fomented the 1830 revolution, the painting was frighteningly realistic. "Was there only this rabble . . . ," wrote one commentator, "at those famous days of July?" The new king, Louis-Philippe, ordered that the painting be purchased by the state, and then promptly put it away so that its celebration of the "rabble" would not prove too inspiring. In fact, the painting was not seen in public again until 1848, when King Louis-Philippe was himself deposed by yet another revolution, this one ending the monarchy in France forever. Apparently attracted to his name, the people of France elected a new Napoleon to lead their new government, Louis-Napoleon, nephew of Napoleon I. Denied by the new constitution to seek a second term, he promptly staged a *coup d'état*. A year later he proclaimed himself Napoleon III, emperor for life. Wrote Karl Marx (1818–1883), author of the *Communist Manifesto*, itself a response to the conditions that had led to the revolutions of 1848, "All history happens twice, the first time as tragedy, the second time as farce." ∎

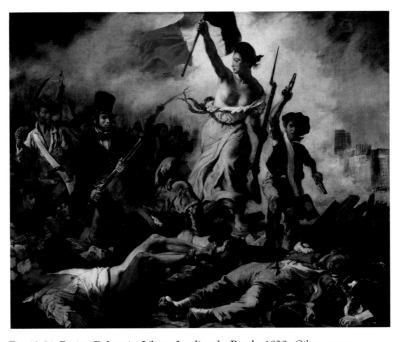

Fig. 12.21 Eugène Delacroix. *Liberty Leading the People.* **1830.** Oil on canvas, 8′ 6″ × 10′ 7″. Photo: Hervé Lewandowski. Musée du Louvre/RMN Réunion des Musées Nationaux, France. SCALA/Art Resource, NY.

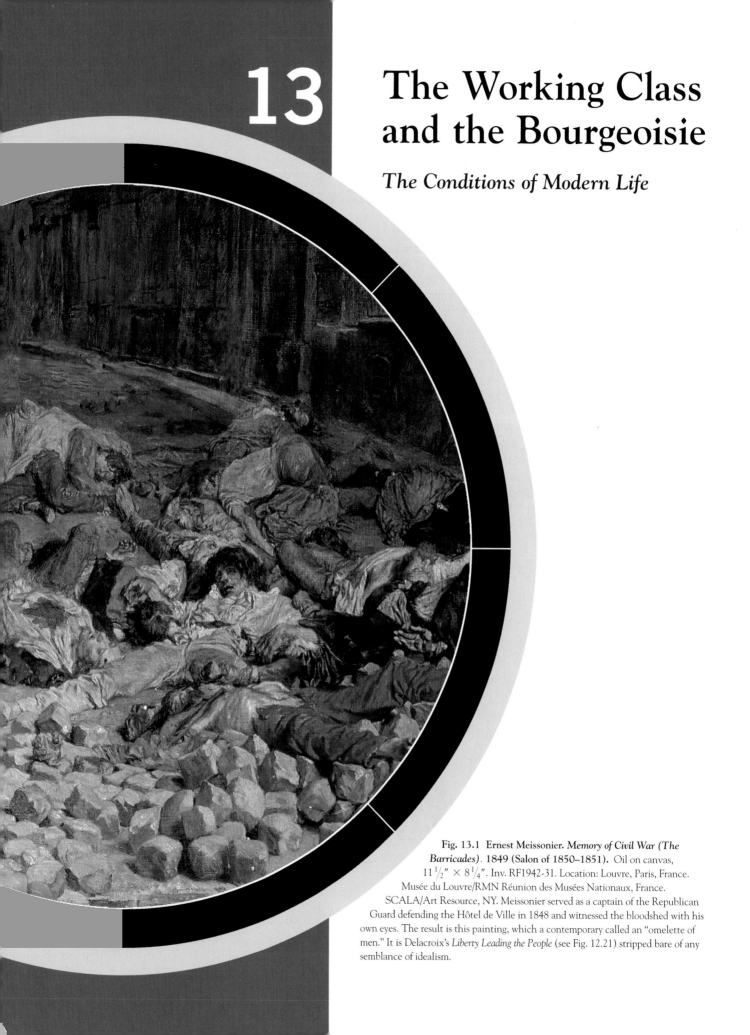

13 The Working Class and the Bourgeoisie

The Conditions of Modern Life

Fig. 13.1 Ernest Meissonier. *Memory of Civil War (The Barricades).* **1849 (Salon of 1850–1851).** Oil on canvas, 11 1/2″ × 8 1/4″. Inv. RF1942-31. Location: Louvre, Paris, France. Musée du Louvre/RMN Réunion des Musées Nationaux, France. SCALA/Art Resource, NY. Meissonier served as a captain of the Republican Guard defending the Hôtel de Ville in 1848 and witnessed the bloodshed with his own eyes. The result is this painting, which a contemporary called an "omelette of men." It is Delacroix's *Liberty Leading the People* (see Fig. 12.21) stripped bare of any semblance of idealism.

" *Thrive, cities—bring your freight, bring your shows, ample and sufficient rivers, Expand. . . .* "

Walt Whitman, *"Crossing Brooklyn Ferry"*

Between 1800 and 1848, the city of Paris doubled in size, to nearly 1 million people. Planning was nonexistent. The streets were a haphazard labyrinth of narrow, stifling passageways, so clogged with traffic that pedestrians were in constant danger. The gutters were so full of garbage and raw sewage that cesspools developed overnight in low-lying areas. The odor they produced was often strong enough to induce vomiting. And they bred rats and fleas, and the diseases they carried, such as cholera, dysentery, typhus, and typhoid fever. One epidemic in Paris during 1848 and 1849 killed more than 19,000 people. Further complicating the situation, no accurate map of the streets existed prior to 1853, so to venture into them was to set out into unknown and dangerous territory.

By 1848, these conditions prevailed throughout urban areas in Europe, made worse by food shortages and chaos in the agricultural economy. The potato famine in Ireland that killed a million people was merely the worst of a widespread breakdown. The agricultural crisis in turn triggered bankruptcies and bank closings, particularly in places where industrial expansion had not been matched by the growth of new markets. In France, prices plummeted, businesses failed, and unemployment was rampant. The situation was ripe for revolution. Soon the streets of Paris were filled with barricades (Fig. **13.1**), occupied by workers demanding the right to earn a livelihood and determine their own destiny. In other European capitals, workers quickly followed the Parisians' lead.

This chapter explores the revolutions of 1848 in Europe and the subsequent rise of an increasingly affluent bourgeois [borzh-wah] (middle class) populace intent on enjoying a style of life far removed from the realities that led to revolution in 1848. At the heart of the revolts that spread across Europe were two ideologies that were sometimes compatible and sometimes not: liberalism and nationalism. Liberal belief was founded in Enlightenment values—the universal necessity for equality and freedom at the most basic level. The nationalist agenda, however, focused on regional autonomy, cultural pride, and freedom from monarchical control, especially that of the Habsburgs, who controlled much of central, eastern, and southern Europe. Liberal politics were transnational; nationalism rested upon claims of distinct regional, even local, ethnic and linguistic identity.

While liberal and nationalist politics dominated all of Europe after 1848, Paris remained the center of revolutionary activity, a focus of world attention, as well as the center of European culture. The realist approach to art that developed in the 1830s and 1840s was integrated into an effort to define the term *modern*, which, after the revolutions of 1848, became a popular characterization of contemporary life. Paris itself was transformed—the labyrinth of ancient streets and dilapidated buildings that were home to the rebellious working class were demolished and in their place wide boulevards with sidewalks and gas streetlights stretched across the city, all lined with some 100,000 newly planted trees. To create these boulevards and a new system of public parks, the government demolished over 25,000 buildings between 1852 and 1859, and after 1860, another 92,000, displacing working class people and along with them all large-scale industry. Paris became a city of leisure, of the good life, surrounded by a ring of industrial and working-class suburbs, as it remains to the present day.

In the 1860s and '70s, writers and painters presented the conditions of life in France's new bourgeois society in sometimes shockingly direct terms, interested not so much in revealing the physical realities, as their predecessors had done in describing the working class, but in examining the social conditions and prejudices of their subjects.

In America, the Civil War—interpreted by Europeans primarily as a contest between liberal and nationalist politics—resulted in a new realism that demythologized the antebellum-era Romantic view of slavery in art and music while also depicting the horrors of war with brutal directness. They also celebrated the good life and the leisure they had come to enjoy. New York City became the epicenter of a new kind of culture and economy in which poor immigrants, wealthy industrialists, ambitious merchants, and flagrantly corrupt politicians struggled to gain a share of the American Dream. This dream—usually expressed in dollars and the things those dollars could buy—was so often built on a framework of fraud and exploitation that writer Mark Twain, the pen name of Samuel L. Clemens (1835–1920), gave this era the compelling name the "Gilded Age." The unprecedented expansion of New York was matched in the country as a whole as agricultural and industrial production, economic growth, and population soared.

As much as the Gilded Age signified prosperity and opportunity, it was also a byword for deceit, corruption, and financial manipulation at every level of government and business. This was especially true of large corporations and trusts (a holding company that controlled many other companies). During the era, an entire class of ultra-rich businessmen emerged, termed "robber barons" because of their use of unethical and anticompetitive methods to gain wealth and power. The rich were notable for their conspicuous consumption and self-indulgent excess, which became fodder for the gossip-hungry press and public. Wealth was on display at every turn. In 1904, Mrs. Stuyvesant Fish, a leader of New York society, threw a dinner party honoring her dog, who wore a $15,000 diamond collar for the occasion. At the time, more than 90 percent of America's families survived on less than $1,200 a year.

The New Realism

Although the working classes suffered most from the miserable living conditions in cities, they were not the initial cause of the revolutionary turmoil of 1848. It was the middle-class political thinkers who most strongly argued for representative government and civil liberties. They considered themselves to be *liberal,* espousing legal equality, religious toleration, and freedom of the press. They generally believed, like Enlightenment writers John Locke and Thomas Jefferson, that government emanated from the people, who freely consented to its rule and had the power to oust unwanted leaders. The people expressed this consent through the election of representatives, and they protected their rights through written constitutions. Many liberals supported the ideas of Adam Smith, who argued that government should keep its nose out of economics and trade. Many were, in fact, self-serving capitalists, partisans of unregulated economic life, and opponents of tyranny of any government that threatened their self-interest. When they allied themselves with the working classes—generally more predisposed to violence—it was more a matter of convenience than conviction. Nineteenth-century liberalism thus expressed the French Revolution's principle, *"Liberté, Égalité, Fraternité,"* in less strident terms, but with the same concern for individual rights and common morality.

Marxism

There were, however, more radical thinkers whose convictions were untarnished by self-interest and who, furthermore, did not shy away from proposing violence to attain their goals. Karl Marx (1818–1883) and Friedrich Engels

[EN-gulz] (1820–1895) were two young, middle-class Germans who believed that since the conditions in which one earns a living determined all other aspects of life—social, political, and cultural—capitalism must be eliminated because of its inherent unfairness. Reform was pointless—only a revolution of the working people would succeed in achieving meaningful change. In fact, Marx and Engels believed revolution was inevitable, following the logic of the philosopher Georg Wilhelm Friedrich Hegel's dialectic. The struggle between the bourgeoisie and the proletariat (working class) amounted to the conflict between thesis and antithesis. (The term **bourgeoisie** generally referred to the capitalist or merchant class—shopkeepers, merchants, and businesspeople—as distinct from the **proletariat**, laborers and wage-earners who lack both ownership of the means of production—tools and equipment—and control over the quality and price of their own work.) The resolution lay in the synthesis of a classless society, a utopian society at "the end of history," since the dialectic forces that drive history would be finally and permanently resolved.

The collaboration of Marx and Engels would ultimately help shape nineteenth- and twentieth-century history across the globe. Their epochal partnership began rather simply in a Parisian café in August 1844, where Marx first met Engels. Marx had been editing a German newspaper and Engels was the heir to his father's textile factory in Manchester, England. The following year Engels published his *Conditions of the Working Class in England,* a scathing indictment of industrial life, and in early 1848 the two had coauthored and published a manifesto for the newly formed Communist League in London. The term *communist* at the time suggested a more radical approach to communal politics than *socialist.* In the *Communist Manifesto,* Marx and Engels argued that class struggle characterized all past societies and that industrial society simplified these class antagonisms. "Society as a whole is splitting up more and more into two great hostile camps, into two great classes directly facing each other: Bourgeoisie and Proletariat."

In its most controversial phrases, the *Communist Manifesto* called for "the forcible overthrow of all existing social conditions," and concluded, "The proletarians have nothing to lose but their chains. They have a world to win. WORKING MEN OF ALL COUNTRIES, UNITE." This simplistic call to arms would gain support steadily through the ensuing decades, even though Marx and Engels failed to anticipate capitalism's ability to adapt to change and slowly improve the lot of "the proletariat." However, the *Manifesto,* as well as Marx's later *Das Kapital (Capital),* offered an important testament of the living conditions of the proletariat and an incisive interpretation of the way capitalism operated. Ironically, this forceful critique of the effects of the free market became an influential factor in advancing reforms in working conditions, as well as providing higher wages and greater social equality.

Literary Realism

The thinking of Marx and Engels reflected a concern widespread among social-minded Europeans and Americans for the plight of working people—and, in America, slaves. Chief among their targets were the economic engine of the industrial state—its desire to reap a profit at whatever human cost—and the unbridled materialism that seemed to drive industrialism's economic engine.

Charles Dickens and the Industrial City   The novels of Charles Dickens (1812–1870) illuminate the enormous inequities of class that existed in nineteenth-century England, with his heroes and heroines, villains and scoundrels, often approaching the point of caricature. While his sentimentalism sometimes verged on the maudlin, Dickens also had an unparalleled ability to vividly describe English reality. In depicting the lives of the English lower classes with intense sympathy and great attention to detail, Dickens became a leading creator of a new type of prose fiction, **literary realism**.

In his earliest published book, writing under the pen name Boz, Dickens describes one of the worst slums in London, on Drury Lane (**Reading 13.1**). A century earlier, it had been a good address, but by the beginning of the 1800s it was dominated by prostitution and gin houses (Fig. **13.2**):

READING 13.1   **from Dickens, *Sketches by Boz* (1836)**

The filthy and miserable appearance of this part of London can hardly be imagined by those (and there are many such) who have not witnessed it. Wretched houses with broken windows patched with rags and paper; every room let out [rented] to a different family, and sometimes two or even three—fruit and "sweet stuff" manufacturing in the cellars, barners and redherring vendors in the front parlours, cobblers in the back; a bird fancier in the first floor, three families on the second, starvation in the attics, Irishman in the passage, a "musician" in the front kitchen, and a charwoman and five hungry children in the back one—filth everywhere—a gutter before the houses and a drain behind—clothes drying, and slops emptying from the windows, girls of fourteen or fifteen, with matted hair, walking about barefoot, and in white great-coats, almost their only covering; boys of all ages, in coats of all sizes and no coats at all; men and women, in every variety of scanty and dirty apparel, lounging, scolding, drinking, smoking, squabbling, fighting, and swearing.

The writing style is pure Dickens. Descriptions pile up in detail after detail, in one long sentence, so that the reader, almost breathless at its conclusion, feels overwhelmed, as the

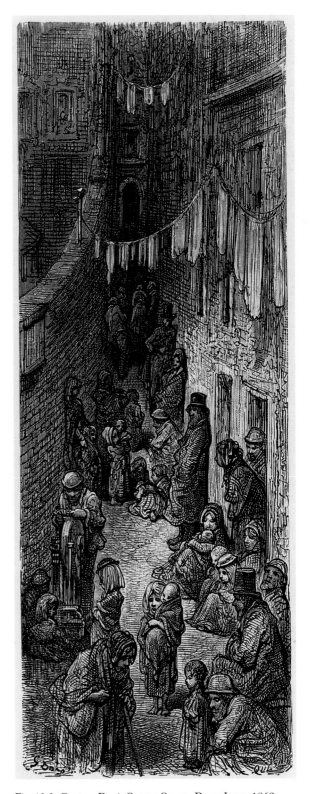

Fig. 13.2 Gustave Doré. *Orange Court—Drury Lane*. 1869. Illustration for Gustave Doré and Blanchard Jerrold, *London: A Pilgrimage*, 1872. Accompanied by policemen from Scotland Yard, Doré went around the city, including the East End and Whitechapel, making sketches on the spot. Though executed some 36 years after Dickens penned *Sketches by Boz*, Doré's drawings capture the poverty that Dickens described, at the same time proving how enduring poverty was.

author tries to make the unimaginable real. His aim is not simply to entertain, but to advocate reform.

French Literary Realism: Balzac and Flaubert In France, realist writers such as Honoré de Balzac [bal-zak] (1799–1850) and Gustave Flaubert [floh-BAIR] (1821–1880) were committed to examining life scientifically—that is, without bias—and describing it in as straightforward a manner as possible. In 1833, Balzac decided to link together his old novels so that they would reflect the whole of French society. He would come to call this series of books *The Human Comedy*. Balzac's plan eventually resulted in 92 novels, which include more than 2,000 characters. Among the masterpieces are *Eugénie Grandet* [er-ZHEN-ee GRAHN-deh] (1833), *Père Goriot* [pair GOH-ree-oh] (1834) (*Father Goriot*), the trilogy *Lost Illusions* (1837–1843), and *Cousin Bette* [koo-ZEHN bet] (1846). The primary setting is Paris, with its old aristocracy, new wealth, and the rising culture of the bourgeoisie. The novel is populated by characters from all levels of society—servants, workers, clerks, criminals, intellectuals, courtesans, and prostitutes. Certain individuals make appearances in novel after novel, for instance Eugène Rastignac [eh-ZHEN RAH-steen-yak], a central figure in *Father Goriot*, who comes from an impoverished provincial family to Paris to seek his fortune, and Henri de Marsay [ahn-REE deh mar-ZAY], a dandy who appears in 25 of the novels.

Balzac drew his characters from direct observation: "In listening to these people," he wrote of those he encountered in the Paris streets, "I could espouse their lives. I felt their rags on my back. I walked with my feet in their tattered shoes; their desires, their wants—everything passed into my soul." The story goes that he once interrupted one of his friends, who was telling about his sister's illness, by saying, "That's all very well, but let's get back to reality: to whom are we going to marry Eugénie Grandet?"

The novel *Madame Bovary*, written by Gustave Flaubert at mid-century, is at its core a realist attack on Romantic sensibility. But Flaubert had a strong Romantic streak as well, for which his Parisian friends strongly condemned him. They suggested that he should write a "down-to-earth" novel of ordinary life, and further, that he base it on the true story of Delphine Delamare [del-MAR], the adulterous wife of a country doctor who had died of grief after deceiving and ruining him. Flaubert agreed, and *Madame Bovary*, first published in magazine installments in 1856, is the result.

The realism of the novel is born of Flaubert's struggle not to be Romantic. He would later say, "Madame Bovary—*c'est moi!*" [say- MWAH] ("Madame Bovary—that's me!") in testament to his deep understanding of the bourgeois, Romantic sensibility that his novel condemns. Toward the middle of the novel, Emma imagines she is dying. She has been ill for two months, since her lover Rodolphe ended their affair. Now, she romanticizes what she thinks are her last moments, experiencing a rapturous ecstasy of the kind portrayed by Bernini in *The Ecstasy of St. Teresa* (**Reading 13.2**; also see Fig. 10.7):

READING 13.2 **from Flaubert, *Madame Bovary* (1856)**

One day, when at the height of her illness, she had thought herself dying, and had asked for the communion; and, while they were making the preparations in her room for the sacrament, while they were turning the night table covered with syrups into an altar, and while Felicite was strewing dahlia flowers on the floor, Emma felt some power passing over her that freed her from her pains, from all perception, from all feeling. Her body, relieved, no longer thought; another life was beginning; it seemed to her that her being, mounting toward God, would be annihilated in that love like a burning incense that melts into vapour. The bed-clothes were sprinkled with holy water, the priest drew from the holy pyx [small box containing the sacrament] the white wafer. . . . The curtains of the alcove floated gently round her like clouds, and the rays of the two tapers burning on the night-table seemed to shine like dazzling halos. Then she let her head fall back, fancying she heard in space the music of seraphic harps, and perceived in an azure sky, on a golden throne in the midst of saints holding green palms, God the Father, resplendent with majesty.

In an 1852 letter describing a dinner conversation between Leon and Emma earlier in the book, Flaubert wrote: "I'm working on a conversation between a young man and a young lady on literature, the sea, the mountains, music—in short, every poetic subject there is. It could be taken seriously and I intend it to be totally absurd." The same could be said of Emma's faint in which her paroxysm of religious experience is as staged as her illness itself. Words and phrases such as "an azure sky, on a golden throne" are examples of what Flaubert called *le mot juste* [leh moh joost], "the right word," exactly the precise usage to capture the essence of each situation, in this case a level of cliché that underscores the dramatic absurdity of Emma's experience. Flaubert felt he was proceeding like the modern scientist, investigating the lives of his characters through careful and systematic observation.

Literary Realism in the United States: The Issue of Slavery The issue of slavery haunted American realist writers. They were inspired largely by the abolitionist movement. While the movement had been active in both Europe and America ever since the 1770s (see chapter 12), it didn't gain real momentum in the United States until the establishment of the American Anti-Slavery Society in 1833. The Society organized lecture tours by abolitionists, gathered petitions, and printed and distributed anti-slavery propaganda. By 1840, it had 250,000 members in 2,000 local chapters and was publishing more than 20 journals.

One of the most important abolitionist texts of the day is the autobiography of Frederick Douglass (1817–1895), *Narrative of the Life of Frederick Douglass: An American Slave*, published in 1845. The book moves from Douglass's first clear memory, the whipping of his Aunt Hester, which he describes as his "entrance into the hell of slavery," to the turning point, when as a young man Douglass resolves to stand up and fight his master. "From whence came the spirit I don't know," Douglass writes. "You have seen how a man was made a slave; you shall see how a slave was made a man," he says before summing up the fight's outcome (**Reading 13.3**):

READING 13.3 from *Narrative of the Life of Frederick Douglass* (1845)

This battle with Mr. Covey was the turning point in my career as a slave. It rekindled the few expiring embers of freedom, and revived within me a sense of my own manhood. It . . . inspired me again with a determination to be free. The gratification afforded by the triumph was a full compensation for whatever else might follow, even death itself. . . . I felt as I never felt before. It was a glorious resurrection, from the tomb of slavery, to the heaven of freedom. My long-crushed spirit rose, cowardice departed, bold defiance took its place; and I now resolved that, however long I might remain a slave in form, the day had passed forever when I could be a slave in fact. I did not hesitate to let it be known of me, that the white man who expected to succeed in whipping, must also succeed in killing me.

More than 100 book-length slave narratives were published in the 1850s and 1860s. Besides Douglass's, one of the other most important of these was the *Narrative of Sojourner Truth*, dictated by an illiterate former slave to her friend Olive Gilbert. Sojourner Truth (ca. 1797–1883) was born Isabella Baumfree to slave parents in Ulster County, New York, and was sold four times before she was 30 years old. In 1843, inspired by a spiritual revelation, she changed her name to Sojourner Truth and became a preacher advocating "God's truth and plan for salvation." She often tied her lessons to her own experiences as a slave, and she championed both abolition and the woman's suffrage movement. Her most famous speech, "Ain't I a Woman?" delivered to a Women's Convention in Akron, Ohio, in 1851, argues that the cause of women's rights is integral to the effort to end slavery. The growing conviction that women—white and black—endured a brand of slavery of their own is one of the most important subtexts of the Civil War.

But the most influential abolitionist tract of the day was the novel *Uncle Tom's Cabin* by Harriet Beecher Stowe (1811–1896). It describes the differing fates of three slaves— Tom, Eliza, and George—whose life in slavery begins together in Kentucky. Although Eliza and George are married, they are owned by different masters. In order to live together they escape

to free territory with their little boy. Tom meets a different fate. Separated from his wife and children, he is sold by his first owner to a kind master, Augustine St. Clare, and then to the evil Simon Legree, who eventually kills him. Serialized in 1851 in the abolitionist newspaper *The National Era*, and published the year after, the book sold 300,000 copies in the first year after its publication. Stowe's depiction of the plight of slaves like Tom roused antislavery sentiment worldwide and it eventually became the bestselling novel of the nineteenth century.

The scene of Little Eva reading from the Bible to Tom (Fig. 13.3) as Stowe sets it up in chapter 22 of the novel is deeply romanticized (**Reading 13.4**):

READING 13.4 from Harriet Beecher Stowe, *Uncle Tom's Cabin* (1852)

It is now one of those intensely golden sunsets which kindles the whole horizon into one blaze of glory, and makes the water another sky. The lake lay in rosy or golden streaks, save where white-winged vessels glided hither and thither, like so many spirits, and little golden stars twinkled through the glow, and looked down at themselves as they trembled in the water. . . .

At first, she read to please her humble friend; but soon her own earnest nature threw out its tendrils, and wound itself around the majestic book; and Eva loved it, because it woke in her strange yearnings, and strong, dim emotions, such as impassioned, imaginative children love to feel.

This passage points to a central mission of the abolitionist movement. Abolitionists felt the duty to enlighten the darkened souls of slaves by asserting Christian beliefs. Notice how light is used as a metaphor in the passage. But the condescension apparent to the modern reader—both Tom and Eva are depicted as children—together with Tom's sentimental attachment to both Eva and her pious Christianity would eventually make the term "Uncle Tom" a derogatory label referring to anyone who is servile or deferential to white people.

A patronizing tone dominates representations of African Americans by whites in the nineteenth and twentieth centuries, and it informs Mark Twain's *Adventures of Huckleberry Finn* (1885), arguably one of the greatest American novels. It tells the story of a young boy, Huck Finn, and Jim, an escaped slave, as they make their way by raft down the Mississippi River from Hannibal, Missouri. They intend to turn north at the juncture of the Ohio River so that Jim might reach freedom in Cincinnati. (Ohio was a slave-free state.) Set in the years just before the Civil War, the book is vigorously opposed to slavery, and portrays those who supported it in a uniformly unflattering light, designed precisely to expose them. When, for instance, Huck and Jim are anticipating arriving at Cairo, where the Ohio meets the Mississippi, Huck is anguished by his role in helping Jim escape (**Reading 13.5**):

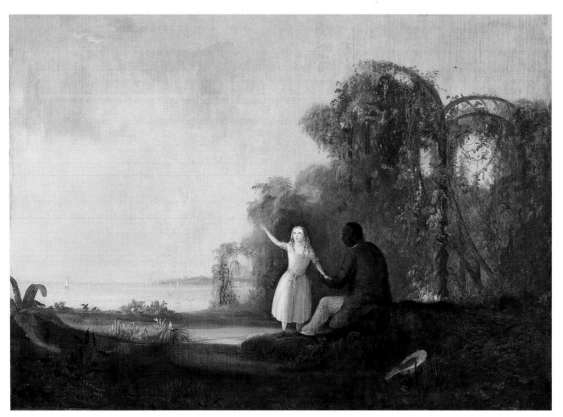

Fig. 13.3 Robert S. Duncanson. *Uncle Tom and Little Eva.* **1853.** Oil on canvas, $27\frac{1}{4}$″ × $38\frac{1}{4}$″. The Detroit Institute of Arts, USA. The Bridgeman Art Library. MI. Duncanson was the first African American artist to receive international fame.

READING 13.5 **from Mark Twain,**
Huckleberry Finn (1885)

Jim said it made him all over trembly and feverish to be so close to freedom. Well, I can tell you it made me all over trembly and feverish, too, to hear him, because I begun to get it through my head that he was most free—and who was to blame for it? Why, me. I couldn't get that out of my conscience, no how nor no way. It got to troubling me so I couldn't rest; I couldn't stay still in one place. It hadn't ever come home to me before, what this thing was that I was doing. But now it did; and it stayed with me, and scorched me more and more. I tried to make out to myself that I warn't to blame, because I didn't run Jim off from his rightful owner; but it warn't no use, conscience up and says, every time, "But you knowed he was running for his freedom, and you could a paddled ashore and told somebody." That was so—I couldn't get around that noway. That was where it pinched. Conscience says to me, "What had poor Miss Watson done to you that you could see her nigger go off right under your eyes and never say one single word? What did that poor old woman do to you that you could treat her so mean? Why, she tried to learn you your book, she tried to learn you your manners, she tried to

be good to you every way she knowed how. That's what she done." I got to feeling so mean and so miserable I most wished I was dead. I fidgeted up and down the raft, abusing myself to myself, and Jim was fidgeting up and down past me. We neither of us could keep still. Every time he danced around and says, "Dah's Cairo!" it went through me like a shot, and I thought if it was Cairo I reckoned I would die of miserableness.

Huck is torn between the tenets of his upbringing, in which slaves were the legal property of their owner, and his affection for Jim as a human being. In helping Jim, he believes he is stealing from Miss Watson, one of the two sisters who have adopted him.

Twain put words into the mouths of his characters that are realistic for the time but offensive today. Thus, when Aunt Sally asks if anyone was hurt in a steamboat accident, Huck replies, "No'm. Killed a nigger." Twain fully intends the word to signify racist dehumanization of African Americans by whites, but Huck is speaking exactly as a young boy raised in the slaveholding South would. Part of Twain's literary achievement is to allow his readers the chance to see the specter of racism rise up in otherwise basically good people, and along with Huck discover that presence in themselves. The triumph of *Huckleberry Finn*, then, lies in the fact that the reader joins Huck in coming to understand and appreciate Jim's humanity.

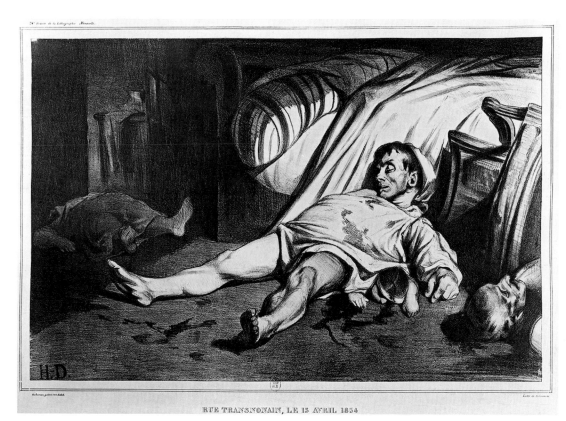

RUE TRANSNONAIN, LE 15 AVRIL 1834

Fig. 13.4 Honoré Daumier. *Rue Transnonain, April 15, 1834.* **1834.** Lithograph, $11\frac{1}{2}"$ × $17\frac{5}{8}"$. Inv. A 1970-67. Kupferstichkabinett, Staatliche Kunstsammlungen, Dresden, Germany. Erich Lessing / Art Resource, NY. A few days after the police killed the residents of 12 Rue Transnonain, Daumier exhibited this image in the window of a Paris store, drawing huge crowds.

Realist Art: The Worker as Subject

One of the leading proponents of a new realist art was Honoré Daumier [DOH-mee-ay] (1808–1879), an artist known for his political satire who regularly submitted cartoon drawings to daily and weekly newspapers. The development of the new medium of **lithography** made Daumier's regular appearance in newspapers possible. He could literally create a drawing and publish it the same day. In his focus on ordinary life, Daumier openly lampooned the idealism of both Neoclassical and Romantic art. No longer was the object of art to reveal some "higher" truth. What mattered instead was the truth of everyday experience, and in Louis-Philippe's France, everyday experience was not always an attractive proposition.

Daumier's *Rue Transnonain* [roo trahns-noh-NAN] is not a cartoon but direct reportage of the killings committed by government troops during an insurrection by Parisian workers in April 1834 (Fig. **13.4**). After a sniper's bullet killed one of their officers, the police claimed it had come from 12 rue Transnonain, and they killed everyone inside. Daumier's illustration shows the father of the family, who had been sleeping, lying dead by his bed, his child crushed beneath him, his dead wife to his right and an elder parent to his left. The strong diagonal of the scene draws us into its space, a working-class recasting of Géricault's *Raft of the "Medusa"* (see Fig. 12.18). The impact of such images on the French public was substantial, as the king clearly understood. Louis-Philippe eventually declared that freedom of the press extended to verbal but not pictorial representation.

In his paintings, such as *The Third-Class Carriage* (Fig. **13.5**), Daumier clearly demonstrates his interest in the daily lives of working people. The painting conveys a sense of unity and continuity with the men gathered in the background apparently engaged in conversation, while a young mother breast-feeds her child, her own mother beside her, a basket (presumably of food) on her lap, and her young son asleep beside his grandmother.

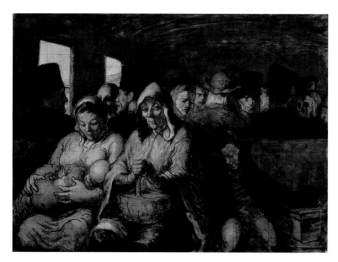

Fig. 13.5 Honoré Daumier. *The Third-Class Carriage.* **ca. 1862.** Oil on canvas, $25\frac{3}{4}"$ × $35\frac{1}{2}"$. Bequest of Mrs. H. O. Havemeyer, 1929. The H. O. Havemeyer Collection. © 1922 The Metropolitan Museum of Art, NY. Without glass windows, third-class carriages were open to smoke, cinders, and the cold.

The subject of Daumier's painting is typical of French realist painting as a whole. By focusing on laborers and common country folk rather than on the Parisian aristocracy and bourgeoisie, the painting is implicitly political, reflecting the social upheaval that in 1848 rocked almost all of Europe. But Daumier's painting is relatively modest in size. When Gustave Courbet [coor-BAY] (1819–1877) exhibited his painting *The Stonebreakers* (Fig. **13.6**) at the Salon of 1859–1861, the public was genuinely astonished by the monumental scale of the painting. Such a grand size was usually reserved for paintings of historical events, but Courbet's subjects were the mundane and the everyday.

A farmer's son and self-taught artist, Courbet's goal was to paint the world just as he saw it, without any taint of Romanticism or idealism. "To know in order to be able to create," Courbet wrote in his Realist Manifesto of 1855, "that was my idea. To be in a position to translate the customs, the ideas, the appearance of my epoch, according to my own estimation; to be not only a painter, but a man as well; in short, to create living art—this is my goal." In fact, he rejected the traditional political and moral dimensions of realism in favor of a more subjective and apolitical approach to art. This new brand of realism would dominate the art of the following generations.

In *The Stonebreakers*, Courbet depicts two workers outside his native Ornans, a town at the foot of the Jura Mountains near the Swiss border. They are pounding stones to make gravel for a road. Everything in the painting seems to be pulled down by the weight of physical labor—the strap pulling down across the boy's back, the basket of stones resting on his knee, the hammer in the older man's hand descending downward, the stiff, thick cloth of his trousers pressing against his thigh, even the shadows of the hillside behind them descending toward them. Only a small patch of sky peeks from behind the rocky ridge in the upper right-hand corner, the ridge itself following the same downward path as the hammer. Together, the older man and his younger assistant seem to suggest the unending nature of their work, as if their backbreaking work has afflicted generation after generation of Courbet's rural contemporaries—"a complete expression of human misery," as Courbet explained it.

Photography: Realism's Pencil of Light

It is no coincidence that the invention of photography coincides with the rise of realism in the arts. The scientific principles required for photography had been known in Europe since

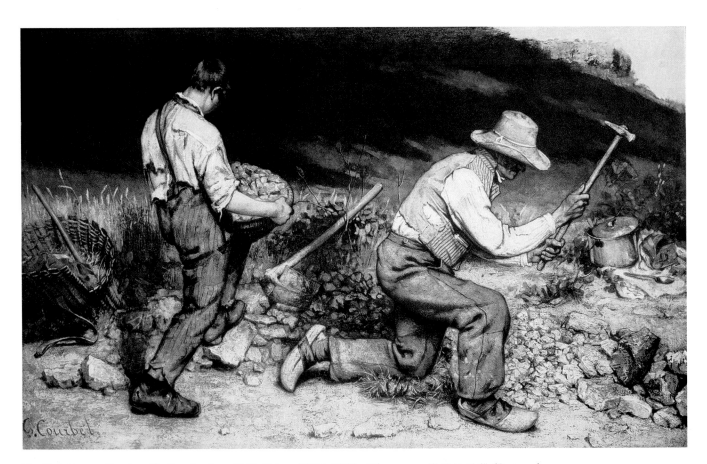

Fig. 13.6 Gustave Courbet. *The Stonebreakers*. 1849. (Salon of 1850–1851). Oil on canvas, 5′ 3″ × 8′ 6″. (Destroyed in 1945), Galerie Neue Meister, Dresden, Germany, © Staatliche Kunstsammlungen Dresden. The Bridgeman Art Library. The painting is believed to have been destroyed during the American fire-bombing of Dresden in World War II.

at least 1727 when Johann Heinrich Schulze (1684–1744), a German physician, showed that certain chemicals, especially silver halides, turn dark when exposed to light. And the optical principle employed in the camera is essentially the same as that used in the *camera obscura*, an instrument that works by admitting a ray of light through a small hole that projects a scene, upside down, directly across from the hole. While the *camera obscura* could capture an image, it could not preserve it. But in 1839, inventors in England and France discovered a means to fix the image. It was as if the world could now be drawn by a pencil made of light itself.

In England, William Henry Fox Talbot presented a process for fixing negative images on paper coated with light-sensitive chemicals, which he called **photogenic drawing**. In France, a different process, which yielded a positive image on a polished metal plate, was named the **daguerreotype** [duh-GAIR-oh-type], after one of its inventors, Louis-Jacques-Mandé Daguerre [duh-GAIR] (1789–1851). Wildly enthusiastic public reaction followed, and the French and English presses reported each advance in great detail.

When the French painter Paul Delaroche [deh-lah-ROSH] saw his first daguerreotype, he exclaimed, "From now on, painting is dead!" Delaroche overreacted, but he understood the potential of photography to seize painting's historical role of representing the world. Photographic portraiture quickly became a successful business, with daguerreotype images of individuals costing 15 francs in Paris. This new medium made personalized pictures available not only to the wealthy but to the middle and working classes. By 1849, a decade after the process was discovered, 100,000 daguerreotype portraits were sold in Paris each year.

At the time Daguerre first announced his discovery, imprinting an image on a metal plate took 8 to 10 minutes in bright summer light. His photo of *Le Boulevard du Temple* was exposed for so long that none of the people or traffic moving in the street left any impression, except for one solitary figure at the lower left who is having his shoes shined (Fig. **13.7**). By 1841, the discovery of so-called chemical "accelerators" had made it possible to expose the plate for only 1 minute, but a sitter could not move for fear of blurring the image. The process remained cumbersome, requiring considerable time to prepare, expose, and develop the plate.

The daguerreotype process resulted in a single, unreproducible image, but the invention of lithography had demonstrated that there was a market for mass-produced prints. Fox Talbot, whose photogenic drawings utilized paper instead of a metal plate, led the way to making multiple prints of an image, and in 1844–1845 he published the first book fully illustrated by photographs, *The Pencil of Nature*. One image

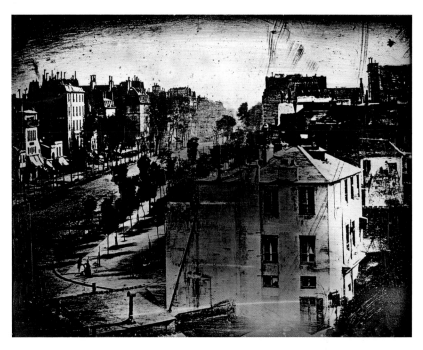

Fig. 13.7 Louis-Jacques-Mandé Daguerre. *Le Boulevard du Temple.* **1839.** Daguerreotype. Bayerisches National Museum, Munich. Daguerre was a painter who made his living producing panoramic dioramas, room-size backlit paintings that appeared to change from daylight to dusk as the illumination behind them decreased. Daguerre composed these large painted scenes with a *camera obscura*, a tedious process requiring hours of tracing. His interest in photography stemmed from his desire to speed up his painting process. This daguerreotype was taken from the roof of the building that housed his diorama attraction.

in the book was accompanied by the following caption: "A painter's eye will often be arrested where ordinary people see nothing remarkable. A casual gleam of sunshine, or a shadow thrown across his path, a time-withered oak, or a moss-covered stone may awaken a train of thought and feelings. . . ." Thus, for Talbot, photography was a realist medium that might evoke Romantic sentiment. But the medium's ability to document current events quickly overshadowed its more artistic possibilities in the public mind.

Mathew Brady's Photographers On September 19, 1862, Alexander Gardner, an employee of the photographer Mathew Brady (1823–1896), visited the battlefield at Antietam [an-TEET-um], Maryland. Twenty-six thousand Northern and Southern troops had just died in a battle that had no particular significance and decided nothing. Until that day, no American battlefield had ever been photographed before the dead were properly buried, but Gardner took many photographs of the scene. He even rearranged the bodies of the dead for photographic effect—in part a necessity created by the technical limitations of photographing on a smoky battlefield. Gardner's manipulation of scenes for the camera was understood as an attempt to record a more accurate sense of the whole. Brady displayed Gardner's photographs in his New York gallery on Broadway in October—and took full credit for them, to Gardner's dismay. Within a month Brady was selling the pictures in both album-card size and stereoscopic views.

In July 1863, Gardner, now working on his own, went to the site of the Battle of Gettysburg with an assistant, Timothy O'Sullivan, who shot the most famous photograph to come out of the war, *A Harvest of Death, Gettysburg, Pennsylvania, July 1863* (Fig. **13.8**). It was published after the war in 1866 in *Gardner's Photographic Sketchbook of the War*, probably the first book-length photo essay. It is a condemnation of the horrors of war, with the Battle of Gettysburg at its center. O'Sullivan's matter-of-fact photograph is accompanied by the following caption:

> The rebels represented in the photograph are without shoes. These were always removed from the feet of the dead on account of the pressing need of the survivors. The pockets turned inside out also show that appropriation did not cease with the coverings of the feet. Around is scattered the litter of the battle-field, accoutrements, ammunitions, rags, cups and canteens, crackers, haversacks, and letters that may tell the name of the owner, although the majority will surely be buried unknown by strangers, and in a strange land.

In O'Sullivan's photograph, both foreground and background are purposefully blurred to draw attention to the central corpses. Such focus was made possible by the introduction of albumen paper, which retained a high degree of sharpness on its glossy surface. "Such a picture," Gardner wrote, "conveys a useful moral: It shows the blank horror and reality of war, in opposition to the pageantry. Here are the dreadful details! Let them aid in preventing such another calamity falling upon the nation."

In Pursuit of Modernity: Paris in the 1850s and '60s

Soon after the stunning events of 1848, Pierre-Joseph Proudhon [proo-DOHN] (1809–1865), the French journalist who first called himself an "anarchist" and famously coined the phrase "property is theft," wrote: "We have been beaten and humiliated . . . scattered, imprisoned, disarmed, and gagged. The fate of European democracy has slipped from our hands." Political and moral idealism seemed vanquished. In their place remained only the banal prosperity of the triumphant bourgeoisie. In fact, the political, moral, and religious emptiness of the bourgeoisie became the targets of a new realism, which critiqued what Proudhon called the "fleshy, comfortable" bourgeois lifestyle.

Charles Baudelaire and the Poetry of Modern Life

The poet Charles Baudelaire [boh-deh-LAIR] (1821–1867) recognized the bourgeoisie as his audience, but their hypocrisy was his constant target. And his poetry, which was

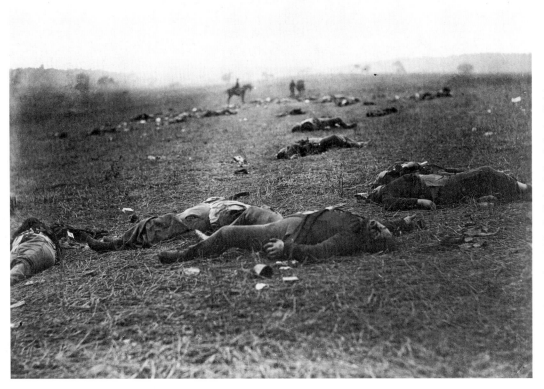

Fig. 13.8 Timothy O'Sullivan (negative) and Alexander Gardner (print). *A Harvest of Death, Gettysburg, Pennsylvania, July 1863*, from Alexander Gardner's *Gardner's Photographic Sketchbook of the War.* 1866. Albumen silver print (also available as a stereocard), $6\frac{1}{4}'' \times 7\frac{13}{16}''$. Location: The New York Public Library, New York, NY/Art Resource, NY. The battle of Gettysburg was the decisive land battle of the American Civil War, a battle that left 51,000 casualties—dead, wounded, captured, or missing—in three days of fighting.

passionately attacked for its unconventional themes and subject matter, was designed to shock bourgeois minds. When Flaubert's *Madame Bovary* first appeared in magazine installments in 1856, its author had been brought to trial, charged with giving "offense to public and religious morality and to good morals." Eight months later, in August 1857, Baudelaire, Flaubert's good friend, faced the same charge for his book of 100 poems, *Les Fleurs du mal* [lay fler doo mahl], usually translated "Flowers of Evil." Unlike Flaubert, Baudelaire lost his case, was fined, and was forced to remove six poems concerning lesbianism and vampirism, all of which remained censored . . . for the next century!

The poems in *Les Fleurs du mal* unflinchingly confront the realities of this "underworld" and of life itself. In the poem "Carrion," for example, Baudelaire recalls strolling with his love one day (**Reading 13.6**):

READING 13.6 **Charles Baudelaire, "Carrion," in *Les Fleurs du mal* (1857) (translation by Richard Howard)**

Remember, my soul, the thing we saw
that lovely summer day?
On a pile of stones where the path turned off,
the hideous carrion—

legs in the air, like a whore—displayed
indifferent to the last,
a belly slick with lethal sweat
and swollen with foul gas.

the sun lit up that rottenness
as though to roast it through,
restoring to Nature a hundredfold
what she had here made one.

And heaven watched the splendid corpse
like flower open wide—
you nearly fainted dead away
at the perfume it gave off.

The poem is an attack on the Romanticized view of death that marks, for instance, Emma Bovary's illusory ecstasy. To look at such reality unflinchingly, with open eyes, is, for Baudelaire, the central requirement of modern life.

Émile Zola and the Naturalist Novel

The novelist Émile Zola [ay-MEEL zoh-LAH] (1840–1902) practiced a brand of literary realism called *naturalism*—that is, in his words, "nature seen through a temperament." It is distinct from realism because it does not pretend to objective reporting. Zola was, in other words, completely aware that the artist's own personality definitively influenced the work and his view of the world (**Reading 13.7**):

READING 13.7 **from Émile Zola, "The Moment in Art" (1867)**

There are, in my opinion, two elements in a work: the element of reality, which is nature, and the personal element, which is man. The element of reality, nature, is fixed, always the same; it is given equally to all men. . . . The personal element, man, is, on the other hand, infinitely variable; there are as many possible works as there are different minds. . . . The word "realist" means nothing to me, since I am determined to subordinate the real to temperament. . . . For it is equally ridiculous to believe that in matters of artistic beauty, there is one absolute and eternal truth. The single and whole truth is no good for us, since we construct new truths each morning and have worn them out by the evening. . . . This means that the works of tomorrow cannot be the same as those of today. . . .

Zola also believed that all human beings (including authors and artists) are products of hereditary and environmental factors over which they have no control but which very much determine their lives. He applied this belief in such novels as *Thérèse Raquin* [tay-REZ rah-KEHN] (1867). The Thérèse of the title begins a love affair with a friend of her husband. The lovers drown the husband, only to find that their guilt makes life together intolerable, leading them to plot each other's murder. Zola described his strategy in the novel's preface (**Reading 13.8**):

READING 13.8 **from Émile Zola, Preface to *Thérèse Raquin*, 2nd edition (1868)**

I set out to study, not characters, but temperaments. Therein lies the whole essence of the book. I chose to portray individuals existing under the sovereign dominion of their nerves and their blood, devoid of free will and drawn into every act of their lives by the inescapable laws of their physical nature. Thérèse and Laurent are human animals, nothing more. I have endeavored to follow these animals through the devious working of their passions, the compulsion of their instincts, and the mental unbalance resulting from a nervous crisis. . . . I had only one desire: given a highly-sexed man and an unsatisfied woman, to uncover the animal side of them and see that alone, then throw them together in a violent drama and note down with scrupulous care the sensations and actions of these creatures. I simply applied to two living bodies the analy- tical method that surgeons apply to corpses.

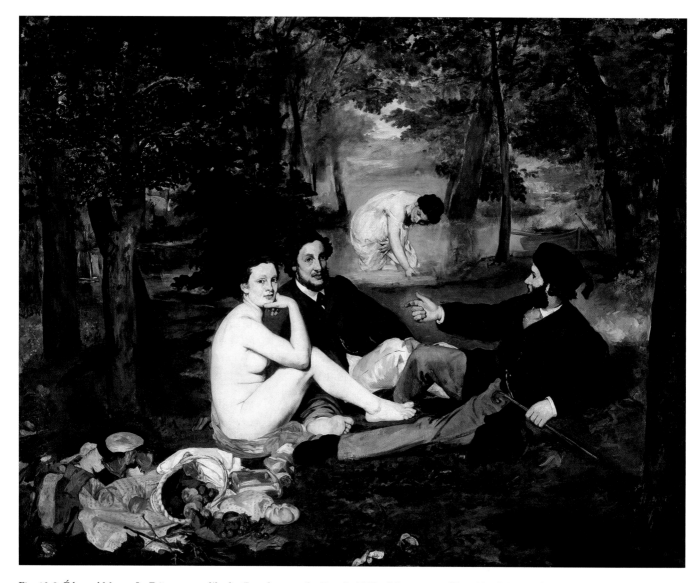

Fig. 13.9 Édouard Manet. *Le Déjeuner sur l'herbe (Luncheon on the Grass)*. **1863.** Oil on canvas, 7′ × 8′ 10″. Musée d'Orsay, Paris. RMN Réunion des Musées Nationaux/Art Resource, NY. © 2008 ARS Artists Rights Society, NY. It seems likely that another source for Manet's painting was Georgione's *Pastoral Concert* (see Fig. 7.36), which was in the Louvre.

Édouard Manet: The Painter of Modern Life

In 1863, Baudelaire called for an artist "gifted with an active imagination" to actively pursue a new artistic goal: describing the modern city and its culture. Zola's close friend, Édouard Manet, most clearly embodies this new vision of the artist as a recorder of everyday city life, since he, like Baudelaire, was a *flâneur*. The *flâneur* was a man-about-town, with no apparent occupation, strolling the city, studying and experiencing it coolly, dispassionately. Moving among its crowds and cafés in fastidious and fashionable dress, the *flâneur* had an acute ability to understand the subtleties of modern life and the ability to create art, according to a definitive essay by Baudelaire (**Reading 13.9**):

READING 13.9 **from Charles Baudelaire, "The Painter of Modern Life" (1863)**

Be very sure that this man, such as I have depicted him—this solitary, gifted with an active imagination, ceaselessly journeying across the great human desert—[aims for] . . . something other than the fugitive pleasure of circumstance. He is looking for that quality which you must allow me to call "modernity". . . By "modernity" I mean the ephemeral, the fugitive, the contingent. . . . This transitory, fugitive element, whose metamorphoses are so rapid, must on no account be despised or dispensed with. By neglecting it, you cannot fail to tumble into the abyss of an abstract and indeterminate beauty.

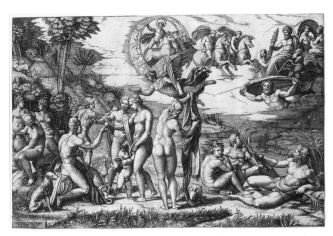

Fig. 13.10 Marcantonio Raimondi after Raphael.
***The Judgment of Paris*. ca. 1520.** Engraving. Inv. 4167LR. Rothschild Collection. Musée du Louvre/RMN Réunion des Musées Nationaux, France. SCALA/Art Resource, NY. Paris judges which of the goddesses—Aphrodite, Hera, or Athena—is the most beautiful. His choice has profound impact, leading as it does to the Trojan War.

According to Baudelaire, the *flâneur* is distinguished by one other important trait: his attitude toward the bourgeoisie. He holds their vulgar, materialistic lifestyle in contempt, and his greatest devotion is to shocking them. "*Il faut épater le bourgeois*" [eel foh ay-pah-TAY leh boor-ZHWAH] ("One must shock the bourgeoisie"), he said. Thus, it came as no surprise to Manet when *Le Déjeuner sur l'herbe* [leh day-zhur-NAY sur lerb] (*Luncheon on the Grass*) was rejected by the jury for the Salon of 1863 (Fig. **13.9**). It was not designed to please them. The

Salon drew tens of thousands of visitors a day to the Louvre and was the world's most prominent art event. The public also reacted with outrage when Manet's painting appeared at the Salon des Refusés [sah-LOHN day reh-foo-ZAY], an exhibition hurriedly ordered by Louis-Napoleon after numerous complaints arose about the large number of rejected artworks. While many of the paintings included in the Salon des Refusés were of poor quality, others, including Manet's *Le Déjeuner sur l'herbe*, were vilified because of their supposedly scandalous content or challenging style. The Paris newspapers lumped them all together: "There is something cruel about this exhibition: people laugh as they do at a farce. As a matter of fact it is a continual parody, a parody of drawing, of color, of composition."

Manet's painting evokes the *fêtes galantes* of Watteau (see Fig. 11.11) and a particular engraving executed by Marcantonio Raimondi [ray-MOHN-dee] (Fig. **13.10**) after a lost painting designed by Raphael, *The Judgment of Paris* (1520). Manet's three central figures assume the same poses as the wood nymphs seated at the lower right of Raimondi's composition, and so Manet's painting can be understood as a "judgment of Paris" in its own right—Manet judging Paris the city in all its bourgeois decadence. It was, in fact, the discord between the seated female's frank nudity—and the fact that she appears to gaze directly at the viewer—and her fully clothed male companions, who seem engaged in a conversation wholly at odds with the sexualized circumstances, that shocked the painting's audience. Manet's assault on his fellow Parisians' sensibilities continued in 1863 with *Olympia* (Fig. **13.11**), though the painting was not exhibited until the Salon of 1865, where once again it was the object of public scandal and ridicule.

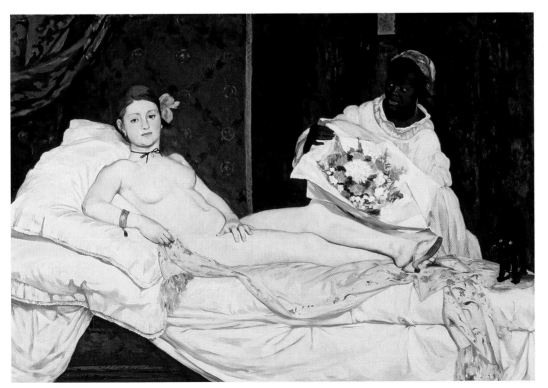

Fig. 13.11 Édouard Manet. *Olympia*. 1863 (Salon of 1865). Oil on canvas, 51″ × 74³/₄″. Inv. RF 2772. Hervè Lewandowski/Musée d'Orsay, Paris, France. RMN Réunion des Musées Nationaux/Art Resource, NY. © 2008 Édouard Manet/Artists Rights Society (ARS), NY. Manet's painting is modeled on Titian's *Venus of Urbino* (see Fig. 7.38). In Titian's painting a dog, symbolizing fidelity, lies at the nude's feet. Here a black cat, symbolizing promiscuity, arches its back as if to hiss at the viewer's attentions.

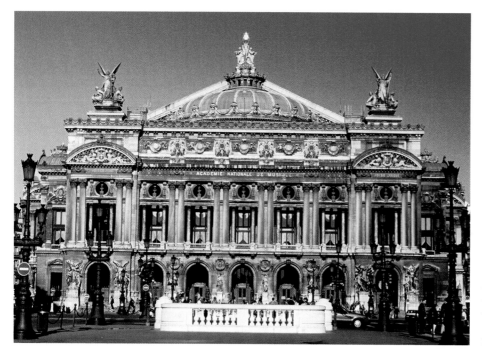

Fig. 13.12 **Charles Garnier. Façade of the Opéra, Paris. 1860–1875.** Construction of the opera building started in 1862, but was slowed because of the high water table under the gigantic stage and fly tower. The water was drained, a massive concrete well was built to carry the stage and fly tower, and it was filled with water to counter the water pressure. This is the underground lake made famous in Paul Leroux's famous play *The Phantom of the Opera.*

Manet's Olympia is a courtesan, or, more properly, not quite a courtesan. For she possesses the slightly stocky body of the working class—a *petite fabourienne* [puh-TEET fah-boor-ee-EN], one critic of the day called her, a "little factory girl." Perhaps she is one of the many factory girls who, in 1863, found themselves out of work in Paris, a casualty of the American Civil War. Unable to get raw cotton from the South, the cotton mills of Paris had to shut down. Many girls turned to prostitution in order to survive. Viewers at the Salon of 1865 were disturbed by her class—a courtesan satisfied upper-class tastes, prostitutes did not—by the position of her left hand, and, above all, by her gaze. Not only is her gaze as direct as the nude in *Le Déjeuner* (Manet used the same model in both); it is confidently directed downward toward us, the viewers. It is as if we have just arrived on the scene, bringing flowers that we have handed to the black maid. We are suddenly Olympia's customers. And if her body is for sale, then we have entered as well into the economy in which human beings are bought and sold—the economy of slavery.

Nationalism and the Politics of Opera

Popular taste in Napoleon III's Second Empire was antithetical to the realism of a Courbet and the naturalism of artists like Manet and Zola. It preferred the Romanticism of an earlier generation, as illustrated by Emma Bovary's voracious consumption of romantic novels. The dynamics of this confrontation between bourgeois taste and what we have come to call the **avant-garde** [ah-vunt-GARD]—artists on the cutting edge—played itself out in the Second Empire most surprisingly at the opera. As a musical form favored by the aristocracy, and increasingly by the bourgeoisie, opera played an important social as well as musical role in Paris. Estab-

lished by Louis XIV in 1669, the *Académie Nationale de Musique* (National Academy of Music) encompassed opera, music, and ballet. The opera was at once a state institution, a symbol of French culture and sovereignty, and a reminder of the country's royal heritage. In a period of rapid change as the aristocracy lost its hold on power throughout Europe, the opera house seemed to be an oasis of conservative stability and aristocratic values. Or ought to be, thought its longtime aristocratic patrons and the *nouveau riche* (newly rich) bourgeois audience.

Yet change did arrive at the opera in the form of the most creative composers of the period, many of whom were associated with the revolutions of 1848 and the fervent nationalism sweeping the Continent. Since the aristocracy and the bourgeoisie were hostile towards liberal nationalism and its notions of social equality and individual rights, a clash between opera's practitioners and audience was bound to happen.

Ever since Beethoven replaced his dynamic and tempo directions written in Italian with German, nationalism had become a growing force in music. Frédéric Chopin, a native of Poland, wrote many mazurkas and polonaises—traditional Polish folk-dance forms—while living in Paris as part of a group of Poles forced into exile after the Russians had taken control of their country. The composer Robert Schumann immediately recognized Chopin's works as political compositions. If the Russian czar "knew what a dangerous enemy threatened him in Chopin's works," Schumann wrote, "in the simple tunes of his mazurkas, he would forbid this music. Chopin's works are cannons buried in flowers."

The confrontation between nationalism and the aristocracy played out, in Paris, at the new Paris Opéra [oh-pay-RAH], designed by Charles Garnier and constructed between 1860 and 1875 (Fig. **13.12**). Its facade is a unique marriage of the

Neoclassical and the Baroque, conceived to reflect a new imperial style. A Corinthian colonnade of paired columns tops a closed arcade of arches at the entrance, the whole embellished with exotic carved decorations. At the head of the new, broad Avenue de l'Opéra running at a diagonal from the rue de Rivoli and the Louvre, the Opéra literally commanded the center of Paris. Its Grand Staircase, rising to a height of 98 feet, is itself a theater within the theater, designed to allow the aristocrats and the bourgeoisie to display themselves. So too were the loges, multi-seat boxes where women typically sat forward, in their finest evening wear, to show off their social position and wealth.

Giuseppe Verdi and the Grand Opera The Italian composer Giuseppe Verdi [VER-dee] (1813–1901) led the way in politicizing opera compositions. Verdi believed that opera should be, first of all, dramatically realistic. No longer were arias, duets, or quartets merely displays of the singers' technical virtuosity; rather, they dramatically expressed the characters' temperament or situation in magnificent sustained melodies. A case in point is Verdi's *Rigoletto* [ree-goh-LET-toh], a tragic opera in three acts, first performed in Venice in 1851, in which the womanizing duke of Mantua [MAHN-too-ah], disguised as a student, pays court to Gilda, who, unknown to him, is the daughter of his hunchbacked court jester, Rigoletto. When Rigoletto learns that the duke has seduced her, he conspires to have him killed by a professional assassin, but the plan goes awry when the assassin's sister, Maddalena [mad-uh-LEH-nah], pleads for the duke's life. Gilda, who has overheard their conversation, sacrifices her own life to save the duke. For Act III, Verdi composed a quartet in which each of the characters conveys contrasting emotions (**CD-Track 13.1**). Two scenes are presented simultaneously. The duke tries to seduce Maddalena inside the inn while Rigoletto and Gilda watch from the outside. Rigoletto is demonstrating to the innocent Gilda the duke's moral depravity, and she reacts with shock and dismay. Here a wide range of human emotion occurs in a single scene.

As Italy struggled to achieve national unity, Verdi's operas came to symbolize Italian nationalism. Any time a female lead in his operas would yearn for freedom, the audience would understand her as a symbol of Italian unification, and it would erupt in a frenzy of applause. Even Verdi's name came to be identified with nationalist politics, as an acronym for the constitutional monarchy, established in 1861, of Victor Emanuel—V[ictor], E[manuel], R[e] d'I[talia], "Victor Emanuel, King of [a unified] Italy."

To have his operas produced in Paris, Verdi was forced to make changes to satisfy the censors, who were sensitive to nationalist references. He had to accommodate French taste as well. Since all Paris operas traditionally included a second-act ballet, he inserted a gypsy dance around a campfire at an appropriate spot in *Il Trovatore* [eel troh-vah-TOR-eh] (*The Troubadour*). *Il Trovatore* (originally premiered in Rome in 1853) was set in Spain and centered on the Count di Luna's young brother, kidnapped and brought up by a gypsy woman, whose own mother had been burned as a witch by the count's father. The second-act ballet was a requirement of the Jockey Club, an organization of French aristocrats who came to the opera after dinner, long after the opera had begun, and expected a ballet when they arrived. As the French journalist Alfred Delvau [del-VOH] explained: "One is more deliciously stirred by the sight of the ballet corps than by the great arias of the tenor in vogue or the reigning prima donna." So Verdi, the most popular opera composer of the day, who also viewed himself as a pragmatist, went along with the idiosyncratic Paris tradition. Considering the large number of Verdi performances in Paris in the 1850s, his changes must have met with success. (In the 1856–1857 season, the Théâtre des Italiens in Paris offered 87 performances—54 of them Verdi operas.)

Wagner's Music Drama Meets the Jockey Club The Jockey Club's ability to dictate taste and fashion—which the bourgeoisie anxiously copied—extended, in a notorious example, to Richard Wagner's opera *Tannhäuser* [than-HOY-zur] in March 1861. Declaring that his was "the art of the future," Richard Wagner [VAHG-ner] (1813–1883) had arrived in Paris in 1859, where Wagner reported that the press found him "arrogant" and guilty of "repudiating all existing operatic music." Nonetheless, he managed to secure Louis-Napoleon's support for a production of *Tannhäuser*, an opera in three acts. Because of the Paris Opéra's rule that foreign works be presented in French, Wagner set about having the opera translated into French.

Tannhäuser's protagonist is a legendary knight minstrel (*Minnesinger*), the German equivalent of a medieval troubadour. When other minstrels gather for a tournament of song in the great hall of the Wartburg [vart-boorg] castle, near the Venusberg [VEH-noos-berg], a hill in which Tannhäuser has taken refuge for a year under the magic spell of Venus, goddess of love, he insists on returning to Earth in order to compete. Once again he meets his beloved, Elisabeth, who sings to him the famous aria *Dich, teure Halle* [dikh toy-ruh hah-leh] ("Thou, Beloved Hall") (**CD-Track 13.2**), welcoming him back to the great hall where he formerly sang. She is excited that this beautiful space will once again resonate with music.

Traditionally, the operatic voice carries the melody and the orchestra provides accompaniment. As a result, Wagner felt, the music overwhelmed the text. So, in order to make the text understandable, Wagner shifted the melodic element from the voice to the orchestra. Elisabeth thus sings in a declamatory manner that lies somewhere between aria and recitative, and the orchestra carries the melody, following Elisabeth's shift in mood from ecstatic welcome to sad remembrance of her year-long loss. So radical was this change, the orchestra more or less taking over from the vocalist the primary responsibility for developing the melodic character of the work, that French audiences found Wagner's music almost unrecognizable as opera.

For a French audience, the music was too new to appreciate fully, and the plot, derived directly from German folklore, was hopelessly foreign. The opera seemed aimed at inflaming French/German animosity. Wagner was informed, furthermore, of the necessity of writing a ballet for the opening of the second act. He refused, though he did agree to *begin* the opera with a ballet. Already unhappy that an expensive production of a German work was to be staged in *their* opera, the Jockey Club was doubly outraged that its composer refused to insert the ballet in its traditional place. Wagner seemed nothing short of a liberal nationalist deliberately trying to provoke his conservative French audience.

As rehearsals progressed, the Jockey Club provided its members with silver whistles engraved with the words "*Pour Tannhaeuser.*" They used these whistles in defense of their aristocratic privileges on opening night, March 13, 1861. With Louis-Napoleon present in his box, the Jockey Club interrupted the music for as much as 15 minutes at a time as they hissed and whistled. "The Emperor and his consort stoically kept their seats throughout the uproar caused by their own courtiers," Wagner noted. The opera received the same reception at both its second and third performances. Paris was divided. The composer Berlioz found no virtue in the music, while Baudelaire admired it. After the third performance, which included several lengthy fights and continued whistling from the Jockey Club, Wagner demanded that the opera be withdrawn from performance. The French government accepted their financial losses and agreed.

Wagner's Music Drama The theme of *Tannhäuser*—the conflicting claims of sexual pleasure and spiritual love—is hopelessly Romantic, which might have appealed to bourgeois and aristocratic French taste, but its music and its approach to the opera as a form did not. Like Verdi, Wagner sought to convey realism, so that his recitatives, arias, and choruses made dramatic sense. And he considered his work a new genre—**music drama**—in which the actions acted out on stage are the visual and verbal manifestations of the drama created by the instruments in the orchestra, "deeds of music made visible," as he put it. This he accomplished by the **leitmotif** [LITE-moh-teef], literally a "leading motive." For Wagner this meant a brief musical idea connected to a character, event, or idea that recurs throughout the music drama each time the character, event, or idea recurs. However, as characters, events, and ideas change throughout the action, so do the leitmotifs, growing, developing, and transforming.

Wagner's greatest realization of the leitmotif idea occurs in four music dramas dating from 1848 to 1874, titled collectively *Der Ring des Nibelungen* [der ring des nee-beh-LOONG-un] (*The Ring of the Nibelung*). The *Ring* forms an epic cycle based on Norse mythology involving the quest for a magical but accursed golden ring, the possessor of which can control the universe. Collectively, it represents Wagner's

dream of composing a ***Gesamtkunstwerk*** [geh-SAHMT-koonst-verk], or total work of art, synthesizing music, drama, poetry, gesture, architecture, and painting (the latter two through stage design). The *Ring* features more than 20 leitmotifs that Wagner weaves into an intricate web, the four music dramas being performed over the course of four days. For instance, the hero Siegfried is associated with his famous horn call, and other leitmotifs represent objects like the Rhine gold and Valhalla (home of the gods), emotional states like love's awakening, and concepts like redemption. The cycle premiered in 1876 in Bayreuth, a small city in Bavaria. Here, with the help of his patron, Ludwig II of Bavaria, Wagner oversaw the building of a *Festspielhaus* [FEST-shpeel-hows], or "festival play house," that he hoped might help to unify Germany both culturally and politically (Fig. **13.13**).

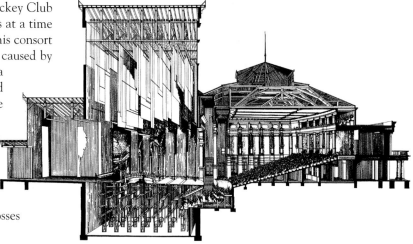

Fig. 13.13 **Richard Wagner. Cross-section of the Bayreuth Festspielhaus. 1872–1876.** From Frederic Spotts, *Bayreuth: A History of the Wagner Festival* (New Haven: Yale University Press, 1994). © 2003 Yale University Press/Spotts, BAYREUTH: A History of the Wagner Festival (1994), image p. 9. The design puts the orchestra beneath the stage, thus drawing the audience closer to the performance and projecting the orchestra's music directly toward it, all resulting in acoustics ideal for the integration of orchestral and vocal parts.

In his appeal for funds to underwrite construction, Wagner makes the political motives of his project plain:

> In Hellas [ancient Greece], the supreme flowering of the State went hand in hand with that of Art; so too the resurrection of the German Empire should be accompanied by a massive artistic monument to the German intellect. In the field of politics, the German mission in the history of the world has recently enjoyed its second triumph [the victory over France in the 1870 Franco-Prussian war]—now its spiritual victory is to be celebrated, through the German Festival in Bayreuth.

It was this spirit of German nationalism that would lead Adolf Hitler to lionize Wagner's music during the Third Reich [rykh] 60 years later.

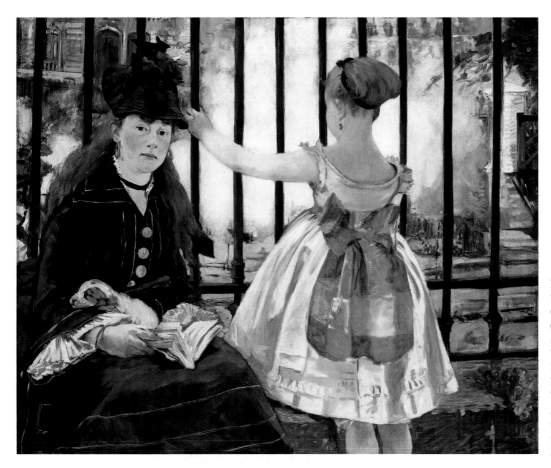

Fig. 13.14 **Édouard Manet.**
The Gare Saint-Lazare. **1873.**
Oil on canvas, $36\frac{3}{4}'' \times 45\frac{1}{8}''$.
Gift of Horace Havemeyer in
memory of his mother, Louisine
W. Havemeyer. 1956.10.1.
Image © 2007. Board of Trustees,
National Gallery of Art,
Washington, D.C. © 2008 ARS
Artists Rights Society, NY. The
model is Victorine Meurant,
who also posed for *Olympia* and
Déjeuner sur l'herbe.

Impressionist Paris

In the early 1870s, Édouard Manet befriended a number of
young painters whom he would deeply influence and who
would in turn come to be known as the Impressionists. Chief
among his new, younger colleagues were Claude Monet,
Pierre Renoir [ruh-NWAHR], Gustave Caillebotte [ky-
BOTT], Edgar Degas, and Berthe Morisot [bert moh-ree-
ZOH], who was married to Manet's brother. Starting in 1874,
the Impressionists organized their own group exhibitions, in
which Manet politely declined to participate, choosing
instead to pursue recognition in the official Salons. Nevertheless, he came to be widely regarded as a pre-Impressionist
if not the first Impressionist.

Manet never abandoned the complex social commentary
that informs his earlier painting. In his *The Gare Saint-Lazare*
[gahr san-luh-ZAHR] (Fig. **13.14**), his model is the same
woman as in *Le Déjeuner sur l'herbe* and *Olympia*. The little
girl is the daughter of Manet's friend Alphonse Hirsch, in
whose garden the scene is set; she gazes through the fence at
the tracks, obscured by the smoke of a passing train in the
new train station of Saint-Lazare. The station was the work
of the Baron Georges Eugène Haussmann [ohss-MAHN],
who was appointed prefect of the Seine by Napoleon III on
June 22, 1853, and charged with the task of "modernizing"
the city by broadening its avenues, demolishing its worst

neighborhoods, and building vast gardens and railway sta-
tions. By 1868, the station was receiving more than 13 million passengers a year, many of whom were workers, clerks,
and laborers commuting in from the suburbs. The station and
the bridge above the surrounding streets would become a
favorite subject of the Impressionist painters. The front door
to Manet's own studio from 1872 to 1878 can be seen
through the railings behind the woman's head. In 1877,
Claude Monet rented a studio nearby in order to paint a
series of views of the station itself.

Manet's painting is a bouquet of contrasts. The little girl is
dressed in white with blue trim, while the older woman,
posed here as her mother, or perhaps her nanny, is in blue
with white trim. The one sits, regarding us; the other stands,
gazing through the fence railing. The nanny's hair is down,
the little girl's up. The nanny's angular collar is countered by
the soft curve of the little girl's neckline. The black choker
around the one's neck finds its way to the other's hair. The
older woman sits with her puppy on her lap, a symbol of her
contentment. The little girl is eating grapes (beside her on
the ledge), which have bacchanalian associations. The older
escapes into her novel, perhaps a Romantic one, while the
younger looks out at the trains leaving the station, possibly
dreaming of adventure.

Manet's painting suggests that the little girl will grow up
into the woman beside her. The painting implicitly portrays

the limits of women's possibilities in French society. As the nineteenth century progressed, women like the Impressionist painters Mary Cassatt and Berthe Morisot would strive to eliminate those limitations as they increasingly demanded equality and respect, not only in their work, but also in their lives.

Monet's *Plein-Air* Vision

From the outset, critics recognized that a distinguishing feature of this new group of painters was its preference for painting out-of-doors, in **plein air** [plen-air] ("open air"). The availability of paint in metallic tubes, introduced between 1841 and 1843, is in part responsible. Now paints could be easily transported out-of-doors without danger of drying. It was the natural effects of light that most interested these younger painters, which they depicted using new synthetic pigments consisting of bright, transparent colors. Before they were ever called "Impressionists," they were called the "École de Plein Air," although the term *Impressionist* was in wide use by 1876, when poet Stéphane Mallarmé [mahl-ar-MAY] (1842–1898) published his essay "Impressionism and Édouard Manet."

Plein-air painting implied, first of all, the artist's abandonment of the traditional environment of the studio. Of all the Impressionists, Claude Monet was the most insistent that only *en plein air* could he realize the full potential of his artistic energy. In rejecting the past, the painters of the Société cultivated the present moment, emphasizing improvisation and spontaneity. Each painting had to be quick, deliberately sketchy, in order to capture the ever-changing, fleeting effects of light in a natural setting. Although Monet habitually reworked his paintings in the studio, he would tell a young American artist: "When you go out to paint, try to forget what objects you have before you—a tree, a house, a field, or whatever. Merely think, here is a little square of blue, here an oblong of pink, here a streak of yellow, and paint it just as it looks to you, until it gives you your own näive impression of the scene before you." It is not surprising, then, that in Monet's *The Regatta at Argenteuil* [ar-zhan-TOY-eh] the reflection of the landscape in the water disintegrates into a sketchy series of broad dashes of paint (Fig. **13.15**). On the surface of the water, the mast of the green sailboat seems to support a red and green sail, but this "sail" is really the reflection of the red house and cypress tree on the hillside. Monet sees the relationship between his painting and the real scene as analogous to the relationship between the surface of the water and the shoreline above. Both of these surfaces—canvas and water—reflect the fleeting quality of sensory experience.

A painting exhibited by Monet in the first Impressionist exhibition offers more insight into this new approach to art. *Impression: Sunrise* (Fig. **13.16**) went a long way toward giving Impressionism its name. The artist applied the paint in brushstrokes of pure, occasionally unmixed, color that evoke forms in their own right. He rendered waves in staccato bursts of horizontal dashes, the reflection of the rising sun on the water in swirls of orange brushstrokes highlighted with white. Violets and blues contrast with yellows and oranges as if to capture the prismatic effects of light. Most of all, one feels the very presence of the painter at work, his hand racing across the surface of the canvas before the morning light vanished. Although Monet would often work and rework his paintings, they seem "of the moment," as immediate as a photograph.

Except for a brief stint in Paris in 1876–1877 when he painted a series of works on the *Gare Saint-Lazare* train station, Monet had continually sought to escape the city for the pleasures of the countryside. In December 1871, he had moved to Argenteuil, an idyllic little village on the Seine downriver from Paris and where he lived for seven years. Then, faced with the suburb's increasing industrialization and urbanization, he moved farther downriver to Vétheuil [vay-TOY], another little town with a tiny population, no railroads, no industry, no pollution, and no weekend Parisian crowds. Finally, in April 1883, he moved farther downriver again, to Giverny [zhee-vair-NEE]. Monet's determined flight from the distraction of crowds is an announcement of the rapid growth of suburbs and outlying towns surrounding Paris (and every other growing metropolis) in the last quarter of the century.

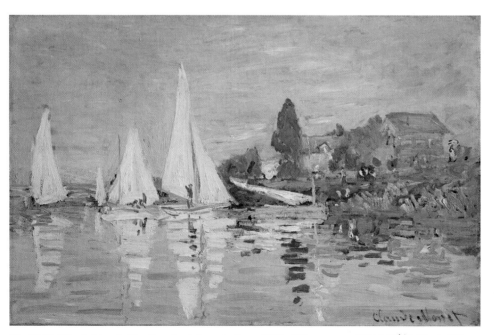

Fig. 13.15 Claude Monet. *The Regatta at Argenteuil.* **ca. 1872.** Oil on canvas, 19″ × 29¹⁄₂″. Musée d'Orsay, Paris, France. Erich Lessing/Art Resource, NY. Monet moved to Argenteuil, a suburb on the Seine just north of Paris, in December 1871.

Monet did not begin painting at Giverny immediately. Instead, he traveled—to the south of France, to the Côte d'Azur [koht dah-ZOOR], to Brittany and the Normandy coast, and to locations all across France. Monet's sojourn through the countryside points to the increased opportunities for leisurely travel afforded by the ever-expanding railroad networks in France. Indeed many of the towns and scenes he painted were tourist locales, frequented by the prosperous Parisian middle class that the Impressionists sought to cultivate. Many of his contemporaries attacked the master of Impressionism for the shallowness of his themes and his apparent instantaneous rendering of light effects. But the painting was anything but instantaneous. "The more I go on," Monet wrote in a letter to a friend, "the more I see that I must work a lot to succeed in rendering what I am looking for: 'instantaneity' ... more than ever I'm disgusted by easy things that come without effort."

In the autumn of 1888, Monet began using a different series format than before, painting the same subject at different times of day and in different atmospheric conditions. In addition to a series on a line of poplar trees and on Rouen Cathedral, he painted a series of grainstacks in the nearby farmer's field. In May 1891, he exhibited 15 grainstack paintings in Paris. They were a spectacular success (Fig. **13.17**). In a preface to the catalog for the exhibition, art critic and Monet's friend Gustave Geffroy describes their effect on the viewer:

> These stacks in this deserted field are transient objects whose surfaces, like mirrors, catch the mood of the environment, the states of the atmosphere with the errant breeze, the sudden glow. Light and shade radiate from them, sun and shadow revolve around them in relentless pursuit; they reflect its dying heat, its last rays; they are shrouded in mist, soaked with rain, frozen with snow, in harmony with the distant horizon, the earth, the sky. . . .

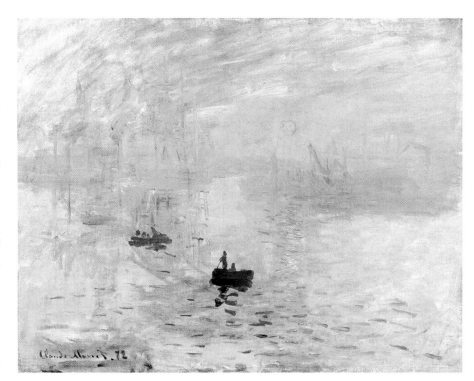

Fig. 13.16 Claude Monet. *Impression: Sunrise.* **1873.** Oil on canvas, $19\frac{5}{8}''\times 25\frac{1}{2}''$. Musée Marmottan-Claude Monet, Paris, France. Erich Lessing/Art Resource, NY. The painting is a view of the harbor in Le Havre, France, on the English Channel.

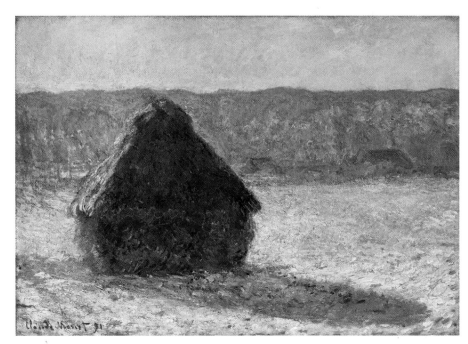

Fig. 13.17 Claude Monet. *Grainstack (Snow Effect).* **1891.** Oil on canvas, $25\frac{3}{4}''\times 36\frac{3}{8}''$. Museum of Fine Arts, Boston. Gift of Misses Aimee and Rosamond Lamb in memory of Mr. and Mrs. Horatio A. Lamb, 1970.253. Photograph © 2008 Museum of Fine Arts, Boston. This painting has a simple geometric structure—a triangle set on a rectangle, both set on a rectangular ground.

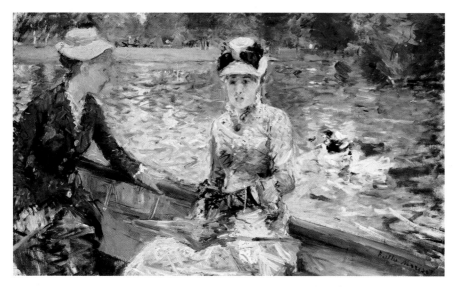

Fig. 13.18 Berthe Morisot. *Summer's Day*. 1879. Oil on canvas, 18″ × 29 3/4″. National Gallery, London. Note the almost arbitrary brushwork that defines the bottoms of the dresses worn by both women, one a set of zigzags, the other a patchwork of straight strokes, emphasizing the distance and difference between the two.

Each painting in the series, then, becomes a fragment in the duration of the whole, and Geffroy's reading of the works transforms Monet into an artist who in rendering nature also depicts his own interior landscape. As he continued to work—almost daily until his death in 1926—he turned his attention to his gardens at Giverny, creating some of the most monumental paintings in the history of art

Morisot and Pissarro: The Effects of Paint

Monet's willingness to break his edges with feathery strokes of paint was even more radically developed in the work of Berthe Morisot. Born to a socially connected bourgeois family (she was the granddaughter of the Rococo painter Fragonard, noted for his rapid brushwork) (see Fig. 11.14), Morisot received an education that included lessons in drawing and painting from the noted landscape artist Camille Corot. She became a professional painter, and a highly regarded colleague to male artists of her generation. Morisot was the sister-in-law of Manet, and it was she who convinced him to adopt an Impressionist technique of his own. But no one could match her "vaporous and barely drawn lines," as one critic put it. "Here are some young women rocking in a boat," writes a critic of her painting *Summer's Day*, ". . . seen through fine gray tones, matte white, and light pink, with no shadows, set off with little multi-colored daubs . . ." (Fig. **13.18**). She drapes her bourgeois figures, out

for a little recreation, in clothing that is often barely distinguishable from the background, like those worn by the woman in the middle of the boat. She shuns outline altogether—each of the ducks in the water is realized in several broad, quick strokes.

If Morisot's paintings seem to dissolve into a uniform white light, Camille Pissarro's landscapes give us the impression of a view never quite fully captured by the painter. In *Red Roofs*, a random patchwork of red and green, orange and blue appears through a veil of tree branches that interrupt the viewer's vision (Fig. **13.19**). Pissarro was deeply interested in the new science of color theory, and he paid close attention to the 1864 treatise of Michel-Eugène Chevreul [shev-RULL] (1786–1889), *On Colors and their Applications to the Industrial Arts.* Chevreul argued that complementary colors of pigment (that is, colors directly opposite each other on the traditional color wheel)—like red and green, yellow and violet, blue and orange—intensify each other's hue when set side by side. Pissarro adopted a later scheme by American physicist Ogden Rood, in which the primary colors of light,

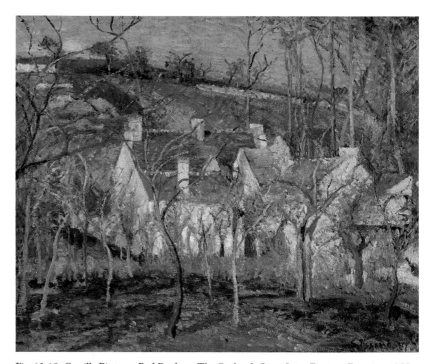

Fig. 13.19 Camille Pissarro. *Red Roofs*, or *The Orchard, Côtes Saint-Denis at Pontoise*. 1877. Oil on canvas, 21 1/2″ × 25 7/8″. Musée d'Orsay, Paris, France. Erich Lessing/Art Resource, NY. When Bismarck advanced on Paris, Pissarro abandoned his home in Louveciennes, on the outskirts of the city, and Bismarck's forces moved in. On rainy days, they created a path across the courtyard with Pissarro's paintings to keep their feet from getting wet. As a result, few of his paintings before 1871 survive.

rather than pigment, were red, green, and blue-violet. In this he anticipated the color theories that would stimulate Neo-Impressionist painters of the next generation like Georges Seurat [suh-RAH] and Paul Signac [seen-YAK] (see chapter 14).

Renoir, Degas, and the Parisian Crowd

While Monet and Pissarro concentrated on landscape painting, August Renoir and Edgar Degas preferred to paint the crowd in the cafés and restaurants, at entertainments of all kinds, and in the countryside, to which the middle class habitually escaped on weekends via the ever-expanding railroad lines. Renoir was especially attracted to Chatou [shah-TOO], a small village on the Seine frequented by rowers. No longer reserved for the upper class, Chatou and other riverside towns became retreats for a diverse crowd of Parisian artists, bourgeoisie, and even workers. Weekend escapes centered on cafés, dance halls, boating, and swimming. Renoir was particularly fond of the Maison and

Restaurant Fournaise [foor-NEZ], a lodging house and restaurant on an island in the river, which served as the setting of *Luncheon of the Boating Party* (Fig. **13.20**). Through the foliage at the back of the painting we can make out two sailboats on the river and, just under the awning, a railroad bridge. We can identify many of the figures from his circle of friends and acquaintances at Chatou, including members of the Fournaise family. To represent such recognizable figures, Renoir had to abandon the gestural brushwork of Monet and Pissarro except in the background landscape. He composed his figures with firm outlines and modeled them in subtle gradations of light and dark, which clearly define their anatomical and facial features. And he carefully structured the group in a series of interlocking triangles, the largest of which is made up of Aline Charigot [shah-ree-GOH], Renoir's future wife, sitting at the table holding her dog. Scholars believe that the painting, begun in the summer of 1880, may represent Renoir's response to Émile Zola's critique in his review of the 1880 Salon charging the

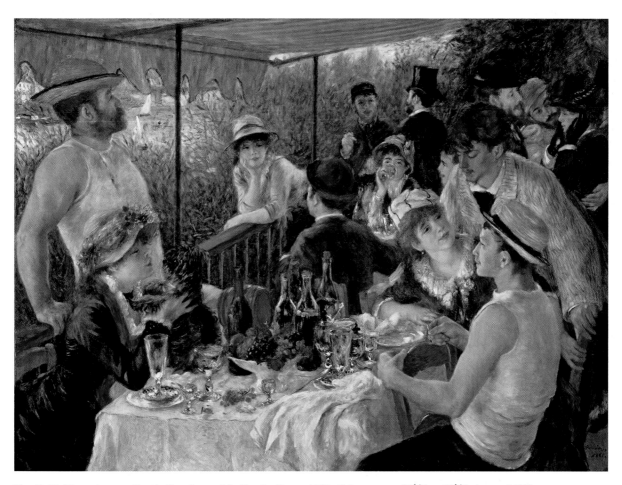

Fig. 13.20 Pierre Auguste Renoir. *Luncheon of the Boating Party.* 1881. Oil on canvas, 51$\frac{1}{4}$″ × 69$\frac{1}{8}$″. Acquired 1923. The Phillips Collection, Washington, D.C. The woman leaning on the railing is Alphonsine Fournaise, the restaurant proprietor's daughter, and leaning against the rail at the left is Alphonse Fournaise, his son. Just below, about to kiss her little dog, is Aline Charigot, Renoir's future wife. The figure leaning over the table at the right—the only one without a hat—is Renoir's friend, the journalist Maggiolo. He addresses an actress by the name of Angèle and the painter Gustave Caillebotte, himself an avid sailor. The man in the top hat at the back of the painting is Charles Euphussi, editor of the *Gazette des Beaux-Arts*.

Impressionists with selling "sketches that are hardly dry" and challenging them to make more complex paintings that would be the result of "long and thoughtful preparation." For this reason, the theory goes, Renoir assimilates into this single work landscape, still life, and genre painting in a manner probably intentionally recalling seventeenth-century Dutch and Flemish paintings like Rubens's *The Kermis* (see Fig. 10.26), which Renoir would have seen at the Louvre.

Edgar Degas was as dedicated as Renoir to the careful construction of his paintings. *Dance Class* depicts 21 dancers awaiting their turn to be evaluated by the ballet master, who stands leaning on a tall cane in the middle ground watching a young ballerina making her salute to an imaginary audience (Fig. **13.21**). The atmosphere is unpretentious, emphasizing the elaborate preparations and hard work necessary to produce a work of art that will appear effortless on stage. The dancers form an arc, connecting the foreground to the middle ground and drawing the eye quickly through the space of the painting. Degas draws the viewer's attention to the complex structure of his composition—that is, to the fact that he too has *worked* long and hard at it.

Work is, in fact, one of Degas's primary themes, and it is no accident that the ballet master leans on a cane—as a former dancer, he is understood to be physically impaired from a dance injury. Degas understood that the young women he depicted were, in fact, full-time child workers. Almost all were from lower-class families and normally entered the ballet corps at age seven or eight when their schooling ceased, leaving most of them illiterate. They had to pass examinations, such as the one Degas depicts here, in order to continue. By the time they were nine or ten, they might earn 300 francs a year (approximately 60 U.S. dollars in 1870, with a buying power of about 400 U.S. dollars today). If and when they rose to the level of performing brief solos in the ballet, they might earn as much as 1,500 francs—more than most of their fathers, who were shop clerks, cab drivers, and laborers. Should they ever achieve the status of *première danseuse* [pruh-mee-YAIR dahn-SUZ], in their late teens, they might earn as much as 20,000 francs, a status like today's richly compensated professional athlete that few reached but all dreamed of. Thus, Degas's *Dance Class* presents young women in a moment of great stress, struggling to survive.

The Gilded Age in America

From 1870 to 1900, New York City was a boomtown of extraordinary diversity. New York's port handled most of America's imports and roughly 50 percent of the country's exports. As the nation's financial center, the city teemed with

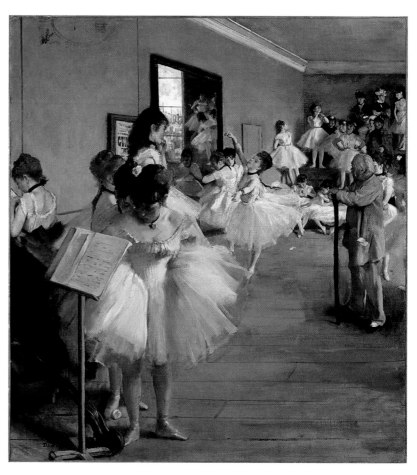

Fig. 13.21 Edgar Degas. *Dance Class.* **ca. 1874.** Oil on canvas, $32\frac{3}{4}'' \times 30\frac{1}{4}''$. The Metropolitan Museum of Art. Bequest of Mr. and Mrs. Harry Payne Bingham, 1986 (1987.47.1). Image copyright © The Metropolitan Museum of Art. The dance instructor is Jules Perrot, the most famous male dancer of the middle third of the century, whose likeness Degas took from a photograph of 1861.

lawyers, architects, engineers, and entrepreneurs of every nationality. In 1892, 30 percent of all millionaires in the United States lived in Manhattan and Brooklyn, side by side with millions of the nation's working-class immigrants. By 1900, fully three-quarters of the city's population was foreign-born, having arrived via Ellis Island, which opened in 1892. Italians, Germans, Poles, and waves of Jews from Hungary, Rumania, Russia, and Eastern Europe sought the unlimited opportunities they believed were to be found in America. Many stayed in New York City. As the twentieth century dawned, these immigrants, and their descendents, would dramatically change American culture.

In order to allow the rapidly growing population to escape the rush of urban life, New York City in 1856 acquired an 840-acre tract of land for a park in the as yet largely undeveloped regions north of 59th Street. It hired Frederick Law Olmsted [OLM-sted] (1822–1903) and Calvert Vaux [voh] (1824–1895) to effect the transformation (Fig. **13.22**). The two men modeled what is now known as Central Park on the English garden (see chapter 11) with, in Olmsted's words, "gracefully curved lines, generous spaces, and the absence of sharp corners, the idea being to suggest and imply leisure,

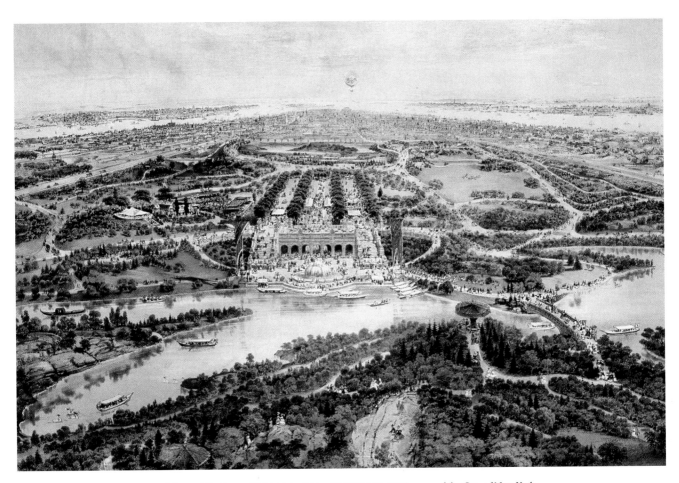

Fig. 13.22 John Bachman. *View of Central Park*. ca. 1870. Color Litho. (fl.1850-77). © Museum of the City of New York, USA/The Bridgeman Art Library. Frederick Law Olmsted and Calvert Vaux designed the park, and construction began in 1857. For Olmsted, the park was an educational environment in which poor immigrants could mingle freely with the upper classes and learn how to properly "comport" themselves.

contemplativeness, and happy tranquility." Here, immigrants from the hundreds of blocks of tenement housing in Manhattan could stroll side by side with the wealthy ladies and gentlemen whose homes lined Fifth Avenue facing the park. Sheep grazed in one area of the park, and in another, the Dairy, children could sip milk fresh from the cows that grazed nearby. In this artificial rural environment city dwellers could forget that they were even *in* the city.

So successful was Central Park that, in 1866, Olmsted and Vaux collaborated on the design of Prospect Park, across the East River, in Brooklyn (see Fig. **13.23**). And after Vaux's dissolution of their partnership in 1872, Olmsted went on to design many other public commons, including South Park in Chicago, the parkway system of the City of Boston, Mont Royal in Montreal, and the grounds at Stanford University and the University of California at Berkeley. Moreover, Olmsted was able to foresee that the increasing population density of cities required the growth of suburbs, a residential community within commuting distance of the city. "When not engaged in business," Olmsted wrote, "[the worker] has no occasion to be near his working place, but demands arrangements

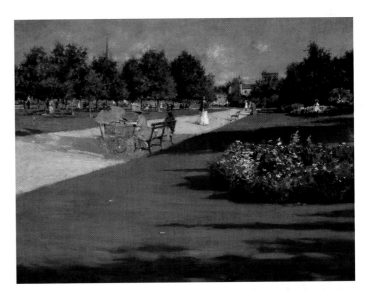

Fig. 13.23 William Merritt Chase. *Prospect Park, Brooklyn*. ca. 1886. Oil on canvas, $17\frac{3}{8}'' \times 22\frac{3}{8}''$. Colby College Museum of Art, Waterville, ME. Gift of Miss Adeline F. and Miss Caroline R. Wing. 1963.040. Benches were everywhere in Olmsted and Vaux's parks. Ten thousand of them were scattered throughout Central Park.

of a wholly different character. Families require to settle in certain localities which minister to their social and other wants, and yet are not willing to accept the conditions of town-life . . . but demand as much of the luxuries of free air, space and abundant vegetation as . . . they can be enabled to secure."

The conditions of town life could be harsh. Widespread fraud and corruption contributed to the impoverishment of the working class, but so did the profit motive that drove the industrial sector of the economy. By 1890, 11 million of the nation's 12 million families had an average annual income of $380, well below the poverty line ($380 would buy about the same as $7,600 in today's dollars). Sudden, unexpected events also precipitated widespread economic hardship, as occurred in September 1873, when a Philadelphia banking firm failed, causing investors to panic, banks to shut down, and the New York Stock Market to close for ten days. Millions of American workers found themselves without jobs in the 1870s, while business owners began cutting wages—an oversupply of employees meant cheaper labor. Many lost their savings as well as their jobs when unregulated banks, insurance companies, and investment firms went out of busi-

ness and federal and state governments stood by. As the unemployment rate in New York and other cities passed 25 percent, famine and starvation in the land of opportunity became a reality.

It should not be surprising that workers developed new forms of collective action in this harsh economic environment. Impromptu strikes, walkouts, and the beginnings of organized labor unions signaled the changing economic and social climate. When the Baltimore & Ohio Railroad cut wages in 1877, its workers staged spontaneous strikes, which spread rapidly to other railroads. In Baltimore, the state militia shot and killed 11 strikers and wounded 40 others.

Owners of railroads and other corporations together with the political leaders they supported made sure wage reductions remained in place. The federal government aided them when the U.S. War Department created the National Guard as a quick reaction force to put down future disturbances. It was an era of unparalleled political unrest, and *The Strike* by Robert Koehler [KOH-lur] (1850–1917) suggests something of the mood of the workers and their bosses, as well as the grim environment of industrial-age America (Fig. **13.24**). The painting depicts an angry crowd

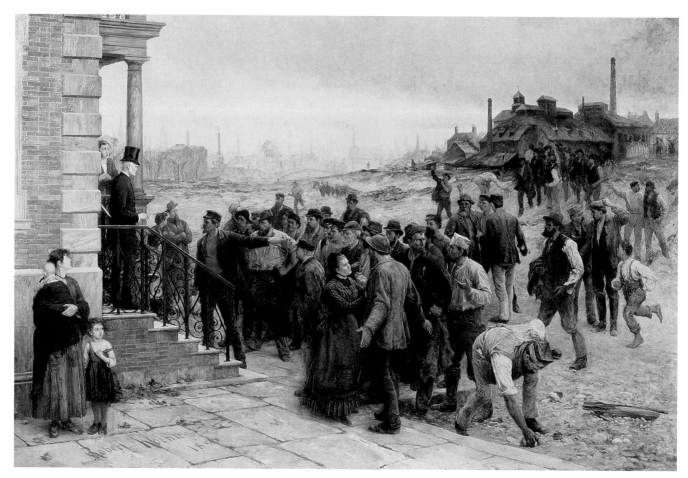

Fig. 13.24 Robert Koehler. *The Strike*. 1886. Oil on canvas, 5' 11⅝" × 9' 5⅝". Deutsches Historisches Museum, Berlin, Germany/The Bridgeman Art Library, NY. Koehler's father was a machinist, and he identified with the plight of the working class. The painting was exhibited at the National Academy of Design in 1886, to general approval.

confronting an employer, demanding a living wage from the stern top-hatted man and a worried younger man standing behind him. An impoverished woman with her children looks on at the left; another woman, more obviously middle class, tries to talk with one of the workers, but behind him a striker bends down to pick up a stone to throw. Koehler's realism is evident in the diversity of his figures, each possessing an individual identity. But the background of the work, with its smoky, factory-filled landscape on the horizon, owes much to the Impressionist style.

The May 1, 1886, issue of *Harper's Weekly* included the painting as its central feature. On the same day a national strike called for changing the standard workday from 12 hours to 8. More than 340,000 workers stopped work at 12,000 companies across the country. In Chicago, a bomb exploded as police broke up a labor meeting in Haymarket Square. A police officer was killed by the blast and police retaliated, firing into the crowd of workers, killing one and wounding many more. Four labor organizers were charged with the policeman's death and subsequently hanged, demoralizing the national labor movement and energizing management to resist labor's demands.

The Song of the Romantic Self: Emerson, Thoreau, and Whitman

The necessity of Olmsted and Vaux's city park movement not only underscores the alienation of the urban worker—an alienation that erupted in the violent protests of the labor movement—but also a national belief in the healing power of the natural world, so remote, it seemed, from the reality of the factory and tenement. In the first half of the nineteenth century, the American wilderness had inspired a sense of wonder at the natural world, with which American writers and artists felt an almost ecstatic communion. In many ways, they were shaped by the nation's emphasis on individualism and individual liberty. Free to think for themselves, their imaginations were equally free to discover the self in nature.

Emerson, Thoreau, and the Transcendental Self In 1834, a 31-year-old minister, disenchanted with institutionalized religion and just back from England, where he had encountered Coleridge and heard Wordsworth recite his poetry, moved to the village of Concord, Massachusetts. Over the next two years, Ralph Waldo Emerson (1803–1882), a Unitarian minister, wrote his first book, *Nature*, published anonymously in 1836. The book became the intellectual beacon for a group of Concord locals, mostly ministers, that became known as the "Transcendental Club." They all felt that the human spirit was possessed of a certain oneness with nature, an attitude that informs the most famous passage of *Nature*, where Emerson outlines the fundamental principle of transcendental thought: In the direct experience of nature the individual is united with God, thus transcending knowledge based on empirical observation (**Reading 13.10**):

READING 13.10   **from Ralph Waldo Emerson, *Nature*, Chapter 1 (1836)**

Crossing a bare common, in snow puddles, at twilight, under a clouded sky, without having in my thoughts any occurrence of special good fortune, I have enjoyed a perfect exhilaration. Almost I fear to think how glad I am. In the woods too a man casts off his years, as the snake his slough, and at what period soever of life, is always a child. In the woods, is perpetual youth. Within these plantations of God, a decorum and sanctity reign, a perennial festival is dressed, and the guest sees not how he should tire of them in a thousand years. In the woods, we return to reason and faith. There I feel that nothing can befall me in life,—no disgrace, no calamity (leaving me my eyes,) which nature cannot repair. Standing on the bare ground,—my head bathed by the blithe air, and uplifted into infinite space,—all mean egotism vanishes. I become a transparent eye-ball. I am nothing. I see all. The currents of the Universal Being circulate through me; I am part or particle of God. The name of the nearest friend sounds then foreign and accidental. To be brothers, to be acquaintances,—master or servant, is then a trifle and a disturbance. I am the lover of uncontained and immortal beauty. In the wilderness, I find something more dear and connate [i.e., congenial] than in streets or villages. In the tranquil landscape, and especially in the distant line of the horizon, man beholds somewhat as beautiful as his own nature.

The sense of the self at the center of experience—the "eye/I"—is also the sense of individualism and self-reliance fundamental to transcendental experience. In fact, in one of his most famous essays, "Self-Reliance," Emerson would declare, "Whoso would be a man must be a nonconformist. . . . Nothing is at last sacred but the integrity of your own mind." Of all Emerson's contemporaries, none fits this description better than Henry David Thoreau [thor-OH] (1817–1862). Educated at Harvard, Thoreau was fiercely independent. He resigned his first job as a schoolteacher in Concord because he refused to inflict corporal punishment on his students. He became one of the nation's most vocal abolitionists and was briefly jailed for refusing to pay a poll tax to a government that tolerated slavery. But most famously, for two years, from 1845 to 1847, he lived in a small cabin that he built himself, on Emerson's property at Walden Pond. This experience spawned *Walden, or Life in the Woods*, a small book published in 1854, dedicated to teaching the satisfactions and virtues of living simply and wisely in communion with nature. Thoreau's woods are the same woods that Emerson extols in *Nature*. Thoreau writes (**Reading 13.11**):

from Henry David Thoreau, ***Walden, or Life in the Woods,*** **Chapter 2 (1854)**

I went to the woods because I wished to live deliberately, to front only the essential facts of life, and see if I could not learn what it had to teach, and not, when I came to die, discover that I had not lived. . . . I wanted to live deep and suck out all the marrow of life, to live so sturdily and Spartan-like as to put to rout all that was not life. . . . Time is but the stream I go a-fishing in. I drink at it; but while I drink I see the sandy bottom and detect how shallow it is. Its thin current slides away, but eternity remains.

The eccentricities of Thoreau's life are matched by the inventiveness of his prose, and in the end Thoreau's argument is for what he calls "the indescribable innocence and beneficence of Nature."

As powerful and as transformative as nature was, Thoreau viewed it as vulnerable to human encroachment, an insight that proved him far ahead of his time. He worried, for instance, that the railroad had destroyed the old scale of distances, a complaint shared by many of his contemporaries. His understanding of the environment's vulnerability and humanity's role in conserving or degrading it illustrates Thoreau's other enduring influence on American literature culture—as a powerful social conscience and spokesman, especially for the environment.

Walt Whitman and the American Self   There is no better human symbol for the restless, ambitious American self in the nineteenth century than the poet Walt Whitman (1819–1892), who revolutionized American literature as he linked the Romantic, Transcendental, and Realist movements. Whitman was a confirmed New Yorker. He eventually gained fame with his portraits of the city's environment and people. He celebrated the sense of urgency and vigor conveyed by the urban atmosphere in "Crossing Brooklyn Ferry" (**Reading 13.12**):

from Walt Whitman, "Crossing Brooklyn Ferry" (1856)

Come on, ships from the lower bay! pass up or down,
    white-sail'd schooners, sloops, lighters!
Flaunt away, flags of all nations! be duly lower'd at sunset!
Burn high your fires, foundry chimneys! cast black shadows at
    nightfall! cast red and yellow light over the tops of the
    houses! . . .
Thrive, cities—bring your freight, bring your shows, ample
    and sufficient rivers,
Expand. . . .

New York City was the very embodiment of the vast American possibilities that Whitman celebrated in *Leaves of Grass*, the long and complex volume of poems that he self-published in 1855 and continuously revised until 1892. It started out as a slim volume of 12 poems and grew to more than 400 as the author's life changed and as he grew into his self-defined role as "the American poet," speaking for the common man. In the first few years, *Leaves* was not received favorably and it did not sell many copies. But within a decade new editions would become a commercial success and the foundation of his growing reputation as the nation's most important poet. In "Song of Myself," the first and eventually longest of the poems, Whitman spoke to his own and the country's diverse experiences (**Reading 13.13**):

from Walt Whitman, "Song of Myself," in ***Leaves of Grass*** **(1867)**

I am large, I contain multitudes. . . .
Of every hue and cast am I, of every rank and religion,
A farmer, mechanic, artist, gentleman, sailor, quaker,
Prisoner, fancy-man, rowdy, lawyer, physician, priest.

I resist anything better than my own diversity. . . .

Whitman openly embraced all Americans in "Song of Myself," from immigrants to African Americans and Native Americans, from male to female, and heterosexual to homosexual. He celebrated all forms of sexuality, a fact that shocked many readers. One early reviewer called *Leaves* "a mass of stupid filth" and its author a pig rooting "among a rotten garbage of licentious thoughts." And in 1865, Whitman, who worked at the U.S. Interior Department as a clerk, was fired by his boss, the Secretary of Interior, for having violated in that work "the rules of decorum and propriety prescribed by a Christian Civilization."

"Song of Myself" consists of 52 numbered sections with the "I" of the narrator serving as a literary device for viewing the experiences of one man as representative of multitudes. *Leaves of Grass* is therefore a subjective epic. "Remember," Whitman would tell a friend late in his life, "the book arose out of my life in Brooklyn and New York. . . . absorbing a million people for fifteen years, with an intimacy, an eagerness, an abandon, probably never equaled."

By the time Whitman issued his final ("deathbed") edition of *Leaves of Grass*, the work had grown from 96 printed pages in the 1855 edition to 438. He would come to anguish over the personal suffering of the soldiers who fought in the Civil War in "Drum Taps," and mourn the death of Abraham Lincoln in "When Lilacs Last in the Dooryard Bloom'd," both added to the 1867 edition. To celebrate the opening of the Suez Canal, he added to the 1876 edition the long

"Passage to India." *Leaves of Grass*, in other words, was as expansive and as ever-changing as its author.

The American Woman

In "Song of Myself," Whitman championed American womanhood:

> I am the poet of the woman the same as the man,
> And I say it is as great to be a woman as to be a man . . .

But women as well as working-class whites and blacks felt the contradictions and limitations of American democracy. In the post–Civil War years, women became the public face of social reform as they led the suffrage movement, aimed at gaining the right to vote, and the Temperance movement, which sought to moderate (or cease) the consumption of alcohol. Both movements met formidable opposition. At the dedication of the Statue of Liberty, officials barred the New York State Woman Suffrage Association from participating. The New York "suffragettes" sailed out to Bedloe's Island anyway and invited the public onboard their ship, where their president, Lillie Devereux Blake, spoke: "In erecting a Statue of Liberty embodied as a woman in a land where no woman has political liberty, men have shown a delightful inconsistency which excites the wonder and admiration of the opposite sex."

In fact, women were making *some* gains. After the Civil War, they had assumed a growing role in education, as state-run schools trained women as teachers. And during the war, many had followed the lead of England's Florence Nightingale (1820–1910), who established nursing as an honored profession during the Crimean War in the 1850s. By the end of the century, nursing schools, usually associated with the nation's medical schools, had opened across the country, although physician training was still reserved for men. By 1900, fully 80 percent of the nation's colleges, universities, and professional schools were admitting women, though in small numbers. And the literacy rate of white women equaled that of white men.

But tensions between the sexes remained high, and with the possible exception of Thomas Eakins's [AY-kinz] *Agnew Clinic* (see *Focus*, pages 412–413), no painting embodies the tension between genders more than Winslow Homer's *The Life Line* (Fig. **13.25**). Immediately recognized as a masterpiece when exhibited at the National Academy in 1884, it depicts a woman's rescue from a ship wrecked in a storm. A review in the *New York Times* summarizes the painting's attraction to its New York audience:

> The coast guard is a well-drawn muscular figure with face hidden. . . . The hiding of his features concentrates the attention very cleverly on his comrade, who has fainted or is numb with fright. She has nothing on but her shoes, stockings, and dress, while the skirt of the latter has been so torn that her legs are more or less shown above the knees. Then, the drenching she has received makes her dress cling to bust and thighs, outlining her whole form most admirable. She is a buxom lassie, by no means ill-favored in figure and face. Her disordered hair, torn skirt, drenched dress, and set face call for sympathy; a redness of the skin, above the stockings hints at a cruel blow, and puts the climax on one's pity; at the same time, one cannot forget her beauty.

This is the very image of the strong, active male in whose embrace the weak, passive female is rescued. And part of her attractiveness is her passivity and vulnerability. That the painting appealed to the prurient interests of its audience—in some other context the couple might be seen as lovers embracing—sealed its success. But above all, the painting positions woman in a condition of total dependency

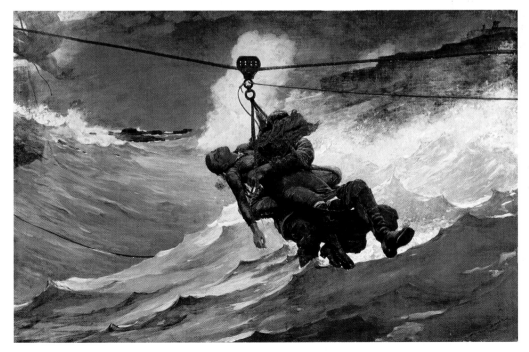

Fig. 13.25 Winslow Homer. *The Life Line*. 1884. Oil on canvas, 28⅝″ × 44¾″. The George W. Elkins Collection, 1924. The Philadelphia Museum of Art, Philadelphia/Art Resource, NY. In the first days that the painting was exhibited, the rescuer's face was visible. However, Homer apparently felt that it detracted from the composition, so he painted in the windblown red shawl to cover him while the exhibition was in progress.

Focus

Eakins's *Gross Clinic* and *Agnew Clinic*

Thomas Eakins (1844–1916) was an American Realist who began teaching at the Pennsylvania Academy of Fine Art in Philadelphia in 1876 and became its director in 1882. Always controversial, he was dismissed from the Academy in 1886 for removing a loincloth from a nude male model in a studio where female students were present. Among his most notable—and controversial—works are two portraits of surgeons, *The Gross Clinic* and *The Agnew Clinic*, painted 14 years apart, in 1875 and 1889 respectively. Although anticipated in seventeenth-century European paintings such as Rembrandt's *The Anatomy Lesson of Dr. Tulp* (see *Focus*, chapter 10), the subject was relatively unknown in American art and so not considered an appropriate subject for a painting. In addition, Eakins's graphic realization of both surgeries shocked the public.

The Gross Clinic is the product of the painter's own desire to paint Dr. Samuel D. Gross (1805–1884) in his surgical clinic, which he had attended when he studied anatomy a year before at the Jefferson Medical College in Philadelphia. It shows Dr. Gross standing in his surgical amphitheater, scalpel in hand, explaining a procedure to his students. Like Rembrandt's *Anatomy Lesson*, the composition is pyramidal in structure, with Dr. Gross at its apex. Light bathes the surgeon's head and hand and the surgery itself, emphasizing the intellectual capacity and physical dexterity of the surgeon. He and his colleagues are in the process of removing a piece of dead bone from the leg of a patient suffering from osteomyelitis, a

Thomas Eakins. *The Gross Clinic*. 1875. Oil on canvas, 96″ × 78½″. Philadelphia Museum of Art and the Pennsylvania Academy of Fine Arts. The Bridgeman Art Library. The brightest color in this painting is the red of oozing blood on the patient's wound and on the surgeon's hands and linens.

bone disease that until the nineteenth century had been treated by amputation. Eakins evidently understood the shock the scene would cause his viewers because behind Dr. Gross he has depicted a woman, probably a relative of the patient, recoiling in horror from the scene. The era's prototypical weak woman, she is a far cry from the stoic nurse who watches Dr. Agnew's surgery in *The Agnew Clinic*.

The Agnew Clinic was a commission from the students of Dr. D. Hayes Agnew (1818–1892), who expected merely a portrait of their retiring mentor. Eakins, however, wanted to survey advances in medicine since his last effort and offered to paint all of Agnew's students and colleagues into a work echoing *The Gross Clinic*. The painting, the largest Eakins ever painted and depicting surgery on a young woman, was rejected by the Pennsylvania Academy—it had asked him to submit it to their annual exhibition—and then subsequently by the Society for American Artists. It was finally displayed at the Chicago World's Columbian Exhibition in 1893. Oblivious to the fact that Eakins was celebrating American medical advancement, one critic wrote: "It is impossible to escape from Mr. Eakins's ghastly symphonies in gore and bitumen. Delicate or sensitive women or children suddenly confronted by the portrayal of these clinical horrors might receive a shock from which they would never recover." Nevertheless, in *The Agnew Clinic* Eakins had replaced the fear and blood of *The Gross Clinic* with professionalism and detachment.

The doctors wear white coats, unlike the surgeons in *The Gross Clinic*. This indicated that in the 14 years separating the two paintings, principles of *antisepsis*—the destruction or minimization of germs and other microorganisms—had been introduced into the surgical arena. The figures are also much better lit by artificial lighting, whereas in *The Gross Clinic* the light enters the auditorium through skylights above.

The figure of Eakins himself stands in the doorway, listening as a colleague of Agnew's whispers to him, possibly explaining the procedure. Eakins's wife Susan added his likeness to the painting.

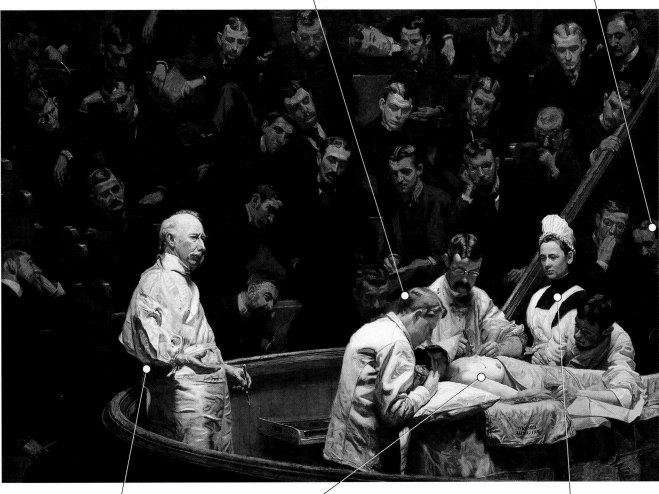

Dr. Agnew was professor of surgery at the University of Pennsylvania School of Medicine. His students described him, according to the Latin motto carved on the finished work's frame, as "the most experienced surgeon, the clearest writer and teacher, the most venerated and beloved man." At Dr. Agnew's request there is no blood shown on him or his patient.

The female patient is undergoing a mastectomy, or breast removal—still an experimental procedure—to combat her breast cancer. The doctor at her head administers chloroform as an anesthetic, another experimental technique. Poor men and women from almshouses were regularly recruited to undergo such experimental procedures in return for free medical care.

The nurse is Mary V. Clymer, at the top of her nursing class at the University of Pennsylvania. She serves a double function: overseeing the propriety of the male doctors' handling of the female patient and representing the new profession of nursing as a whole. While women were still not admitted to medical schools (an exclusion strongly supported by Dr. Agnew), the University of Pennsylvania was one of the first American universities to inaugurate a school of nursing. It was only three years old at the time of Eakins's painting.

Thomas Eakins. ***The Agnew Clinic.* 1889.** Oil on canvas, $84\frac{3}{8}''\times118\frac{1}{8}''$. Philadelpia Museum of Art on loan from the University of Pennsylvania School of Medicine. Today, this painting is reproduced on the diplomas of all graduates of the University of Pennsylvania School of Medicine.

on a man, which is precisely where the American male, in the last quarter of the nineteenth century, thought she should be.

The American Abroad

When American novelist Henry James (1843–1916) remarked, "The world is shrinking to the size of an orange," he meant that it had become easy for Americans to travel to and live in London, Paris, and Rome. In fact, by the end of the nineteenth century there were 17 companies with over 173 steamships regularly sailing between New York and Europe. With the advent of steam turbine engines, screw propellers, and steel hulls, it took less than a week to cross the Atlantic. (Fifty years earlier it had taken two to three weeks, and in Benjamin Franklin's time it took from six weeks to three months.)

Henry James and the International Novel James was perhaps the best-traveled and most cosmopolitan American writer in the nineteenth century. His first years were spent in Paris—his first memory, he claimed, was of the Place Vendome [vahn-DOME] with its Napoleonic column—and he was educated there as well as in Geneva, Switzerland, and Bonn, Germany. American schooling was not up to his father's high standards. On his first European tour, undertaken when he was 26 years of age in 1869–1870, James met the intellectual elite of England. He then traveled on to Paris, to Switzerland, and from there he hiked into Italy, then on to Milan, Venice, and Rome. He took his aunt and sister on a second tour in 1872–1874, returned to Paris in 1875, meeting writers Gustave Flaubert and Émile Zola among others, and then settled in England in 1876. "My choice is the Old World," he wrote in his diary, "my choice, my need, my life."

James often depicted the drama of American innocence confronting European experience in his novels. In *Portrait of a Lady* (1881), for instance, Isabel Archer, a young woman freed by her inheritance to travel wherever she pleases, follows in James's footsteps to England and France, marrying a morally bankrupt American expatriate. Her relationship with him tests every fiber of her innocence and moral being. In *The Ambassadors*, Lambert Strether is sent to Europe to free Chad Newsome, his fiancée's son, from the perceived clutches of the older, more experienced Madame de Vionnet [vee-oh-NAY]. Yet he himself is transformed by his acquaintance, in London and Paris, with Maria Gostrey, an American émigré, and by Chad's new circle of friends. Over a period of weeks, Strether recognizes that Chad has in fact "improved," gaining new sophistication, and knows that something similar has occurred to himself.

Painters Abroad: The Expatriate Vision Henry James was as socially active as a hardworking writer could be. His network of friends and acquaintances included many British and European artists, as well as dozens of American expatriates. *The Ambassadors* began from a germ of an idea that the author captured in his notebook in October 1895 when he recorded how fellow American author William Dean Howells (1837–1920),

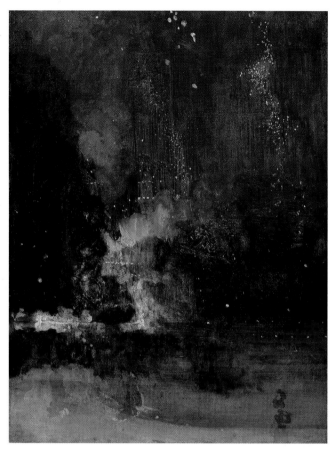

Fig. 13.26 James Abbott McNeill Whistler. *Nocturne in Black and Gold: The Falling Rocket.* **ca. 1874.** Oil on oak panel, 23³⁄₄″ × 18³⁄₈″. The Detroit Institute of Arts. Gift of Dexter M. Ferry, Jr. 46.309. The Bridgeman Art Library. The painting depicts fireworks falling over Cremorne Gardens, the popular resort on the banks of the Thames.

standing in a Paris garden, sermonized to a young man that he must live to the fullest while young. The Parisian home where the garden was located belonged to American expatriate painter James Abbott McNeill Whistler (1834–1903), who maintained a friendship with James for almost two decades.

The painter had notoriously sued English critic John Ruskin for libel after Ruskin published a scathing review of Whistler's *Nocturne in Black and Gold: The Falling Rocket* (Fig. **13.26**). In his review Ruskin berated the artist for asking "two hundred guineas for flinging a pot of paint in the public's face." The trial verged on high comedy, as the jury was shown the offending picture upside down, and "experts" of all persuasions testified to the painting's worth. Whistler eventually won but was awarded only a farthing (the least valuable English coin), a far cry from the cost of the legal action, which eventually drove him into bankruptcy.

The painting at the center of the controversy is a kind of radical impressionistic illustration of a seaside fireworks display, so deeply atmospheric that its subject matter is hard to fathom. Whistler was an admitted **aesthete**—someone who valued art for art's sake—for its beauty, not for its content. In an 1890 collection of essays called *The Gentle Art of Making Enemies*, he explained the philosophy behind **aestheticism**:

> [Art] should be independent of all clap-trap—should stand alone and appeal to the artistic sense of ear or eye, without confounding this with emotions entirely foreign to it, as devotion, pity, love, patriotism and the like. All these have no kind of concern with it, and that is why I insist on calling my works "arrangements" and "harmonies."

Whistler wanted the public to understand that the painter had a right to alter objective truth in order to conform to his or her own subjective standards of beauty. A work created in this way was not incompetent. It was, rather, of the highest order of art.

Certainly Europe, and France in particular, appeared to offer Americans a kind of liberation from the cramped Puritan morality they found at home—and in the stodgy, somewhat old-fashioned attitudes of Ruskin. Their belief in the sort of freedom of thought championed by Whistler led many American artists to work and study on the continent. The painter Theodore Robinson (1852–1896) went to France in 1884 to study with Monet at his home in Giverny. Other Americans came to sit at Monet's feet as well—Phillip Leslie Hale (1865–1931), who stayed at Giverny for four or five summers beginning in 1888; Lilla Cabot Perry, who spent nine summers there; and Theodore Earl Butler (1861–1936), who married Monet's stepdaughter.

Another American painter who spent much of his life in Europe was John Singer Sargent (1856–1924). Born in Florence and trained in Italy and France, Sargent was Whistler's rival, though 22 years his junior. He took Whistler's old studio in London after Henry James convinced the young artist to leave Paris in 1886, and it was there that Sargent did most of his work. Sargent specialized in portraits of the aristocracy and the wealthy, and he was noted for his stylish, bravura brushwork. James and Sargent moved in similar social circles, becoming fast friends after James's review of the 26-year-old painter's work in *Harper's Weekly*.

In the *Harper's* article, James took special note of Sargent's *The Daughters of Edward Darley Boit*, exhibited in Paris at the Salon of 1883 (Fig. **13.27**). The painting depicts the four daughters of an expatriate patrician couple from Boston, Edwin Darley Boit and Mary Louisa Cushing Boit, in the entry to their apartment in Paris. In the foreground, Julia, the youngest child, aged four, sits on the floor with her doll

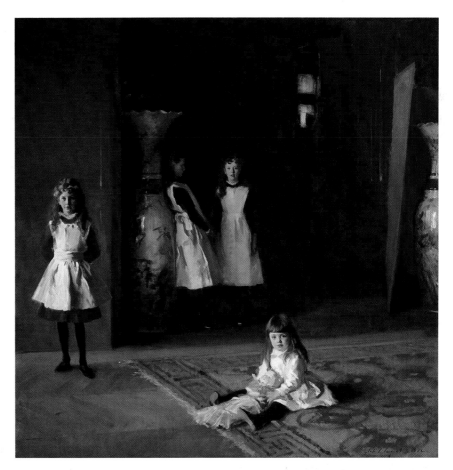

Fig. 13.27 John Singer Sargent. *The Daughters of Edward Darley Boit*. 1882. Oil on canvas, $87\frac{3}{8}'' \times 87\frac{5}{8}''$. Gift of Mary Louisa Boit, Julia Overing Boit, Jane Hubbard Boit, and Florence D. Boit in memory of their father, Edward Darley Boit, 19.124 Photograph © 2008 Museum of Fine Arts, Boston. The unusual, almost square canvas is probably something of a pun on the "Boit" name since *boîte*, in French, means "box."

between her legs. To the left, facing the viewer forthrightly, but gazing just to the viewer's left, is Mary Louisa, aged eight. In the shadows of the doorway, Jane, aged 12, looks directly at us, while Florence, the eldest, aged 14, leans, as if unwilling to cooperate with the painter, against one of two enormous Chinese vases that lend the scene something of an "Alice in Wonderland" effect.

James first described this painting as "a rich, dim, rather generalized French interior (the perspective of a hall with a shining floor, where screens and tall Japanese vases shimmer and loom), which encloses the life and seems to form the happy play-world of a family of charming children." But gradually he perceived in this work the same mysterious depth that he tried to convey in his own fiction—"the sense," he called it, "of assimilated secrets." At least at some level, the painting is a parable of the coming of age of young women in late nineteenth-century society, from the innocence of youth to the privacy and alienation of adolescence. As in James's fiction, there is always more than meets the eye, and this is the lesson that James continually impressed upon Americans who traveled or lived abroad.

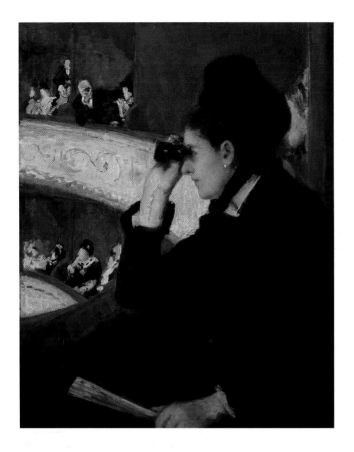

One of the most successful of the American expatriate painters was Mary Cassatt (1824–1926), who moved to Paris in 1874 and was befriended by one of the founders of Impressionism, Edgar Degas. Participating in the Impressionist exhibitions in 1879, 1880, and 1881, Cassatt was a figure painter, concentrating almost exclusively on women in domestic and intimate settings. Among her most famous works are paintings of women at the Paris Opéra. *In the Loge* is a witty representation of Opéra society (Fig.**13.28**). A woman respectably dressed all in black peers through her binoculars in the direction of the stage. Across the way, a gentleman in the company of another woman leans forward to stare through his own binoculars in the direction of the woman in black. Cassatt's woman, in a bold statement, becomes as active a spectator as the male across the way. She is a "modern" woman, and Cassatt celebrates her modernity.

Fig. 13.28 Mary Stevenson Cassatt. *In the Loge.* **1879.** Oil on canvas, 32″ × 26″. Museum of Fine Arts, Boston. The Hayden Collection - Charles Henry Hayden Fund, 10.35. Photograph © Museum of Fine Arts, Boston. This was the first of Cassatt's Impressionist paintings to be displayed in the United States. American critics thought the picture a promising sketch, but not, as the Impressionist Cassatt intended, a finished painting.

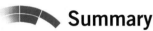 ## Summary

■ **The New Realism** During much of the nineteenth century, industrialization created wealth for a few but left the vast majority of men and women living bleak and unhealthy lives. Humanist writers such as Charles Dickens and Honoré de Balzac described English and French society in realistic terms, describing social issues in minute detail. In the novel *Madame Bovary,* Gustave Flaubert attacked the Romantic sensibilities to which he was himself strongly attracted. In his cartoon work, lithography, and paintings, Honoré Daumier depicted the plight of the French working class, as did Gustave Courbet in monumental paintings that elevated, to the consternation of many, the working class to heroic stature. Finally, the new art of photography arose in the context of the rise of realism in the arts.

■ **In Pursuit of Modernity: Paris in the 1850s and '60s** By the middle of the nineteenth century, living conditions in Paris and across Europe had deteriorated to an intolerable point. In 1848, in Paris, workers revolted, and across Europe other revolutions quickly followed, spawned especially by ethnic nationalist groups trying to assert their independence from monarchist governments. Karl Marx and Friedrich Engels had anticipated these uprisings in the *Communist Manifesto.* Meanwhile, French intellectuals began attacking the bourgeois lifestyle. The poems of Charles Baudelaire purposefully affronted bourgeois taste. Manet's paintings of the 1860s, particularly *Le Déjeuner sur l'herbe* and *Olympia,* shocked his bourgeois

audience, but the naturalist novelist Émile Zola championed them. In music, the nationalist tendencies of the era played themselves out in the Paris opera. Verdi's operas came to symbolize Italian nationalism, while the Parisian Jockey Club ostracized the German composer Richard Wagner on nationalist grounds when he tried to produce his opera *Tannhäuser.*

■ **Impressionist Paris** From 1853 to 1870, Paris was transformed, as working-class districts of the city were replaced with *grands boulevards,* and the working class and industry were displaced to new suburbs. France's younger generation of painters—Monet, Pissarro, Renoir, Degas, and Morisot—the group who came to be known as Impressionists, preferred painting out-of-doors to capture the natural effects of light.

■ **The Gilded Age in America** As New York City grew to over 3 million people in the last decades of the nineteenth century, the country was faced with economic depression and wage cutbacks, which in 1877 resulted in a series of strikes across the country. The plight of the working class contrasted greatly with the extravagance of America's wealthiest people, but poet Walt Whitman celebrated both, announcing an American self able to contain all, a self at one with nature, like the Transcendentalists before him, and the urban environment. Many American artists, seeking to escape the perceived hypocrisy and limitations of the Gilded Age, expatriated to Europe.

A Fair to Remember

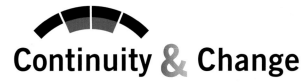

Paris's *Exposition Universelle* of 1889 was a fitting postscript to the nineteenth century as well as a precursor to the twentieth. It commemorated imperial supremacy, modern technology, and national pride one century after the beginning of the French Revolution. As he opened the Fair, French President Sadi Carnot hailed a "new era in the history of mankind" that the revolutionary events of 1789 had initiated, and "the century of labor and progress" that had unfolded since then.

Over 28 million people visited the Paris fair in 1889. They looked with pride on the fair's "colonial" section, where reproductions of housing from around the world attested to the seemingly limitless ambition and power of imperial nations such as France to command the world's resources and peoples (Fig. **13.29**). They excitedly dreamed of the future promised by that marvel of architecture and technology unveiled at the fair—Gustav Eiffel's [EYE-ful] Tower (Fig. **13.30**), a 984-foot-high open-frame structure at the entrance of the fair that dominated the city. Almost twice the height of any other building in the world, the tower was meant "to raise to the glory of modern science and to the greater honor of French industry, an arch of triumph," according to Eiffel. Once the tower was completed, spotlights positioned on the third level illuminated various Paris monuments, an effect even more dramatically realized 11 years later at the 1900 Exposition Universelle, when the entire city of Paris was electrified. Electricity also allowed fair visitors to ascend almost a thousand feet to an observation platform at the top of the tower in a hydraulic elevator designed by the Otis Elevator Company.

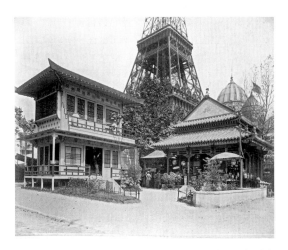

Fig. 13.29 Japanese house (left) and Chinese house (right) in the History of Habitation exhibit, *Exposition Universelle***, Paris. 1889.** Library of Congress, Washington, D.C. LC-US262-106562. The juxtaposition of East and West underscores the growing decentralization of culture at the turn of the century.

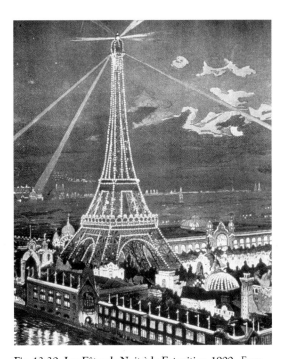

Fig. 13.30 *Les Fêtes de Nuit à la Exposition.* **1900.** From *L'Exposition de Paris* (1900). Smithsonian Institution, Washington, D.C. In 1900, the entire city of Paris was lit for the first time by electric light, and the Eiffel Tower, erected for the Exposition of 1889, was the centerpiece of "les fêtes de nuit," the nighttime celebrations at the fair.

The future was the chief attraction of the Paris Exposition, and *invention* was the key word of the day. In the Palace of Machines, the American inventor Thomas Edison (1847–1931) exhibited 493 new devices, including a huge carbon-filament electric lamp made from many smaller lamps. Edison's phonograph was also a great attraction as thousands of visitors lined up each day to hear the machine. Other inventions fascinated the public—in the Telephone pavilion, one could listen to live performances of the Comédie Française through two earphones that created a convincing stereo effect.

Yet for all the fair's promise, when, in 1789, Carnot hailed the dawn of "a new history of mankind," he had little inkling of the darker side of technology and nationalism that had already been unleashed as European nations competed, in the last decades of the nineteenth century, for imperial control of Africa, the Middle East, Asia, and India. Over the next 50 years more than 60 million people would be killed in two world wars. Ideologies would grow more strident and dangerous in the ensuing decades, becoming virulently transnational in scope. France's president himself would become a victim of a new ideology in 1894 when an Italian anarchist assassinated him to avenge the execution of several French anarchists who had participated in bombings. While nationalism held an increasing, often irrational sway over human behavior, political theories such as anarchism and, later, fascism and communism would also lead to violent and destructive actions by individuals and groups aiming to reshape society to their own standards. A new era had dawned—one of global confrontation. ∎

417

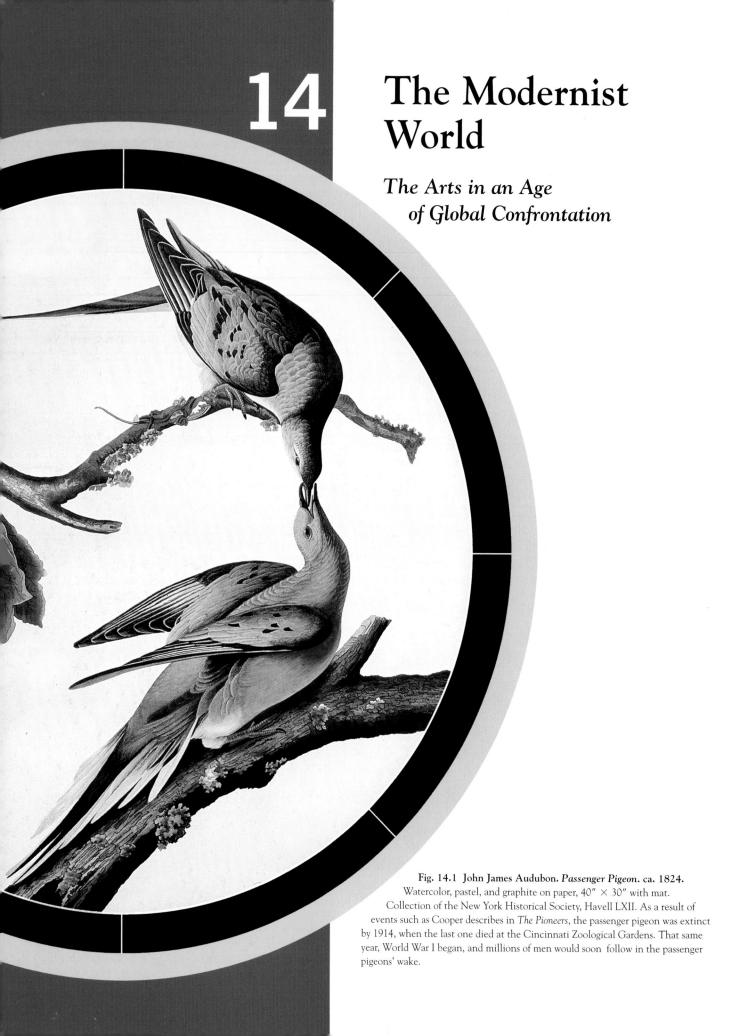

14 The Modernist World

The Arts in an Age of Global Confrontation

Fig. 14.1 John James Audubon. *Passenger Pigeon.* ca. 1824.
Watercolor, pastel, and graphite on paper, 40″ × 30″ with mat.
Collection of the New York Historical Society, Havell LXII. As a result of
events such as Cooper describes in *The Pioneers*, the passenger pigeon was extinct
by 1914, when the last one died at the Cincinnati Zoological Gardens. That same
year, World War I began, and millions of men would soon follow in the passenger
pigeons' wake.

> *Men have gained control over the forces of nature to such an extent that with their help they would have no difficulty in exterminating one another to the last man.*

Sigmund Freud, *Civilization and Its Discontents*

In *The Pioneers*, an 1823 novel by James Fenimore Cooper (1789–1851), Nathaniel "Natty" Bumppo, a white hunter who lives his entire life near the northeast Native American tribal lands of the Iroquois nation, witnesses the wholesale slaughter of passenger pigeons by the residents of Otsego—a fictional town in central New York State modeled on modern Cooperstown. What Cooper's villagers saw to inspire their shooting spree was probably similar to the scene described by the American naturalist and wildlife artist John James Audubon [aw-duh-BON] (1785–1851), author and illustrator of one of the great ornithological books of the nineteenth century, *Birds of America* (1851–1859) (Fig. **14.1**). In 1813, in Kentucky, Audubon calculated that he viewed more than a billion birds pass over him in about three hours. "The air was literally filled with Pigeons," he wrote. "The light of noon-day was obscured as by an eclipse." Natty Bumppo looks on silently at the slaughter, as "the birds lay scattered over the field in such profusion, as to cover the very ground with the fluttering victims," until he is angered into speech by the introduction of a cannon, designed to bring thousands down at a time:

> "This comes from settling a country" he said—"here I have known the pigeons to fly for forty long years, and, till you made your clearings, there was nobody to scare or to hurt them. I loved to see them come into the woods, for they were company to a body; hurting nothing; being, as it was, as harmless as a garter-snake. But now it gives me sore thoughts when I hear the frighty things whizzing through the air, for I know it's only a motion to bring out all the brats in the village at them. Well! the Lord won't see the waste of his creatures for nothing, and right will be done to the pigeons, as well as others, by and by."

Natty clearly relates the fate of the pigeons with the fate of the Native Americans. From Cooper's point of view, the native peoples, so at home in the natural world, must inevitably succumb to the same destructive "civilizing" forces as nature itself. Cooper's story is a premonition of the havoc new technologies would wreak on humanity.

At the dawn of the twentieth century an optimistic spirit of change and innovation permeated Western culture. All this would change. With the eruption of World War I in August 1914, faith in human progress was cast into doubt. The technological fruits of progress seemed to be guns, tanks, poison gas, and, ultimately, the atomic bomb, and the political promise of the nineteenth century's nationalist drive for freedom found its twentieth-century expression in the rise of the new, ultra-nationalist totalitarian state.

The Challenge to Cultural Identity

During the last decades of the nineteenth century, Western nations, revitalized by effective new military, communication, and naval technologies, sought to expand their influence and reap new economic and political power in far-distant lands. As a result of this process of imperial expansion, by the dawn of the twentieth century the tradition and sense of centeredness that had defined indigenous cultures for hundreds, even thousands, of years was either threatened or in the process of being destroyed. Worldwide, non-Western cultures faced fundamental challenges to their cultural identities—not so much a *recentering* of culture but a *decentering* of culture.

The Fate of the Native Americans

The first consistent interactions between Native peoples and Europeans in North America occurred during the seventeenth century and were confined mostly to the eastern part of the continent. In the aftermath of the Revolutionary War and the Louisiana Purchase the movement westward accelerated, first into the Ohio Valley, then the Midwest and South Central regions (Indiana, Illinois, Kentucky), and last, the Great Plains, Rocky Mountain, and Pacific regions. Images such as *The Rocky Mountains, Lander's Peak* (Fig. **14.2**) by Albert Bierstadt [BEER-shtaht] (1830–1902) reinforced in the national consciousness the wisdom of Jefferson's purchase. First exhibited in New York in April 1864 at a public fair, the painting's display was accompanied by performances by Native Americans, who danced and demonstrated their sporting activities in front of it. However, the scenes depicted by the painting were almost entirely fictional. Although commonly believed at the time to be a representation of

419

Lander's Peak in the Wind River Range, the mountain rising in the center of the painting does not bear even a vague resemblance to any Rocky Mountain, let alone Lander's Peak. It is instead an illustration of a mountain from the Alps, a none-too-disguised version of the Matterhorn. Bierstadt presents the American West through a European lens, perhaps because he both understood that view was what his audience expected and saw the world through that lens himself. As Bierstadt wrote in 1859, describing a journey to the American Rockies:

> The mountains are very fine; as seen from the plains, they resemble very much the Bernese Alps, one of the finest ranges of mountains in Europe, if not in the world. . . . The color of the mountains and of the plains, and, indeed of the entire country, reminds one of the color of Italy; in fact, we have here the Italy of America in primitive condition.

By "primitive," Bierstadt means pure, untainted, and unfallen, as if it were another biblical Garden of Eden before Eve ate of the apple of knowledge. The Native Americans in the foreground are similarly "primitive," the "noble savages" that Rousseau so admired, at peace in a place as yet untouched by white settlement. But in the pamphlet accompanying the painting's exhibition as it toured the country, Bierstadt wrote that he hoped that, one day in the area occupied by the Native American encampment, "a city, populated by our descendants, may rise, and in its art-galleries this picture may eventually find a resting-place."

In fact, the populating of the American West was well under way, and Bierstadt knew it. From 1790 to 1860 the population of non-native-born Americans increased from 4 million to 31 million, with nearly half of them moving to territory west of the Atlantic coast states. America's frontier shifted into regions where the possibilities (and natural resources) seemed limitless. "Go West, young man, and grow up with the country," the Indiana journalist John Soule had advised in 1851. The influential New York journalist Horace Greeley (1811–1872) took up the first part of the refrain, and soon it became obvious that the American West would be central to America's self-identity. Unfortunately, the original inhabitants of the lands were only an afterthought to the artists, the political leaders in Washington, and most of all the settlers themselves. Native American culture and tribal identities were almost entirely ignored and disparaged in the process of "going West."

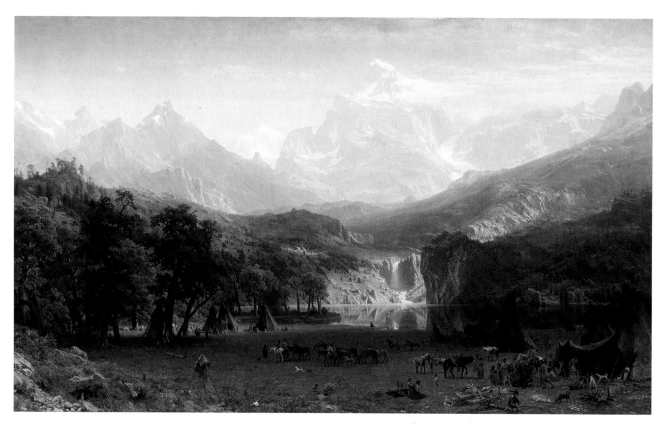

Fig. 14.2 Albert Bierstadt. *The Rocky Mountains, Lander's Peak.* **1863.** Oil on panel, 73 1/2″ × 120 3/4″. The Metropolitan Museum of Art, Rogers Fund, 1907 (07.123). Image copyright © The Metropolitan Museum of Art. This painting established a visual rhetoric that Bierstadt applied in painting after painting—the bucolic foreground with a clear lake at the base of a waterfall that drops from the heights of the mountains beyond. It presented a myth of landscape and of the Native American presence within it.

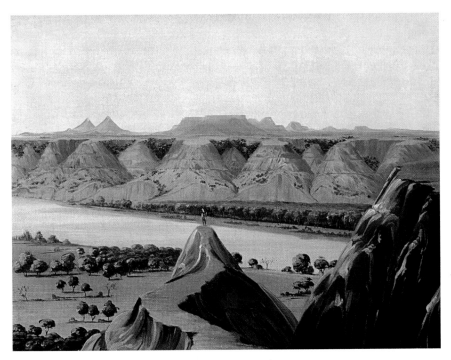

Fig. 14.3 George Catlin. *Big Bend on the Missouri River, 1,900 Miles above St. Louis.* 1832. Oil on canvas, 29″ × 24″. Smithsonian American Art Museum, Washington, D.C./Art Resource, NY. Catlin's lone Indian contemplating the vastness of the landscape is symbolic of a vanishing people and a vanishing wilderness.

twelvemonth before teemed with animal life, was a dead, solitary, putrid desert." It was as if George Catlin (1796–1872), a successful portrait painter from the east coast who in 1830 headed west from St. Louis to record the costumes and practices of the Native Americans, had predicted the demise of the buffalo, and with it the demise of the Indian, when he painted his lone Indian overlooking a Missouri River valley empty of game (Fig. **14.3**). The end of the buffalo signaled the end of Native American culture. A Crow warrior named Two Legs put it this way: "Nothing happened after that. We just lived. There were no more war parties, no capturing horses from the Piegan (tribe) and the Sioux [soo], no buffalo to hunt. There is nothing more to tell."

The British in China and India

While not posing a threat to the actual existence of China and India, Western nations sought to dominate them through aggressive military and economic policies aimed at transferring wealth to their own countries and limiting their sovereignty. During the eighteenth century, the English East India Company and the French Compagnie des Indes [kohm-pahn-YEE dayz-ahnd] (French East India Company) vied for control of trade with India and the rest of Asia even as they engaged in ruthless competition in Europe and North America. India's trade was seen as a stepping-stone to even larger markets in China, whose silks, porcelains, and teas were highly valued throughout Europe and America. Rather than being mutually beneficial, however, trade with the West was a profound threat to local, regional, and national stability in both China and India. Before the end of the nineteenth century, both countries would become outposts in new colonial empires developed by Europeans, resulting in the weakening of traditional cultural practices, political leadership, and social systems.

The European taste for *chinoiserie* (see *Focus*, chapter 11) had created a bustling export economy in China during the eighteenth century, but more important to the Westerners than the Chinese wares was the opium trade. In order to compensate for the gold and silver spent on the purchase of tea, porcelains, and silks, the British East India Company began selling to the Chinese large quantities of opium, a powerful narcotic drug, which it grew in India. Produced at a very low cost, opium was a very profitable trade item for the British. Unfortunately for the Chinese, opium addiction rapidly became a severe social problem. In 1839, after the emperor's son died an opium-related death, the Chinese moved to ban the drug.

Conflict with Native Americans was therefore inevitable during the course of expansion. The most visible dimension of a multifaceted clash of cultures was the fight over land—who owned it and who had the right to live on it. The settlers thought of the land as something to organize, control, and own. They saw the land as central to their own economic well-being and as a resource to exploit to their own benefit. Land was also fungible, like money—that is, it could be traded like any other commodity, and disposed of as well. The Native Americans, on the other hand, saw themselves as one element in the whole of nature, not privileged in relation to the natural world but part of its delicate balance. They thought their primary responsibility was to live in harmony with nature rather than transforming, trading, or altering it in a fundamental way.

The ultimate fate of tribes was inextricably linked to the fate of the buffalo. By the 1870s the military was pursuing an unofficial policy of Native American extermination, and it encouraged the slaughter of the buffalo as a shortcut to this end. Echoing President Andrew Jackson 40 years earlier, General Philip Sheridan (1831–1888) urged that white settlers hasten the killing of buffalo herds, thereby undercutting the Native American supply of food. The effort to build a transcontinental railroad helped Sheridan's wish to be realized, as over 4 million buffalo were slaughtered by meat hunters for the construction gangs, by hide hunters, and by tourists. In the late summer of 1873, railroad builder Granville Dodge reported that "the vast plain, which only a short

The British acknowledged that the Chinese had the right to prohibit the Chinese from using opium, but they considered the ban on trading it an unlawful violation of the freedom of commerce. They declared war and subsequently crushed China, attacking most of its coastal and river towns. In the resulting Treaty of Nanjing [nan-JING], China ceded Hong Kong to Britain and paid an indemnity of 21 million silver dollars (roughly equivalent to $2 billion today). Chinese ports and markets were opened to Western merchants, and by 1880 the import of cheap machine-made products resulted in the collapse of the Chinese economy. It would not recover for over a century.

While British coffers were enriched, the declining Chinese economy produced a chain of unforeseen consequences, typical of the interactions between Westerners and indigenous peoples during this period. First, ever-worsening economic conditions drove many Chinese to emigrate in order to earn a living. Tens of thousands were attracted to California after gold was discovered there in 1849. The Chinese also became an important source of labor for the Central Pacific Railroad as it constructed railroad lines across the Western United States. By 1867, 90 percent of the workers on the railroad were Chinese. Hired for 30 percent less than the cost of hiring whites, they soon organized and struck for better wages. After the Burlingame Treaty of 1868, in which the United States and China established friendly relations, Chinese immigration to the United States increased to approximately 16,000 a year. By 1882, however, the threat to the American workforce posed by immigrant Chinese labor in a time of economic downturn led to the passing of the Chinese Exclusion Act, which outlawed further immigration and denied citizenship to those already in the country.

If the British East India Company's involvement in the opium trade brought China to its knees, it exercised policies in India that crippled that economy as well. In the 1760s, India had been one of the most productive economies in the world. Britain imported most of its best cast steel from India, where hundreds of thousands were employed in mills and mines. But by the end of the eighteenth century, India lost its European markets for finished goods after the British East India Company bought Indian raw materials at exploitatively low prices and then undercut Indian manufacturers by selling finished textiles in India at low prices. Backed by the force of the British Army and increasingly efficient mechanized factories in Britain, English merchants profited handsomely at the expense of traditional economic production in India. So, instead of manufacturing cast steel, India found itself producing only iron ore; instead of manufacturing finished textiles, it exported raw cotton. In this economy, from which manufacturing had been almost completely eliminated, work became a scarce commodity. As its population increased in the second half of the nineteenth century, India experienced an unprecedented series of intensive famines, as well as widespread unemployment and poverty. As a result, over the course of the late nineteenth and early twentieth centuries, nearly 1.5 million Indians sold themselves into indentured servitude. Having produced 25 percent of the world's industrial output in 1750, India by 1900 contributed only 2 percent.

The Opening of Japan

As India was rapidly changing under the British colonial regime in the mid-nineteenth century, Japan sought to accommodate Western industrialization while maintaining the most important aspects of its cultural traditions. Until the American Commodore Matthew Perry sailed into Tokyo Bay on July 8, 1853, Japan had been closed to the West for 250 years. Seeking to gain the Japanese government's assistance in opening trade as well as providing safe havens for stranded sailors, Perry demanded and received concessions. His expedition ultimately led to the Treaty of Kanagawa (1854) and the Harris Treaty (1858) between the United States and Japan, which opened diplomatic and trade relations between the two countries and brought large quantities of Japanese goods to the West for the first time. The Japanese realized that they had to accommodate Perry, the immediate threat, as well as cope with the longer-term challenge from Western nations. Their goal was to modernize along Western lines but maintain their sovereignty as well as their ancient cultural traditions. Visitors arriving in Japan in the late nineteenth and early twentieth centuries had to follow carefully laid out itineraries if they wished to venture beyond the "treaty ports" of Yokohama [yoh-koh-HAH-mah], just south of Tokyo; Kobe [KOH-bee], just outside Osaka; and Nagasaki [nah-gah-SAH-kee]. The Japanese by this means tried to control the image of their country that visitors took home.

At first, Japan focused on closing the technology gap between its army and navy and Western military powers. Samuel Williams, the Perry expedition's interpreter, described the Japanese army as it appeared to him in July 1853: "Soldiers with muskets and drilling in close array," but also, "soldiers in petticoats, sandals, two swords, all in disorder." In order to modernize their society, the government had to industrialize, which they commenced without delay, and by the late nineteenth century, the Japanese economy was booming, as was the art of woodblock printing, called *ukiyo-e* [oo-kee-oh-ay] ("pictures of the floating world"), a tradition that had developed steadily since the beginning of the Tokugawa era (1603–1868). The export trade in prints was a vital part of the economy, and Western artists, particularly the Impressionists, were captivated by the effects Japanese printmakers were able to achieve. Very popular among the urban classes in Edo (Tokyo) since the 1670s, woodblock prints were mass produced and thus affordable to artisans, merchants, and other city dwellers. They depicted a wide range of Japanese social and cultural activity, including the daily rituals of life, the theatrical world of actors and geisha, sumo wrestlers, and artisans along with landscapes and nature scenes. Incorporating traditional themes from literature and history, the prints were also notable for introducing contemporary tastes, fads, and fashions, thus forming an invaluable source of knowledge on Japanese culture over the more than two centuries of its development.

Probably the most famous series of Japanese prints is *Thirty-Six Views of Mount Fuji* by Katsushika Hokusai [HO-koo-sigh] (1760–1849). The print in that series known as *The*

Great Wave has achieved almost iconic status in the art world (Fig. **14.4**). It depicts two boats descending into a trough beneath a giant crashing wave that hangs over the scene like a menacing claw. In the distance, above the horizon, rises Mount Fuji [FOO-jee], symbol to the Japanese of immortality and of Japan itself, framed in a vortex of wave and foam. Though the wave is visually larger than the distant mountain, the viewer knows it will imminently collapse and that Fuji will remain, illustrating both the transience of human experience and the permanence of the natural world. The print also juxtaposes the perils of the moment, as represented by the dilemma of the boatmen, and the enduring values of the nation, represented by the solidity of the mountain. Those values can be understood to transcend the momentary troubles and fleeting pleasures of daily life.

Africa and Empire

During the second half of the nineteenth century, European nations competed with each other in acquiring territories in Asia, Africa, Latin America, and elsewhere around the world. In some cases, their management of these areas was direct, with a colonial political structure supervising the governance of the territory. In other cases, control was indirect, focusing on economic domination. In either case this effort to increase the power of nation-states was termed **imperialism**, and the world is still living with the consequences more than a century later. There is probably no more overt statement of the principle than when the British, in 1858, declared Queen Victoria to be the empress of India.

By the beginning of the twentieth century, Western powers had established cultural, political, and economic hegemony (control or domination) over much of the world. They were motivated by economic and strategic self-interest—that is, the control of natural resources and trade routes. Fierce nationalism, and a Europe-centered belief in the superiority of Western culture (as well as the white race), fueled imperialism, while imperialist philosophy emphasized the humanitarian desire to "improve the lot" of indigenous peoples. By the last quarter of the nineteenth century, the African continent was the focal point of imperialist competition.

The scramble for control of the African continent began with the opening of the Suez Canal in 1869, the shortest route to India, long England's most important and profitable colony. When internal squabbles threatened Egypt's stability in the 1880s, Britain stepped in to protect its interest in the canal, in which it had a major economic investment. Then, to further protect Egypt, it advanced into the Sudan. Beyond Africa's key strategic placement, its vast land area and untapped natural resources proved an irresistible lure for European nations.

France's direct control of Algeria in North Africa dated from 1834, when it formally annexed much of the region. Originally motivated by the desire to thwart piracy in the Mediterranean, France added Tunisia [too-NEE-zhuh], much of West Africa, and Madagascar [mad-uh-GASS-kar] (a large

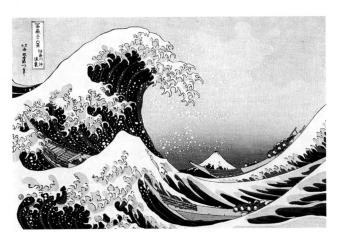

Fig. 14.4 Katsushika Hokusai. *The Great Wave,* from the series *Thirty-Six Views of Mount Fuji*. ca. 1823–1839. Color woodblock print, 10$\frac{1}{8}$" × 14$\frac{1}{4}$". © Historical Picture Archive/CORBIS. The boatsmen can be understood as working in harmony with the powers of nature, something like samurai of the sea.

island nation off the east coast of Africa) to its colonies by the 1880s. Not to be left behind, and motivated by a desire to appear at least as powerful as Britain and France, Belgium, Portugal, Spain, and Italy all began to expand previous colonies or acquire new ones. To counter this expansion, and to protect trade routes around the Cape of Good Hope, Britain expanded into present-day Zimbabwe [zim-BAH-bway] and Zambia [ZAM-bee-uh].

Looking at the situation in Africa, Germany's Chancellor Bismarck decided to acquire Southwest Africa (Namibia [nam-IB-ee-uh]), Togoland [TOH-goh-land], the Cameroons [kam-uh-ROONZ], and East Africa (Tanzania [tan-zuh-NEE-uh]). His motives were purely political, designed to improve his relations with Britain in his never-ending struggles with France and Russia. "My map of Africa lies in Europe," he said. "Here is Russia, and there is France, and here in the middle are we. That is my map of Africa." By and large, European imperial expansion in Africa and Southeast Asia was the nationalist expression of the desire of European countries to assert and expand their own political power.

Darwinian Evolution and the Theoretical Justification for Imperialism

The use of the word "race" in the extended title of the groundbreaking work by Charles Darwin (1809–1887), *On the Origin of Species by Means of Natural Selection, or the Preservation of Favored Races in the Struggle for Life*, became a critical ingredient in the development of a new nineteenth-century ideology, **social Darwinism**.

In December 1831, the 22-year-old Darwin, grandson of Josiah Wedgwood and Erasmus Darwin, founding members of the Lunar Society (see chapter 11), set sail on the HMS *Beagle* to serve as naturalist on the ship's survey of South America. On his five-year journey he kept a daily diary, the basis for his *Journal of Researches into the Geology and Natural History of* the *Various Countries Visited by H. M. S. Beagle* (1839), commonly known as *The Voyage of the Beagle*. There he recorded his detailed observations of the geology, flora, and fauna of the region, from the rain forests of Brazil, "undefaced by the hand of man," to the barren landscape of Tierra del Fuego, and finally, the volcanic islands of Galapagos, just below the equator off the South American coast.

Twenty years later, Darwin would publish his analysis of the vast amount of data he had collected. In *The Origin of the Species,* he concluded that similar flora and fauna, in similar habitats, but isolated from each other, developed in a relatively brief period of time—geologically speaking—into distinct species. Darwin was on the way to understanding the "mystery of mysteries," the origin of life itself.

He further argued that through the process of natural selection, certain organisms are able to increase rapidly over time by retaining traits conducive to their survival and eliminating those that are less favorable to survival. A given species' ability to *adapt to its environment*, then, is fundamental to its survival. A species' ability to repel predators—including environmental challenges such as drought or flood—enhances its chances for procreation and determines its "fitness" to survive. And, in the end, only the "fittest" survive, an idea that, misunderstood and misapplied as social Darwinism, had an enormous impact on social theory late in the nineteenth century.

To those who desired to validate imperialism and the colonial regimes it fostered in Africa and Asia, social Darwinism explained the supposed social and cultural evolution that elevated Europe (and the white race) above all other nations and races. It also explained, in America, the inevitable demise of the Native Americans. Europeans, it was argued, were the "fitter" race, and thus were destined not merely to survive but to dominate the world. Such grandiose thinking would soon characterize the demented ambitions of Adolf Hitler in Germany. Social Darwinism seemed to overturn traditional Judeo-Christian and Enlightenment ethics, especially those pertaining to compassion and the sacredness of human life. It seemed to embrace moral relativism, the belief that ethical positions are determined not by universal truths but by social, political, or cultural conditions (such as the imperial imposition of its values upon another culture). And it was cited in support of the superior evolutionary "fitness" and superiority of the Aryan [AR-ee-un] (or Anglo-Saxon) race.

Darwin himself meant nothing of the kind. Recognizing the ways in which his theories were being misapplied to social conditions, he published *The Descent of Man* in 1871. In it, he offered a theory of conscience that had a distinctly more ethical viewpoint. Darwin contended that our ancestors, living in small tribal communities, and competing with one another ruthlessly, came to recognize the advantages to successful propagation of the tribe. Over generations, the tribe whose members exhibited selfless behavior that benefited the whole group would tend to survive and prosper over

tribes whose members pursued more selfish and individualistic goals. "There can be no doubt," he wrote, "that a tribe including many members who, from possessing in a high degree the spirit of patriotism, fidelity, obedience, courage, and sympathy, were always ready to give aid to each other and to sacrifice themselves for the common good, would be victorious over most other tribes, and this would be natural selection." This was not the ethical philosophy that motivated imperialism.

Darwin's ideas were not the last word on the issue, however, and social Darwinism continually evolved. English philosopher and political theorist Herbert Spencer (1820–1903) offered extensive interpretations of social evolution that were influenced by Darwin but that equated change with constructive progress. Francis Galton (1822–1911) advocated human intervention in evolution, through selective breeding. His theory of **eugenics** focused on eliminating undesirable and less fit members of society by encouraging the proliferation of intelligent and physically fit humans. Galton's theories emphasized eliminating "inferior" humans through increased breeding of the most fit members of society by means of such state intervention as tax and other incentives. Later his theories mutated into the dark ideologies that developed into Nazism in the twentieth century.

The Rise of Modernism

Even as the European states vied for power around the world—imposing traditional Western values upon other peoples as often and as thoroughly as they could—the very traditions that these states embodied were being challenged by new discoveries in science and revolutionary new approaches to art.

In 1900, France had produced 3,000 automobiles; by 1907 it was producing 30,000 a year. The technological advances represented by the automobile were closely connected to the development of the internal combustion engine, pneumatic tires, and, above all, the rise of the assembly line. After all, building 30,000 automobiles a year required an efficiency and speed of production unlike any ever before conceived. Henry Ford (1863–1947), the American automobile maker, attacked the problem. Ford asked Frederick Taylor (1856–1915), the inventor of "scientific management," to determine the exact speed at which the assembly line should move and the exact motions workers should use to perform their duties; in 1908 assembly-line production as we know it was born.

In 1895, in Paris, the Lumière [loom-YAIR] brothers, Auguste (1862–1954) and Louis (1864–1948), had invented the cinematograph, the first motion-picture camera, which also served as a projector; and by 1905, the first motion-picture theater in the world, the Nickelodeon, opened in Pittsburgh, Pennsylvania. In 1903, the Wright brothers, Orville (1871–1948) and Wilbur (1867–1912), successfully tested their airplane: Orville flew for 59 seconds. In 1908, Orville was in the air for 91 minutes, and the following year Louis Blériot [blay-ree-OH] (1872–1936) flew across the English Channel.

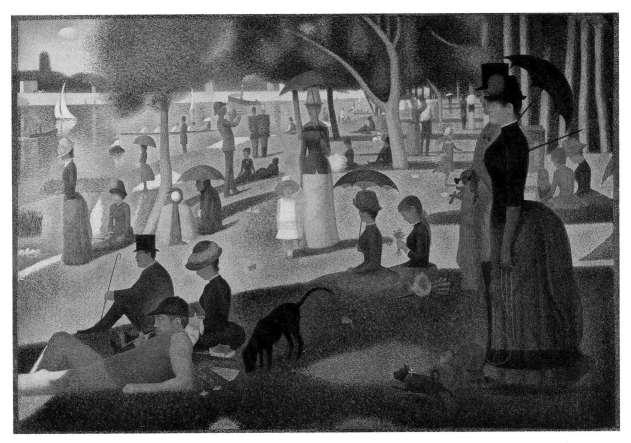

Fig. 14.5 Georges Seurat. *A Sunday on La Grande Jatte*. 1884. Oil on canvas, 5′ 11¾″ × 10′ 1¼″. Helen Birch Bartlett Memorial Collection, 1926.224. Combination of quadrant captures F1, F2, G1, G2. Photograph © 2006, The Art Institute of Chicago. All Rights Reserved. Capuchin monkeys like the one held on a leash by the woman on the right were a popular pet in 1880s Paris.

In 1897–1899, J. J. Thompson (1856–1940), in Cambridge, England, detected the existence of electrons, separate components in the structure of the previously indivisible atom. In 1900, German physicist Max Planck (1858–1947) proposed the theory of matter and energy known as quantum mechanics. By 1913, Danish physicist Niels Bohr (1885–1962) had built on quantum physics to propose a new theory of complementarity: two statements, apparently contradictory, might at any moment be equally true. In 1905, Albert Einstein [INE-stine] (1879–1955) proposed a theory of relativity, and by 1915 he published the *General Principles of Relativity* with its revolutionary model of a four-dimensional space-time continuum. In other words, between 1895 and 1915, the way we understood the physical universe had radically changed. The modern world was born.

Post-Impressionism Painting

The Post-Impressionists were the generation of painters who followed the eight Impressionist Exhibitions in Paris, which ended in 1886. They include Paul Cézanne, Paul Gauguin, and Georges Seurat, all of whom exhibited at various Impressionist shows, but rather than creating Impressionist works that captured the optical effects of light and atmosphere and the fleeting qualities of sensory experience, they sought to capture something transcendent in their act of vision, something that captured the essence of their subject. The Post-Impressionists saw themselves as inventing the future of painting, of creating art that would reflect the kind of sharply etched innovation that, in their eyes, defined modernity.

Pointillism: Seurat and the Harmonies of Color One of the most talented of the Post-Impressionist painters was Georges Seurat [suh-RAH] (1859–1891), who exhibited his masterpiece, *A Sunday on La Grand Jatte*, in 1886 when he was 27 years old (Fig. **14.5**). It depicts a Sunday crowd of Parisians enjoying the weather on the island of La Grand Jatte in the Seine River just northeast of the city. The subject matter is typically Impressionist, but it lacks that style's sense of spontaneity and the immediacy of its brushwork. Instead, *La Grand Jatte* is a carefully controlled, scientific application of tiny dots of color—***pointilles*** [pwahn-TEE], as Seurat called them—and his method of painting became known as pointillism [POIN-tih-lizm] to some, and Neo-Impressionism to others.

In setting his "points" of color side by side across the canvas, Seurat determined that color could be mixed, as he put it, in "gay, calm, or sad" combinations. Lines extending upward could also reflect these same feelings, he explained, imparting a cheerful tone, as do warm and luminous colors of red, orange, and yellow. Horizontal lines that balance dark and light, warmth and coolness, create a sense of calm. Lines reaching in a downward direction and the dark, cool hues of green, blue, and violet evoke sadness.

With this symbolic theory of color in mind, we can see much more in Seurat's *La Grand Jatte* than simply a Sunday crowd enjoying a day at the park. There are 48 people of various ages depicted, including soldiers, families, couples, and singles, some in fashionable attire, others in casual dress. A range of social classes is present as well, illustrating the mixture of diverse people on the city's day of leisure. Although overall the painting balances its lights and darks and the horizontal dominates, thus creating a sense of calm, all three groups in the foreground shadows are bathed in the melancholy tones of blue, violet, and green. With few exceptions—a running child, and behind her a couple—almost everyone in the painting is looking either straight ahead or downward. Even the tails of the pets turn downward. This solemn feature is further heightened by the toy-soldier rigidity of the figures. Seurat's painting *suggests* more than it portrays. As one critic of the time wrote of *La Grande Jatte*, "one understands then the rigidity of Parisian leisure, tired and stiff, where even recreation is a matter of striking poses."

Symbolic Color: Van Gogh Seurat's influence on French painting was profound. Dutch painter Vincent van Gogh (1853–1890), studied Seurat's paintings while living in Paris in 1886–1887 and experimented extensively with Seurat's color combinations and pointillist technique, which extended even to his drawings, as a means to create a rich textural surface.

Van Gogh was often overcome with intense and uncontrollable emotions, an attribute that played a key role in the development of his unique artistic style. Profoundly committed to discovering a universal harmony in which all aspects of life were united through art, van Gogh found Seurat's emphasis on contrasting colors appealing. It became another ingredient in his synthesis of techniques. He began to apply complementary colors in richly painted zones using dashes and strokes that were much larger than Seurat's *pointilles*.

Color, in van Gogh's paintings, becomes symbolic, charged with feelings. To viewers at the time, the dashes of thickly painted color, a technique known as *impasto*, seemed thrown onto the canvas as a haphazard and unrefined mess. And yet, the staccato rhythms of this brushwork seemed to van Gogh himself deeply autobiographic, capturing almost stroke by stroke the pulse of his own volatile personality. A painting like *Portrait of Patience Escalier* is not just a portrait, but the embodiment of van Gogh's feeling for nature (Fig. **14.6**). Escalier's blue coat, though traditional peasant garb, evokes the deep blue skies of the south of France, and the orange background reproduces what van Gogh described as "the furnace of the height of harvest time . . . orange colors flashing like lightning, vivid as red-hot iron." He further explained that ". . . although it does not

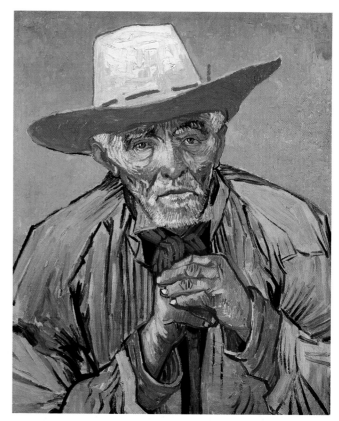

Fig. 14.6 Vincent van Gogh. *Portrait of Patience Escalier.* **August 1889.** Oil on canvas, $27\frac{1}{8}'' \times 22''$. Private Collection/Photo © Lefevre Fine Art, Ltd., London/The Bridgeman Art Library. Van Gogh would comment on the peasants in the south of France, "The natives are like Zola's poor peasants, innocent and gentle beings."

pretend to be the image of a red sunset, [it] may nevertheless give a suggestion of one." Through color, van Gogh calls to mind not just the landscape of southern France, but also the enduring lifestyle and nobility of the peasants who live in it.

Van Gogh understood that in paintings like *Portrait of Patience Escalier*, he was actively abandoning Impressionism. In so doing, he established not only his signature style, but also a vigorous and modern aesthetic sense. As he wrote while working on the painting:

> What I learned in Paris is leaving me and I am returning to the ideas I had . . . before I knew the impressionists. And I should not be surprised if the impressionists soon find fault with my way of working. . . . Because instead of trying to reproduce exactly what I have before my eyes, I use color more arbitrarily, in order to express myself forcibly.

Although his work grew ever bolder and more creative as the years passed, van Gogh continued to suffer from the emotional instability and depression that tormented him most of his adult life. In July 1890, after a number of stays in hospitals and asylums, he committed suicide in the fields outside Auvers-sur-Oise, where he was being treated by Dr. Paul Gachet, who was the subject of several of the great artist's last portraits.

The Structure of Color: Cézanne Of all the Post-Impressionists, Paul Cézanne [say-ZAHN] (1839–1906) was the only one
who continued to paint *en plein air*. In this regard, he remained
an Impressionist, and he continued to paint what he called
"optics." The duty of the painter, he said, was "to give the image
of what we see," but innocently "forgetting everything that has
appeared before." Since the Renaissance, Western art had been
dedicated to representing the world as the eye sees it—that is,
in terms of perspectival space. But Cézanne realized that we see
the world in far more complex terms than just the retinal image
before us. We see it through the multiple lenses of our lived
experience. This multiplicity of viewpoints, or perspectives, is
the dominant feature of *Still Life with Plaster Cast* (Fig. **14.7**).
Nothing in the composition is spatially stable. Instead we wander through the small space in the corner of Cézanne's studio
just as the painter's eye would do. His viewpoint constantly
moves, contemplating its object from this angle, then that one.
The result of this vision is a representation of nature as a series
of patches of color that tend to flatten the surface of his paintings. Note, for instance, how the fruit and onions on the table
are modeled by radical shifts in color rather than gradations
from light to dark (traditional chiaroscuro).

Cézanne returned to the same theme continually—particularly still lifes and Mont Sainte-Victoire, the mountain
overlooking his native Aix-en-Provence [eks-ahn-proh-
VAHNSS] in the south of France (Fig. **14.8**). In the last
decade of his life, the mountain became something of an
obsession, as he climbed the hill behind his studio to paint it
day after day. He especially liked to paint after storms when
the air is clear and the colors of the landscape are at their
most saturated and of uniform intensity. Cézanne acknowledges the illusion of space of the mountain scene by means of

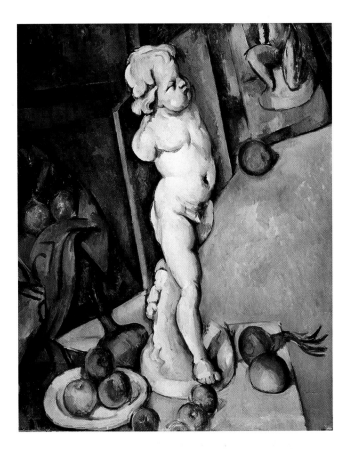

Fig. 14.7 Paul Cézanne. *Still Life with Plaster Cast*. ca. 1894. Oil on paper
on board, 26½″ × 32½″. The Samuel Courtauld Trust, Courtauld Institute
of Art Gallery, London. Cézanne's challenge to tradition is highlighted by the
tension between his radical approach to the representation of space and his
inclusion, at the heart of the painting, of a plaster cast of a seventeenth-
century Cupid sculpted by Pierre Puget [poo-ZHAY] (1620–1694).

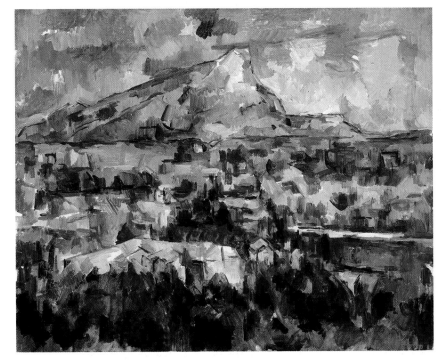

**Fig. 14.8 Paul Cézanne. *Mont Sainte-Victoire*.
1902–1904.** Oil on canvas, 28¾″ × 36³⁄₁₆″. Photo
Graydon Wood. Philadelphia Museum of Art: The
George W. Elkins Collection, 1936. E1936-1-1.
Cézanne painted this from the top of the steep hill
known as Les Lauves, just north of Aix-en-Provence
but within walking distance of the city center. He built
his own studio on a plot of land halfway up the hill,
overlooking the city.

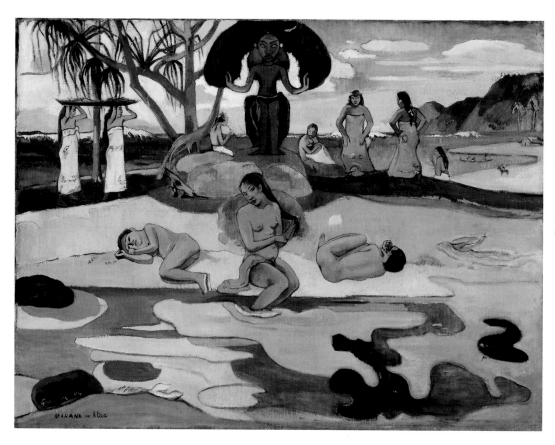

Fig. 14.9 Paul Gauguin. *Mahana no atua (Day of the God).* **1894.** Oil (possibly mixed with wax) on canvas, 26⅝″ × 35⅝″. The Art Institute of Chicago. Helen Birch Bartlett Memorial Collection (1926.198). Photograph © 2007, The Art Institute of Chicago. All Rights Reserved. There is no record of Gauguin ever exhibiting this work. It was first exhibited at the Boston Art Club in 1925.

three bands of color. Patches of gray and black define the foreground, green and yellow-orange the middle ground, and violets and blues the distant mountain and sky. Yet in each of these areas, the predominant colors of the other two are repeated—the green brushstrokes of the middle ground in the sky, for instance—all with a consistent intensity. The distant colors possess the same strength as those closest. Together with the uniform size of Cézanne's brushstrokes—his patches do not get smaller as they retreat into the distance—this use of color makes the viewer very aware of the surface qualities and structure of Cézanne's composition. It is this tension between spatial perspectives and surface flatness that would become one of the chief preoccupations of modern painting in the forthcoming century.

Escape to Far Tahiti: Gauguin In 1891, the painter Paul Gauguin [goh-GAN] (1848–1903) left France for the island of Tahiti, part of French Polynesia, in the South Pacific. A frustrated businessman and father of five children, he had taken up art with a rare dedication a decade earlier, studying with Camille Pissarro and Paul Cézanne. Gauguin was also a friend of van Gogh, with whom he spent several months painting in Arles during the Dutch artist's most productive period. He had also been inspired by the 1889 *Exposition Universelle*, where indigenous peoples and housing from around the world were displayed. "I can buy a native house," he wrote his friend Émile Bernard, "like those you saw at the

World's Fair. Made of wood and dirt with a thatched roof." To other friends he wrote, "I will go to Tahiti and I hope to finish out my life there . . . far from the European struggle for money . . . able to listen in the silence of beautiful tropical nights to the soft murmuring music of my heartbeats in loving harmony with the mysterious beings in my entourage."

Gauguin's first trip to Tahiti was not everything he dreamed it would be, since by March 1892 he was penniless. When he arrived back in France, he had painted 66 pictures but had only four francs (about $12 today) to his name. He spent the next two years energetically promoting his work and writing an account of his journey to Tahiti, entitled *Noa Noa* (*noa* means "fragrant" or "perfumed"). It is a fictionalized version of his travels and bears little resemblance to the details of his journey that he honestly recorded in his letters. But *Noa Noa* was not meant to be true so much as sensational, with its titillating story of the artist's liaison with a 13-year-old Tahitian girl, Tehamana, offered to him by her family. He presents himself as a *primitif*. In French, the word *primitif* suggests the primal, original, or irreducible. Gauguin believed that "primitive" ways of thinking offered an entry into the primal powers of the mind, and he considered his paintings visionary glimpses into the primal forces of nature.

Gauguin arranged for two exhibitions at a Paris gallery in November 1893 and another in December 1894. He opened a studio of his own, painted olive green and a brilliant chrome yellow, and decorated it with paintings, tropical plants, and exotic furnishings. He initiated a regular Thursday salon where he lectured on his paintings and regaled guests with stories of his travels, as well as playing music on a range of instruments.

In this studio he painted *Mahana no atua* (*Day of the God*) of 1894 (Fig. **14.9**). Based on idealized recollections of his escape to Tahiti, the canvas consists of three zones. In the top zone or background, figures carry food to a carved idol, representing a native god; a musician plays as two women dance; and two lovers embrace beside the statue of the deity. Below, in the second zone, are three nude figures. The one to the right assumes a fetal position suggestive of birth and fertility. The one to the left appears to be day dreaming or napping, possibly an image of reverie. The middle figure appears to have just emerged from bathing in the water below that constitutes the third zone. She directs her gaze at the viewer and, so, suggests an uninhibited sexuality. The bottom, watery zone is an irregular patchwork of color, an abstract composition of sensuous line and fluid shapes. As in van Gogh's work, color is freed of its representational function to become an almost pure expression of the artist's feelings.

Gauguin returned to Tahiti in June 1895 and never came back to France, completing nearly 100 paintings and over 400 woodcuts in the eight remaining years of his life. He moved in 1901 to the remote island of Hivaoa [hee-vah-OH-uh], in the Marquesas [mar-KAY-suz], where in the small village of Atuona [aht-uh-WOH-nuh] he built and decorated what he called his House of Pleasure. Taking up with another young girl, who like Tehamana gave birth to his child, Gauguin alienated the small number of priests and colonial French officials on the islands but attracted the interest and friendship of many native Marquesans, who were fascinated by his nonstop work habits and his colorful paintings. Having suffered for years from heart disease and syphilis, he died quietly in Hivaoa in May 1903.

Pablo Picasso's Paris: At the Heart of the Modern

At the turn of the century, the work of artists such as the Post-Impressionists had come to represent a revolt against reason, for to describe the world as it appears is to ignore the subjective experience of human beings—everything from belief and faith to intuition, the creative impulse, and the dream world. Their work represented a sort of return to spirituality, but without formalized religion, and especially its attendant moral rules. What distinguishes this new, increasingly modern self from the Romantic self is that it does not merely seek the truth, even subjective truth—it attempts to *create* it.

In the art world, at the center of this new spirit was the Spanish-born artist Pablo Picasso [pee-KAH-soh] (1881–1973). His studio in Paris was quickly recognized by artists and intellectuals as the center of artistic innovation in the new century. From around Europe and America, artists flocked to see his work, and they carried his spirit—and the spirit of French painting generally—back with them to Italy, Germany,

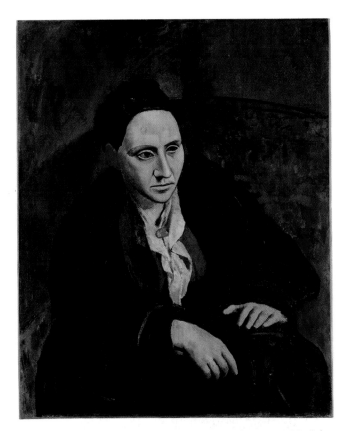

Fig. 14.10 Pablo Picasso. *Gertrude Stein*. Winter–Autumn 1906. Oil on canvas, 39 3/8″ × 32″. Bequest of Gertrude Stein, 1946 (47.106). The Metropolitan Museum of Art, NY. Image © The Metropolitan Museum of Art/Art Resource, NY. © ARS Art Rights Society, NY. According to Stein, in painting her portrait, "Picasso passed [on] . . . to the intensive struggle which was to end in Cubism."

and America, where it influenced the arts there. Picasso's work also encouraged radical approaches to poetry and to music, where the discordant, sometimes violent distortions of his paintings found their expression in sound.

Picasso's Paris was centered at 13 rue Ravignon [rah-veen-YOHN], at the Bateau-Lavoir [bah-TOH lah-VWAHR] ("Laundry Barge"), so named by the poet Max Jacob. It was Picasso's studio from the spring of 1904 until October 1909, and he continued to store his paintings there until September 1912. Anyone wanting to see his work would climb the stairs to the great ramshackle space, where the walls were piled deep with canvases. Or they might see his work at the Saturday evening salons of expatriate American writer and art collector Gertrude Stein [stine] (1874–1946) at 27 rue de Fleurus [fler-OOS] behind the Jardin du Luxembourg [zhar-DEHN due louks-em-BOOR] on the Left Bank of the Seine. If you knew someone who knew someone, you would be welcome enough. Many Picassos hung on her walls, including his portrait of her, painted in 1906 (Fig. **14.10**).

In her book *The Autobiography of Alice B. Toklas* (1932)—actually her own memoir disguised as that of her friend and lifelong companion—Stein described the making of this picture in the winter of 1906 (**Reading 14.1**):

READING 14.1 **from Gertrude Stein,** ***The Autobiography of Alice B. Toklas* (1932)**

Picasso had never had anybody pose for him since he was sixteen years old. He was then twenty-four and Gertrude had never thought of having her portrait painted, and they do not know either of them how it came about. Anyway, it did, and she posed for this portrait ninety times. There was a large broken armchair where Gertrude Stein posed. There was a couch where everybody sat and slept. There was a little kitchen chair where Picasso sat to paint. There was a large easel and there were many canvases. She took her pose, Picasso sat very tight in his chair and very close to his canvas and on a very small palette, which was of a brown gray color, mixed some more brown gray and the painting began. All of a sudden one day Picasso painted out the whole head. I can't see you anymore when I look, he said irritably, and so the picture was left like that.

Picasso actually finished the picture early the following fall, painting her face in large, masklike masses in a style very different from the rest of the picture. No longer relying on the visual presence of the sitter before his eyes, Picasso painted not his view of her, but his idea of her. When Alice B. Toklas later commented that some people thought the painting did not look like Stein, Picasso replied, "It will."

The Aggressive New Modern Art: *Les Demoiselles d'Avignon* In a way, the story of Gertrude Stein's portrait is a parable for the birth of modern art. It narrates the shift in painting from an optical art—painting what one sees—to an imaginative construct—painting what one thinks about what one sees. The object of painting shifts, in other words, from the literal to the conceptual. The painting that most thoroughly embodied this shift was *Les Demoiselles d'Avignon* [lay dem-wah-ZELL dah-veen-YOHN], which Picasso began soon after finishing his portrait of Stein (Fig. **14.11**).

Completed in the summer of 1907, *Les Demoiselles d'Avignon* was not exhibited in public until 1916. So if you wanted to see it, you had to climb the hill to the Bateau-Lavoir. And many did because the painting was notorious, understood—correctly—as an assault on the idea of painting as it had always been understood. It seemed entirely new in every way.

The painting represents five prostitutes in a brothel on the *carrer d'Avinyo* (Avignon Street) in Picasso's native Barcelona. As the figure on the left draws back a curtain as if to reveal them, the prostitutes address the viewer with the frankness of Manet's *Olympia* (see Fig. 13.11), a painting Picasso greatly admired. Also extremely important to Picasso was the example of Cézanne, who, a year after his death in October 1906, was honored with a huge retrospective at the 1907 Salon d'Automne [doh-TUN]. Cézanne, Picasso would say, "is the father of us all." In the way Picasso shows one object or figure from two different points of view, the compressed and concentrated space of *Les Demoiselles* is much like Cézanne's (see Fig. 14.7). Consider the still-life grouping of melon, pear, apple, and grapes in the center foreground. The viewer is clearly looking down at the corner of a table, at an angle completely inconsistent with the frontal view of the nude who is parting the curtain. And note the feet of the nude second from the left. Could she possibly be standing? Or is she, in fact, reclining, so that we see her from the same vantage point as the still life?

Picasso's subject matter and ambiguous space were disturbing to viewers. Even more disturbing were the strange faces of the left-hand figure and the two to the right. X-ray analysis confirms that originally all five of the figures shared the same facial features as the two in the middle left, with their almond eyes and noses drawn in an almost childlike profile. But sometime in May or June 1907, after he visited the ethnographic museum at the Palais du Trocadéro [pah-LAY due troh-kah-DAY-roh], across the river from the Eiffel Tower, Picasso painted over the faces of the figure at the left and the two on the right, giving them instead what most scholars agree are the characteristics of African masks. But equally important to Picasso's creative process was a retrospective of Gauguin's painting and sculpture at the 1906 Salon d'Automne with their Polynesian imagery. At any rate, Picasso's intentions were clear. He wanted to connect his prostitutes to the demonic—and emotionally energizing—forces that Gauguin had discovered in the "primitive." Many years later, he described the meaning of African and Oceanic masks to *Les Demoiselles*:

> The masks weren't just like any other pieces of sculpture. Not at all. They were *magic* things. . . . They were against everything—against unknown, threatening spirits. I always looked at fetishes. I understood; I too am against everything. I too believe that everything is unknown, that everything is an enemy! . . . All the fetishes were used for the same thing. They were weapons. To help people avoid coming under the influence of spirits again, to help them become independent. They're tools. If we give spirits a form, we become independent. . . . I understood why I was a painter. All alone in that awful museum [the Trocadéro] with masks, with dolls made by the redskins, dusty manikins. *Les Demoiselles d'Avignon* must have come to me that very day, but not because of the forms; because it was my first exorcism painting—yes absolutely!

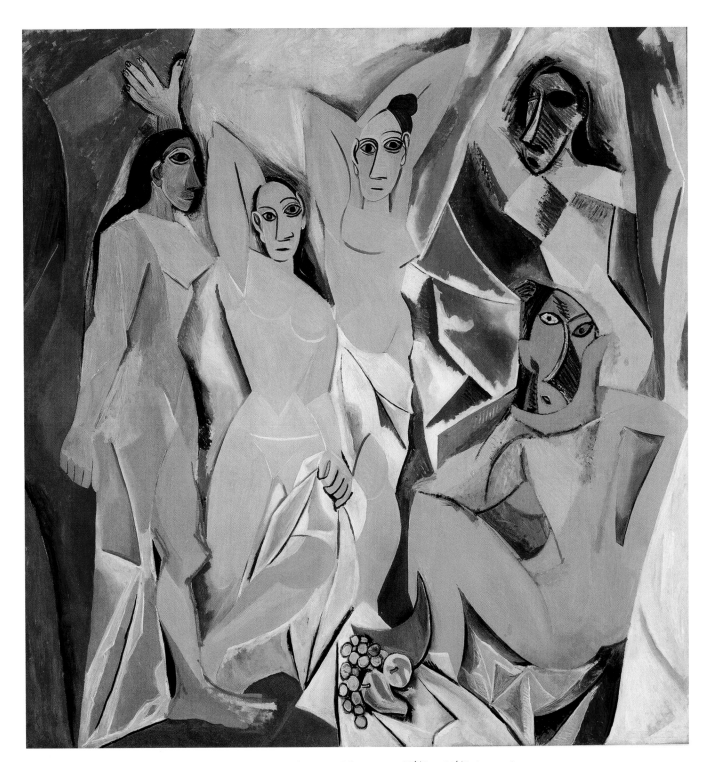

Fig. 14.11   Pablo Picasso. *Les Demoiselles d'Avignon.* May–July 1907. Oil on canvas, $95\frac{1}{8}''\times 91\frac{1}{8}''$. Acquired through the Lillie P. Bliss Bequest. The Museum of Modern Art/Licensed by SCALA/Art Resource, NY. © 2008 ARS Artists Rights Society, NY. Central to Picasso's composition is the almond shape, first used for Gertrude Stein's eyes and repeated in the eyes of the figures here and in other forms—thighs and arms particularly. The shape is simultaneously rounded and angular, reinforcing the sense of tension in the painting.

Les Demoiselles, then, was an act of liberation, an exorcism of past traditions, perhaps even of painting itself. It would allow Picasso to move forward into a kind of painting that was totally new.

The Invention of Cubism: Braque's Partnership with Picasso When the French painter Georges Braque [brahk] (1882–1963) first saw *Les Demoiselles*, in December 1907, he said that he felt burned, "as if someone were drinking gasoline and spitting fire." Like Picasso, he was obsessed with Cézanne, so much so that he planned to paint the following summer in Cézanne country in the south of France. When he returned to Paris in September, he brought with him a series of landscapes, among them *Houses at l'Estaque* (Fig. **14.12**). Picasso was fascinated with their spatial ambiguity and cube-like shapes. Note in particular the central house, where (illogically) the two walls that join at a right angle are shaded on both sides of the corner yet are similarly illuminated. And the angle of the roofline does not meet at the corner, thus flattening the roof. Details of windows, doors,

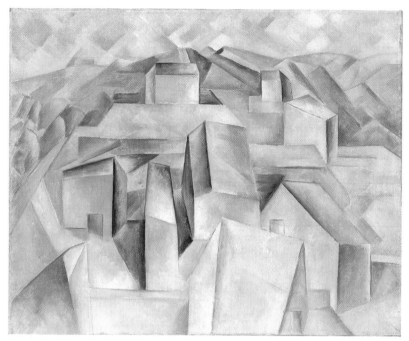

Fig. 14.13 Pablo Picasso. *Houses on the Hill, Horta de Ebro.* 1909. Oil on canvas, 25⅝″ × 31⅞″. Jens Ziehe/Nationalgalerie, Museum Berggruen, Staatliche Museen zu Berlin, Berlin, Germany. Bildarchiv Preussischer Kulturbesitz/Art Resource, NY. © ARS Artists Rights Society, NY. This is one of a series of some 15 paintings executed at Horta de Ebro (known today as Horta de Sant Joan) in the hills above Valencia during the summer of 1909.

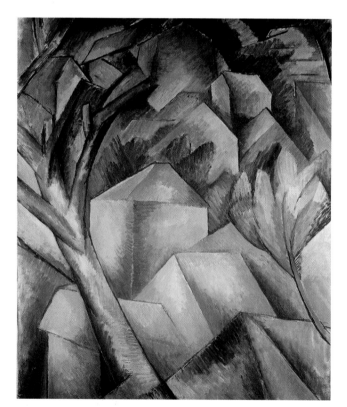

Fig. 14.12 Georges Braque. *Houses at l'Estaque.* 1908. Oil on canvas, 28¾″ × 23¾″. Peter Lauri/Kunstmuseum Bern. Estate of Georges Braque © 2008 Artists Rights Society (ARS), NY/ADAGP, Paris. Hermann and Margit Rupf Foundation. Braque's point of view here underscores the tension between surface and depth, the near and the far.

and moldings have been eliminated, as have the lines between planes so that one plane seems to merge with the next in a manner reminiscent of Cézanne. The tree that rises on the left seems to merge at its topmost branch into the distant houses. The curve of the bush on the left echoes that of the tree, and its palmlike leaves are identical to the trees rising between the houses behind it. The structure of the foreground mirrors that of the houses. All this serves to flatten the composition even as the lack of a horizon causes the whole composition to appear to roll forward toward the viewer rather than recede in space.

Seeing Braque's landscapes at a gallery in November 1908, the critic Louis Vauxcelles [voh-SELL] wrote: "He [Braque] is contemptuous of form, reduces everything, sites and figures and houses to geometric schemas, to cubes." But the movement known as **Cubism** was born out of collaboration. "Almost every evening," Picasso later recalled, "either I went to Braque's studio or Braque came to mine. Each of us had to see what the other had done during the day." The two men were inventors, brothers—Picasso even took to calling Braque "Wilbur," after the aeronautical brothers Orville and Wilbur Wright. When Picasso returned to Paris from Spain in the fall of 1909, he brought with him landscapes that showed just how much he had learned from Braque (Fig. **14.13**).

Picasso and Braque pushed on, working so closely together that their work became indistinguishable to most viewers. They began to decompose their subjects into faceted planes, so that they seem to emerge down the middle of the canvas from some angular maze, as in *Violin and Palette* (Fig. **14.14**).

Fig. 14.14 Georges Braque. *Violin and Palette.* Autumn 1909. Oil on canvas, 36 1/8″ × 16 7/8″. Solomon Guggenheim Museum. 54.1412. George Braque © 2008 Artists Rights Society (ARS), NY/ADAGP, Paris. As in Picasso's *Les Desmoiselles*, the tension in the painting is created by the juxtaposition of rounded and angular forms.

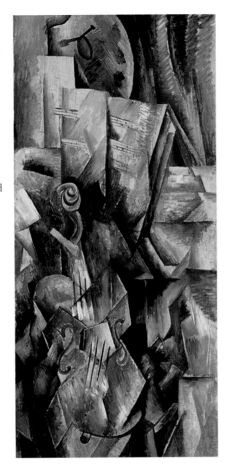

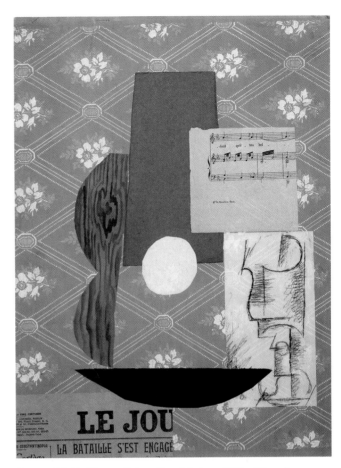

Fig. 14.15 Pablo Picasso. *Guitar, Sheet Music, and Wine Glass.* Autumn 1912. Charcoal, gouache, and *papiers-collé*, 18 7/8″ × 14 3/8″. The McNay Art Museum, San Antonio, Texas. Bequest of Marion Koogler McNay. © 2008. Estate of Pablo Picasso/Artists Rights Society (ARS), NY. The newspaper fragment at the bottom of the painting derives from the front page of *Le Journal*, November 18, 1912.

Gradually they began to understand that they were questioning the very nature of reality, the nature of "truth" itself. This is the function of the *trompe-l'oeil* nail that holds up the palette at the top of the painting. Together with its shadow, the nail announces that the traditional practice of illusionistically representing things in three-dimensional space is no more real than the violin, which is about to dissolve into a cluster of geometric forms. Both are painted illusions, equally real as art.

From 1910 to 1912, Picasso and Braque took an increasingly abstract approach to depicting reality through painting. They were so experimental, in fact, that the subject nearly disappeared. Only a few cues remained to help viewers understand what they were seeing—a moustache, the scroll of a violin, a treble clef.

Increasingly, they added a few words here and there. Picasso used words from a popular song "*Ma Jolie*" ("My pretty one") to identify portraits of his current lover, or "*Jou*," to identify the newspaper *Le Journal*. "*Jou*" was also a pun on the word *jeu* ("play"), and it symbolized the play between the reality of the painting as an object and the reality of the world outside the frame. This kind of ambiguity led Braque and Picasso to introduce actual two- and three-dimensional elements into the space of the canvas, in what Picasso and Braque came to call **collage** [kuh-LAHZH], from the French

coller [koll-AY], "to paste or glue." These elements—paper, fabric, rope, and other material—at least challenged, if they did not completely obliterate, the space between life and art.

Thus in Picasso's 1912 *Guitar, Sheet Music, and Wine Glass* (Fig. **14.15**), at the bottom of the page the headline of *Le Journal* reads, "*La bataille s'est engagé*," "The battle is joined." Literally, it refers to a battle in the Balkans, where Bulgaria attacked the Turks, November 17–19. But the "battle" is also metaphorical, the battle between art and reality (and perhaps between Braque and Picasso as they explored the possibilities of collage). Similarly, the background's trellis-and-rose wallpaper is no more or less real than the fragment of the actual musical score, the *faux bois* [foh-BWA] ("false wood") guitar, and the Cubist drawing of a glass, cut out of some pre-existing source like the other *papiers collé* [pah-pee-ay koll-AY] elements in the work. Collage is the great equalizer in which all the elements are united on the same plane, both the literal plane of the canvas and the figurative plane of reality.

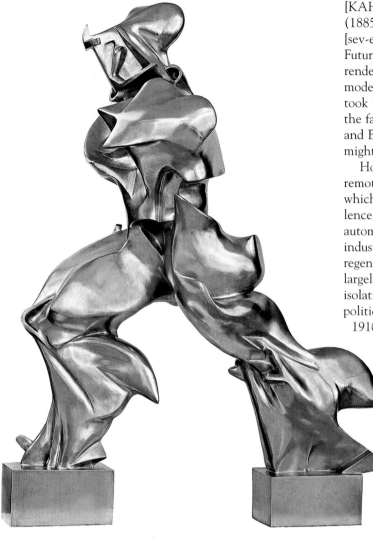

Fig. 14.16 Umberto Boccioni. *Unique Forms of Continuity in Space.* 1913. Bronze, 43 7/8″ × 34 7/8″ × 15 3/4″. Acquired through the Lillie P. Bliss Bequest (231.1948). Digital Image © The Museum of Modern Art/Licensed by SCALA/Art Resource, NY. Between 1912 and 1914, Boccioni made twelve important sculptures. Five have survived, of which this is one.

[KAH-rah] (1881–1966), Luigi Russolo [roo-SOH-loh] (1885–1947), who was also a musician, and Gino Severini [sev-eh-REE-nee] (1883–1966). The new style was called Futurism. The Futurists repudiated static art and sought to render what they thought of as the defining characteristic of modern urban life—speed. But it was not until Marinetti took Boccioni, Carra, and Russolo to Paris for two weeks in the fall of 1911, arranging for visits to the studios of Picasso and Braque, that the fledgling Futurists discovered *how* they might represent it—in the fractured idiom of Cubism.

However, the work they created was philosophically remote from Cubism. It reflected Marinetti's *Manifesto*, which affirmed not only speed, but also technology and violence. In the manifesto, Futurism is born out of a high-speed automobile crash in the "maternal ditch" of modernity's industrial sludge, an intentionally ironic image of rebirth and regeneration. Where the Cubist rejection of tradition had largely been the invention of two men working in relative isolation, the Futurist rejection was public, bombastic, and political. As the Futurists traveled around Europe between 1910 and 1913 promoting their philosophy in public forums and entertainments, their typical evening featured insult slinging and scuffles with the audience, usually an arrest or two, and considerable attention in the press. In fact, it could be said that Marinetti was among the first artists to understand the power of publicity in stimulating public interest, in creating what we have come to call "buzz."

The great masterpiece of Futurist art is Boccioni's *Unique Forms of Continuity in Space* (Fig. **14.16**), a work oddly evocative of the very *Nike of Samothrace* (see Fig. 2.42) that Marinetti in his manifesto found less compelling than a speeding car. Boccioni probably intended to represent a nude, her musculature stretched and drawn out as she moves through space. "What we want to do," he explained, "is show the living object in its dynamic growth."

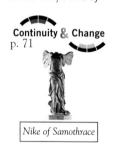

Continuity & Change
p. 71

Nike of Samothrace

Futurism: The Cult of Speed

News of the experimental fervor of Picasso and Braque spread quickly through avant-garde circles across Europe, and other artists sought to match their endeavors in independent but related ways. On February 20, 1909, for instance, the front page of the Paris newspaper *Le Figaro* [fee-gah-ROH] published the *Founding and Manifesto of Futurism*, written by the Italian Filippo Marinetti [mah-ree-NET-tee] (1876–1944). It rejected the political and artistic traditions of the past and called for a new art. Marinetti quickly attracted a group of painters and sculptors to invent it. These included the Italian artists Giacomo Balla [BAHL-lah] (1871–1958), Umberto Boccioni [boch-ee-OH-nee] (1882–1916), Carlo Carrà

The French Fauves and the Expressionist Movement in Germany

By 1910 almost every European artist had turned to Paris for inspiration. German artists were no exception. We call the modernist style they created Expressionism, though no group of artists actually called itself Expressionist. Their immediate source of inspiration was the Parisian painter Henri Matisse [mah-TEESS] (1869–1954).

When Matisse saw Picasso's *Demoiselles d'Avignon*, he is said to have considered it an "audacious hoax," an "outrage [ridiculing] the modern movement." It is little wonder, as the two painters' aesthetic visions were diametrically opposed. Gertrude Stein had introduced the two men in April 1906. Twelve years older than Picasso, Matisse was the favorite of Gertrude Stein's brother Leo. He had established himself, at the Salon des Indépendants in 1904, as the leader of a radical new group of experimental painters known as the Fauves [fohvz]—or "Wild Beasts." **Fauvism** [FOHV-izm] was known for its radical application of arbitrary, or unnatural, color, anticipated in a few of van Gogh's paintings and in the pool of color in the foreground of Gauguin's *Mahana no atua* (see Fig. 14.9).

Picasso and Matisse saw each other regularly at the Steins' apartment, but their relationship was competitive. In fact, it is useful to think of Matisse's monumental *Dance II* (Fig. **14.17**) as something of a rebuttal to the upstart Picasso's *Demoiselles*. For one thing, Matisse's circle dance consists of five figures, like Picasso's five prostitutes. Matisse also replaces Picasso's squared and angular composition with a circular and rounded one. Where Picasso's painting seems static, as if we are asked to hold our breath at the scene before us, Matisse's is active, moving as if to an unheard music. Most astonishing is Matisse's color—vermillion (red-orange), green, and blue-violet, the primary colors of light. In effect, Matisse's modernism takes place in the light of day, Picasso's in the dark of night; Matisse's with joy, Picasso's with fear and trepidation.

Like the Fauves, the German Expressionists' interest in color can be traced to the art of van Gogh and Gauguin. But unlike the Fauves, their subject matter was often drawn from their own psychological makeup. They laid bare in paint the torment of their lives. There were Expressionist groups throughout Europe that encompassed the visual arts and other media, but the most important in Germany was *Der Blaue Reiter* [dair BLAU-uh RY-tuh] ("The Blue Rider"), based in Munich.

Der Blaue Reiter did not come into being until 1911. It was headed by the Russian emigré Wassily Kandinsky [kan-DIN-skee] (1866–1944) and by Franz Marc (1880–1916), an artist especially fond of painting animals, because he believed they possessed elemental energies. They were joined by a number of other artists, and although they shared no common style, all were obsessed with color. "Color," Kandinsky wrote in *Concerning the Spiritual in Art*, first published in 1912 in the *Blaue Reiter Almanac*, "directly influences the soul. Color is the keyboard, the eyes are the hammers, the soul is the piano with many strings. The artist is the hand

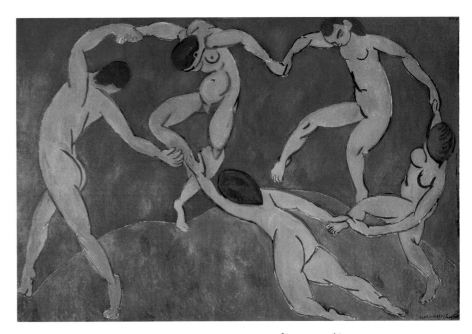

Fig. 14.17 Henri Matisse. *Dance II.* **1910.** Oil on canvas, 8′ 5⅝″ × 12′ 9½″. The State Hermitage Museum, St. Petersburg, Russia. © 2010 Succession H. Matisse, Paris/Artists Rights Society (ARS), NY. This work and another similarly colored painting of musicians called *Music* were commissioned by the Russian collector Sergei Shchukin to decorate the staircase of his home in Moscow.

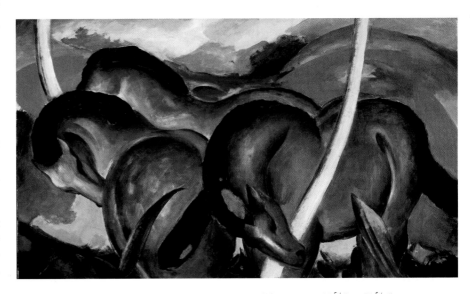

Fig. 14.18 Franz Marc. *The Large Blue Horses.* **1911.** Oil on canvas, 41⅝″ × 71⁵⁄₁₆″. Collection Walker Art Center, Minneapolis. Gift of T. B. Walker Foundation, Gilbert M. Walker Fund, 1942. The painting is meant to contrast the beauty of the untainted natural world to the sordidness of modern existence, very much in the spirit of Gauguin.

that plays . . . to cause vibrations of the soul." The color blue, Kandinsky wrote, is "the typical heavenly color." Marc saw in blue what he thought of as the masculine principle of spirituality. So his *The Large Blue Horses*, with its seemingly arbitrary color and interlocking rhythm of fluid curves and contours, much influenced by Matisse, is the very image of the spiritual harmony in the natural world (Fig. **14.18**).

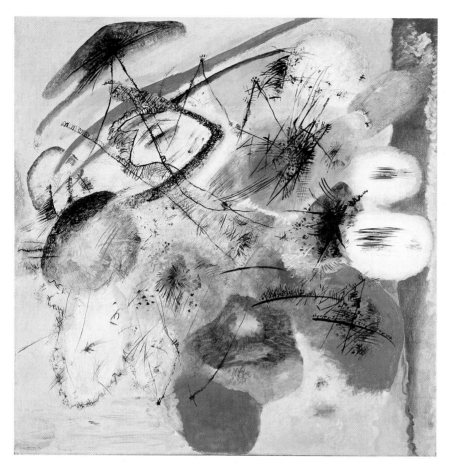

Fig. 14.19 Wassily Kandinsky. *Black Lines*. December 1913. Oil on canvas, 51″ × 51 ⅝″. Solomon R. Guggenheim Museum, NY. © DACS. Giraudon/The Bridgeman Art Library. © 2008 ARS Artists Rights Society, NY. Among practitioners of nonfigurative abstract art, Kandinsky was perhaps unique in not forcing his point of view on his colleagues. If his was what he called "the Greater Abstraction," theirs was "the Greater Realism," equally leading to "the spiritual in art."

Modernist Music and Dance

The dynamism and invention evident in modern painting also appeared in music and dance. On May 29, 1913, the Ballets Russes, a company under the direction of impresario Sergei Diaghilev [dee-AH-ghee-lev] (1872–1929), premiered the ballet *Le Sacre de printemps* (*The Rite of Spring*) at the Théâtre des Champs-Élysées in Paris. The music was by the cosmopolitan Russian composer Igor Stravinsky [strah-VIN-skee] (1882–1971) and the choreography by his countryman Vaslav Nijinsky [nih-JIN-skee] (1890–1950). The performance was a scandal. Together with the Futurists' confrontational performances and, earlier, the public outrage at Manet's *Luncheon on the Grass* and *Olympia* in the earlier 1860s, it helped to define modern art as antagonistic to public opinion and an affront to its values.

The events of that evening surprised everyone. The night before, a dress rehearsal performed before an audience, in Stravinsky's words, "of actors, painters, musicians, writers, and the most cultured representatives of society," had proved uneventful. But on the night of the public premiere the first chords of Stravinsky's score evoked derisive laughter. Hissing, booing, and catcalls followed, and at such a level that the dancers could not hear the music. Diaghilev ordered the lights to be turned on and off, hoping to quiet the crowd, but that just incensed the audience further. Finally the police had to be called, as Stravinsky himself crawled to safety out a backstage window.

What seemed most radically new to Stravinsky's audience was the music's angular, jarring, sometimes violent rhythmic inventiveness. The ballet's story—subtitled *Pictures from Pagan Russia*—centers on a pre-Christian ritual welcoming the beginning of spring that culminates in a human sacrifice. The music reflects the brutalism of the pagan rite with savage dissonance. Part I of the work, The Adoration of the Earth, culminates in a spirited dance of youths and maidens in praise of the earth's fertility. In Part II, The Sacrifice, one of the maidens is chosen to be sacrificed in order to guarantee the fertility celebrated in Part I. All dance in honor of the Chosen One, invoking the blessings of the village's ancestors, culminating in the frenzied Sacrificial Dance of the Chosen One herself (see **CD-Track 14.1**). Just before the dancer collapses and dies, Stravinsky shifts the meter eight times in twelve measures. The men then carry the Chosen One's body to the foot of a sacred mound and offer her up to the gods.

Sometimes different elements of the orchestra play different meters simultaneously. Such **polyrhythms** contrast dra-

Yellow, on the other hand, was the female principle, the earthly as opposed to the heavenly. Kandinsky's *Black Lines* contrasts earthly yellow with heavenly blue, and red with green (Fig. **14.19**). (Red, he wrote, "rings inwardly with a determined and powerful intensity," while green "represents the social middle class, self-satisfied, immovable, narrow.") The black lines, Kandinsky felt, were equivalent to dance, so the painting can be interpreted as a rendering of dance set to music. But it also suggests a landscape with three mountains rising in the distance. In fact, one of Kandinsky's chief themes was the biblical Apocalypse, the moment when, according to a long tradition in the Byzantine church, Moscow would become the New Jerusalem. "Der Reiter," in fact, was the popular name for Saint George, patron saint of Moscow, and the explosions of contrasting colors across *Black Lines* suggest that the fateful moment has arrived. With paintings like *Black Lines*, Kandinsky made the jump from simply using color for its emotional message to abstraction.

matically with other passages where the same rhythmic pulse repeats itself persistently—such as when at the end of the ballet's first part the orchestra plays the same eighth-note chords 32 times in succession. (This technique is known as **ostinato**—Italian for "obstinate.") In addition to its rhythmic variety, Stravinsky's ballet was also **polytonal**: Two or more keys are sounded by different instruments at the same time, and the traditional instruments of the orchestra are used in startlingly unconventional ways, so that they sound raw and strange. Low-pitched instruments, such as bassoons, play at the top of their range, for instance, and clarinets at the gravelly bottom of their capabilities. Integrated across these jarring juxtapositions are passages of recognizable Russian folk songs. Stravinsky's music was enormously influential on subsequent composers, who now thought about rhythmic structure in a totally different way.

If his first Paris audience found Stravinsky's music offensive, Nijinsky's choreography seemed a downright provocation to riot: "They repeat the same gesture a hundred times over," wrote one critic, "they paw the ground, they stamp, they stamp, they stamp, they stamp and they stamp. . . . Evidently all of this is defensible; it is prehistoric dance." It certainly wasn't recognizable as ballet. It moved away from the traditional graceful movements of ballerinas dancing *en pointe* (on their toes in boxed shoes) toward a new athleticism. Nijinsky's choreography called for the dancers to assume angular, contorted positions that at once imitated ancient bas-relief sculpture and Cubist painting, to hold these positions in frozen stillness, and then burst into wild leaps and whirling circle dances.

Meanwhile, in Germany, audiences were equally challenged by the work of Arnold Schoenberg [SHERN-berkh] (1874–1951). Schoenberg was from Vienna, where he led a group of composers, including Alban Berg and Anton Webern, who believed that the long reign of tonality, the harmonic basis of Western music, was over. On January 2, 1911, the *Blaue Reiter* painters Kandinsky and Marc attended a Schoenberg concert in Munich. Marc later wrote to a friend, "Can you imagine a music in which tonality is completely suspended? I was constantly reminded of Kandinsky. . . . Schoenberg seems, like [ourselves], to be convinced of the irresistible dissolution of the European laws of art and harmony."

Schoenberg did in fact abandon **tonality**, the organization of the composition around a home key (the tonal center). In its place he created a music of complete **atonality**, a term he hated (since it implied the absence of musical tone altogether), preferring instead "pantonal." His 1912 setting for a cycle of 21 poems by Albert Giraud, *Pierrot lunaire* [pee-yair-OH lune-AIR], is probably the first atonal composition to be widely appreciated, though to many it represented, as one critic put it, "the last word in cacophony and musical anarchy" (see **CD Track-14.2**). Pierrot is a character from the Italian *commedia dell'arte* [kom-MAY-dee-ah dell-AR-tay], the improvisational traveling street theater that developed in the fifteenth century. He is a moonstruck clown whose mask conceals his deep melancholy, brought on by living in a state of perpetually unrequited desire. (Picasso often portrayed himself as Pierrot, especially early in his career.) In *Pierrot lunaire*, five performers play eight instruments in various combinations in accompaniment to a voice that does not sing but instead employs a technique that Schoenberg calls **Sprechstimme** [SHPRAYK-shtim-muh] or "speech-song." "A singing voice," Schoenberg explained, "maintains the pitch without modification; speech-song does, certainly, announce it [the pitch], only to quit it again immediately, in either a downward or an upward direction." In the *Madonna* section of *Pierrot lunaire*, which addresses Mary at the moment of the *pietá*, when she mourns over the dead body of her son, the lyrics focus on the blood of Christ's wounds, which "seem like eyes, red and open." The atonality of Schoenberg's music reflects this anguish with explosive force.

Creating long works without the resources of tonality was a very real challenge to Schoenberg—hence the usefulness of 21 short works in the *Pierrot lunaire* series. By 1924, Schoenberg had created a system in which none of the 12 tones of the chromatic scale could be repeated in a composition until each of the other 11 had been played. This **twelve-tone system** reflected his belief that every tone was equal to every other. The twelve notes in their given order are called a **tone row**, and audiences soon grew accustomed to not hearing a tonal center in the progression and variation of the tone row as it developed in Schoenberg's increasingly **serial composition**. The principal tone row can be played upside down, backward, or upside down and backward. While the possibilities for writing an extended composition with a single tone row and its variations might at first seem limited, by adding rhythmic and dynamic variations, as well as contrapuntal arrangements, the development of large-scale works became feasible.

The Great War and Its Impact

On July 28, 1914, a young Bosnian nationalist assassinated Archduke Francis Ferdinand, heir to the Austrian throne, in the Bosnian capital of Sarajevo. Europe was outraged, except for Serbia, which had been at war with Bosnia for years. Austria suspected that Serbian officials were involved (as in fact they were). With Germany's support, Austria declared war on Serbia, Russia mobilized in Serbia's defense, and France mobilized to support its ally, Russia. Germany invaded Luxembourg and Belgium, and then pushed into France. Finally, on August 4, Britain declared war on Germany, and Europe was consumed in battle.

Though the Germans advanced perilously close to Paris in the first month of the war, the combined forces of the British and French stopped them. From then on, along the Western Front on the French/Belgian border, both sides dug in behind zigzagging rows of trenches protected by barbed wire that stretched from the English Channel to Switzerland, some 25,000 miles of them. In the three years after its establishment, the Western Front moved only a few miles either east or west.

Stagnation accompanied the carnage. Assaults in which thousands of lives were lost would advance the lines only a couple of hundred yards. Poison mustard gas was introduced in the hope that it might resolve the stalemate, but it changed nothing, except to permanently maim and kill thousands upon thousands of soldiers. Mustard gas blinded those who encountered it, but it also slowly rotted the body from within and without, causing severe blistering and damaging the bronchial tubes, so that its victims slowly choked to death. Most affected by the gas died within four to five weeks. British troops rotated trench duty. After a week behind the lines, a unit would move up, at night, to the front-line trench, then after a week there, back to a support trench, then after another week back to the reserve trench, and then, finally, back to a week of rest again. Attacks generally came at dawn, so it was at night, under the cover of darkness, that most of the work in the trenches was done—wiring, digging, moving ammunition. It rained often, so the trenches were often filled with water. The troops were plagued by lice, and huge rats, which fed on cadavers and dead horses, roamed through the encampments. The stench was almost as unbearable as the weather, and lingering pockets of gas might blow through at any time. As Germany tried to push both east and west, the human cost was staggering. By the war's end, casualties totaled around 10 million dead—it became impossible to count accurately—and somewhere around twice that many wounded.

Trench Warfare and the Literary Imagination

The American novelist Ernest Hemingway (1899–1961) served as a Red Cross ambulance driver on the Italian Front, and on his first day on duty was required to pick up the remains, mostly those of female workers, who were blown to pieces when the ammunition factory at which they worked was blown up. He was himself later wounded by mortar fragments and machine-gun fire while delivering supplies to the troops. "Abstract words, such as glory, honor, courage, or hallow," Hemingway wrote in the novel based on his experiences, *A Farewell to Arms*, "were obscene beside the concrete names of villages, the numbers of roads, the names of rivers, the numbers of regiments and dates." For Hemingway the use of a stripped-down, concrete language became a means of survival.

German soldiers like novelist Erich Maria Remarque, whose best-selling novel of 1928, *All Quiet on the Western Front*, described the horrors of trench warfare in intimate detail, shared similar feelings. The titles alone of the poems that came out of the war speak volumes: "Suicide in Trenches" by Siegfried Sassoon; "Dead Man's Dump" by Isaac Rosenberg, who was killed on the Western Front in 1918; or "Disabled," a poem about a former athlete, with both legs and one arm gone, by Wilfred Owen.

In fact, the poetry of 25-year-old Wilfred Owen (1893–1918), killed in combat just a week before the armistice was signed in 1918, caused a sensation when it first appeared in 1920. "My subject is War, and the pity of War," he wrote in a manuscript intended to preface his poems, "and the Poetry is in the pity." The poems drew immediate attention for Owen's horrifying descriptions of the war's victims, as in "Dulce et Decorum Est," its title drawn from Ode 13 of the Roman poet Horace (see chapter 3), "It is sweet and fitting to die for one's country." But Owen's reference to Horace is bitterly ironic (**Reading 14.2**):

READING 14.2 **Wilfred Owen, "Dulce et Decorum Est" (1918)**

Bent double, like old beggars under sacks,
Knock-kneed, coughing like hags, we cursed through sludge,
Till on the haunting flares we turned our backs
And towards our distant rest began to trudge.
Men marched asleep. Many had lost their boots
But limped on, blood-shod. All went lame; all blind;
Drunk with fatigue; deaf even to the hoots
Of disappointed shells that dropped behind.

GAS! Gas! Quick, boys!—An ecstasy of fumbling,
Fitting the clumsy helmets just in time;
But someone still was yelling out and stumbling
And floundering like a man in fire or lime.—
Dim, through the misty panes and thick green light
As under a green sea, I saw him drowning.

In all my dreams, before my helpless sight,
He plunges at me, guttering, choking, drowning.

If in some smothering dreams you too could pace
Behind the wagon that we flung him in,
And watch the white eyes writhing in his face,
His hanging face, like a devil's sick of sin;
If you could hear, at every jolt, the blood
Come gargling from the froth-corrupted lungs,
Obscene as cancer, bitter as the cud
Of vile, incurable sores on innocent tongues,—
My friend, you would not tell with such high zest
To children ardent for some desperate glory,
The old Lie: Dulce et decorum est
Pro patria mori.

The quotation from Horace in the last lines is, notably, labeled by Owen a "lie." And the fact is, Owen's intent is that the reader should share his horrific dreams. His rhetorical strategy is to describe the drowning of this nameless man in a sea of green gas in such vivid terms that we cannot forget it either.

Before the war, the Irish poet William Butler Yeats (1865–1939) was capable of at least imagining, if not actually experiencing, a reality in which he finds himself attuned to the music and rhythms of nature. But writing in 1919, he can only imagine a much darker world. Apocalypse—if not the literal Second Coming of Christ predicted in the Bible's Book of Revelations, then its metaphorical equivalent—seemed at hand (**Reading 14.3**):

READING 14.3 **William Butler Yeats, "The Second Coming" (1919)**

Turning and turning in the widening gyre
The falcon cannot hear the falconer;
Things fall apart; the centre cannot hold;
Mere anarchy is loosed upon the world,
The blood-dimmed tide is loosed, and everywhere
The ceremony of innocence is drowned;
The best lack all conviction, while the worst
Are full of passionate intensity.

Surely some revelation is at hand;
Surely the Second Coming is at hand.
The Second Coming! Hardly are those words out
When a vast image out of Spiritus Mundi
Troubles my sight; somewhere in sands of the desert
A shape with lion body and the head of a man,
A gaze blank and pitiless as the sun,
Is moving its slow thighs, while all about it
Reel shadows of the indignant desert birds.
The darkness drops again; but now I know
That twenty centuries of stony sleep
Were vexed to nightmare by a rocking cradle,
And what rough beast, its hour come round at last,
Slouches towards Bethlehem to be born?

The poem's opening image, of the falcon circling higher and higher in wider and wider circles, is a metaphor for history itself spinning further and further from its origin until it is out of control. In another poem written at about the same time, "A Prayer for my Daughter," Yeats had asked, "How but in custom and ceremony / Are innocence and beauty born?" Now, he despairs, custom and ceremony, those things that connect us to our origins, have been abandoned and "mere anarchy is loosed upon the world." In their place, a beast resembling the Sphinx at Giza in Egypt rises in the desert, possibly an image of the anti-Christ, the embodiment of Satan who in some biblical traditions anticipates the second coming of Christ himself. This beast is the new Spiritus Mundi [SPIR-ih-toos MOON-dee], or collective spirit of mankind, the specter of life in the new postwar era, insentient, pitiless, and nightmarish.

The other great poem reflecting the pessimism of the postwar era is *The Waste Land*, by the American poet T. S. (Thomas Sternes) Eliot (1888–1965). Eliot had graduated from Harvard with a degree in philosophy and the classics, and his poetry reflects both the erudition of a scholar and the

depression of a classicist who feels that the tradition he so values is in jeopardy of being lost. *The Waste Land's* opening section, called "The Burial of the Dead," is a direct reference to the Anglican burial service, performed so often during and after the war. "April is the cruelest month," the poem famously begins (**Reading 14.4**).

READING 14.4 **from T. S. Eliot, *The Waste Land* (1921)**

April is the cruelest month, breeding
Lilacs out of the dead land, mixing
Memory and desire, stirring
Dull roots with spring rain.
Winter kept us warm, covering
Earth in forgetful snow, feeding
A little life with dried tubers.

The world, in short, has been turned upside down. Spring is cruel, winter consoling. Eliot sees London as an "Unreal City" populated by the living-dead:

Unreal City,

Under the brown fog of a winter dawn,
A crowd flowed over London Bridge, so many,
I had not thought death had undone so many.

The last line here is a quotation from the third canto of Dante's *Inferno* (see chapter 6), an image of the world as hell, populated by the living dead.

Escape from Despair: Dada

Some writers and artists—Picasso, for instance—simply waited out the war. Many others openly opposed it and vigorously protested the social order that had brought about what seemed to them nothing short of mass genocide, and some of these soon formed the movement that named itself **Dada**. The Romanian poet Tristan Tzara [TSAH-rah] (1896–1963) claimed it was his invention. The German Richard Huelsenbeck [HULL-sen-bek] (1892–1972) claimed that he and poet Hugo Ball (1886–1927) had discovered the name randomly by plunging a knife into a dictionary. Whatever the case, Tzara summed up its meaning best:

DADA DOES NOT MEAN ANYTHING . . . We read in the papers that the Negroes of the Kroo race call the tail of a sacred cow: dada. A cube, and a mother, in certain regions of Italy, are called: dada. The word for hobbyhorse, a children's nurse, a double affirmative in Russian and Romanian, is also: DADA.

Dada was an international signifier of negation. It did not mean anything, just as, in the face of war, life itself had come to seem meaningless. But it would prove a potent force in modern art.

Dada came into being at the Cabaret Voltaire in Zurich, founded in February 1916 by a group of intellectuals and artists escaping the conflict in neutral Switzerland, including Tzara, Huelsenbeck, Ball, Jean Arp (1896–1966), and the poet, dancer, and singer Emmy Hennings (1885–1948). At the end of May, Ball created a "concert bruitiste" [brwee-TEEST] or "noise concert," inspired by the Futurists, for a "Grand Evening of the Voltaire Art Association." In March 1917, the group opened the Galerie Dada. Arp's collages (Fig. **14.20**) were among the most daring works on display. They were constructed "according to the laws of chance." Arp had been so frustrated with his painting, which seemed to him totally burdened by conventional technique, that he had torn it apart. When he looked at the random arrangement of fallen pieces, freed of the intervention of his aesthetic sensi-

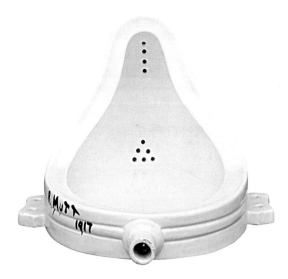

Fig. 14.21 Marcel Duchamp. *Fountain*. 1917; replica 1963. Porcelain, height 14″. Purchased with assistance from the Friends of the Tate Gallery 1999. Tate Gallery, London, Great Britain. © 2008 ARS Artists Rights Society, NY. It is important to recognize that Duchamp has turned the urinal on its side, thus undermining its utility.

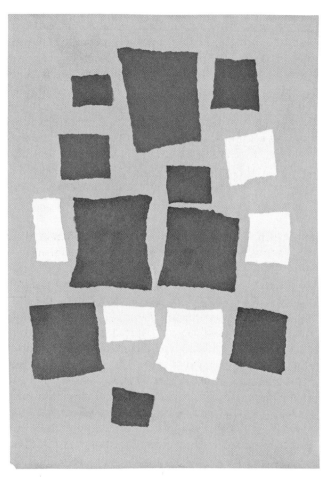

Fig. 14.20 Hans Arp. *Collage Made According to the Laws of Chance*. 1916. Painted paper, 15 ⅞″ × 12 ⅝″. Purchase. (457.1937). Digital Image © The Museum of Modern Art/Licensed by SCALA/Art Resource, NY. © 2008 ARS Artists Rights Society, NY. Arp was from the sometimes German, sometimes French region of Alsace, and spoke both French and German, referring to himself sometimes as Jean (French), sometimes as Hans (German).

bility, they seemed to him more truthful than anything he had created before—and the work was funny, so outrageous that one could only laugh.

Such works, in their willful denial of the artist's aesthetic sensibilities, were considered by many used to thinking of art in more serious, high-minded terms as "anti-art." These more serious minds were especially offended by the so-called "ready-mades" of Marcel Duchamp. The term itself derived from the recent American invention, ready-made as opposed to tailor-made clothes, and Duchamp adopted it soon after arriving in New York in 1915 where he joined a group of other European exiles, including his close colleague Francis Picabia [peh-KAH-bee-ah] (1879–1953), in still-neutral America. The most audacious of his ready-mades was *Fountain* (Fig. **14.21**), an upside down urinal purchased by Duchamp in a New York plumbing shop, signed with the pseudonym "R. Mutt," and submitted to the Society of Independent Artists exhibition in April 1917. The exhibition committee, on which Duchamp served, had agreed that all work submitted would be shown, and was therefore unable to reject the piece. To Duchamp's considerable amusement, they decided instead to hide it behind a curtain. Over the course of the exhibition, Duchamp gradually let it be known that he was "R. Mutt," and in a publication called *The Blind Man* defended the piece:

> Whether Mr Mutt with his own hands made the fountain or not has no importance. He CHOSE it. He took an ordinary article of life, placed it so that its useful significance disappeared under the new title and point of view—created a new thought for the object.

The American photographer Alfred Stieglitz [STY-glitz] (1864–1946), the first person to exhibit both Matisse and Picasso in the United States, immediately recognized in

Duchamp's position the same sensibility that informed photography—in works such as Paul Strand's *Abstraction, Porch Shadows* (Fig. **14.22**), the photographer looks at ordinary articles of life and frames them in such a way that he creates a new thought for the object—and Stieglitz's Gallery 291 soon became the center of Dada in America.

Russia: Art and Revolution

In 1914, Russia entered the war ill-prepared for the task before it; within the year, Tsar Nicholas II (1868–1918) oversaw the devastation of his army. One million men had been killed, and another million soldiers had deserted. Famine and fuel shortages gripped the nation. Strikes broke out in the cities, and in the countryside, peasants seized the land of the Russian aristocrats. The tsar was forced to abdicate in February 1917.

Vladimir Lenin and the Soviet State Through a series of astute, and sometimes violent, political maneuvers, the Marxist revolutionary Vladimir Ilyich Lenin (1870–1924) assumed power the following November. Lenin headed the most radical of Russian post-revolutionary groups, the Bol-

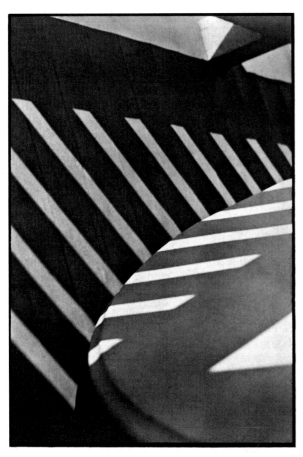

Fig. 14.22 Paul Strand. *Abstraction, Porch Shadows*. 1916. Silver-platinum print, 12$^{15}/_{16}$″ × 9$^5/_8$″. Inv. Pho1981-35-10. Repro-Photo: Rene-Gabriel Ojeda. Musée d'Orsay, Paris, France. Réunion des Musées Nationaux/Art Resource, NY. When Stieglitz published this photograph in the last issue of *Camera Work*, June 1917, he called it "the direct expression of today."

sheviks. Like Marx, he dreamed of a "dictatorship of the proletariat," a dictatorship of the working class. Marx and Lenin believed that the oppression of the masses of working people resulted from capitalism's efforts to monopolize the raw materials and markets of the world for the benefit of the privileged few. He believed that all property should be held in common, that every member of society would work for the benefit of the whole and would receive, from the state, goods and products commensurate with their work. "He who does not work," he famously declared, "does not eat."

Lenin was a utopian idealist. He foresaw, as his socialist state developed, the gradual disappearance of the state: "The state," he wrote in *The State and Revolution* (1917), "will be able to wither away completely when society has realized the rule: 'From each according to his ability: to each according to his needs,' *i.e.*, when people have become accustomed to observe the fundamental rules of social life, and their labor is so productive that they voluntarily work *according to their ability*." But he realized, as well, that certain pragmatic changes had to occur as well. He emphasized the need to electrify the nation: "We must show the peasants," he wrote, "that the organization of industry on the basis of modern, advanced technology, on electrification . . . will make it possible to raise the level of culture in the countryside and to overcome, even in the most remote corners of land, backwardness, ignorance, poverty, disease, and barbarism." And he was, furthermore, a ruthless pragmatist. When, in 1918, his Bolshevik party received less than a quarter of 1 percent of the vote in free elections, he dissolved the government, eliminated all other parties, and put the Communist party into the hands of five men, a committee called the Politburo, with himself at its head. He also systematically eliminated his opposition: Between 1918 and 1922 his secret police arrested and executed as many as 280,000 people in what has come to be known as the Red Terror.

The Arts of the Revolution Before the Revolution in March 1917, avant-garde Russian artists, in direct communication with the art capitals of Europe, particularly Paris, Amsterdam, and Berlin, established their own brand of modern art. Most visited Paris, and saw Picasso and Braque's Cubism in person, but Kasimir Malevich [muh-LAY-vich] (1878–1935), perhaps the most inventive of them all, never did. By 1912, he had created "Cubo-Futurism," a style that applied modernist geometric forms to Russian folk themes. But Malevich was soon engaged, he wrote, in a "desperate attempt to free art from the ballast of objectivity." To this end, he says, "I took refuge in the square," creating a completely nonobjective painting, in 1913, consisting of nothing more than a black square on a white ground. He called his new art Suprematism [soo-PREM-uh-tizm], defining it as "the supremacy of . . . feeling in . . . art."

The "feeling" of which Malevich speaks is not the kind of personal or private emotion that we associate with, say, German Expressionism. Rather, it lies in what he believed was the revelation of an absolute truth—a utopian ideal not far removed from Lenin's political idealism—discovered through the most minimal means. Thus, his *Suprematist Painting, Black*

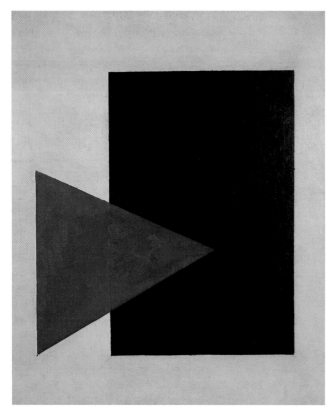

Fig. 14.23 Kasimir Malevich. *Suprematist Painting, Black Rectangle, Blue Triangle.* **1915.** Oil on canvas, $26\frac{1}{8}$" × $22\frac{1}{2}$". Stedelijk Museum, Amsterdam. Erich Lessing/Art Resource, NY. In his 1916 *From Cubism and Futurism to Suprematism*, Malevich wrote, "Painters should abandon subject and objects if they wish to be pure painters."

Rectangle, Blue Triangle (Fig. **14.23**) is about the relation between the two forms (both of which, incidentally, can be read as "shorthand" for the earlier Cubo-Futurist paintings). Note that although the blue triangle is a uniform blue, it appears lighter where it is backed by the black rectangle, and darker where it is backed by the white ground. This phenomenon results from the fact that our perception of a color depends upon the context in which we see it. If the viewer stares for a moment at the line where the triangle crosses from white to black, a subtle visual vibration occurs, and the two parts of the triangle appear to be at different depths. Malevich reveals that in relation these apparently static forms are energized in a dynamic tension.

At the end of the Russian Revolution in 1917, Malevich and other artists in his circle were appointed by the Soviet government to important administrative and teaching positions in the country. Malevich went to the Vitebsk [vih-TEPSK] Popular Art School in 1919, soon becoming its director. In 1921, he wrote to one of his pupils that Suprematism should adopt a more "Constructive" approach to reorganizing the world. By this he meant that art should turn to small-scale abstract works in three dimensions. He considered this "laboratory" work, explorations of the elements of form and color, space and construction, that would eventually serve some practical social purpose in the service of the revolution.

Lazar Lissitzky [lih-SIT-skee] (1890–1941), known as El Lissitzky, was a teacher of architecture and graphics at Vitebsk Popular Art School when Malevich arrived in 1919. El Lissitzky quickly adopted Malevich's Suprematist designs to revolutionary ends. His poster *Beat the Whites with the Red Wedge* (Fig. **14.24**) refers to the conflict between the Bolshevik "Reds" and the "White" Russians who opposed Lenin's party. As in Malevich's *Suprematist Painting*, a triangle crosses over into another form, this time a circle. The wedge is symbolically male, forceful and aggressive as opposed to the passive (and womblike) white circle, which it penetrates both literally and figuratively from the "left." Here design is in the service of social change.

But one of the greatest of Russia's revolutionary innovators was the filmmaker Sergei Eisenstein [EYE-zen-shtine] (1898–1948). After the Revolution, he had worked on the Russian agit-trains, special propaganda trains that traveled the Russian countryside bringing "agitational" materials to the peasants. ("Agitational," in this sense, means to present a political point of view.) The agit-trains distributed magazines and pamphlets, presented political speakers and plays, and, given the fact that the Russian peasantry was largely illiterate, perhaps most important of all presented films, known as *agitkas*. These films were characterized by their fast-paced editing style, designed to keep the attention of an audience that, at least at first, had never before seen a motion picture.

Out of his experience making *agitkas*, Lev Kuleshov (1899–1970), one of the founders of the Film School in Moscow in the early twenties, developed a theory of **montage**. He used a close-up of a famous Russian actor and combined it with three different images—a bowl of soup, a dead woman lying in a coffin, and a girl playing with a teddy bear. Although the image of the actor was the same in each instance, audiences believed that he was hungry with the soup, sorrowful with the woman, joyful toward the girl—a phenomenon that came to be known as the *Kuleshov effect*. Shots, Kuleshov reasoned, acquire meaning through their relation to other shots. Montage was the art of building a cinematic composition out of such shots.

Eisenstein learned much from Kuleshov, though he disagreed about the nature of montage. Rather than using montage to build a unified composition, Eisenstein believed that montage should be used to create tension, even a sense of shock, in the audience, which he believed would lead to a heightened sense of perception and a greater understanding of the film's action. His aim, in a planned series of seven films depicting events leading up to the Bolshevik revolution, was to provoke his audience into psychological identification with the aims of the revolution.

None of his films accomplishes this better than *The Battleship Potemkin* [puh-TEM-kin], the story of a 1905 mutiny aboard a Russian naval vessel and the subsequent massacre of innocent men, women, and children on the steps above Odessa harbor by tsarist troops. The film, especially the famous "Odessa Steps Sequence," which is a virtual manifesto of montage, tore at the hearts of audiences and won respect for the Soviet regime around the world (see *Focus*, pages 444–445).

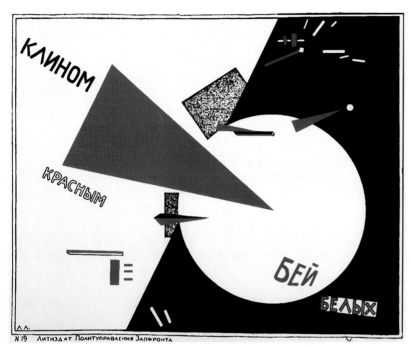

Fig. 14.24 El Lissitzky. *Beat the Whites with the Red Wedge.* **1919.** Lithograph. Collection: Stedelijk Van Abbemuseum, Eindhoven, Holland. © 2007 Artists Rights Society (ARS), New York/VG Bild-Kunst, Bonn. The diagonal design of the composition gives the red wedge a clear "upper hand" in the conflict.

Freud and the Workings of the Mind

Eisenstein's emphasis on the viewer's psychological identification with his film was inspired in no small part by the theories of Viennese neurologist Sigmund Freud. By the start of World War I, Freud's theories about the nature of the human psyche and its subconscious functions were gaining wide acceptance. As doctors and others began to deal with the sometimes severely traumatized survivors of the war, the efficacy of Freud's psychoanalytic techniques—especially dream analysis and "free association"—were increasingly accepted by the medical community.

But Freud understood that free association required interpretation, and increasingly, he began to focus on the obscure language of the unconscious. By 1897, he had formulated a theory of infantile sexuality based on the proposition that sexual drives and energy already exist in infants. One of the keys to understanding the imprint of early sexual feeling upon adult neurotic behavior was the interpretation of dreams. Freud concluded that dreams allow unconscious wishes, desires, and drives censored by the conscious mind to exercise themselves. "The dream," he wrote in his 1900 *The Interpretation of Dreams*, "is the (disguised) fulfillment of a (suppressed, repressed) wish." And the wish, by extension, is generally based in the sexual.

World War I provided Freud with evidence of another, perhaps even more troubling source of human psychological dysfunction—society itself. In 1920, in *Beyond the Pleasure Principle*, he speculated that human beings had death drives (*Thanatos*) that were in conflict with sex drives (*Eros*). Their opposition, he believed, helped to explain the fundamental forces that shape both individuals and societies; their conflict might also explain self-destructive and outwardly aggressive behavior. To this picture he added, in the 1923 work, *The Ego and the Id*, a model for the human mind that would have a lasting impact on all subsequent psychological writings, at least in their terminology. According to Freud, human personality is organized by the competing drives of the id, the ego, and the superego. The **id** is the seat of all instinctive, physical desire—from the need for nourishment to sexual gratification. Its goal is immediate gratification, and acts in accord with the pleasure principle. The **ego** manages the id. It mediates between the id's potentially destructive impulses and the requirements of social life, seeking to satisfy the needs of the id in socially acceptable ways. For Freud, civilization itself is the product of the ego's endless effort to control and modify the id. But Freud's recognition of yet a third element in the psyche—the **superego**—is crucial. The superego is the seat of what we commonly call "conscience," the psyche's moral base. The conscience comes from the psyche's consideration of criticism or disapproval leveled at it by the family, where "family" can be understood broadly as parents, clan, and culture. But since the superego does not distinguish between thinking a deed and doing it, it can also instill in the id enormous subconscious guilt.

Freud's thinking culminated in 1930 in *Civilization and Its Discontents*. In that book, Freud wrote that the greatest impediment to human happiness was aggression, what he called the "original, self-subsisting instinctual disposition in man." Aggression was the basic instinctual drive that civilization was organized to control, and yet, on every count, civilization had failed miserably at its job. In terms that would ring truer and truer as the twentieth century wore on, Freud argued (**Reading 14.5**):

READING 14.5 | **from Sigmund Freud, *Civilization and Its Discontents* (1930)**

The fateful question for the human species seems to me to be whether and to what extent their cultural development will succeed in mastering the disturbance in their communal life by the human instinct of aggression and self-destruction. It may be that in this respect precisely the present time deserves a special interest. Men have gained control over the forces of nature to such an extent that with their help they would have no difficulty in exterminating one another to the last man.

Focus

Eisenstein's *The Battleship Potemkin*, "Odessa Steps Sequence"

The most famous sequence in *The Battleship Potemkin* is the massacre on the Odessa Steps. Odessa's citizens have responded to the mutiny on the *Potemkin* by providing the sailors with food and good company. Without warning, tsarist soldiers carrying rifles appear at the top of the flight of marble steps leading to the harbor. They fire on the crowd, many of whom fall on the steps. Eisenstein's cuts become more and more frenetic in the chaos that ensues.

Eisenstein utilized 155 separate shots in 4 minutes and 20 seconds of film in the sequence, an astonishing rate of 1.6 seconds per shot. He contrasts long shots of the entire scene and close-ups of individual faces, switches back and forth between shots from below and from above (essentially the citizens' view up the steps and the soldiers' looking down), and changes the pace from frenzied retreat at the start of the sequence to an almost frozen lack of action when the mother approaches the troops carrying her murdered son, to frantic movement again as the baby carriage rolls down the steps. Some shots last longer than others. He alternates between traveling shots and fixed shots.

Eisenstein also understood that sound and image could be treated independently in montage, or used together in support of one another. A phrase of music might heighten the emotional impact of a key shot. Or the rhythm of the music might heighten the tension of a sequence by juxtaposing itself to a different rhythm in his montage of shots, as when the soldiers' feet march to an altogether different rhythm in the editing. Eisenstein called this *rhythmic montage*, as he explains:

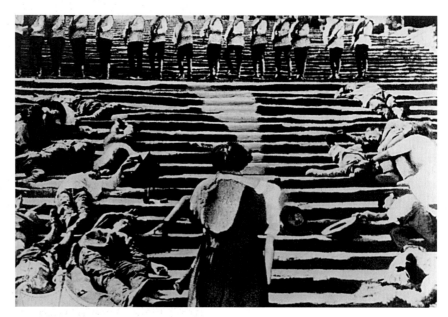

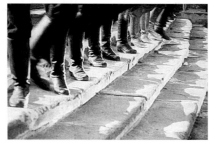
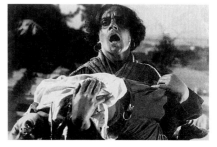

From the "Odessa Steps Sequence" of Sergei Eisenstein's *The Battleship Potemkin*, 1925. Goskino. Courtesy of the Kobal Collection. A mother picks up her murdered child and confronts the troops marching down the steps. At the point where she stands, soldiers in front of her, she is framed by the diagonal lines of the steps and the bodies strewn on each side of her. The soldiers continue to advance.

In this the rhythmic drum of the soldiers' feet as they descend the steps violates all metrical demands. Unsynchronized with the beat of the cutting, this drumming comes in off-beat each time, and the shot itself is entirely different in its solution with each of these appearances. The final pull of tension is supplied by the transfer from the rhythm of the descending feet to another rhythm—a new kind of downward movement—the next intensity level of the same activity—the baby-carriage rolling down the steps.

From the "Odessa Steps Sequence" of Sergei Eisenstein's *The Battleship Potemkin*, 1925. Goskino. Courtesy of the Kobal Collection. The falling body of another mother, shot by the soldiers, falls across her baby's carriage, causing it to roll out of control down the steps. Note the way the diagonals on the steps in the last image at the right echo those of the mother looking up the steps holding her dead child in the earlier scene.

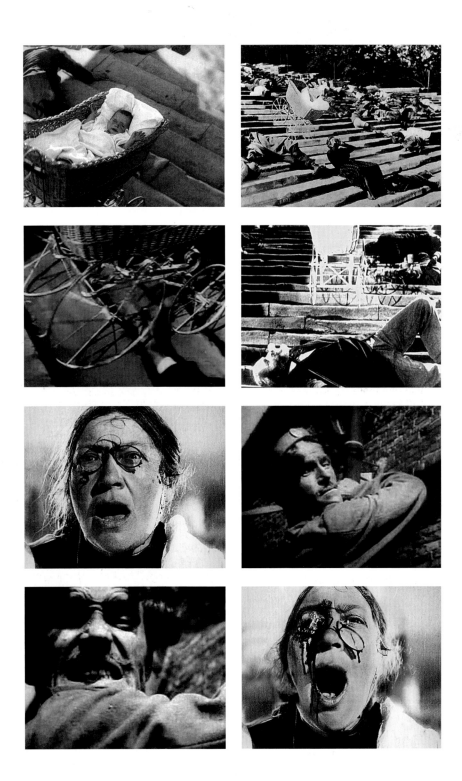

From the "Odessa Steps Sequence" of Sergei Eisenstein's *The Battleship Potemkin*, 1925. Goskino. Courtesy of the Kobal Collection. At the end of the sequence an old woman wearing pince-nez glasses who has looked on horrified as the baby stroller careens down the stairs, is attacked and slashed by a saber-bearing Cossack.

This attention to the rhythm of his film allows Eisenstein to abandon strict temporality. At the start of the baby carriage scene, for instance, the rhythm of the music slows dramatically and the pace of "real time" is elongated in a series of slow shots. The mother clutches herself. The carriage teeters on the brink. The mother swoons. The carriage inches forward. The mother falls, in agony. This is, as has often been said, "reel time," not "real time."

There was, in fact, no tsarist massacre on the Odessa Steps, though innocent civilians were killed elsewhere in the city. Eisenstein's cinematic recreation is a metaphor for those murders, a cinematic condensation of events that captured the spirit of events so convincingly that many viewers took it to be actual newsreel footage.

The Dreamwork of Surrealist Painting

In his 1924 *Surrealist Manifesto,* the French writer, poet, and theorist André Breton [bruh-TOHN] (1896–1966) credited Freud with encouraging his own creative endeavors: "It would appear that it is by sheer chance that an aspect of intellectual life—and by far the most important in my opinion—about which no one was supposed to be concerned any longer has, recently, been brought back to light. Credit for this must go to Freud. On the evidence of his discoveries a current of opinion is at last developing which will enable the explorer of the human mind to extend his investigations, since he will be empowered to deal with more than merely summary realities."

Breton had trained as a doctor and had used Freud's technique of free association when treating shell-shock victims in World War I. As his definition indicates, he had initially conceived of Surrealism as a literary movement, with Breton himself at its center. All of the Surrealists had been active Dadaists, but as opposed to Dada's "anti-art" spirit, their new "surrealist" movement believed in the possibility of a "new art." Nevertheless, Surrealism retained much of Dada's spirit of revolt.

Picasso's Surrealism Breton argued that Picasso led the way to Surrealist art in his *Les Demoiselles d'Avignon* (see Fig. 14.11), which jettisoned art's dependence on external reality. The great founder of Cubism, Breton said, possessed "the facility to give materiality to what had hitherto remained in the domain of pure fantasy." Picasso was attracted to the Surrealist point of view because it offered him new directions and possibilities. Picasso's Surrealism would assert itself most fully in the late twenties and early thirties, especially in a series of monstrous bonelike figures that alternated with sensuous portraits of his mistress Marie-Thérèse Walter (1909–1977), whom he had met when she was only 17 in January 1927. For eight years, until 1935, he led a double life, married to Olga Khokhlova [koh-KLOH-vah] (1891–1955) while conducting a secret affair with Marie-Thérèse.

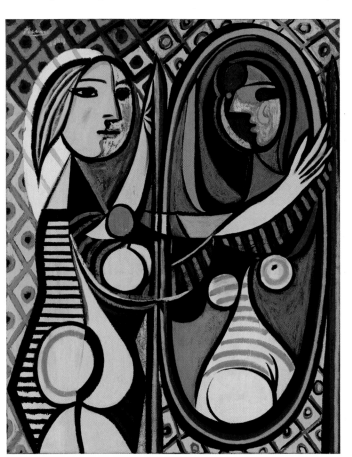

Fig. 14.25 Pablo Picasso. *Girl Before a Mirror.* 1932. Oil on canvas, 64″ × 51¼″. Gift of Mrs. Simon Guggenheim. (2.1938). Digital Image © The Museum of Modern Art/Licensed by SCALA/Art Resource, NY. © ARS Artists Rights Society, NY. The long oval mirror into which Marie-Thérèse gazes, supported on both sides by posts, is known as a *psyche.* Hence Picasso paints her psyche both literally and figuratively.

Picasso was indeed obsessed in these years with the duality of experience, the same opposition between Thanatos (the death drive) and Eros (the sex drive) that Freud had outlined in *Beyond the Pleasure Principle.* His 1932 double portrait of Marie-Thérèse, *Girl before a Mirror* (Fig. **14.25**), expresses this—she is the moon, or night, at the right, and the sun, or light, on the left, where her own face appears in both profile and three-quarter view. Her protruding belly on the left suggests her fertility (indeed, she gave birth to their child, Maya, in 1935, soon after Picasso finally separated from Olga), though in the mirror, in typical Picasso fashion, we see not her stomach but her buttocks, her raw sexuality. She is the conscious self on the left, her subconscious self revealing itself in the mirror. Picasso's work addresses Surrealism's most basic theme—the self in all its complexity. And he adds one important theme—the self in relation to the Other, for Picasso is present himself in the picture, not just as its painter, but in his symbol, the harlequin design of the wallpaper. But the painting also suggests that the self, in the dynamic interplay between the conscious and unconscious selves, might actually be the Other to itself.

Salvador Dalí's *Lugubrious Game* This sense of self-alienation is central to the work of Spanish artist Salvador Dalí [dah-LEE] (1904–1989), who in 1928, at age 24, was introduced to the Surrealists by Joan Miró. Already eccentric and flamboyant, Dalí had been expelled from the San Fernando Academy of Fine Arts two years earlier for refusing to take his final examination, claiming that he knew more than the professor who was to examine him. He brought this same daring self-confidence to the Surrealist movement. Among the first paintings executed under the influence of the Surrealists is *The Lugubrious Game* (Fig. **14.26**). At the lower right, a man wears a suit jacket but no pants, only his soiled underwear. He holds up one hand that clutches a bloodstained cloth, signifying his castration. He stares at the vision in front of him: a cluster of men's hats at the top (probably signifying the father), metamorphosing into egglike forms. Below it is Dalí's own profile, his eye closed in sleep or dream, with a grasshopper perched on his mouth. Below his mouth stretches a bowellike form culminating at the bottom of the stairs in a woman's buttocks seen from the rear. The statue of the male figure on the left reaches out an enlarged hand toward Dalí even as it covers its eyes in disgust.

Dalí, in other words, did not hesitate to confront the "lugubrious"—or mournful and gloomy side—of sexuality. He followed, he said, a "paranoiac critical method," a brand of self-hypnosis that he claimed allowed him to hallucinate freely. "I believe the moment is at hand," he wrote in a description of his method, "when, by a paranoiac and active advance of the mind, it will be possible (simultaneously with automatism . . .) to systematize confusion and thus to help to discredit the world of reality." He called his images "new and menacing," and works such as the famous 1931 *The Persistence of Memory* (Fig. **14.27**) are precisely that. Again, this is a self-portrait of the sleeping Dalí, who lies sluglike in the middle of the painting, draped beneath the coverlet of time. Ants, which are a symbol of death, crawl over a watchcase on the left. A fly alights on the watch dripping over the ledge, and another limp watch hangs from a dead tree that gestures toward the sleeping Dalí in a manner reminiscent of the statue in *The Lugubrious Game*.

By the mid-1930s, Breton and the Surrealists parted ways with Dalí over his early admiration for Adolf Hitler and his reluctance to support the Republic in the Spanish Civil War. To this could be added Dalí's love of money, for which he earned the name Avida Dollars (Greedy Dollars), an anagram of his name created by Breton. In 1938, he was formally expelled from the Surrealist movement.

The Stream-of-Consciousness Novel

Perhaps the most important literary innovation of the era was the stream-of-consciousness novel. The idea had arisen in the late nineteenth century, in the writings of both William James (1842–1910), the novelist Henry James's older brother; and the French philosopher Henri Bergson (1859–1941). For Bergson, human consciousness is composed of two somewhat contradictory powers: intellect, which sorts and categorizes experience in logical, even mathematical terms; and intuition, which understands experience as a perpetual stream of sensations, a duration or flow of perpetual becoming. Chapter XI of William James's 1892 *Psychology* is actually entitled "The Stream of Consciousness." "Now we are seeing," James writes, "now hearing; now reasoning, now willing; now recollecting, now expecting; now loving, now hating; and in a hundred other ways we know our minds to be alternately engaged. . . . Consciousness . . . is nothing jointed; it flows. A 'river' or a 'stream' are the metaphors by which it is most naturally described. *In talking of it hereafter, let us call it the stream of thought, of consciousness, or of subjective life."*

The rise of the **stream-of-consciousness** novel in the twentieth century can be attributed to two related factors. On the one hand, it provided authors a means of portraying directly the psychological makeup of their protagonists, as their minds leap from one thing to the next, from memory to

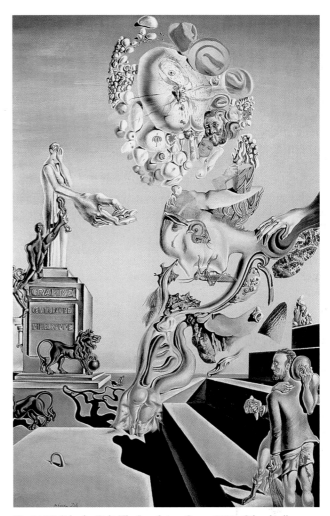

Fig. 14.26 Salvador Dalí. *The Lugubrious Game.* 1929. Oil and collage on cardboard, 17 $\frac{1}{2}$″ × 12″. Private Collection, Paris, France, © DACS. The Bridgeman Art Library. © 2008 ARS Artists Rights Society, NY. Grasshoppers terrified Dalí—hence its nightmarish presence beneath his nose.

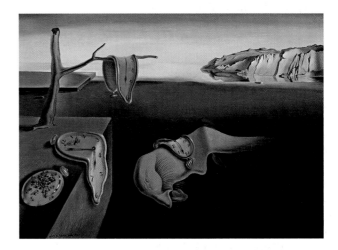

Fig. 14.27 Salvador Dalí. *The Persistence of Memory.* 1931. Oil on canvas, 9 $\frac{1}{2}$″ × 13″. The Museum of Modern Art/Licensed by SCALA/Art Resource, NY. © 1999 Demart Pro Arte (R), Geneva/Artists Rights Society (ARS), NY. Given anonymously. Dalí called such paintings "hand-painted dream photographs."

self-reflection to observation to fantasy. In this it resembles the "free association" method of Freudian psychoanalysis. But equally important, it enabled writers to emphasize the subjectivity of their characters' points of view. What a character claims might not necessarily be true. Characters might have motives for lying, even to themselves. And certainly no character in a "fiction" need be a reliable narrator of events. Nothing need prevent them from creating their own fiction within the author's larger fictional work. Thus, in the stream-of-consciousness novel, the reader is forced to become an active participant in the fiction, sorting out "fact" from "fantasy," distinguishing between the actual events of a story and the characters' "memory" of them.

The most influential stream-of-consciousness novel of the era was *Ulysses* by Irish writer James Joyce (1882–1941). The novel takes place on one day, June 16, 1904, in 18 episodes spread about an hour apart and ending in the early hours of June 17, as its hero, Leopold Bloom, tries to win back the affection of his wife, Molly. Bloom must endure 12 trials—his Homeric Odyssey—in the streets, brothels, pubs, and offices of Dublin. Each character is presented through his or her own stream-of-consciousness narration—we read only what is experienced in the character's mind from moment to moment, following their thought process through their interior monologue.

Other important stream-of-consciousness novels include *Mrs. Dalloway*, by English author Virginia Woolf (1882–1941), which takes place on a single day in post–World War I London as Clarissa Dalloway prepares for a party; the monumental seven-volume *Remembrance of Things Past*, inspired by the childhood memories of Frenchman Marcel Proust [proost] (1871–1922); and *The Sound and the Fury*, by American author William Faulkner, probably the most daring use of stream of consciousness in modern fiction: Faulkner's representation of the mental workings of the intellectually and developmentally disabled Benjy Compson.

Summary

■ **The Challenge to Cultural Identity** The European-American conflict with indigenous Americans mirrored encounters between Westerners and non-Western peoples and cultures during the eighteenth and nineteenth centuries. Western nations began a concerted effort to dominate Asian and African nations with abundant resources or productive economies in order to transfer the wealth to their own countries. Britain proved the most successful at this through the policy of imperialism. China fell victim to Britain's aggressive imperialist tactics in the late 1830s, culminating in the "Opium War" of 1840–1842. India's economy was seriously damaged by the British policies that forced Indians to sell raw materials at exploitatively low prices, and then undercut Indian manufacturers by selling finished textiles at below-market prices. Japan was the only major Asian nation not overwhelmed by the West's policies. After the opening of Japan in 1853, its manufactured products reached the West for the first time as Japan rapidly studied Western ways and adapted them to its society.

■ **The Rise of Modernism** Post-Impressionist painters like Seurat, van Gogh, Cézanne, and Gauguin were dedicated to advancing art in innovative directions. The new century was marked as well by technological innovation: the automobile, the motion picture, the airplane, and, perhaps most of all, by new discoveries in physics. In paintings like his portrait *Gertrude Stein* and the large canvas *Les Demoiselles d'Avignon*, Picasso transformed painting from an optical art to an imaginative construct. The Cubist idiom that he developed with Braque played upon the ambiguous relationship between two- and three-dimensional space—the space of painting and the space of the real world. The Futurists, led by Filippo Marinetti, would introduce the idea of speed and motion into artworks. The German Expressionists employed the exploration of color of Henri Matisse and the Fauves to create an art that centered on the psychological makeup of its creators. In music and dance, composer Igor Stravinsky and the Ballets Russes of impresario Sergei Diaghilev would shock Paris with the performance of *Le Sacre de printemps*, while in Germany, Arnold Schoenberg dispensed with traditional tonality, the harmonic basis of Western music, and created new atonal works.

■ **The Great War and Its Impact** The realities of trench warfare along the Western Front in northeast France and northwest Germany had an immense impact on the Western spirit. The almost unbounded optimism that preceded the war was replaced by a sense of the absurdity of modern life, the fragmentation of experience, and the futility of even daring to hope. Many found the war incomprehensible, and they reacted by creating an art movement based on negation and meaninglessness: Dada. In Russia, political upheaval offered the promise of a new and better life. In painting, a geometry-based art served the revolution in poster and textile design, while in film, Sergei Eisenstein's new montage techniques were created to proselytize a largely illiterate audience through fast-paced editing and composition. The psychological theories of Freud manifested themselves in the Surrealist projects of André Breton and his colleagues, who pursued the undercurrent of Freudian sexual desire that they believed lay at the root of their creative activity.

The Bauhaus: From Weimar to America

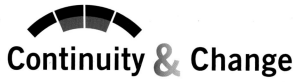

Continuity & Change

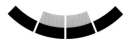

The experimental fervor of the avant-garde did not go forward without meeting resistance. In the Soviet Union, abstract art was banned as the product of "bourgeois decadence," and artists were called upon to create "a true, historically concrete portrayal of reality in its revolutionary development." In other words, artists were expected to create propaganda in support of the Soviet state. In Germany, a similar edict was issued by Hitler, this time motivated by racism. He began a 1934 speech by declaring, "All the artistic and cultural blather of Cubists, Futurists, Dadaists, and the like is neither sound in racial terms nor tolerable in national terms."

A year earlier, Nazi Minister for Popular Enlightenment and Propaganda Joseph Goebbels had inaugurated a program to "synchronize culture"—that is, align German culture with Nazi ideals. To that end, he enlisted German university students to lead the way, and on April 6, 1933, the German Student Association proclaimed a nationwide "Action against the Un-German Spirit." On the night of May 10, 1933, in most university towns, students staged a national march "Against the Un-German Spirit," culminating in the burning of more than 25,000 volumes of "un-German" books, including works by Thomas Mann, Erich Maria Remarque, Albert Einstein, Jack London, Upton Sinclair, H. G. Wells, Sigmund Freud, Ernest Hemingway, and Helen Keller. The events were broadcast live on radio to the nation.

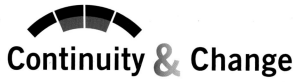

Fig. 14.28 Walter Gropius. Bauhaus Building, Dessau, Germany. 1925–1926.
Photograph courtesy Bauhaus Dessau Foundation, Dessau, Germany.

But the impact on the arts of Hitler's rise to power is nowhere more clearly demonstrated than in the history of the Bauhaus (from the German verb *bauen* [BOW-en (as in "now")], "to build"), the art school created by architect Walter Gropius [GROH-pee-us] (1883–1969) in Weimar in 1919. Its aim, Gropius wrote in the Bauhaus manifesto, was to

> conceive and create the new building of the future, which will combine everything—architecture and sculpture and painting—in a single form which will one day rise towards the heavens from the hand of a million workers as the crystalline symbol of a new and coming faith.

To this end, Gropius recruited the most outstanding faculty he could find. Among them were the Expressionist painters Wassily Kandinsky and Paul Klee [klay] (1879–1940), the designer and architect Marcel Breuer [BROY-ur] (1902–1981), the painter and color theorist Josef Albers [AL-berz] (1888–1976), the graphic designer Herbert Bayer [BY-ur] (1900–1985), and later the architect Ludwig Mies van der Rohe [meez van-der ROH] (1886–1969).

Nazi pressure forced the Bauhaus out of Weimar in 1925, when the community withdrew its financial support due to the school's perceived leftist bent. The school moved to Dessau, closer to Berlin, where Gropius designed a new building (Fig. **14.28**). Although its look is familiar enough today—an indication of just how influential it would become—the building was revolutionary at the time. It was essentially a skeleton of reinforced concrete with a skin of transparent glass. In 1930, the Nazis proposed demolishing Gropius's "decadently modern" building. Although the plan was rejected, the school in Dessau was closed in October 1932 and then reopened by Mies in Berlin as a private institution. Finally, on April 11, 1933, Gestapo (secret state police) trucks appeared at the door. They padlocked the school, and it never reopened.

After the Bauhaus closed, many of its teachers left Germany for the United States. By the early 1950s, they dominated American architecture and arts education. Gropius and Breuer moved to Cambridge, Massachusetts, to teach at the Harvard Graduate School of Design. Gropius would go on to design the Harvard Graduate Center (1949–1950) and Breuer the Whitney Museum of American Art (1966) in New York. Josef Albers would become head of the design department at Yale University in New Haven, Connecticut. Ludwig Mies van der Rohe was appointed head of the architecture school at Chicago's Armour Institute of Technology (later the Illinois Institute of Technology), where he was commissioned to design the new buildings for the campus. Mies would become the foremost designer of the glass-walled skyscraper that today dominates American urban architecture. ■

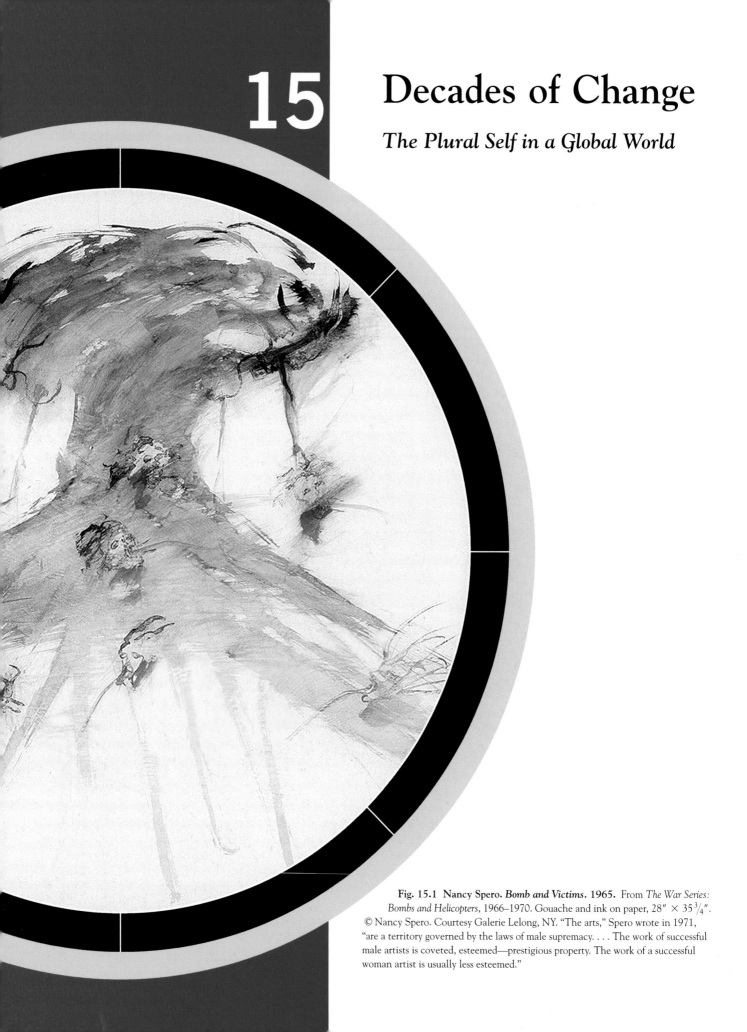

15 Decades of Change

The Plural Self in a Global World

Fig. 15.1 Nancy Spero. *Bomb and Victims*. 1965. From *The War Series: Bombs and Helicopters*, 1966–1970. Gouache and ink on paper, 28″ × 35³⁄₄″. © Nancy Spero. Courtesy Galerie Lelong, NY. "The arts," Spero wrote in 1971, "are a territory governed by the laws of male supremacy. . . . The work of successful male artists is coveted, esteemed—prestigious property. The work of a successful woman artist is usually less esteemed."

> *It is something else again. But what? Not chaos, but a new spatial order.*
>
> Robert Venturi, Denise Scott Brown, and Steven Izenour,
> *Learning from Las Vegas*

World War II and Its Aftermath

Mass Media and the Culture of Consumption

The Ongoing Fight for Civil Rights

The Feminist Movement

The Postmodern Era

In 1969, at the height of the American war in Vietnam, a novel was published by American author Kurt Vonnegut [VON-uh-gut] (1922–2007) entitled Slaughterhouse-Five. It is the oddly narrated story of ex-World War II GI Billy Pilgrim, a survivor, like Vonnegut himself, of the Allied fire-bombing of Dresden [DREZ-den] in February 1945, where 135,000 German civilians were killed, more than Hiroshima and Nagasaki combined. Pilgrim claims to have been abducted by extraterrestrial aliens from the planet of Trafalmadore. At the beginning of the book, the narrator (more or less, Vonnegut himself) is talking with a friend about the war novel he is about to write (*Slaughterhouse-Five*), when the friend's wife interrupts:

> "You'll pretend that you were men instead of babies, and you'll be played in the movies by . . . John Wayne. . . . And war will look just wonderful, so we'll have a lot more of them. And they'll be fought by babies. . . ." She didn't want her babies or anyone else's babies killed in wars. And she thought wars were partly encouraged by books and movies.

In response, Vonnegut creates, in Pilgrim, the most innocent of heroes, and subtitles his novel: *The Children's Crusade: A Duty-Dance with Death*. Pilgrim's reaction to the death he sees everywhere—"So it goes"—became a mantra for the generation that came of age in the late 1960s. The novel's fatalism mirrored the sense of pointlessness and arbitrariness that so many felt in the face of the Vietnam War.

It was not a very great reach for women of the then-emerging feminist movement to see, in the Vietnam War, the very symbol of male oppression. Nancy Spero [SPEER-oh] (1926–) had lived in Paris from 1959 to 1964, but when she returned to the United States she was, she admitted, "enraged." "I was shocked that our country, which had this wonderful idea of democracy, was doing this terrible thing in Vietnam. I wanted to make images to express the obscenity of war." For Spero the male penis is the very agent of war, the bomb its destructive seed. She describes the images in the resulting *War Series* (Fig. **15.1**) as:

> manifestoes against our (the US) incursion into Vietnam, a personal attempt at exorcism. The Bombs are phallic and nasty, exaggerated sexual representations of the penis: heads with tongues sticking out, violent depictions of the human (mostly male) body. The clouds of the Bomb are filled with screaming heads vomiting poison onto the victims below.

For Spero and many others, both men and women, the Vietnam War was symptomatic of a more general cultural malaise for which the culture of consumption and the growing dominance of mass media were both responsible. So was what had come to be known as the military-industrial complex. In his farewell address to the nation in January 1961, President Dwight David Eisenhower (1890–1969) had warned: "This conjunction of an immense military establishment and a large arms industry is new in the American experience. The total influence—economic, political, even spiritual—is felt in every city, every statehouse, every office of the federal government. . . . In the councils of government, we must guard against the acquisition of unwarranted influence, whether sought or unsought, by the military-industrial complex. The potential for the disastrous rise of misplaced power exists and will persist."

By the fall of 1969, Spero had joined with many other artists to form the antiwar Art Workers' Coalition. In a speech at an opening hearing that led to the Coalition's founding, art critic and editor Gregory Battcock outlined how the art world was complicit in the military-industrial complex:

> The trustees of the museums direct NBC and CBS, The New York Times, and the Associated Press, and that greatest cultural travesty of modern times—the Lincoln Center. They own AT&T, Ford, General Motors, the great multi-billion dollar foundations, Columbia University, Alcoa, Minnesota Mining, United Fruit, and AMK, besides sitting on the boards of each other's museum. The implications of these facts are enormous. Do you realize that it is those art-loving, culturally committed trustees of the Metropolitan and the Modern museums who are waging the war in Vietnam?

In other words, museums embodied, in the minds of many, the establishment politics that had led to the Vietnam War in the first place.

As President Eisenhower well knew, those politics had begun to be put in place by the end of the second World War.

451

Furthermore, the horrors of World War II provoked a profound uneasiness in both Europe and the United States, especially the terrible truth of the **Holocaust**, the extermination of around 6 million Jews by Adolf Hitler and the German Nazi government, along with 5 million others whom the Nazis considered racially inferior or otherwise undesirable—particularly Gypsies, Slavs, the handicapped, and homosexuals. In America, the realities of the Cold War with the Soviet Union and what many perceived as the country's crass materialism muted the rapid economic expansion and the sense of well-being that accompanied it. Artists and writers responded by creating a rebellious, individualistic art intended to represent the absolute truth of authentic experience. In the 1960s, a growing dissatisfaction with the status quo inspired an attitude of righteous indignation that manifested itself not only in the anti-Vietnam War movement but in the civil rights movement, the burgeoning feminist movement, and in the atmosphere of youthful rebellion embodied in the rise of rock and roll music and the accompanying use of psychedelic drugs by musicians and audiences alike. In such a world, the very possibility of arriving at definitive answers to the pressing problems of the day seemed more and more unlikely. Everything seemed open to interpretation, and "meaning" itself became contingent and open-ended. By the turn of the century, the increasing globalization of the world's cultures threatened the integrity of indigenous cultures, while even more complex questions began to emerge. Artists in the world's cultures have found themselves in a double-bind—how, they ask, can they remain true to their native personal identities and still participate in a global marketplace? What happens to their work when it enters a context where it is received with little or no understanding of its origins? In the world of global media—motion pictures, television channels such as CNN, or Internet search engines like Google—is the very idea of the "self" threatened by technology and technological innovation?

World War II and Its Aftermath

Ever since the nineteenth century, when Japan, China, India, and Africa experienced social dislocation and upheaval as a result of confrontation with the West, the impact of political events and social issues had become increasingly global in impact. World War I had taken place along a fairly compact front in northeastern France and northwestern Germany. By contrast, World War II was a truly worldwide conflict. No other event of the first half of the twentieth century so greatly increased the growing decenteredness of culture.

The causes of World War II can be traced to the rise of fascism in Europe, itself attributable to the worldwide economic downturn caused by the Great Depression of the 1930s together with a rampant spirit of nationalist pride first fostered in the nineteenth century but manifested, after the crash of the New York stock market on October 29, 1929, as a quest for national unity based on ethnic, cultural, and racial identity. In Germany, Hitler felt that the forces of modernity were determined to destroy the German state, specifically under the leadership of Jewish intellectuals—many of whom were Communists (remember Karl Marx was a German Jew). As far as Hitler was concerned, Jewish economic and political interests were responsible for the Depression itself. By 1932, more than 6 million Germans were unemployed, and thousands of them joined the Nazi party, whose ranks rose from 100,000 in 1930 to over 1 million in 1933.

In Italy, after World War I, peasants seized uncultivated land, workers went on strike and occupied factories, and many felt that a Communist revolution was imminent. In the face of inaction by the government of King Victor Emmanuel III, Benito Mussolini [moo-soh-LEE-nee] (1883–1945) and his followers formed local terrorist squads, called Black Shirts because they always dressed in shirts of that color. These squads beat up and even murdered Socialist and Communist leaders, attacked strikers and farm workers, and systematically intimidated the political left. By 1926, Mussolini had managed to outlaw all opposition political parties, deny all labor unions the right to strike, and organize major industries into 22 corporations that encompassed the entire economy. Although the king remained nominal ruler, Mussolini had established a single-party totalitarian state, declaring himself *Il Duce* [DOO-cheh], "the leader."

The Fascist ideologies that dominated Germany and Italy spread to Spain by the mid-1930s. A strong anarchist movement had developed, resulting in major uprisings, strikes, and full jails. In February 1936, the Spanish Popular Front, a coalition of Republicans, communists, and anarchists that promised amnesty to all those previously imprisoned, was elected to office. This dismayed the *Falange* [fah-LAHN-hay] ("Phalanx"), a right-wing fascist organization with a private army much like Hitler's and that had the sympathy of the Spanish army stationed in Morocco. In July, the *Falange* retaliated, the army in Morocco rebelled, and General Francisco Franco [FRAHN-koh] (1892–1975) led it into Spain from Morocco in a coup d'état against the Popular Front government.

In the civil war that ensued, Germany and Italy supported Franco's right-wing Nationals, while the Soviet Union and Mexico sent equipment and advisors to the leftist Republicans. The United States remained neutral, but liberals from across Europe and America, including Ernest Hemingway, joined the Republican side, fighting side by side with the Spanish.

Hitler conceived of the conflict as a dress rehearsal for the larger European conflict he was already preparing. He was especially interested in testing the Luftwaffe [LOOFT-vah-fuh], his air force. On April 26, 1937, a German air-force squadron bombed the Basque town of Guernica, in northern Spain. The attack was a *blitzkrieg*, the sudden coordinated air assault that the Germans would later use to great effect against England in World War II. It lasted for three and a quarter hours. The stated target was a bridge used by retreating Republican forces at the northern edge of the town, but the entire central part of Guernica—about 15 square

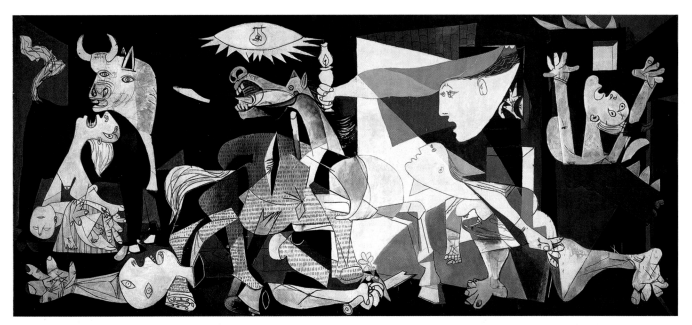

Fig. 15.2 Pablo Picasso, *Guernica*, 1937. Oil on canvas, 11′ 5$\frac{1}{2}$″ × 25′ 5$\frac{1}{4}$″. Museo Nacional Centro de Arts Reina Sofia, Madrid, Spain. John Bigelow Taylor/Art Resource, NY. © 2007 Estate of Pablo Picasso/Artists Rights Society (ARS), NY. *Guernica* traveled worldwide after its exhibition at the Spanish Pavilion in Paris in 1937. It was finally given to the Museum of Modern Art "on extended loan" in 1958. Picasso expressed the wish that the museum return the painting to Spain when and if civil liberties were ever restored in his native land. It was finally returned to Spain in 1981.

blocks—was leveled, and 721 dwellings (nearly three-quarters of the town's homes) were completely destroyed and a large number of people killed. In Paris, Pablo Picasso heard the news a day later. Complete stories did not appear in the press until Thursday, April 29, and photographs of the scene appeared on Friday and Saturday, April 30 and May 1. That Saturday, Picasso began a series of sketches for a mural that he had already been commissioned to contribute to the Spanish Pavilion at the 1937 Exposition Universelle in Paris. Only 24 days remained until the Fair was scheduled to open.

In the final painting, Picasso links the tragedy of Guernica to the Spanish ritual bullfight, in which the preordained death of the bull symbolizes the ever-present nature of death (Fig. **15.2**). The work portrays a scene of violence, helpless suffering, and death. Picasso's choice of black-and-white instead of color evokes the immediacy of a news photo. When the exposition closed, the painting was sent on tour and was used to raise funds for the Republican cause. *Guernica* would become the international symbol of the horrors of war and the fight against totalitarianism.

Meanwhile, in the Pacific, Japan was emboldened by the war in Europe to step up its imperial policy of controlling Asia. It had initiated this policy as early as 1931 with an invasion of Manchuria [man-CHOOR-ee-uh], followed by the conquest of Shanghai [SHANG-high] in 1932 and the invasion of the rest of China in 1937. By 1941, Japan had occupied Indochina, and when the United States in response froze Japanese assets in the United States and cut off oil supplies, Japan responded by attacking Pearl Harbor, Hawaii, the

chief American naval base in the Pacific, on December 7, 1941. The next day, the United States declared war on Japan, even as Germany and Italy, with whom Japan had joined in an alliance known as the Axis, declared war on the United States. World War II had begun.

The beginning of the end occurred two and a half years later, when Allied forces—largely troops from the United States and Great Britain—attacked the Germans on the Normandy coast on June 6, 1944, known as D-Day. Within two months the Allies landed in southern France and advanced northward with little resistance. By the beginning of September they had pushed back the Germans to their own border and had liberated France.

In December 1944, an increasingly desperate Hitler, his oil refineries decimated by Allied air strikes, launched a counterattack on Antwerp, the Allies' port of supply, through the Ardennes Forest of Belgium. Surprise and weather almost won him the day, as the Germans pushed forward into the Allied lines—hence the name, the Battle of the Bulge—but he was turned back. By March the Allies had crossed the Rhine, and the Russians, the eastern arm of the Allied offensive, had approached the outskirts of Berlin. On April 30, 1945, Hitler and his intimates, recognizing that the war was lost, committed suicide in an underground bunker in Berlin. On May 8, the war in Europe came to an official end.

In the Pacific, American troops had advanced as far north as Iwo Jima [ee-woh JEE-muh] and the southern Japanese island of Okinawa [oh-kih-NAH-wah], but the Japanese steadfastly refused to surrender. Faced with the possibility that an invasion of Japan itself might cost one million American lives, the Americans made the decision to drop the newly developed atomic bomb on the city of Hiroshima on August 6, 1945. Two days later, the Soviet Union declared war on Japan and invaded Manchuria. The next day, the United States dropped an atomic bomb on Nagasaki. The power of the atomic bomb, which devastated Hiroshima and Nagasaki, convinced Japan to surrender on August 14, 1945.

Japan after the War: Living with the Bomb

Japan was haunted for generations by the bombing of Hiroshima and Nagasaki. Both cities were civilian sites that contributed almost nothing to the Japanese military effort, and President Truman's motives for bombing them were unclear—to many Americans as well as the Japanese. Some argued that the bombings spared both the United States and the Japanese from a painful and devastating invasion and saved the lives of thousands of American soldiers if the war had continued. Others argued that the bombings were a means of forcing the question of the emperor's fate, a major sticking point in peace negotiations before the bombs were dropped. Still others felt that the bombings were a just retribution for devastation at Pearl Harbor. Truman's archives suggest that the president wanted to demonstrate U.S. military might to the Soviets, whom he recognized would be a threat to world stability after the war. There is probably some truth in all of these points, but none justified the bombings in the eyes of the Japanese.

One of the more interesting ways in which the Japanese came to deal with the atomic bomb and its aftermath is the creation, in 1954, of the movie monster known in this country as *Godzilla*, but in Japan as *Gojira* [go-jee-rah], a hybrid name which joins the Western word *gorilla*—in honor of the 1933 film *King Kong*—with the Japanese *kujira* [koo-jee-rah], meaning "whale." The radiation-breathing monster, born from the sea after an American test of an atomic bomb in the Pacific, was a creation of Toho Studios in Tokyo. This, the first of many Godzilla films, was directed by Ishiro Honda (1911–1993). It was inspired by the success of the 1953 U.S. film *The Beast from 20,000 Fathoms*, in which Rhedosaurus, a giant dinosaur, is awakened from eons of dormancy after an atomic bomb test in the northern polar ice cap. The dinosaur wreaks havoc on New York City, culminating in a showdown with military marksmen at Coney Island amusement park.

Godzilla became for the Japanese a vehicle through which they could confront the otherwise unspeakable significance of the atomic bomb. At the same time they could also shift blame for World War II from themselves to the Americans. Scenes of Tokyo devastated by the radiation-breathing monster leave little doubt as to the symbolic intent of the film (Fig. **15.3**). In its original form, it remains a powerful indictment of the bomb, but that was not the version available in the United States until 2004. *Gojira* was acquired by

U.S. distributors in 1956. They renamed it *Godzilla: King of the Monsters* and completely reedited it. Leaving only its monster scenes, they excised most of the human story, replacing it with scenes featuring a U.S. reporter (played by Raymond Burr, television's Perry Mason) who has come to Tokyo to chronicle the devastation caused by "a force which up until a few days ago was entirely beyond the scope of man's imagination." But, of course, the film represents not the unknown but a force completely within the scope of human imagination—the bomb—a fact that today American audiences can finally appreciate.

Europe after the War: The Existential Quest

The Holocaust and the devastation at Hiroshima and Nagasaki dramatically increased the profound pessimism that had gripped intellectual Europeans ever since the turn of the century. How could anyone pretend that the human race was governed by reason, that advances in technology and science were for the greater good, when human beings were not only capable of genocide, but also possessed the ability to annihilate themselves?

The Philosophy of Sartre: Existentialism During and after World War II, the French philosopher Jean-Paul Sartre (1905–1980) argued for what he termed **existentialism.** "Existence precedes essence," was Sartre's basic premise; that is, humans must define their own essence (who they are) through their existential being (what they do, their acts). "In a word," Sartre explained, "man must create his own essence;

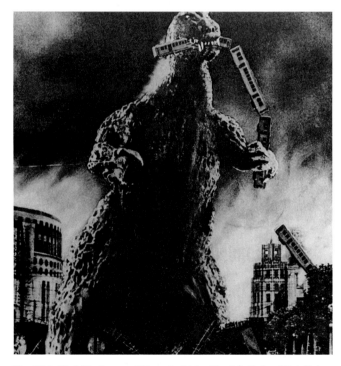

Fig. 15.3 Godzilla destroys Tokyo, in Ishiro Honda's *Gojira* (*Godzilla*). 1954. The Japanese have made at least 27 other Godzilla films.

it is in throwing himself into the world, in suffering it, in struggling with it, that—little by little—he defines himself." Life is defined neither by subconscious drives, as Freud had held, nor by socioeconomic circumstances, as Marx had argued; instead, "Man is nothing else but what he makes of himself. Such is the first principle of existentialism."

For Sartre there is no meaning to existence, no eternal truth for us to discover. The only certainty is death. Sartre's major philosophical work, the 1943 *Being and Nothingness*, outlines the nature of this condition, but his argument is more accessible in his play *Huis Clos* [hwee kloh] (*No Exit*). As the play opens, a Valet greets Monsieur Garcin [gahr-SEN] as he enters the room that will be his eternal hell (**Reading 15.1**):

READING 15.1   **from Jean-Paul Sartre,** *No Exit* **(1944)**

GARCIN (enters, accompanied by the VALET, and glances around him):

So here we are?

VALET Yes, Mr. Garcin.

GARCIN And this is what it looks like?

VALET Yes.

GARCIN Second Empire furniture, I observe . . . Well, well, I dare say one gets used to it in time.

VALET Some do, some don't.

GARCIN Are all the rooms like this one?

VALET How could they be? We cater for all sorts: Chinamen and Indians, for instance. What use would they have for a Second Empire chair?

GARCIN And what use do you suppose I have for one? Do you know who I was? . . . Oh, well, it's no great matter. And, to tell the truth, I had quite a habit of living among furniture that I didn't relish, and in false positions. I'd even come to like it. A false position in a Louis-Philippe dining room—you know the style?—well, that had its points, you know. Bogus in bogus, so to speak.

VALET And you'll find that living in a Second Empire drawing-room has its points.

GARCIN Really? . . . Yes, yes, I dare say . . . Still I certainly didn't expect—this! You know what they tell us down there?

VALET: What about?

GARCIN About . . . this—er—residence.

VALET Really, sir, how could you believe such cock-and-bull stories? Told by people who'd never set foot here. For, of course, if they had—

GARCIN Quite so. But I say, where are the instruments of torture?

VALET The what?

GARCIN The racks and red-hot pincers and all the other paraphernalia?

VALET Ah, you must have your little joke, sir.

GARCIN My little joke? Oh, I see. No, I wasn't joking. No mirrors, I notice. No windows. Only to be expected. And nothing breakable. But damn it all, they might have left me my toothbrush!

VALET That's good! So you haven't yet got over your—what-do-you-call-it?—sense of human dignity? Excuse my smiling.

The play was first performed in May 1944, just before the liberation of Paris. If existence in existential terms is the power to create one's future, Garcin and the two women who will soon occupy the room with him are in hell precisely because they are powerless to do so. Garcin's "bad faith" consists in his insistence that his self is the creation of others. His sense of himself derives from how others perceive him. Thus, in the most famous line of the play, he says, "*l'enfer, c'est les autres*" [lehn-fair, say layz-ohtr]—"Hell is other people." In the drawing room, there need be no torturer because each character tortures the other two.

The Theater of the Absurd Sartre's *No Exit* was the first example of what in the 1960s became known as the Theater of the Absurd. Among its chief proponents were Samuel Beckett (1906–1989), an Irishman who lived in Paris throughout the 1950s, the Romanian Eugène Ionesco [ee-oh-ness-KOH] (1909–1994), the Frenchman Jean Genet (1910–1986), the British Harold Pinter (1930–), the American Edward Albee (1928–), and the Czech-born Englishman Tom Stoppard (1937–). All of these playwrights share a common existential sense of the absurd plus, ironically, a sense that language is a barrier to communication, that speech is almost futile, and that we are condemned to isolation and alienation.

The most popular of the absurdist plays is Samuel Beckett's *Waiting for Godot* [goh-DOH], first written and performed in French in 1954 and subtitled A *Tragicomedy in Two Acts*. The play introduced audiences to a new set of stage conventions, from its essentially barren set (only a leafless tree decorates the stage), to its two clownlike characters, Vladimir and Estragon, whose language is incapable of affecting or even coming to grips with their situation. The play demands that its audience, like its central characters, try to make sense of an incomprehensible world in which nothing occurs. In fact, the play's first line announces as Estragon tries without success to remove his boot, "Nothing to be done." In Act I, Vladimir and Estragon await the arrival of a person referred to as Godot (**Reading 15.2a**):

READING 15.2a   **from Samuel Beckett,** *Waiting for Godot*, **Act I (1954)**

VLADIMIR What do we do now?

ESTRAGON Wait.

That is exactly what the audience must do as well—wait. Yet nothing happens. Godot does not arrive. In despair, Vladimir and Estragon contemplate hanging themselves but are unable to. Then they decide to leave but do not move. Act II takes place the next day, but nothing changes—Vladimir and Estragon again wait for Godot, who does not arrive, and again contemplate suicide. There is no development, no change of circumstance, no crisis, no resolution. The play's conclusion, which repeats the futile decision to move on that ended Act I, demonstrates this (**Reading 15.2b**):

READING 15.2b | **from Samuel Beckett,**
Waiting for Godot,
Act II (1954)

VLADIMIR Well? Shall we go?
ESTRAGON Yes, let's go.
(They do not move.)
(Curtain.)

The promise of action and the realization of none: That is the Theater of the Absurd.

America after the War: Triumph and Doubt

After the War, the United States State Department toured mammoth exhibitions of painting and sculpture by Ameri-

can artists working in a style that came to be known as **abstraction expressionism**. These artists included immigrants like Arshile Gorky [GOR-kee] (1904–1948), Hans Hoffmann (1880–1966), Milton Resnick (1917–2004), and Willem de Kooning [KOO-ning] (1904–1997), as well as slightly younger American-born artists like Franz Kline (1910–1962) and Jackson Pollock (1912–1956). All freely acknowledged their debts to Cubism's assault on traditional representation, German expressionism's turn inward from the world, Kandinsky's near-total abstraction, and Surrealism's emphasis on chance operations and psychic automatism. Together the Abstract Expressionists saw themselves as standing at the edge of the unknown, ready to define themselves through a Sartrian struggle with the blank canvas, through the physical act of applying paint and the energy that each painted gesture reveals. Their work demonstrated, the State Department believed, the spirit of freedom and innovation in American art (and, by extension, American culture as a whole). The individualistic spirit of these artists was seen as the very antithesis of communism, and their exhibitions across Europe—and in Paris, especially—were designed to convey the message that America had not only triumphed in the war, but in art and culture as well. New York, not Paris, was now the center of the art world.

Action Painting: Pollock and de Kooning In 1956, Willem de Kooning commented that "every so often, a painter has to destroy painting. Cézanne did it. Picasso did it with Cubism.

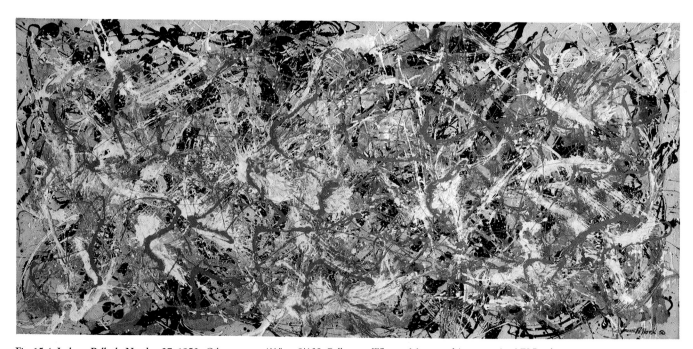

Fig. 15.4 Jackson Pollock. *Number 27.* 1950. Oil on canvas, 4′1″ × 8′10″. Collection, Whitney Museum of American Art, NY. Purchase.
The year *Number 27* was painted, *Life* magazine ran a long, profusely illustrated story on Pollock asking, "Is he the greatest living painter in the United States?" It stimulated an astonishing 532 letters to the editor, most of them answering the question with a definitive "No!"

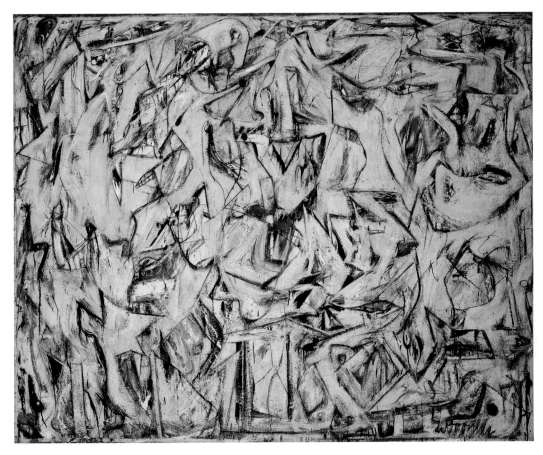

Fig. 15.5 Willem de Kooning. *Excavation.* **1950.** Oil on canvas, 6'8" × 8'4⅛". Unframed. Mr. and Mrs. Frank G. Logan Purchase Prize Fund; restricted gifts of Edgar J. Kaufmann, Jr., and Mr. and Mrs. Noah Goldowsky, Jr., 1952.1 Reproduction, The Art Institute of Chicago. All Rights Reserved. © 2009 ARS Artists Rights Society, NY. This is one of de Kooning's largest paintings. "My paintings are too complicated," he explained. "I don't use the large-size canvas because it's too difficult for me to get out of it."

Then Pollock did it. He busted our idea of a picture all to hell. Then there could be new paintings again." Around 1940, Pollock underwent psychoanalysis in order to explore Surrealist psychic automatism and to reveal, on canvas, the deepest areas of the unconscious. This depiction of a mental landscape soon developed into large-scale **"action paintings,"** as described by the critic Harold Rosenberg in 1942 (Fig. **15.4**). The canvas had become, he said, "an arena in which to act." It was no longer "a picture but an event." Pollock would drip, pour, and splash oil paint, house and boat paint, and enamel over the surface of the canvas, determining the top and bottom of the piece only after the process was complete. The result was a galactic sense of space, what Rosenberg called "all-over" space, in which the viewer can almost trace Pollock's rhythmic gestural dance around the painting's perimeter.

De Kooning was 12 years Pollock's senior and had begun in the late 1930s and early 1940s in a more figurative vein. But by 1950, the surface of de Kooning's paintings seemed densely packed with free-floating, vaguely anatomical parts set in a landscape of crumpled refuse, earth-moving equipment, concrete blocks, and I-beams. None of these elements is definitively visible, just merely suggested. *Excavation* is a complex organization of open and closed cream-colored forms that lead from one to the other, their black outlines overlapping, merging, disappearing across the surface (Fig. **15.5**). Small areas of brightly colored brushwork interrupt the surface.

When, in 1951, *Excavation* was featured in an exhibition of abstract painting and sculpture at the Museum of Modern Art in New York, de Kooning lectured on the subject "What Abstract Art Means to Me." His description of his relationship to his environment is a fair explanation of what we see in the painting: "Everything that passes me I can see only a little of, but I'm always looking. And I see an awful lot sometimes." De Kooning's abstraction differs from Pollock's largely in this. As opposed to plumbing the depths of the psyche, he represents the psyche's encounter with the world. De Kooning's primary concern is the relation of the individual to his or her environment. The tension between the two is the focus of his works.

Fig. 15.6 Mark Rothko. *Green on Blue*. 1956. Oil on canvas, 7′5¾″ × 5′3¼″. Collection of the University of Arizona Museum of Art, Tucson, Gift of E. Gallagher, Jr. Acc. 64.1.1. The religious sensibility of Rothko's painting brought him, in 1964, a commission for a set of murals for a Catholic chapel in Houston, Texas.

The Color-Field Painting of Rothko and Frankenthaler A second variety of abstract expressionism offered viewers a more meditative and quiet painting based on large expanses of relatively undifferentiated color. Mark Rothko (1903–1970) began painting in the early 1940s by placing archetypal figures in front of large monochromatic bands of hazy, semi-transparent color. By the early 1950s, he had eliminated the figures, leaving only the background color field.

The scale of these paintings is intentionally large. *Green on Blue*, for instance, is over seven feet tall (Fig. **15.6**). "The reason I paint [large pictures]," he stated in 1951,

> is precisely because I want to be very intimate and human. To paint a small picture is to place yourself outside your experience, to look upon an experience as a stereopticon view or reducing glass. However you paint the larger picture, you are in it. It isn't something you command.

Viewers find themselves enveloped in Rothko's sometimes extremely somber color fields. These expanses of color

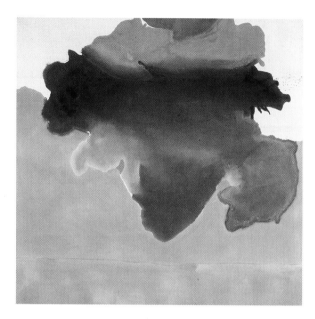

Fig. 15.7 Helen Frankenthaler (b.1928). *The Bay*. 1963. Acrylic on canvas, 6′8¾″ × 6′9½″. The Detroit Institute of Arts, USA, Founders Society Purchase, Dr. & Mrs. Hilbert H. DeLawter Fund/The Bridgeman Art Library. © 2009 Helen Frankenthaler/Artists Rights Society (ARS), New York. This is one of the first paintings in which Frankenthaler used acrylic rather than oil paint, resulting in a much more stable surface.

become, in this sense, stage sets for the human drama that transpires before them. As Rothko further explains:

> I am interested only in expressing the basic human emotions—tragedy, ecstasy, doom, and so on—and the fact that lots of people break down and cry when confronted with my pictures shows that I communicate with those basic human emotions. The people who weep before my pictures are having the same religious experience I had when I painted them.

The emotional toll of such painting finally cost Rothko his life. His vision became darker and darker throughout the 1960s, and in 1970 he hanged himself in his studio.

In 1952, directly inspired by Pollock's drip paintings, 24-year-old Helen Frankenthaler (1928–) diluted paint almost to the consistency of watercolor and began pouring it onto unprimed cotton canvas to achieve giant stains of color that suggest landscape (Fig.**15.7**). The risk she assumed in controlling her flooding hues, and the monumentality of her compositions, immediately inspired a large number of other artists.

The Aesthetics of Inclusiveness In an essay called "The Legacy of Jackson Pollock," written just two years after Pollock's death in an automobile accident in 1956, Allan Kaprow (1927–2006) described Pollock's art, with its willingness to bury nails, sand, wire, screen mesh, even coins in its whirls of paint, as pointing toward new possibilities for the subsequent generation of artists (**Reading 15.3**):

from Allan Kaprow, "The Legacy of Jackson Pollock" (1958)

Pollock, as I see him, left us at the point where we must become preoccupied with and even dazzled by the space and objects of our everyday life, either our bodies, clothes, rooms, or, if need be, the vastness of Forty-second Street. Not satisfied with the suggestion through paint of our other senses, we shall utilize the specific substances of sight, sound, movements, people, odors, touch. Objects of every sort are materials for the new art: paint, chairs, food, electric and neon lights, smoke, water, old socks, a dog, movies, a thousand other things that will be discovered by the present generation of artists. Not only will these bold new creators show us, as if for the first time, the world we have always had about us but ignored, but they will disclose entirely unheard-of happenings and events, found in garbage cans, police files, hotel lobbies; seen in store windows and on the streets; and sensed in dreams and horrible accidents. An odor of crushed strawberries, a letter from a friend, or a billboard selling Drano; three taps on the front door, a scratch, a sigh, or a voice lecturing endlessly, a blinding staccato flash, a bowler hat—all will become materials for this new concrete art.

Young artists of today need no longer say, "I am a painter" or "a poet" or "a dancer." They are simply "artists." All of life will be open to them.

It is hardly surprising that it was Kaprow who founded the **Happening**, a new multimedia event in which artists and audience participated as equal partners. Kaprow's *18 Happenings in 6 Parts* took place over the course of six evenings in October 1959 at the Reuben Gallery in New York. It was inspired by *Theater Piece #1*. Included in the environment were record players, tape recorders, bells, a toy ukelele, a flute, a kazoo, and a violin. Kaprow scored the directions for playing them in precisely timed outbursts that approximated the cacophony of the urban environment. He divided the gallery into three rooms, created by plastic sheets and movable walls, between which audience members were invited to move in unison. Performers played instruments and records, painted, squeezed orange juice, spoke in sentence fragments—all determined by chance operations. The audience, although directed to move according to Kaprow's instructions, was also invited to participate in the work, and Kaprow would increasingly include the audience as a participant in his later Happenings.

In order to add the sounds to his environment, Kaprow had enrolled in a music composition course taught by composer John Cage (1912–1992) at the New School for Social Research in New York. By the mid-1950s Cage was proposing that it was time to "give up the desire to control sound . . . and set about discovering means to let sounds be themselves."

Cage's notorious *4'33"* (*4 minutes 33 seconds*) is a case in point. First performed in Woodstock, New York, by pianist David Tudor on August 29, 1952, it consists of three silent movements, each of a different length, but when added together totaling four minutes and thirty-three seconds. The composition was anything but silent, however, admitting into the space framed by its duration all manner of ambient sound—whispers, coughs, passing cars, the wind. Whatever sounds happened during its performance were purely a matter of chance, never predictable. Above all, Cage's is an art of inclusiveness.

That summer Cage organized a multimedia event at Black Mountain College in North Carolina, where he occasionally taught. Although almost everyone who participated remembers the event somewhat differently, it seems certain that the poets M. C. Richards (1916–1999) and Charles Olson (1910–1970) read poetry from ladders, the 27-year-old artist Robert Rauschenberg [RAUW-shen-berg] (1925–2008) played Edith Piaf [pee-AHF] records on an old windup phonograph with his almost totally "White Paintings" hanging around the room, and Merce Cunningham (1919–) danced through the audience, a dog at his heels, while Cage himself sat on a stepladder, sometimes reading a lecture on Zen Buddhism, sometimes just listening. "Music," Cage declared at some point in the event, "is not listening to Mozart but sounds such as a street car or a screaming baby."

The event inaugurated a collaboration between Cunningham (dance), Cage (music), and Rauschenberg (decor and costume) that would span many years. Their collaboration is unique in the arts because of its insistence on the *independence*, not interdependence, of each part of the dance's presentation. Cunningham explains:

> In most conventional dances there is a central idea to which everything adheres. The dance has been made to the piece of music, the music supports the dance, and the decor frames it. The central idea is emphasized by each of the several arts. What we have done in our work is to bring together three separate elements in time and space, the music, the dance and the decor, allowing each one to remain independent.

So Cunningham created his choreography independently of Cage's scores, and Rauschenberg based his decors on only minimal information offered him by Cunningham and Cage. The resulting dance was, by definition, a matter of music, choreography, and decor coming together (or not) as a chance operation.

The music Cage composed for Cunningham was also often dependent on chance operations. The year 1952 also saw the creation of *Water Music*, a composition for piano using, among other objects, an assortment of whistles (including a siren and a duck call), water, and the radio (**CD-Track 15.1**). Although the real-world sounds are smoothly collaged into the score, no two performances are alike because there is always something different on the radio. For a later collaboration, *Variations V*, Cage's score consists of

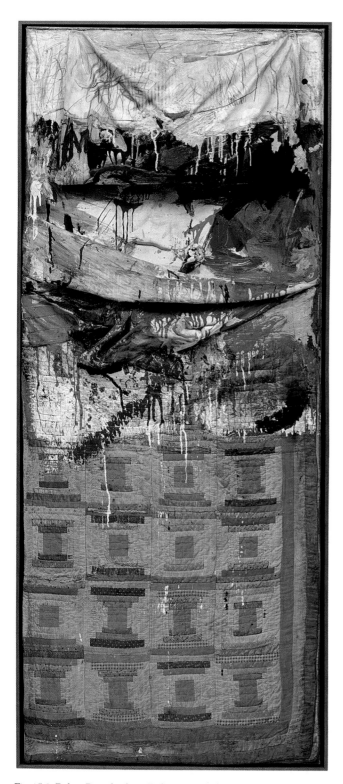

Fig. 15.8 Robert Rauschenberg. *Bed*. 1955. Combine painting: oil and pencil on pillow, quilt, and sheet on wood supports, 75 1/4″ × 31 1/2″ × 8″. Gift of Leo Castelli in honor of Alfred H. Barr, Jr. (79.1989). Digital Image © The Museum of Modern Art/Licensed by SCALA / Art Resource, NY. © Art Robert Rauschenberg Foundation/VAGA, NY. The mattress, pillow, quilt, and sheets are believed to be Rauschenberg's own and so may be thought of as embodying his famous dictum: "Painting relates to both art and life. . . . (I try to act in that gap between the two.)"

sounds randomly triggered by sensors reacting to the movements of Cunningham's dancers. This results in what Gordon Mumma, a member of Cunningham's troupe, called "a superbly poly: -chromatic, -genic, -phonic, -morphic, -pagic, -technic, -valent, multi-ringed circus."

By the mid-1950s, Rauschenberg had begun to make what he called **combine paintings**, works in which all manner of materials—postcards, advertisements, tin cans, pinups—are combined to create the work. If Rauschenberg's work does not literally depend upon matters of chance in its construction, it does incorporate such a diverse range of material that it creates the aura of representing Rauschenberg's chance encounters with the world around him. And it does, above all, reflect Cage's sense of all-inclusiveness. *Bed* literally consists of a sheet, pillow, and quilt raised to the vertical and then dripped not only with paint but also with toothpaste and fingernail polish in what amounts to a parody of Abstract Expressionist introspection (Fig. **15.8**). Even as it juxtaposes highbrow art-making with the vernacular quilt, abstraction with realism, *Bed* is a wryly perceptive transformation of the Surrealist dreamscape.

Mass Media and the Culture of Consumption

The 1950s had been an era of unprecedented prosperity in the United States. In July 1955, Walt Disney opened Disneyland in Anaheim, California, the first large-scale theme park in America. That same year, two of the first fast-food chains opened their doors—Colonel Sanders's Kentucky Fried Chicken (KFC) and McDonald's. In 1953, the first issue of *Playboy* magazine appeared, featuring Marilyn Monroe as its first nude centerfold, and by 1956 its circulation had reached 600,000. Sales of household appliances exploded, and women, still largely relegated to the domestic scene, suddenly found themselves with leisure time. Diner's Club and American Express introduced the charge card in 1951 and 1958 respectively. Both cards required payment in full each month, but they paved the way for the Bank Americard, introduced in 1959 (eventually evolving into the Visa card), which allowed for individual borrowing—and purchasing— at an unprecedented level.

New products proliferated—CorningWare, Sugar Pops, and Kraft Minute Rice (1950); sugarless chewing gum and the first 33-rpm long-playing records, introduced by Deutsche Grammophon (1951); Kellogg's Sugar Frosted Flakes, the Sony pocket-sized transistor radio, fiberglass and nylon (1952); Sugar Smacks cereal and Schweppes bottled tonic water (1953); Crest toothpaste and roll-on deodorant (1955); Pampers disposable baby diapers, Comet cleanser, Raid insecticide, Imperial margarine, and Midas mufflers (1956); the Wham-O toy company's Frisbee (1957) and Hula Hoop (1958); Sweet'n Low, Green Giant canned beans, and Teflon frying pans (1958). Finally, in 1958 as well, Pizza Hut opened its doors for the first time.

Television played a key role in marketing these products since advertisers underwrote entertainment and news programming by buying time slots for commercials. In television commercials people could see products firsthand. Although television programming had been broadcast before World War II, it was suspended during the war and did not resume until 1948. By 1950, four networks were broadcasting to 3.1 million television sets. By the end of the decade, that number had swelled to 67 million. Even the food industry responded to the medium. Swanson, which had introduced frozen potpies in 1951, began selling complete frozen "TV dinners" in 1953. The first, in its sealed aluminum tray, featured turkey, cornbread dressing and gravy, buttered peas, and sweet potatoes. It cost 98 cents, and Swanson sold 10 million units that year. Consumer culture was at full throttle, and Americans quickly took the proliferation of new products and services for granted. Only in Europe, where economic recovery lagged far behind the United States because its industries had been devastated by the war, could the magnitude of American consumption seem obvious. It was in Europe, specifically London, that the first artistic critiques of consumer culture were produced by a group of artists known as the Independents.

The power of the media—television, particularly—to focus on current events crystallized following President John F. Kennedy's assassination in 1963, when audiences watched again and again the replaying on television of Abraham Zapruder's 26-second film of the Kennedy motorcade in Dallas's Dealey Plaza and Jack Ruby's live assassination of Lee Harvey Oswald as Oswald was being transferred to the Dallas jail. But increasingly, it seemed to many observers, American culture had come to look like a vast array of made-for-television events and advertisements.

"The medium is the message," popular sociologist Marshall McLuhan (1911–1980) declared in 1964. A few years later, he had playfully transformed the phrase to "the medium is the massage," implying, at once, that the media "massage" us into belief ("All media work us over completely," he wrote), and that the media are the primary means of expression in the "mass-age." "Mass communication," he argued, is largely a misnomer—that is, "communication" in the mass media is one-directional, sent over the airwaves to a passive receiver who is, for all practical purposes, unable to respond. McLuhan also understood that the mass media exist to make a profit through the sale of advertising. They do not exist to convey information so much as to stimulate consumption of the products they advertise. As a result, McLuhan wrote, "All media exist to invest our lives with artificial perception and arbitrary values." They create a society of desire—the desire to possess and consume what we do not have.

High and Low: The Example of Music

Rock and roll's ascendancy as the favorite music of American popular culture in the 1950s and 1960s underscores a shift in cultural values in which the line between "high" and "low" art became more and more difficult to define.

Rock and roll had gained increasing popularity in the 1950s when the gyrating hips and low-slung guitar of one of its earliest stars, Elvis Presley (1935–1977), made the music's innuendo of youthful sexual rebellion explicit. In the 1960s, led by the Beatles, British rock bands (including Led Zeppelin and the Rolling Stones) transformed rock into the musical idiom of a youthful counterculture that embraced sex, drugs, and rock 'n' roll.

By then, music had become an industry in its own right, perhaps the most fully commercialized medium in the art world. The German company Deutsche Grammophon was dedicated to recording classical music at the highest possible level, and in 1951, it had released the first 33-rpm long-playing records. Now, they owned the Beatles' first recording label, Polydor Records, a company dedicated to recording popular music.

Classical composers had routinely incorporated folk music into their work, but at the same time, classical music was increasingly considered the provenance of elite and intellectual audiences while lighter fare was understood to appeal to wider, more populist tastes. The Boston Pops Orchestra was founded as early as 1885 to present "concerts of a lighter kind of music." Its conductor of over 50 years, Arthur Fiedler (1894–1979), was followed by Academy Award winner John Williams (1932–), composer of the soundtracks to the films *Star Wars* and *Indiana Jones and the Raiders of the Lost Ark*.

In this context, one of the most interesting composers of the era was Charles Ives (1874–1954). Ives had been raised in a military family, son of an army bandleader. Working in a decidedly modern vein—often polytonal and polyrhythmic—Ives composed a body of work in the first 20 years of the twentieth century that incorporates patriotic tunes and marches, hymns, and elements of ragtime. The second movement of his *Three Places in New England*, composed between 1903 and 1911, is intended to reflect a child's impression of a Fourth of July picnic at Putnam's Camp, Redding, Connecticut (**CD-Track 15.2**). A raucous collage of competing melodies and marches—from "Rally Round the Flag" and "Yankee Doodle" to "The British Grenadiers"—a strand of the national anthem dissolves into a jolting discordance at the end of the piece.

The example of Ives is particularly useful because for most of his life his music was largely unknown. Not until after World War II did it begin to attract the attention of an American audience. His third symphony was finally awarded the Pulitzer Prize in 1947, and his second symphony made its premiere at last in 1951, when Leonard Bernstein (1918–1980) performed it conducting the New York Philharmonic Orchestra. It is fitting that Bernstein should have premiered the work since he was himself equally at home in both classical and popular idioms. High and low were distinctions that, in his own work, he tried to ignore, as Mozart had before him. He could write Broadway hit musicals such as *Candide* (1956) and *West Side Story* (1957) and profoundly moving symphonies. His 1963 Third Symphony, *Kaddish*, a musical interpretation

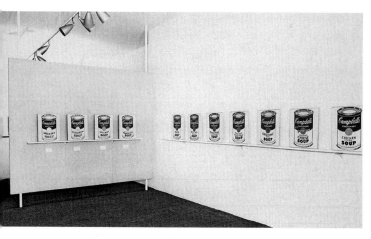

Fig. 15.9 Andy Warhol. Installation view of *Campbell's Soup Cans*, installation at Ferus Gallery. 1962. Founding Collection, The Andy Warhol Museum, Pittsburgh. In order to evoke the way we encounter Campbell's soup on the grocery shelf, Warhol placed the cans on narrow shelves on the gallery.

of the Jewish prayer for the dead, was written for an orchestra, a chorus, a soloist, a children's choir, and a narrator. At its premier performance, in Tel Aviv, Bernstein conducted the Israel Philharmonic. *Mass*, written in 1971, was a full-fledged 80-minute Mass, based on the traditional Catholic liturgy, but which combines Bernstein's classical interpretation of the form with everything from rock-and-roll guitar to a kazoo chorus. Writing in a 1966 book entitled *The Infinite Variety of Music*, Bernstein explained: "As of this writing, God forgive me, I have far more pleasure in following the musical adventures of Simon & Garfunkel . . . than I have in most of what is being written now by the whole community of 'avant-garde' composers. . . . Pop music seems to be the only area where there is to be found unabashed vitality, the fun of invention, the feeling of fresh air." For Bernstein, at least, popular music seemed to have won the day, although the crass commercialization of popular music would later cause him to lose interest in it.

Pop Art

In the early 1960s, especially in New York, a number of artists created a "realist" art that represented reality in terms of the media—advertising, television, comic strips—imagery of mass culture. The term Pop Art quickly became attached to such work. James Rosenquist (1933–) explicitly tied the American military-industrial complex to American consumer culture (see *Focus*, pages 464–465). Inspired by Allan Kaprow's essay "The Legacy of Jackson Pollock" (see Reading 15.3), Claes Oldenberg (1929–) rented a storefront on New York's Lower East Side in 1961 and, in time for Christmas, opened *The Store*, filled with life-size enameled plaster sculptures of everything from pie à la mode, to hamburgers, hats, caps, 7-Up bottles, shirt-and-tie combinations, and slices of cake. "I am for an art," he wrote in a statement accompanying the exhibition,

that is political-erotica-mystical, that does something other than sit on its ass in a museum.

I am for an art that grows up not knowing it is art at all, an art given the chance of having a starting point of zero.

I am for an art that embroils itself with the everyday crap & still comes out on top. I am for an art that imitates the human, that is comic, if necessary, or violent, or whatever is necessary.

I am for an art that takes its form from the lines of life itself, that twists and extends and accumulates and spits and drips, and is heavy and coarse and blunt and sweet and stupid as life itself.

The famous paintings of Campbell's soup cans created by Andy Warhol (1928–1987) were among the first of consumer-based works to find their way into the gallery scene (Fig. **15.9**). In the fall of 1962, he exhibited 32 uniform 20″ × 16″ canvases, at the Ferus Gallery in Los Angeles. Each depicted one of the 32 different Campbell's soup "flavors." Even as the paintings debunked the idea of originality—are they Campbell's or Warhol's?—their literalness redefined the American landscape as the visual equivalent of the supermarket aisle. The works were deliberately opposed to the self-conscious subjectivity of the Abstract Expressionists. It was, in fact, as if the painter had no personality at all. As Warhol himself put it, "If you want to know all about Andy Warhol, just look at the surface of my paintings and films and me, and there I am. There's nothing behind it."

By late 1962, Warhol had stopped making his paintings by hand, using a photo-silkscreen process to create the images mechanically and employing others to do the work for him in his studio, The Factory. One of the first of these is the *Marilyn Diptych* (Fig. **15.10**). Marilyn Monroe had died, by suicide, in August of that year, and the painting is at once a memorial to her and a commentary on the circumstances that had brought her to despair. She is not so much a person, as Warhol depicts her, but a personality, the creation of a Hollywood studio system whose publicity shot Warhol repeats over and over again here to the point of erasure.

The enlarged comic strip paintings of Roy Lichtenstein [LIK-ten-stine] (1923–1997) are replete with heavy outlines and Ben Day dots, the process created by Benjamin Day at the turn of the century to produce shading effects in mechanical printing. Widely used in comic strips, the dots are, for Lichtenstein, a conscious parody of Seurat's pointillism (see chapter 14). But they also reveal the extent to which "feeling" in popular culture is as "canned" as Campbell's soup. In *Oh, Jeff . . .* (Fig. **15.11**), "love" is emptied of real meaning as the real weight of the message is carried by the final "But. . ." Even the feelings inherent in Abstract Expressionist brushwork came under Lichtenstein's attack (Fig. **15.12**). In fact, Lichtenstein had taught painting to college students, and he discovered that the "authentic" gesture of abstract expressionism could easily be taught and replicated without any emotion whatsoever—as a completely academic enterprise.

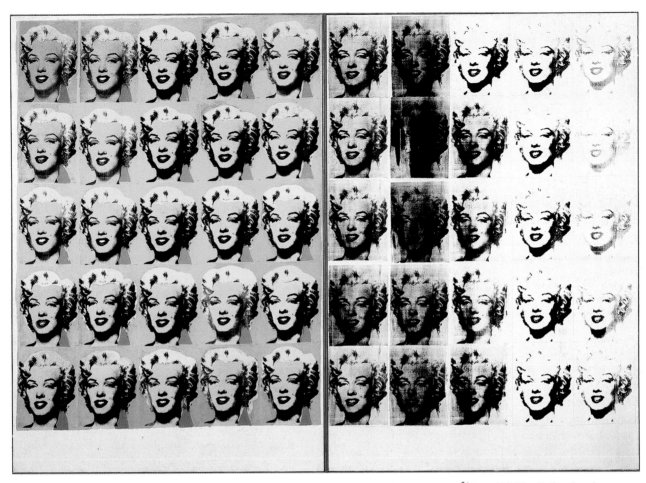

Fig. 15.10 Andy Warhol. *Marilyn Diptych*. 1962. Oil, acrylic, and silkscreen on enamel on canvas, 6′ 8 7/8″ × 4′ 9″. Tate Gallery, London. Art Resource, NY. © 2008 The Andy Warhol Foundation for the Visual Arts/ARS, NY. ™ 2002 Marilyn Monroe LLC under license authorized by CMG Worldwide Inc., Indianapolis, IN. www.MarilynMonroe.com. Warhol was obsessed with Hollywood, especially with the false fabric of fame that it created.

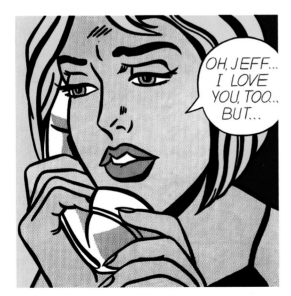

Fig. 15.11 Roy Lichtenstein. *Oh, Jeff . . . I Love You, Too . . . But . . . .* 1964. Oil on magma on canvas, 4′ × 4′. Private collection. © Estate of Roy Lichtenstein. The large size of these paintings mirrors the scale of the Hollywood screen and the texture of the common billboard.

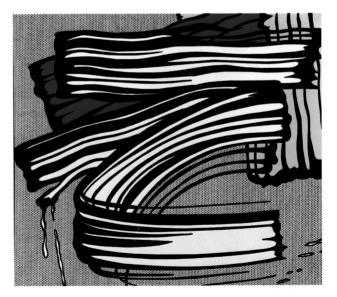

Fig. 15.12 Roy Lichtenstein. *Little Big Painting*. 1965. Oil on synthetic polymer on canvas, 5′ 8″ × 6′ 8″. Purchase, with funds from the Friends of the Whitney Museum of American Art. 66.2. Collection of the Whitney Museum of American Art, NY. This "detail" of an imaginary larger painting is nonetheless a giant in its own right.

Focus

Rosenquist's *F-111*

For Pop artist James Rosenquist the society of the spectacle is above all a society of billboards, which, in fact, he once painted for a living. "Painting," he says, "is probably much more exciting than advertising, so why shouldn't it be done with that power and gusto, with that impact?" The mammoth *F-111* possesses precisely the impact Rosenquist was seeking.

The painting was specifically designed as a wraparound work, like Monet's *Water Lilies* murals, for Rosenquist's first solo exhibition at the Leo Castelli Gallery in New York, where it filled all four walls of the space. It depicts an F-111 fighter bomber at actual scale, "flying," in Rosenquist's words, "through the flack of an economy." In 1964, when Rosenquist was at work on the piece, the F-111, although still in its planning stages, was understood to be obsolete. Nevertheless, production

James Rosenquist. *F-111*. 1965. Oil on canvas with aluminum, 23 sections, 10′ × 86′. Purchase. Gift of Mr. and Mrs. Alex L. Hillman and Lillie P. Bliss Bequest (both by exchange). (00473.96.a-w). Digital Image © The Museum of Modern Art/Licensed by SCALA / Art Resource, NY. © Art James Rosenquist/VAGA Visual Artists Galleries & Association, NY.

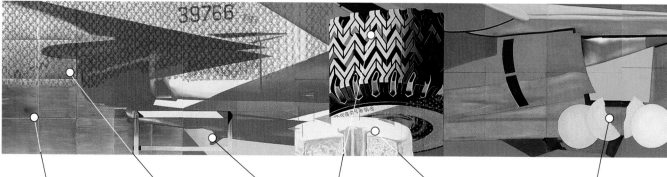

The aluminum panels on this end of the painting would have met up with the strip of aluminum panels at the other end of the painting when installed around the four walls of a gallery. They not only evoke industry, but their reflective quality incorporates viewers into the painting's space, implicating them in the artist's critique of American culture. The scale of the painting makes it impossible to take it all in at once; viewers are always aware that there is more work in their peripheral vision. "I'm interested in contemporary vision," Rosenquist has explained, "the flick of chrome, reflections, rapid associations, quick flashes of light. Bing-bang! Bing-bang!"

The Italian flowered wallpaper, according to Rosenquist, "had to do with atomic fallout."

A runner's hurdle is meant to evoke the arms race.

The Firestone tire, according to Rosenquist, resembles a "crown," becoming a symbol of the supremacy and power of corporate America, the military-industrial complex that Eisenhower warned against. By emphasizing the tire's tread, Rosenquist focuses our attention on the sense of safety that corporate America claimed to provide consumers.

The angel food cake is decorated, stadiumlike, with little pennants listing food additives such as riboflavin and Vitamin D. One even boasts "Food Energy." The chemical manipulation of food is Rosenquist's target here, together with the lack of any real food value in sugar-laden "angel" food.

The three light bulbs can probably best be explained by a comment Rosenquist made in an interview in the *Partisan Review* in 1965: "All the ideas in the whole picture are very divergent, but I think they all seem to go toward some basic meaning . . . [toward] some blinding light, like a bug hitting a light bulb." They also evoke consumer culture and corporations like General Electric or Westinghouse that were also major defense contractors.

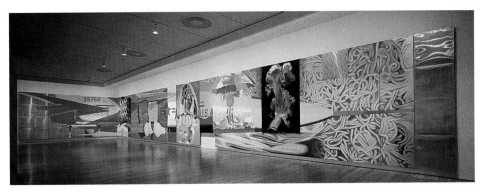

James Rosenquist. *F-111, installation view*. 2000. Oil on canvas with aluminum, 23 sections, 10' × 86'. Gift of Mr. and Mrs. Alex L. Hillman and Lillie P. Bliss Bequest (both by exchange). (473.1996.a-w) The Museum of Modern Art, NY. Digital Image. The Museum of Modern Art/Licensed by SCALA / Art Resource, NY. Art © Estate of James Rosenquist/VAGA, NY. For its MoMA exhibition in 2000, the painting turned one corner to fill two walls, but did not wrap around the viewer on four walls as originally exhibited.

continued on it, by and large to keep those working on it employed and General Dynamics, the company responsible for it, afloat. It is precisely the military-industrial complex about which President Eisenhower had warned, its pervasiveness throughout American consumer culture, that Rosenquist's painting addresses. As the Vietnam War escalated, and the painting traveled to eight museums in Europe, the painting became more generally associated with the antiwar movement. It returned to the United States in 1968, and remains on display at New York's Museum of Modern Art.

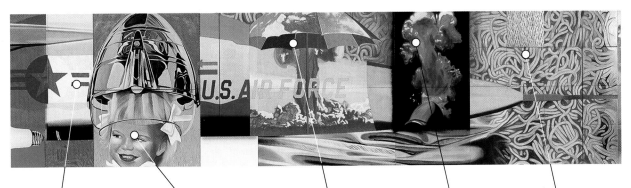

The bars of the Air Force logo, on each side of the hairdryer, function like equal signs in the picture.

"The little girl," Rosenquist says, "was the pilot under a hairdryer." She is also a figure, he says, for "a generation removed, the post-Beat young people. They're not afraid of atomic war and think that sort of attitude is passé, that it won't occur." Thus she smiles happily, her face turned away from the mushroom cloud behind her. She also represents consumer economy, the idea of female beauty, and female passivity in general—the opposite of the phallic jet fighter.

The umbrella, like the Italian flowered wallpaper, is meant to suggest both the defense umbrella of national security and atomic fallout, from which it offers no real protection.

"The swimmer gulping air," Rosenquist explains, "was like searching for air during an atomic holocaust." Visually it echoes the atomic mushroom cloud to its left.

A plate of Franco-American canned spaghetti lies behind the nose of the plane like a pile of entrails. "Franco-American" also suggests French and American involvement in the Vietnam War.

The Ongoing Fight for Civil Rights

In 1954, the U.S. Supreme Court ruled that racially segregated schools violated the Constitution. In *Brown v. Board of Education*, the Court found that it was not good enough to provide "separate but equal" schools. "Separate educational facilities are inherently unequal," the Court declared, and were in violation of the Fourteenth Amendment to the Constitution's guarantee of equal protection. The Justices called on states with segregated schools to desegregate "with all deliberate speed."

Within a week, the state of Arkansas announced that it would seek to comply with the court's ruling. The state had already

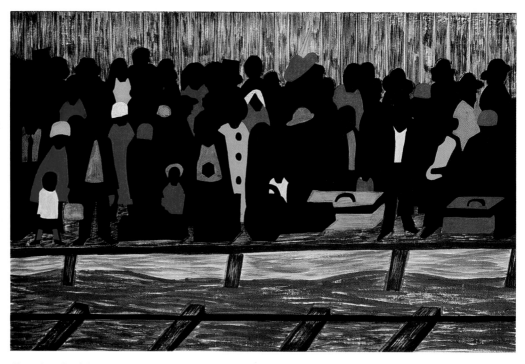

Fig. 15.13 Jacob Lawrence, *The Migration of the Negro,* Panel no. 60: *And the migrants kept coming,* 1940–1941. Casein tempera on hardboard panel, 18″ × 12″. Gift of Ms. David M. Levy. (28.1942.30). Digital Image © The Museum of Modern Art/Licensed by SCALA/Art Resource, NY. © ARS Artists Rights Society, NY. Lawrence's rhythmic repetition of color and form with its abrupt shifts in the direction of line and mass visually imitates the movement of what is perhaps the greatest expression of the Harlem Renaissance—jazz.

desegregated its state university and its law school. Now it was time to desegregate elementary and secondary schools. The plan was for Little Rock Central High School to open its doors to African-American students in the fall of 1957. But on September 2, the night before school was to start, Governor Orval Faubus ordered the state's National Guard to surround the high school and prevent any black students from entering. Faubus claimed he was trying to prevent violence. The nine black students who were planning to attend classes were all turned away by the Guard. Nearly three weeks later, after a federal injunction ordered Faubus to remove the Guard, the nine finally entered Central High School. Little Rock citizens then launched a campaign of verbal abuse and intimidation to prevent the black students from remaining in school. Finally, President Eisenhower ordered 1,000 paratroopers and 10,000 National Guardsmen to Little Rock, and on September 25, Central High School was officially desegregated. Nevertheless, chaperoned throughout the year by the National Guard, the nine black students were spit at and reviled every day, and none of them returned to school the following year.

By April 1963, the focal point of racial tension and strife in the United States had shifted to Birmingham, Alabama. In protest over desegregation orders, the city had closed its parks and public golf courses. In retaliation, the

black community called for a boycott of Birmingham stores. The city responded by halting the distribution of food normally given to the city's needy families. In this progressively more heated atmosphere, the Southern Christian Leadership Conference (SCLC), led by the Reverend Martin Luther King, Jr. (1929–1968), decided Birmingham would be their battlefield. In the spring of 1963, groups of protesters, gathering first at local churches, descended on the city's downtown both to picket businesses that continued to maintain "separate but equal" practices, such as different fitting rooms for blacks and whites in clothing stores, and to take seats at "whites only" lunch counters. The city's police chief, Bull Connor, responded by threatening to arrest anyone marching on the downtown area. On April 6, 50 marchers were arrested. The next day, 600 marchers gathered, and police confronted them with clubs, attack dogs, and the fire department's new water hoses, which, they bragged, could rip the bark off a tree. But day after day, the marchers kept coming, their ranks swelling. A local judge issued an injunction banning the marches, but on April 12, the Reverend Martin Luther King led a march of 50 people in defiance of the injunction. Crowds gathered in anticipation of King's arrest, and, in fact, he was quickly taken into custody and placed in solitary confinement in the Birmingham jail.

The Harlem Renaissance and the Roots of the Movement

Martin Luther King's struggle in Birmingham was the culmination of an ongoing fight to desegregate American society. Soon after Reconstruction, the period immediately following the Civil War, Southern states passed a group of laws that effectively established a racial caste system that relegated black Americans to second-class status and institutionalized segregation. In the South, the system was known as Jim Crow. In the years before the outbreak of World War I, nearly 90 percent of all African Americans lived in the South, three-quarters of them in the rural South. But lured by a huge demand for labor in the North once the War began, and impoverished after a boll weevil infestation ruined the cotton crop, blacks flooded into the North. In the course of a mere 90 days early in the 1920s, 12,000 African Americans left Mississippi alone. An average of 200 left Memphis every night. Many met with great hardship, but there was wealth to be had as well, and anything seemed better than life under Jim Crow in the South.

This Great Migration, as it was called, was later celebrated in a series of 60 paintings by the African-American artist Jacob Lawrence (1917–2000) (Fig. **15.13**), who moved to Harlem in 1924 at the age of seven, into a cultural community so robust, and so new, that the era has come to be known as the Harlem Renaissance. Lawrence was trained as a painter at the Harlem Art Workshop. "Without the black community in Harlem, I wouldn't have become an artist," he later said. Lawrence painted his *Migration* series when he was just 23 years old. It won him immediate fame. In 1942, the Museum of Modern Art in New York and the Phillips Collection in Washington, D.C., each bought 30 panels. That same year Lawrence became the first black artist represented by a prestigious New York gallery—the Downtown Gallery.

"The New Negro" Perhaps the first self-conscious expression of the Harlem Renaissance took place at a dinner party, on March 21, 1924, hosted by Charles S. Johnson (1893–1956) of the National Urban League. The League was dedicated to promoting civil rights and helping black Americans address the economic and social problems they encountered as they resettled in the urban North. At Johnson's dinner, young writers from Harlem were introduced to New York's white literary establishment. A year later, the *Survey Graphic*, a national magazine dedicated to sociology, social work, and social analysis, produced an issue dedicated exclusively to Harlem. The issue, subtitled *Harlem: Mecca of the New Negro*, was edited by Alain Leroy Locke (1886–1954), an African-American professor of philosophy at Howard University in Washington, D.C. He was convinced that a new era was dawning for black Americans, and wrote a powerful introduction to a new anthology. In his essay, sometimes referred to as the manifesto of the New Negro Movement, Locke argued that Harlem was the center of this new arena of creative expression (**Reading 15.4**):

> **READING 15.4** **Alain Locke,** ***The New Negro*** **(1925)**
>
> [T]here arises a] consciousness of acting as the advance-guard of the African peoples in their contact with Twentieth Century civilization . . . [and] the sense of a mission of rehabilitating the race in world esteem from that loss of prestige for which the fate and conditions of slavery have so largely been responsible. Harlem, as we shall see, is the center of both these movements. . . . The pulse of the Negro world has begun to beat in Harlem. . . . The New Negro . . . now becomes a conscious contributor and lays aside the status of beneficiary and ward for that of a collaborator and participant in American civilization. The great social gain in this is the releasing of our talented group from the arid fields of controversy and debate to the productive fields of creative expression. . . . And certainly, if in our lifetime the Negro should not be able to celebrate his full initiation into American democracy, he can at least, on the warrant of these things, celebrate the attainment of a significant and satisfying new phase of group development, and with it a spiritual Coming of Age.

In Locke's view, each ethnic group in America had its own identity, which it was entitled to protect and promote, and this claim to cultural identity need not conflict with the claim to American citizenship. Locke further emphasized that the spirit of the young writers who were a part of this anthology would drive this new Harlem-based movement by focusing on the African roots of black art and music, but they would, in turn, contribute mightily to a new, more inclusive American culture.

Langston Hughes and the Poetry of Jazz As the young poet Langston Hughes (1902–1967) later put it, "Negro was in vogue." Hughes was among the new young poets that Locke published in *The New Negro*, and the establishment publishing house, Knopf, would publish his book of poems, *Weary Blues*, in 1926. Twenty-two years of age in 1924, Hughes had gone to Paris seeking a freedom he could not find at home. He was soon writing poems inspired by the jazz rhythms he was hearing played by the African-American bands in the clubs where he worked as a busboy and dishwasher. The music's syncopated rhythms can be heard in poems such as "Jazz Band in a Parisian Cabaret" (**Reading 15.5**):

> **READING 15.5** **from Langston Hughes, "Jazz Band in a Parisian Cabaret" (1925)**
>
> *Play that thing,*
> Jazz band!
> Play it for the lords and ladies,
> For the dukes and counts,

For the whores and gigolos,
For the American millionaires,
And the school teachers
Out for a spree.
. . . . . .
You know that tune
That laughs and cries at the same time
. . . . . .
May I?
Mais oui,
Mein Gott!
Parece una rumba.
Play it, jazz band!

African Americans like Hughes had been drawn to Paris by reports of black soldiers who had served in World War I, in the so-called Negro divisions, the 92nd and 93rd infantries. Jazz itself was introduced to the French by Lieutenant Jimmy Europe, whose 815th Pioneer Infantry band played in city after city across the country. They had experienced something they never had in the United States—total acceptance by people with white skin. Paris presented itself after the war as the new land of freedom—and opportunity. But Harlem, largely because of the efforts of Johnson and Locke, soon replaced Paris in the African-American imagination.

In Harlem, Hughes quickly became one of the most powerful voices. His poems narrate the lives of his people, capturing the inflections and cadences of their speech. In fact, the poems celebrate, most of all, the inventiveness of African-American culture, especially the openness and ingenuity of its music and language. Hughes had come to understand that his cultural identity rested not in the grammar and philosophy of white culture, but in the vernacular expression of the American black, which he could hear in its music (the blues and jazz especially) and its speech.

The Blues and Jazz

By the time of the Great Migration, jazz had established itself as the music of African Americans. So much did the music seem to define all things American that the novelist F. Scott Fitzgerald (1896–1940) entitled a collection of short stories published in 1922 *Tales of the Jazz Age*, and the name stuck. By the end of the 1920s, jazz was *the* American music, and it was almost as popular in Paris and Berlin as it was in New York, Chicago, and New Orleans. It originated in New Orleans in the 1890s, probably the most racially diverse city in America, particularly in the ragtime piano music of Scott Joplin and others. But it had deep roots as well in the blues.

The Blues If syncopated rhythm is one of the primary characteristics of jazz, another is the **blue note**. Blue notes are slightly lower or flatter than conventional pitches. In jazz,

blues instrumentalists or singers commonly "bend" or "scoop" a blue note—usually the third, fifth, or seventh notes of a given scale—to achieve heightened emotional effects. Such effects were first established in the blues proper, a form of song that originated among enslaved black Americans and their descendants.

The **blues** are by definition laments bemoaning loss of love, poverty, or social injustice, and they contributed importantly to the development of jazz. The standard blues form consists of three sections of four bars each. Each of these sections corresponds to the single line of a three-line stanza, the first two lines of which are the same. In his 1925 poem "Weary Blues," Langston Hughes describes listening to a blues singer in a Harlem club (**Reading 15.6**):

READING 15.6   **from Langston Hughes, "Weary Blues" (1925)**

Droning a drowsy syncopated tune,
Rocking back and forth to a mellow croon,
I heard a Negro play.
Down on Lenox Avenue the other night
By the pale dull pallor of an old gas light
He did a lazy sway . . .
He did a lazy sway . . .
. . . . . .
Thump, thump, thump, went his foot on the floor.
He played a few chords then he sang some more—
"I got the Weary Blues
And I can't be satisfied.
I got the Weary Blues
And I can't be satisfied.
I ain't happy no mo'
And I wish that I had died."

The last lines are the standard blues form (expanded by Hughes to six instead of three lines for the sake of his own poetic meter).

Dixieland and Louis Armstrong in Chicago The bands that played around 1910 in the red-light district of New Orleans, the legendary Storeyville, quickly established a standard practice. A "front line," consisting of trumpet (or cornet), clarinet, and trombone, was accompanied by banjo (later guitar), piano, bass, and drums. In **Dixieland jazz**, as it came to be known, the trumpet carried the main melody, the clarinet played off against it with a higher countermelody, while the trombone played a simpler, lower tune. The most popular forms of Dixieland were the standard 12-bar blues and a 32-bar AABA form. The latter consists of four eight-measure sections. Generally speaking, the trumpet plays the basic tune for the first 32 measures of the piece, then the band plays variations on the tune in a series of solo or collective improvisations keeping to the 32-bar format. Each 32-bar section is called a "chorus."

When Storeyville was shut down in 1917 (on orders from the U.S. Navy, whose sailors' discipline was believed threatened by its existence), many of the bands that had played in the district joined the Great Migration and headed north. Among them was trumpeter Louis Armstrong (1900–1971), who arrived in Chicago in 1922 to play for Joe Oliver's Creole Jazz Band. The pianist and composer Lil Hardin (1898–1971) was the pianist and arranger for Oliver's band, and the two were married in 1924. Soon, Armstrong left Oliver's band to play on his own. He formed two studio bands composed of former New Orleans colleagues, the Hot Five and the Hot Seven, with whom he made a series of ground-breaking recordings. One, *Hotter Than That* (see **CD-Track 15.3**), written by Hardin and recorded in 1927, is based on a 32-bar form over which the performers improvise. In the third chorus, Armstrong sings in nonsense syllables, a method known as **scat**. This is followed by another standard form of jazz band performance, a **call-and-response** chorus between Armstrong and guitarist Lonnie Johnson, the two imitating one another as closely as possible on their two different instruments.

Swing: Duke Ellington at the Cotton Club The same year that Armstrong recorded *Hotter Than That*, Duke Ellington, born Edward Kennedy Ellington in Washington, D.C. (1899–1974), began a five-year engagement at Harlem's Cotton Club. The Cotton Club itself was owned by a gangster who used it as an outlet for his "Madden's #1 Beer," which, like all alcoholic beverages, was banned after National Prohibition was introduced in 1920. The Club's name was meant to evoke leisurely plantation life for its "white only" audience who came to listen to its predominantly black entertainers.

Ellington had formed his first band in New York in 1923. His 1932 *It Don't Mean a Thing (If It Ain't Got That Swing)* (see **CD-Track 15.4**) introduced the term **swing** to jazz culture. (A particularly clear example of a "blue note" can be heard, incidentally, on the first "ain't" of the first chorus of *It Don't Mean a Thing*.) Swing is characterized by big bands—as many as 15 to 20 musicians, including up to five saxophones (two altos, two tenors, and a baritone)—resulting in a much bigger sound. Its rhythm depends on subtle avoidance of downbeats with the solo instrument attacking the beat either just before or just after it.

By the time Ellington began his engagement at the Cotton Club, commercial radio was seven years old, and many thousands of American homes had a radio. Live radio broadcasts from the Cotton Club brought Ellington national fame, and he was widely imitated throughout the 1930s by bands who toured the country. These included bands led by clarinetist Benny Goodman, soon known as "the King of Swing"; trumpeter Harry James; trombonist Glenn Miller; trombonist Tommy Dorsey; pianist Count Basie; and clarinetist Artie Shaw. These bands also featured vocalists, and they introduced the country to Frank Sinatra, Bing Crosby, Perry Como, Sarah Vaughan, Billie Holiday, Peggy Lee, Doris Day, Rosemary Clooney, and Ella Fitzgerald.

The Winds of Change

The sense of ethnic pride and identity developed in the Harlem Renaissance—in its literature and music—was, then, a key contributor to the success of the civil rights movement in the 1960s. But so was the active involvement of young people yearning for change, especially in Birmingham. Alabama, where in April 1963 Martin Luther King had been jailed.

Soon after King's incarceration, the situation in Birmingham had worsened. A local disc jockey urged the city's African-American youth to attend a "big party" at Kelly Ingram Park, across from the 16th Street Baptist Church. It was no secret that the "party" was to be a mass demonstration. At least 1,000 youth gathered to face the police, most of them teenagers but some as young as seven or eight years old. As the chant of "Freedom, Freedom NOW!" rose from the crowd, the Birmingham police closed in with their dogs, ordering them to attack those who did not flee.

Police wagons and squad cars were quickly filled with arrested juveniles, and as the arrests continued, the police used school buses to transport over 600 children and teenagers to jail. By the next day, the entire nation—in fact, the entire world—had come to know Birmingham Police Chief Bull Connor, as televised images documented his dogs attacking children and his fire hoses literally washing them down the streets.

The youth returned, with reinforcements, over the next few days. By May 6, over 2,000 demonstrators were in jail, and police patrol cars were pummeled with rocks and bottles whenever they entered black neighborhoods. As the crisis mounted, secret negotiations between the city and the protestors resulted in change: Within 90 days, all lunch counters, restrooms, department store fitting rooms, and drinking fountains would be open to all, black and white alike. The 2,000 people under arrest would be released.

It was a victory, but Birmingham remained uneasy. On Sunday, September 15, a dynamite bomb exploded in the basement of the 16th Street Baptist Church, a center for many civil rights rallies and meetings, killing four girls—one 11-year-old and three 14-year-olds. As news of the tragedy spread, riots and fires broke out throughout the city and two more teenagers were killed.

The tragedy drew many moderate whites into the civil rights movement. Popular culture had put them at the ready. In June 1963, the folk-rock trio Peter, Paul and Mary released "Blowin' in the Wind," their version of the song that Bob Dylan (1941–) had written in April 1962. The Peter, Paul and Mary record sold 300,000 copies in two weeks. The song famously ends:

> How many years can some people exist,
> before they're allowed to be free?
> How many times can a man turn his head,
> Pretending he just doesn't see?
> The answer, my friend, is blowin' in the wind,
> The answer is blowin' in the wind.

At the March on Washington later that summer—an event organized by the same A. Philip Randolph who had conceived of a similar event over 20 years earlier, this time to promote passage of the Civil Rights Act—Peter, Paul and Mary performed the song live before 250,000 people, the largest gathering of its kind to that point in the history of the United States. Not many minutes later, Martin Luther King delivered his famous "I have a dream" speech to the same crowd. The trio's album, *In the Wind*, released in October, quickly rose to number one on the charts. The winds of change were blowing across the country.

The Feminist Movement

At the same time that the antiwar and civil rights movements galvanized political consciousness among both men and women, "the Pill" was introduced in the early 1960s. As women gained control over their own reproductive functions, they began to express the sexual freedom that men had always taken for granted. The struggle for gender equality in the United States found greater and greater expression throughout the 1960s until, by the early 1970s, a full-blown feminist era emerged.

The Theoretical Framework: Betty Friedan and NOW

In 1963, a freelance journalist and mother of three, Betty Friedan (1921–2006), published *The Feminine Mystique*. In many ways, hers was an argument with Freud, or at least with the way Freud had been understood, or misunderstood. While she admits that "Freudian psychology, with its emphasis on freedom from a repressive morality to achieve sexual fulfillment, was part of the ideology of women's emancipation," she is aware that some of Freud's writings had been misused as a tool for the suppression of women. Latent in Friedan's analysis, but central to the feminist movement, is her understanding that in Freud, as in Western discourse as a whole, the term "woman" is tied, in terms of its construction as a word, to man (its medieval root is "*wifman,*" or "wife [of] man"). It is thus a contested term that does not refer to the biological female but to the sum total of all the patriarchal society expects of the female, including behavior, dress, attitude, and demeanor. "Woman," said the feminists, is a cultural construct, not a biological one. In *The Feminine Mystique*, Friedan rejected modern American society's cultural construction of women. But she could not, in the end, reject the word "woman" itself. Friedan would go on to become one of the founders of the National Organization for Women (NOW), the primary purpose of which was to advance women's rights and gender equity in the workplace. In this, she dedicated herself to changing, in American culture, her society's understanding of what "woman" means.

Feminist Poetry

The difficulties that women faced in determining an identity outside the patriarchal construction of "woman" became, in the 1960s, one of the chief subjects of poetry by women, particularly in the work of the poets Anne Sexton (1928–1974), Sylvia Plath (1932–1963), and Adrienne Rich (1929–).

Sexton's work is exemplary. She was an affluent housewife and mother, living in a house with a sunken living room and a backyard swimming pool in the Boston suburb of Weston, Massachusetts. But she was personally at odds with her life, and as her husband saw his formerly dependent wife become a celebrity, their marriage dissolved into a fabric of ill will, discord, and physical abuse. The poem with which she opened most readings, the ecstatically witty "Her Kind," published in 1960 in her first book of poems, *To Bedlam and Part Way Back*, captures the sense of independence that defined her from the beginning (**Reading 15.7**):

READING 15.7   **Anne Sexton, "Her Kind" (1960)**

I have gone out, a possessed witch
haunting the black air, braver at night;
dreaming evil, I have done my hitch
over the plain houses, light by light:
lonely thing, twelve-fingered, out of mind.
A woman like that is not a woman, quite.
I have been her kind.

I have found the warm caves in the woods,
filled them with skillets, carvings, shelves,
closets, silks, innumerable goods;
fixed the suppers for the worms and the elves:
whining, rearranging the disaligned.
A woman like that is misunderstood.
I have been her kind.

I have ridden in your cart, driver,
waved my nude arms at villages going by,
learning the last bright routes, survivor
where your flames still bite my thigh
and my ribs crack where your wheels wind.
A woman like that is not ashamed to die.
I have been her kind.

Feminist Art

Despite the advances made by women in the arts in the 1960s, real change was slow in coming. Although in 1976 approximately 50 percent of the professional artists in the United States were women, only 15 in 100 one-person shows in New York's prestigious galleries were devoted to work by women. Eight years later, the Museum of Modern Art reopened its enlarged facilities with a show entitled *An International Survey of Painting and Sculpture*. Of the 168 artists represented, only 13 were women.

Faced with statistics such as these, in 1985 an anonymous group of women that called themselves the Guerrilla Girls began hanging posters in New York City (Fig. **15.14**). They listed the specific galleries who represented less than one woman out of every ten men. Another poster asked: "How

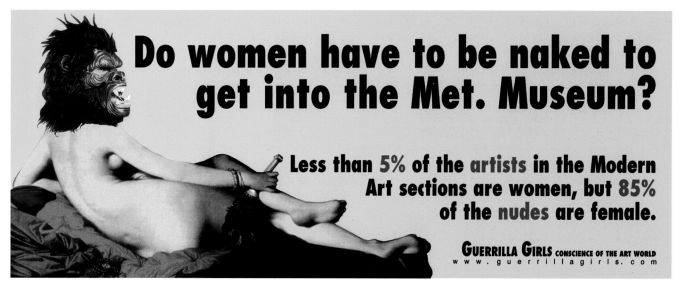

Fig. 15.14 Guerrilla Girls. *Do women have to be naked to get into the Met. Museum?* 1989. Poster. © 1989, 1995 by the Guerrilla Girls, Inc. The figure is a parody of Jean-Auguste-Dominique Ingres's 1814 neoclassical painting, *La Grand Odalisque*, in the collection of the Louvre, Paris.

Many Women Had One-person Exhibitions at NYC Museums Last Year?" The answer:

Guggenheim	0
Metropolitan	0
Modern	1
Whitney	0

One of the Guerrilla Girls' most daring posters was distributed in 1989. It asked, "When racism & sexism are no longer fashionable, what will your art collection be worth?" It listed 67 women artists and pointed out that a collection of works by all of them would be worth less than the art auction value of any *one* painting by a famous living male artist. Its suggestion that the value of the male artist's work might be drastically inflated struck a chord with many.

By the late 1990s, the situation had changed somewhat. Many more women were regularly exhibited in New York galleries, and more major retrospectives were given their work. But, internationally especially, women continued to get short shrift. Where a retrospective by a major male artist—Robert Rauschenberg, for instance—might originate in New York at the Guggenheim and travel to international venues around the world, most retrospectives of women artists remained much more modest—a single nontraveling show at, say, the New Museum in New York or the Los Angeles County Museum of Art.

The Postmodern Era

In 1966, architect Robert Venturi (1925–) issued a "Gentle Manifesto," which offered his criteria for a new eclectic approach to architecture that abandoned the clean and simple geometries championed by Bauhaus architect Mies van der Rohe (see chapter 14), whose mantra "less is more"

described the refined austerity of the modernist glass-walled buildings he designed. Venturi argued for the opposite:

> An architecture of complexity and contradiction has a special obligation toward the whole. . . . It must embody the difficult unity of inclusion rather than the easy unity of exclusion. More is not less.

In their seminal 1972 book *Learning from Las Vegas*, architects Venturi, Denise Scott Brown (1931–), and Steven Izenour (1940–2001) put it simply: "Although its buildings suggest a number of historical styles," they write,

> its urban spaces owe nothing to historical space. Las Vegas space is neither contained and enclosed like medieval space nor classically balanced and proportioned like Renaissance space nor swept up in a rhythmically ordered movement like Baroque space, nor does it flow like Modern space around freestanding urban space makers.
>
> It is something else again. But what? Not chaos, but a new spatial order. . . . Las Vegas space is so different from the docile spaces for which our analytical and conceptual tools were evolved that we need new concepts and theories to handle it.

If anything, since *Learning from Las Vegas* was first written, the collision of historical styles and commercial architecture in Las Vegas has become more pronounced. New York-New York, an enormous hotel and casino, with over 2,000 guest rooms, replicates the New York City skyline. The Luxor Las Vegas is a model of the pyramid and sphinx at Giza. The 24-acre Paris Las Vegas includes replicas of the Eiffel Tower (at 540 feet, more than half as high as the original), the Arc de Triomphe [ark deh tree-OHMF], and Garnier's Opera House. We have come to call the collision of styles and forms epitomized by Las Vegas **postmodernism**.

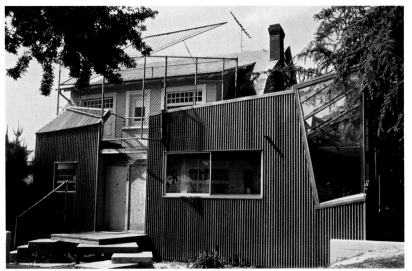
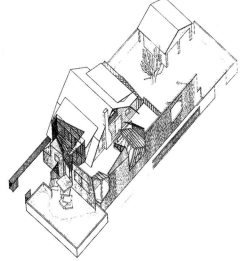

Fig. 15.15 Frank Gehry. Residence, Santa Monica, California, and axonometric rendering. 1977–1978. Photograph by Tim Street-Porter. Gehry's neighbors were not at all pleased with his new house, but Gehry claims that he was trying to use "materials that were consistent with the neighborhood." He explains: "When I built that house, that neighborhood was full of trailer trucks in the back yards, and often on the lawn. A lot of old, aging Cadillacs and big cars on blocks on the front lawn, people fixing their cars. A lot of chain link fences, corrugated metal; I know they didn't use it like I did, and that's the difference."

Architects and builders exemplify the affluent nomads of the new postmodern society. They, like the people they design and build for, inhabit the "world metropolis," a vast interconnected fabric of places where people do business, and between which they travel, work, and seek meaning. Travel, in fact, accounts for nearly 10 percent of world trade and global employment. As nearly 700 million people travel internationally each year, a half million hotel rooms are built annually across the globe to house them.

Today's architect works in the culture first introduced by the Sony Walkman and carried forward by the iPod and iPhone. These are technologies "designed for movement," as cultural historian Paul du Gay describes their function, "for mobility, for people who are always out and about, for traveling light . . . part of the required equipment of the modern 'nomad.'" And architects are also responsible for helping to provide the most elusive of qualities in the postmodern world—a sense of meaning and a sense of place.

Postmodern Architecture: The Example of Frank Gehry

Perhaps the dean of postmodern architecture is Frank Gehry [GHEH-ree] (1929–), whose own home in Los Angeles (Fig. 15.15) is, on the surface, a collision or eruption of parts. In the mid-1970s, still a young and relatively unknown architect, Gehry and his wife moved into a Santa Monica house that fulfilled their main criterion—it was affordable. "I looked at the old house that my wife found for us," Gehry recalls, "and I thought it was kind of a dinky little cutesy-pie house. We had to do something to it. I couldn't live in it. . . . Armed with very little money, I decided to build a new house around the old house and try to maintain a tension between the two." The

new house surrounding the old one is deliberately unfinished, almost industrial. A corrugated metal wall, chain-link fencing, plywood walls, and concrete block surround the original pink frame house with its asbestos shingles. The surrounding wall, with randomly slanted lines and angled protrusions, thus separates not only the "outside" house from the house within, but the entire structure from its environment. The tension established by Gehry between industrial and traditional materials, between the old house and the almost fortresslike shell of his home's new skin, intentionally creates a sense of unease in viewers (one certainly shared by Gehry's neighbors). For Gehry, confronting the "difficult whole" Venturi speaks about is the very project of architecture. Disturbingly unharmonious, Gehry's architecture refuses to be taken for granted. It draws attention to itself *as* architecture.

Gehry's sculptural use of materials—note the steel and wire fencing that extends over the roof behind the front door, which would be "decorative" or "ornamental" were it not so mundane—has continued throughout his career, culminating in his design for the Guggenheim Museum in Bilbao [bill-BOW ("bow" as in "now")], Spain (Fig. 15.16). Working on the models with the Catia computer program originally developed for the French aerospace industry, Gehry notes, "You forget about it as architecture, because you're focused on this sculpting process." The museum itself is enormous—260,000 square feet, including 19 gallery spaces connected by ramps and metal bridges—and clad in titanium, its undulating forms evoking sails as it sits majestically along the river's edge in the Basque port city. But it is the museum's discontinuity with the old town and the surrounding countryside (Fig. 15.17) that most defines its postmodern spirit. It makes Bilbao, as a city, a more "difficult whole," but a more interesting one, too.

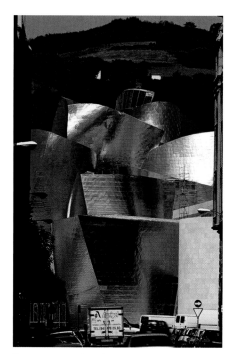

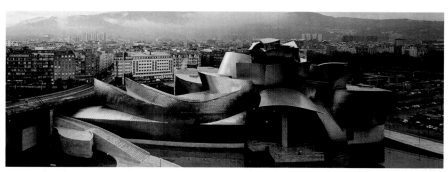

Fig. 15.17 Frank Gehry. Guggenheim Museum Bilbao. 1997. Photo: David Heald. © The Solomon R. Guggenheim Foundation, NY.

Fig. 15.16 Frank Gehry. Guggenheim Museum Bilbao. 1997. Photo: David Heald. © The Solomon R. Guggenheim Foundation, NY. The official description of the building begins: "The building itself is an extraordinary combination of interconnecting shapes. Orthogonal blocks in limestone contrast with curved and bent forms covered in titanium. Glass curtain walls provide the building with the light and transparency it needs . . . the sinuous stone, glass, and titanium curves were designed with the aid of computers. The glass walls were made and installed to protect the works of art from heat and radiation. The half-millimeter thick 'fish-scale' titanium panels covering most of the building are guaranteed to last one hundred years."

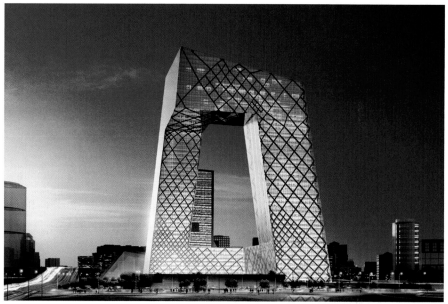

Fig. 15.18 Rem Koolhaas. OMA, New Headquarters, Central Chinese Television CCTV, Beijing, China, competition drawing. 2002. "The irregular grid on the building's facade," according to OMA, "is an expression of the forces traveling throughout its structure," the web of communication that both feed into and emanate from the building.

Architecture in postmodern culture is largely a question of creating distinctive buildings, markers of difference like the Guggenheim Museum Bilbao that stand out in the vast sameness of the "world metropolis," so that travelers feel they have arrived at someplace unique, someplace identifiable. In this climate, contemporary architecture is highly competitive. Most major commissions are competitions, and most cities compete for the best, most distinctive architects. Gehry's design for the Guggenheim in Bilbao was, in fact, stunningly successful, drawing critical raves, massive numbers of visitors, and even concerns that the architecture was so noteworthy that it overshadowed the priceless art within the structure.

East/West, North/South:
Power and Appropriation

Asian cities are particularly challenging to postmodern architects. Unlike American cities, where people tend not to live where they work, Asian cities possess a much greater "mix" of functions. Tall buildings rise in the midst of smaller residential structures. Rem Koolhaas [KOOL-hahs] (1944–), a leading urban scholar and professor at Harvard University, has designed one of the most intriguing new projects in Asia—the headquarters of a Chinese television network (Fig. **15.18**), completed for the Beijing Olympics in 2008. Although 750 feet high, the CCTV tower is, in the words of his architectural firm, "a continuous loop of horizontal and vertical sections that establish an urban site rather than point to the sky." But as Koolhaas's Central Chinese Television project makes clear, architecture as it is practiced on a global scale is, like the Roman imperial architecture of nearly two millennia ago, about power (see chapter 3). The Central Chinese Television building was built to be the focus of world attention during the Olympics, and to function as an advertisement for China's economic might.

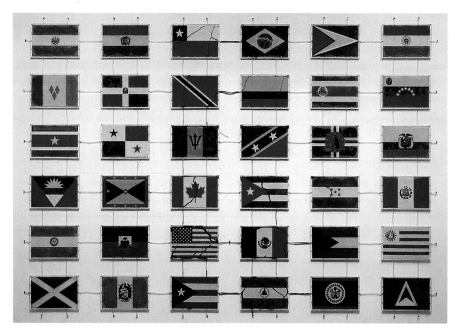

Fig. 15.19 Yukinori Yanagi. *America*. 1994. Ants, colored sand, plastic boxes, plastic tubes, 36 boxes, each 8″ × 12″. Installation view at Museum of Contemporary Art, San Diego, 1994. Collection of artist. "If the travels of the ant show us anything," Yanagi says, "it is that he wanders to resume the task he has been programmed to perform, not to acquire freedom."

America, by Japanese artist Yukinori Yanagi [yah-NAH-ghee] (1959–), is an image of international cross-fertilization (Fig. **15.19**). Creating a grid of plastic boxes, each filled with colored sand in the pattern of a national flag from the nations of North and South America, Yanagi connects each box to the adjacent ones with plastic tubing. When ants were introduced into the system, they immediately began carrying colored sand between flags, transforming and corrupting their original designs. As each flag's integrity is degraded by these "border crossings," a new "cross-cultural" network of multinational symbols and identities began to establish itself. Yanagi's work directly challenges the traditional view that nations are distinct and isolated. Cross-fertilization is everywhere, and every culture is permeable in the age of digital technology.

In *Portrait (Twins)* (Fig. **15.20**), a self-portrait by Japanese photographer Yasumasa Morimura [mor-ih-moo-rah] (1951–),

Continuity & Change
p. 397

Olympia

the artist poses as both Manet's *Olympia* (see Fig. 13.11) and her maid, manipulating the photograph with a computer in the studio, while subverting the idea of ethnic isolationism even more pointedly. On the one hand, he copies the icons of Western culture, but at the same time he undermines them, drawing attention to the fact that the courtesan and her maid share the same identity—they are "twins"—slaves to the dominant (male) forces of Western society. These impersonations place Japanese culture as a whole—and in particular the Japanese male—in the same position, as prostitute and slave to the West.

In Morimura's photograph, transcultural exchange is also a transgendered performance. All boundaries, between East and West, male and female, seem to disintegrate. This blurring of the boundaries in the collision of cultures and multiple identities is epitomized by the controversial painting *The Holy Virgin Mary* by the British-born Nigerian painter Chris Ofili (1968–) (Fig. **15.21**). Ofili portrays the Virgin as a black woman, and surrounding her are *putti* (winged cherubs) with bare bottoms and genitalia cut out of pornographic magazines. Two balls of elephant dung, acquired from the London Zoo, support the painting, inscribed with the words "Virgin" and "Mary," a third clump defining one of her breasts. The son of black African Catholic parents, both of whom were born in Lagos [LAY-goss], Nigeria, and whose first language was Yoruba, Ofili has used this West African culture as a source of inspiration for his art.

The display of sexual organs, especially in representations of female divinities, is common in Yoruba culture, and Ofili's putti are meant to represent modern examples of this indigenous tradition, symbolizing the fertility of the Virgin Mary. As for elephant dung, in 1992, during a trip to Zimbabwe [zim-bah-bway], Ofili was struck by its beauty after it was dried and varnished. He also came to understand it was worshiped as a symbol of fertility in Zimbabwe, and he began to mount his paintings on clumps of dung as a way, he said, "of raising the paintings up from the ground and giving them a feeling that they've come from the earth rather than simply being hung on a wall."

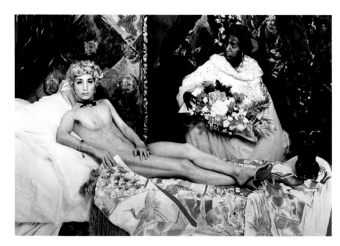

Fig. 15.20 Yasumasa Morimura. *Portrait (Twins)*. 1988. Color photograph, clear medium, 6′10½″ × 10′. NW House, Tokyo. Courtesy of the artist and Luhring Augustine, NY. By cross-dressing—and in this image, un-cross-dressing, Morimura challenges Japanese male gender identity as well.

Fig. 15.21 Chris Ofili. *The Holy Virgin Mary*. 1996. Paper collage, oil paint, glitter, polyester resin, map pins, and elephant dung on linen, 8′ × 6′. The Saatchi Gallery, London. Photo: Diane Bondareff/AP World Wide Photos. While on display in Brooklyn, the painting was smeared with white paint by an angry 72-year-old spectator.

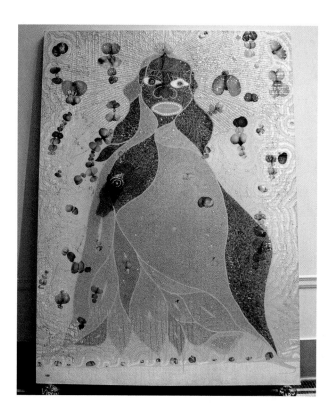

The Holy Virgin Mary artwork thus reflects Ofili's African heritage. But he understood that the association of genitalia and dung with fertility and female divinities would be lost on his Western audience. Indeed it was. When the painting was exhibited at the Brooklyn Museum in late 1999, it provoked a stormy reaction. The Catholic Cardinal in New York called it a blasphemous attack on religion, and the Catholic League called for demonstrations at the Museum. New York's Mayor Rudolph W. Giuliani threatened to cut off the museum's funding as well as evict it from the city-owned building it leased. (He was forced to back down by the courts.) For Ofili, the conflict his painting generated was itself emblematic of the collision of cultures that define his own identity. At the same time, the controversy helped make Ofili even more prominent and improved the marketability of his art. In 2003, he was chosen to represent Great Britain at the Venice Biennale, perhaps the most prominent contemporary global art exhibition.

Similarly, the Pakistani painter Shahzia Sikander (1969–) addresses her heterogeneous background in works such as *Pleasure Pillars* (Fig. **15.22**) by reinventing the traditional genre of miniature painting in a hybrid of styles. Combining her training as a miniature artist in her native Pakistan with her focus on contemporary art during her studies at the Rhode Island School of Design, Sikander explores the tensions inherent in Islam's encounter with the Western world, particularly Christianity, as well as with the neighboring South Asian tradition of Hinduism. In the center of *Pleasure Pillars*, Sikander portrays herself with the spiraling horns of a powerful male ram. Below her head are two bodies, one a Western Venus, the other Devi, the Hindu goddess of fertili-

Continuity & Change
p. 69

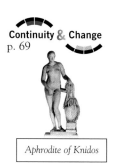

Aphrodite of Knidos

ty, rain, health, and nature, who is said to hold the entire universe in her womb. Between them, two hearts pump blood, a reference to her dual sources of inspiration, East and West. Eastern and Western images of power also inform the image as a lion kills a deer at the bottom left, a direct artistic quote from an Iranian miniature of the Safavid [sah-FAH-weed] dynasty (1501–1736), and at the top, a modern fighter jet roars past.

The cross-fertilization of traditions so evident in Sikander's work, finally, also infuses the art of Latino and Hispanic culture in the United States. From the beginning of the sixteenth century, the Hispanization of Indian culture and the Indianization of Hispanic culture in Latin and South America created a unique cultural pluralism. By the last half of the twentieth century, Latino culture became increasingly Americanized, and an

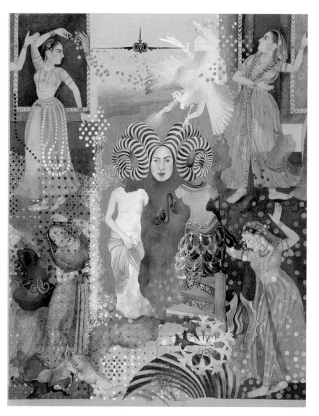

Fig. 15.22 Shahzia Sikander. *Pleasure Pillars*. 2001. Watercolor, dry pigment, vegetable color, tea, and ink on wasli paper, 12″ × 10″. Collection of Amita and Purnendu Chatterjee. Courtesy Sikkema Jenkins & Co., NY. As part of her ongoing investigation of identity, Sikander has taken to wearing the veil in public, something she never did before moving to America, in what she labels "performances" of her Pakistani heritage.

influx of Hispanic immigrants helped Latinize American culture. The situation has been summed up by Puerto Rico-born poet Aurora Levins Morales [moh-RAH-lays] (1954–), in "Child of the Americas" (**Reading 15.8**):

READING 15.8   **Aurora Levins Morales, "Child of the Americas" (1986)**

I am a child of the Americas,
a light-skinned mestiza of the Caribbean,
a child of many diaspora, born into this continent
      at a crossroads.
I am a U.S. Puerto Rican Jew,
a product of the ghettos of New York I have
      never known.
An immigrant and the daughter and granddaughter of
      immigrants.

I speak English with passion: it's the tongue of my
      consciousness,
a flashing knife blade of crystal, my tool, my craft.

I am Caribeña, island grown. Spanish is my flesh,
Ripples from my tongue, lodges in my hips:
the language of garlic and mangoes,
the singing of poetry, the flying gestures of my hands.
I am of Latinoamerica, rooted in the history of my continent:
I speak from that body.

I am not African. Africa is in me, but I cannot return.
I am not taína. Taíno[1] is in me, but there is no way back.
I am not European. Europe lives in me, but I have no
      home there.

I am new. History made me. My first language was spanglish.
I was born at the crossroads
and I am whole.

[1]**Taíno:** The first Native American population encountered by Christopher Columbus (see chapter 9).

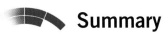 **Summary**

■ **World War II and Its Aftermath** No event underscores the growing decenteredness of twentieth-century culture more than World War II. After the war, Europe was gripped by a profound pessimism. The existential philosophy of Jean-Paul Sartre was a direct response. He argued that the human condition is defined by alienation, anxiety, lack of authenticity, and a sense of nothingness and absurdity, but that this does not abrogate the responsibility to act and create meaning. In America, a note of sincerity was struck by the Abstract Expressionist painters, who applied Sartre's existentialist philosophy to art by defining themselves through a personal struggle with paint and canvas and the gestural energy that struggle revealed. At the same time, a younger, more rebellious generation of artists and musicians like Robert Rauschenberg and John Cage began to explore the possibilities of an art and music of inclusiveness, often generated by chance operations.

■ **Mass Media and the Culture of Consumption** By the 1960s, the attention given events by the media tended to turn them into spectacles. Artists responded by representing American reality in terms of the media—advertising, packaging, television, and comic strips. Pop artists like Andy Warhol, Roy Lichtenstein, Claes Oldenberg, and James Rosenquist represented the commodification of culture in their work and pointed to the marketplace as the dominant cultural force.

■ **The Ongoing Fight for Civil Rights** The civil rights movement gathered momentum when, in 1954, the U.S. Supreme Court ruled in the case of *Brown v. Board of Education* that "separate but equal" educational facilities for whites and blacks violated the Fourteenth Amendment to the Constitution. In 1963, Birmingham, Alabama, became the focal point of the movement, as the Reverend Martin Luther King Jr., galvanized Americans, both black and white, to join the cause. The roots of the civil rights movement go back to the 1920s when the Harlem Renaissance instilled a sense of ethnic pride, identity, and accomplishment among African Americans, evidenced in the art, music, and literature of the era.

■ **The Feminist Movement** Throughout the 1950s and into the 1960s, women artists and writers were equally engaged in asserting their place in an art world from which their work was, if not completely excluded, then demeaned as second rate. By attacking the patriarchal construction of the idea of "woman," these artists sought to change that situation.

■ **The Postmodern Era** The visual confusion of Las Vegas exemplifies a condition of complexity and contradiction that is inclusive, not exclusionary. An appreciation of these contradictions is characteristic of the postmodern attitude. In our increasingly nomadic era, cultures that have been isolated and distinct are now forced to address issues confronting the global community.

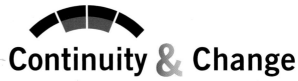
By the end of the nineteenth century, the long-standing cultural traditions of the tribes along the Northwest Coast of the United States and Canada were nearly extinguished. Most of the tribes of the Northwest Coast had ceased to carve *Gyáa'aang*, meaning "man who stands up" in the Haida [HY-duh] language—the tall red cedar poles carved with images and known as "totem poles" by white society (Fig. **15.23**). Oral histories among the Haida culture suggest that the custom of carving the poles is very old, and this is corroborated by descriptions from the earliest white explorers in the region. According to tradition, the Haida learned to carve the poles from a supernatural being. The poles were raised at potlatches, one of the most significant rituals and social occasions among the Haida. The potlatch is a celebration of its host, his social position and his authority. The ceremony was outlawed by the Canadian government in 1883 and remained illegal until 1951, an example of the destructive interference of North American governments on indigenous Americans. Native peoples also began moving from multi-family clan houses into Western style single-family residences in areas that were convenient to employment.

Although some clans secretly continued to celebrate the potlatch between 1900 and World War II, the artistic styles and craftsmanship of the Northwest Coast tribes were almost forgotten. Yet traditions were carried on in small pockets as elders passed on techniques and styles by example to their heirs.

An important stimulus in revitalizing traditional customs in the Northwest occurred in 1970 when tidal erosion uncovered an ancient Makah [mah-

Fig. 15.23 Totem Pole,
probably Tlingit peoples, Pacific Northwest.
Mid-19th century. Wood and pigment. National Museum of Natural History, Smithsonian Institution, Washington, D.C.
The figures on this pole represent, from top to bottom, a man, a bear, and a frog, all symbolic of the authority of the family who erected the pole.

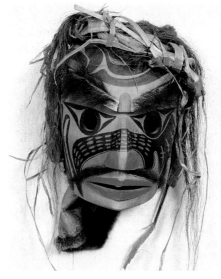

Fig. 15.24 Greg Colfax. *Killer Whaler Mask.*
2003. Cedar, paint, and other materials, 13″ × 15″. Courtesy the Legacy, Ltd., Seattle, WA.
Such a whaler mask might be worn at a potlatch celebrating a successful hunt.

KAW] whaling village on the Olympic Peninsula in Washington, which had been engulfed by a mudslide hundreds of years ago. Over 55,000 artifacts were uncovered, all 300 to 500 years old, and all well preserved. The most spectacular find was a red cedar sculpture, a yard high, carved in the form of a whale's dorsal fin and inlaid with over 700 otter teeth in the shape of a thunderbird holding a snake in its claws. Inspired by the find, a young tribal artist, Greg Colfax, began studying Makah and other Northwest Coast art, using local tribal research resources as well at the University of British Columbia.

Crucial to Colfax's art has been the Makah's identity as a whaling people, and he is especially interested in the ceremonial arts associated with whaling (Fig. **15.24**), which the tribe voluntarily gave up in 1920, recognizing that industrial whaling ships had essentially wiped out the gray whale population. Yet their elders continued to pass on whale-hunting traditions, and the Olympic Peninsula find provided them examples of traditional tools, techniques, and even boats. Nearly 80 years later, when the gray whale population had recovered to about 26,000 whales globally, the Makah Whaling Commission reinstated the hunt, estimating that this population could provide a sustainable population of whales. In May 1999, amid much controversy and protest, the Makah, using traditional boats and techniques, killed their first whale. The Makah are living proof that the forces of globalization can be overcome at a local level and that indigenous traditions, threatened by the leveling forces of the electronic age, can survive. ■

Glossary

a capella Without instrumental accompaniment.

abacus The tabletlike slab that forms the uppermost part of a capital.

absolutism A term applied to strong centralized monarchies that exert royal power over their dominions, usually on the grounds of divine right.

abstract expressionism A style of art practiced by American artists working during and after World War II.

acropolis Literally, "top of the city"; the natural citadel of a Greek city that served as a fortification or religious center.

action painting A term coined by critic Harold Rosenberg to reflect his understanding that the Abstract Expressionist canvas was "no longer a picture, but an event."

adyton The innermost sanctuary of a building housing the place where, in a temple with an oracle, the oracle's message was delivered.

aesthete One who values art for art's sake, for its beauty rather than its content.

aestheticism A devotion to beauty in art.

agency The idea that an object possesses qualities that help to effect change.

agora A large open area in ancient Greek cities that served as public meeting place, marketplace, and civic center.

ambulatory The walkway around the outside of the circular central space of a *central plan* place of worship.

amphora A Greek jar with an egg-shaped body and two curved handles that was used for storing oil or wine.

animal interlace In medieval art, a type of decorative motif featuring elongated animals interlaced into serpentine ribbons.

animal style In medieval art, a style of decoration featuring symmetrical design, interlaced organic and geometric shapes, and animal motifs.

animism The belief that the forces of nature are inhabited by living spirits.

antagonist One who represents an opposing will; an adversary or opponent.

anthropomorphism The practice of investing plants, animals, and natural phenomena with human form or attributes.

antiphonal Musical form of chanting in which one side of the choir responds to the other.

apocalypse The coming of God on the day of judgment.

apse A rounded extension at the end of a Roman *basilica*; the semicircular niche at the end of the nave of a Christian basilica containing the altar.

arcade A succession of arches.

architrave The bottom layer of an *entablature*.

archivolt A curved molding formed by the *voussoirs* making up the arch.

aria An elaborate solo or duet song that expresses the singer's emotions and feelings.

atmospheric perspective This system depends on the observation that the haze in the atmosphere makes distant elements appear less distinct and bluish in color.

atonality The absence of musical key.

atrium An unroofed interior courtyard.

avant-garde Literally, the "advanced guard," this military term is used to describe artists on the cutting edge.

axis An imaginary central line.

bakufu A military-based form of government in Japan that functioned separately from the emperor's government in Kyoto.

ballade In music, a highly dramatic narrative form.

baptistery A building standing in front of the cathedral and used for the Christian rite of baptism.

barrel vault A rounded vault formed when a round arch is extended.

basilica A large, rectangular building with an *apse* at one or both ends.

basso continuo A "continuous bass" line that serves as the supporting accompaniment to the solo or vocal line above it; also, the performers playing that part.

bay The space inside an arch.

bismillah A sacred invocation of the name of Allah.

black figure A style in Greek pottery decoration composed of black figures against a red background.

blank verse Unrhymed iambic pentameter.

blue note A musical note that is slightly lower or flatter than a conventional pitch.

blues A musical genre consisting of laments bemoaning loss of love, poverty, or social injustice; the standard blues form consists of three sections of four bars each.

bodhisattva In Buddhism, a person who refrains from achieving total enlightenment in order to help others achieve buddhahood.

bourgeoisie Middle-class merchants, shopkeepers, and businessmen.

brocateado In the Latin American Baroque, the application of gold leaf to canvas, used especially for creating elaborate brocadelike effects on saints' garments.

buon fresco A type of painting in which pigment is applied to a wet plaster wall.

bushido The code of conduct practiced by the samurai based on fidelity to one's superior, contempt for death, and total selflessness.

buttress A pillar or other support typically built against an exterior wall to brace it and strengthen an interior vault.

caliph A successor of Muhammad.

call-and-response A technique in which two musicians imitate each other as closely as possible on their different instruments.

calligraphy The art of producing artistic, stylized handwriting.

cantata A multimovement musical commentary on the chosen text of the day sung by soloists and chorus accompanied by one or more instruments, most often the organ.

canzona A type of instrumental contrapuntal work increasingly performed in the seventeenth century in church settings.

capital A sculpted block that forms the uppermost part of a column.

carpet page A descriptive term that refers to the resemblance between highly decorated pages of medieval manuscripts and Turkish or Islamic carpets.

cartoon A full-scale drawing used to transfer a design onto another surface.

catharsis Cleansing, purification, or purgation of the soul.

Cavalier The term for the aristocratic royalist supporters of Charles I.

cella The principal interior space of a Greek building, especially a temple; also called a *naos*.

central plan church A circular structure topped by a dome with an ambulatory around the central space.

chador A covering worn by Muslim women that covers the wearer from head to toe and most or all of the face.

chanson de geste A type of French medieval epic poem; literally "song of heroic deeds."

character piece A piano work of relatively small dimension that explores the mood or "character" of a person, emotion, or situation.

chiaroscuro The use of slight gradations of light and dark to create spatial depth and volumetric forms.

chinoiserie A term meaning "all things Chinese."

chivalric code The code of conduct for a knight: courage in battle, loyalty to his lord and peers, and courtesy toward women.

chorale A hymn sung in the vernacular by the entire congregation.

chorus The company of actors who comment on the action in a Greek tragedy.

civilization A culture that possesses the ability to organize itself thoroughly and communicates through written language.

Classical music A style of music that developed in Europe about 1760 and lasted into the nineteenth century as an alternative to and rejection of the Rococo and Baroque; it shares with Greek and Roman art the essential features of symmetry, proportion, balance, formal unity, and, perhaps above all, clarity.

clerestory The topmost zone of the wall of a *basilica* containing windows.

cloisonné A style of decoration in which strips of gold are set on edge to form small cells, which are filled with colored enamel glass paste and fitted with thin slices of semiprecious stones.

cloister A rectangular courtyard in a monastery, typically arcaded and dedicated to contemplation and reflection.

coffer A recessed panel in a ceiling or dome.

collage The technique of pasting cut-out or found elements into the space of the canvas.

column A vertical element that serves as an architectural support, usually consisting of a *capital*, shaft, and base.

combine paintings Works created by Robert Rauschenberg beginning in the mid-1950s that combine all manner of materials.

comédie-ballet A drama that is part *opera* and part ballet.

comedy An amusing or lighthearted play designed to evoke laughter in an audience.

composite view A view that integrates multiple perspectives into a single unified representation.

commune A collective of people gathered together for the common good.

concerto A three-movement secular form of instrumental music.

concert overture A programmatic form that grew out of the eighteenth-century tradition of performing *opera* overtures in the concert hall and that consists of a single movement usually connected in some way with a narrative plot known to the audience.

conch dome A half dome.

contrapposto Italian for "counterpoise;" a term used to describe the weight-shift stance developed by the ancient Greeks in which the sculpted figure seems to twist around its axis as a result of balancing the body over one supporting leg.

conversation piece A work designed to invite discussion of its meaning.

Corinthian order The most elaborate of the Greek architectural orders, distinguished by a *capital* decorated with acanthus leaves.

cosmos In Greek culture, the harmonious and beautiful order of the universe.

counterpoint Two or more independent melodic lines occurring at the same time.

cromlech A circle of *megaliths*, usually surrounding a dolmen or mound.

Cubism An art style developed by Pablo Picasso and Georges Braque, noted for the geometry of its forms, its fragmentation of the object, and its increasing abstraction.

cultural hegemony Cultural domination.

cultural syncretism The intermingling of cultural traditions.

culture The set of values, beliefs, and behaviors that governs or determines a common way of living formed by a group of people and passed on from one generation to the next.

cyclopean masonry Walls made of huge blocks of rough-hewn stone; so called because of myth that a race of monsters known as the Cyclopes built them.

dactyl An element of meter in poetry consisting of one long syllable followed by two short syllables.

dactylic hexameter A poetic verse consisting of six rhythmic units, or feet; each foot is either a *dactyl* or a *spondee*.

Dada A movement that developed among European artists and writers as a result of disillusionment with World War I; its founders claimed that it meant nothing, just as, in the face of war, life itself had come to seem meaningless.

daguerreotype A photographic process developed in the early 1800s that yielded a positive image on a polished metal plate; named after one of its two inventors, Louis-Jacques-Mandé Daguerre.

daimyo Originally any Japanese lord (whether aristocrat or samurai) of a large estate, but by the thirteenth century anyone in control of territory independent even of a shogunate.

deductive reasoning A method that begins with clearly established general principles and proceeds to the establishment of particular truths.

Deism The brand of faith that argues that the basis of belief in God is reason and logic rather than revelation or tradition and, further, does not believe that God is actively involved in the day-to-day workings of the universe.

Deists Those who practice Deism.

deme A division of the Athenian political system composed of small local areas comparable to modern-day precincts or wards.

determinitives In writing, signs used to indicate which category of objects or beings is in question.

dharma In Hinduism, good and righteous conduct that reflects the cosmic moral order underlying all existence.

dialectical method A method of argument that juxtaposes different points of view and seeks to reconcile them.

dialectic method A process of inquiry and instruction characterized by continuous question-and-answer dialogue designed to elicit a clear statement of knowledge supposed to be held implicitly by all reasonable beings.

Divine Office The duty of daily prayer recited by priests and other religious orders.

Dixieland jazz A musical genre in which the trumpet carries the main melody, the clarinet plays off it with a higher countermelody, and the trombone plays a simpler, lower tune.

dogma Prescribed Church doctrine.

domus A traditional Roman house or villa.

Doric order The oldest and simplest of the Greek architectural orders, characterized by a heavy column that stands directly on a temple's *stylobate*.

double entendre A figure of speech in which a phrase can be understood in either of two ways.

dynamics Variations and contrast in force or intensity; more particularly, in music, the notation in a musical score that indicates force (for example, *forte* for loud; *piano* for soft).

ecumenical council A worldwide council of Church leaders.

ego In Freudian psychology, the part of the human mind that manages the *id*, mediating between the id's potentially destructive impulses and the requirements of social life.

elevation The arrangement, proportions, and appearance of a temple foundation, columns, and lintels.

emergence tale A type of narrative that explains beliefs about a people's origins.

empirical method A manner of inquiry that combines inductive reasoning and scientific experimentation.

enchinus The rounded part of a *capital*.

English garden A type of garden design of artificial naturalness that became popular in England beginning in the early 1700s with irregular features and winding walkways.

ennui A French term that denotes both listlessness and a profound melancholy.

entablature The uppermost horizontal elements of an order composed of the cornice, frieze, and *architrave*.

entasis A swelling of the shaft of a column.

epic A long narrative poem in elevated language that follows characters of a high position through a series of adventures, often including a visit to the world of the dead.

epistolary novel A novel made up of a series of epistles, or letters.

epithet A word or phrase that characterizes a person.

equal temperament A system of tuning that consists of dividing the octave into twelve half-steps of equal size.

estate A social rank, namely, the nobility, the clergy, and the common people.

étude In music, a study that addresses particular technical challenges.

eugenics A theory focused on eliminating undesirable and less fit members of society by encouraging the proliferation of intelligent and physically fit humans.

evangelist One who spreads the word of Jesus's life and resurrection.

exedrae A semicircular bay or niche.

existentialism A philosophy that argues that individuals must define the conditions of their own existence and choose to act ethically even in a world without God.

expressionism The attempt to elicit an emotional response in a viewer.

faience A type of earthenware ceramic decorated with glazes.

farce A broadly satirical comedy.

Fauvism A style in art known for its bold application of arbitrary color.

Federal style The term for the Neoclassical style as it appeared in the United States.

feet Rhythmic units in poetry.

feng shui The practice of positioning objects according to certain principles that govern positive and negative effects.

fête galante A gallant and, by extension, amorous celebration or party.

fetish An object believed to have magical powers.

feudal Pertaining to a system of political organization based on ties of allegiance between a lord and those who owed their welfare to him.

feudalism The economic system that prevailed in medieval Europe; it was related to the Roman custom of patronage and was based on land tenure and the relationship between the tenant and the landowner.

fief A piece of land in the *feudal* system.

finial An ornamental top.

flâneur A French version of the aristocratic English dandy. A man-about-town, with no apparent occupation, strolling the city, studying and experiencing it dispassionately.

flying buttress A stone structure that extends from a wall and employs an arch to focus the strength of the buttress's support at the top of the wall.

foot A rhythmic unit in poetry.

foreshortening A technique used to suggest that forms are sharply receding.

framing tale A narrative device that allows a writer to unite different tales under an overarching narrative umbrella.

free organum A type of *polyphony* in which the second voice moves in contrary motion to the bass chant.

French garden A style of formal garden that is characterized by a methodical, geometrical design.

frottola A musical form that usually consists of three parts, with the melody in the highest register.

fugue A contrapuntal work in which a musical theme is played by a series of musical lines, each in turn, until all the lines are playing at once.

genre scene A painting that depicts events from everyday life.

geocentric Earth-centered.

Gesamtkunstwerk A total work of art, one that synthesizes music, drama, poetry, gesture, architecture, and painting.

glazing The building up of color with many layers of transparent oil paint.

Golden Mean Philosophically, the middle ground between any two extremes of behavior.

Golden Section Mathematically, the most beautiful of all proportions, a ratio of approximately 8:5, or, more precisely, 1.618:1.

Gothic A style of architecture and decoration prevalent in the twelfth through the fifteenth centuries in northern Europe, where, it was believed, Classical traditions had been destroyed by Germanic invaders called Goths.

Greek cross A cross in which the upright and transverse shafts are of equal length and intersect at their middles.

Gregorian chant A type of liturgical chant popularized during the time of Charlemagne and still widely used until the twentieth century.

groin vault A vault formed when two *barrel vaults* meet one another at a right angle.

groundling A theatergoer who paid the one-penny base price of admission.

guild An association or group of people with like-minded interests or skills.

hadith The collection of the sayings of Muhammad and anecdotes about his life, accepted as a source of Islamic doctrine.

haiku A form of Japanese poetry consisting of three lines containing usually five, seven, and five syllables.

hajib The Islamic practice of dressing modestly; specifically the requirement that women be covered or veiled.

hajj A pilgrimage to Mecca made as a religious duty for Muslims.

Happening A type of multimedia event in which artists and audience participate as equal partners.

heliocentric Sun-centered.

Hellenistic A period of Greek history that begins with the rise to power of Alexander the Great (356–323 BCE) and extends to the Roman defeat of Cleopatra in Egypt in 30 BCE.

heroic couplet A rhyming pair of iambic pentameter lines.

hijra The flight of Muhammad from Mecca in 622.

hierarchy of scale A pictorial convention in which the most important figures are represented in a larger size than the others; see also *social perspective*.

hieratic style A style in which the importance of figures is indicated by size, so that the most important figure is largest.

hieroglyph A sign used in hieroglyphic writing, a writing system consisting mainly of pictorial characters.

hiragana A purely Japanese writing system that developed in the early ninth century.

Holocaust The systematic extermination of 6 million Jews and 5 million others—particularly Gypsies, Slavs, the handicapped, and homosexuals—by the Nazis during World War II.

homophonic harmony A unison movement of the voices in chords.

homophony A musical technique in which the subordinate voices simply accompany the melody in unison.

hubris Exaggerated pride and self-confidence.

humanism A focus on the actions of human beings, especially political action; more specifically, in the Renaissance, the study of the art and literature of Roman and Greek cultures in order to cultivate one's own unique talents and abilities.

humanist One who practices *humanism*.

hunter-gatherer One whose primary method of subsistence depends on hunting animals and gathering edible plants and other foodstuffs from nature.

hypostyle A vast space filled with columns supporting a roof.

iambic tetrameter The three-beat rhythm consisting of three iambs (short-long).

icon Literally, an image; in Byzantium, a religious image designed to elevate the mind to a higher contemplation of God.

iconoclasm The idea, practice, or doctrine of an iconoclast to destroy or ban religious images and their veneration.

iconography The literal (factual) and figurative (symbolic) significance of an image.

id In Freudian psychology, the part of the human mind that is the seat of all instinctive, physical desire; the principal mechanism of the subconscious.

idealism The eternal perfection of pure ideas untainted by material reality.

ignudi Nude youths.

imperialism The extension of one nation's authority over another by the exercise of its military, economic, and/or political power.

inductive reasoning A process in which, through the direct and careful observation of natural phenomena, one can draw general conclusions from particular examples and predict the operations of nature as a whole.

indulgences Dispensations granted by the Church to shorten a sinner's stay in purgatory.

Industrial Revolution The term used to describe a change in practices of production and consumption that occurred in the nineteenth century.

Inquisition An official inquiry into possible heresy.

intonazione A short prelude.

Ionic order One of the Greek architectural orders, characterized by columns either of caryatids or with scrolled *capitals*.

irony The use of words to say one thing explicitly but implicitly mean another.

Italian sonnet A *Petrarchan sonnet*.

Jacobin A member of a radical minority of France's National Assembly who favored the elimination of the monarchy and the institution of egalitarian democracy.

jamb An upright structural element on both sides of a door that supports the lintel or arch.

jihad The impassioned religious struggle undertaken by Muslims as a religious duty. The *jihad* may take one of two forms: The lesser is a holy war; the greater is self-control over the baser human appetites.

jongleur A professional entertainer or minstrel who performed from court to court.

kami A god or force of nature in Japanese Shintoism.

kenning A compound phrase used in poetry to substitute for the name of a person or thing.

key The central note of a musical composition; also called *tonic note*.

key signature The musical notation indicating the number of flats or sharps per section.

keystone A wedge-shaped stone at the top of an arch.

kiva A Pueblo ceremonial enclosure that is usually partly underground and serves as the center of village life.

knight A chevalier guided by a strict unwritten code of conduct; see *chivalric code*.

koge A scorch, the most prized effect created by firing a ceramic piece for use in the Japanese tea ceremony.

kore (pl. *korai*) A freestanding sculpture of a standing maiden.

kouros (pl. *kouroi*) A freestanding sculpture of a nude male youth.

krater A vessel in which wine and water are mixed.

lacquerware A type of decorative object made by coating it with several layers of lacquer and carving designs into the surface.

laissez-faire Literally "let it happen as it will," this economic policy argues that people should be free to do whatever they might to enrich themselves.

lantern A windowed turret at the top of a dome.

Latin cross The design of a Christian *basilica* with a long arm (the *nave*) and three shorter arms—the *apse* and the arms of the *transept*.

leitmotif In opera, a brief musical idea connected to a character, event, or idea that recurs throughout the work.

liberalism A political theory that argues that people are by nature free, equal, and independent and that they consent to government for protection but not by surrendering sovereignty to a ruler.

libretto The text of a musical work such as an *opera*.

lieder Songs, generally written for solo voice and piano.

literary realism The depiction of contemporary life emphasizing fidelity to everyday experience and the facts and conditions of everyday life.

literati Literary intelligentsia.

lithography Literally "stone writing," this printing process depends on the fact that oil and water do not mix.

liturgy The rites prescribed for public worship.

lyric poem Poetry generally written to be accompanied by a lyre.

madrigal A secular vocal composition for three or more voices.

male gaze A term used especially in art to describe the chauvinistic glance that regards woman as its sexual object.

mana Among the Maori, an invisible, forceful, spiritual substance that is the manifestation of the gods on earth.

mandala The Buddhist diagram of the cosmos.

mandorla An almond-shaped oval of light signifying divinity.

Mannerism A style of art in which the Classicizing tendencies of the High Renaissance were rejected in favor of an artistic display of virtuosity through the manipulation and distortion of the traditional figure.

medieval romance A story of adventure and love that pretended to be a true historical account of Charlemagne, King Arthur, or Roman legend.

megaliths Literally, "big stones"; large, usually rough, stones used in a monument or structure.

melisma A musical passage of many notes sung to one syllable of text.

melismatic In later medieval chant, the practice of singing a single syllable to many notes.

melismatic organum A type of *polyphony* in which the second voice moves in contrary motion to the bass chant or adds numerous notes to individual syllables above the bass chant.

memento mori A reminder of death.

mendicant order A religious order whose members do not hold property or engage in business.

Messiah Anointed One.

messianic Prophesied that the world will end in *apocalypse*.

metaphor A word or phrase used in place of another to suggest a likeness.

metope A square panel between the beam ends under a roof and on a frieze.

Middle Passage The Africa-to-America base of the triangular trade route: Europe to Africa, Africa to the Americas, the Americas to Europe.

minuet An elegant triple-time dance of moderate tempo.

Missa A polyphonic mass.

mode An aspect of musical performance in which, the Greeks believed, different pitches evoked different emotions.

modeling The use of shading in a two-dimensional representation to give a sense of roundness and volume.

modulation The pattern of beginning a composition in a *tonic* key, moving to different keys and then returning to the tonic.

monody A work consisting of a solo voice supported by a *basso continuo*.

monophonic A song in which one or many voices sing a single melodic line with no harmony.

montage An image (whether photographic or cinematographic) made by combining several different images.

mosque A building used for worship by Muslims.

motet A polyphonic form consisting of three (and sometimes four) voices.

motte and bailey A type of castle consisting of a raised earth mound (motte) and the enclosed courtyard at its base (bailey).

moveable type A technology, invented in China in 1045 CE, in which individual letterforms are composed into pages and then printed on a press.

mudra Symbolic gestures of the hands performed by Buddha.

muse One of the nine sister goddesses in Greek mythology who presided over song, poetry, and the arts and sciences.

music drama A musical genre in which the actions on stage are the visual and verbal manifestations of the drama created by the instruments in the orchestra.

music of the spheres The theory that each planet produces a musical sound, fixed mathematically by its velocity and distance from earth, which harmonizes with those produced by other planets and is audible but not recognized on earth.

mystery cult Religious group with secret initiation rituals.

myth A story that a culture assumes is true. A myth also embodies the culture's views and beliefs about its world, often serving to explain otherwise mysterious natural phenomena.

namban A genre of screen painting that emerged in Japan during the Momoyama period and whose imagery was influenced by the arrival by ship of Westerners from the south.

narrative genre A class or category of story with a universal theme.

narthex The entrance hall of a Christian *basilica*.

naturalism In art, representations that imitate the reality in appearance of natural objects.

natural law Law derived from nature and binding upon human society.

nave The central space of a Christian *basilica*, usually flanked by aisles.

Neoplatonist A modern term that distinguishes Renaissance Platonists from their Greek antecedents.

neumatic A simple chant form in which each syllable is sung to two or three notes.

neume A note in traditional Gregorian notation, usually indicated by a small square.

nirvana In Hindusim, a place or state free from worry, pain, and the external world.

nocturne In music, a character piece related to the tradition of the serenade performed outside a loved one's window.

Noh A type of Japanese dramatic play that includes music, chanting, dance, poetry, prose, mime, and elaborate masks and costumes, to create a total theatrical experience.

octave The interval that gives the impression of duplicating the original note at a higher or lower pitch.

oculus A circular opening at the top of a dome.

ode A lyric poem of exaltation, exhibiting deep feeling, often employing elaborate and irregular meter.

one-point perspective A type of *scientific (linear) perspective* in which all lines appear to converge at a single *vanishing point* on the horizon.

opera A text-based musical form.

oral culture A culture that develops without writing and passes down stories, beliefs, values, and systems by word of mouth.

oratorio A lengthy choral work of a sacred or secular nature but without action or scenery and performed by a narrator, soloists, chorus, and orchestra.

orchestra The "dancing space" on which ancient Greek plays were performed.

orchestration A musical arrangement in which each part of the composition has been designated with a specific voice or instrument.

order In Classical Greek architecture, the relationship of an elevation's three vertical elements: platform, column, and *entablature*; see *Doric*, *Ionic*, and *Corinthian*.

organum A type of polyphonic music consisting of voices singing note-to-note in parallel.

origin myth A story that describes the birth of one culture out of another.

orthogonal A diagonal line.

ostinato The continous variation of the same rhythmic pulse

pace A notation in a musical score that indicates rate of movement (for example, *allegro*, for fast; *lente*, for slow).

palatine chapel A palace chapel.

palazzo A palace.

pantheon All the gods as a group.

parados An entranceway through which the chorus entered the orchestra area.

parapet A low wall.

paraphrase Free variation on an existing melodic line in a polyphonic work.

parody A form of satire in which a serious

author or work is ridiculed or mocked in a humorous way through exaggerated imitation.

passion A musical setting, similar to an oratorio, that recounts the last days of the life of Jesus.

patriarch A scriptural father of the Hebrew people.

patrician A land-owning aristocrat.

pediment The triangular area over a porch.

pendentive A triangular curving vault section that supports a dome over a square space.

peristyle A row of columns.

peristyle courtyard A courtyard surrounded by a colonnaded walkway.

persona The voice in a fictional work.

personal essay A form of writing that serves as a vehicle for trying out ideas, testing them even as they are written.

perspectival drawing The use of techniques to show the relation of objects as they appear to the eye and to convey a sense of three-dimensional space on a two-dimensional surface.

Petrarchan sonnet A sonnet composed of 14 lines divided into two parts: an octave of eight lines that presents a problem, and a sestet of six lines that either attempts to solve the problem or accepts it as unsolvable.

philosophes The "philosophers" who dominated the intellectual life of the French Enlightenment and who frequented *salons*.

phonogram In writing, a *pictogram* used to represent a sound.

photogenic drawing A process for fixing negative images on paper coated with light-sensitive chemicals, developed by William Henry Fox Talbot in the early 1800s.

picaresque novel A prose genre that narrates, in a realistic way, the adventures of a *picaro*, a roguish hero of low social rank living by his wits in a corrupt society.

pictogram A stylized drawing that represents an object or being; often combined in hieroglyphic writing to express ideas.

pictorial formula A convention of representation in art.

picture plane The two-dimensional surface of a panel or canvas.

pier An upright structural support.

plainchant Plainsong; a liturgical chant.

platform A raised horizontal surface.

Platonic love The ideal spiritual relationship between two people.

plebeian A member of the poorer classes of ancient Rome.

plein air French for "open air" and referring to painting out-of-doors in front of the subject rather than in the studio.

pointilles Tiny dots of color and the building blocks of the pointillist style.

point of imitation Unit of music in which all the voices of a polyphonic composition take up more or less the same musical idea in succession.

polis The Greek city-state that formed the center of cultural life.

polonaise A stylized version of the Polish dance.

polychoral style A style in which choirs sing to and against each other in increasingly complicated forms.

polyphony Music with two or more lines of melody.

polyrhythms A musical technique in which different elements of an ensemble might play different meters simultaneously.

polytonal Occurs when two or more keys are sounded by different instruments at the same time.

porcelain A type of ceramic made by combining kaolin-rich clays with feldspar and sometimes quartz and fired at a high temperature.

postmodernism A term used to describe the collision of art, literary, and musical styles and forms that followed, and often deviated from, those of modernism. Postmodern works often have multiple meanings and are open to interpretation.

predella The base of an altarpiece.

prehistoric Existing in or relating to the times before writing and recorded history.

pre-Socratics Greek philosophers that preceded Socrates, chiefly concerned with describing the natural world.

primogeniture In the feudal system, the right of the eldest son to inherit all property.

program music Purely instrumental music connected in some way to a story or idea.

proletariat A class of workers lacking ownership of the means of production (tools and equipment) and control over both the quality and price of their own work.

pronaos The enclosed vestibule at the front of a Greek building, especially a temple.

prophet One who serves as a mouthpiece for and interpreter of Yahweh's purposes, which is understood through visions.

proscenium The stage on which actors perform and where painted backdrops can be hung.

protagonist The leading character in a play or literary work.

propylon A large entryway.

psyche In ancient Greek culture, the seat of both intelligence and character.

quadrivium In medieval universities, the mathematical arts, which included music, arithmetic, geometry, and astronomy.

Qur'an The sacred text of Islam, composed of the revelations of Allah to Muhammad.

radiant style A development of the French Gothic style featuring increasingly flamboyant patterns of repeated traceries and ornament.

rational humanism The belief that through logical, careful thought, progress is inevitable.

recitativo A style of singing that imitates very closely the rhythms of speech.

red figure A style in Greek pottery decoration composed of red figures against a black background.

refectory The dining hall of a monastery.

relic An object (bones, clothing, or other possessions) venerated because of its association with a Christian saint or martyr.

reliquary A container used to protect and display relics.

repoussé A metalworking technique of creating a design in relief by hammering or pressing on the reverse side.

revenge play A type of play consisting of a murder that must be avenged by the victim's relative, usually at the request of the murdered person's ghost.

reverse perspective A technique for conceiving of space as extending forward from the picture plane, with parallel lines converging on the eye of the beholder.

rhetorician A writer or orator.

ritornello A musical passage in which an instrument performs episodes that contrast back and forth with the orchestral score.

Romanesque An art historical period so-called because the architecture incorporated elements of Roman architectural tradition.

rose window A round window with mullions (framing elements) and traceries extending outward from its center in the manner of the petals of a rose.

round arch A curved architectural support element that spans an opening.

Roundheads Supporters of the Puritan Parliament who cropped their hair short and dressed plainly.

salon A room designed especially for social gatherings; later, also referred to the social gathering itself.

salon concerts Concerts held in the homes of wealthy music enthusiasts.

salonnière The hostess of a French salon.

samurai The regional warrior clans of Japan.

sarcophagus (pl. **sarchophagi**) A coffin, usually of stone.

satire The literary genre that conveys the contradictions between real and ideal situations.

satyr play A comic play that was one of the three major forms of Greek drama; see *farce*.

scarification Decorative effects made on the face or body by means of intentional scarring.

Scholasticism A brand of theological inquiry based on the dialectical method.

scientific method The effort to construct an accurate (that is, reliable, consistent, and nonarbitrary) representation of the world.

scientific perspective (linear perspective) A technique that allowed artists to translate three-dimensional space onto a two-dimensional surface.

Scientific Revolution A time of major breakthroughs in mathematics, astronomy, geology, physics, chemistry, biology, and medical science, all the result of empirical reasoning.

score A musical composition that indicates what music is to be played by each instrument.

scriptorium The hall in which monks worked to copy and decorate biblical texts.

sect A small, organized group that separates itself from the larger religious movement.

serial composition The principal or prime tone row can be played upside down, so that a rise of a major third in the prime row becomes the fall of a major third in the inverted row; it can be played backwards, or upside down and backwards.

sfumato The process of blurring outlines in painting by subtle tonal variations so that objects in the foreground blend into the background; literally, "smokiness."

shogun The general-in-chief of the samurai.

shoden The main sanctuary of a Shinto shrine.

simile A comparison of two unlike things using the word like or as.

skene Literally, "tent"; originally a changing room for Greek actors that, over time, was transformed into a building, often two stories tall.

social contract An agreement by which a person gives up sovereignty over him- or herself and bestows it on a ruler.

social Darwinism An extension of Darwin's theory of evolution positing that nations and societies advance according to the rule of "the survival of the fittest."

social perspective A pictorial convention in which the most important figures are represented in a larger size than the others; see also *hierarchy of scale.*

sonata form A kind of small form within the larger symphonic form.

Sophist Literally, "wise man;" an ancient Greek teacher or philosopher who was committed to humanism and primarily concerned with understanding the nature of human "knowing" itself.

spandrel The areas between the arches of an arcade.

spondee An element of meter in poetry consisting of two long syllables.

Sprechstimme Literally "speaking tone," a technique between speech and song, in which a text is enunciated in approximated pitches.

sprezzatura For an Italian Renaissance courtier, the undertaking of difficult tasks as if effortlessly and with an attitude of nonchalance.

still life A painting dedicated to the representation of common household objects and food.

stoa A long, open arcade supported by colonnades.

stream of consciousness A type of narration in which the reader reads only what is experienced in the character's mind from moment to moment, following their thought process through their interior monologue.

string quartet A group of musicians playing four instruments from the same family—two violins, a viola, and a cello—thus lending the music a distinctly homogeneous sound.

strophic The same music repeated for each stanza of a poem.

stupa A type of Buddhist burial mound.

stylobate The raised platform of the temple.

sublime The feeing of awe and terror experienced in the face of the infinite and the unknowable.

suite An ordered series of instrumental dances.

summa An authoritative summary of all that is known on a traditional subject.

superego In Freudian psychology, the seat of what is commonly called "conscience," the psyche's moral base.

swing A musical genre characterized by big bands that produced a powerful sound and whose rhythm depends on subtle avoidance of downbeats.

syllabic In music, one note per syllable.

syllogism A type of deductive reasoning consisting of two premises from which a conclusion can be drawn.

symmetrical Balanced on the left and right sides.

symphonic orchestra A large ensemble that organized the orchestra into separate sections according to type of instrument: strings, woodwinds, brass, and percussion.

symphony A musical composition with a strictly defined form consisting of a first movement played in a fast tempo (*allegro*); a second movement that is slow (*adagio* or *andante*) and reflective; a third that picks up the pace again; and a fourth that is generally allegro once again, spirited and lively.

symposium In ancient Greece, a gathering of men initially for the purpose of sharing poetry, food, and wine.

syncretism The reconciliation of different rites and practices into a single philosophy or religion.

T'ai Chi Ch'uan The Chinese martial art that includes both solo forms, or routines, and two-person forms known as "pushing hands."

tempera A type of painting process using a water-soluble material, such as egg yolks, instead of oil paint.

tenebrism An exaggerated form of *chiaroscuro.*

tetralogy A set of four related plays.

tetrarchy The four-part monarchy begun by Diocletian that divided the Roman Empire into two areas ruled by an Eastern and Western emperor, each with a designated successor.

theocracy A state ruled by a god or by the god's representative.

through-composed Used to describe a song in which each line of text is set to new music.

time signature The musical notation indicating the number of beats per measure.

toccata A virtuoso composition, usually for organ, designed to feature both the range of the instrument and the dexterity of the performer.

tonality The key of a composition.

tone row The twelve notes in their given order in a musical composition.

tonic note The central note of a musical composition; also called the *key.*

tragédie en musique An operatic genre that generally consists of an overture, an allegorical prologue, five acts of sung drama.

tragedy A type of drama whose basis is conflict; it often explores the physical and moral depths to which human life can descend.

transept The arm of the *Latin cross* church perpendicular to the *nave.*

triptych A work made of three parts, usually painted panels hinged together.

trivium In medieval universities, the language arts, which included grammar, rhetoric, and dialectic.

trobairitz A woman *troubadour.*

troubadour A class of poets that flourished in the eleventh through thirteenth centuries in southern France and northern Italy.

trumeau The column or post in the middle of a large door supporting the lintel.

tumulus A round structure partially excavated and partly above ground and covered with earth.

twelve-tone system In its most basic form, a system developed by the composer Arnold Schoenberg in which none of the twelve tones of the chromatic scale could be repeated in a composition until each of the other eleven had been played.

tympanum The space created under the portal arch, often filled with sculptural relief.

type A prefigurative symbol.

typology The doctrine of prefigurative symbols, or types, in scriptural literature.

vanishing point The point on the horizon where lines of perspective meet.

vanitas **painting** A type of painting that reminds the viewer that pleasurable things in life inevitably fade, that the material world is not as long-lived as the spiritual, and that the spiritual should command our attention.

vantage **point** The position from which something is viewed.

verism A form of realism in art or literature.

vernacular The language spoken in the streets.

votive A ritual object.

volute A scroll-like motif on a column's capital.

voussoir A wedge-shaped block used to form an arch or vault.

Vulgate The Latin Bible.

waka A form of Japanese poetry consisting of 31 syllables in five lines on a theme drawn from nature and the changing of seasons.

Way of the Tea The Japanese tea ceremony.

westwork An imposing, sometimes monumental entrance of a church made up of two tall towers flanking a multistoried *narthex.*

word painting The effect created when musical elements imitate the meaning of the text in mood or action.

ziggurat A pyramidal temple structure consisting of successive *platforms* with outside staircases and a shrine at the top.

Photo Credits

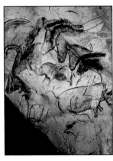

Chapter 1
1.1 Jean Clottes, Ministere de la Culture et des Communications, Ministere de la Culture et de la Communication. Direction Regionale des affaires Culturelles de Rhone-Alpes. Service Regional de l'Archeologie; 1.2 Yvonne Vertut; 1.3 Erich Lessing, Naturhistorisches Museum, Vienna, Austria. © Photography by Erich Lessing/Art Resource, NY; 1.4 Art Resource/Musée du Louvre; 1.5 Aerofilms; 1.6 John Deeks, Photo Researchers, Inc; 1.8 Nik Wheeler; 1.12 SCALA, Art Resource, NY; 1.13 Hervé Lewandowski, RMN/Réunion des Musées Nationaux/Art Resource, NY; 1.15 Staffan Widstrand, Nature Picture Library; 1.16 Werner Forman, Art Resource, NY; 1.18 Bildarchiv Preussischer Kulturbesitz, Berlin, Germany, Art Resource/Bildarchiv Preussischer Kulturbesitz; 1.19 Jürgen Liepe, Jürgen Liepe Photo Archive; 1.20 D. E. Cox, Getty Images Inc.–Stone Allstock, D. E. Cox/Stone/Getty Images; 1.24 "Shiva Nataraja, Lord of the Dance." South India. Chola period, 11th Century. Bronze. 111.5 × 101.65 cm. © The Cleveland Museum of Art, Purchase from the J.H. Wade Fund 1930.331; 1.25 SCALA, Art Resource, NY; 1.26 SCALA, Art Resource, NY; 1.27 Dagli Orti/Archaeological Museum, Naples, Picture Desk, Inc./Kobal Collection; page 22, Art Resource, NY; page 23, Art Resource, NY.

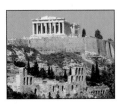

Chapter 2
2.1 Studio Kontos Photostock; 2.2 Sonia Halliday Photographs; 2.3 Figure, Cyclades, ca. 2500 BCE, Marble, height: 15 3/4″ (40 cm). Nicholas P. Goulandris Foundation. Museum of Cycladic Art; 2.4 Nimatallah/National Archeological Museum, Athens, Art Resource, NY; 2.5 Archeological Museum, Iraklion, Crete, Studio Kontos Photostock; 2.6 Erich Lessing, Art Resource, NY; 2.7 McRae Books Srl; 2.8 National Archaeological Museum, © Hellenic Ministry of Culture, Archaeological Receipts Fund; 2.9 Studio Kontos Photostock; 2.10 National Archaeological Museum, Athens/Hirmer Fotoarchiv, Munich, Germany; 2.12 Marco Cristofori, CORBIS–NY; 2.14 Nimatallah, Art Resource, NY; 2.16 © The Metropolitan Museum of Art / Art Resource, NY; 2.17 Greek, Attic, "Statue of a kouros (youth)." ca. 590–580 BC.. Marble. Naxian. H w/o plith: 76 5/8″ (194.6 cm). The Metropolitan Museum of Art, Fletcher Fund, 1932. (32.11.1). Photograph © 1997 The Metropolitan Museum of Art; 2.18 (left), Akropolis Museum, Athens, Studio Kontos Photostock; 2.18 (right), Museum of Classical Archaeology, University of Cambridge, UK; 2.19 Dagli Orti/Acropolis Museum Athens, Picture Desk, Inc./Kobal Collection; 2.22 The British Museum Images; 2.23 With permission of the Royal Ontario Museum © ROM; 2.24 Studio Kontos Photostock; 2.27 Studio Kontos Photostock; 2.28 The Kritios Boy frm the Akropolis. Greek (Archaic), c. 490–480 BCEH: 117cm. Acropolis Museum, Athens, Greece. Nimtallah/Art Resource, NY; 2.29 Dagli Orti/Archaeological Museum, Naples, Picture Desk, Inc./Kobal Collection; 2.30 Reggio di Calabria/Soprintendenza Archeologica della Calabria; 2.34 © The Trustees of the British Museum/Art Resource, NY; 2.35 Penguin Group USA, Inc.; 2.36 Ingrid Geske/Antikensammlung, Staatliche Museen zu Berlin, Art Resource/Bildarchiv Preussischer Kulturbesitz; 2.37 Ruggero Vanni, CORBIS–NY; 2.39 Erich Lessing, Art Resource, NY; 2.41 Art Resource, NY; 2.42 Nike of Samothrace. 3rd–2nd BCE. Hellenistic marble statue. H.: 328 cm. Inv.: 2369. Musée du Louvre/RMN Reunion des Musées Nationaux, France. SCALA/Art Resource, NY; 2.43 The Laocoon group. Roman copy, perhaps after Agesander, Athenodorus, and Polydorus of Rhodes (present state, former restorations removed). 1st c. CE. Marble. H: 2.1 m. Location: Museo Pio Clementino, Vatican Museums, Vatican State, SCALA/Art Resource, NY; page 48 Canali Photobank; page 49 (top left), Nimatellah, Art Resource, NY; page 49 (top right), John Decopoulos; page 49 (bottom), Courtesy of the Library of Congress; page 49 (bottom), Courtesy of the Library of Congress.

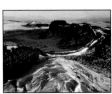

Chapter 3
3.1 Brian Brake, John Hillelson Agency; 3.2 Villa Giulia; 3.3 Museo Capitolino, Rome, Italy. © Photography by Erich Lessing/Art Resource, NY; 3.4 Araldo de Luca, CORBIS–NY; 3.6 Vatican Museums & Galleries, Vatican City/Superstock; 3.7 Foto Vasari, Index Ricerca Iconografica; 3.8 SCALA, Art Resource, NY; 3.9 Dagli Orti/Archaeological Museum, Naples, Italy, Picture Desk, Inc./Kobal Collection; 3.10 SCALA, Art Resource, NY; 3.11 Pubbli Aer Foto; 3.12 Danita Delimont Photography; 3.14 Michael Larvey, Canali Photobank; 3.15 Werner Forman, Art Resource, NY; 3.16 Robert Frerck, Woodfin Camp & Associates; 3.17 SCALA, Art Resource, NY; 3.18 Canali Photobank; 3.20 Hemera Technologies, Alamy Images Royalty Free; 3.21 Henri Stierlin; 3.22 Reprinted with the permission of Cambridge University Press; 3.23 Fotografica Foglia; 3.24 Canali Photobank; 3.25 Araldo de Luca Archives, Index Ricerca Iconografica; 3.26 Bildarchiv Monheim, AKG-Images; pages 258–259, Gilbert Gorski; page 258 (top), Vanni, Art Resource, NY; page 259 (top), Dr. James E. Packer; page 259 (bottom right), Fototeca Unione, American Academy in Rome.

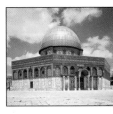

Chapter 4
4.1 A.F. Kersting; 4.2 Erich Lessing / Art Resource, NY; 4.4 SCALA, Art Resource, NY; 4.9 SCALA, Art Resource, NY; 4.10 C. M. Dixon, The Ancient Art & Architecture Collection Ltd.; 4.11 Art Resource, NY; 4.12 © Achim Bednorz, Koln; 4.13 Walter. B. Denny; 4.15 Studio Kontos Photostock; 4.16 Canali Photobank; 4.17 San Vitale, Ravenna, Italy, Canali Photobank; 4.18 San Vitale, Ravenna, Italy, Canali Photobank; 4.19 By permission of The British Library; 4.20 Peter Sanders, The Image Works; 4.22 Peter Langer/Associated Media Group; 4.23 © Achim Bednorz, Koln; 4.24 © Massimo Borchi/© Atlantide Phototravel / CORBIS All Rights Reserved; 4.25 Werner Forman, Art Resource, NY; pages 106–107, Fabbrica di San Pietro, IKONA.

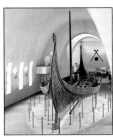

Chapter 5
5.1 Eirik Irgens Johnsen/©Museum of Cultural History - University of Oslo, Norway; 5.3 By permission of The British Library; 5.4 Trinity College Library; 5.5 By permission of The British Library; 5.6 Erich Lessing, Art Resource/Musée du Louvre, RMN Réunion des Musées Nationaux, France. SCALA/Art Resource, NY; 5.8 Fotowerkstatte; 5.9 Erich Lessing, Art Resource, NY; 5.10 Stephen Biesty © Dorling Kindersley; 5.11 Erich Lessing, Art Resource, NY; 5.12 Erich Lessing, Art Resource, NY; 5.13 SCALA, Art Resource, NY; 5.16 © Ruggero Vanni / CORBIS All Rights Reserved; 5.17 © Ruggero Vanni / CORBIS All Rights Reserved; 5.18 Stephen Conlin © Dorling Kindersley; 5.20 Michael Jenner, Robert Harding World Imagery; 5.21 Joanna Cameron © Dorling Kindersley; 5.23 © Achim Bednorz, Koln; 5.24 © Angelo Hornak/Beranger / CORBIS All Rights Reserved; pages 144–145, The Bridgeman Art Library International. With special authorisation of the city of Bayeux, Musée de la Tapisserie, Bayeux, France/The Bridgeman Art Library; page 145 (bottom), Erich Lessing, Art Resource, NY.

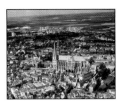

Chapter 6
6.1 Bernard Beaujard; 6.3 © Achim Bednorz, Koln; 6.4 © Achim Bednorz, Koln; 6.5 © Achim Bednorz, Koln; 6.6 Photo Josse; 6.7 Jean Bernard Photographe/Bordas Publication; 6.8 Vanni, Art Resource, NY; 6.10 Interior view of the nave looking towards the West end, 15th century (photo), / Peter Willi, Cathedral of Notre Dame, Reims, France / The Bridgeman Art Library International; 6.11 John Bryson, Photo Researchers, Inc.; 6.13 Angelo Hornak, Angelo Hornak Photograph Library; 6.14 © Achim Bednorz, Koln; 6.15 © Achim Bednorz, Koln; 6.16 SCALA, Art Resource, NY; 6.18 © Achim Bednorz, Koln; 6.19 Good Government in the City, 1338–40 (detail)(fresco), Lorenzetti, Ambrogio (1285–c.1348). Palazzo Pubblico, Siena, Italy. The Bridgeman Art Library; 6.20 View of the church Santa Croce and its surroundings (photo), Allouche, Sylvie (Contemporary Artist) / © Sylvie Allouche, Florence, Italy/ The Bridgeman Art Library; 6.21 ALINARI, Art Resource, NY; 6.22 Canali Photobank; 6.23 SCALA, Art Resource, NY; 6.24 Cimabue (Cenni di Pepi), Index Ricerca Iconografica; 6.25 Galleria degli Uffizi; 6.26 The Art Archive/Duomo Florence/Dagli Orgi, Picture Desk, Inc./Kobal Collection; 6.27 G. W. Scott-Giles; 6.28 The Metropolitan Museum of Art, The Cloisters Collection. 1969 (69.86). Image ©The Metropolitan Museum of Art / Art Resource, NY; 6.29 Snark/Bibliothèque Nationale, Paris, France, Art Resource, NY; 6.30 Erich Lessing, Art Resource, NY; page 178 (top), Alinari, Art Resource, NY; page 178 (bottom), Chapel, Padua, Canali Photobank; page 179, SCALA, Art Resource, NY.

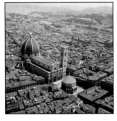

Chapter 7
7.1 © Achim Bednorz, Koln; 7.2 Arte & Immagini srl, Corbis/Bettmann; 7.3 Erich Lessing/Museo Nazionale del Bargello, Florence, Art Resource, NY; 7.4 Erich Lessing, Art Resource, NY; 7.5 SCALA, Art Resource, NY; 7.6 SCALA, Art Resource, NY; 7.7 © Grand Tour/Grand Tour / CORBIS All Rights Reserved; 7.11 Nimatallah/Art Resource, NY; 7.12 SCALA, Art Resource, NY; 7.13 © Achim Bednorz, Koln; 7.14 SCALA, Art Resource, NY; 7.15 SCALA, Art Resource, NY; 7.16 Art Resource, NY; 7.17 Lewandowski/LeMage/Art Resource, NY; 7.18 Leonardo da Vinci (1452–1519), "The Last Supper". 1495–97/98. Mural (oil and tempera on plaster), 15′1 1/8″ × 28′ 10 1/2″. Refectory, Monastery of Santa Maria delle Grazie, Milan, Italy. IndexRicerca Iconografica. Photo: Ghigo Roli; 7.19 SCALA, Art Resource, NY; 7.20 Photo credit: Cameraphoto Arte, Venice / Art Resource, NY, Academia, Venice, Italy; 7.21 Pirozzi, AKG-Images; 7.23 Galleria dell' Accademia, Florence, Art Resource, NY; 7.24 Foto Musei Vaticani; 7.26 Sistine Chapel, Canali Photobank; 7.28 A. Bracchetti/P. Zigrossi, IKONA; 7.29 Galleria degli Uffizi, Florence, Art Resource, NY; 7.30 SCALA, Art Resource, NY; 7.31

ONB, Picture Archive, Vienna: NB 6.673-C; **7.32** Cameraphoto, Art Resource, NY; **7.33** Piero Codato, Cameraphoto Arte di Codato G.P. & C.snc; **7.34** © Achim Bednorz, Koln; **7.35** Cameraphoto, Art Resource, NY; **7.36** Titian (Tiziano Vecellio) (c.1488–1576). "Pastoral Concert." c.1510–11. Musée du Louvre/RMN Reunion des Musées Nationaux, France. SCALA/Art Resource, NY; **7.37** SCALA, Art Resource, NY; **7.38** SCALA, Art Resource, NY; **7.39** The Bridgeman Art Library; **7.40** Erich Lessing/Kunsthistorisches Museum, Vienna, Austria, Art Resource, NY; **7.41** Piero Codato, Cameraphoto Arte di Codato G.P. & C.snc; **7.42** Courtesy of the Library of Congress; **page 192**, The American Institute of Musicology, © American Institute of Musicology. Used with permission; **page 213**, Vatican Museums, Rome, Italy. Scala/Art Resource, NY.

Chapter 8

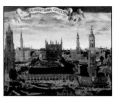

8.1 Pieter Claeissens de Oude, "The Seven Wonders of Bruges (Septem admirationes civitatis Brugensis)." Penel 34$\frac{5}{8}$" × 48$\frac{3}{4}$". Monasterium de Wijngaard, Bruges, Belgium. Private Collection. LUKAS, Art in Flanders, Belgium; **8.3** Art Resource/The Metropolitan Museum of Art, Photograph © 1996 The Metropolitan Museum of Art; **8.4** Art Resource/The Metropolitan Museum of Art, Photograph © 1996 The Metropolitan Museum of Art; **8.6** Jan van Eyck, (1422–1441), "The Portrait of Giovanni Arnolfini and his Wife Giovanna Cenami (The Arnolfini Marriage)." Oil on Wood. 81.8 × 59.7. ©National Gallery, London; **8.7** © Erich Lessing / Art Resource, NY; **8.8** Musée d'Unterlinden, GLMAR; **8.9** Matthias Grunewald, "Isenheim Altarpiece." Closed from the Community of Saint Anthony, Isenheim, Germany. Center Panels: "Crucifixion"; predella: "Lamentation" side panels. Musée D'Unterlinden; **8.10** Albrecht Duerer (1471–1528), "The Large Turf." Graphische Sammlung Albertina, Vienna. ©2004 Nimatallah/Art Resource, NY; **8.11** © 2007 Museum of Fine Arts, Boston; **8.12** SCALA/Art Resource, NY; **8.13** ©The Trustees of the British Museum; **8.14** Erich Lessing, Art Resource, NY; **8.15** Bettmann, Corbis/Bettmann; **8.16** Ruth Schacht, Art Resource/Bildarchiv Preussischer Kulturbesitz; **8.17** Title page of 'Mr. William Shakespeares Comedies, Histories and Tragedies,' engraved by Martin Droeshout (1601–50) 1623 (see also 54369), English School, (17th century)/British Library, London, UK, Giraudon/The Bridgeman Art Library; **8.18** © Dorling Kindersley; **8.19** Palazzo Barberini, Galleria Nazionale d' Arte Antica, Rome, Canali Photobank; **8.22** SCALA, Art Resource, NY; **pages 234–235**, El Bosco (Bosch) (1450–1516), "Garden of Earthly Delights." El Jardin de Las Delicias-Triptico Tabla. 220 × 195. Photo Oronoz. Derechos reservados ©Museo Nacional Del Prado – Madrid; **page 234** (bottom left), Prado, Madrid, Spain/The Bridgeman Art Library; **page 234** (bottom right), Prado, Madrid, Spain/The Bridgeman Art Library.

Chapter 9

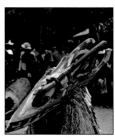

9.1 "Dance of Banda, Baga Mandori." Photo by Frederick John Lamp 1987; **9.2** Museum of Ife Antiquities, Nigeria, Dirk Bakker; **9.4** Stanley Collection, University of Iowa Museum of Art, x1986.513; **9.5** Suzanne Murphy/Stone/Getty Images, Inc.; **9.6** Gina Martin, National Geographic Image Collection; **9.7** Werner Forman Archive, The Image Works; **9.8** The Museum of Modern Art, Licensed by Scala-Art Resource, NY; **9.9** Dr. Merle Greene Robertson; **9.10** AKG-Images; **9.11** Dagli Orti, Picture Desk, Inc./Kobal Collection; **9.12** Justin Kerr/Dumbarton Oaks, Byzantine Photograph and Fieldwork Archives, Washington, DC; **9.13** Photograph © 1995 The Metropolitan Museum of Art; **9.16** Gabinetto Fotografico della Soprintendenza Per I Beni Artistici E Storici, Firenze; **9.17** Bildarchiv Preussischer Kulturbesitz, Art Resource/Bildarchiv Preussischer Kulturbesitz; **9.18** Galileo Picture Services LLC, NY; **9.19** Jon Arnold, Danita Delimont Photography; **9.20** The Nelson-Atkins Museum of Art, Kansas City, Missouri. Purchase: Nelson Trust, 4045.1,2. Photograph by Jamison Miller; **9.22** The Nelson-Atkins Museum of Art, Kansas City, Missouri. Purchase: Nelson Trust, 46-51/2. Photo: Robert Newcombe; **9.23** Kenneth Hamm, Photo Japan; **9.24** The ArtArchive/Laurie Platt Winfrey, Picture Desk, Inc./Kobal Collection; **9.25** Kenneth Hamm, Photo Japan; **9.26** TNM Image Archives Source: http://TNMArchives.jp/DNP (Dai Nippon Printing) Archives.Com; **9.28** Naizen Kano, "Nanban Byobu (Nanban six-panel screen)." Kobe City Museum, Kobe, Japan. 1593–1600. Photo: Galileo Picture Services LLC, NY.

Chapter 10

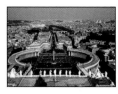

10.1 Tibor Bognar/Alamy Images; **10.4** SCALA/Art Resource, NY; **10.5** Erich Lessing/Art Resource, NY; **10.6** SCALA/Art Resource, NY; **10.7** Canali Photobank; **10.8** Erich Lessing/Art Resource, NY; **10.9** Canali Photobank; **10.10** Canali Photobank; **10.12** Cameraphoto/Art Resource, NY; **10.13** Charles Roelofsz/RKD Images; **10.14** Royal Cabinet of Paintings Mauritshuis, The Hague/Stichting Vrienden van Het Mauritshuis; **10.17** Copyright The Frick Collection, New York; **10.18** Giraudon/ The Bridgeman Art Library International; **10.20** Mickael David/Robert Harding World Imagery; **10.22** Artedia; **10.23** Visual Arts Library (London)/Alamy Images; **10.24** Alamy Images; **10.25** Peter Paul (1577–1640). "The Disembarkation of Marie de' Medici at the Port of Marseilles on November 3, 1600." Oil on Canvas. 394 × 295 cm. Musée du Louvre/RMN Réunion des Musées Nationaux, France. Erich Lessing/Art Resource, NY; **10.28** King Louis XIV of France in the costume of the Sun King in the ballet 'La Nuit,' 1653 (b/w photo), French School,

(17th century)/Bibliothèque Nationale, Paris, France/The Bridgeman Art Library; **10.31** Derechos reservados © Museo Nacional Del Prado – Madrid; **10.33** Testelin, Henri (1616–95), "Jean-Baptiste Colbert (1619–1683) Presenting the Members of the Royal Academy of Science to Louis XIV (1638–1715)." c.1667. Oil on Canvas. Chateau de Versailles, France, Lauros. Giraudon/The Bridgeman Art Library; **page 883** Derechos reservados © Museo Nacional Del Prado – Madrid.

Chapter 11

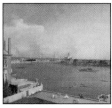

11.1 Goodwood Trustees/The Goodwood Estate Company Limited; **11.2** A.F. Kersting; **11.3** Courtesy of the Bancroft Library, University of California, Berkeley; **11.4** HIP/Oxford Science Archive, Oxford, Gr Br/Art Resource, NY; **11.5** © National Gallery, London; **11.6** Image by courtesy of the Wedgwood Museum Trust Limited, Barlaston, Staffordshire, England; **11.7** Graham Jordan/Britain on View; **11.10** Charles Joseph (1700–77), "Psyche and Cupid." Ceiling panel from the Salon de la Princesse, Natoire. Hotel de Soubise, Paris, France. Peter Willi/The Bridgeman Art Library; **29-03** Erich Lessing/Art Resource, NY; **11.11** Erich Lessing/Art Resource, NY; **11.14** Wallace Collection, London/AKG-Images; **11.17** Hervé Lewandowski/RMN/Chardin, Jean-Baptiste Simeon (1699–1779), "A Chemist in his Laboratory," also known as "The Philosopher Occupied by His Reading. Portrait of the painter Joseph Aved." Oil on canvas, 138 × 105 cm. Photo: Hervé Lewandowski/Musée du Louvre/RMN Réunion des Musées Nationaux, France. SCALA/Art Resource, NY; **11.21** Reproduced with permission. ©2007 Museum of Fine Arts, Boston. All Rights Reserved; **page 347** (bottom), V & A Images/Victoria and Albert Museum/Art Resource, NY.

Chapter 12

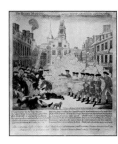

12.1 The Bloody Massacre on 5th March 1770, 1770 (coloured engraving), Revere, Paul (1735–1818). © Massachusetts Historical Society, Boston, MA, USA. The Bridgeman Art Library; **12.3** David, Jacques Louis (1748–1825), "The Oath of the Tennis Court, June 20th 1789." Pen and wash with brown ink, heightened with white, on paper, 1791. MV 8409: INV Dessins. Photo: Gérard Blot. Location: Chateaux de Versailles et de Trianon, Versailles, France. RMN Réunion des Musées Nationaux/Art Resource, NY; **12.4** Giraudon/Art Resource, NY; **12.6** Lebrecht Music and Arts Photo Library/Alamy Images; **12.9** Sir Joshua Reynolds, "Benjamin Henry Latrobe, Tobacco Leaf Capital for the United States Capitol, Washington, D.C." c. 1815. Courtesy of the Architect of the Capitol, Washington, D.C.; **12.10** "A Negro hung alive by the Ribs to a Gallows, from 'Narrative of a Five Years' Expedition against the Revolted Negroes of Surinam, in Guiana, on the Wild Coast of South America, from the year 1772, to 1777," engraved by William Blake (1757–1827), published, Stedman, John Gabriel (1744–97) (after)/Private Collection, Archives Charmet/The Bridgeman Art Library; **12.11** Image by courtesy of the Wedgwood Museum Trustees, Barlaston, Staffordshire, (England); **12.12** Victoria & Albert Museum/Joseph Mallord William Turner (1775–1851), "Transept of Tintern Abbey." Exhibited 1794. Watercolor. 12$\frac{5}{8}$" × 9$\frac{7}{8}$" (32.2 × 25.1 cm). Victoria and Albert Museum/Art Resource, NY; **12.13** The National Gallery, London/The Bridgeman Art Library International; **12.17** Francisco de Goya, (Spanish, 1746–1828). "The Third of May, 1808." 1814–1815. Oil on canvas, approx. 8'8" × 11' 3". Derechos reservados © Museo Nacional Del Prado-Madrid. Photo Oronoz; **12.20** From Jay D. Zorn and June August, Listening to Music, 5th edition, © 2007 Pearson Education, Inc.; **pages 360–361**, C. Jean/Jacques Louis David (1748–1825), "The Lictors bring to Brutus the Bodies of his Sons." Oil on canvas, 323 × 422 cm. Photo: G. Blot/C. Jean. Musée du Louvre/RMN Réunion des Musées Nationaux, France. Art Resource, NY.

Chapter 13

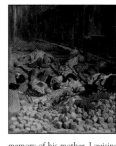

13.2 The New York Public Library, New York, NY USA/Art Resource, NY; **13.5** Honoré Daumier, "The Third-Class Carriage." c. 1962. Oil on canvas. 25 3/40 × 35 1/20 (65.4 × 90.2 cm). Bequest of Mrs. H. O. Havemeyer, 1929. The H.O. Havemeyer Collection. © 1922 The Metropolitan Museum of Art, NY; **13.7** Louis-Jacques-Mande Daguerre, "Le Boulevard du Temple," 1839, Daguerreotype. Bayerisches Nationalmuseum Munchen; **13.12** Robert Harding Picture Library Ltd.; **13.14** Édouard Manet, "The Railway." 1873. Oil on canvas, .933 × 1.115 (36$\frac{3}{4}$" × 45$\frac{1}{8}$"). Framed: 1.130 × 1.327 × .054 cm (44$\frac{1}{2}$" × 52$\frac{1}{4}$" × 2$\frac{1}{8}$"). Gift of Horace Havemeyer in memory of his mother, Louisine W. Havemeyer. 1956.10.1. Image © 2007. Board of Trustees, National Gallery of Art, Washington, D.C. © 2008 ARS Artists Rights Society, NY. **13.16** Claude Monet (1840–1926), "Impression, Sunrise." 1872. Oil on canvas, 48 × 63 cm. Painted in Le Havre, France. Location: Musée Marmottan-Claude Monet, Paris, France. Erich Lessing/Art Resource, NY; **13.17** Claude Monet (French, 1840–1926), "Grainstack (Snow Effect)." 1891. Oil on canvas, 65.4 × 92.4 cm (25$\frac{3}{4}$" × 36$\frac{3}{8}$"). Gift of Miss Aime and Miss Rosamond Lamb in memory of Mr. and Mrs. Horatio Appleton Lamb, 1970.253. Photograph © 2008 Museum of Fine Arts, Boston; **13.18** Berthe Morisot (1841–1895), "Summer's Day." Oil on canvas. 45.7 × 75.2 cm. © National Gallery, London; **13.21** Hilaire-Germain-Edgar Degas

(French 1834–1917), "The Dance Class." 1874. Oil on canvas, $32\frac{7}{8}'' \times 30\frac{3}{8}''$ (83.5 × 77.2 cm). The Metropolitan Museum of Art. Bequest of Mrs. Harry Payne Bingham, 1986 (1987.47.1). Image copyright © The Metropolitan Museum of Art; **13.23** William Merritt Chase, "Tompkins Park, Brooklyn." 1886. Oil on canvas, $17\frac{3}{8}'' \times 22\frac{3}{8}''$. Colby College Museum of Art, Gift of Miss Adeline F. and Miss Caroline R. Wing, 1963.040; **13.27** John Singer Sargent (American, 1856–1925), "The Daughters of Edward Darley Boit." 1882. Oil on canvas, 221.93 × 222.57 cm ($87\frac{3}{8}'' \times 87\frac{5}{8}''$). Gift of Mary Louisa Boit, Julia Overing Boit, Jane Hubbard Boit, and Florence D. Boit in memory of their father, Edward Darley Boit, 19.124 Photograph © 2008 Museum of Fine Arts, Boston; **13.28** Mary Stevenson Cassatt , American, 1844–1926, "In the Loge," 1878. Oil on canvas, 81.28 × 66.04 cm. (32 × 26 in.). Museum of Fine Arts, Boston. The Hayden Collection-Charles Henry Hayden Fund, 10.35. Photograph © Museum of Fine Arts, Boston; **13.30** Smithsonian Institution/Office of Imaging, Printing, and Photographic Services.

Chapter 14

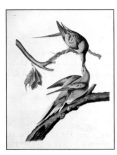

14.1 Victoria & Albert Museum, London/Art Resource, NY; **14.2** Albert Bierstadt (American, 1830–1902), "The Rocky Mountains, Lander's Peak." 1863. Oil on canvas, $73\frac{1}{2}'' \times 120\frac{3}{4}''$ (186.7 × 306.7 cm). The Metropolitan Museum of Art, Rogers Fund, 1907 (07.123). Image copyright © The Metropolitan Museum of Art; **14.3** George Catlin, (1796–1872), "Big Bend on the Upper Missouri, 1800 Miles Above St. Louis." 1832. Smithsonian American Art Museum, Washington, D.C./Art Resource, NY; **14.4** Historical Picture Archive/Hokusai, "The Great Wave off Kanagawa," from the series "Thirty-Six Views of Mount Fuji." 1823–1829. Color Woodcut. 10' × 150'. © Historical Picture Archive/CORBIS; **14.5** Georges Seurat (French 1859–1891). "A Sunday on La Grande Jatte-1884". 1884–86. Oil on canvas. $81\frac{3}{4}'' \times 121\frac{1}{4}''$ (207.5 × 306.1 cm). Helen Birch Bartlett Memorial Collection, 1926.224. Combination of quadrant captures F1, F2, G1, G2. Photograph © 2006, The Art Institute of Chicago. All Rights Reserved; **14.7** Paul Cezanne (1836–1906), "The Peppermint Bottle," 1893/1895, oil on canvas, .659 × .821 (26 × $32\frac{3}{8}''$); framed: 1.057 × .908 ($41\frac{5}{8}'' \times 35\frac{3}{4}''$). Image ©2007 Board of Trustees, National Gallery of Art, Washington. Chester Dale Collection; **14.9** Paul Gauguin, "Mahana no atua (Day of the God)." 1894. Oil on canvas. $27\frac{3}{8}'' \times 35\frac{5}{8}''$ (69.5 × 90.5 cm). The Art Institute of Chicago. Helen Birch Bartlett Memorial Collection (1926.198) Photograph © 2007, The Art Institute of Chicago. All Rights Reserved; **14.17** Henri Matisse, "Dance." Oil on canvas. 260 × 391 cm. Inv. No. 9673. The State Hermitage Museum, St. Petersburg, Rus-sia. © 2010 Succession H. Matisse, Paris/Artists Rights Society (ARS), New York; **14.18** Franz Marc, "The Large Blue Horses." 1911. Oil on canvas. $3'5\frac{3}{8}'' \times 5' 11\frac{1}{4}''$. (1.05 × 1.81 m). Walker Art Center, Minneapolis, Gift of T. B. Walker Collection, Gilbert M. Walter Fund, 1942; **14.20** SCALA/Jean (Hans) Arp (1888–1966), "Collage Arranged According to the Laws of Chance." 1916–17. Torn and pasted paper, $19\frac{1}{8}'' \times 13\frac{5}{8}''$. Purchase. (457.1937). Digital Image © The Museum of Modern Art/Licensed by SCALA/Art Resource, NY. © 2008 ARS Artists Rights Society, NY; **14.22** Paul Strand (1890–1976) © Aperture Foundation "Camera Work." June 1917: Abstraction, Porch Shadows. 24 × 16.5 cm. Inv. Pho1981-35-10. Repro-Photo: Reno-Gabriel Ojoda. Musée d'Orsay, Paris, France. Réunion des Musées Nationaux/Art Resource, NY; **14.27** Salvador Dalí "The Persistence of Memory" 1931, oil on canvas, $9\frac{1}{2}'' \times 13''$. (24.1 × 33 cm). The Museum of Modern Art/Licensed by SCALA-Art Resource, NY. © 1999 Demart Pro Arte (R), Geneva/Artists Rights Society (ARS), New York; **14.28** Vanni/Art Resource, N.Y; **page 444** (top, bottom right), Goskino/The Kobal Collection/Picture Desk, Inc./Kobal Collection; **page 444** (bottom left), Everett Collection; **page 445**, Goskino/The Kobal Collection/Picture Desk, Inc./Kobal Collection.

Chapter 15

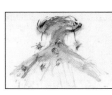

15.3 TOHO/The Kobal Collection; **15.4** Jackson Pollock. Number 27. 1950. Oil on canvas, Collection, Whitney Museum of American Art, NY. Purchase. © 2008 ARS Artists Rights Society, NY; **15.5** Willem de Kooning (American 1904–1997 b. Netherlands), "Excavation." 1950. Oil on canvas, 205.7 × 254.6 cm (81" × $100\frac{1}{4}''$). Unframed. Mr. and Mrs. Frank G. Logan Purchase Prize Fund; restricted gifts of Edgar J. Kaufmann, Jr., and Mr. and Mrs. Noah Goldowsky, Jr., 1952.1 Reproduction, The Art Institute of Chicago. All Rights Reserved. © 2009 ARS Artists Rights Society, NY; **15.6** Mark Rothko (American 1903–1970), "Green on Blue." 1956. Oil on canvas, $89\frac{3}{4}'' \times 63\frac{1}{4}''$ (22.80 × 161.0 cm). Collection of The University of Arizona Museum of Art, Tucson, Gift of E. Gallagher, Jr. Acc. 64.1.1; **15.9** © 2008 Andy Warhol Foundation for the Visual Arts/ARS, New York; **15.13** Jacob Lawrence (1917–2000), "The Trains were Packed Continually with Migrants." 1940–41. Panel 60 from The Migration Series. Tempera on gesso on composition board, 12 × 18". Gift of Ms. David M. Levy. (28.1942.30). Digital Image © The Museum of Modern Art/Licensed by SCALA/Art Resource, NY. © ARS Artists Rights Society, NY; **15.14** Courtesy www.guerrillagirls.com; **15.18** OMA/Ole Scheeren and Rem Koolhaas; **15.19** Yukinori Yanagi, "America." 1994. 12 × 18", each box (36 boxes). Ants, colored sand, plastic box, plastic tube, plastic pipe. Installation view at Museum of Contemporary Art, San Diego, 1994 collection of Artist; **15.20** Yasumasa Morimura, "Portrait (Futago)," 1988. Color Photograph, $82\frac{3}{4}'' \times 118''$. Courtesy of the artist and Luhring Augustine, New York.

Text Credits

Chapter 1

Reading 1.1 Zuni Emergence Tale, *Talk Concerning the First Begining*, THE HEATH ANTHOLOGY OF AMERICAN LITERATURE, Fifth Edition, Volume A, edited by Paul Lauter. Copyright © 2006 by Houghton Mifflin Company. Used with permission. **Reading 1.3** from *The Epic of Gilgamesh* (Tablet VI), From Kovacs, Maureen Gallery, translator. THE EPIC OF GILGAMESH, with an Introduction and Notes. Copyright © 1985, 1989 by the Board of Trustees of the Leland Stanford Junior University. All rights reserved. Used with the permission of Stanford University Press, www.sup.org. **Reading 1.4** from The Hebrew Bible (Dt. 6:6–9), "New Revised Standard Version Bible, copyright 1989, Division of Christian Education of the National Council of the Churches of Christ in the United States of America. Used by permission. All rights reserved." **Reading 1.5** from the *Book of Songs*, Song 156 from THE BOOK OF SONGS translated by Arthur Waley. © by The Arthur Waley Estate. **Reading 1.6** from the *Dao de jing*, From THE WAY OF LIFE by Lao Tzu, translated by Raymond B. Blakney, copyright © 1955 by Raymond B. Blakney, renewed © 1983 by Charles Philip Blakney. Used by permission of Dutton Signet, a division of Penguin Group (USA) Inc. **Reading 1.7** from "The Second Teaching" in the *Bhagavad Gita Krishna's Counsel in Time of War*, From BHAGAVAD-GITA, translated by Barbara Stoler Miller, copyright © 1986 by Barbara Stoler Miller. Used by permission of Bantam Books, a division of Random House, Inc.

Chapter 2

Reading 2.1 from Homer, *Iliad*, Book 24, "Achilles and Priam," by Homer, "Patroclus Fights and Dies" from THE ILIAD by Homer, translated by Robert Fagles, copyright © 1990 by Robert Fagles. Used by permission of Viking Penguin, a division of Penguin Group (USA) Inc. **Reading 2.2a** Sappho, lyric poetry, SAPPHO by MARY BARNARD. Copyright 1958 by UNIVERSITY OF CALIFORNIA PRESS—BOOKS. Reproduced with permission of UNIVERSITY OF CALIFORNIA PRESS—BOOKS in the format Textbook via Copyright Clearance Center. **Reading 2.2b** Sappho, lyric poetry, SAPPHO by MARY BARNARD. Copyright 1958 by UNIVERSITY OF CALIFORNIA PRESS—BOOKS. Reproduced with permission of UNIVERSITY OF CALIFORNIA PRESS—BOOKS in the format Textbook via Copyright Clearance Center. **Reading 2.3** from Book VII of Herodotus, *The Histories*. Translated by Robin Waterfield. Copyright © 1998. Reprinted by permission of Oxford University Press. **Page 73** Virgil, *Aeneid*, Book II, HUMPHRIES, AENEID OF VIRGIL, THE, © 1984 Reprinted by permission of Pearson Education, Inc., Upper Saddle River, NJ.

Chapter 3

Reading 3.1 Cicero, *On Duty*, Trustees of the Loeb Classical Library from CICERO: VOLUME XXI, Loeb Classical Library Volume 30, Cambridge, Mass.: Harvard University Press, 1913. The Loeb Classical Library (R) is a registered trademark of the President and Fellows of Harvard College.

Chapter 4

Reading 4.1 The Gospel of Matthew, "The Sermon on the Mount," "The New Testament," King James Version 1611. Reprinted by permission of Nelson Bibles. **Reading 4.5** Reprinted by permission of Koran USA.

Chapter 5

Reading 5.1 *Beowulf*, From BEOWULF, translated by Seamus Heaney. Copyright © 2000 by Seamus Heaney. Used by permission of W. W. Norton & Company, Inc. **Reading 5.2** *Song of Roland*, From THE SONG OF ROLAND translated by Patricia Terry. Copyright © 1965. Reprinted with permission of Prentice Hall. **Reading 5.3** Hildegard of Bingen, *Scite vias domini*, Excerpts from **Hildegard of Bingen: Scivias**, translated by Mother Columba Hart and Jane Bishop, from THE CLASSICS OF WESTERN SPIRITUALITY. Copyright © 1990 by the Abbey, Inc., New York/Mahwah, N.J. Used with permission of Paulist Press. www.paulistpress.com. **Reading 5.5** Contessa de Dia's "Cruel Are the Pains I've Suffered," from Lark in the Morning: The Verses of the Troubadours, "Lark in the Morning: The Verses of the Troubadours" edited by Robert Kehew. Copyright © 2005. Reprinted with the permission of University of Chicago Press. **Reading 5.6** from Chrétien de Troyes, *Lancelot*, Printed by permission of Everyman's Library, an imprint of Alfred A. Knopf.

Chapter 6

Reading 6.2 from Dante, *Inferno*, Canto 34, translated by John Ciardi. Copyright 1954, 1957, 1959, 1960, 1961, 1965, 1967, 1970 by the Ciardi Family Publishing Trust. Used by permission of W.W. Norton & Company, Inc. **Reading 6.3** from Boccaccio, *Decameron*, THE ITALIAN RENAISSANCE READER, edited by Julia Conaway Bondanella and Mark Musa, translated by Julia Conaway Bondanella and Mark Musa, copyright © 1987 by Julia Conaway Bondanella and Mark Musa. Used by permission of Dutton Signet, a division of Penguin Group (USA) Inc. **Reading 6.4** Petrarch, Sonnet 134, "Sonnet 134" from THE POETRY OF PETRARCH, translated by David Young. Translation copyright © 2004 by David Young. Reprinted by permission of Farrar, Straus and Giroux, LLC. **Reading 6.5** from Chaucer, *The Canterbury Tales*, *From*, Prologue, From THE CANTERBURY TALES by Geoffrey Chaucer, translated by Nevill Coghill (Penguin Classics 1951, Fourth revised edition 1977). Copyright 1951 by Nevill Coghill. Copyright © the Estate of Nevil Coghill, 1958, 1960, 1975, 1977. Reproduced by permission of Penguin Books Ltd.

Chapter 7

Readi[illegible] *renzo de' Medici: Selecti*[illegible] he Pennsylvania State [illegible] y Press. **Reading 7.2** [illegible] Della Mirandola, Giov[illegible] igri Copyright © 1956 [illegible] by special permission [illegible] *Rime, Capitolo* 13, Repr[illegible]

All of his works has been great success w/ powerful ending.
Also Sheri + Albert has also colaberater for 300, Avatar, + Pearl harbor which are very popular movies.

Cha[illegible]

Rea[illegible] from LUTHER'S WO[illegible] Used by permission of A[illegible]

Cha[illegible]

Re[illegible] ILMORE; LITERAR[illegible] 1975 renewed PUP Re[illegible] **4** from Teresa of Áv[illegible] THE COMPLETE WO[illegible] by E. Allison Peers. Ne[illegible] Littlefield/Contin-uu[illegible] *uffe*, Act V (1664) Ex[illegible] slation copyright © 19[illegible] eprinted by permis-sio[illegible] fessionals and ama-te[illegible] he copyright laws of th[illegible] n of Canada, and all ot[illegible] ion and the Interna-ti[illegible] ofessional, amateur, m[illegible], and television are st[illegible] permission for which m[illegible] nal rights (except for a[illegible] ency, 1325 Avenue of t[illegible] ould be addressed to [illegible], Orlando, FL 32887. [illegible] sively by the Drama-[illegible] ateur performance of [illegible] ssion of the Dramatis [illegible] be reproduced in any [illegible] ner.

Chapter 11

Reading 11.2 from René Descartes, *Meditations* (1641), From "The Seventh Set of Objections with the Author's Replies" by René Descartes. THE PHILOSOPHICAL WRITINGS OF DESCARTES. Translated by John Cottingham, Robert Stoothoff, Dugald Murdoch. © 1985. Reprinted with the permission of Cambridge University Press. **Reading 11.4a** from John Milton, *Paradise Lost*, Book 5 (1667), From PARADISE LOST: A Norton Critical Edition, Second Edition by John Milton, edited by Scott Elledge. Copyright © 1993, 1975 by W. W. Norton & Company, Inc. **Reading 11.4b** from John Milton, *Paradise Lost*, Book 5 (1667), From PARADISE LOST: A Norton Critical Edition, Second Edition by John Milton, edited by Scott Elledge. Copyright © 1993, 1975 by W. W. Norton & Company, Inc. **Reading 11.9** [condensed] from Jean-Jacques Rousseau, *The Social Contract*, Book 1, Chapter 4 ("Slavery") (1762), Reprinted by kind permission of Everyman's Library, an imprint of Alfred A. Knopf. **Reading 11.10** [condensed] from Jean-Jacques Rousseau, Discourse on the Origin of Inequality among Men (1755), From A DISCOURSE ON INEQUALITY by Jean-Jacques Rousseau, translated by Maurice Cranston, copyright © 1984 by Maurice Cranston. Used by permission of Viking Penguin, a division of Penguin Group (USA) Inc./Used by permission of Peter Fraser & Dunlop Group Ltd. (Canada).

Chapter 12

Reading 12.8 from Johann Wolfgang von Goethe, Faust, Part I (1808), from Faust, Part I (1952) by Goethe, Johann Wolfgang, edited by MacNeice, Louis (trans). By permission of Oxford University Press, Inc. **Reading 12.9** from Ludwig van Beethoven, Heiligenstadt Testament (1802), FORBES, Elliot; THAYER'S LIFE OF BEETHOVEN 2 VOLUMES. © 1964 Princeton University Press, 1992 renewed PUP Reprinted by permission of Princeton University Press.

Chapter 13

Reading 13.6 Charles Baudelaire, "Carrion," in Les Fleurs du mal (1857) (translation by Richard Howard), From Les Fleurs du mal by Charles Baudelaire, translated from the French by Richard Howard, illustrations by Michael Mazur. Reprinted by permission of David R. Godine, Publisher, Inc. Copyright © 1982 by Charles Baudelaire, translated from the French by Richard Howard, Illustrations by Michael Mazur.

Chapter 14

Reading 14.1 from Gertrude Stein, *The Autobiography of Alice B. Toklas* (1932), From THE AUTOBIOGRAPHY OF ALICE B. TOLKAS by Gertrude Stein, copyright 1933 by Gertrude Stein and renewed 1961 by Alice B. Toklas. Used by permission of Random House, Inc. **Reading 14.2** Wilfred Owen, "Dulce et Decorum Est" (1918), By Wilfred Owen, from THE COLLECTED POEMS OF WILFRED OWEN, copyright © 1963 by Chatto & Windus, Ltd. Reprinted by permission of New Directors Publishing Corp. **Reading 14.3** William Butler Yeats, "The Second Coming" (1919), Reprinted with permission of Scribner, Division of Simon & Schuster Inc., from THE COMPLETE WORKS OF W.B. YEATS, VOLUME I: THE POEMS, REVISED edited by Richard J. Finneran. Copyright © 1924 by The Macmillian Company. Copyright renewed © 1952 by Bertha Georgie Yeats. All rights reserved. **Reading 14.4** from T.S. Eliot, *The Wasted Land* (1921), From The Complete Poems and Plays of T. S. Eliot, 1909–1950. New York: Harcourt Brace, 1952. Reprinted by permission of Faber & Faber. **Reading 14.5** from Sigmund Freud, Civilization and Its Discontents (1930), From CIVILIZATION AND ITS DISCONTENTS by Sigmund Freud, translated by James Strachey. Copyright © 1961 by James Strachey, renewed 1989 by Alix Strachey. Used by permission of W. W. Norton & Company, Inc./ Sigmund Freud © Copyrights, the Institute of Psycho-Analysis and the Hogarth Press for permission to quote from "Civilization and its Discontents" from THE STANDARD EDITION OF THE COMPLETE PSYCHOLOGICAL WORKS OF SIGMUND FREUD translated and edited by James Strachey. Reprinted by permission of The Random House Group Ltd.

Chapter 15

Reading 15.1 from Jean-Paul Sartre, *No Exit* (1944), From NO EXIT AND THE FLIES by Jean-Paul Sarte, translated by Stuart Gilbert, copyright 1946 by Stuart Gilbert. Copyright renewed 1974, 1975 by Maris Agnes Mathilde Gilbert. Used by permission of Alfred A. Knopf, a division of Random House, Inc. and Penguin Books Ltd. **Reading 15.3** from Allan Kaprow, "The Legacy of Jackson Pollock" (1958), From Allan Kaprow, ESSAYS ON THE BLURRING OF ART AND LIFE. Edited by Jeff Kelley Berkeley. Copyright © 1993 University of California Press. Reprinted by permission of University of California. **Reading 15.4** Alain Locke, *The New Negro* (1925), Reprinted with permission of Scribner, an imprint of Simon & Schuster Adult Publishing Group, from THE NEW NEGRO by Alain Locke. Copyright © 1925 by Albert & Charles Boni, Inc. Introduction copyright © 1992 by Macmillan Publishing Company. All rights reserved. **Readings 15.5 and 15.6** Langston Hughes, Selected Poems, "Jazz Band in a Parisian Cabaret," (1925), "The Weary Blues," (1925), from THE COLLECTED POEMS OF LANGSTON HUGHES by Langston Hughes, edited by Arnold Rampersad with David Roessel, Associated Editior, copyright © 1994 by The Estate of Langston Hughes. Used by permission of Alfred A. Knopf, a division of Random House, Inc. **Reading 15.7** Anne Sexton, "Her Kind" (1960), from TO BEDLAM AND PART WAY BACK by Anne Sexton. Copyright © 1960 by Anne Sexton, renewed 1988 by Linda G. Sexton. Reprinted by permission of Houghton Mifflin Harcourt Publishers and SLL/Sterling Lord Literistic, Inc. All rights reserved. **Reading 15.8** Aurora Levins Morales,"Child of the Americas" (1986), From GETTING HOME ALIVE by Aurora Levins Morales (Ann Arbor: Firebrand Books. 1986). Reprinted by permission of Firebrand Books.

Index